CW00432234

Die
GEGEND
um
WIEN.
Nro 125.

Deutsche M. 15. a. 1. 6.

gemeine östreichische Landmeilen eine von
1¼ stunde 20 auf 1 Grad.

Oestreichische Gebürgmeilen eine von
2¼ Stunde und 1¼ auf 1 Grad.

Kagron
Stadlau
Hirschstötten
Anollresdorf
Esling
Rutzendorf
Asparn
Pisdorf
Himerleinsdorf
stadtl
Enzersdorf
Saxengang
Wittau
Antlersdorf
Oberhausen
Mühleiten
Ob. Manewsdorf
Schönau

Mansmirth
Dorf
Fischament
Krob Haslau
Ungarn
Fillend
Kl. Neusidl
Kleine
Un Schw.achat
Kottenhof
Fischa Fl.
Enzersdorf
Rauchenwarth
Schwadorf
Zwölfaxing
Pellendorf
Gallbrun

WIEN
Leopoldstadt
Clacis
Weißgarber
Landstraß
Rennweg
Krob berg
Favorite

Mozart, Haydn
and
Early Beethoven

Mozart, Haydn
and
Early Beethoven

1781–1802

Daniel Heartz

W·W· Norton & Company

New York London

Copyright © 2009 by W. W. Norton & Company, Inc.

All rights reserved
Printed in the United States of America
First Edition

For information about permission to reproduce selections from
this book, write to Permissions, W. W. Norton & Company, Inc.,
500 Fifth Avenue, New York, NY 10110.

For information about special discounts for bulk purchases, please contact
W. W. Norton Special Sales at specialsales@wwnorton.com or 800-233-4830

Book design by Margaret M. Wagner
Production manager: Andrew Marasia and Julia Druskin

Library of Congress Cataloging-in-Publication Data

Heartz, Daniel.
Mozart, Haydn and early Beethoven 1781–1802 / Daniel Heartz. — 1st ed.
p. cm.
Includes bibliographical references and index.
ISBN 978-0-393-06634-0 (hardcover)
1. Mozart, Wolfgang Amadeus, 1756–1791. 2. Haydn, Joseph, 1732–1809. 3. Beethoven, Ludwig van,
1770–1827. 4. Composers—Biography. 5. Music—18th century—History and criticism. I. Title.
ML390.H56   2008
780.9 ′033—dc22

20080025037

W. W. Norton & Company, Inc., 500 Fifth Avenue, New York, N.Y. 10110
www.wwnorton.com

W. W. Norton & Company Ltd., Castle House, 75/76 Wells Street, London W1T 3QT

1 2 3 4 5 6 7 8 9 0

For Bruce

Contents

APPENDICES

List of Illustrations

Preface

AN INTRODUCTION to this book is furnished by its two predecessors, *Haydn, Mozart and the Viennese School, 1740–1780* (1995) and *Music in European Capitals: The Galant Style, 1720–1780* (2003). *Haydn, Mozart,* as it is abbreviated throughout the present volume, concentrated on music in Vienna from the mid-century on, then described the careers and works of both masters up to the turning point of 1780, after which they gradually emerged as leaders of the Viennese school. *Music in European Capitals* cast the net more widely and surveyed the art all over the Continent, beginning with the Galant Style's origins in newer streams of Italian opera during the 1720s and 1730s. In the Preface to *Haydn, Mozart,* I expressed hopes of being able to finish the third volume that would "wind up the careers of Haydn and Mozart, describe Beethoven's first decade in Vienna, intertwined with the tumultuous times surrounding the French Revolution . . ." Behold the third (and final) volume. The story of how three books emerged out of an originally planned one is told in my essay "A Pilgrim's Progress Report Concerning 'Music in the Classic Era,' " in *Music, Libraries, and the Academy: Essays in Honor of Lenore Coral,* ed. James P. Cassaro (Madison, WI, 2007).

Completing this volume took less time than anticipated, thanks partly to habits formed and momentum gathered from writing the first two, also because the material was more familiar to me. The high classic style in music that marked the last two decades of the eighteenth century became manifest in an imposing succession of undisputed masterpieces. During the 1780s Mozart wrote his most famous operas and instrumental pieces. Haydn followed by producing his greatest symphonies, string quartets, masses, and oratorios. Young Beethoven started as a pianist-composer in imitation of Mozart, on whose keyboard sonatas and concertos he patterned his own. Haydn, as well as Mozart, furnished the models when, about the year 1800, Beethoven began composing string quartets and symphonies. The majority of all these great works were old acquaintances of mine. I have been teaching them in the classroom for half a century.

By the early years of the nineteenth century, "Haydn, Mozart, and Beethoven" had become a watchword, a commonplace expression signifying musical excellence. From Vienna, the fame of these composers spread rapidly throughout Western civilization. A survey of music journals in 1804, cited by *Thayer's Life of Beethoven* (revised and edited by Elliot Forbes [Princeton, 1964], p. 361), claimed that critics even then ranked Beethoven as the only musician worthy to stand beside Haydn and Mozart. Many music lovers never relinquished their preference for early Beethoven, although the composer himself moved on to other models and different quests. Their attitude certainly had to do with an abiding love for the music of Mozart and Haydn. E. T. A. Hoffmann was one critic whose tastes *did* move on, by rejoicing in what was specifically new in nineteenth-century music of all kinds, yet at the core of his aesthetic values there remained the same composer-triad: "Haydn, Mozart and Beethoven have evolved a new art . . ." he wrote in 1814. Ten years later a group of Austrian notables imploring Beethoven not to desert them went so far as to tout Vienna's "holy Trinity" in the persons of Haydn, Mozart, and Beethoven.

Readers familiar with the first two volumes may notice that this one lacks color plates, a decision I reached for the following reasons. Of great paintings that could enhance main points in my text I found none. As for colored portraits of the main figures, there are hardly any that have not been reproduced often in other books. The unfinished portrait of Mozart at the keyboard by his brother-in-law, the actor Joseph Lange, reproduced over and over in the literature, springs readily to mind. My search for pertinent and unhackneyed visual material yielded better results among engravings and other black-and-white originals.

In one case, I struck a bonanza. An engraved, little-known map, "Die Gegend um Wien" (The Environs of Vienna), serves as Figure 1.1 and as endpapers. Franz Johann Joseph von Reilly (1766–1820), Austria's most eminent cartographer, published it in 1789. The map can be read by regarding its center, WIEN, the city within the old walls, as the hub of a wheel, whose spokes radiate out into streets and districts. From the top descending counterclockwise, Reilly labels these: Leopoldstadt; then across the Danube canal to Rossau; Waringergasse, where Mozart lived in 1788; Alstergasse, where Beethoven resided during his first years in Vienna (1792–95); and so on down to Mariahilf. Just below the last-mentioned is Gumpendorf, where in 1796 Haydn bought the house in which he died in 1809. Beyond the outer line of fortifications to the west and south of the city are numerous villages and small towns that were summer havens to city dwellers. The names of several villages near Vienna are familiar particularly in connection with Beethoven. Starting at the Danube north-northwest of the city and moving southwest there are, for example, Nusdorf, Heiligstadt, Döbling, and all the way south to the town of Mödling near the map's bottom. Further south beyond Mödling is the spa town of Baden, frequented by Mozart and Beethoven. Routes lead out of the city in all directions. To the east, the Landstras[se] becomes the "Strasse nach Ungarn" (Hungary); to the north, across the Danube, the route to Silesia and Poland diverges from that to Bohemia; to the west lies the "Strasse in das Reich" (Germany); and in the south there are routes to Styria (and Italy) and to Croatia. Tree-lined royal ways (Alees) lead to Schönbrunn and Laxenburg palaces. The river Wien (Wien Fl[uss])) in those days was uncovered except for the many bridges over it.

John Rice acquainted me with Reilly's 1789 map many years ago when he was writing his dissertation here. I somehow managed to keep a copy (among hundreds of other documents) and reminded John of it last year. He knew not only the map but also the identity of a specialist dealer with whom he put me in touch, and from whom I purchased the original engraving reproduced here. As the map leads off the book, so should John lead the list of those thanked in the acknowledgments that follow. He has been one of my most frequent correspondents and of great help with all three books. Another Mozart scholar for whose answers to many queries I am grateful is Paul Corneilson. My colleague Joseph Kerman has been generous in aid of the Beethoven chapter, as has William Meredith of the Beethoven Center at San José State University.

Colin Slim, my near neighbor in Berkeley these last five years, has helped me in many ways. He read the entire work in draft before it went to the press and suggested innumerable improvements and emendations. He has also volunteered to help with the proofs when they arrive. His devoted friendship has sustained me through occasional bouts of dispiritedness and kept me focused on the goal.

I have had but one research assistant, Rebekah Ahrendt, who alone accomplished the feat of putting the entire text on disk over a period of four years as I was writing it (and often rewriting it), all the while making valuable suggestions and corrections. She did this so adroitly, with so much grace and aplomb, as to make the task look easy. I thank her heartily, and also my music typographer, who once again was Michael Zwiebach. My friend, the artist Carol Peale, drew the map of the Rhineland (Figure 7.1) after a rough sketch I made, and together we looked through her vast collection of art books and catalogues until we found an ideal battle scene with which to adorn the dust jacket.

From the publisher's side there was also a major continuity with the first two volumes. I again benefited from the long experience of the inestimable Claire Brook as principal reader. If my text gave her even slightly fewer headaches this time around, I count that as progress—no small thing with such an exacting taskmistress, one to whom I owe so much.

Bruce Alan Brown was central to my finishing the series. By taking on some of my projects he allowed me more time. At my request he relieved me of revising several articles on eighteenth-century music for the second edition of the *New Grove Dictionary of Music and Musicians* (2002). My association with the *Neue Mozart-Ausgabe*, begun with the Attwood papers in the 1960s and continued with my edition of *Idomeneo* (1972), was scheduled to conclude with a critical report on the same. Thanks to general editor Wolfgang Rehm, with whom I have enjoyed most cordial relations over four decades, my requests to transfer responsibility into Bruce's hands were worked out. With the meticulous attention to detail Bruce brings to every scholarly task, his splendid *Kritischer Bericht* on *Idomeneo*, after long hard labor, saw the light of publication in 2005. With profound gratitude for all his help, not only lately but throughout the planning and writing of this series, I dedicate this book to Bruce.

Daniel Heartz
Berkeley, California
September 2007

Mozart, Haydn
and
Early Beethoven

1
Mozart, 1781—1785

Return to Vienna

MOZART was reluctant to leave Munich after the performances there of his *Idomeneo* in early 1781. He still hoped for an appointment to the Bavarian court. For Countess Josepha von Paumgarten, mistress of Elector Carl Theodor, he composed the *scena* and aria K. 369 dated Munich, 8 March 1781. It was his last attempt at persuading Carl Theodor to hire him. His only remaining option was to obey the summons from his employer and liege lord, Hieronymous von Colloredo, prince archbishop of Salzburg, from whose court he had greatly overstayed his leave, as had his father, Leopold.

Colloredo was not in Salzburg at the time but in Vienna, where he had gone to visit his ailing father Prince Rudolf Joseph von Colloredo, vice-chancellor of the Holy Roman Empire. The archbishop and most of his entourage stayed in Vienna at the palatial House of the Order of the Teutonic Knights on the Singerstrasse. To this rather grim building, which incorporated a church that fronted the street, Mozart repaired and was allotted a room of his own. Arrived on 16 March, he wrote to Leopold in Salzburg the next day, the first of a series of letters in which he chafed at his lowly status among the court officials attending the archbishop. Colloredo, understandably miffed with the Mozarts, treated him coldly. Aside from complaining of his lowly station at the communal table, Mozart bewailed his failure to receive extra payment for displaying his talents in the various houses to which Colloredo sent him to perform.

In letters to his father, Mozart painted the situation regarding the archbishop in increasingly bitter terms. He was preparing Leopold for the break that he deemed inevitable. At the same time, he was seeking his father's permission to make such a move. The financial situation of the Mozart family was dire. Leopold had a modest salary at Salzburg and his daughter Nannerl earned no more than a pittance for giving piano lessons there. Moreover, debts remained from Mozart's financially unrewarding trip to Mannheim and Paris two years earlier. He found no appointment at either place. Leopold was reluctant to lose the small but reliable income from his son's position as court organist at Salzburg. In the end Mozart prevailed by getting himself kicked out of the palace on the Singerstrasse. His letter of resignation was scorned, meaning he had no formal release from his duties.

Mozart had last lived in Vienna during the summer of 1773. Having failed to get appointments in Milan and Florence, he and Leopold once again pinned their hopes on the imperial court. Maria Theresa still ruled. Her eldest son, Joseph, was subordinate to her as co-ruler of the Habsburg monarchy since the death of his father, Emperor Francis, in 1765, but supreme in his lesser and more ceremonial role of Holy Roman Emperor in succession to Francis. Even reputable historians have been known to confuse the two roles, and musicologists often get entangled in their complexities. In the first volume of this series, I took the precaution of beginning with a map showing how these political entities intersected and overlapped.[1] It was Maria Theresa, not Joseph, to whom the Mozarts had recourse in 1773. After a visit to Schönbrunn Leopold wrote his wife in Salzburg on 12 August 1773, "Her majesty the Empress was very gracious to us, but that is all."[2]

Maria Theresa died in November 1780 after forty years on the throne of the Monarchy. Four princes were assigned the honor of escorting her coffin to entombment in the Church of the Capuchins on the Hoher Markt. Their names indicate which noble families ranked highest in the court's protocol: Charles von Liechtenstein, Charles Joseph de Ligne, Nicholas von Esterházy, and Georg Adam von Starhemberg. The Prince de Ligne held extensive territories in the Austrian Netherlands and had distinguished himself as an author; Liechtenstein and Starhemberg had stellar careers in the military and diplomatic service respectively; Esterházy, ruler of vast estates in Hungary, was probably the wealthiest prince of all. He also maintained the most elaborate musical establishment, led for decades by Kapellmeister Joseph Haydn. Mozart lacked the temperament that allowed Haydn to remain a court servant over a long period. Yet he aspired to a court

---

[1] "The Habsburg Monarchy and the Holy Roman Empire in 1740," in *Haydn, Mozart and the Viennese School, 1740–1780*, p. xxii.

[2] As in the two previous volumes, I translate all letters cited from the complete edition, Mozart, *Briefe und Aufzeichnungen: Gesamtausgabe*, ed. Wilhelm A. Bauer, Otto Erich Deutsch, and Jospeh Heinz Eibl, 7 vols. (Kassel, 1962–75). The letters will be identified herein only by their date.

appointment that would support himself and his family. He set his sights high, on the new sovereign of the Monarchy, Joseph II.

Soon after arriving in Vienna Mozart made clear his plans to capture, or recapture, the attention of Joseph II. On 24 March 1781, he wrote to Leopold.

> My chief intention here now is to present myself in a polished manner to the emperor, for I am absolutely determined that he should get to know me. I should gladly walk him through my opera [*Idomeneo*] and play him some good fugues, for that is what he likes. Had I known that I would be in Vienna through the Lenten season I would have written a little oratorio and given it for my benefit in the theater, for that is what everyone does here. I could easily have written it ahead of time because I know all the solo voices. How gladly I would have given a public concert here, as is the custom, but—I am not allowed to do so.

Writing on 11 April, he excoriated the in-house concerts he was allowed to give with his fellow court musicians, mainly soprano castrato Francesco Ceccarelli and violinist Antonio Brunetti. "What brought me to near despair was that the very evening we had this shitty house concert [scheis-Musick] I was invited by Countess [Maria Wilhelmina] Thun and who should be there? the Emperor! [Tenor Valentin] Adamberger and [soprano Anna Maria] Weigl were there and received fifty ducats apiece! And what an opportunity!"

Joseph II was aware of Mozart all along, remembering even his first appearances in Vienna as a child prodigy. He took close interest in affairs at the court of Munich and doubtless was aware of the sensation caused there by *Idomeneo*. By the end of April there was talk of Mozart receiving a libretto for an opera from Stephanie, poet of Joseph's German operatic troupe in the Burgtheater. The idea surely came from the Emperor himself, who supervised such matters even while appearing to be above them.

Vienna under the sole rule of Joseph II differed from what it had been under his predecessors, especially as to court ceremonial, much of which he abolished. Diplomatic receptions had to be continued as before but large, purely social, gatherings at court became rare. Joseph reduced his household to a condition more humble than many a family of the high nobility (or wealthy parvenu— think Faninal of operatic fame). Twice a widower, and with no surviving children, Joseph led an austere bachelor existence *chez lui*, went about the city in the plainest attire in the simplest of carriages, and depended for entertainment on a select few friends such as the charming and brilliant Countess Thun.

The time saved from participating in traditional court formalities Joseph spent in governing, sometimes over-governing, his far-flung estates, and in issuing minute regulations affecting education, social welfare, and jurisprudence. His enlightened reforms were often foresighted and achieved long-lasting advances in medical, hygienic, and legal areas. As often as not his reforms ran up against entrenched habits reluctantly abandoned by the very people they were intended to benefit. The law of unintended consequences manifested itself in other ways too. After censorship of most publications was reduced or removed, the streets of Vienna were flooded with pamphlets not worth printing in the first place.

Joseph's restrictions on elaborate music in churches arose from good intentions. They were, of course, resisted by the many musicians whose livelihood, however meager, depended on performing at the numerous churches of the capital. Arguments were waged in print on the pros and cons of the restrictions by several authors, notably Johann Pezzl and Friedrich Nicolai, a visitor from Berlin.[3] The attempt to substitute something akin to Protestant hymns for congregations to sing did not succeed. Elaborate church music returned under Joseph's successors Leopold II and Francis II.

Even so, reforming efforts by Joseph on the domestic front met with more success than did his attempts to wield greater power in international affairs. As his mother's co-ruler and as emperor he had often been more belligerent and territorially aggrandizing than prudence warranted. As long as Maria Theresa held supreme power she reined in her son's ambitions, although not in the shameful case of the First Partition of Poland (1772), when Joseph and their first minister, Chancellor Wenzel Kaunitz, prevailed over her. The later diplomatic crises he provoked are mentioned below following the stand he took against Freemasonry in 1785.

One reform Joseph undertook while still co-ruler with his mother earned him admiration from the populace of Vienna. Close to the city, he opened two royal preserves to the public, the Prater (1766) and the Augarten (1775). This allowed common people to stroll, ride horseback or in carriages through these leafy parks on the island in the Danube directly across from the central city. Reilly's 1789 map "Die Gegend um Wien" (Figure 1.1) shows many locations with important associations for Mozart, Haydn, and Beethoven that will be discussed throughout this volume. Here the emphasis is on those features of Reilly's map that are shown and named on the large island across from Vienna: the suburb of Leopoldstadt, the only settled part, linked with the city by a wide bridge over the branch of the Danube (also called the Danube canal); the Augarten at the northwest end of the island; and occupying the whole southeastern part, the vast Prater (Bratter), on the tip of which, at the end of a long tree-lined Allée, is a "Lusthaus."

Opposite. FIGURE 1.1. Reilly's 1789 map, "The Environs of Vienna."

---

[3] For discussion of this subject see the section "Churches" in "Musical Life in Vienna," ch. 1 of *Haydn, Mozart*, especially pp. 20–23. That chapter was conceived as an introduction to the whole century in Vienna, not just the portion up to 1780.

Die
GEGEND
um
WIEN.
Maßst.

The Augarten and Prater both figure in letters Mozart sent his father in Salzburg. On 25 July 1781, he defended himself against rumors reaching Leopold as to the unsupervised attentions he was paying to an unmarried daughter (Constanze) of Frau Weber, in whose apartment near the Peterskirche he had been renting a room since early May: "We were in the Prater together a couple of times but her mother was along with us." One day in 1783 while in the Augarten he ran into Emperor Joseph, who questioned him about his age when the Mozarts first visited Vienna in 1762 (letter of 20 February 1784). In his letter of 26 May 1784, Mozart wrote that he and his wife went to bed at midnight and rose at five or five-thirty almost every day so that they could go to the Augarten early (their maid had complained to relatives in Salzburg that their hours prevented her from getting enough sleep). During the warmer months, if the weather was clement, the couple spent entire days in the Prater. Mozart's letter of 3 May 1783 is in fact dated "Vienne im Prater ce 3 de may."

> Mon très cher Pére! I can scarcely bring myself to drive back to the city for the weather is far too lovely, and being in the Prater today is so delightful. We have taken our lunch in the open air and shall stay on until eight or nine in the evening. My entire company consists of my little wife, who is pregnant, and her little husband, who is not pregnant but healthily fat.

Another reason that Mozart went to these civic parks was for the summer concert series given in them. In his letter of 8 May 1782 he told Leopold of a series of twelve concerts in the Augarten planned under the aegis of the entrepreneur Philip Martin, with Mozart's cooperation. Martin also owned a restaurant in the Augarten where the composer was welcome. In sum, Mozart made the most of Vienna's two central parks and loved being outdoors in their verdant surroundings.

Further evidence of his rapport with nature, if any were needed, is furnished by his description of a visit to Count Kobenzl's hunting lodge in the hills to the northwest of Vienna, known collectively as the Kahlenberg. On Reilly's 1789 map (see Figure 1.1) the count's particular hill is labeled "Kobenzl." Mozart wrote Leopold on 13 July 1781, "The little house is nothing much, but the countryside!—the forest—in which my host has built a grotto that looks as if Nature herself had fashioned it. That is magnificent and very agreeable." These hills beyond the city provide a background to Bernardo Bellotto's splendid panorama of Vienna from the south.[4]

---

[4] Reproduced on the dust jacket of *Haydn, Mozart.*

Die Entführung aus dem Serail

Opera in Vienna had changed greatly since Mozart's previous visits. These were in 1762, when at age six he witnessed the first production of Gluck's *Orfeo ed Euridice*; in 1767, when the Burgtheater failed to produce his comic opera *La finta semplice*; and in 1773, by which time Antonio Salieri had come to dominate the scene with his operas for the Italian troupe in residence. In 1776, Emperor Joseph II founded a National Theater for plays in German, to which he added a wing for Singspiele two years later. He dismissed the Italian singers. Works in German thus occupied the stage of the Burgtheater, where plays in French and operas in Italian had hitherto held sway.

Joseph II confided overall direction of the German troupe to his advisor and intimate friend Count Franz Xaver Orsini Rosenberg, the court's high chamberlain. Under him was a rotating directorship of five actors. One of them, Gottlieb Stephanie the Younger, had special responsibility for the troupe's Singspiel wing. Stephanie, a prolific playwright, was born in Breslau and came to Vienna as a prisoner during the Seven Years War. Luckily, Mozart enjoyed the good graces of both Stephanie and Count Rosenberg. The latter had invited the Mozarts to visit him in 1770 when they were in Florence, where he was chief minister to Grand Duke Leopold, Joseph II's brother and successor. Stephanie befriended the Mozarts during their 1773 visit to Vienna. Not long after his return to Vienna in March 1781, Mozart showed Stephanie his nearly completed Singspiel *Zaide*, K. 344, written in Salzburg but intended for Vienna. Stephanie rejected it as too serious for the Viennese and promised to find the composer a new libretto to set that would be more to their liking (letter to Leopold Mozart of 18 April 1781). Meanwhile, Mozart introduced Count Rosenberg to *Idomeneo*, which he performed on the fortepiano of Countess Thun (letter of 26 May 1781). On 30 July, Stephanie gave Mozart a libretto with a Turkish subject, by Christoph Friedrich Bretzner, *Belmont und Constanze, oder, Die Entführung aus dem Serail*. The music had been composed by Johann André and was first performed in Berlin only two months earlier.[5]

Idomeneo eased the birth of *Die Entführung*, not only by impressing Count Rosenberg, but also by providing Mozart with an enhanced sense of tonal planning and of expressive possibilities far beyond those in his earlier operas. Some of the most moving passages in *Idomeneo* inspired the music with which Mozart clothed the pair of noble lovers, Belmonte and Konstanze.[6] He emphasized their seriousness by contrasting them with their servants, Blonde and Pedrillo, and with

---

[5] Thomas Bauman, *W. A. Mozart: Die Entführung aus dem Serail* (Cambridge, 1987), p. 10.
[6] This is a major topic in Thomas Bauman's "Coming of Age in Vienna: *Die Entführung aus dem Serail*," in Daniel Heartz, *Mozart's Operas*, ed. Thomas Bauman (Berkeley and Los Angeles, 1990), pp. 65–87.

his Turkish style, assigned particularly to the figure of Osmin. Mozart plays off the brightness these characters bring to the opera, mostly on the sharp side of the tonal spectrum or in neutral C major, against the more subdued and languorous love music of the noble Spanish couple, characteristically set to music on the flat side.

Osmin, the surly overseer of Pasha Selim's country estate, is one of Mozart's greatest dramatic creations, not because the text set this up but because Mozart demanded changes in the libretto. It was the opera's good fortune to have for this role a great bass singer, Johann Ludwig Fischer, who came to Vienna in 1780 after having sung in the German operas for Elector Carl Theodore at Mannheim and Munich. Born in Mainz in 1745, Fischer was trained by the famous tenor Anton Raaff at Mannheim, who created the title role of *Idomeneo*.

In order to exploit Fischer's wonderfully deep voice to the full, Mozart had entire scenes rewritten so as to expand the role, with the result that there is no dramatic exposition at the beginning of the opera. Not until scene four of the first act is it made clear who the characters are and how they got to this exotic locale. Konstanze and Blonde, along with Pedrillo, were captured by pirates and then bought by Pasha Selim and taken to his country house. We learn further, from what Pedrillo tells Belmonte, that the Pasha is not a born Turk but a renegade Christian, one who is too delicate to compel any of his wives to love him. His passions are buildings and gardens. Thus, Pedrillo will introduce Belmonte as an architect.

Mozart ordinarily wrote out the overtures to his operas at the last minute, because they were not rehearsed until then, if at all. In this case, he took a different course. Besides its importance in creating a Turkish ambience, the overture has a middle section that foreshadows the first sung number. It was Mozart's idea to have Belmonte, sung by Valentin Adamberger, begin by singing a short song (No. 1, which he calls a "kleine Ariette" in his letter of 26 September 1781). In it, Belmonte expresses his relief at reaching the place where he hoped to find his beloved (material present in Bretzner only as spoken text). He sings this to simple music in the key of C that had served, though in c, as the overture's short middle section (Example 1.1). The *forte* corresponds to the word "Konstanze!" in

EXAMPLE 1.1. *Mozart,* Die Entführung aus dem Serail, *Overture: middle section*

the sung version. Hearing what was in the minor repeated in the major can only brighten the mood of the audience and urge it to think, "Yes, you will find your beloved Konstanze!"

The exotic tonal coloring of the overture returns as soon as Osmin begins his strophic Lied in g (No. 2). From the end of No. 1, the bass moves one whole tone down from C to B♭, the song's first chord being a first inversion of its tonic chord. This conjunction of B♭ and C occurs many times in the opera, as we shall see. The Lied could as well have been called a Romance, for it has an unusual tonal complexion, hovering mainly between i and v, giving it the archaic character favored for Romances. The text narrates a parable (with self-reference implied), that is sung as conscious song, features also characteristic of the Romance. The tune's several repeated tones, its 6/8 meter, and suggestions of plucked accompaniment (pizzicato strings for the third strophe) all give a foretaste of Pedrillo's delightful equivalent in Act III, No. 18. Mozart saved the term "Romance" for that climactic moment.

Aside from the frequent passing back and forth between C and B♭, the opera often passes from tonic minor to major within and between numbers, which accounts in part for the cheerily optimistic mood it projects overall. Otherwise, Mozart chose to move by intervals of a third or fourth, up or down, in almost all cases, so that successive sections or numbers have a common tone between them. In Act I, he favored several moves up a third.

The move of a major second into and out of the penultimate number comes as something of a surprise, scarcely mitigated by the brief spoken dialogue that separates the end of the brilliant Janissary Chorus in C (No. 6) from the onset of soothing B♭ in No. 7. In opera with recitative such a tonal motion would almost certainly have been prepared with modulation. That the surprise is part of Mozart's overall tonal strategy is evident from his placing a big number in B♭ in the penultimate spot in each of the three acts.[7]

Mozart gave a revealing account of how he made tonal choices in a long letter about the opera to his father dated 26 September 1781. He explains the importance of a particular singer to the project as well.

> Since we assigned the part of Osmin to Herr Fischer, who certainly has an outstanding bass voice (notwithstanding that the Archbishop told me that he sang too low—I assured him that he would sing higher next time). We must take advantage of such a man, especially as he has the entire public here on his side. In the original book, Osmin has only this one little song to sing, and apart from that, he has nothing, except the trio and the finale. Thus, I gave him an aria to sing in Act I and will give him one in Act II as well. I have indicated how the aria will go to Stephanie, and the main portion of the music was finished before he knew a word about it. You have only the beginning of it and the ending, which must have a good effect, for Osmin's rage is made comical by introducing the Turkish music. In working out this aria, I made Fischer's beautiful deep tones shine forth (in spite of that Salzburger Midas). The passage "By the beard of the Prophet" is in the same tempo as before but with quick notes, and as his anger increases more and more, just when the aria seems to

[7] As pointed out by Thomas Bauman, *W. A. Mozart: Die Entführung*, p. 74.

be over the *Allegro assai* arrives in a different tempo and different key, which must produce an excellent effect. For a man in a towering rage oversteps all order, measure, and boundary. He does not know himself and so the music must no longer know itself. But since the passions, be they powerful or not, must never be expressed to the point of disgust, and music, even in the most horrifying situation, must never offend the ear, but must actually please, in other words must remain music, I have chosen a key foreign to F (the key of the aria) but a key allied to it, yet not its nearest relative, D minor, but rather its more distant one, A minor.

Rare is a statement like this, specifying the degree of difference Mozart heard between iii and vi in the context of coming from I. The lesson can be applied to many of the tonal moves in his music. It applies, for instance, to his frequent pairing of E♭ (I) with g (iii). The I-iii pairing also occurs frequently in earlier eighteenth-century music.[8]

There is spoken dialogue following No. 3, but it goes by quickly, as do most spoken passages. Thus the emphatic impression of the key of a minor, made shrill by the jangling Turkish music and obsessive repetitions of the first five tones of that key's scale in the orchestra (eleven times in all!) during a gradual *crescendo*, lingers in the ear when the next tonal move takes place. The angry a minor gives way to a soothing A major.

Belmonte's aria is preceded by an A-major triad played softly by the strings, just as happens in the opening of the third act of *Idomeneo*, coming after storms and calamity there and after Osmin's stormy exit here. Alone for a soliloquy, Belmonte contemplates the joy of seeing his sweetheart once again: "Konstanze! Konstanze! dich wieder zu sehen!" His recitative over sustained string chords, with solo oboe echoing his tones, mirrors the harmonic progression of Ilia's recitative opening Act III but is condensed to nearly half the length. A sudden *rinforzato* brings it to an end with a dominant chord that resolves directly into the aria "O wie ängstlich, o wie feurig klopft mein liebevolles Herz!" (How my love-laden heart beats with fire and anxiety). Mozart explained to his father in the same letter of 26 September how he expressed the throbbing heart, as well as the sighs and whispering that Belmonte imagined hearing from the lips of his beloved. The aria is not long, only 113 measures of *Andante* in 2/4 time, but it conjures up the world of the smitten young nobleman just as does another outpouring by a young lover in the same key, Ferrando's "Un' aura amorosa," No. 17 in *Così fan tutte*. Belmonte's cadential phrase, repeated once, takes the voice up to high A over a I$^6_4$ chord (Example 1.2). It anticipates nearly note for note Ferrando's cadence (mm. 63–67). Like *Idomeneo*, *Die Entführung* contains a fund of riches from which Mozart drew repeatedly during his final decade.

---

[8] Instances are cited in *Haydn, Mozart*, p. 528, and in *Music in European Capitals*, pp. 122 (Pergolesi) and 149 (Jommelli).

EXAMPLE 1.2. *Mozart,* Die Entführung aus dem Serail, *Aria No. 4*

In the penultimate number of Act I, we meet Konstanze in person. She remembers her lost days of love and happiness with Belmonte. Mozart introduces her aria with an *Adagio* in common time of nine measures that could be heard as a slow introduction. Unlike an ordinary slow introduction, its words and music both return in the faster second tempo at the reprise. At the words "Doch wie schnell schwand meine Freude" (how quickly my joy vanished), Mozart switched to *Allegro* in common time. The aria was another piece that he wrote in the first flash of inspiration. At the time, before much thought was given to anything beyond the first act, he may have considered this the only opportunity for the singer portraying Konstanze to show off her coloratura singing, as expected by her partisans. She was the twenty-year-old Caterina Cavalieri, a Viennese-born soprano whose native language was German. Mozart was not altogether satisfied with the text of this aria, nor with his setting of it. To display the heroine's voice he wrote a melisma up to high D on the first syllable of "meinem" thereby violating an Italian ideal, which preferred soft vowels for this purpose. In a letter (26 September) he explained to his father in a kind of apology, "I sacrificed Konstanze's aria somewhat to the agile throat of Mlle Cavalieri . . . I tried to be as expressive as an Italian *aria di bravura* will permit."

A few words are in order concerning the clarinets that figure importantly in Konstanze's aria (No. 6) and throughout the opera. They were played by the brothers Anton and Johann Stadler, Austrian-born artists whose names first appeared in the theatrical accounts in 1779 and who became regular members of the orchestra in 1781.[9] Anton would later win fame and give his own concerts in the Burgtheater. For him Mozart wrote the Clarinet Quintet, K. 581, and Clarinet Concerto, K. 622, as well as the solos for clarinet and basset horn in *La clemenza di Tito,* K. 621. Clarinets figured in *Idomeneo* and had long been included in the famous Mannheim-Munich orchestra for which that opera was composed. They are even more prominent in *Die Entführung.*

Act I ends with a trio of conflict between Osmin and the two Spanish interlopers, Belmonte and Pedrillo. A trio for three men at this time was quite a rarity (excluding cases where one or more of the men sang soprano or contralto).

---

[9] Dexter Edge, "Mozart's Viennese Orchestras," *Early Music* 20 (1992): 64–88; 71.

Mozart did not have another chance to write deep-voiced male trios in opera until the beginning numbers of *Così fan tutte*. This piece, like the previous one, is in two tempos. A vigorous first part in c built on a rising triad theme, *Allegro* in 2/4 time, gives way to an *Allegro assai* as the key changes to C major. There is contrapuntal action between the voice parts, enough so that one of the singers went astray and threw the others off at the second performance, as Mozart reported in his letter of 20 July 1782. The ending, he wrote, is "very noisy—and that is what is needed to end an act—the noisier and the shorter the better, so the audience will not have time to cool off in its applause" (letter of 26 September 1781).

Act II is opened by the only character as yet unheard, Blonde. She speaks a few lines, saying that a European lady like herself cannot be treated as Osmin, into whose care she has been placed, attempts to treat her—that is, as a slave. Strings alone sound a sweetly consonant *Andante grazioso* in 2/4 time and in the key of A that demonstrates the way she insists on being treated, "with tenderness, flattery, pleasantness, and good humor." The phrases are short and simple, providing no competition for Belmonte's sentimental aria, No. 4, in the same key. The absence of winds also marks her lower social status. Yet, Blonde manifests a competitive streak when Mozart gives her coloratura up to high E, one tone higher than her mistress Konstanze in Nos. 6 and 10. Mimicry or not, the feat could not but startle Osmin. Teresa Teyber, the first Blonde, also possessed an agile throat. Her aria is a simple rondo of 102 mm., in which Mozart made a big cut (mm. 38–59). It was the aria that he reported having finished along with the drinking duet, No. 14, before the act was set aside for major text revisions (same letter of 26 September). Blonde's No. 8 is no mere *aria di sorbetto* (as is Arbace's aria at the equivalent spot in *Idomeneo*) but a piece of fine charaterization.

Blonde's plucky independence of spirit becomes the matter of the following dialogue and duet with Osmin, No. 9. She is more than a match for her elderly overseer. She mimics his descent to the lowest tones of his voice with one of her own. It is revealed that she is an Englishwoman, giving Osmin opportunities to rail against the English for allowing women such impertinences. The duet is lively and comical, an *Allegro* in 6/8 time which becomes *Allegro assai* for the last part. Its key of E♭, usually reserved for more solemn numbers, makes its first appearance in the opera here and its choice may have been partly a matter of taking advantage of Fischer's robust low tones, including a sustained low E♭. The duet, along with the drinking duet, was encored at the first performance, according to the composer's letter of 20 July 1782.

After only a few words spoken by Blonde noting the approach of her melancholy mistress, the key of E♭ sounds again, with all traces of the comedic gone. Konstanze receives an obbligato recitative of eighteen measures, very expansive compared to the four measures preceding Belmonte's No. 4, though the plaintive melodic sighs are common to both. In No. 10, the bass moves up slowly by half steps from E to A, which resolves to D, and then to g for the beginning of the Aria, *Andante con moto* in 2/4 time. Before Konstanze sings the first word, "Traurigkeit" (sadness), its melody and harmony are heard from a wind choir of paired flutes, oboes, bassoons, and basset horns. The serious tone of this music, recitative and aria alike, would sound quite at home in *Zaide*, K. 344, or in *Idomeneo*, especially in the role of the love-smitten Ilia. Moreover, there are audible resemblances to the two earlier works. The second subject of No. 10 begins with winds alone and matches the wind ritornello that opens the quartet, No. 15, in *Zaide*, to which the second subject for solo winds in Ilia's aria, No. 11, bears strong resemblance.[10] In Ilia's case, the winds evoked a transformation of that opera's main recurring motif, what I call the "Idamante motif" (Example 1.3). It was never far from Mozart's mind during the years before and after his Munich opera of 1781. In "Traurigkeit," the carryover only confirms that Mozart considers Ilia and Konstanze alike as being overwhelmed by love. The winds seem to plead for them both.

EXAMPLE 1.3. *Mozart,* Idomeneo, *Aria No. 1, Idamante motif*

Some other features drawing the two ladies together are hidden in their music. The technique with which Mozart introduces the reprise in Konstanze's aria, a rising chromatic line in the treble, A B♭ B♮ C C♯ D, which is like the bass rise leading into the aria, has a parallel in Ilia's first aria, "Padre, germani, addio!" Ilia's chromatic rise into the reprise is breathlessly short and concentrated, taking only three measures and a tone (mm. 55–58). Konstanze received a more deliberate treatment (mm. 61–66). Mozart trusted the veteran singer of Ilia's part, soprano Dorothea Wendling, to execute a formal subtlety by anticipating the initial words "Padre, germani" while still modulating, then elide into the first theme at its third measure. He made no such demands on young Cavalieri. Looked at another way, Ilia's elision is something for connoisseurs to savor, while Konstanze's well-demarcated transition and ensuing reprise make the process more clear to those at not quite so high a level of understanding. Not that the public at the Burgtheater was any different for Singspiel than for the Italian opera that preceded and followed its short reign. In the music of Belmonte and Konstanze, Mozart showed that he would surrender none of the advances he had made in Italian serious opera.

[10] See *Haydn, Mozart,* p. 640, ex. 9.14ab.

Mozart ended his long letter of 26 September 1781 on the opera saying that he could go no further with Act II than one aria (No. 8) and the drinking duet already composed because the whole story was about to be reworked. The opera then was set aside for reasons that had nothing to do with him. Its original purpose was the hasty creation of a work to perform before the visiting crown prince of Russia during the fall season. The court decided instead to revive three operas by Gluck, which fully occupied the troupe in the Burgtheater.

The break in composing the opera is confirmed by studies of the paper, showing that Blonde's aria, No. 8, and the drinking duet, No. 14, were written on paper types used in Act I while the rest of the opera used different types of paper.[11] Exactly when Mozart resumed composition is not clear. On 30 January 1782, he wrote his father that the opera had not gone to sleep entirely but was only postponed because of Gluck's operas and "many very necessary alterations to the poetry." He was expecting it to be produced after Easter, which fell on 20 April. Not until 8 May did he play all of Act II to Countess Thun and on 30 May he played Act III for her. Rehearsal began on 3 June and lasted for six weeks until the opera was ready for its premiere on 16 July 1782. On the playbill there is no mention of Stephanie (Figure 1.2).

It was Mozart's intention, as we have seen, to give Osmin an aria in Act II, but he received none. He sings only in the two duets, Nos. 9 and 14. The composer also decided to give Konstanze not only "Traurigkeit" but also its successor, "Martern aller Arten." The latter turned out to be so long and demanding it put all other bravura arias in the shade, including her No. 6 in Act I. It required a new text to serve as provocation for the aria ("motivation" would hardly be correct in this case) for which there is not a hint in Bretzner. Two difficult arias in a row for the same singer was an anomaly in operas of any pretension and Stephanie himself advised against it in the set of rules he proposed in 1792 for writing Singspiel texts.[12] Blonde, who remained on stage during "Traurigkeit," exits after a few words with her mistress and at the sight of the approaching Pasha Selim. When Konstanze rejects his verbal advances, he raises the possibility of forcing her to his will. He goes so far as to end his words with the threat of "Martern von aller Arten" (tortures of all kinds). These key words set off the torrent that follows for full orchestra, which launches into the aria, No. 11, in C as if it were the first movement of a full-fledged sinfonia concertante. After a complete exposition, including a second theme in the tonic, Konstanze begins a second exposition by singing "Martern aller Arten."

Spoken dialogue is at best a poor device to motivate an aria, but an aria of

---

[11] Faye Ferguson, *Kritischer Bericht* to *Die Entführung aus dem Serail*, ed. Gerhard Croll, *NMA* II/5/12 (Kassel, 2002), pp. 34–41.

[12] Bauman, *W. A. Mozart: Die Entführung aus dem Serail*, p. 25.

FIGURE 1.2. Playbill for *Die Entführung aus dem Serail.*

such dimensions and weight as this can only seem incongruous, based on the provocation of a few spoken words. Even the words spoken are likely to be forgotten in the blaze of such a long introduction, sixty measures of *Allegro* in common time. An outburst of this scope deserves at least a dramatic and fiery obbligato recitative to load the charge. Mozart's reasons for writing the aria invite speculation. Possibly, he wanted to anchor the keynote C in our ears midway through the work, just as he did in *Idomeneo* (with a great bravura aria in D for the title role). A sage critic argues that without the aria "Constanze's courage in the final confrontation with death would carry less conviction."[13]

There is also the specific background of Singspiel in Vienna to be considered, and Cavalieri's place within this genre new to the court theater. Ignaz Umlauf's *Die Bergknappen* inaugurated it at the Burgtheater in 1778. Umlauf played first viola in the theater orchestra and was in charge of music for the German troupe's Singspiel wing. Squarely in the middle of his inaugural opera, as the tenth of twenty numbers was a big showpiece for La Cavalieri as heroine—a long coloratura aria in *Allegro moderato*, common time, and in the key of C major—an outburst in which she sang roulades up to high D, exactly as in "Martern." Mozart mentions

[13] David Cairns, *Mozart and His Operas* (Berkeley and Los Angeles, 2006), p. 89.

Umlauf and his music several times in letters to his father, and always with condescension, but Umlauf was nevertheless a serious rival, one who managed to get his successful *Die Irrlicht* (text by Stephanie, adapted from Bretzner) performed ahead of *Die Entführung.* "Martern aller Arten" is a challenge to Umlauf in a kind of duel as to who could best display Cavalieri's "agile throat." The aria remains a challenge to sopranos to this day, as well as a nightmare to stage directors.

Konstanze exits after her great show of *virtù*. At least this rule of traditional opera was followed. The best Selim can muster in response sounds necessarily lame: "Is this a dream? Where did she get the idea to vex me so?"—a remark on a par with the one that had to serve as provocation. He exits.

Blonde enters, followed by Pedrillo, who tells her of Belmonte's arrival and their imminent rescue. He remains while she sings a gleeful aria, No. 13, "Welche Wonne, welche Lust" (What bliss, what joy!), the theme of which Mozart took from the finale of his Oboe Concerto in C (reused in his Flute Concerto in D). This popular, dance-like piece is more like a Lied than an aria and it could furnish no greater contrast to Konstanze's preceding extravaganza. Its folksong style inheres in the repeated tones of the opening and in the simple rhythmic structure of a gay contredanse, *Allegro* in 2/4 time, to which the key of G contributes its popular, Papageno-like verve. After contrasting material, Mozart brings back the first theme, then he embarks on what sounds like a coda in music that also anticipates the giddy *Finale Presto* at the end of the Piano Concerto No. 17 in G, K. 453 (Example 1.4ab). In the aria, Mozart continues on in a leisurely fashion but then made two substantial cuts in order to bring the piece to a speedier end with the return of the initial theme.

EXAMPLE 1.4.

a. *Mozart,* Die Entführung aus dem Serail, *Aria No. 12 (Blonde)*

b. *Mozart, Piano Concerto No. 17, K.453, III*

There is one line of Blonde's second aria that seems to contradict our understanding of her mistress: "Without delay I'll jump and bring the news at once with laughter and jests to her weak and timid heart" (ihrem schwachen, feigen Herzen). How can we believe that Konstanze has a weak and timid heart after

"Martern aller Arten" demonstrates the opposite? Stephanie unwisely chose to repeat the adjective "feiger" in Pedrillo's pseudo-heroic aria, No. 13, in D, "Frisch zum Kampfe! Frisch zum Streite! Nur ein feiger Tropf versagt" (Into the fray! On to the battle! Only a cowardly dolt loses heart). Very few spoken words occur before the orchestra, with trumpets and drums blazing away *forte*, strikes up an *Allegro con spirito* in common time, to introduce the bellicose first theme. The pompous rising triad at the beginning reminds us of its use with truly heroic flair in Konstanze's great aria. Here the military panoply of dotted march rhythm and the treble climbing up to high D are quickly undercut by a soft, indeed timid, continuation. The more Pedrillo tries to gird up his courage in the piece the more the timid phrase takes over; it is even sounded without the words, by the orchestra. The whole aria vacillates between braggadocio and the nagging doubts of this comic servant, whose fears are inherited from such traditional comic characters as Harlequin. The original Pedrillo, Johann Dauer, must have been a fine actor as well as a gifted tenor. Mozart asks him to sing an arpeggio up to high B♮ near the end of this aria.

The spoken dialogue leading up to the drinking duet, No. 14 in C, is truly comic, as Pedrillo cleverly persuades Osmin to imbibe some wine (which has been drugged) despite the strictures of his Muslim faith, which forbids it. Hardly a heroic action this! "Vivat Bacchus! Bacchus lebe! Bacchus war ein braver Man!" is a triumph of both text (Bretzner's) and music, one of the opera's immediately successful pieces. The *Allegro* in 2/4 time begins softly as the piccolo, two flutes, and first violins introduce the saucy main theme. Eventually the full complement of the *alla Turca* band will join in this romp, so that the intoxication overcoming Osmin seems to be growing with the orchestral tumult. Osmin becomes inarticulate. Pedrillo helps him into his house and returns to meet Belmonte. Konstanze appears and the lovers embrace. Pedrillo warns them to be brief because of the danger they are all in. Anyone familiar with opera seria lovers like this pair knew that brevity was out of the question. Their love had to be expressed at length and with appropriately sentimental music. It comes in the form of an aria in B♭ for Belmonte that begins with an *Adagio* in cut time. The orchestra, including clarinets in B♭, intones an eight-measure phrase of the *gavotte tendre* type, with two staccato upbeats. Eight measures are stretched to nine when the winds echo the cadence in the strings. Stephanie concocted a text based on one line from Bretzner and this may well be another case where Mozart gave him the melody first. The opening quatrain sounds almost Wagnerian in its alliteration.

Wenn der Freude Tränen Fliessen,	When tears flow from joy
lächelt Liebe dem Geliebten hold!	Love smiles on the kind lover!
Von den Wangen sie zu küssen	To kiss them from her cheeks
ist der Liebe schönster, grösster Sold.	Is Love's sweetest, greatest reward.

At this slow tempo, Belmonte has ample time to mime this very action. Mozart took great trouble in polishing the piece, as can be seen from the autograph's corrections. Adamberger's rendition of it pleased the public so from the very first performances that it too had to be repeated, according to Mozart's letter of 20 July 1782, where he refers to it as "Belmonte's rondeau."

No. 15 is indeed a fine example of the two-tempo rondò then so fashionable in opera, which typically required octosyllabic quatrains as here. The first was very often set to a slow gavotte theme with a repeated initial tone as it is in this melody (for another example, see the Romance of *Eine kleine Nachtmusik*, K. 525). After repetition of the slow theme following a contrast (second quatrain), there was eventually a faster part (third quatrain), here an *Allegretto* in 3/4 time. This theme sounds like a free variation of the slow one, which is also typical of the form. Its chromatic descent into the word "Schmerz" (pain) corresponds to the chromatic descent in the *Adagio* to depict tears trickling down. Mozart wrote the aria on the long side and then made cuts. The little postlude of the jubilant orchestra anticipates the longer orchestral outpouring to close the sentimental tenor aria in *Così fan tutte* (No. 17). Belmonte's vocal coda, on the other hand, corresponds closely to its equivalent in the love duet of *Idomeneo* (No. 23a).

The ending of Act II required major surgery from Stephanie. Mozart demanded and got an elaborate finale such as had matured in opera buffa by Italian poets and composers, a genre adroitly employed by Mozart himself in *La finta giardiniera* for Munich in 1775. A finale of this type required a little plot of its own and a succession of various poetic meters delimiting each section, set to music accordingly. Stephanie obliged with a fine example of the genre by elaborating on the squabble into which the men got with their lovers, only hinted at in a few lines from Bretzner. It allowed Mozart to pass by stages from serene confidence and celebration at their reunion, to doubts plaguing the men, female solidarity against them, pleas for forgiveness from the men, gradual granting of it to them, then a return to the initial theme of serene confidence, along with a return to the initial key of D. Once can easily hear in this dazzling sequence of pieces a foretaste of the still greater buffo finales to come, beginning with those in *Le nozze di Figaro*.

And yet, the whole finale of Act II marks nothing but a big pause in the dramatic action, making a mockery of Pedrillo's urgings of haste. It represents the triumph of musical needs over those of the drama and one must enter into a state of suspended disbelief—call it Operaland—to accept this glorious music on its own terms and forget about the urgency and danger of the lovers' situation. The finale does help to delineate character still further, particularly of the two women. Konstanze reacts to Belmonte's doubts by a fit of weeping, Blonde to Pedrillo's by boxing his ears. When the men ask forgiveness in an *Allegretto* in cut time and in the key of A, the return to the initial D tonic seems near, but

Blonde complicates the texture by adopting her own 12/8 meter running along simultaneously and refusing to accept apologies, another very effective means of expressing her independence.[14]

Act III gets to the core of the story: the attempted abduction, its failure, and aftermath. But it does not get there directly. Adamberger as Belmonte had to be served with another aria first. He sang coloratura as well as Cavalieri did, was nearly twice her age, and outranked her in salary by nearly two to one. It was his right to have parity with her in the matter of arias. No place for the aria that was his due could be found except at the beginning of the last act. But what could possibly motivate an aria in this place? Very little, it turns out. Pedrillo again urges speed and at the same time tells Belmonte to sing a song, as he himself was accustomed to do at midnight so that the Janissary guards would think all was normal. Meanwhile he would scout the palace. As motivation, this is at about the same level as the spoken dialogue before Konstanze's big bravura aria at the opera's center.

Belmonte is anxious and fearful. He puts all his hope and trust in the power of love. Ergo Mozart gave him another *aria d'affetto* about love, with coloratura extensions. It is a leisurely *Andante* in cut time and in the potent key of E♭, with clarinets in B♭. The piece is strangely lacking in Mozart's usual melodic charm and inspiration although it must be granted that the wind writing is beautiful. Its plodding bass has a strangely old-fashioned ring to it, so much so that it sounds like a throwback to a much earlier Mozart. Just as the transition to the second key begins, there is a melodic outburst that foretells Tamino's "Picture Aria" in *Die Zauberflöte* (another piece in E♭). Yet this fine moment is followed immediately by the infelicity of a doubled A♮ leading tone in the outer voice parts, the bass having resumed its plodding motion (the temptation is strong to speed this moment up by combining mm. 37–38 into a single measure).

Belmonte's No. 17 is often omitted in modern performances. It should be if the lead tenor cannot match Adamberger's technical prowess, demonstrated by the elaborate passagework Mozart gives him. Without the aria, on the other hand, the third act would be too short—it has only five numbers as opposed to seven in Act I and nine in Act II. Act III without No. 17 would also be at a disadvantage by having to begin with a number as slight as Pedrillo's strophic Romance. In tonal terms, it could be argued that E♭, one of the three universal keys like C and D, needs to make another appearance in the opera, not the flighty E♭ of the comic duet No. 9, but the serious E♭ that begins Konstanze's No. 10 and is prominent in the overture's middle section. Mozart may have also welcomed the third relationship between E♭ and the opera's final destination of C. A good substitute

---

[14] Simultaneous conflicting meters were especially characteristic of opéra comique from Philidor to Grétry, a repertory Mozart knew well. See *Music in European Capitals*, pp. 746–52.

for Belmonte's aria, if necessary, would be the Romance in E♭ from the Serenade for thirteen winds, K. 361, which could be played with the curtain down, or with a representation of dusk becoming deep, starry night. The opera needs an intermezzo here as much as it needs E♭.

Pedrillo's Romance, No. 18, has Bretzner to thank for a fine poem, "In Mohrenland gefangen war ein Mädel hübsch und fein" (A fine fair maiden was imprisoned in Moorish lands). It belongs to a specific type of Romance that had begun in opéra comique (and was copied in Singspiels), one that encapsulated an entire plot in the guise of an archaic strophic poem sung on stage as conscious song.[15] Johann André had made little of this piece, setting it in his usual nondescript tonal and melodic style. Mozart, who had witnessed the flowering of opéra comique in Paris from his visits there in the early 1760s and in 1778, was infinitely more resourceful. But he would not necessarily have had to visit Paris to know and prize opéra comique, for it had spread all over Europe before 1780. He always used the French spelling "Romance," and not Bretzner's German equivalent, "Romanze," even in his many instrumental examples of the genre. For Pedrillo he invented a simple modal song that vacillates between major and minor, capturing some of the flavor of exotic Eastern climes; the orchestra imitates the sound of the mandolin with which Pedrillo mimics accompanying himself, by using only plucked strings. The 6/8 meter and singsong nature of the melody, with several repeated tones, have an almost hypnotic effect and belie the sophistication of the unusual turns taken by the harmony. In his last verse, Pedrillo switches from tale-telling to the dramatic situation at hand, by asking the ladies to open their windows. The result is a thrilling, highly theatrical moment that should have audiences on the edge of their seats.

Belmonte descends the ladder with Konstanze. They resume their billings and cooings. Pedrillo cautions them one last time: "Be quick! No gabbing! Else with sighs and long consultations we'll be caught." The watch apprehends both couples in the act of fleeing, which affords Osmin his moment of triumph. The couples are taken away under guard, leaving the stage to Osmin for his aria "O, wie will ich triumphieren," *Allegro vivace* in D and in 2/4 time. Mozart again makes the most of Fischer's vocal range of over two octaves. Majestic D major here has none of the trepidation and holding back of Pedrillo's pseudo-heroic aria No. 13 in the same key. There are also some Turkish touches, abetted by the piccolo on high, such as the streams of sixteenth notes and the repeated appoggiatura G♯ - A emphasizing the tritone. At one point Fischer must sustain his low

[15] An early example of the type is the Romance "Il etoit une fille" in *Annette et Lubin* (1762), attributed to Madame Favart. Its pretensions to antiquity reside in a monotonous accompaniment and modal turns of phrase. See David Charlton, "The Romance and Its Cognates: Narrative, Irony and 'Vraisemblance' in Early Opéra-Comique," in *Die Opéra comique und ihr Einfluss auf das europäische Musiktheater im 19. Jahrhundert*, ed. Herbert Schneider and Nicole Wild (Hildesheim, 1997): 43–92; 76–78. The article is reprinted in facsimile in David Charlton, *French Opera 1730–1830: Meaning and Media* (Aldershot, 2000), item 1.

D for a full eight measures. Out of this splendid piece Mozart took ideas for his "Haffner" Symphony, No. 35 in D, K. 385 (see Example 1.5ab).

The scene changes to a room in Selim's palace. Osmin ushers the noble lovers into the presence of the Pasha. Only at this point do we learn the full identity of Don Belmonte Lostados, scion of an ancient Spanish family and son of the commandant of Oran. Stephanie departs from Bretzner here by making him the only son of Selim's greatest enemy, the person who robbed Selim of everything worth living for. "What," Selim asks, "would your father have done were he in my place?" Abjectly, Belmonte admits that his fate would be lamentable. Selim leaves and bids Osmin follow him, saying he will give orders as to torturing the captives. This sets up the magnificent obbligato recitative and duet for the lovers, No. 20, once again a penultimate piece in B♭.

Idomeneo looms large in this sublime moment, with death threatening both lovers. The strings begin with an *Adagio* in common time and in F, with a bass moving chromatically beneath little outbursts in the first violins and syncopated accompaniment in the seconds and violas. Belmonte enters first, expresses his anguish, and takes all blame on himself, pushing the key to the sharp side, punctuated by diminished-seventh-chord interjections, *forte*. Konstanze enters calmly over a deceptive cadence and says that death is but a transition to eternal rest. The harmony pushes back to the flat side, settling on a cadence in E♭ at her last word (just as it did to paint the word "morte" in the elaborate orchestral recitative with which Ilia begins *Idomeneo*). The strings conclude their discourse by reverting to their opening music and tonally preparing the arrival of the duet proper, which begins with an *Andante* in B♭ and in 3/4 time.

Belmonte commences the duet with a leap of a descending sixth in dotted rhythm from F to A recovered by half-step up to B♭ for the arrival of the tonic (note for note the same as Idamante's "Non ho colpa" beginning his first aria, No. 2, in *Idomeneo*). There is a resonance with a later opera as Belmonte leads the music quickly to the dominant, F, while holding an F pedal against the tremolo upper strings and the bass moving up by step into the cadence, namely the moment in the Trial by Fire and Water of *Die Zauberflöte* when Tamino defies the gates of death (mm. 243–47 of the second finale). Belmonte, in despair, sings the words "Ich bereite dir den Tod!" (I brought you to death's door!). Konstanze turns F into f at her entrance, blaming herself for drawing Belmonte into a death-trap. She then elaborates on the passage so predictive of Tamino's. The music returns to F and the lovers first sing together in response to a wind passage in thirds reminiscent of the second theme of Konstanze's No. 11. The *Andante* proceeds with brief imitations between tenor and soprano. After the wind theme returns, the *Andante* comes to a halt on F as V^7 of B♭.[16]

---

[16] For a discussion of the duet's unusual formal construction, with several musical examples, see Bauman, "Coming of Age," 79–86.

An *Allegro* in common time comprises the second big section of the duet and the return to B♭. Its jaunty theme is related to the woodwind theme in Konstanze's "Traurigkeit," No. 10. The lovers embrace the idea of dying for and with each other. Everything portends a happy love-death. Toward the end, they exchange long-held tones, a climactic device traditional in Italian love duets, including Mozart's. All told, the piece extends to an ample 208 measures and is preceded by the opera's longest recitative.

Selim reappears. Belmonte says, "Take your revenge, I expect the worst and blame you not." The Pasha counters, "Your people must indulge in many injustices since you take them so much for granted. You deceive yourself. I detest your father too much to follow in his footsteps. Take your freedom. Take Konstanze. Sail home." Stephanie thus adopted as a solution the magnanimous Turk topos, one of the trademarks of European dramas of an enlightened stripe, and particularly identified with Voltaire. It makes a much better ending than Bretzner's trite one of having Selim recognize in Belmonte his long-lost son.

To sing the praises of such magnanimity the opera's creators dipped again into the reservoir of opéra comique and brought forth a vaudeville with verses for each singer and a refrain sung by all. It moves along at a pleasant walking gait in the key of F, *Andante* in cut time. Blonde, once again, goes her own way by departing from the praises of Selim in order to berate Osmin, who then overlaps her cadence and cancels the refrain by his still greater departure, in which he excoriates the freed couples and drops from the vaudeville tune halfway through it. He then relapses into the key of a and returns to the angry concluding section of his first aria, No. 3. He storms out. The four Europeans, stunned at first, return the key to F while singing the moral maxim: "Nothing is so hateful as revenge" (anticipating the many sung morals in *Die Zauberflöte*). They end by returning one more time to the vaudeville's refrain, initiated by Konstanze, and joined by the others for an enhanced repetition of the final measures. Without a pause, Turkish music in C bursts forth just as they sing their last word. The vaudeville in F thus serves to provide the opera's end with an enormous plagal cadence. The Janissary chorus sings the praises of their *bassa* (pasha) and wish him a long life while extending "lange" (long) to four full measures of *Allegro vivace* in 2/4 time (see Example 1.6a).

It has been a remarkably coherent tonal arc from the overture in C to this final chorus, achieved in spite of the limitations imposed on the genre by spoken dialogue. One comes away with the impression of the garish Turkish music in C interacting continuously with the softer and suaver love music, mostly in B♭. The break in composition of several months is most evident in Act II, where the previously composed pieces in A and C were followed by pieces in E♭ and D.

No doubt, Mozart would have preferred to write an Italian opera. He said as much in his letter to his father of 4 February 1778. In Vienna during the early 1780s, he had no choice but German Singspiel if he wished to write for the

National Theater, which he most emphatically did. Yet too much has been made of this opera's disunities of style.[17] Not enough credit is given to the steps Mozart took to overcome the disparate French, German, and Italian layers of style and impress his personality on the whole. He turned the public's liking for simple, tuneful ditties to superb account and created complex, unforgettable characters in the persons of Blonde, Osmin, and Pedrillo. But his heart was as much or even more involved in creating his noble lovers, Belmonte and Konstanze. It could scarcely have been otherwise. He was still steeped in the shattering experience of *Idomeneo*, and as he was creating the new opera became involved in his own romantic crisis (with Constanze Weber).

Die Entführung quickly won performances elsewhere throughout German-speaking Europe. Scarcely a city or court that cultivated Singspiel failed to produce the opera. Arrangements of its music reached still wider audiences. More than any other work during the 1780s, it was the one that introduced music lovers to Mozart.

Dramaturgical Concerns

The letters Mozart wrote to his father between 1780 and 1782 concerning the creation of *Idomeneo* and *Die Entführung* are so extensive and detailed that they come close to being a treatise on opera, although this was not their intent. With the earlier opera, Leopold was a go-between who communicated his son's wishes and demands to the librettist, Abbé Gianbattista Varesco of Salzburg Cathedral. Leopold had no such active role in the second opera, but its long genesis, stretching to nearly a year, meant that there was time for Mozart to describe the many changes in the libretto upon which he insisted, and to describe some of the music in detail, as well as the opera's reception at the first performances.

An ultimate lesson from the overly long opera for Munich, which underwent drastic cuts during the final rehearsal, is summed up in Mozart's resigned quotation of a simple adage: "One must make a virtue of necessity" (man muss aus der Noth eine Tugend machen) in his letter of 18 January 1781. Earlier, in a letter of 29 November 1780, he denounced Varesco's long-winded speech for Neptune's Oracle in Act III. "Imagine the theater before your eyes. The Voice must be terrifying and it must penetrate. People must believe that it is real [man muss glauben es sey wirklich so]. How can this work if the speech is too long? . . . If the Ghost's speech in Hamlet were not so long it would be more effective." Unlike

---

[17] Edward J. Dent believed that Mozart was given too free a hand in restructuring the libretto. "The result was an opera which is a succession of masterly and original numbers, but taken as a whole has no unity of style." *Mozart's Operas: A Critical Study*, 2nd ed. (London, 1947), p. 73.

many composers, Mozart constantly envisioned the look of the stage action and its effect on his audience. He strove for the illusion of representing things as they really were. Does that make him a realist in the modern sense? Perhaps. In any case, timing was of the essence for him and was not separable from the visual aspect.

In his letter of 16 June 1781, Mozart made a remark about the importance of the libretto to the success of his promised opera for the Burgtheater: "About difficulties I worry not at all provided that the text is good" (wegen incontrieren sorge ich gar nicht, wenn nur das Buch gut ist). Three days earlier on 13 June, Mozart wrote that Count Rosenberg had commissioned the renowned actor and playwright Friedrich Ludwig Schröder to search out an appropriate libretto that Mozart could set to music. A libretto was soon found, one in four acts that Stephanie rejected because he doubted it would please the count. No more was heard of this libretto and it has never been identified. Mozart, the seasoned dramatist, refused even to look at it. The experience of *Zaide* had taught him not to spend his efforts on something before it had won official approval. He faced this situation again in 1785 when Anton Klein of Mannheim sent him a German play on Emperor Rudolf von Hapsburg for consideration.

At the end of July 1781, Stephanie brought Mozart the libretto of Bretzner's *Belmont und Constanze*. "The libretto is very good," reported Mozart to his father on 1 August, "and the subject is Turkish . . . I am going to clothe the overture, the first-act chorus, and the final chorus with Turkish music."[18] Mozart then relayed the names of the singers who would be cast and that of the actor who would take the speaking role of Selim. He was afire with enthusiasm to compose the work. In two days, he finished two arias and the trio in Act I (this does not necessarily mean written down, much less orchestrated). On 8 August, Mozart reported that Adamberger, Cavalieri, and Fischer were satisfied with their arias and that he had just finished the Janissary chorus (all these in Act I). He played the pieces for Countess Thun, who said she would wager her life on their ultimate success, "but I do not accept praise or criticism from anyone in this matter, not until people have heard and seen everything in its entirety; as of now I am simply following my feelings." The test of an opera according to this statement is seeing as well as hearing it as a whole. This sounds like a simple enough proposition, but it is one that had perhaps never been articulated before. And how was Mozart working toward that goal while proceeding piece by piece? By trusting his intuition as to how it would all cohere. It worked well for him in Act I, less well in the other two acts.

On 12 September, Mozart reported that any hopes for staging an opera of

---

[18] By Turkish music, Mozart meant the complement of piccolo, triangle, cymbals, and bass drum found in Viennese military bands, from which the extra performers had to be hired.

his for the visit of the Russians were dashed, because the singers had to learn two serious operas by Gluck, *Iphigénie in Tauride* in a new German translation by Johann Baptist von Alxinger, and *Alceste* in the original Italian. The opera he hoped they would sing, according to this letter, was not *Die Entführung* but *Idomeneo*, which he would gladly have put in the hands of Alxinger for a German translation, while at the same time revising it so as to accommodate a bass (Fischer) in the title role and making other changes: "The man who translated *Iphigénie* is a superb poet."[19] From this remark, it is again apparent how much importance Mozart attached to the quality of a libretto.

On 19 September, Mozart wrote his sister Nannerl in Salzburg, "You know that I am composing an opera here. What has been written so far has won extraordinary approval, for I know this place, and hope it will come out well, and if it succeeds then I shall be loved here as much for opera as for keyboard music." In his two letters of 26 September and 13 October to his father, he explained how massive changes were being made in the libretto at his request. He made small changes in the wording as well, for instance in Konstanze's first aria, from Bretzner's "Doch wie hui schwand meine Freude" to "Doch wie schnell . . ." (How quickly my joy vanished). "I do not really know what our German poets are thinking of; if they understand nothing about the theater, particularly opera, at least they should not make people talk as if they were herding swine—hui Sau." Unlike the Leipzig businessman Bretzner, Stephanie was a man of the theater through and through, for which Mozart gave him credit. As an actor and as a playwright he was very experienced. His ability as a poet is another matter.

Leopold's answers to Mozart's letters from this particular time are missing, but their content can often be deduced from his son's replies. The revised text of Act I, as well as samples of its music, was in Leopold's hands by September, and he must have complained about some of Stephanie's verses for Osmin, as Mozart's letter of 13 October shows.

> Now to the text of the opera. As for Stephanie's work, you are quite right. Yet the verse is altogether matched to the character of Osmin, who is stupid, coarse, and malicious. I know well that the verse used here is not of the best kind, but it agrees so completely with the musical ideas in my head, even before I had seen the text, that it necessarily pleased me. And I am willing to bet that when it is performed, nothing will be found lacking.

In other words, for a libretto to be good, it did not require the highest class of poetry, but rather, it needed poetry that was easily wedded to music, or in this case born out of preexistent music. This is not the first or last time that Mozart

---

[19] *Haydn, Mozart*, p. 715.

admitted to arriving at his musical ideas of how a piece should go before a precise text was at hand. He had done something similar to prompt the revised text of Ilia's concertante aria in Act II of *Idomeneo.*

Mozart's letter of 13 October 1781 went on to make a few favorable comments on Bretzner's libretto. "As far as the poetry of the original play is concerned, I cannot say anything against it. Belmonte's aria 'O wie ängstlich' could almost not have been written any better for the music. The aria for Konstanze is not bad either, especially the first part, except for the *hui* and *Kummer ruht in meinem schoos* [sorrow rests in my lap], for sorrow cannot rest." In the end, Mozart let this line pass. What comes next is an oft-quoted passage, mostly cited in isolation from its context. "I am not certain, but it seems to me that in opera the poetry must always be the obedient daughter of the music. Why do Italian comic operas please everywhere? This in spite of their defective texts. Even in Paris they have success, as I witnessed myself." The reference is to the season of opera buffa put on at the Paris Opéra under the direction of Niccolò Piccinni in 1778 when several of the best Italian composers were represented: Paisiello, Sacchini, Traetta, and Piccinni himself.[20] Not all their librettos were as defective as Mozart says, yet he decried this Italian company (which included the fine tenor Giacomo Caribaldi) as a "wretched comic opera" (miserable opera buffa) in his letter to his father dated Paris, 11 September 1778. Back then, he was inclined to denounce Italian comedies as a way of annoying his host, Melchior Grimm, who was staunchly pro-Piccinni. Three years later he admits that opera buffa of the Italians was always successful, even in Paris, despite the poor texts, and asks why. He answers his own question: "Because music reigns supreme in them, which makes one forget everything else."

The value of rhymes in poetry for opera is Mozart's next consideration in the letter. "An opera must please all the more if the plan of its story is well worked out, words written suitable for music, rather than to attain some miserable rhyme here or there." At this point, he begins to seethe with irritation on the subject. "Rhymes, by God, contribute nothing, whatever they are worth, to the success of a theatrical performance; rather, they can work to its detriment, words, I mean, or whole stanzas that spoil the composer's entire concept" (die des komponisten seine ganze idèe verderben). Whether opera texts look like good poetry on the printed page is beside the point when it comes to performance in the theater, says Mozart. His notion of the composer's idea taking precedence over text is nothing short of breathtaking.

That the composer had an overall concept of the work to which the poet was subordinate went against all operatic aesthetics since the beginning of the genre. While it is true that some strong musical dramatists before Mozart had made poets do their bidding, rarely had any composer claimed as much in a

---

[20] *Music in European Capitals,* pp. 851–52.

statement. Even Gluck allowed his poet Calzabigi to take the credit for overall conceptions, whether it was true or not.[21] Mozart finished off this remarkable passage by retreating somewhat from such a radical idea. "Verses are probably the most indispensable element for music, but rhymes solely for the sake of creating rhymes are the most detrimental. Those gentlemen who work in such a pedantic fashion will always fail, together with their music."

To crown his bold ideas Mozart described what he imagined to be an ideal collaboration.

> The best thing of all is when a good composer, who understands the stage and is savvy enough to make suggestions, meets an able poet, that true phoenix. Then one need not fear the response even of the uninitiated. Poets almost always remind me of the trumpeters with their professional tricks [Possen]. If we composers were always so bound by our own rules (which were good at a time when no one knew any better), it follows that we would create music as worthless as their librettos.

At this point Mozart dismisses his whole discussion as nothing more than idle chatter, which shows us how much he valued theorizing. Why did he invoke trumpeters? They belonged to guilds of long standing that strictly regulated their number and where, even what, they could perform. They were thus representative of the old rules of a time when no one knew any better. He could also have had in mind the legerdemain by which performers made the impossible seem possible on natural instruments.

Mention of rules by an eighteenth-century composer, and especially of rules that were good for an earlier and less knowledgeable time, also suggests the dichotomy then prevalent between the strict or learned style and the more modern galant style.[22] In the former, rules dictated how dissonances were prepared, suspended, and resolved. The latter gave dissonances more freedom and allowed them to behave more or less as the composer pleased. Mozart took advantage of free dissonance treatment in most of his music. He even took unusual liberties when writing in the strict style, a good example of which is the Fugue for two pianos in c minor, K. 426.

A phoenix Stephanie certainly was not, and Abbé Varesco even less so. *Die Entführung* might have been a stronger, tighter drama had Stephanie stood his ground and followed his own precepts, such as not allowing two arias in a row to the same singer (long and difficult arias in this case). Mozart was too indulgent to his singers but he saw this as the way to captivate the Viennese public on

---

[21] *Haydn, Mozart*, pp. 229–30. Daniel Heartz, "Gluck's *Iphigénie en Aulide*: A Prolegomenon," in *Words on Music: Essays in Honor of Andrew Porter on the Occasion of His 75th Birthday*, ed. David Rosen and Claire Brook (Hillsdale, NY, 2003): 138–51; 145.

[22] *Music in European Capitals*, pp. 19–20, 103, 252, 1005.

the first try. With a little more effort and imagination, Stephanie might have contrived a credible motivation for Belmonte to sing a bravura aria late in the opera. He could at least have suppressed some of Pedrillo's warning to make haste.

Die Entführung was performed for the fourteenth and last time on 10 December 1782, always to full houses and to great acclaim, according to Mozart's letter to his father of 21 December. "Count Rosenberg spoke to me in person at [Prince] Gallizin's and said I really ought to write an Italian opera" (Graf Rosenberg hat mich beym Gallizin selbst angeredt, ich möchte doch eine welsche opera schreiben). This suggestion has been wrongly interpreted as a request or even as a commission to write an Italian opera. "I have already placed orders for the latest librettos of opera buffa from Italy so that I can make a choice but none have yet arrived . . . at Easter a number of Italian male and female singers are arriving here." The remainder of this letter is devoted to a withering critique of one of the Singspiel troupe's last premieres, which says still more about the importance of a good text to an opera's success.

> A new opera or rather a comedy with ariettes by Umlauf was recently produced, entitled *Welch ist die beste Nation?* It is a worthless piece that I was asked to set and I refused, saying whoever composes this without having the text completely revised risked being whistled out of the theater. And had it not been Umlauf this would have happened. It is no wonder, for even with the finest music one would barely be able to stand it. But the music was so poor in this case, that I am uncertain who wins the booby prize, the poet or the composer. To its disgrace it was given a second time, but I believe this will be the *Punctum Satis.*

There was indeed no third performance.[23]

In his letter to Leopold of 5 February 1783, Mozart was not hopeful about the future of opera in German on the stage of the Burgtheater. He derided the poor specimens of it then in production, composed by the long-deceased Florian Gassmann, Johann Mederitsch, and Umlauf.

> It really seems as if they wished to kill off prematurely the German opera, which in any case shall end after Easter; and Germans themselves are doing this—shame upon them! . . . I do not believe that the Italian opera will keep going for long, and besides, I hold with the Germans. I prefer German opera even though it means more trouble for me. Every nation has its own opera, and why not Germany? Is not German as singable as French or English? And more so than Russian?

German opera was more trouble for Mozart partly because good poets were scarce and the norms of the genre were just being established, whereas opera in

---

[23] For a *Spielplan* of the Burgtheater from December 1782 to March 1783, see Otto Michtner, *Das alte Burgtheater als Opernbühne* (Vienna, 1970), pp. 472–73.

Italian had behind it several generations of verbal and musical experience. The situation makes one wish that Mozart could have collaborated with Alxinger, the German poet he so admired. As it was he had no better plan for his next German opera than to have a certain Baron Binder translate for him Goldoni's play *Il servitore di due padroni*.

Joseph II bowed to the wishes of the Viennese public and restored opera buffa to the Burgtheater in early 1783. Singspiel was eliminated but spoken plays in German, representing the core of his National Theater, continued as before. Mozart remained an outsider with no court appointment. His strongest credit with the theater direction was having written a successful Singspiel, which now seemed beside the point. After he had finally managed to get a foot inside the door of the Burgtheater, that door was closed and the lock changed. He had no recent successes in opera buffa to offer the new Italian company. Once he experienced how good the troupe was he gave up his plan to compose another German opera and set about trying to get an Italian libretto. In an engraving of 1783, Carl Schütz conveys the Italian troupe's allure by depicting a couple who consult the billboard on the Burgtheater's facade (Figure 1.3).

Antonio Salieri was still in imperial service and took over the direction of the Italian opera. The return to opera buffa could only benefit him as a composer, since he had several successes in the genre, even in Italy. He chose, not surprisingly, to inaugurate the new company with one of his greatest successes, *La scuola de' gelosi* on a libretto by Caterino Mazzolà, first performed at Venice in 1778 and revived many times there and elsewhere. The choice could also be seen as a compliment to the new prima donna, Nancy Storace, who had sung the seria role of the Countess in this opera during the previous season in Venice and now repeated it in Vienna, her role enhanced by a fine two-tempo rondò crafted in the latest fashion by Vienna's new poet for the Italian theater, Lorenzo da Ponte, and beautifully set to music by Salieri.[24]

La scuola de' gelosi established the tone for what followed, and Mozart took careful note of its ingredients. Besides Storace, whose Countess was plagued by a philandering Count of a husband, played by the Francesco Bussani, the main new singer was the bass Francesco Benucci, who sang the principal male role of Blasio, the bourgeois grain dealer with a flirtatious wife, Ernestina, sung by La Cavalieri. Other German singers added to the Italian troupe besides Cavalieri included Adamberger and Teyber. The remaining roles in Salieri's opera were the chambermaid Carlotte (Teyber), her swain Lunacca, sung by Michael Kelly, and the Lieutenant, sung by the tenor Pugnetti, who makes all things end happily by having the afflicted spouses cause a little jealousy themselves. In all, there were seven roles, four male and three female, ranging from seria and *mezzo carattere* to buffa.

---

[24] John A. Rice, *Antonio Salieri and Viennese Opera* (Chicago, 1998), pp. 357–59.

FIGURE 1.3. Detail from Carl Schütz, "The Michaelerplatz" (1783).

The Easter season opened to critical acclaim on 22 April 1783. Performances of *La scuola* followed on 25 and 28 April, along with many others over the next three years. Count Karl Zinzendorf, who kept a diary with frequent mentions of his theater-going and musical experiences, attended the premiere. His account of that memorable evening in the Burgtheater when the new buffo troupe made its debut is invaluable.

22. Avril: Au Théatre dans la loge de M^es de fekete et de Los Rios. *La scuola de' gelosi.* Melle *Storace*, l'Inglesina, jolie figure voluptueuse, belle gorge, bien en Bohemienne, elle et Bussani chanterant ce duo: Quel visino è da ritratto, mais B. moins bien que

Calvesi a Trieste. Le Buffo *Venucci* [Benucci] tres bon, le primo amoroso *Bussani* moins. L'auditoire fort content.[25]

Zinzendorf typically joined aristocratic friends in their boxes at the theater. These were often women—he was very much a ladies' man, as can be told right away from his description of the "Little Englishwoman," La Storace. Sometimes he mentions individual pieces, as here, and refers to singers he has heard elsewhere, in this case the tenor Vincenzo Calvesi, the future Ferrando in Mozart's *Così fan tutte.* Not infrequent is some remark on how the audience responded to the show. On this occasion, they were "well contented." At a subsequent performance of *La scuola* on 5 May Zinzendorf remarked, "L'Inglesina chanta comme un ange, le buffo [Benucci] est admirable."

A second production of the new troupe in the Burgtheater followed on 6 May 1783: Cimarosa's *L'italiana a Londra* of 1779 on a text by Giuseppe Petrosellini, an intermezzo *a 5* in which Storace and Benucci again won the praises of Zinzendorf. It was not this smaller work with a cast of five that set Mozart searching for a similar libretto, but Salieri's *La scuola*, with its cast of seven. He wrote Leopold at length about the new troupe and his ambitions on 7 May, without mentioning *La scuola* by name.

> The Italian opera buffa has now begun again here, and it pleases greatly. The buffo, whose name is Benucci, is especially good. I have myself looked through easily a hundred Italian librettos, or even more, but have found scarcely one that could satisfy me. To suit me they would have to be substantially altered, and if a poet were willing to do that much, the easier task might be to write an entirely new libretto, which is always preferable anyway.

He was not destined to receive many entirely new librettos even during his last decade, but we know from this statement that he rated original texts higher than derived ones. Originality in all respects formed a part of his operatic creed.

Mozart first mentioned the poet who was to become his phoenix in the following sentences of the same letter.

> We now have here a certain Abbé Da Ponte as poet. He has an enormous amount to do in revising librettos and must also *per obligo* write an entirely new one for Salieri, which will take him two months to finish. After this, he has promised to write a new

---

[25] Dorothea Link, *The National Court Theatre in Mozart's Vienna: Sources and Documents, 1783–1792* (Oxford, 1998), p. 204. To the diary entries for these years, Link adds a performance calendar of the National Court Theater and archival payment records. The diary will be cited here only by the name Zinzendorf and the date.

one for me. Who knows if he will keep his word, or even wish to? You well know how civil the Italians are face-to-face. Enough said. We know them. If he has come to an understanding with Salieri, I shall receive nothing from him as long as I live, and I would love so much to show what I can do in an Italian opera!

The remark about two-faced Italians seems ungracious after all the kindnesses shown the Mozarts in Italy, but we should recall that Mozart was still trying to humor his father into accepting the marriage to Constanze. The remark about Italians may even refer to events as remote as Leopold's bitter experience with his son's *La finta semplice* at the Burgtheater in 1768. As to Da Ponte's collaboration with Salieri, Mozart's comment appears little short of paranoia. What he regarded as collusion was only normal. If the theater's new Italian poet did not work together with the troupe's music director he would not last long in his post.

The point toward which this surprising letter of 7 May 1783 was driving comes next: a tentative suggestion to sound out Abbé Varesco on the subject of writing a comic libretto. Could Mozart have been so disheartened about his status as an outsider that he seriously considered a comic libretto by Varesco? He knew very well that the learned Abbé lacked all experience for the task, and perhaps had never even witnessed an opera buffa. Yet he apparently saw no other recourse.

> Consequently, I wonder if Varesco, supposing he is not still angry with us about the Munich opera [*Idomeneo*] might write me a new libretto with seven roles. You will know best if this is possible. He could start writing now and we could work together when I come to Salzburg. The most important thing about it is that the whole be truly comic. It should include if possible two equally good female roles. One would have to be seria, the other *mezzo carattere*, but in quality both these roles should be absolutely equal. The third role can be entirely buffa, and so could all the male roles if need be.

He has described the seven-role disposition of *La scuola* by Mazzolà and Salieri. His insistence on equality for the second female role has to do with Cavalieri, who would, he assumed, continue in this capacity with the new Italian company. Certainly, he had done his utmost for her in *Die Entführung*. He remained a champion of the German singers who were transferred from Singspiel, to the point of writing substitute Italian arias for them, as described in his letters of 21 June and 2 July 1783.

In his letters to his father, Mozart kept alive the issue of using Varesco, without making any commitment. On 21 May he wrote, "Please pursue the matter of a libretto with Varesco. The main thing is that it has to be comical, for I well know the taste of the Viennese." In one of his lost letters, Leopold communicated an idea from Varesco for a comic opera. Mozart replied in his letter of 21 June 1783 with a favorable first impression, along with comments that reflect poorly on his judgment and even on his ethics.

> Now about Varesco. His plan pleases me very well. I must speak with Count Rosenberg at once to guarantee there will be payment to the poet, but I find it quite insulting that Varesco doubts whether the opera will be well received. I can assure him that his libretto will not please if the music is not good. Because music is the main thing in every opera, and if he hopes for success and a good reward, he must let me alter things and reshape the libretto as much and as often as I wish, not merely following his ideas, for he has not the slightest experience and knowledge of the stage. You can let him know that it matters little whether he wants to write the opera or not. I know the story now, consequently anyone could write it for me as well as he could. And besides, I am expecting four of the newest and best librettos from Italy. Surely, there must be one I can use.

The glib use of Rosenberg's name implies that Mozart had already been commissioned to compose an opera for the new company. Were this true, Da Ponte would have obliged him much sooner. The expected librettos from Italy were perhaps only a feint intended to goad Varesco into action. Treating Varesco and his story as crassly as Mozart suggests is disheartening, to say the least. Whatever the merits of the Abbé, he was a classical scholar and fluent versifier in Italian, one who had served the Mozarts to the best of his abilities in *Idomeneo*. "Music is the main thing in every opera" only restates in simpler terms Mozart's credo expressed in the key statement of 13 October 1781.

L'oca del Cairo (The goose of Cairo) is the opera Varesco proposed and sketched, but apparently not to the end. Mozart began composing it in the fall of 1783, or perhaps as early as his summer visit with Constanze to Salzburg. On 6 December 1783, Mozart wrote his father a long letter with a progress report on *L'oca*.

> My opera's first act is finished except for three arias. With the aria buffa [No. 3], the quartet [No. 5], and the finale [No. 6], I can say that I am fully satisfied, and in fact pleased. Therefore, it would disappoint me if this music has been written in vain, that is, if what is unavoidably necessary fails to be done. Neither you, Abbé Varesco, nor I have reflected that it will have a very bad effect, even cause the opera to fail, if neither one of the two principal female singers appear on stage until the last moment, but must keep walking about on the bastions or on the ramparts of the fortress. The audience might be patient on this point for one act, but they would not stand it for another act. This occurred to me first in Linz. There is no remedy but to introduce them into the fortress in some new scene in the second act.

Mozart goes on to propose quite specifically how this might be done. At the same time, he makes a remark that shows him close to giving up on the whole project. "My only reason for not objecting to this goose story altogether was that two people of greater insight and judgment than myself have not disapproved it, I mean yourself and Varesco." The irony of this statement probably eluded Leopold, so confident was he of his superior judgment in such matters, indeed in all matters, although most of his suggestions about *Idomeneo* the younger Mozart saw fit to ignore. As to Varesco, who had perhaps never even set foot in a theater, Mozart said it all in his letter of 21 June 1783.

However feeble and outlandish the plot of *L'oca*, Mozart continued trying to rescue it in this same letter of 6 December. He diagnosed major failings in the second act and tried to correct them. He closed the letter in a way so as to suggest that the opera was not beyond salvaging.

> Please make my opinion very clear to Herr Abbate Varesco and bid him to be diligent. I have worked very hard at it during this short time. Indeed I would have finished the whole first act had I not needed changes in the words to some arias, but I beg you not to tell him this at the moment. My German opera *Die Entführung aus dem Serail* has been performed very well in Prague and in Leipzig, where it won the greatest applause, as I have heard from people who saw the productions in those cities.

What may seem at first a non sequitur in this passage truly is not because it implies that *Die Entführung* achieved success because Mozart reordered the plot and revised the text. In a postscript to his letter he added, "Please give Varesco a good talking to and urge him to hurry up."

In his letter of 10 December, Mozart wrote only a few words about the project. "Do the best you can to ensure that my libretto comes out well. I wish that the two women could be brought down from the bastion when they sing their arias but will concede that they can sing the whole finale from up there." Varesco did not concede so readily to the need for the women to sing arias. In his next letter of 24 December, Mozart goes into instructive detail about this point.

> Abbate Varesco has written next to the cavatina for Lavinia that it can use the music for the preceding cavatina of Celidora. But this cannot be, for in Celidora's cavatina the words are despairing and hopeless, while in Lavinia's they are trusting and hopeful. Moreover, for one singer to echo the tune of another is a fashion quite out of date and no longer used. At best, it can be used only for the soubrette and her lover, that is, in the *ultime parti*.

This is an important point about the hierarchy of singer's roles. What suited the minor parts sullied the dignity of the principal ones. Mozart himself allowed the maidservant Serpetta a cavatina that was echoed by her lover Nardo in *La finta giardiniera*, Act I, Nos. 9a and 9b. The following passage in the same letter spells out how the principal female roles were to be treated.

In my opinion, the scene should begin with a beautiful duet that can be sung to the same words to which a little addition could be made for the coda. After the duet the dialogue remains as it was. And at the words "e quando s'ode il campanello della Custode" Mlle Lavinia instead of Celidora will have the good grace to absent herself so that Celidora as prima donna has the opportunity to sing a fine bravura aria. In this way, I believe the composer, singer, and audience will be better served, and the whole scene would unfailingly become more interesting.

Here is another way of saying that if anything can rescue an opera, even this one, it is the music. Mozart went on in this lengthy letter proposing correctives to Varesco's ineptitudes, and they are all worth study from the point of view of operatic dramaturgy. A great many changes were necessary, wrote Mozart, perhaps as another signal that the end of the project was approaching.

The next letter from Mozart to his father is dated 10 February 1784, by which time composing the opera had been suspended in favor of other more pressing and financially rewarding works. There is still a sliver of hope held out to Varesco.

If the opera is left lying for a while, it will go better. One sees in the poetry of Herr Varesco all too plainly the haste with which he wrote. I hope that with time he will see this himself. Therefore, I wish to see the opera as a *whole*, however roughly he sketches it out. Then we can make the basic alterations as necessary. We have no need, for heaven's sake, to hurry. If you could hear what I have composed so far, you would wish as do I that it not be spoiled, which happens so easily and so often. The music composed sleeps safely and soundly. I guarantee that of all the operas that will be performed before mine is completed not a single idea will resemble one of mine.

The importance of being original, in music as well as text, finds no stronger statement. These were the last words written about *L'oca del Cairo* that have come down to us. The surviving score consists of incomplete drafts of only six of its numbers, all in the first act.

Lo sposo deluso came into Mozart's hands by 1784 and he began setting it after shelving *L'oca del Cairo*. It was derived from an intermezzo *a* 5 in two acts, *Le donne rivali*, set to music by Cimarosa for the Roman Carnival of 1780. The five characters of the original have been clumsily expanded to seven, four men and three women, the third a buffa. This concoction was formerly ascribed to Da Ponte, although it is plainly unworthy of him.[26] Mozart identified the seven singers he had in mind on a manuscript of the libretto: Signore Benucci, Signora Fischer (the married name of Storace, used only in mid-1784), Signore Mandini,

[26] Andrew dell'Antonio, " 'Il compositore deluso': The Fragments of *Lo sposo deluso*," in *Wolfgang Amadè Mozart: Essays on His Life and His Music*, ed. Stanley Sadie (Oxford, 1996), pp. 403–12. Storace and company arrived in Vienna in early 1783 and not 1784, as the author purports on p. 411.

Signora Cavalieri, Signore Bussani, Signore Pugnetti, and Signora Teiber. These seven are almost the same as those who opened the Italian company's first season in April 1783 with Salieri's *La scuola de gelosi*. The difference is that Mandini replaced Kelly. Mozart composed more of this work than he did of Varesco's goose story, but by early 1785, at the latest, it was also put aside.

Mozart's experiences with these failed operatic attempts confirmed his earlier remark (16 June 1781) about the importance of the libretto being good. No matter how he tweaked and reconfigured Varesco's libretto, it remained unviable. *Lo sposo* was scarcely more viable after the small merit it originally possessed was diluted by the addition of two further parts. What these two failed efforts show clearly is the length that Mozart was prepared to go in order to take advantage of a certain constellation of singers. His stipulation of three female parts in 1783, carefully graded in weight from seria to *mezzo carattere* to buffa, failed at first to produce any completed results, but they remained an ideal for him. Nowhere is this more clear than in *Don Giovanni* of 1787. Donna Anna is a completely seria part, Donna Elvira, her equal in every way, is less serious because of her foibles and follies (i.e., she is *mezzo carattere*), while Zerlina is buffa. By no coincidence did La Cavalieri become Mozart's Viennese Elvira in 1788, or did Teyber, his sparkling Blonde, go on to become a celebrated Zerlina.

In 1784, Mozart's fixation on writing for the new Italian troupe yielded enough to allow a burst of concentrated work centering on the keyboard, which occupied him more completely than in any earlier or later year. We have seen from his letter to his father of 10 February 1784 how he was setting aside Varesco's libretto, partly because he wanted to make money with other works right away. In retrospect, this postponement looks more like a means of letting Varesco down easily without an outright rejection. As he wrote his father a few months later about an inadequate maidservant's behavior, "I would dismiss her at once if I did not hate to make people unhappy" (letter of 26 May 1784). Something of this same temporizing nature appears in his dealing with Anton Klein, an ex-Jesuit and professor of poetry and philosophy at Mannheim, who sent a text for Mozart's consideration sometime before spring 1785.

Anton Klein was the cofounder of the German Society in the Palatinate and the much-maligned librettist of a German opera deemed a success only because of its music by Ignaz Holzbauer, *Günther von Schwarzburg* (1777).[27] Mozart witnessed the opera and in fact was one of the libretto's maligners: "The music by Holzbauer is very beautiful; the poetry is not worth such music" (letter to his father, dated Mannheim 14 November 1777). The work Klein sent Mozart was "Kaiser Rudolf von Habsburg." Like *Günther* it was on a medieval German sub-

---

[27] *Music in European Capitals*, pp. 578–94. See also Daniel Heartz, "Mozart and Anton Klein," *Mozart Newsletter* 10 (2006): 7–10, 18.

ject having to do with the Holy Roman Empire. Emperor Rudolph I lived from 1218 to 1291. His rise to power and territorial acquisitions laid the foundations for the house of Habsburg's eminence in European politics. The possibility of currying favor in Vienna with such a choice of subject surely played a role in Klein's choice.

Mozart wrote to Klein from Vienna on 21 May 1785, with apologies for allowing so much time to lapse before responding. Klein had written two follow-up letters to Mozart before he got his response.

> Most Highly Esteemed Herr Privy Councilor!
> I have been very remiss and I ruefully admit that I was wrong in not acknowledging the safe arrival of your letter and accompanying packet . . . As far as the opera is concerned, I could not tell you then any more than I can tell you now. Dear sir, I have so much to do at the moment that I can scarcely find a minute for myself. As a man of such great insight and experience, you know better than I that one must read this sort of thing with the greatest possible attention and reflection, not just once but many times over. Until now, I have been unable to read it even once without interruption. All that I can say is that I should not like to let it out of my hands yet. I beg you therefore to let me keep the piece [Stück] for a while.

What kept Mozart so busy after Leopold left Vienna to return home on 25 April? The Carnival and Lenten seasons had indeed been busy but not the month of May, as far as we know. It is possible that by this time Mozart and Da Ponte had begun the arduous task of shaping a great play by Beaumarchais into the libretto of *Le nozze di Figaro*. Were this the case, what Mozart says here about the importance of the libretto and of scrutinizing its every detail, considering and reconsidering it as a whole, over and over again, is not only prescient but predictive.

Mozart's letter continues with diplomatic aplomb, asking Klein for more information.

> If I should feel inclined to set it to music, I should like to know beforehand whether its production has actually been arranged at a particular place, for a work of this kind, from the point of view of both poetry and music, deserves a better fate than to be composed to no purpose. I trust you will clear me up on this point.

That Klein was unable to offer any guarantee that the opera would be performed must have been obvious to Mozart at once. Mannheim no longer had the forces to put on much in the way of opera, as Mozart well knew. While trying not to offend Klein, Mozart was clearly seeking to extricate himself from the situation.

Klein's main letter and its follow-ups have not been found so far but he must have asked about the plans to reinstate German opera in Vienna, hoping that the composer could somehow bring about a production in the imperial capital. Mozart's answer to this question was not encouraging.

> I can give you little news concerning the future of the German operatic stage here at the moment, aside from plans for setting aside the Kärntnerthor Theater as a German stage, for things are going very slowly. They say it is to be opened in early October. For my part, I have no hope it will go well. To judge from what has happened so far, it seems to me that they are trying to destroy German opera, which has fallen on bad times but perhaps only temporarily, rather than rescue it and help it to get going again.

His conspiratorial view of the situation had not changed since he wrote his father on 5 February 1783 ("they wish to kill off German opera prematurely"), but this letter gets down to cases, naming individual singers.

> My sister-in-law Madame Lange is the only singer who is permitted to join the Singspiel troupe. Cavalieri, Adamberger, Teyber, all of them Germans of whom Germany can be proud, must remain with the Italian theater and must compete against their own countrymen! It is not difficult to count up the available German singers, male and female. And even if there are singers as good as the ones I have mentioned, or even better ones, which I very much doubt, it appears to me that the theater direction here thinks too much of saving money and yet too little of being patriotic when bringing in expensive foreigners while they have on hand better singers, or at least, equally good ones who could be hired for less. And besides, the Italian company does not need the German singers, as far as numerical strength goes, for they are self-sufficient. The idea is to staff the German opera with actors and actresses who sing only when they must.

In other words, limits were set on the musical demands that could be expected in the new Singspiel, limits that set the genre back to a stage it had reached before *Die Entführung.* Such a company obviously could not produce the kind of grand opera that Klein had in mind.

Mozart blamed Singspiel's ill fortunes in Vienna on its leaders. "Most unfortunately the directors of the theater as well as of the orchestra (Umlauf) have been kept on, those who through their ignorance and lack of spirit had the most to do with the failure of their own enterprise." He exaggerates somewhat in order to persuade Klein how hopeless the outlook was for a German opera on a serious subject in Vienna.

Emphasis on the "patriot" and the "patriotic" appears odd in the overall context of Mozart's letters, the reigning tone of which is cosmopolitan. It can be explained by recalling that Klein was an archpatriot of Germanism, and that Mozart, like his father and many others, was overly inclined to tell people what they wanted to hear. Furthermore, he was trying to sweeten the pill of rejection by letting Klein down easily and gradually. Mozart's final words to Klein are often quoted out of this context (or any context at all).

> Were there but a single patriot to take charge, things would show a different face. Perhaps then, the sprouting of the National Theater would actually come to bloom, and that would be an eternal shame for Germany should we Germans begin to think as Germans, act as Germans, and Heaven forfend, to sing in German!

> Do not take offense, dear Herr Privy Councilor, if in my zeal I have perhaps gone too far. Convinced as I am of speaking to a true German, I have given my tongue so free a rein, which unfortunately is allowed to happen so seldom these days, that after such an outpouring of the heart one might well become inebriated, but without endangering one's health.

Is there a touch of irony here at the last?

Little more is known about relations with Anton Klein, who was surely smart enough to recognize that Mozart's response, no matter how flatteringly couched, amounted to a refusal. Klein continued to tout his play.[28] Had Mozart taken his own words to heart about thinking, speaking, and singing in German, he might have sought less urgently to collaborate with Lorenzo da Ponte. And perhaps he would not have chosen Italian as the language of his famous dedicatory preface to Joseph Haydn a few months later.

Clavierland! Salzburg and Vienna

Vienna was the place for him, wrote Mozart to his father on 2 June 1781, because "it is truly the land of the Clavier!" (hier ist doch gewiss Clavierland!). The phenomenal rise of the fortepiano continued in Vienna as elsewhere.[29] As good instruments became more and more available, a clientele eager to buy music for them emerged, and Mozart was well positioned to take advantage of his skills as a keyboard player and composer. The ample income he predicted therefrom was nevertheless elusive. It is unclear what keyboard instruments he himself had available in his various living quarters.

As a rule, harpsichords were prevalent in the palaces of the great. But Count-

---

[28] Emanuel Schikaneder's troupe of players performed Klein's Trauerspiel *Kaiser Rudolf von Habsburg*, which had been published in 1787, on 20 November 1789; see Otto Erich Deutsch, *Das Freihaustheater auf der Wieden, 1787–1801* (Vienna, 1937), p. 16.

[29] *Music in European Capitals*, pp. 697–700.

ess Thun, one of Mozart's most generous and influential patrons during the first half of the 1780s, owned a fortepiano made by Johann Andreas Stein that Mozart praised. In his letter of 24 March 1781, Mozart regretted that he was unable to play solos in the emperor's presence at a concert in the Burgtheater "on Countess Thun's beautiful Stein fortepiano, which she would have loaned to me." Soon after his arrival in Vienna, the composer became friends with a wealthy bourgeois couple, the Auernhammers, whose daughter Josepha became one of his best pupils. The family owned at least two good pianofortes, matched in quality, it would seem, judging from the superb Sonata in D for Two Pianos, K. 448, that Mozart wrote for her to play with him, which they did often, beginning in the fall of 1781. After leaving Salzburg service, he had to fend for himself in the matter of lodgings. At first, he had no keyboard instrument of his own. In his letter of 1 August 1781, when he was beginning intense work on *Die Entführung*, he mentioned the need to borrow a clavier for his room.

Mozart's main compositional endeavor after the break with the Archbishop in June was the completion of a set of six sonatas for piano and violin intended for publication. This was accomplished in the summer of 1781 and Artaria published the set as Opus II in November of the same year. Mozart dedicated the sonatas to his pupil Josepha, a gesture for which he was presumably well rewarded. When Artaria brought the proofs to her for a trial run, she played the piano part and Mozart played the violin part on a second piano.[30] The choice of a rich bourgeoise marks a striking departure from his earlier practice of dedicating such sonatas to members of the high nobility, whether in Paris, London, Holland, or Germany. His previous set of six (1778) was dedicated to the Electress of Bavaria. The gender of all these dedicatees was the same, confirming that the keyboard remained the special province of women performers.

The "Auernhammer" sonatas were on the whole more ambitious than the previous set of "Palatine" sonatas. They favored a format of three full-scale movements instead of the two that prevailed in the 1778 set. Two of the new sonatas composed in the summer of 1781 were in the key of F. The choice is not surprising, since the most common range of fortepiano keyboards at that time was five complete octaves from low F to high F.[31] Mozart made ample use of these extreme tones in all the sonatas, but especially in the two sharing the key of F.

The Sonata in F, K. 376, was chosen to open the new set. It begins with an emphatic gesture of I - V - I in full chords, spread over two measures of *Allegro* in common time, that serve as a "curtain" preceding the regular four-measure

---

[30] Maximilian Stadler, *Materialien zur Geschichte der Musik unter den österreichischen Regenten*, ed. Karl Wagner as *Abbé Maximilian Stadler*, Schriftenreihe der Internationalen Stiftung Mozarteum 6 (Salzburg, 1974): 72.

[31] The finale of the Sonata in D for Two Pianos K. 448 calls for a high F♯ in the primo part, m. 98, but this single exception may be an oversight.

phrase that follows. This gesture was a well-known beginning for symphonies and concertos, but of course not confined to them. The Church Sonata in C, K. 278 (1777), for organ and orchestra, including trumpet and drums, has this same fanfare-like beginning, a similarity that extends even to the rests between the chords, the tempo, and the rise of the treble 1 - 2 - 3 for the fanfare, then up to 5 for the continuation. So strong a link with a Salzburg composition is noteworthy. There is an aura about K. 376 that makes it sound like an overture to the whole set, just as majestic symphonies served as overtures to whole concerts as well as operas. The curtain reappears to open the reprise and to end both parts of the sonata's taut and cogent first movement. The relaxed middle movement, an *Andante* in B♭ and in 3/4 time, sounding like one of the estival serenades from Salzburg compositions, has no hints of the curtain, but it is a different matter with the finale, a Rondeau in cut time marked *Allegretto grazioso*. The beginning of its theme is stretched over a I - V - I progression occupying two measures, hinting at a possible connection with the first movement. As this harmonic gesture becomes more prominent, appearing on different scale degrees, the hint becomes broader. At last, shortly before the end, the gesture sounds out in full splendor in the home key of F, and then is repeated for good measure. If, as I believe, Mozart composed this sonata specifically to open the set of six, he could not have invented a more appropriate "curtain raiser." The set's other Sonata in F, K. 377, is very different. Its first movement offers a perpetual motion in triplets in counterpoint to a more slowly moving theme, continues with a lovely set of variations on a theme in the key of d, and ends with a *Tempo di Minuetto*.

The sonatas made a welcome addition to the large store of similar works played at home by the Mozart family, with Nannerl at the piano and Leopold as violinist. Before Mozart left Salzburg service in Vienna his violinist partner was Brunetti, of whom he had little good to say. Their association accounts for one of the "Auernhammer" sonatas, the unusual K. 379 in G of April 1781, with its *Adagio* initial movement. Two earlier works included in the set were composed in Salzburg, K. 296 in C and K. 378 in B♭. Who played the violin parts after Brunetti returned to Salzburg? We do not know. The last sonata in the set, K. 380 in E♭, is the most brilliant and posed the greatest difficulties for the piano. Josepha, presumably, was up to them. As Mozart moved from place to place in 1781, he may have had a violin in his possession, or at least available to him, if not yet a piano of his own. A few years later, he certainly took part in playing string quartets, such as those he dedicated to Haydn. Perhaps the public debut of the "Auernhammer" sonatas was shared with the Sonata for Two Pianos, K. 448, first mentioned in November 1781, the same month as the publication. At the Auernhammers on 23 November, Mozart revived the Concerto for Two Pianos in E♭, K. 365, for which he had sent to Salzburg, as well as the new sonata, with Josepha.

Other earlier piano concertos that Mozart revived for himself to play as soloist were K. 246 in B♭ and K. 271 in E♭.

During the Lenten concert season of 1782, the undisputed favorite of the public was the new Rondo in D, K. 382, that Mozart substituted for the original finale of his first piano concerto, K. 175, in D of 1773. He played it at his academy in the Burgtheater on 3 March 1782, in a program that also included excerpts from *Idomeneo*. The Rondo, often denounced by scholars as a vapid and tedious replacement for a fine original, possesses a popular and dance-like nature that guaranteed instant success. With its limited ambitus and many repeated tones, the theme could pass for a folksong with a nursery rhyme text. The entire Rondo, with rather routine variations on so simple a theme, can become a trying experience if heard too often. For the Viennese concert public of that time it was just what they wanted and made good publicity for the first performances of *Die Entführung* on the same stage a few months later.

Leopold Kozeluch was one of Vienna's favorite pianist-composers and teachers of piano at the time. Mozart mentions him in hostile terms in his letter to Leopold of 13 July 1781. Kozeluch made a specialty of piano concertos with finales that consisted of variations on simple, folk-like themes. His well-known Piano Concerto in D that ends with an *Andantino con variazione* in 2/4 time provides a good illustration of the genre.[32] Although this work could be later than K. 382, it may still provide an example of the type of movement Mozart set out to emulate and surpass.

Mozart's many ties with Salzburg were not loosened by his break with the archbishop. Aside from his father and sister, he held Michael Haydn in high regard as he did two close friends of the family, Abbé Joseph Bullinger and Dr. Sigmund Barisani. Other families close to the Mozarts included the Gilowskis, Hagenauers, and Schiedenhofens. Among Salzburg's noble families, the Lodrons had been especially supportive. The Haffners, being a very wealthy merchant family, fell between nobles and commoners. Sigmund Haffner the Elder had become Burgomeister of Salzburg. His son, Sigmund the Younger, who was Mozart's age, had commissioned the "Haffner" Serenade, K. 250, to celebrate the marriage of his sister Elisabeth in 1776. In July 1782, after the senior Haffner died, the younger one was about to be given noble status. Leopold Mozart seized the opportunity to further his links with this wealthy young man. He asked his son to compose a new symphony to celebrate the ennoblement.

July 1782 was a particularly hectic month for Mozart. The first performances of *Die Entführung* were taking place. He was moving from one apartment to another while negotiating a way out of various difficulties with the Weber family over his affair with Constanze. In addition, he was trying to finish a com-

---

[32] Leopold Koželuch, *Konzert D-dur für Klavier und Orchester*, ed. Raymond Meylan (Wiesbaden, 1963).

mission for a wind piece, the imposing Serenade in c, K. 388, and also hastily arranging his new opera for winds so as to forestall arrangements made by others. At the same time, he needed to humor his father into consenting to a marriage of which Leopold disapproved. He wrote Leopold on 20 July explaining his situation.

> I have no small task ahead of me. A week from Sunday I must have my opera ready in an arrangement for winds, otherwise someone else will beat me to it and reap the profits. And now I should compose a new symphony? How would that be possible? You cannot imagine how difficult it is to arrange for winds so that the individual timbre of each shines through while still preserving the music's original effect. So be it. I must work nights. For you, dearest father, the sacrifice will be made. Every post day you should receive something, and I shall work as fast as possible, and insofar as haste permits, write something good.

For a new symphony, Mozart needed more time, not to write it out—for that could be done very quickly, as the case of the "Linz" Symphony, K. 425, of the following year shows—but to think it out, to come up with a new idea for the work. Fortunately, such an idea was close at hand in his new opera.

On 27 July, Mozart wrote Leopold again with apologies, saying he could send only one movement of the symphony.

> You will scowl when you see only the first *Allegro*—there was not time to do more. I had to quickly write a Night Music [K. 388] but restricted to *Harmonie* [wind band], else I could have used it for you. On Wednesday the 31st I shall send the two Minuets and the *Andante,* also the finale. If I can, I shall also send a march, if not: you must simply use the march of the Haffner music [K. 249] which is very little known [notated treble here]. I composed this symphony in D because you like the key so well. My opera was given yesterday [Saint Anne's Day] for the third time to hearty applause in honor of all the Nannerls in the world. In spite of the terrible summer heat, the theater was packed.

The letter continues in this vein then suddenly switches its tone. "Dearest, best of all fathers, I implore you by all that you hold dear in the world to give your consent so that I can marry my dear Constanze."

Four days later, the last day of July, he wrote excusing himself again and saying that, all good intentions aside, he could not do the impossible. "I do not like to just scribble something. The next post day I can send the whole symphony. I could have sent the last movement but I prefer to send it all together for then it will cost only one sum." The finale, finished earlier, provides a clue to the idea that inspired the whole, namely the triumphal aria for Osmin upon apprehending the two Western couples trying to escape.

Osmin's gloating aria in D, No. 14, begins with a fanfare-like descent down the tonic triad, rendered comic by the "Turkish" minor-second appoggiaturas in sixteenth notes upon repetition (Example 1.5ab). The long descent in half notes that rounds out the second theme section (m. 58ff.) will end on the long-held low D when this section later comes back in the tonic. It takes on a more ominous tone with minor-mode trappings meanwhile (m. 87ff.) when Osmin mentions the

EXAMPLE 1.5.

a. *Mozart,* Die Entführung aus dem Serail, *Aria No. 19 (Osmin)*

b. *Mozart, Symphony No. 35 ("Haffner"), K. 385, I, IV*

western marauders creeping like mice around his harem. The upward leaps of an octave here over a descending bass are certainly suggestive of the symphony's majestic opening. The beginning of the aria, moreover, suggests the descending triad theme of the symphony's finale, which also boasts many mocking quick appoggiaturas from below. It is tempting to hear in the symphony, one of Mozart's most popular and often-performed works, the swaggering steps of Osmin after he has caught his prey, or the stealthy stalking of that prey before his triumph. The most hilarious moment in the symphony comes at the very end, when the long descents of the first movement are turned into a chromatically rising passage in the form of a coda.

K. 385 continued to figure in the letters Mozart sent to Leopold. He requested the score or the parts in his letter of 4 January 1783, and more urgently on 5 February: "Please send the symphonies, especially the last one, as soon as possible, for my academy is to take place on the third Sunday of Lent, the 23rd of March, and I must have several duplicate string parts made. If it has not been copied into parts then send me the original score just as I sent it to you and remember to put in the minuets." Two minuets, like the orchestral march to precede and follow the main movements, were part of the original conception of the work as a serenade. Only one minuet survives in the original score, and it is separate from the rest. There is no doubt that it belongs to K. 385: the rise up the octave and stepwise descent of its theme recall the shape of the first movement's theme. A second minuet has not survived. For his concert in March, Mozart revised the score by deleting the march, the repeats in the opening movement, and adding flutes and clarinets to the tuttis of the outer movements. It thus became the "Haffner" Symphony that we know. The concert was a great success, as Mozart reported to his father on 29 March 1783. Emperor Joseph was present and applauded loudly, wrote Mozart, who received 25 ducats as a present from the emperor. A correspondent writing for Cramer's *Magazin der Musik* in Hamburg confirmed the success and said that the concert had brought in an estimated 1600 gulden. Mozart's precise description of the program's content shows it was a typical mixture of vocal and instrumental pieces, including two of his piano concertos, K. 415 and K. 175 (with its new Rondo, K. 382). "I played a little fugue by myself (because the emperor was present) and variations on an aria from the opera [by Paisiello], *Die Philosophen*, and then for an encore played variations on "Unser dummer Pöbel meint" from *Die Pilgrimme von Mekka* [by Gluck]. The last piece was the finale from the opening symphony [K. 385]."

Mozart's letter of 31 July 1782 to Leopold pleaded the case for marrying Constanze in bald terms not used before: "All the good and well-intentioned advice you have sent fails to address the case of a man who has already gone so far with a maiden. Further postponement is out of the question." Constanze's sister Sophie had tearfully declared that her mother would send the police after Constanze if she did not return home (presumably from Mozart's apartment). On 4 August, Mozart wrote to his patroness and confidante Baroness von Waldstätten asking her advice. "Can the police here enter anyone's house in this way? Perhaps it is only a ruse of Madame Weber to get her daughter back. If not, I know no better remedy than to marry Constanze tomorrow morning or if possible today." Mozart and Constanze Weber were in fact married that same day at a side chapel in St. Stephen's Cathedral. Leopold's belated consent and blessing arrived the next day. On 7 August, Mozart wrote thanking his father and described the less-than-gala event. "No one attended the ceremony but her mother and youngest sister [Sophie], Herr von Thorwart as her guardian and witness, Herr von Zetto, district councilor as another witness, and [Franz Xaver] Gilowsky as my best man." A few more remarks described the lacrimose consequences for everyone, including the priest, or so says Mozart. Eventually he returned to musical matters. "I am enclosing a brief march [K. 408 No. 2 (K. 385a)]. May it get there in time and be to your taste. The first *Allegro* must be played with great fire, the last one as fast as possible." He ended the letter saying that his opera was given again the previous day, this time at the request of Gluck, who had paid him many compliments on it and invited him to lunch the following day. The elderly master must have realized that his own Turkish opera *Die Pilgrimme von Mecca*, which had done so much to popularize the genre, had been quite overshadowed.

In the fall of 1782, Mozart began preparing three new piano concertos for the Lenten season of 1783. The first he worked on was the Piano Concerto in A, K. 414. We do well to recall that he had not only the Viennese public to please, but his more fastidious father and sister back in Salzburg, who received and performed his new works as soon as possible. His letter to Leopold of 28 December 1782 describes the new concertos in a passage that is often quoted, but not in the context that I propose. Is it perhaps an admission, albeit tacit, that a style so popular as he used in the egregious Rondo in D, K. 382, compromised his true path?

> There are still two concertos needed to make up the series of three subscription works. These concertos are a happy medium between what is too easy and too difficult; they are very brilliant, pleasing to the ear, and natural, without being vapid. There are also passages here and there from which only connoisseurs can derive satisfaction; but these passages are written in such a way that the less discriminating cannot fail to be pleased, though without knowing why. I am distributing subscriptions for six ducats each.

The concertos themselves amply confirm that the high road taken could also be accessible to many auditors.

In K. 414, Mozart returned to the key of A, which he had not used for a concerto since the stunning Salzburg one of 1775, K. 219, the fifth and last violin concerto. He had never previously used the key for a keyboard concerto, but made telling use of it in his operas for lyric outpourings, for love duets in particular, and most recently for Belmonte's lovely aria "O wie ängstlich." In K. 219, the lyrical is contrasted with the comic poses of his Turkish style, so prophetic of *Die Entführung* and of the *Alla turca* finale of the Piano Sonata in A, K. 331. There are no such exotic moments in the Piano Concerto No. 12 in A. The care Mozart took with it is evident in its every detail, as well as in a sketch for the *Allegro* and a nearly completed alternative finale, the Rondo in A, K. 386, which he rejected.[33]

The first movement of the Piano Concerto No. 12, K. 414, an *Allegro* in common time, begins with a soft main theme that rises through the triad, descends by step, then rises through the triad on ii. The melody charmed Schubert, who used it as the second theme of the first fast movement in his Symphony No. 2

---

[33] K. 386's m. 8 matches m. 8 of the opening *Allegro* of K. 414, which perhaps was a more obvious recollection than Mozart wished.

in B♭. Mozart's continuation employs different rhythm and texture: syncopated half notes in descent, the second violins reinforcing the firsts an octave below. This peculiarly Viennese texture then recurs for all eight measures of the second theme. It goes back to the mid-eighteenth century as a Viennese specialty. Before settling in Vienna, Mozart had used such doubling quite prominently, for example, in the first movement of the Symphony No. 29 in A, K. 201, of 1774 (one of four Salzburg works he requested in score from Leopold by letter on 4 January 1783, the others being K. 182, 183, and 204). With this Viennese piano concerto, it is more prominent than ever. The first movement's closing material offers another lovely idea sung by the first violins, one that nearly matches the music of reconciliation begun by Pedrillo in the same key midway through the quartet-finale of Act II in *Die Entführung*.[34]

Idomeneo also leaves its mark on K. 414. When the piano solo announces a new theme to begin the seconda parte of the *Allegro*, it takes the form of a rapid descent in quick notes slurred from a longer note, that is, the "Idamante motif" (see Example 1.3). On repetition an octave lower, the staccato upbeat quarter note in m. 153 is turned into staccato eighth notes, another trait from the opera, and also prominent in the slow movement of the Sonata for Two Pianos, K. 448. The piano's new theme shapes what development there is, at the end of which the treble rises by half tones to prepare the reprise, as in Ilia's first aria in *Idomeneo*.[35]

The second movement of K. 414, an *Andante* in D and in 3/4 time, presents a very special case. Here Mozart chose to quote a theme by his recently deceased friend and mentor, Johann Christian Bach, a theme that he had used earlier.[36] A venerable critic praised this theme without knowing it was Christian Bach's, saying, "The warmest and most alive movement of this charming little concerto is the *Andante*, with its Schubertian appoggiatura in the cadence" (he then quotes the first four measures).[37] What rewards study is how Mozart diverged from Bach's second four measures, improving them. As the *Andante* reaches its harmonic goals, he did not hesitate to use the *cadence galante*, which lends another nostalgic touch. In both this movement and in the final Rondeau, an *Allegretto* in 2/4 time, there are echoes of the "Idamante motif." All three movements were provided with dual cadenzas, useful aids for the amateur pianist, as well as for Nannerl.

---

[34] As pointed out by Ellwood Derr, "Some Thoughts on the Design of Mozart's Opus 4, the 'Subscription Concertos' (K. 414, 413, and 415)," in *Mozart's Piano Concertos: Text, Context, Interpretation*, ed. Neal Zaslaw (Ann Arbor, MI, 1996), pp. 187–210, ex. 3, which also juxtaposes the passage with themes in K. 376 and the Lied "Nehmt meinen Dank" K. 383.

[35] Compared above with the reprise of Konstanze's "Traurigkeit."

[36] *Music in European Capitals*, p. 928, ex. 9.11a–d.

[37] Alfred Einstein, *Mozart: His Character, His Work*, trans. Arthur Mendel and Nathan Broder (New York, 1945), p. 299. The author goes on to tout the superiority of this *Andante* over the *Larghetto* in K. 413, which he says gives the impression of having been composed earlier.

The Piano Concerto No. 11 in F, K. 413, has elicited mostly bland or feeble descriptions from critics. It begins with an *Allegro* in 3/4 time, a meter rare in the opening movements of keyboard concertos, with the exception of those by Emanuel Bach. Of the early pasticcio concertos for keyboard arranged for Mozart, only the one in G, K. 41, began with an *Allegro* in 3/4 (by Honauer). After the initial chords, the theme is played in unison. Its unusual contours would not have been unfamiliar to keen listeners just coming from performances of *Die Entführung*, for they closely parallel the opera's final chorus, begun by the Janissaries in praise of Selim Pasha (Example 1.6ab). Conductors and piano soloists would do well to

EXAMPLE 1.6.

a. *Mozart, Die Entführung aus dem Serail, No. 21b, Final Chorus*

b. *Mozart, Piano Concerto No. 11, K. 413, I*

bear in mind the operatic connection not only of K. 413's beginning but also of the solo's first entrance, which is not with the Janissary theme but with a tender and leisurely new theme in which the music evokes the chromatic sighs of Ilia's second aria, "Se il padre perdei." Since Ilia and Konstanze have so much in common musically and dramatically, the concerto could be understood to begin by exploring further the dialogues between male ruler and female captive in those two great operas, still so fresh in their composer's mind. One of the oddities of K. 413's opening *Allegro* is that the orchestra in the first exposition strays into the dominant key for its second theme, instead of remaining in the tonic, a course then righted by Mozart's restating the same theme in tonic F. When the orchestra begins to make the same maneuver in the second exposition, which would lead to a premature modulation back to F after C was established, the solo interrupts the orchestra, as if in admonition, deflecting the modulation back to C. This could surely qualify as a moment pleasing non-connoisseurs, yet offering still more to those who understood. Another instance would be the subtle theme of the *Larghetto* in common time and in B♭, which actually moves in 3/2 time at first. The *Tempo di Menuetto* finale offers many contrapuntal refinements and ends by fading away to a surprising *pianissimo*, the last two measures duplicating the first two of the opening *Allegro*.

Mozart, wishing to attract as many subscribers as possible to buy his new concertos, described them as playable by full orchestra or by string quartet. It is true that the strings alone provide what is essential to the musical discourse and the accompaniment of the piano solo, but a lot of lovely wind writing would be lost if the ensemble were limited to strings. The winds add not only color but also tonal and rhythmic emphases at important moments. In the third work, Concerto No. 13 in C, K. 415, the composer added trumpets and timpani as well as oboes, bassoons, and horns. Thus, he conceived of it as a "military" concerto, an equivalent to Symphony No. 34 in C, K. 338, with trumpets and drums, a Salzburg work of 1780 that he revived in Vienna.

K. 415 begins with the rhythm of a military march, *Allegro* in common time with the typical dotted eighth and sixteenth note on the second beat. A single line for the first violins *piano* initially is joined by the seconds in imitation, then by basses building up to a full texture and eventually *forte*, suggesting a march heard first at a distance gradually coming nearer. This is a well-practiced theatrical device used to simulate an approaching crowd, and one need look no further than the march for the embarkation in Act II of *Idomeneo* for an example on the stage. The march rhythm is the same in both, while the slides up and down in sixteenth notes of K. 415 are a carryover from the first theme of K. 414. As in that concerto, the solo part enters the first movement with a new theme of its own.

The middle movement of K. 415 was originally sketched as a dirge in the key of c, very dour of mien, with drooping melodic lines. Perhaps it seemed too gloomy to suit the general purpose of these three concertos. At any rate, Mozart instead wrote a suave *Andante* in 3/4 and in F. He brought the melancholy idea in c back as an episode in the final Rondeau where it sounds so serious as to be comical in the context of this joyous and dance-like *Allegro* in 6/8 time with dotted rhythms, like the intrusion of somberly clad mourners in the midst of a nuptial party. The ending is another *pianissimo*, even longer than in K. 414.

No act of *Die Entführung* ended softly but one act of *Idomeneo* did. In Act II the chorus of fleeing Cretans in d minor leaves an empty stage behind, and the orchestra concludes with an eerie chord of D major, *pianissimo*, with the first oboe (Friedrich Ramm) sustaining his high D. Here the first oboe also sustains the highest tone, in this case C. Mozart commended loud endings as a guarantee of applause when writing about his Turkish opera. He also remembered that sometimes the opposite of what was expected could create a stunning effect.

Subscription to manuscript copies of the three new concertos was announced in local papers beginning in January 1783. For four ducats, the subscriber could obtain from the composer at his lodgings a ticket promising that the concertos would be available in April. In a letter to Jean-Georges Sieber in Paris dated 26 April 1783, Mozart said that he was not very satisfied with the Viennese engraving of his recent set of sonatas for piano and violin, that is, Artaria's printed edition. He offered to send Sieber the three concertos to be engraved for a payment of thirty Louis d'or. Nothing came of the offer. The concertos were engraved instead by Artaria in 1785 as Œuvre IV. Johann Traeg continued to offer manuscript copies of them for sale.

Three sonatas for solo keyboard, K. 330 in C, K. 331 in A, and K. 332 in F, were written as a set in 1783, also intended for engraving and selling. They may have been a kind of peace offering to Nannerl, who reproached her brother for failing to answer her letters and otherwise neglecting her. In 1782, the demands of finishing his opera for the Burgtheater and seeing it through to production had weighed heavily on the composer, not to forget the emotional strains accompanying his marriage to Constanze. 1783 was less hectic.

Mozart claimed he was anxious to bring his bride home to meet his father and sister but he found one excuse after another to postpone the voyage to Salzburg. Finally, after the birth of their first child, Raimund Leopold, the couple traveled to Salzburg in late July 1783, leaving the baby behind. Composition of the solo sonatas may have begun in Vienna before the pair's departure and perhaps continued during the stay of three months in Salzburg (little Raimund died in Vienna on 19 August 1783). In a letter begun on 9 June 1784, Mozart wrote to his father from Vienna, "Now I have given the three solo sonatas that I once sent to my sister, those in C, A, and F, to Artaria to be engraved." The sonatas were published without dedication as Opus VI in the summer of 1784 and went through several subsequent editions.

K. 330 in C is perhaps the most ethereal of all Mozart's solo sonatas. Its first movement, an *Allegro moderato* in 2/4 time, is spun out of the most delicate threads, so that it seems to float in the air like a gossamer in autumn. Could it have been intended as a portrait of Nannerl and her playing? Writing to Leopold on 7 June 1783, Mozart advised his sister not to labor long over Clementi's rapid sixths and octaves lest she "spoil her quiet and even touch, and lose the natural lightness, flexibility, and flowing rapidity of her hand." Portraits in sonatas were not strange to the composer, who stated, for example, that he expressed the character of Rosa Cannabich in the *Andante* of the Sonata in C, K. 309, of 1777.[38] K. 330's middle movement is an *Andante cantabile* in F and in 3/4 time. The melody is truly so *cantabile* it could be sung by a good soprano, unlike the very pianistic first movement. It has a *minore* middle section, which returns as a coda but then transforms into major, a wistful closing thought that is present in the first edition but not in the autograph, and thus literally an afterthought, and extremely touching. The perky *Allegretto* in 2/4 time that closes the work is more like the opening movement in its sparkling arpeggio figures.

K. 331 in A, one of Mozart's most often performed works, begins with a lovely set of variations on a tender original theme, *Andante grazioso* in 6/8 time.

[38] *Haydn, Mozart,* p. 591

The sonata, like its companions, was long assigned to 1778 and the composer's stay in Paris, an incorrect assumption that seemed to be supported by the resemblance of the theme to some of the French songs he chose to vary. As innocent as the theme sounds, it is quite subtly constructed and its treatment is anything but naïve. In the second variation, with flowing triplets and trills, a quick-note minor-second appoggiatura to the main note shows up repeatedly in the bass, a type of ornament used elsewhere to express mockery or derision (for example in Osmin's song of triumph, Example 1.5, or Giovanni's gulling of Masetto in the Act I finale of *Don Giovanni*). Variation four, coming after a *minore* variation, is made very sonorous by the left hand crossing over the right to double the melody on high. Hand crossings are not frequent in Mozart's sonatas. Yet they are carefully depicted by Johann Nepomuk della Croce in the family portrait of ca. 1780 (Figure 1.4). Brother and sister are playing four-hands at the piano, he crossing his right hand over her left hand. The oval portrait on the wall is that of their deceased mother.

The sonata continues with a Menuetto in A that begins with a robust triadic theme in octaves, followed by an unusually elaborate Trio in D, with hand crossings as in Variation four, and the little mocking appoggiaturas that appeared in Variation two (they had also returned in the last variation). Most trios are more

FIGURE 1.4. Oil portrait of the Mozart family, 1781, attributed to Della Croce.

modest than this one, which explodes in a unison passage with octaves in both hands. The double bar in the middle marks a cadence on a modal degree, with descent by step from fifth to tonic. Then a wavering back and forth between 5 and 1 takes place, a foretaste of the exotic music still to come.

The *Alla turca* finale is an *Allegretto* (originally *Allegrino*) in 2/4 time that begins with rising melodic turns in the key of a, then passes into A for the next section, a jaunty refrain with arpeggiated full triads in the bass suggesting a Janissary band (an accompaniment adumbrated in the last variation of the *Andante*). From this, the discourse turns to constantly running sixteenth notes in the right hand, a motion characteristic of Viennese Turkish style. In a brilliant last section marked "Coda," all elements coalesce: the running sixteenth notes, arpeggiated chords, rapid appoggiaturas, and melodic turns. They give this movement a rousing conclusion that also makes a fitting end to the whole sonata. It brought home to Leopold and Nannerl some of the excitement of the Turkish opera they did not have the good fortune to experience on the stage in Vienna. To reinforce the point, Mozart even ends the finale with the wavering between tonic, third, and fifth degrees, similarly to the way he ended his opera—a melodic device that resounds in Hungarian folk melodies called *türökös*.[39]

K. 332 in F sustains the high level of the first two sonatas and is in its own way as theatrical as K. 331. The opening *Allegro* in 3/4 time begins lyrically, continues with what sound like horn calls, then turns to a stormy transition passage full of diminished-seventh chords and dynamic outbursts. The movement has so many disparate components while remaining unified that it has become a favorite display piece for advocates of musical *topoi*. A middle movement in B♭ follows, an *Adagio* in common time with effusions of lyric melody in the right hand over a chordal accompaniment, disposed in the patterns of the Alberti bass or other similar lightweight arpeggiations. The treble cantilena, richly decorated with melodic turns and other ornaments, is supported by subtly evolving harmonies in the left hand, a combination that evokes another aria-like middle movement in B♭, a masterly *Andante* in one of Galuppi's keyboard sonatas.[40]

The finale of K. 332, an *Allegro assai* in 6/8 time, begins with a brilliant passage in sixteenth notes sweeping down from high F. This recurrent passage and others, such as the disjoint rapid sixths in descent, are a little more demanding of the player's right hand than anything in the set of three sonatas. They lend this movement the character of an étude. There is a teasing jest at the end. Hearing the rapid passagework, ascending triads, and emphatic full chords on the tonic that end the first part in C, we are led to think that the sonata is over when at last these return in F. Not so. The three emphatic thuds separated by rests provide the

---

[39] Bauman, *W. A. Mozart: Die Entführung aus dem Serail*, p. 63.
[40] Quoted in its entirety as ex. 3.17 in *Music in European Capitals*, pp. 289–90.

proper punctuation, but the last one is inflected with an E♭ at the top, pointing the music in the direction of IV. What follows is a coda in function but nothing new. It is, in fact, the leaping sixths note-for-note creeping up by chromatic rise of the lower part that originally formed the end of the tonic area before modulation in the first part, a section that had been elided in the reprise. Very little of interest that Mozart states in the first part is not repeated somewhere in the reprise, and in this respect he is unlike Haydn.

Nannerl, an early and probable main recipient of these three sonatas, had technique sufficient to conquer their difficulties, else Mozart would scarcely have posed them in the first place. She was always eager to receive new keyboard works. With these sonatas of 1783, her frequent requests to her brother were richly rewarded. After her marriage in 1784, she lived in near isolation in the village of St. Gilgen some six hours distant from Salzburg, but not without her new fortepiano, which was likely a wedding present from Leopold.[41]

Another solo sonata close to the set of three is K. 333 in B♭. Its first movement, an *Allegro* in common time, begins with a singing melody in the right hand using a motif of which Christian Bach was fond. A convincing argument as to the date, based on paper studies and traits of handwriting, assigns it to November 1783.[42] On his return to Vienna from Salzburg, Mozart passed some time in Linz (where he rapidly wrote out the "Linz" Symphony, K. 425). Each of the three ample movements of K. 333 is rich and challenging either as to technical finesse—there is even a written-out cadenza in the last movement— or as to harmonic subtleties, such as the wrenching progression with which the second part of the *Andante* begins. In its first edition, the sonata was combined with the difficult "Dürnitz" Sonata in D, K. 284, of 1774 and the elaborate "Strinasacchi" Sonata in B♭, K. 454, for piano and violin. Christoph Torricella of Vienna published the three as Opus 7 in the summer of 1784 under this title: "Trois Sonates pour le Clavecin ou Pianoforte. La troisieme est accomp. d'un violon . . . Dediées à son Excellence Madame la Comtesse Therese de Kobenzl." The dedicatee was the wife of Count Ludwig Cobenzl, Joseph II's ambassador to the Russian court. That keyboard sonatas with and without violin could still be published in the same collection shows how close these two genres remained in the 1780s.

The visit to Salzburg in 1783 ended with the performance on Sunday 26 October at Mass in St. Peter's Church of Mozart's unfinished Mass in c, K. 427. This gigantic torso, written to fulfill a vow Mozart made before his marriage, is referred to as a "half-finished score" in Mozart's letter of 4 January 1783. Any further work on it in Salzburg had to compete with a social whirl of visiting friends,

[41] Ruth Halliwell, *The Mozart Family: Four Lives in a Social Context* (Oxford, 1998), pp. 436–38.
[42] Alan Tyson, *Mozart: Studies of the Autograph Scores* (Cambridge, Mass., 1987), p. 80.

excursions, and playing games, all reported by Nannerl in her charming diary entries.[43] Constanze sang one of the soprano solo parts in K. 427.

Mozart composed the "Strinasacchi" Sonata for the virtuoso violinist Regina Strinasacchi to play at her academy in the Kärntnerthor Theater on 29 April 1784 with the emperor present. A tradition of excellent women violinists began with Vivaldi's pupils at the Ospedale della Pietà and other conservatories in Venice.[44] It lived on in this lady, who was born near Mantua in 1764 and was also educated at the Pietà. In Austria, female musicians were nearly all singers or keyboard players, or both, as in the case of Maria Theresia von Paradis. Rare was a woman violinist who was also a professional musician. Writing to his father on 24 April 1784, Mozart announced, "We now have here the famous Mantuan Strinasacchi, a very good violinist who has abundant taste and sensitivity [Empfindung] in her playing; I am writing at present a sonata that we shall play together at her academy in the theater." Five days later when the concert took place, only the violin part was completely written out, as the autograph shows, the piano part having had to be squeezed in under it. Later in the year, Strinasacchi visited Salzburg and played a concert there, earning an unusually glowing tribute from Leopold, who was not easily pleased in matters of violin playing (or anything else). He wrote this reaction in a letter to Nannerl dated 7–9 December 1784.

> I am sorry that you did not hear this very talented young lady, who is petite, polished, about twenty-three years of age, and modest. She plays not a note without feeling, even in the orchestral ritornello she plays everything with expression, and the *Adagio* no one can play with more feeling and more touchingly than she. Her whole heart and soul are in the melody she is playing. Her tone remains so beautiful and so powerful. I find that overall, women with talent play with more expression than men.

This is an extraordinary statement coming from one of the age's finest and most experienced violin teachers, and from an era that was more likely to deprecate than praise professionalism in women.

K. 454 is an imposing work. It begins, like many a symphony, with a slow introduction, *Largo* in common time. These thirteen measures do not rival in length the slow introduction to the "Linz" Symphony of a few months earlier but they do in gravity, and they equal in this regard the slow introduction of the closely contemporary Quintet for Piano and Winds in E♭, K. 452. All three of these introductions alternate loud, forceful chords with soft, pleading melo-

[43] Halliwell, *The Mozart Family*, table 1, pp. 408–23. Extra wind parts only are on Salzburg paper, according to Tyson, *Mozart*, p. 101.
[44] *Music in European Capitals*, pp. 182–83.

dies, mostly falling by step. The introduction of K. 454 continues with a syncopated figure in the accompaniment, repeated as a rhythmic ostinato in support of a broad falling line in the violin, giving full vent to the soloist's vaunted *Empfindung* (Example 1.7). There are parallels between this example and another great work in the same key, the Serenade in B♭ for Thirteen Instruments, K. 361, whose *Largo* introduction in common time begins with similar alternations, and whose first *Adagio* introduces the same syncopated figure as an ostinato accompaniment—exalted company indeed! These stylistic similarities have been used to argue that the wind serenade's composition should have been placed in early 1784, close to the date of Anton Stadler's benefit concert in the Burgtheater on 23 March 1784.[45] In other words, it should not have been placed in the K. 360s with *Idomeneo*, but in the K. 450s, although its paper has been assigned to a year or two earlier.

EXAMPLE 1.7. *Mozart, Violin and Piano Sonata in B♭, K. 454, I*

[45] Daniel N. Leeson, "A Revisit: Mozart's Serenade for Thirteen Instruments, K. 361 (370a), the 'Gran Partita,' " *Mozart-Jahrbuch 1997*: 181–223; 189.

An *Allegro* in common time follows K. 454's slow introduction, one that is rich in melodic ideas and in exchanges between the two instruments, which are treated as absolute equals here and throughout the sonata. The hymnic *Andante* (originally *Adagio*) in 3/4 time and in E♭ is in sonata form, like the first movement. An *Allegretto* in 2/4 time, a sonata-rondo with plenty of brilliant passagework for both players, rounds out the work. Mozart's finest contribution to the genre to date, K. 454, equals in quality and in conversational repartee the six string quartets he began assembling in 1782, those he would dedicate to Haydn. It may not be entirely coincidental that K. 454 was published (by Sieber in Paris) in an arrangement for string quartet.

Joseph II and Other Patrons

THE "LINZ" SYMPHONY

The Thun family, along with Baron Gottfried van Swieten, belongs at the head of any list of Mozart's patrons during his last decade. Returning from Salzburg to Vienna in the fall of 1783, Mozart and his wife stopped at Linz, where they were the honored guests of the senior count Thun-Hohenstein, Johann Joseph Anton, who was a Freemason. Just as an urgent need called forth the "Haffner" Symphony of 1782, another was responsible for the creation of the "Linz" Symphony, K. 425. Each honored a patron and friend, in this case "old Count Thun," as Mozart called him, to whom K. 425 is dedicated. Thun's elder son, Count Franz Joseph, also a Freemason, was the husband of Maria Wilhelmine, whose salon in Vienna was a center of the city's cultural life.[46]

The Mozart couple arrived at Linz on Thursday 30 October 1783 and were escorted at once to the Thun palace. The following day Mozart wrote Leopold, "On Tuesday November 4th I shall give an academy in the theater here, and since I have no symphony with me I am writing a new one at breakneck speed [so schreibe ich über hals und kopf an einer Neuen] which must be ready then." The five days allowed by this scheme, if we are to believe Mozart, were scarcely enough to copy and check the parts of a long and imposing piece for large orchestra such as K. 425, let alone compose such an inventive and path-breaking work. Mozart may have exaggerated for effect, as he often did, and perhaps the time span was not so short, since the Mozarts spent an entire month in Linz. There is no other data confirming a concert on 4 November. If it did take place, then one can only conclude that the composer must have formed the grand design of the symphony in his head well before this time. He used the symphony again for

---

[46] On Countess Thun and her salon, see Volkmar Braunbehrens, *Mozart in Vienna, 1781–1791*, trans. Timothy Bell (New York, 1986), pp. 149–59.

his academy in the Burgtheater on 1 April 1784, and surely it was also played by Count Johann's fine orchestra when the Mozarts visited him in his Prague palace during January 1787.

The large scale of K. 425 and some of its other features proclaim it the gateway to Mozart's greatest symphonies, and as such, it will receive discussion here appropriate to its importance. At the time, concertgoers expected a portentous symphonic movement or a whole symphony to open an academy. They also expected to hear a fifth, G, following an imperious unison rise from C to E, and for the triad to be completed by a further rise to the high tonic. Orderly expectations are derailed in K. 425 by an A instead of a G, which could suggest another route via B♮ up to the high tonic. They are derailed again when the B♮ arrives but at the bottom of a descending seventh, followed by high D two octaves above, then instead of a resolution to C, one down to B♭ (Example 1.8). This rich

EXAMPLE 1.8. *Mozart, Symphony No. 36 ("Linz"), K. 425, I*

and pregnant beginning is made more emphatic by dotted rhythms and rests between the tones so that they are dry and *detaché* (the rests actually make the rhythm double-dotted). The B♭ in m. 3 sets the bass off on a downward journey until it reaches D, the dominant of the dominant. Over this progression, Mozart layers soft, expressive melodies in dialogue between the first and second violins, which begin the process of slowly resolving suspensions in m. 4. After the sudden jolt of *forte* at m. 8 with the V/V chord, a new voice is heard, more expressive still. The poignant tones of the first bassoon alone assert an unprepared minor ninth, E♭ resolving to D, answered in the following measure by the solo oboe with its minor-ninth A♭ resolving to G and the minor-ninth D♭ to C in both oboe and bassoon, spread over three octaves. Note how Mozart takes the trouble to separate the *forte* eighth notes of the contrabasses from the sustained tones of the cellos. Mozart was so fond of this progression by secondary dominants he used it in many other works, and the dissonant ninth in the first bassoon layered above them was nothing less than one of his musical signatures. He had already used this plaintive sound of the first bassoon in its high range intoning E♭ - D as a minor ninth and its resolution in the *Andante* of the "Haffner" Symphony, where there is also an exchange of this figure with the solo oboe. The *Adagio* introduction, after an excursion to the flat side of the tonal spectrum as far as D♭, winds down to a final goal on the dominant, in preparation for the main movement. A great gate has swung open.

The *Allegro spiritoso* is a broadly laid-out movement with many finely wrought details that belie any notion of forced haste in composition or orchestration. It begins with the first violins softly sustaining the tone E for a measure of common time against the pulsating eighth-notes of the second violins, rising to another whole note, F, and then up to the tonic and down to the tones A - G over the chords IV$^6_4$ - I, still soft, but soon to become loud and fanfare-like. The back and forth of these two chords are endemic to Mozart's particular vocabulary for symphonies in C—they can be found as well in Symphony, No. 34, K. 338, and in the "Jupiter" Symphony, K. 551.

The prominence of the third degree in the main theme might be insignificant were it an isolated case but it is not. Repeatedly, the third degree, or the rise from the first to the third degree as at the beginning of the *Adagio*, are made central events. The same is true of the descending seventh leap, so attention-getting in the *Adagio*'s second measure. After 200 measures, the *Allegro vivace* reaches a kind of climax with the first violins reaching up to high E, although the power of this tonic arrival is immediately undercut by a withdrawal of supporting harmony and reduction of the dynamic level. There is another thrust up to E at the end of the coda but only in the bass. It is not until the finale that the importance of high E is allowed its full weight.

The *Andante* following is in the expected key of the subdominant, F, and begins with a seductive melody sung by the violins in thirds and sixths in a lilting 6/8 meter. Contradicting this sweetly innocent main theme is the arrival, an intrusion in effect, of trumpets and drums, rarely heard in slow movements. They accompany the phrase that answers the first idea. Both phrases emphasize the interval of a seventh descending by step. The intruders are pitched not in F but in C (Mozart seems never to have called for trumpets crooked in F, although Haydn did). After the music reaches the dominant it shifts solemnly to the minor, from C to c, as the trumpets and drums repeat their G as a pedal tone, sounding quite ominous. Young Beethoven admired and copied a passage shortly before the reprise (see Example 7.3abc, p. 696). The ensuing Menuetto resumes not only the home key but also the mood of pomp and celebration of the *Adagio* and *Allegro spiritoso*, including fanfares with dotted rhythms. A stately dance, the minuet should certainly have appealed to the older generation of Thuns and Count Johann, who was by then in his early seventies. Its Trio is rustic by comparison and led by a solo oboe, answered by a solo bassoon.

The finale, *Presto* in 2/4 time, begins softly with a singing theme in the violins, answered gruffly by a tutti *forte* in unisons and octaves, a passage that comes to rest on E. At the first firm cadence, the tutti, reinforced by the trumpets and timpani, announce a fanfare theme that proclaims the rise from C to E but with the E appearing in a relatively weak rhythmic position deriving from the shape of the opening soft theme. Nevertheless, it is this jerky motion with its leaps and not any of the more lyric material that Mozart chose to exploit in the development of this extensive sonata form. Not until the very end of the movement, after some four hundred measures, do the violins rise to a high E in a strongly accented position, and at the beginning of a four-measure phrase that is repeated (Example 1.9). The bracketed portion conforms to a treble cadence in the *Allegro spiritoso* (mm. 44–46 passim). Only in the *Presto* are all objectives finally reached. The rise to E places this tone in the strongest possible rhythmic position; the leading tone B♮ coming after a descending seventh, resolves at last to C.

EXAMPLE 1.9. *Mozart, Symphony in C, No. 36 ("Linz"), K. 425, I*

The symphony ends in a way consistent with the very beginning of its wide span so that the first gestures of the slow introduction are made to sound prophetic of the whole. Not even Joseph Haydn had made this point so clearly in his slow symphonic introductions antedating the "Linz" Symphony. There are other ways, too, in which Haydn seems to have taken notice of K. 425, as we shall see. The work written to honor old Count Thun, and through him his family, was no vacation-period, spur-of-the-moment diversion, but Mozart's most masterly symphonic discourse up to that time. The major third in glory at the very end is an unforgettable sonority, just as it is at the end of Beethoven's Symphony No. 8.

BARON VAN SWIETEN

Baron Gottfried van Swieten was Mozart's most steadfast patron throughout the composer's last decade in Vienna. Swieten was born in Leiden in 1733, a son of the eminent physician Gerhard van Swieten, who moved the family to Vienna in 1743 after he was appointed personal physician to Empress Maria Theresa. Gottfried was educated in Vienna's Theresianum by Jesuit scholars and became a Catholic (his father remained a Protestant, an anomaly at the Habsburg court). The boy excelled in his studies, spoke and wrote many languages, and thus became a good prospect for the diplomatic service, in which he worked his way up with postings to Brussels, Paris, and Warsaw before becoming ambassador to Berlin from 1770 to 1777. An informed student and collector of music, he was the composer of an opéra comique for Paris and at least ten symphonies. At Berlin and Potsdam, Swieten, who never married, became an intimate of Frederick II and was probably, like the king, a Freemason. He developed a taste for older music, collecting works of Handel and Bach, as well as the Bach sons. From Emanuel Bach he commissioned the six superb string symphonies of 1773. In gratitude, Bach dedicated his third set of *Sonaten für Kenner und Liebhaber* (1781) to him. After resettling in Vienna, Swieten succeeded his deceased father as prefect of the Imperial Royal Library, housed in Fischer von Erlach's great palace on the Josephsplatz. He was a conduit by which Viennese music reached Berlin and North German music reached Vienna.

Joseph II appointed Swieten President of the Court Commission on Education and Censorship. This, in addition to heading the Imperial Library, made Swieten something like a minister of culture. Together with Professor Joseph von Sonnenfels, he was one of the ruler's chief allies in pursuing the enlightened reforms of the early 1780s. In 1781, the emperor issued a Patent of Toleration that ordered an end to the repression of and discrimination against the main Christian faiths other than Catholicism and removed most of the restrictions against the Jews still in force under Maria Theresa. In matters of trade policy, he followed her reforms. With regard to the established church, he went further than Maria Theresa by suppressing many monasteries and transferring their monks to work in parishes and as teachers. He placed great emphasis on primary education for all. Swieten, "the bastion of Enlightened influence within Joseph's government," urged that authors be protected by copyright, but the emperor rejected the proposal in 1784 for commercial reasons.[47]

[47] Ernst Wangermann, *The Austrian Achievement, 1700–1800* (London, 1973), p. 142.

Swieten played an important role in calling Mozart's attention to some of the treasures of earlier music. Mozart first mentioned him in his letters on 26 May 1781 as one of the auditors, along with Sonnenfels and Count Rosenberg, at the rendition he gave of *Idomeneo* at Countess Thun's, accompanying himself at her fortepiano. Then on 24 November 1781, Mozart mentioned that Swieten and Countess Thun were among those present to hear a concert at the Auernhammers when he and Josepha Auernhammer gave the first performance of the Sonata for Two Pianos in D, K. 448, "specifically composed for the occasion." Around this time, or no later than early 1782, Mozart began attending and performing in the weekly concerts Swieten held in his rooms at the library. On 10 April 1782, Mozart wrote, "Every Sunday at noon I go to visit Baron von Suiten [*sic*] and there we play nothing but Handel and Bach—I am putting together a collection of Bach fugues, that is, Sebastian as well as Emanuel and Friedemann Bach. I am also collecting Handel's."

A few days later, on 20 April 1782, Mozart wrote his sister about the Prelude and Fugue in C, K. 394, he had just written.

> I am sending you here a prelude and three-voiced fugue that will explain why I did not answer you at once, the reason being that I could not finish writing out all the little notes any sooner. It is written down backwards. The prelude should come first then the fugue, and the reason [for their inversion] is that the fugue was already composed and as I was writing it down, I was thinking out the prelude. I only hope you can read it for the notes are so small, and then that you will like it. Another time I shall send you something better [more idiomatic?] for the keyboard. The reason why this fugue came into the world is my dear Constanze.

Mozart spells out here how most pieces with preludial function were surely conceived: subsequent to the more difficult and imposing piece they introduced, or forecast. This is certainly true of K. 394, the fugue subject of which is inspired by the first fugue of Bach's *Well Tempered Clavier*.

Mozart would have us believe that Constanze loved fugues. This was a way of building her up by convincing his sister and father that his choice among the barely educated Weber sisters was astute. Constanze was indeed a singer, although surely less gifted than her older sister Aloysia. And how many singers in any age can manage to concentrate on more than one melodic line at a time? The letter of 10 April continues as follows.

> Baron van Swieten, whom I visit every Sunday, gave me works by Handel and Sebastian Bach to take home with me after I played them through for him. As Constanze heard these fugues, she fell entirely in love with them and now she wants to hear nothing but Handel and Bach, especially in this genre. And as she has often heard me play fugues out of my head, now she asked whether I had written any of them

down? I said no, which led her to scold me and say I was unwilling to write the most artful and beautiful kind of music. She did not relent until I composed a fugue for her, and that is how it came to be. I have purposely written *Andante Maestoso* above it so that it will not be played too fast, for if a fugue is not played slowly one cannot hear the entering theme clearly enough and is consequently without effect. I will compose five more as soon as I have time and favorable opportunity and present them to Baron van Swieten, who has great treasures of good music, albeit in small quantity. Exactly for this reason, I beg you not to renege on your promise. Show it to no one, learn it by heart, then play it. A fugue is not so easily copied by ear.

There are a few fugal beginnings Mozart made about this time that may represent an attempt to build up a set of such keyboard pieces. That they remained unfinished is no great loss judging by the improvisatory nature of K. 394, whose meandering fugue is very free in its dissonance treatment.

That Mozart with more care could compose a really good fugue in the manner of Bach is shown by the Fugue in c for Two Pianos, K. 426 (dating from either 1782 or 1783), although it also has some hair-raising dissonances that would not have been allowed in the strict style. It was surely bound to please Swieten and may have been written especially for his concerts. For Swieten, Mozart probably made some arrangements for string quartet of Bach fugues, K. 405, and later an arrangement for strings of his own K. 426 with a striking prelude, K. 546. He may also have contributed to Swieten's Sunday concerts by playing violin or viola in these works and others like them.

Through Swieten Mozart became more aware of Bach's music and that of other Lutheran masters. He was not unaware of them before. In an excess of enthusiasm about Georg Benda's melodramas he wrote in a letter to his father, dated Mannheim 12 November 1778, that this composer was his favorite among all the Lutheran Kapellmeisters. Music by Handel was put before him to read at sight during his stay in London in 1764–65.[48] Handel's keyboard suites of 1722 were the likely model for Mozart's unfinished keyboard suite K. 399. Too much weight has sometimes been placed on Mozart's turn to older music at the time, even to the extent of speaking about it as a "Bach crisis," as if Mozart had stopped composing in the idioms that were normal to him. Even Swieten promoted Mozart's normal performing activities, as when he helped organize subscribers to the composer's Augarten concerts in 1782. The baron's tastes were not exclusively focused on old music or its style, as his own compositions show. Mozart's shift in attention, however temporary, has sometimes been made to sound like a conversion to the true religion. One scholar warned about this kind of misreading and the cultural biases behind it: "I have the impression that

---

[48] *Haydn, Mozart*, p. 503. The letter cited there as 13 September 1765 should read 1764.

objective grounds have led authors, above all German writers, less than ideo-logical and irrational grounds, to overstress and even exaggerate Mozart's 'Bach experience.' "[49]

Swieten remained a constant supporter of Mozart even during the lean years of the late 1780s, when economic decline took a hard toll on Vienna's concert life. He organized and led a group of aristocratic patrons, called the *Associierte*, who sponsored performances of choral and orchestral works. He commissioned Mozart to arrange for them Handel's *Acis and Galatea* (1788), *Messiah* (1789), and *Alexander's Feast* (1790). These had some bearing on Mozart's own very late works, as well as on Haydn's two late oratorios, written in collaboration with the baron.

FREEMASONRY

A secret society, also known as the Craft, Freemasonry spread rapidly from Brit-ain to the major cities of the Continent by the mid-eighteenth century, particu-larly Paris, The Hague, Brussels, and Berlin. The members of this all-male society called each other brother and worked to further such enlightened ideals as gen-eral education, religious tolerance and the diffusion of knowledge. They met in lodges and followed similar rituals in all countries, which helped forge intellec-tual and social ties along cosmopolitan lines.

Even rulers were known to have joined the society. Francis of Lorraine, elected Holy Roman Emperor in 1744, was initiated into the order at The Hague in 1731.[50] His wife Maria Theresa looked askance at secret societies, as did most other absolute rulers. Moreover, Freemasonry had been condemned by the pope more than once, and Maria Theresa, although a devout Catholic, was deter-mined to reduce the holdings of the church in Austria and her other crown lands, together known as the Monarchy. As a shrewd political ruler in Vienna (Francis was only co-ruler), she worked toward many important reforms, notably sup-pression of some monastic orders; the reforms were carried out more vigorously by their son Joseph II. As to the involvement of her husband, Francis, with the Craft, she mostly looked the other way. There grew to be in consequence a mod-est presence of Masonic lodges in the Monarchy. They were not so numerous or well populated with brothers as in many other lands of the Empire. Freemasonry became especially strong in Prussia, Saxony, and the Saxon dukedoms, where rulers openly belonged to the Craft. It was in the Saxon capital of Dresden in 1781, to celebrate an electoral marriage, that an opera with Masonic themes, *Osir-ide*, was staged, anticipating *Die Zauberflöte* by a decade.

---

[49] Wolfgang Plath, in *NMA* IX/27/2, p. xv, n. 27.
[50] Margaret C. Jacob, *Living the Enlightenment: Freemasonry and Politics in Eighteenth-Century Europe* (Oxford, 1991), p. 80.

After the sudden death of Emperor Francis in 1765, Joseph II became co-ruler of the Monarchy with his mother and also succeeded his father as Holy Roman Emperor. Their joint rule of fifteen years was in fact a triumvirate with Count (later Prince) Wenzel Anton von Kaunitz, state chancellor of Austria. Joseph's views on Freemasonry came to the fore in 1777 when it was brought to the attention of Maria Theresa that her late husband's brother, Prince Charles of Lorraine, regent of the Austrian Netherlands, together with some of his courtiers, were openly frequenting Masonic lodge meetings in Brussels. Kaunitz urged her to suppress the lodges. Joseph sent his opinion to Kaunitz in a letter of 21 February 1777.

> Whatever methods are employed to prevent and harass such clubs tend only to make them more attractive and, since their innocence is recognized by all sensible persons in society, to bring ridicule on governments and on those who, in forbidding things that they believe to be bad simply because they don't know anything about them, endow them with a measure of importance, I therefore very humbly suggest that no action should be taken . . . But if she thinks it appropriate, the leaders of Brussels society could be gently informed that we should prefer them not to amuse themselves so publicly with Freemasonry, but that they should conceal it better, so that the affair won't cause so much talk.[51]

There is a hint here that Joseph considered himself among those "sensible persons" who were knowledgeable about Masonic aims, of which his elders were ignorant. In any case his recommendation could be summed up, not so much as benevolent neglect, but as "sweep it under the rug so it escapes notice." Joseph's attitude remained largely the same during the first half of his sole reign, from 1780 to 1785. Then events took a turn that persuaded him that Masonic "innocence" was not what he had assumed it to be, and that its "importance" could no longer be ignored.

Joseph's first five years as sole ruler saw the number of Viennese lodges increase to eight while the total population of Masons more than doubled. The most reputed lodges were Crowned Hope (Zur gekrönnte Hoffnung), True Concord (Zur wahren Eintracht), and the smaller Beneficence (Zur Wohltätigkeit).[52] An eminent mineralogist, Ignaz von Born, led True Concord and Mozart's Mannheim friend, Baron Otto von Gemmingen, led Benevolence, which was closely allied with True Concord. Mozart applied for admission to Benevolence in November 1784 and was admitted as an Apprentice the following month, presumably with all the usual tests and ceremonies. He was advanced to the second degree, that of Journeyman or Fellow Craft, at a ceremony that took place at

---

[51] Derek Beales, *Joseph II*, vol. 1: *In the shadow of Maria Theresa (1741–1780)* (Cambridge, 1987), p. 486.
[52] These three lodges were located in the northern part of the old city not far from Hoher Markt. For their precise location see the map "Vienna, 1780" in Cairns, *Mozart and His Operas*, pp. xii–xiii.

True Concord in early January 1785 and was further advanced to the third degree of Master sometime later. Perhaps Benevolence appealed to Mozart because its membership was smaller, or because it had mainly non-titled brothers like himself; besides Gemmingen the most prominent noble member was Count (later Prince) Carl Lichnowsky, who was five years younger than Mozart and would later marry Maria Christiana, second daughter of Countess Thun. The average age at this lodge was close to Mozart's, another factor that may have been attractive to him.[53] The lodge had earned a good reputation in 1784, when it lived up to its name with a successful campaign to raise relief funds for that spring's flood victims. Any or all of these factors could have played a role in Mozart's decision to choose Benevolence over True Concord. Haydn chose the latter, which included many leading noblemen as well as two of Vienna's best poets, Alois Blumauer and Johann Baptist von Alxinger, whom Mozart greatly admired.

Biographers have often wondered why Mozart waited so long to become a Mason. During the 1770s, his incidental music to the play *Thamos* by Tobias Philipp von Gebler brought him into contact with Masonic ideas and circles. In fact, he was surrounded by Masons wherever he went: Paris, Munich, Mannheim, or even at home in Salzburg. Mannheim, which Mozart visited twice in 1777–78, was particularly rife with Freemasonry. Elector Carl Theodor, who reigned there, was said to be a Mason himself; like most other Catholic rulers, he deemed it prudent to avoid open connections with an order specifically banned by papal bulls. Nevertheless, the elector chose to surround himself with Masons, whether councilors, diplomats, literary figures, or even musicians. His envoy to the French court, Count Karl Heinrich von Sickingen, was a Mason and a close friend and patron of Mozart's in Paris during 1778. Running the theatrical life at Mannheim were prominent Masons in the persons of Theobold Marchand, leader of the German troupe of players, the aforementioned Gemmingen, playwright and privy councilor, and Wolfgang Heribert von Dalberg, director of the National Theater. Mozart's correspondent Professor Anton Klein was another Masonic privy councilor. Among the chief musicians belonging to the order were first flautist Johann Baptist Wendling, first oboe Friedrich Ramm, and concertmaster Carl Cannabich. When Carl Theodore inherited the Bavarian throne in 1778, most of this group followed him to Munich, where many Masons were already prominent at court, notably Count Joseph Anton Seeau, the intendant of the theaters with whom Mozart had to deal in connection with both *Idomeneo* and *La finta giardiniera*.

Bavaria was also the site of a radical sect loosely tied to the Craft, the Illuminati, who were more secretive and did not keep membership lists, unlike the

---

[53] Heinz Schuler, " 'Mozart von der Wohltätigkeit': Die Mitglieder der gerechten und vollkommenen St-Johannes-Freimaurer-Loge 'Zur Wohltätigkeit' im Orient von Wien," *Mitteilungen der Internationalen Stiftung Mozarteum* 36 (1988): 1–56.

Masons. Professor Adam Weishaupt and Dr. Franz Xaver Bader of Ingolstadt University founded the Illuminati in 1776. The goal of this sect was to make social changes beyond what the authorities deemed permissible. True Masons, as part of their oath, abjured any dabbling in politics. The more militant Illuminati were not so constrained and made many converts, even among the leading Masons in Vienna. Elector Carl Theodore was persuaded, rightly or not, that the Illuminati were conspiring to undermine and perhaps even overthrow his rule in Bavaria. Consequently, he banned all secret societies in 1784. Rumors had reached him that the Illuminati were working in collusion with Viennese colleagues to further the imperial proposal that the elector exchange his rule over Bavaria for possession of the Austrian Netherlands.[54] He required the leaders of the Illuminati to make a formal abjuration of their sect. Leopold Mozart described this situation to Nannerl in the fall of 1785, six months after he himself had joined the Craft in Vienna. His letter is dated Salzburg, 14 October 1785, and in it his concern to downplay the events in Munich is evident.

> From Ramm in person, and already from Marchand's letters, I learned that not even a small fraction of the rumors told here about the Illuminati in Munich are true. Some obstinate individuals [eigensinnige] were banished or departed of their own accord. The rest, who explained themselves to the elector, remained, even Dr. Bader, one of their leaders. The amusing part of it is a list of the members of Bader's lodge that is circulating here naming some seventy persons, many of them priests of high standing, including our Count Spaur, canon of Salzburg Cathedral. According to Ramm, the true Masons, of whom the elector is one, are greatly annoyed at these cranks [sonderlinge], thus their persecution.

Leopold makes no mention of his son in this letter but we may wonder whether Leopold's censure of the over-zealous might also be directed subliminally at Wolfgang.

Mozart's motives for joining the Craft in Vienna were at least in good part altruistic. He truly believed in practicing generosity to those less favored in life and was in sympathy with the emperor's reforms. It cannot be dismissed that he also had some self-interest in mind when joining the brotherhood. There is no inherent contradiction between altruism and self-interest, contrary to what a later age of romantic idealism might wish us to believe. Some young men undoubtedly joined their lodges for reasons that were less than noble-minded. One high official, when attempting to explain to Leopold II how Freemasonry gained such a strong foothold under Joseph, claimed it was one of the best ways to secure government appointments: "This mischief assumed such proportions that many

---

[54] Braunbehrens, *Mozart in Vienna, 1781–1791* (New York, 1986), p. 241.

young people had no hopes of a career unless they became Masons."[55] If advancement had been Mozart's chief concern, he would have quit the order after Joseph turned against it. The best explanation of why he joined it and remained one of its most active members probably lies in the obvious joy he took in its social aspects.

One of Mozart's first initiatives in his lodge was to introduce his father as a candidate for membership. The visiting Leopold, like his son, was promoted rapidly through the three degrees of brotherhood. Another initiative Mozart took was to provide his lodge with new compositions. Musical performance was an integral part of lodge ceremonies. Besides several Masonic songs, Mozart wrote some weightier pieces. To celebrate the achievements of Ignaz von Born, who had just been knighted by Joseph II, he composed the festive cantata *Die Maurerfreude*, K. 471, for tenor solo, men's chorus, and orchestra. Franz Petran, a Mason from Bohemia, wrote the text, which Mozart chose to set in the favorite Masonic key of E♭. Adamberger, Mozart's Belmonte and a member of True Concord, sang the solo part.

Mozart entered *Die Maurerfreude* in his thematic catalogue under the date 20 April 1785. The first performance took place four days later at Crowned Hope, which announced the occasion to the public saying that Born had been honored by a cantata

> written by Brother Petran and set to music by our famous Brother Mozart of the very worshipful lodge Benevolence. It was sung by Brother Adamberger and has now been published by Brother Artaria, together with a drawing by Brother Unterberger and a preface by Brother Epstein. All profits from the sale of this work will be given to the poor, and we hope that you will do all you can to promote its sale in your neighborhood.[56]

Unterberger's title vignette well illustrates the care taken with the edition (Figure 1.5). Under the title in roman and italic letters, a placid stream flows toward the action, in which a female figure crowns the honoree with laurel while another, seated and crowned, with an anchor at her side, lays her hand on his outstretched arm. All three are gowned in the flowing robes of antiquity, not contemporary garments.

Before the year 1785 was over, Mozart wrote another large Masonic piece, *Maurerisches Trauermusik*, K. 477, an elaborately scored orchestral *Adagio* in cut time and in the key of c, calling for three basset horns as well as oboes, clarinets,

[55] Letter dated 29 January 1792 from Count Heinrich von Rottenhan, Burggraf of Bohemia, cited after H. C. Robbins Landon, *Mozart: The Golden Years, 1781–1791* (New York, 1989), pp. 230–31.
[56] Otto Erich Deutsch, *Mozart: Die Dokumente seines Lebens* (Kassel, 1961), pp. 218–19.

FIGURE 1.5. Title page of *Die Maurerfreude*.

horns, and contrabassoon. Questions remain about when the piece was first composed, when revised, and at which ceremonies of mourning it was performed.[57] Mozart took unusual care in this piece with the dynamics, which changed often, sometimes by the measure from loud to soft, and sometimes a *crescendo* or *decrescendo* indicated by hairpin signs within the measures. The piece ends *pianissimo*, with a *tierce de Picardie*.

Music occupied a very large place in the meetings, according to a program at Crowned Hope announced on 9 December 1785. The concert took place on 15 December as a benefit for two visiting lodge brothers from Bohemia, Anton David and Vinzent Springer, virtuosi on the basset horn. The program consisted of:

1. a symphony composed for the event by Brother [Paul] Wranitzky;
2. a concerto for two basset horns performed by Brothers David and Springer;

[57] Konrad Küster, *Mozart: A Musical Biography*, translated by Mary Whittall (Oxford, 1996), pp. 200–204.

3. *Die Maurerfreude* in honor of Brother Born sung by Brother Adamberger;

4. a fortepiano concerto played by Brother Mozart;

5. a suite by Brother Stadler for six wind instruments in which Brother [Theodor] Lotz played the contrabassoon;

6. a second symphony composed for the occasion by Brother Wranitzky;

7. fantasies performed by Brother Mozart.[58]

Mozart entered his Piano Concerto No. 22 in E♭, K. 482, into his thematic catalogue under the date of 16 December 1785, one day after the lodge concert. It could have been the concerto he played there as well as the "new concert" he performed as an entr'acte between the parts of Carl Ditters von Dittersdorf's oratorio *Ester* on 23 December, an Advent concert given by the Musicians' Society (Tonkünstler Societät). Arguments have been adduced that K. 482 was particularly suited to a Masonic event by virtue of its main key of E♭ and slow movement in c minor—the same key as the *Maurerisches Trauermusik*, K. 477—and its use of clarinets for the first time in one of the concertos.[59] Whatever the special significance K. 482 may have had for Mozart's lodge brothers and other Masons, it was also an all-purpose work for the general public, like the other great concertos of 1785–86.

The fortunes of the Craft in the Habsburg realms first took a turn for the worse with the proclamation of Joseph's Freemasonry Act on 11 December 1785. Like the Apostle Peter, Joseph makes a three-fold denial of knowing anything about the subject. This seems not only unnecessarily repetitious but also odd in light of inside knowledge implied by his 1777 letter to Kaunitz quoted above.

> The so-called Freemason societies, whose secrets are unknown to me and whose chicaneries [Gaukeleien] I have until now not taken seriously, continue to multiply and are now spreading to smaller cities . . . [Some] people holding positions of authority fanatically band together and show grave injustice toward their subordinates who are not members of these societies. Previously, in other lands, the Freemasons have been punished or forbidden and their lodges broken up, simply because they would not reveal their secrets. Although I am also ignorant of them, it is enough for me to know that these Masonic societies have engaged in some good work for their fellow men, such as charity and education—more, indeed, than in any other land. Accordingly, I herewith ordain that although I know nothing of their laws and practices, they shall be taken under the protection of the State—as long as their good work continues—and their assemblies shall be officially sanctioned.[60]

---

[58] Deutsch, *Dokumente*, p. 226.

[59] Katherine Johnson, *The Masonic Thread in Mozart* (London, 1977), 90–95. The claimed melodic resemblances between K. 482 and *Die Maurerfreude* are too slight to be more than coincidental. On the other hand, clarinets and basset horns, it must be admitted, were frequently heard at lodge meetings.

[60] Translation from Braunbehrens, *Mozart in Vienna*, p. 243.

The ominous-sounding expressions "state protection" and "official sanction" translated in fact into ongoing surveillance by the police. One scholar sees in this the beginnings of Austria's decline into a totalitarian state terrorized by the secret police of Count Johann Pergen.[61] A full explanation as to why Joseph took this turn in his relations to the Craft has yet to be made. His reference to its suppression in other lands concerns the fate of the Illuminati in neighboring Bavaria. A crisis provoked by his plan to exchange the Austrian Netherlands for Bavaria may be pertinent.

The consequences of the edict were many. Eight Viennese lodges shrank to only two. Benevolence joined Crowned Hope and another lodge to form New-Crowned Hope (Zur neugekrönten Hoffnung); True Concord merged with others into Truth (Zur Wahrheit). Dismayed, Gemmingen left the society, but Mozart remained. Born attempted to go on but after the intense quarrel among the brothers following the edict he also quit. By the end of 1786, the population of Viennese Masons had been reduced to one quarter of its former size.

Joseph II conducted foreign policy as arbitrarily as he treated Freemasonry. His long-standing ambition to acquire Bavaria was supported by no other state. His belligerent moves in the Low Countries in an attempt to add Maastricht to the Austrian Netherlands threatened the peace of Europe in early 1785. Thomas Jefferson, a new nation's ambassador to France, summed up the situation in a letter to James Monroe dated Paris, 14 April 1785.

> War and peace still doubtful. It rather seems that the peace may continue a while yet. But not very long. The Emperor has a head too combustible to be quiet. He is an eccentric character. All enterprise, without calculation, without principle, without feelings. Ambitious in the extreme, but too unsteady to surmount difficulties. He had in view at one time to open the Scheld, to get Maestricht from the Dutch, to take a large district from the Turks, to exchange some of his Austrian dominions for Bavaria, to create a ninth electorate, to make his nephew King of the Romans, and to change totally the constitution of Hungary. Any one of these was as much as a wise prince would have undertaken at any one time. Quod vult, vade vult, sed non diu vult (What he wants he wants badly, but not for long).[62]

The German princes were in a state of panic over Joseph's attempts at aggrandizement and threw themselves under the protection of Frederick II of Prussia— one last triumph over Austria for the wily old monarch, who died the following year. The electors refused to accept Archduke Francis as King of the Romans (hence Joseph's successor as emperor).

---

[61] Ernst Wangermann, *From Joseph II to the Jacobin Trials*, 2nd ed. (Oxford, 1969), pp. 36–43.
[62] Thomas Jefferson, *Travels: Selected Writings, 1784–1789*, ed. Anthony Brandt (Washington, D.C., 2006), p. 25.

Six String Quartets Dedicated to Haydn

Mozart had not written string quartets since his Viennese summer of 1773, when it was a question of compiling a set that would be worthy to stand beside those of Joseph Haydn and would attract the attention of Joseph II, an avid player of chamber music with a penchant for fugues. Leopold Mozart, ever hopeful of an appointment for his son at some Habsburg court, was behind this endeavor. He also tried to sell the 1773 set to publishers, without success. The new set, begun in 1782, won its composer great praise, notably from Joseph Haydn, but it is doubtful whether Joseph II appreciated this aspect of Mozart's art. The emperor still preferred to perform the string quartets of his defunct Kapellmeister Leopold Gassmann.

Haydn's six string quartets of 1781 reached a new level in the genre he did so much to create. They were published by Artaria as Op. 33 in April 1782 and are discussed in chapter 4. For Mozart they were an added stimulation to begin his own set of six new quartets. At the same time, he was still coming to terms with Haydn's earlier sets. In a fragment that has been dated "very probably in spring 1782" he made an attempt to recompose the beginning of Haydn's String Quartet in E major, Op. 17 No. 1.[63] This piece of evidence could mean that from the outset he intended to honor Haydn with a dedication. He warmed his hand to the task of writing quartets again by returning to those of the older master.

In early 1784, a set of string quartets by Ignaz Pleyel came to Mozart's attention. They were published by Artaria and prompted these comments in the letter of 24 April 1784 that Mozart wrote to his father.

> Some quartets have just come out by a certain Pleyel, a pupil of Joseph Haydn. If you do not know them yet do try to get hold of them for they are worth the effort. They are well written and very pleasant. You will immediately recognize who his teacher was. Good and happy the day will be for music if in time Pleyel should be able to replace Haydn for us [uns Haydn zu remplaciren!].

Evident is the high esteem in which both Mozarts held Haydn, also how well they knew and admired his style of composition, so deftly deployed in string quartets. Pleyel's first quartets are indeed attractive and have recently become readily available.[64] Yet no one has ever replaced Joseph Haydn. The case brings to mind an incident a few months later, when Thomas Jefferson arrived in Paris

---

[63] Gerhart Croll, "Remarks on a Mozart Quartet Fragment," in *Haydn Studies*, ed. Jens Peter Larsen, Howard Serwer, and James Webster (New York, 1981), pp. 405–7. In an added remark, Charles Rosen observed that Mozart's Quartet in E♭, K. 428, mm. 5–8, borrowed a moment from the fragment (see Example 1.10, m. 5 below).

[64] Ignaz Pleyel, *Six String Quartets, Opus 1*, ed. Simon P. Keefe (The Early String Quartet, vol. 4; Ann Arbor, MI, 2005). I thank the managing editor of Steglein Publishing, Inc., Mark W. Knoll, for sending me a copy of the edition.

and was greeted as Franklin's replacement. "Sir," he replied, "no one can replace Benjamin Franklin; I am merely his successor."

Mozart dated the Quartet in G, K. 387, Vienna 31 December 1782. He mentioned the quartets as a set of six in his letter of 26 April 1783 to Jean-Georges Sieber in Paris, as an incidental addition to his offer of the three piano concertos, K. 413–415: "Furthermore, I am composing six quartets for two violins, viola and bass. If you wish to engrave these quartets as well, I shall be happy to let you have them, but I could not sell them for less than 50 Louis d'or." There is no telling how far along Mozart was in conceiving the set when he wrote this. At the time, he had written out only K. 387, as far as we know.

Sieber did not reply to Mozart's offer of the six quartets, or else his negative or unsatisfactory reply has been lost. Mozart's terms were high, 50 Louis d'or being the rough equivalent of 550 florins. When the set of six quartets was completed in early 1785, the composer sold them to Artaria for a hundred ducats (450 florins). Publishers liked to see Haydn's name associated in some way with any publication of new string quartets because it increased their salability, or at least reduced the public's sales resistance to an item that was quite expensive. The handsome title page of Artaria's edition states that the works were "composed for and dedicated to Signor Giuseppe Haydn" (Figure 1.6).

K. 387 in G begins with a rather dense first movement, *Allegro vivace assai* in common time. The first violin announces a vigorous theme leaping upward, 1 5 8, and descending by stepwise motion. The other instruments merely accompany the melody for the most part. Dynamics keep changing, with soft and loud measures in alternation, thus producing an almost mechanical effect. Mozart applies the same alternation of loud and soft by the quarter note later in the movement and in the minuet that follows. To counter the nervous and often chromatic character of its first theme, the *Allegro vivace* offers a second theme in the dominant that is more relaxed and is notable especially for its broad harmonic rhythm (two measures per harmony) that contrasts markedly with the rapid chord changes of the first theme. More will be said about this in chapter 4.

FIGURE 1.6. Title page of the String Quartets dedicated to Haydn.

A soft two-measure cadential tag ends the prima parte. Both parts are marked for repetition. In the seconda parte, the music heads for the usual cadence on vi, which is confirmed by the same cadential tag that confirmed V. A lengthy retransition and dominant pedal prepares the reprise. These leisurely proceedings help make the seconda parte more than twice the length of the prima parte (quite unlike Haydn's frequent condensations making the two parts more nearly equal in length).

Joseph II allegedly said to Mozart about *Die Entführung*, "too many notes!" The remark, reported by Niemetschek in 1798, is probably spurious but it points up a common reaction to Mozart's music. Someone who found it to be too complicated and long-winded could readily complain about K. 387, the minuet of which is one of Mozart's longest, extending to ninety-three measures without repeats. The following movement, *Andante cantabile* in the key of C and also in 3/4 time, extends to 106 measures, a more modest number for this type of slow movement, which is largely a cantilena for the first violin. The other parts are kept busy providing a rich harmonic support.

The finale, *Molto Allegro* in cut time, combines contrapuntal artifice with homophonic sections in roughly equal degree. It opens with a four-tone subject in whole notes, initiating a fugato with tonal answers. Acute listeners may guess that the second fugato on a different subject is made so that it will combine with the first, which it eventually does. The delight on hearing this happen does not wear thin no matter how often we experience it. But so learned a movement, stretching to nearly 300 measures, was doubtless too difficult for many listeners of the time. In an effort to sell his own string quartets, Dittersdorf wrote Artaria in 1788 with claims that he had bested not only Ignaz Pleyel but also Haydn and adding that Mozart's quartets dedicated to Haydn were too consistently artful to be bought by everyone. An anonymous critic writing in Cramer's *Magazin der Musik* in 1787 called them "too highly seasoned—and whose palate can long endure that?" It is true that some sections are so liberally peppered with dynamic indications as to make the score appear as if it were sprinkled with them.

Composition of the Quartet in d, K. 421, has been placed in June 1783 on not very convincing grounds. It opens with the first violin jumping down the tonic octave then leaping up a tenth, a span recovered by step, and thus bearing a general similarity to the opening of K. 387. This movement is concise in comparison, an *Allegro moderato* in common time with a prima parte of 41 measures, repeated, and a seconda parte of 77 measures, also repeated. The following *Andante* in 6/8 time and in F takes 68 measures and counters the spirit of unease in the first movement, which was intensified by the slowly descending stepwise bass under the first theme, a device long associated with laments. The descending bass returns to accompany the *Menuetto Allegretto* but this time *forte* instead of *piano*, and intensified by chromatic steps. The link with the earlier theme is also apparent in the prominent dotted rhythms. A delightful Trio in D turns the dotted figures around into Lombard snaps and a simple harmonization consisting mostly of I and V⁷ lends the piece the character of a Ländler. The finale returns to the key of d, as did the minuet. It is lightened by being a siciliana, an *Allegretto ma non troppo* in lilting 6/8 time with dotted rhythms, and by the composer's decision to cast the movement in the form of theme and variations. Both the theme and the set of variations have much in common with the siciliana finale of Haydn's superb Quartet in G of Opus 33, as has often been pointed out.[65] Mozart returns to the key of d after his penultimate variation in D and maintains the minor mode almost to the end—only the last chord introduces F♯, a *tierce de Picardie*. It is preceded by the stepwise descent from D to A in the second violin, the same gesture with which the quartet's bass began.

The Quartet in E♭, K. 428, was the third finished although placed as No. 4 in Mozart's autograph and consequently in Artaria's original print. It is thought to date within a month or so of K. 421 and to have been written out in June or July 1783. Like K. 421, it begins softly and with an octave leap, but this leap is recovered very differently, by smaller leaps down and chromatic rises, until it comes to a seeming point of rest on F in m. 5 (Example 1.10). The expressive components

EXAMPLE 1.10. *Mozart, String Quartet in E♭, K. 428, I*

of the theme have a long history in other pieces by Mozart in the same key. The Quartet in E♭, K. 160, of 1773 includes a passage in which a slurred B♮ - C is followed by A♮ - B♭ on the way down to a prominent F (Example 1.11a). Note the

EXAMPLE 1.11.

a. *Mozart, String Quartet in E♭, K. 160, I*

overlapping groups of three eighth notes between melody and accompaniment. Mozart begins the Quartet in E♭, K. 171, with an *Adagio* that makes the same melodic motifs prominent while the leap down to the F is from a C rather than an E♭ (Example 1.11b). An instructive use of these same motifs occurs in the *aria*

[65] Most recently, perhaps, by John Irving, *Mozart: The Haydn Quartets* (Cambridge, 1998), p. 80.

b. *Mozart, String Quartet in E♭, K. 171, I*

d'affetto from *Idomeneo* when Ilia expresses her love for Idamante in a roundabout way (Example 1.11c). The interlocking groups between melody and bass resemble

c. *Mozart,* Idomeneo, *Ilia's Aria, No. 11*

similar groups in Example 1.11a. Even more similar, and rounding out this little family, are the interlocking groups and melodic motifs at issue as Tamino stammers his inexpressible feelings of love at first sight in the Picture Aria of *Die Zauberflöte* (Example 1.11d).

d. *Mozart,* Die Zauberflöte, *Aria, No. 3*

With this background it is possible to appreciate how emotionally laden for Mozart was the beginning of K. 428, where the same raised tones appear but the lower one first, announced softly but in octaves and unisons as in K. 171. The first four measures take us through nine of the twelve chromatic tones only to land on a prominent F in m. 5, supported by a rich-sounding ii$^6_5$ chord, the same tone and the same chord that Beethoven muses upon to open his Piano Sonata No. 18 in E♭, Op. 31 No. 3. When Mozart repeats the first four measures, while adding harmony to the melody, he uses the other three chromatic tones (F♯, D♭, D♮) and thus employs all twelve in short order. The ii$^6_5$ chord will reappear as the second harmony of the *Menuetto Allegro* third movement, which begins with a leaping octave down from E♭ in inversion of the quartet's beginning (Haydn used this same octave leap down to begin the *Scherzo Allegro* of his Quartet in E♭ of Op. 33).

The second movement of K. 428, *Andante con moto* in 6/8 time, is in A♭, a somewhat rare key for Mozart, who often chose either the key of B♭ or c for the second movement of works with an overall tonality of E♭. The *Andante* is an exercise in minimal melodic motions, mostly conjunct, and subtly shifting harmonies, a movement that has been compared to the prayer-like slow movement in A♭ of Haydn's Quartet in E♭ from his Opus 20 set.[66]

A lighter mood prevails in K. 428 after the *Andante*. The *Menuetto Allegro* dances along for the most part with an easy motion and more cheerily than its counterparts in K. 387 and K. 421. Its Trio begins both of its strains in minor, first c then g, but both end in B♭. The finale, *Allegro vivace* in 2/4 time, is more bantering still. Close to the end, Mozart layers a broader melody in the first violin above the main theme, with chromatic rises, that begins B♭ B♮ C, a faint reminder, perhaps, of the quartet's opening.

Mozart began K. 458, the so-called "Hunt" Quartet in B♭, about the same time as K. 421 and K. 428, that is, in mid-1783, as paper studies reveal. He did not finish it until over a year later, according to the date entered in his thematic catalogue, 9 November 1784. A short while later all six quartets were finished and ready for performance. On 22 January 1785, Leopold Mozart received a short note from his son, the contents of which he reported the same day to Nannerl: "Last Saturday your brother played his six quartets for his dear friend Haydn and several other good friends, and sold them to Artaria for 100 ducats." Leopold was then about to depart for Vienna by way of Munich. From Vienna, Leopold reported to Nannerl by letter of 16 February 1785, "The new quartets were played, but only the three new ones he added to the three we already have [K. 387, K. 421, and K. 428]. They are somewhat easier [etwas leichter] but excellently composed."

K. 458 in B♭ earned its later sobriquet "the Hunt" from the melody in simple 6/8 time with which it begins, *Allegro vivace assai*. For most listeners, even Leopold, the movement would be easier to comprehend, partly because it suggests a widespread topos. It also lacks the chromatic mysteries of K. 428 in E♭. Leopold's description of the last three quartets as a little easier or lighter may have to do with these two specific quartets, because the last two, K. 464 in A and K. 465 in C, could scarcely be considered lightweight or easy to play. Leopold's remark may pertain to certain general characteristics of the earlier quartets: K. 387 was densely worked, tending toward prolixity, and caused its creator an unusual amount of labor and revision; K. 421 in d is somewhat dark and morose; K. 428 has an intense *affetuoso* tone (at least in the first two movements). K. 458 is more airy in texture than the first three quartets, and perhaps this is what Leopold meant. When the second violin and viola repeat the main theme of its opening movement down an octave, the first violin emits a long trill, of the sort often given the piano in Mozart's concertos, then all four parts start warbling

---

[66] *Haydn, Mozart*, p. 341.

a short trill figure that constitutes the second theme. The one rather mysterious passage in this first movement is the sudden hushed moment as all three diminished chords are heard in succession, each prolonged for a measure, shortly after the second theme. In an elaborate and long coda to the movement, the mostly triadic main theme is easily turned into strettos.

The second movement of K. 451 is a *Menuetto Moderato* that pits legato, conjunct melody, and accompaniment (the minuet) against the trio's mostly detached or *portamento* bowing of the melody and constant staccato eighth notes of the accompanying middle voices. The effect of this trio is so light and serenade-like as to evoke the famous "minuet of Boccherini" (from that master's String Quintet in E of 1771 G. 275). The following *Adagio*, in E♭ and in common time, strikes a more serious tone but not at great length: it says its piece in a mere 53 measures. The finale, *Allegro assai* in 2/4 time, is based on a theme with repeated tones and light-hearted banter worthy of Haydn. When the lower strings repeat the cadential figure an octave below, the two violins respond with the tones 5 3 1, which are of course those that began the first movement. Mozart originally introduced imitative entries of the theme at its first appearance. He thought better of this and saved the device for later in the movement. He perceived the contrapuntal possibilities of his theme from the beginning but held back from using them until the piece was well under way, which certainly made things easier for the listener. One recurrent figure from the end of the finale's main theme, an innocent-sounding cadential tag marked *piano*, is repeated so often it becomes a jest. This same cadential tag occurs frequently in the first movement of Haydn's Quartet in B♭ of Opus 33 (Example 1.12ab). It is thus a jest shared by the two composers, but hardly private. We can all hear and rejoice in the wit of Mozart's tribute to his older friend and revered model.

EXAMPLE 1.12.

a. *Haydn, String Quartet in B♭, Op. 33, I*

b. *Mozart, String Quartet in B♭, K. 458, IV*

The last two quartets are in a class by themselves, not only in this set but in all of Mozart's string quartets, of which they are the greatest. It may be that Mozart's tribute to Haydn in the last movement of K. 428 corresponded with the moment he decided to dedicate the set to the genre's pioneer and most innovative master. Some such epiphany would help explain how Mozart then spurred himself on to such great heights.

K. 464 is in A, a key that almost always has special lyrical potential for Mozart, a key of love duets and sentimental outbursts. There is little of either in the opening *Allegro* in 3/4 time. Its main theme evolves out of a melodic turn around the fifth degree from which the first violin alone sings a gentle chromatic descent to the tonic, *piano* (Example 1.13a). As a response, all four voices march in staccato quarter notes from I^6 to V^6_5 in mm. 3–4. The melody repeats in sequence one tone down, the harmonized part projecting V^7- I. There is a slight rhythmic ambiguity to the first violin's solos, which are grouped more readily into 3/2 than 3/4. The answer to this initial eight-measure phrase is a brusque unison, *forte*, using a rising instead of descending sequence in mm. 8–12. The first violin takes charge of the next four-measure phrase, descending gracefully and softly from high A to a full cadence on A an octave below, accompanied by the others. Lurking beneath the surface is the outline of a typical song-form: *a a' b a"*. Each segment begins with the same rhythmic motif, marked x in Example 1.13a and b.

EXAMPLE 1.13 a, b. *Mozart, String Quartet in A, K. 464*

a. *I*

b. *IV*

Almost everything in the opening *Allegro*, a sonata form of 270 measures with both parts repeated, is derived from these opening 16 measures. Transition to the dominant begins by transforming the violin's initial phrase into a point of imitation leading from a minor to C major, which gives way to B major. The second theme sounds new, being a rising chromatic idea for the first violin, 5 ♯ 6 in the new key of E, but its rhythm of half-note, quarter-note, quarter-note is that of the melodic cadence in mm. 15–16. Triplets in response add a new rhythmic motion, spun out further as the motives of the second theme are subjected to contrapuntal elaboration of a very developmental character. This leads to reconfirmation of the second key, E, followed by a codetta weaving duets out of the movement's first theme. There is a closing idea as well but it is derived from mm. 8–12 of the first theme. What is left to develop?

Plenty! The transition of the prima parte is recalled with further permutations followed by the mm. 8–12 segment of the main theme, which is dissected into its constituent parts, such as its rhythm and the individual motifs that make it up—a kind of fragmentation that Mozart rarely employs. Meanwhile, the main theme has been made to combine in new ways with the second theme. This amount of intense working over is unusual for the composer, whose development sections are often mere transitions by means of harmonic sequences. Here the development is nearly as long as the prima parte. All these features point clearly to Haydn, whose rigorous developments often lead to shortened recapitulations. Mozart, on the other hand, makes this recapitulation unusually spacious, especially in its final sections, which are lengthened after the second theme by a new passage, a *subito piano* hush of measure-long diminished chords, reminiscent of those in the first movement of K. 458.

The *Menuetto* second movement of K. 464 goes far beyond the type's dance origins. It is shot through with imitations of all or part of its opening idea, which grows out of the *Allegro*'s mm 8–12, so that the effect is scarcely less contrapuntal than that of the first movement. The trio in E eschews the gruff and stern stuff of the *Allegro* but not its more tender moments, such as the melodic turn and gracious triplet motion.

The heart of the quartet is the long third movement, an *Andante* in D and in 2/4 time that provides the scaffolding for several variations. It begins rather simply with a fall from the fifth to the first degree, like the opening *Allegro*, but with dotted rhythm. The first strain soon foregoes simplicity for chromatic lines, rich harmonies and over-the-bar phrasing before its cadence on V. The second strain keeps pace but seems ready to complete its answer with a matching eight-measure phrase reinstating the tonic when there is more—two additional measures allowing the first violin to climb up to a melodic peak of high D, emphasized by a *crescendo* to *forte*, descending into the cadence.

The variations are figural at first, the thirty-second note filigree of the first violin being transferred to the second violin for the following variation. In the third variation, the viola becomes prominent. The fourth variation features triplet figurations in the minor mode. In the fifth, the theme returns to something close to its original cast but with dotted rhythms more pervasive and with reharmonizations. In addition, Mozart writes out varied repeats of each strain and then repeats the whole. The cello inaugurates the sixth variation, proposing a new drum-like rhythm ♫♫♫♫ combined with a pendulum bass figure, kept up steadily throughout, like an ostinato. A long coda begins as the ostinato figure is transferred to the viola, the second violin, and the first violin, which uses it to ascend up to the highest melodic peak of the movement, high G above its high D to end the theme, and arrived at by another *crescendo* to *forte*. From its high perch the first violin descends, *calando*, to low A, then restates the original theme, abbreviated. There follow brief revisits to some characteristic features of the fifth and sixth variations. Ultimately, the cello transforms its ostinato figure into a tonic pedal and a rising tonic triad. There is no finer set of variations in all the many examples of the form bequeathed by Mozart.

The finale, *Allegro non troppo* in cut time, matches the opening *Allegro*, both being in sonata form with repeats and both beginning with a chromatic descent from the fifth degree sharp (Example 1.13b). Moreover, the rhythmic kernel of the *Allegro* (x) becomes just as important in the finale's theme, albeit slightly masked by the change of meter. A hint of rondo character is lent by a calm and chordal episode in the subdominant midway in the finale. The chromatic descent of the beginning is an ending as well, heard last in the middle voices against the treble's rise to the tonic, *pianissimo*. Haydn used this same chromatic idea rising and falling many times in the fugal finale of his Quartet in C of Opus 20. K. 464 entered Mozart's thematic catalogue with the date of 10 January 1785, his first entry of the new year. Its successor was dated four days later.

Only Mozart could top K. 464, and he did. K. 465 in C begins with an unusual feature for a quartet, a slow introduction, *Adagio* in 3/4 time, resolving on the dominant chord preparatory to the *Allegro* that follows. The tonal meanderings and chromatic layerings of this introduction produce a few tonal clashes that bewildered listeners, hence the misnomer "Dissonant" attached to the quartet.

Slow introductions were rare in Mozart's works up to 1783. The glorious "Posthorn" Serenade in D, K. 320, dated Salzburg 3 August 1779 begins with one but it consists of only six measures and three chords, unlike the kind of motivically pregnant and more gradually unfolding introduction with which Mozart prefaces the innovative "Linz" Symphony of 1783 (see Example 1.8). Similar in plan is K. 465's *Adagio* in that it travels to the flat side of the tonal spectrum and through various chords in minor before resolving to major for the sunny *Allegro*. Both these introductions reflect Mozart's increasing fascination with Joseph Haydn's slow symphonic introductions.[67] Mozart's interest in the device can also be heard in

---

[67] On earlier slow introductions as harbingers of the whole cycle, see the discussion of Haydn's Symphony No. 57 in *Haydn, Mozart*, 368–71, which concludes: "Its slow introduction sets up long-range tensions that require the entire four-movement span for their ultimate resolution."

the slow introduction (K. 444) he added to Michael Haydn's 1783 Symphony in G (Peyer No. 16). The immediate purpose of these slow introductions was to provide a stately and often somber foil for the lively doings that followed.

K. 465's introduction, marked *Adagio* and often discussed in terms of its harmonic and contrapuntal daring, will be considered here for its melodic content. The first violin's melodic sighs A - G and G - F are paramount. After rests, the line continues its downward arc with a protracted F - E and then further down to B, the leading tone that will eventually resolve, after a dominant pedal, to the C that begins the main theme of the *Allegro* (Example 1.14a). This theme gives prominence to the first two melodic sighs but in reverse order, G - F, A - G; the F - E sigh is delayed until the first full cadence in m. 44 (Example 1.14b). These

EXAMPLE 1.14 a, b, c. *Mozart, String Quartet in C, K. 465*

a. *I*

b. *IV*

intervals play an important role throughout the quartet. In its last moments at the end of the finale, Mozart's disporting with them is nothing less than gleeful. To reinforce the F - E melodic sigh he states it in different octaves, with dynamic increase from soft to loud (Example 1.14c). The written-out trill on G - A that

c. *Finale*

begins in m. 401, marked *crescendo* to *forte* and harmonized in the other parts, sounds like a burst of laughter. The same device will signal actual laughter, and ridicule, when used again some sixteen months later by Basilio in the Terzetto No. 7 of *Le nozze di Figaro*, and even more so when used in *Così fan tutte*. The final triumph, and resolution, of the A - G syndrome comes with an insistent A A A D (from the second theme), answered by G G G C in mm. 415–17. They should put us in mind of the long-held A and long-held G with which the first violin began this quartet.[68]

The *Andante cantabile* of K. 465, a movement in F and in 3/4 time, begins with a stately theme that is like a sarabande in both rhythm and melody and that resembles the Sarabande in Mozart's unfinished Keyboard Suite, K. 399. It involves many parallel thirds, lending a sweetness to this song (Example 1.15a). Not only is it singable, but something closely parallel is sung by one of Mozart's operatic characters. Consciously or not, the composer reverts to a theme that began his *terzetto* of farewells in Act II of *Idomeneo* (Example 1.15b). In the same key, meter, and tempo, both themes sink down to the tonic, rise resolutely over subdominant harmony, then descend to the fifth above the tonic via a poignant E♮ appoggiatura. In the opera, this lovely music clothes the words of the young hero Idamante, who, taking leave, seeks to impress a kiss on Idomeneo's paternal hand. The tender thought he expresses accounts for the suave subdominant moment and poignancy after it.

EXAMPLE 1.15.

a. *Mozart, String Quartet in C, K. 465, II*

b. *Mozart,* Idomeneo, *Terzetto No. 16*

---

[68] A parallel that has been proposed between K. 465's slow introduction and the beginning of Haydn's Quartet in C of Opus 33 is considered and rejected below, in chapter 4.

a. (continued)

K. 465's Andante continues as the bass rises from F♯ to G, mm. 5–6 in Example 1.15a, and the treble descends from C to B♭. There are similar motions in Idamante's song but a closer match is a phrase in the third aria sung by Idamante's beloved Ilia at the beginning of Act III, Example 1.15c.

c. *Mozart,* Idomeneo, *Aria No. 19* (original in E)

Her words speak of the faithfulness of their two hearts. Her music adumbrates K. 465 to a remarkable degree. The quartet's third four-measure phrase (not exemplified) rises by step in the treble to a climactic high B♭, *crescendo* to *forte*, before tumbling rapidly down an octave and resuming over subdominant harmony, at which the sweet parallel thirds of the beginning return and push to the cadence with another poignant chromatic tone. The operatic parallel here is also close although the opera had yet to be written. It occurs in Ferrando's *aria d'affetto* "Un aura' amorosa" in Act I of *Così fan tutte,* when he sings of needing no repast other than love (d'un'esca migliore bisogna non ha) in mm. 33–37.

Example 1.15 shows how closely Mozart's works can inform each other regardless of the genre. A soaring climax in the string quartet's *Andante* finds expression with words of love five years later. The *Idomeneo* parallels draw on the sentiments of love and respect for a father, and love between trusting hearts. They could even, at some level of consciousness, express Mozart's feelings toward Haydn, the "father of the string quartet."

The concentrated motivic work Mozart emphasized in K. 464 is no less evident in K. 465, where almost everything in the *Allegro* derives in some way from the first theme, except for a second theme of independent cast, a charming gavotte-like moment for contrast. The pervasive musical sighs of the first theme otherwise dominate. One of the theme's permutations deserves special mention because it is so strategically placed. At the beginning of the seconda parte, the first violin states the main theme with a crucial chromatic alteration and over a different, unstable harmony, with repeated A - G melodic sighs. This moment does not recur until another crucial moment in the overall form, the beginning of the coda, which comes after a double bar with repeat signs. Here the A - G is answered emphatically by a repeated G - F. In the *Andante*, a different sonata form, without repeat signs or a long development, Mozart avoided taking apart his exquisite and ever-so-expressive main theme in search of motifs to develop. Rather, he introduced a new rhythmic cell and put it through innumerable paces, to the extent that it nearly takes over the movement. There is a clear second theme in the dominant, consisting of long melodic sighs layered above a constant murmur of sixteenth notes in the cello, rather reminiscent of the pendulum bass the cello introduced in Variation 6 of K. 464. When the main theme returns it is decorated in a way that suggests the varied reprises of some sonatas by Emanuel Bach.

The *Minuetto Allegro* third movement begins with the first violin sounding a melodic turn around G that is the inversion of the melodic turn with which it began the *Adagio*. A rather long minuet is followed by a Trio in c minor, good for contrast and a reminder that the *Adagio* had tended strongly toward tonic minor. The minuet and trio provide welcome relief from the intensities of the previous movements. The finale, *Allegro molto* in 2/4 time, is jolly and lightweight in theme but complex in structure, being an elaborate sonata form with both parts repeated. As in the last movement of K. 464, the seconda parte, after repetition, is followed by a strong coda as summary.

Artaria advertised the six quartets in the *Wiener Zeitung* of 18 September 1785. He claimed that, because of their genial nature, no cost was spared as to excellent paper and printing in order to give music lovers and connoisseurs an edition of great beauty and clarity. The famous dedication bears him out (Figure 1.7). Mozart follows certain traditions common to dedications such as belittling the author and magnifying the dedicatee. He refers to the quartets as his children and asks Haydn to be their father, guide, and friend, to look with indulgence on any faults that remained hidden to the partial eye of their creator. He also refers to the process of composing them as "a long, laborious effort." This is no cliché, nor is it an exaggeration. Many pages of Mozart's autograph bear witness to the changes, corrections, and rethinkings as these complicated works were polished to perfection. Composing quartets like these posed challenges to any composer. Mozart confirmed this later when referring to his "Prussian" quartets as "this demanding labor" (diese mühsame Arbeit) in a letter to his friend Michael Puchberg written on or before 12 July 1790.

Infinitely more is to be learned about Mozart's quartets dedicated to Haydn from the music itself than from any number of written analyses or from descriptions such as attempted here. On their effect we have the few words Leopold Mozart wrote to Nannerl about that memorable day, 12 February 1785, when he was

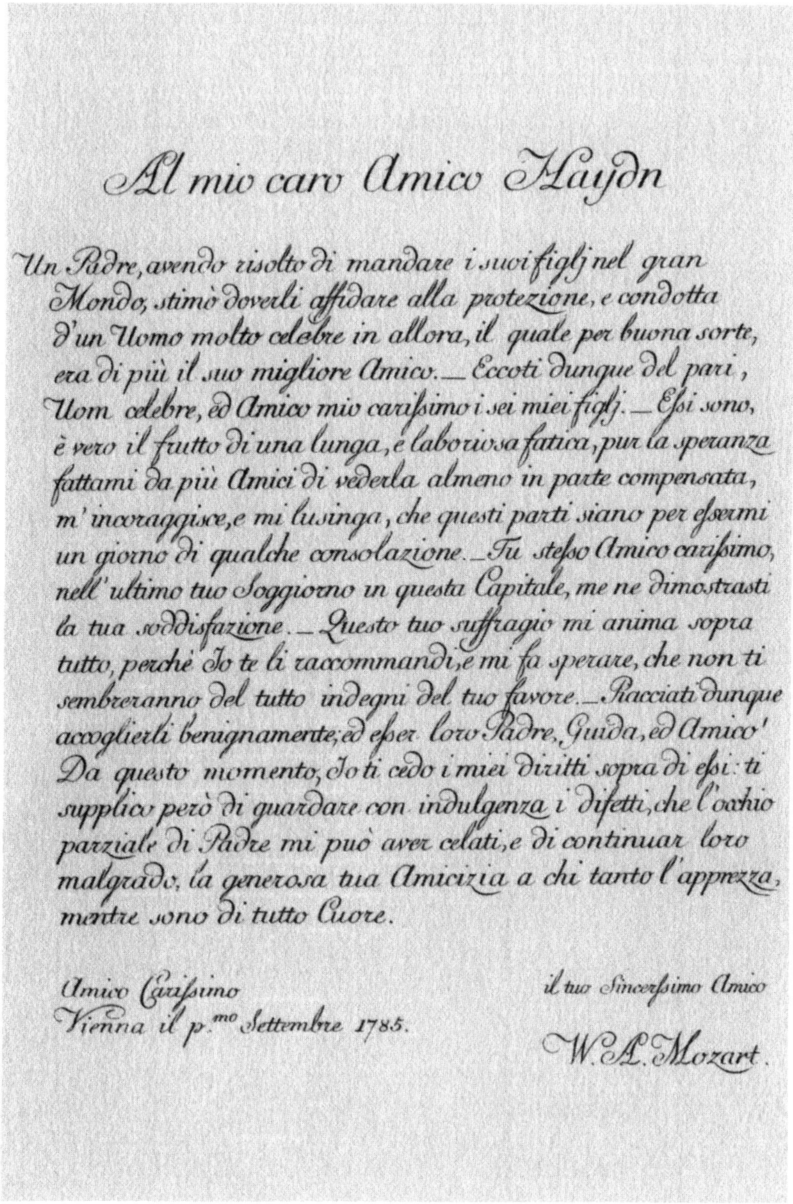

Al mio caro Amico Haydn

Un Padre, avendo risolto di mandare i suoi figlj nel gran Mondo, stimò doverli affidare alla protezione, e condotta d'un Uomo molto celebre in allora, il quale per buona sorte, era di più il suo migliore Amico. — Eccoti dunque del pari, Uom celebre, ed Amico mio carissimo i sei miei figlj. — Essi sono, è vero il frutto di una lunga, e laboriosa fatica, pur la speranza fattami da più Amici di vederla almeno in parte compensata, m'incoraggisce, e mi lusinga, che questi parti siano per essermi un giorno di qualche consolazione. — Tu stesso Amico carissimo, nell'ultimo tuo Soggiorno in questa Capitale, me ne dimostrasti la tua soddisfazione. — Questo tuo suffragio mi anima sopra tutto, perché Io te li raccommandi, e mi fa sperare, che non ti sembreranno del tutto indegni del tuo favore. — Piacciati dunque accoglierli benignamente, ed esser loro Padre, Guida, ed Amico! Da questo momento, Io ti cedo i miei diritti sopra di essi: ti supplico però di guardare con indulgenza i difetti, che l'occhio parziale di Padre mi può aver celati, e di continuar loro malgrado, la generosa tua Amicizia a chi tanto l'apprezza, mentre sono di tutto Cuore.

Amico Carissimo
Vienna il p.mo Settembre 1785.

il tuo Sincerissimo Amico

W. A. Mozart.

FIGURE 1.7. Dedication page of "Haydn" Quartets.

present to hear (and perhaps perform?) the last three quartets. He pronounced them somewhat easier than the first three although excellently composed, as we have seen. Leopold went on to relate what he claimed Haydn said to him: "Before God, and as an honest man, I tell you that your son is the greatest composer known to me either in person or by name. He has taste, and what is more, the most profound knowledge of composition." Haydn may well have said something along these lines as one way of thanking and honoring his hosts. We must remember even so that Leopold, like his son, was given to telling people what they wanted—or what he wanted them—to hear. Nothing was lost in this case if Leopold indulged in a little embellishment, intended to solace the isolated Nannerl. The music, on the other hand, tells only the truth.

The Piano Concertos of 1784

The year 1784 confirmed that Vienna was indeed the promised land for keyboard playing and composition that Mozart prophesized three years earlier. He was never more in demand as a solo player, nor so prolific in composing concertos for piano and orchestra. There were six in all, joined by three more in each of the following two years, a miraculous dozen within a short time span, following which there came only two late stragglers. With the first of these concertos, Mozart began his thematic catalogue, assigning dates to almost all his subsequent compositions.[69] These are the dates cited in Table 1.1.

TABLE 1.1 Piano Concertos, 1784–1791

1784		
No. 14. K. 449 in E♭	9 February	(for Babette von Ployer)
15. K. 450 in B♭	15 March	
16. K. 451 in D	22 March	
17. K. 453 in G	12 April	(for Babette von Ployer)
18. K. 456 in B♭	30 September	(for Theresia von Paradis)
19. K. 459 in F	11 December	
1785		
20. K. 466 in d	10 February	
21. K. 467 in C	9 March	
22. K. 482 in E♭	16 December	
1786		
23. K. 488 in A	2 March	
24. K. 491 in c	24 March	
25. K. 503 in C	4 December	
1788		
26. K. 537 in D	24 February	("Coronation")
1791		
27. K. 495 in B♭	5 January	

[69] Albi Rosenthal and Alan Tyson, eds., *Mozart: Eigenhändiges Werkverzeichnis Faksimile* (London, 1991). Subsequent references in the text will be only to "Mozart's catalogue."

Almost without exception, the concertos were written either in December or in the first quarter of the year, in accordance with their function as main events at concerts during the seasons of Advent and Lent. Dances for the Carnival balls that preceded Lent constituted another kind of seasonal composition. In early 1784, Mozart composed Six Minuets, K. 461, Six Contredanses, K. 462, and Two Minuets with a Contredanse, K. 463.

Stymied as he was in his attempts to write an Italian opera for the new company in the Burgtheater, Mozart increasingly turned to composing for the piano. The "Strinasacchi" Sonata, K. 454, already discussed followed the Concerto No. 17 in G in his catalogue. Preceding it, he inscribed the Quintet for Piano and Winds, K. 452. He entered two sets of variations for solo piano, one on a theme by Sarti, K. 460, dated 8 June 1784, the other on a theme by Gluck, K. 455, dated 25 August, followed by the Piano Sonata in c, K. 457, dated 14 October.

Babette von Ployer was the daughter of Gottfried Ignaz von Ployer, a trade representative of Salzburg in Vienna who figures on the long list of Mozart's concert subscribers sent to Leopold on 20 March 1784 as "Agent Ployer." Asked by Ployer to recommend a violinist for the court orchestra in Salzburg, Mozart suggested a certain Zeno Menzel, who was sent to Salzburg for an audition. The composer promised to send his latest scores to Leopold with Menzel but failed to do so, fearful that they would be copied surreptitiously. The scores, which were sent by the mail coach in May, included four piano concertos, K. 449–451 and K. 453. Mozart cautioned his father to have the concertos copied at home lest dishonest scribes steal them. "No one possesses these new concertos in B♭ and D, and no one but myself and Fräulein von Ployer (for whom I composed them) those in E♭ and G" (letter of 15 May). He added that the Concerto in E♭ would be more use to Leopold "because it can be performed *a quattro* without the wind instruments." Leopold did not normally have wind instruments available for his house concerts. Nannerl was the resident piano soloist until she wed and moved away in August 1784.

Among the new concertos, K. 449 in E♭ is the most idiosyncratic in form and style. Mozart began composing it when he was writing the three subscription concertos, hence he conceived this work too for performance *a quattro*, if necessary. He got no further than m. 170 of the expansive first movement, about half way. Whatever stopped him may have something to do with the special status he assigned to this work. In his letter of 26 May, he wrote about the new concertos, "I am curious to know which of the three in B♭, D, and G you and my sister prefer. The one in E♭ does not belong at all to the same category. It is a concerto of an entirely special manner, composed for a small orchestra rather than a larger one; so we are speaking only of the three grand concertos."

The first movement of K. 449 is an *Allegro vivace* in 3/4 time. Mozart had used triple meter also to begin Concerto No. 11 in F, K. 413, the opening of which K. 449's first theme slightly resembles in its falling melody (Example 1.16). E♭, C, and

EXAMPLE 1.16. *Mozart, Piano Concerto No. 14 in E♭, K. 449, I*

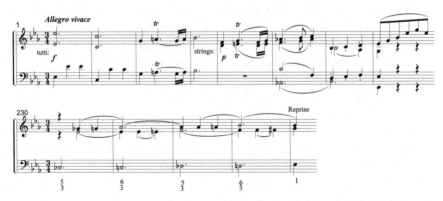

G suggest c minor as well as tones 1, 6, and 3 of the key of E♭, an ambiguity that is also a portent, for c minor plays an important role in the movement. The iambic motion of m. 3 is made more emphatic by a trill on the A resolving up to B♭ and pointing the way back to tonic E♭ (imagine if the A had resolved back to G!). In the *piano* response of mm. 4–8, the iambic motion is repeated, trill included, but softened not only by dynamic change but also by the parallel thirds in place of the *forte* unisons. After two more cadences in E♭, the music plunges suddenly into c minor and stays there for a while before making a transition that prepares the arrival of the second theme, which is in the dominant instead of the tonic customary in first expositions. When tonic E♭ returns, it is with a forceful new idea using dotted rhythms and the ubiquitous trills, but now on the first instead of the second beat. The bass protests with an outburst of strong iambic figures with trills on the second beat. Its descending conjunct fourths in sequence are all the stronger for outlining an angry-sounding diminished fourth in two instances. After inverting this passage, Mozart moves on to strong tonic cadences in E♭ and the entrance of the soloist.

The second exposition proceeds in ways familiar from Mozart's other concertos. To begin the seconda parte, the piano takes up the trilled iambic figures descending a fourth, along with their countersubject. The orchestra responds *forte*, readjusting the descending fourths so as to stretch down a conjunct octave in two measures. The soloist answers with an outburst of ascending arpeggios that sounds rather like a surprised covey of birds flushed into flight. These powerful two-measure exchanges continue between soloist and orchestra in a long harmonic sequence passing by way of c minor, at which point Mozart accelerates so that the answering back and forth come more quickly and the trills occur in every measure, beginning to sound like an orgy of trilling. After a long dominant pedal with many minor inflections the soloist leads in the reprise with an uncanny rising passage, recognizably related to the rising chromatic thirds of mm. 5–6 (and even more to the soloist's version of the same in mm. 97–98), but heightening further the expressive stakes (Example 1.16, mm. 230–34).

Emanuel Bach used this very progression, staggering root position and first inversion triads in upward chromatic motion, as early as the finale of his first Prussian Sonata (1742) and many other composers copied it from him.[70] In fact, the tutelary hand of the Berlin Bach can be heard here inspiring Mozart in a more general way. See, for example, some of Bach's early keyboard concertos, such as the one in d minor of 1748 (Wotquenne 23) with its cranky rhythms and plethora of trills in the outer movements, menacing trills like those on vi in the finale, and those on the second beat of the opening *Allegro* in 3/4 time.[71] These snarling trills can also be related to the overt menace Mozart lends this device in his operas, particularly the threats of the High Priest in *Idomeneo*'s Act III, which are beholden to a similar passage in Gluck's *Alceste*.[72]

One further departure from Mozart's usual procedure cries out for attention. In preparation for a cadenza in the first movement of K. 449, the soloist's customary trill signaling an arrival of the tonic is undercut by a sudden thrust replacing it with c minor for a brief return. The closest parallel Mozart offers to this somber movement is the first movement of his Concerto No. 24 in c, K. 491, the first theme of which is in fact a melodic inversion of K. 449's opening motif.[73]

The tonal choice for a slow movement of a work in E♭ earlier in the century was often the relative minor, c (vi), and so it was for Mozart in K. 271 and K. 364. Haydn and Mozart in the 1780s sometimes chose A♭ (IV) but more often B♭ (V), which was an easier key for most performers. Yet Mozart chose A♭ in some of his greatest works in E♭, including the String Quartet, K. 428, Piano Quartet, K. 493, and above all the Symphony No. 39, K. 543. In his stunning Divertimento in E♭ for Violin, Viola, and Cello, K. 563, a work in six movements, he chose A♭ for the *Adagio* second movement and B♭ for the lighter fourth movement, an *Andante*.

In K. 449, Mozart opts for B♭ in the middle movement, writing a gracious *Andantino* in 2/4 time, beginning with a long-breathed, wayward melody of many parts and a propensity for slipping into c minor. The solo piano at first takes up only a part of this ample material and leads the proceedings to the expected second theme in the dominant. From there the soloist, as if drawn by some magnetic force, slips into c minor momentarily on the way to A♭, where the orchestra begins

---

[70] *Music in European Capitals*, p. 406.

[71] Ibid., ex. 4.25, p. 419.

[72] *Haydn, Mozart*, p. 708.

[73] As pointed out by Philip Radcliffe, *Mozart's Concertos* (London, 1978), p. 30. Simon P. Keefe, " 'An Entirely Special Manner': Mozart's Piano Concerto No. 14 in E flat, K. 449, and the Stylistic Implications of Confrontation," *Music and Letters* 82 (2002): 559–81, posits similarities between K. 449 and K. 491 in the rapid back and forth between orchestra and soloist during the development sections of their initial movements (p. 576).

what sounds like a reprise of the main material. Transposed down a whole tone, the main theme sounds darker and more expressive. This is not a misstep, as rigorists might fear. Heard in broader terms, it is a case of Mozart having the best of both worlds by making use of both B♭ and A♭, as he did in the Divertimento, K. 563. Like the opening *Allegro*, this *Andantino* follows its own laws, or better said, makes them up as it goes along.

The finale, *Allegro ma non troppo* in cut time, begins like an exercise in double counterpoint. Its descending fourths in the treble hark back to the strong tutti passage with trills in the opening *Allegro*. Mozart desists from inverting his treble and bass until the stormy episode in c minor midway through the movement. The finale ends by transforming the main themes into a jolly dance in 6/8 time.

By the year 1784, Mozart could boast of having become Vienna's premier keyboard composer and performer, the goal toward which he had been steadily working since his arrival. His greatest rival for the honor was Leopold Kozeluch. In his letter to his father of 3 March 1784, Mozart listed all the Lenten concerts, a total of twenty-two, at which he had played or was about to play. They included two public concerts in the Burgtheater, three of his own subscription concerts in the Trattner Hall on the Graben, two appearances in concerts given by the pianist Georg Richter, and several in the palaces of Count Johann Esterházy and Prince Galitzin, the Russian ambassador. As if this were not enough to impress his father, in his next letter he sent the long list of subscribers to his concerts, 174 in all, and added, "Thirty more subscribers than the concerts by Richter and Fischer [violinist John Fisher?] combined" (letter of 10 March). The following month, as Richter was leaving Vienna to return to his native Holland, Mozart gave him a note of introduction to his father and wrote concerning him:

> When I played for him he stared all the time at my fingers and kept repeating, "Good Lord, how hard I must work and sweat without winning any applause while to you, my friend, it is all child's play." I replied, "Yes, but I too had to work hard in order to arrive at not having to work hard any longer." Enfin, he is a fellow who may be included among our good keyboard players [letter of 28 April].

This is one of the few statements we have about how Mozart became such a paragon among pianists.

During the spring of 1784, Mozart sent four piano concertos back to Salzburg, along with the score of the "Linz" Symphony. In his letter of 26 May, the one in which he describes K. 449 as being "of a special kind," he characterized the next two concertos, K. 450 in B♭ and K. 451 in D, as being difficult and likely to make the soloist sweat, the former even more than the latter. Then he widened the reference to "the three grand concertos" by including K. 453 in G.

K. 450 made unprecedented demands as well on the orchestral wind players, presumably those in the Burgtheater for Mozart's academy on the first of April, fifteen days after the date assigned the concerto in Mozart's catalogue. Never before had the composer given the orchestral winds so much independence. They begin on their own, sounding the rising conjunct thirds of the main theme, to which the violins provide a response. The winds answer back and forth in repartee with the strings on a basis of equality throughout the movement, an *Allegro* in common time. They are joined by a third equal, the piano solo. The idea of a conversation *à trois* like this is novel.

From this point on, the winds become an indispensable component of Mozart's concertos. At the core of almost all of them are a flute, together with oboes, bassoons, and horns in pairs, to which Mozart sometimes added trumpet and drums in the limited number of keys in which they commonly played. K. 450 well demonstrates the range of wind color at Mozart's command. From the beginning, cheerful clucking sounds emerge from the double reed instruments, especially the staccato tones of the bassoons doubling the oboes an octave below, and perhaps the key was chosen precisely because of the bassoons. This versatile instrument was effective in a number of keys but was nowhere more at home than in B♭, its natural scale, and the key of Mozart's Bassoon Concerto, K. 191, of 1774.

The soloist enters the first movement of K. 450 not with the main theme but with passagework forming an *Eingang*. What led Mozart to choose one or the other way for the soloist to begin is worth pondering. The first exposition consists almost entirely of four-measure phrases. A prominent second theme, marked by syncopations, stretches to eight measures. Yet the closing theme is only six measures long with the result that the piano enters in a rather weak spot in metrical terms, as if it had come in two measures too early. Hence the gradual buildup to the point where the soloist declaims the full eight-measure first theme. Then the solo piano takes charge of the modulating passage to the dominant and announces its own second theme, which is followed by a long stretch of passagework in sixteenth notes for the right hand, then for the left hand, which must raise a sweat in many pianists. In contrast to most of Mozart's second expositions, the orchestra's second theme is not summoned back for restatement in the dominant.

The seconda parte commences with the piano taking up the closing passage and spinning rapid passagework out of it for both right and left hands. Modulations ensue, ranging over a number of keys, some of them in the minor mode. The winds lead in the reprise, answered not by the strings but by the piano. After the soloist's second theme, the orchestra's syncopated second theme is heard, shared with the piano, all in tonic B♭. A *crescendo* passage from the beginning of the movement then reappears, leading to the climactic six-four chord on the tonic with a fermata, signaling that the solo cadenza is to begin. Mozart wrote out a solo cadenza for his sister and made a point of introducing in it the orchestra's second theme, as if making up for its omission in the second exposition. The closing material reappears, now in the tonic but otherwise unaltered except for the addition of a few more cadential chords.

An *Andante* in 3/8 time and in E♭ provides a calm, song-like theme in the strings, copied with embellishments in each of its eight-measure segments by the piano solo. The theme provides an apt framework for the variations that follow. The first variation, mostly for the soloist, is given over to thirty-second note arpeggios in either right or left hands. A second variation begins simply, with syncopations of the theme that cannot but recall the syncopated second theme of the previous movement. The piano is the initiator here and the orchestra responds. Entrusted with the theme alone are the two oboes, while the piano decorates with triplet arpeggios and the strings accompany, pizzicato. The first oboe must climb to the top of its range to sing this long-breathed theme, but not above high C. Mozart employed its penetrating legato tones in the regions of high B♭ to the full here.

For the finale, Mozart adds a single flute, giving him the tones he requires above the oboe from high D to high G. An *Allegro* in 6/8 time, it has a theme that could have easily graced one of the rondo finales of his horn concertos and like them it evokes the hunt. The soloist announces the theme to string accompaniment, then it sounds tutti *forte* to which is added a fanfare-like call, answered softly by a conjunct descent to the tonic in the strings, an exchange reminiscent of the closing idea in the first movement. The winds are less prominent in the finale and much of the time they merely reinforce the strings. One of the most delightful moments in this thoroughly delightful rondo occurs when the tonal preparation for an episode in the relative minor is suddenly deflected by the arrival of the subdominant in its stead, a jest of the pulling-the-rug-out-from-under variety. The movement ends with a long *pianissimo* reiteration of the tonic, with chords rising to the top of the orchestra, yet remaining soft, until a final four measures of *forte* come to surprise the auditors (and make them applaud).

K. 451 in D provides a very different experience. With trumpets and drums in D enhancing its tone of military bluster, the concerto begins like a march, *Allegro assai* in common time, with dotted rhythm on the second beat. Unison Ds throughout the registers, tutti *forte*, sound the call to action (with a single F♯ in the double stop of the second violins). Mozart had made his first original concerto for keyboard and orchestra in D, K. 175, of 1773, do service for a decade in concerts and had even rejuvenated it with a new finale, the crowd-pleasing Rondo in D, K. 382 of 1782. Perhaps he had had enough of the old warhorse in spite of (partly because of?) its tiresome new finale. In any case, K. 451 gave him a military-type concerto that could replace K. 175/382. It shows how far Mozart had come in his skills at managing big orchestral effects over the course of a decade. *Idomeneo* for the Mannheim-Munich orchestra marked an important stage of this evolution. In K. 451, the first violins climb from their low D, *piano*, step by step up the scale until, via a *crescendo*, they reach high D two octaves above. This fine passage is nothing other than the *crescendo* made famous by the Mannheim orchestra and no different in kind from the long rise of the first violins to high D at the end of *Idomeneo*'s Act I. Waves of descending scales in dotted rhythm that ensue resemble those in some of Mozart's military marches in D, such as K. 189 and K. 335. What one misses is anything that might be called a theme in this procession of fanfares, alarums, and preparatory gestures.

A theme of sorts is reached after thirty-four measures when, over a tonic pedal, the horns and oboes intone another fanfare-like call climbing up and down the tonic triad; the call is answered by the more delicate slurred eighth notes of the first violins and flute. The solo piano concentrates almost throughout on showing that it can be just as blustery as the orchestra. It offers no lyric theme of its own and is content to embroider the one offered by the orchestra. Some critics have seen this thematic parsimony as a negative feature, or as downright un-Mozartian, meaning it does not conform to their ideal, formed on the basis of their favorite Mozart concertos. Nevertheless, present in the *Allegro assai* are some contrasts to all the military panoply, notably the passage of slow chords in even half notes over a descending bass of six tones, interjected by the soloist, as if applying the brakes, after the modulation to the dominant in the second exposition. There is no denying the unity of it all. The closing material condenses the rising triad idea that served as second theme (if one concedes that the opening ideas constitute, if not a theme, a thematic constellation in the tonic). Moreover, the same rising and falling triad is present in another guise as the main theme of the rondo finale, an *Allegro molto* in 2/4 time of great jollity. As a coda to the finale Mozart reduced this theme to 3/8 time, making it even sprightlier, much as he did to end the finale of K. 449. There the concluding levity came as relief after a rather somber and serious discourse; here levity is succeeded by greater levity.

No one would mistake the middle movement, an ineffable *Andante* in cut time and in G, as being anything but Mozart of the tenderest and most inimitable kind. The melody wavers gently between chromatic neighboring tones below and above, the second violins doubling the firsts an octave below, a typical Viennese sonority, and the violas providing parallel thirds below the second violins. By the time the theme reaches its half cadence after four measures, it has introduced all twelve chromatic tones. The movement, mostly spun from this magical phrase, provides the perfect foil for the brisk outer movements. Perhaps the composer conceived this gentle *Andante* first and then made its companions as contrasting as possible. Even so, there is one passage in the first movement that is related to the *Andante*'s theme, namely the wavering chromatics above and below the main notes preceding the dominant pedal leading to the reprise. The whole concerto is very much of a piece. It was an early success too, having been printed in Paris ca. 1785 and widely diffused, then republished by Carl Bossler in 1791 in an edition that elicited a favorable reaction from an anonymous reviewer, who called the *Andante* "a kind of *Romanze*, very elegant and touching."[74] The description is apt, especially since Mozart called the rather similar theme that begins the slow movement of Piano Concerto No. 20 in d, K. 466, a Romance.

Spring does not come early to Vienna. Perhaps it had announced a few attempts to arrive in the first part of April 1784, encouraging Mozart to finish a concerto abounding in vernal joy and optimism, K. 453 in G. He inscribed it in his catalogue with the date of 12 April 1784, only twelve days after he inserted the incipit of K. 452 in E♭, the very beautiful but comparatively modest-sized Quintet for Piano and Winds, of which he wrote his father on 10 April, in a burst of enthusiasm, "I consider it to be the best work I have ever composed" (an ill-considered judgment). Aside from the early pasticcio concertos in G for keyboard (K. 41 and K. 107/2), Mozart had earlier written concertos in G for violin (K. 216) and for flute (K. 313). The key is especially favorable to the flute, which can ascend with ease all the way up to high G. A single flute is required by all three of the "grand" concertos of early 1784. The instrument comes into its own in K. 453, often playing a leading role as the treble voice of the winds, truly an equal of the first violins in this respect. Toward the end of the finale it is called upon to run up the scale to its high G, a feat beyond the oboe, and also beyond Mozart's piano.

The opening movement of K. 453, an *Allegro* in common time, is far removed from the martial swagger of K. 451's first movement, yet they have a few things in common, for example a first measure in march rhythm. Unlike its predecessor, this concerto does not begin loudly, repeating the tonic. Its dotted rhythm on the second beat (endemic to marches) is mitigated by a trill and rise by step (Example 1.17a). It sounds like a deflation of military pomp, all the more so when the rhythm and rises are used to heft the melody aloft up to B, preceded by a very galant-sounding chromatic appoggiatura, then coming to momentary rest with a melodic sigh over subdominant harmony. The consequent phrase ends with the same sigh but inverted, adding another chromatic appoggiatura. The winds give their blessing during the interstices with a flurry of four sixteenth notes on the weak beats (a comic opera trait).

The main theme is no ordinary antecedent-consequent phrase, for the dominant chord is lacking. Only tonic and subdominant are heard, lending the proceedings a very soothing and relaxed quality. The dominant chord soon lends

---

[74] *Musical Correspondence of the German Philharmonic Society* (Speyer, 16 May 1792), cited in *The Compleat Mozart: A Guide to the Musical Works of Wolfgang Amadeus Mozart*, ed. Neal Zaslaw with William Cowdery (New York, 1990), pp. 128–29.

its special tensions but the particular mood of blissful ease, once established, is only enhanced by the outpouring of one melodic gem after another in what follows. The orchestra announces its second theme as the broadest of these ideas, a sequence of melodic sighs layered above a descending bass in eleven even half

EXAMPLE 1.17 a, b, c. *Mozart, Piano Concerto No. 17 in G, K. 453, I, III*

notes (cf. the six descending half notes in K. 451:I). Another striking feature of the first exposition follows this theme directly—a big deceptive cadence to ♭VI, with bass movement from D to E♭, which chord is reinforced by its own dominant before the harmony slips back to tonic G. The closing material blossoms into three more melodic ideas, each distinct and memorable, preparing the soloist to run up an octave and launch into the first theme.

The dialogue between winds and strings extends to three equal partners with the soloist's entrance, and nearly beyond counting are the number of different ways they divide up the abundance of musical ideas. These are increased by giving the soloist a separate second theme in the dominant, before recall of the orchestra's second theme, given at first to the solo piano. The seconda parte begins with a big deceptive cadence to ♭VI, with bass movement from A to B♭, leading to a series of modulations, with arpeggiated chords up and down the keyboard for the soloist; the lyrical nature of most of the thematic material did not lend itself to development in the usual sense. To signal the approaching reprise, Mozart gives the soloist a run upwards in sixteenth notes, recalling its first entrance, but this time a dominant seventh chord of tonic G. Everything is eventually restated, the closing material only after the solo cadenza, the big deceptive cadence to ♭VI as a detour on the way to the cadenza.

The *Andante* in C and in 3/4 time begins with a plain five-measure melody sung by the first violins over chordal accompaniment from the other strings. The melody seems timid, not eager to leave the tone G, to which it quickly returns. An inauspicious beginning? The phrase ends on the dominant and is followed by a pause with fermata. There is no proper answer, whereas a consequent phrase moving from V to I would have been expected by Mozart's listeners. Instead, the solo winds change the subject. Flute, first oboe, and first bassoon warble with delight in each other's company, a dialogue that would be quite at home in a sinfonia concertante. They are joined by the strings but only as support, and by the horns playing pedal tones. The soloist enters playing the same initial five-measure theme, without comment or ornament, then plunges into an exploration of g minor that also changes the subject (as well as the key), followed by the concertante dialogue of the winds, which the piano joins. Out of these diverse elements emerges a sonata form that is rich and full of harmonically bold adventures, an unexpected journey after so bland a beginning. Following the cadenza for piano at the end, written out as in the first movement, the woodwinds reiterate the bland initial theme an octave higher than its first statement. They transform it so as to end not on V but on IV, at which point the piano takes over and provides this idea with the conclusion it never had, a consequent phrase ending on I.[75]

The *Allegretto* in cut time that follows proposes a naively simple theme for variations (Example 1.17b). This theme is clearly similar to the opening theme of the first movement, which also outlines the tonic triad from low to high B. As a dance type, it is related to certain contredanses of unmistakably popular nature, such as "Die Strassburgerin," which Mozart quotes in the finale of the Violin Concerto in G, K. 216. Peculiar to the type was the frequent three-fold striking of the tone on the downbeat (most familiar from the famous contredanse by Beethoven that he eventually employed in the finale of his "Eroica" Symphony). The trait has been compared with a stamping of the foot in the dance. Social dancing could not have been very far from the minds (and feet) of the concert's first auditors. Another relative of the tune is the entrance aria for the birdman Papageno, "Der Vogelfänger bin ich ja" in *Die Zauberflöte*.

The variations, like many other sets, proceed by transforming the theme into smaller and smaller note values, then trying it in minor, for which Mozart invents some extraordinary wind sonorities and for which he reverts to the initial quarter notes, making this seem like a slower interlude, also like a development section. The return to major for the last variation is introduced by a five-note slide, *fortissimo*, in the winds, first violins and basses: 5 4 3 2 1. The tonic arrives on the downbeat. This motif may sound familiar because Papageno uses it, also in G, sliding both down and up, when he plays his panpipes. Mozart applies it as punctuation on the offbeats, just as he used the four sixteenth-note comments for the

---

[75] Charles Rosen, *The Classical Style: Haydn, Mozart, Beethoven* (New York, 1971), pp. 223–25, explores the *Andante*'s richness and harmonic boldnesses, with generous music examples.

winds at the beginning of the concerto. The flute is on top here as there and has no difficulty making itself heard in its brilliant high register.[76]

The final variation breaks away from the theme by not concluding. Instead, it winds down to a chord on the dominant, followed by rests with a fermata. Without changing the cut time, Mozart has the violins, *pianissimo*, begin a section marked *Finale Presto*, noted above (Example 1.4b) for its resemblance to a comic aria for Blonde. The bassoons and horns reply with a ludicrous retort, *piano*, either encouraging the folly of the violins or ridiculing them. Out the window flies whatever decorum the finale had before, which was not much except for the variation in minor, and even that in retrospect seems like mockery of a tragic complaint. The Papageno spirit takes over completely as Mozart spins one continuation after another out of these highjinks. When all seems about to end, back comes the theme again, stated by the solo piano, then by the winds. The flute runs up to its highest G at the beginning of a build-up over a tonic pedal that surely signals the end, but proves instead to be a pretext for the piano to come back and stage its own rival *crescendo*. The finale is not over until the piano once again states the theme, inducing a new retort from all the winds, the last tag of which, reiterated, makes the final cadence.

K. 453, like K. 449, was written for Babette von Ployer, whose father presumably paid Mozart well for them. He had a summer estate in the village of Döbling just beyond the city's northernmost fortifications (see map, Figure 1.1). In his letter of 9 June 1784, Mozart described an occasion when she played it.

> Tomorrow Herr Ployer, the [Salzburg] court agent, will be giving a concert in his country house at Döbling. Fräulein Babette will play her new concerto in G and I shall play the Quintet [K. 452] and then we'll perform together the grand sonata for two pianos [K. 425]. I shall fetch Paisiello with my carriage for I want him to hear my compositions as well as my pupil.

It says a great deal about the young lady's skills, and Mozart's pride in them, that he was happy to exhibit her playing before the most famous and popular master of opera buffa.

There is a sense in which K. 453, besides being a wonderful springtime gift to all and sundry, was also a work of personal significance to its composer. On 27 May 1784, Mozart made an entry in his book of expenses recording the purchase of a starling for thirty-four Kreuzer, followed by a notated tune (Example 1.17c). Then he wrote "Das war schön!" The implication is that his bird could whistle something like the theme of K. 453's finale, albeit with a protraction of the sixth

---

[76] In the fifth of his *Sechs deutsche Tänze*, K. 600, of January 1791, Mozart wrote a Trio called "The Canary" in which the piccolo climbs the scale of G up into the stratosphere.

note and a raised G in the following measure. Mozart was a bird lover, and a lover of nature altogether.[77] The chirpings and twitterings that so happily enliven K. 453 from beginning to end could well entitle it to be called the "Avian" Concerto.

One of the three "grand concertos" won preference over the other two in the Austrian capital, according to Mozart's letter of 26 May 1784. "I am eager to know whether your judgment in this matter will coincide with the general opinion in Vienna, which is also mine." From this comment it appears that all three had been publicly performed in Vienna, meaning that Mozart or his pupil had played K. 453 before she performed the solo part at Döbling in June. Can there be any doubt that the last of the three was Mozart's favorite, as well as that of the Viennese? Like *Die Entführung*, its popular aspects, and especially the comic shenanigans of its finale, seemed especially written to please them, comedy-prone as they were. How typical of the composer that he should make a game for his father and sister out of evaluating the three works!

Before the year was over Mozart added two more piano concertos to his impressive roster, No. 18 in B♭, K. 456, and No. 19 in F, K. 459. The former was written for Maria Theresia von Paradis, the blind daughter of imperial court counselor Joseph Anton von Paradis. She was born on 15 May 1759, two days after the forty-second birthday of Empress Maria Theresa, for whom she was named and from whom she received an annual pension beginning in 1774. According to an entry in Nannerl's diary, Maria Theresa von Paradis and her father visited Salzburg in August 1783 at the start of a European tour that would take her to Paris, London, and many other centers, and last until 1786. It was perhaps during the Salzburg visit that the pianist, or more likely her father, commissioned a solo concerto from Mozart, who was then in Salzburg. Visiting Vienna in early 1785, Leopold wrote Nannerl in a letter dated 16 February about a Burgtheater concert at which "your brother played a magnificent concerto which he composed for Mlle Paradis in Paris" (ein herrliches Concert, das er für die Paradis nach Paris gemacht hatte). The sense of "nach" here is debatable. Could it mean, "sent to Paris"? By process of elimination, all candidates for the identity of this concerto except K. 456 have been dismissed.[78] Paradis remained in Paris until November 1784, and then moved on to London. During October, she could have received the commissioned concerto from Mozart, who entered K. 456 in his catalogue with a date of 30 September. No record of her performance of it in Paris, or elsewhere, has yet been found.

---

[77] Daniel Heartz, "Mozart's Sense for Nature," *19th Century Music* 15 (1991): 107–15. The article refutes point by point Alfred Einstein's claims that Mozart had no sense for nature.

[78] By Eva Badura-Skoda, "Zur Entstehung des Klavierkonzerts in B-dur KV. 456," *Mozart-Jahrbuch 1964*: 193–97. She maintains that Mozart uses fewer big leaps in the solo part than usual as an aid to the blind pianist and that a possible link with the composer was the Dutch pianist Georg Richter, Mozart's friend, who was one of her teachers.

Mozart begins K. 456 with the same march rhythm, softly and with a melody that moves almost entirely by step, as if he were thinking what it might be like to start a piece without benefit of sight. The solo part is much less difficult than that of the previous concerto in the same key, No. 15, K. 450. One critic recommended the concerto as a piece pianists could play at home, "since it is easy to read, easy to remember, and grateful to the fingers."[79] Its initial movement, *Allegro vivace* in common time, is more regular in phrasing than is often found in Mozart, but this sameness is atoned for by a mysterious and harmonically rich passage moving to the flat side all the way to C♭ between the first and second themes of the orchestra's exposition. Many of the composer's opening movements, especially in concertos, pass through a circle of fifths progression in lieu of any real development. This one moves with unabated regularity in two-measure segments: A d g c F B♭ E♭. Then comes a long dominant pedal preparing the reprise. Regular phrasing greatly facilitates memorization.

The middle movement is unusual in its choice of the minor mode, the first piano concerto by Mozart to do so since K. 271 of 1777. It is another theme and variations, the form that is the most sectional of all, and hence one of the most easily memorized. The theme falls gently from the fifth degree to the tonic, which it eventually reaches (Example 1.18a). A penultimate variation substitutes G for

EXAMPLE 1.18.

a. *Mozart, Piano Concerto No. 18 in B♭, K. 456, II*

g, also bringing some particularly beautiful wind sonorities before the return to g for the last variation and a long coda, ended by the flute ascending to high G. Perhaps it was this movement that moved Leopold Mozart to tears at the Burgtheater concert of 13 February 1785.

The soloist begins the finale playing repeated tonic triads that would have sounded better on the light-toned fortepiano of that time than they do on its successors (Example 1.18b). The repeated chords recall the finale of another work in

b. *Mozart, K. 456, III*

[79] Arthur Hutchings, *A Companion to Mozart's Piano Concertos* (London, 1948), p. 116.

B♭, Symphony No. 24, K. 182. As if to make up for a certain stiffness in the proceedings, Mozart plunges in one of the episodes of this rondo into the remote key of b, where he has the winds and then the soloist switch to 2/4 time against the 6/8 of the strings, a case similar to Blonde's defiant insistence on triple groupings against the duple ones of the rest in the quartet-finale of *Die Entführung's* Act II. As pointed out above in the discussion of that piece, two against three conflicts were common in opéra comique (an admittedly feeble attempt on my part to connect K. 456 with Paris). Mozart often used them in prior concertos but without changing time signatures. He did use 2/4 time for the soloist against 6/8 for the accompaniment in an episode of the rondo finale of the Oboe Quartet, K. 370, of 1781. Although there is still no way of connecting K. 456 with Mlle Paradis in Paris, we do know something about what she played there.

Leopold Kozeluch, Mozart's main rival in several respects, was Theresia's principal teacher. She played his works exclusively at the Concert Spirituel in Paris, as far as the surviving records allow us to tell. She appeared on this concert series no fewer than ten times between 1 April and 10 June 1784.[80] She is described as playing "a keyboard concerto by Kozeluch" on April 1, 7, 9, 16, 18, and on 10 June (the feast of Corpus Christi, which ended the spring concert season). On two great feast days, Easter (11 April) and Pentecost (30 May) the formula is changed to "a new keyboard concerto by Kozeluch," raising the possibility she received some works he composed for her during her sojourn in Paris. More suggestive still is an item presented on 13 April: "a new Italian *scena* by Kozeluch sung by Mme. Saint-Huberti accompanied by a keyboard obbligato part played by Mlle. Paradis" (bringing to mind Mozart's great aria with obbligato keyboard part, K. 505, inscribed "for Signora Storace and myself"). Saint-Huberti sang the leading female role in Salieri's *Les Danaïdes*, which opened at the Opéra on 26 April. As a principal singer, she was unlikely to have sung the new *scena* unless it was written specifically for her voice. This raises the question of whether Kozeluch himself may have journeyed to Paris and assisted his pupil there. His biographers have nothing to say about any Paris trip but his Symphony in A "à la française" is said to date from ca. 1784. The presence of Salieri in Paris in 1784 is certain. He was surely of help to Paradis, with whose father he corresponded.

All this does little to illuminate K. 456, which Paradis might have played at some concert organization other than the Concert Spirituel, for instance the Concert de la Loge Olympique that commissioned Haydn in 1784 to write his six

[80] Pierre Constant, *Histoire du Concert Spirituel, 1725–1790* (Paris, 1975), items 1120ff. At the concert of 4 April, the description omits Kozeluch's name, but it was likely the same concerto heard three days earlier, for it was usual to give at least two hearings to a newly introduced work. For a general introduction to the Concert Spirituel see *Music in European Capitals*, pp. 611–17.

"Paris" Symphonies (1785–86). Worthy of note in this light is that seven of the ten concerts in which Theresia participated at the Concert Spirituel began with a symphony by Haydn. The richness of concert life in Paris at the time made it a pole of attraction, like Vienna, to musicians from everywhere.

Kozeluch's connection with K. 456, however tentative, can be heard as a kind of ghostly reminiscence in a Piano Trio of 1788 by the Bohemian master (Example 1.18c). His *Allegro* shares the key and melodic outline of K. 456's *Andante*, while

EXAMPLE 1.18.

c. *Kozeluch, Trio in g, I (Poštólka IX: 15)*

its rhythm and meter are similar to the concerto's finale. The concerto was not published during Mozart's lifetime. Possibly Paradis played it or excerpts from it to Kozeluch, who then recreated some of it from memory to form his own theme. Another possibility is that both composers quote from some undiscovered anterior source. Kozeluch was also a music publisher, and one of the composers he published was Mozart.

K. 459 in F entered Mozart's thematic catalogue in late 1784 with a date of 11 December. It begins with the same march rhythm as the previous two but quickly goes beyond the regularity of its main theme into delightful byways. The piano part is no more difficult than its predecessor's and in several respects the two works are twins. They share an unusually high tessitura and achieve a lightness even beyond that of K. 453. In the first movement of K. 459, an *Allegro* in common time, Mozart so delights in the opening motive that he uses it over and over, in ever more imaginative ways. He again writes out a solo cadenza.

For the middle movement, Mozart chose an *Allegretto* in 6/8 time, not in the more usual key of B♭ but in the key of C. Scalar sixteenth-note passages for the winds—one flute, the first oboe, and the first bassoon—treated in concertante fashion, become more and more prominent as the movement goes along. Their delicate traceries forecast those of Susanna's "Deh vieni non tardar" in *Figaro*. It may be the flute, once again, that dictates the key, because it can pursue its scalar ascents all the way up to high G. As a coda to this sonata form without development, the three solo winds add their decorative scales over a broad pre-cadential progression. The harmonies move by the measure, answered by the piano's ascent to high C, after which there is near silence, the strings uttering sparse accompanying chords. But there is nothing to accompany until the piano reenters and provides the final cadence while restating the melody from the very beginning. We were fooled into believing it was just a beginning when it was also an ending, one of Haydn's favorite gems of wisdom about the sameness of beginnings and endings. At least once before, in the *Andante* of the Sonata for Two Pianos, K. 448, Mozart had cut back all figuration in the final pre-cadential area and let a bare accompaniment speak by itself. At the end, the flute bestows its blessing, *pianissimo*, with a final ascent up to C.

The rondo finale, *Allegro assai* in 2/4 time, restores the sprightly character of the first movement as well as its key. It begins with an impish, upbeat-dominated refrain, a theme with subtleties enhanced by minute control of staccato and legato articulation. A pert rondo-theme like this, with its many staccato repeated tones, sounds very Haydnesque and in fact corresponds to a tune that occurs in the major-mode section of the finale to Haydn's Symphony No. 78 in c of 1782.[81] Whether this is another tribute to the old master, at a time when Mozart was just finishing the last two quartets in his honor, or a subconscious recalling of a musical idea that appealed to him, we cannot know. In any case, K. 459's finale has everything going for it, from the near farcical to the pseudo-pomp of a fugato. It has won the admiration of many critics for its blithe combination of tuneful wit with contrapuntal finesse, forces that keep colliding in the most unexpected ways. The composer must have particularly loved this concerto if the posthumous information that he chose to play it at the Frankfurt coronation of 1790 along with K. 537 is correct. Mozart mistakenly described K. 459 in his catalogue as requiring trumpets and drums. Aside from their inappropriateness to the work's witty repartee, he seems never to have used trumpets and drums pitched in F. In the slow movement in F of the "Linz" Symphony, K. 425, he did use trumpets and timpani, but they were in C, as in its other movements.

1785: Leopold's Visit; More Concertos

On his way to Vienna, Leopold Mozart stopped in Munich where he was welcomed by the Marchand family, whose children he had tutored. He traveled on to the imperial capital with his violin pupil Heinrich Marchand, aged fifteen, who was to be presented to the Viennese public as a soloist. The Marchands paid their travel costs. After a grueling trip through heavy snows, they arrived in Vienna on Friday 11 February 1785, the third day of Lent. The concert season was in full swing, and on the very day of his arrival, Leopold attended the first of his son's six subscription concerts on Friday evenings in the Mehlgrube, a concert hall on the Neue Markt.

The Musicians' Society of Vienna had commissioned Mozart in January to compose a choral-orchestral work for its pension concerts at the end of Lent. In

---

[81] Joshua Rifkin, "Ein unbekanntes Haydn-Zitat bei Mozart," *Haydn Studies* 2 (1969–70): 317.

answer to their request, he decided to arrange, or have arranged, portions of his incomplete Mass in c, K. 427, of 1783. The Kyrie and Gloria, but not the two sections of the Credo that had been completed, were fashioned into the Cantata, K. 469, to which an Italian contrafactum, *Davidde penitente*, was affixed. Someone modeled the text of the first aria, "Lungi le cure ingrate," on a quatrain from Metastasio's cantata *Il natal di Giove* that begins "Bell'alme al ciel dilette."[82] The choice has implications involving both Mozarts, father and son. At Munich in 1780–81, Anton Raaff demanded an aria to sing at the end of *Idomeneo's* Act III. He proffered as a little-known text that suited him this very aria by Metastasio.[83] Mozart's letter to Leopold dated Munich 30 December 1780 communicated Metastasio's poem and asked for help. Earlier involvement with the aria text eventually parodied as "Lungi le cure" suggests that one or both of the Mozarts took a hand in compiling the text of *Davidde penitente*. Possibly the Mozart in question was Leopold, who could have saved his son some necessary work at an extremely busy time.

Mozart composed two new arias for *Davidde penitente*, dated 6 and 11 March: the first for Adamberger, his Belmonte, the second for Cavalieri, his Konstanze, in which he again indulged her coloratura and abilities to negotiate wide leaps. He did not enter the work as a whole in his catalogue, only these two arias. The *Duetto*, No. 5 of the Cantata, derived from the "Domine Deus" of the Mass, has an initial cadential section with particular relevance to Piano Concerto No. 20 in d, K. 466, as we shall see below. The new aria for Cavalieri has a bearing on Concerto No. 22 in E♭, K. 482.

Mozart often lent his services to the Musicians' Society for these pension fund concerts given during Advent and Lent. It seemed only natural that he should ask to join the Society, which he did by a (lost) letter of 11 February 1785. The organization's rules required the members to submit their birth certificates. Mozart never got around to doing this so he did not become a member. The concerts in early 1785 were preceded by two rehearsals, one on the morning of Friday 11 March in the Redoutensaal, then a general rehearsal the next morning in the Burgtheater, where the first performance took place on Sunday evening. It did not draw a full house, and its repeat two days later was even more sparsely attended.

The acts of the Society show that Mozart was in charge of the concerts on 13 and 15 March and listed the program of both events, for which the cantata supplied the second half. On 13 March, the concert began with Haydn's Symphony No. 80 in d, presumably Mozart's choice. It continued with a chorus from Gassmann's *Amore e Psiche*, arias sung by Stefano Mandini and Franziscka Danzi

[82] As pointed out by Bruce Alan Brown in his paper, "Singing Lessons in Munich," for the Symposium "L'Europe Galante" at Berkeley on 5 October 2003.

[83] Daniel Heartz, "Raaff's Last Aria: A Mozartian Idyll in the Spirit of Hasse," *Musical Quarterly* 60 (1974): 517–43; 524.

Lebrun, then the storm chorus from Haydn's *Il ritorno di Tobia*, and ended with an oboe concerto with Ludwig Lebrun as soloist (the Lebruns were visiting from Munich). On the second night, it was Heinrich Marchand who played a violin concerto in the same spot. Leopold Mozart surely attended these and all the other concerts in which his son was involved. He was also busy coaching young Heinrich, who made his concert debut at the Burgtheater on 2 March. It was deemed a success, but drew a small audience.

Perhaps the music-loving public was growing weary of the incessant round of Lenten concerts. There were of course other events to distract them. On 13 March, Zinzendorf attended a gala banquet given by the French ambassador for many members of the nobility, including such Mozart patrons as Swieten, Count Wallenstein, and Princess Fürstenberg. Lent obviously did not entail an end of parties and fancy dinners. On Tuesday, the night of Mozart's second concert for the Society, Zinzendorf was out to dinner with another set of aristocrats. As Leopold remarked in his letter of 21 February to Nannerl, rather sardonically, "fasting is unthinkable here."

Leopold wrote several lively accounts to Nannerl about his stay in Vienna, which lasted until 25 April. His first letter is dated 16 February 1785.

> On Friday afternoon around one o'clock, we reached the first-[i.e., second-]floor apartment at No. 846 Schulerstrasse, after traversing streets clogged with snow, ice, shoveling, and all kinds of workers. You can deduce what a fine place, with lovely built-in interior carvings, your brother rented when you hear that he pays 480 florins for it. The same day around six o'clock we drove to the first subscription concert, where a great throng of titled people had gathered.

The building still stands and is known as the "Figaro House," now a Mozart museum (see Figure 2.3, p. 161). The carved decorations that impressed Leopold included the marbled ceiling with stucco figures of cupids and Flora (?) executed by Albert Camesina ca. 1730.

After a few weeks in Vienna, Leopold wrote to Nannerl indicating that, despite the beauties of the apartment, living there was a constant turmoil to which he was ill suited (letter of 12 March).

> We never go to sleep before one at night, or get up before nine in the morning. The main meal is around half-past two in the afternoon. The weather remains horrible. There are academies daily, and what with [Mozart's] constant teaching, making music, and composing, where can I find a niche for myself? If only the academies were over! It is impossible to describe the vexation and upset of everything here. Your brother's grand piano [Fortepiano Flügel] has been moved at least twelve times since I have been here, from the house to the theater, or to some other house. He has had a large pedal board made that stands beneath the piano and that is three spans longer and astonishingly heavy, which must be carried every Friday to the Mehl-

grube and also transported for concerts to the houses of Count [Karl] Zichy and that of Prince Kaunitz.

The key word, *Schererei*, which I translate as "vexation," is effectively sonorous in projecting its meaning. The wonder is that Mozart could find the serenity to complete two great piano concertos, No. 20 in d and No. 21 in C, amidst such a kerfuffle.

As the hours of daylight lengthened, Leopold got out more and looked up many of the friends and acquaintances he had made during earlier visits to Vienna. Among those to whom he paid a call was the aged Giuseppe Bonno, the court Kapellmeister, who had been a supporter of the Mozarts since the ill-fated opera *La finta semplice* in 1768. All this had to be told to Nannerl in detail so that she too could share in the memories and rejoice in the peak of success reached by her brother. There were to be few occasions after this when fortune smiled so completely on Mozart.

Leopold was explicit in his first letter to Nannerl (16 February) about the financing of the Friday concerts, as he was about many matters concerning money. "Every person pays three souverains d'or or three ducats for the six concerts. To rent the Mehlgrube hall your brother pays only half a souverain per concert." In his letter of 21 February, Leopold reported on the high rents paid for lodging by the actor Johann Müller and the playwright Stephanie, citing exact figures. He calculated that the Lebruns would make a lot of money from their concerts in Vienna, wondered whether he should engage Herr Lebrun to play at Heinrich's upcoming concert in the Burgtheater, and estimated its costs at nearly 200 florins, which would have included paying an orchestra. The first half of Leopold's letter of 12 March is devoted to the financial intake and attendance numbers of the various concerts he was hearing, not only Heinrich's but Mozart's. A lost letter of 19 March is quoted only in a problematic citation of one sentence in Nissen's biography of Mozart: "I think that my son can put 2000 florins in the bank if he has no debts to pay: the money is certainly there, and the domestic economy, as far as eating and drinking goes, is economical in the highest degree." Suspicions have been raised that Nissen changed this passage so as to convey the opposite of what Leopold intended.[84]

Leopold had a few things to say about the music he was hearing, fortunately for us. His first letter, of 16 February, contains the memorable passage about the visit of Joseph Haydn on 10 February to the Mozarts' apartment and the three new string quartets. Concerning the first event in the Mehlgrube on the day of his arrival, Friday 9 February, he wrote as follows in the same letter.

> The concert was incomparable, the orchestra splendid. In addition to the symphonies, a female singer from the Italian theater sang two arias. Then came the new and

[84] Halliwell, *The Mozart Family*, pp. 476–77.

magnificent concerto by Wolfgang. When we arrived in the afternoon, the copyist was still at work copying the parts, so that your brother had no time to try out the Rondeau even once because he had to supervise the copying process. You can easily imagine that many acquaintances were encountered who ran to greet me, and many others were introduced.

The concerto was No. 20 in d, K. 466, entered in Mozart's catalogue with a date of 10 February. No doubt, its frantic copying at the last minute was typical. K. 466 was not typical in other ways, above all in Mozart's choice of the minor mode.

Concertos mostly in the minor mode were then very rare in Vienna. Wagenseil left some, mostly forgotten by the 1780s, and his pupil Stefan preceded some of his piano concertos with slow introductions in minor. The standard of comparison with Mozart in the 1780s was neither of them. Rather, it was Kozeluch. Of his twenty-odd piano concertos that have survived, none is in the minor mode.[85] The opening phrases of K. 466 must have puzzled and shocked the Viennese audience. It was one thing to write the String Quartet in d, K. 421, of 1783, a medium for connoisseurs who expected to be challenged. It was something else to present the wider public with a work as demanding as K. 466.

The soft but tumultuous strains that begin K. 466 project unease, portending tragedy. Hearing those syncopated rhythms and ominous slides up to the tonic, the average listeners were likely thrown back upon their operatic experiences for a frame of reference. Such beginnings called up the image of distressed ladies, like the long-suffering Dido or Ariadne. Syncopations like these betokened unrest, nature in turmoil, storm-tossed seas. A benchmark of the last was Leonardo Vinci's shipwreck aria "Vo solcando un mar crudele" in the original setting of Metastasio's *Artaserse* (Rome, 1730), a piece replete from the beginning with multiple syncopations.[86] Mozart wrote an aria of the same kind, "Fuor del mar ho un mar in seno," in his *Idomeneo*. Still more pertinent to the audience of early 1785, and perhaps to Mozart's inspiration for K. 466, was the Storm Chorus in d that Haydn added for the 1784 revival in the Burgtheater of his oratorio *Il ritorno di Tobia*.[87] It was included, as we have seen, in the Society's concerts under Mozart's direction on 13 and 15 March.

Most concertos in those days began with a melody that listeners could seize upon for guidance while entertaining pleasant anticipations of its return. K. 466 begins with a gloomy texture rather than anything an audience would recognize as a theme. The first eight measures elaborate the tonic D in low position by means of sounding its upper and lower neighboring tones: D C♯ E D. The second eight

[85] Milan Poštolka, *Leopold Koželuh: Život a dílo* (Prague, 1964), category IV.
[86] *Music in European Capitals*, pp. 96–97.
[87] *Haydn, Mozart*, p. 384.

measures elaborate the tonic further by exploring the octave above it. Then the full fury of the orchestra, with trumpets and drums, breaks forth with dire pronouncements, as if of doom. A relief of sorts is felt when, without preparation, the relative major arrives as the winds intone a calmer and more melodic idea, F E F in anapest rhythm. Yet this melodic and harmonic relief is more motive than theme because it refuses to stay put in key, rising one whole tone for restatement, then another whole tone. The flute's little answer to the oboes and bassoons consists of an octave leap up, sixth descent by leap and resolution up a half step. It turns out later to be an approximation of the piano's entrance theme. The music returns quickly to d and after more tutti eruptions alternating with calmer passages, the relatively long first exposition comes to a quiet ending. The solo enters with a theme of its own, but spun out of what the solo flute earlier stated, and also related to the initial melodic turn around the tonic. There is wider resonance too with a phrase from Mozart's Mass in c, reused in *Davidde penitente* (Example 1.19ab).

EXAMPLE 1.19.

a. *Mozart, Mass in c, K. 427, Domine Deus; Davidde penitente, K. 469, No. 5*

b. *Mozart, Piano Concerto No. 20 in d, K. 466, I*

Previously, when Mozart gave the soloist entrance music different from the beginning of the movement, it was more of a preparatory *Eingang* than a theme. In this case it is a theme not only by nature of its construction in three four-measure segments that end tonally where they began, but also by way of contrast with the mostly athematic nature of the previous doings, except for the closing theme immediately preceding it. After the piano's entrance theme, the orchestra resumes its rumblings as before, not joined by the piano at first but then accompanied by the soloist's plethora of sixteenth-note figuration. A proper eight-measure second theme in the relative major eventually arrives, first announced by the piano. Display up and down the keyboard occupies much of the remaining prima parte.

The seconda parte begins by reverting to the piano's entrance theme and making three complete, slightly varied statements of it on F, g, and E♭, interspersed by the rumbling, syncopated idea in the orchestra. After suitable modulation and considerable figuration, the piano leads the way to the reprise. Its entrance theme does not return here, which is no surprise after all the use just made of it. Everything else is in place, leading to a cadenza, followed by the closing theme and a few more rumblings of the syncopated initial idea, which dies away to a *pianissimo* final chord of d, with only the violas supplying the faint F that makes the chord minor.

The Romance deserves an exploratory essay in its own right. A few remarks must suffice instead. Its key of B♭ (not F!) and initial fall from the fifth to the third degree match the beginning of Haydn's *Adagio* in his Symphony No. 80 and have the same soothing effect. Mozart continues his melody with falling conjunct tritones answered by falling perfect fifths by step, a passage reminiscent of several in *Idomeneo*, especially No. 30's introduction.[88] The second falling perfect fifth even has the descent followed by staccato afterbeats on the same pitch, a perfect invocation of the "Idamante motif" from that opera, with all it had to say about young lovers ultimately united. This movement is a Romance in many senses. Its stormy episode in the key of g, with rapid sixteenth-note triplets for the piano up and down the keyboard, sounds akin to some of the fiery parts of the outer movements. Mozart restores the initial calm by gradually approaching its original note values as well as its key.

The finale, *Allegro assai* in cut time, is begun by the soloist, who explodes up the tonic arpeggio like a rocket. Aside from its initial upward burst, there is much about the theme that sounds familiar from the first movement, for instance the importance of the melodic turn around D with lower neighbor C♯ and upper neighbor E. Even more evident to the ear is the sixth descent and resolution, A↓C♯↑D, and the eventual leap up to high D and stepwise descent that relates to Example 1.19b. There are other factors as well, such as the movement of the accompaniment in evenly spaced parallel thirds. Mozart makes the connection clear when he condenses the initial theme for the piano's solo statement. And more evident than ever is the genesis of this whole complex in the passage quoted from the Mass in c and *Davidde penitente* (Example 1.19a). Not to be missed is the correspondence of the long-held tone followed by quick triplets descending a fifth in the finale at mm. 65–66 with the same figure in the theme of the Romance (first at mm. 16 and 18). The calm rhythm of the accompaniment is that of the theme first announced by the woodwinds in the opening movement. After the arrival of the relative major in the finale, the winds intone a new theme, lightly provided by the strings with an oom-pah-pah accompaniment. When at length this theme returns in tonic

[88] *Haydn, Mozart*, pp. 713–14, ex. 9.15.

minor at m. 302, it sounds less original and more like another switch on the basic motif of falling fifth to tonic. Its chromatic rises also have a familiar ring. One can easily imagine Mozart's audience and even Leopold, on that memorable Friday evening in early 1785, breathing a sigh of relief when the first oboe softly made a breakthrough by stating the theme not in d but in D, to which the solo piano and then the whole orchestra were gladly converted, the trumpets setting a seal upon the victory by their repeated falling fifths with a major third: A A A / F♯ D.

Mozart drafted thirty-nine measures of a movement related to K. 466 that began like a gavotte with two staccato upbeats and a fall from the fifth to the tonic. It sounds rather staid compared to the explosive beginning of the finale he completed. Yet its basic ingredients are similar: the fall from A to D, the melodic turn around D, and the rise to B♭. Clearly, B♭ is an important tone and tonality throughout the concerto, being the main key of the Romance and the destination of some potent deceptive cadences in the finale. The draft, of which Mozart wrote only first violin and bass parts, rather grimly combines the jaunty gavotte rhythm of the melody with the stolid motion of its bass, more like a counterpoint exercise than an interesting beginning for a movement of K. 466. Yet the draft cannot be denied all possibility of having contributed in some way to the genesis of a masterpiece. The strong claim for being the nucleus of what blossomed into K. 466 remains a small idea from the Mass in c.

Mozart repeated K. 466 four days later at an academy in the Burgtheater for soprano Elisabeth Distler, the sixteen-year old daughter of the theater's *Logenmeister*. Leopold was again present and reported toward the end of his first letter, "Yesterday the 15th there was another concert in the theater given for a little maiden who sings charmingly; your brother played the new grand concerto in D *magnifique* etc. Today we are going to a concert in the house of the Salzburg agent Ployer." Some political news about the emperor's plan to exchange the Austrian Netherlands for Bavaria rounded out this rich letter. In the middle of it, Leopold gave a slightly more detailed account of the Burgtheater concert three days earlier.

> On Sunday evening, there was an academy in the theater for the Italian singer [Luisa] Laschi, who is traveling to Italy. She sang two arias. There was a cello concerto; a tenor and a bass sang an aria apiece. Your brother played the splendid concerto he wrote for Paradis in Paris. I was in a box only two away from the very beautiful Princess of Württemburg and had the pleasure of hearing the interchange of the instruments so superbly that tears of joy stood in my eyes. As your brother left the stage, the emperor waved his hat and cried "bravo Mozart." When he came on to play there was also a burst of applause.

In less than a week Leopold had met Haydn, heard a variety of excellent singers, and attended performances of several of his son's greatest compositions.

Mozart's large and heavy fortepiano with the pedal board earned mention on the handbill distributed to advertise an event one day before his fifth Friday concert:

> Notice. On Thursday March 10, Herr Kapellmeister Mozart will have the honor to give for his own benefit a grand musical academy in the imperial-royal National Court Theater. In it, he will play not only a newly completed piano concerto of his composition but also use an especially large pedal fortepiano in extemporizing [beym Phantasieren].

The concerto was No. 21 in C, K. 467, dated 9 March in Mozart's catalogue.

Improvisations figured importantly on the programs of Mozart's own concerts. He also improvised cadenzas and many other passages in his solo concertos. Since the pedals were there throughout the concert, the temptation would be to use them even when they were not indicated in the score. In the first movement of K. 466, there are a few deep bass notes in the autograph score that could not be played by the otherwise-occupied two hands.[89]

K. 467 breathes dignity, aplomb, and magisterial control over the darker passions that inform much of K. 466, yet the two concertos are alike in some respects, as might be expected from their temporal proximity. From K. 467's soft beginning in the major, we can detect the outlines of a military march, as if heard from a distance. It calls up not so much a regimental parade or the changing of the guard, daily events in Vienna then, as an operatic scene rendering a make-believe replica of the same. Indeed, it suggests what is soon to follow in Figaro's mocking salute to the newly commandeered Cherubino, sending him off to the army with a cheery "alla gloria militar, Cherubino alla vittoria." C major with trumpets and drums suffices for that piece as well.

The first movement of K. 467 bears some similarities to that of Concerto No. 13 in C, K. 415, of 1783, which also announces a march theme, softly, *Allegro* in common time, with a unison figure that climbs upward by degree with various slides up and down. The opening theme of K. 467 also begins in unison. It has the more striking profile and is thus more easily remembered. It also has protean possibilities, can serve as a treble as well as a bass, and can engender imitations of itself and sequences dependent on its head motif, etc. All these happen before the orchestra offers a broadly spun second idea in the tonic, begun by the horns and trumpets. After the orchestra reaches a resounding conclusion using its first measure in canon, there is a quiet passage over dominant harmony with woodwind solos that seem to urge the piano soloist to make an entrance (rather like coaxing a shy child forth to perform).

The piano enters not with the main theme but with an *Eingang* that deploys

---

[89] These are discussed by Hans Engel and Horst Heussner in *NMA*, V/15/6, pp. xiv–xv.

more dominant harmony. Then the main theme sounds again, in unison and soft, like the beginning, above which the piano coyly adds a long trill. Only then does the piano take the continuation of the main theme on itself. As in K. 466, the piano waits for four measures before joining the thematic process of the second exposition. A thematic carryover from K. 466 might be detected in the downward slide of a fourth in a triplet figure following a dotted longer note of K. 467's second measure; it was prominent in both the second and third movements of K. 466, as we have seen. This could be dismissed as mere coincidence, did the piano not make a more substantial reference to K. 466 when entering during the development of K. 467's *Allegro*. It is not merely the falling figure and the rhythm that are similar. The leap up an octave to begin is the same, and even the sixteenth-note upbeat is repeated. Moreover, the accompanying parallel thirds in even rhythm also grace K. 466. However disparate in overall mood the two concertos undeniably are, they also share some features. It is as if Mozart had not completely exhausted the rich potential of a main idea in K. 466 and was still exploring its possibilities. K. 467's *Allegro* ends quietly, as it began, with the winds decorating a descending tonic triad against the rising tonic triads of the strings. The latter have the final word, falling by step down to the tonic with the familiar dotted quarter note and triplet sixteenths, followed by the disjointed tones of the initial measure. Again, the first shall be last.

The gorgeous slow movement of K. 467, *Andante* in cut time and in F, is often praised as one of Mozart's finest, a painting of broad vistas made poignant by beautiful chains of dissonances slowly resolving in long suspensions. Its basic idea comes from a much earlier work, and this is not the first time the composer recalled it for use. Back in 1767, the year Schobert died, the Mozarts included an intriguing *Andante* in F from Schobert's Op. 15 No. 1 Sonata as a middle movement of K. 39 in B♭, the second of the pasticcio keyboard concertos compiled by Leopold to serve as models for his son and as showpieces for him to play. In the *Andante* of Mozart's Piano Sonata in a, K. 310 (Paris, 1778), there is a modulatory passage in which constant sixteenth notes in triplets swathe slowly resolving dissonances in a chain of suspensions over a slow-moving bass with trills, a passage closely parallel to its Schobert equivalent in K. 39.[90] In 1785, the same Schobert model turns up again, this time more clearly. Unlike the *Andante* in 3/4 time of K. 310, K. 467's *Andante* begins, like Schobert's, by having the bass rise up the triad in quarter notes: F A C rest. Mozart starts incessant triplet motion at the very outset, where Schobert had delayed its arrival until his fifth measure. If Mozart's reversion to Schobert's *Andante* was conscious on his part, could this bit of nostalgia have had something to do with Leopold's presence? No surviving words of Leopold pertain specifically to K. 467.

The finale of K. 467, *Allegro vivace assai* in 2/4 time, restores not only the key

---

[90] *Haydn, Mozart*, p. 593.

of C but also the high spirits of the opening *Allegro*. It sounds particularly jolly after the tender reveries of the *Andante*, an aria for the soloist in which the accompanying strings are hushed at first by mutes, and later play mostly pizzicato. Full orchestra with trumpets and drums returns for the *piano* rondo theme that begins the finale. The theme itself borrows its chromatic rises from the opening of the first movement (m. 7 in particular). Among the wittiest moments is the episode in which the piano solo gets into a snarling dialogue with the winds using the head motif of the refrain, at first at a distance of two measures, then shortened to only one measure, with heightening tension, which is resolved as this modulatory passage leads to a long dominant pedal preparing another return of the refrain. The concerto ends, like K. 466, with the piano's rush of rapid octaves up to the final cadence.

Leopold's letters, although they contain no remarks on the composition or performance of K. 467, provide many insights on the concert life of this memorable Lenten season. They also mention several of the people he encountered at concerts. In his letter of 21 February he names, to begin, "Baron van Swieten, whom we also visited at home," followed by Countess Thun and her sister Countess Wallenstein, and Herr von Sonnenfels and his wife. The list also includes, unusually, the names of two Viennese composers, Franz Asplmayr and Joseph Starzer. In addition, two members of the high nobility are mentioned, Prince Wenzel Johann Paar, and Prince Karl Auersperg, both of whom appear on the long 1784 list of subscribers.

The Lenten academies in the Burgtheater were so frequent during 1785 that there was one given even on a Friday (18 February), a day when the theater was otherwise closed during this holy season. There were no fewer than thirty-two academies altogether, twice the number held the previous year. Under this rubric are included the two Society concerts directed by Mozart, a Singspiel *Die Eroberung der Festung*, not staged, of course; an oratorio, *Der tod Jesu*, by the clarinetist Anton Stadler; and Haydn's setting of Metastasio's *L'isola disabitata*, on Saturday 17 March. The last concert, a benefit for Nancy Storace, was held the next day, Palm Sunday. It was attended by Zinzendorf, who commented on her good pronunciation of German in a song based on the Count's serenade "Saper bramate" in Paisiello's *Barbiere*. The Burgtheater remained shut during Holy Week. The day after Easter a play was performed, and the following day an opera.

Leopold Mozart at last had the respite from concerts he wished for. In his letter of 25–26 March, he showed no eagerness to return to Salzburg, pleading that bad weather prevented him. To Nannerl (if not to his employer) he confessed that he would delay leaving in order to take advantage of the post-Easter plays and operas, and this he did, night after night. In a postscript to this letter he added that on the following Friday an actress of his acquaintance, Marianne Lang-Boudet, would make her debut in *Der Hausvater*, by Diderot. She was the wife of the hornist Martin Lang and they were both employed at Munich in the service of Carl Theodor. She did make her debut, and in his letter of 2 April, Leopold praised her, saying that she played the role of Sophie excellently and received great applause. Zinzendorf, also present, was more reserved. He did praise Mlle Catherine Jaquet in the role of Cäcilia: "La Jaquet joua bien, La Lang une nouvelle actrice passablement." The Langs were nevertheless offered a contract in Vienna, with a job for him in the *Harmoniemusik*, but Munich would not release her.

It was expected that the court's vaunted Italian troupe would resume its operatic offerings after Easter, but prima buffa Nancy Storace fell ill following her Palm Sunday concert and apparently could not be replaced on short notice. Zinzendorf explained in a letter to his sister dated 29 March: "Nous voila hors de la monotonie et de nouveau dans les spectacles. Les plus parfaits des nôtres, c'est à dire les operas comiques italiens ne commencent pas encore a cause de la maladie de notre meilleure actrice, que tout le monde aime, parce qu'elle est bonne et chante bien."[91] Thus, the remnants of the German operatic troupe were called upon to substitute with items from their repertory. They had been reduced to giving occasional performances, mainly benefits, in the Kärntnerthor Theater. During Easter week in the Burgtheater, they revived Grétry's *Zemire und Azor* on Tuesday and Gluck's *Die Pilgrimme von Mecca* on Friday. Leopold attended both and reported that Mme Lange, that is, Aloysia Weber, sang and acted outstandingly in them (letter of 2 April).[92] He followed this by saying that "we all dined at the Langes, where Herr Lang from Munich is also lodged, and tomorrow they dine with us." This suggests that the hornist Martin Lang and the actor-painter Joseph Lange, who was Aloysia's husband, may have been related. Leopold then listed where they had dined during the week: on Easter with a banker, Monday with Dr. Rhab, Tuesday with Adamberger, Wednesday with the Langes, and Thursday with Herr von Ployer. He mentions that a new Italian soprano, La Coltellini, would make her debut the following Wednesday, then said that he must close because the floor-polisher was in his room and a warm corner where he could write was not to be found elsewhere in the apartment. Furthermore, he wrote, "it is nearly six p.m. and we are riding to the banker where we ate on Easter in order to play quartets."

Leopold's chatty letters to Nannerl give the best idea of the Mozart couple's very active social life during mid-1785, a time when there are few letters by Mozart

---

[91] Link, *The National Court Theatre in Mozart's Vienna*, p. 59, n. 77, quoted here with a correction of typographical error and realization of abbreviations.

[92] Unmentioned by Leopold was his old friend Emanuel Schikaneder, who made his Burgtheater debut as Schwindel in *Die Pilgrimme*.

himself that survive. With the concert season over, Mozart had more time for his work, even with frequent social outings and entertaining. In April and May, he was able to compose the Masonic Cantata discussed above and several Lie-der. Mozart's long letter to Anton Klein in Mannheim, dissected at some length above, was written on 21 May 1785, after Leopold's departure, which finally took place on 25 April. The Italian opera singers were able to bring a new production, Paisiello's *La contadina di spirito,* to the stage on 6 April. Leopold remarked that its second performance was two days later but he says no more about it. Zinzendorf attended the premiere, at which Celeste Coltellini made her debut, and said she was strongly applauded. Storace reappeared in a revival of Paisiello's *Il re Teodoro* on 20 April, prompting Zinzendorf to write in his diary that she appeared to have suffered, also that she thanked the audience in German.

Leopold's remaining time in April was spent partly in attending Masonic lodge meetings. He was admitted to the first degree of apprentice at Benevolence on 6 April, promoted to the second degree on 16 April, and to the third degree on 22 April. On 24 April, the day before his departure, he and his son were present at the meeting of Crowned Hope when Ignaz von Born was especially honored and the cantata *Die Maurerfreude,* K. 471, was performed. Leopold and his pupil Heinrich Marchand returned by way of Linz, where they were entertained by Count Johann Thun, then on to Munich where Leopold stayed with the March-ands for at least a week. He finally reached Salzburg about 13 May, having been warned that, after stretching his six-week leave to twelve weeks, his salary was about to be stopped.

Mozart began working with Lorenzo da Ponte on the libretto of *Le nozze di Figaro* at some time during mid-1785 after Leopold left Vienna. By the fall of the year, he was being pressed by Count Rosenberg to finish its composition. There was a respite of some kind at the end of the year, probably caused by deferral of the opera from Carnival season until after Easter, that allowed him to return to other kinds of composition. This would explain how he had time to write two big works, both in E♭, before the end of 1785: the Sonata for Piano and Violin, K. 481, dated 12 December, and the Piano Concerto No. 22, K. 482, dated 16 December. Both these works open with movements brimming with one melodic idea after another, as if their creator were relieved to return to compositions unfettered by words and by the kind of concision imposed by opera at its best. All three move-ments of K. 481 are unusually elaborate for a violin and piano sonata.

K. 482 matches the piano concertos of early 1785 in breadth and power. A big piece written to entertain a large audience, it represents the composer's most pub-lic face. At the same time, it belongs to a rather private family of pieces in E♭, with many ties to his other works in this key. He performed it at an Advent concert of the Musician's Society. At these charity affairs, Vienna's professional musicians donated their services, with the result that the orchestra was unusually large, even double or more its usual strength.[93] The orchestra, chorus and soloists were placed on the stage of the Burgtheater, as we know from several descriptions. The main fare of the two concerts was the oratorio *Esther* by Dittersdorf, dating from 1773, performed under the direction of Salieri. Oratorios were written in two parts, and there was a widespread practice of inserting a concerto between them. On 19 December, Joseph Otter played a concerto for solo violin and orchestra as an entr'acte. A special handbill for the second concert on 23 December (the last before the Christmas holiday) announced: "Herr W. A. Mozart will play a new concerto of his composition on the fortepiano."

According to a report in the *Wiener Zeitung*, the event attracted a large gathering, one that included Emperor Joseph, his nephew Francis and wife (Elisabeth of Württemberg), and many members of the high nobility. The report concluded by citing Mozart's piano concerto, "of which the outstanding reception goes without saying because of the great and deserved fame of this master, so well known and treasured by all." Surely the emperor rewarded Mozart well, as he had done on previous occasions like this. If he did so, Mozart may have withheld this news from Leopold in the lost letter dated 28 December, some contents of which were retold to Nannerl (13 January 1786). Instead we hear of other performances: "A letter of 28 December from your brother says that he gave three hastily-organized subscription concerts for 120 subscribers for which he wrote a new piano concerto in E♭ and at which—this is something strange—he had to repeat the *Andante*."

This very *Andante* begins with a theme that bears resemblance to one of the two new arias Mozart wrote for *Davidde penitente* earlier in the year, a cantata that constituted the main fare on the previous program in the Burgtheater given by the Musician's Society. Was it perhaps at their December concert in the same theater that K. 482's *Andante* was encored? (Note that the public, whichever public it was, did not forego applauding after a movement other than the finale). Both the aria and the *Andante* open with themes that seem to grope their way along furtively in a somber setting. The aria's text begins "Amid dark, gloomy shades." In motion and affect, the incipits sound alike. Both depend on minor seconds, ascending and descending, with ties over the barline to increase momentum. In the aria, this gloomy music is a foil to the brilliant *Allegro* in cut time and in C major that follows, with many silvery peals for Cavalieri's "agile throat." K. 482's *Andante* is also a foil, one that sets off the brilliance of the outer movements in E♭, and particularly the carefree finale, a big sonata rondo on a popular-type hunting

[93] The orchestral roster for the Advent concerts has survived. See Dexter Edge, "Manuscript Parts as Evidence of Orchestral Size in the Eighteenth-Century Viennese Concerto," in *Mozart's Piano Concertos*, ed. Zaslaw, 427–60: 429–33 and 448, n. 9. The large orchestra probably played only for the oratorio choruses and was reduced for a work like K. 482. It included six oboe players, two of whom could have played Mozart's clarinet parts.

theme in 6/8 time. There are a few rondo touches in this *Andante* as well, such as the two episodes for winds in the major (E♭ and C); otherwise, it is a theme and variations. The rather stunted theme does not preclude virtuoso passagework for the piano. After a lovely coda, the movement ends softly in the minor.

Assuming that Mozart hit on the character of his *Andante* first, we can understand how he might have wanted to make the fast movements as festive and alluring as possible. Part of the allure is the work's new timbral qualities. For the first time in one of his big orchestral works, oboes are replaced by clarinets, which are prominent in all three movements. There is ample concertante work for the horns, bassoons, and single flute as well. An initial tutti *forte* calls the audience to attention followed by the risky move of handing the discourse over to the two horns, which softly sound a descending passage in even tones from the fifth degree to the tonic (Example 1.20). If the tutti *forte* sounds familiar, it is

EXAMPLE 1.20. *Mozart, Piano Concerto No. 22 in E♭, K. 482, I*

because Mozart used it or a close equivalent in several other works in E♭. Mostly monophonic (only the violins introduce a G in the first measure), with note values that get shorter, dotted rhythm, trills, and the tones of the tonic triad—these are conditions that apply to a whole family of Mozart's incipits in this key.[94] What astonishes is that the descent of the treble voice from 5 to 1 in even tones that follows also occurs in an earlier piece, much earlier in fact, at the beginning of Symphony No. 1 in E♭, K. 16, of late 1764. Mozart's career in terms of lifespan was short but in terms of consistent artistic intentions, it was not. In K. 16, the soft descending passage's treble line is entrusted to the first violins while the horns merely accompany, and there is a simple bass marking the pulse in quarter notes. The chain of suspensions is common to both. Here the staccato tones and leaps of the two bassoons lend more interest and provide the only accompaniment. On repetition, the two clarinets take the place of the horns as the violins assume the lowly task of standing in for the bassoons. One of several striking ideas that follow is a call given to the first horn, doubled by flute and first violins an octave above (m. 51ff.). Emerging here is an idea that also gives shape to the second theme of the overture to *Le nozze di Figaro*, soon to follow.

K. 482's finale has been deemed by some to be overly popular in tone to suit

---

[94] Cuthbert Girdlestone, *Mozart's Piano Concertos*, 2nd ed. (London, 1958), pp. 349–50.

the exaltation of the first *Allegro* and the *Andante*, by which is meant mainly the hunting character of the rondo theme. Tuneful yes, but how cleverly this theme takes the very beginning of the concerto and transforms it. There, a descending unison triad G E♭ B♭ precedes the first horn's B♭; here, inverted, an ascending triad B♭ E♭ G is followed by a gradual climb to the peak tone of B♭. The big episode in A♭ in the middle of the finale, a serenade-like moment with different tempo and meter, *Andante cantabile* in 3/4, is decried as a throwback to the Salzburg years, which it is to the extent that the episode is strikingly like one in the finale of Concerto No. 9, K. 271, also in E♭. The device works equally well here. K. 482 is another omnibus concerto in that it has a little of everything, and something for everyone. Retrospective, if you will, is also the choice of c minor for the slow movement, reflecting a frequent move in earlier works by Mozart in the key of E♭, a practice that goes all the way back to K. 16.

If there is one respect in which K. 482 lacks the appeal of the previous two concertos it is that Mozart, having lavished so much attention on his orchestra, has been less generous in giving enough of interest to the piano solo, that is, to himself. In the first *Allegro*, the solo begins with an *entrata* that strikes this listener as rather vapid. Much of the ensuing passagework is mere commentary on what the orchestra says so eloquently. Even the piano's full-chord insistence on the minor dominant at one point quickly dissipates into yet another reminiscence of the "Idamante motif." The piano's own second theme begins with a somehow pallid rise of an octave by step. All the octaves up and down the keyboard seem less integrated in the whole than heretofore. These reservations apply only to the concerto's first movement.

In its entirety, K. 482 is a marvel of euphony, a sonorous feast for the ears. Few orchestras of that time, and hardly any outside Vienna, were up to the challenges of such a work, and especially some of its completely exposed wind writing. In Vienna itself, the concerto marked an acme of Mozart's career as virtuoso pianist, one who was out to please the public, and who succeeded in doing so. The same issue of the *Wiener Zeitung* of 28 December 1785 that praised the concerto and called its composer a universal treasure included an advertisement by the engraver-publisher Hieronymous Löschenkohl of two new calendars with silhouettes of persons prominent in Vienna. Among them was Mozart.

2
Mozart, 1786—1788

The Approaches to *Figaro*

PIERRE-AUGUSTIN Caron de Beaumarchais was a man of many parts: author, musician, clockmaker, diplomat, and even spy. A jack-of-all-trades, he resembled his most famous fictional character. Better put, Figaro mirrored his creator's checkered career. Born in January 1732, one month before George Washington and two months before Joseph Haydn, he was harp teacher to the four daughters of Louis XV. He pleaded with the French court in 1776–77 to support the American insurgents and then organized a fleet to come to their aid. He wrote several plays before this time, including two serious *drames* modeled on those by Diderot. In 1772, he tried writing an opéra comique for the Parisian Théâtre Italien, *Le barbier de Séville, ou La précaution inutile*, capitalizing on some of his own misadventures in Spain. When this failed to be accepted for performance, he turned it into a mostly spoken comedy with a few songs and as such it was accepted by the Comédie Française in 1775. After initial failure, the play became immensely successful and was performed, printed, and read throughout Europe.

Beaumarchais visited Vienna in the summer of 1774, allegedly searching for the author of a scurrilous pamphlet describing the sterile union of Marie Antoinette and Louis XVI. Maria Theresa and state chancellor Kaunitz suspected he wrote the pamphlet himself and had him put in prison, where he was interrogated by none other than Mozart's patron Joseph von Sonnenfels.[1] He was freed

[1] Alfred, Ritter von Arneth, *Beaumarchais und Sonnenfels* (Vienna, 1868).

at the intervention of the French chargé d'affaires. His questionable behavior in this affair left him in ill repute with the imperial family, but this changed when a brilliant setting of *Le barbier* as an Italian opera buffa by Paisiello, *Il barbiere di Siviglia*, staged at St. Petersburg in 1783, quickly spread to opera houses around the Continent.[2] It became a favorite of Emperor Joseph II, as played by his new buffo troupe in the Burgtheater. Beaumarchais, no less than Paisiello, had triumphed (Figure 2.1).

From the beginning, Beaumarchais maintained that he was creating not one play but a trilogy. True to his promise he created a second play dealing with the same characters, plus some others, a few years later in their lives, *La folle journée, ou Le mariage de Figaro*, which was twice as long, and followed it with a con-

FIGURE 2.1. Saint-Aubin's profile of Beaumarchais, engraved by Cochin.

cluding *drame*, set in a still later time, *L'autre Tartuffe, ou La mère coupable*. After many vetoes by the censors in Paris, *Le mariage de Figaro* was given its first public performance at the Odéon Theater by the Comédie Française on 27 April 1784. Not until after the French Revolution had begun was the third play performed.

Printing presses across Europe could scarcely keep up with the demand for editions of the second play. In spite of its length and complexity, *Figaro* was eagerly adopted by the more enlightened public of the playgoers and by those members of the aristocracy whose pastimes included amateur theatricals. The memoirs of Count Karl Zinzendorf are now largely available as to their musical and thespian contents.[3] They reveal some of the ferment *Figaro* raised in Vienna during the fall of 1784.

Zinzendorf and many other members of the nobility visited their boxes in the Burgtheater on an almost nightly basis. After making an appearance and meet-

[2] *Music in European Capitals*, p. 949.
[3] Thanks to Dorothea Link's *The National Court Theatre in Mozart's Vienna*.

ing with friends for conversation, he would often stay only for a favorite aria, speech, or scene, and then move on to some other social event. In his voluminous diaries, he often says how a given work struck him and why, or how he regarded an individual's performance. Of equal interest to us are some of the conversations he reported having about theatrical matters. On 23 October 1784, he noted "Le Comte Charles Palfy me parla beaucoup de la pièce de Beaumarchais Le mariage de Figaro." At this time, Paisiello's *Barbiere* was being given frequently and on 22 November 1784, he commented on its performance: "charmante musique." Then in a diary entry from early 1785 he wrote: "21 Janvier. A l'opera. Le Barbier de Seville. La Laschi y fait le rôle de Rosine fort bien et fut applaudie . . . Je lus un peu dans le mariage de Figaro." Luisa Laschi replaced Nancy Storace in the role of Rosina often. Of these two women, interchangeably excellent, Laschi would soon become Mozart's slightly older and sadly wiser Rosina as Countess Almaviva, and Storace her maidservant Susanna. Zinzendorf mentioned the two works together perhaps because he was intrigued to learn what happened to Rosina in the sequel.

Another possibility is that Zinzendorf had been "reading a little" in the second play to assess its feasibility for performance in the amateur theatricals that he and his friends, including Mozart's patron Count Pálffy, put on for their own amusement, the so-called Comédies or Théâtres de Société.[4] This seems more than likely after he mentions a third member of his set discussing the play a few days later: "23 Janvier . . . Madame du Buquoy me parla du mariage de Figaro." If they did not stage a private performance it may well have been because of the play's extraordinary length, complexity, and number of characters.

In early 1785, Emanuel Schikaneder petitioned authorities to perform *Le mariage de Figaro* as translated by Johann Rautenstrauch. Joseph II signaled his ambiguous reaction to the minister of police, Count Johann Pergen, in a memorandum dated 31 January 1785.

> I understand that the well-known comedy *Le mariage de Figaro* has been proposed for the Theater at the Kärntnerthor in a German translation. Since this play contains much that is offensive, as I understand it, the censor will either reject it altogether or have such changes made that will allow him to take responsibility for its performance and the impression it makes on the public.

Reject or revise, ordered Joseph, not simply reject, as most authors have said, beginning with Lorenzo da Ponte in his memoirs. Joseph's opinion of the play was also ambiguous in that he allowed the German translation to be printed in full, without cuts. A copy of the translation formed part of Mozart's library,

[4] On these private performances see Link's commentary, pp. 196–203.

recorded in an inventory after his death. The affair concerning the play's performance by a German troupe also caught the attention of the public press and was
duly reported in the *Wiener Zeitung*. Vienna was buzzing with interest in the new
Figaro play during 1785. Thus it seems unwise to say that Mozart "stumbled upon
Beaumarchais's *Marriage of Figaro*" as if it were some *rara avis* or were found only
by accident.[5] One does not "stumble" upon a *succès de scandale*.

Da Ponte claims in his memoirs that he asked the emperor's blessing on the
opera he and Mozart had made of *Figaro* soon after Joseph's instructions to Pergen in January 1785. If this were the case, Mozart would have had to compose the
music in the fall of 1784, whereas he composed it mostly during the fall of 1785.
Da Ponte wrote about his life in Vienna decades later, hampered both by faulty
memories and by excessive desire to enhance his literary reputation. One thing
Da Ponte does not claim is that he came up with the idea of turning the play by
Beaumarchais into an opera. He gives credit for this to Mozart.

Work on the opera may have begun as early as the summer of 1785, but more
likely in the early fall. Leopold knew nothing about the project until it was well
under way in October. His letter to Nannerl telling her about it is the one firm
document we have pertaining to the early stages. The letter is dated 11 November
and tells of a lost letter of 2 November from Mozart saying how overwhelmed he
was in trying to complete the opera.

> He begs forgiveness because he is up to his ears in work since he must finish the
> opera *Le nozze di Figaro* . . . I know the play [piece]; it is a very intricate play [müh-
> sames Stück], and the translation from the French will surely require much revi-
> sion in order to become an opera, if it is to have the effect an opera should have. God
> grant that the action comes off; about the music, I have no doubt. That will cost him
> much running back and forth and arguing until he gets the libretto so arranged as
> he wishes, to suit his purposes. And then he will put things off and lose valuable
> time, according to his lovely habit; now he must go at it seriously because he is being
> driven by Count Rosenberg.

Apparently, Rosenberg was driving them to finish the opera in time to stage it
during the approaching Carnival season. This plan was changed for production
during the spring season after Easter. The case is similar to that of *Die Entführung*, which was also hurried along toward an early production that was then
postponed.

Leopold's remarks on what it would cost Mozart to extract a text that served
his purposes hit the mark. If anyone was well instructed on the composer's ways

---

[5] Georg Knepler, *Wolfgang Amadé Mozart*, trans. J. Bradford Robinson (Cambridge, 1994), p. 111. In the
original German, p. 158, the verb is "stossen."

of getting a libretto made over to his satisfaction it was Leopold. He was the go-between with Varesco and the recipient of detailed accounts of his son's dealings with Stephanie. Mozart's part in shaping the new libretto with Da Ponte is a certainty, not a likely conjecture, as often presented.

The Mozart family was very partial to reading and seeing plays. So it is no surprise that Leopold had read *Le mariage de Figaro*. During his visit to Vienna in 1785, he attended as many plays as operas. Besides observing the visiting players who came often to Salzburg, he witnessed the active theatrical life of Munich, where his friend Marchand directed the court theater's comedians. As for Nannerl, the theater was her favorite secular pastime, aside from music, and she seems to have missed none of the shows brought to Salzburg. Her brother took advantage of playgoing wherever he was. Discussing plays by letter with Nannerl was a frequent way he tried to humor her. He praised the way tragedies were acted by the German players in the Burgtheater when trying to induce her to visit Vienna in 1781. His letter to her of 22 December 1781 brings up specific plays, the first one of which he assumed she had read or seen.

> Do you not think that *Das Loch in der Thur* is a good comedy? But you ought to see it here. *Die Gefahren der Verführung* is also a good play. *Das öffentliche Geheimnis* is only endurable if one remembers it is an Italian play, for the way the princess descends to the level of her servant is really too indecent and unnatural. The best thing about it is truly the open secret, namely the way the two lovers, albeit secretly, make themselves understood to each other.

His talk then turned to actors they both knew.

Unwilling to play the role of servant himself, Mozart had rebelled against his prince. Servants were, he believed, inferior by nature. Perhaps he had a change of heart after Beaumarchais showed him how two women, one the mistress, the other her servant, worked together to thwart a dire threat in *Le mariage de Figaro*. His music for them says that he did.

The complex characters of the three Figaro plays deserve more scrutiny than they usually get. Beaumarchais describes them and how they should appear on stage in some detail. Here are his brief descriptions from the first play: "Le Comte Almaviva, grande d'Espagne, amant inconnu de Rosine; Bartholo, médecin, tuteur de Rosine; Rosine, jeune personne d'extraction noble, et pupille de Bartholo; Figaro, barbier de Séville; Don Bazile, organiste, maître à chanter de Rosine." Note the aristocratic lineage of Rosine, which is confirmed twice in the play's dialogue. "Pupille" does not mean "pupil" but "ward" in the sense of a minor in the charge of a legal guardian ("tuteur" in fact means "guardian"). She is an orphan, aged eighteen, and she has no close relatives, only a cousin, cited in the text as an army officer. There is another female member of the Bartholo household, Marceline, but she is only mentioned, not seen, in the first play. More intelligent than the doctor, it is she who tutors the young noblewoman.

A persistent error in the Mozart literature maintains that Rosine was a commoner, "ein Bürgermädchen."[6] She was from a lower rank of the nobility than Almaviva but they both belonged to the same privileged class. Demoting her to the bourgeoisie wreaks havoc by upsetting the delicate balance of their relationship in the plays and operas. It also betrays a misunderstanding of the rank of Spanish grandee. Almaviva is a man of the highest aristocracy, from an old Castilian family. Moreover, Beaumarchais promotes him in the second play, which takes place three years after the first. He has become "grand corrégidor d'Andalousie," chief magistrate of Andalusia, the southernmost region of the Iberian peninsula. Still a young man, perhaps in his mid-twenties, the Count nevertheless commands a regiment in Catalonia (to which he banished Chérubin by naming him a captain). And there is more. The King of Spain has named him ambassador to the Court of Saint James in London. Such a man, according to Spanish etiquette, could not marry outside his class.

The scene of the second play is the chateau of Aguas-Frescas, located three leagues from Seville. Figaro is described as having become "valet du chambre et concierge au château" and he describes himself as entering his thirtieth year. A more settled life than in the first play has encouraged him to seek marriage with Suzanne. She is described as "première camariste de la Comtesse, et fiancée de Figaro." Marceline is described as "femme de charge." Another servant is Antonio, "jardinier du château, oncle de Suzanne, et père de Fanchette [Barbarina]." To make the second play work, Beaumarchais had to invent a bogus *droit du seigneur*, the lord's right to deflower all virgins in his domain, which existed neither in France nor Spain at the time.

Family plays a considerable role in the second play. Figaro discovers his father and mother in Bartolo and Marcellina (Italian spellings will be used henceforth for the names). Susanna, who like Rosina is bereft of mother and father, at least has her uncle and cousin nearby. There is no mention of seeking parental consent for her marriage. On the noble side, Cherubino, described as "premier page du Comte," has a mother and father to whom the Count threatens to send him back. And at Aguas-Frescas he has a protectress in the Countess, who is related to his family; as she says, "Il est allié à mes parents." She is also his godmother, although at age twenty-one, she cannot be more than four or five years older than he is. In the third play, *La mère coupable*, we learn that the page's full name is Chérubin Léon d'Astorga. The city mentioned is in the province and ancient former kingdom of Leon in northern Spain. It is likely then that Rosina was also from northern Spain. In the first play the Count mentions that he caught sight

---

[6] Stefan Kunze, *Mozarts Opern* (Stuttgart, 1984), p. 245, and Mary Hunter, "Rousseau, the Countess, and the Female Domain," *Mozart Studies* 2 (1997) ed. Cliff Eisen, 1–26; 2.

of her initially at the Prado Palace in Madrid, then scoured the capital city in attempts to find her.

The Viennese public did not lack for new theatrical entertainments in early 1786. During Carnival season, the main operatic novelty in the Burgtheater was *Il burburo di buon cuore* by Vicente Martín y Soler, the text of which Da Ponte had extracted and adapted from Goldoni's French play *Le bouru bienfaisant*. It occupied the boards throughout January and February, the lead singers being Storace and Benucci. There were many other recent productions still in repertory. For example, the Burgtheater reopened on 26 December, the first day of Carnival, with Paisiello's *Il re Teodoro in Venezia*, the Kärntnerthor with Gluck's *Die Pilgrimme von Mecca*, followed by *Die Entführung* on the first of January. Mozart was also represented in the Burgtheater, but only by his two insert contributions to Francesco Bianchi's *La villanella rapita*, which had been performed first on 25 November 1785.

Other operas from repertory performed by the Italian troupe in the Burgtheater at this time were Salieri's *La fiera di Venezia* and *La grotta di Trofonio*, Guglielmi's *Le vicende d'amore*, Stephen Storace's *I sposi malcontenti*, Paisiello's *La contadina di spirito*, Cimarosa's *Il pittore parigino*, and Sarti's *Fra i due litiganti*. This is not a complete list, but it is long enough to show that Mozart was up against a whole phalanx of the best composers of opera buffa.

There was another operatic premiere in the Burgtheater on 20 February 1786, *Il finto cieco* by Giuseppe Gazzaniga, on a libretto by Da Ponte derived from Marc-Antoine Legrand's play *L'aveugle clairvoyant*. French plays were favorites on Da Ponte's work table, for which he was chided by his rival Casti. Zinzendorf attended this premiere and was not impressed: "Musique de Gazzaniga dont peu de morceaux me frapperent." The *Realzeitung* observed that "in spite of some rare beauties in the first act it did not please greatly because too often one was reminded of arias and choruses in other operas."[7] Thus, a perception of originality counted for something when new operas were evaluated.

Zinzendorf made a remark on the performance of Paisiello's *Barbiere* the evening of 1 February 1786 that suggests new interpretations of old favorites were also of interest: "La Storace ne joua point l'innocence de Rosina. Elle et Benucci en font un emoustillée." The last word describes a Rosina who was excited, enlivened, stirred to action. Seconded by Benucci as Figaro, Storace downplayed Rosina's innocence and instead concentrated on her wily and sensuous side, certainly present in the play from the beginning and carried further in the second play. Rosina's plight is central to both, indeed to all three plays. Music could easily paint sensuous qualities in sound, and Paisiello excelled in doing so. Mozart

---

[7] Michtner, *Das alte Burgtheater*, pp. 201–2. Success or not, seven singer-actors of the buffo ensemble as well as the chorus had to work hard to memorize their roles for this full-length new opera during February.

had but to follow his example and outdo him in portraying this same character's evolution from flirtatious ingénue to voluptuous young married lady.

While awaiting the advent of Mozart's Figaro and Susanna in the Burgtheater, connoisseurs received several further demonstrations of the composer's brilliance. Joseph II commissioned from him a work for the entertainments on 7 February 1786 honoring the visit of his sister, Archduchess Marie Christine and her husband Duke Albert of Sachsen-Teschen, regents of the Austrian Netherlands. The German actors and singers of the Burgtheater combined to present a short play with music, *Der Schauspieldirektor,* and a one-act opera, *Prima la musica, poi le parole.* Stephanie wrote the play and Mozart its musical parts, while Casti and Salieri wrote the opera. The centerpiece of this fête was a banquet for the high aristocracy in the Orangerie of Schönbrunn Palace after which the guests moved to a stage at one end of the building to witness the play, then to the other for the opera. The core of the buffo troupe, Storace, Coltellini, Benucci, and Mandini, sang in the latter. Just as the opera was a satire on the Italian troupe and its workings, the play was a lampoon about putting together a touring company of German actors and singers. Thus, they were twin parts of a double bill and were played as such for the general public in the Kärntnerthor Theater three times before the beginning of Lent. The emperor himself had chosen the subjects for both play and opera.

A commission for Mozart's part of *Der Schauspieldirektor,* K. 486, arrived on 18 January. The music was finished in little more than two weeks, by 3 February. The overture is a magnificent *Presto* in common time and in the key of C, worthy of introducing a great symphony—a fully developed sonata form for large orchestra including clarinets, trumpets, and timpani, extending to 204 measures. An almost comic disparity exists between this stately piece and the lightweight situations that follow it, including the four musical numbers that come at the end of the play. Unless Mozart considered this a joke at Stephanie's expense, it could be considered as a call to order introducing not just the play but both of the evening's theatrical spectacles. The two main actors of the play were Stephanie himself as Frank, impresario, and Joseph Weidmann as Buff, his plainspoken advisor. Buff begins by announcing that the troupe landed a commission from (of all places!) Salzburg, eliciting from Frank the disdainful retort, "What, in the paternal home of Hanswurst!" Here Stephanie was obviously playing a little joke on his composer. Buff answers with down-to-earth advice: "Don't make faces! Be happy that some place wants us. When art needs the bread of life any open door will do. But there are strings attached. They request loud, comical plays, ballets, and operas." This sets up the recruiting scenes that constitute the rest of the play.[8]

[8] John A. Rice, *Salieri,* p. 376. K. 486 is neither an opera nor a Singspiel. Its proper title and designation is Schauspiel, meaning "play." The fundamental error of category concerning K. 486 is the fault of the *Neue Mozart-Ausgabe,* which placed it in *Opern und Singspiele,* Series II/5, instead of *Musik zu Schauspielen, Pantomimen und Balletten,* Series II/6.

K. 486's vocal pieces are rather slight, yet they do have some noteworthy interactions with other works by Mozart. Madame Herz (Aloysia Lange) sings the first, an Arietta that begins with a sorrowful song, *Larghetto* in g, reminiscent of Giunia's lament in the tomb scene of *Lucio Silla*. It leads without repetition to an *Allegro moderato* in G that hastens to its end without even modulating to the dominant but still makes room for a burst of coloratura up to high D—it is, after all, a demonstration of her capabilities to director Frank. Mademoiselle Silber-klang (Cavalieri), not to be outdone, exhibits her wares with a more modish choice, a Rondeau (as it is spelled in the text) or Rondò (as in Mozart's auto-graph score). The piece presents an exemplary, albeit brief, demonstration of the two-tempo vocal rondò, a type that was then still the height of operatic fashion. Mozart chose the key of E♭ and set the first part to an *Andante* in cut time, with a short theme in gavotte rhythm that returns after contrast, and concludes on the tonic; then comes an *Allegretto* with livelier vocal writing and bursts of colora-tura almost matching her rival's, as called for by the dramatic situation. Mozart considered, then rejected, a similarly triadic rondò in E♭ for Susanna's final aria in *Figaro*, then replaced it with the sublime "Deh vieni non tardar." The question remains as to exactly when he might have done this. Before, after, or during the composition of K. 486?

Madame Herz takes the liberty of presenting her husband, the actor Lange, her real-life spouse. A tenor appears in the person of Monsieur Vogelsang (Adam-berger), permitting the following trio in B♭. It begins with a quarrel over prece-dence between the two sopranos (adumbrating the quarrel of the Three Ladies in *Die Zauberflöte*). The tenor attempts to pacify them, leading each soprano to give further demonstrations of her vocal capabilities, the first leaping up to a high E♭ and descending in a rapid arpeggio, the second by chains of rapid triplet melis-mas up to high C. "Piano, pianissimo, pianississimo!" pleads the tenor, reconcil-ing the two to merging their talents in the service of art, which they demonstrate musically by rapid parallel thirds up to high F and D. The truce is over in a trice as the sopranos return to singing at each other "Ich bin die erste Sängerin." It is left to the final *Schlussgesang*, a vaudeville finale resembling the one that ended *Die Entführung*, sung as a quartet (with Buff allowed only a small part) to end the dispute. The piece is an *Allegro* in cut time, and it is in the key of C, like the overture.

Zinzendorf called the play "fort mediocre." About Salieri's opera he had no comment except that "La Storace imita parfaitement Marchesi en chantant des airs de Giulio Sabino." This little touch of serious opera in a Vienna bereft of opera seria by decision of Joseph II is worth a digression. Unwilling to pay the high fees of seria singers, the emperor nevertheless allowed Sarti's *Giulio Sabino* to be staged at the Kärntnerthor in August 1785 so as to take advantage of the passage of the great castrato Luigi Marchesi through Vienna on his way to St.

Petersburg. Cavalieri sang the prima donna part and Adamberger the tenor role of Tito. The score was updated by Salieri to include some of his music and also a famous rondò by Angelo Tarchi for Marchesi to sing in the dungeon scene, where the hero bids farewell to his wife and children.[9] Zinzendorf was so enthralled by Marchesi's voice that he missed not a one of the six performances from 4 to 20 August, complaining only about the heat and Cavalieri's shouting. Adamberger had been trained as a seria as well as buffa singer in Italy, as had Storace (a student of Marchesi), and more could have been made of their seria abilities by creating new operas for Vienna had Joseph been willing.

Mozart, it may be recalled, wished to recreate his *Idomeneo* as a serious opera in German with Gluck's librettist Alxinger, with Fischer (Osmin) in the title role and Adamberger as a tenor Idamante.[10] This scheme came to nothing, nor did the composer's keyboard-vocal performance of his Munich opera for the emperor, Countess Thun, Swieten, and others lead to any immediate results. Not until the crowded Lenten season of 1786 was *Idomeneo* heard by an elite public in Vienna.

The *comédies de société* supported by the nobility as one of their most fervent pastimes had a musical equivalent for a time in the operas given by Prince Johann Adam Auersperg in the theater adjoining his palace in the Josefstadt (which building is today a casino). Here *Alceste, Idomeneo,* and Paisiello's *La serva padrona* were performed in early 1786. The first, performed on Sunday 12 February, was attended by Zinzendorf, who says he went to the theater at 5:30, settled in the very cold parterre, and complained that the opera did not begin until 6:45. Inconveniences notwithstanding, he praised Countess Hatzfeld, saying that she sang the title role to perfection. Michael Kelly was also there and recalled the evening in his memoirs: "His Highness also was a great patron of musical performances. He had a beautiful theatre in his palace, at which I saw Countess Hatzfeld perform inimitably well, in Gluck's serious opera of Alceste—she was a charming woman, and full of talent" (see Appendix 1). The orchestra for this kind of performance was largely made up of professional musicians. Mozart had complained earlier (letter of 20 March 1784) that his Burgtheater academy was compromised because Prince Liechtenstein was giving an opera the same evening "and had captured most of the nobility as well as the best performers in the orchestra" in order to put on Vincenzo Righini's *Piramo e Tisbe*, sung by two noblewomen, Anna von Puffendorf and Maria Anna Hortensia von Hatzfeld. These same two sopranos, both accomplished singers, sang the parts of Ilia and Electra in *Idomeneo*. Mozart's close friend Giuseppe Antonio Bridi sang the title role and his pupil Francesco Pollini the role of Idamante.[11] The event took place

[9] Rice, *Salieri*, p. 379. The author reproduces an anonymous print depicting the farewell scene from the Viennese production on p. 380 and in his article "Giulio Sabino" in *The New Grove Dictionary of Opera.*
[10] *Haydn, Mozart,* p. 715.
[11] Elena Biggi Parodi, "Francesco Pollini e il suo tempo," *Nuova rivista musicale italiana* 30 (1996): 333–63; 343–45.

on Monday 13 March, a date of some significance to the imperial family as it was the 45th birthday of Joseph II, and so noted by Zinzendorf, who did not attend. It would be surprising if the emperor himself were not present.

Idomeneo could scarcely have been uppermost in Mozart's mind during the winter of 1785–86, as he was struggling to complete other major works. He could have left its score unaltered. Instead, he revised where improvements were most needed, while working his way back to an amazing degree into the musical world of his earlier masterpiece. He added a new beginning to the second act, a scene between the lovers Ilia and Idamante culminating in a superb new aria for the latter with a concertante violin solo for another amateur performer (and one of Mozart's closest friends), Count Hatzfeld, who was only distantly related to the Countess Hatzfeld singing the part of Electra. It was a full-fledged rondò in two tempos, K. 490, more than twice the length of the rondò in K. 486. He replaced the original, rather childish love duet for two sopranos with a taut, intensely felt duet for tenor and soprano, K. 489, which projects the emotions of two grown-up, mature lovers. He could have adapted the original piece for tenor with a few modifications, as he did with the Act II trio and the quartet in Act III, but opted instead for a new composition using the same key of A and some of the earlier musical material.[12] The skillful Italian texts for the two new pieces were almost certainly by Da Ponte.

It will not have escaped the notice of some readers that in Köchel's list the replacement love duet in A, K. 489, adjoins one of the most beloved of all Mozart's works, the Piano Concerto No. 23 in A, K. 488. The concerto entered Mozart's catalogue with a date of 2 March 1786, joined by the duet on 10 March, three days before its performance. The first performance of K. 488 may have awaited Mozart's Burgtheater academy on 7 April, the next-to-last Friday in Lent. The propinquity of K. 488 to K. 489 is also musical, as might be expected from their sharing the same key as well as time period. Both belong to a group of pieces by Mozart in the key of A that is characterized by a tender lyric quality and sweetness, expressed by chains of parallel thirds. They also show a preference for melodic incipits that descend from the fifth to the tonic, and specifically via 5 3 4 2 1. The concerto and duet propose this beginning with the same harmonic twist of V^7/IV leading to IV^6_4 underpinning tones 3 and 4 (Example 2.1ab). The *Adagio* movement of the concerto has a middle section in which the flute and first clarinet sing in thirds what sounds like a meditation on the first three tones of the incipit, 5 3 4 (Example 2.1a, mm. 35–36).

K. 488 may have been begun a year or two earlier, according to the evidence of paper studies, and originally had oboes instead of clarinets. It may have been set aside for later completion because of the difficulty Mozart had inventing middle

---

[12] For further discussion of K. 489–490, see Heartz, "Mozart's Tragic Muse," in *Mozart's Operas* (1990), pp. 37–63.

EXAMPLE 2.1.

a. *Mozart, Piano Concerto No. 23 in A, K. 488, I, II*

b. *Mozart,* Idomeneo, *K. 489, Duetto (1786)*

and last movements to match the high level of the opening *Allegro*. Ten measures of a piece in D and in 3/4 time, K. 488a, have been designated as an attempt at a middle movement because they share the same scoring (a pair of clarinets in A replace two oboes) as in the first movement. This triadic beginning without tempo marking promised only a rather ordinary *Andante*. The same scoring identifies two attempts to invent a finale. K. 488b consists of twenty-one measures of a piece in A and in cut time that may reflect the opening movement's second theme by its descent of parallel triads in first inversion. K. 488c offers twenty measures of a piece in 6/8 time with dotted rhythm that proved more promising in that it began with a leap from the fifth up to the tonic and then a leap from the fifth down to a fourth. This is perhaps one embryo from which sprang a similar motion beginning the finale of K. 488, although the finale's theme is more closely approximated by the leaps that begin the finale of the earlier Piano Concerto in A, K. 414. It seems that in both outer movements of K. 488, Mozart was revisiting the melodic ideas that generated the equivalent movements in K. 414. The first movements begin by stealing softly on the senses with a lyric melody that starts on the downbeat and explores the same ambitus of a sixth above the tonic and a fourth below it, the low tone reached by stepwise descent. The later melody is plainer while the earlier one is more florid and, with its rhythmic snaps, more galant. A parallel here is evident with the two love duets for *Idomeneo*, the original of 1781 being more florid while its 1786 replacement covers the same ground in simpler, more direct language. Mozart of the *Figaro* years concentrates his expression and achieves more with less.

There is no better example of this than the *Adagio* of K. 488. The slow movement of K. 414 in A had been a lament of sorts, as Mozart took recourse to writing an *Andante* in D on a minuet theme of his late friend and mentor, Christian Bach. The *Adagio* is infinitely more sorrowful, a kind of siciliano in a minor key the composer rarely used, f♯ (Example 2.2). Begun by the solo piano, unaccompanied, the treble sings a melody that starts with the dotted rhythm in 6/8 time, long traditional with this genre. By the second measure, the stakes are raised with poignant and unusual dissonances. The leap down a seventh is expressive

EXAMPLE 2.2. *Mozart, Piano Concerto No. 23 in A, K. 488, II*

enough and made more so because the destination tone B causes the previous A to need resolution to G#, which arrives, but at the expense of making the bass F#, a dissonance that must resolve down to E#. It does so, not in its own register, but an octave lower, a displacement that intensifies the leap of a minor ninth required of the bass. The ambience is set for more suspensions and displacements to follow. These are not the long and leisurely suspensions such as graced the slow movement of K. 467 a year earlier but more intense, more concentrated. The *Adagio* theme comes in three four-measure sections, the second ending on a D triad (VI), the third beginning with the Neapolitan chord N6, as marked in m. 61 of Example 2.2. Exemplified is the return of the siciliano main theme after the celebration of blissful A major in the middle section, with its reminder of the theme with which the concerto began. After visions of paradise like this, the return of the solo piano to its theme, again unaccompanied (with one exception), must necessarily sound all the more disheartened and dispiriting. Mozart extends the third section by a deceptive cadence to VI in m. 64 and here the winds enter to sustain the measure-long chord (the fortepiano had little sustaining power for prolonged tones at this very slow tempo); they seem at the same time to embrace the soloist with an empathic gesture. They also form a bridge by resolving to the N6 chord as the phrase is repeated on the way to the real cadence.

The maximum of expressiveness is achieved when Mozart simplifies the passage at the end of the long-held N6 chord. Instead of rising to a high D via two staccato triads as in m. 62, he takes the soloist down an octave to low G and then leaps up two and a half octaves to the high D. Simpler, yes, but also more intense. The solo singer, the lonely warbler of this sad song, can still be considered in terms of the human voice. A range from low G to high D covers the exact vocal ambitus required by Mozart of the tragic prima donna Vitellia in his last opera, *La clemenza di Tito*. When the piano reaches its inevitable cadence, the melody sinking down to tonic f# in m. 68, the moment becomes one of the most poignant in all Mozart. Its equivalent occurs not in *Figaro* but in the following opera, *Don Giovanni*, when another tragic heroine, Donna Anna, sings the line "Only death will end my tears."

K. 488's finale, *Allegro assai* in cut time, wipes the slate clean of sadness with a brilliant and sometimes even buffo kind of comic interplay between soloist and orchestra. Having plumbed the depths in the *Adagio*, Mozart allows his characters to disport themselves in a merry romp that dispels all gloomy thoughts. The winds once again are treated as equals, often sounding forth without any accompaniment in this witty conversation.

Piano Concerto No. 24 in c, K. 491, was Mozart's other Lenten offering, entered into his catalogue with a date of 24 March 1786. If the Viennese, famous for their addiction to light comedy, were looking for some relief from the rigors of the season, they did not find it here. An initial *Allegro* in 3/4 time offered instead a very disputatious and storm-tossed dialogue. Mozart resorted to c minor again in the first episode of the lyric, Romance-like *Larghetto* in E♭ and in cut time. The finale is a theme and variations in cut time to which Mozart assigned no tempo designation. The lightness often associated with this form is missing. While there is a major-mode variation, which was customary with a minor-mode theme, the general tone remains somber. As in the first movement, no light at the end of the tunnel in the form of a *tierce de Picardie* illuminates the ending, as it did in the finale of K. 466 a year earlier.

K. 491 calls for one of the richest orchestrations Mozart ever used: a pair of clarinets in B♭ as well as two oboes, two horns in E♭, two trumpets in C, timpani, and the usual strings, bassoons, and a single flute. The orchestra resembles that used by Beethoven fourteen years later in his First Symphony, which required two flutes, oboes, clarinets in C, horns, bassoons, trumpets, and timpani, an ensemble that one critic complained was too loud and sounded too much like band music. The two composers were close to the same age when they produced these works, Mozart having turned thirty in January 1786 and Beethoven about to turn thirty in December 1800. There are no surviving complaints that Mozart's orchestration was too weighty for what he had to say in K. 491.

The opening *Allegro* of K. 491 starts softly, like that of K. 488, but with a theme replete with tension—stating the tones of the VI chord in first inversion, then outlining diminished-seventh chords in descent, and ending with a rising chromatic line into the cadential gesture. This much content in an opening theme has some precedent in the beginning of Concerto No. 14 in E♭, K. 449. Mozart extends the first movement of K. 491 to a record 523 measures. The unstable section before the reprise is more truly developmental than is usual with Mozart's concertos, and the peremptory tone of the exchanges between soloist and orchestra reach an intensity even greater than they do in the first movement of K. 449. One critic was tempted to compare this confrontation between soloist and orchestra to the losing battle fought by Don Giovanni against the combined forces of the Statue and the orchestra toward the end of Mozart's opera of over a year later.[13] Where one might expect to find some resonances with *Figaro*, one finds, oddly enough, possible premonitions of death and doom such as haunt *Don Giovanni*.

Lent 1786, which began with Ash Wednesday on 1 March, ended with Easter Sunday on 18 April. Mozart was assigned the last Lenten concert, in the Burgtheater on Friday 7 April, probably the choicest date for an academy, and followed only by the traditional oratorio of the Musicians' Society, in this case *Giobbe* by Dittersdorf, given on 8–9 April, after which both theaters went dark during Holy Week. It stands to reason that Mozart would have performed one or both of his concertos just finished at his concert on 7 April, one of the last of this kind he would ever give. There is no way at present of knowing what was on the program.

Two days after Easter, the Burgtheater resumed its offerings of plays and operas. The Italian troupe performed a relatively light schedule of only six more evenings during April, with no premieres. The reason was surely the need for its singers to commit to memory the longest and most complicated work they had yet encountered. *Le nozze di Figaro*, K. 492, was finally ready for its premiere on Monday, the first of May. Emperor Joseph attended the first night as well as the dress rehearsal two days earlier.

Le nozze di Figaro

The buffo finale reached an unsurpassable peak of perfection in Mozart's first opera with Da Ponte. Big ensemble finales placed at the middle and end of Mozart's most mature operas represent a choice arrived at gradually after trying other solutions. *Idomeneo* has no finales in the opera buffa sense. Each of its three acts closes with an imposing scene complex in the French style, and Mozart decided that each would end in D, the key of the overture. In *Lucio Silla*, his most ambitious serious opera before *Idomeneo*, he had been less insistent on this kind of tonal unity, ending the first act with a love duet in A, the second with a trio in B♭, and only the overture and the final *Ciaconna* for chorus and ballet in D. *Il ré pastore* of 1775, two years later, was more forward-looking in that he set a text that had been reduced to two acts from the three of Metastasio's original; the first he ended with the love duet in A, the second with the usual short *coro* closing the work in C, the key of the overture. The three-act opera buffa *La finta giardiniera* of

---

[13] William Kinderman, "Dramatic Development and Narrative Design in the First Movement of Mozart's Concerto in C Minor, K. 491," in *Mozart's Piano Concertos* (1996), pp. 285–301.

early 1775, on a rather weak text, did at least provide Mozart the opportunity to write two big buffo finales, one in A to end Act I, another in C to end Act II, leaving the short Act III to end with a perfunctory *coro* in D, the key of the overture.

Die Entführung has only one big finale, which Mozart insisted Stephanie add to end Act II, but it was an important step on the way to the medial finales of his later operas. It is not quite accurate to call it a medial finale for it comes more than two-thirds of the way through the three-act opera, followed by a shorter third act. But its dramatic and tonal content provide a precedent for the medial finales of the last five operas, so it can, with a little license, be aligned with them (Table 2.1).

TABLE 2.1 Overall Key Schemes in the Operas of Mozart's Last Decade

	Overture	Medial Finale	End of opera (second finale)
Die Entführung	C	D (Act II)	C
Le nozze di Figaro	D	E♭ (Act II)	D
Don Giovanni	D	C	D
Così fan tutte	C	D	C
Die Zauberflöte	E♭	C	E♭
La clemenza di Tito	C	E♭	C

As the table shows, Mozart used only three tonalities, the three universal keys of C, D, and E♭, as polar centers of attraction in these operas. They are universal in the sense of being keys in which he had available—or chose to use—trumpets and drums, the necessary partners of rousing climaxes and applause-inducing celebrations. Had he lived a few years longer, he probably would have extended this elite trinity of trumpet keys to include B♭ as did Haydn in the 1790s.[14]

The restrictions Mozart observed as to possible keys in overtures and finales relates to a wider one he placed on himself with regard to other set pieces. Very rarely did he choose keys for them that had more than three sharps or flats. In effect then, he confined himself to only seven major-mode keys: C, D, E♭, F, G, A, B♭. It was one way he had of ensuring that his players and singers would sound as much in tune as possible. The main exception was his occasional use of the key of E, mostly reserved for moments or texts that required special color. His favorite minor-mode keys were c, d, g, a, rarely f, and almost never e or b. Even in his music without text, Mozart shied away from keys with many sharps or flats, although here also he had a special penchant for the key of E, but only in chamber music, not in symphonies (unlike Haydn).

Figaro differs from the other operas in Table 2.1 by being divided into four

---

[14] The use of trumpets in low B♭ (*trombe lunghe*), available at Milan for *Lucio Silla* in 1773, is an anomaly; *Così fan tutte*, exceptionally, requires two trumpets in B♭ for "Come scoglio" and the first finale.

acts, although from quite early on it was often given in two long acts. The difference is more illusory than substantial because its medial finale at the end of Act II comes midway in the work, as it does in the following operas in two acts. Nevertheless, Mozart gave his Acts I and III truly climactic and conclusive end-of-act numbers. He did this largely by tonal means, reserving the key of such numbers until last.

Act I uses all seven of the common keys. C major is saved for Figaro's electrifying show-stopper "Non più andrai," the aria that instantly became the opera's biggest "hit," as acted and sung in stentorian tones by the incomparable Benucci. Before this, the action had gradually gathered momentum, beginning with expository *duettinos* for Figaro and Susanna exploring the fragility of their plans to marry. These use the keys of G and B♭, a pair that keeps recurring throughout the opera as adjacent numbers and that recurs during the first act in the *terzetto* of the chair scene in B♭ followed by the peasant chorus in G, which praises the Count for abolishing the (bogus) *droit du seigneur.* Otherwise there is, for Figaro's "Se vuol ballare," sung to an absent Count, the key of F with its prominent horns in F. Next comes a rather short dialogue between Bartolo and Marcellina, leading to Bartolo's blustery call for revenge, "La vendetta," scored for full orchestra including trumpets and drums in the ever-brilliant key of D. Following that is an even shorter dialogue between Marcellina and Susanna, then their *duettino* of competing curtsies in the key of A, usually one of Mozart's most gracious tonalities but here given a sardonic touch. A longer dialogue follows for Susanna and Cherubino, the harmonies of which do not hint at what is coming until the first mention of a canzonetta by the page brings a sudden lurch to the flat side. When Cherubino's infatuation with "every lady in the palace" is about to burst into song there is a quick tonal move to prepare the arrival of a surprising and as-yet unheard key, E♭. Out gushes his "Non so più" in a torrent to the tones 5 4 3 3 2 1 6 5 4 4 3 2. The following *terzetto* in B♭ harbors a delicious musical pun when the inopportunely-arrived Basilio begins with the same pattern but in a different rhythm.[15] Then comes the singsong chorus in G for the peasants, setting up Figaro's grandly martial "Non più andrai" in C major.

Countess Almaviva, alone on stage, begins Act II with a cavatina in E♭, "Porgi, Amor, qualche ristoro," richly evocative of her constant, desperate love for her errant husband, a piece that is indebted for several of its features to Paisiello's aria in E♭ for Rosina in *Barbiere*. The scene is set in her richly decorated bedchamber, the bed itself discreetly placed in the background in an alcove sep-

---

[15] Daniel N. Leeson, "Mozart's *Le Nozze di Figaro*: A Hidden Dramatic Detail," *Eighteenth-Century Music* 1 (2004): 301–4; Ian Woodfield, "Reflections on Mozart's 'Non so più cosa son, cosa faccio,'" *Eighteenth-Century Music* 3 (2006): 133–39; Stephen Rumph, "Unveiling Cherubino," *Eighteenth-Century Music* 4 (2007): 131–40.

arated from the main room by a balustrade (Figure 2.2). Both the play and the opera mention this alcove, so it was clearly not intended that the bed should be front and center stage, as often happens in recent productions (the better to observe whatever vulgarities stage directors ask the Countess to endure around, on, or even in her bed). As Saint-Quentin's illustration for Act II of the play's original edition shows, the Countess should be seated in her armchair. Here she listens to Cherubino sing his love-struck canzonetta "Voi che sapete" accompanied by Susanna playing the guitar (given a perch of its own by Saint-Quentin). This enchanting song in B♭ loses its bearing midway to the extent of descending a whole tone to A♭ as the page tries to describe his feelings of longing and searching, before coming back to repeat the first stanza in its initial key. Once again a number in B♭ is succeeded by one in

FIGURE 2.2. Saint-Quentin's depiction of *Le Mariage de Figaro*, Act II, scene 4. Engraving by Halbon.

G, Susanna's action aria "Venite inginocchiatevi," during which she must try some female finery on Cherubino after first baring his arms, while the Countess remains seated in her chair. The page casts tender glances in the direction of the Countess but that is as close as they get. The Count interrupts the long scene of recitative that follows, already angry to find the door to his wife's chamber locked. Susanna had departed to fetch an article of feminine clothing. Cherubino hides in the dressing closet. A *terzetto* in C follows, Susanna having entered at the back of the room as the Count and Countess argue by the closet door in the foreground. A trio in which two participants are unaware of the third throughout is unusual.

The Count escorts his wife out to search for a key to the locked closet while Susanna hides in the alcove. She hurries to the closet door and urges Cherubino to come out. He does as they sing the tiny *duettino* "Aprite presto." Small though it is in length and time taken, it cost Mozart considerable effort; his earlier beginning for the piece was rather far from the finished one, except in tempo, meter, and key: *Allegro assai* in common time and in G. Susanna tries to stop the page from jumping out the window; his threat to do so is acted out in the music, which goes through a modulatory passage accumulating tension just before he jumps, bringing the piece to an abrupt stop. He scampers away in the garden. Susanna takes his place in the closet in preparation for the return of her master and mistress. Before the finale begins, the Countess confesses that the person in the closet is a boy, Cherubino. The Count waxes furious and in this state begins the great finale, *Allegro* in common time and in E♭.

The Countess insists on the innocence of the boy even if he is in a partial state of undress. Her music leads to firm cadences on the dominant, B♭, hence the ambiguity of the pun on "chiave," meaning both key to the closet and musical key when he portentously outlines the triad on E♭ while proclaiming "Quà la chiave!" Key jokes like this are not rare in opera buffa and there was one, most notably, involving B♭ and E♭ in Act III of Paisiello's *Barbiere*.[16]

Beaumarchais in his plays made a specialty of the *coup de théâtre*, of which there is no more splendid example than the emergence from the dressing closet— to the surprise of both Count and Countess—not of Cherubino but Susanna. Mozart made a specialty of pregnant pauses and memorable transitions, and there is none greater than the four measures that lead from strident E♭, *forte*, to sedate B♭, *piano, Molto andante* in 3/8 time. The new theme is informed by a common minuet rhythm (Example 2.3).[17] Susanna does what any serving maid

EXAMPLE 2.3. *Mozart*, Le nozze di Figaro, *Act II, Finale*

should do when confronted by her lord and lady: she curtsies, as in a minuet. Her curtsy is captured in a print showing the original Suzanne (see footnote 23). The horns have switched crooks from E♭ to B♭ and they enhance the irony of the situation by stating the minuet rhythm on their own. Mozart draws this delectable

[16] *Music in European Capitals*, pp. 961–62.

[17] Mozart owes this musical idea to Grétry's *L'Amant jaloux* (1778), which in Stephanie's translation as *Der eifersüchtige Liebhaber* held the stage in Vienna from 1780 on, one of its performances being in the same month of May 1786 begun by *Figaro*. For Grétry's music, see David Charlton, *Grétry and the Growth of Opéra-Comique* (Cambridge, 1986), p. 169.

moment out as questions are asked and answered cleverly by Susanna. When the Count enters the closet to see for himself that no one else is inside, Susanna quickly explains to the Countess what had happened to Cherubino. The Count eventually asks his wife's pardon, using her first name for the only time in both play and opera. She responds to "Rosina" with an outburst: "Cruel man! I am no longer she but only the miserable object of your abandonment." The Countess after a while forgives her husband, as she will continue to do, for that is her nature. Yet we are left in no doubt as to how deeply disturbed she is.

An exuberant Figaro bursts in upon them. At the end of the *Allegro* in B♭ the horns must quickly change crooks to G. Here there is neither transitional passage nor use of silence. The new key of G sounds forth before the resonance of B♭ has quite faded. In this bright new key Figaro sings to a tune apparently common to Viennese dance halls for a generation or more.[18] His words speak of the rustic pipers who have come to play at his wedding, and one hears them indeed in the music. The Count begins the following section, *Andante* in 2/4 time with a substitution of C major for all the preceding fracas in G, as in a dominant to tonic resolution, which predicts how the rest of the finale will play out tonally. He questions Figaro about the anonymous letter impugning his wife's honor, which Figaro denies having seen. The Count is confused enough by his evasions to lose track of the argument. Figaro, Susanna, and the Countess together urge him to allow the marriage. In an aside the Count worries that Marcellina will not arrive in time with her note stating Figaro's promise to marry her. Just then, after long pedal harmonies in C, the music moves to the next event, which is, predictably, in F. An *Allegro molto* in common time coincides with the arrival of the gardener Antonio, who complains that a man jumped out of the window and landed on his geraniums.

For all his breeding and cleverness the Count is a little slow of mind here in putting two and two together, allowing Figaro time to think up an explanation: he was the one who jumped out the window, and to act out the part he bewails having hurt his foot while doing so. This is sung to a stepwise chromatic descent, the traditional device for laments, which served simultaneously as a transition to the key of B♭.

The new section in B♭ is an *Andante* in 6/8 time. At length, Antonio interjects, "If it was you who jumped these papers must be yours." The Count, acting more speedily than before, seizes them. Figaro now must explain what these papers are and why he has them. The ladies help him find answers, first by recognizing the documents as the page's commission, then providing the reason as to why Figaro should be carrying it: the papers lacked the wax seal proper to them. The

[18] The tune goes back to a vaudeville quoted by Gluck in *Le Chinois poli en France* (Vienna, 1756). See Heartz, *Mozart's Operas* (1990), p. 144, for the music.

lacking seal (*suggello*) was first noticed by the Countess earlier in the act (just before Susanna's aria; Act II, scene 5 of the play).

The Count is foiled again. But this time Marcellina does arrive, together with Bartolo and Basilio. She waves her promissory note and they make a big fuss. Along with them comes the return of E♭, this time clothing a maelstrom of incriminations, charges, and countercharges. The trumpets and drums now weigh in and the battle, an *Allegro assai* in common time, bustles along for nearly a hundred measures, then becomes *Più allegro* for an exhilarating rush to the end. In all, the finale stretches to encompass nearly a thousand measures. It is the *locus classicus* of the buffo finale, thanks partly to the play's impeccable plotting, to Da Ponte's immensely clever adaptation, but mostly to Mozart's tonal planning and abundance of unforgettable musical ideas. Michael Kelly, who sang Basilio and Don Curzio in 1786, declared, "that piece of music alone, in my humble opinion, if he had never composed anything else good, would have stamped him as the greatest master of his art."

Act III is shorter than Act II and comprises only seven numbers, all of them gems. It begins with a long recitative sequence in which the Count remains perplexed by the machinations swirling around him. The Countess tells Susanna to agree to meet the Count in the garden that evening. Dressed as Susanna, Rosina will meet him instead. The Count's assignation duet with Susanna is followed by his angry solo aria after believing he was tricked. The first is the closest thing to a love duet in the opera. Susanna maneuvers her way through the duet's opening section in the key of a minor with evasive answers to his questions and by switching her answers between yes and no. The music sounds like a true love duet when it settles in the key of A and they sing sweetly in parallel tenths, he of his contentment and joy, she asking the audience to be indulgent of her fibs. Michael Kelly, fairly reliable for facts if not chronology, recounted how he visited Mozart the day the duet was composed.

> I called on him one evening: he said to me, "I have just finished a little duet for my opera. You shall hear it." He sat down to the piano, and we sang it. I was delighted with it, and the musical world will give me credit for being so, when I mention the duet, sung by Count Almaviva and Susan, "Crudel perchè finora farmi languir così." A more delicious morceau never was penned by man; and it has often been a source of pleasure to me, to have been the first who heard it, and to have sung it with its greatly gifted composer.

Mozart presumably sang the soprano part. Being able to do so at pitch was just another of his musical gifts, a very useful one when coaching the performance of contraltos and sopranos.

Almaviva's only aria comes after an impassioned obbligato recitative, which already displays the opera seria tinge of what follows. As he did for Bartolo's angry outburst in Act I, Mozart chooses the key of D and uses trumpets and drums. Whereas Bartolo was mocked by such panoply and merely made to sound like an old fool, Count Almaviva sounds much more menacing. His ire is dangerous. The sweeping scales in the strings and their eerie measure-long trill in unisons and octaves would be quite at home in *Idomeneo*. An *Allegro maestoso* in cut time for the first part leads to a faster second part, *Allegro assai*, in which he is even given coloratura flourishes toward the end. Mandini, who had excelled as the Count in Paisiello's *Barbiere*, was a baritone with an extended high range. At the climax of his aria Mozart asks him to prolong a high F$\sharp$. One of Mozart's ways of expressing anger, snapping off two *forte* quarter notes followed by rests, occurs on the last two syllables of the word "audace," a rhythmic trait also used in Bartolo's aria.

The sextet requires a lot of stage action and yet it is musically quite static. Another *coup de théâtre* from the play reveals that Marcellina is Figaro's mother; she points to Bartolo as the father.[19] Figaro's true name is Rafaello. Mozart decided to begin the ensemble only after these revelations, as the newly discovered family members embrace each other, hence the music paints a state of calm and loving bliss, an *Andante* in common time and in the key of F, itself a relaxing choice after the Count's blustery aria in D. Susanna provides the only angry moment when she slaps Figaro upon seeing him embrace Marcellina. The way the composer builds up the responses "Sua madre!" replying to her question "Sua madre?" throughout the texture is akin to the technique of piling up short vocal exclamations in Paisiello's *Barbiere*. Mozart had used another version of it in his great medial finale when the Countess and Susanna pass short answers to the Count's questions on to Figaro.

The Count leaves this scene of bliss disappointed and tormented, accompanied only by the judge, Don Curzio. Omitted from the opera is an extremely witty trial scene. To achieve more concision it had to be sacrificed. After the sextet, the focus shifts back to the Countess and her unhappy marriage.

Countess Almaviva confirms her noble rank with the sublime obbligato recitative that precedes her only aria, "Dove sono i bei momenti." (Her "Porgi amor" to begin Act II was a short cavatina, not an aria). The aria is a rondò in C major of the fashionable two-tempo variety, based on three quatrains of octosyllabic verse, the usual scaffolding of this genre, which was allowed only to the prima donna and primo uomo in serious opera. A melodic sketch survives for the opening *Andantino* in 2/4 time, showing how much effort it cost the composer to invent this seemingly simple and effortless cantilena.

---

[19] On the theatrical history behind this scene, see Stefano Castelvecchi, "Sentimental and Anti-Sentimental in *Le nozze di Figaro*," *Journal of the American Musicological Society* (hereafter *JAMS*) 53 (2000): 1–24.

"Dove sono" is preceded by an expressive and drawn-out Phrygian cadence, with progression from F to E in the bass, then resolving without a break into the aria, V/vi - I. At the beginning of the act, "Crudel! perché finora" commences with this same cadence in the tempo of the piece. By this subtle but easily perceptible correspondence, Mozart can show that the Count is the cause of all the troubles besetting his wife. She expresses her forlorn state and lack of hope twice in the slow initial part, the second time after contrast, as commonly heard in a rondò. The faster final section, *Allegro* in common time, depicts her resurgence. She still hopes that her constancy will kindle a change in her husband's ungrateful heart.

The Letter Duet that follows is a marvel of subtle phraseology. Rosina takes charge by dictating to Susanna what to write the Count. Here many composers would have been satisfied to conceive so lovely a melodic feast and written the duet as a regular exchange, the one echoing the other. Mozart allows only a few outright echoes. More often, he has one pick up the phrase of the other and continue it without literal repetition, showing how these two ladies have become so close that they seem to intuit each other's thoughts. When they finally sing together, two high voices in thirds, an aura of ineffable sweetness and trust descends upon the scene. Another marvel is how Mozart is able to invent a music that sounds so fresh, so unlike anything else in the opera. The *duettino* is in B♭, a straightforward *Allegretto* in a simple, lilting 6/8 meter, without rhythmic complication on the surface. Once again, the composer arrived at this seemingly simple music by dint of hard labor, in this case a complete sketch. Many of his changes were made in search of further simplification. He allowed the piece to peter out at the end rather than come to a firm close. In the little recitative that follows, Rosina gives Susanna a pin to accompany the letter, in lieu of a seal.

The pastoral quality of flowing 6/8 time in moderate tempo is present as well in the next number, "Ricevete, oh padroncina," the modest chorus *a 2* sung by the peasant lasses bearing flowers to the Countess.[20] They intone their rather monotonous phrases not only in 6/8 time, *Grazioso*, but in the key of G, the same combination of choices Mozart made for the peasant chorus in Act I led by Figaro in praise of the Count. Both choruses also deploy drone basses that enhance the rustic coloration. Both come after preceding numbers in B♭, but without the surprise of direct confrontation between these two tonalities. "Ricevete" has enough in common with the Letter Duet to make it sound more like a continuation than a surprise. Besides its meter, tempo, and rhythms, the chorus employs the dulcet sonorities of high voices in thirds, albeit in a plainer, less sophisticated way, fitting to the social status of the singers. One detail of the piece not to be missed is

---

[20] The authority on 6/8 time's pastoral associations is Wye Jamison Allanbrook, *Rhythmic Gesture in Mozart: "Le nozze di Figaro" & "Don Giovanni"* (Chicago, 1983).

how the violins, flute, and bassoon break away from the main melody into flowing sixteenth notes, staccato, that go up and down spanning over an octave, to
mark the first and last cadences. Passages very like these will return to mark the
cadences in the opera's last aria, Susanna's "Deh vieni non tardar."

Among the peasants singing "Ricevete" to the Countess, besides Barbarina,
is her playmate Cherubino in female attire. In the following recitative, Antonio pulls off the page's bonnet. A newly angered Count Almaviva is about to
banish him in disgrace when Barbarina intervenes with a few indiscreet words
indicating the Count's dalliance with her. Cherubino confesses that it was he
who jumped out of the window. Confronted by the Count with this contretemps
Figaro has a clever retort: nothing prevented him from doing the same, he says,
and perhaps we shall start a fashion for jumping one after another, like sheep.

Act III ends with a grand scene of festive rejoicing in the key of C. Mozart
calls this number a finale but it is not one in the Italian sense. Rather, it is a
composite one in the French style, relying on dance, chorus, and spectacle, and
hence of a different temper from what went before. After *Idomeneo*, Mozart was
in total command of such resources. The Count and Countess seat themselves
on thrones and prepare to receive the nuptial couples and place the wedding
veils on the brides (Marcellina and Susanna). A march starts up in the distance
marking the beginning of the ceremonies, as the principals continue their conversations in recitative over its soft strains. In just this way Mozart introduced
the embarkation march in Act II of *Idomeneo*, which is commented on in recitative. By this means, it is possible to suggest the procession beginning to form,
and by increasing the texture and volume bit by bit, to suggest the approach of
a multitude. Moreover, in both marches Mozart begins the piece in the middle,
with the second strain first.

Spanish color is made prominent in the *Figaro* march by stressing the modal
degrees of ii and vi and by their coloration with an exotic-sounding wind figure,
a rapid melodic turn around the fifth degree of these chords. There follows without a break an *Allegretto* in C and in 2/4 time with constant sixteenth notes, to
which two women from the chorus sing, in thirds, the praises of the Count for
abolishing the abhorred old custom. It resembles the *Allegretto* in 2/4 with constant sixteenth notes of the great five-part *Ciaconna* ending Act I of *Idomeneo*. The
four-part chorus comes in briefly, reinforcing the Count's praises in a coda.

The Fandango, another case of Spanish color, is danced by Figaro and others
while the Count receives the note from Susanna. It is an *Andante* in 3/4 time and
in the key of a, a sonority prominent in the march as well as at the very beginning of Act III. As in the march, there is singing over the music as the Count
takes the note and pricks his finger with the pin, occasioning a comment by
Figaro to Susanna. At the close of Mozart's Fandango, which is indebted to that
of Gluck in the ballet *Don Juan* (1761), the Count, in a short but magnificent rec-

itative, declares that further nuptial ceremonies will take place that evening and be celebrated by a rich feast, singing, and fireworks. At this the chorus resumes its praises, ending the act with a blaze of fanfares, trumpets, and timpani.

Act IV begins with a surprise: a little lament in the form of a cavatina sung by Barbarina and performed by twelve-year-old Anna Gottlieb, who would later create the role of Pamina. Just as she was very small, so was the object of her lament: the Count's pin given her to return to Susanna as a sign of his assent. It is a very short *Andante* in 6/8 time with muted violins, sustained violas, and pizzicato basses for accompaniment, so as not to cover her immature voice, in the rarely used key of f minor. Barbarina joins here a select company of distressed young ladies by ending with a plea for sympathy sung to a falling tritone, like Serpina's "Ah! poverina" and Cecchina's "Si maltrata."[21] Figaro and Marcellina come upon the dejected young girl, who with minimal prodding reveals the secret she promised not to tell. This scene had ended Act IV of the play, where it succeeded the ballroom scene. There, the wise Marcellina counsels her newly found son that Susanna may be tricking not him but the Count.

Marcellina had the honor of a soliloquy to end Act IV of the play. How necessary it is, she says, for women to come to each other's aid in defense of "their poor oppressed sex against the proud, terrible, yet slightly foolish [nigaud] masculine sex." Da Ponte picks up only the general idea of women being badly treated and turns it around. His metaphor "Il capro e la capretta" (the goat and she-goat), not dependent on the play, demonstrates how much better females have it in the animal kingdom: he enumerates various species in a kind of catalogue. Audiences today scarcely ever hear his clever poem because the aria is routinely cut, and deservedly so for it is the least interesting music in Mozart's score. A *Tempo di Menuetto* in G gives way to an *Allegro* in common time, both decorated with superfluous coloratura, presumably because Signora Mandini (wife of Stefano) was good at it. Marcellina exits, seria fashion, after her display.

The scene changes from a path leading to the garden to a view of the garden with pine grove in the background and a pavilion on either side of the foreground. Cherubino, Figaro, Bartolo, and Basilio enter, the last two invited by Figaro to witness his degradation. Should he suffer in silence, asks Bartolo, to which Basilio replies that it is better to make an accommodation with the powers that be rather than suffer the consequences.

Basilio's aria is a tribute to the singing and acting abilities of tenor Michael Kelly in the role. Da Ponte concocted a bizarre text, another animal metaphor, this time about hiding in the putrid hide of a donkey in order to ward off attacks

---

[21] The first in Pergolesi's *La serva padrona*, the second in Piccinni's *La buona figliuola*. They are illustrated in *Music in European Capitals*, p. 112, ex. 2.11, and p. 161, ex. 2.25. See also Castelvecchi, "Sentimental and Anti-Sentimental," 13–20.

by predatory beasts. There is no Beaumarchais model here either. For the text of Marcellina's aria he could fall back on Italian madrigal poetry and other pastoral poems; for Basilio's text he was apparently on his own. Basilio's music, on the other hand, is more interesting than Marcellina's. Mozart sets "In quegl'anni" to an *Andante* in cut time and in the key of B♭. He turns to a popular dance type, the gavotte, for its first part, proceeds through a *Tempo di minuetto* section, and ends this long and extravagant tale with an *Allegro* in cut time. There are some amusing moments, as when Mozart makes the wild beasts roar with chromatic descents and ascents in orchestral unisons, anticipatory of the same in Haydn's *Creation*. Yet this concession to Kelly is on the whole a misstep that was rarely sung after the first production. The same is true of Marcellina's aria, which was not even included in the keyboard reduction of the opera advertised in the *Wiener Zeitung* of 1 July 1786.

The arias of Marcellina and Basilio tell us nothing that is vital to the opera's complicated plot. Without them, the action benefits by passing directly from Figaro's anger in Act IV scene 6 to his anguished monologue, an obbligato recitative and aria in scene 10. Da Ponte rejoined Beaumarchais for the recitative's text but took little as to the aria, a diatribe again in the form of a catalogue, this time of women's wiles, sung as a warning to all men. Open your eyes a little, he tells them, "Aprite un po' quegl'occhi." Mozart chooses a *Moderato* in cut time and in the key of E♭. There is much about the piece that is reminiscent of a mocking aria sung by Bartolo to Rosina in Act II of Paisiello's *Barbiere*. Since it was Benucci who played the earlier role to the hilt in Vienna, with great success, it is not surprising to find several correspondences between the two pieces. Both demonstrate Benucci's gift for patter.

Susanna's Garden Aria, the last piece before the second finale, required a lot of effort on the parts of both poet and composer, perhaps more than any other number in the opera. Susanna, dressed as the Countess, takes leave of her mistress. Knowing that Figaro is spying on her from the bushes, she says, "Let us have a little fun, too, and reward him for his doubts." From this point on she sings of her pretended amorous desires while waiting for the Count, beginning with the glorious recitative "Giunse al fin il momento" (At last the moment has arrived). Mozart wrote out a complete sketch for this obbligato recitative in three parts: first violins, voice, and bass. The violins begin with a little night music in tune with the text's pleasant images of smiling nature at dusk. This short ritornello recurs in several different keys in the sketch and leads ultimately to a cadence on B♭, which serves as V, and under which Mozart wrote, "segue rondò." He continued with a two-part sketch for the rondò (he had already made a sketch for voice alone, which also survives).

One of the puzzles about the unfinished rondò "Non tardar amato bene" is the impossibility of a piece in E♭ coming after Figaro's aria in the same key, a succession that contradicts Mozart's entire operatic practice.[22] Could Susanna's "Non tardar" have predated the composition of Figaro's last aria? Ongoing research by Dexter Edge on Mozart's autograph and early copies of it may one day provide an answer. Both pieces came very late in the compositional process. At one stage, still reflected in the ordering of the autograph, Figaro's aria followed Susanna's.

Once Mozart decided to replace Susanna's rondò with a new text, poetic meter, musical setting, and key, he shortened the preceding recitative by ten measures, discarding some of its text as well as several entrances of the violin ritornello. He changed the ending so as to prepare for arrival in F, not E♭. The new verse took images from the discarded part of the recitative and became a beguiling hymn to nature's nocturnal charms: "Qui mormora il ruscel, qui scherza l'aura / Che col dolce susurro il cor ristaura" (Here the brook rustles, the breezes play / With a sweet murmuring that restores the heart). Assuming that this new text preceded the new melody that Mozart first sketched as a single line—which is by no means certain—we can surmise how the music took shape.

"Deh vieni non tardar" requires the lightest of orchestrations: three solo winds (flute, oboe, and bassoon) over pizzicato strings. *Andante* in 6/8 time was a typically pastoral motion. The winds cavort in scalar flights in sixteenth notes, marked staccato, as if in answer to the verb "scherza." The new vocal melody begins by outlining triadic descent through the octave, like the rondò, but it is graceful and unpretentious, unlike its predecessor, while expressing Susanna's essence by incorporating the cadential phrase of the initial *duettino*, as she attempts to focus Figaro's attention on her hat.[23] Mozart makes the aria sound rather capricious by insisting on three-measure phrases almost throughout. Not until her last two lines, "Vieni ben mio, tra queste piante ascose, / Ti vo' la fronte incoronar di rose" (Come to me my love 'midst hidden plants / I wish to crown your brow with roses), does the pattern change to four measures. The strings confirm the change by switching from pizzicato to arco. Here the voice reaches its peak melodic tone (not in the sketch!) before descending as at the beginning. The winds give benediction.

The second finale begins in D after the briefest of recitative passages, accompanying Cherubino's approach to the pavilion at stage left, where the Countess seeks refuge. An *Andante* in common time, *piano*, starts up daintily after the gruff initial tone, a *forte* unison D. The violins play in tenths, with a galant-sounding chromatic rise allocated to the seconds, accompanied only by a triadic figure for

---

[22] Elsewhere I advance several other reasons for discarding "Non tardar." See Heartz, "Constructing *Le nozze di Figaro*," in *Mozart's Operas* (1990), pp. 150–52.

[23] Daniel Heartz, "Susanna's Hat," *Early Music* 19 (1991): 585–89, includes an illustration of the elaborate hat worn by Suzanne in the first production of the play as she emerges from the dressing closet in Act II.

the horns. This is not the lordly key of D projected by the Count in his irate aria, and parodied by Bartolo in his, but a more open, welcoming, and festive sounding key, conjuring the sprightly and mischievous spirit of the Overture. There is a sense here of returning home at last after a long tonal journey—sadly moving, in a way, because it signals the approaching end of the opera, the inevitable close of this "mad day."

The first to sing is Cherubino, eager to take advantage of the situation. He makes advances to the person dressed as Susanna, who rebuffs him. He even makes so bold as to attempt planting a kiss on her cheek, an action that misfires at the intervention of the Count, who receives the kiss instead. Furious, the Count attempts to slap his page but in the semi-darkness hits the spying Figaro instead. Da Ponte took this farcical byplay from Beaumarchais, along with almost all the other moves and countermoves.

A slightly faster section begins, the key having changed to G. The Count attempts to seduce the woman he thinks is Susanna. Figaro is present, unobserved but a potent force because it is the vigorous hammering figure associated with him that dominates the music (see Example 2.9, below). At length Figaro raises an alarum that the two do notice, forcing the Count to retire into the bushes and the object of his desire into the pavilion on stage right.

The music shifts suddenly, via a magical modulatory transition of only two measures. A more lyrical theme follows, a slow minuet in rhythm and in the distant key of E♭. Figaro responds to this *Larghetto* in 3/4 time with the words "Tutto è tranquillo e placido," for which there is no parallel in the play. A veritable seachange seems to have taken place, and it is the composer's doing in order to create a big contrast with all the hectic action, prior and subsequent (cf. the similar slow section in the medial finale of *Don Giovanni* as the maskers pause to contemplate their situation). Figaro reflects sardonically on his role with a classical metaphor, also not in the play: "Enter the beautiful Venus, with the charming Mars, who will be snared by today's new Vulcan." The tempo quickens to *Allegro di molto* while the meter and tempo remain unchanged as Susanna qua Countess enters, altering her voice at first to suggest that of her mistress, then forgetting to do so, revealing her true identity. She eggs Figaro on to seek vengeance, a game he enters with relish, for now he is in the know and she is not.

Figaro plays along, pretending to woo the "Countess," and asks for the lady's hand. Susanna gives it to him in the form of repeated slaps, ending the section in E♭. In the course of their altercation a familiar motif begins sounding, one similar to the theme of "Deh vieni non tardar" (Example 2.4). This reminds us that Susanna tricked Figaro before he tricked her. Figaro then begins a new section, an *Andante* in B♭ and in 6/8 time, as he confesses that he recognized her by her voice and offering to make peace, "Pace, pace, mio dolce tesoro," sung to a triadic figure related to the previous example. Susanna is easily pacified and joins him

EXAMPLE 2.4. *Mozart,* Le nozze di Figaro, *Act IV, Finale*

in singing the "Pace, pace" theme. Enter the Count, who has been wandering the bushes trying to find his prey. The game now becomes one of making him believe that Figaro is seducing the Countess. He is easily fooled and cries out for his people to come and apprehend the miscreants. As in the medial finale, G major arrives with no transition as a surprise after B♭. The horns again had to change crooks in a hurry.

The lively visual action at this point helps revive our attention, which may have been flagging after so many dissemblings. While Susanna qua Countess flees into one of the pavilions, the Count stops Figaro from doing so as he calls out "Gente, gente, all'armi!" the music switching to *Allegro* in common time. Figaro grovels and the others marvel as the Count denounces him as a traitor. From the pavilion, the Count then pulls Cherubino out by the arm, followed by Barbarina, Marcellina, and the disguised Susanna. The Count's ire increases and there are echoes of his earlier outbursts of anger from the end of his aria. The "guilty" couple kneels and asks his forgiveness, echoed by all present. After increasingly testy refusals, the last "No!" comes with the snarling intensity of a measure-long unstable tone, his low C, reinforced in unison by the whole orchestra. Its resolution comes only in accompanying the real Countess as she emerges from the other pavilion and tries to kneel before her husband, singing, "At least I shall obtain pardon for them."

General astonishment is translated by Mozart as a sudden shift from G to g. The dynamic level drops to *pianissimo,* the violins chattering away in eighth notes like startled doves. All this evaporates when the Count begs his wife for her forgiveness as the tempo slows to *Andante* and the major mode returns. Everything now depends on Rosina. In her brief response she reaches a full and satisfying cadence on G: "I am more docile, and say yes." The gentle Rosina, who forgave all Bartolo's faults at the end of *Barbiere,* could hardly do any less than forgive her errant husband once again. In response, all nine characters, including the Count and Countess, join to sing in harmony that comes like a soothing balm, "Ah, we shall all be content thus." The singers are all *sotto voce,* the massed winds *pianissimo.* Only the strings are marked *piano* and *crescendo* as they sound descending broken triads related to "Pace, pace." The voices swell, alternating louds and softs as they repeat the healing words, with a strong emphasis on the subdominant, as in a coda, signaling that the end is indeed nigh.

Music of the serenity and power of the ensemble that follows the reconciliation of the Count and Countess readily persuades us that this marriage has been saved. The plain facts of the Count's philandering throughout the second drama raise doubts on the other hand. Saved for how long? Given an ambiguous situation, we want to believe what the music powerfully tells us. As for the creator of these characters, it took him an entire third play to save their marriage.

After the healing *Andante* (often dragged out *Adagio*), there is no need for a passage to prepare the final return to the home key of D, which could have arrived without one. Yet Mozart provided here one of his greatest transitions in a few measures of *pianissimo* as the strings in unison descend slowly from G as tonic via C♯ to low A, outlining the dominant seventh chord that must resolve to D while the winds sustain. How simple this is, yet how moving.

The play ties various loose ends together, but in the opera, everything explodes in a burst of joy, *Allegro assai*, in relatively few words. "This day of torment, caprices, and madness can only be closed by love. Let the dancing, games, and fireworks begin to the sounds of the march. Let us all run to join the celebration." At the words "corriam tutti" the unison strings begin a running figure in rapid notes, a *piano* with *crescendo* to *forte*, reaching up gradually to the fifth degree from the tonic. The idea proved suggestive for the beginning of the overture, which was written out very late, on a paper type described as the "last paper that Mozart used for *Figaro*."[24]

"Corriam tutti" is not the only music from the opera that has a bearing on the overture. Susanna's repeated pleas in the second *duettino* of Act I, scene 1, to dispel Figaro's suspicions, "Discaccia sospetti," sung to 3 4 1 (Example 2.5),

EXAMPLE 2.5. *Mozart,* Le nozze di Figaro, *No. 2, Duettino*

become a recurring 7 8 5 at the very end of the overture as a climactic reaffirmation of the tonic. It is certainly a central lesson of the whole drama that Figaro should learn to trust his lovely bride, and is thus an appropriate choice to end the overture. The lesson taught the Count is scarcely more important. Amazing as it may seem in retrospect, Mozart had another idea for the overture that would have given it a slower middle section in tonic minor, along the lines of the Overture to *Die Entführung*. The traces of this, crossed out, can be seen on the page of the auto-

---

[24] Tyson, *Mozart*, p. 120.

graph selected to be the first plate in the *Neue Mozart-Ausgabe* score. It was to have been an *Andante con moto* in 6/8 time with dotted rhythm, a siciliana obviously intended to lend a little more Spanish color to complement the Fandango near the end of Act III. Mozart may also have been thinking of the very effective Serenade in Gluck's ballet *Don Juan*, another *Andante* in d and in 6/8 time, with the same scoring of solo oboe and pizzicato strings and the same dotted rhythm.[25] Deleting the siciliana section was a late, perhaps last economy effected by Mozart in tightening up this miraculous score before the premiere on May Day 1786.

Post-*Figaro* Chamber Music

A more leisurely time for Mozart followed the premiere of his opera. He probably presided at the keyboard for the first two performances, according to custom. These took place on the first and third of May. There were further performances on 8 and 24 May, then on 3 June for the court at Laxenburg Palace. Five more performances followed, roughly one a month, during the remainder of the year. The Italian company kept five or six operas in repertory at the same time and ten performances of a work was near the average number per season. After Nancy Storace and Michael Kelly left the troupe to return home in early 1787, the opera was dropped. During its run a revival of *Die Entführung* was being given regularly by the German company at the Kärntnerthor, so Mozart was well represented on the boards of both stages in 1786. No records of box office receipts for either theater have survived for that year. If they had, perhaps they might tell a story not unlike that from 1789–90, from which such records do survive—namely that *Così fan tutte* and the revival of *Figaro* earned the Burgtheater substantial sums because attendance at them was above average. On this basis one scholar has surmised that these two productions were among the most popular then on offer.[26]

Mozart scholars of the last century tended to regard the period after *Figaro* as a dark one in the composer's life, as if he must necessarily have suffered some kind of postnatal depression. One of the most eminent began a chapter dealing with the period between *Figaro* and *Don Giovanni* with this glum statement: "Mozart's external life in Vienna resumed its old miserable rounds as if *Figaro* had never been composed [Mozarts äusseres Leben in Wien ging zunächst seinen alten ärmlichen Gang weiter, als wäre der 'Figaro' nie komponiert worden]."[27] "Miserable rounds" suggests that Mozart resented having to teach students in compo-

[25] *Haydn, Mozart*, p. 185, ex. 3.6. Gluck later used this piece in his *Armide*, where it is called a "Sicilien."

[26] Dexter Edge, "Mozart's Reception in Vienna, 1787–1791," in *Wolfgang Amadè Mozart*, ed. Stanley Sadie (1996), 66–117: 85.

[27] Hermann Abert, *W. A. Mozart, Neubearbeitete und erweiterte Ausoabe von Otto Jahns Mozart,* 2 vols.(Leipzig, 1955–56), 2:306.

sition and piano (from which it is but a step to infer that he was a poor teacher). Another inference is that the opera had somehow failed. One of the most pernicious myths promoted by twentieth-century musical modernism is that great composers were ever misunderstood and rebuffed by their contemporaries. This old saw was a holdover from the nineteenth century, but it took some overly zealous devotees of Arnold Schoenberg to invert the proposition and maintain that misunderstood or despised music must *ipso facto* be great. In truth, Mozart had many partisans who both understood and championed his music when it was new, in Vienna and elsewhere.

The summer of 1786 was probably like those of the previous years in Vienna for the Mozarts. During fair weather, this often meant pleasant days in the Prater or excursions further out into the Wienerwald.[28] From the nature of the charming compositions that came after *Figaro*, it would be difficult to intuit that Mozart was seething with disappointment. The Piano Quartet in E♭, K. 493, the next work in his catalogue, offers a good case in point. It was followed by a new Horn Concerto in E♭, K. 495, for Joseph Leutgeb; the Sonata in F for piano four hands, K. 497; the very jolly and personal Trio for clarinet, viola, and piano in E♭, K. 498 (the so-called "Kegelstatt" Trio); and the blithe String Quartet in D, K. 499 ("Hoffmeister"). To these Mozart added two piano trios, K. 496 and K. 502.

Mozart wrote only two piano quartets, and they surround *Figaro* like a pair of bookends. According to Nissen, the publisher Franz Anton Hoffmeister commissioned three piano quartets from the composer, but this seems odd because the combination of violin, viola, cello, and piano was so new and untried. More likely Mozart experimented with the piano trio texture by adding to it his beloved viola and proposed the idea to Hoffmeister. He may have begun K. 478 in g in July 1785, for he lists it under this date in his catalogue. The autograph, on the other hand, bears the inscription "Quartetto di Wolfgango Amadeo Mozart mp Vienna li 16 d'Ottobre 1785," which was surely the date by which it was finished. Leopold received it in a packet of works from his son on 1 December along with printed violin and viola parts (the cello part, placed under the piano's, could be read from the score). The score Leopold received was probably the autograph because he mentions its precise date in his letter of a day later to Nannerl. Although he was ill, Leopold wasted no time in having the quartet tried out.

K. 478 in g begins with a stark first movement, an *Allegro* in common time dominated by a powerful unison beginning. Rather unusual for Mozart, this theme returns in its entirety in the coda after the repetition of the seconda parte. The remaining two movements are a docile *Andante* in B♭ and in 3/8 time, and an expansive *Rondo* in cut time and in the key of G. One of the odd things about the latter is an appearance at m. 60 of a theme that falls by step 5 4 3 2 1 then by

---

[28] Heartz, "Mozart's Sense for Nature," p. 112.

skips down 4 2 7, one that has parallels in some of Mozart's early works, such as the Divertimento in D, K. 136, of 1772. It matches exactly the theme of the Rondo in D for solo piano, K. 485, the autograph of which is dated 10 January 1786.[29]As the finale sounds likely to be concluding after a climax preparing a big cadence on the tonic, it is not the tonic that arrives but ♭VI, E♭. The same big deceptive cadence marked the first movement of another work in G, Piano Concerto No. 17, K. 453. It may be that in both cases Mozart is showing his admiration for the huge arrival in E♭ late in the first movement of another work in G, Haydn's String Quartet, Opus 33 No. 5.

K. 493 in E♭, the second piano quartet, was entered in Mozart's catalogue with a date of 3 June 1786. This may mean that Mozart was not present at Laxenburg for the fifth performance of *Figaro* on the same day. The work shares certain formal characteristics with K. 478. Its first movement, also an *Allegro* in common time, is followed by a slower movement in 3/8 time. Moreover, both middle movements make prominent use of the minuet rhythm that forevermore will be identified with Susanna's emergence from the dressing closet in the medial finale of *Figaro* (see Example 2.3). In roughly one-third of his instrumental works with a main key of E♭, Mozart chose A♭ for the slow movement, as in this *Larghetto*; in the rest, he chooses either c or B♭. The *Larghetto* ends with a blissful sense of peace, achieved by a floating arpeggio figure in the piano over a wide range (Example 2.6). Coming right after the opera, this cannot but remind us of the "hat motif,"

EXAMPLE 2.6. *Mozart, Piano Quartet in E♭, K. 493, II*

with which Figaro attempts to pacify Susanna in the second finale (see Example 2.4). Note also the rhythmic figure played by the violin and viola. The *Allegretto* in cut time finale, with both main themes in gavotte rhythm, is a rondo movement

---

[29]The theme was perhaps common property to the whole epoch. It was also used by Schobert, according to Abert, *Mozart*, 1:157, n. 2. In K. 478, Mozart does not repeat the theme at the equivalent spot later on, making it seem all the more like a quotation.

of great delicacy yet with flashes of power, as when the strings combine in a *forte* unison figure to challenge the piano, which sounds almost concerto-like. The piano part is so idiomatic and beautifully conceived it is a sheer joy to play it.

There is an earlier piece of chamber music, the Quintet for Piano and Winds in E♭, K. 452, of 1784 that also shares an overall form with the two piano quartets, with the difference that its initial *Allegro moderato* is preceded by a slow introduction. Its middle movement in B♭ and in 3/8 time gives the piano arpeggio figures in thirty-second notes up and down the keyboard similar to those that end the *Larghetto* of K. 493, and its finale is a rondo in cut time on a theme in gavotte rhythm. In scoring K. 452, Mozart placed the four winds above the piano part. In K. 478, on the other hand, he placed the violin and viola parts above the piano part and the cello part below. The autograph of K. 493 does not survive but likely its disposition matched that of K. 478.

Hoffmeister did publish K. 478, which was said to lack many buyers. If there ever was a commission to write three piano quartets, it was dropped at this point. K. 493 was not published until 1787, and not by Hoffmeister but by Artaria. Thus, the genre came to an end for Mozart. It was taken up again by Beethoven and many later masters. Mozart switched his efforts in this kind of chamber music to the more traditional piano trio. He had written an earlier example of it, the Divertimento in B♭ for violin, cello, and piano, K. 254, of 1776 that approached later piano trios by treating the violin as the piano's equal and letting the cello occasionally contribute something other than doubling the piano's bass line.[30]

The Piano Trio in G, K. 496, is dated 8 July 1786 by Mozart in his catalogue. Tellingly, he inscribed the autograph with the word "Sonate," while calling it in the catalogue "Terzett." The piano begins with a long solo in the opening *Allegro* in common time. It certainly sounds like a solo sonata at the beginning when the piano goes on alone for seventeen measures of very idiomatic keyboard work, with fast running passages rising over an octave and arpeggios as well. Approaching the cadence there is a hint of *Figaro* (Example 2.7ab). The violin makes it clear at

EXAMPLE 2.7.

a. *Mozart, Le nozze di Figaro, No. 1, Duettino*

b. *Mozart, Piano Trio in G, K. 496, I*

[30] *Haydn, Mozart*, p. 590.

its first entrance in m. 18 that it too can manage those leaps and runs quite well. In the seconda parte even the cello gets to perform the opening scalar passage, and although it is playable, most cellists will not be grateful to the composer for the challenges posed. Yet much of the development section's interest lies in revealing the cello's prowess in reproducing the piano's running start. The *Andante* in 6/8 time and in the key of C also has fast running passages, thirty-second notes in this case, and all instruments share them throughout. At the movement's end, Mozart shows how he can overlap these fast-note passages in a five-part canon. It is one of the few instances in his works where a show of ingenuity displaces what is natural and idiomatic, for the pianist must manage three of the canonic entries, with only two hands, when three would be useful. The trio ends with a theme and variations on an *Allegretto* in cut time and in gavotte rhythm.

A more endearing work is the Piano Trio in B♭, K. 502, entered in the catalogue with a date of 18 November 1786. Mozart clearly expended much thought and effort here. The opening *Allegro* in common time begins softly with the piano singing a theme in thirds, then in sixths, with chromatic inflections that recall the opening theme of Piano Concerto No. 15 in B♭, K. 450. It is a very galant idea, deployed over a drum bass in the piano's left hand, while the cello mostly holds pedal tones and the violin fills in the interstices of the piano's song. Extraordinary about this movement is how Mozart uses this main theme, modified in several ways, as the basis of nearly every formal function: as transition to the second key, as second theme, in canonic interplay, as closing theme, and, in the seconda parte, as retransition and subdominant substitution after the reprise. Even this list does not exhaust the possibilities derived from a single theme. Concentration on a single melodic-rhythmic kernel, almost to the exclusion of other material, can be found often in Haydn and is quite characteristic of him. For Mozart it seems like an aberration, one that required the kind of thematic intensity typical of string quartets, and we know from his own words how much labor those cost the composer. The slow movement, *Larghetto* in E♭ and in 3/4 time, is extraordinary in another way. Mozart recomposed its entire subdominant episode after writing out an earlier version as a complete melodic line of many measures.[31] Usually, when he changed his mind about the viability of an episode, he made the decision earlier, and often it is possible to intuit what he found wanting in his earlier idea. In this case, what he substituted was quite different, as well as fourteen measures shorter, and the earlier solution seems quite good. Perhaps it was the length of the original episode that induced him to rewrite it completely. The finale is another gavotte type, *Allegretto* in cut time, with spots quite demanding of the pianist, for instance, the rapid parallel third passages first for the right

[31] Ulrich Konrad, " 'In seinem Kopfe lag das Werk immer vollendet . . .': Bemerkungen zu Mozarts Schaffenweise am Beispiel des Klaviertrios B-Dur KV 502," *Mozart-Jahrbuch 1991*: 540–51.

hand, then the left (à la Clementi). The rondo theme blooms into a final swirl of sound, with canons in the violin and cello on the main theme sounding through the rapid scales of the piano.

K. 502 in its entirety gives the impression that Mozart took his time when conceiving and polishing its every detail. For once, perhaps, he was not pressed by a deadline or a demanding recipient. The keyboard part, clearly a showcase for his own dexterity, is as demanding as those in his concertos. This is not to say that trios like these lacked an appreciative buying public. Hoffmeister brought out K. 496 in 1786, and K. 502, joined by the next two piano trios, K. 542 and K. 548, appeared as a set published by Artaria in 1788.

Among Mozart's many pupils at this time, a few can be singled out as having possible connections with some of his chamber music. To the lady pianists who formed the core of his paying pupils must be added Franziska von Jacquin, the sister of Mozart's close friend Gottfried von Jacquin. Mozart called the lady Signora Diniminimimi in the letter to her brother, written from Prague on 15 January 1787, in which he made up jocular names for many of his friends (Gottfried was Hinkiti Honky). On a more serious note, he requested Gottfried to urge his sister "to apply herself in earnest to practicing on her new piano, but this injunction is quite unnecessary for I must admit that I have never had a female pupil who has been so diligent and eager as she is." A witness claims that she was the first pianist to play the delightful Trio in E♭ for viola, clarinet, and piano, K. 498.[32] Mozart entered the work in his catalogue with a date of 5 August 1786, four days after the Sonata for Piano Four Hands in F, K. 497. The clarinet part was presumably played by Anton Stadler, who was given the name Nàtschibinïtschibi in the letter just cited, indication that he too belonged to the composer's inner circle of friends. Although Mozart called K. 498 a "Terzett" as he did the piano trios, the work, less conventional than they, is more like a divertimento, consisting as it does of a short but thematically concentrated first movement, *Andante* in 6/8 time, an expansive Menuetto in B♭ with Trio in g as middle movement, and a light-hearted finale in common time, *Rondeaux: Allegretto*, in which the clarinet is particularly favored. It is very likely that Mozart originally played the viola part himself, for this was his favorite instrument when performing chamber music. "Kegelstatt," as K. 498 came to be called, may have originated by way of osmosis from the Twelve Duos for Two Horns, K. 487 (496a), which date from the same time. They are not included in the catalogue but the autograph is inscribed "Di Wolfgang Amadé Mozart mp. Wien den 27^t Julius 1786 untern Kegelscheiben" (while playing skittles).

A few unlikely clues help tie together Mozart's inner circle with other post-

---

[32] Caroline Pichler, *Denkwürdigkeiten aus meinem Leben* (Vienna, 1844), ed. Emil Karl Blüml, 2 vols. (Munich, 1914), 1:180.

Figaro works. Paper studies show that Mozart's comic trio "Das Bandel," K. 441, the three vocal parts of which are designated on the autograph "Constantz," "Mozart," and "Jacquin," does not belong in 1783 but in 1786, because "its 16-staff paper, most unusual in Mozart's autographs, is a leftover from the Piano Concerto in c, K. 491, of March 1786."[33] Furthermore, the Jacquin-related Notturni K. 436–439, for two sopranos and bass with accompaniments for three clarinets or basset horns, formerly assigned to 1783, have also been advanced in date by at least four years. In Mozart's circle clarinets and basset horns generally signal the Stadlers.

Four-hand piano music can be tied to the same circle by way of Franziska von Jacquin. She likely played the great Sonata in F, K. 497, either with Mozart or with another pupil. There is no proof for this, but for the Sonata's successor, the Sonata in C for Piano Four Hands, K. 521, dated 29 May 1787, there is. Mozart sent the work to Franziska and in an undated note from the same time urged her to study it, "because it is rather difficult." Women usually took the higher part in this kind of domestic music-making, as did Nannerl in the Mozart family portrait (see Figure 1.4). Charles Burney, in his four-hand piano pieces (London, 1777), requested that a lady performer remove the hoops from her skirt and not be alarmed if her left hand occasionally collided with the gentleman's right hand.

K. 497 in F is nearly as difficult as K. 521 and is a more serious work, if only because of the first *Allegro*. The magnificent slow introduction that precedes it, one of Mozart's greatest in the genre, sounds like a harbinger of the slow introductions that preceded two of the last four symphonies. This introduction is an *Adagio* in common time that spans several secondary dominants before reaching a pause on the dominant of F, preparing the arrival of the scintillating *Allegro di molto* in cut time that has something of the rhythmic drive of the Overture to *Der Schauspieldirektor*, particularly in the dramatic dialogue of its development section. Most unlike that concentrated act of orchestral brio is the way Mozart reduces the tension for a contrasting second theme. This memorable theme has a rhythm of its own, more relaxed and broader than what preceded, and also a texture of its own, very like that of a string quartet. In both regards, also in melody and harmony, it sounds like a cousin to a recurring homophonic passage of the Chair Trio in Act I of *Figaro* (Example 2.8ab). The duet passage is shown as recast in the tonic during the reprise and scored as if it were a string quartet (although the second violin obviously could not play the low F in the second measure). This smooth and cantabile bit of chamber music worked its charms on other composers. Christian Cannabich copied it outright in one of his last symphonies.[34]

Mozart's main composition pupil at this time, the young Englishman

---

[33] Tyson, *Mozart*, p. 33.
[34] *Music in European Capitals*, pp. 542–43, ex. 5.24.

EXAMPLE 2.8.

a. *Mozart,* Le nozze di Figaro, *Act I, No. 7, Terzetto*

b. *Mozart, Sonata in F for Piano Four Hands, K. 497, I*

Thomas Attwood, took such examples to heart when writing some of his latest works under Mozart's tutelage.[35] That Attwood, a fine keyboard player (later in life organist of Saint Paul's, London), also had the privilege of playing K. 497 with its composer seems very likely. Many years ago, while editing the free composition part of Mozart's lessons to Attwood, I was struck by how well Example 2.8b embodies principal tenets Mozart was trying to impress on his students. They were taught by direct example as well as by Mozart's correcting their musical efforts, which was done assiduously—no one who has studied these lessons would ever claim that Mozart was a poor or inattentive teacher. Two of his precepts were that the treble must always sing out, and that the other voices must support the treble with the fullest harmonies possible, while not neglecting to sing in their own right. Mozart often showed Attwood how the tenor or viola part might escape its somewhat narrow possibilities by leaping an octave, as happens in m. 241 of the example.[36]

K. 497, subject of the previous digression on Attwood, continues with an *Andante* in B♭ and in common time, based on the same initial idea as the middle movement of the Horn Concerto in E♭, K. 495, dated little more than a month earlier. Leutgeb, the recipient, was an old friend from Salzburg and the butt of many of Mozart's jokes. In K. 495, the movement in question, *Romance. Andante cantabile,* agrees in key but not in meter, being in 3/4 rather than 4/4 time. It is based nevertheless on the same lyric melody, docilely accompanied by parallel thirds or tenths. What made one and not the other a Romance? A simple formal

[35] *Thomas Attwoods Theorie- und Kompositionsstudien bei Mozart,* ed. Erich Hertzmann and Cecil B. Oldman, completed by Daniel Heartz and Alfred Mann (Kassel, 1965). *NMA* X/30/1.

[36] For the latest stage of Attwood's pieces written for Mozart, see in particular his *Rondo Allegretto* in D, *NMA* X/30/1, pp. 225–34, which I discuss in the *Kritischer Bericht* (1969), pp. 90–98. See also Heartz, "Thomas Attwood's Lessons in Composition with Mozart," *PRMA* 100 (1973–74): 175–83.

treatment is characteristic of all Mozart's movements called Romance. This one is a straightforward rondo in which two episodes, one in V (or on V) and a second in vi, are surrounded by statements of the refrain. The *Andante* of K. 497, on the other hand, is a full-scale sonata form, although the development is rather brief. This movement is made longer not only by its form, in which both prima and seconda parti are marked for repetition, but also by the dialogic nature of the texture and thematic process, the two players sharing most of the ideas. Also, in the second theme area, the treatment becomes quite florid, with rapid runs and ornaments. A coda rounds out this substantial movement after repetition of the seconda parte. The two movements demonstrate how Mozart, beginning with the same initial idea, can make two entirely different pieces. Even so the special sweetness of this Romance melody casts an aura of enchantment over both, like a warm breeze from the south on a balmy summer evening. In the finale of the sonata, *Allegro* in 6/8 time, the little swirls of pianism in the *Andante* become a torrent of rapid runs and arpeggios, keeping both hands of the pianists very busy. The movement is a large-scale sonata rondo form that brings this delightful work to a fitting close.

Another work for piano four hands thought to date from the summer or fall of 1786 is K. 497a in G, consisting of an *Allegro* in 3/4 time, continued for ninety-eight measures but breaking off just after the beginning of the seconda parte. A second movement, an *Andante* in 2/4 time, also in G, proceeds for 160 measures of a looser kind of form, a theme and variations with contrasting episodes, before breaking off. Both movements are viable and promising as far as they go. Could Mozart have given them to Attwood or another student as an exercise in composition, the task being to finish them? He used this method on a smaller scale by beginning minuets, not only with Attwood but with other pupils as well. Another possibility is that the second of the two movements was discarded for the winning set of variations on an *Andante* in G for piano four hands that Mozart did finish, K. 501, dated 4 November 1786.

Pupils coming to Mozart for instruction, besides Attwood, included Franz Jacob Freystädtler and the eight-year-old prodigy Johann Nepomuk Hummel. Both Freystädtler and Barbara Ployer received training in music theory, and their notebooks survive to show what this entailed.[37] Freystädtler was born in Salzburg in 1768 and was a favorite, as may be seen from his presence on the list of people to whom Mozart gave nicknames; his was "Gaulimauli." Late in life, Freystädtler said that his instruction by Mozart often took place on a table where "Kegelspiel" was in progress.[38] This need not mean that Mozart was inattentive

[37] *Barbara Ployers und Franz Jacob Freystädtlers Theorie- und Kompositionsstudien bei Mozart,* ed. Hellmut Federhofer and Alfred Mann. *NMA* X/30/2 (Kassel, 1989). Mozart vouched for Freystädtler after he got in trouble with the law for taking one of his pupil's fortepianos. Michael Lorenz, "Mozarts Haftungserklärung für Freystädtler: Eine Chronologie," *Mozart-Jahrbuch 1998*: 1–20.

[38] *Allgemeine Wiener Musikzeitung* 1842, p. 489.

to the lesson, only that the composer could multitask. No doubt Mozart preferred skittles to teaching but that is neither here nor there as a gauge of his efficacy as a teacher. All his life he was very fond of playing games. Attwood told an early biographer of the composer that Mozart "would at any time rather play a game of billiards with him than give him a lesson."[39] To this same pupil Mozart paid high tribute by telling Michael Kelly, "Attwood partakes more of my style than any scholar I ever had."[40] The very lively English coterie surrounding Mozart in 1786 also included Stephen Storace, Nancy's brother, who may have taken some lessons from the master too. Constanze wrote Attwood in 1821 that she still held his memory dear, along with the jolly times they shared in the "Figaro House" on the Dom Gasse (Figure 2.3).

A high point of this fecund time was the String Quartet in D, K. 499, that Mozart entered in his catalogue with the date of 19 August 1786. It has become known as the "Hoffmeister" Quartet because Anton Franz Hoffmeister published it soon after it was completed. It could as well be called the "Figaro" Quartet. The movements are *Allegretto* in cut time, *Menuetto: Allegro*, *Adagio* in G and in 3/4 time, and *Allegro* in 6/8 time. No less learned than the last two Artaria quartets dedicated to Haydn, K. 464–65, it is somewhat lighter in character. The first movement begins softly with the strings in unison intoning a triadic theme that descends from a high third to a low fifth (Example 2.9). The five-fold low A

EXAMPLE 2.9. *Mozart, String Quartet in D, K. 499 ("Hoffmeister"), I*

coming after F♯ and D (marked with brackets) corresponds to one of the main motifs in the second finale of the opera, where its pounding effect is associated with Figaro's anger at seeing what he believes to be the wooing of Susanna by

[39] Edward Holmes, *The Life of Mozart* (London, 1845), p. 259.
[40] Michael Kelly, *Reminiscences of Michael Kelly, of the King's Theatre and Theatre Drury Lane*, 2 vols. (London, 1826; reprint 1968), 1:225.

FIGURE 2.3. The "Figaro House" behind St. Stephan's Cathedral.

the Count. It recurs many times there as a unifying motif for the whole section. Mozart stretched out the moment in the example so that, over a dominant pedal, it becomes a V⁷ chord, to which he then adds a 9th in m. 6. He resolves the accumulated tension, but only after a detour by way of vi and IV. Measures 9–12 (in brackets) duplicate almost exactly the little passage sung in harmony by the four conspirators to conclude the recitative following the Sestetto in the opera's Act III. There the words are "E schiati il Signor Conte al gusto mio" (And let his Lordship yelp to my taste). In the opera, Mozart emphasizes the word "Conte" by marking it *forte* after a *crescendo* from *pianissimo,* and by a deceptive cadence as well as the treble's leap up a fourth, followed by a rest, after which the voices return to *pianissimo.* Those who paid close attention to the opera and had good tonal memories could not fail to have enjoyed the quartet's reminiscences.[41]

Like the first movement of the previous piece, the "Kegelstatt" Trio, K. 498, K. 499's opening *Allegretto* draws almost exclusively on its first theme, which keeps appearing in different guises or different keys. After the beginning, quoted in the example, Mozart continues with a duet for the two violins, echoed by the viola and cello an octave lower, based on the descending sixth leap in m. 1 and the rising fourth leap in m. 10, two salient intervallic features. The upper pair then repeat

[41] They are discussed in Knepler, *Mozart* (1994), pp. 234–36.

their cadence, slightly embroidered in the treble, a one-measure gesture exactly mimicked by the lower pair, then reduced to a half measure and again mimicked. This kind of repartee is as clever as it is humorous. A sudden lurch wrenches the music to a more serious level with the arrival of vi, *forte*, established by its own cadences. This detour turns out to be a momentary delay in the transition leading to the new key of A, a passage peppered with appearances of the main motif from mm. 1–2, now in the outer voices as a canon at one measure's distance between first violin and cello. There is no second theme per se, only more of the canonic interchange as the new key becomes established and is decorated by an emphatic deceptive cadence in its own right, *forte*, after a crescendo, with two quarter notes followed by a rest as in m. 10. After this eruption, the instruments enter softly in imitation of one another and aim toward a cadence on A, only to be shunted aside by another deceptive cadence to vi for a leisurely moment of rest in f♯. Once again, they approach the cadence expected on A and are thwarted by yet another deceptive cadence, this time to the sweetly coy substitution of ♭VI, F major! Schubert, who often used ♭VI in major-mode pieces, surely must have loved this delectable example. The long-sought strong cadences in the key of A finally do arrive, then taper off to a *pianissimo*, over which the violins layer a dainty pitter-patter in staccato eighth notes.

Pitter-patter, pitter-patter, pit—in eighth notes, *piano*, is also the way Mozart ended the prima parte of the *Allegro di molto* of K. 497 for piano four hands, where he continued by transforming this idea from major to minor, but *pianissimo*, to begin the development. After this the eighth notes become a virtual torrent, *forte*, picked up by the primo player when dropped by the secondo, while the harmonies go on a wild spree around the circle of fifths. This is precisely the same course of action taken in the development of K. 499's *Allegretto*. Unlike the sonata, where the eighth notes are slurred, they are *détachés* in the quartet (until just before the reprise) and their mechanistic quality makes them sound like a ticking clock. The chamber pieces that followed *Figaro* not only fish often in the same waters as the opera, they tend to catch many of the same details.

The *Menuetto Allegretto* second movement of K. 499 is only twenty-eight measures in length, briefer than any of the minuets in the six quartets dedicated to Haydn (except that of the "Hunt" Quartet). It is like a Ländler in the way the cello clings to a drone bass for much of it. There is a reminder of the first movement in the prominent move to vi after the double bar in the middle. The Trio is in tonic minor and exploits running triplets throughout.

The *Adagio* in G has an elegiac character, a languishing air from the many thirds and sixths with which the violins sing the melody, which is then duplicated by the lower instruments while the violins provide a kind of commentary. That this is a portrait of Countess Almaviva is suggested clearly at the move to the new key of D, when the first violin sounds the very melody she sings in her Act III aria "Dove sono" at the words "la memoria di quel bene dal mio sen non trapassi" (the memory of this bliss will not quit my breast). After a firm cadence in the new key, there is a sudden eruption of its subdominant, *forte*, with dotted rhythm. This evokes the Count's angry aria in Act III at the words "Ah che lasciarti in pace non vò questo contento" (Ah, I'll not allow you [Figaro] this happiness peacefully).

It sounds as if the triplets of the Trio come back, only faster, in the finale, *Allegro molto* in 2/4 time. Here they are so persistent that for long stretches, the movement sounds like a *perpetuum mobile*, but at the same time it is intricately contrapuntal, and in an elaborately worked-out sonata form. Both parts are repeated, followed by a coda in which the main theme gets a new ending, a device perfected by Haydn.

Many ideas in the *Figaro* score continued to swim in the composer's brain and, whether he realized it or not, to seep into a rather closely-knit family of works. The opera's many musical gems were "wandering around in his head," as he once said about *Die Entführung* (letter of 13 October 1781). An argument could be made that the first movement of K. 499, with its frequent moves from tonic D to vi and its dominant (F♯) has consequences for the "Prague" Symphony, K. 504. The symphony has other reminders that *Figaro* remained a haunting presence. Further shadows of the opera occur as late as the Piano Trio in C, K. 548, of July 1788, which begins with a robust march theme approximating the rising triads in dotted rhythm of "delle belle turbando il riposo," the third line of Figaro's "Non più andrai farfallone amoroso."

The tenth and last performance of *Figaro* in its first production took place at the Burgtheater on 10 December 1786. The English contingent that gathered around Nancy Storace was preparing to quit Vienna, but this did not happen before Mozart gave his Susanna a magnificent token of gratitude and love, K. 505, a concertante rondò for soprano and piano solo on the *Idomeneo* text "Non temer amato bene." Its composer inscribed the autograph with an unusually elaborate heading: "Recitativo con Rondò. Composto per la Signora Storace del suo servo ed amico W.A. Mozart Vienna li 26 di dec^br 1786." In his catalogue the following day he entered "*Scena* con Rondò mit klavier solo. für Mad.^selle Storace und mich." It is the grandest of Mozart's pieces in the rondò genre and at the same time one of his grandest love duets, albeit between an instrument and a voice. What is one to make of the transformation from Mrs. (Signora) to Miss (Mademoiselle) from one day to the next? The woman, whose attractions as a person, as well as a great singer-actress, were captivating, had in fact separated from her husband Fisher. She gave her farewell concert in Vienna at the Kärntnerthor Theater on 23 February 1787. Attwood later stated that K. 505 was on the program and that Mozart also played the Piano Concerto in d, K. 466.[42]

---

[42] Cliff Eisen, *New Mozart Documents: A Supplement to O. E. Deutsch's Documentary Biography* (Stanford, 1991), p. 39.

For some months before, Mozart had been thinking of returning to London, a scheme encouraged by his English friends. Attwood, who had reached his twenty-first birthday on 23 November 1786 and finished his lessons with Mozart, promised to seek concert and operatic opportunities for his master in the English capital. In a lost letter, Mozart proposed that while he traveled, his two surviving children be deposited in Salzburg under the care of their grandfather. Leopold would not hear of it, and wrote to Nannerl of his strong objections in a letter of 17–18 November 1786. Only later did Leopold learn that Johann Thomas Leopold Mozart, born on 18 October 1786, had died within a month.

On the Way to Prague

Mozart's commitment to staying in Vienna was not as strong as is generally believed. As long as he had no court appointment there, his financial situation remained insecure. Joseph II seemed to smile upon him but always favored Salieri when making appointments. Thus Mozart's hopes of becoming the teacher of Princess Elisabeth of Württemberg, affianced to Archduke Francis, were dashed when that position went to Salieri. Leopold convinced his son that the best strategy was to stay in Vienna awaiting the demise of either Bonno, the Kapellmeister, or Gluck, who held a position as Court Composer. Both were aged but continued in their salaried posts. Bonno lived on until 1788, when he died at the age of 77. Gluck was 73 when he died in 1787. Small wonder then that Mozart, while waiting, cast his eyes on the possibilities of returning to the great capitals of western Europe, London and Paris.

Even in the heat of composing *Die Entführung* in the late summer of 1781, Mozart expressed doubts about his future in Vienna. He wrote Leopold on 5 September "If I can see that things are going well for me here I shall stay, otherwise I have in mind to go straight to Paris." A year later, he outlined a more specific plan, writing on 17 August 1782 after his marriage and the success of *Die Entführung*.

> My idea is to go to Paris for the next Lenten season, not without making proper contacts in advance of course. I have already written to [Joseph] Legros about this and await a reply . . . If only I could be affiliated with the Concert Spirituel and the Concert des Amateurs, and in addition, I would have plenty of pupils, which, now that I have a wife, could be supervised more easily and more attentively. Then [there would be earnings] from my compositions and so forth, but especially because of the opera there. I began a little while ago to practice my French, and I have already taken three English lessons. In about three months, I hope to able to read and understand English texts quite well.

In 1783 Mozart did travel, but only to Salzburg.

In 1784 and 1785, Mozart's many appearances as a pianist performing concerts gave the couple money enough to live in style, and the success of *Figaro* in 1786 enhanced his reputation further. Yet there was still no preferment from the court, and concert-giving in Vienna was starting to diminish. Mozart's hopes for greater monetary rewards by going west were rekindled by the Storaces and Attwood, and he anticipated arriving in London in time for the Carnival season of 1787. Prague beckoned him first. Leopold wrote Nannerl on 12 January 1787, "*Le nozze di Figaro* has been such a success in Prague that the orchestra there and a group of distinguished *Kenner* and music lovers have sent your brother a poem in his honor and an invitation to visit Prague . . . Rumors persist in Vienna, Prague and Munich that he will travel to England." A Hamburg paper on 15 December 1786 reported that Mozart planned to go to London in early 1787 by way of Paris.

The needs that would arise during an upcoming concert tour may help explain why Mozart returned to the composition of big orchestral pieces in late 1786. He entered the Piano Concerto No. 25 in C, K. 503, in his catalogue with a date of 4 December, while Symphony No. 38 in D, K. 504, was given a date of 6 December. The two works share an almost identical orchestration of flute (two in K. 504), pairs of oboes, bassoons, horns, trumpets, timpani, and the usual strings.

K. 503 closes the series of grand piano concertos from the mid-1780s. There are ways in which the concerto sounds somewhat retrospective. The breadth of the opening *Allegro maestoso* in common time projects majesty on a grand scale, apparent from the beginning with the dotted rhythms and four measures of tonic harmony spread throughout the orchestra from the flute's high G to the low C of the contrabass. In the fifth and sixth measures, the harmony changes to a ii^7 chord in third inversion, with the dissonant seventh C in the bass, a dissonance which must resolve downward like a suspension, which it does. The whole process is repeated beginning on V and leading back to I. A long-held and eventually resolved bass tone recalls the grandiose beginning of Handel's Coronation Anthem "Zadok the Priest" (1727) and other similar compositions intended to exalt majesty. The closest thing to the concerto's beginning in Mozart's own music is the chorus "Che del ciel, che degli Dei" near the end of *La clemenza di Tito* which deploys the same orchestral forces (plus an additional flute) with suspended bass tone and majestic dotted rhythms, full, slowly-changing chords and rumbling timpani. In this last scene, the stage opens up to reveal a vast and magnificent amphitheater filling with a great procession. The concerto's *Allegro maestoso* paints a similar picture of imperial pomp and splendor, worthy of Kapellmeister Fux and the old "Habsburger Prunkstil." It would have been an ideal choice with which to exalt majesty at the imperial coronation of Leopold II at Frankfurt in 1790, but Mozart did not choose to perform it on that occasion, perhaps because it was too demanding of the meager forces he had at hand.

Everything in the first movement of K. 503 is on as grand a scale as the beginning, and the whole is informed by a chain of suspensions as well as a "knocking" rhythm of three staccato eighth notes as upbeat to a downbeat, a figure often used by the composer (and later, famously, by Beethoven). A second theme, introduced by this rhythm, sounds first in tonic minor for eight measures before changing into tonic major. There are abundant lyric themes as well before the fanfare-like close of the first exposition. To prepare for the entrance of the soloist, the strings lower the dynamic to *piano* and intone a slower V - I cadence after a group of fast ones. The piano enters with an arabesque that leads to a quite bravura exhibition of rapid octaves and scales, all of which Mozart sketched first. Almost every idea in the movement appears in both minor and major guises, which leads to considerable length, 432 measures. At this moderate tempo, these take longer than the 523 measures of rapid triple meter making up the first movement of the work's predecessor in the genre, K. 491.

The *Andante* in F and in 3/4 time is an ingratiating respite from the heroics of the first movement without reaching its very high level in quality. Perhaps no slow movement could have done this. And yet, spoiled as we are by the superb quality of the composer's other concerto slow movements, it seems slightly disappointing for Mozart to revert here to the type of serenade music in which he so excelled during the previous decade at Salzburg. For all its elaborate decoration and fuss with dynamics, that the *Andante* is but a simple minuet is made very clear by the punctuating horns.

The finale is a gavotte in 2/4 time, marked *Allegretto*. It too looks back to a previous time, the refrain being none other than the Gavotte from the ballet music of *Idomeneo*.[43] Critics have been quite severe about this sonata-rondo, some finding it too long and repetitive for its material. The movement foregoes extensive development but not the rondo's two episodes, traditionally in vi and IV, as they are here, the only unusual feature being that the one follows directly upon the other. The refrain occurs four times, perhaps one too many for this old theme.

THE "PRAGUE" SYMPHONY

Symphony No. 38 in D, K. 504, begins with a slow introduction, *Adagio* in common time. This section is long and substantial, filled with strikingly original ideas that nourish the entire symphony, giving it both content and coloring. The "Linz" Symphony's slow introduction, compared above to the swinging open of a great gate, lacks the majesty and mystery of this grander portal.

---

[43] The tune goes still further back, being nearly identical to the gavotte theme that begins the finale of Christian Bach's Symphony in B♭, Op. 9 No. 1 (1772?), as pointed out by Elwood Derr in *Mozart's Concertos* (1996), p. 189.

To begin, a resounding D in unisons and octaves sounds throughout the orchestra from high to low, tutti *forte,* then *subito piano* on the same tones, followed by *forte* slides up to D from the fourth below, then the soft rise through the tonic triad up an octave, with rests after each eighth note giving the impression of tiptoeing. The alternation between loud and soft continues with the loud arrival of the whole orchestra at a non-tonic chord, unprepared, V_3^6/vi, stretched from high F# in the first flute, strongly reinforced in the middle range by both horns and trumpets, C# in the other winds, down to a unison A# low in the strings. It is a striking effect, being the first chord heard as such, leaving aside the lightly outlined tonic triad, and comes as a tonal surprise. The chord resolves as it must to vi, the strings imitate the process down a third arriving at IV, but *piano,* followed by the winds alone down another third to ii. The violins then try to introduce an approach to a tonic cadence but are waylaid in the process, first by ii$_3^6$, then by vi in a deceptive cadence, all this being soft.

What happens at this point is the second big surprise—the whole orchestra including the timpani (repeating its tonic D drum roll from the first measure) landing *forte* on the dominant of the subdominant, V_2^6/IV, with high F# in the winds, plus A, D in the brass (and timpani) and all the strings in unison on the very unstable tone of low C, which must resolve down to B. Once again, the F# at the top of the first flute's range, this time resolving up to G, calls particular attention to itself and sounds quite piercing at this elevation. It is as if Mozart wished to show how many roles F# could play besides being the third of tonic D. Beethoven took notice and explored the same range of possibilities in his "Pastoral" Sonata for Piano in D, Op. 28, and his Second Symphony, also in D and also featuring a long slow introduction, topics treated below in chapter 7.

There is another move toward a cadence on the tonic but it is undercut by being too short and *piano,* hardly an equal to the clamorous arrival on IV$_3^6$ that preceded it. When the tonic does arrive it is still another surprise, for the chord is not D, but d, the minor tonic, for one whole measure, the basses now enunciating the rise through the triad, while the timpani adds a new rhythm in eighth notes, one of them dotted. A measure of *piano* d follows as the violins again ascend the tonic triad, but timorously and bedecked with melodic turns against the pulsating sixteenth-note accompaniment of the seconds and the violas. There is only one sustaining low D below them, provided by the two bassoons. This detail predicts a similar one in another work, the sustaining of only the bass beneath the initial tutti *forte* chord that begins the overture to *Don Giovanni,* Mozart's first opera for Prague.

K. 504's slow introduction presages that of *Don Giovanni's* overture in several respects. The secondary dominant-seventh chord with the unstable tone in the bass while the timpani rumbles on tonic D is also present in the overture (m. 20), where it sounds no less menacing. The whole series of alternating soft and loud passages in the introduction to the overture copies the *Adagio* of K. 504, which proceeds in regular segments, one *forte*, the other *piano*, through the chords of ♭VI (B♭), then its dominant, F, after which the bass rises chromatically: F♯ G G♯ A, ever following the broadly spacious two-measure segments with soft-loud alternations. The overture's bass rises similarly: F G G♯ A B♭. In the symphony's more leisurely progress, arrival on V is not the big event that might have been expected. Questioning minor ninths make it sound troubled and hesitant. Tonic resolution is slow in coming, and the only tonic hinted at in 6/4 chords is d, not D, alternating with V, in a quickening exchange that fades away from *piano* with descending chromatic fourths (more portents of *Don Giovanni*!) to *pianissimo*, the tone F♯ being carefully avoided.

The *Allegro* begins with the first violins intoning a syncopated pedal D beneath which the other strings sing the theme in parallel thirds (Example 2.10).

EXAMPLE 2.10. *Mozart, Symphony No. 38 in D, K. 504, I*

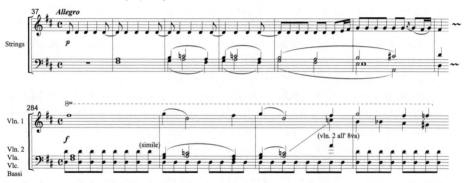

Syncopations were prominent in the introductory *Adagio*, but F♯, while prominent at its beginning was absent at its closing, and is thus welcome here. The theme itself sounds oddly tentative and timid about affirming the tonic, spending time veering off toward IV by way of C♮. So uncertain a theme as this ordinarily could not begin a movement by the mature Mozart. The majestic slow introduction made it possible to open the *Allegro* with a fragile theme seemingly unsure of its tonal bearings. There is a passage quite like it in the first movement of Christian Bach's Symphony in g (1769), a work Mozart might have known (Example 2.11).[44] The similarities as to rhythm and melody are striking, as is Bach's raising the fifth degree from F to F♯ (a device Mozart used on some later occurrences of his theme). Whether Mozart knew or consciously remembered Bach's passage matters not. He liked the idea however he arrived at it. Perhaps he wrote the

[44] The similarity is pointed out by Roger Fiske, *Music in Britain: The Eighteenth Century*, ed. H. Diack Johnstone and Roger Fiske (Oxford, 1990), p. 222.

EXAMPLE 2.11. *Johann Christian Bach, Symphony in g, Op. 6 No. 6, I*

massive slow introduction partly to give a proper setting to it. In any case, this little gem of a theme, modest though it is, returns many times in the *Allegro,* and not just in the normal place at the beginning of the reprise.

Contrapuntal devices enliven the rich store of ideas in the *Allegro,* nearly everything being inverted after its initial statement. Mozart worked out many of the contrapuntal possibilities of his material in careful and detailed sketches that have been preserved. The *Allegro* reaches a true climax in its coda, when the main theme emerges in full glory, no longer timid or hesitant, accompanied by the whole orchestra but shown here only in the string parts (Example 2.10, mm. 284 ff.). The first violins sing a counterpoint to the theme at the top of their range that sounds rather familiar, being one of the many reminiscences of *Figaro* in the score (see Example 2.5).

The *Andante* that follows is a blissful pastorale in G and in 6/8 time. Violins in sixths propose the main theme, which like that of the *Allegro* immediately heads toward IV over a drone-like pedal G in the bass. The three-measure phrase is connected to its repetition by a rising and falling sixteenth-note passage of one measure for the first violins. In m. 8, the strings announce a unison idea, staccato, that becomes a motto for the entire movement, somewhat like the recurrent little figure in the *Andante* of the String Quartet in C, K. 465. Like that motto, this one also rises in a sequence. It is treated as a canon between first violins and bass, a two-part counterpoint with suspended bass resolving by the measure, very like the bass-treble dialogue propelled by suspended dissonances with which the first Duettino begins Act I of *Figaro.* Harking back to the slow introduction is the substitution of d for D when the dominant becomes established, and the subsequent *forte* emphasis on a protracted B♭ chord makes the link stronger. The *Andante*'s second theme is nearly as simple as the first and reverts to parallel sixths between the violins over a drone bass. Adumbrated here is the 6/8 final section of the duet "Là ci darem la mano" in *Don Giovanni.* Generous to a fault, Mozart provides two melodious closing ideas after the second theme.

Like the *Allegro* and the final *Presto,* the *Andante* is a full sonata form, with both parts repeated. These three movements have so much to say and are so intricately wrought that perhaps Mozart thought a minuet would be superfluous. There are no indications in his score or his sketches to show he considered adding one, as he thought to do in Symphony No. 34 in C, K. 338, of 1780. This could be evidence that he was looking ahead to Paris or London, where the norm was symphonies in three movements without minuet.

The *Presto* finale in 2/4 time is pure comic opera, full of jests and surprises. It begins with an upbeat triadic figure reminiscent of the *duettino* "Aprite, presto aprite" for Susanna and Cherubino in Act II of *Figaro*. Here the buffo quality is emphasized by the clipped chords and many repeated notes, patter-like. These features will also enliven the finale of the next symphonic treasure, Symphony No. 39 in E♭, K. 543. At the same time, K. 504's effervescent finale theme sounds the same rising tonic triad idea heard often in the first movement. Instead of leading to V in the first four measures and back to I in the next four measures, as it will later do, the main theme of the *Presto* at first gets sidetracked into spending four measures on the supertonic (recall the prominence of ii in the slow introduction). Another hint of happenings in line with those in the *Adagio* are the emphatic arrivals of d, B♭, and its dominant, as well as the regular exchanges of loud and soft passages. There is a short coda in which the nearly ritual arrival of high D is reached by the first violins, but it is not the result of any "Mannheim crescendo" or other cliché, merely a rise through the tonic triad, like that in the understated rise at the beginning of the *Adagio*. The dynamic finally indicated is *forte*, not *fortissimo*, which occurs nowhere in this symphony. *Pianissimo* is rare too: Mozart calls for it at the end of the *Andante*, the last word of which consists of finally allowing the motto to come to rest on the tonic.

K. 504, composed midway between the premiere of *Figaro* and that of *Don Giovanni*, sounds as beholden to the former as it is prophetic of the latter. Its finale could have been written earlier, in the spring of 1786, according to paper studies. In any case, the whole symphony testifies to a single and unified creative act. The slow introduction already invokes the aura of mystery enveloping the stone guest in *Don Giovanni*. In this sense K. 504, if not written for Prague, perhaps not even performed there before *Don Giovanni*, is nevertheless "on the way to Prague."

Figaro in the Nostitz Theater

Opera in Italian thrived as a nearly continuous phenomenon at Prague during the eighteenth century, although it was rarely state-supported. Typically, local patrons invited and underwrote small, often itinerant Italian companies, such as the one led by Antonio Denzio during the second quarter of the century. Denzio wrote the libretto for the first known operatic treatment of the Don Juan legend, *La pravità castigata* (Prague, 1730).[45] At mid-century, the brothers Angelo and Pietro Mingotti were active in Prague, followed by Giuseppe Bustelli in the 1760s and 1770s. Bustelli alternated between Dresden and Prague, where he leased the

---

[45] Daniel E. Freeman, *The Opera Theater of Count Franz Anton von Sporck in Prague* (Stuyvesant, NY, 1992), p. 132.

theater in the Old Town (Kotce Theater). One of his singers, the bass Pasquale Bondini, succeeded him and continued to work for the Dresden court and in Prague. In 1781, Bondini gave operas in the intimate theater of old Count Thun's palace on the Small Side of Prague. In April 1783, his troupe opened in the splendid new theater built under the auspices of Count Franz Anton Nostitz, which held over a thousand spectators.

The Nostitz Theater, or National Theater, later the Tyl Theater, still stands in Prague, unlike the old Burgtheater in Vienna, which was demolished in the mid-nineteenth century. A handsome building in the neoclassical style (albeit much modified over the years), the National Theater was constricted as to width by streets on either side of it, but unlike many recent theaters it has a very deep stage and an understage space allowing for trap doors, so vital to the infernal plunge of Don Giovanni. A 1793 engraving shows an elevation and floor plan (Figure 2.4).

Bondini's company began performing *Figaro* in late 1786, just as Vienna was

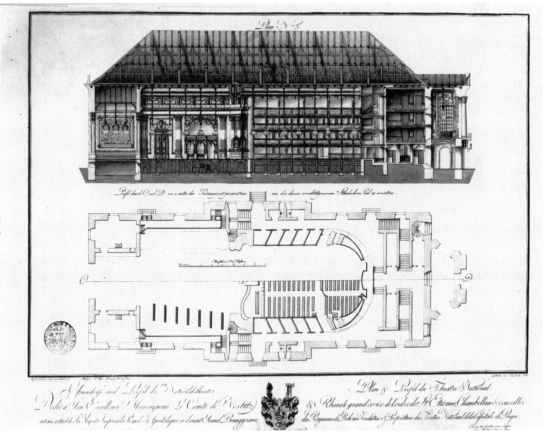

FIGURE 2.4. Floor Plan of Prague's Nostitz Theater, 1792/1793.

seeing the end of the opera's first production. For Prague the opera was modified somewhat, although not much by the standards of that time. It created a sensation, as this review in the *Praguer Oberposamtzeitung* dated 12 December 1786 shows.

> People say commonly here that no work has ever aroused such admiration as this Italian opera, *Le nozze di Figaro*, which has already been performed several times by the resident Bondini company of Italian virtuosi with the fullest applause, and in which Madame Bondini [Susanna] and Herr Ponziani [Figaro] playing the comic roles especially distinguished themselves. The music is by our famous Herr Mozart.

What is meant by calling the composer "our Mozart"? He had never been in Prague. Yet his music was well known there, especially his sacred music. Also, a visiting troupe of German players under the direction of Karl Wahr had performed *Die Entführung* in the Kotce Theater in 1783. Moreover, some of Mozart's staunchest patrons in Vienna belonged to the old Bohemian nobility and had residences in both cities. Closest to Mozart of course was the Thun-Hohenstein family, whose patriarch remained Count Johann Joseph Thun. He insisted that the Mozarts stay with him at Prague during January and February 1787, as he had at Linz in 1783.

The two singers singled out for praise in the review just quoted were each given the profits from one of the opera's performances, she on 14 December, he on 4 January. This favor may hint that the other singers were less admired. All the singers were quite young: Luigi Bassi, the Almaviva, was twenty. The review, while mentioning only two of the singers, went on to sing the praises of another aspect.

> Connoisseurs who have seen the opera in Vienna opine that the one here came out better, very probably because the wind instruments, of which the Bohemians are admitted to be the decided masters, have so much to do throughout the whole work. The duets of the trumpet and horn pleased especially. Our great Mozart must have heard about our orchestra. Rumor has it that he will come to see the opera, to which the well-staffed orchestra and its direction by Herr Strobach has contributed so much.

Bohemia could indeed boast superior wind players, and without doubt produced the best hornists. It should be added, in any comparison between the Prague and Vienna opera orchestras, that the latter had a large contingent of players from Bohemia. The reviewer goes astray in remarking the score's trumpet and horn duets, of which there are none. The horns are nearly omnipresent as usual. What the reviewer could have meant was the sensitive way Mozart treats the trumpets on the occasions when they support the horns. The only place where the trumpets emerge from their subsidiary sustaining role is the end of Act I, where they add a few military fanfares.

The roles most cut in Prague's first production of *Figaro* were those of Susanna, Basilio, and Cherubino. Caterina Bondini's vocal strengths were in the mezzo-soprano range (as the first Zerlina she received but few vocal flurries above it). Some high notes were eliminated in her part as Susanna by cutting the *duettino* with Marcellina in Act I and by giving some of her high notes in other ensembles to the Countess. Marcellina was compensated with a short solo composed by an unknown hand on a new text. A major loss was Cherubino's first aria "Non so più." This was apparently a matter of the text; the impudent boy's amatory desires for every female in the palace were too much for arch-Catholic Prague, or so a censor probably judged. A similar case is the toning down of insults to the priest Basilio, accurately called by Figaro a venal procurer. The part about Basilio carrying a letter to the Count in Act II Scene 9 was cut.[46]

The Mozarts left Vienna on 8 January 1787 and arrived in Prague three days later. The same journal that reported the rumor of his visit welcomed him warmly in a dispatch dated 12 January.

> Yesterday evening our great and beloved composer Herr Mozart arrived here from Vienna. We do not doubt that Signor Bondini will arrange in his honor a performance of *Figaro*, this prized work of his musical genius. Our widely famed orchestra will then be able to give new proofs of its art, and the refined inhabitants of Prague will surely wish to be there in force, although they have already heard the work often. We also wish to be able to admire the playing of Herr Mozart himself.

The wish was soon granted. On 18 January, Mozart gave a concert in the Nostitz Theater. A reviewer, probably the same one, reported briefly on the event in a dispatch dated 23 January, "On Friday last Herr Mozart gave a concert on the fortepiano in the National Theater here. Every expectation one could have formed of this great artist he completely fulfilled. Yesterday *Figaro*, this work of his genius, was performed under his own direction." A later source, of doubtful authenticity, claimed that Mozart improvised three fantasies in response to the enthusiastic reception, the last on "Non più andrai" by popular demand.[47]

Legend has it that this concert also included his latest symphony, K. 504,

---

[46] All these changes are discussed by Alan Tyson, "The 1786 Prague Version of Mozart's 'Le nozze di Figaro,' " *Music and Letters* 69 (1988): 321–33. John Rice kindly informed me by letter of 17 November 2006 that the singers of the Prague operatic troupe in 1786–87 were ten, of whom five were female, and that they are named in an almanac published annually in Milan, reprinted as *Un almanacco drammatico: L'Indice de' teatrali spettacoli, 1764–1823*, facsim., ed. Roberto Verti, for the Fondazione Rossini (Pesaro, 1996).

[47] Abert, *Mozart*, 2:342, n. 9, citing a later director of the theater, Johann Nepomuk Stiepanek.

later dubbed "the Prague," but the story rests on shaky ground. If the concert had employed full orchestra and included a new and very grand symphony, it is odd that the reviewer made no mention thereof. Not until Niemetschek's posthumous biography of Mozart (1798) is there a claim that he was represented by "the great symphony in D," elaborated in the second edition (1808) to include two symphonies, one in D and one in E♭. Mozart had written no symphony in E♭ since No. 26, K. 184, of 1773, and it hardly comes into question here. The superb Symphony in E♭, K. 543, composed in 1788, perhaps obtruded on the author's memory from other, later performances in Prague. As for the Symphony in D performed in January 1787 at Prague, if symphony there was, one piece of evidence suggests that it was not K. 504. Paper studies assign to late 1786 a first trumpet part that Mozart copied for one of his symphonies in D, presumably because this part had been lost and he was preparing a set of parts in anticipation of his tour. The trumpet part belonged not to the "Prague" Symphony but to the "Paris" Symphony.

Prague was one of the great European cities that Mozart had not visited before. On the day of his arrival, Thursday the 11th, he reached the Thun Palace in time for lunch, at which he was regaled with a concert by the Count's excellent private orchestra. That evening Count Joseph Emanuel Canal took him to one of the Thursday balls given by Baron Johann Bretfeld, where the band played numerous dances arranged from pieces in *Figaro*. In his letter to Gottfried Jacquin dated Prague 15 January 1787 Mozart described his reactions.

> I watched with greatest pleasure how everyone was hopping about with heartfelt delight to the music of my *Figaro*, which had been transformed into Contredanses and Deutscher; for here they talk of nothing but *Figaro*; nothing is played, blown, sung, or whistled but *Figaro*; no opera so well attended as *Figaro*; over and over again, it is *Figaro*, certainly a great honor for me.

An idea of how the opera's numbers were turned into dances can be gained from Jan Nepomuk Kaňka's keyboard miscellany, "Balli Tedeschi pro anno 1787. Le nozze di Figaro."[48]

There were musical diversions of another kind for the Mozarts on the following day, Friday the 12th. Count Thun had placed a "very good pianoforte" in the composer's rooms, Mozart reported in the same letter. "We played a little quartet among ourselves." The work could well have been his most recent Piano Quartet, K. 493, in E♭. The travelers accompanying the Mozarts to Prague included the court violinist Franz de Paula Hofer, who married Constanze's sister Josepha.

---

[48] Illustrated in Tomislav Volek and Jitřenka Pešková, *Mozart's Don Giovanni*, exhibition catalogue (Prague, 1987), item 30. Popular diffusion of another kind took place by substituting religious *contrafacta* for many pieces (see item 82 a–d).

They also sang the so-called "Bandel" Trio, K. 441, "Liebes Mandel, wo is's Bandel?" a piece with connections to Jacquin, the letter's recipient.

On Saturday the 13th they visited the Imperial Library and the General Theological Library. After staring at the treasures until their eyes "were almost ready to fall out," they were hungry for lunch at Count Canal's. That evening they attended the opera and it can easily be imagined what a stir was caused by Mozart's first appearance in the Nostitz Theater. "Thus we heard *Le gare generose* [by Paisiello]. Regarding the performance of this opera I can tell you nothing specific because during it I gabbed a lot; why I was gabbing, contrary to my habit can be left without telling—basta." What this may mean is that the composer was so pleased by the greetings of the many people who came to salute him in his box that he broke with his more silent habits in Vienna, where audiences were not quite so warmly enthusiastic about his music. It is certainly not a slap at Paisiello. We have seen how much Mozart treasured his music and him personally.

Further along in this charming and long letter to Jacquin, Mozart wrote that, as much as he has been honored in Prague, which he described as a very beautiful and pleasant city, he was homesick for Vienna and longing to be with the Jacquin family again. "When I reflect that after my return there will be only a short time to enjoy the pleasures of your valued company, after which I must forego this happiness for a long time and perhaps forever, then I realize fully the extent of the friendship and respect I have for your whole family." This can only mean that he was still planning a trip to London, and what is more, possibly remaining there. In a postscript Mozart adds, "On Wednesday next I shall see and hear *Figaro*, if I am not blind and deaf by then."

Mozart did attend a performance of *Figaro* on Wednesday the 17th, then on Friday he was back in the theater to direct a performance of the opera. On this same evening Maria Anna Crux, a violinist aged fourteen who perhaps accompanied the Mozarts to Prague, gave a concert in Count Thun's palace theater, a hall Zinzendorf described in 1791 as "petit, gentil et bien orné." Mozart, too, must surely have performed in it at some point. Since Thun had his own orchestra, it seems only natural that the composer would want to perform for the Count something from among the great store of piano concertos amassed since the Linz visit. It is tempting to believe that he brought with him some of these works in parts for the purpose—parts, moreover, that had been tested in performance, which the parts of the "Prague" Symphony may or may not have been.

Mozart mentioned in his letter to Jacquin that he would likely have to give a second concert in Prague and perhaps he did. In any case, he did not begin the return trip to Vienna until February 8th. Two days earlier is the date he assigned in his catalogue to a set of German dances for full orchestra, K. 509. According to Niemetschek's biography, Mozart came away from Prague with a commission from the Bondini company to write a new opera for the sum of 100 ducats.

There is no other source for this information, and the commission could have come later.

Leopold Mozart was traveling to Munich for the last time as the Mozart couple was returning to Vienna. Communication between father and son had reached a low point. According to Leopold's letter to Nannerl dated 1–2 March 1787, he wrote his son in Prague but received no answer. The only news he had from Vienna, he said, was brought by members of the English contingent who breezed through Salzburg on their way home in late February. They told him that Mozart had made a thousand gulden in Prague, that "little Leopold" had died, and that the composer still planned to travel to England "but before this his scholar [Attwood] must secure something concrete—the contract to write an opera, hold a subscription concert, etc. etc." He blamed the English party for giving Mozart the idea of traveling to London with them, and gave himself credit for fatherly warnings about the risks entailed by the whole venture. He also foresaw, correctly, that the next opera commission from the King's Theatre in the Haymarket would go to Stephen Storace.

Mozart began his last letter to his father, dated Vienna 4 April 1787, with an apology and expressions of annoyance that a letter he had sent had been lost or packed in a trunk by mistake. He had also written from Prague but this letter was perhaps lost, he explained, because one of Count Thun's servants had pocketed the postage money given him, an excuse that rings hollow.

Resettled in Vienna, Mozart continued to take lessons in the English language from a fellow Mason, Johann Georg Kronauer, in whose family album the composer made an entry in English dated 30 March 1787: "Patience and tranquility of mind contribute more tu [*sic*] cure our distempers as the whole art of Medicine." Tranquility hardly described Mozart's hectic professional life, but as a goal, it jibes with some parts of his last letter to Leopold, written after hearing that his father was gravely ill. At this news, after the excuses and some bantering at the expense of musicians they both knew, the letter turned serious.

> Death, closely considered, is the true goal of our life. Over the past few years I have formed such an acquaintance with this true and best friend of humankind that his image holds nothing terrifying for me anymore but instead much that is calming and consoling. And I thank my God for blessing me with this insight (you understand me) that makes it possible to perceive death as the key to our true happiness. I never go to bed without thinking that, even as young as I am, I might not see another day, and yet no one who knows me can say that I am moody or sad to be around, for which blessing I thank my Creator every day, and wish the same for all my fellow human beings.

"You understand me," which Mozart surrounds with repeat signs for emphasis, may refer to their mutual bonds and beliefs as Masons. Some ideas here are tinged with Masonic elements that will surface later in *Die Zauberflöte*. And as often pointed out, the thoughts on death are also related to Moses Mendelssohn's tract *Phaidon, or The Immortality of the Soul*, a copy of which was in Mozart's library. The image of death as a gentle friend strikes an ironic contrast with the two grisly deaths in the opera he was about to compose for Prague. The same contrast is present, moreover, in the two great works he wrote during that spring, the String Quintets in C and g, K. 515–516.

STRING QUINTETS

The Quintet in C, K. 515, dated 19 April 1787 in the composer's catalogue, was followed directly by the Quintet in g, K. 516, dated 16 May. Leopold Mozart died on 28 May. In happier times, at Salzburg in late 1773, Mozart had written his first string quintet with two violas, K. 174, in B♭, a light-hearted divertimento-like piece composed in emulation of some similar works by Michael Haydn and a considerable accomplishment for the seventeen-year-old composer.[49] The new quintets had little to do with the divertimento in form or spirit and belong among the greatest of all Mozart's works, worthy to stand beside *Figaro* or *Don Giovanni*, the latter looming ever closer on the horizon at this point.

K. 515 is dominated by its massive first movement, *Allegro* in common time, which begins with the cello climbing up the triad from its low C over two octaves against the throbbing eighth-note accompaniment of the inner parts. The first violin answers this three-measure segment with a two-measure rejoinder, completing the thought while softening the aura of the cello's imperious rise by a melodic turn that carries it up to high C, which then becomes a suspension resolving down to B in a melodic sigh as the accompaniment switches to dominant harmony. The five-measure process is then repeated (it would be very like Mozart to think of this "fiveness" as related to his chosen medium), but reversing the direction from V to I. The cello then begins again on low C, this time climbing a third higher. Its partner violin answers, following suit, singing its way up to high E, which becomes another and even more expressive suspension, fully harmonized this time and leading into a phrase that ends in a half cadence, taking only four measures. Mozart stretches it to five by adding a measure of silence, with uncanny effect. Now the violin rises, but in tonic minor, and the cello responds with sighs. The interplay of light and shade between major and minor on this large a scale suggests another first movement of Olympian stature, that of the "Jupiter" Symphony, K. 551.

The scale of K. 515's opening *Allegro* is so grand that even before the expected modulation to the dominant for the second group, there is an extensive excursion to the flat side, reaching a tonal realm as remote as D♭ and, moreover, a kind

---

[49] *Haydn, Mozart*, pp. 540–41, 563–64.

of closing theme back in the tonic (concerto-like) before the modulation to V begins. When it does begin, there is further use of the five-measure main dialogue for material, but compressed to four measures by means of overlapping. The second theme is a stream of eighth notes weaving in and about in a constricted range and mostly diatonic, sung first by the first violin but eventually shared by all. The development pursues the main material from the beginning of the movement in its overlapping compressed form, after which the weaving motif of the second theme engulfs the ensemble, rising from bottom to top position. As a dominant pedal predicting the arrival of the reprise sets in, Mozart layers long melodic sighs over one another in the inner parts, akin to those in the replacement love duet for *Idomeneo*, K. 489, of a year earlier. There is a coda to the movement following another measure of silence, and it is devoted to further use of the weaving motif, including stretto. The seconda parte of this huge movement is not repeated, unlike the prima parte.

Mozart took great care to make the succeeding movements of K. 515 worthy of so imposing an *Allegro*. The second is an *Andante* in F and in 3/4 time, beginning with the minuet rhythm indelibly associated with Susanna's emergence from the dressing closet in *Figaro*. High versus low duets, which played a large role in the *Allegro*, reappear in force in the *Menuetto Allegretto*. Noticeable also is its beginning with a *crescendo* leading to a *piano*, like the rising and falling scales at the return of the Commendatore in *Don Giovanni*. The final rondo, without tempo marking, is in 2/4 time and on an apparently simple theme, the complexity of the movement emerging from the inexhaustible store of riches Mozart expends on motivic play, which is as ingenious as it is moving, reminiscent somehow of the end of the "Coronation" Mass in C, K. 317. Totaling 539 measures, the finale becomes one of his longest written up to this date. At the last chord the cello returns to its low C, where this great voyage commenced.

Odysseys for cello cannot help but suggest Boccherini's string quintets with two cellos, the composer's own instrument being very much to the fore. There is no evidence to hand that Mozart knew them, although several were published in Vienna.[50] If nothing else, Boccherini's works expanded the cello's possibilities from its very lowest to highest ranges.

The dark twin of K. 515, K. 516 in g, is as full of pathos as anything Mozart composed, and as such, it too is a harbinger of *Don Giovanni*. Yet there is no mistaking that it shares with K. 515 the same generating idea, namely, a triadic rise answered by a sighing, minor-second descent (Example 2.12a). In this case, there is a whole series of minor seconds in descent. The second measure duplicates the rhythm and articulation of the first, and then the half-step motif is fragmented into little rises and falls before descending into the half-cadence after the trill. The whole theme takes eight measures and is sung by the high trio of voices,

[50] *Music in European Capitals*, p. 988, Table 9.5.

EXAMPLE 2.12 a, b, c. *Mozart, String Quintet in g, K. 516*

a. *I*

with first viola as bass. The theme is repeated by the low trio with the first viola playing the treble an octave lower, making it sound even sadder. This trio goes its own way by extending the theme and introducing a Neapolitan sixth chord where there was none before. An attempt to make the modulation to the relative major is foiled. Its place is taken by another theme in tonic g, a gentle descent at first but then a leap up to an accented minor ninth dissonance, resolved by the descent of a sixth back to the tonic (see mm. 30–33). On repetition, this theme does succeed in modulating to B♭. Most of the development explores the stepwise descending sixth after an accented dissonant tone so that it becomes as much of a main idea as mm. 1–4. In the reprise, Mozart rejects easing into tonic major for the second group, as Haydn preferred to do. The movement ends resigned to tonic minor, and with a long coda, which like its equivalent in K. 515 employs stretto.

A *Menuetto Allegretto* comes next and is also in g. The stepwise descent to the tonic with which it begins relates it audibly to the same in the *Allegro* (Example 2.12b). Only the Trio is in major. The slow movement, an *Adagio ma non troppo*

b. *II*

in common time, is in the key Mozart chose so often to pair with g, sensuous E♭ (Example 2.12c), all instruments playing with mutes. The beginning, small

c. *III*

descents by step in a rising pattern, projects a relative calm and serenity that is soon shattered (see mm. 19–24). A series of descents from an accented tone, familiar from the *Allegro*, sound like entreaties pleading for mercy. In *Don Giovanni*, these will actually become pleas for mercy.

Mozart initially considered writing a minor-mode finale for K. 516 and produced a fragment (K. 516a) that got no further than eight measures. He changed
his mind and replaced it with a major-mode finale with a theme that harks back
to the *Urgestalt* of triadic rise answered by conjunct descent, in this case diatonic,
not chromatic (Example 2.13, m. 39ff). To cushion the shock of the lively and
dance-like finale in G coming directly after the reveries and pleadings of the slow
movement, Mozart took a step very unusual for him. He prefaced the finale with a
long slow introduction, an *Adagio* in 3/4 time and in the key of g, which mediates
between E♭ and G. Some operatic cavatinas are not so long as this imploring cantilena of thirty-nine measures. It is truly a tragic song for the first violin, or better put, a duet, although it ends on the dominant so as to prepare the finale. The
triadic rise of the cello, pizzicato, is answered by the first violin with a conjunct
descent down six tones, the "dying fall" that has become so specific to this quintet and such an expression of suffering (Example 2.13). It is not only the dialogue

EXAMPLE 2.13. *Mozart, String Quintet in g, K. 516, IV*

between bass and treble that harks back to the beginning of the Quintet in C, K.
515, but also the throbbing eighth-note accompaniment of the inner voices.

The pains Mozart took with this *Adagio*'s smallest details may be seen in the
way he slurs the little rises of the second violin and first viola in m. 3. The slurred
leaps upward of the first violin over the barlines in mm. 4–5 and 9–10 have a

familiar ring, having made their impression back at the work's beginning (Example 2.12a, mm. 30–33). The *Adagio* acts as a kind of digest of the quintet's contents and then yields the floor to their final transformation.

Mozart's string quintets, like his quartets, were favorite choices to be performed at home by a close circle of friends. One friend so favored was Abbé Maximilian Stadler (not to be confused with the clarinetist Anton Stadler). When the Novellos visited Vienna in 1829 searching for memorabilia of the composer, they interviewed Abbé Stadler, aged eighty-one. Vincent Novello jotted in his diary, "Mozart and Haydn frequently played together with Stadler in Mozart's Quintettos; [he] particularly mentioned the 5th in D major [K. 593], singing the Bass part, the one in C major and still more that in G minor."[51]

INTERLUDE

Mozart's future as a composer for Vienna's two imperial theaters looked a little dimmer after the appearance of outstanding operas by a pair of relative newcomers during the second half of 1786. The German operatic troupe directed by Stephanie rallied its meager forces with the farce *Doktor und Apotheker* first performed on 11 July. Stephanie adapted the libretto from an obscure French play and the music was composed by Carl Ditters von Dittersdorf, who was not new to Vienna but this was his first musical comedy for the capital.[52] Zinzendorf called the libretto detestable but later admitted that the music was beautiful. The public loved it to the extent that *Der Doktor* quickly became the Singspiel most in demand. Johann Pezzl in his *Skizze von Wien* for 1787 called it the troupe's only outstanding production.[53]

The Italian company had a success of similar magnitude with the premiere on 17 November 1786 of *Una cosa rara, o sia Bellezza ed onestà*, on a libretto Da Ponte adapted from an old Spanish play for the Spanish composer Vicente Martín y Soler. Pezzl wrote of it "this is the opera that brought the city to near madness and at each performance three to four hundred people had to be turned away." Pezzl then mentioned two tunes from which there was no escape in the streets and taverns of the city. The first was from Paisiello's *Barbiere*.[54] The second was a sensational duet from Act II of *Una cosa rara* that Pezzl identified by quoting these lines:

Vieni tra i lacci miei	Come into my embrace
Stringimi o cara ben	Press me tightly my dear

[51] *A Mozart Pilgrimage, Being the Travel Diaries of Vincent and Mary Novello in the Year 1829*, ed. Nerina Medici and Rosemary Hughes (London, 1975), p. 170.

[52] *Haydn, Mozart*, pp. 449–52.

[53] Johann Pezzl, *Skizze von Wien: Ein Sittenbild aus der josefinischen Zeit*, ed. Gustav Gugitz and Anton Schlossar (Graz, 1923), part 3 (1787), section 76.

[54] *Music in European Capitals*, pp. 956–59, ex. 9.15.

>Anima mia tu sei   You are my soul
>Ti vo morir nel sen.   I wish to die on your breast.[55]

Zinzendorf confided that this piece upset him.

The duet in question, "Pace, caro mio sposo!" comes near the end of the opera, as the rustic lovers Lilla and Lubino, with the help of Queen Isabella, have overcome all challenges to their union. Sung by La Storace and Mandini, the piece begins tentatively with a little melody in 6/8 time with dotted rhythm, the tune being passed back and forth between the two, who complete each other's phrases. The lines Pezzl quotes occur as they first sing together in sweet consonances, the harmony being nothing more than a bland descending progression of 6/3 chords, so simple as to give all emphasis to the inflaming text. This does not quite explain why Zinzendorf responded the way he did. At the premiere on 17 November, he commented on the Spanish style of the costumes and some of the music, and pronounced the music charming and strongly applauded by the audience. On 4 December, he singled out this duet: "Le joli Duo de Mandini avec la Storace fut repeté, il est bien voluptueux. J'etois troublé en partant." Then on 17 January 1787 he wrote in his diary: "je trouvois que ce duo si tendre, si expressif de Mandini avec la Storace est bien dangereux pour de jeunes spectateurs et spectatrices, il faut avoir quelque experience pour le voir jouer avec sens froid [sang-froid?]." "To see it performed while retaining one's composure" has to do with the acting of this pair, and surely most to do with that of his favorite, the voluptuous Nancy Storace (Figure 2.5).

La Storace triumphed once again as the beautiful but honest Lilla in *Una cosa rara*. Zinzendorf's reactions to her physical charms were not new. He had

Figure 2.5. De Wilde's portrait of Nancy Storace, 1791.

---

[55] H. C. Robbins Landon, *Mozart and Vienna* (New York, 1991), translates large sections of Pezzl but fails to include the lines identifying these two pieces (p. 137).

been expressing them since her arrival in Vienna, as we have seen, and here is a reminder. At her performance of the female lead in Sarti's *Fra i due litiganti il terzo gode* on 28 May 1783 he confided to his diary: "La Storace joua comme un ange. Ses beaux yeux, son cou blanc, sa belle gorge, sa bouche fraich faisoient un charmant effet." Compare this with Pezzl's rather sour remarks on her departure after four years as reigning prima buffa in the Burgtheater.

> The singers at the opera are select and well recompensed. Mandini and Benucci are the most accomplished buffo actors one can see anywhere. The chief idol in this comic Pantheon was, up to the present, La Storace, of Italian descent, but born in London. She earned over 1000 ducats a year. To tell the truth she sang very well but her figure was not advantageous: a thick little head, without any feminine charm excepting a pair of large and nearly expressionless eyes. Storace returned just recently to England.

Her contract in Vienna ended with the beginning of Lent 1787. London beckoned. With her went an irreplaceable talent: a soprano who excelled at both singing and acting, truly a rare thing at the time. She became strongly allied with Mozart during the course of her stay in Vienna, and her loss multiplied the woes that dispirited the composer during the spring of 1787.

In his last letter to his father Mozart mentioned that his morbid thoughts "had been occasioned by the untimely death of my dearest and best friend, Count [August Clemens] von Hatzfeld. He had just turned thirty-one, my age. I do not grieve for him, but for myself and all those who knew him as well as I did." After Leopold's death Mozart had a serious illness and was treated by his childhood friend Dr. Sigmund Barisani, who himself died within a few months at age twenty-nine. On another level of loss, Mozart buried his pet starling and wrote the bird's epitaph, a poem that is both comic and at the same time touchingly symbolic of other griefs.

During the summer of 1787, as *Don Giovanni* was germinating in the minds of its poet and composer, Mozart wrote two delectable pieces of chamber music that scale the gamut from ridiculous to sublime, "Ein musikalischer Spass," K. 522, and "Eine kleine Nachtmusik," K. 525. In their disparity, even these two light works seem to presage the jostling between the serious and the ludicrous in *Don Giovanni*. K. 522, for two horns, two violins, viola, and bass, was entered in Mozart's catalogue with a date of 14 June, although paper studies suggest it was begun earlier and finished a few months later. K. 525 entered the catalogue with a date of 10 August, its scoring described as "2 Violini, Viola e Bassi," the last interpreted to mean cello and contrabass, to agree with the allotment of the bass to "violoncello e contrabasso" in Mozart's autograph score.

In K. 522, Mozart's verbal sarcasm about incompetent composers and performers, meant to entertain Leopold in that last letter, takes musical shape as a demonstration of how *not* to compose or perform. The work's very incipit suffices to predict the clumsiness of the whole (Example 2.14). It gets off to an

EXAMPLE 2.14. *Mozart,* Ein musikalischer Spass, *K. 522, I, II, IV*

unpromising start, rising timidly before falling back to where it began, a repeat of the first measure. The Menuetto and fugue theme in the finale are equally hapless in their struggle against tonal gravity. Melody is not the only problem. The *Allegro* begins with an anapest that starts on the downbeat, rather than the upbeat (like a gavotte but on the wrong part of the measure). Kirnberger gave this clumsily accented rhythm to a piece entitled "Cossack" in a collection of characteristic dances.[56] Mozart used it elsewhere most memorably to begin and dominate his overture to *Die Entführung* (Europeans lumped Turks and Cossacks together as being both crude and exotic barbarians). Another Mozart melody that skirts the banal by using this rhythm is the famous Rondo in D, K. 382, replacing the original finale of Piano Concerto No. 5, K. 175, wildly popular with Viennese audiences, probably on account of its oft-returning theme. The fugue theme of K. 522's finale parodies that of a fugue that Thomas Attwood wrote for Mozart, none too skillfully, the previous summer.

The earliest edition of K. 522, brought out by Johann André, was illustrated by a hilarious title vignette. An unknown artist shows the six players required by the work, and identifies it by an incipit lying on the table. Two violinists labor over their parts wearing cocked hats, one of them askew, while the violist is conspicuously bareheaded and bald. The bassist makes a face while playing his part. Two hornists look impressive, one very tall, the other very short with his hand in the bell of his instrument (some hand stopping of this kind is required by certain tones in the score). It takes skilled musicians, trained in the art of composition, to plumb all the humor of this elaborate musical joke.[57]

K. 525, "Eine kleine Nachtmusik," is a serenade in G that, in its original form, followed the typical divertimento pattern of two minuets surrounding a slow movement, with two fast outer movements. The first minuet was removed from

---

[56] Johann Philipp Kirnberger, *Recueil d'airs de danse caractéristiques* (ca. 1777), ed. Ulrich Mahlert as *Airs de danse für ein Tasterinstrument* (Wiesbaden, 1995), No. XXVI, p. 32.

[57] For a sophisticated discussion of the work's subtleties see Küster, *Mozart* (1996), ch. 10.

the autograph at some point, perhaps a gift from the composer to the serenade's honoree, whose identity has yet to be discovered. The middle movement in C and in cut time, entitled *Romance. Andante,* is perhaps the most famous of Mozart's several contributions to the genre of the Romance. It has a blithe and simple gavotte-like theme, and like most of the others is in rondo form. Instrumental Romances of this sort probably originated in the symphonies of Gossec and some of his French contemporaries.[58] As simple as this movement is, it does not end before providing a stellar example of how the composer often found some new turn of phrase to enhance the melody at its last breath. The falling sixth by leap and recovery by rising half step that permeates the tonic minor episode of the Romance turns up again in the theme of the rondo finale. This kind of cyclic thinking is similar, on a smaller scale, to that in the two great string quintets of the previous spring.

Don Giovanni

As summer 1787 ended, the imperial court was preparing to celebrate the nuptials of Emperor Joseph's niece Maria Teresa, eldest daughter of Grand Duke Leopold of Tuscany, who was wed by proxy in Florence to Prince Anthony of Saxony. In the old days of her grandmother, Empress Maria Theresa, nothing less than a formal wedding opera would have been deemed fitting for such an occasion. Joseph wanted no extra expenses and decided that the operas already being prepared for the fall season would have to suffice. In Vienna this meant that Maria Teresa would be welcomed at a performance in her honor of the new opera, *L'arbore di Diana* by Da Ponte and Martín y Soler. Since the opera concerns the seduction of the chaste goddess and her nymphs, it is difficult to imagine a less appropriate opera for the virgin princess—unless it was what was being prepared in Prague, through which she was to pass on her way to Dresden.

An incomplete text of *Don Giovanni* reached the Viennese censors at some time before Maria Teresa was due to arrive in Prague. Its deletions betray the fears of the opera's creators that the work was not suitable to celebrate the young princess on her marital progress. The whole second half of the first act, culminating in the ballroom scene in Giovanni's palace and the attempted rape of Zerlina is missing. Maria Teresa and her brother Francis arrived in Prague on schedule by 14 October, but *Don Giovanni* was not ready, or was said not to be ready for performance. A message from on high in Vienna ordered in its stead a repeat performance of *Figaro,* hardly a model of chaste behavior either, but not so flagrant as *Don Giovanni.* Zinzendorf noted in his diary entry for 19 October

---

[58] *Music in European Capitals*, p. 656.

the inappropriateness of *Diana*, saying, "Il etoit peu decent pour feter une jeune epouse. A Prague on lui a donné *le Nozze di Figaro* aussi peu decent."

Mozart and his wife left Vienna for Prague on the first of October, leaving behind their lone surviving child, Carl Thomas, aged three. They arrived on 4 October and stayed at the Three Lions Inn. Old Count Thun was in the last year of his life and perhaps too infirm to receive any further guests. Da Ponte arrived in Prague on 8 October and went about coaching the singers in their stage-action; in his memoirs he wrote, "I spent eight days there directing the singers who were to create the opera." Then, before the premiere, he was ordered back to Vienna by a fiery letter from Salieri, who maintained that the poet was needed to work on the production of Salieri's *Axur, re d'Ormus*. While in Prague, Da Ponte was still revising the text of *Don Giovanni*, as was Mozart.

Mozart described preparations for the opera's first performance to his close friend Jacquin in a letter dated Prague, 15 October 1787.

> You presumably believe that my opera has been performed by now, in which regard you would be a little mistaken. First, the stage personnel here is not quite so capable as in Vienna when it comes to learning such an opera in so short a time. Second, I found on my arrival here so few preparations and arrangements had been made that it would have been simply impossible to give the work by the 14th, yesterday. So instead, they performed my *Figaro,* the theater being fully illuminated and I myself directing . . . *Don Giovanni* is now scheduled for the 24th.

One authority expressed doubts as to whether the poet and composer ever intended to have the new opera performed as the gala event, citing the partial text submitted to the censor as evidence of their fears about its reception.[59]

Mozart resumed writing the same letter to Jacquin on 21 October and explained the cause of further delay.

> *Don Giovanni* had been set for the 24th, but one of the female singers who was taken ill has caused another postponement. Since the company is small the impresario must live ever in apprehension and spare his people as much as possible lest he be plunged into some unforeseeable contretemps and put in the most critical of all critical positions, that of not being able to give any show at all! Therefore things go rather slowly here, and the singers, out of laziness, refuse to rehearse on days when they perform, and the director, out of fear and anxiety, does not hold them to it.

The Italian company in Vienna was larger than Bondini's troupe so that in many cases operas could be double cast. Under the watchful eyes of Joseph II and Count Rosenberg, the singers in Vienna had to earn their salaries or face dismissal.

---

[59] Einstein, *Mozart*, p. 442.

In a third installment of his letter, dated 25 October, Mozart wrote, "the opera will be performed for the first time on Monday, the 29th." This prediction proved accurate. He entered the work in his catalogue with a date of 28 October: "Il dissoluto punito, o, il Don Giovanni, opera Buffa in 2 Atti. Pezzi di musica 24." A dispatch about the premiere appeared in the local paper dated 1 November.

> Monday the 29th the Italian opera company gave the fervently awaited opera of master Mozart, "Don Giovani [*sic*] oder das steinerne Gastmahl." Connoisseurs and musicians both say that never has its like been performed at Prague. Herr Mozart himself directed, and as he stepped into the orchestra, just as when he left it, three cheers were raised. The opera is moreover extremely difficult and everyone admired and wondered at its fine performance after so short a period of preparation. All, stage and orchestra alike, did their utmost to reward Mozart with a good execution. There were also many costs involved, and many choruses and decors required, all of which Herr Guardasoni magnificently provided. The unusual crowds of spectators testify to the general approval of the opera.

On Friday, 4 November, the opera was already receiving its fourth performance.

Da Ponte took credit for suggesting the Don Juan subject to Mozart in his memoirs, first published in Italian at New York (1823–27). He contradicted himself in an earlier partial memoir, translated from Italian into English.[60] In this document he wrote that the Prague management, represented by Bondini's partner Domenico Guardasoni, offered Mozart the *Convitato di Pietro* by Giovanni Bertati, set to music by Giuseppe Gazzaniga for the San Moisè theater in Venice during the Carnival of 1787. Mozart turned it down, says Da Ponte: "Why did Mozart refuse to set to music the *Don Giovanni* (of evil memory) by Bertati, and offered to him by one Guardasoni . . . manager of the Italian theater at Prague?" Da Ponte answers his question with another: "Why did he insist upon having a book written by Da Ponte on the same subject, *and not by any other author?*" (his italics). This prepares the way for Da Ponte to recite at length his superior talents as a librettist. What he does not say here or elsewhere is that he made good use of Bertati's disdained libretto, upon which the first and last quarter of his own are based.

The new libretto gives some indications of having been originally conceived in four acts, like *Figaro*. The clearest hint of this is the finale-like construction of the text and music of the Sextet, No. 19, which gives the appearance of having been conceived as an ending to the original Act III. While this seam is still showing in the two-act version eventually adopted, a similar one between an original first and second act is not obvious. The dramatic pacing of *Don Giovanni* is uncommonly

---

[60] Lorenzo da Ponte, *An Extract from the Life of Lorenzo da Ponte* (New York, 1819), pp. 17–18. See Heartz, *Mozart's Operas* (1990), pp. 158–59. For an astute summary of the relationship between Da Ponte's text and its predecessors see Michel Noiray, "Don Giovanni," in *The Cambridge Mozart Encyclopedia*, ed. Cliff Eisen and Simon P. Keefe (Cambridge, 2006), pp. 138–51.

swift, compared even with *Figaro*. Arranging the whole array of disparate incidents in two long acts has the effect of making it seem even swifter. As in *Figaro*, the action takes place in twenty-four hours, according to the ideals of French classical drama. At least one of the three "unities" is met, that of time. That of place goes by the board. The new opera requires many sets corresponding to different locales, and some quick changes as well. It is possible to claim a unity of action, one death at the beginning leading ineluctably to another at the end.

Bertati's *Il convitato di pietra*, a short one-act opera in two parts, required a cast of ten. Da Ponte eliminated a third noble lady, Donna Ximena, and combined Giovanni's two servants in the character of Leporello. He also made it possible for one baritone to double as Masetto (Bertati's Biagio) and Il Commendatore. This brought the number of singers down to seven, a more manageable one for the limited forces of the Prague company. Gazzaniga had made Giovanni a tenor, a part sung by Antonio Baglioni (unless he sang Ottavio), and who was likely the conduit by which the Venetian libretto quickly reached Prague.

Gazzaniga's score offered a general model in the sense that he assigned the same key (e♭ minor!) to the death of the Commendatore and to his return as a statue at the end. Perhaps this framework was so obvious that any composer would have followed the same plan. In any case, Mozart did so, choosing the key of d for both death scenes, then transferring some of this lugubrious, terrifying music back to the beginning of the overture as a slow introduction. In tonal terms, this constitutes the master narrative. The same is true of it in dramatic terms.

The Overture, instead of ending in D, makes a transition to F for the arrival of Leporello, who sings his labor complaint in this key to begin the *Introduzione*. Then follows quickly the struggle between Anna and Giovanni in B♭, the intervention of her father, the Commendatore, his duel with Giovanni and his death scene, which moves eerily from d to f. The duet of revenge in d for Anna and Ottavio brings the first scene and the *Introduzione* to a close. Recall that Mozart considered the mediant (iii) as closely related to I but not so closely as the submediant (vi), as he explained in describing Osmin's No. 2 in *Die Entführung* (there the key of a was mediant to tonic F). Here, he countenances moves from D (overture) to F, and d to f.

At the other end of the opera, Mozart signals that retribution is nigh by using the same tonal complex involving D, d, F, and B♭. The second finale begins joyously in D, *Allegro vivace* in common time followed by *Tafelmusik* for winds to enliven Giovanni's last supper, music of the kind Mozart praised for accompanying the repasts in Count Thun's palace. The band on stage plays three tunes cleverly chosen for their original texts that either cite a Giovanni by name or say the end is near.[61] To this point the composer placed them in the keys of D, F, and B♭,

[61] Heartz, *Mozart's Operas*, pp. 169–70.

the last being Prague's favorite *Figaro* tune, "Non più andrai," following popular tunes from Martín y Soler's *Una cosa rara* and Sarti's *Fra i due litiganti*. The key of B♭ lingers as Donna Elvira enters and makes a last attempt to save Giovanni from damnation. Leporello, who began the opera in F, now trembles in this key at the approach of the statue. Tonally, there is a sense of backing out of the opera by the way we got into it. (See Table 2.2).

TABLE 2.2. Tonalities at the Beginning and End of *Don Giovanni*

Overture	Leporello	Anna & Giovanni	Act I Introduzione Commendatore	His death	Anna & Don Ottavio
d - D	F	B♭	d	f	d

Giovanni: "Già la mensa è preparata"	Act II Finale Tafelmusik			Elvira	Leporello	Commendatore	Final Scene
	No. 1	No. 2	No. 3				
D	D	F	B♭	B♭	F	d - D	G D

The statue arrives to the same diminished-seventh chord of horror that accompanied the wounding of the Commendatore in the *Introduzione*. There, resolution was jarringly deferred from the expected key of d to the dominant of the remote key of f, to uncanny effect. Here there is no deferral. The diminished chord, tutti *fortissimi* and reinforced by the sepulchral trombones as well as a roll on the timpani, sounds like a clap of thunder, a premonition of doom.[62] At length, as the infernal chorus renders its sentence, Giovanni is pulled down to hell in flames. His last "Ah!" brings the change to D major. Like Gluck at the end of his ballet *Don Juan* (1761), Mozart sends the rake below with a *tierce de Picardie*.

The opera could have ended here and perhaps it did at some stage of Mozart's thinking. It is a possible ending, one he contemplated for its revival at Vienna in May 1788. In Prague, he appended a kind of *Licenza*, giving us a parting visit with the Don's victims, who sing the moral. In tonal terms, this ending, with all its emphasis on the key of G, is like a vast plagal cadence, putting to rest most but not all of the tensions created by the terrors endured.

Mozart returned often in the opera to a few grief-laden melodic contours that intensify its pathos and give more force to its main poetic idea. The most important of these is the age-old symbol of death, the chromatic descent of a fourth (or more), an item his audience knew, even if they were not regulars at the opera house, from the use this figure traditionally saw in the Credo of the

---

[62] The two resolutions in score are juxtaposed as ex. 9.1 in Heartz, *Mozart's Operas*, p. 171.

Mass at the words "Passus et sepultus est." The figure is present from the first tones of the overture and sounded in the bass, to which Mozart calls attention by prolonging its first two tones, D - C♯, beyond the chords sounding above. It is also present in the work's very last tones, after the singers have stopped, in the little peroration softly intoned by the strings. The second violins have the chromatic descent, against which the firsts play a counterpoint, the salient features of which are the rising seconds emphasized by trills (Example 2.15). Winds softly

EXAMPLE 2.15. *Mozart,* Don Giovanni, *Act II, Finale*

join in the chromatic descent, then the final IV - V - I cadence, tutti *forte,* brings down the curtain. The soft passage sounds a distant reminder of the chromatic descents at the death of the Commendatore and of Giovanni himself. In a word, it summarizes the whole drama.

Mozart's orchestra had become so deft a commentator on the action by the time of this opera that he could bring the symbolic chromatic descent to bear as an aside in the most unlikely places. For example, in the seduction duet "Là ci darem la mano" sung by Giovanni and Zerlina, the violins comment with a descending chromatic line after the voices combine to sing "un innocente amor," as if to warn "far from innocent!" At the same moment, the second violins play a counterpoint to the firsts that is essentially the same as between the violins in Example 2.15. Even in the sprightliest of pieces, the chromatic figure can intrude. There is none sprightlier than the aria "Fin ch'an dal vino," which Giovanni sings to Leporello as an order to herd the peasants to his madcap ball. He intones the line "and also bring any girl you may find in the public square" to a chromatic descent of a fourth, but it is the reinforcement of his line two octaves above by the first violins and the flute that we are likely to notice, especially since the composer puts a long slur over it, the first in the piece, as if the orchestra were warning Giovanni. It all sounds so jolly, except that the orchestra seems to be saying repeatedly, "yes, but in fact deadly."

Another melodic idea that Mozart repeats is more specific to this opera. Donna Anna bursts out with a triadic figure to begin the duet of revenge in the Introduzione (Example 2.16a). Distraught at the sight of her father's bloody corpse, as any daughter would be, she berates her fiancé, Ottavio, scarcely recognizing him in her grief: "Flee, cruel man, flee! Let me also die here." To emphasize her distracted state Mozart distorted the melodic line by a protracted first

EXAMPLE 2.16 a, b, c. *Mozart,* Don Giovanni

a. *Act I, No. 2, Duetto*

tone and by strong melodic or agogic accents on the second half of the measure. In the finale of Act I, when Elvira joins Anna and Ottavio in the very palace of the villainous seducer-slayer, Mozart created an aura of unease, perhaps fear, by having Elvira sing Anna's "Fuggi, crudele" motif, but straightened out rhythmically, while urging her friends to have courage (Example 2.16b).

b. *Act I, scene 19, Finale*

The most expressive occurrence of this motif comes in the Sextet of Act II. Elvira sings first of her fears in the dark courtyard (buio loco) to which she has been brought by Leporello masquerading as Giovanni. The piece begins as an *Andante* in E♭ and in cut time. Leporello sings next, lowering the tone from serious to comic by his patter as he seeks to escape and almost does (cadence, but weak, on B♭), when a door opens and there stand Anna and Ottavio in mourning clothes. This is accomplished musically by an augmented-sixth chord on B♭ that resolves as if by miracle to the opera's keynote of D. Prominent trumpets and a timpani roll underscore the couple's high estate. Ottavio begs Anna to dry her tears. His plea would be the most expressive music in the opera were it not topped by Anna's reply, begun over another timpani roll and moving in mode from D to d (Example 2.16c). This time, Mozart distorts the melodic idea by lingering not on the initial tone but the high note, F♮, reinforcing the change from major to minor.

c. *Act II, No. 19, Sestetto*

Anna's words sung to Ottavio are nearly as beautiful as her music: "Lascia alla mia pena questo picciolo ristoro, Sola morte, o mio tesoro, il mio pianto può finir" (To my pain allow me this little relief, Only death, oh my treasure, can end my tears). In the course of her solo, Mozart lowers the tonality from the dark realm of d to the even darker one a whole tone lower, to c minor (as he did with the suffering Electra in the first act of *Idomeneo*). Mozart ends her solo with a descending line, largely chromatic, and arriving via a Neapolitan-sixth harmony at the new tonic (Example 2.16c, mm. 57–61). It is Anna's death wish translated to the highest spheres of poetry, and nothing in all of Mozart sounds more tragic. In the slow movement of Schubert's great String Quintet in C with two cellos, written in the last months of his short life, the composer keeps returning to a "dying fall" phrase with precadential Neapolitan chord that is reminiscent of Anna's lament. Immediately following Anna's last tone, the violins begin a descending chromatic ostinato in dotted rhythm and this descent becomes the prevailing idea to the end of the piece. Thus Mozart brings together in close proximity two of the opera's main melodic motifs, Anna's triadic one and the chromatic descent associated with death.

There is only one piece other than the great sextet of Act II that contains so much of the opera *in nuce*: the overture, written out last, as usual. Transporting the music for the return of the Commendatore as a statue provided the overture with its superb *Andante* worthy of introducing a grand symphony. There was precedent in the slow introduction to the "Prague" Symphony, which seems to breathe the same atmosphere. Some details in the overture reflect moments in the opera other than the Commendatore's return. Mention has been made of the chromatic descent of the bass at the overture's beginning. Above the bass, the treble begins with the leap from high D down to A that comes from the beginning of the second finale, where it is scored similarly for first violins in a triple-stopped D and doubled by flutes. The *Andante* of the overture, after many measures of *crescendo* to *piano*, ends with a climactic Neapolitan chord followed by its dominant, the augmented-sixth chord erected on B♭, mentioned above as occurring in the great sextet of Act II. It occurs earlier, in No. 2, the duet of revenge, with the same resolution to a tonic chord in six-four position and with the same surprise of a *piano* marking, a very Mozartian deception, not in harmony but in dynamics (Example 2.17).

EXAMPLE 2.17. *Mozart,* Don Giovanni, *Act I, No. 2, Duetto*

The *Molto Allegro* section of the overture also dips into the Duet No. 2 for material. Just before Ottavio initially swears vengeance ("Lo giuro"), a moment of recitative interrupts the piece as the basses plunge downward in a strongly articulated *forte*, against the violins rising in an agitated tremolo (Example 2.18a).

Example 2.18 a, b. *Mozart*, Don Giovanni

a. *Act I, No. 2, Duetto*

b. *Act II, No. 20, Aria*

Peremptory tone aside, this descent through a diminished seventh sounds akin to the many pleading descents in the Quintet in g, K. 516 (see Example 2.12), and prefigures an actual plea for mercy sung by Leporello to begin his Aria No. 20 (Example 2.18b). Speeded up and shortened to only five tones, this bass motif provided the overture with what passes for a second theme; it is answered by the soft and cynical response of the violins, which combines the repeated tones of buffo patter with mocking little grace notes (similar to those when Giovanni taunts Masetto in the first finale at "La bella tua Zerlina"). Out of the descending bass motif, Mozart spins most of the overture's powerful development section, where the message is certainly that of conflict. (Recall that the overture to *Figaro* did not even have a development section). Thus the fast part of the overture is woven of both serious and comic material, with a large admixture of the festive, similar to the fanfare-like sounds that enliven the supper scene, which begins the second finale.

The first theme of the overture's *Molto Allegro* is saved for last here because it is so important in determining the coloration of the whole opera. Mozart derived it from Ottavio's plea to Anna in the great sextet of Act II, at the words "Pena avrà de' tuoi martir" (He [the Commendatore] would be pained at your suffering) (Example 2.19). By this choice, Mozart may have wanted to emphasize

Example 2.19. *Mozart*, Don Giovanni, *No. 19, Sestetto*

how important Ottavio is to the drama and particularly to the subject of losing a father. His strongest words as he tries to console her initially in No. 2 are "Hai sposo e padre in me!" (In me you have both father and betrothed!).

Elsewhere in the opera, Mozart and Da Ponte had taken steps that weakened Ottavio. Anna's narration of the attack on her comes after she recognized Giovanni by his voice and leads up to her heroic aria "Or sai chi l'onore rapir a me volse." It is an impassioned obbligato recitative of unforgettable power and it is almost all Anna, with a few meek comments from Ottavio. In Bertati, Duke Ottavio, at the point where Anna says she repulsed the intruder, has a strong speech of several lines berating the villain and saying he will exact a punishment that fits the crime. Da Ponte's Ottavio utters a feeble response here "Ohimè! Respiro!" (Alas! I breathe again!), and that is all. Mozart may have insisted on pressing ahead with Anna's narration, in which the strings work themselves up to what sound like shrieks of distress. He took such care about everything in this scene that he even moved Ottavio's bland interjection "Stelle! seguite" (Heavens! continue) ahead one line in Da Ponte's text.

Bertati had placed Anna's narration in the opening scenes directly after the return of Anna with Ottavio, and it led to a full-fledged aria for the latter. Transferring the narration to later in the act may account for some of Ottavio's deflation by Da Ponte and Mozart but not all. It seems that they intended to portray him as a figure weaker than Bertati's and consequently to raise a doubt in our minds whether Anna truly regards him as "her treasure." At Prague, Ottavio had to wait until after the sextet in Act II to sing an aria. One of the glories of the score, it is the vocally daunting "Il mio tesoro," No. 21. At the revival in Vienna there was a tenor less skilled than Baglioni so No. 21 was apparently scrapped for the easier "Dalla sua pace," inserted after Anna's "Or sai chi l'onore."

By beginning the fast part of the overture with the rising chromatic line to which Ottavio tries to console Anna in No. 19, Mozart may have attempted to somehow compensate this rather forlorn figure. Using Ottavio's music in this way certainly adds to the richness of the overture. In his previous master operas, *Idomeneo, Die Entführung,* and *Figaro,* Mozart had made each overture as individual as the worlds of action and of feeling they introduced. *Don Giovanni's* overture is all that and more, for in it the composer presents a guide as to how he wants us to interpret the strands of comedy and tragedy that collide and overlap throughout the opera. Take the serious parts very seriously, says this guide. Later, he would upbraid an insensitive individual who laughed throughout the solemn scenes in *Die Zauberflöte.*

The success of his opera in Prague, in spite of all its problems and the troupe's limitations, encouraged Mozart, at least for a time. His letter to Jacquin, dated Prague 4 November 1787, testifies to this.

My opera *Don Giovanni* was staged on 29 October with the warmest applause. Yesterday it was performed for a fourth time, and for my own benefit. I think I shall leave here on the 12th or 13th. After I return I shall bring you the aria [?] right away so that you can sing it. I so wished that my good friends, particularly Bridi[63] and you could

---

[63] Giuseppe Antonio Bridi sang the role of Idomeneo at Prince Auersperg's private theater on 13 March

be here if only one evening to share in my pleasure! Perhaps the opera may yet be performed in Vienna? I wish it would be. They are doing everything here to persuade me to stay a few months and write another opera but I cannot accept their offer no matter how flattering it is.

Don Giovanni was performed in the Burgtheater the following spring during the season that began after Easter, for which production the poet and composer made several changes and additions.

The Carnival season of 1787–88 in the Burgtheater was dominated by Salieri's festival opera *Axur re d'Ormus* on a libretto that Da Ponte adapted freely from the composer's *Tarare* (Paris, 1786) on a libretto by Beaumarchais.[64] *Axur* had its premiere on 8 January 1787 in celebration of the wedding between Archduke Francis and Elisabeth of Württemberg. There were several performances before Lent arrived, and the opera remained in repertory for many seasons thereafter. Emperor Joseph was particularly pleased with the work. On 20 February 1788, he raised Salieri to the post of Hofkapellmeister. *Axur*'s initial success surely had a lot to do with the singing and acting of two public favorites: Benucci in the title role of the new king; and as Atar, his disgraced predecessor, the superb tenor Vincenzo Calvesi. The most successful opera new to the Kärntnerthor Theater during Carnival was another tale of royal misfortune, the opéra comique *Richard Cœur-de-lion* by Sedaine and Grétry, transformed into a Singspiel by Stephanie.

The success of *Don Giovanni* and *Figaro* in Prague may have had something to do with Mozart's appointment as Court Chamber Composer with an annual salary of 800 gulden by imperial decree of 7 December 1787. One reason for it was to keep him from seeking employment elsewhere.[65] According to Da Ponte's memoirs, it was Emperor Joseph who asked that *Don Giovanni* be staged in Vienna, rather dubious information, but we can accept fully Da Ponte's blunt description of its reception: "It did not please."

The first performance took place on 7 May 1788. Francesco Albertarelli sang Giovanni; Aloysia Lange, Anna; Francesco Morella, Ottavio; and Catarina Cav-

---

1786. Bridi's musical strengths were lauded by Johann Ferdinand, Ritter von Schönfeld, *Jahrbuch der Tonkunst Wien und Prag 1796*, translated in part by Kathrine Talbot as "A Yearbook of the Music of Vienna and Prague, 1796," in *Haydn and His World,* ed. Elaine Sisman (Princeton, 1997), pp. 289–320; 294. Schönfeld also praises Countess von Hatzfeld (pp. 300–301) and Baroness von Pufendorf (p. 310), who both sang with Bridi in the 1786 *Idomeneo*.

[64] A subject given expert treatment by John Rice, *Antonio Salieri,* pp. 385–420.

[65] Dorothea Link, "Mozart's appointment to the Viennese court," in *Words about Mozart: Essays in Honour of Stanley Sadie,* ed. Dorothea Link, with Judith Nagley (Woodbridge, Suffolk, 2005), pp. 153–78; 170. The appointment was a covert way of giving Archduke Francis his own capella, as argued persuasively by Walther Brauneis, "Mozart's Anstellung am kaiserlichen Hof in Wien: Fakten und Fragen," in *Mozart: Experiment Aufklärung im Wien des ausgehenden 18. Jahrhunderts,* ed. Herbert Lachmayer (Ostfildern, 2006), pp. 559–72. I am indebted to Dorothea Link for a copy of this essay.

alieri, Elvira. Leporello was Benucci; Commendatore/Masetto, Bussani; and Zerlina, Luisa Laschi Mombelli. These were second-tier singers in regard to salary
with the exception of Laschi and Benucci (Cavalieri, for instance, was paid half
as much as Laschi, Lange even less). Moreover, the tenor Morella and baritone
Albertarelli lasted only a short time as court singers in Vienna. Mandini and
Calvesi had left for Naples but the latter returned in 1789.

La Storace wished to rejoin the Viennese buffo troupe for the Easter season
of 1788 and perhaps stay on longer. Joseph did not want her, or rather her salary,
back. Zinzendorf reported in his diary on 31 March 1788 that the emperor was
again having thoughts about dismissing the entire Italian company: "L'Emp. ne
veut pas de la Storace, et est même determiné a renvoyer l'opera Italien." Having
declared war on Turkey in early February, Joseph was off fighting in the Balkans.
Stringent economies on the home front were necessary in order to pay for the
war. The Kärntnerthor Theater was closed again.

Mozart and Da Ponte created three new pieces for the Vienna production
and new recitatives to introduce them. "Dalla sua pace" has already been mentioned. To take advantage of Laschi as well as Benucci, they replaced Leporello's
"Ah pietà, signori miei" (No. 20) with a very buffo duet "Per queste tue manine"
(No. 21a), in which Leporello is tied to a chair. To favor Cavalieri they added an
aria for Elvira, "Mi tradi" (No. 21b), which took the place of Ottavio's aria (No.
21). These three new pieces were entered by the composer in his catalogue with
the dates 24, 28, and 30 April and were thus heard at the premiere on 7 May.
Da Ponte claimed that major changes were made to shore up the opera after its
unsuccessful debut but this cannot be true. The three new pieces appear as texts
in the printed libretto.

All in all, the revisions for Vienna weakened the opera rather than strengthening it. They touched upon the opera's biggest dramatic problem: how to proceed after the shattering experience of the Sextet (No. 19). Instead of solving it,
they made it worse. Da Ponte's friend Giacomo Casanova, living in retirement
near Prague, had also tried to rework No. 20 and its preceding recitative. He
wrote a new text, in which the characters threaten specific punishments for Leporello, who then sings an aria in which he blames the female sex for Giovanni's
excesses (Casanova thus exonerates himself as well).[66] The new duet in Vienna
proved entirely too farcical for this spot.

By canceling Ottavio's big aria (No. 21), the creators left a void in this part of
the opera with respect to lyrical music and vocal charms. They made a big mistake by filling its place with a superfluous aria, preceded by a huge obbligato recitative for poor deluded Elvira, of whose humiliations we have already seen and
heard plenty, and will witness still more in the act's finale. It could be argued that

---

[66] Paul Nettl, "Don Giovanni und Casanova," *Mozart-Jahrbuch 1957,* 108–14.

Anna's "Non mi dir" (No. 23) is, for the same reasons, barely tolerable. Yet it is tolerable none the less, because as prima donna, Anna needed a truly lyric and large-scale aria somewhere and this rondò, preceded by a thematically linked obbligato recitative, provided one. How inept it is even so as dramaturgy! This single aria requires a set change both before and after it. Anna tells us nothing we do not already know about her, yet in order to hear such glorious music we gladly listen. For Elvira to have another grand recitative and aria one number distant from Anna's becomes too much of a good thing. Ottavio's "Il mio tesoro" is more welcome here because it is, for one thing, not another soprano aria, but most of all because it is a different kind of aria, one expressing love, hope, and tenderness.

Don Giovanni's reception in Vienna may have been tepid in high places, but eventually the opera did win over the public. Zinzendorf, in his brief mention of it on the day of its premiere, was not as negative as he often was about works new to him: "La musique de Mozart est agréable et tres variée." At the third performance, on 12 May, he reported a less favorable judgment by the wife of one of the highly placed court officials: "Madame de la Lippe trouve la musique savante, peu propre au chant." On 23 June he wrote, "Le soir je m'ennuyois beaucoup a l'opera *Don Giovanni*." Princess Elisabeth wrote her husband Archduke Francis, "On m'a dit qui'il n'avait pas beaucoup de succès." Joseph, far away on the battlefront, expressed his skepticism to Count Rosenberg: "La Musique de Mozart est bien trop difficile pour le chant." The last performance in Vienna during Mozart's lifetime took place on 15 December 1788. Emperor Joseph, ill after nine months in the field, had returned but did not attend.[67] Altogether, there were fifteen performances of the opera in the Burgtheater during 1788.

1788: Three Late Symphonies

The Mozarts moved from one lodging to another often between 1787 and 1790. On 24 April 1787, they quit their expensive apartment in the Domgasse for a small suburban house on the Landstrasse to the east of the city. Leopold Mozart commented on the move in his letter to Nannerl of 11 May, his last, and thus his last reference to his son: "Your brother lives now in the Landstrasse No. 224 [at present, No. 75]. He writes me but gives no reason for the move. Nothing at all! Alas, I can guess the reason." His guess was probably that they were becoming increasingly insolvent. They now lived in a much less commodious place, costing 150 gulden (compared to 450 for their previous dwelling). In December 1787, the Mozarts moved back to the center of the city to an apartment in the Tuchlau-

---

[67] Joseph Heinz Eibl, *Mozart, Die Dokumente seines Lebens: Addenda und Corrigenda* (Kassel, 1978), p. 58.

ben, where they stayed until June 1788. Here Mozart wrote the three new pieces for *Don Giovanni* in addition to some songs, dances, and replacement arias. The only large work was the Piano Concerto No. 26, K. 537, in D, dated 24 February in his catalogue.

K. 537, known as the "Coronation" Concerto, is very different in character from the many prior masterpieces for piano and orchestra. Its looser facture suggests that Mozart was looking ahead once again to the long-postponed tour and considering the limitations of orchestras less expert than those of Vienna. This shows in the reduced demands made on the winds. The outer movements of the work lack the rich interplay between soloist and orchestra Mozart had previously relished; as for the winds, they mostly double the strings. To make up for these lacks there is an abundance of display for the soloist and of lyrical melodies so cut-and-dried that they court instant popularity. In fact, they suggest the much-maligned Rondo in D of 1783 in some ways. The rondo theme of K. 537's finale skirts the same dangers of over-repetition. Only in the middle movement, a *Larghetto* in A, called *Romance* in a sketch, does the composer seem to be his old self.

Mozart may well have performed K. 537 in Vienna at some Lenten concerts in which he took part, but it is clearly composed for an orchestral situation less ideal than Vienna normally provided. As it turned out, he did play the work in such a situation a year later, at the sadly reduced Dresden court, whose musical establishment he found wanting and said so (letter of 16 April 1789). A year later still he played K. 537 in Frankfurt at a quickly thrown-together concert that was marginal to the imperial coronation of Leopold II. Possibly, Mozart even foresaw two years earlier that there would be call for audience-pleasing festive works to enhance various celebrations of the new emperor.

In mid-June 1788, the Mozarts left the city again and moved to a new dwelling on its northwestern outskirts at No. 135 (now No. 16) Währingerstrasse in the suburb of Alsergrund. In these more tranquil surroundings, Mozart regained his abilities to turn out works of the highest quality very rapidly and in prodigious succession. He probably had fewer pupils coming to this more remote location, but he was counting on financial help to make up the difference from his friend and Masonic brother Michael Puchberg, a rich clothing manufacturer and banker who helped manage sales of Mozart's compositions.

Mozart was initially very pleased with these quieter surroundings. In a letter to Puchberg, undated, but before 17 June, he wrote:

> We sleep tonight for the first time in our new quarters, where we shall remain both summer and winter. They are at least as good as, if not better than, the old ones. As it is I do not have much business to do in the town, and because there will be fewer interruptions from visitors I shall have more time and leisure for work. And if I must

do business in the city, which will certainly be seldom, any fiacre will take me there for ten kreutzer. Moreover, this place is cheaper and during spring, summer, and fall more pleasant, since I also have a garden.

He wrote again to Puchberg, on 27 June, "Do come for a visit; I am always at home. I have done more work in ten days living here than in two months at my previous address." Worries still pressed him, but he held them in abeyance: "If I were not beset so often by black thoughts, which I must chase away forcibly, things would go still better because my apartment is pleasant, comfortable, and *cheap!*"

Mozart's idyllic new residence can be located on Daniel Huber's bird's-eye view of Vienna (Figure 2.6). It is the house on the Währingerstrasse in the middle of the illustration, bordered on the right by No. 134 and on the left by No. 136. Mozart's house had gardens on three sides of it, according to this map. The fresh air this provided must have been a welcome relief from the cramped spaces of the

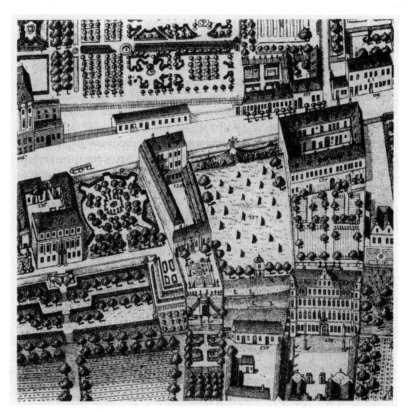

FIGURE 2.6. No. 135 Währingerstrasse from Daniel Huber's map of Vienna, ca. 1770.

inner city. Beyond this refuge on the outskirts, and not very far away, were villages such as Döbling and Grinzing, and beyond them the wooded slopes of the Kahlenberg, lauded by the composer in his letter of 13 July 1781.

The first piece Mozart finished in his new surroundings was the Piano Trio in E, K. 542, dated 22 June in the catalogue, where it is called "Ein Terzett für klavier, violin, und Violoncello." E major had seen little use in Mozart's previous chamber music. Even Haydn, more adventurous in selecting keys with many sharps or flats, made relatively little use of E, choosing it only twice as a main key in his nearly forty piano trios. The key was somewhat difficult for violin and not so easy for piano if only because it was rarely called for. In Mozart's operas, on the other hand, E major has a special place and is associated with rarified natural events or odd locations, like the cemetery scene in *Don Giovanni*. More typical is the "calm seas and prosperous voyage" atmosphere of the embarkation chorus in *Idomeneo*, or that opera's opening of Act III, when Ilia invokes gentle breezes to come to her aid. These two pieces in E predict the magical shimmer Mozart evokes with the sublime trio "Soave sia il vento" in Act I of *Così fan tutte*, another piece in E. One is tempted to imagine that Mozart's response to his leafy new retreat in the Alsergrund had something to do with so idyllic a composition as K. 542.

K. 542 begins with the piano alone, playing a chromatic descent in parallel thirds from the fifth degree, opening the *Allegro* in 3/4 time. Only a month later, Mozart would be setting to paper his most famous descent from the fifth to the first degree with the minuet of the "Jupiter" Symphony. The new trio is of a rare delicacy, unmatched in his other piano trios although approached by the one in B♭, K. 502. Its opening *Allegro* has one harmonic move so bold for its time as to suggest Schubert: a sudden deceptive cadence to ♭VI after the second theme that takes one's breath away. This is not an excursion of a fleeting moment. Once arrived on ♭VI, Mozart lingers there before returning. The *Andante grazioso* in 2/4 time and in A is even more delicate than the *Allegro*. It is a rondo with a winsome *gavotte tendre* as refrain, partly over a tonic pedal, suggesting the drones of pastoral pipes—a genre scene in pastel shades à la Boucher. The concluding *Allegro* initially was to have been a finale in 6/8 time, of which some sixty measures were completed before being discarded for a more vigorous movement in cut time. Here, a steady stream of eighth notes accompanies the *dolce* main theme, which is a singing *Allegro* type that may remind listeners of similar textures in the "Jupiter" Symphony, soon to follow. There is abundant passagework for the instruments, some of it not easily mastered.

Mozart set the bar high for would-be performers of K. 542, although he was in the process of compiling a set of piano trios for sale to the public. He compensated for its demands somewhat in the next work of the kind, the Piano Trio in C, K. 548, inscribed in his catalogue with the date of 14 July. It is in the showy and rather retrospective vein of the Four-Hand Piano Sonata in C, K. 521, of a year earlier. It too glistens with rapid runs and arpeggios, which readily trip off fingers practiced in the key of C. The most winning movement is the *Andante cantabile* in F and in 3/4 time. The concluding *Allegro* is in the light, dance-like 6/8 meter that Mozart tried and rejected as a finale for K. 542. The two new trios were joined by K. 502 in B♭ of 1786 when published by Artaria as the composer's Opus 15 in late 1788.

Many dunning letters by Mozart to Michael Puchberg make for pitiful reading, but they are sometimes leavened by references to the musical gatherings the composer enjoyed with the banker and Frau Puchberg. Thus, in the same letter asking for a huge sum to keep him solvent (dating from before 17 June 1788) Mozart adds in a postscript, "When are we going to make a little Musique again at your house? I have written a new trio." The new trio must be K. 542. The Puchbergs lived in comfort at "Hoher Markt in Walsekischen Haus." In a letter that must date from around 12 June 1790, Mozart requested the return of his viola from the Puchberg's home, where he had left it.

As a violist, Mozart was at the center of one of the greatest works of 1788, the String Trio in E♭, K. 563, entered in his catalogue 27 September and described as "Ein Divertimento à 1 violino, 1 viola, e Violoncello; di sei Pezzi." Six movements indeed it has, including the two minuets sharing the keynote that confirm divertimento form. The expansion comes by adding another slow movement. Exquisite in every detail, K. 563 was laid out as a broad tapestry of contrasting keys, forms, tempos, and meters (Table 2.3). He wrote it for Puchberg.

TABLE 2.3. The Movements of the Divertimento for String Trio, K. 563

Allegro	Adagio	Menuetto Allegro	Andante	Minuetto Allegretto	Allegro
E♭ 4/4	A♭ 3/4	E♭ 3/4	B♭ 2/4	E♭ 3/4	E♭
Sonata form	Sonata form	Trio E♭	Theme and variations	Trio I A♭	Sonata-rondo
				Trio II E♭	

Mozart took extraordinary care with this work in what was for him a new medium (Haydn had cultivated it earlier). Unusually precise are the directions as to its performance. Thus, in the second Menuetto, Trio I was to be followed by the minuet da capo with its repeats, but played *piano*; Trio II was to be followed by the minuet da capo with no repeats, and then by an additional coda of twenty-three measures. The whole movement reaches proportions quite long for a minuet (114 measures not counting repeats). There is a kind of jest encoded in Mozart's own part. The viola takes over the melody near the beginning of the initial *Allegro* by starting on the tone A♭ in its bottom octave. Then in Trio I of the second Menuetto it leads in the second Trio, which is in A♭, beginning with the same tone at the same low pitch. One can guess what will happen in the finale, especially with the knowledge of its equivalent in the *Sinfonia Concertante* in E♭, K. 320e, in which the composer also played the solo viola part.[68] In the development section, the music modulates to A♭, where the viola takes the lead by singing the rondo theme in its rich low register. This episode ends with A♭ becoming a♭, which is then transformed by an enharmonic change to G♯, a switch that anticipates the same in the second finale of *Così fan tutte,* at this point little more than a year ahead. The work would be first published in 1792 by Artaria as "Gran Trio," Opus 19.

Mozart had no reason to believe that the three symphonies he wrote down in the summer of 1788 would be his last nor did he expect to die young. He titled his thematic catalogue in a way that leaves open the possibility of his making additions to it into the nineteenth century: "Catalogue of all my works from the month of February 1784 to the month of _____ 1_____." Even if not intended as a summary statement, the three last symphonies present a sweeping overview of his contributions to the genre. Finished in close proximity to each other they may have been conceived over a period of several years but not finished because he was mainly occupied with the composition of piano concertos and operas. In any case, the symphonies awaited a period of relative peace and tranquility in which they could be completed and written out. By adding three grand symphonies to his portfolio in the summer of 1788, the composer was thinking ahead to future concert seasons, and not just those in Vienna. He had not given up his idea of tours that would take him through Germany to London, or even Paris, the one place he knew by experience paid well for symphonies. Haydn had recently confirmed this anew by his six "Paris" symphonies of 1785–86, which could well have served as an added stimulus. They are in four movements with a minuet. Artaria published Haydn's Symphonies 82, 83, and 84 at Vienna as Opus 31 in 1787. Is it a coincidence that they use the keys of C, g, and E♭? Or that of the three, only Symphony No. 84 in E♭ has a slow introduction?

The least discussed of Mozart's three new symphonies is No. 39 in E♭, K. 543, inscribed in the catalogue with a date of 26 June, three days after that of the Trio in E, K. 542. Their closeness of date obviously does not mean that the composer created or even wrote out K. 543 in such a short time. Like the "Linz" Symphony of 1783 and the "Prague" Symphony of 1786, K. 543 begins with an impressive slow introduction, a feature particularly identified with the symphonies of Haydn. This *Adagio* in common time is longer than Mozart's or Haydn's earlier introductions and more imposing (with the exception of the "Prague" Symphony and the Overture to *Don Giovanni*). It predicts something momentous to follow—the first of the work's many jests is that what does follow sounds like a country dance, a Ländler. The introduction establishes the key of the whole as well as its timbral coloring, which is special, the normal oboe parts giving way

[68] *Haydn, Mozart,* p. 640.

to two clarinets in B♭, thus reinforcing the softer qualities of the key of E♭.

In other respects, K. 543's opening *Adagio* is majestic, clearly akin to the first section of the old French overture because of its abundance of massive chords, dotted rhythms, and rapid scalar *tirades* up and down. All these features recall the grand estate of royal majesty, whether worldly or heavenly. In a passage considered below in its entirety, E. T. A. Hoffmann began his description of K. 543 by saying that "Mozart leads us deep into the world of the spirits."

The initial harmonic progression is like a great curtain slowly sweeping open. It is guided by the rise of the bass in two-measure segments: E♭ F G A♭, and then A♮ B♭. The harmonies erected over G and fleetingly over A♮ are full diminished-seventh chords, the latter resolving to I⁶₄ then V over B♭, a progression that will return for the climactic moment of the first *Allegro* at m. 282, after being adumbrated in mm. 62–70. *Forte* and *piano* in alternation (with the *tirades* in the violins always soft) cease for a long dominant pedal, with all the instruments marked *piano*, including the timpani roll of five measures on B♭. Here the alternation is of *tirades* between the first and second violins by the half-measure accompanying a stately succession of resolving suspensions. *Forte* returns as the lower strings answer the descending scales of the violins with their rising scales. Tonic E♭ is reached in m. 16 but only briefly and *piano*. A harsh dissonant suspension, C against D♭ high in the treble instruments, must resolve before reaching the next goal, which is IV (A♭). The diminished-seventh chord from the beginning recurs and is repeated by the winds alone, with the flute up to high G♭, sounding like a shriek of alarm, then silence (Example 2.20).

EXAMPLE 2.20. *Mozart, Symphony No. 39 in E♭, K. 543, I*

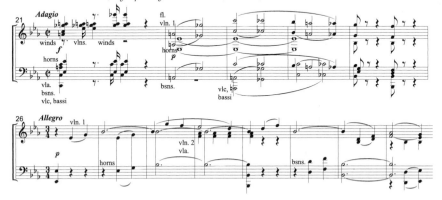

The continuation is *piano*, sustained in even half notes. Wondrous, mysterious even, is the effect of this soft passage. The violins leap up an expressive minor seventh, doubled by the flute an octave above and the first bassoon an octave below, surrounding the long-held E♭ of the horns and imitated one measure later by the cellos and basses. The tritone at the beginning of m. 22, an anomaly, is not immediately resolved. It is heard as a prolongation at a softer level of the previous diminished chord, an exploration of it that begins with only two tones at a time, then three at the beginning of m. 23, transformed magically in its second half to the chord of C♭ (♭VI) in first inversion, then resolving by descending chromatic sixths to the preparatory chords, lightly touched upon, I♯ and V.

The most magical touch of all is the arrival of the tonic as a single tone of E♭, *piano*, an octave lower, in the basses. The violins continue in their octave by softly climbing the tonic triad beginning on the second beat of the new section, *Allegro* in 3/4 time. Mozart's music abounds in the most amazing transitions from one thought to another, but surely none tops the sublimity of this one. From high drama of the *Sturm und Drang* kind through an almost unfathomable transfiguration we arrive at what sounds like a simple waltz within a few measures, from full orchestra to a main theme that is so lightly scored it could have invoked in listeners of those days a small dance band. And yet the new theme is not quite so simple as it first seems. Were it not for the horns' echo of the violins' triad, the tune would be a three-measure antecedent, I - V, and consequent, V - I.

Following the eight-measure main theme, there is a six-measure segment (2 + 2 + 2), a repeat of the first phrase, but inverted. The bass enters first, echoed above by the clarinets, the harmony becoming more chromatic, then the six-measure segment again, also inverted. Next sounds the first tutti *forte* of the *Allegro* announcing a tonic triad in descent, a passage that also becomes chromatic. Wide leaps from high to low in the violins, the harmonic progression, and the *tirades* are all reminiscent of the *Adagio*. They begin a transition to the second key. B♭ is prepared by a strong emphasis on its dominant, F, which arrives with a new motif, a rapid turn around the principal tone using upper and lower neighbor notes in the galloping rhythm of an eighth note and two sixteenth notes. Mozart had used this pert idea before, notably at the end of his first great piano concerto, K. 271 in E♭. It is a figure from comic opera that suggests buffo patter. Mozart played it to the hilt, sounding it on four tones leading from F down to B♭.

The second theme proper is soft, woven out of a continuum of even eighth notes, its first half descending, two measures slurred together, but patterned as a hemiola of 2 + 2 + 2 quarter notes. The cellos answer with a rising line. They are notated separately from the basses here, and repeat a tonic pedal in eighth notes. To solidify the new key of B♭ further, Mozart, with typical melodic generosity, adds a broad lyric theme rising calmly by step in the violins against the pizzicato cellos and basses. It constitutes the closing theme although the end of the prima parte is still some distance away. Tutti passages heard before are marshaled again to put the final closing touches on the triumph of B♭, and last of all, to the galloping motif just before the double bar with repeat sign.

The seconda parte begins with the last item heard (the little galloping motif), a strategy often used by Mozart. This motif leads rapidly to the broad closing theme, now in A♭, enriched by the divided violas joining the violins against the pizzicato accompaniment (cf. the viola's adventures with A♭ in K. 563). From these two ideas, not the first theme or the second theme, most of the development is fashioned, and it does not forego such Haydnesque devices as fragmentation and canonic overlapping while pursuing a course that leads to a strong arrival on G, the dominant of vi in the home key of E♭. The relative minor, vi, is the most frequent goal of developments in major-mode movements with all composers of the time, and hence expected. In this case, there is no arrival of vi. Instead, a soft passage in the winds condenses the mysterious chromatic progression at the end of the *Adagio* and, overtopped by the flute's ascending chromatic sighs, slides smoothly into the reprise, which is little changed until the beginning of the transition, when there is a subdominant substitution. Mozart expands the passage leading up to the final cadence, with the rising strings at one point adopting the hemiola patterning from the second theme. There is no coda and no indication to repeat the seconda parte.

Andante con moto in 2/4 time opens in A♭, the dark coloring of which has already marked the *Allegro*. It projects more nervous energy than the average *Andante*, its main theme giving an important role to sixteenth notes. The rise of the melody up a fifth by step in dotted rhythm, present from the beginning and chosen for extensive development, also ends the movement at the final cadence. When Mozart inverted the figure to a scale sweeping down to the tonic in the bass, it became a clear reminder of the same at the end of the slow introduction. There are several quite somber moments in the minor mode throughout this movement, more hints, perhaps, of Hoffmann's "spirit world." Coming after a movement so melodious as the first *Allegro*, the *Andante* sounds distinctly different, less lyric.

The Menuetto might appear to be almost as pompous as the slow introduction if Mozart had not urged it on with the added marking *Allegretto*. It approaches the first theme of the initial *Allegro* not only in tempo but also in some of its melodic and harmonic material, such as the repeated measure that begins with *mfp* on the first beat and continues with an even more telling descent of the violas C - C♭ - B♭, the same as at m. 50 in the *Allegro*. The relation of this particular chromatic descent to the *misterioso* passage ending the *Adagio* is clear and, once recognized, audible.

The Trio is not mysterious at all but clear and earthy, like a Ländler even to the point of having an oom-pah-pah accompaniment. There was a hint of the same in the first theme of the *Allegro*, but no more than a hint. The Trio's theme comes closer to the eight-measure phrase that opens the *Allegro*, I - V; V - I. This is reshuffled so that the one-measure echo comes not in the middle but at the end, as is more appropriate to country music like this, which sounds almost like the village band in some Alpine locale. Could this same Trio have been an ancestor to the main theme of the *Allegro*?

The *Finale Allegro* in 2/4 time is full of fun and pranks, but not so rustic sounding as the Trio. It is rigorously contrapuntal and entirely monothematic. Together with the Trio and the slow introduction, the finale testifies most clearly that this great work is, among other things, a tribute to the symphonies of Joseph Haydn. The finale's theme has the cut of many a rondo tune by Haydn (see Example 3.4a, p. 234). Like Haydn, Mozart explores this jaunty opening and mines it for all its motivic riches. There is also a jest typical of the older composer encoded in the first seven notes, which initially, and for a long while, seem like only the beginning of a rollicking good tune. They are also an ending, and are called upon as such to end the symphony. The same witticism occurs in the finale of Haydn's "Joke" Quartet of Opus 33, which is also in E♭, and that could be a part of Mozart's jest. Beethoven pays homage to both masters by ending the first movement of his Eighth Symphony with the same trick, using only the first six notes of his theme. The finale of K. 543, for all its jests and surprises, does not fail to return to the mysterious C♭ chord of the *Adagio*, modified by the addition of a seventh to become an augmented-sixth chord on the way to I_4^6 (m. 222). Mozart's high spirits sound worldly to us. To one early critic of music, they conjured up otherworldly spirits.

E. T. A. Hoffmann, the early Romantic composer and critic, in a famous essay on Beethoven's Fifth Symphony first printed in 1810, compared Haydn and Mozart, whom he called "the creators of modern instrumental music." He contrasted Haydn's optimism, perpetual youthfulness, and worldly bliss to Mozart's darker and more spiritual art. (Obviously, in this kind of contrast everything depends on which works are chosen for study.) Hoffmann chose K. 543 to exemplify his argument.

> Mozart leads us deep into the realm of the spirits. Dread lies all about us, but withholds its torments and becomes more an intimation of infinity. We hear the gentle voices of love and melancholy, the nocturnal world dissolves into a purple shimmer, and with inexpressible yearning we follow the flying figures kindly beckoning to us from the clouds to join their eternal dance of the spheres (as, for example, in Mozart's Symphony in E♭, known as the "Swan Song").[69]

Why K. 543? What features of the symphony made him choose it? The mysterious transition passage at the end of the *Adagio* offers a suspect, as does the *Andante*. Another is offered by the very key of E♭. The many authors who wrote

[69] David Charlton, ed., *E. T. A. Hoffmann's Musical Writings: "Kreisleriana," "The Poet and the Composer," Music Criticism*, trans. Martyn Clarke (Cambridge, 1989), pp. 237–38 and p. 97.

on key characteristics at the time were in near unanimity about hearing the key as one of both love and solemnity.[70] Adding clarinets to the mix accentuated the first while trombones would reinforce the second when they joined the E♭ palette of *Die Zauberflöte*. To Mozart's Masonic brothers K. 543 may have sent messages scarcely less powerful and symbolic than his only opera in E♭. As for the A♭ of the symphony's *Andante*, it was often deemed a key so dark and morbid as to be appropriate for funeral processions.

The long alliance between E♭ major and g minor in Mozart's works, and before them in a wide range of vocal and instrumental works by other composers, especially those from the Neapolitan Schools, has been touched upon elsewhere.[71] However long they may have been germinating Mozart brought his two late symphonies in these keys to conclusion within a short time of each other. If it were necessary to choose a single example from Mozart's last decade embodying the symbiosis of E♭ and g, the choice would fall upon the character of Ilia in *Idomeneo*, whose first aria in g showed a person in love but fatalistic and foredoomed, while the second in E♭ breathed devotion and hopes for happiness in love despite all odds.

Symphony No. 40 in g, K. 550, was entered in Mozart's thematic catalogue with a date of 25 July 1788, one month after K. 543. A little-known sketch for the finale of the String Quintet in g, K. 516, unused for that work, provides us with a clue as to how the first theme of K. 550 was gradually taking shape in Mozart's mind (Example 2.21). Already present here are the preoccupations with

EXAMPLE 2.21. *Mozart, Sketch for Finale of String Quintet in g, K. 516*

E♭ - D, then D - C, so central to the later melody, as well as descents by step, in sequence. In the sketch Mozart wavers back and forth, D - E♭ - D, in a way related to the accompanying violins in "Crudeli," an aria in g by Tommaso Traetta for the title role in his opera *Sofonisba* (Mannheim, 1762), sung by Dorothea Wendling, Mozart's Ilia.[72] The aria begins in common time with a measure of shimmering strings playing the accompaniment before the voice enters with the theme, an

[70] Rita Steblin, *A History of Key Characteristics in the Eighteenth and Early Nineteenth Centuries* (Ann Arbor, MI, 1983), ch. 7.

[71] *Music in European Capitals*, pp. 122, 149; *Haydn, Mozart*, pp. 96, 529, 553.

[72] *Music in European Capitals*, ex. 5.26 (p. 556), and pp. 533–35.

exact parallel with the beginning of K. 550. Were this not enough to establish a link, the aria, like the symphony, continues with the rich sound of a supertonic seventh chord inverted so that the seventh, G, is in the bass, a suspension resolving to F♯. For the rhythm Mozart resorted to traditional ones for a *decasillabo* line with anapests, famously illustrated by Cherubino's aria "Non so più cosa son cosa faccio," an *Allegro vivace* in cut time, as against K. 550's *Molto Allegro* in cut time.

Mozart makes much of the initial melodic sigh E♭ - D, played in octaves by the violins, as is the whole first theme. The sigh permeates not only the entire first movement but also makes prominent visits throughout the work. As the main theme begins to repeat, winds are added to the harmonic underpinning in the lower strings. The theme quickly veers off in the direction of the second key, B♭, which is firmly established before the second theme arrives, after a measure of silence. Like the first theme, the second consists of drooping descents, rather mournful in effect but softened by being accompanied in thirds and tenths. There is eventually a sort of closing theme, one that consists of protracted sighs (including E♭ - D), like a duet between lovers.

The seconda parte begins with a rapid modulation to a remote key, f♯, for a statement of the main theme. Bassoons come to the fore in the accompaniment, being the only winds sounding, and the only instruments that sustain long tones. A modulatory dialogue between bass and treble ensues on the first part of the main theme, eventually reduced to only its head motif, with plenty of contrapuntal activity in accompaniment. After a long dominant pedal, the winds alone prepare the return of g with a descending passage similar to the same spot in the Symphony No. 25 in g, K. 183. The reprise begins, sounding the same except that now a single bassoon sighs a very long E♭, two measures in duration, resolving to D. The wistfulness of this single minor ninth is only increased by remembering the minor-ninth appoggiatura sigh of the first bassoon thirteen measures before the end of "Porgi amor" sung by the Countess in *Figaro*. There is a short coda and no repetition of the seconda parte.

Andante in E♭ and in 6/8 time starts gently with an invocation of the old Credo motif 1 2 4 3 in the strings, ingeniously woven into a point of imitation with suspensions. The violins then invoke another of the composer's favorite motifs, 8 ♯6 8 ♮, 5, sung so unforgettably by Ilia in her love-inspired E♭ aria, "Se il padre perdei" (see Example 1.11c). The second tonal area of B♭ arrives without ado, unprepared by transition. As it is about to conclude, a rude interruption of D♭ *forte* delays the process. The sudden tonal departure from routine has a precedent in the previous movement, where there is a similar interpolation of D♭ delaying the cadence of the second theme (at mm. 57ff.). The *Andante* remains intensely serious throughout. In the seconda parte the bass slowly rises by chromatic steps, as it did under the *forte* D♭ interruption in the prima parte, tensions that are calmed only with the onset of the reprise. Both parts are enclosed with repetition signs.

The *Menuetto Allegretto* must have struck listeners as bizarre and scarcely like a minuet at all. Its cranky agogic accents on the second beat and three-measure phrases sound odd by Viennese standards although they are not so odd by French standards. In France there was one kind of old dance in this genre that proceeded by three-measure phrases.[73] K. 550's minuet, after two of these odd units (3 + 3), proceeds by eight measures that can be grouped 2 + 2 + 2 + 2 in a phrase that staggers to the cadence on V to end the first strain. The second strain copies the first metrically by alternating two- and three-measure groupings. One feature that should not be missed is the shrill dissonant suspension of high D in the flute, oboes, violas, and basses against the E♭ of the violins and bassoons. This long-held E♭ resolves, predictably, to D.

The Trio, like that in K. 183, brings tonic major, G, and lots of wind color—in the earlier work, winds alone played it. A look back to the earlier minuet and trio shows how much more Mozart then prized metric regularity, for both dances consist of nothing but four-measure phrases (except for the end of the Trio, where an echo turns four measures into six). In K. 550, the Trio is much simpler than its companion. Yet the first phrase is six measure long (2 + 2 + 2) and its second, for winds alone, takes eight measures, to which the strings append another four. Also, an oddity is that the initial rise up the triad in the violins is likely to sound, at least to untrained ears, as if it begins on the first beat instead of the third, an interpretation not contradicted until the cadence. Thus even the Trio, although not nearly so quirky as the Menuetto, has its moments of sophistication. It could be that this rather crabbed and grouchy Menuetto was intended to provide some kind of comic relief in a symphony that, unlike its two companions, otherwise had none.

The finale, *Allegro assai* in cut time, begins softly in the strings, like the first movement, but here there is a quick retort by the tutti, marked *forte*. First violins initiate the theme by vaulting up the tonic arpeggio from their low D to high B♭, which resolves to A, and on their second sally, up to high E♭, resolving, of course, to D. It is a bold beginning, a rocket that launches another dramatic and serious sonata form (and later on, Beethoven's first piano sonata, Op. 2 No. 1, in f). In addition to looking back in music to the famous Mannheim rockets, we might well look also at some of their Parisian consequences.[74] The second theme attempts to inject a little cheer as well as contrast although its general trajectory is downward, from the fifth degree to the first, like its equivalent in the opening movement.

The *seconda parte* begins with the main theme rocketing up to the accented

---

[73] *Music in European Capitals*, pp. 704–5 and ex. 7.1.

[74] See especially Simon Leduc's Symphony in g, Op. 2 No. 2, of 1767, which begins with the first violins rocketing up to high B♭, followed by A; *Music in European Capitals*, ex. 6.13 (p. 672) and pp. 670–71.

top tone, tutti *forte* (minus the horns), but no longer a triadic arpeggio. This change is minimal in comparison with what comes next. The theme dissolves into only one of its parts, the downward leap of a sixth, the part most clearly related to the upward leap of a sixth at the symphony's beginning. As if gone awry, the downward falls take on a life of their own, transformed into sevenths careening about in space and time. What Mozart has done is excerpt them from a non-existent sequence descending by fourths (Example 2.22ab). Following this

EXAMPLE 2.22 a, b. *Mozart, Symphony No. 40 in g, K. 550, IV*

famous passage is a quieter one with real harmonic sequences, in which the first bassoon shows that it too can ride the rocket in answer to the flute, and does so by leaping up the more important arpeggio that lands it on E♭, followed by D. As in the slow movement, Mozart indicates repetitions for both parts.

At some point during the three years he had remaining, the composer made a version of K. 550 in which he added two clarinets. He rewrote the oboe parts so as to accommodate the fuller harmonies allowed by using both pairs of instruments. The revised second version follows the first in the score published by the *Neue Mozart-Ausgabe.*

Symphony No. 41 in C, K. 551, dated 10 August 1788, acquired the title "Jupiter" after Mozart's death, probably at the hands of the London impresario Johann Peter Salomon, but the name is appropriate to its majesty, which suits the Roman god of the heavens. Each of the last three symphonies in its way looks back to Salzburg. The last brings to the fore the particular brilliance of Mozart's several Salzburg masses in C, particularly the "Coronation" Mass, K. 317, of 1779.

The first movement, *Allegro vivace* in common time, shares features with the last Salzburg symphony, No. 34 in C, K. 338, of 1780. The initial slide up to middle C from G, taking advantage of the violin's lowest tone, also figures in the opening of K. 338, which in addition shares the identical tempo and meter. Swaggering march rhythms with dotted second beats reinforce the bellicose tone. Both emphasize the subdominant chord prior to V - I resolution and indulge in military fanfares for the natural horns accompanied by timpani. An operatic slant on all these trappings is readily at hand in Figaro's aria "Non più andrai," sending little Cherubino off to war, which ends with the very same slides that begin K. 551. To set off the loud clamor of the symphony's tutti passages there are soft, pleading sighs from the strings alone in the interstices. And when the beginning returns *piano* it is topped by a counterpoint of flute and oboe leaping up, then descending by step, forecasting one theme of the finale.

Three thematic complexes provide Mozart with the material to maintain the *Allegro vivace*'s broad span. Roughly described these are the heroic/martial, lyric/galant, and antic/buffo. The second, coming after the modulation to V, offers a soft chromatic rise in the first violins answered and continued up the scale by the violas and basses, with the second violins in the middle providing light accompaniment in even eighth notes. This dainty exchange between treble and bass takes on the qualities of a love duet. Its tender murmurs are threatened by the questioning of a rising sequence that requires an answer. Mozart breaks off the texture completely with a measure of silence. When the answer comes, it is strong—a tutti *forte* outburst on the chord of c minor. The complex resumes but fails to achieve the expected cadence on G. After another measure of silence, the cadence arrives, begun by the basses and violas playing a pizzicato G while the cellos fill in the triad *coll'arco*, another light accompaniment in continuous eighth notes. This is merely support for the new arrival, a catchy tune with staccato repeated notes, as in operatic patter, ending with a pert little leaping figure. In visual terms it is as if a *commedia dell'arte* character, a Harlequin, say, had leapt onto the stage to confront the Capitano and Isabella. The tune's inherent buffo qualities need no further pedigree since it is derived from the comic aria for bass "Un baccio di mano," K. 541, that Mozart had composed only three months earlier.

The seconda parte begins softly with the winds in octaves moving to distant E♭ by the simple expedient of sounding two tones of its dominant, G / F B♭ / E♭. Another of the composer's supremely simple transitions, its rhythm has been heard before at the eruption of c minor in the second-theme area. Moreover, Mozart used this same move to open other development sections in works of the same key, earlier in the first movement of Symphony No. 16, K. 128, later in the overture to *La clemenza di Tito*, K. 621.

For purposes of development, the buffo theme, especially its ungainly leaps at the end, had profile enough to withstand being dissected, reassembled, turned into canonic dialogue, and hustled from place to place without losing its identity. After working it over, the composer reintroduces the main theme in the key of F, sung softly by the strings in the version that had a wind counterpoint on top, played here by the bassoons, which project avian comedy when clucking the staccato descending scale in thirds. In this treatment the main theme moves up the scale by degrees until arrival on vi of the home key, a traditional goal in developments. After more working out and a journey eventually reaching a dominant pedal, the reprise sets in. All elements return in order. The soft version of the main theme with counterpoint above substitutes c for C and initiates a little canonic dialogue of its own on the way to V as preparation for the second theme in I. There are no more surprises, and the seconda parte is not repeated.

Andante Cantabile in F and in 3/4 time, played by the violins with mutes throughout, introduces a quieter, ruminating tone in contrast to the opening movement. Some strongly accented second beats make the theme resemble a Sarabande. A reminder of the opening movement occurs when the tutti *forte* chord of c minor erupts after the main theme is restated by the bass. Equally memorable is the broadly hymnic second idea, rising up in even tones by the quarter-note beat from the first to the fifth degree, reached with a sense of exaltation that is similar to the striving toward G near the end of the "Coronation" Mass. In addition to the Sarabande rhythm, hemiola patterns often regulate the chord progressions and give the movement an almost retrospective cast, one that is reinforced by the many suspensions in the harmony.[75] Another slow movement with a Sarabande-like theme is the *Andante cantabile* of the String Quartet in C, K. 465, and there is an actual Sarabande, unfinished, in the keyboard suite of 1782, K. 399.

Menuetto Allegretto projects a soft, lightly scored chromatic melody, quite like the lyrical and chromatic second theme of the first movement, with its identical pulsating accompaniment in eighth notes for the second violins. The minuet's typical *Prunkstil* steals in softly as early as the third measure with the addition of the horns, trumpet, and timpani, then loudly in the second half of the first strain. In the second strain, these instruments resort to fanfares, clear reminders of the first movement. Not long into the second strain Mozart leaves the ballroom kind of minuet behind and begins developing the simple descending theme with countersubjects, canons, and strettos, a foretaste of the following finale.

The minuet theme shows a family resemblance to minuets in other symphonies by Mozart in the same key (Example 2.23abcd). Their themes begin mostly on the downbeat with a protracted G, descend to the tonic one way or another, and then push on to a half cadence (with the exception of K. 338). Since this characteristic manner of beginning the minuet movement is not shared by Mozart's symphonies in other keys, it follows that there was some linkage in the composer's mind between key, genre, and melodic-rhythmic gesture.

K. 551's Trio starts with the winds alone announcing what is usually an ending, one measure of V^7 harmony resolving to I. Why a cadence first? One expert hears it as the needed resolution of a leading tone, a B♮ that did not get resolved

---

[75] Elaine Sisman, *Mozart: The "Jupiter" Symphony* (Cambridge, 1993), p. 58 and ex. 6.1.

EXAMPLE 2.23 a, b, c, d. *Mozart, Minuet incipits from symphonies in C*

a. *No. 28, K. 200*

b. *No. 34, K. 338*

c. *No. 36, K. 425*

d. *No. 41, K. 551*

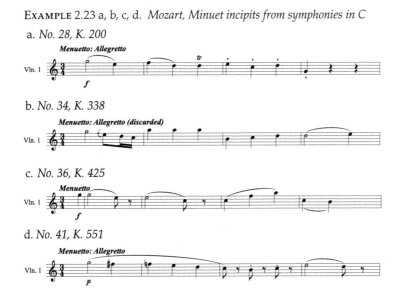

up to C at the close of the soft wind interlude near the end of the minuet's second strain.[76] The Trio's placid first strain ends with a cadence on C in its proper place. A tutti *forte* outburst commences the second strain with a secondary dominant, V/vi, mimicking the cadence beginning the Trio, and continuing on with its disturbance for eight measures.[77] This display of contrariness at the expense of the simple first strain supports measure-long tones in the first violins that explain all. Over these unstable and unsettling harmonies, the violins intone a familiar motif, 1 2 4 3, then reconfigure it in something like an inversion, the last two tones of which, a rising half-step, descend by sequence until they reach B♮ - C, recommencing the Trio from the beginning. The Credo motif 1 2 4 3, having been prefigured in an unlikely place, will now come into its own.

The finale, *molto Allegro* in cut time, assigns the Credo motif to the violins, one whole note per measure, while the seconds play a stream of eighth notes in accompaniment, like those in the minuet's theme and in the second theme of the opening movement; only these go by much more quickly. In this harmonization of C - D - F - E, the third and fourth tones top a deceptive cadence to vi, and the answering half phrase outlines a stepwise descent from A. There is precedent for this in Mozart's "Little Credo Mass," K. 192, of 1774 (Example 2.24ab). The "knocking" rhythm of three short upbeats is still there fourteen summers later,

---

[76] Sisman, *The "Jupiter" Symphony*, pp. 66–67.
[77] Something very like this agitation occurred at the same spot in the Trios of Symphony No. 28, K. 200, and Symphony No. 30, K. 202, as discussed in *Haydn, Mozart*, pp. 573, 575–76.

EXAMPLE 2.24.

a. *Mozart, Credo, Missa brevis in F, K. 192 ("Little Credo Mass")*

b. *Mozart, Symphony No. 41, K. 551, IV*

as is the subdominant underpinning for them and similar melodic descent. In the Mass, expression of the words suggested that "in unum" be subordinate to a (rhythmically) stronger "Deum." The symphony did not need to continue in the same vein, but did so anyway, showing how deeply ingrained certain Salzburg habits remained. The finale's beginning returns, tutti *forte*, with suspensions in the winds layered above, and punctuating slides up to the first beats in the strings below, recalling the very beginning of the symphony. The "in unum Deum" figure takes on great force as the chords on the subdominant are stressed. There is plenty of subdominant at the symphony's opening too, but the abundance of it here signals closing so strongly as to be appropriate only to a finale, not a first movement. Indeed, the ending of this huge movement, and thus of the whole symphony, will use the same passage, which returns to close the coda, after which there is only celebration of the tonic, and a few additional V - I cadences.

Other material reminiscent of the opening movement returns in the finale, such as the stepwise descent of an octave from tonic to tonic, elaborated here by being countered with scales rising an octave, followed by the fanfare-like wavering between V and I before coming to a stop on V. The main theme then starts again beginning on G and is treated as a fugato, begun softly in the strings in the order of second violins, first violins, violas, celli, and bassi, notated separately from the cellos for this purpose. Regularity is avoided by the differing phrase lengths, some of four measures like the theme, others of three because of overlapping.

Modulation to V as tonic (not just its reiteration as dominant) follows the fugato with a new figure rising by step and with a prominent trill on its fourth tone, readily identified in the midst of future contrapuntal skirmishes. The figure is deployed first as a canon between treble and bass, and there would be many more such canons to come. At the same time, it remains a proper transition to the second theme of a regular sonata form. The second theme itself has a distinctive melodic profile, 5 3 6. Familiar textures of continuous eighth-note accompaniments in the second violins persist, as do contrapuntal combinations with other figures previously heard.

The prima parte invents ever new ways to combine its many themes or motifs as it moves toward the double bar with repeat signs. On the way, there is a noteworthy darkening for a moment with the arrival of c minor, presented as iv^6 in the new key of G. This too recalls a moment in the first movement at roughly the same spot. One of the many thrilling things about this movement is Mozart's continual thwarting of the usual four-measure module.

The development would be a challenge for any composer after so much developmental character had already been exacted of this rich store of materials. Mozart's solution is not unusual for him: pursue a broad trajectory around the circle of fifths. This one moves all the way from the chord of A to that of F, then retreats by employing the minor form of these same steps: A D G C F c g d, followed by a long stop on B♮ as V/iii, resolving not to iii but quickly to I for the reprise. The seconda parte is also repeated, after which there is a move up to a resounding V^7/IV followed by a rest.

The famous coda begins with a stretto on the inverted main motif, *piano*, that leads back to C where a fugato starts up on 1 2 4 3, *forte*, decorated with all the thematic strands combined together in various permutations. This is often called a fugue, but it is really just another version of the fugato heard already, with other countersubjects added. The warring themes, subjects, and countersubjects are finally relieved by the familiar upbeat chords on the subdominant supporting a treble A—"in unum Deum" to the rescue, so to speak. With this, the game is over. The great contrapuntal explosion of the coda could be compared to a marvelous pyrotechnic display, an ending to dazzle the ear and outdo all endings ever made. As the Mozarts were fond of saying, "Finis coronat opus."

3
Mozart, 1789–1791

Saxony, Prussia; Chamber Music

URING the spring of 1789, Mozart traveled to Germany in the company of his lodge brother and piano pupil Prince Carl von Lichnowsky, who was five years younger than the composer. Mozart had known Lichnowsky for several years as a frequenter of Countess Thun's salon and may have named his second child Carl, born on 21 September 1784, after him. In late 1788, Lichnowsky married Maria Christiane, daughter of Countess Thun. His family owned estates in Silesia, fealty for which was owed to Prussia after they were wrested from Austria during the mid-century wars. It was thus expedient for the Lichnowskys to visit the Prussian court on a regular basis. The title of prince was a Prussian one, given to Lichnowsky's father in 1773 and inherited at the latter's death in 1788. Lichnowsky nevertheless remained loyal to Austria and resided mainly in Vienna. Mozart, leaving Constanze and Carl behind with the Puchbergs, took only his servant Joseph with him. The party set off from Vienna early on 8 April 1789. The previous evening, Mozart directed a performance of his arrangement of Handel's *Messiah*, K. 572, for Swieten.

Leopold Mozart set a model for his son in the planning of concert tours by laying down a barrage of letters, introductions, and recommendations, and by seeking contacts with officials. The trip north in 1789 was begun with no such preparations. It may have been undertaken on short notice, yet Mozart had the foresight to take with him some orchestral parts, indicating that he anticipated opportunities for performance. His goal was Berlin. Much remains unclear about this trip. Mozart's few letters written while away are often confusing, sometimes by intention, leading one commentator to suggest that the composer took flight, as it were, in order to get away from Vienna and from his wife.[1] Failing the discovery of more information, this can be neither proven nor dismissed.

The traveling party reached Prague on 10 April but spent only a few hours there. Mozart's many friends in Prague were taken unawares by his arrival. Most were not at home. Josepha Duschek, the soprano who was a longstanding friend to the Mozarts, had gone to Dresden. In his letter dated Prague 10 April, Mozart claimed that after finding the impresario Guardasoni he almost concluded an agreement to furnish the Prague theater with a new opera for the following fall, with a promise of generous recompense. Nothing came of the scheme, if that is what it was.

Dresden was the next stop, where the travelers resided in the Hotel de la Pologne upon arrival on 12 April. The city was no longer a great music center, having been reduced by the mid-century wars to a shadow of its former magnificence.[2] Under Elector Frederick Augustus III, expenditures on luxury items, including music, were kept to a minimum in efforts to restore Saxony to economic prosperity. Mozart wrote nothing in his letters about the city or its condition. Fortunately, there is a description of the concert tour of another musician, the young prodigy Johann Nepomuk Hummel, one of Mozart's favorite students, who had passed through Dresden a month earlier, with his father Johann Hummel, who wrote this in his travel diary.

> Dresden is a rather pretty town but there's not much to be done as far as the fine arts go . . . The people promised much and did little, a very hungry people; we weren't even invited to eat because they themselves have nothing to eat, and if you are a guest, there are no more than three courses, soup, beef, and roast; during the day they drink mostly tea . . . The music at the concerts is very poor.[3]

Hummel père kept a record of all financial outlays and incomes, unlike Mozart. It shows that a profit could be made from a concert tour, but only by dint of thrifty habits and inexpensive accommodations.

Mozart appeared unconcerned whether he performed in Dresden or not. Only a year and a half had passed since he had directed a performance of *Figaro* in Prague to honor the passage of Archduchess Maria Teresa on her way to wed Prince Anthony of Saxony. He made no effort to take advantage of this connection, or at least there is no mention of it in surviving letters. What he does say about the quality of music making at the Saxon court agrees with Hummel.

[1] Maynard Solomon, "Mozart's Journey to Berlin," *Journal of Musicology* 12 (1994): 76–84.
[2] *Music in European Capitals*, pp. 346–54.
[3] Landon, *Mozart: The Golden Years*, p. 201.

In his letter dated Dresden 16 April, Mozart wrote his wife that on Monday the 13th he went to the court chapel to hear Mass. The music was by the court's Kapellmeister Johann Gottlieb Naumann, who directed the performance. It elicited two words of comment: "very mediocre" (sehr mittelmäßig). Naumann presented him to "the court's Directeur de plaisirs Herr von König—the sad electoral pleasures" (der traurigen Churfürst: Plaisirs). König asked him if he would not wish to play before the elector. He replied that it would be an honor but that he was not in control of his travel dates and might have to depart before a concert could be arranged. That same day at a lunch given by Prince Lichnowsky a message arrived asking him to play before the court on the next day, Tuesday the 14th, at 5:30 p.m. This was an event quite out of the ordinary, he says, because such invitations were difficult to obtain at Dresden, "and you know I had no thought of playing here . . . I performed my new Concerto in D at court." The reference must be to Piano Concerto, No. 26, K. 537. On the morning after the concert, he received as a reward a "truly handsome box." It contained one hundred ducats, which he neglected to mention—the April issue of a Dresden magazine contained this information. The concert took place in one of the rooms of Electress Amalie.

Mozart arranged for a chamber music session in the court chapel with the organist Antoine Tayber. It included the Bohemian Anton Kraft, first cellist in Haydn's orchestra, who was accompanying his eleven-year-old son and pupil Nikolaus on a concert tour to Dresden and Berlin. "We played the Trio I wrote for Puchberg [K. 563] well enough to be quite listenable [so ganz hörbar executiert] and Duschek sang several pieces from *Figaro* and *Don Giovanni*."

On Wednesday 15 April at a lunch given for Lichnowsky by the Russian ambassador Prince Alexander Beloselki, Mozart played extensively. After this, it was agreed that he would be heard on the organ, and there resulted an impromptu contest with a visiting organist from Erfurt, Johann Wilhelm Hässler, on the Silbermann organ in the Catholic Court Church on the banks of the Elbe. Kapellmeister Naumann was also present.

He [Hässler] is a pupil of a pupil of Bach. His strength is the organ and the Clavier, that is, the Clavichord. People here believe that since I come from Vienna I am unfamiliar with their taste and skills at organ playing. I sat myself at the organ and performed. Prince Lichnowsky, who knows Hässler quite well, persuaded him with some difficulty to play also. Hässler's strong point is his footwork, which is not such a great accomplishment because pedals here are arranged stepwise; otherwise, he has learned the harmonies and modulations of old Sebastian Bach by heart but is incapable of executing a fugue in good order, and his playing technique is not solid. Consequently, he is far from being an Albrechtsberger. After this, we went back to the residence of the Russian ambassador so that he could hear me on the fortepiano. He also played. On this instrument, the Auernhammer girl is just as good, and, as you can guess, his reputation rather sank.

The event was reported in the public press. A dispatch from Dresden dated 17 June 1789 printed in the *Musikalische Real Zeitung* (Speyer) took notice of Mozart's outstanding concerts at court on the fortepiano, also his performances in many private houses of the nobility; it praised his mastery of both clavichord and forte-piano, his incredible sight-reading abilities, and lastly his organ playing, "in which he showed great skill in the strict style [gebundene Spielart]. He goes from here to Berlin."

On the evening of the 15th, the visitors from Vienna attended the electoral opera, which Mozart pronounced "truly wretched" (welche wahrhaft Elend ist). The work they may have seen and heard was Cimarosa's *Le trame deluse*. Mozart's opinion of the elector's music can thus be summed up by his three adjectives "mediocre," "sad," and "wretched." A precious memento of his visit is the fine portrait of him drawn by Doris Stock (Figure 3.1).

The party's next stop was Leipzig, Saxony's second city. They left Dresden on 18 April. Presumably, they arrived in Leipzig a day or so later. On 22 April, according to Johann Reichardt, Mozart gave a recital in Bach's old church with the assistance of its organist, Karl Friedrich Görner, and Cantor Johann Friedrich Doles.

On 22 April, without a prior announcement and without pay-ment, he permitted everyone to hear him play the organ of the Thom-askirche. For a full hour, he played beautifully and artfully for a large audience. The then organist, Görner, and the late Cantor Doles sat along-side him and pulled the stops. I myself saw him, a young modishly dressed man of medium size. Doles was wholly delighted by the per-formance and declared that . . . old Sebastian Bach (his teacher) had risen again. With very good grace, and with the greatest agility, Mozart brought to bear all the arts of har-mony, improvising magnificently on themes—among others on the cho-rale "Jesu meine Zuversicht."[4]

FIGURE 3.1. Portrait of Mozart by Doris Stock, 1789.

[4] Johann Friedrich Reichardt, "Erinnerung an Mozarts Aufenthalt zu Leipzig," *Berlinische musikalische Zeitung* 1 (1805): 132, quoted after Solomon, "The Rochlitz Anecdotes: Issues of Authenticity in Early Mozart Biography," in *Mozart Studies*, ed. Cliff Eisen (1991), 1–59; 29, n. 104.

Around this and other events in Leipzig concerning Mozart's visits there has gathered an accretion of anecdotes that is best ignored, beginning with those of the unreliable Friedrich Rochlitz.

Mozart claimed in his letter to his wife dated Berlin 23 May that he had written her in French from Leipzig the same day as his recital in the Thomaskirche. He also claimed to have written her on 28 April and 5 May from Potsdam, then on 9 May from Leipzig, to which he returned from Potsdam and where he gave a concert in the Gewandhaus, and on 19 May from Berlin. She received none of these four letters and the suspicion is that he never sent them.[5]

The Leipzig concert took place on 12 May. According to a printed program, it consisted of two parts. First part: Symphony, Scene (Mad. Duschek), Piano concerto, Symphony; Second Part: Piano Concerto, Scene (Mad. Duschek), Fantasy on the pianoforte, Symphony. The symphonies listed could have been movements from the same work distributed over the concert. Rochlitz claimed that the concertos were K. 456 and K. 503, but he may not even have heard the concert. By all accounts, the concert, whether from inadequate publicity or whatever, failed to draw a large audience. Mozart, still in Leipzig four days later, wrote his wife and said as much.

Leipzig 16 May 1789

Dearest, best wife of my heart!
What? Still in Leipzig? It is true that my last letter from the 8th or the 9th told you that I would be leaving at two o'clock at night. Yet the numerous requests of my friends prompted me not to make Leipzig suffer on account of the blunders [fehler] of one or two people and to give an academy here on Tuesday the 12th. From the standpoint of applause and honor, the concert was brilliant enough but all the more sparse with regard to profits. Duschek, who happens to be here, sang in it [Duschek welche Sich hier befindet sang darinn].

The casual nature with which Mozart appends Madame Duschek's name, although she was vital to a balanced program, strikes one as odd. Unknown is the identity of the one or two people whose blunders caused an affront to the composer (if this is what he means). The letter continues with excuses for staying in Leipzig so long, and a prediction of leaving very early the next morning.

On the following day, Mozart was still in Leipzig. He wrote down then a short piece K. 574 described in his catalogue, "17 May in Leipzig. A little Gigue for keyboard in the family album of Herr Engel, electoral Saxon court organist in Leipzig." An exercise in imitative counterpoint in a very chromatic style, it bears little resemblance to any of Bach's gigues but manifests a clear resemblance to the

---

[5] Solomon, *Mozart*, p. 444.

Gigue of Suite No. 8 in f of Handel, the last piece in *Suite de Pieces pour le Clave-cin Composées par G. F. Handel* (London, 1720).[6] It shows the composer harking back to the repertory he came to know in Vienna through Swieten. Much has been made of his re-encounter with Bach's music in Leipzig, but mostly based on Rochlitz's unreliable anecdotes.

The return to and lingering in Leipzig defies explanation. In his letter from Berlin dated 23 May, Mozart implicated Lichnowsky in the decision. "My academy at Leipzig fell out badly, as I always said it would, and I made the long trip there and back almost for nothing. Lichnowsky alone is to blame for this, for he left me no peace in the matter: I had to go back to Leipzig; but more on this when we meet."

As strange as Mozart's stays in Saxony are, those in Prussia are still more mysterious. Berlin was purportedly the goal of his trip from the outset. He mentioned it in a little poem to Constanze before leaving that began: "On the Journey in View: When I travel to Berlin / I hope to win much honor and fame." The Prussian metropolis was indeed perhaps the only German city where his genius could have been rewarded both financially and in terms of what it offered in the way of artistic stimulation. After decades of being stifled by the retrogressive tastes in music of King Frederick II, the city's musical atmosphere brightened with the accession in 1786 of his nephew and successor, Frederick William II. This cello-playing monarch had up-to-date tastes in music. Serious opera was no longer to be constrained by the Hasse-Graun corset insisted upon by the old king. There were good reasons for Mozart to think he might win favor with the new king. Haydn and Boccherini had already done so.

In his first letter to Constanze, dated Prague 10 April, Mozart wrote that the Prussian king was eagerly awaiting his arrival. The good news had been stated by his old friend from Mannheim and Munich, oboist Friedrich Ramm, who had just come from Berlin and was passing through Prague on his way home. "Judging from this, my affairs should go well there." Whether Mozart believed this rumor or made it up scarcely matters. Its intention was to give some hope of better fortune to come, not just to Constanze but also to her host and their creditor Puchberg. The husband was eager also to justify to his wife his first and longest absence from her.

When Mozart did enter Prussian territory, the super-efficient border control took note of his name, origin, and occupation, information that then turned up on a report dated 26 April. It was transmitted by the proper authorities in a request for an audience with the king. "One named Mozart, who at his ingress declared himself to be a Kapellmeister from Vienna, reports that he was brought

[6] Tchaikovsky admired K. 574 enough to include it in his Orchestral Suite No. 4 in G ("Mozartiana") of 1887, where it serves as a scherzo.

hither in the company of Prince Lichnowsky, that he desired to lay his talents before Your Sovereign Majesty's feet and awaited the command whether he may hope that Your Sovereign Majesty will receive him." No audience was granted. Instead, Frederick William annotated the petition "Directeur du Port," indicating that Mozart's request was to be shuffled to Jean Pierre Duport, director of the royal chamber music. A famous cellist, Duport was the king's cello teacher.

Mozart had a method of flattering other composers that had often seen use before. He wrote variations on some favorite tune of theirs, thus his variations on melodies by Salieri, K. 180, Paisiello, K. 398, Sarti, K. 460, and Gluck, K. 455.[7] In the same category are his keyboard variations on a minuet by Duport, K. 573, dated in Mozart's catalogue "29 April in Potsdam." This clever maneuver apparently worked. The king eventually received him, it is believed, although there is no hard evidence in proof. The variations in question are like a textbook demonstration of the genre's possibilities. They are easy to play and sound well, if somewhat glib, for which the bland qualities of the original melody can be held responsible.

Court events in Prussia and many other kinds of events as well were documented with ruthless efficiency. Thorough searches there have failed to uncover a single document pertaining to Mozart aside from his request for an audience with the king. The concert activities of young Hummel in Berlin on the other hand are relatively well known. Wherever the young prodigy displayed his talents he was advertised as a pupil of the famous Mozart, and he often played compositions by his teacher. Yet the teacher's fame did not lead to playing concerts at court or for the public, perhaps because Mozart failed to exert himself. In a letter to his wife, dated Berlin 23 May, he claimed that he was to play for Queen Friedericke, but no court document exists to confirm that he did. Unusually for him, he was almost nonchalant in even wishing to play for her. "The queen desires to hear me play on Tuesday but I believe little will come of it. I notified them of my presence only because it was the custom here, and had I not she would have taken it amiss." After endearments to his wife comes the statement, "you will have to be content with seeing me rather than money." Next he mentions a sum, but does not say he has earned it or was about to receive it. "100 Friedrichs d'or are not 900 gulden, but 700, or so I am told." Then followed attempts to explain where his money went.

The explanations were these. "Lichnowsky had to leave early and in a hurry so that I had to pay my own expenses in Potsdam, which is a very expensive place." This leaves open the question of whether the prince accompanied him on the second visit to Leipzig. "I had to lend him [Lichnowsky] 100 florins because his purse was dwindling, and I could not say no, you know why."

---

[7] On K. 180, see *Haydn, Mozart*, pp. 430–31. In his letter to his father of 9 June 1784, Mozart mentioned K. 460 and expressed his admiration for Sarti (see Appendix 2).

It has been assumed that the unstated reason involved the succor that a Mason owed a brother in need. Could Mozart already have been in debt to the prince for larger sums? And does this have anything to do with the legal action Lichnowsky brought against Mozart in 1791 requiring repayment of 1400 florins? Next came the debacle of the Leipzig academy, which the composer blamed on Lichnowsky, who drove him to return there he says. But why would the prince hector Mozart into returning to Leipzig? Only two answers come to mind: he wanted to get rid of the composer, or if he too returned to Leipzig there must have been some urgent reason for him to do so, perhaps of a personal nature.

Josepha Duschek could have been the magnet that helps explain the return to Leipzig. An attractive woman, to judge from her portraits, she had an elderly husband from whom she appeared to live in nearly complete independence. She was said to have affairs, and with members of the nobility. Leopold Mozart in his letter to Nannerl dated Salzburg 14 October 1785 described La Duschek as a mistress of Count Christian Clam-Gallas of Prague. In another letter, dated a week later, he describes the count's twelve-day stay in Salzburg and calls the count "the lover [Anbetter] of Madame Duschek." Perhaps it was not Mozart but young prince Lichnowsky who was smitten with the mature charms of this experienced singer during the spring of 1789 at Dresden and Leipzig.

While explaining why money was scarce in his last letter from Berlin, Mozart remarked in addition that there was not much to be made by giving an academy there, and furthermore the king did not look on such with favor. "You must be content with me and with this: I am fortunate to be in the king's good graces [in gnaden]." Berlin, contrary to what Mozart claimed, was a Mecca for concert-giving artists, and this could not have been the case if the king held the practice in disfavor.

Mozart's relationships with King Frederick William bear further upon the vexed question of commissions from the Prussian court. Once again, there is no confirmation of such from documents in Berlin or Potsdam. In a letter written to Puchberg after the return to Vienna, dated 12 July, Mozart stated, "I am composing six easy sonatas for the Princess Friederika and six quartets for the king which I am going to have engraved by Kozeluch's firm at my own expense; the two dedications will bring in something as well." Scholars have assumed that these works were to be written as a result of orders placed during the composer's visit to Prussia. The outcome lends this view no support. Apparently, Mozart never even began writing the easy sonatas. If only to shore up his credibility with Puchberg and with his wife, perhaps also his faith in himself, he did write a string quartet, K. 575 in D, begun on the return trip, and inscribed in the catalogue under June 1789 as "Ein Quartett . . . für Seine Mayestätt dem könig in Preussen."[8]

---

[8] "King in Prussia," rather than "of Prussia," was the title reluctantly conceded the Hohenzollerns by Emperor Leopold I in 1701. *Music in European Capitals*, p. 296.

K. 575 was joined by two more string quartets the following year, K. 589 in B♭ and K. 590 in F. There were no more, nor any dedications. The three were engraved not by Kozeluch's firm but by Artaria's. Mozart did not live to see the edition. In a letter to Puchberg dating from June 1790, he complained that out of dire economic necessity he had to sell the quartets for a pittance. He did not disguise the second and third quartets with the designation "for the king in Prussia." Even the pretenses remaining from his unfortunate foray to northern Germany had fallen away. The tale of Mozart's refusing a good salary from the Prussian king out of loyalty to Joseph II, the least credible of Rochlitz's anecdotes, should be discarded.

The failures of Mozart to reap much profit from selling his works, or himself as a performer, were exacerbated by bad economic conditions, especially in Austria. The decline began soon after Joseph II went to war with Turkey in support of his Russian ally Empress Catherine, both of them hoping to keep up with the other in territorial gains. In order to finance the war Joseph leveled heavy taxes and these were accompanied by severe inflation and shortages of food. Public unrest spread and conditions in Vienna quickly worsened. A bread riot took place there on 31 July 1788.[9] During this time, Mozart was enjoying his quasi-rural retreat in the Alsergrund and putting the finishing touches on his last three symphonies.

Economic decline affected Mozart nonetheless by 1788. He offered for sale manuscript copies of the two great string quintets K. 515 and 516, joined by an arrangement for string quintet of the wind quintet K. 406 in c minor. These were available by subscription from Puchberg according to an advertisement in the *Wiener Zeitung*. Customers were so few that Mozart inserted a second notice in the same paper on 25 June 1788 saying that he was extending the deadline for subscription until 1 January 1789. In his letter to Puchberg that dates before 17 June 1788, he wrote, "I am putting the date ahead by several months. I hope to find more interested amateurs *abroad* than from around *here*" (his emphases). That he pinned his hopes on support from elsewhere is evident as well from the similar advertisement he placed in the June issue of the Weimar *Journal des Luxus und der Mode*. A critic in this reputed paper for people of fashion reported from Vienna in the same issue, "for lady dilettantes it is Kozeluch who counts the most on the pianoforte." The critic went on to decry attempted performances of a piano quartet by Mozart (K. 493?).

Dilettantes never engaged much of Mozart's attention as a teacher, it is true. He probably lacked the flattering ways necessary with them to become in demand as a teacher to ladies of fashion. He may have ceded this source of income to Kozeluch without a struggle. It is uncertain whether he ever achieved the distinction of being Vienna's favorite pianist, even in 1784, the year of his greatest suc-

[9] Ernst Wangermann, *From Joseph II to the Jacobin Trials*, 2nd ed. (Oxford, 1959), p. 30.

cesses with the public as a keyboard performer and composer. During the same year, Friedrich Nicolai from Berlin published his *Von der Musik in Wien*, in which he claims that the favorite keyboard masters of the Viennese were Steffan and Kozeluch.[10]

Kozeluch was clearly Vienna's favorite pianist. His compositions also found favor in wide circles, while Mozart's did not, or so wrote one unidentified critic visiting Vienna on his return north from a sojourn in Italy.

> The works of this composer [Kozeluch] retain favor and are welcome everywhere, while Mozart's, on the other hand, generally please less. It is also true, and the six quartets dedicated by Mozart to Haydn demonstrate the truth anew, that he has a decided bent for the difficult and the unusual. Yet what great and sublime ideas he has! They betray a keen spirit.[11]

Nevertheless, Mozart continued to vie with Kozeluch for the applause not only of connoisseurs but also of amateurs.

During 1788, Mozart had already shown signs of retreating sometimes from the heights he had reached in chamber music. A month after the ethereal Piano Trio in E, K. 542 he wrote the more robust Piano Trio in C, K. 548, a piece that is brilliant and popular in appeal. Then in October, following these June and July pieces, he wrote the Piano Trio in G, K. 564, which is almost devoid of brilliant passages, and through much of which the pianist need not shift hand positions. A work of many beauties, this trio also shows Mozart's effort to make all three parts simple to play, in other words, to make them more like the music of Kozeluch. This trend is evident as well in Mozart's cultivation of little pieces while at work finishing the three great symphonies. In his catalogue under the date of 26 June 1788, the same given to Symphony No. 39 in E♭, K. 543, he also entered "Eine kleine Marsch" for five instruments, K. 544 (a lost work), and "Eine kleine klavier Sonate für anfänger," K. 545, in C, the miniature jewel that could also be called a sonatina. He followed this on 10 July with "Eine kleine klavier Sonate— für Anfänger mit einer Violin," K. 547, in F.

The nadir for Mozart was reached in the months after he returned from Berlin. Constanze was seriously ill with a foot infection, no small concern in those days. A cure at the sulfurous baths of Baden in the Wienerwald was indicated—an expensive recourse. She was pregnant with their fourth child (the third, Theresia, born in June 1788, died six months later). The couple had resettled once more in the center of Vienna in early 1789. The letter to Puchberg of 12 July 1789, already quoted, strikes a more desperate tone.

---

[10] *Haydn, Mozart*, p. 482.
[11] Cramer, *Magazin der Musik* (Copenhagen, 1789), for July 1789 (Deutsch, *Dokumente*, p. 306).

I must tell you that in spite of my miserable situation I decided to go ahead and give subscription concerts at my house so that I can at least take care of my expenses, which are considerable and frequent, for I was convinced of receiving your friendly help and support; but this plan is not working either. Fate is against me, *but only in Vienna!* [Mozart's emphases]. I cannot earn any money here even when I want to. For two weeks now, I have sent around a list for subscriptions, and there is only one name on it: *Swieten!* It seems to me that my dear wife gets a little better day by day, and so I may yet be able to get back to work, if this crushing blow had not been added.

A concert series gotten up by subscription in the middle of the summer, and at his own house, strains credibility. It was followed by the claim, wishful thinking at best, of writing the easy sonatas for Prussia. Mozart did compose one work for piano, dated July 1789, "Eine Sonate auf klavier allein," K. 576, in D, and far from being easy, it demands greater technical prowess than any of his others.

One reason Mozart felt driven to compose a set of six quartets for the Prussian king may have been the example set by Haydn. In 1787, the older master received a gift from Frederick William and kind words in the king's own hand, thanking the composer for sending a copy of his six Paris Symphonies. This act persuaded Haydn to dedicate to the king the six string quartets of opus 50, brought out in Vienna by Artaria. Haydn did not have an easy time finishing this set, partly because he was so busy at Esterháza as an opera director. On 12 July 1787, Haydn could write Artaria, "Thank God, I am glad I finished them at last." Not even Joseph Haydn regarded the composing of six new string quartets as anything but a laborious, time-consuming burden. Behind Mozart's various apologies to Puchberg, one can sense the added pressure of trying to match their mutual friend Haydn, even if the king had not encouraged him to do so. Once started, Mozart's set dragged on through the various post-Berlin domestic and financial crises that afflicted him.

In December 1789, Mozart wrote Puchberg promising repayment of his loans and added, "I hope to show you by next summer the full extent of my honesty, thanks to my work for the king of Prussia." Then at the beginning of May 1790, while asking Puchberg for a further loan, he wrote, "I must have something to live on until my subscription concerts are settled and until the quartets I am working on have been sent to the engraver." There was no longer talk of six quartets, a goal abandoned earlier. Later the same month, on or before the 17th, Mozart blamed pain and worry about the debts for "having prevented me all this time from finishing my quartets." He then invited Puchberg and his wife to a reading at home of the new quartets. The end of this saga strikes a dismal note. On or about 12 June 1790, Mozart wrote Puchberg, "I have been forced to sell my quartets—this exhausting labor [diese mühsame Arbeit]—just to get some cash in hand with which to meet my present difficulties." Artaria did not publish them until three weeks after Mozart's death.

The three new quartets are rather different from the set of six dedicated to Haydn and the 1786 work (K. 499), mainly because they require a higher level of soloistic virtuosity of all four players. A wish to display the cello in particular may have set loose this showy soloism but in the interests of stylistic cohesion, Mozart extended the same to all the partners. That the emphasis fell often on the cello as leader of the little band was not even a new idea with Mozart, for it happens with stunning success from the very start of the String Quintet in C, K. 515.

K. 575 in D begins with the first violin singing a broad theme, *Allegro* in cut time, a rising triad followed by stepwise descent, a kind of theme that Mozart favored in his earliest quartets, which misled some critics into believing he used old sketches from the 1770s in shaping this theme. If it were a four-measure theme, there would indeed be a resemblance to some of the early quartets. Instead, it is a stretched-out and irregular version of the same, reaching resolution only on the first beat of the seventh measure. The cello sings the second theme in A, beginning with another rising triad, and it follows a broad harmonic progression of I - ii / ii – V, often found in late Mozart.

The second movement is an *Andante* in 3/4 time and in the key of A, often chosen by Mozart to follow D, instead of the more usual subdominant, G, perhaps because A sounded more lyric to him. The second idea, still in tonic A, resembles a lover's duet between treble (first violin) and bass (cello) (Example 3.1). If this dialogue sounds vaguely familiar, even to those without previous

EXAMPLE 3.1. *Mozart, String Quartet in D, K. 575, II*

acquaintance of K. 575, it may be because Beethoven in the *Larghetto* in 3/8 time of his Symphony No. 2 in D also chose the key of A, and at the same spot initiated a quite similar lovers' duet between the clarinets and bassoons in mid-range, answered higher up by the violins, with the same harmonic underpinning. That Beethoven knew and particularly loved K. 575 emerges as well in echoes of the cello solo from its trio in his Piano Trio, Op. 1 No. 3: III (Trio). Mozart makes his *Andante* (73 measures) a lot shorter than Beethoven's *Larghetto* and does not even repeat the second idea later in the tonic, nor does he include a development. The *Andante* ends with a flourish, the first violin's measure-long rise in quick notes answered in kind by the cello, a last gasp of their earlier duet.

For the finale, Mozart again turned to the cello to announce the theme of the movement, an *Allegretto* in cut time that begins with a rising triad on D like the first movement but continues with the melodic motion 4 2 5 that had been prominent in the *Andante*, thus achieving a fusion of previous materials. His earlier idea, crossed out in the autograph, did nothing of the kind. Its theme, titled *Rondeaux*, got only as far as eight measures of a first violin part. It would have been a jolly, rather folk-like finale, another tribute to Haydn, perhaps, beginning like the wonderful finale of Haydn's recent Symphony No. 88 in G. Mozart thought better of it and gave us a finale more consistent with the thematics of the rest of his quartet, a movement consistent also in maintaining the concertante display of previous movements.

K. 589 in B♭ begins with an *Allegro* in 3/8 time. The first violin falls from the fifth degree to the tonic in trochees (like "He shall feed his flock" in Handel's *Messiah*, only decorated with a melodic turn on the third beat). This six-measure phrase (2 + 2 + 2), enlivened with a canonic imitation by the viola, is antecedent to the consequent matching phrase with a melody sung by the cello, against which the first violin adds a free counterpoint in eighth notes. Mozart puts high store upon euphony throughout this quartet, but not at the expense of rapid passagework in quick notes. The cello initiates the *Larghetto* in cut time and in E♭, singing a melody in which, it could be argued, there are too many returns to the tone G. The *Menuetto Moderato* (37 measures) has an unusually lengthy Trio (66 measures) in E♭, which takes the first violin up to B♭ *in altissimo*.

Mozart was not satisfied with an earlier sketch for a finale to K. 589, an *Allegretto* in 6/8 time with dotted rhythm and an incipit rising by step from the tonic, a melody for first violin (all that was sketched) implying a harmonic sequence I - V, then ii - I - V. He crossed this out in the autograph and wrote a different theme, keeping the tempo and meter from the sketch but not the dotted rhythm. He also maintained the importance of the second degree, implying the ii chord, although only the tones C and E♭ are sounded. The advantage of this definitive choice is that it ties in with the falling thirds that begin the first movement. The case is thus similar to K. 575's finale and provides an unmistakable sign that, at this late stage, Mozart sought cyclic unity as much or more than ever. Both finales are weighty in content, perhaps more so than the opening movements, and they are both highly contrapuntal. The coda of K. 589's finale inverts the main theme, giving it a new twist and ending the quartet with a Haydn-like *bon mot*.

K. 590 in F distills some elements of the two previous quartets. A recurrent figure in these works is the rapid scalar descent after a held tone, or after a leap upward, or both. What was to become the beginning of K. 590 occurred to

Mozart earlier as a possible beginning for a Piano Sonata in F, K. 590a, a sketch that according to its paper predates 1790.[12] The crucial similarity of both themes, aside from the key of F and common time, is the rise up the triad followed by rapid scalar descent, first outlining the chord of I, then on repetition the chord of ii or ii$^6_3$, with resolution via V back to I. The fussy dotted rhythms of the keyboard sketch give way in the quartet to a much plainer and more forthright statement (Example 3.2). Mozart condenses the idea to its essence and switches from

EXAMPLE 3.2. *Mozart, String Quartet in F, K. 590, I*

the routine stride of a four-measure phrase to the tighter confines and more challenging premise of a three-measure unit. His six-measure theme can only be heard as 3 + 3. It sounds abrupt, even peremptory, most of all at the snapped-off cadence on the second beat in m. 6 (like the angry cadences of Bartolo or Almaviva). Rhythm is the composer's main preoccupation in this quartet. The slow movement in 6/8 time and in F (*Andante* in the autograph, *Allegretto* in the first edition) concentrates almost entirely on the rhythmic gesture of its opening, the theme of which also moves from I to ii. The *Menuetto Allegretto* begins with phrases seven measures long, its Trio with five-measure phrases.[13]

Mozart once again made an earlier attempt at a finale, this time not in the autograph but on an independent sketch sheet (K. 589b), with a melody in F and in 6/8 time. He opted for an *Allegro* in 2/4 time but kept the initial descent from 5 to 1. Perhaps he thought better of having another movement in 6/8 time, or in terms of the set, two successive finales in this meter. What he produced reflects his admiration for Haydn's finales, particularly those that bustle with nearly continuous sixteenth-note motion, *all'ongarese*. K. 590's finale is at the same time a complex sonata form with both parts repeated. The frequent pauses, effected by rests and fermatas, have a quizzical effect, as if questioning where to go next. They stop the flow, but not for long. The main theme itself has the cut of many a Haydn finale theme (Example 3.3). To add a little spice in the closing area Mozart dwells on the theme's first three tones, repeating them several times against the grain of the meter (m. 121 of the Example), a familiar trick of Haydn's too. The soloistic display so prominent throughout Mozart's set is lacking in this finale. Still very much to the fore is the web of intensely motivic interchange that promotes equality among the partners.

---

[12] Tyson, *Mozart*, pp. 134, 142.
[13] As pointed out by Edward Lowinsky, "On Mozart's Rhythm," *Musical Quarterly* 42 (1956): 162–86.

EXAMPLE 3.3. *Mozart, String Quartet in F, K. 590, IV*

Three quintets joined the three "Prussian" quartets as Mozart's last contributions to chamber music, the Clarinet Quintet in A, K. 581, dated 29 September 1789, the String Quintet in D, K. 593, entered in his catalogue in December 1790, and the String Quintet in E♭, K. 614, dated 12 April 1791. We owe K. 581 to Mozart's admiration for his friend and Masonic brother Anton Stadler, the outstanding clarinetist and basset horn player of his day. The "Stadler Quintet," as the composer himself called it in a letter to Puchberg on or before 8 April 1790, got the full four movements deemed appropriate to string quartets and quintets, not the three movements normally given to trios, or to the earlier quartets for flute or oboe and strings. Moreover, Mozart lengthened the minuet movement of K. 581 by including two trios, one in minor for strings alone, the second displaying the clarinet in a rustic, Ländler-like vein.

All Mozart's works in the key of A, and especially his several love duets, put emphasis on the *cantabile* and revel in the sensuous delight of harmonies rich in thirds and other consonances. There was also a melodic type the composer particularly associated with this key, the fall of a third from the fifth degree. At the time of writing K. 581, *Così fan tutte* was in the offing and perhaps Mozart had already imagined the outlines of the duet in A for the two women, No. 4, the melody of which begins with a languorous fall from the tone E, reminiscent of that at the beginning of Piano Concerto No. 23 in A, K. 488. To begin the Quintet, he used a simpler descent, in even half notes, 5 3 2 1, *Allegro* in common time. The violins sing this in thirds and sixths, while the viola and cello counter descent with a rise in thirds, producing chords in which the third is doubled and providing a rich progression from V⁷ - vi, all in the first two measures. After singing their suave seven-measure statement, the strings pause as if to listen. The clarinet presents itself as a different species of warbler, luxuriating in the concertante while warming up with an arpeggio flourish. The strings repeat their statement, showing the path again to the interloper, a repetition that is slightly modified, mainly in the change of the deceptive cadence from V⁷ - vi to V⁷ - I⅗, the kind of subtle shading in which Mozart delights. The clarinet erupts again, pursuing its arpeggio even higher, and this time the violins respond in kind. Thus is the dialogue begun. The first violin announces the second theme in the new key of E, a chain of smoothly flowing eighth notes under which the harmonies head for an early destination on ii. The clarinet rejoins the ensemble singing the same melody but changing it from E to e, as the strings pulsate in syncopated quarter notes (see Example 7.2). Both parts of this ample sonata form are marked for repetition.

The *Larghetto* in D and in 3/4 time shows how Stadler could sustain a slowly evolving cantilena of great breadth. Its equal is found only in the *Adagio* of the Clarinet Concerto in A, K. 622, also written for him. The Menuetto begins with another version of the descent from fifth to tonic degrees. For the finale Mozart sketched a leisurely rondo, K. 581a, which is related in theme to Ferrando's aria in A, No. 21 in *Così fan tutte*. He pursued this sketch, mostly of the melody, as far as the return of the rondo theme in m. 68. At some point Mozart switched to variations (five, with a coda) on a simple theme, *Allegretto* in cut time, perhaps because it was even more plainly related to the descent from the fifth degree in previous movements. The tune is of a very popular cast, essentially 5 3 4 2 1, and set in the structure most common to German folk melodies ‖:**a a'**:‖:**b a'**:‖.

Brahms pays moving tribute to K. 581 a century later when, near the end of his life and inspired by another virtuoso like Stadler, he composed his Clarinet Quintet in b, Opus 115, of 1891. It begins with the four strings embroidering a descent from 5 to 1, followed by the emergence of the clarinet with a two-octave ascending arpeggio. The slow second movement tenderly proposes as a theme 5 3 2, only later allowing it a few tentative resolutions 5 3 2 1. For his finale, Brahms wrote a theme with five variations and a coda. Thus do great masters speak to each other.

Mozart's last works of chamber music show more than ever his care to fashion cyclical wholes out of disparate movements. Like Haydn, often his model in the task, Mozart avoided overtly obvious ways of making connections between movements. Their restraint in the matter deserves to be called classical as much as many other facets of their work. It seems almost as if they wanted us to uncover for ourselves the subtle ways of tying cycles together and to take even greater pleasure in doing so.

The String Quintet in D, K. 593, begins with that rare thing in Mozart's chamber music (but not in Haydn's), a slow introduction. It comprises some twenty measures in 3/4 time, labeled *Larghetto* in the autograph, but *Adagio* in the thematic catalogue. The implications of this short preparation, both melodic and harmonic, have consequences for everything that follows. To open the proceedings the cello, from its lowest range, rises through the triad of D in dotted rhythm, to which the upper strings reply with a slow chordal unfolding in even quarter notes supporting a *dolce* melody sung by the first violin. Harmonically this opening block moves from I to V. The cello repeats its opening gambit, but up one tone, sounding the triad of ii, and answered by the upper strings with motion from ii back to I. Next the cello states the rising triadic motif on F♯ changing I to i$_3^6$, in answer to which the upper strings also switch to minor and the first violin utters a series of sighing chromatic descents, step by step from A down to D. This stretched-out chromatic descent over a rich harmonic progression sounds tentative, probing, as if seeking an answer. A fully satisfying one arrives only with the onset of the finale, whose theme is a forthright chromatic descent from A to D while its hesitant, sighing form finds many uses in the slow movement, *Adagio* in 3/4 time and in G.

After the *Larghetto* comes to rest on a dominant pedal, the *Allegro* in cut time announces a soft, rather dainty theme, marked by a trill on the first beat. Immediately the calm is disrupted by a *forte* secondary dominant and its soft resolution, V⁷/ii - ii, stated three times, as is the tone E, the goal. More rudely still and right on the heels of E comes a strongly scored *forte* chord on the fourth beat, V⁷/IV. This harmonic non sequitur lasts for two more measures while the first violin scampers down the scale in triplets from high to low. Only then is there resolution, IV - V - I. An eight-measure phrase results, but one of unprecedented shape. Such a richly variegated first theme was nearly sufficient by itself for all the material in the movement, a long sonata form, both halves of which are repeated. Then comes another surprise—the return of the slow introduction, modified, and leading again to the eight-measure *Allegro* theme as conclusion. The theme itself is so fascinating it is heard with pleasure once more. In the finale, *Allegro* in 6/8 time, the signal move from I to ii recurs, as does a precipitous arrival of V⁷/IV, *forte*, followed by a measure of silence, lending it all the more emphasis.

K. 614 in E♭ is less ambitious than the string quintets that preceded it but no less fine. It encompasses an intriguing look backward to one of Mozart's earlier creations, and a final glance at something that had just been created by Haydn. There are two sketch fragments. K. 613a shows Mozart contemplating a quintet in E♭ with a prominent descent from the fifth degree over tonic harmony, answered by a descent from the fourth degree over V - I. In 3/4 time, it eventually became the *Menuetto Allegretto* of K. 614, although Mozart was probably aiming at a first movement in this fragment of 71 measures. This has bearing on the argument, to be made below, that Haydn sometimes composed the minuet before other movements. The fragment's rising-versus-descending scales also found use in the *Menuetto Allegretto*. K. 613b begins with a triadic descent in dotted rhythm *forte*, then a soft rise with trills of the two violins in parallel thirds, more than a little like the first *Allegro* in the previous quintet. K. 614 begins with a duet with prominent trills, but for the two violas, not the violins. The violas, *forte*, start this whirlwind *Allegro di molto* in 6/8 time with their horn-like call. In response, the violins descend in parallel thirds and sixths, down the scale, *piano*, over I - V harmony. The violas, again *forte*, play their call on V, to which the violins respond *piano* with their descent from A♭ over V - I. The whole of this sonata form, with repeats for both parts, depends for material on the initial horn call and scalar descent in response.

The *Andante* in cut time is in B♭, beginning like the most dainty of gavottes, familiar in sound and character as well as key, meter, and melody. It is the sentimental Belmonte who again stands before us here, singing his hymn to love, the Rondeau in B♭ "Wenn der Freude Tränen fliessen" (*Die Entführung*, No. 15). In addition to the beginning, the *Andante* uses the aria's subsequent sighs E♭ - D, G - F at "ist der Liebe." This too is a rondo and in its last episode Mozart creates some exquisite dissonances by piling entries of the gavotte theme's repeated-note beginning on top of each other. The *Andante* does not strive for the depth and intensity of the *Adagio* in K. 593 but it is perfect for the overall tone of lightness and elegance that pervades this last work of chamber music by Mozart.

The finale of K. 614 is another rondo, an *Allegro* in 2/4 time that shows the composer in his most Haydnesque vein again. Mozart's rondo theme bears particular resemblance to a finale by Haydn from the String Quartet in E♭, No. 5 of Opus 64 composed in 1790 (Example 3.4ab). When the tune returns in the lower

EXAMPLE 3.4.

a. *Haydn, String Quartet in E♭, Op. 64, No. 5, IV*

b. *Mozart, String Quintet in E♭, K. 614, IV*

octave, the first violin holds a high B♭ in both pieces. There are other similarities as well. At the last, Mozart inverts his rondo theme, making it sound even more like Haydn's. We can easily imagine the eagerness with which Mozart anticipated playing this latest gem with Haydn, his frequent partner in chamber music. It was not to be, because Mozart died before Haydn returned from England.

The last piano concerto, K. 595 in B♭, belongs in a way among these latest works of chamber music because it is so delicate and refined. Mozart entered it in his catalogue on 5 January 1791, but it may have been begun earlier. Its first and second movements plus the beginning of its finale are written "on a paper-type which is found in dated scores only between December 1787 and February 1789."[14] From this, it appears that Mozart could have laid it aside for later completion.[15] Zinzendorf reported that a few days later, on 9 January, Barbara Ployer was to play the keyboard at a concert given by Prince Auersperg for the visiting King

[14] Tyson, *op. cit.*, p. 156.
[15] Rehm and Plath argue to the contrary, that the handwriting shows the work was written all at one time. *NMA* XV/15/8, *Kritischer Bericht* (1998): 42–43.

of Naples, which may have been the circumstance that prompted Mozart to complete K. 595. A work of surpassing beauty, it is worthy to stand beside the greatest of his compositions in the genre. Its opening *Allegro* in common time begins softly with a lyrical theme rising through the tonic triad, after a measure of anticipatory accompaniment, a feature it shares with the beginning of Symphony No. 40 in g. There is the usual abundance of melodious secondary themes, a veritable cornucopia. When the solo enters it states the initial theme, but ornamented as to its first measure, and lacking the anticipatory measure of accompaniment, thereby throwing the metric organization of the idea into a different light. The development section modulates wildly in getting started, one diminished-seventh chord giving way to another, higher diminished chord, prompting the piano to state the main theme first in b minor, then in C major. The tension between these two diminished-seventh chords is reduced in the finale.[16] A serene *Larghetto* in E♭ and in cut time serves as middle movement, begun by the piano alone. The finale, an *Allegro* in 6/8 time, also begun by the soloist unaccompanied, exudes childlike joy and candor. Mozart used its theme as the tune of "Sehnsucht nach dem Frühling," the first of *Three Spring Songs for Children*, K. 596.

Così fan tutte

1789 was a rather sparse year for entries in Mozart's thematic catalogue. April and May in Germany produced only two. On his return there were, besides the few works already mentioned, several replacement arias. The first of these, K. 577 in F, was "Ein Rondò in meine Oper figaro für Mad:^me feraresi del bene," entered in July. It replaced Susanna's Garden Aria in the revival of *Figaro* that began in the Burgtheater on 29 August 1789 and facilitated the commissioning of *Così fan tutte* (Figure 3.2).

Adriana Ferrarese, born 19 September 1759 and married to one Luigi del Bene, was hired after Joseph II forbade the rehiring of Nancy Storace, who, when she left Vienna in 1787, was paid the high annual salary of 4500 florins. Ferrarese came in 1788 at a still higher salary, 2700 florins for six months. In a letter from his battle quarters dated 14 July 1789, Joseph wrote Count Rosenberg, who was considering hiring her, that "Ferrarese will surely not please at all," a sentiment amplified a week later with comments on the singer's abilities, which he had observed on an earlier trip to Italy: "As far as I remember Ferrarese she has a very weak contralto voice, she knows music very well, but she has an ugly appearance."[17] Disregarding this advice Rosenberg hired her, perhaps because he had

---

[16] As pointed out by Simon P. Keefe, *Mozart's Piano Concertos: Dramatic Dialogue in the Age of Enlightenment* (Rochester, NY, 2001), pp. 152–55.

[17] Rice, *Antonio Salieri*, p. 425.

heard or read of her good reception in London during 1786.[18] Joseph's remark about her knowing music reflects well on her conservatory training in Venice at the Mendicanti, from 1780 to 1782.

La Ferrarese made her Viennese debut as the goddess in the revival of Martín y Soler's *L'arbore di Diana* on 13 October 1788. Zinzendorf, at least, was pleased with her: "Elle chanta a ravir, elle ne joua pas mal." A critic in the public press regretted that her acting was not up to her singing. Music in fact showed her to best advantage because she insisted on having roles tailored to emphasize sustained tones in the low register and rapid coloratura higher up. She had the temperament of an old-time prima donna and managed to get her demands satisfied one way or another. Da Ponte, smitten with her, confesses in his memoirs that he, an ordained priest, had an affair with this married lady.

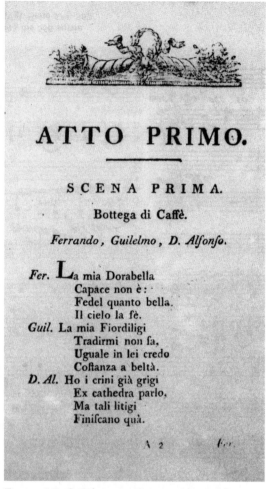

FIGURE 3.2. *Così fan tutte*. First text page of the printed libretto, 1790.

Although I have always in general been most susceptible to amorous passions, I nevertheless made it a very solemn rule of my life never to flirt with actresses, and for more than seven years I had the strength to resist every temptation, and observe my rule rigorously. But at last, to my misfortune, there came a singer, who without having great pretensions to beauty, delighted me first of all by her voice; and thereafter, she showing great propensity toward me, I ended by falling in love with her. She had in truth great merit. Her voice was delicious, her method new, and marvelously affecting. She had no striking grace of figure. She was not the best actress conceivable. But with two most beautiful eyes, with very charming lips, few the performances in which she did not prove infinitely pleasing . . . For her I wrote the *Pastor Fido* and the

---

Cifra with music by Salieri . . . and then the "School for Lovers" [*Così fan tutte*] with music by Mozart, an opera that holds third place among the three sisters born of that most celebrated father of harmony.[19]

There is no reason to doubt what Da Ponte says here, although there is good reason to dismiss many of the self-serving claims elsewhere in his memoirs. What he does not say, or perhaps even remember, is that Salieri, his superior in court service, made an attempt to set the last-named opera and gave up after the first two numbers.[20] Constanze Mozart did remember, and told the Novellos when they visited her in 1829, "Salieri first tried to set this opera but failed."[21] If the idea of a libretto constructed to accommodate many duets and ensembles came from Mozart, as I suspect, Salieri may have pulled rank and preempted the text.

Mozart did not think highly of Ferrarese's singing or acting. After he attended the opera at Dresden, he wrote his wife about the prima donna Maddalena Allegranti, "she is much better than the Ferrarese, but of course that is not saying very much" (letter of 16 April 1789). A few months later, faced with casting Ferrarese as Susanna, he apparently had no choice but to recompose the maid's two arias: that in Act II sung to Cherubino while dressing him in female finery, which demanded acting throughout, and the ever-so-subtle Garden Aria in Act IV. Either the new Susanna's histrionic abilities were too minimal to cope with what he had written for Storace, or Ferrarese simply insisted that she had to have totally new pieces. More than likely, both of these factors entered into the decision. "One must make a virtue of necessity," Mozart's dramaturgical credo, came into play: he sacrificed the original arias for far less appropriate substitutes. Da Ponte provided new texts, which appeared in the 1789 libretto, the printing of which was his job as theater poet. They replaced "Venite, inginocchiatevi" (admittedly a tongue twister) with a strophic song of two stanzas, "Un moto di gioia," K. 579 in G, set as an anodyne little waltz. Mozart did not see fit to enter the piece in his catalogue. In a letter to his wife in Baden dating from late August he wrote, using the double diminutive of "aria": "The *Ariettchen* that I made for the Ferrarese should please, I believe, if she is capable of performing it in a naïve way, of which I have strong doubts. It did please her greatly."

If "Un moto di gioia" could be said to represent the "dumbing down" of Susanna, the other aria, written earlier, could be called the role's "tarting up." It is a display piece, both for her voice and for a concertante wind complement of horn, bassoon, and two basset horns. The text begins with a line Da Ponte had used in *Don Giovanni*, "Al desio di chi t'adora," where it is sung by Anna and

[19] *Memoirs of Lorenzo da Ponte*, tr. Elisabeth Abbott, ed. Arnold Livingston (New York, 1959), p. 89.
[20] Bruce Alan Brown and John A. Rice, "Salieri's *Così fan tutte*," *Cambridge Opera Journal* 8 (1996): 17–43, and Rice, *Salieri*, p. 89.
[21] Vincent Novello in *A Mozart Pilgrimage*, p. 127.

Ottavio in the last scene, and continues with a litany of amorous desire in conventional language. The music conforms to the modish two-tempo rondò, with both slow and fast themes in gavotte rhythm. Both themes return on schedule after contrast. The most interesting part is the transition Mozart writes to prepare the fast theme, which sounds for a moment like its counterpart in the great rondò for the Countess, "Dove sono i bei momenti." The composer asks Ferrarese to sing only up to high A, and this tone is but lightly touched, not sustained. The fast theme, with its leaping figures in arpeggios, indicates that her voice possessed a flexibility readily associated with instruments, especially the clarinet. Before Mozart had convinced Storace to settle for the seemingly simple and truly sublime "Deh vieni non tardar" in F, he toyed with giving her a pathos-laden rondò in E♭, "Non tardar amato bene," the sketch for which shows that it was a forerunner to "Al desio," in both text and music.

With her alluring and showy new rondò, Ferrarese staked out a claim, namely, in the words of *Der Schauspieldirektor,* "Ich bin die erste Sängerin." Indeed that is what Susanna became. The Countess in this production was sung by Caterina Cavalieri, Mozart's original Konstanze, his Madame Silberklang, and his Elvira in the *Don Giovanni* for Vienna. Cavalieri was paid a much lower salary than the new Italian soprano. It was always thus for the German-born Caterina when a rival singer arrived from Italy. Not surprisingly, this soured relations between Cavalieri and Ferrarese. The situation was no different with Dorothea Bussani, the first Cherubino, who apparently retained this role in 1789. Da Ponte, recalling how things stood with these singers in the Burgtheater, had this to say in a continuation of the passage of his *Memoirs* just quoted.

> [Ferrarese's] usefulness to the Opera increased my regard and my attentions to her, especially after I had become the primary cause of her continuance in that city. But the lady had an impulsive, violent disposition, rather calculated to irritate the malevolent than to win and retain friendships. Let alone the envy of other singers, she had angered two especially, the one a German woman [Cavalieri], pushed perhaps a little too far by the good Salieri, the other an Italian *diva* [Bussani] who, though a ridiculous person of little merit, had by dint of facial contortions, clown's tricks, and perhaps by means more theatrical still, built up a great following among cooks, barbers, lackeys, butlers and hostlers, and in consequence was thought a gem.

What Da Ponte implies is that Madame Bussani was a whore. This meant taking a slap as well at her husband, Francesco Bussani, who was twenty years her senior. The first Bartolo and Antonio in *Figaro,* Bussani apparently revived these roles in 1789. He was on very bad terms with Da Ponte. This happy theatrical family, *mirabile dictu,* made *Figaro* more of a success than it had been three years earlier.

Zinzendorf wrote in his diary on the day of *Figaro's* premiere, 1 May 1786, "l'opera m'ennuya," nothing more. Being so long, the opera certainly tired many in the audience. On 4 July, Zinzendorf recorded that he found the music of Mozart "singular, dexterous, without thought." He had little to say about subsequent performances, nothing at all about individual singers or numbers, although he often singled out pieces and individuals in other operas. On 31 August 1789, however, at the second performance of the revived *Figaro*, he recorded a positive comment on the Letter Duet, "Charmant Duo entre La Cavalieri et la ferrarese." On 7 May 1790, with *Figaro* still holding firm on the boards, he wrote, "Le Duo des deux femmes, le rondeau de la ferraresi plait toujours." The production, which lasted until 9 February 1791, racked up twenty-nine performances, nearly tripling the number of the original staging. Without this success, Mozart and Da Ponte might have lacked Rosenberg's support for creating a new opera. Emperor Joseph had relinquished his personal control in such matters.

The Burgtheater had twice preceded *Figaro* in 1786 with performances of Paisiello's *Il barbiere*. Another coupling was afoot in 1789. One of the suburban theaters was preparing a German-language version of *Il barbiere* for which Mozart wrote a replacement of Rosina's aria in the music-lesson scene of Act III, "Già riede primavera." He entered "Schon lacht der holde Frühling," K. 580, in his catalogue under the date of 17 September 1789. K. 580 is in B♭, with a slow contrasting middle section, as in Paisiello's setting, with which it rewards comparison.

Così fan tutte required close coordination because of its many ensembles. Mozart's pupil Joseph Eybler was responsible for coaching the singers and in particular the two leading ladies, Ferrarese and Louise Villeneuve; after mentioning their names, he says that the experience was his "introduction to theatre life, with its disorders, cabals, and so forth."[22] Villeneuve by all reports was as pretty as Ferrarese was plain, cause enough by itself for tantrums and "disorders." Yet the combining of these two voices in duet after duet, with the parallel duets of tenor and baritone, became the glue to hold this opera together, and, as aural wonder, an inventive spring that may have stimulated the process of creation in Mozart's mind. Da Ponte says, as we have seen, that he wrote the opera for Ferrarese, but this does not preclude the possibility that even before he came up with a story of two couples caught in a web of deception and temptation Mozart was beginning to conceive an opera built up from duets. The many and diverse duets pitted against each other in the composer's great string quintets may also have led to imagining a novel kind of opera, different from *Figaro*, from *Don Giovanni*, and from any other opera in its surpassing sensuous beauty.

Mozart was evidently well disposed toward the charms of Villeneuve. He wrote three insertion arias for her to sing during the late summer and autumn of 1789: "Alma grande e nobil core" K. 578 in B♭, a proud, majestic, seria-type piece for a Cimarosa opera, entered in the catalogue under August, and two arias, K.

[22] Bruce Alan Brown, *W. A. Mozart: Così fan tutte* (Cambridge, 1995), p. 23.

582 and K. 583, for Martín's *Il burbero di buon cuore*, dated October. The voice part in all three makes modest demands, moving gracefully with few melismas from the D above middle C to the G a twelfth above (with optional A one tone higher in K. 582), in other words a typical mezzo soprano part with neither high nor low extensions.

Before Vienna, Villeneuve (often called, without any proof, a sister of Ferrarese), sang at the San Moisè theater in Venice, and perhaps she too was trained at one of the city's famous conservatories. She made her debut in the Burgtheater on 27 June 1789, taking over the role of Cupid in Martín's immensely successful *L'arbore di Diana* on a libretto by Da Ponte that has many parallels with *Così fan tutte.*[23] She replaced Luisa Laschi Mombelli, who created the role in 1787. An enthralled critic praised Villeneuve's Cupid for "her enchanting appearance, expressive acting and beautiful artistic singing."[24] Zinzendorf records that he first saw her play this role on 11 July 1789. He called her "une eleve de Noverre," meaning, if true, that she was also trained as a dancer, and consequently moved with above-average grace for a singer. Noverre was in Paris after 1776 (also in London and Lyons) and if his connection with the singer is correct, it strengthens the possibility that she may have been French in more than name. Zinzendorf continued by writing, "Her physiognomy, while beautiful, is less theatrical than [Luisa Laschi] Mombelli." In his entry dated 11 February 1791, he suggested that her beauty roused interest in Leopold II: "On soupçonne l'Emp[ereur] amoureux de la Villeneuve. Il la lorgne a la redoute." Perhaps Empress Maria Luisa noticed this ogling on her husband's part. Shortly afterward Villeneuve was no longer in the imperial service.

Playing opposite Villeneuve's Dorabella was the Ferrando of tenor Vincenzo Calvesi. Mozart wrote for several of the finest tenors of his day, notably Anton Raaff (Idomeneo), Valentin Adamberger (Belmonte), and Antonio Baglioni (Ottavio, Tito). Yet Raaff was then well beyond his prime, and more than one critic noted that Adamberger, for all his good qualities, had a nasal timbre. Baglioni, complained Niemetschek in 1794, had a defective voice that was more of a mezzo-basso and could not cope with Ferrando's arias (but perhaps his voice had darkened).[25] Calvesi topped all others in vocal proficiency and technical brilliance; moreover, his beautiful tone inspired Mozart to a new level of lyric intensity. His vocal quality offers another possible rationale for creating such an opera in the first place. In duets, he was mainly paired with the basso buffo Benucci as

---

[23] Dorothea Link, "*L'arbore di Diana*: a model for *Così fan tutte,*" in *Wolfgang Amadè Mozart: Essays on His Life and His Music,* ed. Stanley Sadie (1996), pp. 362–73.

[24] Brown, *Così fan tutte* (1995), pp. 191–92, n. 14.

[25] "Einige Nachrichten über den Zustand des Theaters in Prag. Im Dezember 1794," *Allgemeines europaisches Journal* (Brno, 1794); *Mozart, Die Dokumente seines Lebens, Addenda und Corrigenda,* ed. Joseph Heinz Eibl (Kassel, 1978), p. 81.

Guglielmo. The nature of buffo singing made this pairing more difficult for the composer than the pairing of the two women. Suffice it to say that Calvesi met his match as to excellence in the non-pareil Benucci, renowned as much for his acting as for his singing.

Calvesi did not go back to the beginnings of the Viennese troupe in 1783, as did Benucci and Francesco Bussani. He arrived, also from Venice, in 1785, when he made his debut as Sandrino in Paisiello's *Il re Teodoro in Venezia*. He sang many other roles but did not appear in *Figaro*, which had no part for a lyric *primo tenore*. From February 1788 to March 1789 he was engaged at Naples, else he surely would have sung Ottavio in the Viennese *Don Giovanni*. He returned in 1789, at which time he was among the highest-paid Italian male singers of the troupe, second only to Benucci. Mozart knew his abilities well, having heard him in many roles and written for him in the ensembles K. 479 and K. 480 of 1785. He made the most of the tenor's strengths from the first numbers in *Così fan tutte*, with Ferrando taking the lead voice in trios with Guglielmo and Alfonso (Bussani). Initially Mozart rewarded Calvesi with three stunning solos, not two as with the other principals, although he later allowed "Ah! lo veggio" (No. 24) to be cut.

The priority Mozart assigned to ensembles in *Così* is evident not only in their sheer number but also in that he began by composing all the duets and ensembles of Act I, leaving aside recitatives and arias until later, as paper studies and early numberings of the pages show. The exceptions are Dorabella's No. 11, "Smanie implacabile" (although its recitative is on later paper), and Guglielmo's original first-act aria, "Rivolgete a lui." The longest ensemble of Act I (aside from the finale) is the Sextet, No. 13 in C, when the two young men begin their masquerade in Turkish disguise. It concludes with many resounding cadences and flourishes, lastly the slides in the violins from low G up to C as at the end of Act I in *Figaro*, rousing the audience to applaud.

In its scenic disposition, *Così* is well planned. The sequence of main events corresponds to set changes in an economical and telling way, as may be seen in Table 3.1.

Table 3.1 Sets and Action in *Così fan tutte*

Act I:	Sets	Bottega di caffè	Giardino sulla spiaggia	Camera gentile	Giardinetto gentile
	Action	The Wager	Seaside Follies	Hysteria, intruders	Despina's Show No. 1: Confusion
Act II:	Sets	Camera	Giardino sulla riva del mare	Camera	Sala richissima illuminata
	Action	Renewed Temptations	Seduction, 1	Seduction, 2	Despina's Show No. 2: Resolution

The Wager was an ingenious way of getting this plot started, and its setting in a coffee shop provides the perfect ambiance. We are in a great port city, Naples, where Vesuvius could be shown smoldering in the background of this outdoor café. How different this is from the rather claustrophobic chateau near Seville for *Figaro*, or the somber city of Seville itself for *Don Giovanni*. Two young officers in the service of the King of Naples are boasting of their sweethearts' fidelity in such extravagant terms that they provoke their elderly and stoical friend Don Alfonso (described in the libretto as "un vecchio Filosofo"), who teases them. Dorabella is as beautiful as she is faithful, insists Ferrando, and is not capable of deceiving; Guglielmo affirms that his Fiordiligi would never traduce him and was equal in constancy and beauty. His music is the same, transposed to the dominant, taking his voice lower. Alfonso responds that his hair is gray and that he speaks *ex cathedra*, and may such disputes end at once. No, answer the officers, speaking as one and taking offense. They ask for proof for Alfonso's doubts, becoming so upset that they put their hands on their swords. This is the first of many instances in the opera where the young lovers, male or female, are made by the musical treatment to seem identical, like peas in a pod. "What a mad desire!" sings Alfonso, literally in the middle between the irate officers' voices, "to seek that fault which, when found, will make one miserable." It is one of Alfonso's many axioms and vital to the lesson he will eventually teach these over-caffeinated young men.

The quarrel continues in the following recitative to the point at which Alfonso asks, "And you expect to find fidelity in women? How pleased I am by simplicity!" One critic compares this with Diderot's mocking "Children!" to reprove lovers' vows of constancy.[26] The recitative cadence on the chord of B major prepares the second trio in E, begun by Alfonso with another axiom, this one comparing fidelity to the Arabian phoenix, a quatrain borrowed from Metastasio. Everyone says it exists, but where? he asks twice. The strings in unison give answer by two falling thirds, *pianissimo*, as if on tiptoes. "No one knows," sings Alfonso to a falling third then a decisive falling fifth back to tonic E. The young men of course have the answer; each propounds the name of his own phoenix. The musical jests of this short trio become increasingly hilarious at every descending third the officers sing, but the last word goes to Alfonso's descending fifth.

Ferrando, the more spiritual of the two officers, derides Alfonso's axiom as "the nonsense of poets," suggesting that he at least knows it is a quotation, while Guglielmo calls it the "folly of old men." Alfonso asks in the following recitative what proof the men have that their lovers' hearts are so invariable. The list tumbles out of them in alternation: "long experience, noble education, lofty thoughts, analogous temperaments, generous souls, immutable characters, promises, pro-

---

[26] Nicholas Till, *Mozart and the Enlightenment: Truth, Virtue and Beauty in Mozart's Operas* (London, 1992), p. 253.

tests." Alfonso interrupts the recital and continues it with "tears, sighs, caresses, faintings—let me laugh a bit." Further enraged, the young men quickly agree to wager a hundred sequins with Alfonso that their ladies are unlike others. He makes them swear that they will not reveal the wager to their Penelopes and they will do exactly as he tells them. To this they agree with enthusiasm and begin to think of how they will celebrate after winning the wager. As the recitative pushes to its end on the chord of G, the full orchestra bursts in resolving G to V^7 of C, then C with trumpets and timpani. Tonally, the three trios tell their own story of falling thirds: G E C.

The third trio differentiates the most between the two officers, a difference set up by the text. Ferrando sings first, as usual, saying he will use the money won to offer a beautiful serenade to his goddess. This noble melody takes his voice up to G, and then a tone higher for the melodic turn before descending into the cadence—eleven measures of lovely cantilena, the salient melodic characteristics of which will return with great effect later. Guglielmo wishes to offer a banquet to his Venus, a more down-to-earth sentiment in a slightly briefer statement sung in his baritone range and with several buffo traits. After Alfonso asks if he will be invited to the feast and the men agree, they settle on a line that all three can sing: repeated toasts to the god of love will they offer. As the words "repeated toasts" recur for the third and fourth time, the strings, as if already giddy from drink, emit a three-part written-out trill in sixteenth notes, for a full two measures, with rise via a *crescendo* from soft to loud. This trill had already been heard, with cadential fall to the tonic, as a main idea of the overture, one that duplicates what the cynical Basilio sang in the Trio, No. 7 of *Figaro*, to the words "Così fan tutte le belle."[27] The trio of men finishes with several more cadences, the tenor up to high A, and then a rousing send-off by the orchestra, thirteen measures of march music in C major, rounded off by the timpani playing a roll on tonic C.

Rapid set changes, common on eighteenth-century stages, permitted the café, presumably played on a short stage, to disappear in an instant and be replaced by a garden on the seashore. The orchestra limns the new atmosphere with a totally different color, gentle A major, in a limpid *Andante* in 3/8 time, the first triple meter to be heard. The passage is made the more unctuous and seductive by the first use of clarinets in A, far gentler than the bright clarinets in C of the overture, and by being given the main theme in thirds, here doubled an octave below by the bassoons.

This new, serenely graceful atmosphere leaves the world of men behind to project an aura of female voluptuousness, as only Mozart could do. The two beauties now sing, Fiordiligi leading off, as she almost always does, asking her

[27] Daniel Heartz, "Three Schools for Lovers, or 'Così fan tutte le belle,' " in *Mozart's Operas* (1990), pp. 216–27.

sister Dorabella to consider the portrait of her Guglielmo and decide whether a more beautiful mouth and noble aspect could ever be found, not ending before a flourish takes her voice up to high A while protracting the "ah" syllable of "ritrovar." The key switches at once to E as Dorabella holds out her portrait of Ferrando and asks her sister to observe the fire in his glance and the flames that dart from his eyes, with a melisma of her own on the "ah" syllable of "scoccar." Their exchanges begin to dwindle in length, a trait well known from love duets. The two voices overlap first in preparing a V⁷ of the A chord in rising parallel thirds. The tempo and meter then change to an *Allegro* in 2/4 time as they sing together a new melody in sixths and thirds. After pauses on the word "Amore" that are given very specific, written-out ornamentation, the singers comes to a short halt. When the ladies resume their singing in thirds Mozart gives them a device found often in love duets: one holds a pedal against the melismas of the other, then they switch roles. Dorabella's pedal is on E, Fiordiligi's on the A a fourth higher. Their words are somewhat prophetic: "May Cupid make me suffer a living torture should I ever change my heart's desire." Although the duet is all about love, rather than the usual message, the music tells us, with its traditional schemes and slightly ridiculous prolongations for billings and cooings in thirds, that these young ladies are no less shallow than their cardboard lovers.

The A major that sheds its radiance on the new scene by the shore also continues the plunge of keys descending by thirds. Indeed, the progression is all the more evident because there is no intervening recitative. Up to this point the opera has moved from number to number only between keys that share a common tone, mostly the third or the fifth of the previous key, beginning with the overture in C. Example 3.5a demonstrates these links by ties between common tones. The move by tonalities down a seventh by thirds can be nothing less than predictive of descent by thirds in the opera's motto-title, as sung in No. 30 (Example 3.5b). If we hear the D of the violins as a continuation an octave above of the bass's and vocal line's descent, there is even a hint of a descending seventh by thirds.

EXAMPLE 3.5 a, b. Mozart, *Cosí fan tutte*

a. *Initial keys*

b. *Motto, No. 30*

The sequence of ongoing common tones from the overture through No. 4 is rudely broken by No. 5, in f minor, Alfonso's little mock-pathetic air in which he feigns grief so strong he cannot bear to utter the truth. After teasing them by delaying the news, he reveals his game: their lovers have been called by royal order to the field of battle. In reaction, the ladies go into paroxysms of despair but avoid fainting. Their young men have been waiting in the wings and appear immediately at Alfonso's call. The Quintet of Farewells, No. 6 in E♭, follows. The lads act their part, Alfonso can barely hide his mirth, and the ladies overreact, asking the men to plunge their swords into the bosoms of their lovers. They behave, in other words, like the heroines of romantic novels, no doubt one of their models. As a spoof of leave taking, it is all so hilarious yet at the same time so breathtakingly beautiful. The men lament the bitter fate imposed upon them and then sing a formal farewell, a *duettino* in B♭, short but not without exchanging pedal for melisma between voices. A drum roll sounds, calling them to embark. Out of nowhere comes a soft military march in D, No. 8, to which a chorus responds "Bella vita militar!" Alfonso, ever resourceful, has moved fast. His little military celebration sets up the Quintet, No. 9. Intended by Da Ponte to be only a recitative, and set to music without key signature, as typical of that genre, it is nevertheless in the key of F and a musical number in its own right, a new kind of multi-voiced arioso. Mozart ran risks of lingering too long on this scene and blowing it out of proportion, but this little number is adorable. "Write me every day," sings Fiordiligi, weeping, one syllable at a time, as if too choked with emotion to manage more. Never one to be outdone, Dorabella raises the stakes with "Twice a day you will write me." The men sing "Addio" to deliciously familiar falling thirds. At the end the cadence on F is followed abruptly by a one-chord transition back to D, the bass moving down a third by step, F E D, for the repeat of "Bella vita militar!"

The ladies wave their handkerchiefs at the *barca* carrying their men out to a waiting galleon. All they can do, with Alfonso in support, is to wish for tranquil seas, kind winds, and that "every benign element corresponds to their desires." For this miraculous *terzettino*, No. 10, Mozart resorts again to the key of E, last heard in No. 2, about the Arabian phoenix. Of all the composer's sea idylls, this is the most famous, eclipsing even "Placido è il mar" of *Idomeneo*, which is also in E. The clarinets in A return to soften the wind complement here, and the violins maintain their sixteenth-note murmuring figure throughout *con sordino*, against the pizzicato of the cellos and basses, leaving among the strings only the violas to play sustained lines in longer notes. The ladies exit. Alfonso muses on his acting talents and cites another aphorism (this one from the poet Sannazaro).

The scene changes to what was perhaps another short stage, a room with various doors, seats, and a little table. The serving maid, Despina, is the first to appear. She has prepared the morning chocolate for the ladies and she begins with a labor complaint not unlike Leporello's at the beginning of *Don Giovanni*, but in rapid recitative. Just as he wants to play the gentleman, she wants to savor and taste the gentlewomen's brew, which she does, whereupon they arrive, Fiordiligi hysterically calling for a knife and poison. Dorabella outdoes her by working her way up, through an impassioned obbligato recitative (with reminiscences of *Idomeneo*) to a furious aria, "Smanie implacabili," in E♭, No. 11. She had presumably observed this kind of behavior on the stage of the Teatro San Carlo in serious operas. It is all parody of course. The more they carry on like this, Alfonso had predicted, the easier they will fall.

Both ladies are desperate and hurl themselves into chairs. "Losing Guglielmo would make me die," whimpers Fiordiligi. Dorabella again goes her one better, "Losing Ferrando, I should die by being buried alive." Despina deflates them with her reply, "One man is as good as another because they are all worthless." Dispensing advice freely, she next urges them to profit from the men's absence by finding other amusements, just as their men are doing. Affronted by this aspersion, Dorabella insists that their men's beautiful souls were incapable of infidelity. That is a tale to tell children, retorts Despina, launching into her aria, No. 12, in F, "In uomini, in soldati sperare fedeltà?" For her giddy exposé of male foibles Mozart resorts to a dance-like *Allegretto* in 6/8 time with dotted rhythm, after opening the piece in 2/4 time. This dance-like kind of 6/8 time, first used here, will recur when Despina's levity gains the upper hand.

The stage empties for Alfonso's entrance. He wonders whether Despina, clever rogue that she is, will be able to recognize the men he has disguised in outlandish Turkish garb and long mustaches. He bribes her to go along and admit the "Turks." She agrees. The men enter as the Sextet No. 13 in C begins, with a comically accented second beat in *Allegro* common time. They pass the test in that Despina, whom they court, does not recognize them. The two ladies enter and are furious with her for letting these strangers into their house (change to 3/4 time and the key of F). Again, they sing as one. The men, led by Despina, sink to their knees to implore the sisters for kindness, in a passage that is mainly in a. Full of fury and scorn, the women pour out a torrent of parallel thirds up and down the scale, made more humorous still by the sudden *fortes* with which the orchestra punctuates their tirade. This last section returns to C major as the tempo becomes *Molto Allegro* in cut time. At 219 measures in length, with several changes of key and meter, the quintet sounds very much like a finale. Its key, on the other hand, being the overall one of the opera, signals that this is not the medial finale, which is still some distance away and in a rival key, as in all of Mozart's last operas.

Alfonso pretends to recognize two old friends in the intruders (not identified as Albanians until the second finale). He has to coach the men sotto voce to play along with him. This encourages their renewed attack. Fiordiligi takes it upon herself to stand firm against them: she and her sister will never betray their oaths of fidelity. To make the point, Da Ponte summoned an old standby of opera seria, the metaphor aria, "Come scoglio immoto resta" (As the cliff remains unmoved by winds and storm, this soul remains strong in faith and love). Mozart responded with a parody of heroic soprano arias, including multiple leaps between high and low, from low A below middle C to high B♭. The orchestra, featuring rarely used trumpets in B♭, announces a pompous beginning with dotted rhythms and a motif climbing the triad, *Andante maestoso* in common time, then *Allegro* after fourteen measures for the second quatrain and return of the first. For the last quatrain, Mozart switches to *Più Allegro*. Here Ferrarese/Fiordiligi got to show off her coloratura in rapid triplets, and her sustained tones. Following this display of her *virtù*, an exit is the only proper action, according to long-standing tradition.

The ladies attempt to flee but are stopped from doing so. Alfonso prevails on them to show some courtesy, and Guglielmo steps forward with an aria boasting of the men's many attributes. Here poet and composer miscalculated by creating a text and musical setting, No. 15a in D, K. 584, so crowded with topical references as to be self-defeating. They replaced it with the much shorter No. 15, devoid of comparisons and in a lighter style.[28] Its allusions to physical attractions are the same as in the original aria and suggestive enough to send the ladies running. Another advantage of the replacement aria is that its key of G did not anticipate the soon-to-begin act finale in D. Joined directly to the aria is a laughing trio for the two men and Alfonso, No. 16, which continues the key of G. After minimal recitative Ferrando sings his sublime *aria d'affetto*, No. 17 in A, for which the clarinets in A make an opportune return. Mozart took this expression of true love so seriously that the aria may represent a turning point at which he began to question Da Ponte's approach. Ferrando comes across as a living and breathing man of passion—no cardboard lover he.

From the "Camera gentile" the action moves to a "Giardinetto gentile." The word "gentile" can mean "pleasant" as well as "pagan" in Italian. Da Ponte may be playing on both senses. He has taken pains to remove any trace of Christian references in the plot and to make it, as nearly as possible, a story without social context. What references he uses from outside are nearly all from pagan antiquity. The garden is apparently a side or back garden off the ladies' commodious villa. On each side, the garden has turf seats, which were in high fashion at the time (Figure 3.3). This was no mean estate inhabited by these two young sisters, whose reasons for being in Naples, alone moreover, remain unexplained, like nearly everything else about them except that they are from Ferrara (a pun on the prima donna's name). They are obviously not poor. Some critics want to

---

[28] Guglielmo's arias are discussed in detail in Daniel Heartz, "When Mozart Revises: The Case of Guglielmo in *Così fan tutte*," in *Wolfgang Amadè Mozart* (1996), pp. 355–61. Edmund J. Goehring, *Three Modes of Perception in Mozart: The Philosophical, Pastoral, and Comic in "Così fan tutte"* (Cambridge, 2004), takes no account of Guglielmo's arias and, consequently, of this essay about them.

FIGURE 3.3. Garden scene from Goldoni's *Arcadia in Brenta*. Engraved by Zuliani.

make them *bourgeoises*, but they have little to go on because Da Ponte has kept class from being an issue.

Scenery can help set the tone for Act I's finale, in accordance with Mozart's orchestra, which paints a serene and beautiful picture before a single word is uttered. The violins and violas are all muted. A murmuring sixteenth-note figure in the second violins accompanies the agreeably lithe and galant melody of the first violins, *Andante* in 2/4 time. The winds enter, overlapping the end of the six-measure phrase of the violins, with two flutes in thirds frolicking up the scale and wavering back and forth like a trill at the top, a fluttering mimicked by the bassoons an octave below. Music like this anticipates a verbal description of zephyrs, gentle breezes, and other natural delights. Yet the two ladies sing to the same music complaining of immutable fate, seas full of torment, unkind stars, pain, languishing, etc., etc. In a case like this, where the music stands in absolute contradiction to the words, we believe what the music tells us. Verbally, the ladies sound like the abandoned Didos and Armidas so cherished on the operatic stage but ludicrously inappropriate to their actual situation. Even they do not believe in these clichés. It is all play-acting, a sham, setting the stage for the next caper, as managed by the experienced and super-efficient Despina.

Mozart needed calm and blissful music at the beginning of the finale, both to paint the garden in sound and to contrast with the tumultuous eruption of the Albanians, threatening suicide by drinking vials of poison, *Allegro* in cut time. They sing from the wings of the stage. In vain, Alfonso begs them to desist. They enter. The ladies, gullible as ever, become frozen by the tragic spectacle before them, played out in the key of E♭. Alfonso urges the women to help them. Instead, they call for help but no one hears them so they call Despina. She arrives and tells the ladies to succor the youths by stroking them while she rushes to find a doctor and an antidote. The ladies relent and gingerly approach the men. "What interesting features," sings Dorabella. They go so far as to feel the men's pulses. Next, they begin to lament the men's fate. The music passes into c minor and their expressions of pity are extended in an ensemble to which the two men also contribute sotto voce, wondering whether this pity will turn into affection.

Despina breaks the spell, or rather the orchestra does, with a bright splash of G major, *Allegro* in 3/4 time, reminiscent of Figaro's bursting in on the scene in the first finale of *Le nozze*. Despina has put on the disguise of a medical doctor. Her mask fools the ladies but not their suitors. She greets the ladies in pseudo-Latin, a language they say is strange to them (so much for "noble education"). Despina as doctor then boasts of all the languages she commands, naming them. She cures the stricken by applying a large magnet to their heads and drawing out the poison, an action painted by the wind instruments with sustained trills, imitating hers. The men come to their senses but pretend to be disoriented, nicely translated into music by moving from G to B♭ without transition. "Are you Venus or Pallas Athena?" they ask. "No! you are my dear goddess." The men make so bold as to kiss the hands of the ladies, who protest, but in asides admit that they are beginning to waver. Again without modulation the music plunges into a key distant by a third, D major, indicating that the end of the finale is near. The men push their luck and demand a kiss from the ladies, who refuse. To great clamor and excitement, with many repetitions, the finale bubbles on to its conclusion.

Act II opens with another short-stage scene, described simply as a room. Despina challenges the sisters from Ferrara to act like real women: "treat love as a bagatelle." She spices her enjoinders with witty sayings and seductive reasonings: "Your Ganymedes have gone off to war." Hence, *Carpe diem*! In the following exchange, she uses the term *Narcissi* for the men, recalling Figaro's description of Cherubino as a little Adonis and a little Narcissus. Invoking Ganymede (comely Trojan youth carried off by an eagle to serve Zeus) and Narcissus (beautiful boy who fell in love with his own image) lends Despina a patina of sophisticated learning but hardly enhances the manliness of the two officers. Rather, it reduces them from men to pretty boys. Despina speaks with such wit and insight throughout this long opening recitative that she is made to sound a lot like Da Ponte himself. His memoirs are replete with such verbal cleverness, as well as with seduction scenes.[29]

Despina, practiced as she is in feminine wiles, proceeds to give a lesson in their use with her aria, No. 19 in G, "Una donna a quindici anni." Like her first aria it is a lilting piece in 6/8 time with dotted rhythm, beginning *Andante* but soon turning *Allegretto*. With its waltz-like oom-pah-pah accompaniment the aria has a lot in common with "Un moto di gioia," K. 579, including its key and prominent melodic turn around the fifth degree. Despina's lesson takes effect, especially on Dorabella, who persuades the more reluctant Fiordiligi to allow a little flirtation with the exotic strangers. Asked which one she might choose for her beau, Dorabella replies that she has already chosen. She begins the duet, No. 20 in B♭, by stating her choice, "Prenderò quel brunettino," that is, the dark-haired one, who, under his disguise, is Guglielmo, her sister's lover. Dorabella takes the lead throughout the duet, by the end of which they are singing together of the pleasures they are going to enjoy. As in their first duet, parallel thirds predominate.

The stage opens up to the opera's grandest scene, a garden on the seashore with turf seats and stone tables. A bark garlanded with flowers bearing the two men glides slowly by. Alfonso has produced this wonder and does not stint its praises to the ladies: "Che allegria! Che musica! Che canto! Che brillante spet-tacolo!" We should not even ask how he got all this up in a trice: ordinary time is suspended in this fantasy opera, in which reality becomes less and less conse-quential. The serenade, No. 21 in E♭, is performed first by a wind band consist-ing of pairs of clarinets, bassoons, and horns, joined later by flutes. They play from the bark on stage as it approaches. Generations of the scenographer's craft went into the making of such scenes, which were accompanied by gently lapping waves, an illusion created by an ingenious machine. Mozart, with all his expe-rience writing serenades for real events, was sure to excel in the stage serenade. The sensuous beauty of the whole scene, greatly reinforced by the music, would be enough to seduce anyone, let alone two such flighty young ladies as Dora-bella and Fiordiligi. The two men sing the serenade Alfonso has given them to words of timeless efficacy, asking the breezes to second their desires and carry their sighs to the goddesses of their hearts. They bear chains of flowers that they present to their ladies, guided by Alfonso and Despina. The astonished women are struck dumb by amazement. Alfonso instructs servants in splendid livery to carry in more sprays of flowers and place them on the stone tables, then motions for them to exit. The moment has come for the men to speak to their goddesses, but they too are struck dumb, to the exasperation of Alfonso and Despina, who begin No. 20 in D, called a quartet but actually a duet, in which Alfonso speaks

[29] Daniel Heartz, "Mozart and Da Ponte," *Musical Quarterly* 79 (1995): 700–19.

for the men and Despina for the ladies; the two men merely echo his words, with very humorous effect. Pleased with this new lesson in wooing and confident of success, Despina and Alfonso withdraw.

The newly assorted couples, still rather tongue-tied, begin to stroll in the garden while making a few trite remarks. Guglielmo suddenly tries a new verbal attack on Dorabella, then presents her with a heart-shaped locket. With little resistance she accepts it, leading to the duet No. 23, "Il cor vi dono," an *Andante grazioso* in 3/8 time and in F. In a few moments they are listening to each other's heartbeats (cf. Zerlina's "Vedrai, carino"). He takes her locket containing Ferrando's portrait and replaces it with his own, as she sings the pertinent aside, "I seem to have a Vesuvius in my breast!" By the time the violins begin adding skittish little runs à la Despina, everything has been decided. The two sing sweetly together of their newly found bliss and exit arm in arm.

Fiordiligi, putting up a fight, sweeps on to an impassioned obbligato recitative as she flees Ferrando, claiming she has had monstrous visions. She calms down a bit as the music moves from g to E♭, the same *Idomeneo*-linked progression used prior to both women's arias in Act I. Ferrando takes her apparent softening as a cue to renew his advances, which take the form of a big bravura aria in B♭, "Ah! lo veggio," No. 24, beginning *Allegretto* and ending *Allegro*, in cut time. His words speak of reading love in her eyes if not in her words, a neutral enough pretext for Mozart to indulge in a tour de force for Calvesi, whose voice is often up around high B♭ and moving consistently by leaps in a high tessitura. Though not called a rondò, the piece has some rondò characteristics: besides the tempo contrast, the slower theme is in gavotte rhythm and returns after a passage in the dominant. The faster final section demands still more vocal heroics. Mozart may have sanctioned the omission of No. 24 because it stole too much thunder from Fiordiligi's bona fide rondò that comes next: another showpiece, indeed the opera's greatest showpiece aria, "Per pietà, ben mio," No. 25 in E. With No. 24 gone, there were still four solo arias in a row at this point.

For "Per pietà" Fiordiligi is alone on stage. She repents having strayed so far into temptation, denounces her weakness, and asks her absent lover Guglielmo to forgive her. Three quatrains of *ottenarii*, typical for a rondò, provide the framework. Unusual is the choice of an *Adagio* in common time for the initial section, the first occurrence of this slow and serious tempo in the opera. Less unusual is the lack of any orchestral music before the voice begins, the way Ferrarese's rondò in *Figaro* also begins. The expected gavotte rhythm shapes the slow theme but is somewhat disguised by dotted rhythms. As the second quatrain dwells on Fiordiligi's horror and shame, Mozart turns to a more agitated style and to minor. On the return of the refrain, two horns in E join her vocal line and then make comments on it. Concertante writing often accompanied the rondò but the choice of two horns as the singer's main partners strikes an uncommon tone. A flute, two clarinets in B♮, and the first bassoon join the dialogue. When the *Allegro moderato* begins, it introduces a more obvious gavotte motion and a melody also typical of this dance to clothe the third quatrain. After contrast, this theme returns. A long and florid coda closes the piece with more vocal display and cavorting of the concertante instruments; this is followed by the heroine's exit, in true opera seria fashion.

Ferrando, having been rejected, tells Guglielmo they have won the bet. He expects to hear his tale of Firodiligi's steadfastness repeated by his friend about Dorabella. Alas for him, the truth comes out, slowly, leading to what was originally planned as a place for Ferrando's cavatina "Tradito, schernito" but instead became the venue for Guglielmo's second aria, "Donne mie," No. 26 in G. This triumph of buffo singing and acting made up to Benucci for the big aria he lost in Act I (No. 15a), borrowing a little from that and some of its excitement from Figaro's electrifying "Non più andrai." The great actor-singer was well served by this slyly humorous piece scolding women for deceiving men.[30]

Ferrando, in a short obbligato recitative marked *Allegro*, works up to his outburst "Tradito," No. 27, an *Allegro* in cut time that is in c minor. A quartet of winds, clarinets in B♭, and bassoons sing a more hopeful and soothing phrase in E♭ all by themselves, as if encouraging him. He responds by singing the same melody to words confessing that in spite of Dorabella's perfidy he still loves her. The emphatic tone of A♭ as dominant seventh, repeated for the word "Amor" and followed by stepwise descent resembles melodic traits in the heroic aria for Pylades to end Act III of Gluck's *Iphigénie en Tauride*, an aria also filled with love and hope.[31] The first part, in c minor, returns briefly and this time is followed not by E♭ but by the winds in radiant C major. Ferrando follows suit, now duplicating Pylades even as to the same pitches. As superb a buffo aria as Guglielmo/Benucci had just received, it is no finer than the seria one for Ferrando/Calvesi that succeeds it, in which the singer's high tenor is set off to glorious effect. His final ascent to G and A before descending echoes the same in No. 3.

After a very long stretch of recitative, Dorabella's giddy aria, No. 28, "È amor un ladroncello" (Cupid is a little thief), returns the opera to the buffo sphere. An *Allegretto* in 6/8 time and in B♭, it is in full Despina mode and makes the point, at too great length, that she has joined forces with her chambermaid, who applauds her pupil. The two exit together, leaving Fiordiligi alone. Still resisting the idea of changing suitors, she has the madcap idea of dressing in military costume and joining her lover at the front. She summons Despina and bids her bring the spare uniforms belonging to the officers from her closet (best not to ask what they are doing there). She hopes that Dorabella will follow her noble example. She begins what seems like an aria, No. 29 in A, "Fra gli amplessi," with an *Adagio* in cut

---

[30] Its components are discussed in Heartz, "When Mozart Revises: The Case of Guglielmo," pp. 355–61.
[31] *Music in European Capitals*, pp. 866–67.

time. Within a few instants, she says, defying all logic, she will be in the arms of her faithful lover. She does not get much further before Ferrando intrudes on her solitude, turning her fantasy into her worst fears.

Musically, and in terms of the drama, Fiordiligi's fall is the opera's high point. Dorabella's came so easily and quickly it provided little interest. By putting up a fight, both with herself and with Ferrando, Fiordiligi throws sparks. No. 29 begins dreamily, with thoughts of amorous embraces. The key of A seems a perilous choice, being the key of Ferrando's ecstatic paean to love, No. 17, but here clarinets in A are lacking. When Ferrando enters her room the key changes first to e then to C as she says that she has been betrayed (by Despina letting him in) and begs him to leave. C major is no less a treacherous place for her than A and to make things worse she sings her pleas to the beautiful phrase Ferrando himself sang as early as No. 3, "Una bella serenata." He picks up her citation and continues it by recalling much of that earlier melody, extending it so that it becomes even more beautiful and forceful.[32] Her former loyalty ebbs with every tone sung. Ferrando takes his time, patiently singing a gorgeous *Larghetto* in 3/4 time, back in the key of A, and singing it "with utmost tenderness" (tenerissimamente). No living creature could long resist the seductiveness of this music, and even Fiordiligi, for all her high principles, is only flesh and blood, as Despina never tired of reminding her.

The actual moment of surrender, "hai vinto" (you have won), coming in the middle of a phrase in dialogue between the two of them, is held together as a continuous line by the nasal tone of the first oboe (Alfonso in absentia) (Example 3.6). It is really only a protracted cadential progression, enhanced

EXAMPLE 3.6. *Mozart,* Cosí fan tutte, *Duetto, No. 29*

by the expressive diminished-seventh chord in m. 98, but this, combined with the melodic turn and the rise to the high tonic of the melody, exerts powerful charms. The rise to high A over a diminished-chord harmony was already present in Ferrando's "Un aura amoroso," No. 17, four measures before the end of its

---

[32] Daniel Heartz, "Citation, Reference, and Recall in *Così fan tutte*," in *Mozart's Operas* (1990), pp. 237–38, ex. 14.2.

extraordinary orchestral postlude. As the solo oboe descends into the cadence in the duet, Fiordiligi sings a rising line to "far di me quel che ti par" (make of me what you will), which answers his offer to be her fiancé, lover, "and more, if you wish" (meaning, presumably, her husband). With the arrival of the cadence, the tempo changes to *Andante* in cut time and the newly-paired lovers embrace, singing in the traditional chains of tenths and sixths of tenor-soprano love duets, along with little imitative exchanges. Guglielmo, observing in the background and beside himself, has to be restrained by Alfonso from fleeing.

The contrast between the two officers here is again telling. Guglielmo had the bad grace to taunt Ferrando after Dorabella's fall by vaunting his superior sex appeal. Now it is his turn to rage and burn. "I shall pluck out my beard, claw my skin, and grow horns. Was that Fiordiligi? The Penelope, the Artemisia of the century?" He calls her by a string of bad names, then "Fior di diavolo." His rant reinforces the coarse and carnal streak in his character that was there from the beginning. He determines to punish the women, but how? Alfonso at once interjects the perfect answer: marry them. Over the men's objections, he persists in promoting his idea as the best, the only solution. "Nature does not make exceptions by creating two women for you unlike all the others. There must be philosophy in all things, and the sooner you learn this, the better for you." Next comes the moral, No. 30, sung to a short *Andante* in cut time and in the keynote of C major, ending with the motto-title of the opera, which Alfonso makes the men repeat after him, to the same descending thirds, deceptive cadence, and final cadence that Mozart placed in the slow introduction of the overture. The oboe solo that begins the slow introduction relates to Ferrando's "bella serenata" music from No. 3 and its derivatives in the duet, No. 29.

Following the singing of the motto, Despina enters, exultant. She will arrange all the details of the marriage she says, including the notary and the banquet. "When Despina undertakes a project it never fails." The second finale, No. 31, starts innocuously in the home key of C, with music of bustle and charm, with little trills in the melody, *Allegro assai* in common time. Continuous fast notes in the accompanying second violins bear a resemblance to the beginning texture of the first finale, No. 18. In a richly lighted chamber, a table is set with silver for four persons; four richly garbed servants are in attendance. Despina has indeed arranged everything in advance, including a band on stage to greet the about-to-be-married couples on their arrival. The band, presumably of winds, is not notated in the score, but doubles the welcoming chorus of servants, directed by Despina. Alfonso enters and praises her efforts. From C major the music plunges with no transition into E♭, duplicating the move up a third in the first finale. The chorus calls blessings down on the wedding couples, who sing, "all is joy, all is love!" A familiar chromatic rise in thirds emphasizes "amore." In this quartet of the couples Fiordiligi cannot resist a burst of song up to high B♭ followed by a plunge down a tenth as further demonstration of her *virtù*, a garnish echoed note for note down an octave by Ferrando, telling us, as only music can, that they really do belong together. She returns the favor by repeating exactly a cadential fioratura he introduces. Did Mozart ever entertain thoughts of changing Da Ponte's conventional ending?

An episode in A♭ after the return of the chorus in E♭ commences with pairs of clarinets and bassoons and is then taken up by the young men. This leads directly to a canonic ensemble, *Larghetto* in 3/4, as the pairs raise their glasses in a toast, also in A♭. Martín's *Una cosa rara* had introduced a vocal canon but it is child's play in comparison. Fiordiligi begins the canon, followed by Ferrando, then by Dorabella, but Guglielmo, when his turn comes, refuses to sing the words or the melody of the canon, uttering instead an Osmin-like aside, "Let them drink poison!" As if in illustration of this proffered change of beverage, A♭ becomes G♯, which turns out to be the major third of the new key of E, *Allegro* in cut time.

Alfonso now appears, announced by the solo oboe, which takes charge of the enharmonic change almost as if its timbre were his calling card, and in this opera it has become as much. He says the matrimonial contract is ready as is a notary, who promptly appears in the person of Despina, disguised once again. She reads the contract in a nasal tone (pel naso) droning on in a formula-bound chant using only two pitches, with the music now in the key of A. The ladies sign the contract. At this, the chord of A turns into a prolonged A⁷ chord preparing D. It arrives as a *Maestoso*, faint and in the distance, but unmistakably the same march that sent the men off to war that very morning. Again the chorus sings "Bella vita militar!" (No. 8) from Act I, which the couples pretend at first not to recognize. Alfonso goes to the window and to his feigned horror announces, to an *Allegro* in E♭ and in 3/4 time, that it is indeed the galleon bearing the officers back from battle. They have already disembarked he says. At this, the servants dismantle the banquet and the stage band vanishes. Laments pour forth from the anguished couples, mostly in the key of g or unstable in harmony. The Albanians are hustled into a side chamber and Despina is led by Alfonso to another room. He tries to reassure the ladies but they remain frenzied, asking what will become of them, to a big cadence in g.

The *scena ultima* provides the answer. "Safe and sane," sing the officers, "we are returned to our most faithful spouses." Their music is a jaunty gavotte tune, *Andante* in cut time and in B♭, sounding rather like the *Andante* in B♭ of their *duettino*, No. 7. They sing as one, in sweet thirds and sixths, with long pauses over key words such as "spose." The chromatic rise in thirds at "spose adorabili" parodies those in the duet, No. 4, sung by the ladies at "Amor mi faccia vivendo penar" (May Cupid make me suffer), and recalls similar chromatic rises sung by them to the word "amore" early in this finale.

The unraveling begins when Guglielmo discovers a cowering notary. Despina takes off her disguise and admits it was only she. The ladies are nonplussed while their officer-lovers act angry and suspicious. Alfonso lets drop the contract, bringing more feigned outrage. Now the game is over, or should be. The men rage on to an *Allegro* in E♭ with rapid scales up and down (cf. Almaviva's anger in Act II of *Figaro*) and try to enter the side room. The ladies stop them with piteous pleas in c minor, saying they are guilty and worthy of death, asking the men to plunge their swords into breasts so undeserving of pity. To this Fiordiligi adds an excuse by blaming Alfonso and Despina as the cruel man and wicked seductress who tricked them. Perhaps poet and composer have stretched the scene out more than is necessary at this point.

Alfonso leads the officers to the adjacent room, from which they come back in their Albanian guise. Ferrando imitates his exotic other with a stiff musical pronouncement in d minor that has no match in the Sextet, No. 13, as it now exists, but probably did at an earlier stage. Guglielmo recalls the Locket Duet, No. 23, and then both men sing the music of Despina as doctor, with protracted trill to boot. The women are stupefied and turn accusingly to Alfonso, who tricked them. "Yes I deceived you," he sings, "in order to undeceive your lovers, who will henceforth behave more sagely." He joins the hands of the original pairs, makes them embrace and be silent. "You should all four laugh over what made me laugh and will continue to do so."

The ladies revert at once to their cloyingly sweet parallel thirds as if they had learned nothing, but the men are chastened enough to admit they wished never again to put them to such a test. Despina, a little confused, writes off the experience saying if she has been fooled this time, it was she who did the fooling many other times. The music has been swaying back and forth between C major and its dominant. With the *Allegro molto* of the last section, there is no doubt about the resolution to C. The final verse begins with a moral that could have ended many another drama of enlightenment: "Fortunate is the man who takes everything for its good side and through all vicissitudes is guided by reason." This was not quite enough for Mozart, who needed another quatrain, sufficiently contrasting to allow a tonal excursion and return. "What makes others weep, for him becomes laughable, and in a world beset with storms he will find peace and calm."

Leopold II: Sacred Music

The production of *Così fan tutte* was brought to a halt by the death of Joseph II in February 1790. Its first five performances, from Tuesday 26 January until 11 February, drew above average audiences.[33] Mozart's demanding new comedy pleased even Zinzendorf, who attended the premiere and called the music charming. Yet

[33] Dexter Edge, "Mozart's Reception in Vienna, 1787–1791," in *Wolfgang Amadè Mozart*, ed. Stanley Sadie (1996), pp. 66–117; 82–85.

its success did little if anything to relieve the composer's financial stresses. All he received was a one-time fee for the work, and this was apparently only half of the 200 ducats he was expecting, according to the weekly ledger payments for the theater from the 1789–90 season.[34]

Throughout January 1790, the emperor's tuberculosis had grown steadily worse. On 29 January, he relinquished all power to a regency council. His condition was pronounced dangerous on 6 February, and two days later his brother Leopold was summoned from Florence. The performance of Salieri's *Axur*, Joseph's favorite opera, scheduled for Saturday 13 February was canceled. On this same day, Joseph received the sacrament of extreme unction. The bad tidings for the imperial family came not single file. On 17 February Princess Elisabeth died giving birth to a daughter. Two days later the emperor died. A period of deep mourning was decreed, and it merged with the Lenten season.

Leopold II did not arrive in Vienna until 10 March. He was solemnly inaugurated as ruler on 6 April, two days after Easter. His coronations (as king of Hungary, king of Bohemia, and Holy Roman Emperor) were deferred until months later. The theaters were allowed to reopen on 12 April but Leopold was too busy with political and economic crises to attend them. Besides the lingering conflict with the Turks, he faced uprisings in the Austrian Netherlands, dissident nobles in Bohemia and Hungary, plus the threat of imminent war with Prussia. Eventually he ended the Turkish War and defused the crises.

Mozart lost no time in sending a petition to the new ruler requesting advancement in the court's service. He mentions his plea in a letter to Puchberg dating from late March or early April 1790. No answer from the court was forthcoming during the month of April. The composer tried to help his case by a written appeal to Archduke Francis, which survives in the form of a draft in his own hand that is not quite complete but gives a revealing glimpse of his state of mind in May 1790.

> Eagerness to gain honor, love of my work, and awareness of my special skills prompted me to apply for the post of second Kapellmeister, in particular because the very skilled Kapellmeister Salieri has never devoted himself to the church style, whereas I have made myself completely familiar with it since my youth. The modest reputation that the world has accorded me for my playing of the pianoforte encourages me to ask His Majesty also for the favor of being entrusted with the musical education of the royal family.

The family in question was in truth large and in need of tutors. Maria Luisa of Spain had produced sixteen children with Leopold, of whom Archduke Francis, aged twenty-one, was the eldest. Mozart still hoped for an affirmative answer

[34] Dexter Edge, "Mozart's fee for *Così fan tutte,*" *Journal of the Royal Musical Association* 116 (1991): 211–35.

from Leopold when he wrote to Puchberg on 17 May, "I now have great hopes at court, for I know reliably that the emperor has not sent back my petition favoring or damning it, like the others. That is a good sign." Mozart had little reason to be this optimistic. His tactic of stressing his experience in the church style as compared to that of Salieri was obviated by the latter's intense cultivation of sacred music since his appointment as Hofkapellmeister in 1788. Moreover, Mozart's reputation as a teacher of amateur keyboard players had not been strongly established. He failed to be advanced to the position of second Kapellmeister.

The Burgtheater brought its second production of *Figaro* back on the first of May 1790, the fourth anniversary of its premiere, and there were several subsequent performances until October. On 6 June *Così fan tutte* returned to the stage, the first of five additional performances spread from 6 June to 7 August, when the opera was dropped. According to a note Mozart sent Puchberg, he himself directed the performance on Saturday June 12, for which the audience was pitifully small. Ticket sales for the summer performances were less than half what they had been for the five showings early in the year, from which it might be deduced that *Così's* enlightening message, approved under Joseph II, was less favored after his death. *Figaro* did better at the box office. Emperor Leopold witnessed neither production. He and the entire royal family first made an appearance in the Burgtheater on 20 September at a performance of Salieri's *Axur*. Three days later, with his wife and two of his sons, Leopold left Vienna for Frankfurt, where the imperial coronation was to take place. He was crowned on 9 October and returned to Vienna by the 22nd.

The number of new compositions entered in Mozart's catalogue during 1790 was sparser than ever. After *Così fan tutte* in January, there were the second and third "Prussian" Quartets, begun earlier, entered in May and June. The catalogue for July mentions the arrangements for Swieten of Handel's *Ode to Saint Cecelia*, K. 592, and *Alexander's Feast*, K. 591. Then nothing at all was added until December, when the String Quintet in D, K. 593, was inscribed. Mozart was ill during the latter part of the summer. He wrote Puchberg on 14 August in even more pitiful terms than usual, saying that his physical illness was made worse by grief and worries.

On 23 September, Mozart left for Frankfurt in his own carriage accompanied only by Hofer and by his servant Joseph. To pay for the trip he had pawned the family silver. Salieri and Umlauf, on the other hand, traveled in the Emperor's retinue along with fifteen chamber musicians in court service; Salieri's *Axur* and *Te Deum de incoronazione* were performed during the official celebrations. The coronation mass was by Vincenzo Righini, maestro di cappella of the prince archbishop and elector of Mainz. This elector's theatrical troupe planned a performance in German of Mozart's *Don Giovanni* for 5 October in Frankfurt but substituted in its stead an opera by Dittersdorf. Mozart was represented on the stage in Frankfurt only by a performance of *Die Entführung* on 12 October, given by the elector of Trier's company under the direction of Johann Böhm. A gala performance of Wrantizky's *Oberon* took place on 15 October.

Mozart no longer expected anything from Emperor Leopold. His hopes were pinned on finding other patrons and a lucrative court appointment somewhere other than Vienna. By the time he returned to Vienna ca. 10 November, these hopes too had been dashed. He did succeed in giving a concert for his own benefit in the municipal theater of Frankfurt on the morning of 15 October. It had been advertised two days earlier. A program survives but it is not very detailed. The first half of the concert consisted of a symphony, described as "eine neue grosse Simphonie," but perhaps merely one of the three for which there were printed parts (K. 297, "Paris"; K. 319, No. 33; and K. 385, "Haffner") and thus not so new. There followed a soprano aria sung by Madame Schick (who sang Countess Almaviva in the *Figaro* at Mainz), a piano concerto, and an aria sung by the soprano castrato Ceccarelli formerly of Salzburg, but by this time at Mainz. The second part began with another piano concerto, continued with a duet for two sopranos, and a fantasy improvised by the composer. A symphony closed the program (perhaps the second half of the one that opened it). The two piano concertos were K. 459 in F and K. 537 in D, as known not from the program but from other sources.

One of the auditors present at Mozart's concert in Frankfurt, Count Ludwig von Bentheim-Steinfurt, recorded his impressions in writing. From him we learn that the composer played a fortepiano made by Stein of Augsburg that had been loaned to him by Mme. la Baron de Frentz. The second piano concerto on the program pleased the count less than the first. He was especially impressed by the improvised fantasy, "dans la quelle il brilla infiniment faisant voir toute la force de son talent." The closing symphony was not performed, he said, because it was already two o'clock and everyone was hungry. He blamed the three-hour length of the concert on the long pauses between pieces. The orchestra was weak, according to him. It consisted of only five or six violins, but these played with precision. Not many people attended: "Il n'avoit pas beaucoup de monde."

Mozart wrote Constanze on the same day in a letter dated Frankfurt 15 October 1790.

> My concert took place today at 11 o'clock. It was splendid in terms of honor but meager in regard to money earned. Unfortunately, some prince was giving a grand dejeuner just at the time of the concert, and the Hessian troops were putting on a big maneuver. Some such obstacles have been plaguing me every day of my stay here. Yet, in spite of it all, I was in good spirits and delighted my audience to the extent that they pleaded with me to give another concert this coming Sunday.

A second concert in Frankfurt did not take place.

From Frankfurt Mozart went by boat down the Main River to nearby Mainz with some young musicians from there, ones who likely played in his concert. He was invited by the elector of Mainz to perform at the post-banquet academy being given in his palace on 21 October. The many guests included Prince Franz Colloredo, Vice-chancellor of the Empire and brother of the Archbishop of Salzburg. In his letter to his wife dated Mannheim 23 October, Mozart mentioned that his meager reward from the elector of Mainz was only 15 Carolin (about 165 gulden). At Mannheim, a high point of his trip, he participated in the dress rehearsal and first performance of *Figaro* sung there (in German translation). His good spirits on the return trip continued in Munich when he met many of his old friends formerly at Mannheim, including the stalwart Christian Cannabich, who had led the performances of *Idomeneo* in 1781, the oboist Friedrich Ramm, and Theobold Marchand, director of the German theatrical troupe. Elector Carl Theodore invited him to perform at Munich before the visiting King Ferdinand of Naples and his Austrian wife, Maria Carolina. In a letter to his wife written from Munich before 4 November, Mozart remarked sardonically, "And what an honor it is for the court of Vienna that the King of Naples has to hear me in a foreign country." Salieri and Haydn were called upon in Vienna to perform for the visiting King of Naples, but not Mozart.

The year 1790 in international politics ended with less danger and chaos than it began. Leopold II started negotiations that would lead to an end of the war with Ottoman Turkey and made some progress in pacifying his Belgian subjects. Moderate reform was in the air for a time in France when Count Mirabeau joined with Louis XVI in an attempt to establish a constitutional monarchy that would end the threat of a return to mob rule. In Vienna Leopold dismantled much of the secret police that the beleaguered Joseph had allowed to form under Count Pergen, who was so thoroughly rebuked that he resigned in March 1791.[35]

Much has been made of a rather cryptic passage in the letter Mozart wrote his wife from Munich.

> I look forward with joy to being with you. And I have so much to discuss with you. I have it in mind to make this tour again with you at the end of next summer. You could visit a different spa thereby, and the entertainment [Unterhaltung], activity [*motion* is the French word he uses] and change of air would do you good, as it has done marvels for me.

Mozart was not a frequenter of spas. His words have been taken as a coded message intended to fool any prying eyes, the meaning of the message being that

---

[35] Paul P. Bernard, *From the Enlightenment to the Police State: The Public Life of Johann Anton Pergen* (Urbana and Chicago, 1991), pp. 175–77.

he had been struck by the new and democratic ideas flowing from revolutionary France into the Rhineland.[36] All the evidence for this argument is circumstantial. Mozart, we are told, responded with enthusiasm to the spirit of independence manifested by the citizens of Mainz, who in 1792 deposed their archbishop and welcomed French troops. Yet in 1790, the revolution in France was still in its first phase and aiming to replace absolute monarchy with a consultative ruling power. The Republic of Mainz was established after Mozart's death, and its existence cannot be pushed back to the time of Leopold's coronation in Frankfurt.[37] In the concert of European royalty Leopold was considered an enlightened prince who was more tolerant of change than most. Among his supporters in Vienna were Swieten, who championed freedom of the press, and Sonnenfels, who had worked out a charter for the Austrian police focusing on public safety and social welfare. Mozart's long and close connections with Swieten and Sonnenfels offer a more promising source of study about the composer's political leanings late in his life than his three days in Mainz.

Mozart's library also offers an opportunity to study such questions. The inventory after decease notes that he possessed all ten volumes of the *Gesammelte kleine Schriften* by Sonnenfels, published at Vienna between 1783 and 1786. Also among his books was a copy of Johann Pezzl's *Faustin, oder, Das aufgeglärte philosophische Jahrhundert*, published in 1783. Pezzl, a Bavarian born ten months after Mozart, was the composer's lodge brother. In light of Pezzl's books and others like them, many attacking monastic abuses, it is possible to believe that Mozart subscribed to the idea, proposed at the end of *Così fan tutte*, about letting reason be our guide through life's vicissitudes. He may even have agreed with the "old philosopher," Alfonso, about the need for philosophy in all things. Perhaps Mozart's books helped him to weather the many vicissitudes of his own life. In any case his last year was to become less bleak in most respects than 1790 had been.

Leopold II lived only a few months beyond Mozart. His twenty-five years spent ruling Tuscany had transformed it into a model state by the lights of his century. Having become an Italian prince, he liked little but Italian music, unfortunately for Mozart. Otherwise, they may have seen eye to eye on many matters. At his coronation in Frankfurt, Leopold was hailed as a new Titus, both just and clement. He tried to save many of the social reforms of his mother and brother Joseph, while undoing some of Joseph's mistakes. If Leopold had not died so soon, and had European politics not turned so violent in 1792, his moderate reforms might have continued. Zinzendorf's epitaph for the emperor was "good, humane, and a peacemaker" (Figure 3.4).

---

[36] Georg Knepler, *Wolfgang Amadè Mozart* (1994), ch. 23: "A Hostile Fate—but Only in Vienna."
[37] T. C. W. Blanning, *Reform and Revolution in Mainz 1743–1803* (Cambridge, 1974), p. 259.

Sacred music stirred Mozart's renewed interest in the late 1780s. In his last letter to his sister, dated Vienna 2 August 1788, the composer asked her to approach Michael Haydn and ask him about lending the music of "two tutti masses and the Graduali." There is no way of knowing which of Haydn's many masses and Graduals these may have been, or why Mozart wanted them. They could have been just objects he wanted to study, or works he wanted to perform, perhaps in the parish church of his neighborhood, at this time the Alsergrund. On 24 August 1788, Mozart received some Danish visitors, who wrote reports about the occasion. The actor Joachim Preisler, one of the visitors, published his account in Danish at Copenhagen in 1789.

FIGURE 3.4. Emperor Leopold II, engraved by Adam after Kreuzinger, 1791.

> Sunday 24 August . . . In the afternoon Jünger, Lange, and Werner fetched us for a drive to see Kapellmeister Mozart. There I experienced my happiest hour of music ever. This small man and great master played fantasies on a pedal piano so wonderfully that I lost awareness of where I was. The most difficult passages and the loveliest themes were woven together. His wife sharpened quills for the copyist, a pupil composed, and a little boy aged four [Carl] ran about the garden singing recitatives. In short, everything surrounding the man was musical. I thought with pleasure of his *Entführung aus dem Serail* that I heard in Hamburg in 1787 and that I knew by heart, but he called this *Operette* a trifle [Kleinigkeit]. It would be unworthy of a man like Mozart to be praised by men who themselves count for nothing so I remained silent. He is writing church music in Vienna and inasmuch as the Singspiel [Operette] has come to an end he has nothing more to do with the theater.[38]

The three men who drove the Danish visitors to the outskirts where the Mozarts then resided included two members of the court's play-acting company, the suc-

---

[38] Deutsch, *Dokumente*, p. 285, gives a German translation from the Danish. I have also relied on the English translation from the original in Deutsch, *Mozart: A Documentary Biography*, 2nd ed. (Stanford, 1966), p. 325.

cessful author Johann Friedrich Jünger, and Joseph Lange, the gifted actor and painter (the Danish party visited the Langes on 20 August, an occasion also described by Preisler). Either Jünger or Lange could have told Preisler about the disbanding of the Singspiel troupe. The third person was perhaps Dr. Karl Werner, the medical superintendent for Lower Austria. While it is true that Mozart received no commission from the court theater until the following year, his *Don Giovanni*, revised for Vienna, was given there twelve times between May and August 1788, thus the statement that Mozart no longer has anything to do with the theater is inaccurate.

The first part of the same statement has Mozart writing church music in Vienna, a claim that has caused some puzzlement. Suggestions have been offered that perhaps the reference was to Mozart's work arranging Handel for Swieten's concerts, which seems unlikely. Mozart noted in his catalogue that his next projects for the baron, an arrangement of *Acis and Galatea* (which could hardly qualify as church music) dated from November 1788 and *Messiah* from March 1789. A recent discovery based on paper studies redates the series of Kyrie and Gloria fragments, formerly assigned to the 1770s and Salzburg, to Vienna and the late 1780s.[39] They confirm that Mozart was turning some of his attention to church music in 1788 and 1789.

Besides strengthening his claim to the post of second Kapellmeister of the court, Mozart also had his eye on succeeding Leopold Hofmann as Kapellmeister of St. Stephen's Cathedral. This could help explain the copies he began making of psalm settings and parts of a Kyrie by Georg Reutter the younger, Hofmann's predecessor. Hoffman's ill health prompted Mozart to take action in early May 1791. He wrote the city council of Vienna offering his services as Hofmann's unpaid assistant and eventual successor. He ended his letter, couched in the subservient style expected of such documents, with a candid assessment: "I deem myself well qualified to take part in the services since I am trained in both the secular and ecclesiastic styles of music." On 9 May 1791, the city council granted his request. With this assurance of future employment, Mozart could regain some of the sense of security he needed and go with greater ease into the huge task of composing his two last operas. He did not expect to be outlived by Hofmann (1738–1793) nor did he expect to die young.

None of the fragmentary church works Mozart began in the late 1780s reached completion (unless there have been losses in this particular area). Why he failed to complete any of them defies easy explanation. It could be that they were not very promising as beginnings in the first place. The musical ideas lack the charm and spontaneity of his most popular mass setting, K. 317 in C of 1779, the so-called "Coronation" Mass, not to mention the profundity of his unfinished Mass in c, K. 427, of 1783. Be that as it may, he turned again to his Salz-

---

[39] Tyson, *Mozart*, pp. 26–27.

burg works when, in the late spring and summer of 1791, opportunities arose to have Masses of his composition performed in church at Baden, the spa town near Vienna where his wife took two lengthy cures before giving birth on 21 July to their sixth child, christened Franz Xaver Wolfgang, who like Carl survived to live a long life.

One bright spot for the Mozarts during this time was their friendship with the Baden choirmaster and schoolteacher Anton Stoll. Mozart loaned parts for the Mass in C, K. 317, to Stoll, then asked for them back by letter of early June from Vienna, apparently because they were needed for a performance. He cited the work by means of a musical incipit, implying that Stoll had more than one mass in C major by Mozart (there were several). The letter with the incipit mentions Anton Stadler as an intermediary in the transaction and shows the composer's confidence in Stoll by having him find rooms for Constanze in Baden. In addition to this practical matter, he asked Stoll to report to him whether the theater in the spa town had opened.

Two weeks later Mozart himself was able to visit his wife in Baden, and there he wrote for Stoll the short and exquisite motet "Ave verum corpus," K. 618, for four voices, strings, and organ, dated Baden 18 June in the thematic catalogue, 17 June on the autograph. On 12 July, in another letter from Vienna to Stoll in Baden, the composer asked for the return of his Mass in B♭, which must be K. 275, "the one we performed last Sunday, and please also return the Gradual in B♭, 'Pax vobis' by Michael Haydn." He wanted the parts back quickly for a performance that was looming in Vienna under his direction. In fine humor, Mozart added a postscript in disguised handwriting pretending to be from Franz Xaver Süssmayer and loaded with obscenities, recalling the Mozart of old, with the threat, "Send back the Mass and Gradual or else you will receive no news of his opera [*Die Zauberflöte*]." Süssmayer was the butt of many of Mozart's ongoing jokes. He was nevertheless a faithful assistant as well as an aid to Constanze in Baden. The Mozarts named their last child Franz Xaver, a choice possibly reflecting gratitude to Süssmayer, or admiration for the bass Franz Xaver Gerl, the first Sarastro, or both.

THE REQUIEM

Demand for new and old works by Mozart increased in his last year. An odd request came to him anonymously from Count Franz Walsegg-Stupach, who was owner and resident of the house on the Hoher Markt where the Puchbergs lodged. Mozart may have been acquainted with Count Walsegg. Puchberg, familiar with the financial conditions of the Mozarts, could have suggested to the Count the possibility of a commission. The young wife of Walsegg had died in February 1791 and he considered ordering a setting of the Requiem Mass in her honor. He had a habit of letting works that he commissioned be passed off as his own, which may explain why the letter delivered to Mozart was unsigned. Niemetschek, who probably got the information from Constanze, says that the letter arrived in the summer of 1791. It inquired if Mozart would consider writing a Requiem, and if so for what price and by what date could it be delivered. Mozart agreed to do it and asked where the work should be delivered when complete. He could not specify a date of completion because of the pressure of other work. He received a down payment as a sign to begin and promise of greater compensation later. All this is secondhand information conveyed by Niemetschek, who is also the source for saying that the messenger who approached Mozart first with the letter reappeared to ask about the work's progress as the Mozarts were entering their carriage in late August for the journey to Prague, where *La clemenza di Tito* was to be staged. Rochlitz further embroidered the tale of the commission in one of his anecdotes. No substantial work on the Requiem was possible until they returned from Prague in mid-September, although Mozart may well have begun exploring musical ideas for it earlier.

The Requiem, K. 626, begins nobly with a beautiful setting of the Introit "Requiem aeternum dona eis, Domine," an *Adagio* in d and in common time. The first sound heard is a point of imitation played by two bassoons and two basset horns. The strings are reduced to accompanimental function, the violins and violas providing offbeat chord tones to the downbeats of the basses. Not many places besides Prague and Vienna could field an orchestra that included basset horns, which lend the beginning an unmistakable tinge of Freemasonry. When three trombones reinforce the cadence, *forte*, joining the basses on the beat, the complexion of the piece changes. Trombones were at home in church and their stern tones were rarely heard elsewhere at that time. Not even the *Maurerische Trauermusik*, K. 477, enjoyed the luxury of trombones, and perhaps Mozart would not have wanted them there because of their strong associations with the church.

After the initial fugal exposition and cadence, the voices of the chorus are heard entering from low to high with a stretto on the initial theme, which they carry through to the words "et lux perpetua luceat eis." Mozart sets these homophonically, leading to a cadence on B♭. The orchestra answers with interjections between choral statements and overlapping them, the strings with the jagged unison figure of a descending arpeggio, reminiscent of how the Quintet in G, No. 5 in *Die Zauberflöte*, begins. The orchestra then introduces a winding figure in sixteenth notes that provides another subject for imitation, against which a solo soprano sings in longer notes "Te decet hymnus Deus in Sion," based on the *tonus peregrinus* of the Magnificat. The choral-orchestral response to this is an outburst in the key of g, with urgent figures in dotted rhythms in the orchestra against the smoother rhythms in the chorus for "Exaudi orationem meum," which sounds less like a supplication than it does an order: "Hear my prayer!" From these several strands Mozart wove a climax with sopranos up to high A intoning the main fugal subject for the return of the initial words (Example 3.7). The movement ends softly with a lingering on the dominant of tonic d.

EXAMPLE 3.7. *Mozart, Requiem Mass, K. 626, Introit*

The Kyrie in d that follows is a substantial fugue, an *Allegro* in common time. Its theme is one of the most common clichés among fugue subjects, familiar to Mozart from "And with his stripes we are healed" in *Messiah* and doubtless many other works as well. At the end there is a pause on the diminished-seventh chord, then the final cadence drawn out at an *Adagio* tempo, just as Handel often did, and did so notably to end "And with his stripes." In technical competence, the Kyrie fugue is impressive, yet the ordinariness of the subject takes something away from it, making it seem like a piece one has heard many times before. Mozart completed only the first movement in almost every detail; he did not live long enough to do the same in the following movements. He supplied no orchestral parts for the Kyrie fugue. In the "Dies irae," a fine flurry of homophonic wrath in the chorus against the raging, tremolo sixteenth notes of the violins, the orchestration remained mostly undone. The subsequent "Tuba mirum spargens sonum" was left even more incomplete.

The wondrous sounding of the last trumpet on Judgment Day Mozart decided would be assigned to a solo on the tenor trombone, in dialogue with successive vocal soloists, from bass up through soprano, concluded by the chorus (see Example 6.15b). Trombone solos were no rarity in Vienna, where Wagenseil had written a concerto for the instrument. They were a commonplace in church services. Friedrich Nicolai of Berlin, visiting Vienna in 1781, heard in the Church am Hof an instance that pleased him: "The Agnus Dei was accompanied throughout by an obbligato trombone that played purely and with understanding, and made a good effect well calculated for the church style." He went on to praise the use of trombones in Austrian and Bavarian churches, deploring their neglect in northern Germany.[40] Long lost today are any associations of the trombone with churchly reverence. Mozart's wandering melodic filigree for the instrument is likely to strike us less like a divine summons than a *morceau de concours* inflicted on some benighted conservatory student. This is unfortunate, but no more so than the music itself.

Mozart's "Tuba mirum" is an *Andante* in cut time in the key of E♭. The trombone solo begins unaccompanied, giving another version of the descending

---

[40] *Haydn, Mozart*, p. 22.

arpeggio (the operatic associations of which extend not only to *Die Zauberflöte* but also to Haydn's *Armida*). The bass solo sings the initial words to the same arpeggio in imitation of the trombone, then sustains the low B♭ at the bottom for three measures while the trombone exhibits its skills by climbing up and down the tones of a seventh chord in its high range. It then begins a kind of dialogue with the solo bass voice, stating a melody that could fit in a Singspiel or any other kind of opera, one that begins with a pretty melodic turn. The vocal solo has an awkward kind of counterpoint to the trombone and is soon matching it rhythmically in overlapping groups of three quarter-note beats, a figure familiar from its beautiful effect in Tamino's Picture Aria, No. 3 in *Die Zauberflöte*, and from many uses in *La clemenza di Tito*. The trombone drops out for a measure, then returns with a conjunct rising passage that introduces the minor dominant, v, a passage familiar from the first movement of the Clarinet Quintet K. 581.

Ghosts of Mozart's secular music were to be expected in the Requiem, but the concentration of them in the "Tuba mirum" is disconcerting. The composer himself perhaps realized that he had taken a wrong or inappropriate turn, for he discontinued writing the trombone's solo at this juncture, where the tenor voice enters, although the instrument's tenor clef continued on in the score, unoccupied, giving indication that he intended to reintroduce it. Süssmayer, when completing this movement, decided to bring back the trombone toward the end of the tenor solo, then he gave up, letting the instrument remain silent. In his hands the trombone passed from being a lead instrument to a mere accompaniment, one in which it acquires the typical drabness of a schoolboy's inner part. Joseph Eybler in his attempt to finish the "Tuba mirum," did not bring back the trombone solo.

These words, harsher than generally allowed here, were written before I ran across even more severe strictures on the subject by a great composer and critic, Hector Berlioz. He knew the Requiem from the edition published by Johann André at Offenbach am Main in 1827. The following passage he wrote about it comes not from hearing it performed but as a digression in his review of Requiems by Cherubini and Le Sueur, performed in 1835.

It is not, in our opinion, that Mozart's Requiem is undeserving of its immense reputation; it contains a multitude of beauties worthy of the immortal creator of *Don Giovanni*. The "Rex tremendae" above all is a model of power and majesty . . . If you reject in a Requiem all dramatic effect while still allowing it to be performed by the means used in theater music you indict Mozart's entire score. This "Dies irae," agitated and trembling, is dramatic; the "Confutatis," menacing and somber, is dramatic; the "Rex tremendae" is dramatic; even the "Pie Jesu" ["Lacrimosa"] is dramatic, for all that is expressive is necessarily dramatic from the moment that you employ the melody, harmony, tonal system, rhythmic patterns, and the instrumental color, even the instruments themselves of dramatic music . . . If, on the other hand, Mozart's "Tuba mirum" is without force as well as without color, it is because the piece is unfinished, badly finished, or a failure; that is all.[41]

Berlioz does not mention the movements that are largely fugal, which include the "Domine Jesu" as well as the first two, but for him, all that Mozart completed of the score was truly dramatic. Yet he could not accept the solo trombone of the "Tuba mirum" even though Mozart chose it, nor its music. For that subject, he said, you needed thirty trombones, or better, three hundred. Berlioz was that rare critic who was in a position to make good on any such threats in his own compositions. He wrote his mammoth Requiem two years later.

Aside from his judgment of the "Tuba mirum," Berlioz had some reservations about Mozart's whole conception of the work and the degree that he would have remained satisfied with it.

> One can, without blasphemy, doubt that, had Mozart lived longer, the Requiem would resemble what we possess. Because, frankly, the "Dies irae," although it contains several beautiful moments expressing alarm, is it conceived largely enough? Is the music truly at the poetic level of its subject? Does it respond adequately to the idea one forms of the universal terror at the arrival of the supreme judge, when Death itself is astonished to see its victims rise, and trembles to see its empire destroyed?

Berlioz goes on to question whether the melodic design of the "Dies irae" is grand enough to thunder in cathedrals, and whether its preoccupation with repeating the same rhythmic formula does justice to the sublimity of the poem's vision. His questions give one much to ponder.

Surely Mozart, with more time, would have taken the trouble to transform the "Lacrimosa" into an edifice as wholly satisfying as the shattering eight-measure opening, which does meet the demands of the poetry.

Lacrimosa dies illa	Day of tearful mourning
Qua resurget ex favilla	When from the ashes will arise
Judicandus homo reus.	For judgment the guilty man.
Huic ergo parce, Deus,	Let him be spared, God,
Pie Jesu Domine,	Merciful Lord Jesus,
Dona eis requiem. Amen.	Grant him rest. Amen.

After a quiet beginning in 12/8 time and in the central key of d, with the violins uttering little melodic sighs on the weak beats, the chorus enters, confirm-

---

[41] Hector Berlioz, *Critique Musicale, 1823–1863,* ed. H. Robert Cohen and Yves Gérard, 5 vols. (Paris, 1996–2004), 2: 249–50.

ing the key chordally, the sopranos outlining the triad of d. Then, to express the verb "resurget," the sopranos climb tentatively in eighth notes followed by two eighth-note rests, step by step up the octave, but their high D is on a weak fourth part of the measure and not the tonic but the fifth of a dominant chord that resolves to c minor to begin the strong word "judicandus" (Example 3.8). From

EXAMPLE 3.8. *Mozart, Requiem Mass, K. 626, Lacrimosa*

this point on the voices sing dotted quarter notes *crescendo* to *forte*, as the soprano keeps rising up to high A for the strongest word "reus," the subject of the sentence. Here Mozart broke off his setting, but what a potent lesson in harmonic-melodic drama he gave us in this short space. Eybler sketched two measures for the soprano in continuation, then gave up. A greatly challenged Süssmayer went on from there.

One masterly detail that is apt to escape notice is the one-chord transition that Mozart made into the "Lacrimosa" from the agitated "Confutatis" in the key of a, but ending with tender music in the key of F. He smoothed the passing into d minor by moving the bass down by step, F E D, and harmonizing the intermediate chord as a V^6_3 of D. This duplicates exactly the transition from F to D, with the same rhythm and pauses, between the Quintet, No. 9, and the return of the March, No. 8, in Act I of *Così fan tutte*.

Constanze hurried the Requiem to completion by Süssmayer so that she could give it to Count Walsegg, who had already made a down payment. She retained copies of the work and one of them served for the concert, performed in Mozart's memory in January 1793 for her benefit and that of the two surviving children, under the auspices of Swieten. Walsegg first directed a performance in memory of his wife in December 1793. He passed it off as his own, and was probably under the illusion that the work was in its entirety by Mozart. His performance is said to have been in church as a part of a liturgical Requiem. The conditions under which orchestral masses could take place in Austrian churches were changing in the 1790s.

Leopold II, at the urging of the archbishop of Vienna, Cardinal Cristoph Migazzi, loosened the restrictions in 1790 against orchestrally accompanied masses that had come into effect during Joseph's sole reign in the 1780s.[42] Under Maria Theresa, elaborate masses with orchestra had flourished and were the delight of the populace. The intellectual reforming zeal of enlightenment ideals saw them in the same light as visual fripperies in church, hence the drive toward "unadorned divine services."[43] In 1792, Francis II, again at the urging of Cardinal Migazzi, lifted the ban on orchestral masses altogether.

Die Zauberflöte

Mozart's last opera in German emerged from an environment very different from that of his other operas, which reflected their origins in court culture and were performed in court-run theaters. *Die Zauberflöte* grew out of the traditions of Viennese popular theater, which had been given many freedoms under Joseph II and flourished in playhouses on the outskirts of the capital. Besides Mozart, an indispensable person in creating *Die Zauberflöte* was Emanuel Schikaneder, the opera's librettist, producer, director, and comic lead singer.

Schikaneder was born at Straubing in Bavaria on 1 September 1751 and educated at the Jesuit school in nearby Regensburg. There he also received musical training as a singer in the Catholic cathedral. During the 1770s, he was an itinerant actor. In 1774, he danced in a court ballet at Innsbruck, where his Singspiel *Die Lyranten*, of which he was poet, composer, and principal singer, was staged the following year. He married an actress in 1777 and became the director of a troupe that appeared in several towns of southern Germany and Austria. In the fall of 1780, he played Salzburg and became intimate with the Mozarts, who rarely missed his shows. Nannerl was a particularly devoted theatergoer, and after her brother's departure for Munich in early November 1780, she informed him of the troupe's doings, as did father Leopold. Even while at work on the arduous task of completing *Idomeneo* for the Munich court theater Mozart kept his promise of supplying Schikaneder with a new recitative and aria for one of Carlo Gozzi's comedies, K. 365a, a work that has been lost. Leopold wrote to his

[42] Karl Gustav Fellerer, *Die Kirchenmusik W. A. Mozarts* (Laaber, 1985), pp. 17, 40.
[43] Fellerer, *Die Kirchenmusik*, p. 39; *Haydn, Mozart*, pp. 20–23.

son in a letter dated Salzburg 2 December 1780, "The comedy with your aria was given yesterday; the comedy is very good, the house was full, the archbishop was also there; the aria was well produced and well sung, or as well as the little time to rehearse it allowed." Nannerl added that Schikaneder was very well pleased with the aria.

Joseph II saw Schikaneder perform at Pressburg in 1784 and invited him to Vienna. With his partner Hubert Kumpf he gave a season of plays and Singspiels in one of the non-court theaters, beginning on 5 November 1784 with *Die Entführung*. The following season, 1785–86, Schikaneder became a regular actor and singer in the Nationaltheater. After that year of court service, he led a company on a tour whose destination was a summer season in Augsburg. One of their stops on the way was Salzburg. On 5 May 1786, Leopold Mozart wrote to Nannerl that Schikaneder had arrived with his troupe, but only the Singspiel wing of it, and would be giving six or eight operas, for which he provided free passes to Leopold and his student Heinrich Marchand. "They sing and act very well," added Leopold.

A week later, on 12 May, Leopold wrote Nannerl that on the following Sunday the troupe would be giving *König Theodor von Corsica* "with the admirable music that Paisiello wrote for Vienna a few years ago." The company must have had several good singers if they did justice to *Il re Teodoro*, a quite demanding score for the Burgtheater regulars. Little attention has been paid to the account Leopold wrote his daughter about how the visitors put together what was apparently the first performance of *Das Urianische Schloss*. Leopold, living as he did across the square from the theater, was in a good position to give an account. Four copyists had been working around the clock for three days to make the premiere possible. All the actors could play either violin or cello, he explained, and helped out by playing through the orchestral parts in search of copyists' errors. There was time for but one serious rehearsal, whereas, according to Leopold, three or four were needed for such an opera.

Leopold's description of the work itself, after this build-up, is a nearly comical letdown, intended to entertain Nannerl of course, but valuable as a clue to Schikaneder's own brand of theatrical show.

> *Das Urianische Schloss* was an astounding foolishness [Kindereyen] in which everything laughable and clownish that ever existed was present: a cat and dog aria, a tailor's song, bears, an innkeeper, Schikaneder dressed as a woman, a composer with a fiddle under his arm, a little contredanse, fireworks, with all the bustle of the people who set them off, peasants with threshers and dung forks, and so on; in short, everything you can possibly imagine. The first performance took in 180 florins, the second only 50, for here one does not like *Kindereyen*. *Robert und Calliste* earned 75 florins. Tomorrow the house will be rather full again. The music of *Urianische Schloss* pleases the ear. It is stolen from many other operas, the main fault being that all the arias,

with the exception of the tailor's song, have two, three, or four different tempos so that no single thought can be pursued. Nary a member of the entire company would say who wrote the music, but I can easily guess who pasted this botch together: Schikaneder himself.

Robert und Calliste, oder, Der Triumph der Treue was an *operette* made from the opera buffa *La sposa fedele* by Pietro Chiari with music by Guglielmi. Leopold included it, along with other works he considered more palatable, such as those by Paisiello, in order to emphasize the low comedy of Schikaneder's own theater pieces. Even so, the music of the latter was still "pleasing to the ear," and not less so for having been stolen from everywhere.

Leopold was often quite severe when judging singers, even those he regarded as friends. Thus of Madame Duschek, who with her husband was visiting Salzburg (where her mother lived) during the same Easter season of 1786, he wrote to Nannerl on 21 April: "She screamed in an astonishing way an aria by Naumann, with exaggerated force of expression, like before, only worse. Good Heavens, she sings so badly I am sorry that she cannot use her voice to any better advantage. And what is the cause of it?" Leopold blamed her husband and teacher, who had convinced her that she alone had the true taste (gusto).

Leopold reacted very differently to another singer, a tenor in Schikaneder's company whom he described in his letter to Nannerl of 26 May 1786.

> The new tenor hired by Schikaneder arrived yesterday. He sings excellently well and has a beautiful voice, with an easy and flexible throat [leicht geläuffige Gurgel] and good technique [schöne Methode]. For this reason another opera, *La Frascatana* [by Paisiello], will be given so that the public can hear him on next Wednesday; perhaps the opera will be given again during the Whitsuntide holidays, before Schikaneder's departure. This man truly sings very beautifully.

The man in question was Bohemian-born Benedikt Schack, Mozart's Tamino, who would become a mainstay of the Schikaneder troupe. He was two years younger than Mozart, of whom he became a great favorite, according to Constanze. Trained at home by his father and later in Prague, he moved to Vienna in 1775 to study medicine and was given further vocal training by Haydn's leading tenor, Carl Friberth.

Schack, like many Bohemian musicians, had many different talents. It was long believed that he actually played the flute on stage as Tamino, an idea now discredited.[44] He was a musician of sufficient depth to be a composer in his own right. Almost all his works were composed for the suburban Viennese theaters

---

[44] Theodore Albrecht, "Anton Dreyssig (c 1753/4–1820): Mozart's and Beethoven's *Zauberflötist*," in *Words about Mozart*, ed. Dorothea Link (2005), pp. 179–192.

on texts by Schikaneder. One of them was *Der Luftballon*, in which Schikaneder capitalized on the public fascination with hot-air balloons during the mid-1780s. Schack often collaborated with the bass Franz Gerl, another member of Schikaneder's troupe and the first Sarastro, in composing new shows. Together they set to music Schikaneder's Singspiel *Der dumme Gärtner aus dem Gebirge, oder, Die zween Anton*, which reopened the Freihaus-Theater auf der Wieden on 12 July 1789 with such great success that it engendered a whole series of Anton operettas. The country bumpkin Anton, rustic cousin of Papageno, was, of course, Schikaneder.

A leading female singer of Schikaneder's troupe in Vienna was Josepha Weber, Constanze's sister and creator of the daunting Queen of the Night role. In 1788 she married the violinist Franz de Paula Hofer, mentioned above as Mozart's companion on his first trip to Prague in January 1787 and also on the trip to Frankfurt in 1790. Josepha joined the Schikaneder troupe in the spring of 1789 as it was preparing to open in the Theater auf der Wieden. For her, Mozart wrote the singing-lesson aria K. 580, a substitute piece in Paisiello's *Il barbiere di Siviglia*, planned for a production in German during the fall of 1789. Mozart entered K. 580 in his catalogue with the date of 17 September 1789: "Eine Arie in die Oper. der balbier [*sic*] von Seviglien. für Mad.^me Hoffer. 2 violini, viole, 2 clarinetti, 2 fagotti, 2 corni e Bassi. Schon lacht der holde frühling." What survives in Mozart's hand is a draft of the score in which, aside from violins and bass, only the voice part is complete, and very demanding with its arpeggios up to high D and rapid coloratura (with two staccato high Ds suggestive of what would follow for her as Queen). The composer did not usually list incomplete pieces in his catalogue, which suggests that the aria may have been completed and this German version performed. Another reason to believe that it reached the stage is that the roles of Schack included a Count Almaviva in German, that is, not Mozart's bass-baritone Almaviva, but Paisiello's tenor one. In any case, Mozart knew well the capabilities of his sister-in-law Josepha Hofer and tried out some bravura high passages for her in K. 580.

The youngest principal singer in the cast was the seventeen-year-old soprano Anna Gottlieb, who created Pamina. She was a veteran of the stage even so, having created the part of Barbarina in *Figaro*. Schikaneder hired her in 1789.

A web of familial and other relationships drew Mozart closer to Schikaneder's circle in the latter part of 1790 and the first months of 1791. Witness the duet that he composed, or assisted Schack to complete in the "heroic-comic opera" *Der Stein der Weisen, oder, Die Zauberinsel* on a text by Schikaneder with music mostly by Schack.[45] It was first performed in the Wiedner Theater on 11

---

[45] David J. Buch, "On Mozart's Partial Autograph of the Duet 'Nun liebes Weibchen,' K. 625/592a," *Journal of the Royal Musical Association* 124 (1999): 53–85.

September 1790. The duet, which was orchestrated in Mozart's hand, was sung by the comic pair played by Schikaneder and, as his wife, Gerl's wife Barbara, who would create the part of Papagena. Having been turned into a cat, she can sing only one word in the duet: "Miau." The story is derived freely from the first volume of Wieland's *Dschinnistan*, the collection of fairy tales that had a direct bearing on *Die Zauberflöte*. *Die Zauberinsel* was the first of Schikaneder's magic operas and in it a serious young couple must surmount various trials. Constanze Mozart remembered Schack as one of Mozart's most intimate friends and claimed that her first husband made some contributions to Schack's opera scores in the period around 1790.[46] She asked Schack in a letter of 26 March 1826 to send some material that her second husband, Nissen, could incorporate in his biography of the master, but Schack died later the same year before complying with her request.

The bass Franz Xaver Gerl had Mozart connections of one kind or another that extended back further in time than Schack's. Born in Upper Austria in 1764, he was an alto chorister in Salzburg Cathedral by 1777 and one of Leopold Mozart's pupils. He made the rounds of various theatrical troupes in the 1780s and in 1787 joined Schikaneder's company at Regensburg, where he sang, among other roles, Osmin in *Die Entführung*. He joined the troupe in Vienna by the summer of 1789. Before the role of Sarastro, Mozart composed for him a concert aria with a concertante part for Friedrich Pichelberger, the virtuoso bass player in the Wiedner Theater's small but excellent orchestra. The aria, "Per questa bella mano," K. 612, entered Mozart's catalogue with a date of 8 March 1791. Gerl's bass had a deep compass but apparently he did not shine in singing the low D that Fischer, the first Osmin, made famous, else Mozart would have used it in K. 612, which is also in the key of D. When the great actor-manager Friedrich Ludwig Schröder returned to Vienna in 1791, he was told not to miss hearing Gerl and Schack. He did hear them both at the Wiedner Theater in a performance of Paul Wranitzky's *Oberon*. He pronounced Gerl's singing of the Oracle "very good" and wrote of Schack in the heroic role of Hüon that he was also good but had an "Austrian accent and suburban declamation."[47]

Directly after his aria for Gerl, Mozart paid a compliment of another kind to Schack. The initial sequel to Schikaneder's *Dumme Gärtner* was *Die verdeckten Sachen*, first staged on 26 September 1789, with music by Schack in collaboration with Gerl and others. Schack was assigned the show's most successful new song, "Ein Weib ist das herrlichste Ding auf der Welt," a pleasant although squarish tune upon which Mozart wrote his last set of keyboard variations, K. 613, of

[46] David J. Buch, "Mozart and the Theater auf der Wieden: New Attributions and Perspectives," *Cambridge Opera Journal* 9 (1997): 195–223.

[47] Peter Branscombe, *W. A. Mozart: Die Zauberflöte* (Cambridge, 1991), p. 147.

March or early April 1791. The eight variations offer little that departs from the composer's usual procedures with this genre, although Mozart slyly showed his friend (and pupil?) how even this simple theme can generate an invertible canon at the octave (Variation 5); how a new consequent to the first four measures could make it more interesting harmonically; how the eight-measure introduction can be combined with the main theme; and finally, how an inversion of the opening can enliven the ending. This set, with its sentiment proclaiming a wife to be the most splendid thing in the world, was likely intended as a tribute not only to Schack but also to Constanze.

In June 1790, Leopold II granted Schikaneder an imperial-royal privilege or license and on 3 August 1791, he and Crown Prince Francis paid a visit to the Wiedner Theater to witness a play. This was a signal honor for one of the suburban theaters, apparently never granted by Joseph II, who supported them only in theory. Niemetschek claimed that Schikaneder requested Mozart to compose *Die Zauberflöte* in order to rescue his theater from financial trouble, but this can hardly be the case because the Wiedner Theater had staged a string of successes. The farces in the Anton series have been mentioned, as has the *Oberon* that Wranitzky composed on a text by Carl Ludwig Gieseke after a drama by Sophie Seyler, which itself was drawn from Wieland's great epic poem *Oberon* (1780). Titled a "romantic Singspiel," it was largely serious in content and set Schikaneder on a path that leads straight to Mozart's opera.

Schikaneder is rarely appreciated today for all the different functions he filled in the creation of *Die Zauberflöte*. If they were to be translated into the context of *Le nozze di Figaro* he could be described as: a Beaumarchais for having put together the story; a Da Ponte for turning the story into prose and verse (with help from Mozart); a Count Rosenberg for having the overall direction of the theatrical troupe that produced it; and lastly a Benucci for having been the actor-singer with the largest part (Papageno) and the greatest contributor to its success with the theatergoing public. Naturally, he tailored the opera to suit his own abilities as a performer. The handbill announcing the premiere and cast, like the libretto, calls the work "Eine grosse Oper" (Figure 3.5). Note that the first singers listed are Gerl and Schack. Both libretto and handbill specify that the work is by Emanuel Schikaneder. Mozart in his catalogue was content to call it "eine teutsche Oper in 2 Aufzügen von Eman. Schikaneder," a statement that by itself should have laid to rest all claims by others to have written the text.

The qualities of the opera's text have been much discussed, with opinions ranging from praise to condemnation. On this question, we can do no better than rely on a great Mozart scholar whose native language was German.

> For the weakness of the libretto—a small weakness, easily overcome—lies only in the diction. It contains a great number of unskillful, childish, vulgar turns of speech.

FIGURE 3.5. Handbill for *Die Zauberflöte*.

But the critics who therefore decide that the whole libretto is childish and preposterous deceive themselves. At any rate, Goethe did not so consider it when he wrote a "Zauberflöte, Part II," unfortunately unfinished, but full of fairy-tale radiance, poetic fantasy and profound thought. In the dramaturgic sense, Schikaneder's work is masterly. The dialogue could be shortened and improved, but not a stone in the structure of these two acts and of the work as a whole could be removed or replaced, quite apart from the fact that any change would demolish Mozart's carefully thought out and organic succession of keys.[48]

The hostile critics, on the other hand, see dichotomy in the diction, with Sarastro and his priests speaking a more proper German, an argument that has been used to support the claim that more than one author was involved. The difference could be used just as well to argue for a conscious effort to characterize the two factions by their diction. That the Queen and her Three Ladies use a cruder language than the Priests tells us from the beginning that they are no better educated than a yokel like Papageno. Mozart did not hold back from criticizing and even changing language for singing that he did not like, as we saw in the case of Stephanie, whose position at the court theater lent him a higher social station than that of anyone who worked in the suburban theaters. It will not do to pretend that Schikaneder was unaware of or incapable of writing proper German. As an actor, he had spoken the parts of serious as well as comic characters and was one of the greatest Hamlets of his day. His theater offered a wide variety of plays, some as high in tone as Schiller's *Don Carlos*.

The text's qualities, or lack thereof, have so occupied critics that they tend to overlook the visual effects that were preeminent in all Schikaneder's shows. *Zauberflöte* requires elaborate sets and quick changes between them, a technique honed over generations of theatrical savvy, a scenic fluidity scarcely possible in subsequent times, as an eminent director has pointed out.[49] Visitors to the Wiedner Theater were particularly struck by its visual effects. Zinzendorf, for example, although not a frequent visitor to the suburban stages, perhaps because of their lower social status relative to the court theaters, was impressed on some rare trips to Schikaneder's theater. In his diary for 8 October 1789, he notes that he was invited there to the box of Countess Kinsky to see "Der bauer aus dem Gebürge," the original Anton operetta *Der dumme Gärtner aus dem Gebirge*. His brief comments tell what his eyes, not his ears, took in: "Le Theatre joli, belle illumination a la fin, le parterre rempli." The parterre was often not full at the Burgtheater. He also noted that Schikaneder sang a couplet honoring Prince Coburg, the field marshal of the Austrian army who had just won a battle over the Turks (an event

---

[48] Einstein, *Mozart*, p. 463.

[49] Anthony Besch, "A Director's Approach," ch. 8 in Branscombe, *Die Zauberflöte* (1991), pp. 178–204; see particularly p. 186.

also celebrated by Mozart's orchestral Contredanse in C, K. 587, "Der Sieg vom Helden Koburg"). It was in the nature of popular theater to comment on current events by tacking on a song or a skit.

Two years later, Zinzendorf made another visit to the theater, this time as the guest of Prince Auersperg. Under the date of 6 November 1791, he wrote, "dans la loge de M. et M^e d'Auersperg. entendre la 24eme representation *von der Zauber-flöte*. La musique et les decorations sont jolies, le reste une farce incroyable. Un auditoire immense." At least the music caught his attention, along with the visual effects and the enormous size of the audience. His comment "unbelievable farce" about the rest suggests he had no taste for fairy tales and Egyptian mysteries (or for Freemasonry).

In his catalogue for 1791, Mozart dated the new opera "Im Julius," meaning that all or almost all of it had been composed by the end of July. Following the flurry of orchestral dances for the Carnival balls in the Redoutensaal in early 1791, the catalogue shows only a few isolated pieces. K. 612 and K. 613, connected with the Schikaneder troupe via Gerl and Schack, were followed by the String Quintet in E♭, K. 614, dated 12 April. Then the listings diminish to a few smaller items: an insertion piece in an opera by Sarti, K. 615; an *Andante* for mechanical organ, K. 616; an *Adagio* and Rondo for glass harmonica, oboe, viola, and cello, K. 617. This takes us to the end of May. The only piece for June is "Ave verum corpus," K. 618.

In May, or perhaps somewhat earlier, the opera must have required intensive labor of both poet and composer. The text was probably finished then, or nearly so, for in June parts of it were being quoted or set to music by Mozart. On 6 June, Mozart wrote his wife in Baden, using French in order to get her to practice the language, that he was taking two guests that evening to a box in the Wiedner Theater, where the fifth installment of the popular Anton series, *Anton bei Hofe*, was being performed. The next day he lunched with Schikaneder, who invited him often—these repasts were likely working sessions as well. In his letter of 11 June, he said he had just composed an aria for his new opera, and ended by quoting, without context, "Death and despair were his reward," the last line of the duet for the two priests, No. 11 in Act II. This presupposes Constanze's knowledge of the text, perhaps the whole text as it then stood. On one of his visits to Baden Mozart took the vocal score of Act I and left it with Süssmayer, who served as copyist as well as Constanze's helper. In his letter from Vienna of 2 July, Mozart instructed her to have Süssmayer send back the score of the first act, from the introduction to the finale, so that he could begin its orchestration.

Schikaneder later felt compelled to defend his work from the mutilations of other poets and in a 1795 preface to another of his operas he defended the integrity of *Die Zauberflöte*, stating that he and Mozart "had thought through the work with all diligence."[50] This applies readily to its story. It also concerns even small details of the text, as has been convincingly argued.

> There is abundant evidence that Mozart took a major part in the shaping and reshaping of the text. That he had a hand in the final stage and in points of detail of *Die Zauberflöte* can be demonstrated not only by the divergences revealed by a close comparison of printed text and autograph score, but also by the superior quality of the libretto to any of Schikaneder's numerous other products.[51]

The import of the last remark bears also on the difference in quality of Da Ponte's librettos depending on whether he was working with Mozart or someone else.

Mozart's contributions to the story might well have been the Masonic layer, much of it derived from the novel *Sethos* by Abbé Jean Terrason. Fairy tales à la Wieland

FIGURE 3.6. Ignaz Alberti's frontispiece for the libretto of *Die Zauberflöte*.

were already well practiced at the Wiedner Theater, but the Egyptian mysteries and ceremonial rites were apparently a new element there. Mozart's lodge-brother Ignaz Alberti printed the libretto and was responsible for its engraved frontispiece, laden with Masonic symbols (Figure 3.6). Schikaneder had once belonged to a Masonic lodge in Regensburg but was apparently expelled for moral turpitude. There is no evidence that he had any connections with the Craft in Vienna. Mozart, on the other hand, remained a devoted adherent to the end. Standing immediately before *Die Zauberflöte*, K. 620, in his catalogue and also dated "im Julius" is "Eine kleine teutsche Kantate für eine Stimme am Klavier" on the text

---

[50] Gernot Gruber, preface to the *NMA* edition of *Die Zauberflöte* (Kassel, 1970), p. xiii; Branscombe, *Die Zauberflöte*, p. 89.

[51] Branscombe, *Die Zauberflöte*, p. 101.

"Die ihr des unermesslichen Weltalls Schöpfer ehrt" (Honor the Creator of the immense universe), K. 619. It was written on commission from E. H. Ziegenhagen, a visiting merchant from Hamburg and fellow Mason, who supplied the text. The very last item in the catalogue is another Masonic piece, dated 15 November 1791, K. 623, "Laut verkünde unsre Freude," for two tenors, bass, and orchestra, composed on a text by Schikaneder to celebrate the dedication of a new temple of Mozart's lodge, Crowned Hope.

The choice of E♭ as the opera's principal key was surely made from the very beginning of the project, when Mozart was mainly shaping the libretto to his satisfaction. Symbolically, the three flats of the key counted heavily, and there was a tradition of pieces with Masonic connections employing E♭ or its relative minor, c. Not by chance does the story rely on three ladies, three boys, three priests, three slaves, and three temples. No allusion is made to the three members of the Trinity, but that is where the key symbolism began. In the opera, c minor, the dark side of E♭, shadows the main key throughout, often preceding or following it. And so it had in several of Mozart's earlier works, for example in K. 271, K. 364, and K. 482, with their somber middle movements in c minor. But the Masonic connection resides most clearly with two works of 1785, *Die Maurerfreude*, K. 471, in E♭ and the *Maurerische Trauermusik*, K. 477, in c minor. Another earlier work anticipating the opera is Mozart's incidental music to the play *Thamos*, K. 345, itself another offspring of *Sethos*.[52]

The opera's overture was completed last as with most of Mozart's other operas. A sketch for it survives showing that aside from its key of E♭ the composer had not decided on its main content until the last moment. A slower chordal introduction, *Andante* in cut time, begins the sketch, followed by an *Allegro moderato* with the prominent descent by step from G down a seventh to A♭, the melodic move that is so expressive in Tamino's Picture Aria. The faster part also harks back to certain details in *Die Maurerfreude*, the first movement of which has a similar leaping figure in the violins. But then he explored other ideas. Another sketch shows Mozart working with the fast theme of what would become the completed overture, a repeated eighth note with a melodic turn in sixteenth notes for the fourth beat of the measure. The flurry of quick notes on the last beat, so characteristic of Papageno and his panpipes, can also be found in the first movement of *Die Maurerfreude*.

The slow introduction of the completed overture became an *Adagio* of fifteen measures in cut time, led in by a progression that is omnipresent throughout the opera: I - vi - I$^6_3$, with bass descending E♭ C G, and just as important, treble rising 1 3 5 (Example 3.9a). It also takes the form of a bass descending by step to support the progression I - V$^6_3$ - vi. Dotted rhythms enhance the majesty of this beginning and

---

[52] On K. 345's several musical links with the opera, see *Haydn, Mozart*, p. 679. For further uses of the *Thamos* music, see Neal Zaslaw, "Mozart's Incidental Music to *Lanassa* and His *Thamos* Motets," in *Music, Libraries, and the Academy: Essays in Honor of Lenore Coral*, ed. James P. Cassaro (Middleton, WI, 2007), pp. 55–63.

provide for the quick upbeats to the second and third chords, a rhythm that prevails almost to the end of the introduction. When the *Adagio* chords return at the end of the first part they are static and consist only of the dominant B♭. They sound three times, interrupted by rests with fermatas. Each blast now has its quick note preparation. Not to be missed is what the treble sounds on top: 1 3 5. At the opera's end, the circle is completed when the treble rises to the tonic: 3 5 8 (Example 3.9b).

EXAMPLE 3.9 a, b. *Mozart,* Die Zauberflöte

a. *Overture*   b. *Final Chorus*

Mozart does not emphasize the key of the relative minor in the overture's development, where it makes only passing appearances. No doubt he wanted to save the full force of the c minor menace for the moment when the curtain goes up to reveal Prince Tamino in a chaotic setting of cliffs and overgrown plants, pursued by a dragon. The lower strings throb in eighth and sixteenth notes in this *Allegro* in common time, as if to portray the youth's trembling. The violins sound 1 3 5 in c minor as their main tones above all the churning motion. Tamino begins to sing, calling out for help. He seems near the point of expiring from fear as the tension builds toward a cadence. In the first of several memorable deceptive cadences throughout the opera, the Three Ladies appear and divert the seemingly inescapable resolution to c minor by substituting a surprising A♭, singing the unforgettable words "Stirb Ungeheur, durch unsre Macht!" (Die, monster, through our power!).

Tamino conveniently faints. The Ladies tout their heroic deed as a triumph. With Tamino prone and inert, poet and composer can take the time to characterize the Ladies, who are seized with instant pangs of love for the beautiful youth. They resolve to hurry to the Queen to tell their story but then quarrel as to which one can stay behind and watch over the prince. We get the picture quickly that these Ladies, behind their veils, are no nymphs, and will later be told as much outright (by Papageno). The scene enlarges upon that of the quarrelling sopranos in *Der Schauspieldirektor.* It is carried out until they sing multiple farewells to the youth, mounting to a resounding cadence in C major, the conclusion of this *Introduzione* (the spelling adopted by Mozart in his catalogue). The creators of the opera make the point at once that, far from being one of those German operas consisting of simple songs and an occasional aria, their opera would profit from the wondrous ensemble scenes that Mozart had created in his Italian operas with Da Ponte, such as the *Introduzione* to *Don Giovanni.*

After Papageno sings his introductory birdcatcher's song, No. 2 in G, a strophic Lied, the Ladies return and present Tamino with a picture of the Queen's daughter. Tamino is smitten with love at first sight and in this opera love, like beauty and wisdom, means bringing back the keynote of E♭. Rapt with gazing at her enchanting visage, he sings No. 3, "Dies Bildnis ist bezaubernd schön," short and condensed to the essence from Mozart's lifelong effort to enhance these same expressive devices (see Example 1.11d). E♭ returns in No. 7, another paean to love, sung as a strophic duet between Pamina and Papagena, "Bei Männer welch Liebe fühlen." Mozart does not bring back c minor for an important reappearance in Act I, but it recurs in the finale, used twice for particular text painting, and in confrontation with E♭.

The Finale in C, No. 8, begins as the Three Boys lead Tamino before three temples. He is driven back by the voices of the priests from within the temples of Nature and Reason. That leaves the middle temple of Wisdom, from which the Old Priest emerges and asks him what he seeks in this holy place. Love, and Virtue, he answers. These words bring forth E♭ and the progression so associated with the priests: I - V$_3^6$ - vi, etc. (Example 3.10). Only four lines later the Old Priest

EXAMPLE 3.10. *Mozart,* Die Zauberflöte, *Finale, Act I*

tells him that he was not led here by Love and Virtue but was inflamed by Death and Vengeance (Example, mm. 93–94). His words unleash a plunge into c minor for a jagged melodic line in dotted rhythm. The diminished fourth between B♮

and E♭ is memorable and destined to return. Later in the finale when Sarastro answers Pamina's tender mention of her mother, Mozart brings back c minor, the jagged melodic line and diminished fourth to express, "You would lose all hope if left in the hands of your mother" (Example, m. 429). The implication is clear that Death and Vengeance impel the unhappy Queen of the Night. These hints become explicit threats in Act II.

Mozart saved the grand confrontation of E♭ with c minor until the final crisis. The finale, No. 21, begins in E♭ with a noble trio sung by the Three Boys as they descend to the stage in their flying machine (shades of *Der Luftballon*). Pamina, in despair at what she believes is Tamino's rejection of her, determines to kill herself. She starts singing in the key of c, continues in f, then g, the key of her only aria, the tragic "Ach, ich fühl's, es ist verschwunden," No. 17. Just as she is about to stab herself, the Three Boys intervene with a deceptive cadence that turns the key toward E♭. They then work around to singing the loveliest of all the opera's beautiful moments: "Two hearts burning with love can never be separated by human weakness." In E♭, it is waltz-like and seemingly simple, colored in loving terms especially by the two clarinets' responses. Mozart, in the course of the opera, breaks up many words by inserting rests, a practice frowned upon in serious opera, although used nonetheless in his *Tito*. Here he breaks in two "Zwei Her - zen" and even "Men - schen." This lighthearted ensemble is followed directly, with no transition and only minimal exit music from the orchestra, by the stern sounds of c minor, *forte*, proclaimed by the strings and three trombones, answered by the winds. They accompany the instantaneous transformation to one of the opera's grandest scenes.

Two large mountains appear, one with a roaring waterfall, the other spitting fire. The first is surrounded by black mists; the second is seen against a bright red horizon. Schikaneder's very specific stage directions throughout were so much a part of the show, it seems fitting to include at least mention of these for this scene. The wings to the sides of the stage represent rocky cliffs. Each mountain has a grating through which fire and water can be seen. Directions for the costumes of the Two Men in Armor who patrol the scene are equally specific. The early depiction of this scene from the smaller stage at Brno/Brünn adheres to some but not all these specifications.[53]

[53] The opera was performed at Brno in 1793 by Karl Hain's company. Two years later, there appeared in the Brno monthly *Allgemeines europäisches Journal* between January and July 1795 six illustrations of scenes from the opera engraved by Joseph and Peter Schaffer. They are reproduced in Otto Erich Deutsch, ed., *Mozart and his World in Contemporary Pictures*, tr. Peter Branscombe (Kassel, 1961), nos. 540–45. The roaring waterfall on a mountain suggests the grotto that Count Cobenzl built at his estate on the Kahlenberg, praised by Mozart in his letter of 13 July 1781; see Annette Richards, *The Free Fantasia and the Musical Picturesque* (Cambridge, 2001), pp. 214–16, with illustration of the grotto from 1810, figure 6.2, and John A. Rice, *The Temple of Night at Schönau: Architecture, Music, and Theater in a Late Eighteenth-Century Garden* (Philadelphia, 2006), p. 165; for the scenic designs of Karl Friedrich Schinkel, see pp. 176–77.

The solemn chordal opening of the scene, *Adagio* in cut time, resembling the opening of the *Maurerische Trauermusik,* gives way to an equally serious contrapuntal stroll in the form of an old-fashioned trio sonata. As if in a chorale prelude by Bach, the two Armed Men enter singing the cantus firmus in longer notes, and in octaves. Their melody is the old Lutheran chorale "Ach, Gott, vom Himmel sieh darein," which Luther translated in 1524 from Psalm XI, "Salvum me fac." The words they sing, on the other hand, come from *Sethos:* "Whoever wanders this path alone and burdened will be purified through Fire and Water, Air and Earth. Whoever can overcome the Fear of Death will rise from Earth to Heaven." There is no more serious moment in the entire opera, and it is made even more sublime when Pamina is allowed to join Tamino, and then to lead him through the trials as he plays his flute, the key of c having given way to C major.

The last eruption of c minor is the most powerful. It portrays an attempted coup d'état. Accompanied by her minions, the Queen advances by stealth into the lower floor of the temple, plotting the overthrow of Sarastro and his Priests. Their music is dominated by a motto that sounds ominous yet is very simple. It was more complicated as Mozart earlier drafted it (Example 3.11ab). This is one of

EXAMPLE 3.11 a, b. *Mozart,* Die Zauberflöte, *Finale, Act II, scene 30*

a. *Draft of Quintet, "Nur stille, stille"*

b. *Final Version*

several cases in which the composer gained immeasurably by reducing the complexity of an earlier version. In the draft, he brought back the false interval of the diminished fourth from E♭ down to B♮ (see Example 3.10), in which it conveyed death and revenge. Here they appear incarnate in the persons of the Queen, the Three Ladies, and Monastatos, who has thrown in his lot with the dark powers of Night (perhaps the reason he was made a black person in the first place). To paint their malevolence in the clearest way, Mozart changed to a more direct statement by removing the diminished fourth and repeating the same fourth leap down from C to G. This way he enhanced the bleakness of the moment and did not detract from the sinister quality of the slightly accented second beat, marked *mezzo forte*, followed by the *piano* trill, which in this context sounds like something between a sneer and a snarl. After the second trilled tone, Mozart used the falling diminished fourth between A♭ and E♮, an interval all the more effective here for not having been anticipated. Such attention to detail marks the entire score. Sometimes it even comes down to the use of staccato articulations either by strokes or by dots. He replaced the strokes with dots for the first upbeats of the two versions and then made use of dots to lighten the penultimate measure of equal eighth notes in comparison with the two quarter notes and octave leap that follows, articulated by strokes. There is both menace and tip-toe stealth in that penultimate measure, which is much improved in overall expression by Mozart's smoothing out the line with the change of a single tone from C to G.

The same intense scrutiny of detail pertains to the opera's few recitatives. There is a long melodic sketch for the scene in Act I in which Tamino stands before the three temples. At this point in the drama, he is still the deluded would-be hero intent upon rescuing the abducted maiden at all cost. "Pamina's rescue is my duty," he sings twice, to a rising sequence that parallels a passage in which Zerlina describes her beating heart in *Don Giovanni* No. 18. As in the previous musical example, Mozart decided to simplify, using fewer different tones (Example 3.12ab). The result intensifies Tamino's calling out the beloved's name, aided by the fermata on the second syllable.

EXAMPLE 3.12 a, b. *Mozart, Die Zauberflöte, Finale, Act I*

a. *Sketch*

[Tamino: Pa-mi - nen ret-ten, Pa-mi - nen ret-ten ist mir Pflicht.]

b. *Final Version*

Pa - mi - nen ret - ten, Pa - mi - nen ret - ten ist mir Pflicht

The opera summarizes much of Mozart's long-evolving use of tonality to denote specific emotional states. Experts have not hesitated to discuss it in terms of the intentions behind the composer's choice of keys. There is, for instance, this often-quoted general assessment.

The key of the mystical and fundamental idea of the opera is E♭. That of the world of the Priests is F, while that of the sinister and light-deprived powers is c minor. G is reserved for the bright world of the comic figures, while g minor is the key of suffering. At high points of the action, the advocates for both warring parties switch from their tonal spheres to sharper keys, the Queen by adopting d minor, Sarastro by singing in E major.[54]

In general, with a few qualifications to be added, the points are well taken. The particularly buffo and folk-like qualities Mozart attached to G major were honed long before 1791, and nowhere more clearly than in an avian comedy such as the finale to Piano Concerto No. 17 in G, K. 453. Obvious as well is the special radiance the key of g minor held for Mozart and how often he used it to portray sorrow-stricken women, whether Giunia, Ilia, Konstanze, Madame Herz, or Pamina. Much has been said on the subject, including how the music of these suffering heroines spills over into non-vocal works, such as the String Quintet in g, K. 516.[55]

Most in need of qualification is the association of the key of F with the world of the Priests. At the beginning of Act II this is clear for the March of the Priests, No. 9 (like the overture a late addition to the score), followed by their chorus, No. 20, "O Isis und Osiris." Both pieces portray a hushed solemnity appropriate to worship and the temple. Timbral color as much as or more than key lend these two numbers their solemnity when combined with their slow and dignified motion. The march has an initial harmonic motion of I - V[7] –vi, topped by the 3 5 1 treble and bearing strong resemblance to the March of the Priests in Act III of *Idomeneo*. What is novel is the orchestration: flute, two basset horns, bassoons, horns, strings, and three trombones (instruments that in *Idomeneo* appear only with the oracle). The chorus No. 10 uses the same band minus the flute, violins, and contrabasses. Removing the basset horns and the trombones restores the key of F for use as a more all-purpose vehicle, fitting choice for instance, in the same Act II, for Papageno's Lied "Ein Mädchen oder Weibchen," No. 20, with its perky Glockenspiel solos. Similarly, C major is an all-purpose key, one that can serve equally well the buffo patter of Monastatos, the close harmony of the Three Boys, and the act-ending jubilation in praise of Sarastro.

The choice of the rather rare key of E for Sarastro's "In diesen heil'gen Hallen," No. 15, is indeed a deviation. Another composer might have put it in F, like the other priestly music, and thereby spared the poor bass at least by a half tone in his lowest range. Mozart avoided F here because it is too closely related to the key of the previous piece, the Queen's hellish revenge aria "Der Hölle Rache kocht in meinem Herzen," No. 14, in d minor. For Sarastro's dismissal of revenge and his praises of love, forgiveness, and brotherhood in its stead, a

---

[54] Abert, *W. A. Mozart*, 2: 687, n. 2.
[55] Steven Jan, "The Evolution of a 'Memeplex' in Late Mozart: Replicated Structures in Pamina's 'Ach ich fühl's,' " *Journal of the Royal Musical Association* 128 (2003): 330–70.

key so near the previous aria as the relative major would be inappropriate. The Queen's music is so powerful that the intervening spoken dialogue cannot erase it from our tonal memory. For Mozart's thoughts on the nearness of the relative minor to a major key there are his words explaining why he avoided it in order to project Osmin's rage.

Another question that has been raised concerns the appropriateness of choosing G for the Quintet, No. 12, when the Three Ladies invade the temple and tempt Tamino and Papageno to break the silence imposed upon them. Why choose the key so indelibly associated with Papageno since his entrance song about his bird-related activities? Moreover, the music begins with the I - V$_3^6$ - vi progression central to the whole opera. Here, it could be argued, the women use key and progression in an attempt to deceive the men. Papageno, easily hood-winked after hearing his familiar key, cheerily breaks his vow and resumes chattering. Tamino, not so easily fooled by their use of a progression to which he himself had sung of love and duty, remains steadfast. Eventually all five sing a kind of moral, namely that a man of resolve thinks before speaking. At this point, an unseen chorus of men turns the cadential G to a resolute E♭ on the way to a cadence in c minor as the Ladies, having profaned the temple, are ejected.

More about Mozart's ways of moving tonally between pieces can be learned from the several sets of orchestral dances he composed in early 1791 for that season's Carnival balls in the Redoutensaal. These are not suites. Neither are they randomly ordered as to key succession. The composer's main strategy was to select a key that shared at least one chord tone with its predecessor. In other words, he moved by the interval of a third or fourth up or down, not by a second, which would provide no common tone. Exceptions are *Six Ländler*, K. 606, all in the same key, and *Five Contredanses*, K. 609, in which he twice moved by the interval of a second, from E♭ to D to C. In the first act of the opera, there are no exceptions. His choice is to follow one number, or section, within the *Introduzione* and finale, with another that has a shared common tone.

In the second act, some pieces arrive with no common tone shared with the previous number. The Queen's violent aria in d minor, No. 14, succeeds the giddy aria of Monastatos in C and is followed by Sarastro's aria in E. As the distance grows between the bickering factions, so does the tonal divide. After the Three Boys sing their second trio in the key of A, No. 16, there follows, with only brief dialogue intervening, Pamina's despairing lament, No. 17, in g. Another factor must be considered here. Sworn to silence, Tamino cannot speak to her. Instead, according to a stage direction, he communicates by playing his flute. What does he play? The usual choice, and a good one, is the tune from his blithe solo in the first finale, "Wie stark ist nicht dein Zauberton," a piece in limpid C major. It sounds familiar and reassuring. In addition, it serves to mitigate tonal distance, having the third degree with which it starts in common with the fifth of No. 16 in

A, and its fifth degree, the tune's first melodic goal, in common with the tonic of No. 17 in g. Pamina does not grasp this message but we, the audience, can learn to do so.

Poet and composer conceived the opera with an important role for spoken dialogue, some of it necessary for characterization. There is a long stretch of it at the beginning of Act II to commence the rites of initiation. Mozart took the scene very much to heart, as we know from his letter to Constanze of 8–9 October 1791.

> [Name crossed out] had a box this evening and applauded everything with vigor. He, the know-it-all, acted so much like a Bavarian I could not remain there or I would have had to call him an ass. Unfortunately I happened to be with them just when the second act began, thus at the solemn scene. He laughed at it all; at first, I was patient enough to draw his attention to some of the speeches. He made fun of everything. Well, it was too much for me. I called him a Papageno and left the box. I doubt that the dolt understood what I meant by this.

One attempt to decipher the obliterated name tentatively came up with "Adamberger," the tenor who was in fact a Bavarian.[56]

Mozart's words about "the solemn scene" should caution directors of the opera not to reduce the spoken dialogue beyond the bounds of comprehensibility. Pantomime can convey some of the dialogue's important messages but it cannot replace them entirely. Mozart was not seeking volleys of applause with this work, as he admitted doing in *Die Entführung*. In a letter dated a day earlier, 7–8 October, he wrote that several numbers were encored, "but what pleases me most is the silent approval!" (was mich aber am meisten freuet, ist der *Stille beifall!*) His audiences had learned, like Tamino, that silence could be golden.

With *Die Zauberflöte*, Viennese Singspiel reached its zenith. It was such a hard act to follow that none of the many attempts made by Schikaneder to duplicate the original recipe enjoyed more than ephemeral success. He enlisted several composers in the attempt, among others Süssmayer, Johann Schenk, and Peter Winter. Goethe sought out Paul Wranitzky as the most appropriate composer to set his *Zauberflöte Zweite Teil* (1796) but the project was abandoned. Only Beethoven's *Leonore* (1805) combined spiritual message and sublimely great music to the extent of becoming a worthy Viennese operatic heir of *Die Zauberflöte*.

---

[56] John Arthur, " 'N. N.' Revisited: New Light on Mozart's Late Correspondence," in *Haydn, Mozart, and Beethoven: Studies in the Music of the Classical Period: Essays in Honour of Alan Tyson,* ed. Sieghard Brandenburg (Oxford, 1998), pp. 127–45; 145.

La clemenza di Tito

Mozart had completed *Die Zauberflöte* except for its two instrumental pieces by midsummer 1791, when he began intensive work on his last opera. Naturally, his head was full of his German opera (K. 620), and the consequences of this can be heard often in *Tito* (K. 621). The two magnanimous rulers in particular, Tito and Sarastro, have much in common.[57] One way in which the two works differed greatly was in their treatment of dialogue. Opera in Italian hardly ever permitted spoken dialogue, least of all in a work for a festive court occasion. Time for completing the new opera was inadequate, so the composer had to delegate composition of the simple recitatives to another, traditionally thought to have been his pupil and assistant Süssmayer, who accompanied the Mozarts to Prague in order to help ready the score and parts.

In his thematic catalogue, Mozart entered *Tito* with the date of 5 September 1791, the day before its premiere. He described its function as a coronation opera for Leopold II and specified that it was an opera seria in two acts, reduced to a true opera (ridotta a vera opera) by Signor Mazzolà, "poet of His Highness the elector of Saxony." He honored the librettist here not only in the positive way in which he describes the revised version of the text, Metastasio's famous three-act opera of 1734 for Vienna, but also by the way he cites his poet's name and title. He never did as much for Da Ponte in his catalogue.

Guardasoni was by this time in sole charge of the National Theater in Prague. Eighteen months after *Don Giovanni*, Mozart encountered him again when he passed through Prague on the way to Berlin. In his letter to his wife dated Prague 10 April 1789, he informed her that he had met with Guardasoni "who almost promised me [fast richtig machte mir] to pay 200 ducats and fifty more in travel money [1150 florins] for writing an opera for this coming fall." This plan may have been nothing more than a fib told to cheer up Constanze. In any case, it cannot be linked with the coronation opera of 1791.[58]

Leopold II, after being crowned both emperor in Frankfurt and king of Hungary in Pressburg in the fall of 1790, was in no hurry to undergo coronation as king of Bohemia (a ritual Joseph II had evaded altogether). The Bohemian Estates, presided over by Count Heinrich Rottenhahn as Burgrave, were also dilatory. By the time they got around to signing an opera contract with Guardasoni on 8 July 1791 there were scarcely two months remaining before the coronation

[57] Daniel Heartz, "La Clemenza di Sarastro: Masonic Beneficence in the Last Operas," in *Mozart's Operas* (1990), pp. 254–75.
[58] The link was posited by Tomislav Volek, "Über den Ursprung von Mozarts Oper 'La Clemenza di Tito,'" *Mozart-Jahrbuch 1959*: 274–86. It has since been refuted, in greatest detail, by Sergio Durante, "The Chronology of Mozart's 'La clemenza di Tito' reconsidered," *Music and Letters* 80 (1999): 560–94.

was scheduled to take place. Plans were already under way in Vienna for a coronation opera, it seems, probably even before the signing of this document.

At the beginning of 1791, Leopold had taken firm control of opera in the Burgtheater. Previously he had allowed Count Rosenberg to continue running the court theaters. Rosenberg, who was raised to the status of prince at the imperial coronation, was replaced by Count Wenzel Ugarte, for whom the title of Musikgraf, long in disuse, was revived. Prince Adam Starhemberg, the Obersthofmeister, wrote to the emperor on 15 January 1791 reminding Leopold that the Musikgraf had always been subordinate to his office. Leopold returned his letter with a note saying yes, but "in matters concerning the management of the theaters he will be under my sole direction."[59]

In the spring of 1791 Leopold went to Italy. There he became deeply involved in the attempted flight in June of his sister Marie Antoinette and her husband Louis XVI, along with the political repercussions from its failure.[60] Leopold left Vienna in mid-March. At the same time both Da Ponte and Ferrarese were dismissed. To replace them, Count Ugarte began hiring new personnel. Irene Tomeoni came as prima donna buffa and made her debut in Vienna on 24 April in Guglielmi's *La bella pescatrice*, with notable success, according to Zinzendorf. Another new arrival was Caterino Mazzolà of Dresden, who was given temporary leave from the Saxon court so that he could replace Da Ponte for a few months. At the Viennese court theater he was paid 100 florins a month from May through July (Da Ponte never rose above 600 per annum). Crown Prince Francis, in lieu of his father, received Mazzolà on 13 May. There were no premieres of new operas given by the Italian court singers during Mazzolà's stay, raising the question of what he did to earn his salary. The answer could be that he was surreptitiously working on a coronation opera. Not even the emperor knew about it. When Leopold learned in Italy of Mazzolà's appointment he made his disapproval known by a protocol of 25 May saying the Dresden poet was unnecessary and superfluous since only old operas would be given in the summer.[61] Furthermore, on his way back from Italy he told Ugarte by letter of 15 July not to make any further appointments in the theater until his return.

Mazzolà, with the likely approval of Ugarte and Guardasoni, expertly trimmed Metastasio's old court opera down to a manageable size, cutting it by about a third. He reduced the number of arias and recitatives greatly, while adding several ensembles and new arias, often cobbled from Metastasio's recitatives.[62] Mozart

[59] Rice, *Salieri*, pp. 495–96.

[60] Munro Price, *The Road from Versailles: Louis XVI, Marie Antoinette, and the Fall of the French Monarchy* (New York, 2002), pp. 239–41.

[61] Helga Lühning, "Nochmal zum Titus (Erwiderung)," *Die Musikforschung* 28 (1975): 211–14.

[62] Helga Lühning, *Titus-Vertonungen im 18. Jahrhundert: Untersuchungen zur Tradition der Opera seria von Hasse bis Mozart* (Laaber, 1983), pp. 79–108, and John A. Rice, *W. A. Mozart: La clemenza di Tito* (Cambridge, 1991), pp. 31–44.

presumably took a hand in the process, as he had with all his librettists.

Mazzolà was no newcomer to opera seria. Like his protégé Da Ponte, who was five years his junior, he hailed from the Veneto. Before being named poet to the Saxon court in 1780, he had written serious operas for Venice. Librettos for opera seria were not much in demand at Dresden, which in its straitened post-war circumstances could afford few seria singers. But for special occasions they could be imported. To celebrate the first marriage of the electoral prince in 1781, Mazzolà wrote the Masonic opera seria *Osiride*, set to music by Naumann. His opera seria *Elisa* from the same year was revived in 1788 at Prague, to which the poet traveled and for which he wrote a new opera buffa. He and Guardasoni were thus well acquainted.

Theatrical connections between Dresden and Prague were strong at the time and had been since mid-century. Mazzolà must also have been aware of the latest operatic fashions in Vienna. *Axur* by Da Ponte and Salieri was produced at Dresden in 1789. Salieri claimed that he was the first choice of composer for *Tito*. This would have been only normal because of his position as the imperial court's Kapellmeister, but there are reasons to doubt his claim.

The contract Guardasoni signed with the Bohemian Estates on 8 July 1791 begins by specifying that the work in question be an opera seria. It could hardly be anything else, given the preference of Leopold II for the genre and the precedent set by the coronation opera of 1723, Fux's *Constanza e Fortezza* for Charles VI, Leopold's grandfather. Guardasoni promised that, for a fee of 6000 florins, he would procure the services of a first-class *musico*, that is a castrato, and should he be able to get Luigi Marchesi the sum increased to 6500; a prima donna of equally high standing would be hired. The second point of the contract stipulated that he would have the poetry of the libretto written on one of the two subjects furnished to him by the Estates and have it set to music by a distinguished composer. A revealing caveat about the subject of the libretto was added: if time were too short, Guardasoni would supply instead a newly-composed opera on the subject of Metastasio's *Tito*. With this, the clandestine planning came out into the open. The time was, of course, too short to do anything but produce the opera apparently already under way in Vienna. Guardasoni thus extricated himself from his obligation to accept the subjects he was given. He also promised to have new costumes made "especially for the leading roles," and two new changes of scenery.[63]

The Estates for their part guaranteed money for the impresario to travel to Vienna and Italy, plus certain specified sums if the opera were to be canceled. The agreement does not say what Guardasoni was to do in Vienna, but implied that the librettist and "a distinguished composer" would be hired there, to match the leading singers hired in Italy. Guardasoni left for Vienna upon signing the con-

[63] Sergio Durante, "Le scenografie di Pietro Travaglia per 'La clemenza di Tito' (Praga, 1791): Problemi di identificazione ed implicazioni," *Mozart-Jahrbuch 1994*: 156–69.

tract. Salieri injected himself into the story about this time by claiming in a letter to Prince Anton Esterházy, undated but probably mid-August 1791, that the
impresario begged him to compose the opera and did this in the course of five
visits, while showing the composer the sum of 200 *zecchini*.[64] A man hurrying on
to Italy had time to pay Salieri so many visits? The whole tale sounds concocted
and designed to show how busy Salieri was at the Burgtheater, where there had
been an unpleasantness about allowing the prompter to take part in the festive
cantata for the installation of the new prince at Esterháza. This event took place
on 3 August 1791, with music by Salieri's pupil and assistant Joseph Weigl (in
place of Kapellmeister Haydn, who was in London).

Mozart put some ideas for the opera on paper by drafting the first and third
numbers, both on texts by Mazzolà, and both involving the primo uomo, Sesto,
whose part he wrote for a tenor voice and in keys other than those of the final versions. The simplest explanation for the choice of tenor for Sesto is that Mozart's
drafts antedate the contract or communication of its contents to the composer.
Both drafts show ideas in common with the final versions yet are quite distinct
from them. They are written on Paper Type I along with other pieces among the
first to be composed.[65]

The early drafts for Nos. 1 and 3 are complete as to the vocal parts and the
bass line, to which a few cues in the violins have been added, and in the case of
No. 1, a conclusion for the violins. Mozart chose for this first number the key of
C and placed the tenor part in its highest range (Example 3.13a). The final ver-
sion is in the key of F and composed after he knew he would have a contralto
Sesto (Example 3.13b). There are several similarities between the two in general

EXAMPLE 3.13 a, b. *Mozart,* La clemenza di Tito, *No. 1, Duetto*

a. *Draft*

[64] "The Acta Musicalia of the Esterházy Archives (Nos. 101–152)," *Haydn Yearbook* 15 (1984), No. 14, pp.
153–57. The original letter in Italian is given with English translation and commentary. Salieri's "è stato
cinque volte da me" is mistranslated "the impresario came five times from Prague to Vienna." His letter in the original is also quoted in *Dokumente: Addenda, neue Folge,* ed. Cliff Eisen, *NMA* X/31/2 (Kassel,
1997), pp. 70–71.
[65] Tyson, *Mozart,* pp. 48–60; 54; other pieces using this type of paper are the ensembles Nos. 7 and 10.

b. *Final Version*

motion and text setting. Both versions reach their melodic peak for the repetition of the word "tutto"; both versions break into *Allegro* for the final section and there are other similarities as well. Pairs of slurred eighth notes are frequent in both. They also figure prominently in Don Ottavio's "Il mio tesoro" in *Don Giovanni*, written for the Prague tenor Baglioni. This and the high tessitura of the draft argue that Mozart first imagined the part of Sesto for him. The final version of the first duet is more agitated and exciting than the draft, as can be seen even by comparing their beginnings. To emphasize the imperative "imponi" (command me), Mozart snaps it off at the second beat in both versions, but in the second he repeats it a step higher, creating an extra measure, breaking the regular phrasing of the draft. The editor of the critical edition believed there was sufficient distance in substance between the two versions that the draft could be dated early in 1791; his critic rejects the idea saying it suits none of the scenarios as to how and when the composer began setting Mazzolà's text.[66]

The *duettino* for Sesto and Annio, No. 3, Mozart drafted as an *Andante* in the key of F. The text begins "Deh prendi un amplesso amico mio fedel" (Receive, my faithful friend, a tender embrace), which Mozart set to a lilting rhythm in 6/8 time. He diluted the effect somewhat by imitation between the voices and by chromatic motion. Both of these complications are nearly eliminated in the final version, which attains within its tiny compass a pastoral quality of repose and contentment quite similar to the first number of *Il re pastore* K. 208, another three-act opera by Metastasio that had been cut down to two acts. The beauty of Metastasio's language, exact or paraphrased by Mazzolà, shines through *Tito* in a way that perhaps reminded Mozart of his Salzburg opera of 1775, of which there are several echoes in *Tito*.

Vitellia is one of Metastasio's most compelling characters. The daughter of Emperor Vitellius, she is a captive of her pride who believed her rightful place was at Tito's side as empress. Both spitfire and seductress, Vitellia is much the liveliest of the characters. Such a humane and forgiving ruler as Tito certainly won Mozart's sympathy. So did the scheming Vitellia, whose musical portrait in this opera is worthy to stand beside that of his spiteful Electra, or the Queen of

[66] Franz Giegling, ed, *La clemenza di Tito*, NMA II/5/20 (Kassel, 1970), p. XII. The critic is Helga Lühning, "Zur Entstehungsgeschichte von Mozarts 'Titus,'" *Die Musikforschung* 27 (1974): 300–318; 316, n. 79.

the Night at her most violent. There is no denying the composer's gift for making scorned women come alive. His music tells us that he found Vitellia just as fascinating as those other vipers and perhaps a little more interesting than Tito the Just, whose clemency was so predictable as to become almost boring.

From her entrance in the very first number, Vitellia spells trouble. After the relative calm of the plea with which Sesto begins, her music is stormy and seething. The strings become agitated with tremolo sixteenth notes and jerky figures in dotted rhythm, while the harmony becomes unstable. Her vocal line is as extravagant as her words. She wants the miscreant dead before sunset she says, and adds, "Know that he usurped an empire." Mozart translates her words into vocal fireworks (Example 3.14a). At the most urgent words, "estinto" and "usurpa," he gives her vocal melismas that descend precipitously, as if into the abyss. "Usurpa" elicits a plunge down nearly two octaves to low A, then a great leap up. The draft of No. 1 contains nothing of the kind, from which it may be deduced that Mozart by this time believed or had hopes that the prima donna hired would be well-endowed in vocal equipment.

EXAMPLE 3.14 a, b. *Mozart,* La clemenza di Tito, *Vitellia's melodic style*

a. *No. 1, Duetto*

The same aggressive arpeggio figures mark Vitellia's solo aria in G, No. 2, and receive even more violent expression in the *terzetto*, No. 10, which is more like another aria for her than a trio. Having dispatched Sesto to kill Tito she learns that she has become Tito's choice for bride after all. She freezes with horror, as she says, at her dire predicament. The first time through this text, which is not Metastasio's, she leaps up to a *forte* high B♮ for the melodic climax (Example 3.14b). Upon the text's return at the end this becomes a startling leap from F♯ up to a *forte* high B♭, followed by a stunning capper: transfer of the triadic arpeggio from No. 1 up to G, taking her voice up to high D.

b. *No. 10, Terzetto*

Vitellia concentrates a strong dose of torment in her music and vocal line. Mozart allowed a little of her melodic flaring to rub off on Tito when, in his aria No. 6 in "her" key of G, he sings of a ruler's torment to a downward arpeggio. Even Sesto catches the virus from her in the *terzetto*, No. 18, as he is led away to prison, when he is given a long-held "Oh Dio!" followed by a descending arpeggio. In the *terzetto* No. 14, sung by Vitellia, Sesto and Publio, prefect of the Praetorian Guard, Vitellia is chastened somewhat by remorse for her own follies. Sesto sings first, in music remaining firmly in the tonic. Yet when her turn comes to sing, the mood darkens just as in No. 1. The strings begin their tremolo sixteenth notes while the harmonies become somber and unsettled.

Vitellia's final aria is the famous rondò "Non più di fiori vaghe catene discenda Imene ad intreciar" (No more charming wreaths of flowers will Hymen descend to weave). The desperate arpeggios return, as does the low A, and there is even a low G in the rondò's fast section. Rarely does a soprano have these low-lying tones as well as the ability to reach the high D required in No. 8. Maria Marchetti Fantozzi, the prima donna hired for the role, came close to having both capabilities, as a study of several of her previous roles has revealed.[67]

"Non più di fiori" makes a stunning culmination of Vitellia's role. Yet its tessitura is lower than the rest of her part, which led scholars to suspect that it had originally been written for a different soprano. Later studies, relying on the paper and inks used by Mozart in writing the piece down, as well as other kinds of evidence, have removed most doubts: the aria was added to the score in the late stages of its composition.[68]

Vitellia's rondò had an elaborate concertante part for Anton Stadler. In this case, his instrument was a basset horn, which weaves lovely chains of florid melody in supporting her, in line with the "vaghe catene" of the text. The earlier two-tempo rondò that most closely approaches this combination of voice with a solo instrument providing florid concertante accompaniments is Idamante's "Non temer amato bene," K. 490, of 1786, for tenor and violin. In both arias music of the slow part returns, quickened, as a subdominant episode in the *Allegro*.

Mozart wrote no other arias for soprano and basset horn solo, as far as is known. Suspicions fell upon an aria sung by Josepha Duschek at her Prague concert of 26 April 1791, described on the program as a "Rondo by Mozart with obbligato basset horn."[69] The problems of identifying this with "Non più di fiori" are manifold. One is that Mazzolà's text, cleverly drawn from a few words

[67] John A. Rice, "Mozart and His Singers: The Case of Marchetti Fantozzi, the First Vitellia," *Opera Quarterly* 11 (1995): 31–52.

[68] John Arthur, "Some Chronological Problems in Mozart: the Contribution of Ink-Studies," in *Wolfgang Amadè Mozart*, ed. Stanley Sadie (1996), pp. 25–52: 45 ff.; and Durante, "The Chronology of Mozart's 'La clemenza di Tito' reconsidered," 574–75, 588–90.

[69] Volek, "Über den Ursprung von Mozarts Oper 'La clemenza di Tito,'" 275.

in recitative by Metastasio and beautifully attuned to Vitellia's situation at this moment of the drama, could scarcely have been written so early. Another is that Mozart's good friend Josepha lacked the very low tones required by "Non più di fiore." In two concert arias Mozart composed for her, K. 272 of 1777 and K. 528 of 1787, her low range ended with the D above middle C. Later, after Mozart's death, she made a specialty of singing Vitellia's rondò in concert, but we shall never know to what extent her rendition matched the demands of Mozart's vocal part.

Marchetti Fantozzi in 1791 was about thirty in age and had been singing leading roles for several years, particularly at Naples. Acclaimed for her acting as well as her singing she specialized in portraying tragic heroines. Less than two years after *Tito* in Prague, a Berlin critic wrote with high praise of her abilities.

> The compass of her voice is not big; the low register is rough and dull and the upper reaches are such that she can reach high C only in passing. Yet her otherwise full voice is completely at her command; her tone is quite pure, and she has the Italian expressivity with its good aspects and without too much exaggeration; she sings with great feeling, and, when it is necessary, with considerable virtuosity, although it requires much effort of her. . . . But her acting, her delivery, are masterful; they are such as only she, the best actress on the operatic stage, can have.[70]

Singers' voices can change quickly. Mostly they contract in range with age and overuse. It is possible that, even in the course of a couple years, the soprano lost some of her top voice or her vocal flexibility.

Leopold II submitted to the long ordeal of coronation on 6 September 1791. That same evening and night, he and his weary court attended the premiere of *Tito*. Marchetti Fantozzi made a better impression on Zinzendorf than did the opera as a whole. He wrote, "La Marchetti chante fort bien, L'Empereur en est entousiasmé." This suggests that, whatever it cost her in effort, she got through the role with aplomb—arpeggios, high notes, and very low notes notwithstanding. Of the opera's overall impression, Zinzendorf wrote, "On nous regala du plus ennuyeux Spectacle *La Clemenza di Tito*." Empress Maria Luisa was more severe still in a letter the following day to her daughter-in-law Maria Theresa de Bourbon.[71]

For the primo uomo part of Sesto, Guardasoni brought from Italy another experienced and widely-praised singer, the castrato Domenico Bedini. Before going to Prague, he had sung in all the Italian centers of opera. Emperor Leopold

---

[70] *Berlinische musikalische Zeitung* 2 (9 February 1793), as quoted in translation by John A. Rice, *Tito*, p. 52.

[71] "Au soir au Theatre la grande opera n'est pas grande chose et la musique très mauvaise ainsi nous y avons presque tous dormi. Le Couronnement est allé a merveille." Rice, *Tito*, p. 165, n. 31.

well knew his talents for Bedini had performed in no fewer than six operas at Florence during the 1780s. He was especially noted for singing grand specimens of the two-tempo rondò.

Sesto's role in the drama is pivotal. He also has the most music to sing and plays the most prominent part in several ensembles. Moreover, he has two huge arias plus an enormous obbligato recitative at the end of Act I. His first aria, No. 9, is sung to Vitellia on the traditional text by Metastasio, "Parto, ma tu ben mio."[72] The piece has a florid concertante solo for Stadler on the basset clarinet in B♭, the key of the piece. Although not a rondò, the aria comprises both an *Adagio* in 3/4 time and an *Allegro* in common time. Again, as in No. 1, Sesto begs Vitellia for a glance to send him inspired on his mission of death. One musical feature forecasts her rondò, No. 23: the slow part returns in text and melodic incipit as a subdominant episode in the fast part. There is a still faster third section, *Allegro assai*. It begins with whirling sixteenth notes in the strings up and down in contrary motion, suggestive of chiming bells and similar to passages that Mozart put into the overture, probably written last. This excitement is in the nature of an implied stage direction: she finally gives her lover the glance he begged and it sets him together with Stadler off into competing chains of triplet melismas, a rousing climax to end this tour de force.

Vitellia has little time to react. In a short recitative, Publio tells her that Tito has named her his choice. Astonished, she begins the agitated *terzetto*, No. 10 in G, before the long stretch of B♭ has had a chance to dissipate. This sounds a little shocking, although Mozart has prepared our ears for third relationships in the overture (E♭ directly after G) and between Nos. 3 and 4 (from C without transition to E♭). These tonal plunges into *terza minore* and *sesta minore*, to become favorites of Rossini, show Mozart moving with the times and keeping abreast of the latest fashions in Italian opera seria.

The last four numbers of Act I make up a tonal complex that is driven by dominant to tonic propulsions, much like the second act of *Idomeneo* (Table 3.2). As one critic has put it, "Mozart creates a great musical arch, of wide span, that holds the last four pieces of the opera's Act I together."[73]

TABLE 3.2. *La clemenza di Tito*, Act I

No.	9	10	11	12
	Sesto's Aria	Terzetto	Sesto's Monologue	Quintet with Chorus
	B♭	G	c - f - B♭	E♭

[72] For several examples of other composer's settings of "Parto," beginning with Caldara's in 1734, see Lühning, *Titus-Vertonungen*, pp. 376–422.

[73] Lühning, *Titus-Vertonungen*, pp. 421–22.

Comparisons with *Idomeneo* are more apt here than those with buffo finales, which have their own poetic and musical requirements. Choral and scenic horror work together to end *Idomeneo*'s second act, with its monster, storm, and flight of the populace. They also combine to end *Tito*'s first act, showing the burning of Rome, attempted assassination, and general panic. Metastasio had banished such vivid actions to mere mentions, but they returned on stage in Italian serious opera via a massive infusion of French models.

The change of scene to the Campidoglio corresponds with the beginning of Sesto's monologue, No. 11. This incomparable obbligato recitative is much longer than Idomeneo's between the two choruses. It has moments of softening as Sesto asks himself how he could possibly kill his friend and benefactor, moments when the music turns melting in its tenderness. Such mood swings also have precedents in *Idomeneo* and in Gluck's tragedies. *Tempo primo* ultimately prevails over these *Andante* musings by restoring the brisk *Allegro assai* in common time with which the monologue opens. Also restored is the brusque orchestral motto that dominates the whole number and also left its mark on the overture. The motto self-destructs at the end of No. 11 by going into a paroxysm of rising disjunct thirds, suggesting the action of going up in smoke and flames, exactly what the Campidoglio is described as doing in a stage direction at just this point (see Example 7.16b, p. 766). A depiction from 1795 shows how one artist envisaged the scene with costumes and architecture in the then-modern neoclassical style (Figure 3.7).

The *Quintetto con coro*, No. 12, begins in exultant tones, as Sesto climbs a tonic arpeggio to convey Rome's splendor and his wish to preserve it. More typical of Sesto's music is confusion and grief to the point of near madness. Mozart had risen to the challenge of expressing Roman splendor mixed with grief and choral dirges once before, in the tomb scene of *Lucio Silla*.[74] Here the case is more dire and consequently the music more impassioned. Asked where he is going by his friend Annio, Sesto stammers a few words as the music staggers uncertainly in direction, passing from E♭ to the distant realm of G♭ with almost no preparation. This is the same G♭ Sesto sang at the end of No. 10, a long-held tone, left unresolved, to express "too late!" (ahi! tardo). Annio, as much in reaction to the move up a *terza minore* as to Sesto's confused words, responds, "I do not understand" (Io Sesto non intendo). This is followed by the orchestra's insistence upon c minor, reinforced by the violins' ominous slides from their low G up to C (also used to begin and end the overture). Servilia expresses fears of arson and an evil plot.

The chorus enters singing the expression "Ah!" on a diminished-seventh chord, topped in the orchestra by a *sforzato* high D♭ in the first violins, which then shiver down throughout the tones of the chord in quick notes before reaching a

[74] *Haydn, Mozart*, pp. 552–55.

FIGURE 3.7. *La clemenza di Tito*: Act I, final scene ("Burning of the Capitol") from a 1795 score.

resolution in the key of f. Publio enters, announces that a conspiracy has broken out, and fears for Tito's safety. This brings another "Ah!" from the chorus on a different diminished chord, and soon another, then another as the music pushes to the key of g. Vitellia enters. The chorus and soloists answer back and forth while the harmonies lead in a new direction, A♭, for a long solo passage for Sesto, who asks the earth to open up and swallow him. At this point Mozart took the liberty of interjecting five measures of recitative for Sesto and Vitellia, followed by an *Andante* in which the other three question Sesto. He almost confesses, until she silences him in another burst of recitative. The *Andante*, now sung by all five, serves as a transition to the final chorus. Mazzolà's words here are, "The star is extinguished, gone is the bringer of peace" (Ah dunque l'astro è spento, è spento di pace apportator). They were well chosen to honor Emperor Leopold, another bringer of peace.

"Oh nero tradimento, oh giorno di dolor" are the sonorous words with which Mazzolà finishes the scene. They are enough for Mozart to paint a grim picture of black treason commingled with sorrow. The chorus begins this dirge, with punctuations by the orchestra. Then the words are tossed back and forth between chorus and soloists in overlapping groups of three beats, a device that occurs frequently over the whole course of the work. A cadence on E♭ is averted twice, lastly by a prolonged diminished-seventh chord *tutti forte* as the two groups hurl "tradimento" at each other. The act ends softly, as did Act II of *Idomeneo*, making the horror of the scene even greater. Nothing could be further from the hullabaloo required to end a buffo finale.

One of Mozart's contemporaries found the ending of *Tito's* Act I so shattering he invoked not only parallel scenes in *Idomeneo* but also Shakespeare in response. "[It] displays so unmistakably and with such hair-raising intensity Mozart's Shakespearian, omnipotent power for the grand, the magnificent, the terrifying, the monstrous, the staggering."[75] Rochlitz has been rightly chastised for inventing many biographical comments about the composer, but on the music itself, his reactions sometimes provide valuable insight.

Sesto's rondò, No. 19, is another of the opera's high points and provides a magnificent climax for the flawed hero, who pleads to kiss the emperor's hand one last time before he dies. Mazzolà's text is of the usual construction: three quatrains in *ottonaria* lines, to which a pair of additional lines is added. Sesto asks Tito to recall for an instant the love that had bound them. The very word "amor" was perhaps sufficient to prompt Mozart to use the key of A, as he did so touchingly in Act I for the duet, No. 7, between Annio and Servilia. The initial *Adagio* in common time was originally barred so as to begin on the third beat, like most gavottes, then changed to begin on the first beat (Example 3.15). This slow

EXAMPLE 3.15. *Mozart,* La clemenza di Tito, *No. 19, Rondò (original barring)*

theme returns following tonal contrast, after which it is time for the fast theme. In a sketch that he rejected, Mozart inserted a short transition here, then opted for a longer one. All of a sudden, the orchestra launches into an *Allegro,* an ominous-sounding *crescendo,* with minor-mode inflections, and a scurrying motif like the beginning of the overture to *Figaro.* It leads not directly to the expected faster theme of the rondò but instead lurches unsteadily into C major (*terza minore*).

---

[75] Solomon, "The Rochlitz Anecdotes," No. 21, pp. 32–33.

There he sings, "I go in desperation to meet death."[76] The orchestra's vigorous commentary takes the form of thrusting lines in contrary motion, mostly up in the treble and down in the bass, a passage that pleased Mozart so much he included it in the overture. This long and powerful transition eventually comes to rest on V of A, preparing the fast rondò theme, which is a true gavotte and very sprightly (Example 3.15, m. 53ff.). It is initially played only by the two violin parts, the seconds making horn fifths with the firsts, and is rendered more piquant by having the two horns in A reinforce the staccato quarter notes and the cadence. This theme, clearly related to its slow counterpart, was found by some critics of the time to be too cheerful for a man going to his death, an objection dismissed by Carl Maria von Weber, who defended the aria and the whole opera in the warmest terms.[77] In fact, the lighter parts of the piece throw the grim ones into even greater relief. Sesto does not fear death, he says; he suffers only for having betrayed his friend. What he does not say is that he goes to his death with the consoling thought of having saved Vitellia by his silence.

At the first episode after the fast rondò refrain, the piece offers another surprise. The violins leap up to a high B♭, *sforzato*, a dissonant tone from which they shudder down in a sixteenth-note run to a resolution in F major (*sesta minore*). The gesture comes from No. 10, as does Sesto's ensuing melody. Another transition leads back to A major for a return of the refrain with more extensive orchestral accompaniment. The last section offers more surprises still. The tempo increases with a *Più Allegro* and the bass adds punch by rocking back and forth in quick notes. Sesto holds a pedal while the orchestra plays the speeded-up refrain, then he sings it again, leading to the final cadence.

The grand two-tempo rondò, exemplified at its most dramatic and powerful by No. 19 for Sesto and No. 23 for Vitellia, formed a potent legacy to Italian serious opera of the waning eighteenth and early nineteenth centuries, up to Rossini and beyond.[78] This type of aria in fact became the forerunner of the kind of climactic aria that proceeded from a slow, *cantabile* opening to a lively and repetitious cabaletta. Lichtenthal assailed the type with wry humor: "After a little *Andante* or *Andantino*, Queen Cabaletta opens her smiling mouth and emits a kind of waltz, with extraordinary rhythm and word setting."[79] He describes the next part, citing specific tonal goals. "To the languishing cries of 'Si!' and 'No!' she modulates to the favored *terza* or *sesta minore*." (Mozart's two rondòs in *Tito* encompassed

---

[76] An astounding parallel to this passage in a 1782 rondò by Cimarosa has been located by Friedrich Lippmann, "Mozart, Jommelli, Cimarosa: Zu einigen Arien," *Die Musikforschung* 59 (2006): 31–48; 44.

[77] Abert, *W. A. Mozart*, 2: 613, n. 3.

[78] Daniel Heartz, "Mozarts 'Titus' und die italienische Oper um 1800," *Hamburger Jahrbuch für Musikwissenschaft* 5 (1981): 255–66.

[79] Peter Lichtenthal, "Rondò," in *Dizionario e bibliografia della musica*, 4 vols. (Milan, 1826). The original is quoted in the article just cited.

both.) "The chorus and subalterns applaud their Queen, and she, all complacent, returns suddenly to rebless her faithful subjects by repeating the celestial melody." An expert and original voice has this to say in a recently published book.

> Both the obbligato recitative and the two-tempo rondò harnessed musical language in the interests of narrative continuity and expressivity in a way that neither the more sectional and rounded da capo nor the dal segno could do, nor even the younger genre of through-composed sonata-like aria. And they did so with a compelling musico-dramatic force that was to continue expanding into the nineteenth-century scena composed by the likes of Mayr, Paer, Donizetti, Bellini, and Verdi.[80]

To this last trio of great composers one can only say "Amen!" while adding the reservation that Rossini too deserves a place in the same hierarchy.

Tito contains four arias in Act II for the secondary characters, of which Annio received two, Nos. 13 and 17, and Publio one, No. 16; Servilia is at last served with a short but exquisite *Tempo di Minuetto*, No. 21. Otherwise, there are two great trios, Nos. 14 and 18, in both of which Sesto predominates vocally. Tito was awarded a very grand aria in the old-fashioned ternary form, a setting of Metastasio's poem "Se al impero è necessario un cor severo," No. 20. It shows that Mozart trusted the tenor Baglione to exert the same breath control and vocal agility required of Ottavio in "Il mio tesoro" four years earlier. Both arias are in B♭ and there are other similarities, even as to details of the melismas.[81] Tito's two arias in Act I, Nos. 6 and 8, the latter a late addition, are in comparison to No. 20 short and undemanding. In addition, Tito received a solo within the chorus No. 15, one that recalls some features of Idomeneo's prayer with choral refrain (No. 26 in *Idomeneo*). One searches Mozart's comments in vain to find any praises for Baglioni's vocal contributions to *Tito*.

The climax of the opera was reached with Sesto's rondò, No. 19, Tito's brilliant aria No. 20, and Vitellia's obbligato recitative and rondò, Nos. 22–23 (before which Servilia's modest and tender plea, No. 21, acted as a foil). These three arias secured the opera's place as a public favorite and as a vehicle for great voices in the last years of the eighteenth century and first decades of the nineteenth. Rochlitz claimed in his 1798 articles on Mozart that the composer was forced by circumstances to make only the main pieces in *Tito* very good, while writing the less important ones "readily with a light touch and merely following the tastes of the multitude at that time."[82] His description fits best the three arias for Tito.

---

[80] Martha Feldman, *Opera and Sovereignty: Transforming Myths in Eighteenth-Century Italy* (Chicago, 2007), p. 325.

[81] For a fine comparison, see Rice, *Tito*, pp. 54–59.

[82] Anecdote 21: "ganz leicht hin und blos dem Zeitgeschmack des grossen Haufens gemäss zu bearbeiten." For a different translation, see Solomon, "The Rochlitz Anecdotes," p. 33.

No. 20, his main aria, is old-fashioned in form (not style), while No. 8 adopts the "shorthand" or pendulum bass accompaniment, a timesaving device favored by Paisiello and other Italians.[83] Tito's No. 6 shows signs of haste too, although more in terms of text setting—for example, long notes on the weak second syllable of "alla"—than of harmony or texture.

The pressures of time on Mozart are also evident in the similar vocal incipits of Nos. 16, 17, and 18. His other operas avoid such parallels in successive numbers. Rochlitz's suggestion that he wrote the secondary arias superficially must nevertheless be rejected. As short as is Publio's No. 16, Mozart took the trouble to give it a beautiful postlude based on its main theme. There are many fine postludes in *Tito*, which ranks in this regard close to *Don Giovanni* and *Die Zauberflöte*. Annio's No. 17 has been shown to be a well-polished creation having melodic affinities with an aria of 1780 by Galuppi.[84] Servilia's lone aria carries her role to a level far from the superficial. The same is true of her lovely duet with Annio, No. 7, a refined outpouring of sentiment in the traditional key for love duets, a piece superior in its every detail, including its postlude, a delightful reharmonization of the main idea. The sweep of the first violins up to the third above the high tonic to begin and end the duet occurs in an earlier aria in the same key of A, No. 11 in *Il re pastore*, where it concludes the piece. Nostalgic glances at his heroic operas for Salzburg and Munich lend added poignancy to his last opera of all.

Anton Stadler's exceptional skills as a clarinetist contributed greatly to Sesto's "Parto" and Vitellia's "Non più di fiori." Stadler, a close friend and lodge brother of the composer, may have traveled with the Mozarts to Prague. Whereas the performances of *Tito* after the first, like other theatrical events in Prague, suffered in attendance because of competition from the coronation balls and other celebrations, the tenth and last performance, given on 30 September, was a resounding success, according to a letter Stadler wrote Mozart.

The Clarinet Concerto, K. 622, written for Stadler was surely a reward for his devotion to Mozart and for his stellar role as a soloist in *Tito*. It can be considered an extra bonus deriving from the opera. Its roots may have been planted somewhat earlier than the opera. The first movement exists as an extensive draft (199 measures out of 354) in the key of G and for basset horn. Present in the draft already is a passage for the soloist that moves to the minor mode and is almost identical with a similar passage for Stadler in the *Allegro* of Vitellia's rondò. The concerto's slow movement, *Adagio* in D, begins like the *Larghetto* in D of the Clarinet Quintet, K. 581, but soon goes its own way. Mozart did not finish K. 622

[83] Heartz, *Mozart's Operas*, pp. 314–16. *Music in European Capitals*, pp. 265–66.
[84] Reinhard Wiesand, "Ein 'einfaches Sekundariestück, ohne individuelle Züge'? Tradition und Erfindung in der Arie 'Torna di Tito a latò,'" *Mozart-Jahrbuch 1984/85*: 134–44. The quotation is from Abert, *W. A. Mozart*, 2: 611.

until after he returned from Prague in mid-September. His letter of 7–8 October to Constanze brings together the concerto and *Tito* in a way that reinforces their connections. He began writing late on the evening of Friday the 7th.

> I told Joseph to get Primus to fetch me some black coffee, with which I smoked a splendid pipe of tobacco, and then I orchestrated almost all of Stadler's Rondò. Meanwhile I have received a letter Stadler sent from Prague. All the Duscheks are well. Mme Duschek seems to have received none of your letters, and that I can scarcely believe! Enough. They have already heard about the splendid reception of my German opera. The strangest coincidence is that the evening my new German opera was performed with such great approval, *Tito* was given for the last time in Prague, with extraordinary success. All the pieces were applauded. Bedini sang better than ever. The little duet in A for the two maidens [No. 7] was repeated. And had not the audience wanted to spare Madame Marchetti, her Rondò would have been gladly repeated too. Stadler writes, "What a wonder for Bohemia! Cries of Bravo! rang out for me from the parterre and even from the orchestra. Indeed I really gave my best."

Evident from this is that the composer took as much satisfaction and pride in *Tito* as in his German opera.

Servilia's short aria, No. 21, surrounded by the grand final arias for Sesto, Tito, and Vitellia, makes an effect out of all proportion to its means.[85] The aria text and preceding simple recitative are by Metastasio and are a tribute to his powers. Servilia pleads with Vitellia for her brother Sesto: "Quell'infelice t'amò più di se stesso" (That unfortunate man loves you more than himself). By contrast, Vitellia loves herself more than any other and thinks only in selfish terms—up to this point. Marked *Tempo di Minuetto*, the piece starts softly, its key of D far from the heroic tone often associated with this key. The violins mark the pulse with eight notes while building up the triad of D. She begins "S'altro che lacrime non tenti, tutto il tuo piangere non gioverà" (If you have no more than tears for him, all your weeping is to no avail). Mozart was adept at painting words like "lacrime" and "piangere," but there is none of that here. The simple message projected by this heartfelt music suggests what, to the contrary, will be of avail: unselfish and unconditional love.

The aria's closing phrase and generous postlude sum up its essence (Example 3.16). If measures 35–38 sound familiar it may be because their like occurred in *Don Giovanni* when Zerlina presses Masetto's hand to her heart at the end of her

---

[85] Servilia was sung by a young Polish soprano later famous in Vienna under the name Antonia Campi, who in 1791 married Gaetano Campi, the first Publio. Walter Brauneis, "Wer war Mozarts 'Signora Antonini' in der Prager Uraufführung von 'La clemenza di Tito'? Zur Identifizierung der Antonina Miklaszewicz als Interpretin der Servilia in der Krönungsoper am 6. September 1791," *Mitteilungen der Internationalen Stiftung Mozarteum* 47 (1999): 32–40.

EXAMPLE 3.16. *Mozart,* La clemenza di Tito, *No. 21, Aria*

aria "Vedrai, carino" and sings "Sentilo battere" to a rising sequence (see also Tamino's "Paminen retten," Example 3.12). Another resonance with Servilia's aria is the *Adagio* of the Clarinet Concerto, the beginning of which pulsates softly with an eighth-note accompaniment in the same meter and key. The second half of its main theme descends a fifth in a rising sequence like the aria's "piangere" (Example 3.17). Their cadences are nearly identical. The aria's postlude, with its

EXAMPLE 3.17. *Mozart, Clarinet Concerto, K. 622, II*

long dying falls from high A by step down to the tonic, also has some affinity with the melodic descents of the Adagio. One could even hear the Adagio as a further meditation on the unconditional love and tenderness projected by the aria.

La clemenza di Tito, like *Die Zauberflöte,* ends with a blaze of glory. Mozart took infinite care with the concluding "Sestetto con coro," No. 26, an *Allegretto* in cut time proclaiming the eternal majesty of C major. In his 1798 biography, Niemetschek declared, "Among all the choruses that I have heard none is so flowing, so sublime and full of expression as the closing chorus of Act II in *Tito.*" It begins somewhat in the manner of a Vaudeville finale, with separate verses sung by Sesto, then Tito, with Vitellia, Servilia, and Annio forming a high trio in praise of the emperor's goodness and generosity (Publio comes in later). The chorus adds its blessings as well. Tito returns for another verse, by the end of which the other soloists and the chorus sing rejoinders at ever-shorter time intervals. The frequent overlapping groups of three quarter notes, so striking throughout the opera, have their greatest impact at this point. When the soprano voices march by step up to their high A over subdominant harmony, closure is all but achieved. The orchestra finishes the process with a postlude, the treble parts climbing in syncopated triads over a pendulum bass until the cadence.

Unison slides, like those that end the overture, put period to the whole.[86]

Composing this last opera and the Requiem took its toll on Mozart's health. His ever-frail constitution broke down. He suffered a rapid collapse and died on 5 December 1791. The opera's honoree, Leopold II, lasted a scant three months longer, his robust health done in by a lifetime of mental and physical overexertion. Haydn, who was soon to turn sixty, was in distant London and disconsolate upon hearing the news of Mozart's death. He abandoned his hopes of retiring in Mozart's favor and resolved to go on. Young Beethoven, aged twenty-one, could no longer aspire to study directly with Mozart. In 1792 he came to Vienna to study under Haydn, determined to become the successor of both Haydn and Mozart.

---

[86] The climactic final chapter of Jessica Waldoff, *Recognition in Mozart's Operas* (Oxford, 2006), is devoted to *Tito*, with admirable results.

4
Haydn: The 1780s

DURING the 1780s Haydn continued to serve as Kapellmeister to Prince Nicholas Esterházy. The administrative offices of the vast Esterházy domain remained in the town of Eisenstadt, where Haydn owned a house. Increasingly, Prince Nicholas chose to reside much of the year at his new summer palace of Esterháza, about twenty miles distant, where Haydn and his wife occupied three rooms (his orchestra members, with the exception of concertmaster Luigi Tomasini, were not allowed to bring their families). The Prince usually elected to spend only the winter holidays, from Christmas to early February, at his city palace in Vienna, which was about fifty miles distant from Esterháza, or a whole day's journey.[1]

Haydn's musical responsibilities changed with the gradual withdrawal of Prince Nicholas from playing his favorite instrument, the baryton, in chamber music created especially for him. The last few of Haydn's 130 or so Baryton Trios date from the mid-1770s. At this point in his sixties, the Prince became less of a participant in music-making and more of an auditor-spectator. Sporadic operas at Esterháza to celebrate gala occasions had taken place since its opera house was inaugurated in 1768. In 1776, regular operatic seasons began, requiring the importation of many scores, which Haydn had to tailor to the local forces, then direct in performance from the harpsichord. This consumed ever larger portions of his time as the Prince's appetite for new operatic entertainments grew apace

[1] A map created to the purpose showing the relative position of these localities may be found in *Haydn, Mozart*, p. xxvii.

and the opera seasons lengthened. Perhaps as a reward for his good service, the Prince made a major change in his contract when it came up for renewal in 1779: no longer was Haydn restricted from composing for other patrons or from selling his music to publishers.[2]

In about 1780, Haydn's personal life underwent as big a change as did his professional career. In 1779, his musical forces had been augmented by the arrival of an Italian couple, Antonio and Luigia Polzelli, he an elderly violinist, his wife a mezzo-soprano of modest talent, aged nineteen. Prince Nicholas, unimpressed by this pair, did not renew their short-term contracts for low-paying jobs in his service. Haydn insisted that they remain and remain they did, throughout the 1780s. He had fallen in love with Luigia. The operas he was constantly adapting for the troupe allowed him to adjust a few minor parts for her and he put considerable effort into composing several new insertion arias that made the most of her voice. As we know without a doubt from letters that he wrote her later from London, she became his mistress. Her husband was consumptive and soon left the orchestra but lingered on until early 1791 when he died.

Maria Anna Haydn née Keller, whom Haydn married in 1760 when she was thirty-one, three years his elder, was a second choice after her younger sister Therese refused him (the parallel with Mozart and the Weber sisters is inescapable). The match proved unsatisfactory to both wife and husband, but only Haydn's side of the story is known. He was attracted to many other women, and to his surprise, women were attracted to him. Haydn's most prominent features were dark brown eyes, a long nose, and thin face (Figure 4.1). For a faithful Catholic of only modest means like Haydn, divorce was not an option to escape an unhappy marriage.

String Quartets, Opus 33

Haydn began to take advantage of his new freedom to dispose of his works freely by selling six keyboard sonatas to Artaria, who published them in 1780 as *Sei sonate per il Clavicembalo o Forte Piano*, dedicated to the sisters Caterina and Marianna von Auenbrugger. In 1781, Artaria brought out twelve Lieder by Haydn for solo voice and keyboard accompaniment. Like keyboard sonatas, Lieder were almost invariably dedicated to women, and the dedication of these songs figured

---

[2] *Haydn, Mozart,* "The Turning Point of 1780," pp. 400–406. As in that volume, our two major sources of biographical information are Haydn's interviewers Griesinger and Dies, who are cited after *Joseph Haydn: Eighteenth-Century Gentleman and Genius,* A Translation with Introduction and Notes by Vernon Gotwals of the *Biographische Notizen über Joseph Haydn* by G. A. Griesinger and the *Biographische Nachrichten von Joseph Haydn* by A. C. Dies (Madison, WI, 1963). This exemplary edition has a detailed index.

FIGURE 4.1. Detail of Mansfeld's
1781 portrait of Haydn.

in the correspondence between composer and publisher. Haydn wanted to confer the honor on the mistress of his prince, Mlle Elisabeth Clair.[3] In his letter to Artaria dated 27 May 1781, he proposed her as dedicatee adding, "Just between us this young lady is the goddess of my prince. You will easily understand what an impression such a move would make!" Yes, especially on the prince's wife, the still vigorous Marie Elisabeth, née von Weissenwolf. The plan was aborted. Instead, Haydn dedicated the songs to Francisca von Kreutzner, whose father, the military officer Anton Liebe von Kreutzner, then commissioned the composer to write his second *Missa Cellensis*.

Determined to make the most of his new freedoms, Haydn decided to sell a new set of string quartets not only to Artaria, but also on an individual basis to many wealthy music lovers by subscription. He sent letters over his signature to a number of prospective buyers offering correctly written copies of the parts at a fee of six ducats for a set of six quartets, "composed in an entirely new and special way, because I have written none in ten years" (auf eine gantz neue, besondere art, denn zeit [*sic*] 10 Jahren habe Keine geschrieben). This wording is from his letter of 3 December 1781 to Prince Kraft Ernst of Öttingen-Wallerstein. A similar letter of the same date went out to the learned Johann Caspar Lavater of

[3] *Joseph Haydn: Gesammelte Briefe und Aufzeichnungen*, ed. Dénes Bartha (Kassel, 1965), p. 96. Letters will be cited henceforth from this edition solely by date or by number. All translations are my own.

Zürich, personalized to the extent that Haydn began by writing, "I love and read your works. I am also not unskilled, according to what is said, heard, and written, and my name is given great credit in all countries." Only three letters of this kind survive but there were apparently many more; the third was addressed to Robert Schlecht, abbot of a monastery in the then-Habsburg province of Baden in southwest Germany.

Haydn composed the new quartets in the summer and fall of 1781. On 18 October he wrote Artaria explaining why he was behind in finishing the Lieder: "A little trip and the present work on the six new quartets that must be ready in three weeks kept me from the songs," and then in a postscript, "of the new quartets four are already done, which task has further delayed me slightly." According to this schedule the new quartets were to be ready for Artaria (and individual buyers) by November. The Lieder appeared in December, when Haydn was again in Vienna, but he was apparently not in close touch with Artaria, although his abode, the Esterházy palace in the Wallnerstrasse, was only a few minutes away from the publisher's shop in the Kohlmarkt. The quartets were still not ready by year's end but Artaria went ahead and advertised them, which infuriated the composer.

Any publisher in possession of a treasure the magnitude of these quartets would attempt to bring them out as soon as possible, unless enjoined otherwise by the composer. Haydn had given no such instruction. Artaria consequently added to the announcement of the Lieder in the *Wiener Zeitung* of 29 December 1781 this statement: "There are also six entirely new quartets by this great man in the press and it is hoped that they will be published in about four weeks." Haydn reacted in his letter of 4 January 1782. Instead of his usual formal salutation of several words, he addressed Artaria with a single word.

> Monsieur! With astonishment I read in the local paper that you will publish my quartets in four weeks. You did not even show me the consideration of waiting until I had left Vienna [some of Haydn's subscribers were Viennese]. Such a proceeding puts me in a most dishonorable position and damages me greatly. It is a very base action on your part. At least you could have waited with the announcement until the whole work was completed, for I have not yet satisfied all my subscribers. Herr Hummel also wanted to be a subscriber but I did not send them to him in Berlin out of friendship and thoughts of further transactions with you, and by God you have cost me more than 50 ducats since I have still not filled the orders of numerous subscribers, and cannot possibly do so for those living abroad. Nevertheless, our commerce under way must continue. I entreat you to have an exemplar of the Lieder bound in red taffeta and sent to Herr von Liebe, an ordinary one sent to my brother-in-law, and three to me. You can charge these against the second dozen [Lieder, published in 1784]. Otherwise, I remain with all respect Your most obliged servant, Joseph Haydn.

Haydn's letter made its point. Artaria withheld publication of the quartets until April, when they appeared with the designation "opus 33." Haydn wrote again on 20 January and admitted that his previous letter had been hasty and irate in tone; another time, he added, they would both be more wary. Yet more misunderstandings or disagreements like this were to follow.

The troubles Haydn foresaw as a result of Artaria's premature announcement of the quartets persisted. One Conrad Breunig, a composer in Mainz, acquired a manuscript copy of the quartets with the understanding that they were to remain unpublished for some time to come. Breunig wrote a "most impertinent letter" to Haydn, who turned it over to Artaria in his letter of 15 February to the publisher. Another letter, addressed to Haydn by an official of the Prince of Öttingen-Wallerstein, dated 18 February, complained that the quartets ordered by subscription had not arrived. Very few of the subscription copies have survived, raising the question of how many of the original subscribers ever received their copies. An undated letter (No. 45) that Haydn sent Artaria in the summer of 1782 again bemoaned the situation caused by the overly hasty public announcement: "among many others I have heard from Baron van Swieten, who made it clear that henceforth I should dedicate my compositions to the public." Haydn's contacts with this key figure in Viennese musical life dated from at least as early as 1776, when Swieten visited Vienna while still serving as ambassador to Berlin.

The winter of 1781–82 in Vienna was marked by the arrival of foreign visitors of great distinction, with consequences for both Haydn and Mozart. Crown Prince Paul of Russia with his wife Maria Feodorovna were sent by Empress Catherine II to return the compliment of Joseph II's visit to her in 1780. Formally, this was not a state visit, because the couple traveled as the Count and Countess of the North, but it was treated as if it were one. The countess was a sister of Princess Elisabeth of Württemberg, affianced to Joseph's nephew Archduke Francis, so that ties with that German state were being strengthened as well as the Russian alliance. Maria Feodorovna was a skilled keyboard player, and while in Vienna had some coaching lessons from Haydn. It was largely to entertain her that Joseph arranged a keyboard competition between Mozart and the visiting Roman virtuoso Muzio Clementi. The emperor is said to have wagered with her on Mozart's winning the contest. It took place on Christmas Eve and is reported in two of Mozart's letters to his father. On 12 January he wrote, "Clementi plays well, with regard to right-hand technique. His specialty is passages in thirds. Otherwise he hasn't a trace of feeling or taste, in a word, he is a mere mechanic." Four days later he described the contest again, at which, he says he used the fortepiano loaned him by Countess Thun when playing alone.

> He is a good cembalist. With that all is said [he then repeats the above]. After compliments aplenty were exchanged the emperor told him to begin, saying *La santa chiesa Catholica*—for Clementi is a Roman. He played a prelude and then a sonata. His Majesty said to me *allons drauf los*. I also played a prelude and then variations. Next the Grand Princess gave us a sonata by [her teacher] Paisiello (miserably writ-

ten in her own hand) from which I had to play the *Allegro* and Clementi the *Andante* and *Rondò,* then we took a theme out of it and treated it further on two pianos.

Haydn was later more generous than Mozart in his remarks on Clementi, as we shall see. This could have been the occasion when Haydn first saw and heard Mozart play, although it is unlikely that they were presented to one another. The Mozarts, father and son, held Joseph Haydn in such high regard that the son surely would have told his father had he actually met the famous Haydn, if only to further cajole Leopold at a time when every letter he sent pleaded for paternal consent to marry Constanze.

Joseph II decided that the best way to impress the Russian visitors, while showing off pieces composed by a musician in Habsburg service, was to stage three gala productions of serious operas by Gluck: *Orfeo, Alceste,* and, in a new German translation, *Iphigénie en Tauride.* The emperor disdained serious opera because it cost so much but in this case, with his imperial prestige at stake, he relented and paid for it.

Haydn was also pressed into service although he had no official ties with the imperial court and his renown, while great, was not yet so great as that of Gluck. On 26 December, there was a concert under Haydn's direction in the palatial apartment assigned to Maria Feodorovna. A report on it appeared in the *Pressburger Zeitung* dated 12 January 1782.

> [The Emperor and Archduke Maximilian] attended a grand concert on 26 December in the chambers of the Countess of the North. The author [Verfasser] of it was Prince Esterházy's Kappellmeister, the famous Haydn. At this occasion there was presented a quartet [Quartetto] played by Herrn Luigi Tomasini, Asplmayer, Weigl, and Huber. The illustrious company honored it not only with their gracious applause, but also bestowed on Haydn, as composer, a magnificent enameled box studded with diamonds; the four other artists named received a golden snuffbox apiece.[4]

Surely the quartet performed was one from the new set of six, and it would not be surprising if the choice had fallen on the Quartet in G, the first in order and most stunning of the set.

The connection of Op. 33 with the concert over which Haydn presided is strengthened by the appearance in some copies of the print with an inconspicuous dedication placed at the bottom of the first music page of the Violino primo: "Dediés au gran Duc de Russie." The editors of the critical edition surmise that "the dedicatee received the work with a less inconspicuous dedication, either

---

[4] Marianne Pandi and Fritz Schmidt, "Musik zur Zeit Haydns und Beethovens in der Pressburger Zeitung," *Haydn Yearbook* 8 (1971): 165–266; 182. On the quartet's performers, see *Haydn, Mozart,* pp. 324–25.

in printed or manuscript form and perhaps the Grand Prince even received the autograph [since lost] at the December concert."[5]

The grand ducal couple left Vienna on 5 January and began their descent into Italy. At Venice the aged Galuppi presented the Grand Duchess with six new harpsichord sonatas. By summer, they were laying plans for the trip home by way of another visit to Vienna during October 1782. On this stop Artaria's print, along with a special dedicatory page, could have been presented to Prince Paul. Van Swieten's wish that Haydn henceforth dedicate his works to the public, dating from the summer and quoted above, would make more sense if the dedication of Op. 33 to a foreign prince had already been known earlier in the year, before the return of the Russian grandees.

Why Haydn suddenly took up the composition of a set of string quartets in mid-1781 after a long hiatus defies easy explanation. It could be that the impending visit of the eminences from Russia in the fall of 1781 had something to do with his decision. Or his avowed affinity for the genre he did so much to create might be reason enough by itself. "Because I have written none in ten years" bespeaks an awareness of some responsibility to continue, also of the worth of those created earlier. "Composed in an entirely new and special way" shows both pride of accomplishment and a will to advertise the product. The one does not preclude the other. Henceforth Haydn often touted his works to potential buyers.

In his three sets of string quartets Opp. 9, 17, and 20, Haydn had established the four-movement form with a single minuet. In the first two of these sets he placed all the minuets as second movements, then in Op. 20 of 1772 he staggered placement of the minuets with three as second movements and three in third place (in his autograph score Nos. 1, 3, and 5 have second-movement minuets, a pattern followed by Mozart in his six quartets dedicated to Haydn).

The dance movements of the new set offer the most obvious example of what is "new and special" about it. Haydn labeled them all Scherzo and gave their trios no label at all. Otherwise, they are no different from his other minuets and trios. "Scherzo" may imply a faster tempo to us but did not necessarily do so to him and besides, he qualified the term by adding *Allegretto* in three cases, as he did with many minuets before and after Op. 33. There are two instances of qualifying Scherzo with *Allegro* and one with *Allegro di molto* and these truly are different in implying a tempo much faster than the typical minuet's moderate speed. In two quartets, those in G and D, he placed these dance movements third, in the others, second.

Artaria's original edition of 1782 ordered the quartets as follows: G, E♭, b, C, D, B♭. Pleyel's complete edition of 1801–2 reordered them so that they came out

---

[5] *Streichquartette "Opus 20" und "Opus 33" (Joseph Haydn: Werke* XII/3), ed. Georg Feder and Sonja Gerlach (Munich, 1974), *Kritischer Bericht*, p. 22. This edition will henceforth be *JHW*.

in the sequence 3, 2, 4, 6, 5, also adopted, unfortunately, in Hoboken's thematic catalogue.[6] The new critical edition has wisely gone back to the original order.

The Quartet in G begins with a misplaced cadence, *pianissimo*, which assumes its correct function as a true cadence at the end of the eight-measure phrase (Example 4.1a).[7] The *Vivace assai* will end with this same cadence in mm. 301–2,

EXAMPLE 4.1 a, b. *Haydn, String Quartet in G, Op. 33*

a. *I*

preceded by an extension of the motivic play on the rising conjunct fourth motif, the first thing heard. Exactly as at the beginning, the viola takes the seventh in the V[7] chord on its way to resolution. Then all four parts sound the rising motif in unison and octaves. To end the finale, a set of variations on an *Allegretto* theme in 6/8 time, Haydn wrote what starts out to be the fourth variation, but changed to *Presto* and reduced to half of its sixteen-measure length. The *Presto*, after quickly reaching the theme's cadence, spins off into a little coda and repeats that cadence twice. It sounds familiar, being the same rise of a fourth up to the tonic that initiated the whole cycle (Example 4.1b). Two more IV - V - I cadences add emphasis and at the very end the viola takes the 7th in V[7] - I, *forte.*

b. *IV*

Each movement of the quartet has the same tonic. The slow second movement is in g. A *Largo cantabile*, it is an aria or an extended arioso for the first violin to which the other instruments provide a stratified, never-changing accompaniment (Example 4.2). Coming after the witty conversations of the *Vivace assai*, the *Largo* sounds like an operatic *scena*, as if a prima donna or primo uomo castrato

---

[6] Anthony van Hoboken, ed., *Joseph Haydn: Thematisch-bibliographisches Werkverzeichnis*, 3 vols. (Mainz, 1957–78), 1: Gruppe III, Nr. 37–42, pp. 393–401.

[7] Gretchen A. Wheelock, *Haydn's Ingenious Jesting with Art: Contexts of Musical Wit and Humor* (New York, 1992), pp. 98–103, offers a good discussion of this "putting the cart before the horse."

EXAMPLE 4.2. *Haydn, String Quartet in G, Op. 33, II*

had strayed into a jolly company playing a drawing-room comedy. In melodic contour, the *Largo* bears a strong resemblance to the oboe solo that unifies the arioso "Che puro ciel" in Act II of Gluck's *Orfeo ed Euridice*, a work performed under Haydn's direction at Esterhazà in 1778.[8] Since *Orfeo* was one of the operas by Gluck revived to entertain the visiting Russians in 1781–82, the famous arioso melody was not part of the forgotten past. It could be that Haydn with his related melody was paying another tribute to the older master he revered.[9]

Haydn's *Largo cantabile* is also operatic in its employment of a ritornello figure for punctuation, sounded to divide his song into parts, first softly, then tutti *forte* in unison, as well as in its full-fledged cadenza for the solo voice of the first violin. After the modulation to B♭ (III), the melody (Example 4.2, m. 26) leads back to g for the reprise with a phrase that is reminiscent of a transition in the hauntingly beautiful flute solo that Gluck added as a trio to the "Dance of the Blessed Spirits" in his *Orfée et Euridice* for Paris in 1774 (Example 4.3). Haydn's

EXAMPLE 4.3. *Gluck,* Orfée et Euridice, *Ballet des Ombres heureuses*

rising chromatic line makes the same link from II back to i as Gluck's flute solo, and against the same murmuring accompaniment of non-stop sixteenth notes. This raises the question of whether the flute solo added for Paris was also added to the revival of *Orfeo* at Vienna in 1781–82. Gluck was present then and played a supervisory role at the revival of his three operas.

The *Largo cantabile* ends with the ritornello figure that climbs by step from 1 to 5, then subsides, before a final unison pizzicato G. It is followed directly by the rude eruption of the *Scherzo Allegro*, which also rises, as if in mimicry, up the tonic triad, but in major, deflating the solemnity that went before. By transforming one of his motifs into a jocular dance, strongly accented, and with the contrariness of

[8] For some of the prior incarnations of "Che puro ciel," see *Haydn, Mozart*, p. 148, ex. 3.1.

[9] *Haydn, Mozart*, p. 338.

hemiola cross accents, Haydn returns the quartet to the levity of the first movement. He also gives his dance a soft and sustained cadence, V⁷ - I, with the viola
taking the 7th, as if asserting the cyclic nature of the whole.

The Quartet in G bears more resemblance to the previous Op. 20 set of quartets than does most of its companions in Op. 33, particularly in its diversity of
forms and styles. A specific parallel is the *Adagio* second movement of the Quartet in f from Op. 20, which is in tonic minor, and another operatic *scena*, although
more obbligato recitative than aria. The Quartet in D of Op. 20 offers a set of variations on a slow theme in the parallel minor as its second movement. The other
quartet of Op. 33 with a slow movement in the parallel minor is also the one in
D, its *Andante* being an impassioned oration for the first violin beginning with a
long *messa di voce*.

What sets the Quartet in G of Op. 33 most apart from its companions is
the extent and shape of its first-movement sonata form, 305 measures of tightly
organized, motivically saturated argument, with both prima and seconda parti
indicated for repetition. The nervous intensity of the first theme, of the whole
first-theme area, comes to a stop with an emphatic landing on the dominant of
the dominant, which chord is repeated, followed by a pause with fermata. The
first violin blithely continues on the same tone A, turning it into the beginning of
the most lyrical moment yet heard, with chromatic waverings and a soaring up to
high F♯ before a *legato* stepwise descent down a seventh to G, whence the process
is repeated over dominant harmony in the new key of D (Example 4.4). The second

EXAMPLE 4.4. *Haydn, String Quartet in G, Op. 33, I*

violin reinforces the first a tenth below while the lower voices sustain drones.
Haydn countered the tense, energetic first theme, centered in mid-range, with a
suavely relaxed cantilena marked *dolce*, supported by harmony over four octaves,
and with a broad harmonic rhythm that traverses only two harmonies in support of an eight-measure period. There are other happenings later that contribute to making the movement so successful, such as the broad deceptive cadence
to ♭VI toward the end of the reprise (a moment that recalls the same maneuver
in the first movement of the composer's early Symphony No. 8 in G, "Le Soir").
Yet nothing remains in the memory so much as the sharply defined difference in
mood between the primary material and the second theme.

Haydn did not often favor a highly contrasting second theme in opening movements at any time in his long career. It was only one of many ways he went about building sonata forms. Historians of musical form during the nineteenth century regarded thematic contrast as an inviolable norm. Other composers following Haydn's example helped make it so. The immediate consequences of Op. 33, and the Quartet in G in particular, are apparent in Mozart. Not only did he begin to compile his set of six quartets dedicated to the older master with a quartet in G, K. 387, dated 31 December 1782, he also constructed its first movement as a counterpoise between opening material of a nervous, motivically saturated nature in rapid harmonic rhythm and a broader second theme that moves in stately fashion over a few chords. Like Haydn, Mozart deploys little chromatic waverings in his second theme and it almost seems as if he chose the third of the chord for this effect rather than the fifth so as not to sound too much like Haydn.

Another composer greatly beholden to Haydn for the same idea was not so reticent about resembling his teacher. Young Beethoven in his Piano Sonata in G, Op. 14 No. 2, begins with a first theme that is a paragon of rhythmic nervousness. After a long pedal on V/V, Beethoven yields to the delights of a second theme that luxuriates in a slower harmonic rhythm, deployed over a greater range, with wavering chromatic thirds in the treble followed by a long descent in thirds (Example 4.5). One advantage of so prominent and distinct a second

EXAMPLE 4.5. *Beethoven, Piano Sonata, Op. 14, No. 2, I*

theme is that it can expect instant recognition in the development section. Haydn began his seconda parte by casting the first theme into tonic minor, then midway through the long development section he brought back the entire second theme verbatim, also in minor, in this case the relative minor, e. Beethoven followed suit by beginning his development section with the first theme in tonic minor. After several measures devoted to fragmenting the first theme, he brought on the second theme, in B♭ but otherwise unchanged until the bass begins to rise chromatically at its close. Both composers made the most of the strong contrast set up between the primary thematic material and their more relaxed second themes.

The finale of Haydn's Quartet in G, consisting of variations on a gentle siciliana melody in 6/8 time with dotted rhythm, has a close counterpart in the variations on a siciliana tune of similar cast that end Mozart's Quartet in d, K. 421, as noted above. Exemplified in Chapter 1 are some passages in common between the finale of Mozart's K. 428 in B♭ and the first movement of Haydn's Op. 33 Quartet in B♭ (see Example 1.13ab). Other connections as well have been posited between the two sets of quartets, some untenable.

A parallel has been proposed between the slow introduction to Mozart's Quartet in C, K. 465, and the beginning of the first movement of Haydn's Quartet in C from Op. 33.[10] Mozart's *Adagio* moves a whole tone down to ♭vii for the repetition of its opening four measures. Haydn's *Allegro moderato* in common time moves a whole tone up to ii for the repetition of its first six measures. Yet the two pieces sound totally different. Haydn began with a motoric repetition in eighth notes of E and C, the two bottom tones of a tonic triad in first inversion, to which the first violin, coming in a measure later, supplies G, at first a whole note, then as half notes preceded by F♯ grace notes, making the first of many chirping sounds that account for this quartet's nickname, "The Bird." This soft beginning swells to *forte* as the cello enters and robustly climbs up the tonic triad through two octaves. Haydn repeated the process one tone higher with no modulatory link between tonic and supertonic chords. There is a piece by Mozart with a similar beginning: it is not K. 465 but the String Quintet in C, K. 515, of 1787.

Haydn's bold beginning to the Quartet in C continues to surprise by offering a third segment not six measures in length but five, the chord this time being v$^6_3$, first inversion of the minor dominant. Then the proceedings quickly return to tonic C in m. 18. The first seventeen measures, identified as an introduction in the article cited, cannot be one because they constitute the main theme and are recapitulated as such, albeit with reharmonization of some of the first violin's original melody. What followed it in m. 18, which was called the first theme following an introduction, is not even recapitulated.

Several other features of this charming quartet make "The Bird" a favorite with players and listeners alike. At the reprise in the first movement, the first violin starts its song while the chord of the mediant still lingers from a big cadence on iii, as if entering a little too early. This "mistake" is quickly rectified as the harmony returns to tonic C. Another surprise is the way Haydn ended the movement as abruptly as it began, eliminating only the first measure before the vio-

---

[10] Mark Evan Bonds, "The Sincerest Form of Flattery? Mozart's 'Haydn' Quartets and the Question of Influence," *Studi musicali* 22 (1993): 365–409; 383.

lin came in. The *Scherzando Allegretto* begins by having ii follow I as in the first movement; its Trio pursues the chirping topos with many trills for the first violin in a duet with only the second violin for accompaniment. The following *Adagio* in F and in 3/4 time, which occasionally anticipates some sarabande-like features of Mozart's equivalent slow movement in K. 565, has as its most striking feature a decorated restatement of the whole first part. There is room for only a minimal passage before the reprise, six measures during which the cello rises chromatically up to the tone C (as dominant). In the finale, *Rondo. Presto* in 2/4 time, Haydn's high spirits come into play again in a scintillating game that begins with the first violin on the same G that inaugurated the whole quartet (Example 4.6).

EXAMPLE 4.6. *Haydn, String Quartet in C, Op. 33, IV*

Note that the first destination after I is ii, via V/ii. In the coda the violins play tag with the viola and cello leading to a climax with *crescendo* up to V^7/IV, then a pause, followed by soft, then softer, cadences of V^7 - I. The first violin's last tone is not C, but G.

The Quartet in E♭ begins in rather staid fashion, with a singing *Allegro* melody for the first violin, confined mainly within an octave (Example 4.7a). The

EXAMPLE 4.7 a, b. *Haydn, String Quartet in E♭, Op. 33*

a. *I*

accompaniment is simple, the cello supporting each chord with its root, the inner voices playing eighth notes. Regular harmonic rhythm makes the proceedings sound even more ordinary, except for the cadence in m. 4, which is speeded up and makes the end of the theme sound abrupt. Bridging over to the second half of the theme is an expressive raised fifth degree up to C, from which the melody falls down to the tonic. The condensation of m. 4 is melodic as well as harmonic, as the tune falls quickly to the tonic with the same tones that took longer from m. 2 to m. 3. The theme may not seem rich in possibilities but Haydn mines it to the extent of deriving nearly the entire movement from two of its melodic-rhythmic motives—the initial upbeat skip of a fourth and the descent to the cadence in m. 4. Moreover, the rondo refrain of the finale transforms two of its salient melodic features, the fall from 5 to 1 and a chromatic rise in the middle, into a giddy *Presto*

(Example 4.7b). When this refrain returns for what we guess is a final time, after a protracted V⁷ chord and then a rest with fermata, the quartet should be over.

b. *IV*

Instead, an *Adagio* stretches out two portions of the tune. How quaint, we think, it closes like a Handelian "Amen." But there is more. The first two measures, I - V - I, of the *Presto* refrain return to provide the final cadence. Final it is not. The players remain poised for more. Haydn brings back each two-measure segment of the theme after a lengthy pause. The fourth segment again makes the cadence. There cannot be more than this, surely. Yet the players still remain poised to play. After a pause three times as long as the previous ones, the initial segment returns *pianissimo*, I - V - I. It is no wonder that posterity has given this quartet the nickname "The Joke." The jest is not broad but subtle. Consider, for instance, how the quartet begins by compressing time in m. 4 and then ends the finale by expanding it greatly.

The Quartet in D offers a lovely first movement, *Vivace assai* in 6/8 time, one that is spacious, airy in texture, and lighthearted. Occasional drones in the bass or treble enhance its pastoral feeling. The drones offer one feature that continues in the next movement, an *Andante* in common time and in tonic minor that seems like a meditation. It is short, without repeats, and ends in tonic major in its final measures, like a *tierce de Picardie*. The *Scherzo Allegro* and its unnamed trio have melodic links with both the first movement (descent by step from 5) and the last (melodic turn around the cadential goals). The finale is a double theme and variations, *Allegretto* in 2/4 time. The double variation, to which Haydn became very partial, lends variety to Op. 33. It sees use only here.

Pleyel strangely chose to open his score edition of Op. 33 with the one quartet that has an ambiguous beginning, with a little duet for the violins in which the second accompanies the melody of the first (Example 4.8). We are led to hear the initial D as the tonic until the second violin surprises us with an A♯. The cello enters with an F♯ and emphasizes the tone with a melodic turn around it, reiterating the four descending sixteenth notes of the first violin in mm. 1–2. The chords built up above it are alternately V⁷ or V⁹ of b minor, which should arrive after the *crescendo* to *forte* but is replaced by a deceptive cadence to VI. Throughout this build-up, the cello staunchly insists on A♮ against a repeated A♯ above it. The delayed cadence on i does not arrive until m. 11, after a series of evasions, lastly

EXAMPLE 4.8. *Haydn, String Quartet in b, Op. 33, I*

by way of a Neapolitan chord. This material becomes richer and more intense as it goes along. When the second key, D, arrives, it supports the same theme as the opening, as if Haydn were saying, "You could have been right about the key, as I now demonstrate." For the reprise in the seconda parte, he ups the ante of his main theme with an added A♯ in the first chord, turning it into an augmented triad (Example 4.8, mm. 59–60). Pleyel took liberties by canceling the sharp before A and transferring this three-part chord and the next one back to his m. 1. The regularization gains nothing and loses a lot. It has prevailed in subsequent printings for two centuries and still persists.[11]

Haydn's astute augmented chord at one of the most prominent returns of his main theme perhaps emboldened Mozart to raise A to A♯ when repeating the main theme in the opening *Allegro* of his "Prague" Symphony of 1786. Pleyel's proffered correction of his teacher brings to mind an anecdote related by Griesinger on the subject of faultfinding.

> He [Haydn] once read a review of one of his compositions in which he was charged with a false fifth. "These gentlemen may think themselves very wise in such discussions. Ach! if I wished to take up criticism, how much I should find to criticize!" He also told me that once in the presence of K. [Kozeluch] and Mozart, he had one of his new quartets played over, in which several bold passages appeared. "That sounds strange," said K. to Mozart. "Would you have written it that way?" "Hardly," answered Mozart, "but do you know why not? Because neither you nor I should have come upon this idea."[12]

[11] For example, in H. C. Robbins Landon, *Haydn: Chronicle and Works*, 5 vols. (Bloomington, IN, 1976–80), 2:580. Landon's indispensable multi-volume work will be cited henceforth only as Landon, *Haydn*, then the volume and page numbers. It is greatly indebted to the earlier fundamental study of the life and works by Carl Ferdinand Pohl, *Joseph Haydn*, 3 vols., vols. 1–2 (Leipzig, 1875–82); vol. 3, ed. Hugo Botstiber (Leipzig, 1927).

[12] *Joseph Haydn*, ed. Vernon Gotwals, p. 36. For full citation, see note 2 above. Subsequent references to Dies and Griesinger are to this edition and are made without page citations.

The Quartet in b was perhaps the work that occasioned this anecdote. There is a passage in its slow movement that may have reinforced the boldness mentioned. An *Andante* in 6/8 time and in the key of D, it is also in sonata form. Upon reaching the key of A at the end of the prima parte Haydn leaned heavily on a dissonant passing tone on the way to the cadence, repeating it several times. Perhaps it is no coincidence that the emphasized tone is A♯.

The Quartet in b is the most serious of the set, not just by virtue of its being in the minor mode. Its Scherzo (renamed Menuetto by Pleyel) has little dance character and is in tonic minor, with tonic major for the unnamed trio. The finale, a *Presto* in 2/4 time, is another sonata form. It begins and ends in tonic minor. This is something Haydn was more likely to do ten years earlier than in the 1780s, when endings of minor–mode sonata forms usually turned into tonic major.

The Quartet in B♭, the last of the six in the original edition, has been encountered above in connection with Mozart, who seemed to acknowledge a little recurrent tag in Haydn's opening movement, *Allegro moderato* in common time, by taking it over in the finale of his own Quartet in B♭, K. 458, the fourth of those he dedicated to Haydn (see Example 1.13ab). The second movement, Scherzo *Allegretto*, has a Trio in b♭ labeled *Minore* with which Pleyel tampered, changing its first strain from nine measures to eight, presumably because he favored 4 + 4 regularity in phrase structure. Haydn provided such regularity in the theme of his slow movement, a *Largo* in 3/4 time and in E♭. The finale is a jolly rondo, a *Presto* in 2/4 time with many repeated notes in its refrain. There is a surprise ending as all the players reiterate the rondo theme softly, pizzicato.

What impressed players and listeners of that time as new and special about Op. 33? Compared with his last set, the Op. 20 quartets, which provided so hearty a diet to his admirers that it took them a decade and more to digest, the new quartets are on the whole lighter in tone, more consistently playful, witty, and charming. One feature alone, Haydn's rondo finales, summarizes much about his new quartet style. The rondo finale was honed in his symphonies.[13] It became indelibly associated with his quartets as well, beginning with Op. 33. In this new set Haydn combined great emotional range with technical prowess, without depending on fugal forms such as he resorted to in the quartets of Op. 20. He composed three more sets of six quartets each during the decade, Op. 50 of 1787, Opp. 54–55 of 1788, and Op. 64 of 1790. In his subsequent sets, he sometimes looked back to Op. 20 and before, but mostly he followed and deepened the course chartered in Op. 33.

---

[13] For example, in Symphony No. 68 in B♭ of the mid-1770s. See *Haydn, Mozart*, p. 372. The three Haydn chapters of this book were written before publication of *The String Quartets of Joseph Haydn* by Floyd Grave and Margaret Grave (Oxford, 2006). They give a finely nuanced account of Op. 33 in their ch. 11.

Sacred Music and Opera

In late 1790, the impresario Johann Peter Salomon and Haydn set out for London from Vienna.[14] They traveled by way of Bavaria, the Rhineland, Brussels, and Calais. At Bonn, where Salomon was born in 1745, they stopped for a few days. Maximilian, Maria Theresa's youngest son, ruled there as archbishop and elector of Cologne. He had known Haydn since at least 1773, when the imperial family visited Esterháza and heard Haydn's *L'infedeltà delusa*. Salomon made Haydn's presence known to the elector, and plans were laid to honor the composer with a performance of his music. Dies recorded the following as having been told to him by Haydn on 29 November 1805.

> Salomon took Haydn on Sunday to the court chapel to hear Mass. Hardly had they entered the church and found themselves a good place, when the High Mass began. The first sounds announced a work of Haydn's. Our Haydn supposed it a coincidence that was so obliging as to flatter him, but it was very pleasant to him to hear his own work. Toward the end of Mass, someone approached and invited him to go into the oratory, where he was expected. Haydn went there and was no little astonished to see that the elector Maximilian had summoned him there, took him immediately by the hand, and presented him to his musicians with the words, "Thus I make you acquainted with your much-celebrated Haydn." The elector gave both parties time to get acquainted, and to give Haydn convincing proof of his own esteem, invited him to his own table.

Salomon had already ordered a little dinner to be served to Haydn and himself in their rooms and they made their excuses. The elector accepted these and then trumped his offer by transforming their little dinner into a large one for twelve persons so that the "ablest of the musicians" could remain with Haydn. Beethoven, court organist and viola player in the court orchestra, had just turned twenty and was likely among them; another member of the band, the identically aged flautist Anton Reicha, later recalled that he first met Haydn in Bonn at this time.

Which of Haydn's many masses sounded in the court chapel at Bonn on this pleasant occasion? An authority on them has suggested that, of the several written before 1790, the most likely candidates were the first *Missa Cellensis*, a work begun in 1766, or the second *Missa Cellensis*, composed in 1782.[15] The great length and uneven quality of the earlier work leave no doubt that Haydn would have been more agreeably surprised (which was the whole point) by hearing his

---

[14] A fine 1791 oil portrait of Salomon by Thomas Bush Hardy is reproduced in Landon, *Haydn*, 3: Color Plate III.

[15] Carl Maria Brand, *Die Messen von Joseph Haydn* (Würzburg, 1941), p. 216.

latest and more skilled Mass of 1782, which was cogent from first note to last and represented a triumph over the long-winded, discursive style of earlier days. Its duration has been estimated at about thirty minutes, as against seventy-five in the case of its predecessor.[16]

The first *Missa Cellensis* had not nearly the diffusion throughout the Catholic parts of Germany as did the second. For all their differences, the two Masses do have several points in common, besides their connection with the pilgrimage church of Mariazell in Styria, one of Austria's principal shrines, or with the services in honor of Our Lady of Mariazell in several Viennese churches. The most important common factor is their key, C major, the overall tonality of both Masses. Jubilant C major, colored by trumpets and drums, had long been an Austrian favorite for High Masses. The scoring of these works is otherwise quite similar, in 1782 involving four-part strings, two oboes, two bassoons, and possibly organ as well, although there is no longer a basso continuo part, nor a figured bass. Both works begin with a slow introduction to which the first "Kyrie eleison" is sung. The introductions function in both like slowly-drawn curtains opening a tonal vista of what is to come.[17]

THE SECOND *Missa Cellensis*

The basses begin the Mass softly, intoning "Kyrie" to an *Adagio* in common time, followed by the tenors and altos building the tonic triad, above which the sopranos add a B♭ that turns the chord into V^7/IV, resolving to IV^6_4. The next chord is V^6_5, *forte*, which resolves to I, with strong agogic accent on the middle syllable of "e - lei - son" (Example 4.9). The orchestra supports the choral build-up while

EXAMPLE 4.9. *Haydn, Second* Missa Cellensis, *Kyrie*

[16] Bruce C. MacIntyre, *The Viennese Concerted Mass of the Early Classic Period* (Ann Arbor, MI, 1986), p. 111.
[17] This point is explored at length in the discussion of the earlier work in *Haydn, Mozart*, pp. 296–305. For a continuation of the discussion about the work's date, see Bruce C. McIntyre's review of the critical edition in *Notes*, March 1995; he suggests 1766 for the Kyrie and Gloria, ca. 1773 for the rest.

throbbing in a sixteenth-note accompaniment. Their basses cling to a pedal C even when the choral basses substitute the leading tone, B♮, for C at the beginning of m. 3. In m. 4 the voices begin again softly with "Kyrie," like the initial two measures but with a new harmony, vi, followed by its dominant and a diminished-seventh harmony for the accented middle syllable of "e - lei - son," *forte*, as before. With the resolution of this chord to ii^6, one can sense that a return to tonic C is near, but one could not predict how Haydn got there. On the last beat of m. 5 the chorus and orchestra land in full force, *fortissimo*, on the chord of ii in root position, with the sopranos up to high A, the peak melodic tone for them in the entire mass. From their high perch, the sopranos descend by step, with *diminuendo* indicated in the orchestra by a hairpin curve. Then Haydn repeats the move one step lower to restore the tonic, from which there is a brief detour to V in order to prepare the following *Vivace*. Aside from the 4 - 3 suspension in the soprano part at the end there is nothing specifically church-like in this dramatic introduction.

The slow introduction, *Largo* in common time, of the first *Missa Cellensis*, although harmonically rich, lacked the force and theatrical flair of its successor. It had no interruptions by sudden accents of its smoothly flowing progression and in fact no dynamic indications at all. It made much of the 4 - 3 suspension, of which there were several. The setting of the word "Kyrie" is rhythmically the same in both. They both end with the sopranos singing their 4 - 3 suspension, but the *Largo* sounds a churchly tone throughout. There is a lot of slow-moving music in the earlier work, and not much in its successor.

Haydn repeated the *Adagio*'s contrast between tonic and supertonic as the Kyrie continues, *Vivace* in 3/4 time, with a solo soprano over soft accompaniment, a four-measure phrase that proceeds from I to I$^6_3$ and back, followed by an identical phrase one tone higher, from ii to ii$^6_3$ and back. It takes only another four-measure phrase for the soprano to complete a return to the tonic, descending by step as in m. 7 of the *Adagio*. The cadence overlaps the initial measure of the chorus, which repeats the whole twelve-measure main idea. By overlapping, Haydn gains an urgency that would have been missing had he made a full stop before beginning the choral repetition.

The guiding principle behind the remainder of the *Vivace* is sonata form. After a transition in which the chorus is divided into sopranos and altos answering back and forth with tenors and basses, there is a clear second theme in G, continuing the antiphonal dialogue. Then a closing theme is stated with the sopranos holding a long high G as a pedal while the other voices wind around below it. Here the orchestra alone adds its punctuation, like a ritornello.

It is left to a solo alto to introduce the "Christe eleison" part of the text, which Haydn did by reverting to the main theme in the new key of G, a very common way of beginning a *seconda parte*. The first two of the four-measure phrases return verbatim, but a modulatory patch for chorus overcomes the third phrase, leading to a cadence in a. The closing material is heard again, this time with the sopranos holding a long pedal on their high A. After a quick transition the reprise begins, shortened by elimination of the soprano solo—Haydn often compressed this section by deleting repeated material, regardless of the medium. The secondary thematic material returns in C as expected, and likewise the closing material, the sopranos settling on a long C pedal. The *Vivace* could easily come to an end here. Instead, Haydn postponed closure by his favorite stall, a long-held secondary dominant with fermata, V^6_3/V marked *tenuto*.[18] What follows is cadential material that has been heard before and could be considered a coda. The musical discourse has been straightforward and to the point, neither too long nor too short for the material at hand. It makes Haydn's frequent discursiveness in earlier sacred music seem overlong by comparison. At 156 measures including the *Adagio*, the Kyrie approximates in length one of the composer's symphonic first movements with slow introduction, that of the contemporaneous Symphony No. 75 in D.

Having set the Kyrie straight through after its slow introduction, Haydn broke the Gloria and Credo into different and contrasting sections. He divided the first into four sections: *Allegro con brio* in common time for "Gloria in excelsis Deo," with clear melodic ties to the Kyrie; a soprano solo in **A B A** form for the "Gratias," an *Allegro* in 3/8 time and in the key of F, joined without a break to "Qui tollis peccata mundi" in the same meter and tempo but in f minor and for chorus; C major returns for "Quoniam tu solus Sanctus" in common time and marked *Allegro con brio*, followed by a concluding fugal "Amen."

The Credo is also divided into four sections and through a sleight of hand takes no longer than the Gloria in spite of its much longer text. "Credo in unum Deum" begins with the voices and orchestra sounding the tone C in unisons and octaves, a single tone being one way of expressing "unum" that was often used. The tempo is again *Vivace* and the meter 3/4 time as in the Kyrie. "Et incarnatus est" brings a tenor solo contrasting in key and motion, a *Largo* in common time and in a minor. By way of the relative, C, Haydn works around to c minor, then E♭, and even further into the flat side when the chorus sings "Crucifixus" in imitative counterpoint. Drooping chromatic lines clothe "passus et sepultus est," as they very often do. The movement ends softly in c minor. C major, *Vivace*, and 3/4 time return for "Et resurrexit," sung by the sopranos, while the other three parts simultaneously sing different later parts of the text. This curious setting may be liturgically dubious but it accomplished a quick traversal of the wordiest parts of the text. Simultaneous polytextuality was nothing new in music. In medieval motets it was tolerated in the belief that no detail could possibly elude the divin-

---

[18] The same device appears near the end of the "Domine Deus" in the first *Missa Cellensis*, as pointed out in *Haydn, Mozart*, p. 299.

ity. The first person singular of "Credo" throws quite a different light on this rush through the items of belief in the Nicene Creed. In musical form the result is convincing because Haydn recapitulates material from the beginning of the Credo. There is a vigorous fugue in 6/8 time, *Vivace*, for "Et vitam venturi saeculi." The countersubject is a rising chromatic line that sounds very secular, especially after becoming rising chromatic thirds. Although short, this is a rollicking example of the jig-fugue and predicts the "tipsy fugue" in fast 6/8 time that, nearly twenty years later, will bring "Autumn" to a rousing C major conclusion in *The Seasons*.

The Sanctus returns to the *Adagio* in the triple meter of the initial Kyrie, with which there are other similarities (Example 4.10). Most suggestive of the Kyrie is

EXAMPLE 4.10. *Haydn, Second Missa Cellensis, Sanctus*

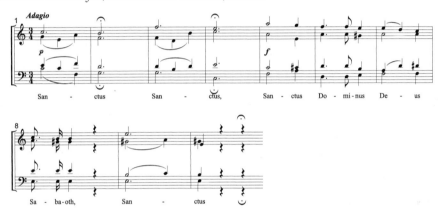

the *forte* outburst in m. 5, with the sopranos up to their high A, then descending by step, with harmonic progression from IV to V/vi. Remembering the Kyrie, we anticipate a similar descent from G sinking to the tonic. Instead, Haydn lingers on E major, savoring its wonder. If Beethoven were there and heard this it might have inspired the distant beginnings of his preoccupation with the major triad on the third degree, so characteristic of his own Mass in C of 1808. After the silent pause with fermata, Haydn resumes by repeating the soft beginning of the Sanctus, this time followed by a loud and harmonically rich progression that leads to a big cadence in the tonic, with 4 - 3 suspension in the tenors. There may have been something nostalgic for Austrians about the beginning of the Sanctus. The melody, sung by the altos and tenors in thirds, doubled an octave above by the oboes, is part of "a Marian pilgrimage song of considerable antiquity," or so it has been claimed.[19] This could be the reason why the music of the first four measures is more sweetened by thirds than it normally is in Haydn.

---

[19] Landon, *Haydn*, 2:559.

"Pleni sunt cœli" and "Osanna" Haydn set to a jubilant C major, *Allegro* in 3/4 time, after which the Benedictus sounds an uncommonly somber tone, being an *Allegretto* in g minor and in 2/4 time. Haydn borrowed this music from an aria sung by Ernesto, one of the serious characters in his setting of Goldoni's *Il mondo della luna*. The original text, "Qualche volte non fa male," throws no light on the choice. In many masses, the Latin text is set to a pleasantly ambling gait in order to express the verb of motion in "Benedictus qui venit." The aria's second theme, in the relative major, ultimately in tonic major, conveys more of the expected mood, with a flowing sixteenth-note accompaniment to a melody that was a long-time favorite of the composer's, one that descends by step from the upper tonic.[20] It was to become the melodic climax of his famous "Emperor's Hymn" of 1797. The soloists reappear for the final section of the Benedictus in a placidly flowing G major, making for an easy V - I progression back to C for the necessary repetition of "Osanna."

The Agnus Dei begins with an *Adagio* in common time and a return to the c minor last heard at the end of the "Crucifixus." The tenors first sing the words "qui tollis peccata mundi," and they do it to a melodic line that goes by step from E♭ down to B♮, which is how Haydn set these words in the Gloria of the first *Missa Cellensis*.[21] After some twenty measures of this gloomy music, C major returns in the form of a fugue for "Dona nobis pacem," *Vivace* in common time. As the fugue moves toward its conclusion it begins to sound more like the homophonic and antiphonal exchanges that enlivened the Kyrie's *Vivace*. To remind us even more of that movement, Haydn applies the brakes tonally with another protracted stall, here intensified by being a diminished-seventh chord. With its resolution to V[7] the end is not far off. It comes after the chorus and orchestra in unison soar in a flurry of sixteenth notes up to high A followed by a resounding cadence. The last chord is devoid of a third in the chorus, as it was at the end of the Kyrie.

Haydn wrote the mass for Anton Liebe, a retired military commander who wished to celebrate his elevation to the nobility as Edler von Kreutzner. It had good reason therefore to be, on the whole, jubilant, and "an assertive, forthright work."[22] These qualities are shared with another commissioned work of 1782 that celebrated a family's ennoblement: the "Haffner" Symphony, K. 385. In comparison with Haydn's earlier sacred music the mass shows the definitive overcoming of a sluggishness that plagued the *Stabat mater* of 1767 and some sections of the

[20] The pattern appears in some of Haydn's earliest sacred music, dating from the 1750s; *Haydn, Mozart*, pp. 241–42.

[21] *Haydn, Mozart*, p. 300, ex. 4.12.

[22] H. C. Robbins Landon and David Wyn Jones, *Haydn: His Life and Music* (Bloomington, IN, 1988), p. 189. Landon wrote the chapters on his life and Wyn Jones those on his music. Landon's are condensed from his five-volume *Chronicle and Works*.

first *Missa Cellensis*. In the Great Organ Solo Mass of ca. 1770, Haydn found a way around this trait by inserting frilly organ solos that have been compared with the stucco ornaments in Rococo churches, then at their finest in southern Bavaria.[23] The Benedictus of the first *Missa Cellensis*, on the other hand, was so devoid of ornamentation as to seem downright neoclassical. But that great woolly mammoth of a mass was far from being stylistically consistent throughout. By the time Haydn came to write its successor he was able to make it both concise and learned, as well as consistently direct and powerful. In these respects it stands up well in comparison to the plain, neoclassical buildings springing up in Vienna during the Josephine decade, such as the General Hospital (1784) and the Academy of Military Surgery (1785).

Orlando Paladino

In July 1781, Prince Nicholas appointed the poet Nunziato Porta director of the Italian opera company at Esterháza. Porta remained in this post, supplementing his meager annual salary of 150 gulden by copying music, until the troupe's dissolution in 1790. At his request, two scores were purchased from Vienna in 1781: *Orlando paladino* by Guglielmi and others, and Traetta's *Il cavaliere errante* (*Stordilano*), both belonging to the category of *dramma eroicomico*. Porta's task was to adapt existing librettos and write the texts for insertion arias when they had to be new. This happened with Traetta's opera, which was produced in March 1782, and under normal circumstances would have happened with the pasticcio *Orlando* score that went under Guglielmi's name, on a libretto by Porta himself. In the summer of 1782, Prince Nicholas was alerted that the returning grandees of Russia would be visiting Esterháza in the fall. He was not about to allow his court opera to be represented by an old work, seen before in Vienna, and already in preparation by his forces. Nothing less than a work by his Kapellmeister would do. Thus, Haydn was forced to compose *Orlando paladino* in a hurry on a poor libretto that, given time for study and reflection, he might have rejected. He mentioned the project as something newly thrust upon him in his letter to Artaria dated ca. 24–25 July 1782: "Now I have to compose an entirely new Italian opera because the Grand Prince with his wife, and possibly His Majesty the Emperor too, will come down to visit us." The visit was canceled when the Russians had to leave Vienna earlier than expected. Thus, the case of Haydn's *Orlando* duplicated that of Mozart's *Die Entführung* a year earlier—begun in haste to entertain the visitors from Russia, then postponed. *Orlando* was first performed on 6 December 1782 in celebration of Prince Nicholas's name day.

Ludovico Ariosto's epic poem *Orlando furioso* engendered countless librettos. *Orlando paladino* was one and it had a typically checkered history. Porta based it

---

[23] *Haydn, Mozart*, p. 312.

on a comic libretto by Carlo Francesco Badini, *Le pazzie d'Orlando*, which was set by Pietro Guglielmi for the King's Theatre in London (1771). The ragings of the mad knight take an amusing turn in this opera when the sorceress Alcina turns Orlando into stone to calm him down, then says that her spell can be broken only by the sounds of soothing music. Medoro, satirized as a Parisian fop, tries singing a French air, identified in the libretto as one of Rameau's, to no avail.[24] Angelica breaks the spell by singing "Che farò senza Euridice" from Gluck's *Orfeo ed Euridice*. Porta got rid of this witty combat between rival musical styles. He made Angelica and Medoro into stereotypical seria lovers, Orlando into a *mezzo carattere* part that is neither heroic nor comic, and shunted the farcical situations to Orlando's squire Pasquale. Some of Guglielmi's music remained in Porta's *Orlando* as performed in 1774 at Prague, where it received new pieces by Guglielmi as well as borrowings from Jommelli, Piccinni, and Paisiello.[25] This score was then used for the *Orlando paladino* at Vienna that had twelve performances in 1777.

To introduce the new opera Haydn wrote a Sinfonia, consisting of a single *Vivace assai* in cut time in the key of B♭—the composer's first one-movement overture and a promising sign that economy was on his mind. The opening has two components, an eight-measure, fanfare-like *Intrada* and a lightly scored lyric idea sung by the first violins to the constant eighth-note accompaniment of the seconds. This theme rather resembles that of the *Vivace* in cut time that begins the composer's Symphony No. 77 in B♭ of 1782. Nevertheless, the *Vivace assai* could not be confused with the first-movement sonata form of the symphony. The *Intrada* keeps returning, for one thing, and there are no repeat signs and little development. Similar in length, both movements project comic verve, but the *Intrada*, pompous and ceremonial, conveys other aspects of the drama to follow, if not exactly "heroic," at least other than comedic.

Two newly hired singers played the seria roles of the lovers, soprano Matilde Bologna and tenor Prospero Braghetti. Their hiring indicates that the Prince was looking with favor on expanding his almost exclusively comic repertory to include seria elements and even opera seria itself. Less than a year after *Orlando paladino* the Esterháza stage witnessed its first full-length opera seria, a production of Giuseppe Sarti's hugely successful *Giulio Sabino*, that is to say two years before this opera was revived at Vienna as a showpiece for Luigi Marchesi in 1785

[24] Bruce Alan Brown, "*Le Pazzie d'Orlando, Orlando Paladino*, and the Uses of Parody," *Italica* 64 (1987): 583–605. The author identifies the French air as being not by Rameau but from *Tom Jones* by François-André Danican Philidor.

[25] Hoboken, 2:415. Karl Geiringer, "From Guglielmi to Haydn: The Transformation of an Opera," *Report of the Eleventh Congress [of the IMS], Copenhagen 1972*, ed. Henrik Glahn, Søren Sørensen, and Peter Ryom, 2 vols., 1:391–95, and Helen Geyer-Kiefl, "Guglielmis 'Le Pazzie d'Orlando' und Haydns 'Orlando Paladino,'" *Bericht über den internationalen Joseph Haydn Kongreß 1982*, ed. Eva Badura-Skoda (Munich, 1986), pp. 403–15.

(see p. 129). *Orlando* and *Giulio Sabino* paved the way for Haydn to create, as his last opera for the prince, a full-length opera seria of his own, *Armida*.

Among the many operatic treatments of Ariosto's characters Angelica, Medoro, and Orlando were Quinault's *Roland* for Lully in 1685 and Handel's *Orlando* for London in 1733. Any hopes Haydn entertained for doing justice to this great tale of romantic love won and lost sank because of Porta's unwieldy and poorly focused libretto. Porta showed incompetence on several levels. His Orlando elicits little sympathy as he wanders uncomprehendingly in and out. As one expert has written, "The weaknesses in the characterization of this central figure are typical of the opera as a whole: the number of constituent elements, often attractive in themselves, fail to combine to form a convincing drama."[26] Orlando shows no qualities that make him worthy of his adored Angelica. His heroics are mocked by his groom and outdone by the boastful Rodomonte, King of Barbary. Medoro, the lyric first tenor, lucky in having secured the love of Angelica, is not very happy either in this opera, during which he does a lot of complaining. Worse still, he is a ditherer, the kind of indecisive bungler that opera can scarcely tolerate. One wonders what Angelica, a very sensitive high soprano caught up in a turmoil of *sensibilité*, could have seen in the boy (as she calls him) in the first place. A merely carnal attraction seems to be the answer, and it does not suit the composer's musical personality very well. Porta's strongest contribution to the libretto is his sympathetic shepherdess Eurilla, a clever go-between who is loved by Pasquale. She sees through her ridiculous suitor, who sings two delightful and boastful catalogue arias, one about his travels, the other about his musical skills. She loves him whatever his faults, a trait that endears her to audiences. Porta enhanced the role of Pasquale especially for this version of his libretto and perhaps at the behest of Haydn, who shone brilliantly in setting Pasquale's rodomontades.

Porta's management of the stage action leaves a lot to be desired. Characters wander off for no particular reason then soon return for no better reason. Act II goes through many of the same situations already seen in Act I. The long finales ending both acts become tedious, in spite of Haydn's wonderful music, which sadly lacks momentum from one section to the next.[27] Many changes of scene are required (an expense that had to be approved by the prince) but they rarely correspond to the opera's mood swings. Too often, these are only variations on a basic mood of fear and desolation. Pietro Travaglia, Esterháza's masterful scenographer, was kept busy. His set design for the very first scene, "a snow-covered mountainous landscape," survives and shows an attractively irregular concep-

[26] Landon and Wyn Jones, *Haydn* (1988), p. 185.
[27] For the best case that can be made in these matters, see Caryl Clark, "Orlando paladino," in *The New Grove Dictionary of Opera* (1992).

tion of the bleak wasteland, with a waterfall surmounted by a rickety-looking bridge (Figure 4.2).

Haydn strove valiantly to impose some unity on the work by his choices of key and characteristic motion. He favored the key of E♭ for the title role. Orlando enters for the first time in scene 8, midway in Act I, rather late after having been talked about so much. He begins with an obbligato recitative, an *Adagio* in E♭, which becomes agitated as he refreshes himself by a fountain and then spies the names of Medoro and Angelica carved on a tree. He draws his sword and destroys the fountain and some trees. Then he sings a lively aria in E♭ in which he repeats the fatal carved words: "Medoro felice!—Angelica amante!" He returns in the ensuing finale and at last confronts not Medoro but Rodomonte, whom he threatens to slay but is prevented when Alcina turns Rodomonte into Beelzebub and then confines Orlando in an iron cage. Toward the end of Act II, Orlando again attempts to pursue the lovers but is stopped by Alcina, who produces a monster. Frightened, Orlando sings another aria in E♭ that begins "Cosa vedo! Cosa sento!" (Porta's text is filled with clichés such as "Che giornata è questa qua," to which he resorts in both Acts I and II.) Orlando's third aria is his most interesting musically. It comes at the beginning of the brief Act III after he wakes up in a changed state, his madness washed away by the waters of the river Lethe.

FIGURE 4.2. Travaglia's stage design for *Orlando paladino* ("Snowy Mountain").

This, his last aria, is distant from E♭. "Miei pensieri, dove siete?" is an *Adagio* in common time and in the key of E. It begins off-tonic with a hesitancy that is effective, and continues in a languorous style that suits the text, which is about silence and sleep.

Angelica sings some of her music in the soothing and melodious realm of A major, the traditional key of love duets and of this opera's love duet. She first enters near the beginning of Act I with a slow cavatina, an *Adagio* in A and in 3/4 time. Her big aria toward the end of Act I is in D, with coloratura. For her most moving aria, "Aure chete" in Act II, Haydn also chose D. This is a two-tempo piece consisting of an *Adagio* in cut time, the theme of which returns after contrast, then a *Vivace* with conspicuous gavotte rhythm (Example 4.11a). It approaches the

EXAMPLE 4.11 a, b, c. *Haydn,* Orlando Paladino

a. *Aria, Angelica, Act I*

fashionable two-tempo rondò, without embracing all the mannerisms of that genre, which Haydn must have known well from directing so many Italian operas by other composers. The text brings together pictures of smiling nature, with quiet zephyrs, green laurels, and calm waves, then an outburst in the fourth line, "amici orrori" (friendly horrors), as she despairs of finding Medoro. Haydn employs two oboes in thirds to mediate between her statements and suggest her next pitch (cf. Rosina's "Dove sono i bei momente" in *Figaro*). The *Vivace* commences at m. 59 and continues to use the conjunct descent of a third as a melodic springboard (unhappy me! where shall I go?). Desperate, she prepares to throw herself off a cliff into the sea. Medoro appears. They embrace and the love duet begins (Example 4.11b). It has the same rhythm and falling motif, 5 4 3, that

b. *Duet, Act III*

began her "Aure chete" and was a late addition to the score. Orlando surprises the lovers and eventually sings his second aria, bringing his world of E♭ to bear on their love music in A, and he also sings their motif (Example 4.11c).

c. *Aria, Orlando, Act II*

Act III offers little of interest after Orlando's aria. A group of wild men chase Angelica and seriously wound Medoro. Orlando and Rodomonte pursue their quarrel and actually come to blows, for which Haydn provides a *Combattimento* in D. Angelica sings a despairing and dirge-like aria about losing Medoro, a lengthy *Largo* in B♭ and in cut time. To the rescue once again comes Alcina, who heals Medoro's wounds and reunites the lovers, while a confused but docile Orlando looks on. At this, the rest of the cast join them in a vaudeville final. Orlando begins singing "Son confuso e stupefatto." They all sing the refrain "Se volete esser felice," which recurs after each character (except Pasquale) sings a solo verse. The text goes back to Badini's original and was set as a vaudeville final by Guglielmi, called "Coro Rondeau." Haydn may have taken a cue from Guglielmi in framing his catchy refrain in gavotte rhythm.[28]

Haydn may also have been responding to the stunning vaudeville final of *Die Entführung*. Mozart's superior vaudeville ended a Singspiel with many touches of its opéra comique heritage in evidence. Coming at the end of *Orlando*, a work firmly in the Italian style and tradition, a vaudeville final sounds out of place, but it was not Haydn's first use of the form.[29] There is a certain tonal logic in Haydn's choosing the key of A for his last number, especially coming after Angelica's big aria in B♭. At the beginning of the opera, the overture and *Introduzione* in B♭ were followed by her cavatina in A. Clumsy plot though it has, *Orlando paladino* pleased Prince Nicholas, who ordered many repetitions. Translated into German it also achieved productions far and wide, which says something about the dearth of good original works being created in German-language opera houses at the time.

Armida

In a postscript to his letter of 18 June 1783, Haydn wrote Artaria, "Regarding the clavier sonatas [trios] with violin and bass you must be patient for I am just now composing a new opera seria." It was only a month after the success of Sarti's opera seria *Giulio Sabino* at Esterháza. *Armida, dramma eroico*, shaped partly on the model of Sarti's opera, benefited from an almost leisurely period of gestation.

---

[28] Bruce Alan Brown informed me by letter of 27 July 2004 that Guglielmi's *Orlando* also uses gavotte rhythm and has "a first phrase that (coincidentally?) shares the first seven notes with Haydn's melody."

[29] Herbert Schneider, "Vaudeville-Finale in Haydns Opern und ihre Vorgeschichte," in *Bericht über den internationalen Joseph Haydn Kongress 1982*, ed. Eva Badura-Skoda (1986), pp. 302–9.

Travaglia on 6 August 1783 estimated costs for the scenery, then on 13 October Prince Nicholas approved estimates for the costumes, including changes of costume for the three principals. Parts were copied from the score throughout the following January and up to the premiere on 26 February 1784, the opening night of the new season.

The singers for whom Haydn created *Armida* were, with the exception of the bass, the same as those who had sung in *Giulio Sabino*: soprano Matilde Bologna (Armida), tenor Prospero Braghetti (Rinaldo), tenor Antonio Specioli (Ubaldo), bass Paolo Mandini (Idreno), soprano Costanza Valdesturla (Zelmira), and tenor Leopold Dichtler (Clotarco). Many extras were employed to impersonate warriors, demons, nymphs, and furies. The production was so successful that it had to be given fifty-four times in the next five years, far more than any other opera at Esterháza, either by Haydn or anyone else. Beyond the princely theater, it had some success when translated into German and was revived in a 1797 concert performance at Schikaneder's Theater auf der Wieden. Artaria brought out a collection of favorite numbers from the opera in 1787.

Haydn was justly proud of *Armida*. After its second performance he wrote Artaria on 1 March 1784 saying, "it received general approbation and people are saying that it is my best work to date." *Armida* in fact has many claims to being the best of all his operas.

The libretto was derived, presumably by Porta, nearly word for word from an anonymous *Rinaldo* composed by Antonio Tozzi for Venice (1775).[30] Feeding into the anonymous libretto were others on the same subject that had been composed by Sacchini (Milan, 1772) and Naumann (Padua, 1773). Rinaldo's incursion into Armida's enchanted garden in Porta's Act III is taken from the *Armida abbandonata* set by Jommelli (Naples, 1770). Absent from Haydn's opera is any use of the most famous of all librettos on the subject, that of Philippe Quinault for Lully, which inspired its own line of descent, leading to Traetta's *Armida* (Vienna, 1761), Salieri's youthful *Armida* (Vienna, 1771), and Gluck's *Armide* (Paris, 1777), the greatest of all operas on the subject.[31] The costume sketches in rococo style attributed to Travaglia, formerly thought to have been for Haydn's *Armida*, are now assigned to Salieri's *Armida* of a decade earlier.[32] They have always seemed out of step with the artistic ideals of the 1780s. For the 1784 *Armida* one should imagine costumes and decors in a more neoclassical style.

A glance at Sarti's *Giulio Sabino* may help provide context at this point. Created for Venice in 1781 on a libretto by Pietro Giovannini, Sarti's opera ratified

[30] Marita P. McClymonds, "Haydn and his Contemporaries: 'Armida abbandonata,' " in *Bericht über den internationalen Joseph Haydn Kongress 1982*, pp. 325–52.

[31] *Music in European Capitals*, pp. 830–42. Rice, *Salieri*, pp. 162–75.

[32] Caryl Clark, "Fabricating Magic: Costuming Salieri's *Armida*," *Early Music* 31 (2003): 451–61.

the dominance in opera seria of the prima donna and primo uomo at the expense of everyone else. Their superior station was canonized by sole possession of the rights to singing the most fashionable kind of aria, the two-tempo rondò, and to singing the love duet. Sarti's prima donna, the hero's wife Epponina, sings her rondò "Con qual core" in Act II. Its *Andantino* is in 2/4 time and in G, in the expected rhythm of a gavotte, with the theme returning after contrast; the *Allegro assai* in common time is also in gavotte rhythm and similarly structured, with the added feature of a return to the initial stanza to pad the fast section. Eventually Sabino, condemned to death as an enemy of Rome, sings an expressive aria in E♭, "Cari figli," as he bids goodbye to his children. This piece has some rondò-like features but it is not *the* rondò. That famous piece is saved for Act III, after the death knell of the *Marcia funebre* in c minor has sounded. Sarti makes splendid use of obbligato recitative between the two occurrences of his funeral march. The rondò proper for Sabino, "La qual barbaro momento," is in the key of A (cf. Sesto's rondò in Mozart's *Tito*). It starts in the usual slow gavotte rhythm, a *Largo* in cut time that is repeated after a move to V. An *Allegro* in common time, also in gavotte rhythm and structured so as to return after contrast, almost completes the aria when it dissolves into an obbligato recitative as his wife attempts to perish with him. The tension is high throughout the opera and gets higher in Act III, but after Sabino's rondò, poet and composer brought the drama to a rapid conclusion. The Roman commander Tito forgives all in simple recitative and a happy little *coro* sends the audience home relieved of stress and glad to stop weeping. This final homophonic *coro* is not a real chorus, of course, but merely an ensemble for the singers in the cast. The other ensembles are only two in number, the duet of Sabino and his wife ending Act I and a trio for them and Tito ending Act II. Tito also loves Epponina, who spurns him. The emphasis on conjugal love and a simple line of action are departures from the Metastasian tradition of multiple amatory intrigues. Such directness could be seen to reflect neoclassical values and is linked with the rescue operas of the French tradition, which lead to Beethoven's *Leonore*. (For an anecdotal description of Sarti's visit to Haydn in 1784, see Appendix 2).

Armida elicited from Haydn his finest opera overture. Forceful, majestic, and concise *Vivace* sections frame a middle *Allegretto* that anticipates the magic-grove music of Act III. The whole is in a flowing C major, in which the first aria will be sung. In the first scene, there is a short recitative dialogue between Armida, Rinaldo, and Idreno, King of Damascus, who is Armida's uncle and betrothed to Zelmira. This leads quickly to Rinaldo's bellicose aria in C, "Vado a pugnar contente," followed, after another short recitative, by Idreno's aria promising to cede the kingdom to Rinaldo if he is successful in restoring peace. These are both exit arias, leaving the stage free for Armida's first big soliloquy. Obbligato recitative makes the first of many appearances in Haydn's score here, as she muses on her lover's departure, the dangers he faces, and his possible death. Her situation is not unlike that of Angelica, who consulted her book of magic and invoked the sorceress Alcina to help her. Armida, further advanced down the path of necromancy, is herself a sorceress. She invokes her pagan gods to protect Rinaldo. The text of her aria, "Se pietate avete, oh Numi," was set up to require a ternary or da capo aria, with repeat of the first of its two quatrains after contrast. Haydn chose the key of A major and an *Adagio* in cut time for the first part, using gavotte rhythm. He does not repeat the slow theme after contrast, but he does use the same theme for the first part, *Allegro* in common time, so that the effect is that of an unhackneyed kind of rondò. Armida's aria stretches to over six minutes in length, longer than any other, and if taken together with the preceding recitative, to nearly ten minutes.[33] No aria comes close to it in expressiveness in Haydn's setting until Rinaldo sings his big rondò in the middle of Act II.

Haydn chose for the love duet that concludes Act I, "Cara, sarò fedele," the key of B♭ (the same chosen by Mozart for his tenor-soprano love duet in *Die Entführung*). Rinaldo begins, swearing fidelity to Armida by her beautiful eyes (Example 4.12). His supple melodic line first takes his voice up to a G, then reaches

EXAMPLE 4.12. *Haydn,* Armida, *Duet, end of Act I*

that same G again via a chromatic rise in mm. 6–7 before sinking quickly to the cadence in m. 8. A modulation to the dominant follows, joined in the example at mm. 12–13. Having established the new tonic, F, with a cadence in m. 13, Haydn again took the voice up an octave, and with melismas in m. 14 repeats the chromatic rise to G, then to high A, the melodic peak, before descending to the cadence in the lower octave. The little two-note melodic sighs, separated by rests in m. 15, could not be more Italian. They are found in a similar pre-cadential passage in Sacchini's opera seria *Mitridate* (London, 1781).[34] Haydn intensified the next octave descent to the tonic by employing two additional chromatic tones, C♯

---

[33] As sung by Cecilia Bartoli in the complete performance of *Armida* recorded in 2000 under the direction of Nikolaus Harnoncourt (Teldec 8573–81108).

[34] *Music in European Capitals,* p. 924, ex. 9.10.

and B♮, before the final trill and cadence. His florid melodic line, so beautifully ornamented, would do credit to any composer of opera seria, even Mozart. To make his melisma on the word "vedrai" in m. 14 sound still lovelier, he put off the final "i," giving the voice the much-preferred open vowel sound of "ah." "You will see, my idol, how my heart adores you" is acted out in this lyrical effusion, which becomes more and more expressive as it goes along. Armida is properly impressed and sings the same music herself but her words still express doubt. Rinaldo overlaps her cadence with renewed assurances and then their entries begin to accelerate. By the time of the Allegro in 2/4 time she is convinced to the extent of joining him in sweet warblings on loving thoughts, up and down in parallel tenths. It makes a very effective act ending.

Mozart thought highly of the duet. He revised it on a surviving sheet, perhaps for one of his concerts, an alternate version that spared the soprano some of the coloratura and any tones above A♭ (K. 506a, hs4). The soprano in question could have been Nancy Storace.

Rinaldo's rondò in Act II is not labeled a rondò. Yet its text of three *ottenaria* quatrains sets up this form. Ubaldo, nothing if not faithful to duty, has previously persuaded the hero that he must leave Armida to join his fellow crusaders for the imminent battle. Rinaldo wavers (he does little but waver throughout the opera). He bids her farewell, upon which she faints and lies motionless on a rock. In an obbligato recitative even longer than the preceding ones he ponders whether it is just to leave her in such a state (the situation recalls "Se cerca, se dice" in Metastasio's *L'Olimpiade,* sung over the prostrate body of the prima donna, who has swooned).

Cara, è vero, io son tiranno	My dear, it is true, I am cruel
nel doverti abbandonar.	in having to leave you.
Tanto amore e tanto affano	So much love and so much anguish
già mi fa vacillar.	already make me hesitate.
Ma il dover, la gloria, il fato	But duty, glory, fate
la mia fede . . . Oh Dio! Non so . . .	my faith . . . Oh God! I know not . . .
Se la lascio, io son ingrato . . .	If I leave her, I am ungrateful . . .
Se qui resto . . . ah, non si può.	If I remain . . . No, it cannot be.
Giusti Dei, che fiero instante	Just gods, what a harsh moment
il dovermi allontar.	decrees my departure.
Chi mai vide un core amante	Who ever saw a loving heart
tante pene a sopportar?	suffer so much pain?

The piece begins as an *Adagio* in E♭ and in cut time for the first quatrain. Haydn avoided Sarti's favorite gavotte rhythm but not the return of the initial theme after contrast. For the second quatrain, Haydn switched to an agitated *Presto* in common time. Ubaldo comes running back to this music—it is unusual for one character to enter during the aria of another, but Ubaldo embodies Rinaldo's Christian conscience so it is not inappropriate for him to return here. Haydn disregards the expected form by bringing back the slow section, words and music, in the middle of the *Presto*. He is no slave to fashion. After the aria has achieved great length and a stunning conclusion, the knights exit.

Armida conveniently comes back to life. At first, she thinks that Rinaldo is still present. She upbraids him for his treachery in another highly charged obbligato recitative, "Barbaro!" When she realizes he has gone she waxes even more indignant and works up to the point of bursting into a wonderful rage aria in e minor, "Odio, furor, dispetto." This showpiece is worthy of Mozart's Electra or the Queen of the Night at their most furious. Unlike those ladies, Armida does not call for revenge—that she does only at the end. Haydn's choice of e minor after so much E♭ major expresses the personal conflict in an effective tonal way, much as Sarastro's anti-revenge aria in E major, coming after the Queen's outburst in d minor, expresses irreconcilable difference.

The seconda donna, Zelmira, plays a moderating role with regard to the opera's various conflicts. Somewhat like Eurilla in *Orlando* in her instinctive dignity and decency, she is given the first aria in Act II but it is no *aria di sorbetto*. In it she reproaches Idreno for the treachery he is planning in order to trap the Christian knights. He refuses to listen to her. She pleads with him in the aria "Tu mi sprezzi, e mi deride." In setting it, Haydn came very close to the melody of one of Sarti's secondary characters (Example 4.13ab). Whether it is the rhythmic cut

EXAMPLE 4.13 a, b.

a. *Haydn,* Armida, *Aria, Zelmira*

b. *Sarti,* Giulio Sabino, *Aria, Tito*

chosen for the *settenaria* lines, the melodic course, or the harmonic one, these beginnings are nearly identical. Their close correspondence does not continue beyond this. The scholar who discovered this and many other similarities between the operas of Sarti and Haydn does not claim that the latter necessarily knew he was quoting.[35] He summed up the similarities as being what might have

[35] John A. Rice, "Sarti's *Giulio Sabino,* Haydn's *Armida,* and the Arrival of Opera Seria at Esterháza," *Haydn Yearbook 15* (1984): 181–98; 197.

happened naturally when one composer was so steeped in preparing a production of the other's work, then directing it in performance; "Haydn had no need to imitate Sarti's music; his mind was full of beautiful musical ideas." In strikingly similar terms, Gluck reproved critics for charging composers with plagiary: "M. Sacchini, genius that he is, and full of beautiful ideas, has no need to pillage others."[36]

Ubaldo is a one-issue character focused on bringing Rinaldo back to his duties in Godefroi's army. He sings two arias, in Act I as he attempts to penetrate the magic spell surrounding Armida's mountaintop palace, and in Act II as he harps on military glory to Rinaldo. He takes an equal role in the grand *terzetto* that closes Act II, when he and Armida tug Rinaldo in different directions. His henchman Clotarco, a Danish knight, has only one aria, in which he readily submits to Zelmira's charms.

Critics weaned on opera buffa always complain of the lack of ensembles in opera seria. They too readily dismiss what makes *Armida* such a strong representative of its genre. Haydn packed great tension into every act, partly by uncommon tonal moves into and out of the set pieces and partly by writing continuous music over several scenes, working up to the climactic ensembles that end the acts. He took great pains to heighten the tension in the enhanced orchestral language of obbligato recitative, of which there is more here than in any of his previous operas. Simple recitative served as a foil for preparing these lengthy and complex passages of orchestral agitation that must have cost the composer many days at his work desk. Haydn also delighted in orchestral painting of references in the text to storms and other natural or magical phenomena. In Act III, as Rinaldo finally fights his way out of Armida's enchanted garden, these orchestral depictions reach their acme.

Porta is usually given credit for the libretto of Haydn's *Armida*, yet little was done to change the anonymous text inherited from Tozzi's opera. Ubaldo's role was scaled back by cutting one aria and his duet with Rinaldo in Act III. Also cut were all references to dancing in Act III—dancers were not on hand at Esterháza. Tozzi's happy ending for the lovers was changed by leaving their future in doubt. Armida remains furious and wishes Rinaldo dead, but he departs with a conciliatory word for her and hopes for his return. The others draw the moral, or try to:

Oh sorte inique avara,	Oh grudging, unjust fate,
oh divisione amara	oh bitter separation
ch'all'alme innamorate	that to loving souls
d'esempio ognor sarà.	will ever be an example.

[36] *Music in European Capitals*, p. 32.

It did not take much of a poet to write this verse. In sum, the changes to Tozzi's libretto were such as the composer might almost have made himself. As for the music, the opera ends with a short ensemble, ninety-three measures in C major lasting about three minutes. Compared with ca. nine minutes for the love duet and ca. seven for the *terzetto*, this cannot help but sound somewhat perfunctory. Yet it is a better closure than the triteness of a happy ending. Sarti began and ended his opera in C major, and so did Haydn.

Haydn wrote no more operas for Prince Nicholas after *Armida* but he did revive his *La vera costanza*, the score of which had been lost in the opera house fire of 1779; possibly the new version of 1785 was heavily revised.[37] It, along with *Orlando* and *Armida*, ensured that Haydn's own music was well represented on Esterháza's stage during its last lustrum.

THE *Seven Last Words*

By 1780, Haydn's music became so widely known that his fame had spread even to the Iberian Peninsula. The Spanish poet Tomás de Iriarte had sung Haydn's praises in "La música" (1779). In 1781, King Charles III of Spain sent Haydn a golden snuffbox studded with diamonds; it was presented by the head of the Spanish legation in Vienna, who made a special trip to Esterháza to do so. In February 1781, Luigi Boccherini, then in the service of the king's brother, Infant Luis, sent a letter to Artaria professing his esteem for Haydn in the highest degree—these two events may be related.[38] From Cadiz came the order to compose several orchestral pieces appropriate to meditations on the last words of the crucified Christ, as handed down in Scripture. The letter commissioning the *Seven Last Words* has not survived, nor has the autograph, which Haydn may have sent to Spain. The time of composition was approximately the same as the six Paris Symphonies, 1785–86. Thus, Haydn was occupied simultaneously with one of his most worldly works, for the City of Light, and one of his most solemn sacred works, appropriate to Holy Week rites in a darkened Spanish church.

Accounts differ as to the exact nature of the devotional services and their location. Haydn told Griesinger what he remembered of the commission fifteen years later. He told Dies much the same. The former sticks to the point while the latter, prone to digressions, sometimes wanders from it. Griesinger's account follows.

> A canon in Cadiz requested Haydn, about the year 1785, to make an instrumental composition on the Seven Words of Jesus on the Cross which was to be suited to a solemn ceremony that took place annually during Lent in the cathedral of Cadiz.

---

[37] *Haydn, Mozart*, pp. 394–96.
[38] *Music in European Capitals*, pp. 986–87.

On the appointed day the walls, windows, and piers of the church were draped with black, and only a single lamp of good size, hanging in the middle, illuminated the sacred darkness. At an appointed hour all doors were locked, and the music began. After a suitable prelude, the bishop mounted to the pulpit, pronounced one of the Seven Words, and delivered a meditation upon it. As soon as it was ended, he descended from the pulpit and knelt down before the altar. The music filled in this pause. The bishop entered the pulpit a second, a third time, and so on, and each time the orchestra came in again at the end of the talk.[39]

Griesinger had used this information before, in nearly the same form, to serve as a preface to an edition of Haydn's oratorio version of the work on a text by Joseph Friebert emended by Swieten, published by Breitkopf and Härtel (Leipzig, 1801). In his *Notizen* of 1810, Griesinger closed his remarks by writing, "It was indeed one of the most difficult tasks to make out of thin air, with no [sung] text, seven adagios following one another that would not weary the listener but would stir in him all the feelings inherent in each of the Words uttered by the dying Saviour. Haydn oftentimes declared this work to be one of his most successful."

Haydn wrote his London publisher William Foster a letter dated 8 April 1787 that included a description of the work. He offered other works for sale as well: "6 Prächtige Sinfonien" (the Paris Symphonies) and "3 ganz neue niedliche Notturni" (i.e., from the Lire Concertos, Hob. VIIh:1–5. See note 75 below). Compared to the "magnificent" symphonies and the "dainty" notturni, the other species of composition on offer was much more unusual.

An entirely new work, consisting solely of instrumental music [bestehen in blosser Instrumental Music], divided into seven sonatas, each lasting seven or eight minutes, together with an introductory prelude, and to end, a Terremoto, or earthquake. These sonatas are arranged and measured to the words Christ our Savior spoke on the Cross. [He lists them]. Each Sonata, or each text, is expressed solely through instrumental music but in a way that makes a profound impression on the souls of even the most inexperienced listener. The work in its entirety lasts a little more than an hour. Each sonata is set apart by a pause, so that one can ponder ahead of time the following text. Copying the whole would occupy a little more space than one of my symphonies, in total about 37 folios. The instrumentation is the same as in my symphonies.[40]

Instead of having the instrumental sonatas follow the declaimed and explicated text, as at Cadiz, Haydn proposed that the listener meditate on the word, then lis-

[39] Translation from Gotwals, *Joseph Haydn*, p. 21. Hoboken, I:845, relates another version told him by Spanish sources that places the devotion in an underground grotto of the parish church of Santo Rosário in Cadiz, which was under the care of the cathedral canon Marqués de Valde Inigo. Haydn's work requires a large orchestra, making it unlikely to have been performed originally in any but a large church.

[40] Haydn ended the letter by writing, "Please reply in French." His English, like Foster's German, had not reached a serviceable level.

ten to the matching music. He included the text in his letter probably because he wanted it communicated in some fashion to the listeners, perhaps by a program note. In the first edition, brought out by Artaria in Vienna during July 1787, Haydn made clear what he meant by "measuring" his sonatas to the biblical words by carefully placing each text under the first violin part. Moreover, these unspoken, unsung texts were known by the first auditors in Vienna even before the appearance of the original edition. Zinzendorf wrote in his diary for 26 March 1787 that he attended a Lenten concert given by Prince Adam Auersperg: "au Concert de hayden sur les 7 paroles de notre Seigneur sur la croix. La seconde du Paradis, la derniere du dernier soupir me parut bien exprimée." In fact, the *Seven Last Words* began to challenge the traditional passion oratorios as Lenten fare.

Artaria entitled his edition *Musica instrumentalis sopra le sette ultime parole del nostro Redentore in croce, o siano Sette sonate con un introduzione ed al fine un terremoto* followed by the long list of instruments required. On 7 July 1787, he advertised it and also an edition of Haydn's version of the same for string quartet, to be available shortly, plus a version for solo keyboard verified by the composer. By year's end, Foster had published his edition, *The Passion of Our Saviour Expressed in Instrumental Parts for a Grand Orchestra, Concluding with the Earthquake, Composed by Joseph Haydn of Vienna.* Other music publishers soon followed. Like Haydn's quartets, symphonies, and trios, the *Seven Last Words* generated business for composer and publisher.

If sacred music can be defined by its association with liturgical or religious texts it follows that this work, however unusual, cannot be denied a place among Haydn's sacred scores. It bears some relationship to his *Stabat mater* of twenty years earlier, also dealing with the Crucifixion and also a composite work made up of individual texts, in that case sung. Haydn imposed a loose tonal plan on the earlier work so that the initial sequence of keys returned in the second part and the ending was on the same tone.[41] The dangers of an overall sluggishness, not always overcome in the *Stabat mater*, were miraculously avoided in the *Seven Last Words*. Variety of key, affect, dynamics, instrumentation, and even motion (within the limitations imposed by the slowness of the pieces) was deployed in so masterly a fashion that a listener remains enthralled throughout. The initial theme, shaped by the sound and rhythm of the Latin texts, intensifies the meaning of the words upon various returns and transformations. Thus, the texts impress the soul (as Haydn said) in ever deeper ways. It helped, of course, that Haydn had deepened his art so much by the 1780s.

As in the original Artaria parts, the critical edition correctly places the Latin texts under the violino primo part as Haydn wished.[42] This is not the case with

---

[41] *Haydn, Mozart*, pp. 305–9.

[42] *JHW* IV, *Die Sieben letzten Worte unseres Erlösers am Kreuze: Orchesterfassung (1785)*, ed. Hubert Unverricht (Munich-Duisburg, 1959).

almost all other modern editions. The seven texted themes are given here along with incipits for the introduction and final movement (Example 4.14). From the

EXAMPLE 4.14. *Haydn,* Seven Last Words, *Incipits*

beginning with a majestic and pathos-laden *Adagio* in d minor Haydn traversed seven keys—B♭, c, E, f, A, g, E♭—before returning to c for the Terremoto. The *Introduzione* already predicted c minor by restating its opening down one tone, with no preparation. A complete melodic sketch for the Terremoto shows that

Haydn's earlier main theme derived from the "Dance of the Furies" in Gluck's *Don Juan*. It takes the original full-orchestra version to do justice to this music and much else in the work.

Sonata I emerges smoothly from the *Introduzione*, the B♭ triad sharing two tones with that of d minor. "Father, forgive them" is soothing in comparison, appropriately, with an almost sweet chromatic appoggiatura for "them" (illis). Sonata II promises the repentant thief his reward, "Today thou shalt be with me in Paradise." The initial c minor soon gives way to E♭, in the reprise to C major, a lovely kind of reward indeed with flowing sixteenth notes in the second violins accompanying the broad diatonic song of the first violins (more hints of the "Emperor's Hymn" to come). For this vision of paradise Haydn required four horns, two in E♭ and two in C basso. Sonata III brings a stunning tonal change for "Woman, behold thy son"—radiant E major, stated softly three times as a tonic chord, then the simplest of melodies, 5 3, 4 2, 1, with the violins in parallel thirds during the descent. As his thoughts turned again to Mary, Queen of Heaven, Haydn perhaps remembered that early in his career he had chosen similar music for his *Salve regina* in E (assigned by the composer to the year 1756).[43] Haydn used two horns in E sparingly in the "Mulier," mostly for pedal tones; the predominant wind color is provided by a solo flute lending an airy sheen high in its range, when playing the main theme. Sonata IV marks the turning point of the work, the mark of despair and incomprehension. "My God, why have you forsaken me?" turns from the key of four sharps to the key of four flats, a far remove, and yet the third of E major, G♯, corresponds to the third of f minor, A♭, and they even sound at the same pitch near the beginning of both themes. Haydn put strong emphasis on the "why?" (utquid) by making it the highest tone and the only leap in an otherwise conjunct theme, by placing a *sforzato* on this normally weak beat, then bringing in the basses and cellos with another *sforzato* on D♭ two octaves below, which turns the "quid" of "utquid" into a dissonant seventh in need of resolution. The bass D♭ is so much a part of the theme it becomes recognizable in its own right during the subsequent proceedings, which end where they began, in f minor. When Haydn turned the *Seven Last Words* into a vocal-orchestral work he divided it into two parts, as was customary in oratorios, the break coming after Sonata IV.

Sonata V in A major is the only one that begins with a nearly complete phrase before the characterizing scriptural expression occurs, in this case the single word "Sitio" (I thirst). The word is layered on top of the pizzicato theme played by the second violins and violas in parallel thirds and sixths, and overlaps their cadence. That measure-long E in the first violins resolving down a third to coincide with the arrival of the tonic, were it for voice, would be a *messa di voce* (and has a par-

---

[43] *Haydn, Mozart*, pp. 241–42. For music example, see Landon, *Haydn*, 1:159–65.

allel with the entry of the voice in the 1756 antiphon with a long-held "Sal - ve"). Haydn interrupted his idyll with an eruption of e minor, bringing staccato eighth notes in the treble *fortissimo* against a striding bass with leaps reminiscent of the *Introduzione*. When this turbulence subsides, the main motif is in an unusual position against a higher pedal, and it is not just 5 3, but 5 3, 4 2, 4 2, 3 1, clear reference to the beginning of Sonata III. And at this point the harmony clears away to the secondary key of E, the main key of "Mulier." The suggestion Haydn makes is inescapable: "Mulier" and "Sitio" are addressed to the same person, Christ's mother. "Sitio" is the only Sonata in which he did not indicate a repeat of the prima parte. Every movement, including the introduction and even the earthquake, is in sonata form, often treated quite freely. In none does Haydn place repeat signs around the seconda parte.

Sonatas VI and VII employ the keys of g minor and E♭ major, a pairing central to Haydn's *Stabat mater* and used often in his other music, including the contemporaneous Symphony No. 83 in g of the Paris set, with its slow movement in E♭. Haydn decided on an even-toned theme to match the five syllables of "Con-sum-ma-tum est," quite unlike any of the other themes. These tones, 8 6 4 5 1, are sounded tutti *unisoni* and imply the tonal cadence of IV - V - I, lending a compelling sense of finality to "It is finished." The first violin continues by transforming this motto into a more tortured, soft descent to the tonic, reached by the minor second beneath it. This second motif also sounds related to the rough outburst in minor in "Sitio." Sonata VI resumes *forte* with a chain of four rising minor seconds emphasizing the tones B♭ G E♭ D; similar descents with minor-second grace notes are found often in settings of "Crucifixus" in the mass. They also appeared in the despairing Sonata IV, but there were sounded *pianissimo*, like the plaintive cry of a distant voice. After a big cadence on D, full chords *fortissimo*, the last a full measure prolonged by a fermata, we certainly expect to return for more g minor. Instead, Haydn moved on without ado to a gentler lyric theme in the relative major, B♭, with the same chromatic appoggiatura heard in the first theme of Sonata I, which this theme slightly resembles. It sounds as if Haydn were summarizing here. This gentle theme in major (built though it is above the bass of the stern initial motto) projects a sense of release from suffering. The idea becomes ever stronger when the reprise begins with the lyric material in the brighter tonal world of G major and ends there, softly.

The E♭ of Sonata VII, coming after the long stretch of G, makes for a lovely third relationship, the descending major third being one of the composer's favorite tonal moves. "Into Thy hands, Lord, I commend my spirit" inspired Haydn to create an elegant and relatively tranquil movement, the violins playing with mutes and the first violins singing throughout in a nearly aria-like way. An air of resignation hovers over the whole. It ends by dwindling into silence over a long tonic pedal. The violins sound a last 5 3 in parallel thirds, doubled by the flutes and then by the bassoons an octave lower. The two horns in E♭ hold on to a tonic pedal for five measures, marked *sempre più piano* and given in addition a long hairpin sign. Doubling them above is only the first flute. Off come the mutes. *Attaca subito il Terremoto.*

The onset of the earthquake furnishes the greatest contrast of the work, but there were strong contrasts in some of the Sonatas as well. In spite of the limitations imposed by concentrating on the emotions aroused by the scriptural words, Haydn managed nearly throughout to exploit the polarized feelings inspired by the words in order to suit his sonata forms.[44]

Symphonies

Throughout the 1780s Haydn, like Mozart, explored possibilities of earning money in or from the two great metropolises of London and Paris. With London, this usually meant garnering an invitation to compose for the Italian opera in the King's Theatre; with both cities it meant profiting from the many music publishing firms. Instrumental music had become a great commercial success for publishers. The symphonic genre even experienced a spurt in public sales, fueled by the ever-widening circle of amateur orchestras. In his *Magasin der Musik* in 1783, Carl Friedrich Cramer reviewed Haydn's Symphony No. 73 ("La chasse"), which had been issued at Vienna in July 1782 by the firm of Christoph Torricella. Cramer lavished praise on the "great master, who seems to be inexhaustible in ideas," at the same time warning amateurs to study the work before attempting to perform it because "there are in this, as in all his symphonies, difficulties and unexpected progressions."[45] Nevertheless, Cramer hoped that "Heydn [*sic*] will crown this great epoch of the symphony with more such wonderful pieces, and thereby reduce all bad writers of symphonies to silence, or to improving their superficial products, through which none but themselves can derive any pleasure." Crown this great era of the symphony was indeed what Haydn was about to do. Perhaps no one except Mozart fully understood the true magnitude of Haydn's achievements in the genre. Supreme though Haydn was as a symphonist, it is to be doubted that he reduced "all bad writers of symphonies to silence." But he certainly did inspire many imitators.

Symphonies Nos. 75–81

Haydn composed several symphonies ca. 1780 that elude more specific dating. Of these, No. 75 in D has special claims to attention. A few years after its composi-

---

[44] For a sensitive discussion of this point with citations from critical reactions at that time, see Richard Will, *The Characteristic Symphony in the Age of Haydn and Beethoven* (Cambridge, 2002), pp. 103–110.

[45] Landon, *Haydn*, 2:479.

tion Mozart jotted down the first theme of the opening *Presto* in common time, which follows an impressive slow introduction. Mozart labeled his incipit simply "Sinfonia" (Example 4.15). The chromatically raised first degree was bound to

EXAMPLE 4.15. *Haydn, Symphony No. 75, Presto*

Incipit in Mozart's hand, *K. 387d, I*

catch Mozart's attention (the incipit of Haydn's Symphony No. 62 in D notated by Mozart on the same fragment shares this feature). Recall the importance of D D♯ E that begins the fast theme of the overture to *Don Giovanni* (see Example 2.19). Another feature that could have intrigued Mozart is the leap up an octave for the double-stopped *forte* outburst coming after a *piano* beginning in which the tune meekly traverses a limited space step by step. Haydn's slow introduction had begun by outlining the tonic triad softly after a unison D, *fortissimo* (Example 4.16). The reply, which should complement I - V with V - I, begins as if this would

EXAMPLE 4.16. *Haydn, Symphony in D, No. 75, I*

happen, with a *fortissimo* C♯ unison but then answers the initial three-measure unit with six measures, leisurely expanding beyond the expected cadence in m. 8 to include a lovely chromatic rise A A♯ B before falling back down to D. The answer then returns tutti *fortissimo* in unison and another rise through the triad, but *forte* and in d minor, topped by the violins utilizing double-stops for the first time: | ♭ 6 - 5 - ♮ | followed by a soft continuation by step down the tones of the minor scale, coming to rest on the leading tone C♯. The rest is dominant pedal preparing for the arrival of the *Presto* in tonic D, and enlivened with two of Haydn's favorite descending-seventh leaps in the first violins. Not only has tonic D been prepared, but also the outburst that is the *Presto*'s most prominent dynamic, melodic, and rhythmic figure (Example 4.15, m. 4). Any doubts about the importance of that outburst are dispelled by the development section, where Haydn inverted the motif, moved it from place to place, combined it in various ways with the rest of the first theme, and found still other uses. After this, he gave short shrift to the main theme in the reprise, but invented another canonic treatment of it in lieu of a second theme.

The second movement of Symphony No. 75 consists of four clear-cut variations on a simple binary theme of eighteen measures, a hymnic *Poco Adagio* in G and in 3/4 time, played by the first violins *con sordino*. It had a profound effect when played at a concert in London on 26 March 1792, as described by the composer in his notebook: "An English preacher was present who fell into the most profound melancholy on hearing the Andante [incipit] because he had dreamt the previous night that this piece foreshadowed his death. He left the company at once and took to his bed." Later he added, "Today, the 25th of April, I heard from Mr. Barthelemon that this Protestant clergyman had died." Both Griesinger and Dies include the anecdote, the latter with embroidery. In all three sources the notated incipit is labeled *Andante* and consists of the first three measures of the first violin part, Haydn with two added ornaments, Griesinger with a wrong note, and Dies with a different ornament and no articulation. Haydn linked the theme of the *Adagio* with the slow introduction's prominent sarabande rhythm (Example 4.16, mm. 12–13) by using the rhythm no fewer than seven times. The second strain of the *Menuetto Allegretto* coyly introduces the little lyric flourish with the raised fifth degree from mm. 8–9 of the introduction.

The *Finale Vivace* in cut time is a light-hearted frolic in a loose rondo form. Its theme assumes rounded binary form with repeats of both halves. This refrain at first seems innocent of motivic connections with prior material and yet the prominent conjunct descent in its melody 5 4 3 2 sounds vaguely familiar, and the pre-cadential leaps of the melody down a seventh hint at the same nearing the end of the slow introduction. An episode in tonic minor follows the refrain, which then returns, followed by a section that wavers between being an episode in vi and a development section (which has misled some to call the movement a sonata rondo). In the ensuing refrain Haydn gives the second strain to winds alone, which are rudely interrupted by a tutti *fortissimo*, three hammerstrokes on a diminished-seventh chord, followed by a rest. The theme returns and is elaborated in a coda, bringing another instance of three hammerstroke chords plus a rest, this time with tones 6 7 8 up to the high tonic, followed by a soft and mysterious delaying passage with the harmonic rhythm slowed to one chord per measure. The head motif of the refrain makes a timid return, *piano*, accompanied by two horns the first time, by two bassoons the second, playing softly, like a distant hunting call 1 2 3 𝄽, setting up the *fortissimo* third statement with the horns *forte* doubled by the trumpets cutting through the texture with their 3 2 1 𝄽. The final cadence corresponds with what Mozart notated as m. 4 in Example 4.15. A single cell, at once melodic, rhythmic and harmonic (I - V^7 - I), can be heard to unite the outer movements.[46]

Symphony No. 75 demonstrates many features of Haydn's late symphonic style: a slow introduction replete with ideas that nourish subsequent movements (or, if composed last, digests some of their features); intricate thematic development in the fast movements; a hymnic slow movement as theme and variations; and a saucy rondo finale with some sonata-form elements. No wonder Mozart was impressed with the work to the extent of jotting down an identifying theme, perhaps because he wanted to study it further, or perhaps as a reminder to include it in one of his concerts.

Long before Haydn set foot in London, his symphonies were in demand there in public and private concerts. William Foster published Symphony No. 74 in E♭ that he received directly from Haydn in 1781. On 20 February 1782, Foster advertised its performance at one of the last concerts given by Carl Friedrich Abel, who continued the Bach-Abel concerts for a short time after Johann Christian Bach died on 1 January 1782. During 1781, their concert series had included Haydn's well-traveled Symphony No. 53 in D ("L'imperiale"). In 1782, Haydn's future friend the Earl of Abingdon assumed control of these concerts and advertised a series of twelve more, to be given in the Hanover Square Rooms.

Not only were Haydn's symphonies eagerly sought but their composer was as well. In 1782, various reports in the public press announced that Haydn had been engaged and would soon arrive to preside over his works in concerts. There is confirmation of this from Haydn's side. He had prepared three new symphonies specifically for presentation in London, Nos. 76–78, as we know from a letter he wrote to the music publisher Boyer in Paris in answer to a request for his works. The letter is dated 15 July 1783.

> I composed last year three beautiful, magnificent, and by no means overly long symphonies requiring 2 violins, viola, basso, 2 horns, 2 oboes, 1 flute and 1 Fagott [*recte:*

---

[46] For an entirely different reading of Symphony No. 75, one that sets out to show that there are no connections in musical materials among its movements, see Ethan Haimo, *Haydn's Symphonic Forms: Essays in Compositional Logic* (Oxford, 1995), ch. 6.

2 bassoons], nevertheless all very easy, and without much concertante [nicht viel concertirend], for the English gentlemen, and I intended to bring them over myself and produce them there, but a certain circumstance hindered the plan . . . I assure you that these three symphonies will have a huge sale.[47]

Boyer wanted autographs and exclusive rights to print them, also a written contract specifying as much. Haydn cannily dodged all three demands. He claimed, "You must rely on my word of honor and not believe a scrap of paper." Boyer got burned by doing so, as did many other publishers dealing with Haydn.

Haydn's letter to Boyer points up some matters of general interest. By stressing modest length, ease of performance, and little concertante, Haydn may have intended to woo markets where orchestral playing could not be assumed to reach the virtuoso level of his own band or those in the Viennese theaters. Various visitors to London could have told him what to expect of orchestras there. It is also possible that Haydn was reacting to criticisms that his symphonies were too long, too technically demanding, and too concertante in nature for amateur performers. Nevertheless, Symphonies Nos. 76–78, when considered in this light, look scarcely different from his works in the genre that came before and after them.

Symphony No. 76 in E♭ opens with an *Allegro* in 3/4 time that, while it may lack thematic ideas as memorable as those in Symphony No. 75, suggests its own Mozart connection. Haydn's movement foreshadows some devices used by Mozart in the *Allegro* in 3/4 time of his Symphony No. 39 in E♭ of 1788, most obviously flurries of sixteenth notes that serve as punctuation. These and other similarities may be mere coincidence but they raise the question of whether a wider syndrome is involved when two movements by contemporaries share the same key, meter, and tempo. The finale, an *Allegro, ma non troppo* in cut time, offers more of interest than the other movements. It is a sonata form with both parts repeated.

Symphony No. 77 in B♭ makes a better impression. The first movement is a *Vivace* in cut time that has been compared with Haydn's lively overture to his *Orlando paladino*, also composed in 1782. At the beginning of the second movement, *Andante sostenuto* in 3/8 time and in F, Haydn planted an odd chromatic descent, G G♭ F, as an unusual way of connecting the first eight measures with their repetition. The G♭ is eventually elaborated late in the movement, when it is interpreted as a seventh resolving to the chord of D♭ to provide a new harmonization of the theme's beginning. Instances like this, of which Haydn was fond, provide a distant ancestor to the famously intrusive C♯ in the finale of Beethoven's Symphony No. 8 in F. Haydn follows his *Andante* with a charming *Menuetto Alle-*

[47] The original letter in German was not available in full until published in Armin Raab, "Haydns Briefe an den Verleger Boyer," *Haydn Studien* 8 (2003): 237–52; 237–38.

gro with lots of cross rhythms. The finale, *Allegro spiritoso* in 2/4 time, has generated a literature of its own. One scholar claimed it was a pioneer in Haydn's creation of his own kind of sonata rondo finale.[48] Another rejected the claim, saying that the theme is merely in rounded binary form with both strains given a written-out repetition, while use of the first theme as material for the second is nothing unusual for Haydn; in sum, "The finale of Symphony No. 77 has little claim to be considered a rondo of any kind."[49] Nevertheless, the movement appeared in a widely used anthology as the only representative of Haydn.[50] The simple cut of the main theme and its many repeated tones give it the homespun charm of a folksong, and there is a nice twist to end the movement when Haydn condensed the tune's eight measures to four.

Symphony No. 78 in c begins as if it were going to be another minor-mode saga of struggle and toil like the Symphony No. 52 in c of ca. 1770.[51] The opening movement of that work is an *Allegro* in common time. This one is a *Vivace* in 3/4 time, but the first three tones, C E♭ B♮, are the same in both. In 1782, Haydn continued with a diminished-seventh leap up, contracted to a sixth in two subsequent leaps while becoming *piano*, then *pianissimo*, as the treble outlines a Neapolitan-sixth chord before proceeding smoothly to the cadence. It is a prediction that the whole symphony will take a less rugged stance than does Symphony No. 52. This symphony, in line with Haydn's general description of the three, is less challenging to performers and auditors alike. Instead of struggle there is a rather graceful contest as to which would prevail, minor or major, E♭ or E♮. The *Vivace* ends in c. It is followed by an *Adagio* in 2/4 time and in E♭, a lovely movement with a theme initiated by a falling third, 5 3, like movements III and V in the *Seven Last Words* of three or four years later. Without further ado, the *Menuetto Allegretto* turns E♭ into E♮, the first tone of the rising upbeat triadic figure with which the first violins introduce the melody. Not far into the second strain the same melody returns but in E♭, before turning back via c minor to C major. A falling third, G E♭, initiates the perky *Finale Presto* in 2/4 time and in c. This rounded binary form with repeats gives way to a shorter section in the same form and on the same theme, but in C major. Haydn's finale is truly a sonata rondo by virtue of an impressive development section. Approaching the end there are some teasing delays and long pauses, as if the belle of the ball were trying to decide which of her two beaux to accept. Will there be one more return to c minor before the end? Certainly not! C major prevails.

---

[48] Malcolm S. Cole, "Haydn's Symphonic Rondo Finales: Their Structural and Stylistic Evolution," *Haydn Yearbook 13* (1982): 113–42, summarizing the author's earlier writings on the subject.

[49] Stephen C. Fisher, "Further Thoughts on Haydn's Rondo Finales," *Haydn Yearbook 17* (1992): 85–107.

[50] *Norton Anthology of Western Music* [1st ed.], ed. Claude V. Palisca (New York, 1980), 2 vols., 2:112.

[51] *Haydn, Mozart*, pp. 292–94.

Haydn followed the symphonies of 1782 with another three of similar cast, again with one of them beginning in the minor mode, Symphonies No. 79 in F, No. 80 in d, and No. 81 in G. He may have thought of these six symphonies as a set since he repeated no key from the first triad in the second. A letter he wrote on 25 October 1784 to the firm of Boyer and Nadermann in Paris offered the latest symphonies: "You accepted three symphonies I composed and now I am offering you three more, entirely new, diligently composed [fleissig bearbeitet], neatly and correctly copied, for fifteen ducats, on offer through the end of November. If you accept I shall hasten to send you at the first opportunity the keyboard works requested in your last letter." The symphonies did not appear under these auspices, as far as is known. Perhaps these publishers discovered meanwhile that Haydn had sold Symphonies Nos. 76–78 in triple copies and that the editions of Torricella in Vienna and Foster in London during 1784 actually preceded their own Paris edition (dated 1785).

Symphony No. 79 in F begins with the first violins, doubled an octave lower by the first bassoon, playing a gentle cantilena—the kind of singing *Allegro* theme of which Haydn had lately made only occasional use. At the reprise, the flute joins the violins in singing it. The theme then passes into the minor whence it slips off into a tour of related cadences on chords of two, three, and four flats. Another feature of the theme is the strong pentatonic flavor of its beginning, an emphasis that will return in the finale's theme. The second movement, an *Adagio cantabile* in 3/4 time and in B♭, has a theme in rounded binary form with repeats written out. The theme breaks into short segments separated by pauses that are then bridged over by the winds on repetition. After varied restatements of this long theme Haydn plunges abruptly into a section in cut time marked *un poco allegro*. Here he introduces a comic-opera kind of theme, replete with patter-like staccato repeated notes, also in rounded binary form with repeats, and sounding as if it might be quoted from some popular song. One expects the *Adagio* to return with its more soulful song but it does not. Comedy triumphs in a kind of coda with one more go-around for the comic tune, which then disintegrates into a *pianissimo* statement with pauses before an exultant *fortissimo* cadence. Formalists may look at this movement askance while others can just enjoy it as good fun and even high drama. The comedy continues with the *Menuetto Allegretto* that also plays with pauses, while its trio alludes to the popular-sounding tune in the previous movement. The *Finale Vivace* in 2/4 time is a jolly rondo.

Symphony No. 80 in d does not long remain faithful or return often to the minor mode of its opening, *Allegro spiritoso* in 3/4, which is stormy and features the bass climbing up a tortuous path in quarter notes against the torrent of sixteenth notes holding a tonic pedal in the treble. It is usual after beginnings like this to dwell for a time on the dignified appearance of the relative major as a counterbalance to all the turbulence. Here the relative F arrives as a continuation of the stormy music and when something finally arrives that might be considered a theme, it is a little Ländler tune of seven measures, with pizzicato oom-pah-pah accompaniment. The tune ends lamely, in what is a four-measure antecedent followed by a three-measure consequent, as if the cadence came too soon. After repetition of the prima parte, the seconda parte begins with two measures of silence. Then, like Harlequin in an improvised farce, the Ländler tune appears, accompaniment and all, in an unexpected place—D♭. Perhaps it was not so unexpected to those accustomed to Haydn's ways, for the composer often dropped down a third at this crucial juncture. In the development the stormy initial theme fights it out with the cheerful and oddly-shaped Ländler, the combat taking them to a variety of keys. D minor returns but just in passing during this long development. When the reprise begins, it is not in d but in D, and considerably abbreviated. This comedy ends with the light touch of the Ländler, in D and is completed by the additional measure it always lacked, a mere duplication of its cadence.

One critic uses harsh words for the Ländler, calling it "this cheap tune," "trivial sounding" and "not even a decent antecedent-consequent period," one that pops up "in all manner of peculiar keys."[52] Denigrating language and a moral stance such as this may convey something of what is involved but misses the fun with which Haydn deflates his own heated rhetoric. The *Adagio* in cut time is in B♭. It begins with a melodic turn around the fifth degree, 5 6 5 4 3, that may remind listeners of the famous Romance in Mozart's Piano Concerto No. 20 in d, K. 466, a movement that is also in B♭. Both bring a nocturnal quality of reverie to contrast with their respective first movements in d. The Menuetto reverts to d minor and has the same march of the bass upward against the treble as the beginning of the first movement. It is followed by a Trio in D with constant triplet motion accompanying a melody with strong emphasis on the tone F♯. This same tone initiates the *Finale Presto* in 2/4 time. The offbeat beginning may fool listeners into hearing as a downbeat what is an upbeat, at least until the half cadence brings them up short. The development of this sonata form ends on the triad of F♯, V/vi. From there Haydn slips directly into the reprise. There are countless cases in which he makes the same leap from V/vi to I.

Symphony No. 81 in G starts softly with a tonic pedal and iterated eighth notes in the bass, over which Haydn piled one dissonance after another, at first a flat seventh, F♮, then above that a C. Double dissonances like these hint at the proximity of Mozart's so-called "Dissonant" Quartet in C, K. 465, completed in January 1785. The melodic sighs produced by the resolutions of these dissonances also bring Mozart's slow introduction of the quartet to mind. Haydn's *Vivace* in common time is a lot faster, but he prolonged the dissonant tones so that the

---

[52] James Webster, *Haydn's "Farewell" Symphony and the Idea of Classical Style: Through-Composition and Cyclic Integration in His Instrumental Music* (Cambridge, 1991), p. 167.

effect is not so different. Another piece that resembles the symphony's beginning is Haydn's String Quartet in B♭, Opus 50, No. 1, which starts with a throbbing tonic pedal in the bass against which various non-chord tones are deployed. To begin the seconda parte of the *Vivace*, Haydn descended a minor third from D to B (V/vi). Where the reprise should begin, he elided into material following the main theme and saved this striking idea for use as a coda. For his second movement the composer chooses not C but D and an *Andante* in 6/8 time, a rounded binary theme with repeats that gives rise to four variations, the second a *minore*. The *Menuetto Allegretto* reflects the *Vivace*'s most striking feature by insisting on a dissonant F♮ in the bass, although it conflicts with the F♯ in the treble, and then a dissonant C♮ to begin the second strain. The Trio, also in G, takes an unusual course by ending with eight measures in g. The unity of the whole work is subtly reinforced by the theme of the *Finale Allegro, ma non troppo* in cut time, giving rise to another large sonata form, like the *Vivace*. It begins with a long-held note in the treble against eighth-note motion in the bass, which lands on a tone that turns the treble into a dissonant seventh in need of resolution. On a structural level, there is a similarity between outer movements in the way the seconda parte begins by dropping down a minor third from D to B.

Haydn also composed a few solo concertos with orchestra during the first half of the 1780s. The *Journal de Paris* dated 26–28 April 1784 announced that Maria Theresia von Paradis would play a new keyboard concerto by Haydn at a forthcoming *concert spirituel* ("Mlle Paradis exécutera un nouvelle Concerto de clavecin de M. Haydn"). But in the preserved records of keyboard concertos by Viennese composers during 1784 at this renowned concert series only Kozeluch is mentioned. On the other hand, Boyer announced publication of a *Second Concerto pour le clavecin où le forte-piano . . . exécuté au Concert Spirituel par Mademoiselle Paradis composé par J. Haydn.* The "second concerto" in question was the one in G, Hob. XVIII:4, apparently brought by the blind pianist, or sent to her from Vienna, to join her many concertos by Kozeluch and Mozart's Piano Concerto No. 18 in B♭, K. 456. Boyer's "first concerto" by Haydn was his well-known Keyboard Concerto in D, Hob. XVIII:11. This is the work that concludes with the great Gypsy Rondo, called in Boyer's edition (which may be the first) "Rondo Hongrois," a piece with such modal delights as the sudden chordal slippages of a tone from e to D and Hungarian "Turkish" specialties such as the alternation of tones one and five. Another solo concerto that matches this one in excellence is the Cello Concerto in D of 1783. It is thought to have been written for Anton Kraft, first cellist in Haydn's orchestra, and if so, he must have been a fine player in order to meet the work's technical demands. These aside, the concerto is in Haydn's suavest and most melodious manner, almost as if he were competing with the very galant cello concertos of Boccherini.

What Paris most wanted from Haydn was nevertheless his symphonies, and hardly a concert took place there that did not begin with or include one of them. Parisian publishers and dealers did their best to keep up with the demand. In this light it seemed only a matter of time before some French maecenas commissioned a whole set of new symphonies from the composer.

Contexts for the Paris Symphonies

Empress Maria Theresa had put great store by her alliance of the Habsburg Monarchy with the French realm against Prussia and England during the 1750s, with consequences from the Seven Years' War (1756–63) that were disastrous for France. Nevertheless the alliance continued and was sealed by a marriage of state. In 1770, the Empress sent her youngest daughter, Marie Antoinette, born in 1755, to be married to the Dauphin Louis, heir to the French throne, who was only a year older. The young pair acceded to the throne in 1774 at the death of Louis XV. French foreign policy was henceforth in the hands of the formidable minister Count Charles de Vergennes. At the instigation of Beaumarchais, Vergennes persuaded Louis XVI to support the American colonies in their War of Independence from Great Britain. While French armed and naval forces were engaged abroad, affairs on the Continent were roiled by the expansionist policies of Emperor Joseph II, Maria Theresa's son and co-ruler. The policies had begun in the 1770s at the expense of Poland, then aimed at absorbing Bavaria, and followed with designs on territories in the Balkans ruled by Turkey. For many generations France had been allied with the Ottoman Empire. Vergennes was a former ambassador to the Sublime Porte and remained a steadfast ally. So did Maria Theresa, who was grateful to the Turks for their support during the troubled times of her succession. After her death in late 1780, Joseph, as sole ruler, struck an alliance with Catherine II of Russia, who was bent upon dismembering the Ottoman Empire. The Franco-Austrian alliance became increasingly precarious as a result of this. Joseph pressured his sister Marie Antoinette to sway French policy in favor of his schemes.[53] His overbearing ways were considered demeaning to her station as Queen of France and mother of "les enfants de France."

Joseph II counted heavily on the Austrian ambassador to the court of Versailles, Count Mercy-Argenteau, a Liègeois, to intimidate Marie Antoinette. Count Mercy was thirty years her senior and had acted as a father figure to her since she arrived in France. During the 1770s, he made sure that Gluck, her former teacher, retained her favor and was offered a lucrative court appointment. Not only did Gluck reside in the Count's mansion near Saint Sulpice when in Paris, he also wrote three title roles for the soprano Rosalie Levasseur, who also

---

[53] Antonia Fraser, *Marie Antoinette: The Journey* (New York, 2001), pp. 195–98. Derek Beales puts the emperor in the best possible light in *Joseph II* (1987), 1:304–5.

resided there as the Count's mistress. In the 1780s, after Gluck had won over the Parisians, his disciple Antonio Salieri, the favorite composer of Joseph II, came from Vienna to replace him at the Opéra. The emperor sent Mercy specific instructions on how to manipulate public opinion in favor of Salieri.[54] A clearer case of cultural politics than this could hardly be found. Haydn never won the emperor's favor. But Vienna could only smile at the great success his symphonies enjoyed in France and bask in the further prestige this lent Austrian music and, by extension, Austrian policies. One of his new symphonies for Paris, No. 85 in B♭, quickly overtook the others in popularity and had the honor of being dubbed upon its first edition "La Reine de France."

The commission for the Paris Symphonies came from a dashing young military officer, scion of an old noble family, Claude-François-Marie Rigolet, comte d'Ogny, who was born at Dijon in 1757.[55] He was the eldest son of Jean Rigolet, Intendant Général des Postes, and became adjunct postal director of the realm in 1785. In Paris the Rigolets inhabited a fine house on the rue Coqueret (or Coq-Héron) next to the Hôtel Royal des Postes on the rue Plâtrière, near the church of Saint Eustache.

Count d'Ogny was a cellist and music lover who used his social standing and great wealth to further a series of concerts given by the Masonic *Loge Olympique de la Parfaite Estime*, which was chartered by the Grand-Orient of France in 1779. As a collector D'Ogny amassed one of the richest musical collections of the time, of which he had a catalogue made.[56] He is remembered most for enriching the repertory of his lodge's famous orchestra by getting Haydn to compose six works known as the Paris Symphonies, Nos. 83–87 in 1785–86, and three more, Nos. 90–92, in 1788–89.

The Loge Olympique had its official seat in the arcades of the Palais Royal at No. 65. Its members numbered 200 gentlemen and 102 ladies. The men paid an annual fee of four Louis d'or to belong, the ladies less. To be eligible for membership candidates had first to belong to another Masonic lodge (in Paris women had their own *Loges d'Adoption*). An almanac of the Palais Royal for the year 1786 describes their formal activities and adds a few words about their concerts.

> The meetings strike one by their éclat and brilliance. They are remarkable above all for the tone of grandeur, decency, and politeness that reigns there. Besides the sessions at the Palais Royal, the society gives extraordinary entertainments. In 1785 there were several concerts in which the most famous foreign virtuosi joined those

---

[54] Rice, *Salieri* (1998), pp. 312–14.

[55] For an engraved portrait of him in profile, see László Somfai, *Joseph Haydn: His Life in Contemporary Pictures* (London, 1969), p. 97.

[56] The collection was dispersed by sale in 1791. See Barry S. Brook, *La symphonie française dans la second moitié du XVIIIe siècle*, 3 vols., 1:341–49.

of the capital. Concerts were given in the rue Coqueron [chez Rigolet?]. But hence-forth the Society has obtained a hall in the Tuileries Palace for their concerts and balls during the winter. Among the events they gave in 1785 all Paris noticed the one at the Menus with distinguished foreign guests.[57]

"Menus" refers to the Salle des Menus Plaisirs du Roy in the rue Berger, one of the finest Parisian theaters.[58] There is an engraving that shows the interior of a small theater, with stage, boxes, and benches, labeled "Salle de Spectacle de la Société Olympique."[59] It comes from the rather crude series of popular engravings enti-tled *Vues de Paris* dating from ca. 1795. This same series included a little hall with the caption "Salle de Concert de la Société Olympique" (Figure 4.3). The room is empty except for one couple standing on the floor, another depicted looking down from an encircling gallery above, and several tall music stands to the left side. A space this small would be reason enough to move the well-attended concerts and balls to the sought-after hall in the Tuileries Palace. There they took place in the large Salle des Gardes adjacent to the Salle des Cent Suisses, where the Concert Spirituel had held forth since its founding in 1725 until April 1784.[60] Thus, Haydn's new symphonies for Paris were first performed next door to where Mozart heard his "Paris" Symphony, K. 297, in June 1778.[61] When the royal family was forced to move to the Tuileries in October 1789, all concert functions there ceased.[62]

Concerts of the Société Olympique were supported by a distinguished list of subscribers and advisors, twenty-four "free associates" who were non-paying auditors. In 1780, the subscribers included Baron de Bagge, well-known for his own concert-giving, and Chabanon, writer on music and member of the august Académie Française, Jean-Benjamin de La Borde, and the composers Étienne Méhul and Giovanni Battista Viotti. The free associates included Nicolas-Marie Dalayrac, Giuseppe Maria Cambini, Nicolas-Étienne Framery, Louis-Joseph Francoeur, and François-André Danican Philidor.

The orchestra was a large one by the standards of the time, more than double the size of Haydn's at Esterháza. Its 65 members numbered 14 first and 14 sec-

---

[57] *Almanach du Palais-Royal pour l'année 1786*, cited by Jean-Luc Quoy-Bodin, "L'Orchestre de la Société Olympique en 1786," *Revue de Musicologie* 70 (1984): 95–105; 96.

[58] *Music in European Capitals*, p. 610 and p. 707, fig. 7.2.

[59] Reproduced in Brook, *La symphonie française*, 1:340. Fully-staged operas were the prerogatives of the royal theaters, but semi-staged works could be performed elsewhere. Luigi Cherubini wrote two dra-matic cantatas for the Société Olympique, *Amphion* (1786) and *Circe* (1789). He was a member of the society.

[60] Warwick Lister, "The First Performance of Haydn's 'Paris' Symphonies," *Eighteenth-Century Music* 1 (2004): 289–300. See the diagram of the main floor of the Tuileries Palace, p. 293, fig. 3.

[61] Historian John Rogister reports on proposals in Paris to rebuild the Tuileries Palace in the *Times Literary Supplement* of 19 March 2004: 12–13). The ruins of the old palace were demolished in the 1870s.

[62] *Music in European Capitals*, p. 617.

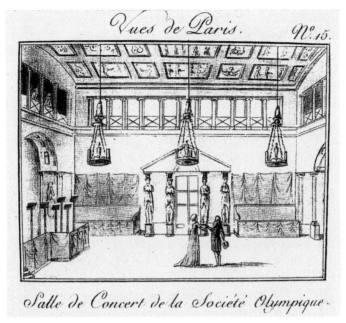

FIGURE 4.3. Concert Room of the Société Olympique, Paris.

ond violins, 7 violas, 10 cellos, 7 contrabasses, 4 horns, three flutes, and pairs of oboes, bassoons, clarinets, and trumpets, plus timpani. Some of the most famous players in Paris belonged to it. The first flute was François Devienne. Jean Bréval and Jean-Louis Duport were cellists. Julien Navoigille was the first violin, and an associate member of the society. First horn Jean Le Brun and first clarinet Michel Yost were then reputed to be the best in Paris. The second violins included Marie-Alexandre Guenin and Jean-Jérôme Imbault, the prominent music publisher who brought out the first edition of Haydn's Paris Symphonies, which he inscribed "from the Repertory of the Loge Olympique."[63]

An intermediary between Haydn and the Count d'Ogny is said to have been the Chevalier de Saint-Georges, the glamorous mulatto swordsman also known for his exploits with the violin.[64] His connection with either Haydn or the Count is not supported by any solid evidence. Saint-Georges, because of his European reputation and experiences, would at least have been a credible go-between. He is not known to have been a Freemason, yet because so many prominent musicians in Paris were, it seems likely that he too followed the fashion, as did so

---

[63] For more details on the subscribers, associates, and orchestra members, see Jean-Luc Quoy-Bodin, "L'orchestre de la Société Olympique en 1786."
[64] *Music in European Capitals*, pp. 680–85.

many prominent musicians in Vienna. And that brings us to another subject, one that can be deferred no longer: Haydn and Freemasonry.

Requests from the Loge Olympique for the symphonies probably reached Haydn in late 1784 or early 1785, close to the time when he was proposing himself for membership in Vienna's foremost Masonic lodge, whose members included the distinguished humanist Joseph von Sonnenfels. On 29 November 1784, Haydn wrote to the Master of Ceremonies of True Concord stating that he wished to join the brotherhood and moreover, that he had long admired it. His request begins: "The favorable impression I have of Freemasonry awakened in me long ago the most sincere desire to be admitted to this order on account of its humane and wise principles." His petition was successful. He was balloted white by the lodge on 24 January 1785 and invited to present himself for initiation on Friday four days later. Mozart, initiated into the Beneficence Lodge on 14 December 1784, as we saw above, came with thirty other guests to True Concord on the appointed day for Haydn's initiation, but Haydn did not because the invitation failed to reach him in time. As it happened, Haydn was initiated on Friday 11 February 1785. Mozart certainly would have been present had he not that very evening been giving the first of six successive Friday concerts by subscription in the Mehlgrube. On the following day, Saturday 12 February, the famous quartet party took place in Mozart's lodgings, when the latest three of the six string quartets Mozart dedicated to Haydn were performed. Two of Haydn's lodge brothers, the barons Anton and Barthomeus von Tinti, filled out the quartet (probably on cello and second violin). Leopold Mozart's enthralled description of the occasion is well known. As to the coincidence between Haydn's becoming a Mason and the commission from Paris, the least that can be said is that, given the international links specifically prized among all lodges, Masonic brotherhood could only have furthered a desire to cooperate in both parties. Masonic circles in Paris continued to honor their Brother Joseph in Vienna to the end of his life.

We lack verifiable knowledge of the commission sent or brought to Haydn or what he was paid. The only source that has ever been cited on these questions is late and demonstrably marred by errors. It claims that the Société Olympique paid 25 louis for each of the six symphonies, "which seemed a colossal sum to Haydn, who had up to this point earned nothing for his symphonies."[65] The sum was so colossal in fact as to be quite unbelievable. Such a sum for all six would have been closer to the going rate for that time. Mozart considered five louis a handsome fee for his "Paris" Symphony. Haydn, as we have seen, was already earning tidy sums for selling his symphonies to several publishers. Claiming that he had earned nothing only throws more doubt on the rest: "The Chevalier de

---

[65] Henri Barbedette, "Haydn, sa vie et ses œuvres," *Le Ménestrel* 38 (1871): 27, cited in Brook, *La symphonie française*, 1:378, n. 6.

Saint-Georges, then first violin and director of this society, was in charge of the negotiations and he deducted five louis per symphony for himself on the publication of the symphonies by Sieber." Saint-Georges was neither first violin nor director of the society. The first publisher of the symphonies was not Sieber but Brother Imbault.

Imbault's first edition bears a printed title on the violino primo part of Symphony No. 85: "La Reine de France." The work, which was by far the most popular of the set, to judge by its many reprints and arrangements, many bearing the title "La Reine," included a second movement that Haydn called a Romance, an *Allegretto* in gavotte rhythm. Mozart had written several Romances by 1785 but for Haydn this was apparently a first. C. F. Pohl in his ground-breaking work on Haydn, described the movement as "charming variations on a well-loved Romance," and provided a texted song to a nearly identical melody as evidence, "La gentille et jeune Lisette."[66] Pohl cites no source for this song and none has been found since. It is most unlikely that the text predates Haydn's music. Any French lover of Haydn's music with a bent for making up verse could have added these simple lines in the pastoral tradition. The practice was sanctioned by no less a figure than Grétry in the first volume of his memoirs, which came out in 1789, one year after the six symphonies were published and about two years after they were first heard in concert. "Quelle amateur de musique n'a été saisi d'admiration, en écoutant les belles symphonies d'*Haydn*! Cent fois je leur ai prêté les paroles qu'elles semblent demander."[67]

The question remains whether this Romance or its text had any connection with Marie Antoinette. Her penchant for the rural and pastoral expressed itself most famously in the little model village she had built behind her favorite residence, the deceptively simple and supremely elegant Petit Trianon, designed by the royal architect Anges-Jacques Gabriel and given to her by her husband.[68] More to the point here were the amateur theatricals she loved to perform with her courtiers in the theater at Le Petit Trianon, where she often sang the roles of country lasses as innocent as the young maiden described in "La gentille et jeune Lisette." These theatricals, when studied, may provide a link between "La Reine" and the Romance of "Jeune Lisette." Besides cultivating her voice, Marie Antoinette played the harp, guitar, and keyboard instruments. She was severely criticized by some for whatever she did, including allowing herself to be portrayed by Elisabeth Vigée-Lebrun unadorned, in a plain white muslin dress deemed too simple for a queen of France.

---

[66] C. F. Pohl, *Joseph Haydn*, 3 vols. (Leipzig, 1875–1927), 2:275.

[67] André-E.-M. Grétry, *Mémoires, ou, Essais sur la musique*, 3 vols. (Paris, 1789–94; reprint 1971), 1:348.

[68] Wend von Kalnein, *Architecture in France in the Eighteenth Century* (New Haven, 1995), pp. 155–56.

THE PARIS SYMPHONIES, NOS. 82–87

Imbault's prime edition of the six symphonies stems directly from Haydn's autographs. Nos. 82, 84, and 86 bear the date 1786, Nos. 83 and 87 the date 1785, as No. 85 did originally (the autograph does not survive intact). Imbault published the scores in order as he received them from D'Ogny, and the Loge Olympique autographs were numbered at this point from one to six as follows: 83 (g), 87 (A), 85 (B♭); 82 (C), 86 (D), 84 (E♭). Intentionally or not this produced the tonal sequence of two identical minor thirds rising by step, an unwonted symmetry. Sieber of Paris secured Haydn's permission or "concession" to reprint the symphonies (the person who reviewed the case for the French authorities regarding such moves was none other than Grétry). The order is the same in Sieber's edition except that No. 85 "La Reine" was moved to first place. In a letter dated Esterháza 2 August 1787, Haydn asked Artaria to print them in the order 87, 85, 83; 84, 86, 82. He also told Artaria to delay publishing the last three (those dated 1786), so as not to precede Imbault's publication. Artaria disregarded Haydn's wishes and published the symphonies in the order that has since prevailed.

There is a merit in considering the earlier symphonies apart from those dated 1786 and we follow Haydn's suggested order. Symphony No. 87 in A is the least performed of the set and with some reason. The opening *Vivace* in common time charges forward with a burst of energy in nearly constant eight-note motion and frequent upbeat patterns that make it sound rather like the Haydn of an earlier time. Indeed, they bring to mind Haydn's Symphony No. 28 in A of 1765, which also switches back and forth between tutti *unisoni* and four voice parts in its first movement (albeit in 3/4 time). The 1765 work required only strings, while winds lend color and play an important thematic role twenty years later. The *Adagio* in D and in 3/4 time gives still more prominence to the winds, with solos for flute and the first oboe, and an eight-measure passage for winds alone at the close of the prima parte; after a short transitional passage the winds are given the honor of ushering in the reprise. A long concertante-style duet for the flute and oboe, ended by the solo bassoon's entrance, sounds like a written-out cadenza. Mozart's use of wind solos in his piano concertos of 1784 spring readily to mind and perhaps it was Mozart who told Haydn that the wind players in Paris were particularly strong and reliable. One of Mozart's favorite cadential figures, 5 6 1 ↓ 7 ↑ 1, occurring in both middle movements of his "Paris" Symphony, occurs also in the slow movements of Haydn's Symphonies 28 and 87. The very galant Menuet of Symphony No. 87, replete with three-note slides and triplets, uses the same melodic figure for its cadence. In the Trio the solo oboe shines again and pursues its line all the way up to high E, one tone higher than Mozart recommended to Attwood as appropriate for an orchestral oboe. The *Finale vivace* in cut time renews the driving rhythms of the first movement. In sonata form, the seconda parte begins with a harmonic surprise by dropping down a minor third (from V^7 to V^7/vi). Before the end, Haydn introduced one of his favorite stalling moves, a sudden V^7/V with fermata giving way to a similarly held V^7 (both chords in inversions). To end Haydn stressed the same climb up and down the tones of the tonic triad that began the symphony.

Symphony No. 83 in g starts with another climb up the triad, but on the way to the fifth above the tonic there is a shockingly dissonant C♯ appoggiatura in strong metric position. The consequent phrase beginning over dominant harmony offers an even more grinding dissonance in the equivalent spot. Parisians had heard earlier symphonies in the key of g that began with an emphatic rising triad, such as the one by Simon Leduc.[69] Perhaps none had been so angry in tone as the beginning of this *Allegro spiritoso* in common time. It was the soft second theme in the relative major, with a perky little tune, lightly accompanied, that apparently drew the most attention. Almost every tone of the melody is preceded by an appoggiatura of a rising minor second, as if in parody of the exaggerated rising-second appoggiatura of the main theme. On repetition, the solo oboe accentuates this comic theme by a stuttering repetition in dotted rhythm of B♭ on every quarter-note beat. This device suggested to the French, whether intended by Haydn or not, the clucking of a hen laying an egg, hence the sobriquet "La Poule" that they applied to the whole symphony. If nothing else, it was an imaginative response that shows they were really listening. The seconda parte begins by dropping down a minor third to state the grim opening theme, then quickly giving way to the comic second theme before getting down to the serious business by putting the main theme through a long and very contrapuntal development. The reprise, correspondingly, makes short work of this theme before relaxing into G major for an encore of the delightful second theme, the mimicking solo oboe perching this time on its high D. In accord with a strong tradition of works in g minor, operative in France as elsewhere, Haydn chose E♭ for his completely serious slow movement, a lyrical *Andante* in 3/4 time that has features in common with the *Andante* of Mozart's great Symphony No. 40 in g minor.[70] Unlike Mozart, Haydn did not return to g minor for the remaining movements. His joyous *Menuet Allegretto* and trio are both in G, as is the *Finale Vivace* in the rather rare 12/8 time. There is a sing-song, folklike quality to this finale in sonata form that makes one wonder if there is a French equivalent to the nursery song "Three blind mice," for Haydn parallels the tune of "They all ran after the farmer's wife." In his violin tutor of 1756, Leopold Mozart belittled the compound meters of 9/8 and 12/8 as "worthless stuff."[71] Mozart himself, on the other hand, put both meters to good use.

[69] *Music in European Capitals*, p. 671, ex. 6.13.
[70] Landon and Wyn Jones, *Haydn*, pp. 226–27.
[71] Leopold Mozart, *Versuch einer gründlichen Violinschule*, trans. Edith Knocker (London, 1948), p. 32.

Symphony No. 85 in B♭, "La Reine," is one of three works in the set that begins with a slow introduction, and perhaps a crucial one in the composer's decision that, thenceforth, nearly all his symphonies would begin thus. Majestic chords are outlined by unison rises in dotted rhythm to start this *Adagio* in cut time, in order I, vi, IV, I. Upon regaining the tonic the first violins add sweeping upward scales to the progression's varied repeat, which lands the music on V, a pedal over which many more dotted rhythms are deployed. It could be that both the sweeping scales and dotted rhythm are meant by Haydn to suggest the old French overture.[72] The *Adagio* passes smoothly into the *Vivace* in 3/4 time as its final protracted C descends to B♭, a held tone in the treble resolving eventually as a suspended dissonance, while the B♭ in the bass leads off a lightly tripping plunge down seven tones to C, making necessary the treble's resolution to A (I - V) (Example 4.17). On repetition (V - I), the treble resolves from C to B♭ by way of

EXAMPLE 4.17. *Haydn, Symphony in B♭, No. 85 ("La Reine"), I*

an *échappée*. From this invertible counterpoint in two parts (the violins in unison, the violas and basses in octaves) Haydn constructed nearly the entire *Vivace*. After the soft main theme, *forte* returns, as do the rising scales of the *Adagio* and its I - vi - IV - V progression. A return of the main theme, reorchestrated, is followed again by the loud passage with rising scales, leading this time to a transition that makes elaborate preparations for the arrival of the second key. What arrives, surprisingly, is not F but f minor, a *fortissimo* outburst that parallels the beginning of Haydn's Symphony No. 45 in f♯ minor. The "Farewell" Symphony of Haydn was well known in Paris at the time, having been recently performed there. It ended the last program of the *concert spirituel* in the Salle des Cent Suisses on 24 April 1784, presumably with the same theatrics of leave-taking as at Esterháza. For the knowing few, hearing reference to it in "La Reine" must have provided a delicious irony.

The *Vivace*'s true second theme in the dominant, which is merely the main theme again reorchestrated, restores the movement's placid temper. The seconda parte, just as in the first movements of Symphonies 87 and 83, begins by dropping down a minor third from F to D (V/vi). Haydn brings back the stormy syncopa-

[72] For an early symphony that updates the older French overture, see François Martin's Overture in D of 1751, in *Music in European Capitals*, p. 648, ex. 6.7.

tions from the "Farewell" Symphony in the development but mostly he puts his main theme through its paces until coming to a very long pedal on D, V/vi, which is not resolved but is followed directly by tonic B♭ and the reprise. Haydn was partial to following a big statement of V/vi directly by I all his life. In one of his last works, the "Creation" Mass in B♭ of 1801, he achieves a sublime effect with this progression between the last two sections. In the *Vivace* of "La Reine," he makes short work of the reprise, as usual, and signals a repeat of the seconda parte.

The *Romance Allegretto* is in cut time and in E♭. Its lengthy and loving treatment of a simple song offers the symphony's only plateau of relaxation. The *Menuetto Allegretto* is as robust and sturdy as its Ländler-type Trio is fresh and winsome, a bassoon solo that evokes rural Austrian bands. For the *Finale Presto* in 2/4 time Haydn chose a rondo-sonata hybrid form. Not long after the rondo theme makes its first return he unleashed a development section nearly as tense as that in the opening *Vivace*. It begins with the progression I - vi - IV, familiar from the symphony's outset, and includes a long stretch of V/vi before heading back to I for the refrain. After a short coda, emphatic cadences bring the symphony to a close with three resounding tonic chords, evenly spaced. Every one of the Paris Symphonies ends with the same three tonic thumps. Or are they three knocks? And did they possess Masonic significance?

Symphony No. 84 in E♭ is prefaced by a weighty slow introduction, about double the length of the *Adagio* that begins "La Reine." This *Largo* in 3/4 time flows smoothly and presages the more mystical introductions of some of Haydn's latest symphonies, especially No. 103 ("Drumroll"), also in E♭. Here there is nothing so dramatic as a timpani solo, but the steady tread in even quarter notes is common in both. Much will be made of the treble's conjunct descending fourths that end with an ascent of a second. They pass into the bass in a slightly condensed form with chromatic enhancement, lending a sense of unease, even mystery to the proceedings (Example 4.18). The following *Allegro* in cut time presents a

EXAMPLE 4.18. *Haydn, Symphony in E♭, No. 84, I*

blithe and singing main theme, a regular period divided into 4 + 4 measures. The second tonal area in the dominant begins with the same idea but sung by the winds instead of the first violins. After this the music becomes more chromatic and after a *fortissimo* arrival of the ♭VI chord (G♭) the first violins shudder down in eighth notes on the tones D♭, C♭, B♭, A♮, B♭, recalling the slithering chromatics of the bass in the example, mm. 5–10. The seconda parte begins without tonal disjunction, merely continuing on in the dominant, B♭, where there is another statement of the main theme that gets derailed. Again, Haydn develops his material at length, so that the seconda parte ends up being nearly twice the length of the prima parte. Both parts are repeated. The *Andante* in 2/4 time is a set of variations on a theme that has melodic links to the slow introduction. The *Menuet Allegretto* sounds free of these links, but not its Trio, nor the substantial *Finale Vivace* in 2/4 time and in sonata form.

Symphony No. 86 in D begins with the set's longest and most splendid slow introduction, a lyrical *Adagio* in 3/4 time for an orchestra fleshed out with two trumpets as well as two horns, timpani, and the usual complement of strings and winds. Haydn made an extensive sketch for the *Adagio*, continuing on far into the *Allegro* (not labeled as such).[73] It shows that, at least in this case, and at this stage of creation, he wrote the introduction first—whether he conceived it first is another matter. Certain, on the other hand, is the joint nature of their conception, for without the leisurely introduction establishing and reconfirming the key of D Haydn would not have been able to begin the *Allegro spiritoso* with a soft, off-tonic theme, a secondary dominant, V/ii - ii. It is answered by the same moved down to V - I, whereupon the whole orchestra, trumpets included, bursts in with three tonic taps in eighth notes, as if signifying approval. The three taps actually end the introduction, there separated by rests, *piano*, and on V, in preparation for the fast theme. For the next movement Haydn provided an enchanting *Capriccio Largo* in G and in 3/4 time. It commences with the unison rise through a triad up an octave in even eighth notes followed by rests. This gesture refers back to the pizzicato bass at the very beginning of the slow introduction. The *Capriccio* is like a reverie, much of it in florid discourse for the first violins, pursuing their every whim. It has a parallel in this regard with the *Adagio* of Symphony No. 102. The movement ends as it began, with the simple rise through the triad up an octave, after a rhapsodic coda. The *Menuet Allegretto* makes ample use of the secondary dominant and its resolution that began the *Allegro spiritoso*.

A most charming lesson to be learned from Haydn's sketches for Symphony No. 86 pertains to the Trio, a little dance that seems as if it had been arrived at without effort. The sketch shows just the opposite. Haydn jotted down a more complicated-sounding Trio that yielded almost nothing he finally accepted. What sounds so folklike and frolicsome in Haydn's music sometimes took him a struggle to achieve, which he did in this case by refining and simplifying. Seeming naiveté could be hard won.

The *Finale Allegro con spirito* in common time begins with the first violin

---

[73] The sketches are reproduced in *JHW* I/13, *Pariser Sinfonien 2. Folge*, ed. Sonja Gerlach and Klaus Lippe (Munich, 1999), pp. 163–69.

stating five staccato high Ds, the first an upbeat, an idea Haydn had used earlier to begin the stunning and very different finale of Symphony No. 70 in D, which also had trumpets. In this 1786 finale, a full-scale sonata form, there are no great surprises. Unusually, Haydn did not ask for the seconda parte to be repeated. He began it by slipping up a tone from A to B, as the root of V of e, the supertonic, the same chord that set going the *Allegro spiritoso* at the symphony's beginning.

Symphony No. 82 in C was perhaps second in popularity only to "La Reine" with audiences in Paris. It is a work of boisterous high spirits, which reach their zenith in the drones of the finale, a kind of music associated with the bagpipers who accompanied dancing bears in street entertainments; hence the very early nickname "L'Ours" (the Bear). A keyboard arrangement of the finale in Heinrich Bossler's *Anthologie* of 1788 already calls it "Bärentanz." The work needs no slow introduction. It starts boldly, with a tutti *unisoni* sweep up the tonic arpeggio to high E, then down in two-note bursts separated by rests. Even the first oboe is asked to play this high E, both here and in the related theme that begins the pompously old-fashioned Menuet. The finale theme makes quick work of reaching up to the E, but here only the flute and not the oboe has to play this tone, apparently so squealing in sound then that Mozart avoided it in orchestral works and even in the solo part of his Oboe Concerto in C (but not in his Oboe Quartet). In the opening movement Haydn moved into the seconda parte with a harmonic non sequitur over the bar line, leading down a tone from the cadence on G to a cadence on F. He did the same thing in the finale, which is also in sonata form. In a work verging on overstatement in its outer movements and minuet, the understated second movement, *Allegretto* in F and in 2/4 time, comes as a relief. It is a set of double variations that begins so slyly that an unwary listener might think the first two measures were in g minor rather than F. In a lengthy coda, Haydn even more slyly harmonizes the opening of the theme as if it were in g minor, then pulls back to F by way of its subdominant. The final cadences are soft, then softer still, the lower strings playing pizzicato.

Paris was not the only city where concertgoers were swept off their feet by this set of six symphonies. Reactions were similar everywhere, and edition followed edition in the centers of music publishing. Haydn's international fame, confirmed by the success of the String Quartets of Opus 33 in 1782, reached an even higher level with these ebullient new symphonies of 1785–86. In consequence, no composer of the time exceeded Haydn in popular favor, and no musical luminary gained so much credence with the critics and the erudites of music theory.

Symphonies Nos. 88–92

It may be that Haydn's two symphonies of 1787, Nos. 88 and 89, were also composed for Paris, to which Johann Tost, a violinist in Haydn's orchestra, took them.

He sold them to Sieber there, also to Longman and Broderip in London. This commerce embroiled Haydn in disputes and correspondence that involved Tost, Sieber, and Artaria, who first published the symphonies in Vienna. The next three symphonies, Nos. 90–92, dated 1788–89, were written on another commission from D'Ogny. Haydn showed his appreciation to this patron on the title page of two autographs: "Sinfonia in Es Pour Mons: le Comte d'Ogny di me giuseppe Haydn mpria 788" (No. 91); "di me giuseppe Haydn mp. 789—Pour S: Excellence Monsaign. le Comte d'Ogny" (No. 92). This did not deter the composer from selling them at the same time as originals to another patron, Prince Krafft Ernst von Oettingen-Wallerstein, who complained about receiving copies instead of autographs. In defending himself, Haydn fibbed that his autographs were illegible.

Symphony No. 88 in G later became one of Haydn's most loved works but at the time was not as popular a favorite as "La Reine." In it, the composer concentrated on a few specific melodic motifs in all the movements, for example, prominent emphasis on the third scale degree, with frequent recurrence of the figures 1 3 and 5 3. The slow introduction moves beyond even its parallels in the Paris symphonies by condensing the work's essence into a mere sixteen measures. It begins by the move up a major third in slow triple meter, as does the introductory *Adagio* of Mozart's "Linz" Symphony of 1783, and this is not the only similarity between the two symphonies. Both introductions are propelled by dotted rhythm and emphasis on the second beat of three, found often in sarabandes and chaconnes. Haydn's opening melodic gesture, unlike Mozart's, states four tones, G B C A, that will recur in the *Allegro* theme (Example 4.19).

EXAMPLE 4.19. *Haydn, Symphony in G, No. 88, I*

In the *Adagio*, when the opening gesture returns for the second time Haydn reharmonized it, changing I - V$^6_5$ - V^7 to I - IV$^6_3$ - V$^6_5$. Near the end of the finale, *Allegro con spirito* in 2/4 time, Haydn applies the brakes to this jolliest of contredanses.[74] He brings back the part of the *Adagio* that lands on IV$^6_3$, which he stretches out to five measures in one of his characteristic stalling moves, followed by a fermata. Resolution comes with a coda of whirring scales and orchestral brio to bring the symphony to an end. Recurrence of the progression from the intro-

---

[74] The tune may not have begun as a contredanse but it became one, as shown by Sarah Bennet Reichart, "The Influence of the Eighteenth-Century Social Dance on the Viennese Classical Style" (Ph.D diss., City University of New York, 1984), p. 198.

duction at the very end shows that Haydn intended the *Adagio* to foreshadow not just the following *Allegro,* which it does motivically, but to serve as a frame for the whole work.

Much has been written about this altogether winning symphony. Its fast movements could win for it the title of being Haydn's "symphony of the dance" (as Wagner called Beethoven's Seventh Symphony). The glorious slow movement, *Largo* in D and in 3/4 time, a freely treated theme and variations, begins with a 5 3 5 8 melodic motion that duplicates at pitch the first four tones of the *Adagio* in Mozart's Violin Concerto in G, K. 216, of 1775. That is no doubt a coincidence, but perhaps the choice of D rather than the more usual C for the slow movement of a work in G is made for similar reasons, which could include the greater fervor and brilliance that strings can project in the key of D. The Symphony's *Adagio* includes a surprise appearance of trumpets and drums (in D), which did not normally play in slow movements. Yet there was a symphonic precedent for this, in Mozart's "Linz" Symphony. One little detail that might escape a listener's attention is that the fluttering little sighs in descending melodic seconds marking the first variation of Haydn's *Largo* were planted earlier in the slow introduction.

Haydn departs from the six Paris Symphonies in reverting to his more usual *Menuetto* instead of *Menuet* (qualified by *Allegretto* in Nos. 83–86, as in No. 88). It is a case of "a rose by any other name . . . " because No. 88's Menuetto is as sturdy and pompous an example of the old court dance as the Menuet of No. 82 ("L'Ours"). The audiences that enjoyed the squealing drones of the rustic pipes in the finale of "L'Ours" had even more to admire in the rustic comedy of No. 88's Trio, which brought the exotic sounds of the Hungarian countryside to life as an unlikely companion to one of Haydn's most courtly minuets. The finale is a superb example of a rondo with development.

Symphony No. 89 in F runs the risk of sounding inferior in scope and depth to its immediate predecessor but it has its own delights, albeit more modest ones in comparison. Haydn saved himself some effort here by borrowing its second and fourth movements from the middle and final movements of Concerto V for two lire and orchestra (the last indebted furthermore to the finale of Symphony No. 78). The five lire concertos had been composed for the King of Naples a year earlier.[75] Haydn changed the orchestration of the borrowed movements and added some passages to the finale of Symphony 89 but the result sounds similar, like light music for entertaining otherwise occupied guests. Without introduction, the initial *Vivace* in common time begins with a fast "curtain" consisting of five tonic chords, *forte,* with the treble climbing up and down the tonic triad. Only then comes the main theme, *piano,* an eight-measure antecedent-consequent phrase

[75] The *lira organizzata* was a kind of hurdy-gurdy that had a brief vogue in the 1780s and was a particular favorite of Ferdinand IV of Naples, whose queen was Archduchess Maria Carolina of Austria.

that turns the triadic descent into a lyric theme. A nice touch in the consequent is the chromatic rise in the viola, doubled by the bassoons (5 ♯ 6 over IV) answered three measures later by the first violin's 2 ♮ 3 over I. This kind of detail may sound rather Mozartian but Haydn used it long before Mozart. The prima parte takes only 58 measures, rather short by Haydn's symphonic standard of the 1780s, but the seconda parte is nearly three times as long, including changes in the reprise that give it the character of a further development. Before ending the movement, Haydn employed one of his favorite delaying devices, an emphatic V_3^4/V that slows down the cadential process. He repeated the gesture at the end of the finale. The newly composed *Menuet Allegretto* and Trio, especially the latter, share melodic material with the *Vivace*.

Symphony No. 90 in C, the first of the new set for D'Ogny, shares features in addition to its key with Symphony No. 82 of the earlier set. Besides a pompous Menuet in each, the slow movements in F are both in 2/4 time and make similar use of Haydn's by-now-standard double variation form with two sections in tonic minor. No. 82 has no slow introduction, a big difference. The *Adagio* in 3/4 time that introduces No. 90 represents something unusual for Haydn. After a tutti *fortissimo* call to order on unison C and the three following measures, the violins and violas softly state in slow motion what the main theme of the *Allegro assai* that follows will be, actually a cadential progression in which the treble, after repeated Gs, falls gently to the tonic and reaches it after a melodic turn on D. The movement will end with this cadence, as might have been predicted, first verbatim, then dissected and recombined, with the repeated Gs and descent to the tonic going to the bass under the D with melodic turn in the highest voice, assigned to the flute. Although the movement as a whole is dominated by this main theme or its derivatives, there is room for a clearly articulated theme after the dominant is reached, a lithe antecedent-consequent phrase of eight measures sung by the flute (solo oboe in the reprise). In a sense, it is more of a theme than the truncated main idea's four measures of consequent without an antecedent. In his intense development, Haydn made good use of both themes as well as subsidiary material. This section ends with a long statement of V/vi, leading into the reprise by moving from E chromatically up to the repeated Gs of the main theme.

The *Andante* of Symphony 90 could almost be exchanged with the *Allegretto* of Symphony No. 82 because they are so similar, even as to the accented tone D in both themes. Here, unlike in Symphony No. 82, there is no mystery about how this tone will be harmonized. It is accompanied on first appearance by a IV chord *sforzato*, the fifth of which in an inner voice rises F F♯ G (a move adumbrated in the slow introduction). The *minore* variations startle us with the shock of an unexpected Neapolitan chord tutti *fortissimo*, coming after *pianissimo* offbeats. This grand surprise, also the way it is prepared, like a trap being set, predicts some moments in the London symphonies, looming ever closer on the horizon. The *Allegretto* has an expansive coda, with leisurely tour in the regions of ♭VI before coming to a quiet close.

The *Finale Allegro assai* in 2/4 time seems jaunty and lightweight at first but attains surprising tension through Haydn's inexhaustible powers of development. After some grand-sounding tonic fanfares following the reprise of this sonata form, closure seems near. Four measures of silence probably fooled some listeners into believing it had been achieved. Haydn started up again in remote D♭, with the strings softly initiating the theme to which the solo oboe pipes in retort the fanfare rhythm, last heard at the fracas on the tonic. The dialogue of these two figures continues in a modulatory fashion, like a second development section. Back in C at last, the oboe and bassoon announce the beginning of the theme again and this time the flute, which has a starring role throughout the symphony, responds with a new retort that inverts their descending figure to a rising one. Saucy new retorts to head motifs in order to cap a finale are a Haydn specialty. It would be difficult to surpass this one in sheer giddiness. The coda goes on grandly with many more orchestral fireworks, extinguished at length only after a plagal harmonic move.

Symphony No. 91 in E♭ opens with an introductory *Largo* in 3/4 time that has many conjunct thirds, rising or falling, slurred and soft, or détaché and loud, like the very beginning. The *Largo* winds down with a long descent in conjunct thirds over a dominant pedal, then elides into the main theme of the *Allegro assai,* where the rising and falling conjunct thirds answer back and forth to each other in a two-part counterpoint that is then inverted, after an eight-measure antecedent (Example 4.20). Haydn was particularly eager to use this symphony in London

EXAMPLE 4.20. *Haydn, Symphony in E♭, No. 91, I*

and it is easy to see why. In one respect, it is a continuation of certain preoccupations in his previous Symphony in E♭, No. 84 (note the slurred conjunct motion in Example 4.18 above). In a lost letter of July 1791 sent to Maria Anna von Genziger, Haydn asked her to retrieve this symphony from his rooms in Vienna and send it to London. He repeated his request to her in a letter of 17 September, then more urgently on 13 October by notating the beginning of the *Allegro*'s theme (in the treble of Example 4.20, mm. 20–21), saying, "Since I do not remember the little *Adagio* [*sic*] at the beginning of the Symphony in E♭, I take the liberty of noting the beginning of the following *Allegro*." It may seem strange that Haydn forgot the beginning of his *Largo* of three years before, but not so strange as Mozart telling his father (letter of 15 February 1783) that he had forgotten every single note of his "Haffner" Symphony, K. 385, composed only six months earlier. The *Largo* and *Allegro* are so closely tied together that the latter could not begin thus without the former preparing the way. It is clear nevertheless that for Haydn the *Allegro* theme was the main event while the *Largo* was composed to accommodate it. The rising chromatic line that is the nucleus of the *Allegro* theme, G A♭ A♮ B♭, is already present, at the same pitches an octave lower, in the *Largo* introduction to Symphony No. 84 in E♭. This main theme dominates the entire *Allegro assai* of Symphony No. 91 and suffices, with an added counterpoint, for its second theme.

The *Andante* in B♭ and in 2/4 time presents a gavotte-like theme in two strains, each repeated, as a subject for a theme and variations. It avoids rounded binary form in that, where a return to the beginning would normally occur in the second strain, the music goes astray tonally and lands in D♭, whence it is called back to order, first softly, then loudly. Haydn toys with us here and the joke approaches the parody Mozart created when rude tonal corrections were necessary after the players went hopelessly astray in *Ein Musikalischer Spass*, K. 522. The variations on Haydn's theme dutifully observe its contours, aberrations and all. The *Menuet Un poco Allegretto* first outlines a rising diatonic third (like the *Largo*), then continues softly by outlining a rising chromatic third covering the same span, evidently a link with the diatonic versus chromatic thirds so prominent in the *Allegro assai*. The *Finale Vivace* in cut time starts softly with a perfectly regular antecedent-consequent theme, lightly accompanied, then bursts into a tutti *fortissimo* emphasizing the rise E♭ F G, like the beginning of the *Largo*. It is an ample sonata form with both parts repeated. After several more urgent requests to Vienna for Symphony No. 91's score, the parts arrived instead (letter of 2 March 1792).

Symphony No. 92 in G, the last of the symphonies for Paris, is known as the "Oxford" Symphony because Haydn is said to have chosen it for performance in connection with ceremonies at Oxford University in July 1791, when he was awarded an honorary doctorate in music. There is no firm evidence tying the work to this event. Its *Adagio* in 3/4 time begins with three light taps on the tonic triad, with the fifth in the treble. Haydn told Dies a story that concerns this beginning and its rehearsal with his London orchestra, quoted in chapter 5. The soft beginning, unusual for an introduction, with descents of the treble like "dying falls," provides the material for the theme of the following *Allegro spiritoso*, also in 3/4 time, and supported by three eighth-note taps in accompaniment. There is no tonic arrival for this tentative-sounding main theme until the fifth measure of the *Allegro* and then it is vigorous, with the violins leaping up a tenth onto an accented second beat, another, and very prominent, recollection of the chaconne rhythm. This gesture begins the transition to the new key, which involves a clamorous tour via d, B♭ and g, before arriving at a tiny second theme in D, of only four measures, really a mere cadential tag. After a vigorous working out and clash of the main ideas, loudly argued, the reprise creeps in softly. Haydn rewrites a great deal, with further development of the chaconne idea and a big deceptive cadence on ♭VI. The tonal surprise might be interpreted as part of a coda, but this cannot be, for the little closing tag has yet to sound. Haydn saves it for the very end, then indicates a repeat for the seconda parte.

The slow movement is the heart of the work, a calm *Adagio* in D and in 2/4 time, far removed from the jaunty sectional movements marked *Andante* in the previous two symphonies. It can be no coincidence that Haydn's most recent symphony in the same key, No. 88 in G, also had a true slow movement in D, the moving *Largo* with variations, or that both bring out the rich sound of the strings in low range and emphasize in particular the third degree, F♯. Aside from their warm sonorities these two movements have an intense lyricism in common. *Cantabile* is the direction placed over the first violins, a long cantilena joined for much of its course by the flute, at the reprise by the first oboe. A large ternary form, the *Adagio* has a stormy *minore* middle part in the key of d, ample pretext for bringing back the whole first part and even expanding it with a gorgeous section for winds alone.

The *Menuet Allegretto* of Symphony No. 92 shares a few details with its parallel movements in Symphony No. 88 but the two trios are very different. In No. 88 the rustic theme dominated; here it is a rhythm that fools the listener into thinking at first that the accented third beats are downbeats, before this deception is undercut. The finale is a *Presto* in 2/4 time that might sound initially as if it would generate a rondo, but instead inaugurates a grand sonata form of ample extent. As in so many other finales, Haydn withheld a trump card to the very end. On the final page, he made the initial theme into a phrase that completes its business in eight measures instead of sixteen, a compression that serves as a fare-thee-well. In Symphony No. 88 there was a similar surprise at the end, with compression of the main theme into the embryo of a descending triad.

String Quartets

Early depictions of a string quartet in performance are rare. One such is the anonymous silhouette of four court musicians from the cappella of the Prince of Oettingen-Wallerstein, one of Haydn's principal patrons and a client for his Op. 33 Quartets (Figure 4.4). The musicians play their parts, which are in oblong format and arrayed on independent music stands, all standing except the cellist, who holds the instrument (lacking an endpin) between his knees.

Haydn first mentioned composing a new set of string quartets in a letter to Artaria of 5 April 1784. He agreed to the offer of 300 florins for them with the provision that Artaria be patient until July, "by which time all six should be finished, and secondly I request to receive either twelve copies or my choice of the dedication." On 18 May Haydn wrote, "matters can wait with regard to the quartets," then went on to state his wish, unfulfilled, to see a complete edition of his opera *Armida*. The new string quartets were set aside, apparently. In his letter of 5 April, Haydn had mentioned other projects under way, and notably "those half-finished quartets I am currently working on—they are very small, consist of only three movements, and are for Spain." These mini-quartets are believed to have been commissioned by the Duchess of Benavente-Osuna through the intermediary of the poet Tomás de Iriarte.[76] A lone string quartet by Haydn, known as Op. 42, may be a survivor of this project. In the key of d minor, it qualifies by being small in scope, limited in technical demands, and simple in structure, albeit in four short movements rather than three. The dance movement is placed second, as in four of the Op. 33 quartets, and is a Menuet with Trio. This solitary work, the autograph of which is dated 1785, was first published by Hoffmeister.

Several events in late 1784 and early 1785 conspired to deter Haydn from dashing off a new set of six string quartets at top speed, if that was ever his intention. He gradually experienced the rich feast of the six quartets dedicated to him by Mozart. Concurrently, and perhaps with the encouragement of the younger composer, he became a Freemason. Two important commissions arrived from abroad, one for the six Paris Symphonies, the other for a new and very demanding kind of work, the *Seven Last Words*. Not until these obligations were met and the works dispatched do we hear any more about composing a new set of six string quartets. Then, in February 1787, as the quartet arrangement of the *Seven Last Words* was reaching completion, the subject of the new set came up again.

Opus 50

The Op. 33 quartets of 1781 had renovated the genre, as Haydn himself maintained. It would be too much to say that with Op. 50 of 1787 he reinvented the

[76] Ludwig Finscher, *Joseph Haydn und seine Zeit* (Laaber, 2000), p. 412.

FIGURE 4.4. Silhouette of a string quartet from the Oettingen-Wallerstein court.

genre once again, and yet there is a grain of truth in this claim, for he adopted quite a different approach. The new quartets were composed in the order of their eventual publication, with the exception of Quartet No. 5, completion of which lagged behind No. 6. The first two quartets, in B♭ and C, were finished before a new and potentially lucrative opportunity for a dedication presented itself. Artaria enquired of the Prussian ambassador to Vienna, Herr Konstantin Jacobi, about dedicating some works of Haydn to Frederick William II, the new king of Prussia who succeeded his uncle Frederick II in mid-1786. This cello-playing monarch had already shown his largesse as crown prince by appointing Boccherini as his chamber composer in absentia. Haydn heard directly from Jacobi about Artaria's approaches. On 27 February he wrote Artaria saying he hoped that the works being considered for Berlin were not the *Seven Last Words* in either original orchestral or quartet version, for this would be "altogether counter to common sense" (wider alle Raison), presumably on account of their lugubrious nature. "If it should concern the new quartets, as I believe, then I approve." The letter confirms that the quartets were begun before the idea of a Prussian dedication reached Haydn.

Communications between composer and publisher were fitful. In his letter to Artaria of 7 March 1787, Haydn stated that he had written Herr Jacobi saying that, as far as he knew, the works dedicated to the king would be the new quartets. With this letter, he took the unusual step of including a specimen, derived from the first movement of Quartet No. 3 in E♭. One odd thing about the third quartet is that its texture lacks the intricacies of the first two quartets; also, its movements are shorter. Haydn began the second movement, a freely organized theme and variations, with an odd choice: the cello states the theme, accompanied only by the viola beneath it. More than in almost any other quartet Haydn imposed a kind of melodic unity here, by shaping the trio and finale themes to match the opening of the first movement.

On 21 April, Haydn heard directly from his exalted new patron. Frederick William thanked him for the present of his Paris Symphonies. This letter of praise signed by His Majesty included as an additional token of approval a golden ring, as intimated by Haydn to Artaria in his letter dated 2 May. In his letter of 19 May, Haydn informed Artaria that the fourth quartet in f♯ minor had been finished and would soon be sent. He reaffirmed his decision concerning dedication of the quartets to the king and confirmed the present of a golden ring.

The work went slowly. Throughout the summer of 1787, Haydn labored on the set, which was still not quite complete by September. At last, the lacking finale of the fifth quartet was ready. On 7 October, Haydn reported that he was having the quartets played through from the printed parts (in order to spot any errors needing corrections). Finally, Artaria published the parts in a handsome edition adorned with the approved dedication and ornamented with the Hohenzollern coat of arms: *Six quatuors pour deux violons, alto et basse composés et dédiés a sa majesté Frederic Guillaume II Roi de Prusse par Joseph Haydn. Oeuvre 50me*. At least Quartets 3–6 were composed specifically *for* the king. He presumably played the cello part in performance with members of his cappella.

Opus 50 resembles Opus 33 in plan while overall being a little weightier and more serious. All quartets have four movements and are more regular in the sense that all the minuet movements (no longer called *scherzi*) are placed third, as in Haydn's symphonies. A greater seriousness and intricacy is particularly evident in the minuets of the new set. These often move far from their dance origins in the direction of being intervallic studies, and in some cases, their motivic material is pertinent to the whole four-movement cycle. The other movements that were most changed are the finales, which are all in sonata form (a couple tinged with rondo traits), as opposed to only one (the Quartet in b) from the 1781 set. In Quartets 1, 3, and 4, Haydn chose to write in the form of theme and variations, or the double variation, his specialty. As in Op. 33 one quartet is in the minor mode and placed in the middle of the set, No. 4 in f♯. To a greater degree than in the earlier set, also than in the more recent Paris symphonies, Haydn explored the possibilities in his sonata forms of deriving both primary and secondary thematic materials from a single idea. Only in Quartet No. 2 does the opening movement follow the model of Op. 33 in G by having a long preparatory wait on V/V, then a distinctive and clearly periodized second theme in the dominant. This device, so important for Beethoven, was always at Haydn's beck and call, but was just one possible choice among many. Haydn's drive to effect greater thematic economy in sonata form is often called "mono-thematic," which hardly does justice to his ingenuity at wresting multiple uses out of primary material.

Quartet No. 1 in B♭, like the Quartet in G, No. 1 in the original edition of Op. 33, begins with a closing gesture, there a V - I cadence, here *Allegro* in cut time with a larger cadential moment, V - I, followed by the plagal IV - I, all underpinned by the cello softly sounding quarter-note pulses on tonic B♭. The cello begins these alone, two measures before the upper voices come in. In continuation of this odd beginning the four parts break into a flurry of triplets, reaching a firm V - I cadence only in mm. 11–12. The cello resumes its lonely tonic pedal and the upper voices restate their material, but with chromatic enrichment of harmony and melody. Haydn ended this first group with a move very unusual for him, a full stop on the tonic followed by a pause. Only then does the transition to the second key begin. There is a second group, if not a second theme, consisting of further exploration of the triplet motif. To begin the seconda parte Haydn dropped down a third from F to D (V/vi in B♭) leading to an expansive working out of the material. The reprise greatly condenses the first group, nearly eliminating the initial part but bringing it back whole to end the movement—that is to say, it finally assumes its proper role as closing gesture. Haydn used this same material as a closing gesture to end another work of the same year, the finale of Symphony No. 89 in F.[77] The *Adagio* in E♭ and in 6/8 time gives a chance for the second violin to sing the theme in the first variation, while the first violin both mimics and nearly overwhelms it with flashy scale passages in quick notes. The cello shines in the third variation by imitating these runs. The minuet may have provided Haydn with the motivic kernel out of which he spun the broader melody of the *Adagio*. The closing *Vivace* in 2/4 time has the jaunty cut of a rondo theme, and it might fool the ear into believing that it is a rondo, which is belied by its division into two parts, both repeated.

Quartet No. 2 in C begins softly, like No. 1, with an even subtler proposition (Example 4.21). A Hummel or a Pleyel might have been happy to turn the first

EXAMPLE 4.21. *Haydn, String Quartet in C, Op. 50 No. 2, I*

[77] As pointed out by Janet Levy, "Gesture, form and syntax in Haydn's music," *Haydn Studies* (1981), pp. 355–62.

two measures into a sequence alternating harmonies between I and V, with a lunge up to high A over IV before ending with a cadence in the conventional eight measures of a regular period. Haydn avoided routine by rhythmic disruption, an accented offbeat in the third measure, richer harmonies, and a surprise F in the first violin—a dissonance needing resolution to the E that might have been expected at the beginning of m. 5. His climb up to the exultant high A with *sforzato* is tortuous, making it seem like an accomplishment to arrive there. The phrase takes nine, not eight, measures. It is followed by an uncanny unison fall, *piano*, from fifth to third degree, as if in verbal comment on the preceding phrase. But what are the instruments agreed upon saying? It could be "Ohimè!" or some other droll comment in two syllables, but coming so soon after the *Seven Last Words* it also sounds like a profanation of "Si - tio." Whatever the sense, Haydn plunges next into a loud and unexpected V/V chord resolving to V, which is then stretched out for five measures with *crescendo* to *fortissimo* and with scalar and chordal repetitions to the point of absurdity. If the beginning of the previous quartet was loath to leave the tonic, this beginning plunges with indecent haste into the realm of the dominant. Haydn softened the three hammerstroke chords on G to three *piano* chords on V^6_5 as a preparation to return to the beginning. The whole first theme is repeated, enriched by melodic and harmonic changes. The continuation starts out as before but this time leads to a long stay on V/V, preparing a proper second theme in the dominant that is *cantabile* and periodic. Normal comportment here tends to emphasize the audacious oddities of the main theme and the intricate contrapuntal treatments it will receive. An *Andante cantabile* in F and in common time is an old-fashioned solo for the treble voice, sung first by the second violin, then by the first, against the pulsating chords of the other instruments. The cadential fall of this florid solo melody approximates mm. 7–11 of the preceding *Vivace*. The cello's emphasized C♯ D to begin the Menuetto ties in with the prominence of these tones at the beginning of the *Vivace*. These tones recur even more prominently in the finale toward the end, as does the descent from G to E, a clear reference back to the work's beginning.

Quartet No. 3 in E♭ has already been mentioned for its concision and thematic unity. Quartet No. 4 in f♯ minor is perhaps the simplest of the set. Instead of bringing increased pathos and greater chromatic and dissonant means to bear, as might be expected in the minor mode, it is one of the set's most consonant and straightforward works. The three knocking upbeats of the initial *Allegro spiritoso* in 3/4 time pervade every part of the movement, the content of which can be summed up as stating the principal idea (in its second-theme version) in several different keys and finally in tonic major. An *Andante* in A and in 2/4 time presents a double theme and variations, the alternating parts being in a. Tonic major (F♯) recurs for the minuet as does the descending triad of the first movement's main theme, while its trio, predictably, is in f♯ minor. The last movement, entitled

Fuga. Allegro moderato, is in 6/8 time, one of the lighter meters, which mitigates fugal severity somewhat, as does the movement's sonata form. The finale ends where it began, in f♯ minor, after the short span of eighty-seven measures, without repeats. Critics have been rather severe on this quartet, calling it variously "impersonal," "unsensuous," and even "perfunctory."[78] They preferred passion along the lines of the earlier minor-mode symphonies, while what it offers is more in line with the recent ones. Its finale is actually a better fugue than the one ending Op. 20's quartet in f minor.

Quartet No. 5 in F commences with an *Allegro moderato* in 2/4 time that is as nimble in theme as many a finale of Haydn's. Its main attraction is the play between different textures. The main idea is rather retrospective, as shown by a comparison with rhythmically similar material in the *Scherzando* movement in 2/4 time from the Quartet in F, Op. 3 No. 5, by pseudo-Haydn, the 1770s set attributed to Roman Hofstetter.[79] One critic sees a further trait of the older style in the movement's recourse to decorative passages in sextuplets. One of the lessons learned after the autograph was discovered is that Haydn, as an afterthought, inserted the first of these sextuplet passages early in the movement so as to prepare for their recurrence later. The *Poco Adagio* in B♭ and in 3/4 time struck some players and auditors as being of such a dreamy character that they gave it the nickname "Ein Traum." Perhaps it was the frequent exploitation of scalar moves in contrary motion between treble and bass that suggested this. Approaching the end, the first violin sweeps all the way up to the stratosphere (B♭ *in altissimo*), and back down against the ascent of the others, which may have suggested the ladder leading up to heaven that Jacob saw in his dream (Genesis 28:12). The passage reminds this listener of the great sweeps in contrary motion from top to bottom of the orchestra ending the Credo, also in B♭, of Beethoven's *Missa Solemnis.* *Menuetto Allegretto* has a trio that transforms the minuet theme into the minor mode, a rare occurrence in Haydn's music. *Finale Vivace* in 6/8 time is the last movement of the set to be finished, also its lightest. Unlike the crotchety minuet, its harmonic rhythms are broad and regular. Haydn took care to end its main theme the same way he ended the *Allegro*'s first theme.

Quartet No. 6 in D opens with an *Allegro* in common time that begins with a puzzling off-tonic start by the first violin alone, which plunges from a held E down a sixth by step to land on a held G, the seventh of V⁷ as it turns out, but on first hearing not so clear (Example 4.22). Resolution of the implied and unstable chord comes quickly, at first weakly, then strongly. Thus the first and last quartets

---

[78] The first by David Wyn Jones, the second by Sutcliffe, and the last by Tovey. See W. Dean Sutcliffe, *Haydn: String Quartets, Op. 50* (Cambridge, 1992), pp. 88–89, who takes issue with Tovey's comments.
[79] Sutcliffe, *Haydn: String Quartets, Op. 50,* pp. 95–96 and ex. 15. On Hofstetter, see *Haydn, Mozart,* pp. 261–62.

EXAMPLE 4.22. *Haydn, String Quartet in D, Op. 50 No. 6, I*

have unconventional beginnings and they put one in mind of the subtly unstable beginning of the first *Allegro* of Mozart's "Prague" Symphony, K. 504, with its seventh in need of resolution and its plagal emphasis, a work Mozart surely showed Haydn with pride after it was completed in December 1786. Haydn took his time in firmly establishing the dominant in the course of his *Allegro*, postponing its arrival by a big deceptive cadence on F instead of A. There is a hint of Mozart perhaps in the repeated D in syncopation given the second violin on the first page (K. 502 again) and also in the way the expressive chord of ii$^6_5$ is protracted at this same spot, while the cello has a sixteenth-note flurry on the fourth beat, getting quite close to an effect on the first page of Mozart's Quartet in E♭, K. 428. To begin the seconda parte, Haydn brought back m. 1 verbatim at pitch but then reharmonized m. 2 so as to point in the direction of b minor (vi), which is then elided by another deceptive cadence.

A *Poco Adagio* in 6/8 time brings the tonic minor, d, a choice that could be heard as a souvenir of earlier times (e.g., Op. 20), although the Quartet in G of Op. 33 had an extremely theatrical *Largo* in tonic minor. This *Adagio* is less theatrical but does project a hint of the stage, like a ballad from olden time sung by a troubadour to a fancy accompaniment. Just before the reprise the first violin rapidly descends a sixth after a longer tone, recalling the quartet's very beginning, a figure also recalled at the end of the finale. The *Adagio* ends by turning the main theme into tonic major, D, where the minuet begins. This is the set's only case where Haydn adds *Allegretto* to *Menuetto*, contrary to modern editions that routinely add it to every minuet. The Trio is long and begins with a flurry of four sixteenth notes on the upbeat, as in the *Allegro*'s very beginning.[80]

The finale of Quartet No. 6 is a tour de force for the players. An *Allegro con spirito* in 2/4 time, it asks the first violin to stagger rapid repetitions of the tone A, later the tonic D, between open and stopped strings. It is a kind of *bariolage* that lends its stamp to the entire movement, at the close of which the three higher instruments all play the tonic triad this way. The cello does not have a choice of strings with which to sound its low D so it gets a trill instead, which must be executed *pianissimo* just as the higher strings are. It was perhaps the less secure techniques of the second violin and viola in some amateur performances that made their imitation of the violin *en bariolage* sound like the croaking of a frog, and thus arose the soubriquet for the whole quartet: "The Frog." To begin the

---

[80] Finscher, *Haydn* (2000), p. 413, says that Mozart made reference to this trait in the minuet of his String Quartet in D, K. 575, of 1789 dedicated to the king of Prussia.

finale's *seconda parte* the cello adds a rising chromatic fourth to the first violin's *bariolage* on D. At the very end, the cello turns this chromatic rise to a chromatic descent down to its final low D. This sonata form is one of the few in the set in which Haydn chose to write a distinctly different second theme. It is not distinct from all else in the quartet; its held tone followed by a conjunct descent in rapid notes down a sixth reflects the opening of the *Allegro*.

Artaria advertised the published quartets in the *Wiener Zeitung* on 19 December 1787. Other editions soon followed in Paris, London, and Berlin. A public eager for new quartets by Haydn rose to the challenge of these sophisticated and often difficult works. Haydn had again enriched and deepened the genre. In this respect, he was responding to the challenge posed by the quartets Mozart dedicated to him. An expert on the quartets of both masters puts it this way: "Perhaps the biggest contrast with Op. 33 lies in the strong chromaticism of melody and harmony, and the consequent richness in dissonance and in thick textures; at least as to these traits can one imagine an influence of Mozart."[81]

MOZART AND HAYDN

December 1787 was a month in which Haydn and Mozart could have gotten together again for the first time in a year. The opera season at Esterháza usually kept Haydn occupied there from February through November, and this was the case in 1787. Mozart returned to Vienna after the creation of *Don Giovanni* in Prague in the second half of November 1787. The imperial court appointed him chamber composer with a small salary of 800 florins in succession to the deceased Gluck, on 6 December. In the same month he and Constanze moved to an apartment on the Tuchlauben in the inner city, where their daughter Theresia was born on 27 December. The two composers had many new works to show each other, Op. 50 in Haydn's case, and as for Mozart, his two great string quintets K. 515 in C and K. 516 in g, composed the previous spring but unpublished, not to mention *Don Giovanni*. One participant in their musical soirées, Abbé Maximilian Stadler, lived long enough to tell of them to the visiting Novellos from England much later.

> Haydn and Mozart were like Brothers. Mozart delighted in Haydn's writing and owned repeatedly that he was much indebted to him in forming his style. Stadler said that on his first arrival in Vienna and becoming acquainted with Haydn's work, Mozart naturally changed his manner of composing. Haydn was not a great Pianoforte player (his best instrument was the Violin) - but he delighted in hearing Mozart play the pianoforte. Haydn owned Mozart's superiority and said "he was a God in Music" (Stadler exclaimed to me "Mozart est *unique*; il etoit universel et savoit *tout*.") Mozart and Haydn frequently played together with Stadler in Mozart's Quintettos;

[81] Finscher, *Haydn*, p. 513.

particularly mentioned the 5th in D major, singing the bass part, the one in C major and still more that in G minor.[82]

Stadler probably did not know about Mozart's earlier stays in Vienna, or if he did, he surely meant Mozart's 1781 settling in Vienna and the subsequent quartets dedicated to Haydn. Stadler's precise reference to the quintets by key confirms the veracity of the whole passage. K. 515 in C and K. 516 in g are the likely candidates for their musicales in late 1787–early 1788; K. 593 of December 1790, cited by incipit as well as key, must refer to a session of chamber music three years later. Stadler also related to Novello that he played second viola in these sessions while either Mozart or Haydn played first viola in turn.[83]

To December 1787 is assigned a letter largely concerning Mozart that Haydn sent Franz Rott of Prague, a government functionary and wealthy patron of music. The request does not survive, nor does Haydn's letter, except for a fragment printed in Niemetschek's Mozart biography of 1798. Its authenticity has not been questioned, although the spelling and prose style diverge from Haydn's normal vernacular. Niemetschek may have polished both, but he would not have dared invent such a document with Haydn still very much alive and flourishing in Vienna. The translation here attempts to be as literal as possible.

> You request an opera buffa from me. Very gladly, if you wish one of my vocal compositions for yourself. If you mean for performance on the Prague stage, then I cannot serve you because all my operas are too bound to our personnel (at Esterháza in Hungary), and moreover would not create the effect that I calculated according to this locality. It would be a totally different matter were I to have the immeasurable luck to compose an entirely new book for the theater there. Even then I should be daring too much, since the great Mozart can hardly have anyone else at his side.

Too daunting for Haydn was the prospect of having to share the same Prague stage with *Le nozze di Figaro*, and henceforth *Don Giovanni* as well. Haydn concluded this letter with an outpouring of praise for his friend, and pleas on his behalf.

> If only I could convince every friend of music, but especially the great, to comprehend and intuit the inimitable works of Mozart, so marked by deep, interior feeling, as I understand and feel them, then would nations vie to possess such a treasure within their walls. Prague should hold this dear man fast, but also reward him, for without this the story of great geniuses is sad and gives posterity little encourage-

---

[82] Vincent and Mary Novello, *A Mozart Pilgrimage*, p. 170.

[83] Vincent and Mary Novello, *A Mozart Pilgrimage*, p. 347, n. 123. In an 1805 visit to Haydn, Carl Bertuch quoted the master in praise of Mozart, "whom he, whenever he was in Vienna, saw almost daily and with whom he lived in the most complete harmony." Cited after Landon, *Haydn*, 5:338.

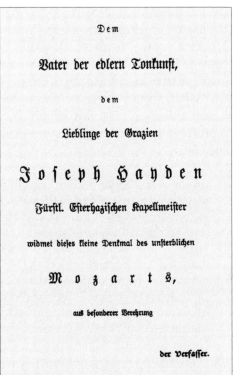

FIGURE 4.5. Title and dedication pages of Niemetschek's Mozart biography, 1798.

ment to strive further, and that is why so many promising talents stumble. It angers me that this unique Mozart is still not engaged by some imperial or royal court. Forgive me if I get derailed; I hold the man so dear. I am etc., Joseph Hayden [*sic*]. P.S. My most respectful compliments to the Prague orchestra and the virtuosi there.

Haydn means engaged as Kapellmeister, not as imperial chamber composer with a pitifully small salary, referring to Mozart's appointment of 6 December 1787. It was perhaps this slight that angered Haydn. Calling Mozart "unique" here helps substantiate the choice of this term by Stadler in trying to convey to the Novellos what Haydn had said to him about Mozart.

Franz Niemetschek met Mozart at Prague in 1791 and remained in close touch with Constanze thereafter. He published his biography of the master in 1798.[84] It begins with a stirring tribute to Haydn. In fact Haydn's name on the dedication page receives larger print than that of Mozart (Figure 4.5). Translated, the tribute reads, "The author, in deepest homage, dedicates this small memorial of

[84] Franz Xaver Niemetschek, *Ich kannte Mozart: Die einzige Biographie von einem Augenzeugen*, ed. Jost Perfahl (Munich, 2005). This edition incorporates readings and additions from the second edition of 1808.

the immortal Mozart to Joseph Haydn, father of the noble art of music, darling of the muses, and kapellmeister of Prince Esterházy." Following what he says about Mozart's youth, Niemetschek relates that the composer after settling in Vienna became personally acquainted not only with Gluck but also "with the great and incomparable Joseph Haydn, who was even then the pride of our music, and now that Mozart is no more, remains our favorite and our delight. Mozart often called him his teacher." The last remark confirms what Stadler told Novello: Mozart repeatedly asserted his indebtedness to Haydn. Niemetschek then becomes more specific:

> In the year 1785 he [Mozart] gave his six masterly quartets to be engraved, with a dedication to his friend Kapellmeister Joseph Haydn—a handsome expression of his esteem for this great man. Thus is Haydn's fame increased by the tribute of a man like Mozart. This gesture made us esteem even more the lovable heart of such an artist, whose own genius commands the admiration of all. Certainly, Mozart could have chosen no better work than these quartets to honor Joseph Haydn as they are a treasury of the most beautiful ideas, a model and school of composition. Connoisseurs regard this work as the equal of any opera composed by Mozart. Everything in them is thought through and perfected! One sees from these quartets what an effort he made to win Haydn's approval.

Niemetschek's remarks only gain force when we recall that it was Haydn who virtually created and perfected the genre in the first place.

Opera 54–55

Haydn returned to composing string quartets in the summer of 1788, a time when Mozart had moved out of central Vienna to Alsergrund, where he composed his three last symphonies. The greatest of Haydn's new quartets, Op. 54 No. 2 in C, reflects to a remarkable degree the profound impression left upon him by Mozart's String Quintets in C and g. The quartet's *Vivace* in common time commences with a sustained tonic chord *forte*, the lower instruments holding while the first violin descends the tones of a tonic arpeggio for three measures, a little wavering passage of a measure, a V^7 chord with two soft afterbeats occupying a fifth measure, and then a measure of silence. Almost the same description would fit the beginning of K. 515 in C, although there the strident voice sounding an arpeggio in quarter-note beats is the rising cello. The resemblance is too close to be fortuitous. Mozart moved on eventually by beginning the initial process again, following a measure of silence, but in tonic minor. Haydn went him one better by turning still further to the flat side with a statement of the initial idea in the key of A♭. After suitably abundant emphasis on V/V, Haydn introduced a lyric second theme of more ordinary shape than the first. The antecedent four measures could easily be mistaken for Mozart but the consequent, with its ungainly downward leaps of a seventh, as if making fun of the lovely antecedent, is Haydn at his most characteristic.

An odd thing about the development of this movement is the way it begins in and returns to F, the subdominant; it is of relatively short duration as Haydn's developments go. Before the seconda parte is finished, the cello sings the first violin's arpeggio theme, and in tonic major, which sounds even closer to K. 515. Moreover, the *Vivace* exploits the cello's low C at the close, suggestive of the very end of K. 515, when the cello returns to the low C with which it began.

Haydn's second movement, an *Adagio* in c minor and in 3/4 time, sounds quite different from Mozart's *Andante* in 3/4 time and in F, but both feature elaborate decorations of their simple themes. With Haydn, this movement passes directly into the *Menuetto Allegretto* in C, which bears little apparent resemblance to Mozart's *Menuetto Allegretto*, except for the return to the keynote. Haydn surprises us by following the minuet and trio with an *Adagio* in 2/4 time and in C major, its slow melody unfolding into a series of embellished restatements, like a free variation. To support the second statement of this melody the cello climbs up the arpeggio of C major beginning on its low C and then does the same on the dominant chord, reminding us of the first movement (and K. 515). Is this a slow introduction? Probably not, we think, when this theme is put into c minor with the cello lending appropriate support to a c-minor arpeggio up from its low C. A slow introduction would scarcely have sprung to mind as a possibility here had not Mozart done exactly this in his Quintet in g, K. 516, in which the *Adagio* following the minuet brings reminders of the first movement. Yet after thirty-nine measures it ends on the dominant, resolved by the onset of the fast finale in G major. Haydn's *Adagio* also ends on the dominant, after its minor mode section has stretched the movement out to fifty-six measures. Then comes a fast movement, *Presto* in 2/4 time back in tonic C major, with a merry rondo-like character to its theme. But this turns out to be only a mini-movement before the *Adagio* theme, once again in C major, returns to interrupt the jocular doings, provide a coda, and bring this strange finale to an end. One critic called the assemblage a dream vision interrupted by a fairy round dance ("Elfenreigen").[85]

Haydn's Op. 50 Quartets of a year earlier were inspired to some extent by the quartets Mozart dedicated to his older friend. The new quartets of Opp. 54–55 sound as if they share the more spacious and sonorous worlds of Mozart's string quintets, and like them put more emphasis on drama and surprise. Op. 54 No. 2, in C provides no better example of expansion in the direction of theatrical amplitude than the end of the minuet. When you think it has reached a conclusion with a satisfactory cadence, once repeated, it adds an expansive further gesture

[85] Pohl, 2:299–300.

in which all the instruments march in unison up two octaves by step for three measures, encompassing the gamut from the cello's low C to the first violin's C *in altissimo,* from which it plunges down to its open G string after a *crescendo* to *fortissimo.* A nearly symphonic grand gesture like this had hardly ever been heard in Haydn's previous quartets. It predicts the symphonic grandeur of gesture often present in Haydn's quartets of the 1790s.

The Quartet in G, Op. 54 No. 1, does not fall behind its companion in C in sonorous amplitude. Yet there are some features that sound a little old-fashioned coming after the Op. 33 and Op. 50 quartets. The opening *Allegro con brio* in common time jogs along mostly as an accompanied solo for the first violin. Compare the first movement of Haydn's Quartet in G from Op. 9, an *Allegro moderato* in common time in which the bass and often all three lower parts keep on chugging in a seemingly endless stream of what Burney called "iterated quavers," supporting a florid first-violin part. Another surprising trait in the later *Allegro* is articulation of the arrival at the dominant with three chordal whomps, the trait that served as an unmistakable signal to soloists in arias and concertos, but rarely heard in Haydn's most recent quartets. The following *Allegretto* in 6/8 time and in C major also has a lot of chugging along in eighth-note accompaniments but it is more charming than the first movement. An adequate but hardly inspired minuet and trio reinforce the impression that Haydn is coasting in well-known waters, turning out another work for sale to the avaricious publishers so eager to market his works. The *Finale Presto* in 2/4 time is a rondo with an irrepressible refrain. Near the end, there is a flashy unison passage in sixteenth-note arpeggios, *fortissimo,* in its effect rather like the passage that ends the previous Quartet's minuet.

These works are sometimes called the first set of "Tost" quartets, wrongly said to have been dedicated to Johann Tost, a confusion with the set of six quartets Op. 64 of 1790 that Tost claimed Haydn did dedicate to him. With the Opp. 54–55 quartets Tost was merely the intermediary who took the set to Paris, along with Symphonies 88 and 89, and sold them to Sieber, who published them in two series of three each, calling them Op. 54 and Op. 55 (advertised on 13 June 1789). At the same time either Tost or Haydn apparently sold another copy to Longman and Broderip in London, also printed in two sets, with the Quartet in C preceding the Quartet in G, an order followed by Hoboken. The grand Quartet in C may be the manuscript quartet performed with acclaim to open the Professional Concert led by Wilhelm Cramer in the Hanover Square Rooms on Monday 2 February 1789. Unlike in Paris and Vienna, public concerts in London by the later 1780s regularly included string quartets, mostly led by first violin Cramer or by his rival Salomon, and their composer was Pleyel twice as often as Haydn.[86] One change

---

[86] Meredith McFarlane and Simon McVeigh, "The String Quartet in London Concert Life, 1769–1799," in *Concert Life in Eighteenth-Century Britain,* ed. Susan Wollenberg and Simon McVeigh (Aldershot, 2004), pp. 161–96.

in performance practice about 1785 surely pertinent to the subject was the perfection of the "Tourte" bow, which was stronger than its predecessors and in concave rather than convex shape. The main inventor was François Tourte in Paris and credit is given as well to English maker John Dodd and to Wilhelm Cramer, both in London.[87]

Quartet No. 3 is in E, a key Haydn had not chosen to use in the genre since Op. 17 No. 1, of 1771. The *Allegro* in common time begins as the second violin, in thirds with the viola, proposes a smoothly rising and descending turning figure (*x*) to which the first violin responds with a descending arpeggio figure (*y*), V^7 - I. A four-measure antecedent ends with a half cadence followed by a four-measure consequent and full cadence—the vaunted *période* of French critics. These euphonious and clearly measured sounds pleased the composer so much he lingered on I, as the cello initiates a long pedal on low E under the next eight measures; then he made several additional cadences, the last decorated by triplets in the first violin. After another half cadence that could lead either back to E or on to the new key, the second violin and viola take charge and opt for the latter, where they invert their initial melodic turn *x* to form a new theme, eliciting a different response from the first violin, which eventually confirms the key of B with whirling triplet figures answered in kind by the second violin. There is a lovely feint to G major ($\flat$VI in B) before the arrival in B. The seconda parte begins charmingly by going directly back to G major, using the main theme in its entirety. After many modulations, the music settles down on a long pedal G$\sharp$ (V/vi in E) but does not reach vi. Instead, the reprise sets in simply when G$\sharp$ is transformed into the third of tonic E. Upon restatement, the main theme is inverted so that *x* is on top and *y* below. Some material is then eliminated but Haydn was in a very expansive mood here so that in this case the seconda parte is more than double the length of the prima parte.

The *Largo cantabile* in A and in 3/4 time offers an elaborately decorated rounded binary form with repeats, a *minore* middle part, and a return of the first part with even fussier ornamentation. For the minuet Haydn resumed a practice cultivated in the early *Divertimenti a quattro*: violins in octaves (e.g., Op. 2 No. 2 in E). In this case, the viola and cello are also cast in octaves. The *Finale Presto* in 2/4 time has a rondo-like theme but becomes a sonata form, with a return of the long tonic pedals for cello heard in the opening movement. Virtuoso treatment of the first violin, brilliant concertante treatment of all parts, and a popular tint (not just the waggish finale but also the dance-hall octave doublings in the minuet) add up to an attractive whole.

Opus 55 No. 1 in A begins with an *Allegro* in cut time that is short on origi-

---

[87] David D. Boyden, *The History of Violin Playing from Its Origins to 1761 and Its Relationship to the Violin and Violin Music* (London, 1965), pp. 327–28. The violinists and violist in Figure 4.4 (ca. 1780) play with pre-"Tourte" bows.

nal ideas but long on extended triplet passages for the first violin that sound as if they were employed for lack of a better idea. There is a distinctive secondary theme following the long passage in triplets that incorporates a sequential passage V/ii - ii / V - I, used also in both minuet and trio, and in the *Finale vivace* in cut time, lending a feeling of unity to the cycle. Following this passage in the *Allegro* Haydn again resorts to doubling the violins in octaves. The gem of the quartet is the second movement, an *Adagio cantabile* in D and in 2/4 time on a simple, periodically regular theme, a haunting melody that keeps recurring with everdifferent ornaments and accompaniments.

Quartet No. 2 in f departs from standard design by placing first what is usually a second movement, an *Andante più tosto Allegretto* in 2/4 time cast in double variation form. An *Allegro* in cut time, also in the key of f and cast in sonata form, follows. In the *Andante* the alternate theme for variation is in F, and is derived from the principal theme in f, in which the Neapolitan chord plays a climactic role. The *Allegro* projects a melody with a long descending arc, as does the *Andante*, and makes ample use as well of the Neapolitan chord. The *Andante* ends in tonic major, as does the *Allegro*, after a greatly condensed reprise that is entirely in F. Haydn may have been thinking back to his Symphony No. 49 in f, "La passione," in which he placed the *Adagio* before the *Allegro* and unified them thematically. In that work of 1768, the subsequent minuet and finale were also in f, F being restricted to the trio. Twenty years later Haydn released us from the gloom of f minor sooner and granted us not only a minuet in F (with only its trio in f) but a finale too, a joyful *Presto* in 6/8 time. The quartet acquired the nickname "the Razor" from the legend that the English music publisher John Bland, visiting Haydn at Esterháza in 1789, induced the composer to sell him some music, in part by sending as a present some razors and a watch.[88]

Quartet No. 3 in B♭ is the slightest of the six making up Opp. 54–55. A *Vivace assai* in 3/4 time starts the proceedings with a trochaic melody rising softly in unisons and octaves: 1↓7 / 4 - 3 / 6 - 5 / 4 - - /. The consequent is *forte*, an octave above, harmonized, and mostly descends before reaching a half cadence. A second theme in the dominant is spun out of the first, following which there is an interesting passage in which the cello creeps up the scale chromatically with offbeat accents against the pulsating accompaniment of the violins. *Adagio ma non troppo* in E♭ and in 2/4 time brings variations on a theme in rounded binary form. The *Finale Presto* in 2/4 time, although short, is a complete sonata form. Like the opening *Vivace* it begins with a monophonic passage, a descent played by the first violin taken up in unison by the others, with the same material that opened the quartet rearranged but still stressing tones 8, 6, and 4. From this whirligig of a theme Haydn spins a gossamer fabric that suggests a *Kehraus*—the

---

[88] Landon and Wyn Jones, *Haydn*, pp. 177–78; Pohl, 2:235, quotes a more explicit but unverifiable anecdote.

last dance that sweeps all away in a burst of joy. It cannot be a coincidence that Haydn ended the last quartet of his Op. 9 set, No. 6 in A, with a fast finale in 2/4 time built from scales that cascade down, placing emphasis toward the end on degrees 8, 6, and 4. That last dance has been compared to "a merry 'Bon soir' to the assembled company at evening's end."[89] This one suggests a nostalgic revisit, albeit more sophisticated, of the one many years earlier that ended Haydn's first set of true string quartets.

An anonymous critic of the time chided the composer for departing in Opp. 54–55 from the true quartet style, as invented by Haydn himself: "Almost all main ideas or concertante places are given to the first violin, the other instruments are largely reduced to accompaniments. . . . To a Haydn it must nevertheless be little trouble to write real quartets."[90] From the vantage point of all Haydn's works of the time we observe that the more showy and popular traits in these quartets approach his language in the Paris Symphonies, finished a year earlier. As for the greater use of concertante elements we do well to be aware of the evolving French *quatuor concertant* and *quatuor brilliant* championed notably by Giovanni Battista Viotti in his two sets of *Six Quatuors concertans* (Paris, ca. 1783–85). Haydn's overall course as creator and perfecter of the string quartet needs to be a constant frame of reference here. His foremost critic today illuminates the issue in a comparison of Op. 50 with Opp. 54–55. Of the latter he writes, "The works are, while of the same size, more easily accessible than Op. 50, more friendly in tonal language [Tonfällen], simpler, broader in construction [im Satz], while the form of the movements and the cyclical form show greater variety. Correspondingly the minuets return to decidedly dance-like inflections."[91]

Opus 64

Haydn considered composing another set of string quartets as early as August 1788, when he wrote Artaria offering a choice of new quartets or keyboard trios. Artaria chose the latter, which was in greater favor with amateurs. He sought a wide clientele for his music and art prints, and Carl Schütz, in a detail depicting Artaria's shop front on the Kohlmarkt, shows the public response (Figure 4.6).

No later than the summer of 1790, Haydn must have begun writing another set of quartets. He finished in the fall. His intention was not just making a quick profit from publication but also having something new ready for a trip abroad, long bruited about in the London press and finally coming to pass in late 1790.

The composer took with him to London the autographs of the six new quar-

[89] *Haydn, Mozart*, pp. 331–32.
[90] *Allgemeine deutsche Bibliothek* 111/1 (1792): 121–22, cited after Georg Feder, *Haydns Streichquartette* (Cologne, 1998), pp. 76–78.
[91] Finscher, *Haydn* (2000), p. 415.

tets. Parts had presumably been copied and tested, very likely in his circle of Viennese friends, including Mozart. The first edition of the parts, made not by Artaria but by Kozeluch's firm in early 1791, gives every indication of being unauthorized. Its readings stem from a copy divergent from the autograph and do not match the authorized version Haydn sold to Bland in London. Kozeluch's edition bears the printed mention "Composés et dediés a Jean Tost par monsieur Joseph Haydn." The claim is dubious on more than one count. Whatever Haydn's dealings with Tost had been, they left the composer in an angry frame of mind. Why would he then write quartets "for and dedicated to" Tost? It is no longer in doubt that the former violinist in Haydn's orches-

FIGURE 4.6. Detail from Carl Schütz's "The Kohlmarkt," showing Artaria's shop, 1786.

tra named Johann Tost was the same person as the Hungarian industrialist of this name in the 1790s.[92] When Kozeluch reissued his edition in 1793, after Haydn's return to Vienna, the dedication was missing, nor did it appear in any of the other early editions of which there were several dated 1791. The appellation Op. 64 comes from Sieber's edition, advertised in the *Journal de Paris* of 9 June 1791.

Haydn numbered the individual quartets by hand to show the ordering he intended: C, b, B♭, G, E♭, D. Strikingly, the tonalities he chose exactly match those of the six quartets in Op. 33 of 1781. It is as if the composer resolved to end the decade as he had begun it. Another unmistakable sign that Haydn was thinking back to his breakthrough of ten years earlier concerns the Quartet No. 2 in b, which begins in the same indefinite way as does its counterpart in Op. 33, keeping us guessing whether it is in major or minor. Other quartets clearly on Haydn's mind when he wrote Op. 64 were the six dedicated to him by Mozart.

[92] Sonja Gerlach, "Johann Tost, Geiger und Grosshandlungsgremialist," *Haydn-Studien* 7 (1998): 344–65.

Quartet No. 1 in C begins with two measures that duplicate the incipit of the *Vivace* of a Piano Trio in A of 1785 (see Example 4.26b, p. 402). This kind of head-motif migration is not uncommon with Haydn. Once the springboard got him started he continued by writing a different theme altogether, smoother, broader, and more gracious, without the leaping about of the trio's theme. In the quartet, he changed the inverted dotted rhythms to less fussy ordinary dotted rhythms. Both themes climb the tonic triad then descend identically, preceded by a leap up a fourth as upbeat. Rising chromatic seconds play an important part in the quartet theme, an *Allegro moderato* in cut time. The first statement of the theme ends with an appoggiatura rise to the third, $\hat{2}$ 3. This is apt to sound quite Mozartian to us but Haydn was using the trait long before Mozart did. For his second theme, Haydn generated a different continuation from the original springboard. He began the seconda parte by repeating the figure that ended the prima parte, transferred from first violin to viola. Although the development is not long, and the "second theme" is missing from the reprise, Haydn stretches the seconda parte out with another quasi-development of the closing theme so that its overall length nearly doubles that of the prima parte. Earlier he made more efforts to keep the two parts close to parity. Before ending the movement, Haydn brought back the springboard of head motif as a point of imitation, using stretto. A contrapuntal showing such as this suggests the Op. 20 quartets more than those of Op. 33.

Haydn placed the dance movement second in the Quartet in C, as he did also in Op. 64 No. 4 in G. Throughout this opus, he labeled these movements Menuet, using the old French spelling that modern editions regularly transform into Menuetto. The one in C begins with an upbeat leap of a fourth to a rising tonic triad, linking it in theme to the *Allegro*. Also, the *Allegro*'s closing figure comes back to end the first strain of the Menuet, or, if Haydn conceived the Menuet first, vice versa. The Trio is like a variation in the minor of the Menuet, using the same rising triad theme preceded by an upbeat leap of a fourth. The third movement uses another variant of this beginning. It is in F but is hardly a slow movement, being an *Allegretto scherzando* in 2/4 time, a theme and variations. With its regular pulse in eighth notes it provides a slight foretaste of another non-slow movement, the metronome caricatured in the *Allegretto scherzando* in 2/4 of Beethoven's Symphony No. 8 in F. Haydn's *Finale Presto* in 6/8 time escapes the common beginning of a rising fourth upbeat although it does begin with an upbeat. The first violin sounds initially only the tone C to the rhythm ♪ |♪ ⸴ ♪ ♪ ⸴ ♫ |♪. This catchy motif, sounding a little like Morse code, provides Haydn with material for much of the development of this rollicking sonata form. Here it is Beethoven's enhancement of a rhythmic motto as a musical element in its own right that seems to be adumbrated, especially notable in his Rasumovsky Quartets, Op. 59, of 1808. Never to be forgotten in this regard, moreover, is the cello's drumbeat rhythm in the final variation of Mozart's Quartet in A, K. 464, dedicated to Haydn.

Quartet No. 2 in b has an odd beginning, a solo for the first violin that intones a D, then a turn around it, in a way that would convince almost any listener it is the tonic, until the other parts come in and prove it is not. D is but the third of the key of b and is so harmonized upon the beginning's repetition. A little motivic carryover exists between the closing idea of the previous quartet's *Allegro*, there A G B C, here G F♯ C♯ D, that is, falling step, leap up, rising step. The second theme leaves little to remember it by. It is only a pedal on D providing the necessary stay on the relative major. A resounding Neapolitan chord in this new key then gives way to a curious passage in which the note values diminish from half notes to quarter notes to sixteenth notes, on the way to a cadence on D. At a total of 108 measures, this movement, *Allegro spiritoso* in common time, is on the short side but so was the equivalent movement in Op. 33. The *Adagio* in 3/4 time that follows captures what is most characteristic of the quartet as a whole: the transformation of tonic minor into tonic major, and in this respect it departs from its Op. 33 counterpart. The Menuet is in the key of b and begins with an upbeat leap of a fourth, another link with the previous quartet; its Trio substitutes B for b and begins similarly. The *Finale Presto* in 2/4 time also begins with the upbeat leap of a fourth followed by the tones 1 2 3. Its key is b, and the reprise remains in tonic minor up to the point when it comes time for the secondary material. Then, after a dominant pedal, Haydn brought back the main theme in tonic major. The sense of relief is so strong that one critic goes so far as to refer to it as a kind of tonal salvation.[93] The first violin does indeed seem to climb heavenward to close the movement softly, all the way up the triad of B to high B *in altissimo*, the same climb that ended the first movement but *forte* there.

Quartet No. 3 in B♭ commences as if in the middle of a phrase, with three eighth-note upbeats followed by a downbeat resolution of three more eighth notes (Example 4.23). The oddly shaped seven-measure phrase alternates these two

EXAMPLE 4.23. *Haydn, String Quartet in B♭, Op. 64 No. 3, I*

figures and reaches a cadence in m. 5, then returns to the beginning for an additional two measures. There is a strong emphasis on the third and fifth degrees.

---

[93] Finscher, *Haydn* (2000), p. 417.

Haydn, once again at his most waggish, seems to have been thinking back to the comic play on 5 4 3 and 5 5 3 that figured so prominently in starting Op. 33 in B♭, to which Mozart then responded by making jocular reference in the finale of the "Hunt" Quartet in B♭, K. 458 (see Example 1.13ab). Instead of pursuing his initial idea Haydn allowed it to be overwhelmed by a veritable gallop, a profusion of dactyls in all four parts simultaneously and in quick notes. The initial theme returns to lead in the second key area of V but sounds less like a second theme then does a broader passage with the violin singing a *dolce* melody in more sustained tones. To end the prima parte of sixty-nine measures the nervously charged initial theme returns again. This theme and the dactylic figures contest the development section of fifty-five measures. A mere forty-five measures suffice the reprise, in which Haydn eliminates the *dolce* lyric idea. He reduced the dactyls to only a few occurrences, but they come back to inaugurate the finale, *Allegro con spirito* in 2/4 time, a sonata form of 245 measures that ends with these same dactylic figures.

An *Adagio* in E♭ and in 2/4 time offers an expansive ternary form with a middle section in tonic minor acting like a variation on the main section. The Menuet is an *Allegretto* with a one-beat upbeat. To end the first strain the first violin uses double-stops to render a little fanfare with horn fifths, ornamented with trills. Viola and cello respond by mimicking the violin an octave lower to begin the second strain, the viola under the cello playing 5 3, 5 3, 5 3, a passage suggestive of the way the two violas begin Mozart's last chamber work, the String Quintet in E♭, K. 614.

Haydn's Quartet No. 4 in G likewise continues the dialogue with past accomplishments in the same key. Its initial *Allegro con brio* in common time is on a smaller scale than the first movement of Op. 33's Quartet in G, the one with the very expansive and lyric second theme. Here the material of the main theme provides also for the thematic statement in the dominant, as happens more often in Haydn. The somewhat denser and more chromatic web of this *Allegro* points less to Op. 33 than it does to the first movement of Mozart's Quartet in G, K. 387, the first of the set dedicated to Haydn. In particular, its raised fifth and tonic degrees seem haunted by the raised fifth in Mozart's initial theme. Haydn began his seconda parte with a point of imitation on the closing theme (played *sopra una corda* by the first violin). After threatening to make a big cadence on vi, he diverted tonal direction so as to lead in the reprise. In this instance, he did bring back the second-theme version of the main material, but not before another big diversion, a typical halt to the proceedings called by a suddenly deflected cadence, a protracted V_3^6/V followed by V_5^6. Haydn applied the brakes, as it were. The *Menuet Allegretto* comes next (as it does in K. 387). Its Trio is a Ländler melody with pizzicato accompaniment that inverts the rising tonic arpeggio with which the quartet begins. An *Adagio sostenuto e cantabile* in 2/4 time and in the key of C follows. This is another broad ternary movement with a middle section in the minor on the same theme. The first six tones of the finale duplicate the incipit of the *Adagio*'s melody. In this sonata form, *Presto* in 2/4 time, once again the first violin dominates the discourse, as it does often throughout the quartet. The emphasis on the melody (first violin) and subordinate accompaniment can be heard as a nod back toward textures favored in the Op. 17 quartets.

The greatest gems of Op. 64 are the two last quartets, No. 5 in E♭ and No. 6 in D. Kozeluch's edition scrambled the order of the two, an inversion that can still be seen in some modern editions. Hoboken went further astray by ignoring Haydn's numbering on the quartets. Quartet No. 5 in E♭ begins with a quiet and reflective theme, *Allegretto* in common time, with an ordinary antecedent structure of 4 + 4. What becomes of this ordinariness in the course of the movement is of a richness and variety that well illustrates what makes Haydn so treasurable. The theme projects a diminution of note values after the half notes of its first measure. The D♭ picked out for emphasis by a *sforzato* at the end of the theme will become one main goal of the development, and, after it is established, the dominant of another goal, G♭. Perhaps the least significant aspect, we think at first encounter, is the rhythm of the cadential measure. It will become an obsession in the development, and so as to better prepare us for that, Haydn repeats it, not once, but twice, and then stretches it into two measures, so that the V - I cadence occurs four times in all. For a second theme, the first serves well, and this time it is imitated by the cello at the distance of a measure, and at a fourth below. Repetition of an identifiable thought, as asserted in closing the prima parte, is carried by the first violin into a frenzy that involves not only diminution of note values but also a mad pre-cadential figure that is stated eight times. The seconda parte shows that the main theme is good for a stretto at the half-measure, leading to further contrapuntal elaborations of this theme. The reprise begins after an unresolved V/vi. Haydn economized on restatements of the theme as he often did, yet he introduced new treatments as well as those already heard.

After the intense first movement of the Quartet in E♭ Haydn opted for a pleasant, leisurely *Andante* in B♭ and in 3/4 time, without rhythmic complications and quite idyllic in effect. There is a movement much like this in Michael Haydn's Symphony No. 4, an *Andante* in 3/4 time that moves in the same even eighth notes and projects similar melodic sighs. The quartet's *Andante* is in a simple ternary form, with the middle part in minor, impassioned, and quite Schumannesque. With the *Menuet Allegretto* we return to the indisputably Haydnesque. A sudden accent on a B♮ resolving to C lends greater significance in retrospect to the choice of this same turn of events after the first statement of the main theme in the opening movement. In fine good humor, the composer provided two versions of the Trio, marking the second "in case it should ever please you to repeat it" (Trio per la seconda volta, caso mai se piacesse a replicarlo). He may have meant another return of the whole Trio followed by another repeat of the main dance, as Beethoven later would often request. The Trio itself is an airy Ländler with slurred grace notes from the upbeat to the main beat, interpreted by some performers as a portamento slide that creates a tipsy effect. In the optional Trio, the return of the melody in the second strain goes to the second violin while the first violin plays an accompanimental part high up in its range. *Finale Presto* in 2/4 time is a rondo with a pert theme resembling one Mozart later wrote (see Example 3.4ab). It ends with a witticism that only a Haydn would likely think up: a rhythmic augmentation of the rondo theme, thus a reversal of the many diminutions heard in the opening movement.

Quartet No. 6 in D has an unforgettable beginning. An *Allegretto moderato* in cut time commences with a nicely turned, satisfactory eight-measure phrase for the three lower parts playing staccato and marking the beat with even pulses. It turns out to be only the accompaniment of what comes next: a beautiful sustained phrase, soaring high above in the first violin, a flight so graceful that it earned for the work as a whole the title of "Lark" (Example 4.24). There is precedent for

EXAMPLE 4.24. *Haydn, String Quartet in D, Op. 64 No. 6 ("Lark"), I*

such a beginning in the way the accompaniment prepares the entry of the first violins in "Sitio" from the *Seven Last Words*, but there the treble melody joins in at the cadence of the first phrase. After the quartet's entirely diatonic initial phrases Haydn introduces a descending chromatic line on the way to preparing the second key area, which gets along without any second theme. A unison rise, mostly chromatic, up an octave, prepares the cadence that ends the prima parte. The seconda parte uses the main material, the initial theme and accompaniment sounding first in G. Haydn left an elaborate and nearly full sketch for this whole development section, which shows how much care he took with its every detail. He was loath to dissect so lyric a theme as his soaring violin melody. Only the figure in dotted rhythm at the end (mm. 17–19) is excerpted for use here and there. After stating the initial complex in a reprise, followed by discourse on the chromatic rises and triplet figurations, Haydn returned to the lyric idea and stated it again in its entirety, an unusual treatment but very welcome because of its great beauty.

The following *Adagio cantabile* is in the key of A and in 3/4 time. It wanders off into the region of F♯ before returning to restate the initial hymn-like song. The form is ternary with a middle section that begins in tonic minor but quickly turns to C major for a restatement of the beginning. The celestial melody of the main section is further varied upon repetition.

A minuet marked *Allegretto* gets the quartet's second half under way. It begins with a simple eight-measure first strain ending on V. The second strain takes more time, with a deviation to B♭ intervening before the repeat of the beginning, then elaborations of the precadential area before the final cadence. The Trio takes off from the scalar figures in eighth notes ending the minuet and becomes a kind of chromatic study on the same, very far in nature from the folklike Ländler of the preceding quartet. As if to restore himself and his listeners after such intellectual rigors, Haydn provides a finale, *Vivace* in 2/4 time, of a type familiar and very welcome in his circle, where it would have been recognized instantly as one of his delightful essays *all'Ongarese*. It commences with a swirl of sixteenth notes running up and down in seemingly nonstop fashion. When the first violin switches to eighth-note motion, as if to catch its breath, the second violin takes over the quicker note values, a *minore* episode that momentarily displaces the rondo theme. At last the first violin moves up an octave to restate the refrain a final time and we can more easily perceive that its rush of notes encapsulates something important we have heard before, namely the high F♯ E D of its soaring melody back at the very beginning of the quartet. A coda continues the unstoppable flow until just before the final cadence, which then arrives with a final rush up and down the scale to D as the chords sign off with an emphatic V - I. The breathtaking rush of sixteenth notes in the finale of Mozart's last string quartet, K. 590 of June 1790, sounds somewhat similar, but its tone does not impress one as being quite so "Gypsy" in style as Haydn's finale.

Piano Sonatas and Trios

The first keyboard works Haydn composed in the 1780s were two dozen Lieder "für das Klavier" published in two installments by Artaria in December 1781 and April 1784, both volumes dedicated to Francisca von Kreutzner. For the most part these strophic songs are quite simple. With few exceptions they use only two staves, one for voice and right hand employing soprano clef, the other in bass clef for left hand.[94] With these works Haydn joined other Viennese composers who published vernacular songs in collections designated "für das Klavier." Joseph Anton Steffan was the first, in 1778, followed by Carl Friberth, who sang tenor in Haydn's opera company until 1776, and Leopold Hofmann. The last appears to have provided the direct stimulus for Haydn. In his letter to Artaria of 20 July 1781, Haydn says he recomposed three texts on which Hofmann had made settings that possessed "neither ideas, expression, nor, much less, melody"; Hofmann, moreover, had tried to disgrace Haydn in the Viennese salons where such songs were sung, or so Haydn was told, perhaps by his friend Friberth.[95] A quarter of the songs in Haydn's two dozen bear no dynamic markings. As many others make minimal use of them. The rest are liberally sprinkled with *forte* and *piano* markings, plus many *sforzato* signs and a rare *crescendo* (in No. 19). They presuppose that the instrument of choice was the fortepiano rather than the harpsichord. Throughout Haydn makes ingenious use of instrumental preludes, interludes, and postludes, thus emphasizing the difference between the Viennese Lied and the more primly accompanied Lieder of the North German School.

One of Haydn's songs, No. 9, "Trost unglücklicher Liebe," stands out for its expressive power and wonderfully idiomatic treatment of the piano. It is an *Adagio* in cut time and in the key of f minor, one that Haydn chose seldom but endowed with great depth when he did, as in Sonata V of the *Seven Last Words*. There are other similarities, notably the way accented offbeats turn into melodic sighs and the plunge without ado into the relative major for a second key. The song depends on a triplet accompanimental texture throughout and in this regard foretells some well-known songs by Schubert, for example, "Wohin?" "Trost" is not only a great song, but also a splendid short piano piece as a "song without words." In recital it would make a gorgeous prelude to Haydn's sublime Variations on a Theme in f minor of 1793 (Hob. XVII:6). Haydn resorted again to an agitated f minor to paint the last stages of despair in the cantata *Arianna a Naxos* for voice and piano of

---

[94] *JHW* XXIX/1, *Lieder für eine Singstimme mit Begleitung des Klaviers*, ed. Paul Mies (Munich-Duisburg, 1960). The soprano clef is replaced by treble clef in this edition.

[95] *Haydn, Mozart*, pp. 471–72; A. Peter Brown, "Joseph Haydn and Leopold Hofmann's 'Street Songs,'" *JAMS* 33 (1980): 356–83, provides the parallel settings by both composers of the three texts in question.

late 1789 or early 1790, Hob. XXVIb:2.[96] He chose it as well for the later orchestral solo cantata, the well-known "Scena di Berenice" composed in London for Brigida Banti in 1795.

The 1780s were not as rich as the previous decade in Haydn works for solo keyboard, but a few of them are masterpieces. Whereas in the 1770s he compiled three sets of solo sonatas, a substantial trove capped by the collection for the Auenbrugger sisters published by Artaria in 1780—the set that ends with the well-known Sonata in c minor—there are a mere handful from the 1780s by comparison, no more than six altogether. The earliest is the Sonata in e minor, Hob. XVI:34, published in London in 1783, an unauthorized edition that also includes the Sonata in D, Hob. XVI:33 (dated 1778 in a Viennese MS), and a Sonata in A♭, Hob. XVI:43, the authenticity of which has been challenged.[97]

The Sonata in e begins with an austere *Presto* in 6/8 time that has some qualities of an étude. Dynamic markings in it are so rare as to be almost nonexistent, yet Haydn achieves the effect of swelling and reducing volume by textural changes. In other words, it makes a fine piece for the harpsichord.[98] The middle movement is an *Adagio* in G and in 3/4 time, a floridly decorated melody over calm and slow-moving chordal accompaniment, until it is time for the final cadence, which blossoms into a full-voiced and rhythmically active transition to prepare the return of the initial key. Tonic e arrives with the onset of the *Vivace molto* in 2/4 time marked with the curious direction *innocentemente*. Again the right hand sings the melody to the chordal accompaniment of the left hand, in this case an Alberti bass for the refrain, the three statements of which, repeated with slight variations, surround two statements of a similar theme cast in the parallel major, which also undergoes variation. At first, the major section foregoes the Alberti bass, and then, as if converted by the intervening refrain, adopts it. Thus the movement provides an example of rondo-variation, one of Haydn's favorites, and used with even greater effect to close the Divertimento in D, Hob. XVI:19, for harpsichord, dated 1767.[99]

For a very different instrument are the three sonatas that Haydn composed and dedicated to a young princess about the same time. They are deceptively easy to play, yet sophisticated, and consist of only two movements apiece. Moreover, they take full advantage of fortepiano dynamics. This instrument alone is

---

[96] Julian Rushton, "Viennese Amateur or London Professional? A Reconsideration of Haydn's Tragic Cantata *Arianna a Naxos*," in *Music in Eighteenth-Century Austria*, ed. David Wyn Jones (Cambridge, 1991), pp. 232–45.

[97] By László Somfai, *The Keyboard Sonatas of Joseph Haydn: Instruments and Performance Practice, Genres and Styles*, trans. the author with Charlotte Greenspan (Chicago, 1995), pp. 163–64.

[98] Only by special pleading can it be placed in a category of pieces "conceived in a *tentative fortepiano* idiom," as in Somfai, *The Keyboard Sonatas of Joseph Haydn* (1995), p. 23.

[99] *Haydn, Mozart*, pp. 316–17.

named on the title page: *Trois Sonates pour le pianoforte composées et dediées à son altesse Madame la Princesse Marie Esterházy née Princesse de Lichtenstein par son trés-humble et trés-obéissant serviteur Joseph Haydn.* The firm of Heinrich Bossler at Speyer in the Rhineland brought out the first edition in 1784, hence, the works are sometimes called the Bossler Sonatas. They are believed to have been offered to the young lady as a wedding present. At age fifteen, she married the grandson and namesake of Prince Nicholas. Later, as reigning Princess Marie Hermene-gild, she would figure as the person whose name day Haydn celebrated in his last masses.[100] He may well have been her main piano teacher.

The Sonata in G offers a charming bucolic scene in 6/8 time, as if limning a portrait of the young lady (Example 4.25). How music can suggest innocence, as

EXAMPLE 4.25. *Haydn, Piano Sonata in G (Hob. XVI: 40), I*

requested in the tempo indication, remains unclear, but perhaps a pastoral vision is conveyed by the choice of key, meter, melody, and harmony, with a drone bass on tonic G reinforcing the picture. The theme is framed as a rounded binary form with both strains repeated, and gives rise to variations, of which the second and fourth are in tonic minor, the third and fifth in major. The surprise *sforzati* that Haydn injected on the second half of m. 3 and on the last beat of m. 4 are followed by several other surprises at different spots in the subsequent variations. At the very end there is a *forte* punctuation of the tonic chord spread out between the two hands as seven-voiced harmony—a foretaste of the famous effect to come a decade later in the "Surprise" Symphony. The movement requires a dynamic range from *pianissimo* to *fortissimo*, a *diminuendo* (*calando*), and instant changes of dynamic by the beat, all showing that this music is indeed "pour le pianoforte." The finale is a *Presto* in common time, a ternary form with a middle section in

[100] Jeremiah W. McGrann, "Of Saints, Name Days, and Turks: Some Background on Haydn's Masses Written for Prince Nikolaus Esterházy II," *Journal of Musicological Research* 17 (1998): 195–210.

g, and both sections in rounded binary form. Variation enters here too, as the reprise of the main section is elaborated with so many running sixteenth notes that it takes on a hint of "Turkish" music.

The other two Bossler Sonatas, in B♭ and in D, are no less attractive than the first. No. 2 begins with a substantial *Allegro* in common time cast in sonata form; to begin the seconda parte Haydn makes one of his favorite harmonic moves by descending a major third without preparation. The ensuing *Allegro di molto* in 2/4 time is in ternary form with the middle section in tonic minor. Sonata No. 3 consists of variations on a theme, an *Andante con espressione* in 3/4 time followed by a *Vivace assai* in 2/4 time in an unusual binary form, tonic arrival being greatly delayed in the second strain, which grows to many times the length of the first strain. Two-movement sonatas like these have their limitations, the biggest being lack of a contrasting key, but these works are by no means simple sonatinas. Within the limits Haydn imposed on himself he asks much of the performer and he added many details increasing their value, such as phrase extensions and eloquent perorations. Another occasion to compose a solo sonata apparently did not arrive until 1789.

Keyboard trios, or as Haydn usually called them, accompanied sonatas, had not occupied the composer for many years when in 1784 he again began writing a few. William Foster of London, having published several Haydn symphonies with success, asked the master for some works in this light genre that had such great attraction to amateur musicians. Haydn sent him three. As if to underscore his low esteem for the genre he sent works, only one of which was his own, the other two being trios by his former pupil Pleyel, who may have submitted them to him. Unfortunately, Longman and Broderip in London bought the same trios from Pleyel and published them under his name. The matter of the disputed trios went to law and was settled out of court only in 1794.[101] The trio in G, Hob. XV:5, which *was* by Haydn is a work of three movements all in the same key, an *Adagio non tanto* in 3/4 time, *Allegro* in common time, and a minuet marked *Allegro*. The work shows that Haydn persisted in thinking of the genre in terms closer to the divertimento than to his more serious chamber music, such as the string quartets.

In 1784–85, Haydn grouped three trios together—Hob. XV:6–8—and sold them to Artaria, who brought them out with a dedication to Countess Marianne de Vicsay, a niece of Prince Nicholas who lived near Esterháza. She may also have been a pupil of Haydn, who wrote Artaria on 26 November 1785 asking if these "sonatas" were already engraved and saying he wished to visit the dedicatee on her estate before leaving for Vienna "in a fortnight at the latest." On 10 December, having received a copy, he wrote again complaining in minute detail about errors of every kind in the engraving—a most instructive letter and a balm

---

[101] Landon, *Haydn*, 2:379.

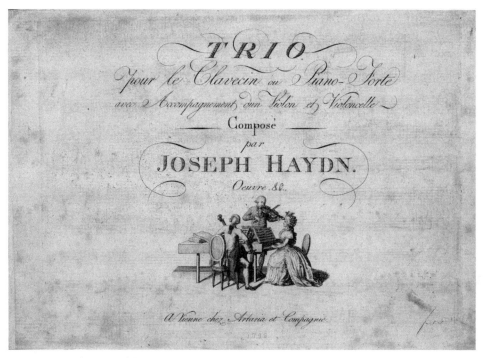

FIGURE 4.7. Title page of the Piano Trio, Hob. XV:10, published by Artaria.

to anyone who has ever had to deal with such problems. Artaria had the works engraved all over again.

The trios for Countess Vicsay are on a small scale. The genre as a whole reminds us that it, like solo keyboard sonatas, lingered for Haydn in the realm of *Damenmusik*, and indeed most of the illustrations of it in performance that come down to us show women at the keyboard (Figure 4.7). The first work, a Trio in F, and the third one, in B♭, are in two movements, the second of which is a Tempo di Minuetto. In the second trio, in D, Haydn opts for three movements, an initial *Andante* in 2/4 time, an intermediate *Andante* in d and in 6/8 time with dotted rhythm, like a siciliana, and an attractive finale, *Allegro assai* in 2/4 time, a ternary form whose middle section ends up on F♯ (V/vi), which tone then becomes the third of tonic D to begin the return of the main part. Here Haydn displays an interest greater than in the other two trios, and it will continue to grow as he gradually warms to the genre's challenges and possibilities.

Haydn's next set of three trios was sent to Foster in London, where it arrived by the end of December 1785. The first one, a Trio in A, has some endearing features well worth study. The second, in F, is a revised and extended version of a Baryton Trio of many years earlier. The third, in E♭, begins very promisingly, with ideas and textures that suggest Haydn's string quartets. It does not manage to continue to the end at this high level. The cello part, as usual, remains a mere reinforcement of the pianist's left hand bass part. Cellists often complain of this lack of independence and consequently balk at playing Haydn's trios, having been spoiled by Haydn's generous treatment of them in his quartets.

The Trio in A of this set shows that Haydn did not always assign the cello a mere doubling role. In the initial *Adagio* the piano begins with an expansive I - V - I statement, then pauses while the violin and cello, in parallel tenths, provide a response and a link to the next chordal statement of the piano (Example 4.26a).

EXAMPLE 4.26 a, b. *Haydn, Piano Trio in A (Hob. XV: 9)*
a. *I*

This leisurely slow movement is in sonata form with both parts repeated and is spun out to a total of sixty-six measures, lasting several minutes at this slow tempo.[102] Haydn ties it together with the following *Vivace* in cut time by using a similar melodic incipit (Example 4.26b). The composer's impish disposition

b. *II*

emerges in his favorite downward leap of a seventh from upbeat to downbeat going into m. 5, then a ninth leap before approaching the cadence. For a pithy earlier example of such downward leaps, we need look no further than the start of the String Quartet in g of Op. 20, which plunges from a flurry of leaps into a premature cadence.[103] In the trio, upward leaps answer the downward ones and while the cello mostly doubles the bass line, sometimes it provides chord tones otherwise lacking. The peak of playful jests with the leaping figures comes in the

---

[102] For a full discussion of it and complete musical illustration, see W. Dean Sutcliffe, "The Haydn Piano Trio: Textual Facts and Textural Principles," in *Haydn Studies*, ed. W. Dean Sutcliffe (Cambridge, 1988), pp. 246–90.

[103] *Haydn, Mozart*, p. 339, ex. 5.4. The descriptive word used there is "grotesquery."

reprise when Haydn extends the figure further (Example 4.26b, mm. 143–48).

Haydn's penchant for such leaps may have something to do with the grotesque style of dancing and its great proponent Gennaro Magri who worked for the Kärntnertor Theater in 1759, when Haydn wrote for the same troupe *Der neue krumme Teufel*.[104] Even before Haydn went to London his works evoked unfavorable comparisons with circus clowns. Charles Dibdin called him "a rope-dancer, who, though you cannot but admire how prettily he frisks and jumps about, keeps you in a constant state of terror and anxiety for fear he should break his neck."[105]

After 1785, Haydn stopped publishing trios and sonatas for a few years while his energies, those that remained to him after preparing and directing operas for his prince, mostly went into two big commissioned works, the Paris Symphonies and the *Seven Last Words*. Short of money again in 1788, he wrote Artaria on 10 August proposing to compose before year's end either three new string quartets or "three new keyboard sonatas with the accompaniment of a violin and violoncello." Artaria opted for the trios and sent an advance of twenty-five ducats, acknowledged by Haydn in his letter of 17 August, saying his zeal in composing the desired sonatas would be a guarantee of his wish to retain Artaria's friendship. On 26 October, he wrote again, saying he was still short of money, "as happens even to learned people," and stated, "In order to compose your three Klavier sonatas especially well I was forced to buy a new fortepiano." Therefore he asked Artaria to transfer thirty-one ducats directly to the organ- and instrument-maker Wenzel Schantz, saying he would repay the money by the end of the following January. The new instrument is believed to have been a fortepiano grand, which Haydn acquired at a special price, and which he later resold for two hundred ducats.[106] The Schantz brothers Wenzel and Johann were of Bohemian origin, active in Vienna from about 1780, the same year their rival Anton Walter settled in Vienna.

The three new trios, Hob. XV:11–13, were half composed, Haydn claimed in his letter to Artaria of 16 November, but on the following 8 March he was still making excuses. "The abrupt decision of my prince to quit Vienna, which he hates, caused my hasty departure for Esterháza. . . . On the day of my departure I was seized by a bad cold that made me useless for three weeks but now that I am better, thanks be to God, I promise to send the third sonata within a week."

[104] Bruce Alan Brown, "Magri in Vienna: The Apprenticeship of a Choreographer," in *The Grotesque Dancer on the Eighteenth-Century Stage: Gennaro Magri and His World*, ed. Rebecca Harris-Warrick and Bruce Alan Brown (Madison, WI, 2005), pp. 62–90.

[105] Charles Dibdin, *The Musical Tour of Mr. Dibdin* (Sheffield, 1788), p. 182, cited after Roger Fiske, "Concert Music II," in *Music in Britain: The Eighteenth Century*, ed. H. Diack Johnstone and Roger Fiske (Oxford, 1990): 205–60; 253.

[106] Somfai, *The Keyboard Sonatas of Joseph Haydn* (1995), p. 11, n. 31.

Haydn finally sent it on 29 March and Artaria published the three trios as Op. 57 in July 1789. Trio No. 1 is in E♭, like the one that preceded it, and also begins with an *Allegro moderato* in cut time; their initial themes bear some resemblance. For a second and final movement the new trio adds a Tempo di Minuetto. Trio No. 2 is more substantial. In the key of e minor it begins with another *Allegro moderato* in cut time and is followed by an *Andante* in 6/8 time and in E major, which is retained for the finale, a *Rondo. Presto* in 2/4 time that extends to 237 measures. Trio No. 3 likewise begins in minor and ends in major, in this case c/C. The movements are an *Andante* in 2/4 time and an *Allegro spiritoso* in 3/4 time that is spun out by variations to 259 measures.

In his letter of 29 March 1789 that accompanied the third trio, Haydn wrote, "I have recomposed it with variations, to suit your taste. Please get the engraving done as soon as possible because many people are achingly awaiting them." The same could be said of many music publishers elsewhere for Haydn's trios sold very well, unlike Mozart's chamber music. The public obviously loved the theme and variation form. Haydn used it often and hardly needed prompting from Artaria in this matter. Ideally one would like to play these trios, or hear them played, on a Schantz fortepiano like the one the composer claimed he had to buy in order to compose them "especially well" (besonders gut).

Artaria published the Trio in A♭, Hob. XV:14, by itself as Haydn's Op. 61 and advertised it in the *Wiener Zeitung* of 20 October 1790 as "splendidly written for the Klavier." The opening *Allegro moderato* in 2/4 time is built from a broad main theme into a rich sonata form, following which one might expect a slow movement in the relative minor, f. Instead Haydn provided an *Adagio* in 3/4 time in the remote key of E major, ♭VI to A♭. The finale, *Rondo. Vivace* in 2/4 time, effected the return to A♭.[107] More and more in his remaining years Haydn came to favor such mediant relationships between movements. Beethoven surely took notice. He used the same drop down a major third for the slow movement of his Piano Concerto No. 1 (Op. 15). With this very fine trio, one can discern Haydn's increasing interest in the genre as a vehicle for some of the deeper content he had come to invest in string quartets.

Haydn composed another set of three trios, Hob. XV:15–17, at the behest of John Bland, who visited him at Esterháza in November 1789. These are special because the first two require a flute instead of a violin; the third specifies either one or the other. The first two are truly flute sonatas and are exquisitely written to take advantage of the instrument, long familiar to Haydn as the soprano of his wind choir. Haydn picked keys especially favorable to the flute of his time, G and D (the keys of Mozart's two flute concertos), and themes that make the most of the instrument's lustrous tones. Both are in three movements, with broad first

---

[107] For a discussion of the Trio in A♭ see Landon and Wyn Jones, *Haydn*, pp. 210–11.

and third movements surrounding a middle one that is slower and in tonal or modal contrast.

The Trio in G begins with a two-measure "curtain," making the cadence before the flute enters to sing the six-measure theme (Example 4.27). The "curtain"

EXAMPLE 4.27. *Haydn, Piano Trio in G (Hob. XV:15), I*

shows its true colors when it ends the movement, which at 245 measures is very spacious. An *Andante* in 6/8 time and in C major follows, a ternary form with a middle section thematically related to the main section. The flute is just as prominent here, and reaches up to its high F♮ at a prominent moment in the theme. With his great sense for spinning one theme out of another, Haydn takes the fourth, fifth, and sixth tones from the treble of the *Allegro*'s beginning (B F♯ G) and transforms them into a stream of eighth notes comprising the theme of the finale, *Allegro moderato* in cut time, a capacious rondo of 171 measures. Not long before the end the flute gratifies us by vaulting up to its high G, the tone that makes it the shining star of both Haydn's and Mozart's orchestral winds.

The flute trio in D is only slightly less attractive. Its initial *Allegro* in sonata form and in common time again gives the main theme to the flute. For the middle movement Haydn chose an *Andantino più tosto Allegretto* in 6/8 time and in d minor, and then a rondo, *Vivace assai* in 2/4 time. The third trio, in F, reverts to normal texture and to the two-movement format most common before this time.

An *Allegro* in common time and in sonata form gives way to a routine-sounding *Finale. Tempo di Menuetto*. When Haydn returned to the composition of piano trios four years later and wrote his most famous works in the genre he favored the three-movement format.

In addition to this spate of trios at the end of the decade, Haydn composed two more solo sonatas. Christoph Gottlob Breitkopf, the Leipzig publisher who had met Haydn in Vienna in late 1786, wrote him on 10 January 1789 requesting a new fortepiano sonata, for which the composer was to name his own fee. Neither the request nor Haydn's reply are extant. Breitkopf specified delivery by March, a deadline almost met by the composer, who sent the work by 5 April, for which he received in advance a payment of ten ducats. The sonata, Hob. XVI:48, is in two movements, with an initial double variation, *Andante con espressione* in 3/4 time and in C major alternating with a related theme in c minor. Haydn's flair for coaxing original textures and dynamic contrasts out of the fortepiano was never more in evidence than here. Surpassing even this movement is the finale, a *Rondo. Presto* in 2/4 time that compares favorably with the great finale of Symphony No. 88 in G of some two years earlier. Like that gem, this one too features the two quick repeated-note upbeats of the *Gavotte gai*, and is disposed in a large five-part **A B A C A** form with teasing waits before the returns of the refrain. Some chordal spacings in this movement, such as the octaves with a third in the middle (1 3 8) moving rapidly up in the left hand, as well as the rapid runs in thirds for the right hand in the first movement, suggest a possible link with Clementi's keyboard style, of which Haydn was well aware. In his letter of 18 June 1783, he thanked Artaria for the *Clavier Sonaten* by Clementi and said, "They are very beautiful."

By 1789 at the latest, Haydn had become acquainted with the family of Dr. Peter von Genzinger, personal physician to Prince Nicholas. The Genzingers lived in Vienna at a house in the Schotten-Hof, where they held musicales. Madame Maria Anna von Genzinger, who was born in 1750, developed a cordial relationship with Haydn. She wrote him on 10 June 1789, enclosing an arrangement for keyboard of "a beautiful *Andante* from your so admirable composition, which I made from the score myself, without the help of my teacher." She asked Haydn to correct any errors and expressed the hope of seeing him again soon in Vienna, conveying her kindest regards, also from her husband and children. Haydn replied from Esterháza only four days later warmly praising her work, her handwriting, her kind words, etc. He also supplied the correct tempo of *Adagio* to her transcribed movement and asked whether she had to take the trouble of scoring the parts before making her arrangement. Of his most recent symphonies, only No. 92 in D ("Oxford") has an *Adagio* as slow movement (excluding *Adagio* slow introductions) and before that, Symphony No. 87 in A of the Paris set. Mme von Genzinger wrote again on 15 September sending the first movement of "the symphony, the *Andante* [*sic*] of which I sent you some months ago" but this letter is lost and known only from her reference to it in her follow-up letter of 29 October, which included the symphony's last movement. Haydn replied on 7 November begging her pardon for the delay in returning her "laborious and admirable work" with the excuse that during a cleaning of his rooms his copyist mislaid the first movement in an old opera score. Anyone working with many open scores lying about can readily sympathize with this explanation.

Haydn closed this letter of 7 November 1789 in an unusually personal tone: "I assure you that, in my frequently depressed moods, nothing cheers me so much as the flattering conviction that your memories of me are pleasant; for which favor I kiss your hands a thousand times." The lady answered him on 12 November acknowledging his letter and closing hers with, "I look forward with greatest pleasure to the happy day when I shall see you in Vienna." On 18 November, Haydn wrote again sending her a copy of the *Musikalischer-Potpourri* volume published by Breitkopf that included his Piano Sonata in C as well as a keyboard arrangement of Symphony No. 79 in F (lacking the minuet). "If the arrangement of the Symphony in it is yours, Oh! then I shall be doubly pleased." If not, he asked her to send him one of the symphonies she had arranged, which he would then send to Leipzig to be engraved. Too much should not be made of their small talk, consisting mainly of *formes de politesse*. Yet it does seem that the composer was trying to get more closely acquainted by drawing her in as a kind of accomplice to his labors.

In late 1789, Haydn was detained longer than usual before being allowed to go to Vienna for his annual winter visit. Dated December in his hand are several pieces for a new musical clock constructed by the prince's librarian, Joseph Niemecz, which were perhaps a holiday offering to the prince.[108] On 30 December Haydn authenticated with his name a bill presented to him for copying music for the opera company. From Vienna comes evidence about this time of Haydn's presence there. In a letter that has been assigned to Tuesday 29 December, Mozart wrote Michael Puchberg another request for money to which he added that he could not entertain Puchberg for chamber music on the following day as had been agreed because he had too much work, and asked him to tell this to Zistler (violinist Joseph Zistler). "But Thursday I am inviting you (and you alone) to come to me at ten in the morning for a small opera rehearsal—I am inviting only you and Haydn to it." The opera being readied was *Così fan tutte*. Besides its score, Mozart was finishing at this time several orchestral dances for the Carnival balls in the Redoutensaal.

The Mozarts were again living in the inner city, on the Judenplatz. It was no great distance from Puchberg, who lived in the Hoher Markt, or Haydn in the

---

[108] There is an extensive literature on Niemecz and mechanical musical instruments, summarized by John A. Rice, *The Temple of Night at Schönau* (2006), pp. 122–27.

Walnerstrasse. On Wednesday 20 January 1790, Mozart wrote again to Puchberg requesting more monetary aid and saying, "Tomorrow is the first orchestral rehearsal in the theater. Haydn will go with me to it . . . come to me about ten in the morning and we shall all go together." The premiere took place on Tuesday 26 January and it would be surprising if Haydn were not also present at it, and perhaps he attended the repeat performances on 28 and 30 January as well. Writing Mme von Genzinger on 23 January, Haydn told her of arrangements for a little quartet party on the following Friday (29 January). He mentioned a violinist by the name of Johann Baptist von Häring, who was a local banker. Mozart may have been too busy with duties in the theater on the 29th to participate in chamber music, but if he did, we can imagine that they played some of the latest quartets composed by both masters, K. 575 in D, and those from Haydn's Opp. 54–55.

Besides seeing *Così fan tutte*, Haydn almost certainly must have attended performances of the revised *Figaro* in the Burgtheater on 8 January and 1 February. He had *Figaro* under study for performance at Esterháza and had received the score and vocal parts from Vienna the previous summer. It is also the opera he mentions in a letter to Mme von Genzinger after returning, with great reluctance, to Esterháza in February 1790. They may well have witnessed one of the performances together. On 3 February, Haydn wrote her declining her invitation for that evening and wishing her many happy evenings, forever and ever the most pleasant of gatherings. As for himself, he said, those evenings were over, because he had to return to his sad loneliness in the country. "May God only grant me good health, but I fear the contrary, for today I am feeling not well at all."

Such is the background against which Haydn's last piano sonata of the decade took shape, Hob. XVI:49 in E♭, the "Genzinger" Sonata. He began it in mid-1789 with his favorite lady in mind, and finished it in the spring of 1790, the *Adagio* middle movement having been revised last. Because of the correspondence between them, we know more about the composition of this piece than any other by Haydn.

Haydn's most famous letter of all is surely the one he wrote her from Esterháza on 9 February 1790, beginning: "Well, here I sit in my wilderness, forsaken like a poor waif, almost without any human society, sad, full of the memories of noble days past. They are gone alas, and who knows when they will return? Those beautiful social gatherings, where the whole circle was of one heart, one soul, all those beautiful musical evenings . . ." For a composer so little given to self-dramatization this language is striking. It could almost have come from one of the opera libretti he was constantly perusing.

> I found everything at home in confusion, and for three days I knew not whether I was Capell-master or Capell-servant. Nothing could console me, my whole quarters were in confusion, my fortepiano that I usually love so much was perverse and dis-

obedient, it irritated rather than calmed me. I could sleep only a little and even my dreams persecuted me. Just when I was happily dreaming that I was listening to the opera *Le nozze di Figaro* the fatal north wind woke me and nearly blew the nightcap off my head. I lost twenty pounds in weight in three days, for the good Viennese food I had enjoyed disappeared on the journey. Alas, I thought to myself as I was eating in the commons here, instead of that tasty slice of beef, a chunk of cow fifty years old.

Haydn continued with this amusing description of the food served him in the court officers' refectory at Esterháza, as opposed to the delicacies he had been enjoying in the metropolis. We must not take him too seriously. He was writing to amuse and delight, a role in which we know him so well from his music, but hardly at all from his prose. And why is it *Figaro* rather than *Così* that he tells her of hearing in his dreams? Aside from studying *Figaro* for future performance as he was, it could also be that she knew it well too, a knowledge perhaps beginning with the first production in 1786, whereas she may not yet have heard the new opera.

Events at Esterháza took a turn that kept Haydn busier than ever, leaving him little time to feel sorry for himself. Princess Esterházy, the consort of Prince Nicholas for some four decades, died on 25 February, a few days after the death of Joseph II in Vienna. The prince was crushed, as Haydn wrote to Mme von Genzinger on 14 March, a letter in which he describes all the extra music making intended to console him, including a revival of Gassmann's *L'amor artigiano* especially at the prince's wish, a production for which Haydn rapidly composed three new arias. Mention is also made in this letter of a teacher of the French language coming to Esterháza, whose appointment apparently had something to do with Mme von Genzinger, or at least in which she took an interest.

There are hints in Haydn's subsequent letters that the frequency of their correspondence was the cause of gossip. On 13 May, he wrote her of his concern that one of his letters went astray and promised that "for greater security in the future and to put a stop to disgraceful curiosity I shall enclose all my letters in an extra envelope addressed to our porter." In closing this letter he asks, "When shall I have the inexpressible happiness of seeing Your Grace at Esterháza?" She evidently accompanied her husband occasionally on his trips to the castle.

Haydn's letter of 30 May laments the disappearance of his previous letter to her, in which he informed her about the production of his opera *La vera costanza* at the newly opened Theater in the Landstrasse, and told her more about the aforementioned French teacher. There are the expected praises of her towering virtue "which is acknowledged by all men," and a plea to keep writing him.

Do not be frightened away from consoling me occasionally by your pleasant letters, for they comfort me in my wilderness and are a highly necessary balm for my heart, which is so often deeply hurt. Oh could I but be with Your Grace for a quarter of an hour to unburden my troubles and to breathe in your comforting words. I suffer many annoyances under our current regime and must do so in silence. My only consolation is that I am healthy, praise God, and have a lively desire to do my work.

This last brings him up short, for he has not found the time to work on the symphony he promised to write for her in his letter of 13 March. He apologizes for this and also explains why he could go so rarely to Vienna: he had not the heart to insist on receiving permission for fear of offending his prince. "This time too will pass and the time come when I shall have the inexpressible pleasure of sitting beside Your Grace at the Clavier, hearing you play Mozart's masterpieces and kissing your hands for so many beautiful things." Physical propinquity by her side at the instrument suggests that the hand kisses here exceeded, at least in his mind, mere *formes de politesse*. Give Mozart credit for another seduction scene. Except this lady was innocent and Haydn was and remained dutifully bound elsewhere. He did not again in his letters to Her Grace come so close to crossing a certain line dictated by propriety.

The genesis of the "Genzinger" Sonata is complicated by ambiguous data. A certain young lady of high station in the Esterházy household, Anna de Jerlischek, also known as Nanette, ascended after the death of Princess Maria Elisabeth to be head housekeeper of the castle. She owned property and was related to Mme von Genzinger. Haydn treated her with great deference and inscribed the piece in question "Sonata per il Fortepiano Composta per la stimatissima Signora Anna de Jerlischek." It was composed for her only in the sense that she sponsored it. On 6 June 1790, Haydn reported excitedly to Mme von Genzinger, sparing neither capital letter nor exclamation point.

> JUST BETWEEN US! Your Grace should know that our Mademoiselle Nanette has commissioned me to compose a new Clavier sonata for you, which may not come into the hands of anyone else. I consider myself fortunate to have received such an order. Your Grace will receive this sonata in two weeks at most. Said Mademoiselle promised me a payment for it. Your Grace will easily understand that I shall refuse any; your approval will ever be the greatest reward for me.

The story has a concocted ring to it. Why did the composer need an excuse to compose such a sonata? It could be that Mlle Nanette was being used as a go-between so as to deflect further suspicions of his paying Her Grace too many attentions. In his letter to her of 20 June, Haydn gives a contradictory account of when and how the work was composed.

> The sonata is in E♭, entirely new, and forever meant only for Your Grace. How wonderful though that the sonata's last movement contains the very Menuet and Trio

that Your Grace requested from me in your latest letter. This sonata was already intended for Your Grace a year ago. Only the *Adagio*, which I recommend to Your Grace most highly, did I recently complete, and it has a lot of meaning, which I shall explain to Your Grace when the occasion permits. It is somewhat difficult but full of feeling [Empfindung]. What a pity that Your Grace does not have a fortepiano by Schantz, with which so many effects could be created.

A very personal matter indeed has this sonata become. Its minuet finale was already known to the lady, who made a special request for it, while the *Adagio* expressed feelings so deep they had to be explained to her in person.

At the beginning of this same letter, Haydn related how he had delivered the sonata to Mlle Nanette and was awaiting her command to perform it for her. He wondered whether Her Grace had already received it by mail. At the letter's end in an extended kind of postscript, there is still more, and it suggests that Haydn was afraid his ruse involving Mlle Nanette might unravel.

> N. B. Mlle Nanette must not learn that this sonata was already half finished since she might get other ideas that could be damaging to me. I must be very careful not to lose her good will. Meanwhile, I count myself fortunate that I can at least be the means of giving her some enjoyment, especially as the offering is made to you, my dearest Frau von Genzinger. Oh, if only I could play this sonata [for you] a couple of times, then I could reconcile myself to staying longer in my wilderness. I have so much to say to Your Grace, so much to confess, things no one but Your Grace alone may hear. What cannot be now will, I hope to God, come this winter, and the time is almost half over until then.

He ends this letter with most obedient respect to her husband and all her family. Finally, "Your Grace I kiss 1000 times—on the hands."

Haydn did not have the greatest confidence in his abilities as a keyboard player, as is evident in his next letter to her, dated a week later and describing his first performance of the sonata for others.

> Your Grace will surely have received the new keyboard sonata, or if not, will do so in the same mail as this letter [dated 27 June]. Three days ago, I had to play the sonata at Mlle Nanette's in the presence of my most gracious prince. I was doubtful at first whether I would win approval because of the sonata's difficulty, but was then convinced of the opposite when I received from her own hand a gold snuffbox as a present. Now I wish only that Your Grace will be satisfied with it, so that I can obtain greater credit with my benefactress. For this reason I ask Your Grace to let her know, if not personally at least through your husband, that I have been unable, for joy, to conceal her generosity, the more so since I am convinced that Your Grace shares pleasure at all boons bestowed on me.

This is a far cry from the composer's earlier disdain of any monetary reward for the sonata. He continued the letter by again recommending the purchase of a Schantz fortepiano to replace her still serviceable *Flügel*, which he suggests she give to her daughter Peperl. "Your beautiful hands and their facility in execution deserve this and still more. I know that I should have written this sonata for your type of Clavier, but it was just impossible because I am not at all used to it any more." *Flügel* normally meant a wing-shaped harpsichord, but it could also mean a large wing-shaped fortepiano. The instrument that Haydn no longer used and urged her to replace was probably a Walter fortepiano. We know that Walter was called to Esterháza in 1781 to work on the fortepianos as well as the harpsichords.

Haydn's next letter to Her Grace, dated 4 July, has much more on the choice of instrument for her and introduces a surprising twist, again involving Mlle Nanette. Prince Nicholas had agreed to finance a new fortepiano for Madame. "I am somewhat the cause of this because I repeatedly begged Mlle Nanette to persuade your husband to buy you one. Now the decision depends entirely on Your Grace to choose one that suits your touch and taste." Next comes the most often-quoted passage in this letter, comparing the different makers of instruments and their products.

> Certainly, my friend Herr Walter is very famous, and I receive from him every year many civilities. But between us and to be candid, among ten of his products sometimes there is but a single instrument that one can rightly call good, besides which they are exceptionally expensive. I am acquainted with the fortepiano of Herr Nikl, which is first rate, but too heavy for Your Grace's hand, and one cannot play everything on it with the appropriate delicacy, therefore I wish Your Grace to try one made by Herr Schantz. His fortepianos have an entirely special lightness and an agreeable action. A good fortepiano is greatly needed by Your Grace, and my sonata will win so much therefrom.

In a final paragraph, Haydn thanked Her Grace for exercising the caution he suggested with regard to Mlle Nanette. He mentioned the gold box she had given him (which was tarnished) and hoped that his recommendation of Schantz will be acted upon, else she might receive a fortepiano "beautiful on the outside but with a stiff action within."

The Sonata in E♭ at the base of all these discussions and recommendations may seem somewhat eclipsed by the verbal onslaught. Yet the more one gets to know the work the lovelier it becomes. The first two movements, *Allegro* and *Adagio*, plumb levels of expressiveness from which the *Finale. Tempo di Minuet* at first seems remote. We should bear in mind that this "Menuet and Trio," as Haydn called it in his letter of 20 June, carried meaning from earlier as a bond between composer and recipient. If composers banned finales on preexistent material of a light nature, we would be deprived of another finale in the same key of E♭, that of the "Eroica" Symphony. The "Genzinger" Sonata compares well with Haydn's most ambitious piano trios of 1789–90 in having amply proportioned movements in a pattern of fast, slow, and finale of dance-oriented character.

The *Allegro* in 3/4 time deploys an upbeat beginning of four sixteenth notes in the right hand answered by a smooth descent in sixth chords and eighth notes, outlining I - V in four measures, repeated in the following consequent as V - I⁶. It continues as the upbeat figure climbs higher and then leads to a full cadence (with a falling melodic seventh in the treble leading the way into it). After the modulation, Haydn modified the initial theme to serve in the new key. He introduced another secondary theme in the bass, requiring the right hand to cross over the accompanying sixteenth notes of the left hand. This is not the first time the composer had called for hand crossings but he had been sparing in their use. Aiming toward the goal of a big cadence on B♭ to end the prima parte, the harmony gets derailed to the chord of A♭, a tone lower, which is then exploited for its color before giving way through an augmented-sixth chord to the expected tonal goal and an attractive closing idea in flowing eighth notes related to those in the initial theme. The seconda parte starts in the same place by repeating the material just heard, treated in canon, then in a long chain of suspensions moving to a resolution on c minor, vi of the original tonic. After briefly exploring the key of D♭, Haydn heads in leisurely fashion back toward E♭, combining various elements in new ways and introducing another chain of suspensions, this time in four voices instead of three. After a generous amount of dominant seventh preparation and wispy hints of the first theme, a long run from the top of the keyboard meanders down *a suo piacere* to the tenor range for the reprise, which is quite regular. The part that required crossing hands before does not do so here. The descent one whole tone to A♭ there brings D♭ here. Then comes a lovely peroration on the closing idea (Example 4.28a). A rapid run for the right hand up to a G above tonic E♭ resolves the last of a series of V⁷ - I cadences, an optimistic gesture, lacking the finality that a run up to the tonic note itself would have projected.

EXAMPLE 4.28 a, b. *Haydn, Piano Sonata in E♭ (Hob. XVI: 49)*

a. *I*

Adagio e cantabile in B♭ is also in 3/4 time, an unusual move by Haydn. As the designation implies, the movement is pure song with harmonic accompaniment throughout. Its large ternary form provides another difference with the opening *Allegro*. The middle section in tonic minor contrasts strongly with the main section. It has its own texture consisting of an accompaniment in sextuplets for the right hand in the tenor range supporting a dialogue between gruff octaves in the deep bass answered by crossing the left hand over the right to play a more lyric plea in the high soprano. Such a dialogue could easily be heard in terms of an intransigent male voice to which a pleading female voice replies. Was this the message that Haydn wanted to explain to Her Grace in person? In any case, another composer achieved very much the same effect by a rustling mid-level accompaniment with dialogue between high and low achieved by hand crossings, namely Schubert, in the middle section of his Impromptu in f minor from Op. 142. When Haydn's main section returns it is more exquisitely decorated by embellishments than ever. The movement ends *pianissimo*, dying out in the high tenor range, which must have sounded particularly beautiful to the composer on the Schantz fortepiano he vaunted for its delicacy.

The finale, with its *Tempo di Minuet*, adds another movement in 3/4 time, which is even more unusual. It is perhaps this as much as anything else that has caused some adverse criticism. A wiser reaction would be to regard the movement as completing the portrait of its graceful recipient, Mme von Genzinger. One purely musical feature that enhances the feeling of completion arrives with the minuet's descending sixth chords like those of the sonata's very beginnings; another is that the Trio resembles in theme the closing idea of the *Allegro* (Example 4.28b). Furthermore, after the minuet returns, shortened to its first strain

b. III

only, there is a second Trio in minor with incessant triplet motion that cannot help but recall the middle section of the *Adagio*. When it subsides, the Minuet returns a last time, complete, and finally adopts a flowing triplet accompaniment. The sonata ends quietly after a short coda.

The correspondence was not quite over even after the sonata had been delivered to the source of its inspiration. There were thanks to be rendered, comments to be made, and even a complaint. Mme von Genzinger wrote on 11 July acknowledging receipt of his last letter of 4 July and saying that she agrees to leave the choice of an excellent fortepiano up to him, also that Mlle Nanette will give him the payment order signed by the prince. She finds little to say about the work itself.

> The sonata pleases me exceedingly well. Yet one thing I would like changed (if it could be done without altering the piece's beauty) is the passage in the second part of the *Adagio* where the hands cross over, because I am not used to this, so it is difficult for me. Please let me know in what way it could be changed.

The complaint seems odd, hardly explicable unless she is just carping in order to have something concrete to say about the work. Hand-crossings like this were quite common in keyboard music of the time. Note that she did not complain about the similar technique required in the *Allegro*. If crossing the left hand over the right for a short passage was new to her, she was obviously unfamiliar with its telling use in Mozart's Sonata in A, K. 331. Haydn's passages are easier to play than Mozart's because more time is allowed for the left hand to find the notes in the high range. Haydn himself acknowledged that the sonata was difficult (letter of 27 June). More likely what he had in mind were the passages in three- and four-part counterpoint in the development of the *Allegro*.

In the same letter of 11 July, Her Grace made cursory mention of two further works. She was returning to him another "Sonata" he had lent her to copy (Trio in F, Hob. XV:17) which she pronounced "sehr schön." Her terse comment on the run-of-the-mill Trio would have been better applied to the sonata especially written for her. She continued by reminding the composer of the symphony he promised to write for her and her alone, saying she hoped it had not been displaced by the sonata. After all his labor over the sonata, and all the cares taken to please her with it, this remark seems petulant. The promise of a symphony composed just for her was one that Haydn regretted having made. He apologized profusely in his letter of 15 August, saying that it had long haunted his mind but the pressures of work precluded its being written. He wrote this on her name day (Assumption BVM) in an attempt to assuage her and held out the thought that a happier time was approaching. What he could not have known then was that the greatest change in his life was about to occur with the death of Prince Nicholas on 28 September 1790.

At least one more reference to the "Genzinger" Sonata occurs in the correspondence. On 2 March 1792, Haydn wrote Her Grace from London to express his dismay on learning that the sonata destined for her alone had appeared in print: Artaria published it as Op. 66 in August 1791. "I was alarmed not a little when I had to read the unpleasant news about the sonata. By God I would have rather lost 25 ducats than to hear about this robbery." Haydn's business dealings with publishers leave us somewhat doubtful of his protestations. He blamed his copyist (Johann Elssler?) and added, "But I hope to make good this loss and in fact again through the hands of Mme Tost for I do not wish to give her any reason for reproaching me." Mlle Nanette, aged 25, married Johann Tost on 14 December 1790, bringing him a dowry of 6,000 gulden plus joint rights to a much larger capital, which he proceeded to decimate. A daughter was born to them in 1792 whom she attempted to protect financially in her will before dying in 1796.[109]

Departure

By the year 1790, Haydn had passed nearly three decades in the service of the Esterházys. He became Vice-Kapellmeister in the spring of 1761 under Prince Paul, who died a year later and was succeeded by his brother Nicholas. In 1766, Haydn advanced to the position of Ober-Kapellmeister. He remained loyal to Prince Nicholas while chafing at the many restrictions imposed on his freedom. He was treated very generously by the prince, who twice rebuilt Haydn's house in Eisenstadt after it was destroyed by fire.

Prince Nicholas, at age seventy-seven, may have been failing in the summer of 1790. Performances at his opera house stopped suddenly at the beginning of September, when the season was at its height. He made the move, unusual for this time of year, of going to Vienna, perhaps in need of more medical attention. He died there on 28 September. In his will, he left provision that Haydn should get an annual pension of one thousand gulden. Two other musicians of long service were also rewarded with life pensions, the tenor Leopold Dichtler and concertmaster Luigi Tomasini. Prince Anton, who succeeded his father, was less interested in music and glad to eliminate the huge expenditures required by Esterháza's opera company, which he dismissed. Of his instrumental musicians he retained at first only the wind band (*Feldharmonie*) needed for the hunt and parades; Haydn interceded for the orchestral winds and saved their jobs too. Both Haydn and Tomasini remained in princely service and received wages in addition to their pensions but they were free at the same time to accept other engagements. Haydn considered going to Naples at the invitation of its king, Ferdinand IV, who was visiting Vienna in 1790 and for whom he had composed the several notturni, or lire concertos. Another more challenging offer won him over instead.

For Haydn these events meant a big rupture in his life and career. He sold his house in Eisenstadt and went to Vienna, where he took an apartment on the ramparts overlooking the Glacis (today's Stadtpark) on the eastern side of the

[109] Gerlach, "Johann Tost," pp. 363ff. Tost turned out to be a prodigal and died poor.

city. Here he and his wife spent the rest of the year until he left for London on 15 December 1790. His mistress Luigia Polzelli, dismissed along with the rest of the opera troupe, also moved to Vienna. When Haydn wrote to her from London on 14 March 1791, a long news-filled letter in Italian, her address was "Madame Polzelli à Vienna im Starnbergischen Freyhaus auf der Wieden Nr. 161," which made her a close neighbor of Schikaneder's theatrical company. She had begged Haydn for money and sent the news that her husband Antonio was at death's door, her son Pietro ill. He sent her a sum of 100 florins by way of one of the Esterházy officials in his confidence, insisting that the sum appear to come from Luigia's sister in London. Apparently he did not wish to have his liaison with Luigia known to Prince Anton.

Johann Peter Salomon, renowned German violinist and London impresario, hastened to Vienna upon hearing of the death of Prince Nicholas. Dies and Griesinger differ slightly on Salomon's itinerary. Griesinger says that "he was in Cologne on his way back to London after he had engaged several German musicians for Gallini," and that Gallini "had gone to Italy for singers." Dies states that Salomon was "en route to Italy." John Gallini, formerly Giovanni Gallini, was an Italian dancer, choreographer, and impresario who had worked his way up in English society, marrying the eldest daughter of the Third Earl of Abingdon, whose brother was one of Haydn's patrons. Gallini was said to have been awarded a knighthood of the Order of the Golden Spur by the Pope and in London was styled "Sir John." As manager of the King's Theatre in the Haymarket, he commissioned Haydn to write an opera and moreover, paid the composer in advance for it.

Haydn had long been urged by Gallini (prompted by Charles Burney) to come to London as Opera Composer of the King's Theatre.[110] To Gallini's offers in 1783 Haydn replied with a request for £600. Negotiations faltered but were the subject of renewed enquiries from Gallini in 1787. The contract that Salomon, acting for Gallini, worked out for the 1791 season in London guaranteed Haydn £300 for an opera, £300 for six symphonies, and further sums for publications rights, for other compositions, and for directing performances of his works. These potent monetary arguments won Haydn over.

Dies and Griesinger offer characteristically divergent reports of what took place before Haydn's departure. Griesinger is terse in recounting what Haydn told him about his last meeting with Mozart.

> Mozart said to Haydn, at a happy meal with Salomon, "You will not bear it very long and will probably soon come back again, because you are no longer young." "But I

---

[110] *The Letters of Dr. Charles Burney, Volume 1 (1751–1784)*, ed. Alvaro Ribeiro (Oxford, 1991), pp. 382, 401; Ian Woodfield, *Opera and Drama in Eighteenth-Century London: The King's Theatre, Garrick, and the Business of Performance* (Cambridge, 2001), pp. 213–14.

am still vigorous and in good health," answered Haydn. He was at that time almost fifty-nine years old, but he did not find it necessary to conceal the fact. Had Mozart not hastened to an early death on December 5, 1791, he would have taken Haydn's place in Salomon's concerts in 1794.

The last item of information does not occur in Dies or elsewhere. It was Haydn's intention after his return to Vienna to retire in favor of Mozart, or so he told Griesinger.

Dies elaborated more on what Haydn told him, or perhaps he was able to coax the master into saying more. This account stems from his Eleventh Visit on 21 November 1805.

> "If it pleases my prince," said Haydn, "I'll go with you to London." Prince Anton granted permission for the journey at once, but it was not all right as far as Haydn's friends were concerned, the ones who had so often before tried to persuade him to leave Vienna. They reminded him of his age (sixty years) [*sic*], of the discomforts of a long journey, and of many other things to shake his resolve. But in vain! Mozart especially took pains to say "Papa!" as he usually called him, "you have had no training for the great world, and you speak too few languages." "Oh!" replied Haydn, "my language is understood all over the world!"

Whether he ever made such a witty and perceptive response to Mozart matters not: it was true. But it was so much more true after Haydn's London works and monumental successes like *The Creation* and *The Seasons* that we can forgive Dies if he made it up nearer the time of his writing, or Haydn did in 1805. We could trust Dies more readily if he did not make small errors like misstating Haydn's age in 1790. As for the universality of Haydn's music, there is a curious echo of the idea in the text of *The Creation*, as we shall see in Chapter 6.

Dies continues with some reflections of his own bearing on the rarity of close and friendly relations between two great masters of the art.

> The pointed expression of both composers, the unrestrained utterance of the truth, many readers might take for intentionally offensive raillery; for, in the usual course of events, two artists like Haydn and Mozart ought to hate and persecute one another. No doubt, too, both would have indulged in fury if they had been ordinary men. Nature, however, was pleased to make, as it were, extravagant use of the harmonic stuff necessary in the formation of two such superior beings, so I find it no wonder that they valued one another highly and were joined by a bond of sincere friendship.

Indeed, the extreme rarity of such a close relationship between two composers of the greatest genius challenges one to come up with any other examples of such a phenomenon.

Haydn was a man of caution when it came to money, as years of poverty and hunger as a youth had properly taught him to be. Dies explains some of Haydn's monetary concerns for his family upon leaving, then concludes as follows.

> Salomon had to agree to deposit in the Fries and Company Bank 5,000 gulden as indemnity for any untoward event. When Haydn had settled this and his household affairs, he fixed his departure and left on December 15, 1791 [*sic*] in company with Salomon. Mozart on this day never left his friend Haydn. He dined with him, and said at the moment of parting, "We are probably saying our last farewell in this life." Tears welled from the eyes of both. Haydn was deeply moved, for he applied Mozart's words to himself, and the possibility never occurred to him that the thread of Mozart's life could be cut off by the inexorable Parcae within the following year.

It might be thought that this reference to the Fates of Roman mythology by Dies was more literary than would ever have been used by Haydn himself. On the other hand, he had, after all, been dealing with opera librettos for most of his long creative life, and they were replete with such references.

Griesinger confined his few further remarks on the older composer's relationship to Mozart in a paragraph that begins with Haydn's generosity in praising several other composers, coming after one about his pride in his humble beginnings and his modesty about his own works.

> No one also was more inclined to do justice to the merits of others than Haydn. He openly acknowledged that most of what he knew he had learned from Emanuel Bach.[111] Likewise, he always spoke of Gluck, of Handel, and of his earlier teachers with the most grateful respect. "Where Mozart is, Haydn cannot appear!" he wrote, when he was invited at the same time as Mozart to Prague for the coronation of Emperor Leopold II; and he repeated with deep emotion and tears in his eyes, "Mozart's loss is irreparable. I shall never in my life forget his clavier playing. It touched the heart."

Something is amiss here. The significant clue after the first quoted exclamation is "he wrote." Haydn must have been referring to his written reply in response to a request to send one of his operas to Prague, quoted above, and dating from December 1787, as Griesinger himself affirms in his final paragraph, after which he quotes Haydn's letter. Somehow Griesinger mixed this up with the Prague coronation of October 1791. That Haydn was in England throughout the entire year 1791 was well known to the entire world of music. What Griesinger did was

---

[111] In a more reliable document, his autobiographical letter of 1776, Haydn says he learned "the true fundamentals of composition" from Porpora and does not mention Bach. *Haydn, Mozart*, pp. 237–38.

paraphrase Haydn's remarks in the 1787 letter and boil them down to a terse "Where Mozart is, Haydn cannot appear!"

The Salomon party first traveled to Munich, where Haydn made the acquaintance of Christian Cannabich, one of his warm admirers among symphony composers and music directors. Griesinger gets the location right but Dies says Mannheim, where Cannabich had formerly been concertmaster of the famous orchestra. From Munich, they made a brief visit to Wallerstein Castle so that Haydn could meet his patron Prince Krafft Ernst von Oettingen-Wallerstein. Then they hurried on to Bonn, Salomon's native town, where they rested for a few days. The honors paid to Haydn there by archbishop and elector Maximilian are recounted above. They made rapid passage through the Austrian Netherlands, recently pacified by the concessions of Emperor Leopold II, via Brussels to Calais, the only patch of French territory that they touched. Haydn surely would have welcomed the chance to visit Paris and meet his most fervent admirers in musical and Masonic circles there, which the relatively calm political climate of the year 1790 would have permitted, but the opening of London's winter concert season did not. From Calais, they made a nine-hour crossing of the Channel on the first day of January 1791. The next day they arrived in London.

5
Haydn in London,
1791–1795

NTIL he left Vienna in late 1790, Haydn had spent his entire life within a short radius of the imperial capital. The furthest he got from it was his early service to Count Morzin in Bohemia, near Pilsen. To the jumble of impressions made on him by his rapid journey through southern Germany, the Rhineland, and the Austrian Netherlands, were added in quick succession his first experience of the sea, travel through the English countryside, and, at last, the great metropolis of London.

He wrote two letters back to Vienna, both dated 8 January 1791, six days after arriving in London: an account of his professional doings to his employer Prince Anton, and a longer, chattier account of his experiences to Mme von Genzinger, to whom he had already written a short note from Calais before embarking on a stormy crossing of the Channel. In his January letter to her, he recounted the voyage in some detail. "I remained on deck during the entire passage so as to observe to my full that monstrous beast the ocean [um das ungeheure Thier das Meer satsam zu betrachten]." He had witnessed operatic storms of course, even taken part in creating them, along with the wave machine and other theatrical marvels, but this was the first time he had actually experienced any body of water larger than the shallow and marshy Neusiedler See. As the winds grew ever stronger and the waves more mountainous, he was a little afraid, he admitted to her, and a little indisposed, but not sick, unlike most of the other passengers. "I did not feel the effects of the passage right away and went on to London but then it took me two days to recover."

He first visited his friend and publisher John Bland at No. 45 High Holborn, opposite Chancery Lane. Meanwhile Salomon was preparing an apartment for him close to his own at 18 Great Pulteney Street in Soho, near Golden Square, a bustling part of town just north of Piccadilly Circus. The location was convenient for them, being about equidistant between the Hanover Square Rooms for Salomon's concerts and the King's Theatre in the Haymarket, where Haydn was contracted to Gallini for an opera. Near their residence, on the other side of Great Pulteney Street, was the music shop of John Broadwood, who offered Haydn a room in which to compose, which was probably not nearly soundproof enough to suit the composer. Haydn could attend Mass nearby at the Catholic chapel of the Bavarian embassy on Golden Square.[1]

The First Months

Haydn had prepared for his arrival in London with his usual care for propriety and detail, quite in contrast with Mozart's helter-skelter descent on Berlin in 1789. He requested letters of introduction from Vienna to diplomats in London and carried them with him, one from Swieten (in French) to the Austrian ambassador Count Johann von Stadion, another from King Ferdinand of Naples to his ambassador Prince Castelcicala. In his January letter to Mme von Genzinger he wrote that following a few days' rest and some sightseeing, he delivered the letters. "After looking at this endlessly huge city of London, the various beauties and marvels of which have quite astonished me, I soon paid the necessary calls, such as to the Neapolitan Ambassador, and to our own; both called on me in return two days later, and four days ago I lunched with the former." The local newspapers, carefully primed by Gallini and Salomon, were filled with notices of his arrival, as he wrote her in the same letter: "My arrival caught the attention of the whole city and for three days the story was dragged out in all the newspapers. Everyone wants to make my acquaintance." Haydn's innate caution came to his rescue. "I had to dine out six times already, and if I wished I could be invited out every day, but I must consider first my health, and secondly my work." He set limits on receiving visits. "With the exception of Mylords I accept no callers until 2 p.m. and about 4 o'clock I dine at home with Monsieur Salomon. I have a neat, comfortable, but also very expensive lodging." He was very concerned about prices. "My landlord is Italian and at the same time a cook who serves me well with four meals a day. We each pay, without including wine or beer, 1 fl. 30 kr. a day—everything here is frightfully expensive."

[1] Philip Olleson, "The London Roman Catholic Embassy Chapels and Their Music in the Eighteenth and Early Nineteenth Centuries," in *Music in Eighteenth-Century Britain*, ed. David Wyn Jones (Aldershot, 2000), pp. 101–18.

In the same letter to Mme von Genzinger he relates how he was taken to a "grand amateur concert" at which he was led to the front and roundly cheered by the audience. The event was a concert of the Academy of Ancient Music in Freemasons' Hall led by Samuel Arnold. It was followed by a banquet for 200 in an adjoining room where he was toasted with Burgundy wine. "All this, my gracious lady, was very flattering and yet I wished after a time that I could flee to Vienna in order to have some quiet for my work, for the noise made here by various street criers selling their wares is unbearable." And next he added a very few words about that work. "Because the libretto for the opera is not fully ready I am now working on symphonies. In order to have more quiet I shall have to rent a room in the suburbs." He did so, hiring a room where he could work daily in the then rural hamlet of Lisson Grove to the northwest of London, near Paddington. Here he "found the necessary quiet for composing," says Dies, "and respite from the constant visits of the curious."

Writing to Prince Anton perhaps a few days later, although under the same date, 8 January, he was far more brief. Whereas we might expect him to elaborate on his diplomatic visits, he was cursory about them, and what he did say more about is a subject of much greater interest—his opera. Some informed source told him the opera's name and the general content soon after his arrival.

> The new opera I am to compose is entitled *Orfeo* and is in five acts. I shall not receive it for a few days yet. It is said to be entirely different from the one by Gluck. The prima donna is called Madame Lops. She is from Munich and a pupil of the famous [Regina] Mingotti. The seconda donna is Madame Capeletti. The celebrated tenor [Giacomo] Davide will create the primo uomo part. The opera has only three persons, Madame Lops, Davide, and a castrato reputed to be nothing very special. Otherwise, the opera is said to be dotted with choruses, ballets, and many big changes of scene.

Whoever told Haydn this must have been close to the librettist Carlo Badini, or to Gallini, if not one or the other of these in person. A choral-balletic-scenographic kind of spectacle suggests that Gluck's masterpiece was having some effect on imagining the new work, even if the poet was trying to distance himself from such an iconic opera by bringing forth an "entirely different" drama on the same subject. The three characters Haydn reported would rather confirm the limitation Gluck and Calzabigi imposed by restricting their characters to Orfeo, Euridice, and Amore. Oddly, Haydn named four singers for only three roles, but perhaps Capeletti was only a backup if needed. The libretto at this unfinished stage apparently had not acquired its third most important role: Euridice's father Creonte. Two of Creonte's three arias are on turgidly moral or "philosophical" texts, which may help explain how the opera gained its alternate title "L'animo del filosofo." Possibly Badini delayed finishing the libretto because the addition of this role was a late idea about how to further distance his version of the legend from Calzabigi's.

In closing his letter of 8 January to Prince Anton, Haydn relayed some concrete details that might point to Gallini as his informant. "In two weeks the first opera, *Pirro* by Paisiello, will be given." Then he added that Salomon's concerts would begin on 11 February, "of which I shall give Your Excellency a full account." Was Prince Anton more interested in music than has been generally assumed? More likely, Haydn wished his professional doings to be known in some detail to his principal employer, looking ahead to the time when he should report back to work.

What Haydn did not know at this time was that a conspiracy at the highest levels of power had been formed to prevent Gallini and William Taylor from reopening the King's Theatre in the Haymarket. Taylor had nearly finished rebuilding the theater after it burned in 1789, but meanwhile a rival company and theater had been set up in the Pantheon on Oxford Street. The main conspirators behind it were the Prince of Wales (the future George IV), the Duke of Bedford, and the Marquis of Salisbury. Playing a particularly sordid game was the last of these—as Lord Chamberlain he was responsible for licensing the theaters, a scandalous conflict of interest were his part in the conspiracy to become known; a way out of this impasse was later found by having the Pantheon conveniently burnt down.[2] The Prince of Wales was scarcely less duplicitous since he appeared to support Gallini and Haydn strongly while allowing Bedford and Salisbury to guarantee a license to the rival opera company of the Pantheon. Charles Burney, another Haydn supporter, had invested heavily in the Pantheon; he privately predicted that Taylor's theater in the Haymarket would be abandoned "for want of money to go on, or for want of a license, should it be finished."

What should have been a triumph for Haydn's opera eventually came to naught. Instead of a reopening of the King's theater in the Haymarket that included *Orfeo ed Euridice* as the new opera of the season, following Paisiello's *Pirro*, it was the Pantheon opera company that opened. This company also aimed high, while attempting to please the well-known tastes of the London public. It hired as prima donna the experienced German soprano Gertrude Mara, as primo uomo the even more famous Gasparo Pacchierotti, soprano castrato. Several less renowned Italian singers, three of whom reserved the right to appear also in buffo operas, completed the company, along with some famous dancers. Wilhelm Cramer led the Pantheon's orchestra. The manager of the company was one Robert O'Reilly, who had written to Mozart on 26 October 1790 inviting him to provide two operas, either serious or comic, acting on the information that Mozart

---

[2] Curtis Price, "Italian Opera and Arson in Late Eighteenth-Century London," *JAMS* 42 (1989): 55–107. His findings resulted from a discovery of Bedford's papers.

was about to arrive in London. The letter begins, "Par une personne attachée à Son Altesse Royale le Prince de Galles j'apprends votre dessein de faire un voyage en Angleterre." The offer in financial terms was not very generous: £300, compared to Haydn's receiving a similar amount for one opera. Whether Mozart ever replied to the letter, or even received it, is not known. As its house composer the Pantheon settled for the not very distinguished Joseph Mazzinghi, an English-born Corsican. Paisiello was invited to fill this position. He declined but did compose for the company a new *dramma giocoso*, *La locanda*, which he sent from Naples. Financial problems dogged the Pantheon opera almost from the start, and manager O'Reilly was forced to take the fall for its failure; before the end of 1791 he fled to Paris to escape imprisonment for debt. In his favor it should be said that besides inviting Mozart, he gave William Turner his first job, painting stage sets.[3]

Haydn's third surviving letter from London was sent to his mistress Luigia Polzelli in Vienna. The autograph says 4 March 1791 but this must be a mistake for 14 March. Luigia had written him asking for money to help her deal with a dying husband and a sick son, Pietro. Haydn began his reply by commiserating with her troubles and wishing Pietro a speedy recovery. He mentions seeing Luigia's sister, the soprano Cristina Negri, in London, and regrets that he has not been able to see her more often recently because he is weighed down with work preparing his opera and concerts, also because he is constantly annoyed by having to attend other concerts. (In London there was a concert of some kind every night of the week, and Haydn was under pressure to honor by his presence the more important ones, such as the Professional Concert). Then he turned to news of Gallini's company, which had just given an open rehearsal of the first opera.

> Until now our theater has not been allowed to open since there is no license from the king. Signor Gallini will open with a kind of subscription, if not he will lose £20,000. I shall lose nothing because the money has already been deposited with the banker [Moritz] Fries in Vienna. My opera, entitled *L'anima del filosofo*, will go into production at the end of May. I have already finished the second act; there are five acts, and the last two are quite short. Signor Gallini, in order to show our theater, opera, and ballet to the public, has adopted a strategy of treating the general rehearsal of the opera as if it were a premiere. He distributed four thousand tickets and more than five thousand persons showed up. The opera entitled *Il Pyhro*, by Paisiello, pleased rather well [ha piaciuto assai]. Unfortunately, our prima donna is a nitwit [salame] and I shall not take her for my opera. The ballet was a great success [il Ballo è andato alle stelle]. Now we must wait to see whether the king says yes or no to our theater.

[3] Judith Milhous, Gabriella Dideriksen, and Robert D. Hume, *Italian Opera in Late Eighteenth-Century London*, vol. 2: *The Pantheon Opera and its Aftermath, 1789–1795* (Oxford, 2001), pp. 51–54.

The whole subject of reopening the theater and Haydn's opera presents a maze that can trap even reputable scholars. Exception must be taken to a recent work in which it is stated that the King's Theatre was scheduled to reopen with Haydn's *Orfeo and Euridice*.[4] The plan was always to open with Paisiello's *Pirro*, which happened after a fashion, giving Haydn the time to take the measure of the soloists and orchestra while finishing his score.

Haydn continued his letter of 14 March to Luigia with a few remarks on the Pantheon Opera relative to a performance of their pasticcio of Sacchini's *Armida*, which opened the company's season on 18 February. "When our theater opens, the other theater, that is our opponent, will have to remain closed, because the large castrato [castrone] and the prima donna are too old, and their opera in fact did not please at all." His words concern the principal singers Mara (aged 42) and Pacchierotti (aged 51). It is true that Mara reached her peak when she sang in Paris from 1782 to 1784. Trained at first as a violinist, she was more technically skilled in music than most singers but never was much of an actress. The year 1791 saw the last of Pacchierotti's several London seasons stretching over many years.

Rosa Lops, the rival prima donna of Gallini's company, was no nymph herself. A reviewer in the *Morning Chronicle* said of her appearance at the open rehearsal of *Pirro* on 23 February that she was "a good and finished singer; she has every accomplishment but youth and beauty."[5] Little is known about her except that she was from Munich and was a pupil of Regina Mingotti. There was a family of string players named Lops in the service of the Bavarian court through much of the century and Rosa might have married one of the two violinists active there in her time, Joseph and Anton Lops. As for Mingotti, who sang in London in the 1750s and early 1760s, she ended her stage career at Munich in 1767, aged 45. Lops was perhaps the same age when she disappeared from view in London in 1791. If Haydn had truly finished the first two acts of *Orfeo* by early March, most of the prima donna's role was composed. Having died by the end of Act II, Euridice is absent from Act III and only briefly resurrected in Act IV. His deprecation of Lops notwithstanding, Haydn may have had little choice as to the casting. His position of house composer at the opera did not give him his former rights as Kapellmeister in assigning roles. Perhaps he maligned his leading lady to Luigia partly in order to give a little encouragement to his mistress of long standing but few musical accomplishments.

---

[4] John Spitzer and Neal Zaslaw, *The Birth of the Orchestra: History of an Institution, 1650–1815* (Oxford, 2004), p. 24, n. 23. It is dubious whether *Orfeo* ever reached the stage of a general rehearsal, as the authors also claim.

[5] Cited from Landon, *Haydn*, 3:39. A strong feature of Landon's third volume, *Haydn in England*, is the amassing of many press reviews, which will be cited here henceforth only by event and newspaper title.

Orfeo ed Euridice

Badini set his story further back in Ovid's Orpheus myth relative to Calzabigi's telling. He began with the attempted rape of Euridice by Aristeus (Arideo). King Creonte promised to marry his daughter to Arideo against her wishes. She flees and is about to enter a hostile wood when a chorus warns her of its dangers. Beast-like creatures threaten to capture and kill her. The chorus sends for Orfeo, who subdues the creatures by the beauty of his singing. Creonte, informed, agrees to the union of Orfeo and Euridice. Act I ends happily with their love duet.

In Act II hostile forces erupt again, distracting Orfeo, who leaves Euridice unattended. An emissary of Arideo attempts to abduct her, and while trying to escape she is fatally bitten by a poisonous snake. Orfeo returns, finds her lifeless form, and laments. Creonte decrees revenge on Arideo and sounds the alarm to rouse his forces.

Act III commences with general mourning (at the point chosen by Calzabigi and Gluck). Orfeo consults the Sibyl, who sends Genio (Gluck's Amore) to bid the Thracian singer pluck up his courage and follow him to the abyss if he wishes to see his spouse. Furthermore, Genio tells Orfeo that tears are of no avail and that to remedy his loss he must put his trust in Philosophy. "Philosophy," scoffs Orfeo, "in order to make me happy must bring back Euridice to my forlorn heart." On this slender thread, apparently, hangs Badini's fancy title "The Philosopher's Spirit." Haydn makes little of this scene, setting it in a short simple recitative that is over in a trice, thus undercutting Badini's pretentious title. Act III ends with a request sung by a chorus asking Orfeo to let justice reign in his heart and to respect divine power.

Act IV opens with a chorus of unhappy shades on the banks of the Lethe. Genio leads Orfeo to Charon's bark and they are attacked by a band of Furies. Orfeo does not win them over gradually by his singing as in Gluck. They quickly agree, as does Pluto. A chorus tells Orfeo his pains have ended but if he looks back upon his spouse while still in the netherworld he will lose her. Genio urges him to heed their warning. Euridice appears and in a brief recitative—quite inadequate to the situation, which should be a climactic moment—is lost again when the admonition is not heeded. Alone in the infernal fields Orfeo laments and is given a text so trite it would dispirit any composer: "I have lost once more the heart of my heart. Whatever will become of me?" Thus ends Act IV, scene 4, with Orfeo making an exit after his aria. What is called Act IV, scene 5 begins with him on stage again, either a gross ineptitude or a hint that something is amiss or lacking here. The scenery has changed to a seashore, which could be used to argue that this was conceived as the beginning of an Act V. The Bacchantes arrive and attempt to entice Orfeo. After he rejects their blandishments and forswears all feminine company, they poison him and he dies. They celebrate but their revels are curtailed by a mighty storm and a shipwreck.

The libretto is as inept as any Haydn ever set. It founders on poor management of stage action and inconsistencies affecting character and plot. Badini was all too eager to show off his classical learning, which did nothing to redeem the work. Haydn was scarcely in a position to do much about the situation in which he found himself. He never lamented the failure to achieve performance, as far as we know, but it must have rankled. When he entered the opera in his thematic catalogue after returning to Vienna it was in the most laconic terms and without Badini's name or his fancy alternate title: "Orfeo. In England. 4 Acts."

The overture gets the opera off to a good start. After a short introduction in c minor, it launches into a winningly lyric *Presto* theme which Haydn spun into a monothematic and cogently argued sonata form without repeats (Example 5.1a). To begin the seconda parte the music slips down a third from G to E♭ for a

EXAMPLE 5.1. *Haydn,* L'anima del filosofo

a. *Overture*

resounding repeat of the first theme (in its second-theme guise). The reprise turns the tonic E of V/vi into the third of tonic C, a device used very often by the whole generation but of never failing charm (Example 5.1a, mm. 104–6). This theme matches one from Orfeo's big aria in Act II as he sings of having lost his consort (Example 5.1b). The text setting seems odd, as if words were being fitted

b. *Aria, "In un mar d'accerbo pene"*

to a previously existing melody, and the music sounds too cheerful for the meaning of the words, but no more so than Gluck's famous "Che faro senza Euridice" with the same message and placement in the drama. Haydn's pert melody, it should be understood, is a second, contrasting theme of an intense aria of mourning in f minor. It occurs first in A♭ and only near the end as here, in C major, which then becomes c minor (the reverse of the overture) and leads back to f minor for the conclusion. At 256 measures in length, the aria is complex and in grand style, the high point of the opera. The sparkling overture was later used to precede Salomon's vernacular entertainment *Windsor Castle,* whence its subsequent title "Overture to an English Opera."

If Haydn's attractive melody and its passage back and forth between major and minor sound rather familiar it may be because Mozart anticipated several of its traits in one of his most widely performed works, the *Coronation* Mass in C, K. 317 of 1779 (Example 5.2). This theme occurs after the slower choral introduction

EXAMPLE 5.2. *Mozart, Mass in C, K. 317, Kyrie*

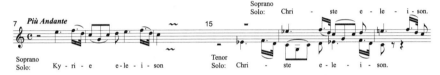

marked by features of the old French overture with its dotted rhythms and rich harmonies (Haydn's slow introduction to the overture has the same general features but does not bear any relationship to Mozart's opening). Haydn's *Presto* theme comes close to duplicating K. 317's Kyrie, especially when, in the aria, he puts it into minor, as in Mozart's "Christe." The resemblance takes nothing away from Haydn's overture or his magnificent aria for Orfeo in mourning. It would be pleasant to imagine, nevertheless, that Haydn was unconsciously thinking about the music of the younger genius left behind in Vienna, not knowing of course that he would never see him again.

Euridice bears the brunt of the solo singing in the early scenes. After entrance with a short recitative and exchanges with the chorus warning her, she sings a coloratura aria comparing herself to a nightingale, "Filomena abbandonata." Haydn begins the aria with an *Adagio* in F, in gavotte rhythm in cut time, followed by an *Allegro* with volleys of rapid scale passages stretching up to high C and down to low A. A similar passage at the end of the aria is quite ungrateful for the voice. Its complicated passagework would be more proper to an instrument like the clarinet. Haydn here, in his mind's ear, was perhaps still savoring Fiordiligi's pseudo-heroic "Come scoglio" sung by La Ferrarese in *Così fan tutte,* to which Mozart took him just a year before in early 1790. That aria shares some traits with "Filomena" and the same vocal range from low A to high C. Moreover, following a pompous slow introduction with dotted rhythms, the faster theme of "Come scoglio" resembles the previous two musical examples (Example 5.3).

EXAMPLE 5.3. *Mozart,* Cosí fan tutte, *Aria, No. 14, "Come scoglio"*

Orfeo has by far the best solo music in the opera. For this we can thank the tenor Giacomo Davide (or David), whose fine technique and powerful, expressive voice Haydn put to good use. Paisiello created the title role of his *Pirro* specifically for Davide, in an opera on a libretto by Giovanni de Gamerra for the San Carlo at Naples on 12 January 1787 to celebrate the birthday of King Ferdinand. Davide repeated the role in productions at many other theaters in Italy before and after singing it in London to open Gallini's doomed 1791 season. *Pirro* marked an important milestone in the gradual triumph of tenors over castrati in taking over the role of primo uomo; Davide was also praised for the intensity of his acting. This drama represented a breakthrough to a more adventurous type of opera than was customary in Naples, for it integrated several ensembles and considerable spectacle into the usual round of arias, forcibly reduced in number. Badini's *Orfeo* followed it by requiring even more extensive stage spectacle. It was lavish too in its musical demands, not with ensembles, of which there is only the love duet ending Act I, a long-standing staple of opera seria, but in its wealth of choruses. It went far beyond Haydn's previous operas in this respect. Ballets were also originally intended, according to the first letter Haydn wrote Prince Anton, describing the opera as "dotted with choruses, ballets and many big changes of scene."

Haydn set Creonte's large role for a baritone. He wrote some of the part using tenor clef, the rest in bass clef. His treatment of the voice was cautious, not exceeding the range of an eleventh in any of the three arias, as if he were not sure who would sing the role. The texts for Creonte with which he had to work in Acts I and III were not so much philosophical as moralizing, more appropriate to oratorio than to opera, whereas Creonte had to conclude Act II with a "Sound the trumpet" kind of aria, a blatant applause trap. Gallini's troupe did include a baritone in the person of Francesco Albertarelli, whom Haydn would have known from Vienna, where the singer belonged to the Burgtheater company in 1788–89—he sang the title role in the Viennese version of *Don Giovanni.*

Genio appears only in Acts III and IV and was given one aria in the former, a demanding one with coloratura. The part may have been intended for the castrato mentioned in the letter to Prince Anton, or for the seconda donna, Madame Capeletti. Aside from Davide, the cast, or likely cast, can hardly be described as of the first rank. Madame Lops may not have lasted as prima donna beyond March—a hard blow both for her and her venerable teacher Regina Mingotti, who is said to have accompanied her to London.

The choruses gave Haydn an opportunity to show himself to advantage. Even a composer as experienced as Paisiello was less practiced at choral music than Haydn. Badini asked the chorus to play many different roles, sometimes as characters in the drama, at other times as commentators on the action, almost in the sense of ancient tragedy. Correspondingly, Haydn composed many different kinds of pieces. Different choral textures ensured a variety of effects that is one of the opera's strengths. The choruses in Act I are for men only (T - B). They warn Euridice and sing in response to her pleading, an exchange reminiscent of Gluck's great scene in which Orfeo pleads with the recalcitrant Furies. This gloomy piece in c minor has a bright counterpart in the next chorus in C major, sung in praise of the power of harmony revealed in Orfeo's previous song to his lyre that tames the wild creatures of the wood. Act II gives a turn for women's (and boys'?) voices to shine. These high voices (S - S) represent little Cupids (Amorini) and sing some of the lightest music in the opera, a gavotte-type *Allegretto* in A that Haydn borrowed from his *Orlando paladino*. When the two lovers join together and sing the refrain, later a verse in alternation with the chorus, the result sounds very much like a vaudeville final from some opéra comique.

A chorus representing young maidens (S - S) and men (B - B) opens Act III with a minuet-like *Andante* in E♭ that resembles the *Duetto con Coro* in the second act of *Così fan tutte* (No. 21). There the men serenade the ladies, also in E♭ and minuet-like (the way a descending triad in the horns is used to link phrases is identical in both). In *Orfeo*, this lavishly orchestrated feast for the ears takes place at the bier of the dead Euridice and is directed to her—Haydn's choice of musical raiment might have been deemed inappropriate had it reached performance. There is no more gorgeously sonorous moment in his score. The high voices sing first, followed by the high ones again, then the men come in with a shorter phrase before they all sing together, a magical moment since it is the first choral sound *a 4* in the opera. The first four-voiced chorus of the usual S A T B texture is saved for the exuberant end of Act III, enjoining Orfeo to be steadfast (at least its forthright music, an *Allegro* in 2/4 time and in D major with predominantly chordal texture, suggests that is the intention of the muddled text).

The chorus (S A T B) has its greatest moment when it begins Act IV by representing the unhappy shades on the banks of the Lethe, an *Andante* in 6/8 time and in the key of f minor notated with only three flats in the signature. They lament their sorry lot which will "last long and never be pitied" (senza mai trovar pietà) to a dirge that begins in imitative counterpoint and reaches expressive climaxes, intimated when the tenors cling to a long pedal on "mai," and reached when at the end of the same phrase all motion stops in order to prolong two chords sung to the word "mai." Haydn raises the expressive stakes of this climactic moment near the end by making the second prolonged chord a *fortissimo* diminished seventh. The voices drop out one by one to end the piece, uttering the single word "mai," in descending order. The last "mai" is low F for the basses, the only vocal resolution of the dangling leading tone E♮ left unresolved by the "mai' of the tenors a major seventh higher. A chorus of the Furies for men (T - B) soon follows and sounds appropriately angry, a *Vivace assai* in common time and in d minor with prominent descents by step outlining diminished intervals (4ths and 7ths), suggestive of the overture's slow introduction. The orchestra conveys ferocity with rattling tremolos and particularly with a heavily inflected version of a melodic minor scale made out of matching tetrachords A G♯ F♮ E | D C♯ B♭ A, as choral parts answer back and forth to each other approximating the dying falls in the orchestra. A very brief men's chorus "Trionfi oggi" after Orfeo succeeds in entering Hades is in D major and partly in octaves for the voices. Haydn took little trouble here. The S A T B version of the same piece is used to warn Orfeo of the conditions under which he may have Euridice back.

The Bacchantes in Act IV, scene 5 (or Act V) are sung by high voices (S - A), a chorus with which Haydn took even less trouble. They beckon Orfeo with another minuet-like piece, this one of a sugary sweetness in A major, *Allegretto*. They poison him to the same treacly tune, which ends with, of all things, a *cadence galante*, from which Haydn departs on a modulatory tour of several other keys while the sky darkens and Orfeo dies. The Bacchantes end the segment in F major. They celebrate his demise in the same key and embark for the island of delight. Finally, delight turns to the terror of a storm in d minor, ending with their shipwreck. Haydn was very experienced in writing storm choruses—he had added one of his best to the oratorio *Il ritorno di Tobia* in 1784. The cataclysmic ending of the *Seven Last Words* with an orchestral earthquake also served him in good stead. Like the catastrophe that overtakes the Bacchantes, it is in rapid triple meter with many orchestral unisons. Endings like this were ultimately beholden to the final Dance of the Furies in Gluck's ballet *Don Juan.* The Bacchantes' demise certainly seems to belong to this tradition in the way the music trails off gradually to its conclusion. In Gluck, the flames flicker down until d minor finally gives way to D major. Haydn used some of the same progressions that Gluck did to calm the waves, leading to a single tone of D with neither F nor F♯ to go with it.

Scholars have tried to find any examples of influence Gluck's *Orfeo* may have had on Haydn, and one such that has been claimed is the beginning of Euridice's recitative before her second demise (Example 5.4). This is related, we are told, to

EXAMPLE 5.4. *Haydn,* L'anima del filosofo, *Act IV, scene 3*

"Che farò senza Euridice" in the 1762 opera: "Though brief, the quotation—in the original key of E♭ major—is unmistakable."[6] The original key of "Che farò" is C, not E♭. A better case could be made that Haydn's Euridice parallels here a famous moment in *Don Giovanni*, the beginning of the voice part in Elvira's entrance aria, "A chi mi dice mai qual barbaro dov'è?" which does share the key of E♭. This parallel applies to Haydn's complete thought, not just the first measure. In general, Haydn made a point of distancing himself from Gluck's opera of the same name, just as Badini did with Calzabigi's poem. Haydn knew Gluck's *Orfeo ed Euridice* by heart—he had conducted performances of it at Esterháza in 1776. In one form or another it was also well known to London audiences, whereas Mozart was almost totally unknown to them. Haydn made less effort to distance himself from Mozart in his *Orfeo*.

Haydn's orchestral imagination, an area in which he was truly supreme, went far beyond that of Italian opera composers, even the most genial of them such as Sacchini and Paisiello. In London, Haydn had at his disposal the large band led by Salomon in both theater and concert hall, the disposition of which is discussed below. For his opera, the score calls here and there for additional instruments beyond the usual complement of winds and strings. A harp introduces Orfeo in Act I. Euridice's death scene in Act II begins with an obbligato recitative that recalls Orfeo's harp by its slow sextuplet accompaniment figures and the key of B♭; there is also a hint of the melody that is common to the overture and to Orfeo's great aria in f (Example 5.5). Haydn could have brought back the harp

EXAMPLE 5.5. *Haydn,* L'anima del filosofo, *Act II, scene 2*

but perhaps that struck him as too obvious. He alludes to it by giving the sextuplets to the violas doubled by bassoons while violins in octaves play the melody. The cavatina for Euridice following this recitative is a *Largo* in cut time and in E♭ into which he introduced two English horns, instruments he had used before in this key for texts about dying.[7] The primo player is given the task of finishing the cavatina in a little postlude, *pianissimo*, after Euridice's last sigh. The serenade-

[6] Curtis Price, Judith Milhous, and Robert D. Hume, *Italian Opera in Late Eighteenth-Century London,* vol. 1: *The King's Theatre, Haymarket, 1778–1791* (Oxford, 1995), pp. 599–600 and ex. 9.1.

[7] At least as early as his *Stabat Mater* of 1767 (*Haydn, Mozart,* pp. 305–7). He used English horns earlier in Symphony No. 22 in E♭ ("The Philosopher") of 1764. Two years earlier still, Gluck called for them in his *Orfeo*.

like chorus at the beginning of Act III calls for two clarinets in B♭, whose dulcet sonorities enhance the soothing effect of this piece in E♭. To give body and *terribilità* to the chorus of Furies in Act IV, Haydn called for two trombones in addition to the two horns and two *trombe*. For the drowning cries "Oh, che orrore!" of the Bacchantes at the very end, in d minor like the Furies, he calls again on these six brass instruments. Had this music reached audition it surely would have struck terror in all.

Dies mentioned the opera twice during his visits to the elderly composer. In his Thirteenth Visit on 9 December 1805 he stated, "The Opera seria, *Orfeo e Euridice*, was the first of Haydn's output in London." On the Fifteenth Visit of 14 January 1806, Haydn cut Dies short on the subject by saying simply, "The opera was not performed." There followed an explanation of how the new theater was constructed without royal permission and of Gallini's consequent failure to secure permission to perform Italian operas. Then Dies recounted an attempt to rehearse the opera.

> The theater now stood there completed and the orchestra was already assembled to rehearse the opera *Orfeo*. Haydn had distributed the parts, and hardly had forty measures been played through when official persons entered and in the name of the King and of the Parliament ordered that the opera should under no circumstances by played, not even once in rehearsal, and so on. Even single arias might nowhere be sung or played. *Orfeo* was, so to speak, declared contraband, and what was worse, the playing of all operas in the Theater in future was forbidden.

So dramatic an account of a *concentus interruptus* did not strike present-day authorities on the subject of the King's Theater as anything more than an invention, a yarn spun by either Haydn or Dies. If anything of the kind had happened, they suggest, it would have caused public scandals, upon which the press delightedly pounced.[8] Moreover, Haydn's fame was increasing in the spring of 1791 because of his successes—triumphs even—at Salomon's concert series in March and April. Whatever befell Haydn in the long struggle between the two opera companies was a matter of intense interest to Londoners.

The question remains why Taylor and Gallini failed to put on *Orfeo*, or excerpts from it, in one of their concerts, which they continued to give, paired with a half evening of ballet, to end the spring season in 1791. If Dies was correct at least in saying that all the music was declared contraband, it would provide one answer. Haydn wrote the opera so much around the gifts of Davide there seemed little chance of an adequate performance after the tenor left London for good the fol-

---

[8] Price, Milhous, and Hume, *The King's Theatre, Haymarket 1778–1791* (1995), p. 600, n. 1: "There is nothing to corroborate this obviously embroidered and sensationalized account. Had such a rehearsal been planned and then interrupted, it would surely have been reported to the newspapers."

lowing summer. Gallini owned Haydn's score and possibly could have tried other means of bringing it to the public in subsequent seasons if he remained in managerial control of the Haymarket theater. Taylor wrested control from him and he was not the man to spend what was needed to do justice to the opera's vocal and scenic demands, even had Gallini allowed him access to the score. Haydn apparently washed his hands of the whole affair, content to know that they were clean, because he had kept his part of the bargain. Under Taylor's aegis again from 1792 on, Italian opera in London declined.[9]

Salomon's 1791 Concerts

Gallini managed the King's Theatre in the Haymarket until mid-1791. He was also the proprietor of the Hanover Square Rooms, London's main concert hall. Opened in 1775, the hall then belonged to the partners Gallini, Christian Bach, and Carl Friedrich Abel, but the two composers sold their shares to Gallini the following year. The famous Bach-Abel concerts had taken place in the Hanover Square Rooms. They ended when Bach died at the beginning of 1782 and were followed at the same locale by the Professional Concert (1783–93). These were led by the Mannheim violinist Wilhelm Cramer, a pupil of Johann Stamitz and Christian Cannabich, who settled in London in 1772 after a few seasons at the Concert Spirituel in Paris. Cramer's greatest rival was Salomon, who began his own series of subscription concerts there in 1786. The Hanover Square Rooms accommodated 500 auditors comfortably.[10] Filling the same space with well-paying subscribers was the concern of both Cramer and Salomon, whose rivalry reached its peak in 1791–92. Informed opinion generally gave the palm to the Mannheim-trained Cramer as orchestral leader but favored Salomon in string quartets.[11]

The Professional Concert had the advantage of starting first, before Salomon was able to open his series. It possessed another advantage in the services of Elizabeth Billington, London's favorite female soprano. At his first concert on Monday, 7 February, Cramer paid Haydn the compliment of including both a symphony and a string quartet by the famous visiting composer; which ones are not known, but they must have already been in circulation. Haydn attended this as well as many other concerts besides Salomon's in London, delighted, at

[9] Price, Milhous, and Hume, *The King's Theatre*, p. 436. "Had Gallini rather than Taylor emerged as proprietor of the new King's Theatre in 1792, London might have continued to flourish as a center for Italian opera."

[10] Simon McVeigh, *Concert Life in London from Mozart to Haydn* (Cambridge, 1993), pp. 20, 168.

[11] Ian Woodfield, *Salomon and the Burneys: Private Patronage and a Public Career* (Aldershot, 2003), pp. 15–16.

least initially, to have a free pass to all, something he remarked to Griesinger had never been the case in Vienna. At Cramer's opening concert he met for the first of many times Dr. Charles Burney and thanked him in person for the gift of the three-volume *History of Music*, also for his poem, "On the ARRIVAL OF *HAYDN* IN ENGLAND." Burney complained to a friend that Haydn thus saved himself the trouble of writing a letter (something Burney could have added to his epistolary treasures). Salomon had announced in early January that his series would begin on 11 February, the Friday following the first Professional Concert, and the same date Haydn quoted in his letter to Prince Anton. On 15 January, Salomon put an invitation to subscribers in the newspapers saying his concerts would take place on twelve successive Friday evenings and that "Mr. HAYDN will compose for every Night a New Piece of Music, and direct execution of it at the Harpsichord."[12] Such a task would have proved daunting even to a Haydn, and even if he were not occupied composing a new opera. If the qualification "new to London" is allowed, which in fact pertained to most of the pieces advertised as new, then Haydn was able to comply.

On 26 January, Salomon released another statement naming many of his forces. As performers already engaged he listed Signor Davide, Signora Capeletti, Miss Abrams, and Signora Storace. Among the principal instrumental soloists he listed were himself, violin; Breval, cello;[13] Jan Ladislav Dussek, pianoforte; Harrington, oboe; Johann Graeff, flute; Mr. Eley, clarinet; Mr. Holmes, bassoon; and Madame Krumpholtz, pedal harp. Continental instrumentalists figured importantly in his band. They had settled in London after seasons in Paris, like Salomon himself. He was forced to delay opening his series, he then announced, because Davide and Capeletti were prevented by the authorities from singing in public "at any place previous to their Appearance at the Opera." Thus the squeeze being put on Gallini's opera company by the Lord Chamberlain, which prevented these singers from appearing there, also extended to Salomon's concerts. From this double bind there was no easy exit. Salomon put the best face he could on the situation, announcing that he had "postponed his First Concert, which was advertised for the 11th, to the 25th Inst., that no Opportunity might be lost of hearing those eminent Singers."

Salomon next announced his intended program for the opening night. It began with an Overture (i.e., a symphony) by Rosetti, a song sung by Storace, an oboe concerto played by Harrington, a vocal piece sung by the banned Davide, and ended with a violin concerto by Salomon. That was just Part I. Part II started

---

[12] Landon, *Haydn*, 3:43. Landon's year-by-year Chronicle of concert life in London touching Haydn is used here as the source of all further citations of newspaper accounts.
[13] Could this refer to the eminent Parisian cellist Jean-Baptiste Bréval? He did not go to London, as far as is known.

with a "New Grand Overture" by Haydn (in the choice spot), another piece for Storace, a concerto for the harpist Krumpholtz, another aria for Davide (also a choice spot), and finally ended with a "Full Piece" (another symphony?) by Kozeluch. The program is typical of London concerts at that time in contents and order: always a symphony to begin both parts, and always vocal music sprinkled among instrumental pieces, with a predominance of solo concertos in this category.

The first concert had to be delayed again and was given on 11 March. Davide sang in spite of the ban, but not Capeletti. In the event, the authorities looked the other way. Instead of playing a solo concerto himself, Salomon graciously yielded his spot on the program to a Madame Gautherot, a French refugee, who played a violin concerto by Giovanni Battista Viotti, then the dominant violinist-composer in Paris. Otherwise, the program previously announced was followed, except that Giovanni Tajana, a secondary tenor in Gallini's opera company, sang the first vocal piece in Part I instead of Storace. Davide concluded Part I with a recitative and aria by a certain Rusi (Rossi?). Part II opened with Haydn as promised, continued with an unidentified recitative and aria for Storace, followed by what is described as a Concertante for Pedal Harp and Pianoforte for Krumpholtz and Dussek (who composed it), a rondò for Davide identified by a critic as being by Gaetano Andreozzi, and concluded with the Kozeluch full piece.

Salomon's choice of instrumental compositions here and throughout the series shows a predilection for the younger masters of the Austro-Bohemian School, those then most in vogue, not Haydn's contemporaries as much as those closer in age to Mozart. Beginning the series with a symphony by Rosetti pays appropriate honor to a master of the genre in the front rank of those followers who took Haydn as their model. Born in Bohemia ca. 1750, Anton Rössler—or Antonio Rosetti as he became known—triumphed as a symphonist at the Concert Spirituel during 1780 and had at least a dozen symphonies printed subsequently in Paris. Some four dozen symphonies by him have survived. He had no known connection with London. Most of the Continental composers selected by Salomon for performance came to London by way of Paris. This was the case with Jan Ladislav Dussek, born at Čáslav in 1760, and Adelbert Gyrowetz, born at Česke Budějovice in 1763, a symphony by whom opened Salomon's fourth concert on 1 April. Paul Wranitzky was also favored by Salomon. The dean of these Bohemian composers was Kozeluch, whose music was as popular in London as it was in Paris and Vienna. Such earlier Viennese favorites in London as Vanhal, Hofmann, and Dittersdorf had largely disappeared from concert programs. The Austrian-born Ignaz Pleyel, Haydn's pupil, would soon arrive from France to swell the contingent of younger composers from the Viennese orbit.

Haydn brought with him to London, among many other works, two of his most recent symphonies, No. 90 in C and No. 92 in G. He intended to bring

No. 91 in E♭ as well but it was left behind by mistake or lost in transit, hence his urgent requests to Mme von Genzinger to have it sent to him. The work that Haydn selected to introduce himself to the London public on 11 March was likely Symphony No. 92, the last of the nine that he wrote for the Count d'Ogny, known to posterity as the "Oxford" Symphony. Several kinds of evidence have been used to arrive at this supposition.[14] Dies in his Fifteenth Visit, after discussing Haydn's unperformed opera, explained that it had taken nearly all Haydn's time during the first months in London and consequently how useful were the works he brought with him for concerts. In the Thirteenth Visit, having gotten Haydn onto a favorite subject, namely the importance of winning over players in rehearsal, Dies illustrated by an example how Haydn ingratiated himself with the band led by Salomon.

> He had set out a symphony that begins with a short adagio, three identical-sounding notes opening the music. Now when the orchestra played the three notes too emphatically, Haydn interrupted with nods and "Sh! Sh!" The orchestra stopped and Salomon had to interpret for Haydn. Then they played the three notes again but with no happier result. Haydn interrupted again with "Sh! Sh!" In the ensuing silence, a German cellist quite near to Haydn expressed his opinions to his neighbor, saying in German, "If he doesn't like even the first three notes, how will it be with the rest!" Haydn was happy to hear Germans speaking, took these words as a warning, and said with great courtesy that he was requesting as a favor something that lay wholly in their power, and that he was very sorry he could not express himself in English. Perhaps they would allow him to demonstrate his meaning on an instrument. Whereupon he took a violin and made himself so clear by the repeated playing of the three tones that the orchestra understood him perfectly.

The reference can be to only one work, Symphony No. 92, the slow introduction of which, labeled *Adagio*, begins with three lightly touched triads on tonic G for first and second violins plus violas, marking the beats of 3/4 time. Most slow introductions before this, including Haydn's Symphonies Nos. 88, 90, and 91, began loudly, so that the soft beginning of Symphony No. 92 was in fact an innovation, perhaps taking even Salomon by surprise. The initial dynamic marking is *piano*.

Haydn's first appearance in London presiding at the keyboard over one of his symphonies made a sensation. The *Morning Chronicle* reported the next day, 12 March, in a tone of excitement that belies British reserve. "The First Concert under the auspices of HAYDN was last night, and never, perhaps, was there a richer musical treat." The composer was then compared to Shakespeare for his power to move the passions. "His *new Grand Overture* was pronounced by every scientific ear to be a most wonderful composition; but the first movement in particu-

---

[14] Landon, *Haydn*, 3:53–55.

lar rises in grandeur of subject, and in the rich variety of *air* and passion, beyond any even of his own productions." The reviewer went on to state, "The Overture has four movements—An Allegro - Andante - Minuet - and Rondo. They are all beautiful, but the first is pre-eminent in every charm, and the Band performed it with admirable correctness." If the Symphony was indeed No. 92, the account is accurate enough for a first impression by ear. It lacks mention only of the slow introduction, calls the big slow movement, marked *Adagio*, an *Andante*, and designates as a Rondo the final *Presto*, which is an elaborate sonata form with a few rondo-like features. A review in *The Diary; or Woodfall's Register*, also dated 12 March, reported, "A new grand overture by HAYDN, was received with the highest applause, and universally deemed a composition as pleasing as scientific. The audience was so enraptured, that by unanimous desire, the second movement was encored, and the third was vehemently demanded a second time also, but the modesty of the Composer prevailed too strongly to admit a repetition." Haydn himself confirmed repetition by demand in his letter three days later to Luigia Polzelli: "I made a sensation with a new symphony; they called for repeating the adagio [io ho fatto furore con una nuova Sinfonia, loro hanno fatto replicare l'adagio]." This helps confirm that the work, new to Londoners, was indeed Symphony No. 92, which has an *Adagio* slow movement.

An eyewitness to Salomon's concerts with Haydn, Charlotte Papendiek, preserved some valuable sidelights on them in her memoirs, written much later.[15] She was an attendant of Queen Charlotte, and lived at Windsor with her husband Christopher Papendiek, a professional flautist who was a music teacher to the royal children. She described the Haydn work heard at the first concert as "a symphony of Haydn's that he brought with him, but was not known in England." This sounds like privileged information of the kind that her husband would have known or found out—earlier he had been a soloist in Vienna where Haydn may have known him, and he was long associated with Salomon, having played a concert with him as far back as the violinist's London debut in 1783. Her impressions are particularly valuable for the precise description of how the orchestra was seated, which has enabled a modern scholar to reconstruct a plan using all the evidence available (Figure 5.1).[16] Salomon sat on a raised platform close to Haydn, placed so that all players could take their cues from his bow arm. Haydn could easily scan the entire orchestra, although the principal wind players, so important in his scores, were rather distant. Salomon usually set the tempo for all pieces but allowed Haydn to do so for his own compositions. Burney said that Haydn was censured for this and defended him on the point.[17] It was wise of

---

[15] Charlotte Papendiek, *Court and Private Life in the Time of Queen Charlotte: Being the Journals of Mrs. Papendiek, Assistant Keeper of the Wardrobe and Reader to Her Majesty*, ed. Vernon Broughton, 2 vols. (London, 1886–87), cited after Landon, *Haydn*, 3:50–53.

[16] McVeigh, *Concert Life in London* (Cambridge, 1993), p. 212, Plan 3.

[17] Rosemary Hughes, "Dr. Burney's Championship of Haydn," *Musical Quarterly* 27 (1941), 90–96; 95.

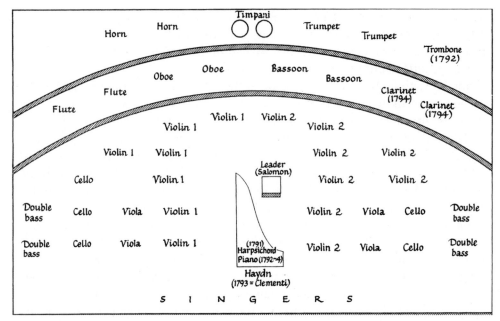

FIGURE 5.1. Simon McVeigh's hypothetical seating plan, Hanover Square Rooms.

Salomon to let Haydn do this, which is to say to function the way he always had when Kapellmeister.

Once begun, the concerts continued regularly on Friday evenings. The second on 18 March was attended by the Prince of Wales and featured as the novelty a "New Quartetto" by Haydn performed by Salomon, Dahmen, Hindmarsh, and Menel. It was new to London in any case and surely from Haydn's latest set, Op. 64. On 10 June 1791, Bland published Nos. 3, 6, and 5 from Op. 64 as "Performed at Mr. Salomon's concert." The vogue for chamber music like this in a large concert setting was specific to London. Part II of the concert began with a repetition of the symphony heard a week earlier "By particular Desire" of the subscribers. The "full piece" that ended the concert was by Pleyel, whose music was heard also at the third concert (a string quintet with two violas). Haydn was represented on this program by a "Grand Symphony" in the usual spot, meaning one of his old symphonies. The novelty by him was a "New Cantata" sung by Storace, a piece that has eluded precise identification, or has been lost. The fourth concert had a "New Grand Symphony" by Haydn performed from manuscript parts (No. 90?). The fifth concert offered a "New Divertimento" for flute, oboe, and strings, an arrangement by Haydn of one of his recent *Notturni* for the King of Naples, while the sixth offered another new string quartet by Haydn. Thus, Haydn was able to sustain the promise of a new piece on every program.

The subscription concerts were half over with the sixth, on 15 April. There was a respite of one week for Good Friday and Easter, then they resumed on 29 April. Haydn was probably done with his opera, or nearly so, by the end of March, thus he had more time to devote to truly new works for Salomon. He finished two new symphonies under these conditions, Nos. 95 and 96, one of which was probably the "New Grand Overture MS. Haydn" that opened Part II of the seventh concert. The next evening Haydn presided at the keyboard over one of Gallini's concert and ballet offerings in the Haymarket Theater, and for this one a program survives. Several of the singers in the opera company performed (but not Mme Lops) and Haydn figured as the composer of two symphonies. The eighth concert on 6 May offered another new string quartet by Haydn and a repetition of the new symphony. Storace reappeared singing a Cantata by Haydn, perhaps the same as on the third concert. The female singers who had replaced her since the third concert were Miss Abrams, Signora Teresa Negri (same as Luigia Polzelli's sister Cristina Negri?), and Miss Corri. On 16 May, Haydn had his benefit concert and composed for it a new aria for Davide with oboe and bassoon obbligato, a piece that is lost although reported to have been an outstanding success. Another boon to the audience, and perhaps a surprise when they read the announcement in the press, was that Signor Pacchierotti of the Pantheon Opera would appear and sing a cantata by Haydn (actually the aria "Ah, come il core" from *La fedeltà premiata*) and end the program by singing a duet with Davide. On 19 May, Gallini's company put on another concert and ballet evening in the Haymarket Theater, this one as a benefit for the poet Badini. Albertarelli sang a Hunting Song by Philidor, which must be the famous pictorial aria from *Tom Jones*, then followed Haydn's "Hunting Symphony," No. 73, in D, the composer presiding. To end the evening the ballet performed *Orpheus and Euridice* (the music being a pasticcio by Vincenzo Federici and others).

At the tenth concert on 20 May the novelty by Haydn was another of his *Notturni* for the King of Naples arranged for small orchestra. On this concert, after the Haydn symphony that began Part II, was a sonata for pianoforte, a distinct oddity at the time in large public concerts. Dussek, who composed and performed it, was on good terms with Haydn, who praised him in a letter to Dussek's father. The eleventh concert on 27 May had a "New Grand Overture" by Haydn, which was perhaps Symphony No. 95 or 96; otherwise there was no novelty by the composer on the program. The twelfth and last concert, on 3 June, announced several favorites and the main novelty appears to have been the first appearance of Mme de Sisley, another French refugee, who sang an aria. Part I had begun with an Overture by Gyrowetz and included a new piano concerto by Dussek. It ended with an aria sung by Davide and a violin concerto played by Salomon. "By Particular desire the New Grand Overture—Haydn—as performed last Friday, will be repeated." This began Part II, followed by another aria for Mme de Sisley, a harp concerto by Mme Krumpholtz, a scena sung by Davide, and a Finale by Kozeluch. The series had been an overwhelming success.

Madame Krumpholtz played in the last concert, as in the first, in the choice spot close to the end of the program, as she had in five other concerts in the series plus in Haydn's benefit concert. Obviously a favorite with the public, with Salomon, and with Haydn, she deserves a little biography here. Born Anne-Marie Steckler about 1755 in Metz, she was a pupil of the great harp maker and composer-performer for the instrument, Jean-Baptiste (originally Jan Křtitl) Krumpholtz, born in 1742. He performed as a solo harpist in Vienna's Burgtheater in 1773 with success, after which Haydn accepted him as a pupil in composition. After touring widely on the Continent, Krumpholtz settled in Paris, where he played often at the Concert Spirituel from 1778 to 1788. He married Anne-Marie, his young pupil from Metz, and they had three children. She also performed regularly at the Concert Spirituel in harp concertos by her husband. On 8 April 1784, for instance, she is mentioned as playing a solo concerto published as his Opus IV, then on 10 April the couple played one of his concertos for two harps. Harmonious concord eluded their private lives. She is said to have taken a young lover and eloped with him to London by 1788. Legend has long had it that he was young Dussek, who did indeed compose as many as three surviving harp and pianoforte concertos for them to play together. Legend also has Dussek fleeing Paris for London at the outbreak of the French Revolution in 1789. In fact, he was in London before the storming of the Bastille because he played as a soloist on 1 June 1789 in the Hanover Square Rooms. Mme Krumpholtz became a widow on 19 January 1790 when her husband, still in Paris, drowned himself in the Seine. Dussek did not marry her but did marry another female soloist in Salomon's concerts, the soprano, pianist, and harpist Sophia Corri, daughter of the composer and publisher Domenico Corri from Rome. She first sang as Miss Corri at the sixth concert on 15 April, at which Dussek also played one of his compositions for pianoforte, a sonata accompanied by Salomon, Hindmarsh, and Menel. They married a year later. Mme Krumpholtz continued to perform in public until 1803. She remained in London and died there in 1813.

Child prodigies were as popular in London concerts as elsewhere, the most famous example being Mozart in the 1760s. Master Hummel and Master Clement had a joint benefit concert on 13 June 1791 led by Salomon and Haydn, whose original orchestral version of the *Seven Last Words* supplied the middle of this three-part occasion. Franz Clement, aged eleven, played a solo violin concerto of his own composition to end Part I (in 1806 Beethoven wrote his Violin Concerto for Clement). Johann Hummel, aged thirteen, opened Part III playing a solo concerto for fortepiano. Sophia Corri was only fifteen when she made her debut in Salomon's sixth concert. George Bridgetower, a mulatto born of an African father and European mother, was a violinist who made his debut as a soloist, aged ten, at the Concert Spirituel on 13 April 1789. Subsequently in London, he often played in concerts. Master Bridgetower appeared on Salomon's sixth concert directly after Miss Corri, playing a violin concerto. For him Beethoven later wrote his Violin Sonata in A, Op. 47, known as the "Kreutzer Sonata" (from its later dedication to the famous violinist Rodolphe Kreutzer).[18]

The choice of music and performers for his series was Salomon's prerogative, although it is clear that his vocal soloists mostly sang Italian music of their own choice, probably pieces already memorized. Haydn may have had a hand in persuading Salomon to welcome so many younger composers from the Austro-Bohemian school to present instrumental music on the programs. Some were Haydn's former pupils and almost all were his followers in a stylistic sense. Gyrowetz actually came to London and became close to Haydn. He was adept in several languages and no doubt his excellent French and English were a help when he accompanied Haydn to functions in high society. Gyrowetz was proud to say in the memoirs he wrote much later that he patterned his music after Haydn's. Other composers, not already mentioned, from the Viennese circle whose music was chosen by Salomon included Wenzel Pichl and Franz Anton Hoffmeister, Mozart's friend and publisher. Another Viennese connection was provided by the two basset horn players who performed a concerto on the fourth concert, Vincent Springer and Divorsack (an English attempt to spell Dvořák). Springer was also Bohemian by birth and a Freemason who had played basset horn in the first performance of Mozart's *Masonic Funeral Music* (K. 477) in 1785. The press often mangled foreign names. An Overture that opened the second concert (18 March), identified by *The Times* as by "Mozart," was attributed to "Mazant" in the *Public Adviser*. Of Mozart's symphonies that were in print, either the "Paris" or "Haffner" would have made excellent concert openers.

Haydn participated in many concerts besides Salomon's. Soon after his arrival, he attended a Court ball accompanied by Gallini and Salomon, on 18 January at St James's Palace in honor of the Queen's birthday. Here he first encountered the Prince of Wales, who startled everyone there by bowing to Haydn, an event duly reported in the press. The following morning Haydn received an invitation from the Prince to a concert at his residence of Carlton House. Musicians present besides Haydn included Salomon, Giornovichi, and Davide. There were many other concerts like this arranged at the instigation of the Prince, who had his own private band. Haydn described one such concert in November (letter of 20 December 1791 to Mme von Genzinger) in which the Prince sat next to him on his right and played along on his cello as Haydn was directing his symphonies from the keyboard; "The Prince of Wales is the handsomest man on God's earth, has an extraordinary love of music and much feeling, BUT LITTLE MONEY."

---

[18] Another famous and widely traveled violinist, Giovanni Giornovichi, played a concerto (gratis) at Haydn's benefit concert on 16 May. He had made his debut at the Concert Spirituel in 1770.

In late 1791, the Prince of Wales commissioned John Hoppner to paint Haydn's portrait. The impressive result still graces the Royal Collection. At the same time John Bland commissioned a rival oil portrait from Thomas Hardy, who himself made a fine engraving from it (Figure 5.2).

SYMPHONIES NOS. 95–96

It was an accomplishment for Haydn to have completed two new symphonies in the spring of 1791, given the pressures put on him by his social life, and most of all by the exhaustive work of composing an entire opera since his arrival. He sent copies of these two symphonies back to Vienna later in the year. Whoever compiled the catalogue of his symphonies for his friend Bernard von Kees entered their incipits as they were received and on each made the comment "NB Von London gekommen."[19] They are the last two entries of the catalogue, in which the works are numbered from 1 to 94. The Symphony in D, later given the number 96, is inscribed first, followed by the Symphony in c, later No. 95. Preceding them are incipits for Symphonies in C and in D, Nos. 90 and 92 in the Breitkopf and Härtel list compiled by Mandyczewski that became standard; at the bottom of the previous page is the incipit of No. 91 in E♭, reflecting the order received, and perhaps composed.

Similarly, placing No. 96 in D before No. 95 in c may indicate the order in which they were composed, or first performed. It stands to reason that Haydn would be eager to add a new symphony in D to his roster. The key was his most frequent tonal choice over the long span of his symphonies. In the standard list of 104, twenty-four are in D, twenty in C, and twelve in G. No. 96, furthermore, offered some melodic similarities with his Symphony No. 53 in D ("L'Imperiale") of the late 1770s, a work that was a great favorite in England. Both slow introductions descend the tonic triad in a stately 3/4 time, tutti *forte*, and continue with a *piano* rejoinder for strings alone. Perhaps an astute few in Salomon's 1791 audience even recognized and welcomed this resemblance to the old favorite.

The *Adagio* that begins No. 96 adds an arresting feature not found in the earlier introduction (but found in that of Symphony No. 75 in D), namely a restatement of the opening tutti on tonic minor, a move that has repercussions later in the work. The descending triad of the very beginning will resound through all the movements in various guises. Equally ubiquitous is the rising triad that follows and its upbeat rhythmic motif of three eighth notes, a pattern that dominates not only the introductory *Adagio* but also the whole *Allegro* in 3/4 time that follows, even to the point of initiating its first theme. The V^7 chord that ends the *Adagio* returns an octave higher at the end of the prima parte of the *Allegro* to prepare its repetition. What comes next to begin the seconda parte is a surprise.

---

[19] Jens Peter Larsen, *Three Haydn Catalogues*, 2nd rev. facs. ed. (New York, 1979), p. 49.

FIGURE 5.2. Portrait of Haydn painted and engraved by Thomas Hardy, 1792.

It is loud and a tonal non-sequitur (V^6_5 of vi in D) that places the three upbeat "knocks" as a downbeat beginning the measure. The rhythmic shift is not without preparation because the movement's gentle main theme beginning with the upbeats ended its antecedent with the same motif on the downbeat. Resolution to vi brings with it the main theme in minor and inverted, with the original accompaniment in the bass placed above the theme (an example of Haydn's automatic thinking in double counterpoint). The development seems to end with the same secondary dominant with which it began, but in root position. After a pause, the resolution is not to tonic D but via a deceptive cadence to G for the main theme, a *fausse reprise* that probably fooled many listeners. A few measures more bring the harmonic progression around to a dominant pedal and the real reprise. At the point in the prima parte where the composer began introducing little flurries of chromatic motion in both bass and treble taking the place of a distinct second theme, he expands to the extent of working up to a climactic *fortissimo* outburst of the tonic minor and a descending triad reminding one of the *Adagio,* after which comes a quick conclusion and repetition of the seconda parte.

An *Andante* in G and in lilting 6/8 time makes a pleasant contrast. The three-note upbeat persists, now as three sixteenth notes. The theme is playful, and lightly scored with a few upbeat chirpings from the winds, but followed by more menacing tutti *forte* sounds that involve even the timpani and trumpets (a first in this kind of movement since Symphony No. 88). This rude interruption is dissipated little by little and the initial, gracious part returns, rounding off a small ternary form. Overlapping its cadence, which is in g minor and *forte,* Haydn begins a fugato, for which he changes the key signature to two flats. Its subject, with accompanying countersubject, enters in the strings from high to low (the second entry is un-fuguelike by beginning on the same pitch as the first). This *minore* section (not labeled as such) remains in fine contrapuntal fettle throughout, providing ample foil for the return of the whole first section. As the returned first part nears conclusion there is a I^6_4 chord, tutti *forte,* with fermata, the customary signal for a solo cadenza. It is provided by two violins, surely Salomon and Dahmen, the head of the second violins. Their cadenza transmutes into a longish coda with more modulation before final resolution. A sketch sheet survives that shows Haydn working over a few figures in this cadenza and demonstrates how carefully he went about paying honor to his new orchestra and its leaders. The length and ostentation of the contrapuntal display in the middle of the movement is somewhat unusual for Haydn. Was he courting those who preferred the music of generations past? In England, there were many who still swore by "that old-time religion" represented by Corelli, Geminiani, and Handel. Haydn had attended a concert of the Society for Ancient Music soon after his arrival in London. He observed how recent English music was often marked by resonances from the past. He was well aware that George III's only favorite was Handel.

The *Menuetto Allegretto* is relatively straightforward compared to the *Andante* and quite pompous. After firmly establishing the pulse and meter, all the violins in unison rush up the octave to high D, a run that also occurs several times in the *Allegro*. The Trio sounds quite rustic. It is a lovely solo for the first oboe, Mr. Harrington, who was one of the first desk players that Salomon singled out for mention in his press release of 26 January, and who performed an oboe concerto on the first and tenth concerts. He was a key player in the arrangements Haydn made of his Notturni for these concerts. In this Trio, Haydn gave him a simple oom-pah-pah accompaniment for strings, providing a nice contrast with the stately formality of the minuet, as trios often do.

A delightful rondo finale, *Vivace* in 2/4 time, concludes the work. It hews closely in spirit and form to the finale of Symphony No. 88. The head motif of the refrain is a descending triad that ties it to the beginning of the slow introduction, also the very end of the *Allegro*, as the winds play a rapid descent of an octave through the triad. The refrain is in rounded binary form with repeats, and at the return of the beginning the first flute joins the violins in playing the theme (the flute also figured importantly in the *Andante*). Salomon's first flute was Herr Graeff, also announced in January, and the performer of solo concertos at the second and ninth concerts. The finale's first episode is in tonic minor followed by a return of the refrain that quickly goes off the track tonally into a development, preparing the complete return of the refrain, followed by a coda with appearances of the solo wind instruments. At the end of the movement all that is left of the theme is its head motif, which serves as closure. Instead of the usual three evenly spaced tonic chords to signal the end and invite applause, Haydn sounded the tonic chord in dotted rhythm.

Symphony No. 96 acquired the nickname "The Miracle" at some unspecified time, but only in England. A story was circulated relating to the performance of one of Haydn's symphonies, unspecified as to which, that once a crowd pressed forward to regard him close up, vacating a part of the floor upon which a large chandelier then fell. Dies asked Haydn about this anecdote. The composer replied that he never heard of it, reason enough why it should be suppressed.

An instinct that guided Haydn to make such a showy fugato in one of his truly new symphonies in the spring of 1791 may have prompted him to choose the minor mode to begin the other. Sir John Hawkins in his last published writing, a preface to the second edition of *W. Boyce: Cathedral Music* (London, 1788), pined not only for "the solemn and pathetic *Adagio*, the artful and well-studied Fugue," but also for the "sweet modulation of the keys with the minor third."[20] One of the three symphonies, No. 78 in c that Haydn wrote "for the English gentlemen" a decade earlier, was also a work that began, like Symphony No. 95, with

[20] *Music in European Capitals*, p. 905.

a loud tutti *unisono,* followed by a softer continuation. Symphony No. 78 was not so doggedly committed to c minor as Symphony No. 52 of the early 1770s, although less prone than Symphony No. 95 to turn minor into major at nearly every opportunity.

The main theme of Symphony No. 95's opening *Allegro moderato* is in cut time (not common time as indicated on the last item of the Kees Catalogue). It consists of the jagged head motif in unison *forte* (winds) and *fortissimo* (strings) followed by the soft, *dolce* answer given by the first violins, accompanied chordally by the other strings. While the head motif descends majestically, the continuation, after a silence, struggles meekly upward with a dotted rhythmic figure and leads, a few measures later, to the reiteration of the head motif, *forte.* This time the continuation is a soft reiteration of the rising minor second from m. 2, descending in sequence after pauses. These three figures, head motif, rising continuation, and descending sequence of little minor second rises, are almost enough for Haydn to construct a taut and often contrapuntal movement. No time is wasted in reaching the relative major E♭, which arrives by m. 16, with a version of the main theme in the bass and counterpoint above. Then follows a stretto imitation on the head motif leading quickly to a truly contrasting theme in E♭. This jaunty idea is broadly laid out and colored by the two horns pitched in E♭ on first statement, by other winds as well on its full repetition. From here to the double bar is taken up with the cadential material, the whole lasting only sixty-one measures, very few by the standards of Haydn's other symphonic first movements of the last two decades. The prima parte is repeated as usual.

The seconda parte starts softly with the head motif in E♭ then slips quickly back to c minor and, in a passage saturated with the head motif, the harmony reaches a loud climax on the chord of C major, followed by a pause. Without preparation, it slips down to A♭ for the soft continuation of the main theme. From A♭ a modulation prepares the arrival of B♭ and the broad second theme, which is wide ranging and does not quite finish before modulation sets in again. The head motif is heard over and over against various counterpoints, the climax coming with its reappearance in c minor, which could suggest the beginning of a reprise, or just another stop on the modulatory tour. A pedal begins on G as if preparing for the real reprise and it comes, but in the form of the soft, rising continuation of the head motif, which very quickly dissolves into C major for the sounding of the broad second theme. Haydn could have had his trumpets in C take the place of what his horns in E♭ played on the first appearance of this theme, but apparently he did not trust them to such an extent. The trumpets come in at the end of the theme but only to double the horns (now in C) for the triumphal cadential celebrations of C major. Even so, Haydn reorchestrates the second theme considerably, giving a bigger role to the winds and decorating it with little tags for Salomon to play solo. The seconda parte is not marked for repetition, for its passage from stern and gloomy c minor to bright C major can hardly exert its magic in full more than once; besides which, quite enough has been heard of this main theme and its very contrasting second theme. The marriage of dour lessons in counterpoint with luxuriant sonorous beauty is not entirely happy and seems to go on for a long time even though it is the briefest first movement of all twelve London symphonies.

An *Andante* in 6/8 time and in E♭ presents a brief binary theme with repeats, the first strain being only four measures long and ending on the tonic. The second strain is lengthened to six measures by an internal repetition, also ending on the tonic. Variations on the theme ensue. The first begins with a solo cello (Herr Menel) playing the theme; the second is in tonic minor; the third has figuration in smaller note values. A return to the unadorned but reharmonized theme begins Variation 4, which turns into a coda after the first strain. The movement may suffer because the theme itself is too anchored in the tonic.

Haydn calls the third movement simply *Menuet* and it is a rather plain exemplar of its species, begun in c minor, moving to E♭ for the end of the first strain, and back to tonic minor in the second. There are hints of the first movement's head motif in the minuet's melodic line, for example, the A♭ F♯ G before the return to c minor at the end. The Trio resorts to C major and a solo for the first cellist, as in the first variation of the *Andante*.

The *Finale Vivace* in cut time continues the oscillation between major and minor, beginning in cheerful C major. Like the first strain of the *Andante*, the *Vivace*'s refrain in rounded binary form with repeats has a first strain that does not modulate, which lends it a rather cut and dried effect upon repetition. Three movements in a row so dependent on the small repeating forms of dance music do not seem like a good way to maintain interest. Following the refrain there is a fugato serving as a development, modulating to E♭, which arrives with a bang, a *fortissimo* explosion of maximum orchestral sonority, and just before this a long descent reminiscent of the third part of the *Allegro moderato*'s main theme. The reprise begins with one of Haydn's promised arrivals that turns out to be a non-arrival. V/vi makes a big preparation for vi only to be undercut by the coy reappearance of I, the E in the bass becoming the E as third of tonic C to begin the refrain. A big return to tonic minor could be expected in order to match that of E♭ earlier. It comes and sounds like an even bigger explosion, one on the scale of the whole symphony, not just its finale. C major then replaces c minor and the end can be sensed approaching. There is one typically Haydnesque delaying tactic by means of V_3^4/V and V/V, leading to a final statement of the refrain, reharmonized. The rest is cadential celebration.

Besides their overt show of contrapuntal acumen, Symphonies 95 and 96 have similar eruptions of tonic minor in common. In Symphony No. 96, an outburst of tonic minor marks the slow introduction and comes again near the end of the *Allegro*. The effect of these tutti *fortissimi* moments is quite similar, and similar too is the spacing of the tonic triad throughout the orchestra, with the third on top. They must have jolted the original listeners, and that was presumably Haydn's intention. This bursting forth might have struck some as merely quaint, like one of Jove's thunderbolts, while to others it may have sounded like a bomb exploding. One critic does not hesitate to invoke a connection with the struggles in the political arena unleashed in 1789 and slowly growing, like a long *crescendo*, with each passing month and every new arrival in London of refugees from the Continent.[21] Then again, there may be too much hindsight in this idea. Early 1791 was still a long ways from the Terror that reigned in 1793–94. Nevertheless, Londoners were alarmed, as was the entire kingdom, at the spread of popular meetings in support of revolutionary ideas and at the number of republican clubs that had sprung up by 1791.

The London Notebooks

During his two stays in London Haydn filled four notebooks with random jottings, occasionally, and of most interest to us, about performances he gave or attended. The first two notebooks correspond with his visit of 1791–92, the last two with that of 1794–95. In the second notebook Haydn copied the affectionate letters he received from Mrs. Schroeter, thus preserving them from the fate of almost all other personal correspondence of this nature directed to him. He made the notebooks available to both Dies and Griesinger, for use in their biographies. Notebooks one and two eventually came to the Austrian National Library, the third notebook to the Mozarteum at Salzburg. Book four has been lost, and its contents are known only from the quotations made by Griesinger and Dies.

The surviving notebooks waited long for a complete scholarly edition. They appeared first in English translation, along with all the correspondence, in H. C. Robbins Landon's *The Collected Correspondence and London Notebooks of Joseph Haydn* (London, 1959). The many documents discovered or collected by Landon were then passed on to Dénes Bartha for his edition with commentary of the letters and notebooks in their original languages, *Joseph Haydn: Gesammelte Briefe und Aufzeichnungen, unter Benutzung der Quellensammlung von H. C. Robbins Landon* (Kassel, 1965). I have regularly consulted both editions. My English translations are made from Bartha's edition. As with the letters, most of the notebook entries are in German, yet they are peppered with words and quotations in other languages, as might be expected of someone from a polyglot culture like that of Vienna and the Esterházy court. There are many verses in Latin and anecdotes of all sorts, some ribald.

---

[21] Finscher, *Haydn* (2000), p. 362.

At one time it was customary to refer to these commonplace books as Haydn's London Diaries. They lack such basic qualities of a diary as chronological sequence, provision of dates, and regularity of entries. Sometimes Haydn provided a date, or the approximation of one. Early in the first notebook Haydn recorded his experiences at the Lord Mayor's banquet to which he was invited in November 1791. Its first two sentences will give the reader an idea of the problems faced by the modern editor. "Den 5ten 9ber war ich Gast zu Mittag bey dem Fest von Lord Mayor. an der ersten Tafl Nro 1 speisete der neue Lord Mayor sammt seiner Frau, dan der Lord Canceler, die beide Scherifs, Duc de Lids, Minister Pitt und die übrige Richters von ersten Rang." Ordinary editorial practice would require applying *sic* several times. Bartha wisely leaves Haydn's spelling as is, with only [Leeds] provided after "Lids"—an example of how Haydn transliterated English words into German.

Haydn goes on to describe this popular festival with a keen eye and ear for detail. He mentions how the Lord Mayor was accompanied to his seat and from it by a procession ordered by rank to the sound of trumpets accompanied by a wind band ("unter Trompeten begleitet mit eine Harmonie Music"). In the dancing after the feast, he observed another separation by social rank. In a smaller room where the nobles assembled, one couple began the dance, then others joined according to rank, as is done at court on the King's birthday (4 June).

> Nothing but minuets are danced in this room. I could not stay there longer than a quarter of an hour, first because the heat from so many people crammed into a small room was too great, second because of the bad dance music, in which only two violin and a cello constituted the whole orchestra; the minuets were more Polish than our kind or the Italian kind. I went from there to another room, which was more like a subterranean cavern, where they danced the English way and the music was somewhat better because a drum played along and covered the misery of the fiddlers. I went next into the great room where we had all eaten, and here the band was more numerous and more bearable. They danced English fashion, but only on the high platform where the Lord Mayor and the other notables had dined. The other tables were all occupied by men, who as usual drank heartily the whole night long. [Haydn uses the verb "sauffen," which is appropriate for beasts].

The din grew great with the many toasts shouted out to roaring approval. Haydn described many more details of drunken revelry, which seemed to amaze him. After a blank page he made a one-line entry: "Mtris Schroeter No 6 Bukinghamgate." He left many pages empty, perhaps intending to fill them later as leisure allowed. After some statistics on England's national debt, which was staggering, and two more names of persons with their occupations, comes a witty saying, perhaps told him by Salomon or some other German-speaking friend: "In France maidens are virtuous, wives are whores; in Holland maidens are whores, wives are virtuous; in England they remain lifelong whores." Landon's translation deflates the punch line with "In England they stay proper all their lives."

Haydn used the notebooks often as *aides-memoires* and to preserve verses he later set to music, or considered for possible use. With the long descriptive passages such as those about the Lord Mayor's banquet or the horse races at Ascot (in June 1792), he was perhaps storing up tales to tell upon his return home.

Following his detailed account of the Ascot races Haydn expressed amazement at the severity of punishments in the English criminal code, also at the inability of the King to mitigate them.

> If someone steals two pounds he is hanged, yet if I loan someone 2000 pounds and he carries them off to the devil, he goes free. Murder and forgery cannot be pardoned; last year a clergyman was hanged for the latter notwithstanding the best efforts of the King himself to intervene . . . When a wife murders her husband she is burned alive, while the man murdering his wife is hanged. The penalty for murder is increased by giving the body up for dissection after death.

Certainly there were many differences between British law and the direction in which the penal code for Austria was evolving after 1770. Maria Theresa abolished torture in 1776. Religious toleration was on the increase under Joseph II, who restricted capital punishment to crimes against the state, such as treason.

On 9 June 1791, Haydn attended a religious service in St. Paul's Cathedral that left a profound impression on him.[22] The Charity Children of London, several thousand strong, both girls and boys, assembled annually in Christopher Wren's vast edifice where they lined up, tier upon tier, on special bleachers erected under the great dome. There was always a large and fashionable attendance at this end-of-the-season public event. Haydn described it in his notebook and notated by ear the chant by cathedral organist John Jones to which they sang a hymn in unison.

> Eight days before Pentecost I heard in St. Paul's Church 4000 children sing the following song. One performer gave the tempo. No music in my entire life moved me so strongly as this devotional and innocent

Example 5.6. [Melody sung by the Charity Children as taken down by Haydn]

---

[22] Ian Spink, "Haydn at St. Paul's—1791 or 1792?" *Early Music* 33 (2005): 273–80. The author eliminated the rival date in June 1792 because Haydn was then going to the races at Ascot.

N. B.: All the children are newly clad and enter in procession. The organist first played the melody in good and simple style, then all began to sing at once.

Haydn was not the only genius to record being overcome by the sight and sound of the poor waifs, all orphans or indigents. William Blake depicted and wrote a poem about the same experience in 1788. Berlioz in his more wildly enthusiastic style described the same event during his London visit of 1851, devoting many lines to what Haydn expressed in so few. Haydn's genius for creating broadly spun slow movements in hymnic style, which reached a first peak in the *Largo* of Symphony 88, could only deepen as a result of this new inspiration.

Haydn's warm response to the event at St. Paul's contrasts sharply with his reluctance to say anything about Handel's music either in his London Notebooks or to Griesinger and Dies. It has been widely assumed without any proof that Haydn attended the Handel Festival in Westminster Abbey that took place on 23, 26, 28 May and 1 June 1791. All Haydn said about the event came a year later, in his first notebook. "On 30 May 1792, the grand Widow's Concert that was given for the last time a year ago in Westminster Abbey with 885, took place in St. Margaret's Church, because of the great expense involved. There were 800 persons at the rehearsal and 2000 at the actual performance. The King gave 100 guineas each time." This sounds less like direct observation than hearsay, as is true of much else in the notebooks. Haydn repeated some of the same information in the second notebook: "Anno 1791 was the last grand concert with 885 persons in Westminster. Anno 1792 it was transferred to St. Margaret Chapel with 200 performers. Criticism of this was made to me." He did not even say what was performed (in this case it was *Messiah*). At least once he admitted that he was in direct competition with the English idolatry of Handel's music. In the lost fourth notebook there is a passage quoted by Griesinger relative to a concert given by the Duke of York on 1 February 1795, the entire royal family being present, at which Haydn directed his own compositions from the piano and at one point was asked to sing. "The King, who hitherto could or would hear only Handel's music, was attentive."

Toward the end of Griesinger's account there is a passage in which Haydn praised Italian song and Italian singers, which led to this comparison: "Handel was great in his choruses but mediocre in song." A few pages earlier came the passage in which Griesinger wrote that Haydn always spoke with respect of Gluck, Handel, and his earlier teachers yet "most of what he knew he had learned from Emanuel Bach." Giuseppe Carpani, on the other hand, described how Haydn was struck dumb upon hearing Handel's music in London. Carpani took much of what he wrote in *Le Haydine* (1812) from the 1810 publications of Dies and Griesinger but not this. His credibility does not extend beyond what he actually witnessed and his fervent testimony in this case is suspect, to say the least. So are other later sources purporting to quote Haydn's opinion of Handel's music. Carpani was probably unaware of how much Handel was heard in Vienna at Swieten's concerts before Haydn went to London.

Summer 1791–Winter 1792

Haydn's success at the Salomon concerts prompted several honors and invitations to stay at country estates from members of the nobility and gentry. In July, Oxford University made him an honorary Doctor of Music. The London press was full of the elaborate proceedings, which were also related at length by Haydn to Dies and Griesinger. Dies gives this lively account.

> Dr. Burney was the instigator. He persuaded Haydn to this course and even traveled with him to Oxford. At the ceremony in the University Hall, the company present was stirred by an address to honor with the doctorate the service of a man who had risen so high in music. The whole assembly gave Haydn an ovation. Then Haydn was dressed in a white silk gown with sleeves of red silk and a small black hat, and thus arrayed he had to sit in the doctor's seat.

Griesinger wrote, "The doctors dress in a ruffle and a little mantle and turn out in this costume for three days. 'I really wished that my Vienna acquaintances had seen me in this outfit!' La Storace and several other musical friends waved to him from the orchestra." Cramer, Davide, and Salomon were also among those who traveled to Oxford to give the celebratory concerts that followed. Some slender evidence connects Symphony No. 92 with one of these concerts, hence it became known as the "Oxford" Symphony.

Haydn spent almost all of August and part of September at the country estate of banker Nathaniel Brassey near Hertford, north of London. After he returned to London, he wrote to Mme von Genzinger on 17 September a letter that is one of his most revealing. He began by expressing his regrets that he had had no reply from her to the letter, with music, he had sent her on 3 July (lost), then he goes on to more personal matters.

> My dear lady, how does your fortepiano? Is a Haydnish thought renewed at it by your fair hand from time to time? Does my good Miss Pepi occasionally sing the poor Ariadne? Oh yes, I hear it reaching even here, especially during the last two months when I have been living in the country at one of the most beautiful places, owned by a banker whose warm-heartedness and that of his whole family is like that of the Genzinger home, and where I lived as if I were in a monastery.

In what follows, Haydn expressed himself with a candor and directness not frequent in his prose, though it is in his music.

I worked hard and every morning early, as I was walking alone in the woods with my English grammar, I thought of my Creator, of my family and all my friends left behind, among whom I prize your family the most. I admit that I hoped to see you sooner but my situation—destiny, in short—decrees that I remain in London for another eight or ten months. Oh my dear lady, how sweet indeed tastes a certain freedom! I had a good prince, but had to depend sometimes on base souls. I often sighed for release, and now I have it to a certain extent; I recognize the good sides of this though my spirit is burdened with more work. The awareness of not being a bonded servant makes amends for all my efforts, yet, so dear to me as is this liberty I shall still request on my return to be taken into the service of Prince Esterházy again, if only for the sake of my family.

Haydn meant by his family, besides his wife, his siblings and their descendants. He was also concerned for the welfare of the underlings who worked for him. He continued his letter expressing doubts whether Prince Anton would have him back, revealing that he had received a summons from the prince. "Whether my request will be favorably received is doubtful, for in his letter my Prince objects strenuously to my long absence and demands absolutely my swift return. I cannot comply with this because of the new contract I have made here. Now, sadly, I await my dismissal. Yet I hope that God will give me the grace to lighten the burden somewhat by my industry."

Haydn continued to send money and letters to Luigia Polzelli. On 4 August, just before leaving for Hertfordshire, he wrote expressing condolences on the death of her husband and made the clearest statement to survive concerning the seriousness of the relationship that had existed between them. He almost suggested that they might still have a future together, although perhaps mostly to comfort her during this trying time. "Maybe the time will come, which we both dreamt of so often, when four eyes will be closed. Two are now closed but the other two—enough of this, it will be as God chooses." Frau Haydn, the remaining pair of eyes, lived on.

Another reason in Haydn's mind for remaining in London may have been personal. Sometime during the spring concerts he met and accepted as a pupil a wealthy widow, Rebecca Schroeter. Her husband, Johann Samuel Schroeter, had come to England with his family as a young man in the 1770s in order to concertize. An elegant composer in the galant style, he wrote some concertos for fortepiano that caught the attention of Mozart, who supplied some cadenzas for them.[23] Schroeter eloped to Scotland with his pupil Rebecca and was allowed to marry her only after her family insisted that he stop performing in public, which he did. He became Music Master to Queen Charlotte after the death of Christian Bach in 1782 and died young in 1788, leaving Rebecca both ample funds and a fine house in the best part of London's West End. It was from this address that she wrote

[23] *Music in European Capitals*, p. 919.

Haydn on 29 June, saying that she was back in town and eager to resume her lessons. Her friendship with Haydn became more intimate as the months went by. Haydn preserved her notes to him and took them back to Vienna. He told Dies, when asked by him about these letters in English, that she was "although already sixty [more likely forty] years old, still a beautiful and amiable woman whom I might very easily have married if I had been free then."

Haydn was in correspondence all along with his wife. None of the letters survives although he occasionally mentioned in other letters what she had written him. He began his letter of 13 October to Mme von Genzinger with a request that she immediately advance 150 fl. for a short time as a loan to his wife, who must have convinced him of some urgent need. Frau Haydn tended to be a spendthrift and the frugal composer perhaps kept her on a short leash in financial matters. She was not above spreading gossip in retaliation, as a later passage in the same letter suggests. Rumors reached the ears of Herr von Kees that prompted him to make inquiry of Haydn, who wrote in the same letter of 13 October:

> He would like to know about my circumstances here in London because there are various stories about me circulating in Vienna. I was exposed from youth on to envy and therefore am not surprised that people try to suppress my modest talents altogether, however the Almighty is my support. My wife writes me, but I cannot believe it, that Mozart has spoken very ill of me. I forgive him. It is certain that I have a crowd of people envious of me in London and I know almost all of them. Most are Italian but they cannot harm me because my credit with the common people [Credit bei den Volck] has been firmly established for many years. Your Grace should rest assured that if I had not received fitting approbation I would have returned long ago to Vienna, and that, aside from the Professors, I am appreciated and loved by everyone. As for my remuneration, Mozart should ask for information from Count Fries, with whom I deposited £500 and from my prince, an additional 1000 fl., in total nearly 6000 fl. I thank my Creator daily for this beneficence and flatter myself that I can take home a few thousand more, notwithstanding the great expenses that I have, and notwithstanding the travel expenses.

By "the Professors" Haydn meant the Professional Concert which, unable to pry him away from Salomon, was beginning to slander him.

In November, Haydn was again in the country north of London, this time for two weeks at the estate of Sir Patrick Blake. Then he was invited by the Prince of Wales to visit Oatlands, an estate owned by the second son of George III, the Duke of York. This prince had just married the eldest daughter of Frederick William II of Prussia, Frederica Charlotte, whose musical skills as pianist and singer impressed Haydn. He wrote, "We played music for 4 hours in the evening, that is, from 10 o'clock till 2 o'clock in the morning." In mid-November Haydn and Salomon visited Cambridge to hear the Dutch cellist and gambist Johan Arnold Dahmen or Damen, presumably related to violinist Johan Dahmen, who played with Salomon in string quartets and led the second violins in his orchestra. Both Dahmens were engaged for the upcoming subscription concerts at Hanover Square. The cellist was also referred to as "Dahmen jun."

Haydn's months of respite were given over to composing the works that would nourish the new concert season soon to begin. Before the year ended, he had completed at least two new symphonies, No. 93 in D and No. 94 ("Surprise") in G. Both autograph scores bear the date 1791. He may also have started work on their successors, Symphonies No. 97 in C and 98 in B♭, both dated 1792.

In Haydn's last letter of the year to Mme von Genzinger, dated 20 December, he wrote in answer to her taunting him about preferring London to Vienna. "I do not hate London, but I would be incapable of spending the rest of my life here, even if I could amass millions." In fact, Haydn found much to his distaste in the metropolis, aside from its noise. He was shocked by the rowdy behavior of people in the theaters as well as in the streets, also by the widespread public drunkenness, and the harshness of judicial punishments. In this same letter, he reacted with disbelief to the first, unconfirmed reports of Mozart's death.

Haydn did not mention Mozart's death in the letters he wrote to Luigia Polzelli and Mme von Genzinger on 14 and 17 January 1792 respectively, although he must have known by this time that the rumors were true. His first known reaction is in a letter, presumably from late January, written to a mutual friend of the composers, their lodge brother Michael Puchberg. The letter exists only as a fragment and it is somewhat dubious since it did not emerge until nearly a century later.[24] But the anguish and generous thoughts, if not the language and grammar used to express them, sound as if they could have come from a grief-stricken Haydn.

> London, January 1792
>
> For some time now I was quite beside myself about his death and could not believe that Providence would dispatch such an irreplaceable man to the other world. I regretted only that he was not able to convince the still unenlightened English of his merits, about which I preach to them every day. You will, good friend, have the kindness to send me a catalogue of pieces unknown here. I shall give myself every conceivable trouble to promote such works for the widow's benefit. I wrote the poor lady three weeks ago to the effect that, when her dear son [Carl] reaches the appropriate age I shall teach him composition gratis to the best of my abilities so that he might to some degree fill his father's position.

It is hard to understand how Puchberg in Vienna could be expected to supply a list of Mozart's pieces unknown in London, a task for which Haydn was better

---

[24] Gustav Nottebohm, *Mozartiana* (Leipzig, 1880).

placed. Whatever efforts Haydn made to see that Mozart's mature works were published in London had few immediate consequences. When he returned to Vienna, Haydn remained close to Constanze Mozart and her family. He was instrumental in the education of both sons, Carl Thomas, born 1784, and Franz Xaver, not born until 26 July 1791 and hence not yet known to Haydn in London. Haydn took a supervisory and supporting role in the musical education of the sons but apparently never taught them himself.

Franz Xaver Mozart had become a formidable pianist and prolific composer by 1826 when he visited Salzburg to see his mother and his aunt, Nannerl, who by this time was blind and mostly confined to her bed. The Novellos were also in Salzburg then and seized the chance to interview Franz Xaver. They asked him which of his father's colleagues "seemed most completely to appreciate his incomparable genius?" Mary Novello noted his answer: "Haydn he thinks his father's greatest admirer, and he never saw him as a child but he wept." Her husband Vincent noted the same and more.

> Spoke highly of Haydn—never saw him but he wept. [Especially his] Seven Last Words and the Vocal Quartets and Trios. Haydn told him that if he (Mozart) went to England first (as Salomon at one time wished) it would be of no use for him (Haydn) to go there as 'nothing would do after Mozart's compositions.' Haydn often visited them and repeatedly declared that Mozart was the greatest musical genius that ever existed.[25]

This suggests that there were negotiations between Mozart and London (Gallini and his agent Salomon) about which we know nothing, and that the letter from O'Reilly of the Pantheon Opera to Mozart was a rival offer. In a later conversation with Franz Xaver, Vincent Novello asked him which of his father's compositions he liked the best. He named two piano pieces, the Fantasia in c minor (K. 475), and the Rondo in a minor, K. 511, then mentioned Symphony No. 41 in C, K. 551: "Mozart's son said he considered the Finale to his father's Sinfonia in C—which Salomon christened the Jupiter—to be the highest triumph of Instrumental Composition, and I agreed with him." How would Franz Xaver know this information about Salomon giving the symphony its nickname? Probably because Haydn told him as much. Otherwise it could be read as an interpolation by Novello. There is confirmation of the story that Haydn did not want to follow Mozart to London in what Abbé Stadler told Novello in Vienna: "Mozart always declared his style greatly indebted to Haydn, though this latter thought so superiorly of him that he begged to go to London first, otherwise he should not dare to succeed Mozart, the English would not tolerate him."[26]

[25] *A Mozart Pilgrimage*, p. 92.
[26] *A Mozart Pilgrimage*, pp. 174–75.

In London, at the beginning of 1792, Haydn had to contend not only with his grief at Mozart's death but also a contretemps intended to rival or even replace him in popular favor. The Professional Concert, smarting over Salomon's coup in bringing over Haydn and the successes this entailed for Salomon's concerts, tried desperately to win Haydn's services for their series. Haydn refused to budge from his allegiance to Salomon. At this juncture the Professional Concert turned to Pleyel, whose music was already a great favorite at London concerts. Pleyel agreed to come over for the twelve 1792 subscription events of the Professional Concert. It was, in a way, a further compliment to Haydn to see his former pupil so courted and honored. But the intention clearly was to supplant Haydn in public esteem. Pleyel arrived in London on 23 December 1791 and promptly invited his old teacher to dine with him on Christmas Eve, which Haydn did. From this cordial renewal of their acquaintance onward, they behaved a lot like father and son in a happy family. Yet the competition set up by others was potentially embarrassing to both composers.

If Haydn was annoyed by this maneuver of the Professional Concert he did his best not to show it. He wrote Luigia on 14 January 1792 a letter that contains among other things a pertinent comment on the situation. "The Professional Concert has had my pupil Pleyel fetched to face me as a rival but I am not afraid because last year I made such a great impression on the English, and hope therefore to win their approval this year too." He was more explicit in his letter to Mme von Genzinger dated 17 January.

> At present I am working for Salomon's concerts and I am making every effort to do my best, because our rivals, the Professional Concert, have had my pupil Pleyel come here from Strasbourg to conduct their concerts. So now a bloody harmonious war will commence between master and pupil. The newspapers are full of it, but it seems to me that there will soon be an armistice, because my reputation is so firmly established here. Pleyel behaved so modestly toward me upon his arrival that he has won my affection again. We are very often together, and this does him credit, for he knows how to appreciate his father. We shall share our laurels equally and each go home content.

Their behavior does great credit to both of them, to the fatherly master, who did not allow himself to be overly perturbed, only stimulated by the presence and products of one of his best pupils, no less than to the young phenomenon who remembered where he had received both training and inspiration. How tempting it would have been for two more ordinary humans to have acted with less civility. The newspapers, to which Haydn was not insensitive, would have loved to tell of squabbles or worse between them had they so behaved.

Salomon made his first announcement of the new season in January, sending out to various newspapers what would now be called a press release. It announced, "Dr. Haydn, who is engaged for the whole season, will give every night a New Piece of his Composition and direct the Performance of it from the Piano Forte." The various concert series got under way in February. The Ancient Concert was the first to start, on Wednesday 8 February. Haydn mentioned the event in his notebook, although he left blank the space for the program, meaning that he may not have attended it. On Monday 13 February, the Professional Concert began, with a bow to Haydn in the form of one of his symphonies to open Part I. The event of the evening was "Grand Symphony, composed for the occasion, Mr. Pleyel." Pleyel brought many of his works with him that had not been heard or printed in London and there was no way for the audience to know whether this was one of them, or actually composed for the occasion. Cramer played a violin concerto on the first half and Mrs. Billington, the vocal star of the series, sang on both halves.

Salomon's 1792 Concerts

On Friday 17 February, as promised, Salomon opened his series. In a bow to his rivals he began the first half with a symphony by Pleyel, followed by the debut of a soprano castrato new to London, Signor Calcagni, the other singers being the established soprano Miss Corri and a Mr. Nield. To open Part II there was a true premiere. The "New Grand Overture M.S. Haydn" was Symphony No. 93 in D.

Salomon's practice was to repeat a premiere by Haydn the following week and it happened at the second concert on 24 February, at which the promised novelty by Haydn was "The Storm," a cantata for four voices, chorus, and orchestra on a short poem by John Wolcot, alias Peter Pindar, who called it a madrigal, as did Haydn. It was his first composition on an English text, intended to flatter his audience and did just that. On 2 March, there was another entirely new symphony by Haydn, No. 98 in B♭, taken out of turn, as it were, since he completed No. 94 in G sooner, to judge by the date 1791 on the autograph, and No. 98 only within the previous weeks, because it bears the date 1792. As we shall see, the slow movement of Symphony No. 98 gives one of the clearest indications of how Mozart's music was haunting Haydn's mind in early 1792. The audience showed its appreciation of the new symphony by demanding encores of its first and last movements, according to Haydn's notebook.

On the same day as Salomon's third concert, Haydn wrote again to Mme von Genzinger. He thanked her for the arrival, at long last, of the score to Symphony No. 91. This is also the letter, already quoted, in which he lamented the appearance in print of the piano sonata in E♭ of 1790 written for her alone. Then there is another assessment of the contest with Pleyel.

> My labors have been increased by the arrival of my pupil Pleyel, brought by the Professional Concert. He came here with a lot of new compositions, but they had been

composed long ago; he promised to present a new work every evening. When I saw this I realized at once that this whole crowd was against me, and so I announced publicly [i.e., through Salomon] that I would likewise produce twelve different new pieces. In order to keep my word, and to support poor Salomon, I must be the sacrifice and work the whole time, no matter what it really costs me. My eyes suffer the most, and I have many sleepless nights, though with God's help I shall overcome it all. The people of the Professional Concert wanted to tweak my nose because I would not go over to them. The public nevertheless is just. I enjoyed a great deal of success last year, but still more this year. Pleyel's presumption is sharply criticized, yet I love him just the same. I always go to his concerts, and am the first to applaud him.

It seems that Pleyel's promise to compose twelve new works was aired in the press as a first salvo, perhaps even before his arrival at Christmastide. Salomon's announcement in January that Haydn would do the same returned the fire. One cannot but admire Pleyel's audacity in challenging the master to whom he owed nearly everything about his modern style, as did an entire generation of younger composers. How moving it is, moreover, to read that Haydn pushed his enormous creative powers still further in response to Pleyel's challenge.

The fourth concert on 9 March brought forth Haydn's most direct response to Pleyel, a new "Concertante" in B♭ for four soloists and orchestra. The symphonie concertante was a colorful genre that flourished in the last third of the century, especially in Paris.[27] Its chief composers included the second-generation Mannheimer Carl Stamitz, the international Italian favorite Giuseppe Cambini, and Christian Bach, who wrote his mainly for a Paris audience while in London. By the 1790s, the principal heir to this tradition was Pleyel, who composed several symphonies concertantes calling upon various solo instruments. His *Sinfonie Concertante* in B♭ (1791), which may be one of the non-specified works in the genre on the 1792 programs of the Professional Concert, required as solo instruments violin and viola, the most traditional choice ever since the genre's beginnings, and the one Mozart chose for his superb *Sinfonia Concertante* in E♭ of 1779, K. 364.

As soloists in his only contribution to the species Haydn chose violin, cello, oboe, and bassoon, that is to say, Salomon, Menel, Harrington, and Holmes. Haydn's instrumentation had always favored a certain amount of concertante solo playing, especially evident in the "Time of Day" Symphonies of 1761, Nos. 6–8. In London too he took full advantage of the array of fine soloists Salomon had gathered, both in *Orfeo* and in the new symphonies. Still, a Concertante Symphony was something else, a concerto-like display piece for multiple soloists from its start to its finish. As a part of this devilish bargain, some more serious parts of the normal symphony, such as the frequent developmental passages that Haydn relished placing everywhere, not just in development sections, had to give way.

[27] *Music in European Capitals*, pp. 676–79, 684–85, 916.

The *Concertante*, as Haydn called it, perhaps to avoid the choice between "Sinfonia" and "Symphonie," was confined to three movements, fast - slow - fast, as was quite typical of the genre, showing its closeness to the concerto. At the premiere a critic for the *Oracle* wrote of the "New *Concertante*—the third movement of which seemed expressly calculated to shew the brilliance of SALOMON'S, and the sweetness of his tone." To further enhance his part Haydn even gave him a pathetic instrumental recitative. Possibly the *Concertante* resulted from a request by the astute Salomon. The critic continued, "The prevailing manner of this Master pervaded every movement—it had all his usual grandeur, contrasted with the levity of airy transition, and the sudden surprises of abrupt rests." The work has all these things and more. It makes for a pleasant listening experience, if not heard too often. The concerto was never Haydn's forte. On the other hand, it may well have been the style of work best suited to Pleyel.

A study of Pleyel's works on the programs of the Professional Concert would be of great help in assessing their relationship to those of his teacher. One scholar has gone so far as to suggest that Haydn's use of ominous-sounding slow introductions in the minor mode to three of his London Symphonies (Nos. 98, 101, and 104) "was an idea perhaps learnt from a Pleyel Symphony (B. 147) performed at the Professional Concert in 1791."[28] Haydn had been using such introductions long before Pleyel. They served him well in overtures such as those to *Il ritorno di Tobia* (1775), the *Seven Last Words* (1787), and indeed, *Orfeo*. Pleyel's *Symphonie Concertante* in F (B. 113) for a large complement of solo instruments can be identified as the Concertante on the Third Professional Concert on 28 February. The critic of the *Oracle* wrote of it, "The novelty of the evening was a Concertante by PLEYEL for six instruments, The subject extremely easy, airy, and well calculated for the *obbligati* of the different Instruments which succeed each other—all varied with profound skill, and producing the most delightful effects." Then came a kind word for the concertmaster: "CRAMER led the first Performance with that consummate ability which has placed him in our esteem the first of the Leaders." The critic concluded, "of this Concertante it will be sufficiency of praise to say, that HAYDN might own with honour these works of his Pupil. It was the triumph of both—the Master was there, seemingly proud of his Work; the Scholar, himself only second, was very sensibly affected by the applause." Pleyel published it later in Paris (Figure 5.3).

Salomon's fifth concert on 16 March offered a new recitative and an aria by Haydn for Signor Calcagni, a piece left unnamed that could possibly have come from *Orfeo*, in which case it would necessarily appear incognito. As noted by the critic in the *Morning Herald* there were no fewer than six pieces by Haydn

---

[28] McVeigh, *Concert Life* (1993), p. 143. B. 147 refers to Rita Benton, *Ignaz Pleyel: A Thematic Catalogue of His Compositions* (New York, 1977), p. 61.

SIMPHONIE

CONCERTANTE

Pour Violons, Alto, Violoncelle,
Flute, Hautbois et Basson Obligés

Avec Accompagnement d'Orchestre

Composé pour le Concert d'Hanover
Square de Londres.

Par

IGNACE PLEYEL

Propriété de l'Auteur.

PRIX 9ᵗ

A PARIS

Chez PLEYEL, Auteur et Editeur de Musique Rue Neuve des Petit Champs.
Nᵒ 1286, vis-à-vis la Trésorerie Nationale.
520

FIGURE 5.3. Title page of Ignaz Pleyel's Symphonie Concertante in F, B. 113.

on the concert, which began with his "Overture [Symphony] from last year," and continued with a string quartet performed by Salomon, Dahmen, Hindmarsh, and Menel, perhaps another one from Op. 64. Calcagni's new aria closed the first half. Part II began with a "New Concerto for Piano Forte" composed and performed by Johann Wilhelm Hässler, with whom Mozart had vied at Dresden on 15 April 1789, continued with an unspecified cantata by Haydn sung by Miss Corri, the *Concertante* ("by desire"), and "The Storm." The same critic opined, "Of these admirable works, the Concertante and the Storm, were certainly the best."

With the sixth concert on 23 March Haydn's first London visit reached the pinnacle of success. Its new work was his Symphony No. 94 in G, very soon afterward to be dubbed the "Surprise." A critic of the *Oracle* wrote, "The Second Movement was equal to the happiest of this great Master's conceptions. The surprise might not be unaptly likened to the situation of a beautiful Shepherdess who, lulled to slumber by the murmur of a distant Waterfall, starts alarmed by the unexpected firing of a fowling-piece. The flute obbligato was delicious." As naïve as this may sound it is certainly not inapt. The simple theme, its rising tonic triad answered by the falling tones of a V^7 chord, with almost every tone repeated instantly, like nursery song in character, could easily be made to sound like a sleep-inducing lullaby. Its charm is a pastoral plainness, softly projected, that could understandably convey the image of a shepherdess at rest reclining by her flock. When the shockingly loud chord on G comes in at the half cadence, it is marked *forte* in all the winds, *fortissimo coll'arco* in all the strings (after a *pianissimo* pizzicato repeat of the theme's first strain), and signally, *fortissimo* for the timpani, which Haydn insisted be struck *con tutta forza*, earning the work its other nickname, "with the drum stroke." It must indeed have sounded like a gun shot because of the way Haydn has set it up, by lulling audience expectations. And yet this very identifying feature of the symphony, the shockingly surprising loud chord, was not a part of his original draft. This work alone so captivated London that, even though Salomon's concerts were only half over, there was no longer any doubt that Haydn had won the "harmonious war" with Pleyel, and Salomon likewise over Cramer.

The seventh concert was deferred until 13 April because of the delayed arrival of Mme Mara, its vocal star. It began possibly with Symphony No. 91 in E♭, the long-sought score of which had recently arrived. Mme Mara did not appear but a new tenor, Giuseppe Simoni, made his first appearance in London, winning press plaudits. The critic of the *Morning Chronicle* described him as "a vocal performer who has gained great acclaim at the *Theatre de Monsieur* in Paris, and who will justly be ranked as one of the finest voices we have in England." On 20 April at the eighth concert, the new piece by Haydn was his fine Piano Trio in A♭ of 1790, with Master Hummel at the keyboard. Piano trios were a rarity in public concerts, and this exception was apparently granted on account of the pianist's youth. By the time of the ninth concert on 27 April Mme Mara did appear, singing solos at the end of the first part and next-to-last on the second. The new piece by Haydn was a divertimento, another London arrangement of one of the notturni for the King of Naples. Both parts began with Haydn symphonies, Part II including "By particular desire, the Favourite Overture, —Haydn, As performed last season, on the First and Second Nights." This was almost certainly Symphony No. 92, and no clearer proof remains of what a great public favorite it truly was. At Haydn's benefit concert on 3 May he may have given the first performance of Symphony No. 97 in C, which was probably the same as the "New Overture M.S. Haydn" on the tenth concert the next night.

For the two remaining subscription concerts, on 11 and 18 May, Mme Mara retained her choice spots on the program and the new pieces by Haydn were two more London arrangements of the notturni. A critic in *The Times* on 14 May reproached Mara for her deportment: "Turning her back, and leaning on the harpsichord has too much the air of negligence and contempt. We are sorry to observe, that most of our principal singers need to be often reminded in this respect." Mr. Hässler's "New Concerto Piano Forte" (as announced) annoyed this quite acerbic critic, who advised Salomon to banish his concertos: "His performance on the harpsichord was the most wretched attempt we ever heard. There might be skill, but harmony was wholly forgotten." The critic's naming of the instrument as a harpsichord might be just a habit from the past of so naming all large keyboard instruments, particularly if the writer belonged to the older generation.

Toward the end of this concert season, on 24 April, Haydn wrote Mme Genzinger saying he regretted not having the opportunity to compose more choral pieces in English besides "The Storm." He explained that it was impossible to have any boy choristers on the days their concerts were given (Fridays). He also summed up the results of the rivalry with Cramer's Professional Concert.

> Despite the great opposition and my musical enemies, who are so set against me and who together by means of my pupil Pleyel went to great lengths to dethrone me this

past winter, I have (praise God!) recovered the upper hand. But I must admit that because of so much work I have become quite exhausted and wearied, and look longingly forward to the peace that will very soon descend on me.

Haydn does not exaggerate—he rarely does. The Professional Concert tried everything to triumph over Salomon's concerts with Haydn but did not succeed in doing so. It collapsed after the 1792 season. Haydn had indeed won.

In the same letter of 24 April, Haydn renewed his protests of devotion to Her Grace and thanked her for the advice not to go to Paris, which he may have told her earlier was his plan.

> There are various reasons why I do not intend to go to Paris, of which I shall tell Your Grace when I arrive. I am awaiting word from my Prince, to whom I wrote recently [on 10 April] as to where I should go. It could be that he will have me come to Frankfurt [for the coronation of Francis II as Holy Roman Emperor]. If not, between us, I shall go by way of Holland to Berlin for a visit to the King of Prussia, and from there via Leipzig, Dresden, and Prague, finally to Vienna in order to embrace all my friends.

Frederick William II, the cello-playing dedicatee of the Prussian Quartets, Op. 50, still ruled in Berlin (until 1797) and had extended an open invitation to Haydn, perhaps renewed by his daughter in England, the Duchess of York. Following the defensive alliance of February 1792 between Prussia and Austria relations between them were more cordial than usual.

Symphonies Nos. 93–94

Symphony No. 93 bids fair to be considered the most wryly comic work of all twelve London symphonies, which did not deter Haydn from using it to open the 1792 subscription concerts. It begins with a typical call to order, detached *fortissimo* Ds in dotted rhythm tutti *unisoni*. An *Adagio* in 3/4 time, the introduction continues with a tender legato melody in the first violins, *piano*, and partly accompanied by the other strings. The legacy from other slow introductions to symphonies in D (especially Nos. 53, 75, and 86) could not be more clear. Instead of resorting to an eruption of the minor mode, as happens so powerfully in No. 96, Haydn did something more adventurous. The harmony slides up by half a tone from D to E♭, the Neapolitan chord, sounded in its first inversion after the move to V. Descending thirds, already present in the first soft rejoinder, quite monopolize the discourse until the harmony settles on a dominant pedal in preparation for what follows. Half-tone slides had become increasingly attractive to Haydn. They drew Beethoven's special attention, as did this entire symphony.

The *Allegro assai* is also in 3/4 time, another feature in common with the first movement of Symphony No. 96. Just as the violins began their soft lyric song in the *Adagio* with the sweetness of the major third, so do they begin the main theme of the *Allegro,* an octave lower this time and gradually rising rather than falling. It is broadly laid out as sixteen measures in antecedent-consequent form. After a long and vigorous transition, a strong *sforzato* accent on the second beat appears to signal the definitive cadence on the new tonic, A. Another truly lyric theme begins, with the tones 5 3 1 in the new key, sung by the first violins to the light accompaniment of the other strings. This theme is another perfectly regular antecedent-consequent shape, but only half the length of the main theme. A solo flute restates the second theme an octave higher, to its own accompaniment of clucking bassoons in thirds, staccato. Haydn interrupted the consequent by repeating a single upbeat figure in it, two eighth notes slurred to a quarter note. He did not develop either lyric theme per se. Rather he created a potent kernel mined from small features of both themes (Example 5.7). It is this figure that

EXAMPLE 5.7. *Haydn, Symphony in D, No. 93, I*

dominates the entire development, in a manner suggestive of how Beethoven was often to operate in similar situations. When there comes at last a respite from Haydn's oft-repeated motif, we hear the second theme in the key of C. It gets only half through before modulatory instability recommences, leading back to tonic D via a protracted V⁷ chord. Haydn does not merely repeat everything, tonally adjusted to stay in the tonic, he keeps rewriting his material and giving it new twists. Before reaching the powerful final cadences, he revisits a detail at the end of the *Adagio* as the treble slips a half tone, from G♯ to G♮. The seconda parte is not repeated.

In his notebook Haydn jotted down, "At the first concert the *Adagio* of the new Symphony in D was encored." This can only mean the *Largo cantabile* of No. 93, which is in G and in cut time. Its opening theme provides material for nearly everything that happens in the movement, and keeps returning, albeit by different approaches and with different instrumental colorings. The score requires trumpets (in C) and timpani, unusual for slow movements at the time, but pioneered by Mozart in his "Linz" Symphony, K. 425, of 1783. In both of these movements the trumpets and drums enter to reinforce a rather menacing turn to the minor mode. Haydn saved one of his most flagrant teases for the coda. As he begins to state the theme a final time it dissolves into wispy little descents of parallel thirds in dotted rhythm, tossed back and forth and then fragmented to a single descent of a third, and then to just a third with no descent. The answer to this withering away comes with a mighty blast from the two bassoons, *fortissimo* on their low C. Only after this untoward event does the theme come, for the first time, to a cadence. In polite society this kind of noise, emitted willy-nilly, is called an eructation or breaking wind—more vulgarly, a belch or fart. Perhaps it was this raucous moment that induced the audience to demand the movement's encore. The surprise in this case is more complex than the famous surprise of Symphony 94, because of the way Haydn prepared it, how he set us up for his lusty prank, which has become known as the great bassoon joke.

Menuetto Allegro is lusty too, and as vigorous a dance as could be wished, with strong accents of every kind on the first beats. Familiar from the first movement's second theme is the stream of staccato eighth notes up and down in thirds to accompany the exuberant melody. The Trio is very far from the rustic scene we have come to expect from Haydn. Instead he commenced in military fashion, with the winds pounding on tonic D with triplet upbeats. A mild answer in the strings is a curious non sequitur in the wrong place, b minor (vi) and with a nod to the main theme of the slow movement. Winds sound their call again, to which the strings answer by moving their response down a third to G (IV). To the next call the strings answer with their own tattoo, moving the harmony to repose on V. The second strain begins as the winds proclaim A, to which the strings rejoin by moving their soft response down a third to F♮, then modulating so as to end on a dominant pedal. All join together to conclude this romp, with mighty second beat accents reminiscent of those in the *Allegro*. The returning minuet by contrast seems straightforward.

Finale Presto ma non troppo in 2/4 time reverts to a melodic beginning clearly related to the F♯ D A descent in the violins that began the slow introduction. The continuations are also similar in emphasizing B G E. In a case like this we cannot know which came first to Haydn's mind. Possibly, the *Largo*'s theme represents a digest of the finale's main theme, which is another perfect antecedent-consequent shape of sixteen measures. This theme is in an ample rounded binary form with both parts repeated, often the indication of a rondo to follow. What follows is a sonata form without repeats. A hint of the first theme leads in the secondary key, which is confirmed by a clear second theme having both a similar melodic shape to the *Allegro*'s second theme and its familiar accompaniment, also heard in the minuet. Following a short development the modulation settles on a C♯ pedal (V/vi), hammered home by the two eighth-note upbeat figures in repeated tones that begin the movement. After a measure of silence this is followed by the slide up a half tone from C♯ to D, with the same upbeat figure and octave leap, now tutti *fortissimo*. The massive tonal slippage between F and F♯ in the finale of Beethoven's Eighth Symphony could well have been inspired by this moment. A complete reprise follows, in which the second theme is reassigned to the solo oboe, well suited to playing it in its tonic guise (there was another prominent oboe solo in the coda of the *Largo*). The coda of the finale begins after another silence and makes use of the melodic turn prominent in the main theme. It finally simplifies the main theme into a plain statement of D F♯D↓A that brings it even closer to the beginning of the slow introduction. Haydn apparently dedicated this symphony to Mme von Genzinger and in his letter of 2 March regretted that he could not yet send it to her because he needed to improve the finale, which was otherwise too weak in comparison with the first movement. What we have may be the improved version, at least it shows nary a sign of weakness and is quite worthy of the *Allegro.*

Symphony No. 94 follows two other beloved symphonies by the composer in the key of G, No. 88 and No. 92. Both made prominent use of the solo flute, which was in its element in this, its most fitting key, being the only common instrument among the winds that sounded well up in the regions around high G. In No. 94 Haydn took the extraordinary step of commencing its *Adagio* introduction with winds alone. It is in 3/4 time and begins with a soft, caressing melody in thirds to which the strings give response, also *piano.* On repetition the two flutes take over what the two oboes initiated, an octave higher, pushing the first flute up to high G. These exchanges give way to a modulatory passage for strings that introduces darker shadings, with a slow chromatic rise in the violins from G to D. This initiates the dominant pedal that will be resolved only by the onset of *Vivace assai* in 6/8 time, which begins rather timidly on a secondary dominant (V/ii), then rights itself by moving down a tone. The tune is short, lasting only four measures, but memorable. The entire orchestra joins in confirming the tonic, as if expressing its approval. Haydn had used this V/ii - ii, V - I progression in the same spot and with the same kind of theme descending in sequence to begin the *Allegro* of Symphony 86. The second theme area of the *Vivace assai* is unusually rich in new material, as if to make up for the shortness of the main theme. Its second theme proper is not so much a theme as a rhythm and texture, involving *sforzato* accents on the weak third and sixth beats of the measure. A more melodic idea over a tonic pedal in the new key of D serves as a closing theme. The prima parte ends with a series of repeated tones on B that leads back for its repetition and forward, with a different resolution to C major to begin the seconda parte. There follows a tonal chase around the circle of fifths before the reprise sneaks in. Haydn saves some new treatments of his main theme for its subsequent statements, and for the first time harmonizes it fully in four voice-parts. Then he rewrote this statement and extended it in a passage for winds alone, followed by the closing theme. He did not repeat the seconda parte, nor did he do so in any of the opening movements of the remaining London symphonies. This move freed him in the sense that he no longer had to think about how the end of the seconda parte would make a good connection with its beginning for the repeat.

The celebrated *Andante* "with the drumbeat" that ensues is in C major and 2/4 time; a marking above the first violin part adds *semplice.* The theme is indeed simple. In rounded binary form, it has a naïve directness that makes it unforgettable. Haydn's treatment of it in the subsequent variations brings more variety than one would have thought possible. The movement by its nature could not savor the depths of expression reached in the slow movements of the two previous symphonies in G. The *Andante* was intended to captivate and did so. It played a role in his decisive besting of Pleyel. Gyrowetz recalls in his memoirs visiting Haydn as he was completing it. We can be wary in general of the type of anecdote describing how the author was there when this or that famous piece was composed. Gyrowetz tells his tale at least with charm, and it is but one of many variations on the same tale.

> The concerts often lasted until well past midnight so that sometimes the ladies fell asleep. This prompted Haydn to compose something that would arouse them from their nap. And so he composed the celebrated *Andante* with the drum stroke, which resulted in shocking them awake, and from some elicited a loud cry. As Haydn was just composing this *Andante* Gyrowetz arrived for a visit. Haydn was so pleased and delighted with his own idea that he forthwith played the *Andante* on his square pianoforte, laughing as he did so, and predicting: "There the women will jump."[29]

Are we to believe that it was only the ladies who fell asleep at long concerts? That British men had no trouble staying awake, or if they did fall asleep were too stolid as to be awakened by loud noises? More likely, Haydn just preferred to think about women. The symphony did not come late in the evening. Like Haydn's other new symphonies for London, on first performance it began the second half. One other point relevant to Gyrowetz's veracity is that Haydn added the surprise only after composing an earlier version without it. Easily lost from view is the effectiveness of the movement as a whole. The first variation does not change much, but the second is impetuous and in the minor mode, the third features prominent wind solos, including the two flutes, often in thirds as was so characteristic of the slow introduction. The review in the *Oracle* singled out the flute solos as "delicious."

The anecdote about Haydn waking up the auditors, once launched, has seen no end of variants and retellings. Dies embellished the tale after his fashion, then on one of his visits to the master asked him directly about it. Haydn denied its truth.

> I asked him once in jest whether it was true that he had composed the Andante with the Drum Stroke to awaken the English who fell asleep at his concert. "No," came the answer, "but I was interested in surprising the public with something new, and in making a brilliant debut, so that my student Pleyel, who was at that time engaged by an orchestra in London (in 1792) and whose concerts had opened a week before mine, should not outdo me. The first Allegro of my symphony had already met with

[29] Adalbert Gyrowetz, *Biographie des Adalbert Gyrowetz* (Vienna, 1848); later editions ed. Alfred Einstein (Leipzig, 1915); R. Fischer-Wildhagen (Stuttgart, 1993).

countless Bravos, but the enthusiasm reached its highest peak at the Andante with the Drum Stroke. Encore! Encore! sounded in every throat, and Pleyel himself complimented me on my idea.

This explanation rings truer. Not to be outdone by the easily accessible music of his young disciple, Haydn went out of his way to create something that could not fail to reach every last member of his audience.

Relative to the *Largo cantabile* of Symphony 93, the famous *Andante* is scarcely a slow movement at all and sounds best when it moves along briskly, with strict attention paid to the *tenuto* marks placed in the theme. Haydn marked the minuet in that symphony *Allegro*, an unusual tempo for a minuet, but in this minuet he went even further, calling for *Allegro molto*. Effectively he destroyed any lingering feeling for the old courtly dance, which moved at a stately *moderato* pace. Then why did he call it by its original French name *Menuet*, not even *Menuetto* as in No. 93? Perhaps this is intended as another surprise, or even a joke in its own right. In form, Haydn adhered to tradition, just as he did in the *Scherzi* of his Opus 33 String Quartets. At this very fast tempo the piece nevertheless suggests parallels with the Beethovenian scherzo. The Trio is particularly jocular, largely given over to the first bassoon, which doubles the first violin an octave below. Perhaps in performance Haydn relaxed his very fast tempo in the Trio, if only out of consideration for the solo bassoon.

Symphony No. 94 gives the impression of a constant *accelerando*. An unusually brisk *Andante* gives way to a faster-than-ever minuet, capped by a still livelier finale, a sonata rondo that demonstrates anew the intoxicating power of rhythm. It may not be faster than the minuet when measured by the pulse of the quarter-note beat, but it sounds faster, especially at the end, when it whirls into a wild explosion of orchestral fireworks. Haydn, like Mozart, kept prodding orchestras to keep them from slowing down. On 10 December 1791 he attended an English opera, *The Woodman*, by his friend William Shield. It was performed at Covent Garden, another royal company, one at that time not allowed to give Italian opera. He had little good to say of the experience. "The Theatre is very dark and dirty, and almost as large as the Vienna Court Theatre." The singers displeased him except that he did praise the scandal-prone Mrs. Billington, while decrying the scandalous behavior of the gallery. What he wrote last in his notebook was close to his heart and he emphasized it by using capital letters: "THE ORCHESTRA IS SLEEPY."

Symphonies Nos. 97–98

The largest new works finished in early 1792, as confirmed by the date on their autographs, were these two symphonies, along with the *Concertante*. Their completion coincided with Haydn's sure knowledge that Mozart had died, and this has a possible bearing on both symphonies. No. 97 in C was his first symphony in this common key since No. 90 of 1788. Its slow introduction, *Adagio* in 3/4 time, goes no further than the first measure, with its loud, hortatory unison C, before introducing an expressive cadential progression. The melody rises softly by step up to C over diminished-seventh harmony, then falls an octave over the chords I$^6_4$ - V - I (Example 5.8). The second violins add a 4 - 3 suspension over V but this

EXAMPLE 5.8. *Haydn, Symphony in C, No. 97, I*

implies no churchly ties here. Melody and harmony duplicate verbatim a passage from an opera of 1790 in Vienna's Burgtheater. In January of that year Haydn accompanied Mozart to a rehearsal of the new opera in preparation, *Così fan tutte.* The moment in question was the very climax of the opera, when Fiordiligi, after putting up a valiant resistance, yields to Ferrando and the sensuality of Mozart's music (see Example 3.6). Haydn has condensed the passage slightly by omitting the melody corresponding to Mozart's m. 99 yet keeps the exact same harmonic progression. Even the ornaments used by Mozart's solo oboe to enhance this ravishing melody are the same in Haydn. What we have here may be more than just another case of Haydn putting the ending of a phrase before its beginning. Possibly he chose this particular cadential phrase because it had great meaning for him after Mozart used it so beautifully in what may be the last work by the younger composer that Haydn heard under its creator's direction.

Haydn treats the precious melodic-harmonic cadence in ways that show how much he valued it. Not unexpectedly it finishes the introduction by assuming its true cadential identity. And the next arrival on tonic C coincides with the onset of the blustery *Vivace* in 3/4 time, which begins like a fanfare. After a pleasantly contrasting second theme, thinly accompanied by an oom-pah-pah accompaniment, Haydn closes the prima parte by using the familiar cadence in rhythmic augmentation to prepare the definitive cadence on G. The seconda parte bursts upon us with the fanfare in E♭ coming directly after G. It provides all that he needs for material to develop. The reprise wends its way through most of the same materials until brought to a halt by a measure of silence. Softly, the initial cadence reappears, giving rise to an elaboration of it that leads back to E♭, then pushes as far as D♭ before settling on a dominant pedal. This coda sounds like a quiet meditation on the movement's most memorable idea, the one in common with Mozart.

An *Adagio ma non troppo* in cut time in the expected key of F introduces a smoothly flowing theme that is treated to variations, the first in triplets, the second in minor, and the third in sixteenth notes, rounded out by a coda. The *Menu-etto Allegretto* that comes next is in the ponderous old style, with heavy textures and harmony changing by the quarter-note beat. It serves to set up a charming Ländler-like Trio, with portamento slides up to the main beats, a reference, it would seem, to rural dance bands. The last time around for the tune is a solo violin part an octave higher marked "Salomon Solo ma piano."

The *Finale Presto assai* in 2/4 time begins with a tune related to that of the Trio. This refrain is in a rounded binary form with both strains marked for repetition. While the movement has frequent moments of development it is more rondo-like than is the finale of Symphony 94, for instance, because it has no clear second-theme function. The main goal reached in the middle of the movement is E♭, of which much is made. After restoration of the refrain in its entirety and more celebration of the tonic, a coda coyly tries to prolong the piece with pauses and cadences stretched out by fermatas. It does not succeed. The last thing heard, preceding two final chords, is an unexpected chromatic slide in the bass from G up to C, a retort to a chromatic slide from D down to G in the second strain of the refrain. Haydn often saves some piquant little touch for the very end. As a whole, this symphony, after its first movement, does not maintain the high level of interest throughout that is found in some others, notably Nos. 93 and 94. No. 98, on the other hand, exceeds even them.

Symphony No. 98, first performed on 3 March, marked Haydn's first use of trumpets in B♭. His previous symphony in B♭, No. 85 ("La Reine") did not use them and earlier they seemed to be altogether rare. The trumpets crooked in B♭ that Mozart required in *Così fan tutte*'s "Come scoglio" have been mentioned. Once Haydn adopted them he began to use them frequently. A week following the premiere of Symphony 98 came the first performance of the *Concertante* in B♭ with two trumpets. The instruments became a mainstay in his later choral music.

An *Adagio* in cut time begins the symphony with accented tones evenly spaced climbing up the minor triad from the tonic like the bold strides of a giant. This rise in half notes is followed by a jagged descent in quarter notes down to A♮, all this in unison until the violins add tones F and C to the A♮, in a dotted rhythm, a strident call to attention followed by a quarter-note rest with fermata. If this were an opera, one could expect some angry and impassioned recitative to follow. Haydn softens the continuation here, making it another rise, C E♭ A♭, *piano* and legato, with similar descent, also legato, leading to A♭, turned by the chords in dotted rhythm into V_3^6/III. III (D♭) promptly arrives with its own imperious rising triad, followed by the arrival on F for the dominant pedal that ends this bold and unusual introduction. It takes place in the relatively brief span of fifteen measures (only thirty beats in cut time), notably shorter than the previously discussed triple-metered introductions, which far outnumber those in duple meter.

A listener hearing the work for the first time has a lovely surprise when the *Allegro* opens by turning the *Adagio*'s beginning into a rising major triad, with a descent in quarter notes similar to the jagged one at the opening, becoming here a soft and pleasant-sounding theme. The descent then serves as a counterpoint to a melodic sigh in longer notes above. Haydn had never done this before with any of his slow introductions merging into fast main movements. The closest he came was to plant the *Allegro* theme of Symphony 90 in the middle of the slow introduction, yet there was no contrast between major and minor there. Less close is No. 97's planting of the initial movement's closing gesture in the slow introduction, at both beginning and end.

There is so much motivic potential in the first theme of the *Allegro* Haydn needs little else to generate an entire movement. It is one of his tautest and most economical sonata forms. When the first tutti arrives to confirm the tonic it brings an emphatic stomping rhythm associated with the contredanse: tap tap tap rest. Here Haydn adds his two trumpets in B♭ to the horns and all the rest. They color the whole symphony with their special tint. Arrival at the dominant gives Haydn a chance to dress the main theme with some different raiments and continuations. To begin the seconda parte he drops down a third from F to D, states the main theme there softly over a D pedal, then resolves it up a half tone to E♭ for the same theme *forte*. From here a merry chase ensues, with the rising triad motif treated in various canons while subjected to modulations that end with a climactic arrival on D (V/vi). After tentative resolution to g, the pull of gravity inevitably leads back to B♭ for the reprise, and this time the initial measures are not *piano* but *forte*. Before the movement ends there are two more returns to the main theme in the tonic, the second and last getting the most vigorous and foot-stamping version of all. The trumpets, horns, and most of the rest of the band play the rising triad *forte* in unisons and octaves while the remaining instruments play offbeat chords, marked *fortissimo* in the second violins, violas, and basses. With a few more cadences the end is quickly reached. The single flute high above all signs off 5 3 1.

The *Adagio* in 3/4 time and in F begins with one of Haydn's hymn-like melodies and is marked in the first violin part *cantabile*. It moves at first only to the closest melodic intervals and would be a perfect antecedent-consequent phrase of eight measures except for the internal repetition, modified, of two measures within the consequent. In repeating the antecedent Haydn changes the harmony so that it quickly leads to V/V, preparing the remarkable second idea in C. Tovey was perhaps the first to insist that what follows is Haydn's clearest invocation of Mozart. Many astute listeners over the years since 1792 must have recognized this, and many more agreed to its significance, with Tovey's prompting. Haydn's tribute to the genius he mourned took the form of a near approximation of the second theme in the slow movement of Mozart's Symphony No. 41 in C ("Jupiter") of 1788. As we have seen, it was probably Salomon who gave that symphony its nickname. Thus there is possibly more than one poetic justice at work that his concert series should introduce Haydn's poignant testimony to his departed friend. This is no superficial resemblance involving a melodic, harmonic, or rhythmic trait, but a matter of all these, and more importantly, phrase structure (Example 5.9). Tovey lets this musical example speak for itself. To strengthen his

EXAMPLE 5.9. *Haydn, Symphony in B♭, No. 98, II*

point he could have added a few details. Mozart repeats the fifth through seventh measures of the example. So does Haydn. A most personal signature of Mozart is the minor ninth appoggiaturas added to the melody on repetition, which Haydn introduces in an accompanying part. Tovey instead seized on the main point of difference between the two passages and what it means.

> He [Haydn] has not caught the cross-rhythm which in Mozart compresses the chromatic sequence and leaves room for a broader expanse before the close. On the other hand, Mozart's more highly organized paragraph is intended to be capped by a formal cadence-theme, whereas Haydn's purpose is to plunge dramatically into a strenuous development. The contrast between the two masters is thus seen even where Haydn is most touchingly docile towards his spiritual son, who has left him alone in the world of earthly music with only the awkward and stubborn young Beethoven to fill the void.[30]

The last sentence says so much so well it discourages further comment. I add only a thought about how Haydn could have known the music of Mozart's last symphony. He probably encountered it during their personal contacts when its

---

[30] Tovey, *Essays in Musical Analysis*, 6 vols. (London, 1935–39), 1:153–54. For comments by James Webster and Charles Rosen, see *Haydn Studies* (1981), pp. 412–13.

composer could have showed him the score or played it for him at the piano. An orchestral performance in Vienna was unlikely, as is the possibility that Haydn owned the score or saw it in London. Meetings between the two composers could have taken place in Vienna at the turn of 1788 into 1789, in January 1790, or in the fall of 1790 before Haydn's departure.

The *Menuet Allegro* brings us back from reverie to celebration, specifically to the big sound of B♭ tutti *forte* with trumpets and timpani. Also reminding us of the opening movement, the main idea outlines the tonic triad, not 1 3 5 as there but 5 3 1 preceded by an upbeat (recall the flute's 5 3 1 to end the *Allegro*). In the second strain of this fast dance 1 3 5 also makes several appearances. There is a fall by step of nearly two octaves in the first strain. The second strain outdoes this by a boisterous fall by leaps down two and a half octaves in unisons and octaves to a low G, *forte*, resolved, *piano*, by the chord of A♭, the first violins then climbing up triads 1 3 5 in different octaves. The Trio begins with a soft lilting melody in the first violins doubled by a single bassoon an octave below. Its second strain erupts with a loud burst, V/vi (D) resolving to vi (g), reminiscent of the harmonies that begin the *Allegro*'s seconda parte. Related too, perhaps, is the unexpected outburst of V/vi to begin the second strain of the Trio in the "Jupiter" Symphony.

The *Finale Presto* in 6/8 time is a jig-like dance cast as a large scale sonata form. Its tune is launched by a 5 3 1 figure following an upbeat, like the minuet, but much faster. This theme is completed in only eight measures and there is no hint of the usual rounded binary form. Rather, a ringing tutti for the whole band, including trumpets and timpani, leads to the new key of F, where the main theme gets started again only to go off the tonal track before being called to order by several cadences. Then comes a clear second theme, twice as long as the main theme but just as chatty, yet more relaxed because of its pauses for breath. After more cadences Haydn interrupts closure with his first call for *fortissimo* in the finale, as the strings in unison execute a chromatic turn around C, C D♭ B♮ C. Now we know why Haydn picked out a similar chromatic twisting motion in the slow introduction with his first *fortissimo* there and, moreover, why he introduced a *subito piano* to single out the passage in measure-long tones C C♯ D B♮ C, before closing the prima parte of the *Allegro*. In the finale a similar chromatic passage, partly *fortissimo*, occurs a few measures before the end of the prima parte. Here the seconda parte begins with a move from F to A♭ (cf. the slow introduction). The discursive second theme next takes over, and to make it chattier still, it is given to a solo violin—Salomon, of course. This sets the stage for a later solo appearance of the orchestra's other leader, Haydn himself sitting at the keyboard. Following the solo violin passage there is a big tumble of descending intervals that winds up with a deceptive cadence to A, a moment that cannot help but recall a similar one in the minuet's second strain. Haydn clearly wants this finale to be a mirror of the whole symphony, and that it becomes. His final surprise, in the long coda, is to include a tinkly accompaniment in sixteenth notes for his right hand to play as the main theme makes its last stand in the first violins. Haydn marked this "Cembalo solo" but almost all indications point to the pianoforte as his instrument of choice in directing these concerts. Just before his solo appearance he exhibits his signature "jam on the brakes!" maneuver: IV^6 - silence - V^6_5, with trumpets blazing and timpani pounding. This is just another instance of how this great symphony, besides being irresistible, is unusually personal.

Interim in Vienna

When Haydn left England in late June or early July 1792 he expected to return for the 1793 concert season and had signed an agreement to this effect with Salomon. His plan was to restock his supply of new compositions for the following season during the fall spent at home. Moreover he anticipated having Beethoven come to Vienna for study with him, then taking him along to London in early 1793. Haydn was not able to write very much new for London, partly because of exhaustion from his previous exertions and his travels. Also of importance to his plans were the worsening travel conditions on the Continent resulting from war.

The French monarchy teetered on the brink of collapse after the attempt of the royal family to flee from Paris was foiled at Varennes in June 1791. The failed escape attempt had been planned from Italy by Emperor Leopold, in collusion with the two brothers of King Louis XVI, who were living in luxurious exile. Returned to Paris, the king, Marie Antoinette, and their family were held as virtual prisoners in the Tuileries Palace. Moderate political forces that worked to rehabilitate the king as a constitutional monarch were gradually displaced by the Girondists. They forced Louis to sign legislation requiring all priests to swear allegiance to the government, then obliged him to declare war on Austria in April 1792, a month after the death of Leopold II, whose last diplomatic move had been to form an alliance with Prussia.

Haydn at the bidding of Prince Anton attended the Frankfurt coronation of Leopold's eldest son as Francis II, Holy Roman Emperor, in July 1792. He also undertook a brief trip down the Rhine to Bonn, where, it is believed, he met Beethoven and made an agreement to take him as a student. As for Haydn's earlier plan to go to Berlin and visit the Prussian king, it foundered. Frederick William II was about to lead the Prussian army in an invasion of northern France. Battle was joined with the French army at Valmy near Verdun in September, with the result that the Prussian army retreated back to the Rhineland. At the same time France officially became a republic. Two months later the Austrian army was routed at the battle of Jemappes, with chaotic consequences for the Austrian Netherlands. All hope of rescuing the royal family in Paris vanished. In January 1793 came the trial for treason of Louis XVI, his conviction, and his death sentence by a narrow majority of the Assembly. England's declaration of war against France soon followed. Marie Antoinette was executed in October 1793.

In Vienna, where Haydn arrived in late summer 1792, the beginning of a long and disastrous series of reversals for the imperial armies could scarcely be detected as fall passed into winter. The usual round of social pleasures went on as if there were no war, or no defeats. They reached a climax in the Carnival season of 1793 with the traditional balls and court galas. Haydn composed little new music but he did contribute twelve German Dances and twelve Minuets, Hob. IX:11–12, which were heard in the Redoutensaal at the charity balls for the widows and orphans of deceased artists. He was always generous in such matters, regardless of how parsimonious he could be otherwise.

Vienna became a lonelier place for Haydn after the death of his beloved Mme von Genzinger on 20 January 1793, aged only 42. Two short letters between them are all that survive from the latter half of 1792, both from him to her, one dated 4 August soon after his return, and this one dated 13 November.

> Gracious Lady!
> Besides wishing you a good morning I ask Your Grace to give the bearer of this note the last great aria in f minor of my opera, which I must have copied for my Princess, and which I shall return in two days at the latest. Today I take the liberty of inviting myself to visit at midday, when I shall have the opportunity of kissing the hands of Your Grace in return.

The aria in question is the climactic one for Orfeo in Act II. The Princess Esterházy for whom it was to be copied was Marie Therese née Hohenfeld, wife of Prince Anton, to whom Haydn would dedicate his next set of piano trios.

The short reign of two years enjoyed by Emperor Leopold II, more than half of which Haydn missed by being in London, had reinforced the domination of Italian opera in Vienna's court theaters. Leopold's tastes ran to serious opera and dramatic ballets, for which he was willing to expend the sums necessary, unlike Joseph II. He will be remembered nonetheless for hiring a new poet for comic operas, Giovanni Bertati, and the perfect musical partner for him, Domenico Cimarosa. Together they created *Il matrimonio segreto*, which had its premiere in the Burgtheater on 7 February 1792, before Leopold died. For decades it was the most successful opera buffa of all in Vienna, far outstripping in number of performances any opera by Mozart. Da Ponte derided Bertati's verses to no avail. They are well made for music. *Il matrimonio* as a whole is well concocted, with interesting characters and situations. Bertati derived it from the play *The Clandes-*

tine Marriage by George Coleman the Elder and David Garrick, along with some French imitations thereof. Cimarosa's music deserves its reputation for a melodic inventiveness that ensured immediacy of effect and a positive response from the general public. Only because we are so accustomed to the richer harmonic weave of Haydn and Mozart does this sparkling work often seem to lack something in substance—specifically, enough accompaniment to fill the sometimes empty sonic spaces between treble melody and supporting bass.

Goethe encountered comic operas by Cimarosa in Italy during his Italian tour in the late 1780s and praised their music in the entertaining book he made out of his adventures on his return. He also had kind words for their librettos, and specifically for one poet.

> It is the fashion to find fault with Italian libretti for repeating phrases over and over again without thinking about what they mean. They are light and easy, one must admit, and make no more demands on the composer and the singer than either is willing to give. Without enlarging on the subject, I will only mention the libretto of *Il Matrimonio Segreto*. The name of the author is unknown, but whoever he was, he was the most skillful of those who worked in this field up to that time.[31]

Even Da Ponte, who berated Bertati for nearly every aspect of his work, had to admit that his clarity and concision in handling plots came over well in the theater. The hedonism of the times in Vienna favored what was "light and easy."

Haydn's successes in England did little to enhance his reputation in a Vienna intoxicated by Cimarosa's tuneful charms, and captivated as well by the irrepressible Papageno and Papagena. At length, during Lent 1793, a concert was gotten up in the small Redoutensaal for Haydn's benefit (15 March). No newspaper account reported the event. It is known only that three of his most recent symphonies were played and that Irene Tomeoni, the prima donna of the Italian troupe, and the famous tenor Vincenzo Maffoli sang. Zinzendorf was present and called it "un Concert de Haydn," and remarked, "Il etoit charmant, un Adagio surtout. Maffoli et Tomeoni chanterent." There is only one real slow movement (as opposed to slow introductions) marked *Adagio* in the six London symphonies completed to this date, not the *Adagio ma non troppo* of Symphony No. 97 in C, but the *Adagio cantabile* of Symphony No. 98 in B♭. It would be deeply satisfying to believe that Haydn chose this particular work, with its connections to the "Jupiter" Symphony, as a way of bringing home to Vienna his personal tribute to Mozart.

Vienna, although far smaller than London, offered some of the same vexations to Haydn, or perhaps to any composer needing solitude and absolute quiet.

---

[31] Johann Wolfgang von Goethe, *Italian Journey (1786–1788)*, trans. W. H. Auden and Elizabeth Mayer (San Francisco, 1982), p. 417.

He took refuge from it (and from his wife) by going to Eisenstadt. There he presented Beethoven to Prince Anton in May. He also took with him his ward and pupil Pietro Polzelli, who was apparently a well-behaved young man, one who even managed to escape the wrath of Frau Haydn. In a postscript to a letter Pietro wrote to his mother on 22 October 1792 from Vienna Haydn added, "Your son has been received quite well by my wife, and I hope this continues." Few letters from 1793 survive. The one Haydn wrote Luigia in Bologna on 20 June is lengthy and gives the best indication we have of Haydn's uncertain plans.

> I am at present in Eisenstadt with your son, alone [without his wife]. I shall remain here for some time in order to enjoy the air, and to have a rest. You will receive with mine another letter from your son. He is quite well and kisses your hands for the watch [a gift from her]. I shall remain in Vienna until the end of September, and then I am inclined to travel with your son, and perhaps, perhaps go to England again for a year but first it would be necessary for the theater of war to shift, and if not, I'll make another tour, perhaps, perhaps to Naples. My wife is in poor health most of the time, and always in the same bad humor, but I don't give a damn [io mi non curo di niente]. These woes will end one day . . . Before your departure for Naples I hope for a reply.

Recall that in 1790 the composer considered accepting an invitation from King Ferdinand to visit Naples. Evidently it was still open. Haydn's other long letter surviving from this year was written on 23 November to Maximilian, elector of Cologne, in support of Beethoven, and its study will be deferred until Chapter 7.

In mid-1793 Haydn and his wife signed the contract to acquire a small house and garden in the suburb of Gumpendorf (see Figure 1.1, at about 8 o'clock from the city center). Dies relates that the property was discovered by Haydn's wife, who wrote to her husband in London asking for the money to buy it so that she would have "the house to occupy in future when she was a widow." Dies says that Haydn smiled at this remark, which later writers have used to further blacken the woman's character. Many people around Haydn, including Mozart, thought Haydn, because of his age, would not likely survive the rigors of a trip to London and back. In the event, it was Frau Haydn who died first, in 1800, and the widower who lived to the end of his days in this charming house, which he had extended by adding a second story. Dies quotes Haydn directly as saying, "I did not send her the requested money but waited until my return to Vienna. When the time came, I inspected the little house myself. Its quiet and solitary situation pleased me. I bought it." The Haydns did not occupy their renovated house until 1796, after the master's second return from London. Today it survives as the Haydn Museum of Vienna, expertly restored and kept up by the Museum der Stadt Wien.

Haydn agreed to direct the Advent concerts of 22–23 December 1793 in the Burgtheater for the benefit of musicians' widows and orphans. Three of the London symphonies were performed, as well as a chorus composed in England ("The Storm," translated into German). For once the Viennese commentators took notice and acknowledged the composer's stature. In the *Wiener Zeitung* a critic wrote, "Haydn himself conducted the orchestra, which consisted of over 180 persons [including the chorus?] and the excellent performance moved the public, which appeared in large numbers, to show its complete satisfaction by often repeated and vigorous demonstrations of its undivided approval." A writer for the *Oesterreichische Monatschrift* made more extensive and searching remarks.

> They gave the newest symphonies which the great Haydn had performed in London, and gave them as well as they had there, as even Englishmen assured us. The house was extremely full and the success extraordinary. If there is a musician of whom his fatherland can be in every respect proud, it is Haydn. A great, creative, and ever productive genius is in him combined with the most pleasant manner and a modesty which is almost exaggerated; not to speak of a most noble generosity in all that concerns his art! The late Mozart had no warmer friend, no more ardent admirer. There is only one great artist we know whom Haydn will allow no fair judgment and that is—himself.[32]

This may be the first time that a critic drew together Haydn and Mozart as being in a class by themselves at the summit of Vienna's musical Parnassus.

Caroline von Greiner, the poet and memorialist who was a daughter of Haydn's friend Franz von Greiner, frequent host of musicales where Haydn's Lieder were sung, wrote an execrable poem entitled "On hearing the six new symphonies completed in England." In describing them she writes, "the thund'rous tones of the timpani and the trumpet's bright clangor that inspires the swelling breast and incites courage and boldness in us to face the enemy, and hear the loud battle cries with pleasure" (my translation, with thanks to John Dryden's "Ode to Saint Cecilia," the one so memorably set by Handel). She makes one reference that seems specific to the "surprise" in Symphony No. 94. To end the poem she expresses her fears that Albion would claim Haydn for good after his approaching second visit. This shows that the visit was widely rumored by December 1793.

The best account of the deliberations surrounding another trip to England was gathered from Haydn during the Twenty-Fifth Visit by Dies, who says that Prince Anton was less willing to let Haydn go than he had been in 1790.

> When Haydn asked Prince Anton . . . for permission to undertake a second journey to London, he found great difficulties to overcome. The Prince, to be sure, required no services of Haydn, but took pleasure in his presence, and was of the opinion that

---

[32] Landon, *Haydn*, 3:226.

Haydn had acquired for himself fame enough. He should therefore be content, and at the age of one-and-sixty no longer expose himself unprotected to the dangers of a journey and the consequences of jealousy stirred up in London. Haydn recognized, to be sure, that all these expressions of Prince Anton's were proofs of his noble disposition; nevertheless, since he felt keenly his own strength and preferred an active life to the quiet in which the Prince had placed him, it was natural that the wishes of the Prince did not coincide with his own.

There may have been a general opinion in Vienna about his first foray abroad that if the journey did not kill him his enemies would. This might help explain what Luigia Polzelli jotted down on Haydn's first letter to her from London of 14 March 1791: "He will die—an enemy has followed Haydn to London to overthrow him." The passage from Dies implies that Haydn recounted to Prince Anton some of the opposition he met from Italian musicians resident in London. Dies continued this passage with explanations that strike closer to the truth than any noble sentiments of either party.

> There was the added fact that Haydn on his first stay in London had cleared 1200 gulden, and in addition knew that the English public still greatly favored his muse. Also he had contracted with Salomon, who was now no longer under contract to Gallini, to write six more symphonies; he had besides made very profitable contracts with various publishers. All these and other points were compelling reasons for going against the wishes of the Prince, who ended by giving up his own will to Haydn's profit and granting him the permission of the journey, which ensued on January 19, 1794.

Of the contracts, none mentioned has survived. It is clear nevertheless that during 1793 Haydn was working toward the creation of some new works for his second sojourn in London. He had made some progress on the symphonies and had even finished six new string quartets destined for Salomon.

String Quartets, Opera 71–74

Haydn wrote the new set of string quartets in Vienna with a view to their public performance in London. They are dated 1793 on the autographs and known as the "Salomon Quartets," also as the "Apponyi Quartets" because they are dedicated to Count Anton Apponyi, the Hungarian magnate who had stood as sponsor to Haydn when he was initiated as a Freemason in 1784. Count Apponyi paid Haydn 100 ducats for the quartets and received in return sole use of them for a year. Publishers in London and Vienna brought them out in groups of three during 1795–96, under various opus numbers that coalesced into Nos. 71 and 74 by the time of Pleyel's complete edition of the quartets. At least two and perhaps three of the new quartets were performed by Salomon on his 1794 subscription concerts. Haydn held the rest for the following season but the change of management to the Opera Concert, with increased emphasis on vocal music, may account for their lack of presence on the 1795 programs. Haydn perhaps began writing the first two quartets in the fall of 1792. That he did not rush the set to completion suggests that he already had doubts about returning to London in 1793.

The Quartet in B♭, Op. 71 No. 1, announces a new way of getting attention, two measures of *fortissimo* staccato chords, I - IV - I$^6_4$ - V^7 - I, supporting a descending treble melody 5 4 3 ↓ 7 | 1, the full sonorities accomplished by double- and triple-stops on the three higher instruments. They function like a slow symphonic introduction, only in miniature. Also they are not slow but in the tempo and meter of the whole movement, *Allegro* in common time. The melody that follows is a typical singing *Allegro* for the first violin, with light chordal accompaniment, all parts being marked *mezzo voce*. This main theme is short and simple, easily grasped, and if not impressed on every listener at first hearing, certainly it would be after nearly verbatim repetition, *forte*, a few measures later. Then it gives way quickly to the second key area, where the first theme mutates from its head motif of a falling triad into the second theme. The harmonic rhythm is mostly regular, often changing harmonies by the measure, or two measures, with few of the quirks and surprises abundant in Haydn's earlier quartets. Yet there is a welcome surprise just before the end of the prima parte, a sudden *pianissimo* diminished-seventh chord held for an entire measure before the big cadence. Mozart did something similar in two initial movements of the six quartets dedicated to Haydn, K. 458 in B♭ and K. 464 in A. The seconda parte begins in the most conventional of ways, with the main theme in the dominant. Then it is heard again in the subdominant. Haydn calls for a repeat of the seconda parte, as he does in all six quartets, and composes its beginning and ending accordingly. There is a brief nod to the rhythm of the introductory chords with rests between them to end both parts.

An *Adagio* in 6/8 time and in F begins with a main theme in rounded binary form with repeats indicated by signs. The form of the movement could not be simpler: ternary, with the middle section a little shorter than the main section. The *Menuetto Allegretto* is also brief and regular in form, moving steadily in quarter notes, with a penchant for *sforzato* accents on the third beat. The Trio counters with a soft and even flow of eighth notes from beginning to end. For the finale Haydn writes a *Vivace* in 2/4 time that begins with a catchy tune of the contredanse variety, with the typical repeated tones to mark the cadences (Beethoven comes very close to this music in his most famous contredanse, the one that ended up as the finale of the "Eroica" Symphony). Haydn's finale might turn into a rondo with a beginning like this but it turns instead into a sonata form with both parts repeated. Looking back over Haydn's earlier sets of string quartets we observe that this is the first to begin with a work in B♭, which was to become his most favored key.

The Quartet in D, Op. 71 No. 2, brings another imposing introduction, this one *Adagio* in common time, with contrasting dynamics and a full antecedent phrase packed into its four measures, making it even closer than that of the preceding quartet to Haydn's symphonic slow introductions. Brilliance is built in to this most resonant key for the strings, and Haydn capitalizes on it when he begins the *Allegro*, also in common time, with *forte* leaps down an octave for each instrument entering in turn from low to high and spelling out the tonic triad. The first violin continues by stating a theme that begins F♯ E D C♯, the same conjunct fourth in descent with which the cello accompanied the beginning of the *Adagio*. The leaps and succeeding material give Haydn plenty of substance for the whole movement. In this case there is also a memorable second or closing theme, with a catchy upbeat figure that is very dance-like. It is this figure in particular that supplies momentum in the development. The *Allegro* is shorter than many other Haydn first movements of the time, but so packed with interest as to seem longer than its 125 measures would suggest.

The *Adagio cantabile* is in 3/4 time and in the key of A, not so common a choice for works in D as is G. Even so, Mozart chose it many times when he wanted a more lyrical rather than pastoral kind of slow movement for a work in D. Haydn's melody, made out of rising triads beginning on the fifth degree, is simple and easily retained by the ear. It suffices as well for the melody of the second key area, E major. In the course of this exploration, tonic E suddenly turns into the third of C major, whence the discourse wends its way back to A for the reprise, which is heavily decorated with florid passagework for the first violin. The *Menuetto Allegro* is forthright with its ascending versus descending triads spanning octaves, reminiscent of the *Allegro*. Both it and the Trio are quite short, apparently a part of the set's overall strategy. The *Finale Allegretto* in 6/8 time provides a delightful rondo, with an episode in d minor and final return of the refrain in faster tempo, *Allegro*.

Quartet No. 3 in E♭ of Op. 71 commences without a tempo marking in 2/4 time, with a single tonic chord projected by double-, triple-, and quadruple-stops, a quarter note followed by a rest, then a measure of silence with fermata. After this call to order comes the double bar, with repeat signs and the indication *Vivace*. The meter remains the same. Violino primo sings the theme, an eight-measure antecedent and consequent phrase stretched to twelve measures by two little tags after each half. Haydn again makes sure listeners grasp the theme by repeating it exactly, here an octave higher. The second theme is made out of the first, as happens very often in his music. After the seconda parte is repeated there is an added coda that, like the beginning of the development, slips into e♭ minor, then ends with a vigorous reassertion of tonic major.

The *Andante con moto* in B♭ is also in 2/4 time and offers variations on a theme that misbehaves by reaching a cadence on iii where one expects V, and spends half of the second strain on V/ii before returning to I. Tonic minor occupies the first variation, while the second is content to state the theme unaltered except for the lack of repeats, very odd but perhaps justified because the harmonic structure of the theme is even odder and listeners need this added exposure to it. Variation 3 parades the first violin in a steady stream of sextuplet sixteenth notes. The fourth variation begins in tonic minor but ends with the return of tonic major, in celebration of which the piece breaks into a strange dance in sixteenth notes, staccato and at first *piano*, like a fairy round, into which the first violin attempts to introduce the theme, and eventually succeeds. A coda winds up this spree. The *Menuetto* bears no *Allegro* or *Allegretto* qualification, not surprising since the *Andante con moto* turned into a quasi-scherzo. It too is harmonically strange, by spending almost all its time in the first strain on V or V⁷ of E♭. A cadence on tonic E♭ first arrives midway through the second strain. The *Finale Vivace* in 6/8 time is a rondo that flirts with variation form. Its refrain, in rounded binary form with repeats indicated, displays the same tendency to shun the tonic and a similar choice of harmonies as the minuet. In sum, the work is more whimsical than the first two quartets of the set.

Opus 74 No. 1 in C has great breadth, spacious textures, and concertante display aplenty, along with harmonic richness and subtlety of detail. Here the introduction consists of two loud, thickly scored chords, V⁷ - I, followed by a pause. Then comes the double bar with repeat signs and tempo indication, *Allegro moderato*, continuing on in common time, with a soft main theme over a tonic pedal (Example 5.10). The theme comes in three segments, the first two of four measures each, with the first becoming louder and more chromatic on its way to a weak tonic cadence. The second, with a burst of first violin *forte* up to high C and E, rapidly descends in quick notes down to its lowest point, while the lower voices introduce the same chromatic rises heard in the first segment. Its cadence is the same weak one on the tonic, an octave lower. The third segment begins again like the first, then takes off with another *crescendo* up to high C in mm. 13–14 and a broader descent that doubles the phrase length. If the second rise to high C, over diminished-seventh harmony and decorated by an expressive melodic turn, sounds familiar, it may be because it duplicates the main idea in the slow introduction to Symphony 97 in C (Example 5.7) interpreted above as related to Mozart's use of the same idea in *Così fan tutte*. The big cadence after a broadening of the harmonic rhythm, the cadenza-like heroics of the first violin over a I⁶₄ chord, the 4 - 3 suspension over V in the second violin, and the not-to-be-neglected return of the cello to the booming low C with which it began, all make for a grand effect. The first theme is so rich it serves well, hardly changed, as the second theme, and then as the closing theme. To begin the seconda parte Haydn heads from G down to E♭, where he states the majestic first theme again. After a leisurely tour, there is the usual emphasis on V/vi - vi

EXAMPLE 5.10. *Haydn, String Quartet in C, Op. 74 No. 1, I*

on the way back to the tonic after an ample dominant pedal decorated by the first violin with a stream of sixteenth notes. A fugato in stretto puts the main idea through paces Haydn surely had in mind when he designed this theme. To close the movement, after a rousing detour to A♭, all players pounce on the theme and play it in unison and octaves, a climax fit to shake the floorboards.

The second movement of the Quartet in C, *Andante grazioso* in 3/8 time and in G, is one of the lightest dances of the set, and to emphasize its popular character Haydn uses the typically Viennese dance-hall practice of violins in octaves for one of its themes. The second theme offers sweet little duets in thirds and sixths, a high pair answered by a low one. The seconda parte of this sonata form gets a little more serious when it pushes suddenly to E♭ for the main theme. In the coda, Haydn adds a wry twist when the harmony wanders into the unlikely realm of c♯ minor, but only for a moment. The *Menuetto Allegretto* is full-blooded (many low Cs for the cello) and rather old-fashioned sounding. Yet the consequent phrase of the opening melody has a chromatic rise, C C♯ D F ↓ B♮ C♮, that sounds related to the main theme of the first movement. The second strain opens with a move to A♭, then b♭ minor, and offers further harmonic enrichments when it comes back to the main idea of the minuet, not once but twice, the second time with the all-stops-out fullness of C major climaxes in the opening movement. It is more than three times the length of the first strain, making for one of the composer's longer minuets, the longest in this set at sixty measures. Its Trio moves off without ado in the direction of the sharp side, introducing A major as its key without the slightest preparation. Haydn deems a transition necessary after the Trio, but it does not modulate, merely settling on V of A, the chord of E major, which then by the single tone E becomes the third of C major and leads in the minuet's return. Third relations like this have intrigued Haydn so much that they begin to challenge the norm of dominant to tonic convention.

The *Finale Vivace* in 2/4 time is in sonata form, and its main theme seems to ponder aspects of the first movement's main theme, like the minuet. A crucial chromatic rise to D from C stamps the end of the theme. With this motif, the quartet will end in triumph many measures later. On the way, a second theme in G is made out of the first and becomes a subject of contrapuntal treatment. The closing theme waxes very sweetly in duets, as in the second movement, and this is followed by the violins in octaves pouring out a deliciously rustic final dance over drone harmonies. The seconda parte indulges in further contrapuntal flights. When the drones return at the very end, they are of course in C major and could remind one of those in Symphony No. 82 in C ("The Bear").

The introduction to the Quartet in F, Op. 74 No. 2, is unlike any of the others, being a flourish of triads up and down, first on I then ending on V, in the tempo and meter of the movement, *Allegro spiritoso* in common time. It lasts for eight measures, then comes the double bar with repeat sign and the beginning of the sonata form. The first theme also sounds a rising triad, although *piano* instead of *forte*, and climbs up to high C for two descending triads. The answer to this long antecedent phrase is not a consequent at first but the same antecedent stated in the supertonic (ii), and finds its way back to the tonic only at its conclusion. A second theme is made out of the same material and given contrapuntal treatment. The seconda parte begins after a two-note transition with the main theme in A major, another descending-third progression, coming after the repeated tone C before the double bar. The rising triad idea may have worn out its welcome even before its long manipulation through various keys in the development. It certainly does not engender the fascinating changes Haydn lavished on the more complex main idea of the preceding quartet. The *Andante grazioso* in B♭ and in 2/4 is a theme and variations of only moderate interest. A *Menuetto Allegro* revives attention. Its Trio moves without ado from F down to D♭. A modulatory transition connects it with the return of the main dance. The stamping rhythm of the contredanse marks the *Finale Presto* in 2/4 time, which begins with a rounded binary form, the second strain of which takes a hint from the main theme of the initial movement by starting on the supertonic (ii). What ensues is a sonata form, or close to it. The second theme sounds curiously exotic by wavering between major and minor over drone harmonies. It may have evoked music heard in the Hungarian countryside by Count Apponyi. Neither prima nor seconda parte is repeated. A long sketch for this Finale that survives shows the care Haydn took with details, even the routine final cadence.

Connoisseurs, among them the dedicatee Apponyi, would have expected Haydn to include at least one quartet in the minor mode, as he had in previous sets. They were not disappointed, only made to wait for it until the last quartet, contrary to the custom of tucking it in the middle. The Quartet in g, Op. 74 No. 3, is the first in this key since Op. 20 No. 3 of 1772, and Haydn rarely used the key in symphonies (Nos. 39 and 83). The quartet's *Allegro*, qualified *ma non troppo* on the first English print, begins with the striding motion of unison leaps up the octave on the second and third beats of 3/4 time. It is unclear how or when the work acquired the nickname of "Der Reiter," which may have been suggested to some player or listener by the motion of this opening or by the persistent offbeat eighth-note accompaniments in the rapid finale. The eight measures that open the first movement and end on V could be an introduction. Or do they form the antecedent phrase of the first theme? Since they are followed by eight quarter-note beats of silence and not answered by a consequent phrase, it is best to hear them as another fast introduction, which is confirmed by their disappearance at the beginning of the reprise. On the other hand, Haydn introduces the leaping octaves briefly at the start of the seconda parte, after which they are heard no more. The repetition of the seconda parte may help explain why Haydn restricted this figure to no larger role on his stage. Its disappearance could be used to argue that the more potent reason this quartet became "The Rider" in some people's minds resides in those persistent rhythms of the finale, which suggest galloping horses.

The main theme of the initial *Allegro* is not so much a theme as a contrapuntal web of voices, entering from low to high. Haydn does not remain long in g minor before moving off to its relative major and preparing for a truly folk-like second theme. It is a kind of Ländler first sung by the violino primo and consists of legato leaps up a sixth on the first beat, like a parody of the angry-sounding octave leaps at the beginning. These have been made more popular by sliding up the sixths in a *portamento*, suggested by the indication *sull'una corda*. This phrase is perfectly square, 4 + 4 measures, quite unlike the amorphous first theme. For its reappearance at the end of the seconda parte in tonic major, Haydn changes the key signature to one sharp, thereby avoiding a lot of accidentals.

There is no more sublime slow movement in all of Haydn's vast output than the *Largo assai* in common time that follows. Acute listeners experienced in his ways would have expected, after the wash of G major at the end of the *Allegro,* a soothing C major to come next, as if in temporary resolution. What they heard instead was a bold plunge down to the key of E major, a striking example of how Haydn was lately changing his ways in favor of third relationships. The piece belongs to a long series of hymn-like slow movements marked *Largo* or *Adagio*. They made a deep impression on his listeners everywhere, not least on Londoners. This movement begins like something they might have heard sung in church, then quickly soars to other realms, propelled by harmonic means and a *crescendo* to a powerful, measure-long augmented-sixth chord, *fortissimo*, with texture enriched from four to seven tones in a marvel of chord spacing (Example 5.11). Descent from the climax in m. 8 to the half cadence requires several

EXAMPLE 5.11. *Haydn, String Quartet in g, Op. 74 No. 3, II*

additional beats. A rounded binary form of small proportions, and with repeats, suffices this large **A** section of the overall ternary form, the phrases perfectly regular except when Haydn stretched the first strain from eight to ten measures to accommodate the explosion in m. 8. The middle section of the movement, **B**, is in tonic minor. Haydn simply inverted the initial falling conjunct third in m. 1 as a way of arriving by step at the same A of m. 2. Portents of Beethoven multiply wherever one looks in these quartets, and why not, since the apprentice composer worked with Haydn during the year when they were being created. In Haydn's rising fourth one could hear approaching, by similar tread, the rising fourth motif in c minor that becomes a fugato toward the middle of the *Marcia funebre* in the "Eroica." Haydn's large **A** section returns unchanged except for elaborate embellishments of the first violin part and a few other small changes. Haydn further employs the conjunct third idea as a tiny coda in which he combines features of **A** and **B**, while leaving the melody completely unadorned, to great expressive effect.

Menuetto Allegretto is short and affable, choosing G not g, and celebrating the conjunct third in other ways. Its Trio brings tonic minor and some reminders of the octave leaps that opened the *Allegro* as well as of the prominent motif D E♭ C♯ D. The *Finale. Allegro con brio* in common time is a clear sonata form. Like the initial *Allegro* it passes from g to G for the last return of its rollicking second theme. Haydn foregoes repeating the seconda parte, perhaps thinking that he had already milked to the limit the pleasures of hearing tonic minor transformed into tonic major. Before conveying the quartets to Apponyi, Haydn would have tried them out in his own circle to find any notes that needed correction. We can easily imagine that Beethoven did not miss an occasion such as this. He might possibly have participated as one of the players—in the Bonn court orchestra his instrument was the viola.

Warfare raged intensely on the northern and eastern border regions around France during 1793. First one side gained the advantage, then the other. Having swept through the Austrian Netherlands in late 1792, the forces of the French Republic were pushed back by reverses in 1793, as they were in Beethoven's Rhineland home area, to which he would never return. But then the tide turned again. Nevertheless, Haydn decided to risk the dangers of travel. His trip was expedited by Swieten, who gave him "a comfortable traveling coach," according to Griesinger. Little is known about the route that he took. According to an anecdote related by Dies, he stopped on the way at an inn in Wiesbaden, where he encountered some officers of the Prussian army, one of whom was heard in another room playing the celebrated *Andante* of Symphony No. 94 in G. This spa town was a few miles inland from the Rhine and five miles north of Mainz, a city that itself had changed hands between the belligerents more than once. Contrary to earlier plans, neither Beethoven nor Pietro Polzelli accompanied Haydn on the journey. He was joined by his faithful servant and copyist Johann Elssler, who would be most useful for the task ahead in London, namely, to furnish six new symphonies that could somehow surpass the first six.

Salomon's 1794 Concerts

Haydn arrived in London on 4 February and must have been occupied at once by rehearsals for Salomon's first concert six days later. On arrival in 1791 he had to compose an entire opera. Without this burden he could now direct all his energies to providing music for Salomon's twelve subscription concerts. He took lodging in the elegant quarter of St. James at No. 1 Bury Street. At this address he was close to Carlton House, the residence of the Prince of Wales off Pall Mall, and to the King's Theatre in the Haymarket. Not by chance perhaps, his new residence brought him closer to the house of Rebecca Schroeter, No. 6 St. James St., Buckingham Gate. Nearby Green Park and St. James's Park presumably made for better city air and a quieter environment than at Salomon's in Soho. No letters of any kind survive between Mrs. Schroeter and Haydn from this second London sojourn. Almost certainly she resumed her piano lessons with him, if only because of a fine set of piano trios he composed and dedicated to her, first published by Longman and Broderip in 1795. Haydn made friends in England with persons from all walks of life, from the highest levels of society to tradespeople, including one wine merchant. As a foreigner of great distinction who was entertained by the royal family it behooved him to represent his country and his profession with dignity. A residence in St. James helped project an aplomb that was natural to him anyway and doubtless raised him in the esteem of some West London patrons. Haydn's addresses of Pulteney Street (1791–92) and Bury Street (1794–95) are signaled by stars on Figure 5.4.

By 1794 Salomon was the sole impresario putting on a full concert season of new music, the Professional Concert under Cramer having failed in 1793. He announced his plans for the new season in January and they were printed in several newspapers: "His concerts will open on Monday the 3rd of February next, and continue on every succeeding Monday (Passion and Easter Week excepted). Dr. Haydn will supply the Concerts with New Compositions, and direct the Execution of them at the Piano Forte. Principal Vocal Performers are, Madame Mara, and Mr. Fischer." Ludwig Fischer, Mozart's first Osmin, had settled in Berlin after leaving Vienna and was first bass at the Prussian court. His choice by Salomon was daring. It was one thing to substitute for the traditional male soprano another high voice like the famous tenor Davide, quite another to opt for a low male voice, traditionally associated with comic roles. High society, which made up the bulk of Salomon's subscribers, could well have objected. As it turned out they were *éblouis* by Fischer's extraordinary vocal and emotional range. Salomon promised the participation of instrumental artists in concertos and concertantes including, besides himself, Viotti, Dussek, Harrington (oboe), Ashe (flute), and Mme Krumpholtz (pedal harp). The price of subscription remained as before, twelve concerts for five guineas.

The concerts could have begun without the presence of some of these luminaries, but not without Haydn, so Salomon postponed his first concert until the following Monday, 10 February. As in 1791 it began with a symphony by Rosetti, whose music Salomon often favored, deservedly so. Mme Mara and

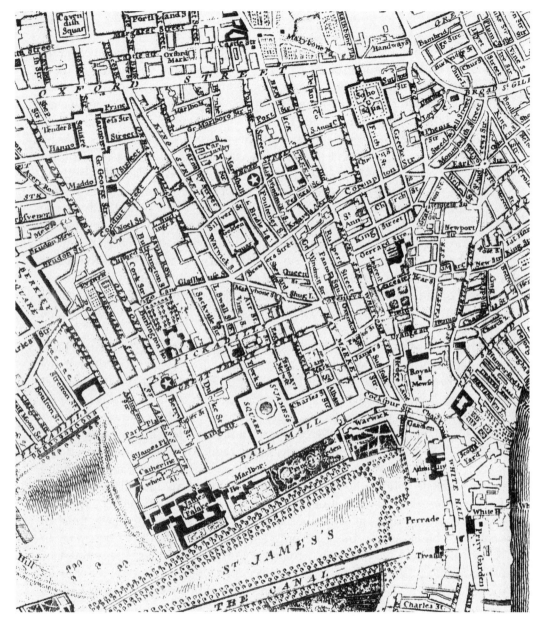

FIGURE 5.4. Districts where Haydn resided, from a London map by John Rocque.

Dussek were featured on the first half, and filling in for Fischer, not yet arrived, was a Mr. Florio, jun., a young man said to be Mme Mara's lover, and with whom she concertized widely. The "New Grand Overture" by Haydn that opened the second part was indeed new, and while very grand, also surprisingly intimate, being Symphony No. 99 in E♭. Viotti played one of his violin concertos at the midpoint of Part II.

At the second concert on 17 February, the new symphony was repeated. In addition, Haydn was represented by a new string quartet, surely one of those composed the previous year in Vienna. Since Mme Mara was ill and Fischer had still not arrived, replacements were summoned in the persons of Mme Ducrest and Mr. Huttenes, both having fled Paris. In 1793, Salomon had given a benefit concert for Mme la Marquise Ducrest; Huttenes was a professional musician who had held a royal appointment in France (what a social leveler was the concert stage!). The presence of these two refugees, who sang arias by Paisiello, Sacchini, and Sarti, gave newspaper correspondents an opportunity to vent their rage at the horrors and iniquities of the French Revolution. Viotti played in his same spot, followed only by Mme Ducrest and the orchestra's "Full Piece." The critic of the *Morning Chronicle*, who outdid the others in giving details about the music and in being a perceptive listener, said that Viotti's concerto was in the minor mode. Possibly it was No. 22 in a, subsequently such an international favorite and admired by Brahms. The same critic said, "in style it was neither perfectly ancient or modern, though it partook of the beauties of both." This concert began with a symphony by Kozeluch.

The third concert of 24 February began with a symphony by Wenzel Pichl who, like Rosetti and Kozeluch, was born in Bohemia and who had written many baryton pieces for Prince Nicholas I Esterházy. It was followed by a flute quartet by another Bohemian, Gyrowetz, long departed from London. Haydn's advice could have played a part in selecting these fine composers from the Austro-Bohemian school, and so could British support for its Austrian allies, whose armies bore the brunt of the war with France, being regularly beaten for their efforts. Ludwig Fischer at last made his first appearance at this concert and won high praise from the critics, who were astonished by his nearly incredible low tones. The symphony by Haydn that opened the second part is assumed to have been one of his older ones. He carefully spaced the premieres of the newly finished ones. Also by Haydn on the third program was a revival of the *Concertante* in B♭ from 1792, his most direct reply to one of Pleyel's specialties. The savvy critic of the *Morning Chronicle* identified the piece for us beyond a doubt by praising the tenderness of Salomon's solo violin in the finale's passages of instrumental recitative.

At the fourth concert on 2 March, Mme Mara still being indisposed, Mme Ducrest sang again, and in duet with Fischer, a piece assigned to Ferrari (Paisiello's pupil Giacomo Gotifredo Ferrari), who had left Paris for London in 1792, when he first met Haydn, under circumstances he described in his memoirs. The great event of this concert was the premiere of Symphony No. 101 in D ("The Clock"). The *Morning Chronicle*'s critic seized at once on the feature that would give the work its sobriquet: "The management of the accompaniments of the *Andante,* though perfectly simple, was masterly," and at the fifth concert the symphony's repetition evoked from the same critic, "The charming Andante of the new overture was encored." Also repeated was the new string quartet by Haydn "as performed on the Second Night." Mme Mara returned for this concert. Her rondò on the second half followed Viotti's solo concerto, his fifth consecutive appearance in this spot, winning higher-than-ever praises from the *Chronicle's* critic and the remark about Mara that "she was evidently inspired by what she had just heard." The concert began with a symphony by Reichardt, who like Fischer was in Prussian service. On the fields of battle, Britain's Prussian allies were doing no better than the Austrians.

The sixth concert, on 17 March, began with a symphony by Wenzel Pichl, continued with a song by Mr. Florio, a cello concerto by Mr. Dahmen jun., an aria by Mme Mara, and a *terzetto* sung by her, Florio, and Fischer. The Haydn symphony that began Part II was described by a critic as having "the second movement, as usual, encored," meaning probably Symphony No. 101. On the second half was another novelty with Viennese connections, a quintet with Glass Harmonica solo by Marianne Kirchgässner, who was blind from birth and the recipient of Mozart's Adagio in c and Rondo in C, K. 617, from the spring of 1791. It is not unlikely that the piece she played in London was this very quintet, with flute, oboe, viola, and cello accompaniment. The critic of the *Morning Chronicle* opined that it was very fine but nearly inaudible in a hall the size of the Hanover Square Rooms, and covered by the accompaniment no matter how softly they tried to play. The same critic wrote of Mara's Cavatina at the last, "We could wish she would not too often repeat the same songs, however beautiful; especially as she is a thorough musician, and finds no impediment from the labour of learning new airs. The Concert altogether was by no means the equal to that of the Monday before."

On the seventh concert of 24 March, a symphony by Gyrowetz commenced the program. The novelty by Haydn was another string quartet played from manuscript. Apparently Symphony No. 101 was heard yet again—"The Andante Movement of the Overture was universally encored," according to the *Morning Chronicle.* There were two concerts to go before the hiatus surrounding Easter. Haydn reserved for these concerts what he must have known would be an enormous success with the public, Symphony No. 100 in G ("Military"). In the midst of a war being waged on land and sea, the sensation made by such a work was not surprising. Its second movement, an *Allegretto* in C, required the addition of clarinets in C plus the percussion instruments of the typical "Turkish" battery in military bands. Very early the symphony was identified as the one "with the Militaire movement." (Actually the military instruments reappeared in the finale, but not the clarinets in C). At the eighth concert, on 31 March, Haydn was also represented by a repeat "by desire" of the string quartet heard the previous Monday. A symphony by Pleyel opened the program.

Viotti appeared in his usual spot with a violin concerto of his own, having missed only the sixth concert on 17 March. He also played in the ninth concert on 7 April. Of the latter performance the critic in the *Morning Chronicle* wrote, "Though his Compositions partake of the Old French School, there is yet a rich-ness, unity and grandeur to them." This remark may be compared with the ear-lier one about combining the beauties of both old and new compositional styles, regarding Viotti's concerto in the minor at the second concert. It is unclear what is meant by the Old French School, but perhaps Viotti's penchant for the minor mode reminded some of Leclair. Viotti came to London in 1792 after nearly a decade in Paris, where he was quickly acknowledged to have become Europe's greatest violinist. Salomon deferred to this artist by assigning him a role he might occasionally have filled himself. Viotti must have known at least Haydn's Paris symphonies before coming to London. Once there he was surrounded by Haydn's new music concert after concert, with Haydn directing it from the piano, an experience that intimidated many another composer. Instead, Viotti profited from it. A good case has been made that he absorbed some of Haydn's style in his own.[33] The two composers enjoyed friendly personal relations and Viotti per-formed on Haydn's benefit concerts in both 1794 and 1795.

There remained three Monday concerts in Salomon's series after Easter Week. At the tenth concert, on 28 April, an older symphony by Haydn began both the first and second parts (or "acts," as they were often called by the press). The sym-phonies described as played from manuscript parts could have been any of the six from 1791–92, of which Salomon owned the autographs and parts. Fischer and Dussek did the solo honors as did two players of the French horn performing for the first time in England. Viotti did not appear. Nor did the promised Mara, who was replaced by Miss Parke. Symphonies by Haydn played from manuscript opened both parts of the eleventh concert, on 5 May, as well. Viotti resumed his accustomed place on the second half. The critic of the *Morning Chronicle* described an echo effect achieved by the two new horn players, praised Miss Parke again, and said "Fischer was in full voice, and at each descending note the Audience could not but enquire, What! deeper yet?" The description fits Osmin's "Oh wie will ich triumphieren," which is not to say that Fischer kept that showpiece in his repertory, but he surely had some pieces like it; a display of his deep tones in descent likely inspired Mozart to write Osmin's aria in the first place. On Haydn's work the critic wrote, "The overture of the second act was the favourite one two years ago, and was heard with infinite delight; the last movement was encored."

[33] By Chappel White, *From Vivaldi to Viotti: A History of the Early Classical Violin Concerto* (Philadelphia, 1992), pp. 345, 348.

It could have been No. 98, with the unusual keyboard solo for Haydn at the end.

The final concert of the series, on 12 May, began with a symphony by Haydn played from manuscript parts, and to begin the second part, "The Grand Overture with the Militaire Movement." At the bottom of the announcement of this concert sent to the press was a note saying, "Mr. Salomon is extremely sorry, that Madame Mara's indisposition still continuing, prevents her from fulfilling her engagement to perform at the Concert." Miss Parke again took her place. Master Bertini, a pupil of Clementi, played a fortepiano concerto that was, according to the *Morning Chronicle*, "of his own composition." The first part also included a concertante for winds by Gyrowetz. Fischer sang an aria in the middle of the second part and Miss Parke a rondò at the end, surrounding a manuscript duo for two violins played by Viotti and Salomon, a fitting climax to the season.

One noticeable difference between this season and Salomon's concerts of two years earlier was the near disappearance of two names prominent then. Clementi was represented only by his young pupil and Pleyel by one symphony, and it can scarcely be by chance that it was placed on the same program as the premiere of Haydn's massive "Military" Symphony. The disappearing act of Mara, for whatever reason, was followed a year later by a subscription series without her.

Haydn's benefit concert fell on Friday, the second of May. It was very like one of the last few subscription concerts, with major roles played by Fischer and Miss Parke, and concertos played by Dussek as well as Viotti. Haydn symphonies opened both parts, and it is no surprise that the second was "By desire, the Grand Overture with the Militaire Movement, as performed at Mr. Salomon's concert." Tickets "at 10s 6d each to be had of Dr. Haydn, No.1, Bury-street, St. James," and at other specified addresses.

During this season, Salomon also directed the concerts of the Academy of Ancient Music. He managed to introduce some of Haydn's music even there, despite the strictures against works by living composers. These concerts were held at Freemasons' Hall, which was slightly larger than the concert hall in Hanover Square.[34] Haydn had no connections with these concerts and apparently kept his distance from English Freemasonry.[35] Cramer, who was an active Freemason, remained in demand as a leader after the collapse of the Professional Concert. He was favored by the new management running the King's Theatre in the Haymarket. Their large concert room was the locus of entertainments at which Cramer led the orchestra, including at his own benefit concert on 8 May. Like almost all such events in London it commenced with a Haydn symphony.

[34] On the dimensions of the various venues for London concerts see McVeigh, *Concert Life in London*, pp. 56–57.

[35] Simon McVeigh, "Freemasonry and Musical Life in London in the Late Eighteenth Century," in *Music in Eighteenth-Century Britain*, ed. David Wyn Jones (Aldershot, 2000), pp. 72–100; 81. For a depiction of Freemasons' Hall, see p. 87.

SYMPHONY NO. 99

On 10 February 1794, Haydn reintroduced himself to his London public at Salomon's initial concert with Symphony No. 99 in E♭. He had finished it in Vienna and dated the autograph 1793. It is probably the only one of the three new ones that was ready for presentation so early. One of the loveliest of his works, whatever the medium, it abounds in special qualities and will be taken up separately. For the first time Haydn calls for clarinets in one of his symphonies. He had done so earlier in his score for *Orfeo* (1791), so they were not strange to Salomon's orchestra. Clarinets appear in all the movements and lend the work its particularly suave character. They are in B♭ except for the slow movement in G, where he substitutes clarinets in C. All movements also use trumpets and drums, giving the work a tinge of the heroic and celebratory throughout. The astute critic in the *Morning Chronicle* understood something of the symphony's multifaceted appeal: "It is one of the grandest efforts of art that we have witnessed. It abounds with ideas, as new in music as they are grand and impressive; it rouses and affects every motion of the soul. It was received with rapturous applause."

The introductory *Adagio* in cut time alternates massive tutti chords, marked *fortissimo* in the strings and *forte* in the winds, with tenderly lyric *piano* passages for the strings. A half-tone rise above the dominant lands the music on C♭ for a whole measure, with fermata and a *tenuto*. The soft answer takes this as a signal to alter harmonic direction, changes C♭ to B♮, and moves off in the direction of the sharp side all the way to G, where it settles and is reinforced by the loud tutti. The introduction seems to end with a long pause on G (V/vi?). It is not quite the end because the winds softly intone V⁷ of E♭, with the seventh, A♭, on top, begging for resolution. Daring, yes, and surely a little confusing to first-time listeners.

The *Vivace assai* in common time commences with a soft melody of the singing *Allegro* type, with light, pendulum-bass accompaniment in eighth notes. It is organized as four two-measure segments, **a b b' c**, and is immediately repeated, tutti *forte*. Motives from the slow introduction bestrew the transition to the second theme, which is made out of the first. A closing theme offers another lyric gem, lighter still, and this is what Haydn chooses to develop: it and a syncopated figure, an accented B♭ followed by an accented C♭, clearly related to the same half-tone movement in the preceding *Adagio*. The prima parte ends with three strong chords on B♭. After the repeat sign comes the soft chord of G major, that is, the reverse of these same triads, going from the introduction to *Vivace assai*—there G *forte* - B♭⁷ *piano*; here B♭ *forte* - G *piano*. Moreover, at the end of the Trio in C major, Haydn uses these same two chords in a transition back to the minuet by making a G⁷ chord plus flatted ninth mutate into the top three tones of a B♭⁷ chord. He may have had this clever idea at the initial conception of the minuet, perhaps of the whole symphony, and it may relate to the choice of G as the main key of the slow movement. Whatever the case, his fascination with third relationships has moved up a notch to encompass both within and between movements. In the development of the *Vivace* the main theme nearly disappears, except for a brief appearance at the very beginning, making it all the more welcome when it shows up to begin the reprise, loudly proclaimed by the whole orchestra.

The *Adagio* in G occupies that key as if in a dream or magic spell that began when the slow introduction firmly settled on G as its seeming goal. The *Adagio* theme is sung by the first violins, marked *cantabile*. They begin serenely then pause, with the effect of raising a question or a doubt; the end of the theme is then echoed by the winds alone an octave higher. On a second try, the theme, inflected, gets further but still fails to make a full cadence before moving off to the dominant, where the winds take over and explore the first theme all by themselves. This little choir, consisting of first flute, the two oboes, and first bassoon attracted the attention of the same critic for their long and enchanting solo quartet (one week later on the repeat performance).

> The Overture, being performed with increasing accuracy and effect, was received with increasing rapture. The first movement was encored: the effect of the wind instruments in the second movement was enchanting; the hautboy and flute were finely in tune, but the bassoon was in every respect more perfect and delightful than we ever remember to have heard a wind instrument before. In the minuets, the trio was peculiarly charming: but indeed the pleasure the whole gave was continual; and the genius of Haydn, astonishing, inexhaustible, and sublime, was the general theme.

Following the ethereal quartet for solo winds, the strings return, the violins singing another beautiful theme, one that harks back to the opening of the slow introduction (Example 5.12ab). It is broadly supported by the rest of the orchestra and

EXAMPLE 5.12 a, b. *Haydn, Symphony in E♭, No. 99*

a. *I, Introduction*

b. *II*

comes to an abrupt end with strong punctuation, an accented chord on the second beat, like a chaconne. After the repeat, a development starts up by turning D into d. This leads to a statement of the broad closing theme in C, softly but for full orchestra, even the trumpets and drums, which Haydn pitched in C precisely for this moment. The harmony moves toward another strong cadence on the triad of B♮, arrival of which is punctuated with the same chaconne-like accent. This is, of course, V/vi in the home key of G. As in so many other instances at the end of Haydn's development sections, there is no resolution to vi. Tonic G returns in its stead, with the initial theme softly stated. Strings take over the lovely point of imitation that the winds had made of this theme and duplicate it with little change, except for the key, now tonic G. The closing theme comes back for two statements in G separated by a dramatic rise to a climax, which is followed by a long dominant pedal. A chaconne cadence closes the curtain and ends the enchanted vision.

One of the most striking moments in this rapturous slow movement occurs in the protracted V⁷ pedal before the final statement of the closing theme, reaching closure for the first time. The violins, doubled by the trumpets and horns, pulsate in quick notes on a dissonant interval, D and C together at the top of the V⁷ chord, while the bass strides up and down in dotted rhythm. This parallels a frequent texture in the slow movement of Mozart's Symphony No. 39 in E♭, K. 543, with even sixteenth notes coupled with figures in dotted rhythm. It makes one wonder if the experience of that whole symphony by Mozart was not on Haydn's mind when he wrote Symphony No. 99. Mozart used clarinets in B♭ throughout and prominently. They do much to color both works with their soothing tones. Mozart wrote a long, slow introduction to his symphony that wanders off into distant tonalities involving C♭. And at the other extremity, the finales have themes that sound as if they belong to the same giddy family.

The *Menuet Allegretto* has been mentioned. It is quite straightforward and is constructed on a descending arpeggio theme. Haydn being Haydn, the theme appears often in inverted form. "Particularly charming" is the Trio, declared our critic. Part of its charm resides in its third relationship with the main dance. The *Finale Vivace* is no less charming. Its theme is so typical of Haydn that it could serve as the perfect model of his rondo refrain (Example 5.13a). The movement

Example 5.13

a. *Haydn, Symphony in E♭, No. 99, IV*

in its entirety is one of the clearest examples of Haydn's perfected combination of rondo and sonata forms. It is more like a rondo than many of his late finales because it has a mid-movement return of the complete refrain in the tonic. When compared with Mozart's finale in Symphony No. 39, which is always described as one of his most Haydn-like, the badinage of sallies up and down sound remarkably similar. The little figure of four conjunct sixteenth notes rushing to two staccato eighth notes is shared with Haydn's theme (Example 5.13b).

EXAMPLE 5.13

b. *Mozart, Symphony in E♭, No. 39, IV*

SYMPHONIES NOS. 100–101

Symphony No. 100 in G ("Military") became Haydn's most popular of all twelve for London with early audiences, perhaps reflecting their concerns about the ongoing war. It made a striking impression even on first hearing, just as the composer had planned. This and the companion work, No. 101 in D ("Clock"), were begun in Vienna, to judge by the Italian paper on which their minuets are written—one of the clearest indications that Haydn was occupied by minuets early in the process of creation. Whichever of the two symphonies was first ready for performance, Haydn deemed it wise to have No. 101 go first, on 3 March, and held back No. 100 until four weeks later, knowing it would provide the climactic point of the whole season.

An *Adagio* in common time begins No. 100 with a soft and pleasant theme in the strings, one that hardly forecasts the boisterous nature of what was to follow but does anticipate the main theme of the following *Allegro*. Its calmness is perturbed momentarily by a menacing switch to tonic minor with the brass instruments added over a timpani roll, as the whole orchestra swells via a *crescendo* for a brief show of force. The music quickly subsides, passing through E♭ back to the tonic, the most challenging progression being no more than an augmented-sixth chord on the way to the dominant pedal, which is held long enough to have all good ears on the alert for the resolution that follows. A main theme in the mellow tenor range might have been predicted from the end of the introduction. Instead Haydn shifts the range to high in the winds, where the first flute and two oboes announce an *Allegro* in cut time with a cheery, almost chirpy theme, | 5-6 8 | 5 over I - IV$^6_4$ - I. The flute goes up to its high G in the very first measure, sounding there like a piccolo (a military instrument in origin). Some listeners may have been reminded that their previous favorite among Haydn's symphonies, No. 94 in G, began with similar sounds, with the flutes in thirds at the top of their range: 5 8 6 | 5 (over I - IV$^6_4$ - I). In Symphony No. 100 the strings play the theme in turn, an octave lower, and resolve it with a full cadence. After an ample transition to the new key of D, the wind trio returns to sing its theme a fourth lower, making it serve the function of a second theme. Then Haydn provides a new melody as a distinct theme for the closing function. It is preceded by its accompaniment, a steady stream of eighth notes in the second violins and violas, over bass pizzicatos, to which the first violins add a bouncy upbeat tune of a comic opera kind, quite repetitious, like patter. (Cf. the actual aria buffa cited by Mozart and similarly located in the first movement of the "Jupiter" Symphony, a tune also preceded by its steady harmonic accompaniment.) At the beginning of the seconda parte are two measures of silence. One could easily have predicted what Haydn would do next: sound the buffo tune down a major third, if only because that is what Mozart did at the same spot. Buffo material lends itself so much better to development than lyrical material, as both cases demonstrate. In the reprise, Haydn condenses, then expands with an explosive move to E♭. This too could almost have been predicted from various other first movements in the same key, his Symphony No. 8 and String Quartet in G from Op. 33 among them, not to forget Mozart's Piano Concerto No. 17 in G, K. 453.

The *Allegretto* in cut time and in C is a very simple melody that Haydn borrowed verbatim from the *Romance Allegretto* of his Lira Concerto in G of 1786, Hob. VIIh:3. Ready for action, as a few observant members of the audience perhaps noticed, were some extra musicians and instruments, namely triangle, cymbals, and bass drum: the *musica Turca* of Viennese military bands. If the audience did not notice them at first, their ears soon told them all, when this crew plus timpani added their raucous sounds to a *forte* episode in c minor that followed the many repetitions of the anodyne main theme. The *Romance* returns in tonic major and on its repetition with fuller scoring also suffers the added battery of percussion. The flutes on top here sound the melody in high range, which takes them again up to their piercing G. When the movement appears to be over, or nearly so, a single trumpet sounds a call, an alarum before the battle, as it were. A timpani roll of two measures on tonic C makes a *crescendo* into the tutti *fortissimo* chord of ♭VI, A♭, which is resolved by the simplest means at hand, by becoming an augmented-sixth chord on the way to I$^6_4$. The movement is a large ternary form, **A B A** plus coda, easily grasped by everyone, even those "long ears" that exasperated Mozart. Its simplicity of content nevertheless stirred up terrible visions in those first audiences. On this point the *Morning Chronicle*'s critic waxed eloquent after the work's repeat performance at the eighth concert, on 7 April.

> The middle movement was again received with absolute shouts of applause. Encore! encore! encore! resounded from every seat: the Ladies themselves could not forbear. It is the advancing to battle; and the march of men, the sounding of the charge, the thundering of the onset, the clash of arms, the groans of the wounded, and what may well be called the hellish roar of war increased to a climax of horrid sublimity! which, if others can conceive, he alone can execute; at least he alone has effected these wonders.

Battle symphonies and other battle pieces were no rarity in concert halls of the time. They were all the rage. But Haydn's proved lasting while others were quickly forgotten. His mastery of timing and of orchestration worked near miracles here with the simplest of materials.

After the uproar of the *Allegretto*, the *Menuet Moderato* restores a tone of stately decorum, and the *moderato* implies that this is just what Haydn wanted. The other two Haydn symphonies new this season say *Menuet Allegretto*. This one, at a more moderate pace and with regular phrases, becomes almost danceable to the traditional steps of the old court dance. The Trio is a modest duet for solo flute and solo oboe.

A *Finale Presto* in 6/8 time concludes the work. Its main theme is a rounded binary form with repeats but the movement as a whole is closer to sonata form than to a rondo. The popular nature of the theme is apparent from its jaunty rhythmic character and its many repeated tones. It approaches certain traditional jig tunes, such as "The Irish Washerwoman." Part of the development begins what sounds as if it would become a fugato but soon dissipates into a less contrapuntal discourse. Toward the end the audience perhaps noticed that the battery of percussion was preparing to resume its attack, which it did and remained prominent up to the final cadence.

With Symphony No. 100, Haydn closed his legacy of late orchestral masterpieces in the key of G, a tetralogy made up of Symphonies Nos. 88, 92 ("Oxford"), 94 ("Surprise"), and this work. For whatever reasons, his successors avoided G as a main key in their symphonies, as if Haydn had exhausted its greatest possibilities. Neither Beethoven nor Schubert adopted G for any of their symphonies. They were followed in this regard by Brahms, Schumann, Mendelssohn, and Tchaikovsky. Antonín Dvořák broke the chain with his brilliant Symphony No. 8 in G of 1889, soon followed by Gustav Mahler's Symphony No. 4 in G. Dvořák agreed with Haydn's lesson that in this key, the flute shines with particular luster. He assigned the vibrant main theme of his first movement to solo flute, or, better put, he created this theme especially to take advantage of the instrument.

Symphony No. 101 in D begins, like Symphony No. 98, with a slow introduction in the tonic minor, there in duple meter, here an *Adagio* in 3/4 time. Its rising scale in the lower range may not seem to promise much. Nevertheless, the rising conjunct passage is an idea basic to the whole symphony, present in the minuet and Trio, also in the sketches for them, hence early. The Trio in particular seems to have shown the way to such rises at the beginning of the *Adagio* and in the main theme of the following *Presto* in 6/8 time. In the *Presto*, Haydn manipulates his main theme to provide both transitional and secondary thematic material. The *Adagio* harbors other motifs that see use in the *Presto*, for instance, the intervallic play among A, B♭, B♮, and C♯ at the top of the initial rising figure, translated into A♯, B♮, C♯ in mm. 93–95 of the *Presto*. The seconda parte begins without resorting to any unusual juxtapositions. Haydn saves those for the *Andante* in 2/4 time and in G. Its light accompaniment in staccato eighth notes up and down the interval of a third provided the feature that suggested to listeners the ticking of a clock. A loud exploration of tonic minor follows the soft main theme and serves as a development section leading back to the main theme. At this point the theme is very delicately rendered, being sung by violino primo with only a flute and a bassoon to provide the tick-tock accompaniment. After this the music stops for a measure of silence. The second violins softly strike up the clock motion with staccato eighth notes G B♭ G B♭, hinting at a return of tonic minor. Yet it does not return. Instead those tones become 3 5 3 5 over E♭, where the first violins begin singing the theme. An augmented-sixth chord smoothly resolves to I$^6_4$ of tonic G for the return of the entire main theme in glory, its jubilation celebrated by the full orchestra, including the two clarinets in A, which are present in all four movements, mainly used to give greater sonority to passages like this. The movement ends softly as if the clock had run down, with three final ticks in rhythmic augmentation. It is another feat of orchestration.

The *Menuet Allegretto* and Trio were sketched on a large sheet that has miraculously survived.[36] The top half contains jottings for the Trio and begins not with the rising octave by step so central to the whole symphony but with a subsidiary passage near the beginning of the second strain. This unison descending passage in sequence goes against the meter with its units of five eighth notes, which took Haydn many tries before he got them exactly the way he wanted. Only then did he sketch the Trio's beginning, which starts with the repeated tones of F♯ for four measures (a tonic chord in the completed score and a kind of "vamp until ready"), followed by the rising octave scale for solo flute meant for Haydn's London friend Andrew Ashe. Finished with the Trio, he sketched the minuet—of course, in his mind he may have conceived them in the order in which they were to occur. The *sforzato* on the E that begins the minuet's second measure is already there in the sketch, alerting us to hear the first tone of every measure as this dance's take on the rising scale of D.

The *Finale Vivace* in cut time steals softly on the ear with 3 4 5, etc. in D, as if Haydn willfully withheld from us the first two tones of the scale. A symmetrical and short refrain in rounded binary form initiates what is to be a clear rondo form with mid-movement return of the refrain in the tonic, giving way to an episode in tonic minor. The head motif of the refrain then returns as the subject of a fugato, leading to the theme's soft final appearance, for strings alone like its first appear-

[36] *JHW* I/17: 57a, Kritischer Bericht; *Haydn-Studien* II/3 (1970); and H. C. Robbins Landon, *Critical Edition of the Complete Symphonies*, 12 vols., rev. 2nd ed. (1981), 12:406–7.

ance, and as a coda over a tonic pedal. In answer, a vigorous tutti *forte* begins climbing the scale of D from the bottom 1 2 3 4. By beginning on the third degree the finale merely confirms a trait common to the Trio's "vamp" and the *Andante's* tick-tocks.

The Minuet and Trio in Symphonies 100–101 were scored by Haydn on Italian instead of English paper, unlike the rest of these works. They were apparently composed first and most likely when he was still in Vienna awaiting return to London, as is certain in the case of Symphony No. 99, which he dated 1793 on the autograph, written entirely on Italian paper. The inference is that a good minuet could prime the way to creating the rest of a larger work. Possible confirmation for this idea exists in a remark Haydn made to Griesinger on the subject of rules governing strict composition.

> Someone told Haydn that Albrechtsberger wished to see all fourths banished from the purest style. "What does that mean?" replied Haydn. "Art is free, and will be limited by no pedestrian rules. The ear, assuming it is trained, must decide, and I consider myself as competent as any to legislate here. Such affectations are worthless. I would rather someone tried to compose a really *new* minuet."

More than anyone else responsible for confirming four-movement form with minuet in quartets and symphonies, Haydn was not about to abrogate at least this rule of composition.

Other Events of 1794

Italian opera in London furnished the principal entertainments of a musical-dramatic kind to the English nobility and gentry in 1794, as they had long done and would continue to do. Sheridan and his Royal Theatre in Drury Lane (patented to perform only in English) attracted a more plebeian audience. By the end of 1792, William Taylor had regained the royal license for and monopoly on opera in Italian. To recoup his losses he leased the opera house in the Haymarket to Sheridan and his company while the theater in Drury Lane was being fully rebuilt and enlarged in 1792–93. The Italian company limped along in the smaller theater across the Haymarket, and employed at least two very good singer-actors in Nancy Storace and Michael Kelly, who also sang leading roles with the Drury Lane Company in the English operas of Stephen Storace and others. Making things still more complicated, Taylor, as manager of the Italian company, delegated authority in artistic matters to Kelly, Stephen Storace, and Vincenzo Federici as *maestro al cembalo*. By 1793 Badini had died. His successor as opera poet was a far greater librettist, Lorenzo da Ponte. Any hopes for improvement on an artistic level of the Italian offerings were doomed nevertheless by inherent weaknesses germane to the pasticcio practice.

Da Ponte and Federici mainly revised old operas, comic and serious, for London. These included Cimarosa's *Il matrimonio segreto* (11 January 1794), Gazzaniga's *Il Don Giovanni* (1 March), and Paisiello's even older *La Frascatana* (5 June). Da Ponte revised the serious opera *La vendetta di Nina, o sia, Semiramide*, composed for Naples in 1790 by Francesco Bianchi, who actually came to London and prepared his own music revision (18 March 1795 as *Semiramide*). It was performed forty-one times over six seasons. Bianchi prepared several more works for the King's Theatre in collaboration with Da Ponte. The leading ladies during Da Ponte's tenure were prima donna Brigida Giorgi Banti and prima buffa Anna Morichelli, the latter known earlier to the poet because she had sung at the Burgtheater in Vienna during 1787–88.

Da Ponte's memoirs can take over at this point. They make up in verve what they lack in accuracy.

> The opera season [of 1793–94] was almost half over when two famous rivals came to London: the Banti woman, at the time one of the most celebrated singers in Europe in serious parts, and *la* Morichelli, equally celebrated in comedy. They were neither of them any longer young [both were about forty], and never had they been enumerable among the great beauties: but the one was much sought after and exorbitantly paid for the splendors of a glorious voice, the single gift she received from Nature: the other, for her acting—she gave a performance that was true, noble, carefully worked, and full of expression and grace. They had therefore both become idols of the public but the terrors of composers, poets, singers and impresarios. One of them alone was enough to make any theatre where she was engaged tremble at her name. I leave my good readers to imagine, therefore, what the situation at the Italian Opera in London must have been at a time when both these stage heroines were engaged contemporaneously.[37]

Da Ponte is merely warming up here to the task of telling anecdotes of side-splitting drollery about the clash of these two ladies. Banti had sung in London before and spoke some English, an advantage over her rival, who had sung nearly everywhere (besides Italy and Vienna, in Paris, Madrid, and St. Petersburg) but was making her first trip to England. "The moment they arrived in London, they joined battle for the possession of the manager's heart." William Taylor, whose gruesome portrait Da Ponte drew in garish colors, succumbed to Banti, who then set her sights on several other conquests, including Da Ponte himself, to hear him tell it. For her lover, Morichelli settled on the composer Vicente Martín y Soler, famed for his comic operas with Da Ponte for Vienna, especially *Una cosa rara*.

---

[37] Da Ponte, *Memoirs*, trans. Elisabeth Abbot (1959), p. 126.

Their two operas for London were *La scuola dei maritati* (27 January 1795) and *L'isola del piacere* (26 May 1795). Haydn went to the latter and dismissed it in his notebook as "a lot of old stuff from *Cosa rara*." Both Banti and Morichelli sang in Haydn's 1795 concerts.

In Paris, the most violent phase of the Revolution reached its peak in 1794. The Terror unleashed by Robespierre and his cohorts sent many of the country's greatest to the guillotine, including Lavoisier, the famous chemist. André Ché-nier, poet, perished on 25 July aged 32, three days after music patron, collector, and author Jean-Benjamin de La Borde. Two days later Robespierre himself met the same fate on the guillotine, hastening an end to the Terror. The war conditions under which a violent group had achieved political supremacy were not so easily ended. In 1793, the harvest had been very poor in France and many parts of the country were consequently threatened with famine. The worst was averted when large shipments of grain from America escaped British naval pursuit and reached Brest in June. Thereby hangs the tale of a famous battle, with consequences that touched Haydn.

The admiral of the English Channel Fleet was Richard Lord Howe, an aged hero of both wars in North America (1756–63 and 1776–83). Much of the French Atlantic fleet was sent to protect the convoy of over a hundred ships that had set sail from Chesapeake Bay in early April. Lord Howe sailed in May with twenty-five ships of the line, nearly matching his adversary in gun power. With daring tactics he hurried to intercept the French fleet and the slower grain ships off the coast of Brittany. Battle was joined in late May and went on for days. It reached a climax on the first of June. By the end Howe had sunk one warship and captured six others, a great victory, yet more tactical than strategic since most of the grain ships reached port and the First French Republic survived.

It took several days for the news to reach England, where it created a national euphoria. After bad news for months about the battles on land, the nation was ready to celebrate this battle, dubbed "The Glorious First of June." London saw many giddy reactions to the victory, on the stage and in the streets. Da Ponte hastily wrote a cantata, "La Vittoria," that could be sung to the music of Paisiello's *La serva padrona*, which had been scheduled. Banti ended the evening by singing "Rule Britannia" to shouts of acclamation. This was on 23 June. Earlier still, according to the press, when the electrifying news first reached London on 10 June, Paisiello's *La Frascatana* was in midcourse, with Morichelli in the title role singing an interpolated aria of her own choosing. She was interrupted for the announcement from the stage, at which the orchestra struck up "Rule Britannia" and played it over and over. At one point Banti was persuaded to come down from her box and sing "God save the King," lending a new twist to the battle of the sopranos. Not to be outdone, the Theatre Royal in Drury Lane put together an afterpiece, *The Glorious First of June*, with music by Stephen Storace partly drawn from patriotic songs. The show, first performed on 2 July, ended with fire-works and the audience singing "Rule Britannia."[38]

Haydn made an entry in his notebook recording the events.

> On the 11th of June the whole city was illuminated to celebrate the taking of seven French warships. Many windows were broken. On the 12th and 13th again the whole city was lit up. The common people [Pöbl] behaved very violently. In every street small arms as well as big guns were shot off, and this lasted the entire night.

One can imagine the composer stopping his ears or putting his head under a pillow. In a different place he jotted down information about the Earl of Chatham, first Lord of the admiralty, on learning of the victory. "He was so drunk for three days that he could not even sign his name, which prevented Lord Howe from leaving London and his fleet from sailing." Whether this was true or not, it jibes with Haydn's disapproving comments on the drunkenness he had observed at the Lord Mayor's annual banquet in 1791.

In the summer of 1794, fashionable Londoners rushed to see the wrecks of the captured French battleships brought to Portsmouth. Haydn too was swept along in the enthusiasm to see them and the great naval port. He was fascinated by all manner of naval lore and by seamen. His diary recorded many jottings that show this, none longer than the following.

> On 9 July I left at five in the morning for Portsmouth 72 miles from London and arrived in the evening about 8 o'clock. 14 miles before the port city there stands a small fortification near a camp of 800 men, one mile further a barracks with 3500 French prisoners of war. I observed all around the fortifications, which are in good condition, especially those opposite Gosport, which have lately been completed by the governors. I climbed aboard the French ship of 80 cannons named Le juste, one of those captured by the English, that is by Lord Howe. (The cannons of the fort are 36-pounders). The ship is pitifully shot up; the great mast, which is about 10 feet 5 inches in circumference, was cut off at the bottom and stretched out on the ground. A single cannonball that passed through the captain's cabin killed 14 sailors. I made the acquaintance of the famous painter Lauterburg.

This apparent non-sequitur deserves comment. The Alsatian-born and Paris-trained Philippe de Loutherbourg, a member of the Royal Academy in London, was famous for his paintings of shipwrecks, storms, and catastrophes, among

---

[38] Jane Girdham, *English Opera in Late Eighteenth-Century London: Stephen Storace at Drury Lane* (Oxford, 1997), pp. 215–18. On the other side of the Channel, the gallantry of one warship that went down fighting rather than surrender became the subject of legend in folk tellings, songs, and visual illustrations. See Herbert Schneider, "Le mythe du vaisseau *Le Vengeur* de 1794 à 1951: Textes—Images—Musique," *Acta Musicologica* 77 (2005): 71–121.

other preferred subjects. Eight years Haydn's junior, he was just the sort of person that one could expect to encounter clambering about the wrecked ships. Another leading representative of the increasingly violent and tormented tableaux so much in fashion was the Swiss-born Henry Fuseli, also a member of the Royal Academy, who was especially famous for his depictions of nightmares (Goethe loved them) and ghoulish apparitions such as the witches in *Macbeth*, engravings of which Haydn brought back from London—they figure in the catalogue of his large picture collection (1809).

Haydn continued his entry saying he would have gladly visited the great dockyard, its magnificent buildings, and seen the newest ship of the line, the 110-gun Prince of Wales, but as a foreigner he was not allowed to do so. "The King with his family visited the dockyard, spending three days in the governor's house." He did visit the Isle of Wight, where he was invited to stay at Fernhill, the pseudo-Gothic governor's mansion "with splendid views of the ocean." Scattered mentions of the Isle of Wight in the third London Notebook apparently refer to a visit made in July 1794. Returning to London via Southampton, Haydn visited Winchester, location of "a beautiful great gothic cathedral [eine schöne gotische grosse Cathedral kürche] with altarpiece by West." The American-born Benjamin West was president of the Royal Academy of Art in succession to Sir Joshua Reynolds, who died in 1792. Haydn was more interested in and knowledgeable about visual art than he is usually given credit for. He was an avid collector of prints.

Compared to his uneventful summer of 1791 in England, that of 1794 was frequently devoted to seeing the sights. On returning to London from Portsmouth he was taken to view the Bank of England and described that in his diary at some length. On 2 August he left very early for a visit to Bath accompanied by Andrew Ashe, Salomon's first flute, and the Venetian composer and singing teacher Giambattista Cimador. He stayed at the country estate near Bath of the soprano castrato, composer, and harpsichordist Venanzio Rauzzini, who had functioned in several capacities at London's Italian opera.[39] Remarkably detailed is his description of Bath's situation, architecture, city planning, and tourist industry, the high season of which, when visitors flocked to the town to take the waters, extended from October to mid-February. Everything invited the composer's interest, down to the stone from which the houses were made and where it came from. "Bath is one of the most beautiful cities in Europe." From here he went on to spend a few days with an acquaintance in Bristol, a very different kind of town, being a busy center of business and shipping, all described by Haydn in his notes. "The churches, of which there are very many, are all in the old Gothic taste, as also at Bath." He returned to London soon after this.

Haydn almost never allowed himself to write anything in letters, or even in

[39] Price, Milhous, and Hume, *The King's Theatre* (1995). See the exemplary index, under "Rauzzini."

his notebooks, about the religious question, but once, in terms that are only nostalgic, not bitter, there emerges an inkling of what it must have been like for him to live in an overwhelmingly Protestant society for the first time in his life:

> On 26 August 1794, I went to Waverley Abbey, forty miles from London, to visit Baron Sir Charles Rich, a rather good cello player. Here are the remains of a monastery that already stood for 600 years. I must admit that, whenever I looked at this beautiful wilderness [of ruins], my heart became oppressed that all this once stood under my religion.

He was likely aware of at least some of the virulent anti-Catholic bias directed against him in the London press when attempts to bring him to England failed in the 1780s. It would be surprising if he did not encounter the same, one way or another, while he was there. Was this one of the things about London that made him reluctant to stay, matters he could not put in writing to Mme von Genzinger but had to tell her in person? (Letter of 20 December 1791). Could it also help explain why he remained aloof from English Freemasonry? He did not do so with regard to French Freemasonry.

Haydn stayed in London for most of the fall. He was busy with preparations for the upcoming season, composing three more grand symphonies. He worked also on piano sonatas and piano trios. His two major publications of songs in English with piano accompaniment came out in 1794 and 1795, *VI Original Canzonettas*, volumes 1 and 2. The first volume contained songs set to poems by his friend Anne Hunter and such favorites as "My mother bid me bind my hair." The second volume of 1795 began with a rousing "Sailor's Song," the anonymous text of which tells of the "vessel high bounding o'er the raging main," becoming more specific in the second stanza: "the roaring cannon loudly speaks, 'tis Britain's glory we maintain." The accompaniments were much more elaborate than those in Haydn's two sets of Lieder for Vienna in the 1780s, and consequently cost their composer much more work. One text from the second set came from Shakespeare's *Twelfth Night*: "She never told her love." Haydn's presence at a performance of *Hamlet* on 13 October at Covent Garden was cited in a newspaper review but not in Haydn's notebooks. Little by little his spoken English improved, to the point where it became minimally usable in daily discourse.

When Haydn returned to London in early 1794 he was contracted to provide for Salomon six more symphonies, meaning in effect two seasons' worth, 1794 and 1795. There never seemed to be any doubt that Haydn would remain for at least two seasons. The death of Prince Anton soon after Haydn left Vienna loosened him from any ties binding him to return to Esterházy service. The situation changed when Haydn heard sometime in the summer of 1794 from an official writing in the name of the new Prince Nicholas II that the orchestra was to be reconstituted and that Haydn had been named its Kapellmeister. The news was welcome in that it gave the composer a sense of security about his future.

Piano Trios and Sonatas, 1794–95

During his first sojourn in London, Haydn wrote nothing for keyboard aside from a few small works in which it functioned as accompaniment and the small solo for himself at the end of Symphony No. 98. His second stay of a year and a half, on the other hand, was richly productive of works for piano, mostly of the kind accompanied by violin and cello, known to posterity as piano trios (although he called them sonatas). He grouped them mainly into four series of three works apiece. All four sets were dedicated to women, two Esterházy princesses among them: Princess Marie Therese, widow of Prince Anton, and the reigning Princess Marie Hermenegild, who was later to become one of his strongest supporters. These, along with the String Quartets, Opp. 71–74, dedicated to Count Apponyi in 1793, suggest that the composer was concerned with maintaining his sources of patronage at home—furthermore, that he never seriously considered remaining in London.

The London piano trio of the time was greatly in demand by amateur keyboard performers, whose efforts were sustained in performance by the accompanying instruments, the violin sometimes in duetlike fashion, the cello most often only doubling the bass played by the pianist's left hand. Music publishers in London fed the demand for such pieces with trios by a legion of composers, mostly Continental but also English. Artaria in Vienna was no less susceptible to the lure of this market. Recall that when Haydn in 1788 offered him either new string quartets or new piano trios, Artaria chose the latter. An important factor bearing on the London trios was the rapid improvement of pianos built in England, which increased in quantity as well, so that publishers and piano makers could make common cause and reap great profit.

Both of the Princesses Esterházy were keyboard players themselves, in fact they may have both been pupils of Haydn. Marie Hermenegild, for whom he had written the "Bossler" Sonatas published in 1784, was almost certainly his piano pupil. Haydn's regard for her predecessor Marie Therese makes it a reasonable conjecture in her case too. In his letter to her husband Prince Anton dated London, 8 January 1791, Haydn made a point of sending "submissive handkisses to the most beautiful Princess." She was indeed an attractive woman, according to an oil portrait of her.[40] Also, as a widow she was wooed by and subsequently married to Prince Karl Philipp Schwarzenberg. Widow Rebecca Schroeter was with-

[40] Reproduced as Plate 25 in Landon, *Haydn*, 3, between pp. 321 and 322.

out a doubt Haydn's pupil in London and emotionally attached to him. The third set of trios is dedicated to her and was published shortly after Haydn departed London for good on 15 August 1795. The fourth recipient was Therese Jansen Bartolozzi, a pupil of Clementi's and a very accomplished pianist to whom both Clementi and Dussek dedicated publications. Table 5.1 groups Haydn's late piano trios according to the four dedicatees.

TABLE 5.1 Haydn's Sets of Piano Trios, 1794–95

Hob. XV:	*Diletto Musicale:*	Key	Published in London on:	Dedicatee:
18	32	A	15 November 1794	Marie Therese née Hohenfeld, Dowager Princess Esterházy
19	33	G		
20	34	B♭		
21	35	C	23 May 1795	Marie Hermenegild née Liechtenstein, Princess Esterházy
22	36	E♭		
23	37	d		
24	38	D	9 October 1795	Mrs. Rebecca Schroeter
25	39	G		
26	40	f♯		
27	41	C	20 April 1797	Mrs. Therese Jansen Bartolozzi
28	42	E		
29	43	E♭		

The trios of all four sets consist of works in three movements, relying almost totally on the fast - slow - fast (or dance) pattern. They continue trends evident in Haydn's trios of the late 1780s by bringing the genre closer to his quartets in seriousness. Yet they retain a few traits typical of the lighter divertimento styles.

The initial trio of the first set, Hob. XV:18, relies on tonic minor for its middle movement, and the final *Allegro* in 3/4 time relates to a particular dance in style, the polacca, which is typically in a syncopated triple meter with prominent accents on the second beat or second half of the first (cf. the polacca in Bach's First Brandenburg Concerto). The finale also displays another exotic touch at some main cadences by using the Hungarian *Turökös* close, 5 8 5 and 1 5 1 with little appoggiaturas. This trio may have been begun or even finished in 1793 when Haydn was working on the String Quartets, Opp. 71–74. It begins with massive chords I - V - I, like an opening "curtain," and in this respect resembles the Quartet in B♭, Op. 71 No. 1. The trio's first movement, *Allegro moderato* in cut time, closes with these emphatic chords, in the same rhythm.

The second trio, Hob. XV:19, opens with a plaintive *Andante* in g minor and in 2/4 time, a double variation alternating major and minor, to end which Haydn switches to 6/8 time for the longer final variation in major.[41] A florid *Adagio ma non troppo* in E♭ and in 3/4 time serves as the slow movement, followed by a sprightly *Presto* in 6/8 time and in g minor that switches to G major for the reprise and ends there. Trio No. 3, Hob. XV:20, in B♭ impresses from its outset with a sweeping descent of the piano from its high F, doubled an octave below by the violin in legato quarter notes against the left hand's ascent from low B♭, and doubled by the cello an octave above in staccato eighth notes. This *Allegro* in common time is a brief but powerful and brilliant sonata form with both parts repeated. Haydn chooses G major for the second movement, *Andante cantabile* in 2/4 time. An oddity here is that he writes the theme of these variations for the pianist's left hand alone ("Solo con mano sinistra"). The *Finale Allegro* in 3/4 time returns the key to B♭ and begins V^7 - I. It resembles a minuet with a *minore* trio in form and for the return of the minuet brings back the first movement's brilliant runs up the scale of B♭ in the pianist's right hand.

Three Trios dedicated to Marie Hermenegild came ten years later than the three Sonatas dedicated to her in 1784, when she was a fifteen-year-old Princess Liechtenstein and the bride of Prince Nicholas II. The still-young couple acceded a decade later. The earlier set began with a Sonata in G that opens with a charming pastoral movement in 6/8 time (see Example 4.25). It may be no coincidence that Haydn commences the Trio in C, Hob. XV:21, with six measures of *Adagio pastorale* in 6/8 time, possibly even a reminder of the earlier work and thus something like the composer's calling card. All three instruments rise in unison on the tones of the tonic triad, then on the subdominant, ending this unusual slow introduction with a pause on the dominant. The ensuing *Vivace* in 6/8 time also relies on triads in the melody, some suggesting a yodeling model. The *Adagio*'s melody sounds idyllic compared to the boisterous *Vivace*, suggesting country music and bearing resemblance to the triadic tunes heard over drone harmonies in Christmas pastorales.[42] The following *Molto Andante* in G and in cut time presents a discourse on its theme, which reappears in tonic minor and relative minor, suggesting a loose variation form but cast as a sonata form without repeats. The *Finale Presto* in 2/4 time has a rondo-like theme but is another sonata form.

Trio No. 2, Hob. XV:22, in E♭ is conceived more broadly and has a more serious mien. The first movement, *Allegro moderato* in 2/4 time, stretches to 234 measures not counting the repeats of both parts. Haydn selects G major for the lovely second movement, *Poco Adagio* in cut time.[43] It requires the pianist to make rapid

---

[41] Rosen, *The Classical Style* (1971), pp. 82–88, illustrates the two major-mode variations of the first movement at length and shows how they relate to each other.

[42] One cadential figure (mm. 154–56) approaches the "Ranz des vaches" quoted by Rousseau in his *Dictionnaire de musique* (1768), which is described as being appropriate for bagpipes (cornemuse).

[43] For a facsimile of the piano part from the first edition, see Landon, *Haydn*, 3:429.

leaps of the right hand over the left. In juxtaposing E♭ and G, Haydn reiterates the main key contrast of Symphony No. 99 in E♭ of 1793. The constant triplets of the trio's *Adagio* and its wandering melodic line give it the rapturous qualities of a fantasia, anticipating the *Adagio* of the better-known Trio in f♯ minor (reappearing in Symphony No. 102). The *Finale Allegro* in 3/4 time makes for another movement of substantial length, which like the first is a sonata form with both parts repeated. The Trio in d minor, Hob. XV:23, begins with an *Andante molto* in 2/4 time that is a double variation, minor mode alternating with major. There follows an *Adagio ma non troppo* in B♭ and in 3/4 time, with another wayward mel-

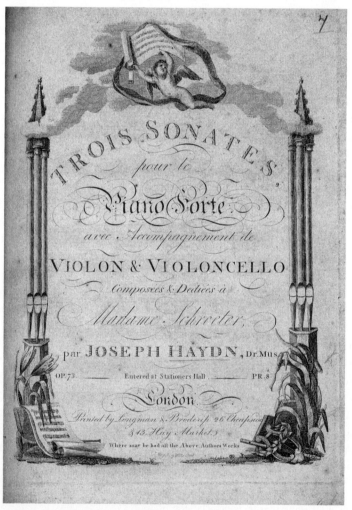

FIGURE 5.5. Title page of the Piano Trios dedicated to Rebecca Schroeter.

ody luxuriating in florid embellishments. The *Finale Vivace* in 3/4 time reclaims D major, where it begins and ends.

The set dedicated to Rebecca Schroeter shows that she, like the two princesses, must have been a good player, if not in a virtuoso class with Therese Jansen. Longman and Broderip printed the original edition with a fancy title page (Figure 5.5). A single *forte* chord in the tonic, standing outside the repeat signs, begins the *Allegro* in cut time of the first trio, Hob. XV:24. There is a similar single-chord introduction to the Quartet in E♭, Op. 71 No. 3. In both cases it allows Haydn to begin softly, the first theme in this case being intimate and tender. A slight resemblance links the main themes of quartet and trio. The trio remains in character unlike the quartet, which quickly adopts a buffo tone. If this reading of the trio's character is correct it would certainly suit the emotions shared by the composer and Mrs. Schroeter as indicated by her letters to him of 1791–92. One trait of this tender *Allegro* that also helps give it an individual character is its frequent dramatic pauses. The second movement is an *Andante* in tonic minor and in 6/8 time that is equally lyric in quality. The concluding movement in 3/4 time restores D major and is marked *Allegro ma dolce*.

Of all Haydn's trios, the middle one of the set for Mrs. Schroeter, the Trio in G, Hob. XV:25, became the most popular, largely because of its wildly successful Gypsy Rondo, called in the original edition "Finale. Rondo, in the Gypsies' Style." It appears in many subsequent editions as "Rondo all'Ongarese. Presto." Haydn's crowning success with a keyboard piece in Viennese "Turkish style," it is equivalent to the "Rondo alla turca" in Mozart's Sonata, K. 310. The running sixteenth notes of Haydn's melody provided its most "Turkish" element while the immediate move of the harmony to a modal degree (ii) also lends an exotic tinge. The trio begins with a lovely *Andante* in 2/4 time, a cross between rondo and variations, with episodes in both tonic and relative minor. For the slow movement, Haydn indulges in his favorite and still fresh tonal move down a third, where the key of E major (VI) is home to an *Adagio* in 3/4 time, a ternary form. The middle part is in A (IV), with a sustained melody given to the violin throughout. (Because most of the melody exists also in the accompanying triplets of the pianist's right hand, this beautiful lyric outpouring is almost complete without the accompanying instruments. This is true for the entire trio.) None of the movements is in sonata form and each contributes to make the work a success with performers and listeners. Hand crossing is not required but is present in the first and third trios of the set. Apparently, the procedure did not unsettle Rebecca Schroeter to the extent it did Mme von Genzinger.

The third trio of the Schroeter set is no less worthy of adulation than its predecessor. The Trio in f♯ minor, Hob. XV:26, shares its rarely used key with the composer's "Farewell" Symphony, No. 45, and String Quartet, Op. 50 No. 4. The Trio is no stormy odyssey in the manner of the Symphony but more of a reflective, gentle expression, like the Quartet. Symphony, String Quartet, and Trio all stress the relative major A as well as the tonic major F♯. The Trio's opening *Allegro* in common time moves to the key of A after only eight measures and remains there for the rest of the prima parte. The many parallel sixth chords impart a rather melancholy tone to this movement. In the seconda parte the tonal journey around the circle of fifths goes so far afield that Haydn switches the signature from three sharps to three flats and back. Both parts are marked for repetition. An even more extraordinary movement is the *Adagio cantabile* in F♯ major, a floridly ornamented cantilena that could as well be called Capriccio or Fantasia. This seamless piece, in which the main idea reappears midstream in A major and which takes only forty-four measures in 3/4 time, became the *Adagio* second movement of Symphony No. 102 in B♭—not just the melodic or harmonic idea or the main theme, but the entire movement, something so unusual it may be unique in the composer's vast oeuvre. Older views believed that the Trio's *Adagio cantabile* was derived from the Symphony's *Adagio*, but these have been corrected after close examination of the latter's autograph.[44] To close the trio, Haydn reverts to the initial f♯ minor in a rather dainty but extensive *Finale Tempo di Minuetto*. The right hand of the pianist crosses over the left in the second strain of this dance after a leisurely stay in A major. The movement has a Trio (not called such) in F♯ major. Haydn writes out the repetition of the main dance, which would ordinarily be indicated only by *da capo*, and adds a CODA (so named and spelled), led in by a deceptive cadence V –VI. He resolutely avoids the temptation to end in tonic major. Anyone hoping for a *tierce de Picardie* at the very end is bound to be disappointed.

The finesse with which Haydn treats every detail of this great trio may be interpreted as pains taken for a special person in his life. It suggests that the loving notes from the lady in 1791–92, although nothing of the kind survives from 1794–95, in between, or thereafter, indicated the true state of their relationship during both of Haydn's London sojourns. If it is true that music can say much more than words, Haydn's choice of her *Adagio cantabile* for the centerpiece of one of his greatest symphonies says it all. That they remained in touch after their final separation is demonstrated by two pieces of evidence that do survive. In August 1796 Schröter served as witness to a contract between Haydn in Vienna and Frederick Hyde of London, representing Longman and Broderip,[45] and in 1799, she was a subscriber to the first edition of *The Creation*.

The fourth set of trios introduces another female pianist, a virtuoso of the

---

[44] Two scholars arrived independently at this same conclusion—A. Peter Brown, *Joseph Haydn's Keyboard Music: Sources and Style* (Bloomington, IN, 1986), p. 54, and Irmgard Becker-Glauch, edition of the Trios in *JHW* XVII/3 (1986), pref.

[45] Jens Peter Larsen, "A Haydn Contract," *Musical Times* 117 (1976): 737–38.

keyboard. She could have become a professional performer like her teacher Clementi or her friend Dussek, but that was considered socially demeaning and was eschewed by most women (other than singers). Therese Jansen was born around 1770, the daughter of a celebrated dancing master at Aachen who brought her and her younger brother Louis to London. They both became sought-after teachers of dance and music, from which they made a good livelihood. Haydn included her name on his 1791 list of prominent London keyboard players and composed for her his great Piano Sonata in Eb, Hob. XVII:52, dated 1794.

Ambitious young people in the arts or in business made marriages with other successful people of similar station. Dussek wed Sophia Corri, the Miss Corri active as a pianist in Salomon's concerts and daughter of the publisher Domenico Corri, whose firm later became Corri and Dussek. Therese Jansen married the son of the very distinguished artist Francesco Bartolozzi, engraver to George III, a Florentine who had apprenticed at Venice with one of the greatest eighteenth-century engravers in Italy, Joseph Wagner. Through Burney, Haydn became friends with Bartolozzi, who engraved one of his portraits and also designed the frontispiece of William Napier's *A Selection of Original Scots Songs in Three Parts. The Harmony by Haydn* (London, 1792). Bartolozzi's son Gaetano, born in Italy in 1757, came to London with his father in 1764 and also became an engraver and publisher, eventually taking his father's place. On 16 May 1795 in the fashionable church of St. James on Piccadilly, Miss Jansen wed Gaetano Bartolozzi, an event at which the two male witnesses were Bartolozzi senior and Haydn. Possibly the set of trios Haydn dedicated to her were intended to celebrate her wedding. She owned Haydn's autograph, which she was in no hurry to see published. Given the difficulty of the piano parts, so much beyond what was expected in the genre, publishers were perhaps not very eager to print them. In any case they waited until 1797 for Longman and Broderip to bring them out as *Three Sonatas for the Piano-Forte with an accompaniment for violin and violoncello. Composed and Dedicated to Mrs. Bartolozzi by Joseph Haydn Mus. D.* The same year the Bartolozzis had a daughter, Lucia, destined to become a famous contralto singer, actress, and theater manager under her married name of Madame Vestris.[46]

Nothing in Haydn's other trios quite prepares the pianist for the shock experienced when trying to play the trios (and sonatas) written for Therese Jansen Bartolozzi. In the first of the trios, Hob. XV:27, the right hand must play rapid octaves in sixteenth notes, then faster in sextuplet sixteenth notes, and make swift crossings over the left hand, while the left hand is required to stretch a tenth and also play quick chords in a 1 3 8 position. Difficulties like these can be found in Clementi's works for piano, which we know Haydn admired, and here he had a Clementi-trained pianist who could execute them. The first movement

---

[46]Lucia married a member of the Vestris clan, a veritable dynasty in the world of dance.

of this Trio in C is an *Allegro* in common time with the treble climbing rapidly up the tonic triad to high E and with arpeggios along the way to provide more density to the texture. The weightier-than-usual effect at which Haydn aimed also resulted in giving the cello more to do than was customary in London trios. To begin, the cello plays a rising triad of its own in a figure not given to the pianist's left hand, which is otherwise busy repeating chords. At various points in the *Allegro*, the cello supplies the only bass to chords. Ending the movement it makes ample use of its low C. The result of giving the cello more independence and the fuller textures bring the ensemble closer to the Viennese piano trio evolved by Mozart and continued in early Beethoven. In this first-movement sonata form, Haydn does not call for repetition of the seconda parte. The last two, very full, chords of the *Allegro* have E and C at the top. The *Andante* in 6/8 time that follows is in A major, one of Haydn's favorite tonal moves by the mid-1790s. Its melody falls from E after an ornamented upbeat consisting of a rapid melodic turn, 4 3 2 3 4 | 5. The *Andante* is in a large **A B A** form with a middle section in tonic minor. The *Finale Presto* in 2/4 time has a main theme that ascends rapidly up to high E, recalling the main theme of the *Allegro*. A rondo could easily emerge from the rollicking refrain, with its impish upbeats propelling it forward (two sixteenth notes going to an eighth note as in the finale of Symphony No. 102). Two large parts, with modulation to V and back, each repeated, confirm sonata form, not rondo, as predominant. Nevertheless there is a strong residue of rondo discourse in the impish refrain itself and in the way it climbs a final time up to high E to end the seconda parte.

Trio No. 2 in E, Hob. XV:28, is a more delicate work in comparison and less difficult for the pianist, though no less interesting and complex as a composition. An *Allegro moderato* in common time sounds a lightly scored theme in the piano, accompanied by pizzicato strings. On repetition this main theme is harmonically enriched and further decorated. It easily provides material for a second theme in V, following which there is also a closing theme. The seconda parte acquires many double sharps as it goes along and eventually makes an enharmonic switch, from G♯ to A♭, where the first theme appears in strength as the movement's climax. Haydn again decides against repeating the seconda parte. An *Allegretto* in 3/4 time and in the key of e minor produces an entirely different effect. Its main idea is a nonstop bass in eighth notes, sounding like a *seicento* ground bass, against which there appears as countersubject a declamatory theme with chaconne-like accents on the second beat and many dotted rhythms, giving the whole a rather stilted character. There is something decidedly retrospective about this movement, over which the shade of Emanuel Bach seems to hover.[47] The finale, an

---

[47] For a more detailed description of the movement and the whole Trio, see Rosen, *The Classical Style* (1971), pp. 359–60.

Allegro in 3/4 time, returns the trio to E major and decisively to the *settecento* in style, and even to a surprisingly galant aspect of the style. Sweet-sounding parallel thirds abound, as do typically galant chromatic inflections. Emanuel Bach favored vivid contrasts between movements and "split personality" discourses. Was Haydn possibly paying his respects here to the keyboard master who died at Hamburg in 1788?

The Trio in E♭, Hob. XV:29, begins with a single tonic chord *forte*, a silencer that allows Haydn to begin with a soft main theme, *Poco Allegretto* in 2/4 time. The theme is in a rounded binary form with repeats and is subjected to variations, bound to appear at least once in any set. In the course of the theme Haydn thickens the texture, even asking for triple-stops from the cello. There is an abundance of dotted rhythm in the theme and in the rest of the movement, giving it a rather galumphing effect. For the middle movement Haydn chooses the key of B major, down a major third, and 6/8 time. He marks it *Andantino et innocentamente* (recalling the *Allegretto innocente* in 6/8 time of the "Bossler" Sonata in G). It is another movement with enharmonic switches in the middle and many delicate chromatic shadings in melody and harmony, one that ends with a V^7 of E♭ and elides with the onset of the finale (*attaca subito*). "Finale. Allemande (in the German Style). *Presto assai*" is the complete title in the original edition, often abbreviated in subsequent editions. "In the German Style" reminds us of "In the Gypsies' style" for the finale of the Trio in G. A fine example of a Ländler in 3/4 time, it has a simple rhythmic accompaniment that supports a wandering, quasi-improvisational melodic line in eighth notes above. Its country-dance flavor can be found in the Trio of Mozart's Symphony No. 39 in E♭ and in many trios of Haydn's quartets and symphonies. Some drone effects and half-step appoggiaturas before the beat suggest the Dudelsack of rural bands and predict the ultimate apotheosis of this folk-like strain of dance and music in the drinking chorus that ends "Fall" in *The Seasons*.

With the three Bartolozzi Trios, Haydn's contributions to the genre were nearly at an end. The most substantial addition to them is the Trio in E♭, Hob. XV:30, which the composer sent to Breitkopf, who acknowledged its receipt by letter in 1796 and printed it in 1797. Its second movement is in C major and ends on its dominant, from which the music passes directly (*attaca subito*) to the finale in E♭. A Trio in the rare key of e♭ minor, Hob. XV:31, dated 1795 in the autograph consists of an *Andante cantabile* in theme and variations form, followed by an *Allegro* in E♭. Haydn dedicated it in Artaria's print to Magdalena von Kurzbeck, a former pupil and close friend. Another two-movement work is the Trio in G, Hob. XV:32, an *Andante* theme and variations and *Allegro* finale, published at London in 1794.

Haydn wrote at least two solo sonatas for Therese Jansen. The Sonata in E♭, Hob. XVI:52, is inscribed on the autograph "Sonata composta per la Celebra

Signora Teresa de Janson . . . di me giuseppe Haydn mpria Lond. [1]794." The
work's technical demands are on a par with those in the Trio in C of the set dedicated to her, prompting one scholar to argue, persuasively, that he composed the
trios too in 1794.[48] As with the trios presented to her, she was in no hurry to have
this great sonata printed, which was done by Longman and Clementi in 1799
from the autograph, perhaps after she had seen the edition printed by Artaria
at Vienna in 1798 with a dedication to Magdalena von Kurzbeck. The other solo
sonata for her does not survive in autograph. The Sonata in C, Hob. XVI:50, was
first printed at London ca. 1800 under the title *A Grand Sonata for the Piano Forte
composed expressly for and dedicated to Mrs. Bartolozzi by Haydn.*[49]

The Sonata in E♭ of 1794 creates an effect strikingly different from that of
the Genzinger Sonata of 1790. Even someone with no knowledge of music could
observe that, unlike the earlier sonata, the later one darkens the pages with many
more notes per measure. Aside from being in the same key and in three movements with an *Adagio* in the middle, the two works have little in common. In the
technique required of both left and right hands there is no comparison. For the
performer the difficulty is even greater in bringing all the various motions of the
1794 opening *Allegro* under control, and it is conceptual as well as technical.

The *Allegro* begins with thick chords and with dotted rhythm on the second
beat, typical of the march (Example 5.14 mm. 1–2). The commanding nature of this

EXAMPLE 5.14. *Haydn, Piano Sonata in E♭, Hob. XVI: 52: I*

harmonic move to IV and back sustains the entire movement. To preserve the
swagger of a march, the chords should be articulated crisply with no legato. If
Haydn had wanted them slurred together he would have so indicated. A legato

[48] Brown, *Haydn's Keyboard Music*, pp. 46–47, 128.
[49] Some (all?) copies were signed on the title page "T. Bartolozzi." One such title page is reproduced (from
the author's copy) in Brown, *Haydn's Keyboard Music*, plate VII, p. 52.

echo of m. 2 in m. 3, *piano*, comes with the left-hand accompaniment made even more detaché by rests. The effect is proud and solid, like a weight-bearing pillar that supports the whole edifice. After eight measures the beginning gesture is repeated an octave higher; it returns again after another eight measures to confirm the arrival of the second key, B♭, and yet again toward the end of the prima parte, with 1 3 5 in the treble instead of 1 3 4. In the last case, reversion to the main idea calls the movement back to order after various diversionary second-theme materials. The most memorable of these secondary ideas is a soft passage with horn fifths in the left hand decorated by dotted rhythm in the right hand, the whole being of a gossamer lightness that contrasts admirably with the weighty pillars of the main idea. The effect is so pianistic as to be hardly transferable to any other instrument or ensemble. On the way to a big cadence that ends the prima parte, there is nevertheless a moment that does resemble some of Haydn's symphonic writing, namely the sudden appearance of soft, barren octaves (Example 5.14, mm. 38–39). A soft cryptic passage in long notes like this appears at the end of Symphony No. 75 in D of ca. 1781.

After the repeat the seconda parte announces itself with the same soft passage in half notes, with descent in the bass but chromatic rise in the treble (Example 5.14, mm. 44–45). Here the passage leads not to the final rush up the tones of a pre-cadential I$^6_4$ chord but to a whole measure on the chord of G major, protracted by fermata signs. This chord is resolved by the arrival of the horn fifths idea in C major. After a thorough working out of the various ideas, Haydn returns to the full measure of G major triad with fermatas, in lower position on the keyboard but with G still as the top tone. Knowing Haydn's ways of slipping from V/vi directly to I for the reprise one could anticipate that he might change that G into the third of tonic E♭ major and thus ease into the reprise. This kind of mild surprise hardly qualifies as startling anymore since Haydn has done it so often. In this case he does give us a real surprise, a tonal jolt that is most unsettling. The elfin dance of the horn fifths arrives, as dainty as ever but in the impossibly distant realm of E major. From there Haydn moves rather quickly, by means of a descending sequence, back to the flat side for the reprise. The usual economies are effected by deleting some repetitions of the main idea; the horn fifths now return in tonic E♭ when expected. Before the tonic 6/4 chord leading to the final cadence returns, there is another of the cryptic soft passages in octaves, longer than before and even more cryptic (Example 5.14, mm. 109–11). This one wrenches our tonal bearings once more. Translated into enharmonic equivalents the tones are C B♮ A♮ G♯ A♮, leading to—what? Heard as a melodic turn around A♮, the tones might suggest as a natural goal a return to B♮, the fifth of the E major that so surprised us in the middle. Having baffled us once, Haydn is amused to do so again in a mysterious climax to the *Allegro*. The tone reached is not B♮ but a half tone away—B♭, the bass of the precadential I$^6_4$ chord, resolution of which ends the movement. No repeat of the seconda parte is called for, placing this sonata in a league with the late symphonies.

The *Adagio* is in 3/4 time. Haydn has prepared us for the shock of its key, E major, by presenting one of the main ideas of the *Allegro* in E, then hinting at this key's return at the end with a cryptic passage that defies easy explanation. The arrival of E is still a shock, and players should perform it as such by not delaying its appearance. There is no more striking slow movement in all Haydn than this magical *Adagio*, with its theme of placid yet fervent striving upward, tinged by deep longing. From a simple motif in dotted rhythm the striving idea suddenly intensifies its arc in a *crescendo* accompanied by dense chords, until reaching a climax nearly two octaves above where it started, then falling back slightly for a half cadence, all this in the space of four measures. Beginning again, another four measures follow the same trajectory and reach momentary repose on the dominant. So goes the first strain of a rounded binary form, the plainest and oldest of all those available. The second strain, **b**, continues with the same intensity and richness, making its way through distant C major in another four measures that prepare the return of the beginning, or **a'**. Decorated and extended to six measures, it is changed in order to bring the theme home to a cadence on tonic E. The cadential measure and the climactic one, two measures before, clarify the basic rhythm, which is that of a slowly moving chaconne, with a strong accent on the second beat that is at once agogic, harmonic, and melodic. This main section of the *Adagio*, **A**, is closely related to the equally expressive and explosive *Largo assai* in E of the "Rider" Quartet, Op. 74 No. 3 (see Example 5.11).

The **B** section, like that of the *Largo* in the Quartet, is in the parallel minor, e. It is short but intense, and not free from the slow chaconne rhythm, or from melodic references to the main motif of **A**. The clearest of these is in the left hand as the section passes through G major on the way back to e minor. It ends with a declamatory passage in octaves that dissolves into an arpeggio sweeping up the chord of V^7, which turns into an anguished diminished-seventh chord, vii^7, left unresolved. Resolution comes like a soothing balm with the return of E major and the whole **A** section, intact and further decorated. There is a short coda on an E pedal with low E sounded by the right hand crossing over the left.

Haydn plays "bait and switch" with us once more at the beginning of the *Finale Presto* in 2/4 time. A soft, repeated G♮ sounds all alone at first, making us wonder whether it is a reminder of the stormy middle part of the *Adagio*, perhaps as an added codetta. The performer must make it sound as if e minor could possibly return in order to make Haydn's point clearer. His intention emerges only when he gives G♮ as bass not of E but of E♭. Another half-tone switch has beguiled us. The tonal play continues as he repeats the beginning up one whole tone in f minor (ii), starting with a repeated lone A♭ (so recently celebrated as its enharmonic equivalent G♯). After this, and only after this, is tonic E♭ firmly established. It is celebrated fully then, in an ample sonata form of 307 measures, with prima but not seconda parte repeated. Normality seems to triumph at last. Yet so lengthy and serious a finale as this was by no means normal to Haydn's solo sonatas or piano trios. The late Sonata in E♭ for Therese Jansen has no equals among the composer's keyboard sonatas, not even the Genzinger Sonata.

The Sonata in C, Hob. XVI:50, is as demanding technically, but not musically, as the Sonata in E♭. Its opening *Allegro* in common time, with a head motif of 8 5 1, is beautifully wrought and tightly constructed. Comparatively unadventurous in harmonic terms, Haydn begins the seconda parte, for instance, by changing G to g and placing the head motif in the left hand as a bass under running counterpoint. He enlivens the main theme by ending it with one of his signature traits, spicy descending seventh leaps. Throughout he is at his most witty. Both the prima and seconda parti are marked for repetition. Some details point to the rapid strides being made by English piano makers. One such is the request "Pianissimo open Pedal" in the *Allegro*, a special effect used to highlight the arrival at A♭ as a central goal in the middle of the development and again to emphasize tonic C major with some similar music in the middle of the reprise. The marking is thought to be a request for a shift by pedal to *una corda* or *due corde*.

The *Adagio* in F major and in 3/4 time offers a fine specimen of lyric invention combined with idiomatic embellishment, rather conventional compared to the *Adagio* just discussed, yet effective. It existed separately from the rest of the work in a version only slightly different from that printed by Artaria in June 1794, hence it was composed before Haydn left for England in January.[50] The Sonata is a compilation, then, or so it appears, and indeed there is no sign of an overall vision governing the three movements as that found in its companion. An *Allegro molto* in 3/4 time serves as a finale and uses rounded binary form with repeats, expanded here and there by tonal derailments that sound quite like some of those favored by Beethoven. As a short rollicking dance movement, it is good fun and serves its purpose. Notable is the extension of the top range of the piano up to high G and high A, beyond the high F still standard on most grand pianos of the 1790s, another English advancement.

The Sonata in D, Hob. XVI:51, is a curious piece in two movements. A sprawling *Andante* in cut time, in loose sonata form without repeats, gives way to a very short *Finale Presto* in 3/4 time in the same key and in a rounded binary form with repeats. It is a study in the working out of one motivic-rhythmic feature, so obsessive it suggests the completion of an assignment in composition. The *Andante* begins with I - V - I used as a gateway, less original than the way this device was utilized in the Sonata in C. It continues with a rather attractive idea,

---

[50] It is also close to the *Adagio* beginning of the Trio in A of 1785, Hob. XV:22, as pointed out by Sutcliffe, "The Haydn Piano Trio" (1988), pp. 281–82.

a melody in octaves for the right hand against the left hand's triplet accompaniment (Example 5.15). This passage never returns. Odd-sounding for Haydn is the

EXAMPLE 5.15. *Haydn, Piano Sonata in D, Hob. XVI: 51: I*

chord spacing in m. 13, specifically the tripling of the third degree in both chords, the second chord omitting the fifth of the triad (as Schubert so loved to do). Later there are other chord spacings and doublings that verge on the careless. Moreover, the multiple repetition of the same cadence pattern involving a diminished seventh wears out its welcome (albeit similar to one beautifully used by Haydn in the slow introduction and following *Allegro* of Symphony No. 97 in C). Could this be some student copying features admired in Haydn? The provenance of the work is not reassuring as to its authenticity. No autograph has been found. It was printed in Leipzig by Breitkopf and Härtel in 1803 as *Sonate pour le Pianoforte Composée par Joseph Haydn*. Griesinger sent it to them from Vienna saying that it was "An Andante and Finale that Haydn composed in England for a Lady who kept the original manuscript." Haydn may have told something like this to the faithful Griesinger. He was adept at inventing reasons why his original manuscripts were not sent. One of his students, who could have written a passage as sonorous as the one illustrated, was, of course, Beethoven. Indeed, Beethoven used this same texture of quarter notes in octaves in the right hand for the melody against triplets in the left hand for the rondo refrain of the finale to his Piano Sonata in E, Op. 14 No. 1, dating from 1798–99. There is, on the other hand, one confirmation that the Sonata in D is by Haydn. A passage nearly identical to the example quoted in its melody and wedge shape (treble rising, bass descending) occurs in Haydn's cantata for soprano and piano "Lines from the Battle of the Nile" (1800).[51]

---

[51] See Landon, *Haydn*, 4:603, the piano solo part marked *dolce*.

The Opera Concerts, 1795

The subscription concerts that began in early 1795 differed from those of previous years in locale and leadership. William Taylor, manager and principal owner of the King's Theatre in the Haymarket, took over the series that had been run by Salomon and moved it from Hanover Square, where he would have had to pay rent, to his own building—though not into the large amphitheater for opera but into a spacious concert hall in the same structure rebuilt after the fire. As impresario of both opera and concert series, Taylor could use the services of all the Italian singers contracted for the opera without new agreements. This does not mean that they went unpaid for extra services in the concert hall, merely that he was saved the expense of hiring additional singers and bringing them to London. Like Gallini before him, Salomon was squeezed out of his impresarial role by Taylor. Salomon still continued to be represented in the subscription series as a solo performer. Willingly or not he gave up his former functions as leader of the band to Cramer and that of music director (responsible for choosing the program) to Viotti. Salomon put the best face possible on the situation in a gracious notice to the public that was printed in various newspapers, dated "Hanover Square, January 12, 1795."

> Mr. Salomon respectfully presents his acknowledgements to the Nobility and Gentry who have hitherto done him the honour to support his Concert: he feels the most lively sentiments of gratitude for the protection which they gave him in the arduous undertaking; and it is with real regret that he is under the necessity, from circumstances which he is not in his power to control, to decline the further continuation of the establishment.
>
> In the present situation of affairs on the Continent, Mr. Salomon finds it impossible to procure from abroad any Vocal Performers of the first talents, but by the influence of terms which an undertaking like his could by no means authorize him to offer; and it would be a presumption, of which he is incapable, to solicit the patronage of the Nobility and Gentry to an inferior entertainment.[52]

Salomon went on in this vein, displaying tact and verbosity. He expressed his pride in what his series had achieved in the past and said that he intended to bend his efforts toward furthering "The plan of a National School of Music becoming the taste and grandeur of this kingdom, in a quarter which necessarily possesses the means for that purpose." Apparently he intended by this the Hanover Square Rooms, which remained under his management and Gallini's ownership.

---

[52] The announcement is quoted in full in Landon, *Haydn*, 3:280.

The proposed plan could refer to Burney's earlier idea to establish a public music school along the lines of the Venetian and Neapolitan conservatories of music.[53] Burney and Salomon were on good terms and both were probably aware that, although such hopes made but small progress in London, they were fast laying the foundations for the first great national conservatory of music, that in Paris.

Salomon closed his remarks with a generous salute to his successors. "As a professional man, he wishes well to the new establishment of a grand and regular Concert at the Opera," which "many eminent masters" and he himself had been invited to join. He names two masters in particular who had made his successes possible, Haydn and Viotti, renders thanks to them and all the other Professors who assisted him, and rejoices that they have entered into agreement with the new enterprise. Haydn may have done so with some misgivings about the Royal Opera and Taylor, a natural consequence of the debacle he endured in 1791 with his opera *Orfeo*. In his notebook he refers to Taylor as "that miserable cur [Hundsfud]." Salomon in private surely shared his opinion.

The King's Theatre Room was large for concert halls of those times. Hanover Square Rooms had a hall 32 × 79 feet, while the King's Theatre Room was 48 × 97 feet.[54] Nearly a quarter larger, the newer hall was intended to seat eight hundred spectators, three hundred more than the older one. Both fitted in larger numbers on some occasions. In 1795, the basic orchestra was expanded to sixty in number, not counting soloists or extra performers as needed (e.g., in Haydn's "Military" Symphony). It remains unclear at what point Haydn became aware that the 1795 concerts would take place in the larger hall. He does seem to have taken account of the fact in his last three symphonies, which are even more sonorous and broadly laid out than the three of 1793–94. Despite the overall increase of operatic content in the 1795 concerts it was Haydn's symphonies that dominated more than ever. What disappeared from the programs for this larger hall was instrumental chamber music, even Haydn's string quartets.

The concert series was reduced from twelve to nine Monday evenings and cost four guineas per subscription. In general these concerts were less publicized than Salomon's had been, and less critical comment in the press was devoted to them. This could be a sign that interest in subscription series was waning. After Haydn's departure it declined markedly in spite of (because of?) its greater dependence on stars from the operatic stage. The Opera Concerts, combining forces from Cramer's defunct Professional Concert and Salomon's Concert, lasted only a few years and did not arrest the general decline in London's musical life.[55] Salomon made one more attempt to revive his own series in 1796 and then gave up.

[53] *Music in European Capitals*, pp. 184–85.
[54] McVeigh, *Concert Life in London* (1993), p. 57.
[55] McVeigh, *Concert Life in London*, p. 18.

The first concert, which took place on 2 February, offered several oper-
atic excerpts sung by leading figures in the resident Italian company: Banti and
Morichelli, sopranos; Luigi Brida, tenor; Carlo Rovedino and Giovanni Morelli,
basses. They sang vocal pieces by Bianchi, Cimarosa, Gazzaniga, and Piccinni.
Michael Kelly, who was attached to the King's Theatre in various capacities, joined
with the others for two vocal ensembles, one by the resident composer Martín y
Soler. Otherwise Mr. Holmes played a bassoon concerto by François Devienne,
Dussek a piano concerto of his own, and Viotti a new violin concerto he composed. An old Haydn symphony began the first part. The pièce de résistance of
the evening began the second part, Haydn's "New Grand Overture, composed
for the Occasion," being the first performance of Symphony No. 102 in B♭.

Subsequent concerts in general followed the outline of the first, and at all
of them Haydn presided on the piano. In his notebook about this time he jotted down the names of some of the singers, composers, and instrumental players involved: "Banti, Rovedino, Morichelli, Morelli, Brida, [Prospero] Braghetti;
Bianchi, Martini [Martín], Ferlendis,[56] Dragonetti, Harrington [oboe]; Taylor,
impresario; Neri, poor castrato." Possibly he was considering which singers and
players to use in one of his own compositions or not use. La Banti, who leads his
list, was one for whom he did choose to compose.

The second concert on 16 February began with a symphony by Vincenzo
Federici, whom Taylor employed as a musical assistant and accompanist at the
opera. Da Ponte had scathing words for Federici in his memoirs, which make him
out to have been a hack composer who patched together the works of others and
claimed them as his own, and who was one of Morichelli's lovers. Otherwise, the
first part included a Duetto Concertante performed by Viotti and Salomon, and
ended with a "New Symphony for the occasion" by Clementi. Haydn occupied his
usual spot at the beginning of the second part, in this case, a symphony described
as one "introduced by Salomon's Concert last year . . . The second movement was
encored" (The *Sun*). This may point to No. 101 with its very popular tick-tock second movement. The piece that drew the most attention in the press was Banti's
newly composed cantata at the end of the program, with Bianchi the composer,
"who sat at the harpsichord." It would have been his privilege as composer to
replace Haydn at the keyboard if he so chose, and he might also have required a
harpsichord rather than the standard fortepiano. The critic of the *Morning Chronicle* had the most specific things to say of the new pieces, indicating that it was
probably the same writer as in previous seasons. About Clementi's new symphony this critic wrote, "The slow movement was a canon, in four; and which in
this species of composition is very rare, [it] was no less sweet than scientific; and

---

[56] Giuseppe Ferlendis was the composer of oboe concertos in which he was the soloist. He may have
passed off the concerto Mozart wrote for him (K. 271k) as his own.

the last movement, continuing the same subject in rapid time, exhibited great learning, and perhaps too much contrivance."[57] When Burney uses "learned contrivance" he often meant fugue and it was not intended by him as a compliment. The other two critics whose reviews survive ignored Clementi's symphony.

At the third concert, on 23 February, the opening symphony was by Reichardt. The first part included, besides several vocal numbers, a cello concerto performed by Mr. Lindley, and to close it, Gluck's overture to *Iphigénie en Aulide* of 1774, which long enjoyed favor in England.[58] The second half opened with the ever-favorite "Great Militaire Overture M.S. Haydn." All the London symphonies remained in manuscript at this point and were owned by Salomon, another reason that made his collaboration essential. Madame Banti ended the program by repeating her new Cantata from the previous concert.

The fourth concert, on 2 March, again opened with Reichardt, continued with a vocal piece ("Song") sung by Signor Morelli, identified as being by "Mozzart." In 1791 Morelli had sung "Non più andrai" from *Figaro* at a concert, and this may have been a repeat of it. Mr. Ashe played a flute concerto of which he claimed to be the composer. The critic in the *Sun* wrote, "His second movement was [Stephen] Storace's pretty Air of *Lullaby*, to which the variations by Ashe are beautiful." Morichelli sang a piece by Haydn, and the first half ended with the overture to *Démophoon* by Johann Christoph Vogel.[59] The event of the evening was the premiere of Haydn's Symphony No. 103 ("Drumroll") in E♭. Its slow introduction, Haydn's longest and most mysterious, at once caused comment. In the *Morning Chronicle* of 3 March the music critic wrote, "The Introduction excited the deepest attention, the Allegro charmed, the Andante was encored, the Minuets, especially the Trio, were playful and sweet, and the last movement was equal, if not superior to the preceding." From its origins as a short passage written to silence the audience and prepare the key of the important business to follow, the introduction had come a great distance in Haydn's hands. The second part of the concert contained another instrumental work that drew comments from the same critic, Viotti's *Concertante* for two violins, performed by the composer and his young pupil Mr. Libon, described as having "an ear uncommonly chaste and delicate."

No program announcement has survived for the fifth concert, on 16 March. The review in the *Morning Chronicle* compensates for the loss. "Among other

---

[57] Symphonies by Clementi are lost, for the most part. Two that survive as Op. 18 of 1787 are described and exemplified by Leon Plantinga, *Clementi: His Life and Music* (London, 1977), pp. 120–26. Plantinga, p. 149, mentions the 1795 one but does not use this criticism.

[58] The Overture's beginning appears incised beneath the orchestra in a satirical London print depicting one of Noverre's ballets, reproduced in *Music in European Capitals*, p. 489, fig. 5.6.

[59] Vogel was born at Nuremberg in 1756. His *Démophoon* played by the Opéra at Paris in 1789 was revived in 1793; its Overture figured in the repertory of the Concert de la Loge Olympique. Vogel died at Paris in 1788.

delightful pieces, for the selection of which the subscribers are indebted to the director, Viotti, we again were charmed, or rather shaken, by the grand opening symphony to Demaphoon." And surely it was Viotti, too, arrived in London from Paris in mid-1792, who served as a conduit for this and other recent pieces of French provenance. "Morelli had a comic song in his usual bold and characteristic stile, and was encored." It could have been another piece by Mozart or the same one sung before. Banti and Morichelli also sang. Salomon performed a violin concerto which won great praise, as did Clementi's "New Overture" (end of the first part?). The Haydn symphony chosen was the first of the new ones for this season, i.e., No. 102. "The best judges seem to doubt whether Haydn himself ever surpassed it. The last movement was encored; and the Adagio still more deservedly ought to have been."

At this point in mid-season, just before the end of Lent and the Easter holidays, there were a number of benefit concerts. Mme Mara gave hers on 24 March in the Hanover Square Rooms, and it attracted Haydn's attention. In his notebook he wrote, "Mr. Clementi sat at the pianoforte and gave his new Grand Symphony, without applause." He was reporting this secondhand, it appears. "She had no more than sixty persons and one said she never sang better." In quite a gossipy vein, unusual for Haydn, he reported that at the supper she gave after the concert in an adjoining room, her husband appeared and asked for a glass of wine; he was raging, to the extent that her lawyer ejected him. "Mme Mara recently went to Bath with her *cicisbeo* Mr. Florio, and I rather think that her willfulness [Eigensinn] makes her despicable to the whole nation." Mr. Florio, her lover, was a tenor and composer whom she took with her to Germany in 1803 and sang pieces by him there. In her declining years in London she did not disdain to sing in ballad operas.

A few days later Haydn attended an opera at the King's Theatre and wrote an unusually detailed account of it in his notebook.

The 28th of March 1795 I saw an opera Aci and Galatea by Bianchi. The music is very rich in wind instruments, and it seems to me that if they were fewer the main melody could be better heard. The opera is too long, especially since Banti alone has to sustain it. Brida, a good youngster with a beautiful voice but very little musicality, Rovedino, and the good Braghetti, plus the miserable seconda donna, earned and deserved not the slightest applause. The orchestra this year is richer in numbers but just as mechanical and badly placed as it was before, and indiscreet in accompanying. In short, this was the opera's third representation and everybody was dissatisfied. It happened that when they started the second ballet the whole audience was so displeased that they began shouting: "Off—off—off!" They wished to see the new ballet that was produced for the benefit of Mme Hilligsberg two days earlier. Everyone was embarrassed. There was an interval that lasted half and hour until finally a dancer came forward and announced submissively: "Ladys and gentelman!" Mr. Taylor cannot be found but the whole ballet company promises to perform the desired ballet next week, for which the impresario must pay Mme Hilligsberg £300. With that the people were satisfied and cried "go on—go on." The old ballet was then performed.

Haydn found nothing to say about Bianchi's music except that it was overscored as to the winds. He had performed three of Bianchi's operas at Esterháza, *La villanella rapita* (1784–87), *Alessandro nell'Indie* (1787–88), and *Il disertore* (1787–89). Bianchi was one of the most adventurous Italian composers of the time, with the double advantage of having been trained by Jommelli and of spending three years in Paris, where he worked at the Théâtre Italien, home of the original *Déserteur* by Sedaine and Monsigny.

A few remarks about Haydn's night at the opera are in order. Braghetti was surely identical with Prospero Braghetti, who sang with the opera troupe at Esterháza from 1781 to 1790, and hence Haydn's familiar "the good Braghetti." The tenor Luigi Brida is not to be confused with Mozart's friend Giuseppe Antonio Bridi (or Brida), also a tenor, who was a merchant from Rovereto. In his memoirs, Michael Kelly tells of paying a visit to Haydn "accompanied by a friend of mine of the name Brida, a young Tyrolese merchant."[60] That Banti gave *Aci e Galatea* the only sustaining power it had according to Haydn is of interest because he was soon to write—or had already written—for her one of his greatest vocal works, the cantata known as *Scena di Berenice*. The composer's reaction to the unruliness of London audiences he had expressed before about a performance at Covent Garden. The King's Theatre in the Haymarket was not immune to the same.

The social season reached a peak of excitement in early April with a royal wedding, duly reported by Haydn in his notebook.

> On the 8th of April, the marriage took place between the Prince of Wales and the Princess of Brunswick. On the 10th I was invited to a musical soirée at the Prince of Wales's residence, Carlton House. An old symphony [of mine] was performed, which I accompanied on the pianoforte, then a quartet, and afterwards I had to sing some German and English songs. The Princess sang with me too; she played a concerto on the pianoforte rather well.

Salomon led this concert, according to reports in the press, and the quartet heard was likely one of Haydn's latest, from Opp. 71–74.

Princess Caroline of Brunswick was in the unfortunate situation of marrying a man already wed. That the Prince of Wales was secretly married to Mrs. Fitzherbert, a Catholic, could not be revealed without disbarring him from the throne. The official marriage was, if not happy, at least blessed with a child, Charlotte, named

---

[60] Kelly, *Reminiscences*, 1:218, and Appendix 1 of the present volume.

after the Queen. In celebration of the nuptials there was a special entertainment entitled *Windsor Castle. Grand Masque.* Haydn attended a performance. "I was at Covent Garden Theater to see the great spectacle [Spectacul], Windsor Castle, the music by Salomon, quite tolerable [ganz Passable]. The decorations, costumes, machinery, crowd of people are excessive [übertrieben]. All the Gods of Heaven and Hell, everything that lives on earth are included." What Haydn does not say is that the overture was his and was identical with that attached to his opera *Orfeo ed Euridice.* Critics of the Masque recognized the overture as Haydn's.

The subscription concerts at the Haymarket resumed their course with the sixth one, on 13 April, for which there is no press notification. A sparsity of announcements for the remaining concerts could be due to Taylor's parsimony; perhaps he reckoned that since the series was fully subscribed there was no need to advertise contents of the individual programs. According to the critic in the *Morning Chronicle*, the sixth concert offered a striking vocal quartet by Cherubini sung by Brida, Morelli, Morichelli, and Rovedino. The piece could have come from Cherubini's very successful *Lodoïska* (Paris, 1791), parts of which Stephen Storace adapted in his opera of the same name for Drury Lane in June 1794.[61] It may be relevant also that Viotti and Cherubini were closely associated in Paris. Haydn was represented on the program by one of his earlier symphonies. On 20 April at a charity concert "for the relief of decayed musicians, their widows and orphans, residing in England," Haydn presided at the fortepiano while Cramer led the orchestra. The second part began with a "Grand Symphony, M.S.—Haydn—and performed under his immediate direction."

Advertisement in the press of the seventh concert, on 27 April, was limited to a reminder telling subscribers that it would take place, and that the two remaining concerts on the series would be on 11 and 18 May. The critic in the *Morning Chronicle* made up for the lack of program details elsewhere with an unusually detailed critique. The program included Gluck's overture to *Iphigénie en Aulide,* a duet by Giacomo Gotifredo Ferrari for two men, Rovedino and Morelli, a new flute concerto by Ashe, "well written and well performed, especially the middle movement," two arias sung by Banti composed by Guglielmi and Cimarosa, and "an air of the ballad kind, by Mozart sung by Morichelli." Some kind of strophic form is implied by "of the ballad kind," a condition that does not suit many arias for female voice by Mozart, but does suit Cherubino's "Voi che sapete" from *Figaro*, which would also match the singer's mezzo soprano range. There was again a new violin concerto by Viotti and a symphony by Clementi, "performed before, but re-written and essentially improved (the best musical judges allow it to be a masterful performance, full of passion and rich in thought, but in some places somewhat too abrupt in its modulations)." The unstated term of compari-

---

[61] Girdham, *English Opera* (1997), pp. 215–16.

son is, of course, Haydn, and the younger master would seem to be struggling to compete with him in the symphonic domain. The critic arrives there in his next mention: "and another Overture, by the great master of the art, Haydn, which had been performed once before, and was repeated with additional effect and pleasure." Heard once before, on the fourth concert, was Symphony No. 103. "The Room, though the largest in London, was crowded. No wonder, the musical powers of all Europe are at present there collected."

Benefit concerts were still advertised with full announcements of the program. Cramer's took place on the first of May, Haydn's three days later. "Dr. Haydn's Concert" became the zenith of Haydn's musical activities in London.

On this momentous day, 4 May 1795, the first public performance of Haydn's last and perhaps greatest symphony, No. 104 in D ("London") took place. The program is documented not only by the usual announcement and musical criticism but also by a handbill, of the kind given to members of the audience—the rarest kind of evidence to survive.[62] Moreover, the handbill is annotated by the concertgoer, allowing us to identify more music on the program than usual. And even more unusual is Haydn's own commentary on the evening in his notebook, providing further insights. From these various sources we have a better idea of this concert than any other of the time. The following remarks proceed by going back and forth between the sources, item by item.

The announcement began with the customary formula. "Dr. Haydn most respectfully begs leave to acquaint the Nobility and Gentry, that his concert is fixed for Monday Next, the 4th of May. Part I. Overture M.S.—Haydn." The handbill begins "NEW ROOM, KING'S THEATRE. Dr. HAYDN's Night." Next to "Overture, MS. —*Haydn*" the anonymous concertgoer, henceforth "the subscriber," wrote, "Very good."[63] In his notebook Haydn wrote: "On the 4th of May 1795 I gave my benefit concert in the Haymarket Theatre. The hall was full of a select company. a) First part of the Military Symphony . . . " This specific bit of information confirms what has been hinted at before about symphonies being broken up and their movements distributed over different parts of a concert. In this case, apparently, the slow introduction and initial fast movement of Symphony No. 100 were performed to begin the concert. Splitting a symphony like this suggests that in many of the subscription concerts, going back to Salomon's 1791 season, where Haydn or another composer was listed for the Overture to Part I, and where the concert ended with an unidentified "Final" or "Full Piece," the latter parts of the same symphony were sounded.

The concert continued with a "Song, Sig. Rovedino—Ferrari," dismissed

---

[62] The handbill was one of many precious documents owned by the late Albi Rosenthal.

[63] For a facsimile of the page, see H. C. Robbins Landon, *Supplement to the Symphonies of Joseph Haydn* (London, 1961), facing p. 48.

curtly by the subscriber with the single word, "nothing."[64] There followed a Duetto for Morichelli and Morelli by Haydn, identified in the text below as "Quel tuo visetto Amabile" and the characters as Eurina [*sic*] and Pasquale; its source, unidentified, was Haydn's 1782 opera *Orlando paladino*. In his notebook the composer wrote, "Duett (Morichelli and Morelli) von mir." The two had sung this duet to a different text in Martìn's *Il burbero di buon cuore* in the King's Theatre. Who but the composer himself would have restored the original text? The subscriber wrote next to the printed text, "Morichelli's short part diverting in the buffo stile." The critic, as we shall see, used this duet paired with the cantata in the serious style in order to enlarge upon Haydn's many-sided genius. The first part ended with "New Overture—Haydn," which elicited from the subscriber two words: "very noisy." There is no doubt as to what this was because of Haydn's description: "A new Symphony in D, namely the twelfth and last of the English ones." Choice of this spot rather than the usual one was due to special circumstances. For one thing, this was nearly an all-Haydn concert; secondly, Part II began with the "Military Symphony," or rather, continuation of the same, with that great crowd pleaser, the *Allegretto* with the Turkish instruments, and it elicited from the subscriber "grand but very noisy." Haydn confirms it in his description, "zweyter Theil der Militär symphonie."

Following the great crowd pleaser and the tumult of cheers that always ensued could have been no enviable task, and it fell to Mme Morichelli. She sang an aria by Paisiello, the text of which began "Crudelle, or colei piangi," annotated by the subscriber, "Nothing more than a decent second opera singer." Next came a violin concerto composed and performed by Viotti, annotated by the same, "Most delicate execution but very little music in the composition." How difficult it was for even a very good composer to measure up against Haydn on the same program! Haydn's turn came next, with "New Scena, Madame Banti," as announced, "Scena nuova von mir" in the composer's own words. From Italian and German he proceeded with a comment in English, "She sang very scanty." The subscriber next to the lengthy text for the "Scena di Berenice," derived from Metastasio's *Antigono*, showed that, if not exactly a connoisseur of instrumental music, he or she, like most of the patrons of these concerts, was quite at home in the world of opera. Next to "Berenice che fai?" the subscriber wrote, "Recitative very finely composed." Then next to the beginning of the aria, "Non partir bell'idol mio," the comment was, "Something of a pleasant air"; further on, next to "Me infelice che fingo?" "Recitative I think" (which was correct); and finally: "Ends with an air in the minor key" (also correct). "Banti has a clear, sweet,

---

[64] At the bottom of the handbill, texts of the vocal pieces are quoted. This one began "Or dell'avverse sorte amata Berenice," an interesting choice, on the same subject as the last vocal piece, Haydn's "Berenice che fai?"

equable voice, her low and high notes are equally good. Her recitative admirably expressive. Her voice rather wants fullness of tone; her shake is weak and imperfect." Haydn's "scanty" about her singing may relate to these technical shortcomings, or she may not have been at her best that particular night. The program ended with "Finale," appearing both on the announcement and the handbill, in all probability the *Finale Presto* of Symphony No. 100.

The critic of the *Morning Chronicle* rose to the occasion to deliver a broad assessment of the composer's achievements.

> More than half the pieces performed were of Haydn's composition, and afforded indubitable marks of the extent and variety of his powers. Nothing was ever more truly comic, or more in the Italian Buffo stile, than his Duet, sung by Morelli and Morichelli. The Scena [di Berenice], by Madam Banti, was no less Italian, and still more masterly; because the stile of composition is of a grander kind. He rewarded the good intentions of his friends by writing a new Overture for the occasion, which for fullness, richness, and majesty, in all its parts, is thought by some of the best judges to surpass all his other compositions.

Implied by this astute overall view is a kind of progression from the buffo style, mastered so early by Haydn, through the grander seria style, to full richness and majesty in the last symphonies. In terms of their slow introductions alone we can fathom how true an observation this critic has hit upon, and from there extend the concept by pondering how very central the slow introductions are to the individual character of the entire work in these late symphonies. It is fashionable with most historians of the present day to see only the opera buffa antecedents of Haydn's achievement, and yet so much is lost by not taking into account the contributions of the seria style to forming the grand synthesis—call it the classic pinnacle, classic moment, or what you will.

The Opera Concerts under Viotti's direction had been so successful that two additional ones were added after the final two on 11 and 18 May, to take place on 27 May and 3 June "at the request of a very great number of the Subscribers," according to a note appended to the handbill for Haydn's benefit concert. Precise announcements and critical comment on the two remaining regular concerts are almost totally lacking, but not so with the two additional concerts, the dates of which were changed to 21 May and 1 June.

The program of the additional Opera Concert on 21 May was announced as beginning with "Overture, double Orchestra, MS. Bach." Perhaps it was Christian Bach's Symphony in E♭, Op. 18 No. 1, for double orchestra, a very attractive work that went back to the Bach-Abel concerts of the late 1770s.[65] The second

---

[65] For the incipit, see *Music in European Capitals*, p. 915, ex. 9.8.

concert, on 1 June, was announced as beginning with the same piece, but at the actual concert, an Overture by Vogel was heard in its place, indication enough that even one of the best symphonies of a generation earlier no longer could compete. Haydn was represented as usual by a symphony to begin the second part, on the program for 1 June specified as "Grand Military Overture." The high point of these concerts, it seems, came near the end, on 21 May with a piece for Mme Banti accompanied on the English Horn by Mr. Ferlendis, and on 1 June with a Concerto on the English Horn by Ferlendis. The critic in the *Chronicle* wrote on 25 May:

> Of the two additional Subscription Concerts, the first was distinguished by the introduction of an instrument called (we know not why) the English Horn; the power, tone, and utility of which we are persuaded are highly excellent. It is a tenor instrument, new (as far as our enquiries could extend) to the musical world, or at least only partially known; but with a sweet, full and articulate tone. Signor Ferlendis performed both on this and the Hautboy, with great feeling and effect.

The cor anglais was long known on the Continent, as we have seen. Haydn wrote for it in his score of *Orfeo ed Euridice,* meaning he expected to find a player of the part, or had one, in London. As one of Banti's several lovers, Ferlendis came in for ridicule by Da Ponte, who described the oboist in his memoirs as "a great player of the transverse flute (Milady Brigida's favorite instrument)."[66]

Brigida Giorgi Banti, Da Ponte's many ribaldries at her expense notwithstanding, must have been a phenomenal soprano, arguably the greatest for whom Haydn ever wrote. Mount Edgcumbe greatly admired her, composed his *Zenobia* for her in 1800, and called her "far the most delightful singer I ever heard"; in his memoirs he described her voice as "of most extensive compass, rich and even, and without a fault in its whole range—a true *voce di petto* throughout."[67] Surely this was the voice that inspired Haydn to compose his "Scena di Berenice" for her in the first place, no matter that she, for whatever reason, held back at its first performance and "sang scanty."

Toward the end of the concert season there was another spate of benefit concerts, which were traditionally allowed to all solo performers, vocal or instrumental. At such events the beneficiary was also the principal soloist, or, in Haydn's case, composer. At all these concerts Haydn was expected to attend and preside at the piano. It is no wonder that he may have become overtired by June. He did not accept every obligation of the kind. Invited by Dr. Samuel Arnold to participate

---

[66] Elizabeth Abbott, in her translation, p. 133, compounds Da Ponte's error by rendering flauto traverso as "cornet."

[67] Richard Edgcumbe, earl of Mount Edgcumbe, *Musical Reminiscences* (London, 1824), cited after Bruce Carr, "Banti, Brigida Giorgi," in *The New Grove Dictionary of Opera.*

on 30 March at a huge charity concert in the vast Freemason's hall, spelled by the composer in his notebook "Free Maisons Hall," he refused. "One of my big symphonies was to have been performed under my direction but since they allowed me no rehearsal I declined and did not appear." At the first of the two additional Opera Concerts, on 21 May, the *Chronicle*'s critic reported, "Haydn was indisposed, and could not conduct his grand sinfonia [No. 104?]; the middle movement of which was most deservedly encored." He was apparently well enough to participate in the second concert, on 1 June, and two days later at a benefit for the violinist Hindmarsh. Two days later still, he was a guest of Burney and his daughter, Fanny, on which occasion Haydn gave her a musical memento. Then on Monday 8 June he participated in a benefit concert for his friend Ashe, the flautist. This concert is the last to be recorded from his second stay in England. There were still several weeks remaining before he departed England on 15 August. Unlike the summer of 1794, which was varied by trips outside London, there are no records or mentions of his leaving the city before his final departure.

The question remains as to what Haydn was doing, besides tidying his affairs, packing his trunks and the like during his last two months in England. Negotiations with music publishers must have occupied some of his time. London publications of his music in the fall of 1795 included the Trios for Mrs. Schroeter, the String Quartets of Op. 74, and the second set of *VI Original Canzonas* (the first set of six came out in 1794). No scraps of music survive to give an indication of what he was working on in June and July of 1795. Of those pieces being readied for publication, the Trios for Mrs. Bartolozzi offer likely candidates. Bearing on them is a letter Clementi wrote to a lady in the country allegedly dated "London March 29th 95."

> Madam,
> There seems to be a great scarcity of musical works of late, so that I am reduced to the poverty of a single Concerto by Cramer and my op. 37th which I sent this evening by the Expedition Coach from the Bell and Crown, directed as you desired. Pray, Madam, have you Haydn's twelve Symphonies printed for Salomon adapted for the Piano-Forte from those which used to be performed at his Concerts? You certainly have Haydn's 3 last Sonatas I think. The first is in C; the 2nd in E, and the 3d in E♭ with the last movement in the German style beginning thus [incipit]. I have the honor to remain Madam, your bbt. st. Muzio Clementi. Please to turn over. [Verso:] One of the symphonies of Haydn mentioned in the preceding page contains this andante [incipit of No. 94: II] another has this Rondeau [incipit of No 96: IV] another has this 1st Allegro after the Introduction [incipit of No. 93: I] another is this Rondeau [incipit of No. 102: IV].[68]

[68] Muzio Clementi, *Epistolario, 1787–1831*, ed. Remo Giazotto (Milan, 2002), Letter 6, pp. 115–17. There are no annotations of the individual letters, only Italian translations of those not written in Italian.

A March 1795 date of "Haydn's 12 Symphonies" is manifestly impossible. The "Twelfth and last of the English" had not even seen its first performance by then. The "5" in the quoted date must be a misreading or a slip of Clementi's pen. A mere glance at any list of Clementi's works would reveal that his Op. 37 Sonatas were not published until 1798, a date that also accommodates Haydn's Bartolozzi trios, first published in 1797. It agrees also with the published arrangements of Haydn's symphonies for piano trio brought out by Corri and Dussek, the first set of six in 1796, the second set in 1797.

Clementi's choice of symphonies for the incipits he dashed down in this quick letter to one of his clients (perhaps a former pupil) may betoken the first that came to his mind. Three are from the first set of 1791–92. No surprise attends the first, that unforgettable *Andante* of the "Surprise" Symphony. Unexpected, on the other hand, are the "Rondeau" of Symphony No. 96 and the first *Allegro* of Symphony No. 93. These may have been works that made a particularly strong impression on the younger composer when hearing them, under Haydn's direction, for the first time. Only one incipit recalled a work from the second set of 1794–95. Not the irrepressible "Military" Symphony that so pleased the public, not the "London" Symphony, nor the "Drumroll" either, but the "Rondeau" of Symphony No. 102 in B♭.

SYMPHONY NO. 102

Symphony No. 98 of 1792 anticipated some of the features of the grand symphony that followed in the same key. Their instrumentation is the same or nearly so, marked by horns and trumpets in B♭, plus timpani, the only difference being two flutes in No. 102 instead of one. These works consequently have in common their characteristic sound, which signals the arrival of B♭ as a festive, all-purpose key, a bright new color in Haydn's tonal palette. Both slow movements choose the key of F, not E♭. It may be recalled that in the *Adagio* of No. 98 Haydn paid personal tribute to Mozart by recalling moments in the slow movement of the "Jupiter" Symphony, Mozart's last. The *Adagio* of No. 102, also in 3/4 time, is a memento of a different sort, connected with the lovely Mrs. Schroeter; nevertheless, it is another personal gesture of respect and devotion. While the earlier *Adagio* is in Haydn's hymnic style, the later one is rhapsodic. After each, the composer placed an unusually fast minuet, *Menuet Allegro*, putting a distance between the 3/4 time of the *Adagios* and that of the dance movement while making them seem even slower by comparison. The *Finale Presto* in 6/8 time of No. 98, with its extended solo appearances for both Haydn and Salomon, seems by the end to become a Shandean jest in contrast with the directness of the *Finale Presto* in 2/4 time of No. 102, the movement that sprang to Clementi's mind. A difference in scope can be heard predicted even in the slow introductions of the two works. The earlier one (*Adagio* in cut time) is theatrical sounding, with its angry minor triad and flat-sixth dramatics carried out in unison by the strings, with alternating light and shade as if threatening a *dramma serio* to follow. It leads in fact to a comic, almost buffo *Vivace*, also in cut time. The main thing predicted by this introduction, aside from the arrival of tonic B♭, turns out to be a ubiquity of rising triad motifs throughout.

The *Largo* in cut time that opens Symphony No. 102, on the other hand, is like a slow curtain. Its first tone is a single B♭ sounded throughout the orchestra to a whole note with fermata, swelling and diminishing as indicated by a sign that appears also on the timpani's B♭, which must be rolled in order to extend for a measure. Simple as this opening is, it portends a world. The upper strings alone next announce an equally simple idea, a lyric phrase sung by the first violins that will nourish much of the thematic material to follow (Example 5.16). After

EXAMPLE 5.16. *Haydn, Symphony in B♭, No. 102, I*

its half-cadence in m. 5, *pianissimo*, the unison B♭ returns, as does the halo-like shimmer of the high strings, beginning the same way but leading quickly, with the aid of more chromatic alterations, to a cadence not *on* V but *in* V. The perfect symmetry of 1 + 4 measures repeated begins to break down when the cellos overlap the cadence in m. 10, transferring to the bass line the head motif 5 8 7 6 | 5. Contrapuntal answering like this was already begun in m. 3 by the violas. The cellos lead the way in pushing to the flat side, smoothly supporting the chord of ♭VI on the way to ♭III, with *crescendo* to *forte* and a filling out of the harmony in the other strings and in the woodwinds. This is the same route taken to prepare the dominant pedal as in No. 98's slow introduction but with more subtle a course. The *Largo* of No. 102, at twenty-two measures, is not much longer than its equivalent in No. 98 yet it seems twice as long because there is so much fine detail to savor along the way. In richnesses of every kind and orchestral refinement the *Largo* speaks Haydn's London language, while the slow introduction to No. 98 seems by comparison not very distant from the finest pre-London introductions, such as those to Symphonies Nos. 86 and 92.

From the head motif of the *Largo* bursts the main theme of *Vivace* (Example 5.16, mm. 23–26), which arrives like a shout of joy, tutti *forte*. It is a slightly decorated version of the same basic 5 8 7 6 | 5 skeleton, transformed into exuberant conjunct falling fourths. Also the same is the procession of 6/3 chords descending that leads to a half cadence on V.

The spacious temper of the *Vivace* emerges especially in the closing area, after the second key of F has been firmly established. At this point Haydn sounds a *fortissimo* A, a powerful intrusion that may remind listeners of the work's first measure and may also sound to them on first hearing like the third of the triad on F. It is not so interpreted by what follows, which is the root of a secondary dominant, V/vi in the new key of F, presaging modulation to an extent not typical at this stage of the prima parte. Haydn follows up by repeating the procedure with a unison D, V/ii, even louder, because the trumpets and horns join in. This move leads quickly back to F. The closing area is marked by offbeat syncopations and *sforzati* heaped upon various conjunct fourths marching up and down, and they grow from the *sforzato* quarter note to the *sforzato* half note. The orchestral unison outbursts continue this rhythmic augmentation up to the level of the whole note syncopation at the measure-level, coming with even stronger accent after an accented measure (Example 5.17). The bass has been singled out in this example because it is

EXAMPLE 5.17. *Haydn, Symphony in B♭, No. 102, I*

the material that is particularly chosen for working over in the development section that follows. The treble is mostly a simultaneous inversion of these same passages in the bass. After the double bar and repeat, the seconda parte gets under way with another of the stentorian unison and octave calls, this one on G, which soon turns into the third of E♭. The development has everything one has come to expect of late Haydn, including a false recapitulation. The intensity of these long, loud stretches may sound like Beethoven at times, and the movement is indeed one from which Haydn's pupil learned much that he would put to his own use.

After the rugged temperament of the first movement the *Adagio* comes as a great contrast. Above it Haydn wrote "In nomine Domini," which he otherwise placed only at the beginning of multi-movement works, indicating that it may have existed as a symphonic piece before the rest, in which case he would have written the first movement as a foil for its interior kind of reverie. He had to transpose the movement from the Trio's version in F♯ down a half tone to F, and there are traces of the process left in the symphony's autograph. The original version was a large rounded binary form, with the first strain enclosed by repeat signs. He wrote out this repetition with changed orchestration in the symphony but there are no changes in the music's essence. The marvel is how the delicate traceries of this elaborately ornamented melody, so natural to the pianist's right hand, was orchestrated so as to lose none of its feathery lightness and quality of caprice. Trumpets (in C) and drums (C, F) are added to the repeat of the first strain. Most of the time they play softly but occasionally they erupt with menacing sounds, for example, just before the initial melody returns in the second strain. In the measure preparing the return, the treble ascends by chromatic steps against the chromatic descent of the bass. This, too, is present in the original trio version. The diverging lines correspond loosely to the long chromatic rise up to B♭ against a bass descent in the slow introduction.

The *Menuet Allegro* breaks the spell of the nocturnal *Adagio* with as robust and sunny a specimen of this dance as it is possible to imagine. Trumpets and drums in B♭ return and make their presence felt from the initial downbeat, which is made more emphatic by a melodic turn, another trait that may come from the practice of actual dance bands. The resulting emphasis on the downbeats gives the piece a particular vigor, one that seems remote from the stately minuets of old. Before the first strain is over, there are some *forte* unisons in the orchestra, like loud knocking, recalling the strong unisons that interrupted the first movement. They return in even more powerful form, *fortissimo,* by the end of the second strain. To reinforce the return of the initial tune in the second strain, Haydn adds a descending line in the flutes and bassoons as a countermelody against the rising theme (Example 5.18a). The Trio is, by comparison, demure and subdued.

EXAMPLE 5.18 a, b. *Haydn, Symphony in B♭, No. 102*

a. *III, Menuet*

It begins with the 5 3 descent proposed by the countermelody in the example and ends both strains with the same falls from 5 to 3, protracted.

The *Finale Presto* in 2/4 time begins with a theme that relates to the minuet's initial rise up the triad (Example 5.18b). Every detail of this idea is subjected to

b. *IV, Finale*

jocular treatment, especially the ta-ta-dum rhythm of two quick notes rushing to a downbeat with which it begins (as does the main theme of the first movement). Its melodic content of 3 4 5 appears in inverted form quickly and often. The entire refrain is, as usual, a rounded binary form with repeats. Confirmation of tonic B♭ is followed quickly by modulation to F, where the head motif of the refrain generates a different theme, followed by lengthy confirmation of the new key. The return of the refrain in its entirety (without repeats) and in tonic B♭ affirms the rondo credentials of the finale (which Clementi called a "Rondeau"). The expected episode in the minor then follows, but it is more a development section than a closed episode. It includes a fugato on the way back to the refrain in B♭, of which only the conclusion of the second strain is heard here, followed by material originally heard in V now appearing in I (the sonata form legacy). A few more teasing attempts to start the refrain end abruptly with cadences. The wedge shapes first presented in the introduction appear twice before the tonic pedal sets in to stay, enlivened by the timpani's ta-ta-dum four times and then a final roll of four measures as the winds and strings toss back and forth the original cell 3 4 5 as 5 4 3. Finally, 3 2 1 ends a work that has everything, in abundance.

Symphony No. 103

The two London symphonies in E♭, Nos. 99 and 103, share less than do the two in B♭. Yet No. 103 has one feature in common with No. 99 that is not to be missed, namely, the importance they both assign to the tone G and the triad on G. Both slow introductions break off by reaching not the dominant, as in almost all of Haydn's other symphonic introductions, but G, arrived at in a way so as to sound like V/vi. In No. 99 this elaborate preparation and arrival of c minor is deflected at the last moment from G, tutti *unisono* and *forte*, to a soft V⁷ of E♭ in the winds that prepares the gentle beginning of the *Vivace*. The G triad returns to begin the seconda parte of the *Vivace*, and the glorious *Adagio* that follows takes G as its principal key. The introduction to No. 103, far bolder, does without the nicety of a transition in passing from *Adagio* to *Allegro*. The G that ends the *Adagio* sounding like V/vi transforms directly into G as the third of tonic E♭, the tone that begins the *Allegro*'s theme. Better put, the alternation of soft, repeated Gs with loud, accented A♭s, ending A♭ - G, reverse position when the *Allegro* tune begins in 6/8 time, G G A♭ | G G F E♭. The ultimate consequence of all this emphasis on G arrives in the finale, one of Haydn's grandest. Its long and complicated development section is brought to a halt by a tutti *fortissimo* climax that turns A♭ into G, first as a triad, then as a single tone, followed by a pause with fermata. After this comes the reprise (or refrain). None of Haydn's other symphonies, not even No. 104, surpass this in achieving a high level of tonal integration over the whole cycle. Nos. 103 and 104 make a pair in shifting the greatest weight among movements to the finale. Also, neither has a real slow movement in the middle. Their introductions remain the only parts that are truly slow.

The *Adagio* introduction of No. 103 takes longer and is more idiosyncratic than any of Haydn's previous symphonic introductions. The slow introduction that began No. 97 in C featured a recurrent cadential figure, one that shows up later in the fast movement. In No. 103 Haydn recalls a much longer segment, a complete twelve-measure phrase at the original slow tempo near the end of the *Allegro*. In addition, he uses parts of the phrase integrated in various ways thematically into the *Allegro*. Furthermore, he calls attention to the *Adagio*'s first phrase by preceding it with a portentous attention-getter so striking that it lent its name to the whole work: a solo drumroll. It is a measure long, protracted by a fermata. There is a similarity here with the *Largo* that opens No. 102. There, the drumroll, also the first measure with fermata, supports a massive tutti of unison and octave B♭ throughout the orchestra, marked *piano* and with a swelling and diminishing indicated by wedge signs. In the autograph of No. 103 Haydn placed no dynamic marking or signs to indicate how he wanted the timpani to sound the initial measure. Presumably the same timpanist played in both works and could have taken his cue from No. 102, which had its premiere exactly four weeks before that of No. 103. Or, since Haydn was right there at the piano, he could have indicated what he wanted.

Another person who was there on that memorable night of 2 March 1795 at the first public performance of No. 103 was surely Salomon. As supervisor of the arrangements for trio and quintet destined for publication and perhaps himself their arranger, he necessarily provided guidance to a wider set of performers. In the trio arrangement he authorized for the first measure wedge signs like those at the beginning of No. 102. The quintet arrangement differed by indicating a *fortissimo* attack followed by a *diminuendo*. However performed by the timpanist, the reaction of the first audience must have been astonishment, or unease, as if to a roll of thunder. Not exactly comforting either was the immediate aftermath, a slow dirge deep in the orchestra, played in barren octaves and lacking a clear metrical pattern, at least initially.[69] Haydn takes his time in letting this sink in by repeating the whole twelve-measure antecedent-consequent phrase in a higher and slightly varied form. Only then does the clear establishment of tonic E♭ become threatened by a move to what sounds like V/vi and a close on those insistent tones of A♭ and G.

The hopping nimbleness of the sprightly *Allegro* in 6/8, peppered with staccato articulations, contrasts drolly with the lumbering pace of the *Adagio*'s legato melody in 3/4 time. Haydn nevertheless has the *Allegro* absorb melodic motifs from the *Adagio* at various points. Once under way, the *Allegro* makes brief work of the prima parte but atones in intricate thematic work for what it lacks in breadth. The main theme spins off into a tutti *forte* proclaiming the power of E♭ and reinforcing

[69] For a more detailed discussion of the slow introduction, see David P. Schroeder, *Haydn and the Enlightenment: The Late Symphonies and Their Audience* (Oxford, 1990), pp. 190–94. The author calls attention to the resemblance of the *Adagio*'s beginning to the plainchant setting of the words "Dies irae" in the Requiem Mass.

it with a descending sequence of 6/3 chords through the octave. Recourse to this device is common when Haydn wished to extend and confirm a key, and there are plenty of other examples in his most recent works in the key of E♭. Here the second key arrives quickly and with little ado. Everything is so concise that one could wish for a memorable contrasting idea before the end of the prima parte. Haydn provides it in the form of a speeded-up Ländler or Waltz (*Deutscher*) with oom-pah-pah accompaniment. He resorted earlier to waltzlike closing themes like this in the first movements of Symphonies 93 and 97, all cases using only the simplest common chords. When this dance returns in the tonic during the reprise, the horns show that they too can play along (Example 5.19). What they play here (bracketed) anticipates their horn call that begins the finale.

EXAMPLE 5.19. *Haydn, Symphony in E♭, No. 103, I*

To begin the seconda parte Haydn avoids tonal surprise. The key remains, however briefly, the same B♭ established before the double bar. His ingenuity resides in making a fugato out of what had been the second violin's accompaniment of the main theme. With intricate working of small motifs from this theme, he modulates quickly back through E♭ to c minor and stops on its dominant, G (V/ vi again!), emphasizing the moment by a short rest with fermata. Direct quotation of the *Adagio*'s melody in E♭ follows, at the original low pitch but accelerated to *Allegro*. From the next pause with fermata it would have taken only adjustment of a chord tone or two in order to arrive back at E♭ for the reprise. Instead, Haydn moves off to the flat side for a statement of the waltzing theme in D♭, almost complete, breaking off just before the end so as to begin a tonal maneuver that does bring in the reprise. D♭ as destination of the development's most ear-catching junket, just before the reprise, corresponds to a similar choice in the middle of the finale, where Haydn makes a point of insisting on D♭ at length as bearer of the second theme. This is another feature that makes the finale sound familiar, even when heard for the first time.

A Hungarian march might be the best description for the second movement. It is in 2/4 time and is marked *Andante*, bringing it close to the *Allegretto* march in the "Military" Symphony, a cousin in some other respects as well. This march is a set of variations on an alternating theme, long one of the composer's favorite forms, and here he is generous to the point of providing two variations instead of his usual one on the second theme. *All'Ungarese* (as in his Keyboard Concerto in D) and "Gypsies' Style" (as in the Trio in G dedicated to Mrs. Schroeter) meant the same thing to Haydn. In this instance he apparently wanted to demonstrate for Londoners the so-called Gypsy scale, with its prominent raised fourth degree: C D E♭ F♯ G A♭ B♮ C. The first theme begins with its initial four tones, which probably struck his audience as no less exotic than the raised fourth at the beginning of Symphony No. 83 ("La Poule") hurled at Parisian ears a decade earlier. Following the first theme's nearly symmetrical strains, each repeated, comes the second theme, in major but "infected" by the same raised fourth of the first theme, of which it is a loose copy. It sounds nearly as exotic.

In the first variation Haydn is restrained, adding only a few dabs of wind color in counterpoint to the first theme. The first major variation is a long and elaborate solo for violin, presumably played by Cramer at the premiere (unless the honor went to Salomon). The second minor variation unleashes a military march with all the trappings, a moment that surely reminded the public of its favorite movement in the "Military" Symphony, which had been revived for a performance only a week earlier. The second major variation offers a delightful contrast—a rural idyll with bird-like chirpings in the winds. A coda on a tonic pedal begins by repeating the closing phrase of the major theme's second strain, adding a descent made poignant by suspended dissonances gracefully resolving (Example 5.20). Whether

EXAMPLE 5.20. *Haydn, Symphony in E♭, No. 103, II*

Haydn knew it or not this lovely passage duplicates one in his favorite Mozart opera, *Figaro*: a moment of calm in the second-act Finale when, over a pedal C, Susanna, the Countess, and Figaro implore the Count to allow the marriage ("Deh signor nol contrastate" mm. 449ff.). Haydn goes on from this moment to modulate rapidly until reaching the chord of E♭, in 6/3 position, tutti *fortissimi*, including the timpani executing a roll on its G. The tonal progression resembles that in the first-movement coda of Symphony 97. From E♭ the music makes its way gradually back to C for a final, compressed statement of the major theme, which ends with a burst of exultation over a long timpani roll on C.

The *Menuet* intensifies first-beat accents by rapid melodic turns, as did its counterpart in No. 102. Besides these, to make the rhythm still more biting, Haydn uses Lombardic rhythm, or, as his London public would have experienced it, Scotch snaps. Their twofold echo in the winds ending the first strain sounds quite impudent, as if more in sarcasm than compliment. The same falling fifth, without the snaps and legato, *piano,* leads off the second strain which veers suddenly to the flat side and lands the music in ♭III. From there the *forte* leaps of the minuet's beginning, fortified by the rapid melodic turns and the descending seventh leaps, with Scotch snaps, in canon between treble and bass, make a strong showing on the way to B♭, preparing the return of the beginning. The two clarinets (doubled by the strings) with one bassoon are featured in the better-behaved Trio, in which all the eighth notes are even.

The *Finale Allegro con spirito* in cut time begins with the horn call adumbrated in Example 5.19 and continues with the same as an accompaniment to a counter-melody, three knocking upbeats going to a melodic sigh for the first violins with answering phrase supported by clarinets alone, one of the few times Haydn trusts his clarinets to this extent (Example 5.21). The continuation places these knocking

EXAMPLE 5.21. *Haydn, Symphony in E♭, No. 103, IV*

upbeats in the bass on the weak fourth measure of the preceding phrase, imitated in canon by the treble so that the theme starts a rhythmic struggle with itself as to which measure is strongest. After a long dominant pedal occupied by the same back and forth of the canon, the beginning section or refrain returns in its entirety. The movement is a large-scale rondo with four statements of the refrain. At the same time it has traits of sonata form, such as the transition to the second key of B♭. Duly prepared, the second theme coyly appears in the bass, preceded by four measures of static accompaniment in the strings. It is the first theme, yet altered in overall metric shape so that the knocking upbeats start on a weak fourth measure (Example 5.22). The change entailed a readjustment in the harmony too, from I - V - I - I to I - V - V - I. A similar play between strong and weak beginnings of the main idea was first explored in the initial *Allegro.*

EXAMPLE 5.22. *Haydn, Symphony in E♭, No. 103, IV*

The second theme is followed by a return of the main theme in tonic E♭, the kind of return expected in a rondo. It is not long before the return bursts into an impassioned development, calmed at first by the arrival of the second theme, preceded by its static accompaniment, in the key of D♭, as remarked above. This theme also gives way to more development before arriving at the pause after the big arrival of G as V/vi. Without resolution of this chord, as at the end of the slow introduction, E♭ softly begins with the first theme. To conclude the finale Haydn brings in his trumpets to reinforce the repeated horn calls, ending the symphony in a burst of triumph. The final two tones that the violins insist upon are high G descending to E♭, the same two tones on top of the double-stops they played to end the first *Allegro*.

SYMPHONY No. 104

In choosing the key of his last symphony, Haydn reverted to his favorite symphonic key of D major. Two of the previous symphonies, Nos. 98 and 101, also began with slow introductions in the minor mode that led to fast movements in the major. Both, like No. 104's *Adagio*, made a brief visit to the relative major (III) before returning to the minor. No. 101, also in D, offers an *Adagio* beginning that is soft and smoothly flowing, completely unlike the introduction to No. 104, which begins with a jagged clarion call to shake the rafters. The entire orchestra, which includes two flutes, two clarinets in A, and two trumpets in D, plays in unisons and octaves, *fortissimo*, using double-dotted rhythm to proclaim the imperious command. Ominous timpani rolls reinforce the awe and splendor of the moment (Example 5.23, mm. 1–3). If the dirge following the timpani roll at

EXAMPLE 5.23. *Haydn, Symphony in D, No. 104, I*

the beginning of No. 103 reminded some cowering listeners of the "Dies irae," similarly gloomy imaginations may have reacted to this beginning as if it were a summons to the Last Judgment. Not until the third measure of the Example does the F♯ appear that announced d minor. Although soft, the second violins, using the same double-dotted rhythm, provide another interval, D E, that will become as central to the whole work as the initial rise of a fifth. The tutti blast is heard twice more, on F at midpoint and toward the end again on D, but this time the rise of D up to A is answered with an eerily *pianissimo* falling fifth instead of a falling fourth, D G. The last tone lingers to become the sounding bass of the Neapolitan-sixth chord on the way to I$^6_4$ and its resolution (Example 5.23, mm. 14–16).

The *Allegro* theme sinks gracefully down from F♯ to D, then rises up to A for repeated quarter notes marked staccato and a slurred B A in half notes, followed by a descent in half notes with suspensions resolving to form 6/3 chords (Example 5.24). Three melodic motifs, marked *x*, *y*, and *z*, make up the antecedent half

EXAMPLE 5.24. *Haydn, Symphony in D, No. 104, I*

of the main theme. Each has a high profile and is rife with possibilities for further treatment. In the consequent phrase, the chordal descent in 6/3 chords is replaced with a chordal rise, the treble climbing up to G. Subsequent phrases confirm the tonic with several IV - I cadences, initiated by the dactylic rhythm of *x*. Then the IV - I cadences are stated differently, with the treble descending from D with a few chromatic shadings on the way down, actually a version of *z*, with rhythmic augmentation from two measures to four. The same suspended D resolving to C♯ that led into the *Allegro* in m. 16 recurs again twice, first at the same pitch, then an octave higher, and these cadential preparations are also augmented to double their original length, lending further solidity to the as-yet-uncontested reign of D major. Then the bass begins another descent from D down the octave (*z*). Appearances of G♯ suddenly contest the tonal stability and prepare for a modulation to the new key. The path is smooth and undramatic, made smoother by further resort to the dactylic head motif (*x*). An old convention dictated that important demarcation points, such as the arrival of the new key, be announced by three chordal blows as a kind of sonic guide. Haydn indulges his audience with the same here. The second theme itself, as we have come to expect of him, is the first slightly transformed. At first, the new guise is restricted to the sparse addition of a few winds doubling the strings (antecedent), but then it blossoms into harmonic changes and enrichment by way of secondary dominants (consequent). Confirmation of the key of A, as earlier of D, involves a suspension-laden descent in 6/3 chords as well as IV - I cadences. After several V - I cadences in A, there is an additional closing theme, begun by a little exchange between the first violins and the seconds. The prima parte closes with more cadential reinforcement. It has lacked the raw power and drama of its equivalent in No. 102, or the rhythmic subtleties and close motivic work of that in No. 103, yet it is richly developmental in its own smooth-flowing way, and we welcome the chance to hear it repeated so as to savor more of this richness.

No sudden harmonic jolt or other surprise inaugurates the seconda parte, merely a quiet secondary dominant, V of b minor, supporting motif *y*, heretofore neglected. The mood becomes ominous nevertheless as *y* is repeated in various ways and ever more insistently, leading to one key after another, all of them minor. After the abundant major-mode radiance of the prima parte, this turbulence sounds threatening, as if clouds had suddenly obscured the sun. There is a brief respite from *y* as the head motif is softly explored in c# minor and then on to E, which becomes e for a moment that is another version of 6/3 chords in descent with suspensions (Example 5.25). The repeated tones in the treble may suggest *y*,

EXAMPLE 5.25. *Haydn, Symphony in D, No. 104, I*

but there are three of them instead of four and they lead not to the rise of a second but to a melodic sigh beginning on the same tone, that is to say, they duplicate the motif so important to the great finale of No. 103, whose spirit seems close. Motif *y* soon asserts itself again, and the peak of vehement insistence on it is reached with the arrival at b minor, at which point Haydn adds both horns and trumpets doubling winds and strings in hammering out *y*. They play it first as D D D D | E D over I⁶ in b minor, the first key intimated in this breathtaking development section. From the relative minor of D it is but a short step to a dominant pedal preparing the arrival of D itself.

The reprise begins with the main theme played softly by the strings as before. This time the consequent phrase, with treble and accompaniment inverted, goes to the winds alone. The corroborating phrases with the IV - I cadences follow in order, then Haydn begins condensing and consolidating. The long transitional path is shortened to a few measures, at the end of which comes a surprise. The full orchestra reinforced by the timpani launches into a harmonized version in D of D D D D | E D, repeated for good measure. If this sounds like a great moment of triumph, and it does, the reason is that we heard these same tones not long before, harmonized in b minor as the climax of the development. Apotheosis of motif *y* is at hand and it banishes all doubts and anxieties created by its treatment in the development. The result of turning this motif into so positive and trium- phant a moment is to quite overshadow everything else in the *Allegro*, even the head motif. From this peak of excitement Haydn climbs down, while assuming a more modest demeanor so as to prepare for the second theme, again the first theme in different guise. It is totally rewritten but recognizable from the coloring lent by its secondary dominants. The closing theme follows, as expected, leading to another triumphant appearance on high of D D D D | E D with full orchestra, made more sonorous by the busy running eighth-note filler of the flutes and vio- lins at the top.

Some fifteen years earlier Haydn composed another festive Symphony in D, No. 70, performed to celebrate both the name day of Prince Nicholas I on 6 December 1779 and the laying of the cornerstone to the new opera house at Esterháza. No. 70 concluded with a powerful finale built mainly around a fugue in d minor on a subject that began D D D D | E↓A | F F F F | G↓C | A.[70] This theme, switched to major and converted from polyphony to homophony at the end, lends the work a triumphant character not unrelated to the experience of resurgence just described.

Quite retrospective is Haydn's choice of an *Andante* in G and in 2/4 time for the second movement of his last symphony. He had done the same in No. 101, and for that matter in No. 1 in D, dating from 1759 or earlier, thus he could hardly have made a more conventional choice. This *Andante* is in a large ternary form and moves along with a march-like swagger enhanced by dotted rhythms, much like its equivalent in No. 103, if a little less rapidly. There it was a case of tempering minor-mode statements by one in the major. Here, too, there are aspects of dou- ble variation evident. A minor version of the initial theme in the major begins the large middle section, after which the section turns mostly to development. There are also hints of the famous "tick-tock" *Andante* of No. 101 in the way the return to the initial music is preceded by the return, first, of its rhythmic accompaniment. As in other second movements of these last symphonies, a rich and full orchestral panoply, including trumpets and drums, clothes Haydn's thoughts.

The *Menuet Allegro* returns to familiar ground not only in the tonal sense. Its forthright declaration of a rise up the tonic triad from D to A recalls the slow introduction's powerful beginning and the rise to A in the *Allegro*'s main theme. Possibly the minuet theme occurred to Haydn before these other ideas did. The way its A, once reached, is surrounded by accented neighboring tones above and

[70] For further discussion, see *Haydn, Mozart*, p. 374.

below raises the question of whether it could have originated in the composer's mind as a further byproduct of the nimble theme in 6/8 time of No. 103's first *Allegro*. His famous penchant for humor, otherwise not much in evidence here, emerges in the second strain, when two measures of silence are preceded by what sounds like a hiccup. The Trio is all modesty and discretion in comparison, a flow of even eighth notes without distorting accents. Not so ordinary is the choice of B♭ for its key, after a beginning that seemed to promise d minor. Even this little dance affirms the central idea of rising to the fifth degree. Haydn's fascination with third relationships, especially with ♭VI, finds final symphonic expression here. The Trio is followed by a proper and leisurely transition back to D for the repeat of the minuet.

The *Finale Spiritoso* in cut time begins by invoking a rural scene. Drone octaves sound D in the horns reinforced by the cellos and basses providing the only accompaniment for the tune above—a *Dudelsack*—or bagpipe—kind of music (Example 5.26). The tune's initial moves, 5 4 2, 4 3 1 are certainly the stuff of folk

EXAMPLE 5.26. *Haydn, Symphony in D, No. 104, IV*

songs and nursery songs, yet not unknown to Haydn's vast melodic store and used as recently as the introduction to Symphony No. 101. Claims that he copied this melody from folk songs remain unproven. More likely, folk songs sprang up from copying Haydn. The only difference that separates his antecedent phrase from its consequent is the final tone D instead of E, a very simple construction that is also folklike, as are the restriction to so few tones and their gravitation toward the tonic. Someone in his original London audience may have noticed that 5↓2 3 1 in mm. 5–6 and 9–10 duplicated the tones in the bell chimes William Crotch wrote for Cambridge University in 1794, later known as the Westminster Chimes.[71]

---

[71] Percival Price, "Chimes," in *The New Grove Dictionary of Music and Musicians* (2001) (cf. the middle of the third quarter past the hour in Westminster Chimes).

The finale Haydn builds from this material is less complex in formal shape than its predecessor in No. 103 but no less monumental in scope. It is a generously proportioned sonata form with repeat of the prima parte and an unusual reluctance to reach closure in both parts. Transition to the second key brings some strong offbeat accents, so gruff that they sound like Beethoven, and *sforzato* accents on the second tone of a rising second in half notes (equivalent to the main theme's unaccented m. 6). The second theme is the first with added countersubjects and the same *sforzato* accents. In the cadential area Haydn delays coming to a close by backing away via a secondary dominant. Then just as the big cadence is set to arrive, he pulls away again by means of more secondary dominants, this time in a soft, sustained, and gently wistful passage in longer notes, quite an unusual step at this stage of a movement in sonata form. When closure arrives, it is replete with more rises of a second to an accented tone.

The seconda parte begins by working over the head motif 5 4 2 and other material heard before. Development seems ready to end with the arrival of V/vi, as happens so often in Haydn. The measure of silence following almost guarantees that it will happen again here. Instead, Haydn returns to the quiet, reflective music over secondary dominants until it comes to rest over a C♯ pedal in the basses supporting a chord that is V/III in D, *pianissimo*. He resolves this by slipping up a half tone, like a deceptive cadence. The tell-tale sound of the horns' low D in octaves here, *piano*, leads again to the main theme, a reprise that seems to have snuck in by the back door. Economies are effected immediately by Haydn's eliminating the first statement of the theme as mere melody over drone and proceeding directly to the second, harmonized version of the theme. The strong syncopations of offbeat chords and the *sforzato* accents to emphasize the second tone of a rising second recur, but the second-theme version of the main theme is suppressed, unlike the soft, wistful passage. For the coda Haydn pulls out all the stops to obtain maximum sonority and brilliance. The main theme reappears in full glory, and this time the equivalent to m. 6 acquires the *sforzato* on the second tone, D - E, stated in octaves unlike the rest of the theme. He sharpens the point by repeating this part. And the point, we realize, is a correspondence with the triumphant motif that emerges in the course of the first movement. To make sure we have not missed this point he ends the symphony by augmenting D - E from one measure to two, eliciting the final answer A - D, either rising or falling (Example 5.27). Now those

EXAMPLE 5.27. *Haydn, Symphony in D, No. 104, IV*

imperious tones that begin the slow introduction come into full focus. Never has Haydn achieved a stronger sense of finality than here.

Later, in Germany, No. 104 was sometimes called the "Salomon" Symphony, which was of a piece with its more widely used appellation of "London," in the sense that all twelve works are both Salomon and London symphonies. Haydn called them his English Symphonies. He drew attention to the special status of the last in his notebook: "eine neue Symphonie in D und zwar die zwölfte von den Englischen," which was unusual as was his detailed description of the whole benefit concert on 4 May 1795. Ordinarily, specific programs have to be pieced together from reports in the press and other sources. Unparalleled, moreover, is his inscription on the autograph of No. 104, in English: "The 12th I have composed in England." This extraordinary circumstance, taken together with the work's emphatic closing gesture and its entire character, have raised the question as to whether he intended to signal then and there the end of his contributions to the genre he did so much to shape and perfect. Subsequently, having returned to Vienna, he declined requests to compose further symphonies, and for that matter, further sonatas.

It might have turned out differently had Vienna possessed an organized concert-giving institution such as those that had commissioned the Paris and London symphonies. Vienna's only approximate equivalent was Swieten's Associated Society, which put on oratorios and the like, the expense shared by several members of the high nobility. Their concerts lacked a stable orchestra, location, and musical leadership. Yet they, and the wish of Prince Esterházy to honor his wife with newly composed Masses on her name day, were largely responsible for Haydn's return to composing Masses and oratorios, a move prompted also by his desire to make greater contributions to vocal music. Like Mozart, Haydn composed almost entirely on demand, which is to say that both retained creative processes typical of their time.

> The terms on which Haydn undertook so long a journey and so responsible a duty, were, three hundred pounds for composing six grand symphonies, two hundred for the copyright to them, and of a benefit, the profits guaranteed at two hundred pounds. The latter produced three hundred and fifty pounds, and as Haydn refused to pay the band, the expense fell on his enterprising countryman [Salomon].[72]

The same editor published another account describing the agreement of 1793 with Salomon: "His [Haydn's] next engagement was on the same terms, exclusive of the copyright of the six last symphonies; which, being left in the hands of a lady by the composer when he quitted England, were afterwards delivered

---

[72] *Harmonicon* 8 (1830), p. 45, cited after Schroeder, *Haydn and the Enlightenment* (1990), p. 106.

FIGURE 5.6. Charles Gore. Drawing of a ship entering Hamburg harbor, 1792.

to Salomon, on his paying the further sum of three hundred pounds."[73] If these documents are not mere concoctions, the lady with whom Haydn left the scores of Symphonies 99–104 was surely none other than Mrs. Schroeter, who is known to have ratified a contract for him after he left. Confirmation of a kind could be inferred from the dates on which Haydn gave Salomon future rights to the symphonies. Two days before leaving England, he signed such a document for the first six. Only after returning to Vienna did he sign, on 27 February 1796, the similar agreement for the last six. The payment mentioned could have been transacted between these two dates.

Haydn left England for good on 15 August 1795. He sailed on a ship that carried him to land at the free imperial city of Hamburg where he arrived after a voyage of about five days (Figure 5.6). Ahead lay a creative phase even more genial than his previous ones.

[73] *Harmonicon* 5 (1827), p. 7, cited after Schroeder, *Haydn and the Enlightenment*.

6
Haydn: Late Harvest

Vienna, 1795–96

Hostilities on the Continent continued to go badly for England and her allies during 1795. Prussia withdrew from the conflict in March and made a separate peace with France. In June a British expeditionary force reinforced by French émigrés landed at Quiberon in Brittany with the intention of supporting counter-revolutionary forces in the Vendée. Battle was joined on 16 July with an army of the Republic led by General Hoche. They defeated the invaders, took many of them prisoner, and slaughtered the émigrés as traitors. Another general, Pichegru, led an army north to battle the Dutch and forced Holland to capitulate. Stadholder William V and his family fled to London. With all of the Low Countries under French control and much of the Rhine valley as well, Haydn had to find a different route between England and Austria. What remained of Dutch trade with England was mostly relocated north, to the port of Hamburg. Haydn went home this way.

Although Haydn's stay in Hamburg was brief, he did meet with Anton Reicha, who had fled from Bonn in 1794 after it fell to the French. Reicha recalled later that he encountered Haydn on his way to England in 1790 and on his return to the Continent in 1795. Haydn wished to pay respects to the family of Emanuel Bach, probably expecting to meet Bach's widow, but she had died a month earlier. He found only Bach's daughter living in the family home, the two sons also having died. According to Dies, "Haydn at this time traveled back by way of Hamburg expressly to make the personal acquaintance of C. P. E. Bach. He came too late; Bach was dead and of the family he found only the daughter living." Haydn was not so out of touch with the world of music as to be ignorant of Bach's death seven years earlier.[1] He would have known about it soon after the event if only because of his close links with Swieten, Bach's patron and staunch supporter. Griesinger, while relating Haydn's repeated assertions of respect for the music and teaching of Emanuel Bach, makes no mention of Hamburg in this connection.

Haydn's arrival at Hamburg is documented in press accounts, albeit sparsely.[2] It took place either on 20 or 21 August. He stayed with a publisher-bookseller, Johann Heinrich Herold, who had printed music by Emanuel Bach. One account in the press, dated 22 August, regretted that his stay was so short, "since he continues his journey to Vienna tomorrow." Haydn was apparently in a hurry to return home. Instead of going east to Berlin, where he had been invited and hoped to visit, he took a more southerly route, perhaps by way of the Elbe valley. He passed through Leipzig where he met Rochlitz and possibly Breitkopf. Dies writes that he stopped in the Saxon capital: "In Dresden he visited Naumann but did not find him home." Encountering only a domestic servant cleaning the premises, Haydn asked if he could at least see a portrait of Naumann, which was arranged. He collected many portraits of musicians, as recorded in the catalogue of his pictures made after his death in 1809 (none specifically names Naumann). From Dresden it would have been a relatively easy journey to Prague and through Bohemia south to Linz on the Danube, or to Passau, a short distance upriver, where he is said to have made a stop.

Sigismund von Neukomm, one of Haydn's favorite students, described how the master was surprised to hear one of his own works performed at Passau. Neukomm was born at Salzburg in 1778, studied music theory there with Michael Haydn, and went in 1797 to Vienna, where he became Haydn's student in composition for four or five years. Much later he wrote a few pages of addition to the *Biographische Nachrichten* by his friend Dies, saying that his personal conversations at table with Haydn were earlier than Dies's interviews and belonged to a time when Haydn was still strong enough to create a gigantic work like *The Seasons*.

On his second return from England Haydn passed by way of Passau, where he decided to stay overnight. He learned on his arrival that on that very evening a per-

---

[1] Ernst Fritz Schmid, "Joseph Haydn und Carl Philipp Emanuel Bach," *Zeitschrift für Musikwissenschaft* 14 (1932): 299–330; 308. The author doubts that Haydn was unaware of Bach's death in 1788.
[2] Robert von Zahn, "Haydns Aufenthalt in Hamburg 1795," *Haydn-Studien* 6, no. 4 (1994): 309–12. Most of this article concerns the unconfirmed tale of a refugee, Mme de Genlis, about hearing a burial chant for trumpet sounded from the tower of St. Catherine's, supposedly composed by Haydn on his passage through Hamburg.

formance of the *Seven Last Words* was taking place and that the Kapellmeister there had composed vocal parts to the work. Haydn was satisfied with the performance but added to the telling, with his usual modesty, simply "the vocal parts, I believe, I could have handled better." As soon as he arrived in Vienna he undertook and completed the clarifying addition of vocal parts, for which arrangement Baron van Swieten took care of the German text and Carpani the Italian one (a free translation).[3]

The neatness of this explanatory excursion raises suspicion, for history can rarely be so simple a case of cause and effect. In favor of it nevertheless are two factors: Neukomm's unarguable closeness to his teacher, and his good will toward both Dies and Haydn in setting down a few additional details to enhance the work of Dies, without seeking credit for himself.

Die Sieben letzten Worte

Haydn arrived back in Vienna during the last days of August. The claim made by Neukomm that Haydn immediately set about work on a vocal text to his 1786 orchestral version of the *Seven Last Words* is acceptable if modified to allow time for the text to be put in final form by Baron van Swieten. From this moment on, the Baron played an increasingly important role in Haydn's career (Figure 6.1).

On 10 August 1799 Haydn wrote a letter to Cornelius Knoblish, music director of a monastery in Silesia whose abbot had ordered a copy of *The Creation* by subscription. Haydn, after expressing his gratitude and promising to send the copy as soon as it was printed, mentioned the mass settings he had composed on order from his prince, and another work as well:

> Your Reverence has only half enjoyed the *Seven Words of Our Savior,* because three years ago I underlayed a new four-voiced vocal music throughout, without changing the instrumental part. The text was written by an experienced (sehr geübter) music canon at Passau, and corrected by our great Baron van Swieten. The effect of this work surpassed all expectation. If before my end I should travel in your region I would take the liberty of performing it for your Abbot. At present no one possesses it except our monarchy [i.e., Empress Marie Therese].

The music canon at Passau is usually assumed to have been Kapellmeister Joseph Friebert. But was he in fact a canon of the cathedral? Three years earlier than this letter would be August 1796, yet the new version was performed already at Lenten concerts early in 1796. Haydn in fact made several changes in orchestration for the oratorio version. He discarded Friebert's obbligato recitatives, added ritornellos, and substituted an unmetered and unaccompanied choral setting of

---

[3] Horst Seeger, "Zur musikhistorischen Bedeutung der Haydn-Biographie von Albert Christoph Dies (1810)," *Beiträge zur Musikwissenschaft* 1, no. 3 (1959): 24–31; contains "Bemerkungen Neukomms zu den Biographischen Notizen von Dies," 28–31.

each Word in German translation to precede the choral-orchestral numbers.

Judging from his letter to the Silesian cantor in 1799, Haydn considered the vocal version a completion of the original score for orchestra alone. Others were less sanguine. Griesinger sniffed at the Passau text, which he deprecated as "patched together [geflickt] out of church songs by a Passau clergyman." Dies was reserved to the point of saying that he would let others judge if it were an improvement on the original version, an unusual reticence on his part. One's response to the text depends on how much tolerance can be mustered for the exaggerated language and emotional fervor that was characteristic of Pietism. The late eighteenth century in general saw a withdrawal from the *Empfindsamkeit* so typical of the midcentury and exemplified

FIGURE 6.1. Portrait of Gottfried van Swieten by P. Fendi, engraved by J. Axmann.

by Karl Ramler's passion oratorio *Der Tod Jesu,* set to music by Carl Heinrich Graun (1755). The editor of the oratorio version in *Joseph Haydns Werke,* who also edited the original version, confined his criticism of the text to saying that it reflected "a certain influence of Gellert's *Odes and Songs.*"[4] This editor also pointed out the influence of *Der Tod Jesu* on the text. Swieten did nothing to lessen it. In fact he discarded the Passau text altogether for the Earthquake, the final number, and substituted verses 261–69 of *Der Tod Jesu.*

Haydn's work in piecing together the new version required weeks, as opposed to the months of labor that went into the first version. He had an orchestral score compiled from the parts printed by Artaria in 1787, gave directions that the third and fourth horn parts be omitted, and left room for the addition of two clarinets, two trombones, and the four vocal parts. This score survives. He filled in these

---

[4] *JHW* XXVIII/2, *Die Sieben letzten Worte unseres Erlösers am Kreuze,* ed. Hubert Unverricht (Munich-Duisburg, 1961), Vorwort, p. vii. The facsimile that serves as frontispiece gives the first page of Sonata 1 as copied out, with parts added in Haydn's hand.

parts when making his own vocal version from the original, depending rather strongly on Friebert's score at first, then becoming more independent. He made many revisions, showing the care he exerted over all details, even in the performing parts copied by Elssler.

One entirely new piece was added by Haydn, besides the new choral intonations: an *Introduzione* for wind band in the middle of the work. The band of twelve instruments comprises one flute, pairs of oboes, clarinets in C, horns in C, trombones, and bassoons, plus contrabassoon. The two trombones and first bassoon state the theme of the piece after the chords initiating this *Largo e Cantabile* in 3/4 time and in the key of a minor. It serves to prepare the A major of Sonata No. 5 ("Sitio"). Oratorios were customarily divided into two parts, so the division here emphasizes the new generic aspirations of the work, while demonstrating Haydn's wonderful ways with wind coloring. The piece is substantial, its seventy-one measures at this slow tempo taking several minutes. It serves to replace the introductory intonations of the Word for Sonata 5. The sung text begins "Jesus rufet: Ach, mich dürstet!"

Whatever gains are made by having the explanatory texts sung are outweighed by the many awkwardnesses of this particular text. The overabundance of words tends to diminish the force of the short scriptural quotations. Haydn composed all the sonatas in response to themes suggested to him by the Latin incipits (see Example 4.14). Much is lost by adding texts of the incipits in a different language, with explanatory texts following. Many compromises had to be made in the switch from Latin to German. For instance, the forceful cadence of Sonata 6 ("Consumatum est") that serves as its main theme had to be reduced from five tones to four to accommodate the four-syllable replacement "Es ist vollbracht!" To accomplish this Haydn had the first tone of the motto played but not sung, with consequent loss of force. Under the onslaught of a sea of words, some of them bordering on the trivial, Haydn's daring and demanding original conception could only suffer.

It is difficult to accept that Haydn really believed his oratorio version somehow completed the original. He was doubtless swayed by the success of the choral version, and content to know that what he considered to be one of his greatest compositions had been injected with new life after being largely forgotten. One expert who took a different view was his friend Abbé Stadler, who told Novello that he "preferred these beautiful compositions without the words just as they were originally conceived by their author."[5] When the choral version was first published by Breitkopf and Härtel in 1801, a contrary claim was made in the introduction, saying that the instrumental sonatas without commentary "would never be able to make the Savior's words understandable to everyone." The key word here is

[5] Novello, *A Mozart Pilgrimage*, p. 172.

the last one. In a question as delicate as this, it is best to rely on scholars who are native speakers of the language. In this category, there is no more telling summary of the subject than what an eminent Haydn scholar has recently written.

> Truly it is easy to see why the oratorio version was so much more popular in the nineteenth century than the original orchestra version: it demanded no straining of the intellect, no binding of meditative and structural listening, but invited instead an emotional identification with the text through the medium of music. This becomes very clear in places where the borders of triviality become permeable, as in the texting of the horns' motif in the Seventh Sonata.[6]

Haydn's pious wish to have his *Seven Last Words* reach out to wider circles and to non-connoisseurs of music can be understood most sympathetically for its intention to instruct while still managing to please, a concept so typical of the composer, and of the Enlightenment in general.

The new oratorio version was first performed in the city palace of Prince Joseph Schwarzenberg on the Neue Markt on 26 March 1796, at a concert financed by Swieten's Company of Associates, of which Schwarzenberg was a member. A libretto dated 1796 was printed in Vienna by Mathias Andreas Schmidt. Zinzendorf is our only witness of the performance who left a mention; he was also present for the performance of the original version on 26 March 1787. At that earlier event he recorded that the second and seventh Words seemed to him well expressed. Nine years later to the day, he maintained the same opinion: "Au grand Concert de Haydn chez le Prince Schwarzenberg sur les 7. dernières paroles de notre Seigneur. Le second et le septiême me plurent davantage. Il fesoit bon effet dans ce salon."[7] Zinzendorf was pleased or intrigued enough with the work to return for the repeat performance the following day (assuming it was not some social reason that drew him): "De nouveau au Concert. Toujours la 7me parole. Vater, ich befehle—me plait le plus et davantage que Es ist vollbracht." Here he cites the pieces not after Swieten's text but from the preliminary intonations of the scriptural words translated into German. In the case of No. 7, his "Vater, ich befehle" corresponds only loosely with "Vater, in deine Hände empfehle ich meinen Geist." Perhaps he did not purchase a copy of the libretto.

Haydn had not far to go to the concerts of 26–27 March. He was then renting a lodging in the city at the Hoföbstlerischen House on the Neue Markt, while he and his wife waited for their suburban house in Gumpendorf to be readied for occupation. The concerts presaged the circumstances surrounding *The Creation* two years later, namely Swieten's textual role and the first performance in the Schwarzenberg palace, sponsored by Swieten's Company of Associates.

[6] Finscher, *Haydn* (2000), p. 328.
[7] Edward Olleson, "Haydn in the Diaries of Count Karl von Zinzendorf," *Haydn Yearbook* 2 (1963/64): 45–63; 51.

The oratorio version anticipated the direction that Haydn would take in his last works, which are predominantly vocal or choral-orchestral. In the light of his entire career the shift is not so marked, because from his earliest years he was greatly involved with composing for the operatic stage and for church services. Changing circumstances account for some shifting. The ban on most church music of an elaborate kind under Joseph II during the 1780s meant a diminishing of his efforts in sacred music. The death of Prince Nicholas I in 1790 put a stop to his operatic labors for the Esterházys. If *Orfeo* had reached performance in London and won success, his operatic career might have continued. Even without operatic works Haydn continued to write a lot of vocal music, for instance, the occasional *scena* for a special occasion or a particular singer, many songs, and many delightful part-songs. After his return to Vienna, Haydn kept on writing part-songs and, as an arranger, folk song settings commissioned from abroad. Still, the overall impression left by the London works was that Haydn was primarily an instrumental composer. This was simply untrue in the light of his whole career. It was perhaps in reaction to the growing legend about him that Haydn related to Griesinger what appear to be his regrets on the subject. Coming close to the end of Griesinger's *Notizen*, the remark takes on all the more significance: "Haydn sometimes said that instead of many quartets, sonatas, and symphonies, he should have written more vocal music."

Griesinger's next remarks might have been expected to contradict the master by mentioning the greatness of the last masses and oratorios. Instead it takes the reader in a direction that surprises. "Not only might he have become one of the foremost opera composers, but also it is far easier to compose along the lines of a text than without one." Or is this Haydn still speaking? It was very unlike him to vaunt his own deeds or capabilities. As for difficulties, when was Haydn ever known to shun those or seek easy solutions?

The direction of the conversation as reported by Griesinger takes an even more surprising turn in what follows. The opera under consideration was not Italian, the language of almost all of Haydn's works for the theater, but German.

> He complained, moreover, that our German poets do not write musically enough, for a melody that suits the first stanza will seldom do for the following one. Often the sense fits in one line but not in that which should correspond to it. They are not careful in the choice of vowels. Haydn was only a little acquainted with the poets of the latest period, and he readily confessed that he could no longer find his way in their sequence of ideas and in their expression.

This suggests that Haydn might have considered writing opera for the German-language companies flourishing in Vienna after his return, if anyone had asked him to do so and if the poets could have provided language and metrics he considered appropriate for music. Schikaneder could have done so but, as far as is known, there was no move on his part to involve Haydn anew with music for the stage, nor from any other quarter.

Neukomm added an anecdote to Dies indicating that Haydn realized how great was his contribution to vocal music in his late works. The successful Singspiel composer Wenzel Müller, music director of the Marinelli troupe at the Leopoldstadt Theater, brought a foreign guest one day and introduced him to Haydn. The visitor praised Haydn's works excessively, "which the master bore with his usual modesty." When Müller interrupted saying "it must be true that Haydn in quartets is incomparable!" the venerable composer replied with a typically wry comment: "It is sad enough, my dear Müller, that otherwise I have learned nothing more." Neukomm concludes, "I heard this anecdote from Haydn's own mouth."

The three late oratorios may serve as pivotal works around which it is convenient to group the other works of the composer's last creative period. Table 6.1 lists them first, beginning with the *Seven Last Words*, here given Haydn's title for the oratorio version.

TABLE 6.1 Three groups within Haydn's last works

Oratorios	Masses	Other
Die Sieben letzten Worte (1795–96)	Sancti Bernardi (1796)	Trumpet Concerto (1796)
	In tempore belli (1796)	Emperor's Hymn (1797)
Die Schöpfung (The Creation)	In angustiis ("Nelson")	String Quartets Op. 76
(1796–98)	(1798)	(1796–97)
	"Theresien" (1799)	String Quartets Op. 77 (1799)
Die Jahreszeiten (The Seasons)	"Schöpfung" (1801)	Te Deum (1800)
(1799–1801)	"Harmonie" (1802)	String Quartet in d (Op. 103) (begun 1803)

Neukomm speaks of Haydn's "last and glorious" period in connection with the masses and mentions their connection with the name day celebrations of Princess Marie Hermenegild Esterházy. All except the Missa "In tempore belli" were composed expressly for this purpose, and it too was used in connection with the event, which took place annually on or near St. Mary's Day (8 September) at Eisenstadt.

Missa Sancti Bernardi de Offida ("Heiligmesse")

Haydn completed two masses in 1796, this one and the Missa "In tempore belli." Arguments have been advanced at various times as to which came first, with general scholarly opinion inclining toward the former. The Saint Bernard in question was an Italian Capuchin monk who lived from 1604 to 1694 and devoted his life to caring for the poor in or near his native town of Offida, in the March of Ancona. The long process leading to his being proclaimed a saint was reaching culmination in 1795 when he was beatified by Pope Pius VI. Perhaps Haydn learned of the saint because he lived near the Capuchin Monastery in the Neue Markt, where he may also have participated in some devotions. It is assumed that he composed the mass in Vienna during the summer of 1796 and took it with him to Eisenstadt, where it was performed as a name day celebration for his Princess on 11 September in the Bergkirche. The musical forces necessary may have been partly recruited for the occasion, likely from the theatrical troupe of Johann Karl Stadler, recently hired by the Prince.

The mass is in B♭ and requires a complement of strings, oboes, clarinets (used sparingly), bassoons, and organ, plus two trumpets and timpani. The trumpets in B♭ help give the work its opulent sheen and festive character. A few years later Haydn added horns and gave an expanded role to the clarinets. Breitkopf and Härtel published an edition of the original version in 1802 that was greeted by an enthusiastic and informed review written by Friedrich Rochlitz: "the trumpet and drums (not used sparingly to be exact) are, because of their low pitch, of the greatest strength, dignity, and gravity."

As in the *Missa Cellensis* of 1782, the Kyrie begins with a slow introduction, *Adagio* in 3/4 time in both, ending on V and followed by a sonata form in 3/4 time, an *Allegro moderato* in the latter case. This *Adagio* occupies twelve measures and moves in stately chordal fashion, the harmonies enriched almost from the beginning by two non-diatonic tones, A♭ and G♭, both of which will become important (Example 6.1, mm. 1–6). Accompanying strings emphasize the dissonant chord

EXAMPLE 6.1. *Haydn,* Missa Sancti Bernardi de Offida, *Kyrie, beginning and ending*

in m. 5 with a *sforzato*. The slow trochees of the *Adagio* become faster in the *Allegro moderato*, which begins 3 2 | 1, a melodic progression already present in the tenor in mm. 4–6. The fast theme is so simple it sounds folklike, constituting a perfectly symmetrical eight-measure phrase (2 + 2 + 2 + 2). The initial chordal section gives way to a fugato with the voices entering from low to high, the main feature of the theme being a flat seventh, A♭, descending to G, clearly set up by the altos' A♭ - G in m. 3 of the introduction. Another chordal section follows the fugato and takes the music to an arrival in the dominant, its most salient moment being the rise of the sopranos up to A♭ resolving to G then F, transformed into A♮ G F (i.e., like the descending conjunct third that begins the fast theme). The fugal subject returns, and receives a little tonal confirmation by the orchestra alone, and then it is on to the Christe eleison, marking the division between the prima and seconda parti. The chorus begins softly but becomes *forte* as a modulatory section begins, in the middle of which "Christe" is replaced by "Kyrie." When tonic B♭ returns, so does the soft first theme. The fugato as such is absent except for its head motif. On the climactic drive to a tonic cadence, the bass descends in measure-long tones A♭, G, G♭, F, the last two chords being an augmented sixth giving way to I⁶₄. In the final measures, the sopranos again climb up to high A♭ and descend while the altos sing the head motif of the fugato (Example 6.1, mm. 150–57). The sopranos also invoke G♭ - F, as do the tenors, twice, the second time prolonging G♭ for an entire measure before sinking into the final chord of B♭. The lesson here is clear: pay attention to every detail of slow introductions.

Haydn did not have to search far for a good beginning to the Gloria. He used the same rhythmic-melodic motive for the first four words as in his mass of fourteen years earlier (Example 6.2ab). Others may well have used it before him, for

EXAMPLE 6.2 a, b.

a. *Haydn, Second* Missa Cellensis (1782), *Gloria*

Soprano: Glo - ri - a in ex - cel - sis De - o, glo - ri-a, glo - ri - a in ex - cel - sis De - o.

b. *Haydn,* Missa Sancti Bernardi (1796), *Gloria*

Soprano: Glo-ri-a in ex-cel-sis De - o, glo-ri-a in ex-cel-sis, glo-ri-a in ex-cel - sis, in ex-cel - sis De - o

it deftly sets "excelsis" higher than "gloria," and "Deo" higher still and longer. As in other cases where he used an earlier incipit as a springboard, the continuation, while similar, begins diverging into a quite different piece.

A melodic sketch survives for the Gloria, Credo, and Benedictus of the St. Bernard Mass. The high B♭ in m. 7 of Example 6.2b stands alone in the sketch while in the score Haydn gave an option of taking the tone an octave lower. The higher tone, which makes the most sense musically, was clearly the composer's preference, yet he bowed to practical considerations and allowed that a leap up to it at the beginning of the Gloria might strain some of his sopranos, hence the choice offered of the lower tone. Later, and especially in the final moments, with the chorus fully warmed up, he does not spare the sopranos a leap up to high B♭, which sounds all the more satisfying if it is an aural revisit to the movement's beginning.

The Gloria is divided into three parts, with *Vivace* in common time movements for the outer parts and a more subdued movement for "Gratias agimus tibi" in the middle, an *Allegretto* in 3/4 time that begins in g minor and moves to E♭ before "Qui tollis peccata mundi" and back to g minor for its final section on this text. "Qui tollis" often brings a slowing down, but here Haydn marks it *"Più Allegro."* Perhaps he was worried that the considerable length of this triple-metered middle part was taking too much time or it was in danger of losing momentum (recall his complaint about a London orchestra becoming "sleepy"). Rochlitz found the request for more liveliness "very strange," and then offered good reason why in this case it was deemed necessary: "The same flowing motion might prove too long for the listener." Soloists appear rarely in this mass, one of the places being at the start of the "Gratias." By inference, it appears that the soloists were not specially hired but were drawn from the chorus. They do not appear at the end of the Gloria, after the double fugue on "In gloria Dei Patris" and its countersubject "Amen, amen."

The Credo begins, *Allegro* in common time, with an exultant descent through the tonic triad, chorus and orchestra in unison, thus inverting the Gloria's initial climb up the same chord. This descending figure will recur in the orchestra at the end of the first section, appropriately, to illustrate the words "descendit de coelis." There is an odd circumstance about the section that follows, an *Adagio* in E♭ and in 3/4 time for "Et incarnatus est." It is a canon for three soloists, two sopranos and an alto, a piece that is also used in one of the composer's secular canons with the text "Gott im Herzen, ein gut Weibchen in Arm, jenes macht selig, dieses g'wiss warm" (God in the heart, a good little wife in one's arms—the one makes holy, the other quite warm). The secular canon's date cannot be ascertained, yet it appears to be earlier since Haydn copied this text into his first London Notebook (1791–92). For the Crucifixus, sung by two solo tenors and bass, the music becomes chordal and passes into tonic minor. Haydn does not change the key signature to five flats, perhaps to avoid alarming his singers unduly. The chorus sings "Passus et sepultus est" to a chromatic progression and alternates with the three solo men singing "Crucifixus." All sections are based on the melody first introduced as a canon. In its soft, homophonic final statement by the chorus in E♭ major, the music takes on the character of a lullaby.

"Et resurrexit," usually set in the major mode following the minor-mode ending of the previous section, here elicits c minor following the cadence of the last "sepultus est" in E♭ major. The new section continues in 3/4 time, but *Allegro*. It passes into g minor and comes to a halt on its dominant, D (V/vi). Haydn's plan then becomes clear when he springs from this chord to an outburst of tonic B♭ for "judicare vivos et mortuos," which he often prefers to emphasize in these late mass settings. He withholds his trumpets for the bigger climax yet to come at the end of the Credo. The text is rapidly dispatched following "et exspecto resurrectionem mortuorum," where there is another protracted V/vi chord. "Et vitam venturi saeculi, amen" brings another return to tonic B♭, now *Vivace assai* and cast as a double fugue. Soloists are lacking here too, as at the end of the Gloria. What does reappear in the climactic drive to end the Credo fugue is a climb of the sopranos up to high A♭ (cf. the end of the Kyrie in Example 6.1), which is prolonged for a measure with a fermata, over a timpani roll on B♭. Resolution brings the sopranos down to G, and by step down to B♭, followed by the final cadences.

The Sanctus, which begins by repeating the first word for four measures of *Adagio* in common time, offers a clue to the work's possible gestation. There is a familiar melody lurking in the parallel thirds between the alto and tenor parts (Example 6.3). It corresponds to an old vernacular Sanctus melody that was current

EXAMPLE 6.3. *Haydn,* Missa Sancti Bernardi, *Sanctus*

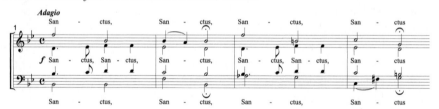

in Austrian and South German churches, "Heilig, heilig, heilig. Heilig über heilig."[8] Perhaps congregations sang the simple melody in thirds. In any case Haydn's work became known very early on as the "Heiligmesse." Appearance of the old hymn tune in Haydn's Sanctus called attention to itself at once by the different rhythm with which the middle voices are set. On textual restatement the familiar melody repeats almost exactly. The music moves in a forward direction by modulating, which entailed Haydn's using two non-diatonic tones, A♭ and F♯ (alias G♭). The beginning and ending of the Kyrie used these same two tones, and besides that, the Kyrie begins with the altos and tenors in parallel thirds singing a melody akin to the traditional "Heilig," over which the sopranos are confined mainly to the

[8] Landon, *Haydn,* 4:151–52.

single tone of B♭, as if chanting. Haydn ended the choral part of the Sanctus with only four more measures, a consequent phrase in answer to the antecedent quoted in the example. Perhaps the perfect symmetry seemed too foursquare to him in the context of the whole. He added another two measures for orchestra that moved the harmony back to V/ii, where it had been in m. 4, and sounded the "Heilig" tune in the first violins, like an echo or a commentary. He resolved V/ii to ii for the onset of "Pleni sunt coeli et terra," an *Allegro* in 3/4 time. It too is short, only eight measures for chorus plus two for orchestra (which sounds the descending tonic triad from the Credo), then chorus and orchestra launch into a longer imitative section for "Osanna in excelsis," and it too is quickly over at this *Allegro* pace.

Benedictus makes up for the brevity of the Sanctus with a leisurely processional type of movement, a *Moderato* in 2/4 time and in E♭. To reach the climactic cadential arrival of tonic E♭ for good took some one hundred measures. The music of "Osanna" heard before usually recurs at this point, but here only the text, as required by the liturgy, comes back, draped over a few cadences in E♭ to finish the Benedictus.

Agnus Dei begins in tonic minor, *Adagio* in 3/4 time, and continues for a long stretch in this key, far on the flat side of the tonal spectrum. Haydn scored the initial sections for chorus, strings, and organ only, for which Rochlitz in 1801 offered this explanation.

> This Agnus Dei is again an uncommonly beautiful movement. It dispenses with all ornaments and is scored only for the four vocal parts and the usual strings. This is good, because it is placed between sections which are rich in wind instruments; moreover, it takes into consideration the difficulty of wind players to perform in correct intonation when in B♭ minor, in which key the movement is placed. The very key itself, so remote, from which the composer does not stray far, only to D♭ major and E♭ minor, assists in giving the whole something solemn and deeply felt.[9]

The specific progression mentioned is a rising sequence for the "Agnus Dei . . . miserere nobis," from b♭, to D♭, to e♭, making each imploration sound more intense, so that after the last, when the text changes from "miserere nobis" to "Dona nobis pacem," we are ready for, and demanding of, relief. Haydn provides it with a joyous outburst of B♭ major, *Allegro*, for the entire chorus and orchestra, not omitting the trumpets and timpani. It sounds not like another request but an answer, a request granted, a positive response to all the pleas heard throughout the entire work. Such jubilation should convince anyone that Haydn believed in an all-forgiving, peace-granting Deity. There are quieter moments and questionings of the ultimate tonal goal along the way as this sonata form unfolds, but they only

[9] Landon, *Haydn*, 4:161.

allow Haydn to reach that goal with more finality than ever. Some of the questioning comes in the form of nondiatonic tones in need of resolution, such as the G♭ to F (here F♯ to F♮) and A♭ to G, motions that hark back to the very first phrase of the Kyrie. The stunning and beautiful unity of the whole would be characteristic of all six of these late masses by Haydn. His advanced age notwithstanding, he remained an amazingly youthful and fiery creative spirit.

Missa in Tempore Belli

The year 1796 saw clashing armies surge back and forth across southern Germany. More ominous still for Austria were the French successes in Italy, where Napoleon Bonaparte emerged as a leader of the French armies and rapidly gained fame equal to that of other generals. He was a young artillery officer who came to prominence in 1793, aged 23, for his part in the reconquest of Toulon from the British. In 1795 he became commander-in-chief of the Republic's Army of Italy. By April 1796 he had conquered Piedmont, the proud Kingdom of Sardinia ruled from Turin, and forced it to sue for peace. A deeper disappointment for Vienna was his subsequent conquest of Austrian Lombardy, which soon followed his forcing his way across the bridge over the Adda River at Lodi on 10 May 1796. His victory at Lodi was celebrated in a sweeping battle picture by one of the participants, Louis-Albert Bacler d'Albe.[10] Five days after the defeat of the Austrians at Lodi, Napoleon entered Milan in triumph. Among the Milanese who fled to Vienna at this time was Haydn's biographer Giuseppe Carpani. Pope Pius VI tried but failed to rally support from the Dukes of Parma, Modena, and Tuscany; his desperate appeal to Vienna for the safety of the Italian principalities, including, of course, his own Papal States, evoked little sympathy.[11] Austria's high command staked all on holding the fortress of Mantua in order to stem the sweep of Napoleon's army across Italy. Repeated attempts to relieve Mantua came to an end at the battle of Rivoli Veronese on the Adige, just north of Verona, fought on 14 January 1797. Napoleon's victory cleared the way for advancing into Austria proper, which happened with incursions into Styria.

Haydn's "Mass in Time of War" possibly saw its first performance in Vienna near the time of Austria's defeat at Rivoli. On St. Stephen's day, 26 December 1796, a performance of a mass by Haydn took place in the church of the Piarists in the Josephstadt. It was described as a war Mass (Kriegsmesse) and celebrated

[10] Reproduced on the dust jacket of this book. It is discussed in *Poussin, Watteau, Chardin, David: Peintures françaises dans les collections allemandes, XVIIe-XVIIIe siècles*, ed. Pierre Rosenberg and David Mandrella. Exhibition Catalogue, Paris, Munich, Bonn, 2005; pp. 342–43.

[11] Alan J. Reinerman, "The Papacy, Austria, and the Anti-French Struggle in Italy, 1792–97," in *Austria in the Age of the French Revolution*, ed. Kinley Brauer and William E. Wright (Minneapolis, 1990), pp. 47–68. Austrian diplomats excoriated the meager efforts of the papacy and other Italian states to defend themselves.

the ordination of Joseph Hoffmann, son of a government official who was head of the financial department of the War Ministry. An undated letter from Haydn to a financial officer of Prince Nicholas confirms that Haydn was busy composing a new mass about this time. In the letter Haydn says that he has been in Esterházy service for thirty-six years, which would place the letter in 1797. Possibly the "new mass" in the Piaristenkirche on 26 December 1796 was actually an older mass. One of the striking things about the new Mass in C was its prominent use of solo sections, especially those for the bass and soprano soloists. These soloists would necessarily have been imported for a performance in the Piarist's Church. From various sources it has been deduced that money was not a consideration in hiring talent and making the performance a festive event.

The Mass in C is scored for pairs of oboes, bassoons, and trumpets that alternate with horns, as well as timpani, organ, and the usual strings. A slow introduction of ten measures, *Largo* in common time, moves to a *forte* chord on IV_3^6 after softer statements of tonic and dominant. The descent of the basses, C B♭ A, then continues down to A♭ supporting a iv_3^6 chord that soon turns into an augmented-sixth chord resolving i_4^6 - V - i - V, with a little wavering motion in the upper voices, resolved with the beginning of the *Allegro moderato* in common time.

The solo soprano sings the main theme, a pleasant melody and a rather frilly, galant one. At the solo's cadence the chorus enters, repeating the second half of the phrase in a manner that might remind some listeners of the choral encouragements given to soprano soloists in Italian opera. After modulation to the dominant is assured, the solo alto enters singing the main theme beginning the seconda parte, which quickly becomes modulatory. The only use of the words "Christe eleison" occurs here, and the two words are repeated only once, just before the reprise, which is given to the solo soprano. The material is collapsed and has little interjections by all four soloists, after which the chorus concludes, with the sopranos up to high A. It is all very light-hearted, particularly when compared to the mass just discussed. The text setting suggests it was the soprano's flowery solo, that is, the main theme, that first occurred to the composer.

C major was long the favorite key for festive masses with the Austrian-Bohemian school. There is little else that is traditional in this mass setting. To begin the Gloria, Haydn reverts to an idea related to the rise up the tonic triad to G in his Mass in C of 1782 (see Example 6.2), but with the differences that here the meter is triple and that on the way up the tonic triad there is a raised fourth, F♯, which could be compared to the strongly accented raised fourth in the rising triad that begins Symphony No. 83 in g ("La Poule"). Haydn neutralizes this foreign tone by substituting F♮ in the consequent part of the phrase. The chorus sings in unisons and octaves except for its harmonizations of the word "Deo," which is a simple and effective way of making it stand out above the others.

The Gloria has a strong sense of unity, aided by the recurrence of an orchestral ritornello of four measures. It first occurs close to the beginning, between the last "bonae voluntatis" and the first "Laudamus te." After the modulation to the dominant it occurs in G before "Domine Deus," a section that quickly turns modulatory. When it next sounds, the ritornello coincides with the return of C major and the imminent end of the section. From the final tonic chord the only link with what comes next is the third E, which becomes an upbeat as the fifth introducing the key of A major. Selection of a key a major third below the overall tonic is a move that Haydn made a specialty of in the 1790s. This instance begins with a lovely solo for cello carrying the melody of an *Adagio* in cut time. The bass solo enters, singing "Qui tollis peccata mundi" to the cello's theme, while the cello offers little commentaries on the voice part, an exchange that develops into a regular concertante dialogue between equals, the kind of texture one might expect from an operatic love duet. Most settings of this text are dark and foreboding, but not this one, even when the chorus comes in chanting "miserere nobis" and becomes a third party to the conversation between bass and cello. The pleasant and leisurely tone persists until the bass darkens the color by singing the main theme in the key of a minor. The movement dies away on a final unison A. By a leap up a third, the music returns to C major, *Allegro* in 3/4 time, as the chorus sings "Quoniam tu solus." The orchestral ritornello also returns. To liven the proceedings further Haydn indicates *più stretto*. There is no fugato for this final section, although there is choral polyphony and a musical stretto based on the descending conjunct fourth motif that begins the ritornello. For the final repetitions of "amen," the customary reentry of the soloists is restricted to a brief solo by the soprano.

The Credo begins with a fugato, perhaps the deciding factor in omitting one at the end of the Gloria. The subject is a strongly profiled descending figure, 8 5 6 4 3 2 5 1, that will come into its true significance when it is used to paint "descendit de coelis" ending the first section, which gets through the long text in an economical thirty-three measures. "Et incarnatus est" features the soloists. They sing an *Adagio* in 3/4 time and in c minor, to which the strings provide an introduction that sounds like what might precede a dramatic obbligato recitative in an opera. The solo bass enters with the same rise up the minor scale from the tonic. Over a dominant pedal the soprano sings "ex Maria Virgine." The winds are prominent, consisting at this point of oboes, clarinets in B♭, bassoons, and horns in C alto. They provide the main accompanying chords as the tenor sings "et homo factus est," followed by the alto. Haydn exploits the coloristic possibilities of clarinets in ways he had scarcely done before, apparently satisfied at last that the instruments were in the hands of good players. The ethereal texture of the soprano's descending line at "et homo factus est" owes some of its uncanny effect to the clarinets and some to the unusual harmonic choices, especially the augmented chord in m. 54 (Example 6.4). The predicted cadence on E♭ is undercut by

EXAMPLE 6.4. *Haydn,* Missa in Tempore Belli, *Credo*

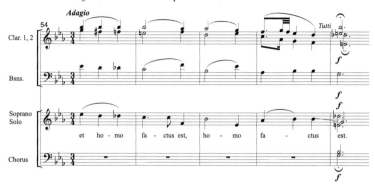

a tutti *forte* diminished chord starting the next text repetition. After another tutti *forte* interruption by a seventh chord on D comes resolution to E♭ for "Crucifixus." Haydn returns to c minor for "passus et sepultus est." One last *forte* interruption brings the chord of D♭, the Neapolitan, which becomes a descending chromatic bass on the way to resolution in a protracted chord of c minor, *pianissimo.*

An orchestral sunburst, *Allegro* and *forte,* with the rising scale of C major in the strings, is joined at the top by the chorus singing "Et resurrexit." This is one of Haydn's passages from darkness to light that foreshadows his grand gesture of the kind in *The Creation,* which was already beginning to take shape in his mind during 1796. The text rushes by quickly after this beginning, with no particular attention paid to "judicare vivos et mortuos," as it is in other late mass settings. *Allegro* becomes *Vivace* in cut time for the fugue at "Et vitam venturi," a rare case of strict rather than tonal answer being used as the choral voices enter from high to low. The soloists make their wonted appearances for two sections of "amen," and the chorus then concludes, descending in unison through the tonic triad with a majestic final gesture.

An *Adagio* in common time and in C major is allotted to the Sanctus, the strings announcing a soft initial phrase continued by the solo alto. The chorus then enters *forte,* the basses first, singing the same descent down the tonic triad that ended the Credo. Since the entire Sanctus takes only thirteen measures and ends on V, it sounds like a slow introduction to the outburst of C major resolution for "Pleni sunt coeli," at which trumpets and timpani return. The solo tenor begins singing "Osanna," continued by the chorus using the same theme.

Benedictus commences in c minor as a rather tuneful *Andante* in 6/8 time that ambles along, taking its time, with intrusions that hint at darker happenings ahead. From the long orchestral prelude, the impression arises that whoever is coming ("qui venit") is in no hurry. The soloists come in singing the same music in c minor, then in E♭, where ample cadences are made, followed by the soprano commencing the main theme yet again in E♭ to begin the seconda parte. A return to c minor is prepared. There arrives instead the main theme in C major, a lovely turn of events. "Osanna" is added as a coda, sounding like the music of its previous setting but in fact new.

Agnus Dei begins calmly as an *Adagio* in 3/4 time and in F major, sung by the chorus to a rhythmic pattern of trochees alternating with iambs, often used to set these first two words. The harmonic progression is rich and appropriate, beginning I –V^7 | vi - | ii - V^7/ii | ii - | and ending with IV - | I$^6_4$ V | I$^6_4$ V - |. At this second half-cadence, with the harmony perched on the dominant, something unusual sounds: the timpani on C, alone at first, with a rhythm of thirty-second notes as upbeat to the downbeat. The pattern is maintained over several measures as the strings enter softly, the bass rising by step. Then the chorus enters singing "miserere nobis" with the same progression continuing over the dominant pedal. A gradual buildup of chorus and orchestra suddenly becomes a *crescendo* to *forte* as the inexorable timpani beat switches from C to G.

From a faint rumbling in the background, the timpani has come to suggest the menace of an enemy army on the march and fast approaching. This is no flight of interpretive fancy. Haydn told Griesinger that the passage was to be performed to create an illusion "as though one heard the enemy coming already in the distance." These are the drums of war and the precise reason why Haydn called his work "Mass in Time of War." The cadence brings the timpani and all the rest from G back to c minor, in which the chorus recommences singing "Agnus Dei." The harmony comes to rest on V/V in c minor, and the winds, dominated by the trumpets, seize on D and keep repeating it until the violins and chorus come around to making a cadence in d minor. Here the chorus begins singing "Agnus Dei" again, then modulates to a pedal G, as the timpani softly returns with its pattern of rapid upbeats to downbeats, now on G. At this point the chorus replaces "miserere nobis" with "dona nobis pacem," sung tentatively, one word at a time separated by rests, as if posing the question "is peace possible?"

The answer comes with a fanfare in C major for timpani, trumpets, and other winds, *Allegro con spirito*, to which the chorus enters singing a prolonged G on "Dona." It resolves to C for the arrival of an even longer "pacem," making it sound like "PACEM!" Haydn leaves no doubt that the pleas have already been answered by the Deity. The rest is primarily cadence-driven, although there is a tonal excursus away so that we can come back to C. After another feint away from the tonic, the return is even more solid and satisfying. The last "pacem" has the sopranos singing not 5 1, but 5 3.

Haydn presumably had an expert player on timpani for so daring and novel a passage as this. It has been argued that it was Ignaz Manker, later the timpanist of the Theater an der Wien and a cellist in the Esterházy orchestra.[12]

---

[12] Theodore Albrecht, "The Musicians in Balthazar Wigand's Depiction of the Performance of Haydn's *Die Schöpfung*, Vienna, 27 March 1808," *Music in Art* 19 (2004): 123–31; 129.

The Trumpet Concerto

About the same time that Haydn made a stunning advance in orchestration with the timpani part of his Mass in C, he was endowing another solo instrument with a concerto that represents a feat just as daring. His Trumpet Concerto in E♭ for Anton Weidinger featured a keyed trumpet that could play an entire chromatic scale, an instrument then in the process of being invented. Weidinger, a trumpet player in the imperial court orchestra, was a friend of the composer and apparently a close one, for Haydn served as witness to the marriage of Weidinger's daughter in early 1797. The concerto, dated 1796 on the autograph, may be linked with the wedding celebration. It survives only by way of the autograph, which slumbered unedited and forgotten for several generations until a score was published in 1931. After this, thanks to early recordings, the work soared to wide acclaim and became the composer's most popular concerto.

Weidinger had been working to perfect a keyed trumpet since 1793, or so he claimed in the announcement of the musical academy he gave in the Burgtheater on 28 March 1800, four days before Beethoven's first benefit concert there. He promised to present to the world for the first time "an organized trumpet he had invented and brought to perfection after seven years of hard and expensive labor; it will be displayed in a concerto especially written for this instrument by Doctor of Music Joseph Haydn." The program also included two symphonies by Haydn and other works especially written for Weidinger and his chromatic trumpet by Ferdinand Kauer and Süssmayer. Perhaps he was waiting until these pieces were ready before displaying his invention. Or it could have been the daunting nature of Haydn's concerto for him that made Weidinger delay so long before presenting it in public. He may have been working all the while on being able to do it justice by perfecting the new instrument as well as his playing technique.

The sound of the new instrument apparently still left something to be desired in 1800. A critic wrote of the concert that "through using the keys, the trumpet tone loses something of its characteristic and prominent strength, and approaches the tone of a strong oboe." The tones of the modern valve trumpets that have been heard by this listener on modern recordings are so coarse as to suggest that sounding more like an oboe might be an improvement.

Haydn scored the work for large orchestra including horns, ripieno trumpets, and timpani. The resulting amplitude in sonority helps explain why it caught on with listeners used to the full scoring of Mozart's largest concertos and those of Beethoven. The work profits from Haydn's expansion of his orchestral palette in the London symphonies and especially in the *Concertante* in B♭ of 1791 for London, which agrees with the Trumpet Concerto in overall form and style. Both consist of three movements: *Allegro, Andante, Allegro*. In both, the *Andante* is a movement in 6/8 time of a simple, song-like nature, while the first *Allegro* is in a forthright common time with no preliminary upbeat; and the finales are scintillating examples of the sonata rondo type of movement, both in 2/4 time. The emphasis is on virtuoso display of the soloist, or soloists in the case of the *Concertante*. Neither is the place to look for the intricacies of expression and depths of feeling that emerged in the late choral works or the string quartets of Opus 76. Just as the *Concertante* is best appreciated if not heard too often, so the same can be said of the Trumpet Concerto. It is enough to celebrate this work as opening up new coloristic possibilities for an instrument long relegated mostly to mere supporting roles. That Haydn ventured to write the *Andante* of this concerto in A♭ major, calling extensively on the solo instrument's newly possible chromatic tones, was an exciting breakthrough at the time. A few years later the work inspired a successor in Hummel's Trumpet Concerto in E, also for Weidinger, which became even more popular for a few years, partly because it quoted tunes that were then well known.[13]

String Quartets, Opus 76

Our main source of information about the genesis of these six quartets is the Swedish diplomat Frederik Silverstolpe, who was chargé d'affaires at the Swedish embassy in Vienna. He arrived in May 1796 and first met Haydn on 1 April 1797 at a performance of Handel's masque, *Acis and Galatea*, as an oratorio in Prince Schwarzenberg's palace. In May, Haydn moved into town in order to be near Swieten as they were working together on *The Creation*. Silverstolpe wrote in his dispatch to Stockholm on 14 June 1797 as follows:

> A few days ago I went to see Haydn again, who now lives right next to me since he gave up his customary winter and spring lodgings in one of the suburbs and moved a whole quarter-of-a-mile away. On this occasion he played to me, on the piano, violin quartets which a certain Count Erdödy had ordered from him and which may be printed only after a number of years. These are more than masterly and full of new thoughts. While he played he let me sit beside him and see how he divided the various parts in the score.[14]

If Haydn finished the quartets in the first half of 1797 he probably began them in 1796. The period of private use by Count Johann Erdödy must have been two years, for the *editio princeps* did not begin to appear until 1799 and was sold to Longman and Clementi in London for publication. Another edition, dedicated to Erdödy, was printed by Artaria almost simultaneously (Figure 6.2). The arrange-

---

[13] John A. Rice, "The Musical Bee: References to Mozart and Cherubini in Hummel's 'New Year' Concerto," *Music and Letters* 77 (1996): 401–24.

[14] Carl-Gabriel Stellan Mörner, *Johan Wikmanson und die Brüder Silverstolpe: Einige Stockholmer Persönlichkeiten im Musikleben des Gustavianischen Zeitalters* (Stockholm, 1952), p. 318.

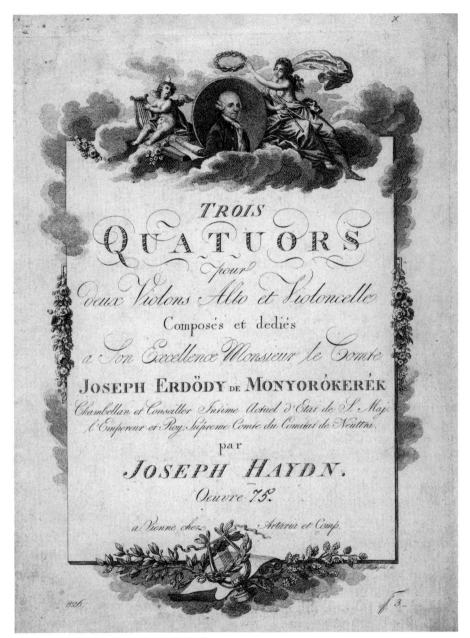

FIGURE 6.2. Title page of the Erdödy Quartets, Op. 76, published by Artaria.

ment with the dedicatee did not preclude Haydn's personal use of the quartets. In the fall of 1797 music from them was heard at a social reception in Eisenstadt castle, as reported by the diarist Joseph Carl Rosenbaum, an official in Esterházy service. Under the date 27 September 1797 he wrote, "New quartets by

Haydn were played, [of which one was] based on the hymn 'Gott erhalte Franz den Kaiser.' "[15]

Quartet No. 1 in G opens with three *forte* chords separated by rests, requiring double-stops on the violins and viola. The chords are I - V[7] – I, with conjunct rise of the top line 1 2 3. This kind of loud "curtain" figured often in the previous set, Opp. 71–74, written in Vienna in 1793, with the obvious intention to silence chatter and capture attention in the concert halls of London. The continuation is in the same tempo and meter, *Allegro con spirito* in cut time. The cello announces a four-measure phrase, as if beginning a fugue or fugato. In fact, it is the antecedent half of a theme, the consequent of which is appended by the viola. Then the second violin takes a turn at the antecedent, accompanied by the cello, followed by the first violin's consequent to the viola's accompaniment. A continuation over a tonic pedal further confirms the key and leads up to the transition. Arrival at the new key of D coincides with a new idea, a descending conjunct stream of eighth notes, legato, that soon turns staccato in the first violin. After a few tonal wanderings, D is restored and confirmed by a lyric closing theme, another eight-measure symmetrical construction. After the repeat of the prima parte the viola restates the main idea in D. It sounds quite different because of its countersubject, which is nothing other than the descending eighth notes from the second theme, indeed, the same tones played there by the viola an octave lower. Such motivic intricacy goes by so quickly there is hardly time to savor the finesse of its invention. The staccato eighth notes also come into play as the music moves from place to place, as if searching for the right landing. It is soon found after a dominant pedal culminating in a V^9_7 chord. The reprise features canons at close range, as could have been predicted from the nature of the triadic theme itself. The continuation over a tonic pedal is in place along with all the rest, except that the second theme is shorn of its two initial measures with the falling conjunct eighth notes, perhaps because they saw use at the beginning of the reprise. Like the prima parte, the seconda parte is repeated. There is a reminder of the "curtain" in the first violin's final melodic gesture 1 2 3, to which is added 5 3.

The *Adagio sostenuto* in C major and in 2/4 time has the broad, hymn-like character often found in the truly slow movements of the late works. After a varied repetition of the theme, the middle voices provide an even-pulsed accompaniment in sixteenth notes as the cello takes the lead with an idea in the same rhythm, answered by the first violin climbing the scale with a flutter of thirty-second notes (Example 6.5). The *Andante cantabile* of Mozart's last symphony, K. 551 ("Jupiter"), has a very similar moment that also comes directly after the main theme. It cannot be coincidence that Haydn, in the slow movement of his Symphony No. 98,

[15] Rosenbaum, Joseph Carl, *The Diaries of Joseph Carl Rosenbaum, 1770–1829*, ed. Else Radant, *Haydn Yearbook* 5 (1968): 25–26.

EXAMPLE 6.5. *Haydn, String Quartet in G, Op. 76 No. 1, II*

seemed to muse on the second theme of the same *Andante cantabile* by Mozart. Haydn may have been unaware how that movement lurked at some level of his consciousness, yet the impression remains that he was somehow haunted by its beauty. There is still more in this *Adagio* that resemble features in Mozart's *Andante*, namely the chains of tiny, thirty-second-note offbeats for the first violin on the way to the first big cadence in the dominant. There is no repetition sign here, and the movement as a whole is more like a rondo than a sonata form.

The *Menuet Presto* owes nothing to Mozart. It is terse and robust, and if Haydn truly intended it to be *Presto*, it must have flown by like a real scherzo. The Trio, surely meant to be taken at a more relaxed tempo, is like a Ländler, with an acrobatic and mainly triadic tune for the first violin against the pizzicato accompaniment of the others. Except for its great compass, the tune sounds like an entry in a yodeling contest.

The surprise of the *Finale Allegro ma non troppo* in cut time is its key, g minor. It too is vigorous and begins by mimicking one particular descending triad in the Trio. The theme is stated at first in unison, then by the viola with the two violins accompanying, with slightly parodistic resemblance of their falling minor-second melodic sighs to the repeated and exaggerated melodic sighs with trills that end the theme. The movement is a regular sonata form, with repeat of the prima parte, and returns to g minor after a dynamic development. Only then does g minor yield to G major. For a coda the music turns still lighter and more dance-like, the theme in the first violin transformed into a closing gesture against the return of the pizzicato accompaniment heard in the Trio. At the end, the first violin plays the 1 2 3 motif in various guises, reminding us how this quartet began.

Aside from the Trio, there had been few lighter moments in the quartet before the finale, compared, for example, to the many such moments in the Opus 33 quartets, and notably in the dominating Quartet in G from that path-breaking set. When the end of the new Quartet in G for Erdödy brought with it such a light touch, it may have reminded some dedicated string quartet players and listeners of that earlier tour de force in G major. The Erdödy family was large and musically inclined. Count Ladislaus Erdödy, head of the elder, Pressburg branch, was a long-time patron of Haydn, to whom he had sent Ignaz Pleyel as a boy for years of study in the 1770s. Count Joseph headed a younger branch of the family and was presumably a fine string player. He would have had to be a fine violinist if he attempted the violino primo part of this quartet.

Quartet No. 2 in d minor is widely known as the "Quintenquartett" because of the successive descending fifths A↓D E↓A in half notes that begin the work. They provide a motif prominent throughout the quartet. Without a transition following the first theme and only twelve measures into the *Allegro* in common time, the music moves to the relative major, F, where the viola states the main idea against a rising figure in quicker notes for the first violin. The whole second theme area is developmental. Endemic to the four-tone motif itself, when used sequentially, is modulation. To begin the seconda parte, the cello, low in its range, inverts the motif to D↑A G↑D. Other devices are applied to it as well, including stretto and diminution, to the extent that it is almost omnipresent, and aurally perceptible no matter what dress the fifths put on. The movement is not long, and one welcomes the repetition of the seconda as well as the prima parte.

An *Andante o più tosto Allegretto* offers a lilting theme in 6/8 time and in D major is sung by the first violin to the pizzicato accompaniment of the other strings (first strain), repeated, then presented *coll'arco* after the double bar, alternating with pizzicato. The second strain of this rounded binary form is also repeated. Haydn makes a tease out of the return to the theme in the second strain by making us wait an extra measure for it. The first variation, not named as such, begins as if in the minor tonic, as expected, but this is another tease as he lops off the first tone of A↓F↓D and turns it into F↓D B♭. This becomes tonic for a while before it is displaced by rapid modulation, leading somehow back to D, whose arrival is preceded by another extra measure of teasing anticipation of the opening motif. Variation three restores the theme to D at first as a close replica of its original form, then decorated by nearly constant thirty-second-note passagework for the repeat of the first strain and for the rest of the theme. After this barrage of figural bravura for the first violin we await, somewhat resignedly, another variation, perhaps in the minor. Haydn spares us this and goes on to provide an ample coda. Even those with limited tolerance for long theme-and-variation movements could not fault this one for overstaying its welcome.

The *Menuet Allegretto* (to which *ma non troppo* was added in the first edition) restores d minor. Haydn opts here for a sure-fire standby from his vast arsenal, the two-part canon at the octave. The violins play in octaves at the top, the viola and cello in octaves below. The effect is strong and could also easily become tedious if Haydn had not kept it quite short. This kind of minuet in canon casts a glance back to the flurry of minor-mode works of ca. 1770, in particular the canonic minuet of Symphony No. 44 in e. The Trio, in D, seems to take a leaf from the finale of Symphony No. 70 in D, which also plays with the tonic as a single tone that can change into either d or D.

In the *Finale Vivace assai* in 2/4 time, a theme in binary form with repeats indicated by signs, which in earlier works often signaled a rondo to follow, is here the first theme of a large sonata form lacking repeats of both prima and seconda parte. The theme itself makes a point of emphasizing the interval of the fifth, first by climbing from D up to A, reached by way of a prominent raised fourth, lending an unmistakable exotic accent to the proceedings and reminding us that the Erdödys were indeed Hungarians. On the way to the second key of F major there is a pedal on C, with the cello booming out its lowest tone and the violin doing what sounds like a Hungarian country dance on high. When F finally does arrive, it is to a falling chain of thirds, comically prefiguring a more famous finale's "alle Menschen, alle Menschen, alle Menschen" in another chain of falling thirds. Equally comic and the quintessence of Haydn's wit is the way he caps this plunge with a leap upward and one of his favorite downward leaps of a seventh, this one exaggerated to the size of an octave and a seventh. After a relatively small section devoted to development, the reprise begins in d minor, which soon dissolves into another dominant pedal preparing a welcome reprise in D major, with all the subsequent material in proper order.

Quartet No. 3, the most renowned of the set, is known as the "Kaiser" or "Emperor" Quartet because it incorporates variations on the patriotic melody Haydn wrote in early 1797. The story of how this text and musical setting came about can be summarized quite briefly. The idea probably went back to Swieten, who asked a higher government official, Count Franz Joseph Saurau, to commission a poem and musical setting that would urge the populace to rally around their sovereign and boost lagging support for the seemingly endless war. Lorenz Haschke drafted four stanzas of a poem beginning "Gott! erhalte Franz den Kaiser, Unseren guten Kaiser Franz!" these two lines recurring at the end of each stanza. Haydn, asked to set them to music, quickly did so. The result was printed and distributed throughout the realm in time for the public celebrations of the Emperor's birthday on 12 February 1797. Zinzendorf attended the celebrations in the Burgtheater and was touched by the spectacle. Of the hymn he wrote, "The verses would be good, without Schelm und Bubenstreich, because they are simple. The music is very simple." He refers to lines in the third stanza that say "may every trick of scoundrel [Schelm] and scamp [Buben] be uncovered." The reference may be to the sedition laws and purges in Austria in the wake of the notorious Jacobin trials. Saurau himself was the leading denouncer of the "Jacobin conspiracy," and a proponent of continuing the war at any price.[16] Haydn chose the key of G for his hymn, which is also the standard key to which "God Save the

16 Wangermann, *From Joseph II to the Jacobin Trials*, pp. 188–90.

King" was and is sung. The Quartet is in C, providing a frame for the hymn as a slow second movement in G. Unlike "God Save the King," Haydn's hymn begins like a stately gavotte, which gives it a somewhat lighter or less ponderous gait (Example 6.6). The closing, a graceful descent through the octave from 8 to 1, has

EXAMPLE 6.6. *Haydn,* Kaiserhymne

many precedents in older tunes and in Haydn's own melodies, but the entity as a whole is new and original, well suited to its purpose: it is eminently singable by the public because of its restricted range and largely stepwise melodic motion.

Haydn began the first movement of the quartet with a short phrase of four measures that seems to be related to the hymn melody in some subtle way (Example 6.7). The first gesture in both melodies is to descend to the tonic, the smooth

EXAMPLE 6.7. *Haydn,String Quartet in C ("Kaiserquartett"), Op. 76 No. 3*

4 3 2 1 of the hymn having its equivalent in the *Allegro*'s 3 4 2 1. According to one ingenious theory, the tones G E F D C that begin the *Allegro* are an anagram for the first letters of "<u>G</u>ott <u>e</u>rhalte <u>F</u>ranz <u>d</u>en Kaiser (<u>C</u>aesar)."[17] This descent to the tonic lends initial solidity to both melodies. The *Allegro* melody goes on to be exuberantly nonvocal in stretching over nearly two octaves, with some staccato articulations, and with Haydn's trademark leap of a seventh down (mm. 3–4) exaggerated to an octave and a seventh, as in the previous quartet. Note that the melody ends the way it began with G E.

[17] László Somfai, "Learned Style in Two Late String Quartet Movements by Haydn," *Studia Musicologica* 28 (1986): 326–49; 328.

In fact, the motif G E permeates this four-measure theme and the movement as a whole. When other members of the quartet take up the theme's head motif, it is accompanied by a vigorous counterpoint in sixteenth notes, a rising scale in dotted rhythm. This becomes independent of the theme and turns into the tune of a wild rustic dance supported by the others harmonically, with the cello at the bottom on its low C. The texture remains full and very busy as these two features, main theme and sixteenth-note figures, suffice almost by themselves to satisfy all the functions of the prima parte, before the end of which there is an excursion to E♭ for a softer interlude based on the main theme. The seconda parte takes off in a new direction, with a pedal E in the cello supporting chords that predict an arrival in the key of a minor, undercut by a quick return to C major, which initiates a series of modulations that lead to E major. This tonality is made the biggest event of all, emphasized by the open fifths E B passed back and forth between cello and viola, supporting the even wilder dance of the two violins in the octaves above riffing on the sixteenth-note figure in dotted rhythm. Haydn continues this harmonic stasis on E major for an indecorous ten measures, from which he slips into a softer e minor and from there into the reprise. The critic just cited does not hesitate to suggest that this seeming inebriation with E is a symbol for "Erdödy," and hence for Hungary.

Haydn triumphs in the second movement by making his "very simple" hymn the inspiration for an equally simple and unadorned set of variations. He marks the movement *Poco adagio cantabile* and sets it in cut time, meaning it should move along and not dawdle, as it is sometimes played in an attempt to gain greater expressiveness. To underscore the special character and meaning of the tune, Haydn adopts an unusual strategy of simply passing it from instrument to instrument, unadorned and always the same. In succession violino primo, secondo, cello, and viola intone the melody, with repeats written out, the whole neither shortened nor lengthened. In other words, it is treated like a cantus firmus. Variation 1 consists from beginning to end of sixteenth-note figuration for the first violin accompanying the melody, sometimes below, more often above it. Variation 2 surrounds it with a slightly more elaborate counterpoint, which is worked out further in Variation 3. In the fourth and last variation, a rich four-part harmonic web emerges as the tune is once again assigned to the first violin. Five additional measures of tonic pedal conclude.

The *Menuet Allegro* is a quite ordinary specimen of its genre. Besides restoring C major, it reverts to Haydn's pet leaps down, which grow here from a sixth to a seventh, then to a ninth. The Trio is in a minor, except for the *pianissimo* part in the middle, which is in A major. The *Finale Presto*, in common time, begins in c minor, which is hardly a surprise since the first two quartets of the set have finales that begin in tonic minor. Its theme, like that of the *Allegro*, harbors some hints of a melodic resemblance to the 1 2 | 3 2 beginning of the hymn. Modulation to the relative major, E♭, reveals a few more hints of the hymn's melody. The piece is a sonata form with the prima parte repeated. As in the finale of Op. 74 No. 1, there is a reprise in tonic minor, followed by one in tonic major.

Quartet No. 4 in B♭ opens quietly with an *Allegro con spirito* in common time that spreads the tonic triad over four measures, the first violin making a graceful climb up an octave and a half decorated by minor-second preparatory tones before the chord tones. The first phrase is an antecedent that concludes with ii^6 - V$^4_3$/ii - ii, taking an additional two measures. The consequent phrase begins with a long-held dominant chord with the treble climbing successively to the 5th, 7th, and 9th scale degrees, followed by the chords vi - V^7 - I. The treble rises have prompted the silly nickname "Sunrise" for the quartet. Rich in possibilities, the opening supplies Haydn with nearly everything he used to construct a broad movement in sonata form. A small detail such as the interaction of chord tone and minor-second auxiliary tone generates a transition that is a steady stream of sixteenth notes, a passage so attractive it seems to have inspired the young Mendelssohn to copy it when inventing the brilliant Scherzo of his Octet in E♭, Op. 20, of 1825. The second theme in F is prepared by the busy work in sixteenth notes coming to a big stop on V/V, and when it arrives, it is the cello's turn to play the main theme, inverted to become a descent (a "sunset" already?). After a few tonal detours and more sixteenth-note chatter there is a distinct closing idea in which the high pair is pitted against the low pair on the offbeat. To begin the seconda parte Haydn drops down a third from F to D and places the main theme in d minor, which leads to g minor, then E♭, and so on to the eventual reprise. The sixteenth-note figure is rarely absent from the modulations. After a mighty climax and a long-held chord of V$^6_5$/IV comes resolution in the form of a short coda, with no repeat indicated.

An *Adagio* in 3/4 time and in E♭ follows. The effect may be hymn-like but its close melodic movement of minor seconds is not lyrical, that is, does not inspire the wish to sing. A stronger resemblance to the *Allegro*'s main theme is this theme's construction as an antecedent ending on ii and a consequent ending on I. On the way to the second key the first violin takes flight in some rhapsodical passagework in quick notes, answered briefly by the cello imitating the same. When the second key does arrive, with a bow to the first theme and in stretto, it is merely a short preparation for the return of the tonic, which arrives not as E♭ but as e♭ minor, a false reprise. The true reprise brings with it more complicated strettos, and the movement fades away to *pianissimo*, still haunted by the initial motif up to the end.

Menuet Allegro is another case in which the dance movement offers a pithy simulacrum of the first movement's initial theme. It is fruitless to speculate which version came first to the composer's mind. Near the end of the second strain, there are some IV$^6_4$ - I affirmations that sound close to those at the identical place in the minuet of Symphony No. 102, which shares the same favorite key of B♭. The minuet's beginning with a triadic rise could also have had a bearing on the triadic rise used to initiate this quartet's first and third movements. The Trio begins with a descending theme that incorporates the minor second E♮ F, the initial sounds of the first violin to begin the quartet and the only minor-second interval missing in the theme of the minuet. Otherwise, it features a winding melodic line, the two violins in octaves over a drone bass, made even more exotic by the descent in octaves of all the instruments through A♭ G♭ F E♭ F, in lieu of a half cadence (the E♭ instead of E♮ here sounds especially strange).

Finale Allegro, ma non troppo in cut time begins with a rounded binary form with repeats, of the type that often yields a movement in rondo form. Before the return of the beginning in the second strain there is a teasing delay of six measures, a wait on a V^9 pedal, perhaps a reminder of the prominence of V^9 in the main theme of the first movement. The playfulness of this moment is enhanced by an eightfold sounding of an obstinate little figure of three eighth notes, 9 8 7, going against the grain of the meter. They anticipate the 5 4 3 beginning of the theme. Rather than a rondo, Haydn opts for a large ternary form followed by two codas. The **B** section is in tonic minor, for which the key signature is changed to five flats. This section is also in rounded binary form. Upon return to B♭ major, the main theme is modified by changing it in the second half of the first strain into a constant stream of eighth notes: 5 4 | 3 5 4 3 2 4 3 2 | 1 3 2 1 . . . As the second strain is about to finish, there is an interruption delaying the final cadence, in place of which, to a *Più allegro*, Haydn has the first violin take off on the streaming eighth-note version of the theme, this time legato instead of staccato. These constant eighth notes are next distributed in an airy texture by being tossed from one voice to another. In a still faster section, *Più presto*, the first violin tries again with the theme in its perpetual motion guise and gets through the whole rounded binary form nearly to the end. In another interruption the tension builds to its highest point in a *crescendo* to *fortissimo* (Example 6.8). The reference made by the

EXAMPLE 6.8. *Haydn, String Quartet in B♭, Op. 76 No. 4, Finale*

first violin, as could not be more clear, is to the very opening of the quartet. When the cadence is finally reached, all instruments in unison play the rapid eighth-note figure, plunging down to a low C, then rising in a longer-note chromatic rush back up to F, from which are launched the final chords, V - I, thrice repeated. There is so much to admire throughout every movement of the quartet, it wins our palm for being the most beguiling among its five fellows.

Quartet No. 5 in D begins with an *Allegretto* in 6/8 time, a lighthearted kind of theme that swings along with dotted rhythms and invites variations. The movement is a loosely articulated series of restatements of this theme without indications as to where each section begins. A tonic minor variation occupies the middle of the movement, after which the theme returns to tonic major. There follows an *Allegro*, based on the head motif of the theme, that serves as a long coda. The sweeping scalar passages at the end have been heard earlier in the movement.

The *Largo Cantabile e mesto* in cut time is in the unexpected key of F♯ major (six sharps). Odd choices like this continued to attract Haydn, perhaps because they posed a challenge, as they surely did to early performers. The initial theme in the first violin rises, from the fifth below the tonic up an octave, by the notes of the triad and then further up to the high tonic in stressed position, intensified by a *crescendo* to *forte*. This peak tone is harmonized by a IV$^6_4$ chord, a combination of melody and harmony that, when emphasized as here, has associations with many maudlin nineteenth-century themes. His *Largo* puts the main idea through many keys before returning home, in a movement that can take as much as ten minutes in performance. It is certainly *cantabile* but hardly *mesto* (mournful). The minuet, as usual, returns the tonality to the original key, in this case D, easily forgotten after the tonal meanderings of the *Largo*. Haydn marks it *Menuet Allegro*; it is a quite normal example of its species and is of modest length, like the other movements (excepting the *Largo*). The Trio in d minor is built over a quasi-ostinato bass in the cello part, above which the other parts keep repeating the identical V- i cadence. The same repetitions (V - I, V - I, etc.) that begin the *Finale Presto* in 2/4 time will, as we have come to expect, end it. Once again Haydn has put the cart before the horse and the jest remains just as witty as it was in the Quartet in G of Op. 33. The finale delights in scampering motions up and down, the parts leading each other on a merry chase. It helps the quartet as a whole that the finale, although lacking a repeat sign in the middle, is a full-fledged sonata form, the only one in the work.

Quartet No. 6 in E♭ also begins with an *Allegretto* in variation form, this one in 2/4 time. Unusual for Haydn are first movements in adjacent quartets sharing the theme-and-variations form. Moreover, both movements end with an *Allegro*. This theme has more to offer than its singsong equivalent that opens the previous quartet. It is in rounded binary form with repeats, starting with two balanced eight-measure phrases, then swelling to double length for the return and final cadence of the first phrase. The return goes off the track when the first violin begins musing on the leap of a fifth down from offbeat to downbeat in the first strain. The leap is expanded and, indulging in several of Haydn's signature leaps down a seventh, is followed by a cadence, which is expanded by a codetta over tonic pedal, an added stability felt necessary perhaps because of the caprices of violino primo. The variations do not immediately begin by ornamenting or changing the theme. Rather, it is kept intact and passed around from one instrument to another, the same technique used in the variations on the Emperor's Hymn in Quartet No. 3. In Variation 1 the theme goes almost entirely to the second violin, then is given to the cello in Variation 2. In Variation 3 the first violin again plays the theme and begins embroidering it with sixteenth-note passagework, then surrenders it to the second violin. Connoisseurs may have expected a minor-mode variation next. Instead, the *Allegro* begins, still in major, and it is not a variation but an ample fugato on the theme's head motif (mm. 1–4), steadily accompanied by its countersubject. The rising conjunct third in the head motif, 3 4 5, calls to mind the similar rise in the theme of the finale of Symphony No. 101 ("Clock"), which at one point is also put through its paces in a broad fugato. There is a final variation in the guise of a coda, in which the theme goes, appropriately, to the viola, the one instrument heretofore denied the chance to sing it.

An *Adagio* in a remote key is Haydn's choice for the slow movement, as it is in the previous quartet. Here the meter is 3/4 and the title is unusual: *Fantasia Adagio*. There is no key signature yet the music starts out with a regular antecedent-consequent phrase that is clearly in B major. The sinuous melody, cast mostly in quarter notes, is almost completely in conjunct motion. The accompanying parts are closely woven and also move mostly by step. Upon repetition there is modulation to c♯ minor, after which the first violin, without accompaniment, plays a rising sequential passage in even eighth notes that one expects may lead back to B major. It leads instead to E major, where the main theme begins, changed to e minor in the consequent, which modulates then to G. The wandering, unaccompanied passage in eighth notes goes next to the cello and again leads to an arrival a minor third above, B♭ major, for the main theme's antecedent, turning to b♭ minor in the consequent followed by a quick modulation to B major. After more modulation, the theme begins in A♭ major and is allowed to cadence there after the full antecedent-consequent idea is stated. The decision to use no sharps or flats as a signature becomes understandable. Haydn's theme displays an unusual degree of tonal wanderlust. After the complete statement in A♭, another of those wandering eighth-note passages in the cello lands the theme back in B major, where it began. To signal this arrival further, Haydn places before it the appropriate signature of five sharps, which will remain until the end of the movement. This is no ordinary reprise, on the other hand, for the theme begins receiving treatment as a fugato in its consequent phrase. Imitative texture continues at some length and even sports an augmentation of the theme in the first violin. Approaching a broad and definitive IV - I$^6_4$ - V^7 - I cadence in B major, the instruments break into sixteenth notes, an excitement sounding rather like a written-out cadenza. Clearly, the aged Haydn is still experimenting and pushing the limits of his tonal language, with deeply expressive results. Fantasia indeed!

The *Menuet Presto* returns to the overall tonic by the simple expedient of turning the last sounding tone in the treble of the *Adagio*, D♯, into its enharmonic equivalent, E♭. The dance thus begun is so swift and strongly accented by offbeat accompaniments, it will probably remind listeners of some of Beethoven's liveliest scherzos. This piece, a scherzo in all but name, pulls out of its many fits of leaping about with rapid scale passages to end both first and second strains. The Trio, called *Alternativo*, takes up the scales and makes a new trochaic theme out of them in a dance that is a little more sedate but need not be any slower. Perhaps Haydn was reluctant to call it Trio because it defies traditional form by never modulating.

The *Finale Allegro spiritoso* is also in 3/4 time, and moreover, is built on a main theme that is another derivative of the scales in eighth notes that end the minuet. Like the theme of the opening movement, the first tonal move of this theme is from I to ii, and the tune itself takes the *Allegretto*'s 3 4 5, 2 3 4, and makes sport by turning them upside down into 5 4 3 . . . 4 3 2. As in Quartet No. 5, the finale is the only movement in sonata form, here more overtly because both the prima and seconda parti are marked for repetition. Strong chords on the second beat accompany the main theme, played by the first violin, and these offbeat accents are reminiscent of those in the minuet. The minuet's theme also made much of the supertonic. For a second theme in the finale, Haydn merely called on the first and puts it in a different light as well as a different key, with the two violins in octaves pursued at a close distance by the viola and cello in octaves. The overall effect is of scampering characters in a comic romp.

One of the early commentators on Opus 76 was Haydn's learned friend in London, Charles Burney, who by this time was very advanced in age, being six years older than Haydn. On 19 August 1799, Burney responded positively to a request Haydn made to him in a lost letter of 15 July, saying he would be delighted to find English subscribers to the proposed edition of *The Creation*. Opus 76, Nos. 1–3 had appeared in the first edition of Longman and Clementi during June 1799. Burney, after answering Haydn's request, reported hearing a good performance of them shortly after publication.

> I had the great pleasure of hearing your new quartetti (opera 76) well performed before I went out of town, and never received more pleasure from instrumental music: they are full of invention, fire, good taste, and new effects, and seem the production, not of a sublime genius who has written so much and so well already, but of one of highly-cultivated talents, who had expended none of his fire before. The Divine Hymn, written for your imperial master, in imitation of our loyal song "God save great George our King," and set so admirably to music by yourself, I have translated and adapted to your melody, which is simple, grave, applicating, and pleasing. La cadenza particolarmente mi pare nuova e squisitissima.

Italian was the language the two correspondents usually used with each other, so it is no surprise to see Burney lapse into Italian in order to say that the end of the hymn melody seemed to him particularly novel and exquisite. Burney wrote, furthermore, that he addressed Haydn in English only after seeing how well Haydn used it in a letter to a mutual friend of theirs. What Burney says about the originality and fiery character of the first three quartets of Op. 76 applies equally well to the second three, which did not appear in print until a year later. By this time the master was beginning to doubt that he would be able to compose another set of string quartets that could reach the level of Opus 76.

The Creation

Haydn's two trips to London were made to earn handsome monetary rewards in partnership with Salomon, which he did. Salomon figured that they could profit still more were Haydn to compose an oratorio in English. To this purpose, he procured an old English libretto, one said to have been intended for Handel. The project foundered upon Haydn's admitted inadequacy in English. Griesinger is our best source on its initial stages.

> The first idea for the oratorio *The Creation* belongs to an Englishman, Lidley by name, and Haydn was to have composed Lidley's text for Salomon. He soon saw, however, that his understanding of the English language was insufficient for this undertaking; also the text was so long that the oratorio would have lasted close to four hours. Haydn meanwhile took the text back with him to Germany. He showed it to Baron van Swieten, the royal librarian in Vienna, who arranged it as it now stands. Salomon was going to sue Haydn for this, but Haydn protested to him that he had used only Lidley's ideas and not his words; Lidley moreover was already dead, and so the matter was dropped.

He could have added that, if anyone deserved royalties, it was the Milton of *Paradise Lost*. Haydn protested too much in this case, for many of the English libretto's expressions did survive in *The Creation*, as has been shown by clever deductions made in the absence of the old libretto itself, which does not survive.[18] It is generally accepted in recent Haydn scholarship that "Lidley" was a misspelling of "Linley," and that the person in question was Thomas Linley the elder (1733–1795), who was an impresario at the Drury Lane Theater in London, where the tradition of performing Handel's oratorios persisted from their composer's day to the time of Haydn's stays in London. Linley was not the author of the old libretto

---

[18] Edward Olleson, "The Origins and Libretto of Haydn's *Creation*," *Haydn Yearbook* 4 (1968): 148–68.

but rather its proprietor and transmitter to Salomon, hence he retained some legal claims to it.

Dies relates the same information as Griesinger does, without mentioning Lidley/Linley, which may mean no more than that he forgot the name, obscure to him, cited by Haydn.

> The talk turned to *The Creation*. The first suggestion for this work came from Salomon in London. Since he had been fortunate in so many musical undertakings up to then, and Haydn had contributed no little to this fortune, his courage for new undertakings was always greater. Salomon resolved to have a great oratorio written by Haydn, and delivered to him for that purpose an already old text, in the English language. Haydn had doubts about his knowledge of the English language, did not undertake it, and finally left London on August 15, 1795.

Haydn then forgot about the English text, says Dies, until Swieten said to him shortly after his return to Vienna, "Haydn, we are eager to hear another oratorio by you!"[19] Another, that is, beyond *Die Sieben letzten Worte*, the text of which Swieten had a hand in during 1795–96. Haydn "informed the Baron of the state of affairs," continued Dies, "and showed him the English text. Swieten offered to make an abridged free translation of it into German. Once this was done, he also knew how to push Haydn so that he had no choice and earnestly resolved to compose the German text."

Swieten described the process by which the work began to take shape in a letter to the *Allgemeine musikalische Zeitung* dated Vienna, end of December 1798, and printed in early 1799.

> . . . and now a few words on the poem you choose to call *my* Creation. My part in the work, which was originally in English, was certainly rather more than mere translation; but it was far from being such that I could regard [the libretto] as my own . . . [It is] by an unnamed author who had compiled it largely from Milton's *Paradise Lost*, and had intended it for Handel. What prevented the great man from making use of it is unknown; but when Haydn was in London it was looked out, and handed over to the latter with the request that he should set it to music.[20]

Haydn saw merit in the libretto, says Swieten, but declined to make any decision about setting it until later, after further consultation. Swieten rejoiced that "such an exalted subject would give Haydn the opportunity I had long desired, to

---

[19] This is my translation of "Haydn, wir möchten doch noch ein Oratorium von Ihnen hören!" Gotwals has "Haydn, we have still to hear an oratorio of yours!"

[20] The translation of Swieten's letter is from Olleson, "The Origin and Libretto of Haydn's *Creation*," 149–50.

show the whole compass of his profound accomplishments and to express the full power of his inexhaustible genius." If Swieten were ever of a mind to claim debts owed by Haydn to Handel's music, this would have been a good place to do so. Silent on this issue, he went on to further define his own role.

> I therefore encouraged him to take the work in hand, and in order that our Fatherland might be the first to enjoy it, I resolved to clothe the English poem in German garb. In this way my translation came about. It is true that I followed the plan of the original faithfully as a whole, but I diverged from it in details as often as musical progress and expression, of which I already had an ideal conception in my mind, seemed to demand. Guided by these sentiments, I often judged it necessary that much should be shortened or even omitted, on the one hand, and on the other that much should be made more prominent or brought into greater relief, and much placed more in the shade.

As Haydn was writing the music, the libretto was taking shape accordingly, Swieten seems to be saying with the phrase "as musical progress and expression demanded." Librettist and composer apparently worked closely together, which throws the work in a light different from Haydn's previous librettos. In London he was not in a position to make many demands at the Royal Opera. As Esterházy Kapellmeister, he had so many duties that he was often less exigent or selective about librettos than he should have been.

The Swedish diplomat Silverstolpe, already encountered above in connection with Haydn's String Quartets, Op. 76, mentioned in a letter of 14 June 1797 that Haydn had moved from Gumpendorf into town for the winter and spring. In his much later memoir, published in 1838, he gave more precise reasons for the move, saying that Haydn "only rented this lodging for a short period to be near Baron van Swieten."[21] This makes sense and can be believed, but the subsequent direct quotation from Haydn becomes less credible as it goes along: "I find it necessary [said Haydn] to confer often with the Baron, to make changes in the text, and moreover, it is a pleasure for me to show him various numbers in it, for he is a profound connoisseur who has himself written good music, even symphonies, of great value." His last remarks sound like a series of diplomatic niceties. Haydn told Griesinger directly what he thought of Swieten's eight symphonies; they were, he said, "as stiff as he was." In the memoir of 1838, Silverstolpe often elaborates on his own early letters in ways that strain belief.

Nevertheless, the closeness with which Swieten and Haydn worked on the text and musical expression is apparent from the numerous suggestions Swieten made in the margins of his German text as to how the music should go.

---

[21] C. G. Stellan Mörner, "Haydniana aus Schweden um 1800," *Haydn-Studien* 2, No. 1 (1969): 1–33; 24.

Haydn followed most of them, and he would not have done so had they been less than expert. He felt no compulsion to heed all of them. Working together, Haydn and Swieten developed an effective integration of text and music, one close to Mozart's exacting standards. Recall what Leopold Mozart wrote in the fall of 1785 about his son's work with Da Ponte on *Figaro*: "That will cost him much running back and forth, and arguing, until he gets the libretto so arranged as he wishes for his purpose."

Haydn first met Silverstolpe on 24 March 1797 at a concert performance of Handel's serenata *Acis and Galatea*, one of the works Swieten had Mozart arrange. It took place at Prince Schwarzenberg's palace and was given by Swieten's Company of Associates. In his letter back to Stockholm of 1 April, Silverstolpe expressed his pleasure at what he called "an Oratorio [*sic*] by the famous Handel," and described it as "among the finest things I have heard." About Haydn he gave his initial impressions, saying, "He is a modest man and does not receive compliments gladly." Haydn invited him to the next concert, scheduled for 7 April, at which he would conduct *Die Sieben letzten Worte*. "I could never praise myself," said Haydn, "but as far as that work goes it is not without merit, et je me flatte que c'est le meilleur ouvrage que j'ai fait." Apparently they conversed in a mixture of French and German. In his 1838 memoir, Silverstolpe elaborates, "We had just heard *Acis and Galatea*. This work at first provided us with a topic of conversation. 'It was well performed,' said Haydn, 'but in Westminster, with an orchestra of 500 or 600 persons, the way the works of this great master ought to be heard, there it moved me most.' " The idea of performing *Acis and Galatea* with these forces is preposterous, even more so that of Haydn's enjoying such a performance. Handel's oratorios, of which *Acis* is not one, were then being played by very large orchestras, but not that large. According to more trustworthy sources, Haydn remained silent about the "bloated" forces of the English Handelian tradition.[22]

Both Dies and Swieten say that Haydn worked at first with the German text. Swieten was no more expert in English than Haydn was, but together they pieced together an English text to match the German one, much of it taken from the text Haydn brought from London. Their intention from the start was to create a bilingual oratorio. German was, of course, appropriate to the "fatherland," as Swieten put it. England, on the other hand, remained Austria's constant ally, indeed one of its few hopes, in the ongoing war. Mercenary thoughts of making profits from an oratorio in English were not necessarily in conflict with loftier ideals.

Haydn began composing the music of his new oratorio, at least in his mind, by the latter part of 1796. His close and greatly esteemed friend Albrechtsberger wrote a letter to Beethoven in December 1796 congratulating him on his birthday

---

[22] Landon and Wyn Jones, *Haydn*, p. 334, speak of the "bloated Handel performances then customary in London."

and mentioning a visit by Haydn. "Yesterday Haydn came to me. He is carrying around in his head the idea of a big oratorio that he intends to call 'The Creation' and hopes to finish it soon. He improvised some of it for me and I think it will be very good." At this stage the text was likely still a work in progress. The composition must have occupied Haydn almost entirely in 1797, a year when there was no new mass composed for Eisenstadt. Silverstolpe wrote his father in Stockholm on 10 January 1798, "Two grand concerts will be given at Prince Schwarzenberg's, the music for them being prepared by Haydn, who played me a part of it. It promises to give me great pleasure and is an oratorio called *The Creation*." The intention was for these first semi-private performances to take place during Lent. As it happened they were delayed until the very end of April, perhaps because more rehearsal was needed. Finally, they took place on 29 and 30 April. The audience was restricted mainly to the nobility, court functionaries, and the diplomatic corps. Entrance was by invitation. To pay for the work Swieten leveled a fee of 50 ducats apiece on his Associates, raising a sum that allowed Haydn to be paid a handsome honorarium of 500 ducats. The first truly public performances did not take place until a year later, in the Burgtheater.

Several witnesses left their impressions of the event in one form or another. A particularly well-informed one was Princess Eleonore von Liechtenstein, who recorded her impressions in letters to her daughter, Countess Josephine von Harrach. Her informant was Count Marschall, an insider, since he was a member of Swieten's Associates, according to Dies. In her letter of 1 May, she wrote, after expressing her astonishment at the grandeur of the subject and the music, that Haydn brought back the poem from England and Swieten had adapted it, "que le Baron a travaillé et sans lui rien oter je crois à-peu-près traduit." In other words, "the Baron worked on it, and I believe, without taking anything away from him, had more or less translated it."[23] Princess Liechtenstein went on to describe precisely how Haydn "directed" the work: "La musique à été parfaitement executée, dirigée par Haydn qui donait la mesure des 2 mains." Seated at the pianoforte for the performance was Salieri. Another auditor at this event was Carpani, who would become the work's translator into Italian. He claimed that the performance commanded the perfect silence and scrupulous attention of the audience for the two hours that it lasted.[24]

Zinzendorf was present for the performance on 30 April and wrote in his diary, "a 6ʰ 1/2 au Concert de Haydn a la maison de Schwarzenberg intitulé die Schöpfung, tiré de la bible et de Milton, traduit par le B. Swieten, la musique faite

---

[23] The phrase has been mistranslated by applying "sans lui rien oter" to the poem, which would require "sans en rien oter" (Landon, *Haydn*, 4:118, and Nicholas Temperley, *Haydn: The Creation* [Cambridge, 1991, p. 21]). Temperley has "Swieten had almost finished translating it without leaving anything out." Swieten made clear in his statement of December 1798 that, of necessity, he left a lot out.

[24] Giuseppe Carpani, *Le Haydine, overro, Lettre sulle vita e le opera del celebre maestro Giuseppe Haydn* (Milan, 1812), p. 165.

express pour les paroles pour 500 Ducats." It was his custom in entries like this to list next, with little or no comment, numbers or passages that pleased him, if any. He listed in this case no fewer than fourteen.[25] His enthusiasm for the work and for the performance was such that he procured tickets to return for the repetitions on 7 and 10 May.

Haydn's triumph was even greater when, during the following Lenten season of 1799, the new oratorio had its first public performance in the Burgtheater, an event often called the summit of his career. The date chosen was 19 March, a day that had special significance, for it was the Feast of St. Joseph, thus special to Haydn, and honored as well the patron saint of Austria. Emperor Francis and his entire family attended. Perhaps it was already the custom, in the emperor's presence, to initiate an event with the communal singing of Haydn's "Gott erhalte Franz den Kaiser!" and if so, the portentous unison C throughout the orchestra that began the oratorio had a preliminary dominant, G, preparing it.

In this larger venue, with a more diverse audience, there was a chance that listeners would not be so well behaved as those who attended the semiprivate performances in Prince Schwarzenberg's palace. Haydn took no chances and had a notice printed and distributed to the audience requesting that they hold their applause after the individual numbers, "because otherwise the exact connection between the separate parts, from whose unbroken succession the effect of the whole should stem, would necessarily be destroyed, and thus the pleasure received would become noticeably diminished." No clearer verbal statement of the composer's artistic goals exists. It challenges us anew to inquire how the succession of individual movements or pieces fit together to form a whole.

The opening *Largo* in cut time represents Chaos. Haydn's earlier oratorios, *Tobia* and *Die Sieben letzten Worte*, had begun with orchestral pieces that were actually overtures in closed musical forms. The *Largo* depicting Chaos follows their example and at the same time owes something to the mysterious awe with which Haydn envelops slow introductions to his latest symphonies, especially the last two, No. 103 ("Drumroll") and No. 104 ("London"). This tone of mystery is already present in the slow introduction of the overture to *Tobia*, a *Largo* in common time, beginning with a loud C in unison, but it goes on for only thirteen measures. In the "Drumroll" Symphony on the other hand, the introductory *Adagio* in 3/4 time stretches to thirty-nine measures, near the end of which the unearthly opening passage returns. It provides a closer parallel to the tortuous passage that frames Haydn's depiction of Chaos, for which he made multiple sketches in full score.[26] They differ only slightly from one another, almost as if

---

[25] Olleson, "Haydn in the Diaries," 53.

[26] They are transcribed in Landon, *Haydn*, 4:357–73, where they are broken up into seven parts. A. Peter Brown, "Haydn's Chaos: Genesis and Genre," *Musical Quarterly* 73 (1989): 18–59, reproduces the original sheets and argues that they constitute only three different attempts.

he were trying out his conception more than once or twice to see if any different ideas struck him during the process of putting notes on paper.

Haydn drew almost the entire *Largo* out of a few intervals at the beginning, and these were present in the sketch representing the earliest stage (Example 6.9). The crucial intervals are descending minor seconds, the procedure that of

EXAMPLE 6.9. *Haydn, "Chaos," The Creation, Early Sketch (reduced to main voices)*

layering them on as suspensions, properly prepared and resolved downward, producing musical sighs. Mozart exploited a similar beginning using layered suspensions, and in fact, with the same resolutions C↓B♮, A♭↓G, to initiate the slow introduction of his String Quartet in C, K. 465 ("Dissonant"), the last of the six he dedicated to Haydn (Example 6.10). This precedent stands out because of its close

EXAMPLE 6.10. *Mozart, String Quartet in C, K. 465, I*

personal associations with Haydn and because it comes from a time when both friends were eager new members of the Masonic Order. We quote Mozart here from the entry he made in his thematic catalogue (with slurs not quite matching those of his autograph and the original printed parts). Similarity between the two examples exists in several particulars. In each, the bass protracts C and provides the foundation of all that will follow. In both, the A♭ enters next and resolves down a half-step, like the initial C. Mozart's E♭ also resolves as a melodic sigh down to D. In Mozart the first aberrant behavior occurs in m. 2, when the treble startles us by entering on A♮, but it too then resolves down to G, bringing a different kind of gasping fall, yet remaining a musical sigh. In Haydn's most finished draft ("sketch C") the initial C in the bass is stretched out for another whole measure, by a *forte unisono* (Example 6.11). The E♭, as in Mozart, now joins the C

EXAMPLE 6.11. *Haydn, "Chaos,"* The Creation, *(sketch C: main voices only)*

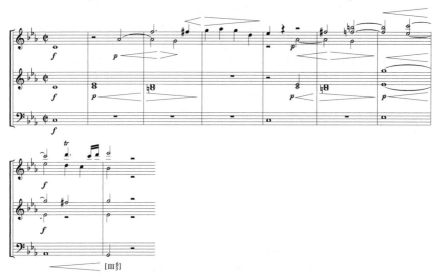

and resolves downward with it. Haydn's aberrant behavior begins in m. 3 of this draft, when the F, instead of resolving down as in his earlier sketch, moves up to F♯, then G. When Haydn repeats the first four measures he squeezes them together, making them even more aberrant. The F♯ that was a passing tone enters suddenly as a dissonance that cannot be explained. It resolves in a sense but only to what is another dissonance, F♮, and then down to E♭. What Haydn begins to suggest is the descending chromatic tetrachord, that age-old symbol of grief, death, and darkness. The same descent down a fourth from C to G is limned in the bass lines, although not fully chromatic. When the G does arrive at the bottom of the chord it forms a part of neither a V nor a i$^6_4$ in c minor but the third of a surprising resolution to E♭ (III$^6_3$). The next arrival, a few measures later, is even more surprising, a plunge down a whole tone to D♭ (cf. Mozart's eerie progression down one tone from c minor to b♭ minor). As Haydn's *Largo* returns to c minor and concludes with the initial material, the chromatic descents are ever more black and despairing. Ultimate blackness is the very essence of Chaos. In *Paradise Lost*, Milton describes Chaos among other things as "utter darkness."[27]

    The beginning of Genesis in the Bible is of great beauty and power, whatever the language used to convey it. Haydn enhanced both beauty and power as only music can. Leading up to "And there was light," all has been hushed, with the strings muted since the first measure of the Introduction (Einleitung). Hov-

---

[27] Bruce C. MacIntyre, *Haydn: The Creation* (New York, 1998), pp. 74–75, quotes the passage at length. The author's many comparisons of Milton's work with the oratorio's text reward study.

ering between c minor and E♭ major in the initial recitative, Haydn manages to withhold the single tone of E♮ that will burst forth in the choral tenors, after an upward leap of a sixth, on the word "light." Off come the mutes on the strings as the chord of C major emerges throughout the orchestra, tutti *fortissimo*. The first violins take the E♮ and outline the tonic chord by climbing up an octave to high E. Haydn has been very economical with orchestral power until this shining moment. To complete the initial recitative he switches narration from the solo bass Raphael to the solo tenor Uriel, ensuring that the vocal peak tones E and F for the word "God" emerge with ringing luster. The passage from darkness into light is a crucial element in the Masonic ritual of initiation and would have had special significance here to members of the Craft. At the same time it is nearly a universal symbol and still works its magic on every listener, of whatever creed, as Haydn surely intended.

Following the C major moment of glory comes a tonal surprise, a move to a third-related key, A major, without proper preparation. Third relationships were still a vivid means of expression then, a novel device. Although Haydn had exploited the device often and in many contexts, he never did so more effectively than here. The connection with what went before is provided by the single tone E, the only tone common to both C major and A major. It sounds forth brightly to begin the descending arpeggio of A major in the first violins, doubled an octave above by the first flute, providing a kind of halo for this *Andante* in cut time. Uriel follows, singing "Now vanish before the holy beams" with the same A major triad in descent, beginning with the E he sang on the word "God." The text continues immediately with contrast, providing the subject of the verb "vanish": "the gloomy shades of dark." Haydn paints these with a writhing chromatic line, then repeats both lines to related but different music. He will find still darker shades to express gloom in the course of the piece. When the text gives him the sinking of hell's spirits down to the deep abyss, he modulates quickly from E major (as V) back to the c minor of Chaos and speeds up the tempo to *Allegro moderato*. Uriel paints the fall with an ascending and descending arpeggio encompassing his whole vocal range, an arpeggio that provokes the violins to whirr in chromatic climbs and falls in quick notes. There is a cadence on c minor at "to endless Night," which is overlapped by the chorus, entering from low to high with a point of imitation well suited to the vivid text "Despairing, cursing rage attends their rapid fall." Again Haydn paints the fall by descending triads, this time in modulating sequences, so that tonal uncertainty adds to the picture of anxiety and wrath. Tonal stability returns after a long pedal on E, preparing the return of A major in chordal harmony, *sotto voce*, with soothing effect for "A new created world springs up at God's command." It is novel in a purely musical sense in that the return to A major brings with it a new theme, not just a reprise of Uriel's first section. Haydn goes through the same process again, bringing back hell's black throngs for a brief last stand. He does not go all the way back to c minor, only to a minor, whence he returned easily for a final "new created world" music in A. Thus ends creation's first day. From the first tone of Chaos to this point has been a single, unified tone painting. How wise were Haydn's words enjoining listeners to pay attention to the exact connection between the different parts.

In the following sections the narrative gives Haydn a chance to paint dreadful storms, which he does with running scales up and down in d minor, then lightning, thunder, and other natural phenomena, leading to the heavenly choir's praise for the work of the second day. This is another solo with chorus. Here it is the soprano Gabriel who leads the celestial singers, "The marv'lous work behold amaz'd the glorious hierarchy of heaven." The German is less hierarchical with "der Himmelsbürger frohe Schar" (the joyful crowd of heaven's citizens). Exchanges of solo singing with choral homophony like these invite comparison with the final number of Mozart's *Tito*. When they are done praising, the bass Raphael returns with a recitative and aria. To begin them the basso continuo moves from the C ending the previous chorus up to C$\sharp$, resolving as the bass of a V$^6_3$ chord up to D and a chord of d minor. Mozart often made the first harmonic movement in a recitative predict the tonality of the following number, as is the case here.

The storm-at-sea aria in d minor, "Rolling in foaming billows," projects a full-scale tone painting of the watery depths in upheaval, only hinted at in the previous recitative. Syncopated rhythms take over, and sixteenth-note scales rush up and down. Perhaps Haydn had flashbacks while creating this storm to the choppy seas he weathered in crossing the Channel on 1 January 1791. He created many other agitated storm pieces in this same key of d minor, and there is also, by way of comparison, the first movement of Mozart's Piano Concerto in d, K. 466 (which comes directly after the "Dissonant" Quartet, K. 465, in his thematic catalogue). Two London works by Haydn that offer analogues are his cantata "The Storm" in d, and the end of his opera *Orfeo*, as the bacchantes are drowned in a storm surge. At the very end of *Orfeo*, d minor gives way to D major, and so it does on a far grander scale in this aria, as the raging waters end by becoming "the limpid brook" coursing "through silent vales." Relative to the tumult before, the music at least approaches silence, and the murmuring triplet motion in eighth notes of this D-major brook describes how it "softly purling glides on." In every sphere where there are precedents clearly at hand in Haydn's previous works they are excelled.

A brief recitative starts in D and moves rapidly through the circle of fifths to prepare the following key of B$\flat$. From storm topos we move to pastoral topos, which has even more parallels in Haydn's previous oeuvre. Gabriel's aria "With verdure clad the fields appear delightful to the ravish'd sense" Haydn sets to a lilting melody, *Andante* in 6/8 time with dotted rhythms, in the manner of a siciliano. The effect is sweetened by predominantly consonant harmonies with emphasis on the major third throughout—the final chord consists of only tonic and third. The shortest of all the recitatives, only four measures long, begins with a D$^6_3$ chord like the previous recitative, and the bass moves up F♯ G G♯ A (V/D). The chorus elides the recitative cadence by coming in on the same A and resolving it to D to begin an exultant "Awake the harp, the lyre awake!" Representing the heavenly host, it renews the Creator's praises, this time, after the initial chordal acclamations, to a vigorous fugue with the parts entering from low to high. Haydn allows a little of his great learning and contrapuntal dexterity to show in this essay. At one point the basses declaim the theme in rhythmic augmentation. Toward the end there is deft use of stretto, then it is back to choral homophony for a rousing conclusion. The sequence of root-position chords alternating with sixth chords in descent marking the climax hint at Mozart's *Die Zauberflöte*. Haydn's admiration for that work will emerge even more clearly in what follows.

The key of D persists for the beginning of the elaborate obbligato recitative, painting the rising of the sun with an appropriately majestic swagger, so typically masculine in contrast with the moon, which glides upward more meekly and slowly to a rising scale beginning on low G, with "softer beams and milder light." It was Haydn's intention to close the fourth day with another chorus of praise in D. Then he changed his mind, perhaps to avoid too much tonal sameness. He reverted to C major.

Psalm 18 ("Caeli enarrant") provided the text for the grand chorus "The Heavens are telling the Glory of God. The wonder of his works displays the firmament." In the English translation used, the two following lines can be puzzling ("it" refers to "the Glory of God" in line one). "To day that is coming speaks it the day; The night, that is gone, to following night." Haydn assigns these lines to the three soloists, who enter after the choral outburst of the beginning, *Allegro* in cut time, which, like the previous chorus, "Awake the harp," has no orchestral prelude. Both resolve the previous recitative by beginning 5 1. This kind of beginning conveys an impetuous, brook-no-delay impression. To accompany the chorus, Haydn at first uses all the winds and his large brass complement of horns, trumpets, three trombones, and bass trombone (doubled by a contrafagotto). He withholds the violins so that they give fresh color to the orchestral restatement of the choral-orchestral first phrase. The tonal language is straightforward and entirely diatonic, but when Haydn reaches the word "night" he at once plunges into c minor and puts the solo soprano in low range and close harmony with the tenor and bass. C major returns for a choral repetition of the first two lines to different music, which is followed by the soloists with a shorter interlude to the lines "In all the lands resounds the word, never unperceived ever understood." The German here is more concrete and preferable: "In aller Welt ergeht das Wort, jedem Ohre klingend, keiner Zunge fremd" (sounding in every ear, strange to no tongue). This resembles what Haydn supposedly told Mozart at their parting in 1790 about his language being understood the world over. Haydn emphasizes "keiner Zunge fremd" by multiple repetitions, even bringing all to a stop with a fermata at one point after "keiner," almost enough to convince one that Haydn remembered his bon mot.

Allegro becomes *Più Allegro* after the pause for "keiner," as the reinvigorated chorus brings back the music from its second appearance, leading to a pedal on the dominant, G. At this point the basses commence a fugato on the subject of the conjunct sixth, a figure derived from the consequent part of the first phrase. The voices enter from low to high then begin to use stretto imitations of one another, also inversions, sung to the second line of verse, as Haydn displays the firmament of his own contrapuntal skills. When the power of this fugal section appears to have reached the highest degree of tension over a dominant pedal, with the tenors up to their high A, there are still more and even narrower strettos and more ingenious combinations of simultaneously descending and ascending sixths. With these the listener might think the peak of glory has been reached. Yet there is more. The basses start up their conjunct sixth as before, from C to B♭, but this B♭ does not resolve down as previously, rather, it resolves up as the sopranos hold a pedal on E (Example 6.12). The basses keep pushing up by chromatic

EXAMPLE 6.12. *Haydn,* The Creation, *Chorus, "The Heavens are telling"*

degrees until they reach D, forcing the sopranos to resolve their now dissonant E down to D. The final cadences follow this climax as if revealing a wonder.

In Part II, the soloists receive an aria apiece, abundant recitative, and a Terzetto that is ended by a chorus ("The Lord is great"). In the final chorus ("Achieved is the glorious work"), the soloists have a substantial middle section, a full movement. The work's success depended partly upon them. In the original performances of 1798, the soprano was Christine Gerardi (Gabriel and Eve), a young woman who was just about to get married and move away. The tenor Mathias Rathmayer (Uriel), another amateur singer with experience performing in Swieten's concerts, was a legal scholar. Rathmayer sang Tito in a concert performance of Mozart's *La clemenza di Tito* given by Constanze (in which she also sang) two days before the premiere of *The Creation,* on 27 April 1798. The bass Ignaz Saal (Raphael and

Adam), was a professional singer and actor. At the public performances of the oratorio a year later, Gerardi was replaced by Therese Saal, the seventeen-year-old daughter of Ignaz Saal. She was a great beauty, to judge by the oil portrait of her as Eve painted by Friedrich Heinrich Füger, director of Vienna's Art Academy. She is portrayed in a low-cut antique-style gown holding a lyre in one hand and musical sheets titled "EVA" in the other.

Part II flows smoothly from one item to the next, largely because of the tonal connections made. The initial recitative has the orchestra strike up three chords on C major in first inversion, picking up where Part I left off. The chords resolve to F, thus forecasting the location of the following set piece, Gabriel's aria "On mighty pens [Federn] uplifted soars the eagle aloft." Haydn complies with a melody that climbs upward to begin this *Moderato* in cut time. Besides soaring eagles (reminding Viennese audiences of the Emperor's double-eagle device), the poem offers the "merry lark," cooing doves, and the "nightingale's delightful notes." The lark greets the morning as painted by a solo clarinet's song while the first violins below begin with a signal call for morning that will also see use in *The Seasons*. The pair of doves obligingly warble in thirds in the two bassoons. As for the nightingale, it is represented by a florid passage for the flute. The aria is a long one and needs to be to accommodate this feathered flock. Mozart's avian caprices may have helped pave the way for this particular tone poem, which Zelter called the most beautiful aria in the work.[28]

The single tone of A (third of F) carries over to the following recitative as an A^6_3 chord. The Terzetto in A will eventually follow, after God has enjoined all creatures to be fruitful and multiply, which Haydn's music ingeniously suggests by moving slowly in the low strings alone, with violas and cellos both divided into two parts. *Moderato* in A and in 2/4 time, the Terzetto has a melody that begins exactly like the duet "Là ci darem la mano" in *Don Giovanni* (also in A and in 2/4 time, *Andante*). A sketch Haydn made for the melody shows he did not begin with the resemblance to Mozart but only ended up with it.[29] This tone poem, with flowing accompaniments in sixteenth notes, gives us gently sloping hills "with verdure adorned," as well as fountains and "the cheerful host of birds." It leads directly into the *Vivace* in common time for the soloists, then the chorus to proclaim over and over, "The Lord is great." The soloists come in finally to enliven the latter sections, much as they do in Viennese settings of the Gloria and Credo of the Mass. The solo soprano and solo tenor both touch high B♭s in their melismatic passages in sixteenth notes. Thus ends the fifth day.

Day six begins with a simple recitative that proceeds from A to D, which will eventually be the locus of Raphael's aria. First comes an enormous obbligato rec-

---

[28] Carl Friedrich Zelter wrote a sensitive critique of the oratorio's published score in the *Allgemeine musikalische Zeitung*, 3 (1800). It is translated in full by Landon, *Haydn*, 4:592–97.

[29] Transcribed in Landon, *Haydn*, 4:380.

itative, the largest in the work, depicting the emergence of various members of the animal kingdom, such as the lion (orchestral roars), the tiger (leaping to a *Presto* in 6/8 time), followed by the nimble stag, the "sprightly steed," and grazing cattle. For the last Haydn modulates from D♭ via an enharmonic switch to A major for an *Andante* in 6/8 time with dotted rhythm, as pastoral as can be. Then come bleating sheep, swarms of insects, and lastly the lowly worm, which slowly moves "with sinuous trace" and reaches resolution in D major. After this extended recital Gabriel sings an aria in D, *Maestoso* in 3/4 time, "Now heav'n in fullest glory shone." There is more cataloguing of the menagerie and other natural phenomena, "but all the work was not complete." Something rather stiff and old-fashioned about this aria makes it sound unlike Haydn, as if he were holding something back until the moment of fulfillment, when the work will at last be complete.

Uriel next sings, beginning with a simple recitative that moves at once from G to C, which it will do again to end. The aria is an *Andante* in common time in a plain diatonic language that is rather reminiscent of "The Heavens are telling." Its first verse describes what was missing up to this point.

In native worth and honour clad,	Mit Würd' und Hoheit angethan,
With beauty, courage, strength adorn'd,	Mit Schönheit, Stärk' und Muth begabt,
To heav'n erect and tall he stands a man,	Gen Himmel aufgerichtet, steht der Mensch,
The Lord and King of nature all.	Ein Mann und König der Natur.

These words derive mainly from Milton's *Paradise Lost* at the point where Satan first glimpses Adam and Eve; the fourth line has been traced also to Genesis.[30] The German text, derived from the English, clearly shapes Haydn's theme (Example 6.13). There is nothing elaborate about the melody with which he chose to clad these plain words.

EXAMPLE 6.13. *Haydn,* The Creation, *Tenor aria, "Mit Würd' und Hoheit"*

---

[30] MacIntyre, *Haydn: The Creation*, pp. 162–63.

After a concise orchestral introduction, Uriel sings the same music, which starts broadly with two measures of tonic harmony followed by two measures of dominant seventh. Then the harmonic rhythm quickens until in m. 18 chords change regularly by the half measure. The pulse quickens too, with activity on every beat, and the little dotted figure in the bass on the offbeats lends a special propulsion to the act of standing up described by the words. Note also how the first violins take over from the vocal line in m. 17. The full orchestra, including horns, trumpets, and timpani in C, erupts briefly after the cadences, as if applauding the sentiment expressed. A middle stanza allows Haydn to modulate to the dominant. Just when the new key of G seems about to be confirmed with a full cadence, Haydn modulates far afield and substitutes an arrival in A♭, a surprise and yet only a big extension of the precadential augmented-sixth chord already touched momentarily in m. 29. A dominant pedal prepares the reprise, which harbors a surprise. The text is not a repeat: it is, instead, devoted to the first woman. By means of music, Haydn has made woman equal to man. There is an ample coda and yet the whole aria is remarkably concise, only 103 measures in length. This is not only the last aria in the work but the favorite one of many. Haydn has indeed saved the best for last. As we shall see, it was the last piece performed for him in the spring of 1809, shortly before he died.

A simple recitative of eight measures heads toward the flat side preparing Part II's final destination of B♭ for the first singing of the chorus "Achiev'd is the glorious work." It is a *Vivace* in common time with active bass line that resembles the kind of motion favored by Haydn in the Credos of his late masses. Mostly homophonic, it celebrates the special euphony of B♭ major with the entire orchestra, including the three trombones and contrabassoon. This short version of the chorus serves as a tonal springboard to the leisurely E♭ Terzetto that follows for the soloists, *Poco Adagio* in 3/4 time. The winds first sing the simple four-measure theme, which is repeated as the soloists begin singing the text, derived from Psalm 104, then continue on in dialogue and accompaniment, with unmistakable echoes of some of the wind sonorities in the hymn-like moments of *Die Zauberflöte*. The theme itself can easily be imagined as issuing from the Three Boys in that deeply spiritual work. There is a contrasting middle section to the Terzetto assigned to the bass Raphael, of darker tonal hue and with orchestral shudders to accompany thoughts that all bliss would vanish if breath were withdrawn from the newly created beings by divine displeasure. After the reprise, sung to a different text, as "life with vigor fresh returns," and a little orchestral transition, the chorus recommences its *Vivace* in B♭, which is extended by an Alleluia final section. Only three measures long, the transition is not really necessary, any more than is the little transition with descending bass that connects the last two numbers of Mozart's *Figaro*. Such tiny gestures in the guise of transformation are superbly expressive for being where they are, and saying so laconically what they say.

Part III begins with a radiant sonority not heard before, E major, one that, coming after the long sojourn in B♭ and E♭, represents the greatest tonal disjunction in the work. Beginning the third and last act of an opera with a zephyr piece in E major was not unheard of—witness Mozart's *Idomeneo*. Another piece in this key that comes to mind, although placed in mid-act, is the blithely atmospheric Trio "Soave sia il vento" in *Così fan tutte*. Haydn's *Largo* in 3/4 time paints the Garden of Eden in the bliss of early morning. A heavenly sonority sounds forth from the solo flute singing a melody on high, accompanied by two other flutes and pizzicato strings. This music swells and subsides to repose in E major, where Uriel begins with a recitative describing the first morning in Paradise as "harmony descends on ravished earth." Interspersing the recitation are some recalls of the flute music with a prominent role for two horns in E, one of the rarer sounds from Haydn's palette (he had not written a symphony in E since No. 29 of 1765, and it too required horns crooked in E). The recitative ends on G so as to prepare the following Duetto with Chorus in C, "By thee with bliss, o bounteous Lord." Solo soprano and bass have become Eve and Adam. Their slow hymn of praise, *Adagio* in cut time, is introduced by an oboe solo accompanied by continuous staccato triads in triplet motion in the second violins, easily imagined as paradisiacal harps. Duets for soprano and bass were rare in opera, nearly unheard of in serious Italian opera, although not so uncommon in opera buffa. The challenge for Haydn was to avoid any buffa overtones during this leisurely stroll in Paradise Garden. He averted them. To enliven interest further in the first section of the duet he introduced an orchestral effect from his *Mass in Time of War* (1796): timpani adding a soft rapid-note punctuation of the V and I chords. Are we invited to hear this as a warning of danger ahead as it was in the Mass?

If warning it was, the charmed couple pay no heed and launch into an *Allegretto* middle section in F and in 2/4 time, a sprightly piece, rather Lied-like, over an active bass line reminiscent of that in the chorus "Achieved is the glorious work." The chorus joins in, providing an episode ending on V, whereupon Eve sings the refrain to different words. Adam responds by beginning an episode in IV, which turns modulatory in response to "ceas'less changes" in the text. The chorus takes over, changing the subject back to divine praises but keeping up the flatward drift and confirming it by cadence in A♭ where the refrain recurs, at first in the winds, then sung by Eve. Adam responds with another modulatory section, in which the chorus joins in, this one leading to a return of the refrain in the key of G. The piece is clearly a rondo, but of an unusual kind, in which the refrain returns in various keys. G is an opportune preparation for the chorus to push for and achieve the return of the initial key of C. The tempo remains the same, the pleasantly ambling *Allegretto* of the rondo theme, while the texture changes to the choral homophony remembered from earlier acclamations. Haydn manages to create dramatic effects and a sense of impending climax as he pushes the sopranos up to their high A, to emphasize "ever more" (Ewigkeit), followed soon after by the tenors up to their high A for the first time since the end of Part I. There is a reliving of the climactic moment at the end of "The Heavens are telling" with a long chromatic rise up to C, followed a little later by the orchestra's chromatic rise up to B♭ against a choral pedal of C on a long-held "Ewigkeit." This unleashes the first of several powerful cadences. A very long piece because of its long text, in fact, the longest in the composition, it marks one of the work's two conclusions and bids farewell to C major.

Adam begins a simple recitative initiating the last complex, saying "Our duty we performed now, in off'ring up to God our thanks, Now follow me dear partner of my life!" The accompanying chords move from F via B♭ to E♭, signaling the key of the next set piece. After the word "thanks" in the first sentence, Haydn interjects, in B♭, then in E♭, a literal quotation in the continuo, marked *Allegro*, of the rising bass line that began the choruses of praise in B♭ ending Part II. This serves to remind us that B♭ has become another home tonic along with C. After ringing so many changes on the idea of thanking and praising the Almighty, Swieten turns to the subject of human love. Eve, told by Adam to follow his lead, makes appropriately deferential bows to him (at least, they were deemed proper in Haydn's time) and they move on to their next duet, this one in E♭. It begins with an *Adagio* in 3/4 time, Adam singing "Graceful consort!" The head motif B♭↓ D | F E♭ is note-for-note the same as Euridice's cavatina "Del mio core" in Haydn's *Orfeo*. Eve enters, singing the same music in B♭, an octave and a fifth higher, and then they begin singing together. How like the love duets of opera seria, knowing listeners must have thought, but what this pair cannot do is warble in parallel thirds together the way two high voices did in that genre. They reach a cadence in E♭ and the same listeners, experienced as they were in hearing the two-tempo rondòs of Italian opera, could anticipate that a faster cabaletta would follow. What followed, *Allegro* in 2/4 time, had to be faster to accommodate the text "The dew-dropping morn, o how she quickens us all!" Yet there is nothing Italianate about the new theme, which is announced *forte* by a pair of horns first, then sung by Adam, and punctuated by an orchestral commentary that makes it sound even more like a contredanse. It was risky of Haydn to resort to another *Allegro* in 2/4 time for the fast section, having done so in the previous piece. At least it must be granted that this *Allegro* is quite different, being in an overtly popular style as compared with the drawing-room Lied character of the other. This one also goes on for a very long time, too long perhaps, for a position so close to the oratorio's end. It requires ideal performers and an ideal performance to sustain interest.

Uriel follows the duet with a short simple recitative that has caught the attention of many, both at that time and ever since. The English is strained and probably represents Swieten on his own, not the original London libretto. "O happy pair, and always happy yet, if not, misled by false conceit, ye strive at more, as granted is, and more to know, as know ye should!" To make it more intelligible and closer to the German, substitute "too" for "yet," delete the comma after "not" and replace the two occurrences of "as" with "than." A premonition of Original Sin, at least in so many words, was probably lacking from the original libretto given to Haydn in London. What we may have here is a case of Swieten nudging the text a little closer to traditional Catholic beliefs than was typical of English Deism. One critic has written that Haydn "gave great weight to this warning through his forebodingly dark harmonization."[31] I demur, first, because a simple recitative of a mere seven measures, which are over in an instant, cannot pull such weight, and second, because two minor chords, amounting to six quarter-note beats altogether, versus twenty beats for several major chords, do not add up to dark foreboding. If anything, Haydn underplayed the verbal warning.

The final chorus, "Sing ye voices all!" begins with an introduction for chorus and full orchestra, *Andante* in common time. The key, B♭, had become the composer's favorite for large late works for a variety of reasons having to do with ideal choral sonorities, his partiality for trumpets in B♭, and B♭'s being the natural home of trombones, bassoons, and contrabassoon. Following the brief, homophonic *Andante* ending on V, the altos announce an *Allegro* fugue subject beginning with a rising fourth, 5 1, the same interval with which the sopranos began the *Andante*, there 1 4. The fugue subject starts with three eighth notes as upbeats, giving it good definition in the contrapuntal web that ensues. While the altos sing "The Lord is great, his praise shall last for aye," the tenors enter with a more flowing countersubject sung to the single word "Amen." An A♭ in the subject, resolving to G, implies subdominant harmony, which has a closing effect appropriate to a finale. After an ample exposition of the fugue subject and countersubject, the soloists come in, now four in number, S A T B. They sing roulades on the sixteenth-note figures from the countersubject, quite in the manner they often did in the closing moments of Viennese Glorias and Credos. The choral fugue resumes and builds in tension, culminating in a long dominant pedal; thereupon the soloists reappear, and exchanges between the two groups become more rapid. With the climactic "his praise shall last for aye," in which the orchestra, tutti *fortissimi*, reverts to the initial rising fourth, followed by the chorus, which expresses "Ewigkeit" (a better choice than "last for aye") by sustaining an E♭ pedal for four measures, the rising fourths rampage down in sequence in the strings (Example 6.14). Haydn pulls out of the sequence and its aftermath by a harmonic surprise, a secondary dominant, V^6/ii, resolving to ii, then in sequence, V^6 - I. Those eager to show how much Haydn admired Handel's *Messiah* could scarcely find a better analogue than the passage of rising fourths at the end of the "Hallelujah Chorus" at the words "For he shall reign for ever and ever." Handel was content with only three rising

[31] Finscher, *Haydn* (2000), p. 477.

EXAMPLE 6.14. *Haydn,* The Creation, *Final Chorus*

fourths in a sequence falling by thirds. By using his orchestra, Haydn extended the sequence to include three more. In conclusion, Haydn has all the parts sing the original fugue subject in unison. It was, of course, born to be an ending. Two chordal renditions of "Amen" end the oratorio. Both are V - I cadences, over which the sopranos sing 2 3, then 5 3.

The Creation is a Handelian oratorio in the sense that its text is constructed on models like *Messiah* and *Israel in Egypt.* In almost every other way it is a work in the musical style of its own time. That is to say, it is a towering monument in the classic style that Haydn, more than anyone else, created.

Griesinger had some hard words about Swieten as a poet but not about his organizing abilities. Dies got Haydn to talk about Swieten (who died in 1803) and reported it in his Twenty-Eighth Visit of 21 November 1807:

> Baron van Swieten was a great admirer of Haydn and Mozart. His knowledge height-ened his birth, and both supported his inclination to elevate music as much as pos-sible. He was the power by which the high aristocracy was often spurred on to ally itself with great undertakings and to produce things that without Swieten would

perhaps never have been realized. Industry was also a great merit of Swieten's that no one could deny him.

Was this particular praise of his industry (Fleiss) perhaps ironic on the part of Haydn? He made a detrimental remark to Griesinger about Swieten's verse in *The Seasons* that began "O Fleiss, o edler Fleiss." Dies on Swieten continues as follows:

> He showed it [industry] particularly this time, and through him was brought about a union of twelve persons of the highest nobility who got together an honorarium of 500 ducats for Haydn's composition of *The Creation*. These noble persons were the Princes N. Esterházy, Trauttmannsdorf, Lobkowitz, Schwarzenberg, Kinsky, Auersperg, L. Liechtenstein, Lichnowsky, the Counts Marschall, Harrach, Fries, Barons von Spielmann and Swieten.

Of these thirteen names, Griesinger omits Marschall, Spielmann, and Swieten himself; he adds four names: a Prince Sinzendorf and Counts Czernin, Erdödy, and Apponyi.

The oratorio, if not Swieten's text, had a jubilant reception nearly everywhere that elaborate concert music of its kind was performed. Christoph Martin Wieland, with Goethe and Schiller one of the triumvirate of great German poets at Weimar, celebrated the work with verses that "gave the composer much joy," says Griesinger, who quotes them, as does Dies. Perhaps from this encounter arose Haydn's desire to collaborate with Wieland in producing an oratorio on the Last Judgment. The poet, who was only a year younger than Haydn, resisted all blandishments from Vienna to write such a libretto.

Nowhere did the oratorio receive a warmer reception than in Paris, not even in Vienna. Griesinger describes what happened after the first performances in France.

> In August 1801, Haydn received a highly flattering token of the creditable reception of his oratorio *The Creation* in Paris. The assembled musicians of the great Opera in this capital sent him a large gold medal engraved by N. Gatteaux, with a lifelike portrait bust on one side and on the other an antique lyre over which hovers a crown of stars. The inscription reads: *Hommmage à Haydn, par les musiciens, qui ont exécuté l'oratorio de la Création du Monde au théatre des Arts l'an IX de la République Française ou MDCCC.*

The long central sentence of the accompanying panegyric conveys the exalted tone of the whole.

> Il ne se passe pas une année qu'une nouvelle production de ce compositeur sublime ne vienne enchanter les Artists, éclairer leurs travaux, ajouter aux progrès de

l'art, étendre encore les routes immenses de l'harmonie, et prouver, qu'elles n'ont point de bornes, en suivant les traces lumineuses, dont *Haydn* embellit le présent et sait enrichir l'avenir; mais l'imposante conception de *l'Oratorio* surpasse encore, s'il est possible, tout ce que ce savant compositeur avoit offert jusqu'ici à l'Europe étonnée.

The letter was signed by the orchestra director and all the performers, a total of 142 signatures. This was the first of a series of medals and eulogies that Haydn received from France. Griesinger summed them up as follows: "Haydn was likewise elected a foreign member and honored with medals by the French Institut National, by the Conservatory of Music, by the Amateur Concert, and by the Societé Academique des Enfants d'Apollon in Paris." Honors, medals, or both also arrived from Amsterdam, St. Petersburg, and Sweden. Not to be outdone altogether, the city of Vienna presented Haydn with its Salvator Medal and made him an honorary citizen in 1803. Carpani ended *Le Haydine* with a print depicting some of these medals (Figure 6.3).

FIGURE 6.3. Medals awarded to Haydn. From Carpani, *Le Haydine*, 1812.

Sacred Music, 1798–1800

The great princes of the Habsburg realms attempted some economies at their lavish country estates and Viennese palaces during the relatively peaceful months that followed the humiliating Treaty of Campo Formio in October 1797. French forces used the lull to occupy the Papal States and Switzerland, then Napoleon turned his attention to Egypt in hopes of disrupting the British Empire's lifeline to India. Prince Esterházy dissolved his battalion and donated 120 of its horses to the Emperor. He also dismissed his wind band (Feldharmonie). This left Haydn with a small orchestra, reduced to strings and organ, to which he was able to add three trumpets and timpani. The restrictions inspired rather than hindered him, as often happened with great composers. For these reduced forces, he prepared in the summer of 1798 his annual tribute to Princess Marie Hermenegild, "Missa in Angustiis" (Mass in Straitened Times), a title that comes from his Entwurf Katalog. It acquired the title "Nelson" Mass later.

MISSA IN ANGUSTIIS ("NELSON" MASS)

Haydn made precise annotations on the autograph when he began and finished the new mass: "1798 10 July at Eisenstadt," and "31 August." Thus, the work of composing and scoring took fifty-three days in all. Near the close of his *Biographische Notizen*, Griesinger related what Haydn told him regarding the time various genres required. For each of the twelve symphonies for London "he spent, of course amidst other occupations, one month, on a mass three months. He also remembered, however, having written one in one month, because he could not go out, on account of sickness." It has been suggested that the reference is to the mass of 1798.[32] A passing remark with no data to back it up has been used to bolster this argument; it purports that after the first performances of *The Creation* in April and May 1798, "Haydn experienced a letdown [Entspannung] and even had to remain confined to his rooms [in Vienna?] on account of sickness."[33] This could also be an invented elaboration relying on Griesinger's testimony. Certain, only, is that Haydn composed the work in Eisenstadt.

The first performance took place on 23 September, not in the Bergkirche but in the town's large parish church. By this time the news had reached Austria of Admiral Nelson's great victory of 1 August over the French fleet he surprised in anchorage at Aboukir in Egypt. The new work was not called the "Nelson" Mass at that time, but it may have been so identified two years later if it was performed in honor of the admiral when he visited Eisenstadt in the fall of 1800. A very wel-

[32] Brand, *Die Messen*, p. 321.
[33] Pohl-Botstiber, 3:132.

come visitor at the first performance in 1798 was someone Haydn had not seen in twenty-seven years, his brother Michael. He arrived after a slow trip from Salzburg, made slower by the honors paid him at several churches and monasteries on the way. He was a celebrated composer in his own right, especially loved for his masses and other sacred music. The third Haydn brother, Johann, still served as a tenor in the Esterházy cappella.

The new mass is in d minor initially and again at crucial moments throughout, yet the festive parts in D major are more numerous and longer. D major is above all a trumpet key, and Haydn took great advantage of this in his writing for the three trumpets. He had written no Mass in D before this, and in point of fact, D was far less common than C for masses composed in the Austrian-Bohemian sphere. Among Mozart's many masses for Salzburg only one was in D, K. 194 of 1774. From Mozart's last year, on the other hand, came his most famous sacred work of all, K. 626, the Requiem in d (but often in D). It was performed widely in the 1790s and was certainly known by Haydn. His new mass of 1798 in d/D has some specific points of contact with K. 626. In the original scoring, Haydn made up for the lack of woodwinds with solo passages for organ, which he played himself at the first performance. The traditional woodwind parts were provided soon afterward and before the score was printed. Another odd feature of the work was the lengthy and elaborate concertante parts for the vocal soloists, especially for the soprano, for which no explanation has yet been found.

From the very first tones of the Kyrie, Haydn serves notice that the work will be as serious as if it were a Requiem. Although in 3/4 time, there is nothing lightweight about this *Allegro moderato*. It sounds grim and wrathful, punctuated as it is with insistent *forte* Ds in the trumpets and timpani, repeating the same rhythm ♫.♫♫|♩ 𝄾 𝄾 |. The violins outline a triadic descent through the octave from D to D and then give out strident, double-stopped chords projecting such melody as there is, while the violas keep restating the octave fall, 8 1. The chorus enters singing "Kyrie" in dotted rhythm to more 8 1 descents. Given the severity of this music, the words could just as well be "Dies irae, dies illa." Mozart's "Dies irae" is not similar in rhythm, being in common time, yet its d-minor fury seems of a piece with Haydn's Kyrie, and there is a slight similarity in the way both composers use the minor second below the main note (for example at Mozart's setting of "quantus tremor est futurus").

In Haydn's Kyrie the soprano solo comes to the fore in the first section, then leads in the "Christe eleison," which is in the relative major. The other soloists join in accompanying the soprano's florid solo, and the chorus confirms the key of F with a more imitative texture, bringing back the word "Kyrie" and serving as a long transition back to the austere initial music. At the moment of reprise the soprano produces a roulade that carries the voice in rapid notes up to high B♭, a thrilling moment, indeed. It requires a voice powerful enough to compete with the tutti *forte* of chorus and orchestra, including the three trumpets, which probably rules out a boy soprano. That high B♭ takes on a thematic and dramatic significance that could not have been guessed merely from the top note of double-stopped chords in the violins. The movement remains ultra-serious to the end. The choral sopranos also have to climb up by step to high B♭. This could be heard as the climax of the movement, after which there is a gradual retreat into submission, momentarily interrupted by an eruption of B♭ major via a deceptive cadence. As the chorus clings to a pedal D as third of B♭, it is challenged by assault from below of the rising chromatic bass and the strings in unison, forcing the chorus to yield to d minor. The device resembles that used so powerfully to end "The Heavens are telling" in *The Creation* (see Example 6.12).

The Gloria begins in D, *Allegro* in common time, with the solo soprano presenting the theme, which is immediately taken up by the chorus, an exchange that continues to the end of "in excelsis Deo." For the softer "Et in terra pax hominibus," the soprano soloist is joined by the tenor and bass, who begin singing over a low D pedal, which then becomes an E pedal. The tenor's tessitura is high, and there are some lovely duet moments with the bass in thirds, then in sixths. Haydn is demanding of all his soloists in this work. He also makes more demands on his Eisenstadt chorus than he did on the chorus in Vienna for *The Creation*, for example, the leap up to high B♮ that he requires of the sopranos on "glorificamus te." The *Allegro* is in a binary form with modulation to V and back. Left out at the beginning, the solo alto is given the honor of leading in the first theme, on V, that initiates the second half. After a broad cadence on D there are three beats rest and then a sudden and dramatic arrival on a *fortissimo* unison B♭ in the orchestra, commencing an *Adagio* in 3/4 time for "Qui tollis."

"Qui tollis" is a bass solo that begins like another bass solo, the "Tuba mirum" of Mozart's Requiem. The tonal move from the bare octave of D to B♭ marks both, and this is not the only similarity. Haydn has his solo bass start the plea for mercy "Qui tollis peccata mundi miserere" with a stately descent through the tonic triad, like that in the Kyrie but different because here there is an added tone a third above the higher tonic (Example 6.15ab). He makes no effort to disguise

EXAMPLE 6.15 a, b.

a. *Haydn,* Missa in Angustiis *("Nelson," 1798), Gloria*

b. *Mozart,* Requiem, *Dies irae*

his model. Clearly it is Mozart's bass solo, which also touches the high D before descending through the octave to a sustained low B♭. Mozart also has a solo trombone that leads the way. Haydn's big arrival on B♭ to begin the "Qui tollis" throws a different light on the runs up to high B♭ and the grand deceptive cadence to B♭ in the Kyrie. Possibly the inspiration of K. 626 was what ignited Haydn's imagination at a very early stage of conceiving this mass in d minor.

There have been many highly dramatic moments in Haydn's previous mass settings but nothing more dramatic than several moments in this mass. The second "miserere," sung by the bass, is greeted by a poignant minor ninth appoggiatura in the solo bassoon and first violins (a sonority that has its own Mozartian resonances). Soon after this, the chorus joins in a soft chanting in unison of "miserere nobis," quite similar in effect to the choral chanting in *The Creation*'s chorus "By thee with bliss." Upon repeating his solo and moving on to the second part of the text, the bass is joined briefly by the soprano soloist, who sings the single word "Suscipe," imploring the Deity to "hear our prayer." The chanting chorus supplies "deprecationem nostram," moving the tonality to g minor, where the solo bass again sings the descending octave idea. From g it is but a short distance to d minor, where the *Adagio* ends on V of d, which can also be V of D, as it turns out to be.

An *attaca* cadence brings back D major and the *Allegro* in common time, also the same music, sung here by the solo soprano to "Quoniam tu solus." This makes for an uncommonly unified and cogent setting of this hallowed text, more compelling even than Haydn had achieved in his previous two mass settings. Such a movement deserves a good fugue to cap the whole with "In gloria Dei Patris, amen." It arrives as the basses announce a theme that contains two descending triads, followed by the other sections in ascending order. The nature of the theme makes various strettos possible, and Haydn's skill is applied to making this an exciting process as the entries get closer and closer together. In good Viennese tradition the soloists return to decorate the ending, which is made more blazing still by the trumpets. The final cadences are like those in *The Creation*, two V - I chords with the sopranos singing on top 2 3, then 5 3.

The Credo commences as a rugged canon that conveys the rock-firm beliefs of the faithful in a novel way, a tour de force in *Allegro* cut time. The higher voices, tenors and sopranos, are paired in octaves and pitted against the altos and basses in octaves, who follow them in canon a fifth below at the distance of a half measure. The octaves express the oneness of "in unum Deum," and the dogged pursuit indicates the rigor and inevitability of the faith. Pursuing this path like a force of nature, the ineluctable canon is made to modulate from and return to tonic D while traversing the long text in an economical manner up to the words "descendit de coelis," which are repeated to end the canon and are stated again as the choral parts coalesce in four-part harmony and then in unisons and octaves.

Having dispatched the wordiest part of the text in about two minutes, Haydn lingers more than twice as long on the radiant "Et incarnatus est" that forms the middle part of the Credo. He sets it as a soprano solo of great tenderness, a *Largo* in G and in 3/4 time offering a vision that has its painterly equivalent in the frescoes of his contemporary Franz Anton Maulbertsch, "the Austrian Tiepolo." The chorus begins to repeat the solo soprano's twelve-measure phrase but departs from it by modulating to D, continuing on to the word "crucifixus," which is set to a *forte* unison with a turn toward g minor. At this point Haydn brings in trumpet and drums, which sound a soft D pedal, as if in admonition, using a rhythmic pattern similar to what they played so often in the Kyrie. Instead of an arrival in g minor, the harmony is deflected to B♭, in which chord the trumpets keep sounding their D pedal. The other soloists join the texture, then the choral sopranos sing the descending fourth by step that is so characteristic for "crucifixus, passus, et sepultus est." The section ends meekly in G major, with the chorus hushed to *pianissimo*.

It was traditional for "Et resurrexit" to arrive with a burst of major following on a minor-mode closing. In a switch from the usual Haydn followed a major-mode closing with a minor-mode resurrection. There is a burst of energy in place of major, *Vivace* in common time. The unexpected key of b minor is only a feint that is quickly transformed into its relative major D, which is reinforced by trumpets, drums, and all else to emphasize the words "gloria" and "judicare vivos, et mortuos." With the help of a few modulations Haydn sustains the jubilant tone to the end of the text, without recourse to the usual fugue. Traditional, on the other hand, is the reappearance of the soloists before the end, adding their blessings to the proceedings. The solo soprano is treated specially, with a lovely descending sequence sung softly to "et vitam venturi saeculi. Amen." The show of contrapuntal skill to begin the Credo may have convinced Haydn to end it without a fugue.

The Sanctus is an *Adagio* in common time for the chorus, a homophonic setting that begins I - V⁷ - vi; IV - V⁷/ii - ii, with the treble falling by step, 3 2 1, 6 5 4. It lasts only twelve measures and ends by preparing d minor. What arrives instead is a vigorous D major for "Pleni sunt coeli," *Allegro* in 3/4 time, ending with an elated "Osanna in excelsis." One of the most memorable features of the Sanctus is the swelling and diminishing of tonic and dominant chords, as directed by wedge signs, and the punctuation of the loudest point by an offbeat *forte* D from the trumpets and timpani. The last "excelsis" is tempered somewhat by the introduction of B♭ into its penultimate chord. It could be heard as a signal of what is ahead, also a reference to the very beginning of the Kyrie.

The Benedictus restores d minor and proceeds in a walking tempo, *Allegro moderato* in 2/4 time. The timpani and trumpets punctuate here too, and loudly, beginning in the fourth measure. There is quite a long discourse before any words are sung. These are assigned at first to the solo soprano, echoed *forte* by the chorus. The soloist is indulged on second appearance with some melismatic passagework as the music turns to the relative major, F. The other soloists enter, turning the progression around, from F back to d, where it seems the movement is about to reach an ending, with the soprano up to high B♭ over iv$^6_4$ harmony. The expected cadence is withheld. Instead the orchestra pounces on B♭ and D, *forte*, reminiscent of how the bass solo began "Qui tollis" in the Gloria. At this moment the three trumpets and timpani enter with their fiercest alarum on D and persist in maintaining it, to which the chorus responds, also *forte*, swelling to *fortissimo*. The cadence comes suddenly as the choral sopranos, having ascended to high B♭, descend quickly by step down to D, the top of a final chord in the chorus that has tonic and fifth but no third. The return of "Osanna," after the orchestra's cadence, brings with it the F♯ of D major and a quick conclusion. An outburst such as Haydn allows his trumpets, drums, and chorus in the Benedictus stamps the entire Mass, intensifying the anguished moods projected from the beginning.

The Agnus Dei reverts for its beginning back to the softly lyrical understatement of "Et incarnatus est." Another slow movement, here *Adagio* in 3/4 time and in the key of G, it seems almost like a continuation of, or further reflection on, the earlier movement. There are melodic similarities too with the 3 2 1 beginning of the Sanctus. For once it is the solo alto who leads, followed by the soprano entering at the cadence and overlapping the alto. The soprano's music quickly turns toward D in what amounts to an obbligato recitative, the orchestra providing an accompaniment in dotted rhythm. This is not the only moment in the work that sounds rather operatic. Throughout, the soprano has verged on becoming a prima donna on display. The other soloists join in as the music moves toward a cadence in b minor, ending with a long pedal on F♯ as dominant of b for the first singing of "Dona nobis pacem." Resolution comes quickly, not to b minor, but to D major, in an *Allegro vivace* in common time, the chorus entering in imitative fashion singing the same words. The music makes the text sound less like a plea than an exuberant celebration of a plea granted and peace achieved. Haydn exposes the theme to quite elaborate treatment and then does the same in the dominant. The violins keep up a steady chatter in sixteenth notes that would be equally effective in an operatic finale's climactic moments. A giddiness then seizes the first violins to start playing little offbeat twiddles up and down, with very dance-like, not to say buffo, overtones. This charming music must, of course, come back in the tonic, which it does. The movement may be the composer's most scintillating setting of "Dona nobis pacem."

Haydn has outdone himself again in order to end his mass with an encouraging message. What an adventure it has been from the darkly dramatic Kyrie to the irrepressible joy of the finale. One could intuit from the journey Haydn's defiant response to his country's "straitened times."

"Theresienmesse"

Haydn wrote his next mass for the name day of Princess Esterházy in the summer of 1799. It is in B♭, and it was first performed in the Bergkirche at Eisenstadt, presumably on 8 September. On the same day there was a grand banquet at the castle at which many healths were drunk. "The Prince also drank Haydn's health, to general concurrence," as reported by Rosenbaum, who recorded in his diary too how the eve was celebrated: "There was Turkish music in the square, then a French play. At the end there was a decoration with the Princess's portrait."[34] The mass is scored for three trumpets in B♭, timpani, two clarinets in B♭, strings, and organ (plus two bassoons to double the continuo bass, not in the score but the original parts), and the usual four soloists and chorus. The designation "Theresienmesse" is said to have come from its association with Empress Marie Therese, about whom more will be said in the following section on the Te Deum that she commissioned from Haydn. A copy of the parts, and a score for this mass copied from the autograph, are extant in the vast collection of masses and other sacred music amassed by the Empress, who was one of the most important music patrons of her day.[35] It has not been possible so far to date the title "Theresienmesse" any earlier than 1815 (she died in 1807). Possibly Haydn gave her a copy of the mass. She could also have sung the solo soprano part in a performance, as she was very active as a performer in sacred and other music—operas, cantatas, oratorios, etc.—but not in public, it goes without saying.

The Kyrie begins with a slow introduction, as the violins rise up the tonic triad to the octave before sinking down by step via A♭ to G, initiating this *Adagio* in cut time. Entering in m. 4, the chorus softly intones "Kyrie" to a unison-octave F, after which the orchestra begins again, this time joined by the soloists singing the initial music. The alto introduces a new motif, 3 5 3 1, imitated by the soprano, followed by the tenor, who turns the first and third tones into minor thirds (D♭), and that is answered by the soprano with G♭. At this the basses enter *forte* with "Kyrie" sung as an octave drop 8 1 in dotted rhythm, and this is not the only echo from the Kyrie of the previous year's Mass in d. The trumpets and timpani enter on the same B♭, *forte*, with dotted rhythm involving two sixteenth notes, similar

[34] *Haydn Yearbook* 5 (1968): 68.

[35] John A. Rice, *Empress Marie Therese and Music at the Viennese Court* (Cambridge, 2003), pp. 240–41.

to their oft-stated pattern in the Kyrie of a year earlier. The basses then leap up a minor sixth to G♭ and resolve it downward. Brief this menacing moment may be but it sounds a portent of further such disturbances ahead.

As a whole, the mass is not as "noisy" as the "Nelson" Mass of 1798. It often has a gentle, yearning character, setting off the more dramatic moments all the better. The initial *Adagio* wends its way to a final V⁷ chord at a length of twenty-eight measures. There follows a robust fugue, *Allegro* in common time, begun by the tenors on a theme that begins 8 ♭7 6, familiar from the *Adagio*. It also sounds like a digest of the great fugue in B♭ ending *The Creation*. As in that piece there is a running countersubject mostly in eighth notes, with two sixteenth notes in an upbeat position, a feature already present in slower guise in this Kyrie's introductory *Adagio* when the trumpets and drums make their momentary intrusion. Haydn puts the short theme and omnipresent countersubject through their paces. The soloists take over after the second key of F is established, singing "Christe eleison" to the same motif introduced by the alto in the *Adagio*: 3 5 3 1, to which the solo soprano responds with a more florid passage (involving two sixteenth notes as upbeat), which all the soloists then adopt. The fugue returns, abbreviated, and at the end the *Adagio* also returns like a framing song, for which there is precedent in the opening movement of Symphony No. 103 in E♭.

The Gloria is divided into three large sections, with very lively movements in B♭ surrounding a more complex and slower middle section. An *Allegro* in 3/4 time begins the piece, announced by the orchestra, which has its own theme, with strong accents on the second beats of many measures, countering the different rhythms of the chorus. While the orchestra provides the equivalent of a Polonaise the chorus sings more sedately, in chordal texture. The familiar 8 ♭7 6 motif appears, first in the orchestral basses, later in the choral parts. Also appearing in both is the flat 6th, G♭ (marked *sforzato*), resolving to F. Before the chorus has finished with "Gloria in excelsis Deo," there is an amiable passage for the tenors and basses moving smoothly in parallel thirds, copied an octave above by the altos and sopranos. For "Et in terra pax" the orchestra makes a transition to the relative minor g, where the chorus begins singing in its previous lyric vein. The harmony slips from G up to A♭, like a deceptive cadence. A modulatory passage lands the music back in g minor, at which point the orchestra recommences its ritornello, leading quickly back to B♭ for "Laudamus te," etc. To enhance these praises Haydn brings back the fanfare instruments to play the same tattoo with which they interrupted the Kyrie. There is more duetting in thirds with high voices paired against low voices, leading eventually to a climax in which the sopranos climb by step up to high B♭ (a surer way to get there than lunging up a sixth, as they must do in order to sing the fugue theme in its highest position during the Kyrie). This brings the *Allegro* close to its conclusion, after which there is a little transition preparing the next key. The usual choices would be F or E♭.

Instead, Haydn chose C major, perhaps because it suited the alto and bass solos he had in mind for beginning "Gratias agimus tibi."

In a nine-measure prelude, the orchestra lays out the theme, *Moderato* in cut time, and it is surprisingly galant, with emphasis on sweetly consonant harmony over a static bass, the second chord being a whole measure of IV$^6_4$. The melody nearly weeps with melodic sighs. There are many cases like this in late Haydn, and they suggest nothing so much as the forlorn heroines of sentimental nineteenth-century operettas yet to be written. The result will not be to everyone's taste even though it was prophetic. When the bass sings the tune, the alto accompanies him, mainly in sixths and tenths. Modulation carries the music to d, then the orchestra prepares F, where Madame Soprano herself sings the treacly tune. More modulation leads to g minor for the tenor to have his turn at it. All four soloists unite in the following passage, preparing for the arrival of c minor, *forte*. The orchestra introduces constant triplets against the singing of the chorus in plodding quarter notes, "Qui tollis peccata mundi." At this moderate tempo the triplets achieve the effect of making the movement sound as if it were in 12/8 time. A threatened lap around the circle of fifths is happily averted. Otherwise of note, the sopranos layer a series of suspended longer tones on top of the texture, at the risk of making the section sound like an overextended counterpoint exercise. There is modulation aplenty yet it cannot allay fears that the section goes on far longer than its musical interest warrants. Finally, after 174 measures, the orchestral triplets stop and the chorus chants a cappella one final "miserere nobis" softly, low in their ranges, departing on the chord of G major as V of c minor.

What arrives next, with a flash of brilliance from the orchestra, *Vivace* in common time and without preparation, is the initial key of B♭ for "Quoniam tu solus." The orchestra is once again at full strength, including the trumpets and timpani. The theme, taken up by the chorus, is made out of a melodic turn around the tonic followed by a rise up to the third and fourth degree before falling by step back to the tonic. First treated as a treble melody with monophonic accompaniment, it eventually becomes the head motif for a fugal passage when the word "amen" is reached. Haydn restates it so often, in various guises, one wonders if he may not be quoting a plainchant. The soloists appear in the middle and again at the end to round things off, singing, among other passages, a descent of three parallel diminished chords, doubled by the strings playing pianissimo (for which the singers were doubtless thankful). In response to this little episode the chorus produces the most robust sound in the whole Gloria, as if applauding: the high duet of sopranos and altos in thirds up and down, doubled (not followed) by the men's voices an octave lower. This is an unusual sonority for Haydn and suggests the swagger in some of the great choruses to come in *The Seasons*, already occupying his mind.

The Credo begins as did the Kyrie and Gloria with orchestra alone, announcing what the chorus will sing in unison for their first measure, as if it were an old chorale tune (an effective way to express "unum"). In this *Allegro* in common time, the orchestral basses keep up a steady stream of eighth notes to support the violins' stream of running sixteenth notes. The walking bass and active texture above are typical for Haydn in beginning the Credo, as are the meter and tempo. They convey an old-fashioned solidity, implying the firmness of belief. The first part of the text passes rapidly, taking less than two minutes. It helps that Haydn omits some of the words, perhaps out of forgetfulness. The chorus repeats the last two words of "descendit de coelis" in unison for the cadence, ending the *Allegro* as they began it. For the central mysteries of the faith beginning with "Et incarnatus est" Haydn chooses the rare key of b♭ minor (five flats). An *Adagio* in 2/4 time, it commences with the soprano soloist and is soon joined by the other soloists. The music shifts to the relative, D♭, where "Crucifixus" is eventually sung. Repetition of short motifs at length in this section conveys a sort of transfixion in response to the story being told. The treatment is subtle compared to the usual one of invoking the most mournful strains in the whole service. "Passus et sepultus est" brings a return to the key of b♭ minor but not the usual chromatic descents. Instead, the bass moves up by half steps. On reaching the cadence Haydn brings in the timpani for punctuation, another unusual step, calling attention to the resemblance of this music to the beginning of the Kyrie at the moment when major turned into minor and the basses leapt up a minor sixth to G♭.

Haydn downplays "Et resurrexit" by denying it the usual clamor of tonic major exultation after a minor mode cadence. Instead he sets it in the relative minor of the main key, exactly as he did a year earlier in his previous mass. Otherwise it is fast, *Allegro* in common time, a texture like the first *Allegro*. He saves the full force of tonic major, tutti *fortissimi*, for "judicare vivos et mortuos," again as in the "Nelson" Mass. The rest of the text passes rapidly by, with just enough tonal diversion to make a final, more imposing return to tonic major necessary. On the way, there is an irresistible fugue, *Allegro* in 6/8 time, on a subject that rises a fifth by step, partly chromatic and partly in dotted rhythm, which gives it a jig-like character. Contemplation of life in the centuries to come ("et vitam venturi saeculi") inspired Haydn with visions of joy, perhaps of a Paradise filled with angels dancing, as in paintings of old. Toward the end, his fugue becomes less traditional and more exuberant as the sopranos and altos take to singing the subject in parallel thirds. The soloists then echo the same and spin it further, ending after the basses enter and sing the fugue subject, then extend it upward to encompass a tenth, after which the final gestures toward the cadence are set in motion and achieved. Haydn is truly in his element in this fugue, which prepared him well for the even grander, jiglike fugue that ends "Autumn" in *The Seasons*.

The Sanctus returns to more gentle tones in an *Andante* in 3/4 time involving both chorus and soloists. The former takes sole possession of "Pleni sunt coeli . . . osanna in excelsis," which increases its speed to *Allegro* while remaining in triple meter. The sopranos end by falling a third, F D, and on that same D, the treble of the Benedictus begins, but in G, not B♭. Its pleasant strains unfold, *Moderato* in cut time, with calm assurance, interrupted only by a IV$^6_4$ - I passage from the "Gratias" of the Gloria, which becomes interjections from the chorus when the solo soprano takes up the orchestral melody. On repetition the other soloists enter and modulate so as to prepare the second key. The alto sings the initial material in D, a fourth below the soprano's statement, and we seem about to return to G when there is a sudden turn to g minor, and then an interruption, as the tutti are summoned to sound the chord of B♭ *fortissimo*. The chorus sings the main material in B♭ and it is left to the solo soprano to return it back to G, with the same choral interjections, extended. What follows could be considered a coda, but if so, a very long one. The bass and tenor echo in thirds some of the previous chorus, followed by a longer passage in thirds for the soprano and alto, soaring up to high B♮ and G. Haydn's indulgence of his singers is by no means over. It continues in leisurely fashion until the Benedictus reaches a long-postponed conclusion. The liturgy demands that "Osanna" return but Haydn forswears bringing back its music and treats the words only as another coda to the music of the Benedictus. Such extended treatments of the thematically related "Gratias" (ca. seven minutes) and Benedictus (nearly as long) assure that these two lyrical movements lend the mass its predominating character.

Agnus Dei begins in g minor with a stark figure sounded by the chorus and orchestra in unison, without benefit of orchestral introduction, the only large section of the mass to lack one, or at least a preliminary chord to give the pitch to the singers. Its starkness is very much inherent in the nature of this figure, striding at first in half notes down a fourth, up a minor second, then down a diminished seventh (Example 6.16). The beginning is reminiscent of many old fashioned

EXAMPLE 6.16. *Haydn, "Theresienmesse," Agnus Dei*

fugue subjects, well exemplified by the Kyrie of Mozart's *Requiem*. Coming after the idyllic and quite worldly tableau painted in the Benedictus, the stern, Old Testament severity of the Agnus Dei sounds otherworldly. Of course in an actual Mass it would not have followed directly. In between came the Consecration and Elevation of the Host and the Pater Noster recited or chanted by the priest. (There were also breaks between the Gloria and Credo as well as the Credo and Sanctus, which helps explain why they can all be in the same main key whereas a sequence of like-sized movements in the same key would be unlikely in a symphony.)

"Agnus Dei . . . miserere" is sung with minimal repetition. The text returns along with the music of the beginning for a unison statement on D and once again on tonic G, harmonized this time. Then the music subsides to a soft closing on V of g minor, or V/vi in the overall home key of B♭. This key bursts forth without further preparation as a tutti fanfare leading in the *Allegro* in 2/4 time for "Dona nobis pacem." With the exultant return of the keynote the issue of pleading for peace is regarded as a settled issue, the gift accepted with alacrity and joy, reason enough for protracted celebration (158 measures!). Clearly Haydn was scaling his finale to the dimensions of the whole mass, and in this sense he was thinking of the work as a musical whole, like a symphony.

The Agnus Dei began with a fugue-like subject sung in unison that never turned into a fugue. At the same time it was not totally forgotten in the headlong rush of celebration. After proceeding through the equivalent of an exposition and development of the fast music for "Dona nobis pacem," with episodes and brief fugato sections, plus alternations of soloists and chorus aplenty, Haydn returns to B♭ for the initial fanfare, like a reprise, but this time the chorus sings over the fanfare in measure-long unisons descending a fourth that cannot but remind us of how the Agnus Dei began (Example 6.16, mm. 135–36). He does not continue with that earlier subject here, yet some ten measures further, with B♭ securely established, the sopranos sing another fragment of that beginning, in tones lasting two measures, recalling unmistakably the rise of a second and fall of a seventh in the original (Example 6.16, mm. 164–68). There is a final transformation, after the tonic has long been established and confirmed in all its majesty. The initial fall of a fourth at the end generates two more such falls within the tonic triad, 3 1, and a more protracted 5 3, with which the mass ends (Example 6.16, mm. 194–201).

Te Deum Laudamus; ADMIRAL NELSON

Haydn composed his late *Te Deum* in C for large chorus and orchestra at the instigation of Empress Marie Therese, the second wife of Emperor Francis and his first cousin (Figure 6.4). She was the eldest child of King Ferdinand of Naples and Maria Carolina, his Austrian consort who was a sister of Leopold, father of Francis. She is called Marie Therese in order to distinguish her from her grandmother Empress Maria Theresa (also her husband's grandmother). Like the grand sovereign for whom she was named, Marie Therese was a musician, and a good one. She sang soprano and played several instruments. More to the point she was a central figure in the musical life of the Viennese court as patron and collector. Haydn's employer Nicholas II was not very musical yet out of pride he attempted to keep the services of his famous Kapellmeister to himself as much as possible. In August 1797 the Empress paid a visit to Esterháza and Eisenstadt, where she

FIGURE 6.4. Leonard Posch. Engraved portrait of Empress Marie Therese.

was welcomed by the Prince and his family. It was perhaps at this time that she requested Haydn to write something specifically for her. A request from so high a personage could scarcely be refused. Griesinger, in one of his first letters from Vienna to his friend Gottfried Christoph Härtel in Leipzig, wrote on 25 May 1799 that "it was impossible for him [Haydn] to promise three new sonatas because he was overwhelmed with business and still has back orders to fill for the Empress, Prince Esterházy, and many wealthy Viennese."[36]

Haydn's *Te Deum* composed for Marie Therese probably dates from 1799 or

[36] Olleson, "Georg August Griesinger's Correspondence with Breitkopf & Härtel," *Haydn Yearbook* 3 (1965): 5–53; 9. Olleson quotes the original German, from which we translate here and in all subsequent references to the correspondence."*Eben komme ich von Haydn—*": *Georg August Griesingers Korrespondenz mit Joseph Haydns Verleger Breitkopf & Härtel, 1799–1819*, ed. Otto Biba (Zürich, 1987) offers a model annotated edition of the letters.

1800. The autograph likely cited a precise date but it has been lost. There is evidence that suggests a performance under Haydn's direction at Eisenstadt during the September 1800 festivities celebrating the name day of Princess Marie Hermenegild.[37] They coincided with the visit to Eisenstadt of Admiral Nelson and the Hamiltons. At this point it is opportune to backtrack to 1798 in order to fill in the picture regarding them.

The months following the Battle of the Nile were not so glorious for either Nelson or the allies. Napoleon eluded capture and returned to France. King Ferdinand of Naples, Haydn's former patron, was improvident enough to declare war on France without winning prior approval from Vienna. His army melted away as the French advanced to the south of Italy, entering Naples without a fight on 20 January 1799. Nelson in his flagship carried the King, Queen Maria Carolina, and their court, including British Ambassador Lord Hamilton and his second wife, Emma, to refuge in Palermo, Sicily. The ignominy of this retreat was lost on no one. The love affair between the married Admiral and Emma Hamilton began at about this time. An open secret, it tarnished Nelson's reputation. Worse still Nelson lingered in Palermo contrary to orders from London. Still, as an English war hero, one of not very many at that time, he got away with it. In 1799 the tides of war changed as France's Army of Italy suffered reverses at the hands of the Austrian and Russian armies. Ferdinand returned from Sicily to Naples and had hundreds of his republican adversaries slain. Napoleon crossed the Alps and regained ground lost (Battle of Marengo, 14 June 1800). Nelson still tarried contrary to orders. In disgrace with his superiors at the Admiralty, he was given leave to return home but no ships with which to do so.[38] In July 1800 he traveled north overland in the company of Maria Carolina and the Hamiltons. He was feted everywhere he went. They reached Austria by late summer and after Vienna received them Nelson and Emma visited Eisenstadt, where they arrived on 7 September, just in time for the name day celebrations of Princess Esterházy. They stayed four days.

Haydn was swept up in the Nelson phenomenon like everyone else. In 1798 after the naval battle at Aboukir, Miss Cornelia Knight, daughter of another British admiral, had written a poem entitled "The Battle of the Nile." From this ode, which ends "Eternal praise, great Nelson!" Haydn excerpted several lines and composed a short cantata for soprano and piano entitled "Lines from the Battle of the Nile." He dedicated it to Emma Hamilton. It consists of an intricate recitative in the grand style that commences in c minor, leading to an aria in Haydn's now favorite key of B♭ major, and ending there with another patch of recitative.[39] The aria's main theme is heroic and not particularly memorable (like the words).

[37] Landon, *Haydn*, 4:562.
[38] Edgar Vincent, *Nelson: Love and Fame* (New Haven, 2003), pp. 370–71.
[39] Haydn, *The Battle of the Nile*, ed. H. C. Robbins Landon (Vienna, 1981).

The secondary theme that follows, on the other hand, first announced softly by the piano, is striking, and this very progression with bass and treble diverging by step so beautifully is encountered also in the late Piano Sonata in D (see Example 5.15). Thus Haydn's paternity in the case of that sonata, questioned above, receives confirmation here. Miss Knight, who accompanied the Hamiltons from Italy, had this to say in her memoirs about their stay in Vienna.

> We had often music, as the best composers and performers were happy to be introduced to Sir William and Lady Hamilton. I was much pleased with Haydn. He dined with us, and his conversation was modest and sensible. He set to music some English verses, and, amongst others, part of an ode I had composed after the battle of the Nile, and which was descriptive of the blowing up of L'Orient . . . Haydn accompanied Lady Hamilton on the piano when she sang this piece, and the effect was grand. He was staying at that time with Prince Esterházy, and presided over the famous concerts given by that nobleman at his magnificent palace in Hungary . . . It did not appear to me that the English nation was at all popular at Vienna. The people generally were opposed to the war with France, which had proved so unfortunate to them.[40]

Emma Hamilton was well known for her singing as well as her dancing. Responses to both varied greatly, from praise to ridicule. Of her devotion to Haydn there is no question. Griesinger wrote Härtel on 21 January 1801 that "Haydn found in Lady Hamilton a great admirer. She paid a visit with Nelson to the Esterházy estates in Hungary but she bothered very little with their highnesses and never left Haydn's side for two days."[41] In his Biographical Notes Griesinger wrote, "When Lord Nelson traveled through Vienna, he asked for a worn-out pen that Haydn had used in his composing, and made him a present of his watch in return." Two engraved portraits of Nelson were in Haydn's portfolio of pictures along with an engraved view of the Battle of Aboukir.

Whether the Mass in d minor of 1798 was performed at Eisenstadt under Haydn's direction in the presence of Nelson is a question that cannot be resolved. The most that can be said is that if it had been performed then, there would be at least a good explanation of how the work came to be called the "Nelson" Mass. Firm evidence points to the likelihood that the late Te Deum was performed on this occasion; namely, that Haydn paid a bill at the time for its copying.

There is an early setting of the Te Deum by Haydn that survives. It dates from ca. 1762 and is also in C major with trumpets and timpani. The two works provide a capsule view of how Haydn's style evolved over the nearly four decades separating them. Some things remain the same in spite of all the changes that

---

[40] *The Autobiography of Miss Knight*, ed. Roger Fulford (London, 1960), p. 73, cited after Landon, *Haydn* 4:561.

[41] Olleson, "Griesinger's Correspondence with Breitkopf & Härtel," 17.

enabled him to achieve broad and sweeping tonal climaxes in the later work. Aside from the key and the trumpets there are similar means of rhythmic propulsion from early to late. Also, he divides the text the same way, into three parts, fast-slow-fast, as if it were a concerto.

The late work is scored for flute, pairs of oboes, bassoons, and horns, three trumpets, timpani, strings, organ, and mixed chorus. One early source also included three trombones ad libitum. They are not accepted as authentic in the most recent critical edition of the score.[42] Another difference among early scores is that some lack the opening eight-measure ritornello for orchestra alone. The chorus begins singing in unison, doubled by the winds and accompanied by the rest of the orchestra, "Te, te Deum Laudamus," *Allegro con spirito* in common time, with a version of the Eighth Gregorian Psalm Tone, which is used in many other settings of the text as well. Haydn rarely asks the sopranos to sing above high G and generally the work is less difficult and demanding than are his late masses. Perhaps he trusted the musician of the imperial chapel less than those under his own direction at Eisenstadt.

The initial *Allegro* after eighty-two measures winds down to a dominant pedal, with blazing fanfares from the trumpets and drums. There follows an *Adagio* in c minor for the middle part of the text, "Te ergo quae sumus, famulis tuis subventi . . . " (Help us then, we implore thee: help thy servants whom thou hast ransomed with thy precious blood). The winds and brass are silent here, while the strings mostly throb in sixteenth-note chords. At the words "quos pretioso sanguine," Haydn places the symbol of lament, a descending chromatic tetrachord, in the bass. The *Adagio* takes only nine measures, rather like the medial interlude in some early eighteenth-century concertos. *Allegro con spirito* in C major with new music resumes for the rest of the text. Haydn sets the first part homophonically with some duetting, which well suits the first person plural of the choral pleas. Arriving at the last two lines he unleashes a double fugue, the sopranos singing "In te Domine speravi" against the countersubject of the altos singing "Non confundar in aeternum." Eventually the choral parts become fixated on a single diminished-seventh chord built up from a bass B♮ for four measures, creating great tension as they call back and forth to each other. Then they move up to a higher diminished-seventh chord built up over a bass C♯. Most of the orchestra moves by another whole tone up to E♭ from which it plunges down in sequence by a series of leaps: E♭↓A♭, C↓F, A♭↓B♮, followed by the chorus singing in unison and in canon two beats later. The effect is similar to and just as thrilling as the climactic sequence of falling fourths in the last chorus of *The Creation*. As in that chorus, the final cadences soon follow. The whole Te Deum has taken 193 measures, for a duration of about twelve minutes, surely one of the shorter settings of the many collected by Empress Marie Therese.

[42] Haydn, *Te Deum for the Empress Marie Therese* (1800), ed. Denis McCaldin (Oxford, 1992).

The Empress found in Michael Haydn a composer less occupied with other work and more willing to comply with her requests for new sacred music. By 1802 his older brother Joseph was suffering from nervous exhaustion brought on by his strenuous efforts to complete *The Seasons*. In view of Joseph's impending retirement from Esterházy service Prince Nicholas invited Michael to replace him as Kapellmeister. After a lengthy period of deliberation Michael decided he was better off in Salzburg under its new ruler, Archduke Ferdinand, formerly Grand Duke of Tuscany and dispossessed there by the French (as he would be in Salzburg after a short rule). In the draft of a letter to Michael dated 23 January 1803 Joseph expressed his regret at the decision, saying also that he understood it: "Both [Princes] are great, but the Archduke's love for and understanding of music are greater than those of my Prince." These few words say a world about the difference between Nicholas II and his grandfather, Nicholas I.

String Quartets, Opus 77

The reviewer for the *Allgemeine musikalische Zeitung* who attended the first public performance of *The Creation* on 19 March 1799 sent back a report dated five days later to which he added that Swieten was preparing a successor based on Thomson's *Seasons*, of which he had already completed "Spring," the first part. He added further that "Haydn is at work, as he himself informed me, on six new quartets for the Hungarian Count K." Haydn was indeed working on new string quartets, but only two emerged bearing the date 1799 and they were printed in 1802 by Artaria as Op. 77, dedicated not to a Hungarian Count K, but to Prince Joseph Franz Lobkowitz, a member of Swieten's Associated Company of Cavaliers. This prince was born in Bohemia in 1772, just two years after Beethoven, of whom he became a major patron and dedicatee of many works, among them the Op. 18 Quartets. Whether Lobkowitz originally commissioned Haydn's Op. 77 Quartets is unclear.

Haydn was finding that composition caused him more and more nervous reactions. The six new string quartets planned dwindled to three, finally to two. Griesinger wrote to Härtel on 12 June 1799 that Haydn had also promised to write a set of quintets for Count Moritz von Fries, a genre that he had not cultivated before, which makes the information appear somewhat suspect. On the other hand, he probably promised to write something for and dedicated to Fries, which he did, although it amounted to only the two movements of a string quartet he was able to finish in 1803, published as Op. 103. Also bearing on the question is Beethoven's splendid String Quintet in C with two violas, Op. 29, composed in 1800–1801 and dedicated to Count Fries, who presumably favored the genre. The same day Griesinger wrote to Härtel, 12 June 1799, Haydn himself addressed a letter to Christoph Breitkopf (son of Johann Gottlob, who died in 1794). He apologized for leaving an earlier letter unanswered, then goes on to explain how he was overwhelmed by work, and business (by which he meant mainly writing letters to secure subscribers to *The Creation* in published form).

> The older I get the more business I have to transact daily. I only regret that on account of advancing age and (unfortunately) the decrease of my mental powers, I am able to dispatch but the smallest part of it . . . Every day the world pays me compliments on the fire of my works, but no one will believe the effort and strain it costs me to produce them. There are some days on which the weakened memory and failing nerves so bring me down that I fall into the saddest condition and thus am quite incapable for many days at a time of finding even a single idea until at length Providence revives me, and I can sit down at the keyboard and begin to scratch away [kratzen]. Enough of this.

Later letters often repeated these sad and alarming tales of nervous exhaustion.

The Quartet in G, Op. 77 No. 1 reveals none of the problems of which Haydn complained. Rather, it proclaims his strength of mind, ready wit, and a profound command of his art on a par with any of his previous works. G major can become, among other things, a fertile ground for jesting and banter in the opera buffa sense. Consider in this light the opening Duettino for Figaro and Susanna in Mozart's opera, an *Allegro* in common time with propelling dotted rhythms on some offbeats. This quartet's *Allegro moderato* in common time has the same spirit and the same propelling offbeat dotted rhythms. Furthermore the music in both cases has a higher rhythmic and harmonic propellant, namely that which forces the initial G of the bass line to become a dissonance that must resolve down to F♯. On the second pass through his delightful first theme, Haydn has the cello respond to the flighty dotted figures of the first violin. Much of the movement turns out to be a game between these two instruments, while the two middle parts stand by and accompany the action.

If this were an actual opera buffa scene one could say of it that the pert chambermaid takes the lead over her slightly dense suitor, yet the latter gets in some good licks in return. There is scarcely another melodic idea besides the first that is needed to construct the whole movement, or dialogue, as it might well be called. The sustained passage of seven measures in D midway in the prima parte has sometimes been considered a second subject. While Haydn makes much of it in the extended development section he excludes it entirely from the reprise; in other words, it lacks one of the defining features a proper second theme should contribute. The seconda parte is so long without it that Haydn does not call for repetition. It ends, as did the prima parte, with a little tag in which dotted rhythm appears on all four beats of the measure before the cadence. Mozart ended both parts of the initial movement of his String Quartet in G, K. 387, first of the six he dedicated to Haydn, with the same little ending gesture in the identical place, the penultimate measures.[43] If Haydn is in dialogue with any other composer here it is certainly Mozart, and not, as has occasionally been claimed, his former student Beethoven, whose Quartets Op. 18 were composed between 1798 and 1800 (published 1801).

For the second movement Haydn wrote an *Adagio* in cut time and chose the key of E♭. The third relationship, and this particular one, a descent to ♭VI, can hardly surprise after so many superb examples of the same in his late works. The first idea, announced by all the parts in unison, is striking and dominates the entire movement: 8 3 6 | 4 2 ↓ 7. Brahms, a great admirer of Haydn, made of this same idea, in a more decorated form, the first theme of one of his late works, the Sonata for Clarinet and Piano in E♭, Op. 120 No. 2. Haydn's *Adagio* theme comes into full bloom when played by the cello deep in its range, changing the continuation so as to begin the transition to a second key, confirmed when the cello sounds the theme again in B♭. There is an enchanting moment when all the instruments come to rest on C, the cello on its lowest tone, a full measure and more of C, protracted by a fermata. The next move is bold, although once digested it seems inevitable. As if in a deceptive cadence, the harmony slides up a half step to D♭ where the first violin plays the head motif, accompanied by the others, all playing *pianissimo*. At the reprise we are back in E♭ with the first violin sounding the theme in a version that is fully harmonized. In the movement's final chord the viola provides the third, the G below middle C.

The *Menuet Presto* begins with the same G, now restored to being the tonic. The speed, vast leaps, and many syncopations of this manic-sounding dance have evoked comparisons with Beethoven, but up to this date no scherzo by the younger master has behaved so frantically at such breathtaking speed as this so-called minuet. Its Trio is in E♭ and is undeserving of its title in the sense that there is no hint of three-part texture. It is scarcely less wild than the main dance. The first violin plays all there is in the way of a melody, the other parts tag along following the leader, as if trying to keep up. Haydn writes out the repeats and at the end adds a transition back to the key of G.

The *Finale Presto* in 2/4 time is another large sonata form, comparable to the first movement in scope. It has a unison beginning, like that of the *Adagio*, and perhaps some thematic connection with the downward plunge of that movement's main idea. Here the tonal material is more exotic, with emphasis on a raised fourth in accented position (Example 6.17). The two leaps down a fifth in

EXAMPLE 6.17. *Haydn, String Quartet in G, Op. 77 No. 1, Finale*

[43] This correspondence, hardly a coincidence, was pointed out by Finscher, *Haydn* (2000), pp. 423–24, in a short section entitled "Das Ende: opus 77 und 103" that is full of valuable insights.

particular call to mind the plunging 4 2 ↓ 7 of the *Adagio*'s theme. The raised fourths bring up the possibility of being regarded as "in the Gypsies' style," as do the later streams of sixteenth notes.

Opus 77 No. 2 in F offers many puzzling features. Its opening movement is in common time, marked *Allegro moderato*, a combination of meter and tempo characteristic of the composer's earlier quartets, not his later ones. In fact, first movements in common time marked *Moderato* or *Allegro moderato* in Opp. 9, 17, 20, and 33 prevail by a margin of nearly two to one over other types of movement yet they are almost lacking after Op. 33. It is not just this type of movement that seems retrospective. The loose-jointed and square phrasing, concertante character, and above all the relegation of second violin, viola, and cello mainly to a role of harmonic underpinning, seem like a step backward. This kind of texture was typical of Op. 9 and Op. 17. Compare, for instance, the opening movement of Op. 17 No. 2 in F, which offers a *Moderato* in common time with an abundance of passages in which the cello jogs along in eighth notes, helping to mark the pulse but otherwise providing little interest.

Can the movement possibly be an earlier composition that Haydn pulled out of a drawer where it had lain neglected? No it cannot. There are too many features present showing how advanced it was for the time around 1800. The first idea promises little, being a kind of cliché of the lighter, serenade type of movement, especially sweet because of its parallel thirds and IV$^6_4$ - I progression (Example 6.18a). Mozart used this turn of phrase with apparently satirical intent

EXAMPLE 6.18 a, b.

a. *Haydn, String Quartet in F, Op. 77 No. 2, I*

when he had Leporello further taunt Elvira to begin the last and slower part of the Catalogue Aria (Example 6.18b). Leporello's voice is doubled by the violas

EXAMPLE 6.18

b. *Mozart,* Don Giovanni, *Catalogue Aria*

playing in thirds an octave above, and by the violins in thirds an octave above the violas, rendering the effect all the more saccharine. Haydn's beginning corresponds only to the "egli ha l'usanza" part, and not as sung by Leporello but as ornamented by the strings, without the doubling thirds. Haydn begins, that is, where Mozart has put the musical equivalent of an exclamation point, a sudden *forte* on the D. He avoids using the accompanying thirds against the violin's descent and instead has his second violin ascend against the first, which results in rather acerbic intervals of an eleventh followed by a seventh. On the second statement of the theme Haydn almost yields to allowing the consonant thirds in descent but not quite, then he becomes more intricate by introducing the head motif in the inner voices, then in the cello.

When it is time for the second key to arrive Haydn prepares in an old-fashioned way, with a flourish on V/V then a stop. The second idea, as so often with Haydn, is but the first in a new guise. It appears in the middle of the texture with a chromatic rise above it in the first violin C D D♯ E (Example 6.18a, mm. 37–40). At a moderate pace, and slurred as marked, this *sotto voce* passage cannot help but resemble what used to be called "close harmony," of the kind associated with barbershop quartets and the like. An admirable nineteenth-century composer, Antonín Dvořák, did not hesitate to begin one of his loveliest Slavonic Dances (Op. 72 No. 6) with a slow passage very like this. The point is that Haydn is anticipating a kind of music that is more characteristic of the nineteenth century than he is usually credited with (or blamed for). Another detail in which his *Allegro moderato* seems in advance of its time is the way he goes so far afield tonally, to e♭ minor, transforming it into e minor, and then getting gradually back to F for the reprise.[44]

Haydn places the minuet next, as he often did in his earlier quartets, much less often in his later ones. He marks this piece *Menuet Presto.* Its brusque

---

[44] László Somfai, "A Bold Enharmonic Modulatory Model in Joseph Haydn's String Quartets," in *Studies in Eighteenth-Century Music: A Tribute to Karl Geiringer on his Seventieth Birthday*, ed. H. C. Robbins Landon and Roger E. Chapman (New York, 1970), pp. 370–81.

counter-rhythms make it seem like a scherzo of a slightly later time, although it is not quite so wild as the dance movement of the previous quartet. For the Trio Haydn slips from F down to D♭ after rests for four beats. He has made this move down a major third without modulation so familiar there is little surprise involved for us, but that was scarcely the case in the 1790s. Here the mood of ser-enade music that inspired the main theme of the first movement returns. Paral-lel thirds up and down by step over drones in the cello provide a kind of lighter music in relief of the main dance, as Trios often did. As in the previous quartet's dance movement there is a transition added to prepare the return of the first dance, da capo.

An *Andante* in 2/4 time and in the key of D follows, a rounded binary form with repeats, foretelling variations to come. Arrival of the first variation is delayed by an interlude of seventeen measures mostly prolonging the dominant, A. Then comes a proper variation, with the theme assigned to the second violin in the middle of the texture, the first violin providing comment above. Haydn was wise to do away with the repeats, for variation cannot lend much interest to a theme that has so little to begin with (it keeps repeating 3 2 1). Variation two begins in tonic minor, shortening the theme quite drastically, and could be regarded as merely a transition on the way to a full-scale return of the theme, played now by the cello with the first violin executing thirty-second note arabesques nonstop from beginning to end. Such an old-fashioned device as this sounds mechanical and routine at so late a stage in Haydn's music, although it would not have been thought so in Op. 9 or Op. 17. The first violin abandons its frenzy of quick notes and after a pedal on A and a dramatic preparation, plays the original theme *pia-nissimo*, fully harmonized for the first time.

The *Finale Vivace assai* returns to F. It is in 3/4 time with strong accents on the second beat (or on the second half of beats), with a great deal of syncopation. As a dance type it is familiar from the finale of the Piano Trio in A, the first of the set of three dedicated to the dowager Princess Esterházy. Like that movement this one has strong Hungarian overtones. In this large-scale sonata form only the prima parte is repeated. The seconda parte begins with a series of canonic imita-tions based on the first theme, the four instruments offering cascading versions of an upbeat-begun figure descending stepwise from the fifth degree. There are many passages like this in Haydn's latest instrumental compositions and they often, as here, bear some kinship with the powerful canons in the development of Symphony No. 102's first movement. Those canons were also built on a conjunct descent of several tones beginning with an upbeat that gives them great rhythmic momentum, and they moved from place to place tonally in a similar way.

Although Op. 77 No. 2 finishes with a strong finale, some of the more puz-zling aspects in the other movements, as well as their sequence of keys—odd even for very late Haydn—cannot but raise suspicions that the work gave its creator uncommon trouble. This might have had something to do with its lack of a direct successor. More likely, Haydn left off composing quartets mainly because he was so pressured by other compositional tasks, besides all the business he was conducting. By summer 1799 he was working on another mass ordered by the Prince to honor his wife's name day. Also, much of the work on the new oratorio with Swieten occurred in 1799. It is not surprising then that these labors began taking their toll on his health.

The Seasons

A somewhat happenstance set of circumstances had accounted for *The Creation*'s genesis: an old English oratorio text was given to Haydn in London; remembering it in Vienna some months later he consulted Baron van Swieten as to its feasibility; they decided to go ahead and attempt the project. *The Seasons* was planned carefully from the start so as to capitalize on the success of *The Creation*. It is unclear whether Haydn or Swieten came up with the idea to make a German text, *Die Jahreszeiten*, by adapting Thomson's *The Seasons*. Certainly both worked together to fashion a vehicle displaying many of Haydn's strengths that had so impressed the public in *The Creation*: climactic choruses of praise and thanks to the deity; orchestral tone paintings on a vast as well as tiny scale; a quasi-operatic narrative allowing for the customary format of recitatives and arias.

James Thomson of Scotland lived from 1700 to 1748 and wrote his epic poem on country life in the 1720s, inspired by Milton's *Paradise Lost*. The succession from one oratorio to the next was foreordained in a way since Milton's poem was a mainspring of *The Creation*. Singing the praises of a humble life close to nature was quite out of step with Rococo sensibilities at the time in which Thomson wrote. Consider the cases of two of his main contemporaries on the Continent: Metastasio, born in 1698, who despised life in the country; Boucher, born in 1703, who opined of Nature that it was "too green." Thomson's poem first came out in installments and its reception encouraged him to branch off into some very wordy digressions as he continued. The final version amounted to a grand total of over 5000 lines.[45]

Swieten was on his own in the task of drastically condensing Thomson's poem down to a reasonable 650 lines. Fortunately the subject matter itself provided a strong framework of four sequential actions of equal duration, beginning with "Spring." He selected what would most likely interest Haydn, with an eye on what had particularly pleased in *The Creation*. Where Thomson did not provide narrative or pictorial matter appropriate for music Swieten supplied it, relying on

---

[45] Landon, *Haydn*, 5:93–94.

other poets in some cases. The great choruses that end each season with grand celebrations of one sort or another owe much to their equivalents in *The Creation* and sometimes even surpass them. Swieten was not up to the task of providing an English text that would fit the same music nearly as well as the German. With the previous oratorio he could fall back on the original English libretto for wording. His English version of *Die Jahreszeiten* often went beyond the quaintly odd to the scarcely intelligible. Many attempts have been made to redress the situation with better English. Such multiplicity makes it advisable to refer here to the individual numbers usually by their German texts. This is not meant to take any credit away from the good Baron, without whom we would lack Haydn's glorious final oratorio. Swieten provided not only an English singing text for the first publication of the work by Breitkopf and Härtel but also a French one, whereupon two scores were printed, German-English and German-French. Apparently the French version was as impossible as the English one. Instead of helping to ensure the success of the oratorio abroad these singing translations achieved the opposite, effectively impeding the initial reception in France and England. The setting invoked by Swieten's text was not Thomson's Britain but the mountainous lands of central Europe ruled by the Habsburgs, with their lofty snow-covered peaks and lush green valleys for farming and hunting.

What we know about the early stages of the work come mainly from Haydn's two diplomat friends Griesinger and Silverstolpe. The beginnings of the new oratorio coincided loosely with the public performances of *The Creation* in the spring of 1799. Griesinger arrived in Vienna that year as the tutor to a son of Count von Schönfeld, the ambassador from Dresden, and he remained in Saxon service to become Secretary, then Councilor, to the legation. His friend Härtel in Leipzig asked Griesinger to help him gain access to Haydn. Griesinger's letter to Härtel dated Vienna, 12 June 1799 mentions that "Haydn will compose a counterpart to his *Creation* about the four seasons; Van Swieten is writing the text for it." On 4 February 1800 Griesinger wrote Härtel, "Haydn is rather far along on his four seasons." Silverstolpe confirmed this in his report back to Stockholm dated 5 April: "The 'Spring' is already done and Haydn is writing with new zeal, since he has recently had the good fortune to lose his spiteful [böse] wife. She followed Frau Gluck, who died recently—they had quite different characters." Then on 1 July 1800 Haydn himself wrote Härtel relaying his belated thanks for a gift and his regrets for not being able to oblige him by composing a new piano sonata (probably meaning a piano trio): "The difficult task that I now have of composing *The Seasons*, along with my weakened physical state, do not permit me to work on two things at once."

The same Viennese soloists who sang *The Creation* were called upon to perform *The Seasons*: Mlle Saal, soprano, her father, bass, and Rathmayer, tenor. Initial performances took place as semi-private ones at the Schwarzenberg Palace under the auspices of Swieten's Company of Associates, beginning on 23 April 1801. The first public performance was in the large Redoutensaal a month later on 29 May, after the end of the concert season and general exodus of the nobility. The house was not full. Rosenblum estimated an audience of 700, roughly half the hall's capacity. The scant month between first private and public performances did not allow for the excitement to mount as it had for *The Creation*.

Zinzendorf was present at the performance on 23 April and names in his diary several members of the high nobility who attended, including Archduke Ferdinand, Beethoven's patron Archduke Maximilian (d. 27 June 1801), and Prince Starhemberg, the Obersthofmeister. He wrote more than usual in describing the music.

> Le *Printems* a de la musique douce, un Freudenlied et un Hymne qui plait. L'*Eté* exprime bien la langueur generale qu'occasione le chaud. L'orage est rebattu. L'*Automne* est tres varié, un hymne au travail. Les noisettes, l'amour des champs, le limier, la chasse au lièvre, la chasse à courre, les vendanges, un tapage incroyable. L'*Hyver*, la chanson des fileuses, la romance d'Annette, de la morale et un Hymne. Cela est long.

That the work is long cannot be denied, perhaps a third longer than *The Creation*. Zinzendorf's point about the variety of "Autumn" is well taken, and his choice of words is apt in describing the way it ends: "an incredible racket." The initial performance he attended began at 7 p.m. and lasted about three hours. Griesinger was also there and sent a detailed critique of the work to Leipzig for the *Allgemeine musikalische Zeitung*, which printed it on 2 May 1801. It will be cited here in part as some of the individual pieces come up for discussion.

"The Introduction presents the passage from winter to spring" (Die Einleitung stellt den Übergang vom Winter zum Frühling vor). Each of the four parts has such an introductory prelude. This one is also a powerful overture to the whole work. It begins with a *Largo* of four measures in common time with an initial unison G for strings, bassoons, and timpani, all marked *fortissimo*, followed by similarly marked whole notes F, E♭ (trilled), and D in the strings. On this last tone Haydn places a fermata and makes it more ominous by adding a roll on the timpani's D. Beethoven was struck by the power of this opening, as is evident from the beginnings of his second and third Leonore Overtures.

What will come next is uncertain, at least on first hearing. It could be C. In fact it is g minor that arrives on the next downbeat, initiating a sonata form that is on the scale of Haydn's largest symphonic opening movements. This *Vivace* in common time sounds angry and menacing. It portrays winter's stormy behavior upon departing and its lurking power to wreak more havoc. The first theme is a canonic exchange between treble and bass at the octave that firmly establishes the reign of g minor. As a dialogue the canon sounds more like a combat than a conversation. The relative major arrives eventually, bringing little contrast of mood at first, only more latent forms of menace, with a few brief moments of lighter fare in a playful interchange among solo winds. At the cadence the lower strings hurl their offbeat responses to the first violin and wind chords on the beat. The seconda parte plunges from B♭ to b♭ minor, beginning a chase pursued through several keys until the reprise. There are rushing passages in sixteenth notes that could suggest wintry gusts not yet ready to depart. As the movement winds down the harmony comes to linger on a *fortissimo* diminished-seventh chord built up over B♮ in the bass, held for nine measures, whereupon the bass Simon enters singing in recitative "See how winter flees." After resolution to c minor the retreat is described with vivid commentary by the orchestra, making this one of Haydn's grandest obbligato recitatives.

An orchestral softening occurs after the tenor Lucas enters and describes the melting snow falling from cliffs, with a tonal move to A♭. E♭ is suggested next as the soprano Hanne enters and announces a balmy southern wind replacing wintry blasts, the messenger of "Spring." With this the E♭ chord is transformed into an augmented-sixth chord resolving to D, the harmony implied wavering between D and g minor. Swieten, having used the word "Frühling," employs another lovely word meaning "spring" for the chorus that begins "Komm holder Lenz!" just as Haydn saves B♮ from any appearance before the tender melody in the first flute, reinforced softly an octave below by the first violins. "Come, gentle spring!" is charming and begins Thomson's poem. "Komm holder Lenz!" is even better, more euphonious, and a perfect match for Haydn's melody.

Of Haydn's many pastorales in the key of G major, with lilting 6/8 time and frequent drone harmonies, this one deserves the crown. There is a challenger even so, exemplified above in the *Allegretto e innocentemente* of the first piano sonata for Princess Marie Hermenegild as a young bride in 1784 (see Example 4.25). The chorus is also marked *Allegretto*. To make its point fully it must be extended and challenged tonally so that a complete reprise is necessary and desirable. Swieten obliges with a text Haydn sets as an episode in C major for the sopranos and altos, divided into four parts and representing Wives and Maidens. This is followed by an episode in c minor for the subdivided tenor and bass sections, for which Swieten provided a warning against premature celebrations, as the chill blasts of winter could still return. Instead, the reprise begins. To make its ending more climactic Haydn employs rising chromatic progressions akin to those he perfected in *The Creation*.

Simon sings the first aria after a very short, simple recitative. It is an *Allegretto* in C major and in jaunty 2/4 time, like a contredanse. The text describes how the husbandman begins his work in tilling the field while whistling a happy song. The orchestra then quotes the tune he whistles, and it is Haydn's greatest "hit" tune of all, the *Andante semplice* of the "Surprise" Symphony No. 94 in G (with *Andante* conveniently in C). There are several instances in this last oratorio where Haydn casts a nostalgic glance backward over his career. Griesinger in his long review of *The Seasons* identifies the quotation in Simon's aria and says of the piece that it "breathes the air of unaffected sprightliness." The aria's jaunty character is reinforced by the orchestration. The bassoons play quick notes staccato in their most jocular vein, and the country air of the whole is reinforced when the basses intone a drone with minor second appoggiaturas from below, suggesting bagpipes. Ways are found in text and music to stretch this aria out to considerable length.

The Prayer (Bittgesang), or Hymn as Zinzendorf called it, comes next, for which Haydn selected the key of F and *Poco Adagio* in 3/4 time. Lucas begins the serene melody and the chorus responds by singing the same broadly framed entreaty to Heaven for its blessing. The general message is the same as the Agnus Dei of the Mass and so it is no surprise to hear that the music resembles some actual settings of that prayer. Composers often favored slow 3/4 time for the initial section of the Agnus Dei and a trochee-iamb setting of the first two words. Such was the case in Mozart's "Coronation" Mass, K. 317, for a melody that was used later to begin "Dove sono" in *Figaro*. A very similar beginning is used by Haydn to begin the Agnus Dei of his last mass setting in 1802 (Example 6.19abc). Note

EXAMPLE 6.19 a, b, c.

a. *Mozart, "Coronation" Mass, K. 317, Agnus Dei*

b. *Haydn,* The Seasons, *Aria, "Sei uns gnädig"*

c. *Haydn, "Harmoniemesse," Agnus Dei*

how the two halves of the phrase are connected by an instrumental tag in all cases. In "Sei uns gnädig" the other two soloists join Lucas and have various interchanges with the chorus. Eventually the piece becomes a fugue, the subject of which closely resembles that of "Quam olim Abraham" in Mozart's Requiem. This final section is marked *Un poco più moto* and has a running bass in sixteenth notes through most of it.

"Spring" has so far been a series of dominant to tonic resolutions: g/G → C → F → ? Haydn avoids the predictable here and opts for a third relationship, to A major, for the following recitative and chorus plus solo voices, begun by Hanne, an *Andante* in 2/4 time. It is described as a *Freuden-Lied* (the same expression as in Zinzendorf) for a chorus of youths. The text lists various natural beauties springing to new life, giving mention in the final section to buzzing bees, birds on the wing, and the gamboling of lambkins, all duly painted in the orchestra, though briefly. The piece ends not on A but on D, giving Haydn one of his favorite progressions of all, from D to B♭ for the final sunburst of "Spring" (i.e., V/vi passing directly to I). Swieten had suggested changing to a key markedly different so as to enhance the solemn and devotional aspects of the textual cries. Haydn complied.

The orchestra at its most powerful leads the way with a unison tutti *fortissimo* on B♭, joined by the timpani. They repeat the tone in faster note values and with dotted rhythm, to which the chorus responds, also in unison, "Ewiger," falling a fourth from B♭ to F. The orchestra next sounds B♭ and D to the same pattern, which elicits from the chorus "mächtiger." Then the orchestra sounds the full tonic triad. The chorus, instead of following suit, sounds a full V^7 chord with electrifying effect, resolving to I for "gütiger *Gott*!" The original translation, "Endless God, mighty God, merciful God!" counters the buildup in which "God" is saved until last, along with resolution to the tonic. Two additional three-syllable words are needed, such as "E'erlasting, Powerful, Merciful God!" Haydn's inspiration for this passage may well have been the beginning of Act II in *Die Zauberflöte*, "the solemn scene" as Mozart called it. After the opening March of the Priests, Mozart has his winds intone a three-fold blast on B♭, with dotted rhythm and a treble that climbs up the triad 1 3 5 (a passage he later altered in harmony and used to begin the Overture). Both Haydn and Mozart use three trombones to enhance the power and solemnity of these passages. Many listeners in Vienna at that time must have noticed the similarities, which shed a particular light upon Haydn's fanfare to honor three attributes of the divine. Some listeners thought they detected certain Masonic elements in *The Creation*. Yet the kinship of this passage with Mozart's *Die Zauberflöte* is clearer than anything in the previous oratorio.

The mighty fanfare and choral response constitute a slow introduction ending on V to what could be considered the main introduction, a *Poco Adagio* in 3/4 time that begins simply, with a song-like antecedent phrase for the two clarinets playing in sixths with the two bassoons supplying the bass. The trio of soloists then takes up the same half-phrase to a text about how the Lord's abundance has comforted us. This prompts the choral tenors and basses to interject "Mächtiger Gott!" supported by the full orchestral tutti, *fortissimo*. Only then does the consequent phrase for the soloists arrive. The exchanges continue until this second slow introduction comes to rest on a protracted F. An *Allegro* in common time then transforms the F into the first tone of a fugue, begun by the basses, followed by the other parts in ascending order. Haydn treats this vigorous fugue subject at length, demonstrating how many different ways he can make it combine with itself, and modulating enough to prepare a great climax on the return to the tonic. To cap the excitement he deploys a very long chromatic line rising in the basses, one that competes with the passage doing the same and similarly placed near the end of "The Heavens are telling," which closed Part I of *The Creation*. Here Haydn pushes still further. He has twice taken his sopranos up to high A♭ in the course of the piece, then takes them by an octave leap up to high B♭ and has them sustain it for nearly two measures. After this moment of exhilaration he returns to the fanfare music of the first introduction and repeats the initial acclamations. Haydn's late works have many great choruses of praise in B♭. None tops this one.

"Summer" begins softly with an introduction painting the twilight before dawn. Marked *Adagio* and in common time, it soon becomes an obbligato recitative for Lucas, at the end for Simon. As unlike the music for "Spring" as can be, the music creeps slowly along, beginning in c minor, with a winding chromatic line that struggles to rise. The text is both pictorial and sonic, mentioning the gloomy sounds of night birds returning to their caves, and a bright-sounding call in C major for solo oboe that suggests the cockcrow, harbinger of day. This is the signal for the countryman to assemble his flock and lead them to pasture. A dawn song for solo horn commences the aria for Simon, an *Allegretto* in 6/8 time and in F. What the horn plays is actually a signal call that was widely recognized as such at the time (Example 6.20). Griesinger in his review refers to it as a traditional

EXAMPLE 6.20. *Haydn*, The Seasons, *Aria, "Der munt're Hirt"*

(Horn signal for the herds to go out.)

call. Haydn had used it near the beginning of his first "Times of Day" set of symphonies, No. 6 in D ("Le Matin").[46] The aria is short, a scant sixty measures before its final tone turns into a modulation introducing an obbligato rec-

---

[46] *Haydn, Mozart*, p. 270, ex. 4.6. There he gives the call to the solo flute to begin the prima parte, then transfers it to solo horn just before the reprise.

itative for Hanne. She announces that rosy dawn is approaching and describes the mountain peaks as already tipped with fiery gold. Haydn was experienced in the orchestral painting of sunrises: Symphony No. 6 begins with one as a slow introduction. *The Creation*'s sunrise is also in D and slow. Here he writes a *Largo* in common time and in D. The violins begin a long climb to the high tonic, described by the soloists, then the chorus, at the sun's gradual rise. Resolution brings an *Allegro* as the first violins reach high D in accented position, then run up to high F♯ while the chorus sings "Heil, oh Sonne, Heil!" To extend the piece after it has reached a big cadence on V in the middle, the soloists begin an *Andante* in 3/4 time that provides contrast before the original *Allegro* returns. The soloists thank the Creator for such a wonder of Nature, which is greeted by the chorus with shouts of joy.

"Summer" is the only season to be treated as the progress of a single day from dawn to dusk. In this sense it covers the same span as the "Times of Day" Symphonies of forty years earlier. The subject was perfect for the young Haydn, no less than for the composer at the peak of his powers.

Swieten quickens the passage of time so that in the following recitative, reaping scythes (*semplice*) and a trembling in the muted strings (*obbligato*) accompany mention of the midday sun beating down on the land under a cloudless sky. He allowed himself some images that are rather too complicated for what has to be sung, for instance, "On the scorched plains floats, steaming below, a blinding sea of light and reflection" (in the original English "O'er th'arid grounds and parched fields of gleaming and reflected rays a dazzling deluge reigns"). This precedes a Cavatina for Lucas in E major, *Largo* in common time, on a text about how man, beast, flowers and all else wilt in the raging heat. Strings remain muted and predominant, with only a few cadential reinforcements from the flute and oboe. A short piece, it has an active bass, lending a retrospective cast. The E of the final chord connects by third relationship to the following piece in C, an obbligato recitative for Hanne, *Poco Adagio* and, what is an unusual occurrence in recitative, in 3/4 time. With its shady groves and murmuring waters, the text offers respite, pastoral images that Haydn translates into woodwind colorings. The piece is nearly an arioso for orchestra, with voice declaiming in typical recitative formulas (cf. "Che puro ciel" in Gluck's *Orfeo*). Its cadence on B♭ prepares the locus for the substantial aria that follows, sung by Hanne. "Welche Labung für die Sinne" (O what comfort for the senses) begins slowly as an *Adagio* in 3/4 time, with commentaries from the solo oboe. An *Allegro assai* in common time comes next, displaying some obvious similarities to Mozart's *Tito*. Hanne's big two-tempo aria is not a rondò although it is close to one. Its fast section is a display piece with coloratura. The solo oboe keeps up with the vocal acrobatics and even outdoes them. There is no reason why an oratorio should not have its operatic moments, and good precedents abound.

It is time for the tempest. In simple recitative over a bass with chromatic turns that project unease, Simon describes how the heavy air has ascended to the mountain tops and how the sky darkens. Lucas responds to a dull roaring that has just sounded from the valley (his reaction caused by a soft roll on the timpani's G). The strings enter *Poco Adagio* in 3/4 time plucking disjunct chords as Hanne expresses anxious anticipation. Nature pauses, she sings, no leaf or creature stirs. When the progression reaches c minor the timpanist again rolls the G very softly. "Deathly silence [Todesstille] reigns," she concludes, unaccompanied. In a flash, *attaca subito*, the storm erupts with a bolt of lightning.

The Times of Day Symphonies of 1761 featured a storm that waits until the finale of No. 8 ("Le Soir"), where it occupies the whole last movement, entitled "La Tempesta." There Haydn had the flute descend in a jagged arpeggio representing lightning (Example 6.21a). Forty years later the choice is still the same, but the jagged descent is more terrifying, because it is a diminished-seventh chord in outline instead of a major triad (Example 6.21b). The effect is similar and part

EXAMPLE 6.21 a, b.

a. *Haydn, Symphony in G, No. 8, Finale, "La tempesta"*

b. *Haydn, The Seasons, Chorus "Ach! das Ungewitter naht"*

of it was certainly visual, for the jagged paths traced by the notation even looked like forked lightning. This kind of *Augenmusik* remained a potent stimulus. Surely it originated in operatic storms and remained in fashion on the stage far into the nineteenth century.

When the flute's lightning bolt strikes bottom on middle C, it is smothered by the entire orchestra (minus the trombones) *fortissimo* on the same C. After their bout of pizzicato the strings use their bows, the same switch that proved so powerful at the creation of light in the previous oratorio. There it was the chord of C major that over-powered listeners, here the single tone C. More overpowering is the entrance of the chorus in the following measure on a diminished-seventh chord strengthened by the three trombones and the timpani roll on C. The chorus calls on Heaven for help and asks "where shall we flee" (Wo flie'n wir hin!). Any country person would have known that indoor shelter was a better idea than under the nearest tree. Be that as it may, a piece of music with such a beginning has to roll on to an appropriate length, and the chorus as protagonists have to remain on stage, as it were, and suffer through the whole of it. A good, rip-roaring thunderstorm cannot make a sudden departure. At the height of the storm, Haydn doubles the tempo to *Allegro* in cut time and does what comes naturally to him in one of these great homophonic choruses. He resorts to fugue. It has a drooping chromatic subject, appropriate to suffering, sung to a strong text: "The earth convulsed reels to the very bed of the sea" (original: "Convulsed is the globe till in the boundless deep"). With this the piece achieves the desired length and gravity. As it winds down, the chorus resumes singing "Weh' uns" in block chords alternating with the orchestra, and the music subsides gradually, with a final descending chromatic fourth. The orchestra adds a little postlude of its own in which the last chord is not c minor but C major.

Chorus and soloists rejoice after the storm in F major, a destination that could have been guessed. The vehicle is an *Allegretto* in 2/4 time, of the same jaunty contredanse character exploited twice before. The sun peeps out from behind the clouds before setting, sings Hanne, who follows Lucas. The cattle return to their accustomed stalls, adds Simon. Gentler nature takes the stage again as the quail calls to its mate, crickets chirp, and in the marsh frogs croak, these last critters requiring a digression, although painted orchestrally by Haydn only briefly and quite unobtrusively. Suffice it to say here that the ending parts of "Summer" are charming. Modulations prepare the final chorus in E♭, in which the evening bell tolls. Praises are sung of the stars that shine from above, inviting all to gentle sleep.

There was a tiff between Haydn and Swieten about one instance of the work's tone paintings. Griesinger recounted it as follows in his *Biographical Notes*.

> *The Creation* and *The Seasons* have been criticized for depicting objects foreign to the nature of music, which is inherently subjective and not objective, and this imitation is indeed not unconditionally commendable. In the midst of so many excellences, however, such passages are only minor blemishes, and Haydn himself set small store by them. When in correcting the clavier edition of *The Seasons* he found the croaking frogs too strongly expressed, he observed that this place really belonged to Grétry, and Baron van Swieten wanted it that way. In the full orchestra this vulgar notion would disappear soon enough, but it would not do in the clavier edition.

A comparison of the two passages shows that the keyboard version in fact prolongs and emphasizes the offending trill, which is scarcely noticeable in the orchestra. According to Dies, Haydn "sensed something base about it and tried to keep it from being heard. Swieten took him to task on this account, produced an old piece [by Grétry] in which the croaks were set with prominent display, and tried to talk Haydn into imitating it." Haydn was insulted and let his ire surface in a letter to August Müller, the Leipzig arranger of the keyboard version, when he corrected the passage on a separate sheet and jotted down "this whole passage imitating a frog did not flow from my pen: I was forced to write down this French croak [Quark]." To his consternation, these words found their way to a hostile critic who reported them in print. Swieten was furious when he saw them but the rift was soon patched. Haydn had high respect for Swieten in general, and rightly so. He also respected French musicians, who did him many honors during his last decade, more than those of any other nation. One of his fondest hopes, never to be realized, was to take *The Seasons* to Paris and direct performances of it there, and thus pay his respects to some of his most ardent supporters.

"Autumn" begins with an introduction that paints the countryman's delight at the rich harvest. An *Allegretto* in 3/4 time with abundant dotted rhythm and in the key of G, it is a modest-sized ternary form in which a bassoon and a flute join the violin melody in alternation. After the cadence Hanne begins in recitative and is joined by Lucas. The chorus in C that follows, *Allegretto* in common time, praises the labor that brought such abundant rewards. The text verges on the stilted. A typical line is "O Fleiss, o edler Fleiss, von dir kommt alles Heil [Oh work, noble work, from thee comes all prosperity]." Haydn protested to Griesinger that he had been a hard worker all his life though unconvinced that industriousness per se could be a subject for music. Unsurprisingly his music for this chorus and the three soloists can scarcely redeem the text. Eventually it breaks out in a fugue, *Più Allegro*, on the line quoted, meaning we hear it repeated countless times. Trumpets and drums add fanfares to end the piece.

A section for Hanne and Lucas follows that leads coyly up to their love duet, with country images of little children at play and a young swain spying on his beloved shepherdess. The duet begins as an *Allegretto* in 2/4 time and in B♭, a folklike tune with many repeated tones, its rustic character reinforced by the bassoons doubling the violins, all playing staccato. The lovers sing each other's praises, and when the piece moves to an *Adagio* in 3/4 and in C major, they praise true love, then return to the jaunty manner in B♭, *Allegro,* to conclude. Writing a tenor-soprano love duet meant fewer challenges for the composer than the bass-soprano one of Adam and Eve in *The Creation*. The result is no better. They are both quite comic-opera oriented.

Simon's recitative that follows has a confusing text: the countryman does not mind if unbidden guests (insects? poachers? wild animals?) consume whatever is left behind in the cornfield because he does not wish the remains to cause his censure for having profited too much. He regards this as a boon "and willingly joins in the hunt that delights his good master," Swieten's non-sequitur attempts to paper over the discrepancy between his country folks and the aristocratic pastime of hunting that was denied to them, or allowed them to participate only in the most menial ways. Truer to life was the outraged farmer whose garden was ravaged by his lord's hunting party in the opéra comique *Le jardinier et son Seigneur* by Sedaine and Philidor.[47]

The first hunting piece is an aria in a minor, *Allegro* in common time, sung by Simon. It concerns shooting birds with the aid of a hunting dog to track them down (referred to by Zinzendorf as a "limier," i.e., a bloodhound). The text could not be more pictorial. The dog lopes through the grass in search of traces, and nearing its quarry, stops in its tracks, standing motionless as a stone. Haydn depicts the idea with a bass in constant eighth-note motion, increasing the excitement to a sixteenth-note ostinato passage, *Più moto*, just before the dog stops, depicted by the music coming to a virtual halt. At this point Haydn switches to A major as the bird is flushed and tries to rise in flight. One shot brings the prey down. The loud noise of the gun's discharge is captured by a *fortissimo* tutti chord with timpani. Opponents of tone painting had much more to complain about here than they did with the frogs. Opponents of blood sports (and curiously, James Thomson was among the few who were) could only have been as outraged then as they are now. Swieten was an avid hunter, and so was Haydn after he had risen high above his original status. The same must also have been true of a large majority of their Viennese audiences.

Next comes the hunting of hares, with a pack of hounds rousting them from their burrow, dispatched quickly in an obbligato recitative marked *Allegro*, with the strings chasing after each other in little spurts up and down, and falling only at the end as the hares succumb and are "laid out in rows with delight." The cadence in A is joined without a break to the beginning of the Hunting Chorus, one of the work's most famous pieces, as the first of the horn calls sounds, beginning unaccompanied on A. Van Swieten suggested using some of the traditional calls associated with the stag hunt, which Haydn did, many of them in fact.[48]

Haydn uses four horns. They are crooked in D for the first part of the chorus and all of them play the unison call to begin the piece, *Vivace* in 6/8 time, the typical meter of the *Chasse par force* on horseback (Zinzendorf calls it "Chasse à courre"). Audiences of those times would have had their joy redoubled at recognizing in the horns' initial call "La Queste," traditionally sounded to alert all participants, huntsmen, servants, horses, and dogs, that the hunt was about to begin.

Four horns playing in unison make a very strong impression, in accordance with the first line of the text, "Listen to the loud tone that resounds throughout the forest!" The horns remain in unison as they sound various calls inter-

[47] *Music in European Capitals*, pp. 749, 767.

[48] Daniel Heartz, "The Hunting Chorus in Haydn's *Jahreszeiten* and the 'Airs de Chasse' in the *Encyclopédie*," *Eighteenth Century Studies* 9 (1976): 523–39. Independently of my essay, Landon later published similar findings based on some of the same sources. See Landon, *Haydn*, 5:167–70.

spersed among the choral entries describing the progress of the hunt. Three-note slides in the orchestra are explained immediately after they sound as the barking of the hungry hounds. The piece is not stagnant tonally in spite of the tonic-bound horn calls. Toward the end of the first section two horns play a two-part call (i.e., two tones sounding at once). A rapid modulation takes the key up a half step to E♭. The horns change crooks and two of them initiate the new key with a two-voiced call, at which the chorus interjects "Now he [the stag] has fooled the hounds, and disordered they run amok." The tonal move from D to E♭, like a deceptive cadence, provides a tonal equivalent. It is necessary to call the scattered hounds together and get them back on track. This is accomplished by sounding the age-old cry "Ta-jo!" (i.e., "Tally-ho!").[49] The chorus sings it to the traditional rising-fourth interval. Beyond merely describing the hunt, the chorus here impersonates the hunters. The new key of E♭ remains in control. Haydn works up to a climax, eventually calling on all four horns, as the hunters and reunited dogs regain the advantage. There is a sudden dropping down of the dynamic from *fortissimo* to *piano* accompanying a move to the subdominant, A♭. This momentary wave of tenderness can be interpreted as one of pity for the cornered stag. The original English text says "Surrounded now from ev'ry side, his spirits and his rigour lost, exhausted drops the nimble deer."

"Halali!" the shout of victory, one of the best known calls of all, sounds forth in the horns, punctuated by the three-note slides of the barking dogs rendered by strings and trombones. The men of the chorus proclaim "of sounding brass the conqu'ring tune, of hunters the loud triumphant shouts: Halali." They stretch out the last word on its middle syllable as the call is heard again in the horns, doubled by other sections of the winds. Use of this call as a triumphant conclusion to hunting pieces has quite a history in opera. Two salient examples must suffice. The Hunting Aria in Philidor's *Tom Jones* (1765), an opera encountered by Haydn in London, ends with "Halali" as a climax after a soft interlude.[50] Étienne Méhul's 1797 opéra comique *Le jeune Henri* was preceded by an overture that was so popular it had a life of its own as *La chasse du jeune Henri*, which charts the progress of the hunt and ends with "Halali." The overture was welcomed by E. T. A. Hoffmann with a lengthy review saying "this excellent composer . . . has furnished in his brisk and brilliant hunting-piece a reliable model for those who wish, in striving to conjure forth particular pictures from the imagination, to paint in music."[51] Possibly Haydn was among those to whom he furnished a model in this case.

---

[49] Michael Kelly in his memoirs tells an amusing story involving these two terms and a confused Emperor Joseph II, a passage included in Appendix 1.

[50] *Music in European Capitals*, p. 757.

[51] Ernst Hoffmann, *E. T. A. Hoffmann's Musical Writings: Kreisleriana, The Poet and the Composer, Music Criticism*, tr. Martyn Clarke, ed. David Charlton (Cambridge, 1989), pp. 296–300. See also Patrick Taïeb, "*La Chasse du Jeune Henri* (Méhul, 1797). Une analyse historique," *Revue de Musicologie* 83 (1997): 205–46.

Another horn call is heard at the end of Haydn's chorus, rounding out and completing the picture, "Le retour de la chasse."

If this were an actual painting, instead of a musical one relying on descriptive words and the traditional calls, stretched over a massive orchestral canvas, it would be called a genre scene. Hunts were a favorite subject of genre paintings at the time, and one artist even specialized in the hunt, the Bavarian painter Johann Elias Ridinger. Five of his pictures were selected and engravings made from them to illustrate the article "Chasse" in the *Encyclopédie*.[52] Figure 6.5 shows two of them, at the top the "Chasse par force" in full swing, with hounds and two mounted hunters following, the lead rider playing a large cor de chasse. The lower one depicts the stag dismembered and the hunters dismounted, four of whom sound the appropriate call on their horns, in all probability "Halali."

One grand genre painting in music deserved another. Swieten's text provided for it with what Zinzendorf referred to as *Les vendanges*. Fall, season of the hunt for aristocrats and their servants, was for the common folk a festival of harvesting the grapes and making wine.

Gathering and pressing the grapes could have been elaborated as a ritual akin to the hunt. Instead these labors are passed over quickly in a simple recitative for the soloists, asking us to "look at the mountainside all aswarm with people!" The chorus then proceeds directly to celebrating the wine after it has been pressed. Haydn complained about the text of this chorus to both Dies and Griesinger. He protests too much considering how great a genre painting he made from it. Swieten may have actually extended this scene in order to give Haydn more scope. If Haydn was embarrassed by the text, as he claimed, it could have been because of the rustic nature of the scene. Specifically local was the Austrian *Heuriger* in celebration of the new wine, familiar to Haydn since he was a child, and still common in villages surrounding Vienna. Perhaps Haydn was a little wary of the opinions of his stalwartly Protestant publishers in Leipzig and their mostly central and northern German clients. For whatever reasons, he sought to distance himself from certain exclamations of the chorus, some of them admittedly silly (or inebriated?), such as "Long live the wine! Long live the cask in which it is kept! Long live the jug from which it flows!"

The chorus does not work up to a celebration, it begins with one. A simple harmonic progression using the most common chords and a four-measure phrase inaugurates the piece, stated with explosive force by the entire orchestra, including the three trombones and timpani. The chorus comes in overlapping the cadence, then sings the same phrase, resulting in a seven-measure period. Their words are simple: "Juhhe, juhhe! der Wein ist da." It is difficult to find a two-syllable expression in English meaning "shout for joy!" to match the dialect

---

[52] Heartz, "The Hunting Chorus in Haydn's *Jahreszeiten*" reproduces all five.

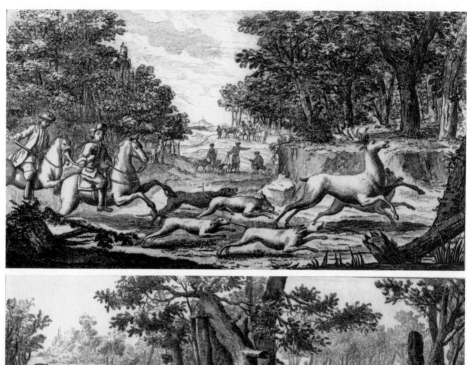

FIGURE 6.5. Johann Elias Ridinger. Two prints of the stag hunt.

word "Juhhe!" (Example 6.22). The word is crucial because Haydn soon reaches a melodic climax on it as the sopranos are required to accent with a *sforzato* and then a portamento slide up to high A (m. 14) before the cadence. The original score's printed English "Hey-day, hey-day!" not being dialect and rather pale in comparison, does not attain the desired result, which would ideally have the same "o͞o" sound (as in "hoot"). The sopranos should sound as if someone had just pinched them, and even more so at the last climax of the piece as they sing

EXAMPLE 6.22. *Haydn,* The Seasons, *Drinking Chorus*

this cry in rhythmic augmentation and one tone higher, taking them up to high B♭ (mm. 218–22).

The excitement accrues little by little, for instance, when the first violins start playing a rapid figure against the syncopations of the second violins while the men sing "Let us drink now!" to which the voices representing women respond "Let us sing now!" By this time the second key of G has been reached and momentarily secured. A series of modulations using the original main theme suggest a kind of development before a return, not to C but to G, in preparation for the next event: the symbolic arrival of the rustic players who will start the dances (the regular orchestra imitates their sounds). The meter changes to 6/8, the tempo to *Allegro assai,* and the text provides colorful descriptions of the noises made by the folk instruments.

1) Nun tönen die Pfeifen	Now the pipes are playing
2) und wirbelt die Trommel,	And the drum is beating,
3) hier kreischen die Fiedel	Here the fiddles are scratching
4) da schnarret die Leier	There the hurdy-gurdy rasps,
5) und dudelt der Bock.	And the bagpipes drone.

Haydn translates the words into sounds by (1) non-stop sixteenth notes for the first oboe, joined by the first clarinet; (2) a roll on the timpani's C; (3) harmonic slippage to a modal degree (a minor); (4) a drone on G and chromatic descent from it; (5) prolonged G as drone in the basses, with appoggiaturas of a minor second below. What an advantage his rustic origins gave him here!

The dance is a Deutscher, or fast Ländler. The young of all ages join it, says the text, little ones, boys, and maidens on the arms of their swains—all are hopping and jumping. From G the music moves down a third to e minor, which becomes unison E to lead in a new variant of the oboe's fast tune in A major as the grown women take part in the dance. With little preparation, the music switches to an even more vigorous and loud F major as the men call out for refills of their tankards. Haydn's tonal strategy of moving by falling thirds is evident, as is the very daring one of daubing his canvas with large swatches of bright color, here a patch of A major, there a bit of F major, etc. Out of the melee he returns to G major where we started this kermis, and even changes the key signature to one sharp.

Rather inconspicuously, the second violins introduce a new theme into the tumult, one familiar-sounding nevertheless because of its descending thirds, strongly marked by syncopations. The choral voices pay little attention to it at first and keep on with their jubilant shouts. When the first violins enter with the same theme a fifth above, it becomes clear that a fugue has started, and is lurching forward propelled by all its syncopations. The orchestral basses enter next with the theme and are joined by the choral tenors at least for the first half of the subject. And so it goes through a series of modulations, with the fugue taking place in the orchestra and the chorus singing along in snatches here and there, as if too tipsy to do more than this. Another unsteady factor is the theme's struggle against the downbeats, giving it a staggering gait. The dance comes to a first climax with the return of C major (the sharp in the signature is canceled). As the fugue theme comes home to tonic C major, played on high by the winds and doubled below by the second violins, the sopranos sing it too, but in a version with the syncopations ironed out of it. The other voices accompany chordally. To increase the excitement Haydn brings in the tambourine and triangle as well, and they play to the end. Straightening out the choral rhythm to flowing eighth notes helps prepare for the second great climax, taking the sopranos up to high B♭ over diminished-seventh harmony (Example 6.22, mm. 218–22). After a brief pause the final cadences begin. There is one more climactic drive, with the chorus in unison rising chromatically from C to G with most of the orchestra, then three V - I progressions, to the last of which the sopranos sing "Juh, juh!" to 5 3.

Haydn's vast canvas is his equivalent to the ballroom scene in Mozart's *Don Giovanni*, only the locale here is not a palace but a country tavern or perhaps a village green on a fine fall day, with the populace assembled for a *Heuriger*. The signal Haydn used to begin the dancing, a low repeated tone with under-appoggiatura, is the same that Mozart used to introduce the last and most humble of his three dances, the lowly "Teitsche," which is Austrian dialect for "Deutscher." All due praises to Mozart aside, it must be admitted that, when it comes to painting a rustic genre scene such as ends "Autumn," no composer surpasses Haydn.

That Haydn achieved what he did here at such an advanced age is another cause for wonder. One critic who seized on the last three numbers of "Autumn" to point this out claims that this "amazing series of pieces that concludes Autumn . . . alone could ensure Haydn's premiere place with Titian, Michelangelo, and Turner, Mann and Goethe, Verdi and Stravinsky, as one of the rare artists to whom old age brings the gift of ever bolder invention."[53]

"Winter" begins with an introduction more striking than any of the three

---

[53] Michael Steinberg, in program notes for *The Seasons* performed by the San Francisco Symphony under the direction of then–Music Director Edo de Waart, in the fall of 1982. This is perhaps the place to admit that the Hunting and Drinking Choruses first led me to study Haydn's music more extensively beginning some forty years ago, and that no music has elated me more in old age than *The Seasons*.

others. The heading says that it "describes [schildert] the thick fog with which winter begins." Whereas "Spring" had begun with an agitated movement depicting winter's blustery departure, the season before us is characterized as one of increasing darkness and cold. Haydn resorts to an *Adagio ma non troppo* in common time and the key of c minor. At first one hears only the tonic chord in the strings, then the first violins announce the motif that will dominate the whole, Eb B♮ C (followed by Ab, sometimes G). The motif appeared often in Haydn's music of three decades earlier, whether for stormy beginnings such as the particularly forceful Symphony No. 52 in c of 1772, or in more sedate and pensive mode pieces such as the "Qui tollis" and Benedictus of the first *Missa Cellensis* finished at about the same time.[54] One thing strikingly different in this very late work of the master is the prominent role he gives the winds, and especially the solo clarinet, in spinning the web of motivic discourse. Otherwise many of its elements are similar to those in his minor-mode pieces of thirty years earlier: reliance on Neapolitan harmony, diminished-seventh chords, and melodic sighs (although here, when given to lower voices, they sound more like groans). The piece winds down gradually to a cadence followed by a coda, begun by solo winds with a cry of minor-second misery and taken over by the strings midway (Example 6.23).

EXAMPLE 6.23. *Haydn,* The Seasons, *Introduction to Winter: Thick Fogs*

The motif is reduced to its smallest component of a rising minor second until after its final rise up to G for the descent into the cadence. This passage is foreshadowed in uncanny detail by the veritable orgy of grief-stricken minor seconds let loose by the strings in Mozart's *Idomeneo* Act III, after the king admits that the sacrificial victim is his own son (just before the chorus of mourning "O voto tremendo!" No. 24 in c minor).[55]

---

[54] *Haydn, Mozart*, p. 300, ex. 4.12, and p. 303, ex. 3.14.
[55] Heartz, *Mozart's Operas*, p. 11, ex. 1.1B.

An extensive obbligato recitative follows, using the prelude's main motif to comment on Simon's words about how the old year is sinking, as mists surround the mountains and the plains. A quiet cadence on D♭ is superseded by a loud arrival on the chord of A major (D♭ becomes C♯) a major third below, introducing Hanne, who speaks of icy blasts from the caves of Lapland. The key of A major is confirmed by the time of the cadence, which points to D as a subsequent destination (we think) for the set piece to follow. What arrives is F major, another drop of a major third (as before, what was tonic becomes the third of the new key). Hanne's Cavatina begins in gavotte rhythm, *Largo* in common time, and describes how light and life are weakening, how long dark nights follow upon sullen days. Time hangs heavy. Yet the combination of F major with the slight lift of a dance-like phrase, even if slow, endows the music with more cheer than the text suggests. There is a very soft ending, and the final tones are protracted so as to depict the long-lasting nights. Lucas follows with a recitative that is still more dour as to the text, with mentions not only of natural phenomena in decline but also of a cadaverous pallor and of the earth becoming a grave, where strength and charm lie buried. This recitative begins by going back to D♭, the tonality abruptly quit at the arrival of Hanne. Haydn works the modulation so that it ends on the chord of B major, preparing the arrival of Lucas's aria in e minor.

The text tells the tale of a wanderer who loses his way in the snow. Its music has a rather old-fashioned ring, with frequent figures in dotted rhythm, *Presto* in common time. The violins have jerky little figures exchanged rapidly between firsts and seconds, lending a nervous quality to the texture that projects unease. One interior phrase, at the words "he finds himself still more astray," bears resemblance to the beginning of the bass aria "The people that walked in darkness" in Handel's *Messiah*. Complaints of the wanderer about weariness and cold bring a string of repeated tones as the strings shiver along with him. This comes shortly before a dominant pedal that should lead in the reprise and the doom to which Thomson consigned his wanderer. At this point Swieten takes a turn made to order for Haydn. The wanderer perceives the sudden appearance of a light shimmering in the distance. Instead of the expected e minor, E major takes over (cf. the similar outcome of the aria "Rolling in foaming billows" in *The Creation*). The tempo of the new section is *Allegro*—"lively" well describes the way the wanderer's heart beats at the sight of a hut to which he hurries. The whole tale can be read as a metaphor appropriate to an oratorio, or, it can be taken as a secular drama closer to opera. Haydn seems to point in the latter direction with his music. To express his joy at the end the wanderer bursts into coloratura and before he is done scales the melodic peak of high B♮.

Lucas resumes singing in recitative, "See how he approaches through howling winds a place from which bright voices reach his ear." Hanne enters and explains that he has reached a little hamlet and a warmed meeting room where the villagers gather. Some weave baskets, others mend nets. The old men tell tales while the women spin the distaff as their daughters operate the rotary wheels, the spinning of which is heard in the orchestra even before verbal mention. Smoothly legato in sixteenth notes up and down, this figure sets up the following chorus and runs through it from beginning to end.

The Spinning Chorus, with solo participation of Hanne, is an *Allegro* in 6/8 time. Its key is not so clear and that is one of its many odd charms, making it one of the most memorable pieces in the work. For its text Swieten turned to an outside source, a *Spinnerlied* by Gottfried August Bürger. In a large strophic form, as if it were a folk song, the piece is constructed as a choral refrain that keeps returning to frame different solo episodes for Hanne. A strong flavor of "olden times," of customs passed on from generation to generation, inheres in it, enhanced by the many modal turns in the harmonic progressions. The first chord proclaims d minor, as prepared by the recitative, yet there is an immediate cadence in a minor, making us wonder if perhaps it is the tonic. We can easily picture such a spinning scene in our minds, and that is another of the piece's attractions. Visually, at least, there were spinning scenes in earlier operas of the Singspiel variety, for example in *Die Jagd* by Johann Adam Hiller on a text by Christian Felix Weisse, derived from the opéra comique *Le roi et le fermier* by Michel-Jean Sedaine, from which we have a depiction showing a spinning wheel as a stage property.[56]

The chorus sings at first in only two parts, sopranos and altos, initially at the octave. Their refrain is only four measures long and is ground into the memory by frequent repetition. Hanne sings episodes of longer duration and takes the harmony to different points of rest to C major, but ending in a, which turns quickly into A to prepare for the unchanged refrain. The next solo episode leads from C to e. The chorus pays no heed and sings its refrain as before, a charming effect that lends a character somewhere between stolid and exotic. These alternations go on further until at last there is a big break from the hypnotic routine that has been established and the chorus begins singing in four parts (men's voices added) and takes up the melody previously sung by Hanne. It sounds as if the piece wants to end in A, then with a jolt it ends in d, the last of its many tonal surprises. The tonal uncertainties throughout and the unorthodox final cadence remind one of Pedrillo's Romance in *Die Entführung*. Another charming effect is the way the spinning motif runs down at the end by lengthening its notes before stopping altogether, like the clock's running down in the *Andante* of Symphony No. 101 ("Clock").

Swieten set his composer a challenge by placing one strophic descriptive piece directly after another, with only the link of a short recitative between to describe how the villagers gather around Hanne as she begins to tell a story. A seemingly

---

[56] *Music in European Capitals*, p. 771, fig. 7.8.

unrelated narrative placed within the larger framework of the main body of the text is a characteristic that defined many operatic Romances.[57] Swieten originally titled this text "Romance" then apparently switched it to "Märchen." He derived it from the Romance "Il etait une fille d'honneur qui plaisait fort a son Seigneur" in the opéra comique *Annette et Lubin* by Marie Duronceray Favart (Mme Favart).[58] Zinzendorf in the diary entry from the first performance quoted above refers to the piece with the single word "Annette." Sung on stage by Annette (originally Mme Favart), the Romance has five stanzas and tells the tale of a village girl fancied by her Lord, who catches her alone while out riding; he dismounts and begins his assault, to which she seems to yield in order to gain time, then distracts his attentions and rides off on his horse.

Haydn could have adopted the modal twists that characterized the 1762 Romance of Annette and many other stage Romances. Since he had used these to emphasize the venerable age of the previous Spinning Song, he decided to use his own style and set the stanzas of Hanne to a sprightly contredanse kind of melody, with repeated tones to give it a folkloric shading, *Moderato* in common time and in the key of G. Even so one of the stanzas turns to the minor, as happens often in *Romances*. The most interesting parts of the piece are the choral comments on each stanza, and especially the laughing chorus at the end.

From the merry laughter that greets the end of Hanne's song the text moves swiftly back to the dread consequences of winter, described as a grim tyrant who has won the battle with Nature. Haydn sets it in a simple recitative of a mere eleven measures. Some critics have seen, in this rapid juxtaposition of comic and serious, an aspect of Shakespearean theater. There is no denying that *The Seasons* reaches its most serious point immediately after its most highly comical one in the last three numbers of "Winter." Swieten did well in Simon's aria, the penultimate piece, to evoke the times of year as parallels for the times of a mortal lifespan: "Behold, deluded man, the portrait of your life. Your brief spring has lost its bloom; your summer's strength is exhausted; your autumn is fading into old age. Pale winter draws nigh and shows you the open grave" (my translation). Swieten's English original is fussier though his points are undeniably well taken. The placement of "grave" at the end has the virtue of paralleling a famous line in Thomas Gray's immensely popular "Elegy Written in a Country Churchyard" (1750): "The paths of glory lead but to the grave."

Haydn chooses one of his most expressive keys, E♭ major, to clothe Simon's peroration. In a *Largo* in 3/4 time that contrasts smooth cantilena with loud and

[57] Daniel Heartz, "Beginnings of the Operatic Romance: Rousseau, Sedaine, and Monsigny," *Eighteenth-Century Studies* 15 (1981–82): 149–82; reprinted in Heartz, *From Garrick to Gluck: Essays on Opera in the Age of Enlightenment*, ed. John A. Rice (Hillsdale, NY, 2004), pp. 188–209.
[58] David Charlton, "The *Romance* and Its Cognates," essay 1, ex. 12.

abrupt interjections, Simon sings the words to what sounds more like an arioso, or extremely elaborate obbligato recitative, than it does an aria. The voice pauses after "summer's strength" for an orchestral commentary that cannot be other than a reference to the drooping scales in inverted dotted rhythm in the *Andante* (also in E♭) of Mozart's Symphony No. 40 in g minor, K. 550. It could be that this music came to Haydn's mind while he was musing on the fate of the genius whose life was cut off after the equivalent of only two seasons, spring and summer. No moment of the oratorio is more moving than this extraordinary *memento mori* evoking Mozart, so private in a way, and yet unmistakable. Zinzendorf referred to this aria as "de la morale" and he got it right, for it embodies what Haydn would teach us, his listeners.

As the Mozartian orchestral commentary continues, it accompanies the voice and travels to various tonal goals (c, b♭, e♭) before settling on an unharmonized tone of B♭ as the text reaches "das off'ne Grab." An orchestral outburst on a diminished-seventh chord follows, *Allegro molto* in 2/4 time, to which the voice responds in recitative style, "Where are they now, those lofty plans?" The exchange continues between orchestral outbursts and questioning mentions of a series of human vanities. "All have vanished like a dream." The upper winds alone prepare for the final recitative cadence with slow chords that sound like an ascent to the heavenly sphere, lending a halo to the last words: "Nur Tugend bleibt!" (Only virtue remains). As Simon holds the last tone of B♭, the orchestra resolves with force to E♭ in two vigorous V - I chords. A simple recitative continues with Simon still on B♭: "She alone remains" (*Tugend* is a feminine noun). "She, unchangeable, leads us through changes of time and the yearly seasons, through sorrow or joy, on to the highest goal." This little recitative takes only six measures, enough for Haydn to change keys in order to prepare the final tonal goal of C major, reinforced when the winds and trumpets begin with what sounds like a solemn processional, *Allegro moderato* in common time.

Swieten found what he wanted for the beginning of the final number in Thomson's poem. The passage in question spells out the parallel between the resurrection of Nature and humankind, made more specific by slipping the word "uns" (us) into the third line.

Thomson:	Swieten:
'Tis come, the glorious morn! the second birth	Dann bricht der grosse Morgen an,
Of heaven and earth! awakening nature hears	Der Allmacht zweytes Wort
The *new-creating word*, and starts to life,	Erweckt zum neuen Daseyn uns,
In every heighten'd form, from pain and death	Von Pein und Tod auf immer frey.[59]
For ever free.	

[59] Landon, *Haydn*, 5:111–12.

Haydn's trumpet intrada is majestic and novel in tone color (no strings). It sets the tone for this grand double chorus with participation of the three soloists. Simon begins by singing the trumpet tune, modified at first to suit the words just quoted, then going beyond it to descend by a seventh and rise a minor second on the words "pain and death." The other two soloists enter and sing lines describing how the heavenly gates will swing open to reveal the holy mountain beyond, crowned by the Lord's dwelling place, where peace and joy reign. At this, Chorus I enters impetuously with the question, "Who may pass these gates?" Haydn gives the treble a jagged line of chromatic seconds and leaps, at the top of which are D E♭ B♮ C, the same motif with which he began "Winter." The answer comes serenely from the soloists: "Who shuns evil and does good." For this Haydn brings back the woodwind halo, led here by the clarinets, forming the only accompaniment. He also brings back E♭. The moment is strongly reminiscent of the questioning of Tamino by the Priest in *Die Zauberflöte* (Act I, beginning of the Finale) also in E♭, where a clarinet-led halo of calmly moving chords responds to the word "Heilig-tum" (sanctuary) (see Example 3.10a). The questions and answers, back and forth between the two choruses, last for several exchanges, allowing Haydn the modulatory scope necessary to sustain such a grand edifice as this becomes. The text at length begins to resemble a child's catechism lesson in its incessant questions and answers, but it is rescued by Haydn's inspired music.

Tonic C major returns, prepared by its dominant to express "Oh see, the glorious morning is near!" Arrival coincides with "It is already brightening," and then more firmly with both choruses, and the orchestra tutti *fortissimi* for "The gates of Heaven swing open," revealing the wonders that have been promised. In quick exchanges between the two choruses, mention is made of life's winter storms having passed and disappeared, replaced by eternal springtime and boundless happiness as virtue's reward, sung together by both choruses. It remains for the soloists to rejoin the grand tableau: "May we too receive such reward!" With the two choruses, staggered, they sing "Let us strive," "Let us battle," "Let us expect," then all together: "to gain the prize!" More emphasis on the dominant leads us to expect something new yet to come.

That something is, of course, a fugue. What better musical metaphor for striving and doing battle? It is expected also because of the precedents set by the other great choruses in these last two oratorios. The final stanza of the text begins "Lead our hand oh God! Lend us strength and courage." The basses of the now-combined choruses lead off with a magnificent subject that consists of a falling tonic triad, down to C, a rise by step to A, by leap from D to B♭, which arrives in strong rhythmic position, and a concluding rise by step up to C. The B♭ will eventually play an important role at the end of the piece. Haydn puts the subject through all kinds of contrapuntal and harmonic adventures in what must be one of his most forceful contributions to the genre. One of the last entrances goes to the basses, whose rise up a sixth by step then a leap up a sixth is answered immediately by the sopranos leaping up an octave, first to high G, then to high A. There is a momentary settling on IV, reinforced by the whole orchestra, leading by way of a dominant pedal to the first solid cadence on the tonic. The instrumental fanfares return in even greater majesty. "Then shall we sing" proclaims Chorus I, answered by Chorus II singing "Then shall we enter." Both: "in Thy realm's glory. Amen." Here the sopranos mount up to high B♭ and hold it. The resolution to IV occupies two full measures, with prolongation of the last chord by fermatas, followed by rests with fermatas. Only then is the final cadence begun by the orchestra, to which all respond "Amen." The sopranos, in the first of the V - I progressions, sing 2 3, then in the last measure of this heaven-storming chorus, they sing their "Amen" to 5 3, Haydn's favorite way of expressing not only finality but hope. Never has it assumed greater transcendence than here.

E. T. A. Hoffmann expressed reservations about Haydn's Masses but almost none about the two late oratorios. The Masses for him were insufficiently "pure" as models for church music, compared with those of earlier times. Such scruples vanish from his assessment of the last oratorio.

> There is no more splendid or colourful picture of human life than that which the composer has delineated in *The Seasons*; and the playful wit only colours more vividly the motley figures from life who dance about us in brilliant circles. This wonderful music is charged with the same constant alternation of gravity, awe, horror, jollity, and exuberance as that which mundane activity gives rise to, and it relates to the church only to the extent that pious reflections play a part in the affairs of everyday life.[60]

In the following paragraph he tempers even his criticism of the Masses by blaming the worst excesses of "theatrical gaudiness" on Haydn's innumerable followers. "How often the great Haydn has been imitated, or rather aped; but these so-called church composers merely nibbled at the shell without penetrating to the kernel, and the deeper spirit of harmony contained in his works never dawned on them."

Valediction

Schöpfungsmesse

On 28 July 1801, Haydn commenced a new mass for the name day of Princess Esterházy. It was first performed in the Bergkirche at Eisenstadt on 13 September. He began the Kyrie of this, his third mass in B♭, with what is clearly a revisit to the "Theresienmesse" of two years earlier, his most recent addition to the series.

[60] E. T. A. Hoffmann, "Old and New Church Music," pp. 370–71.

Both masses treat the Kyrie as a slow introduction followed by a substantial fast movement. A rising triad in the first violins serves as the incipit of both compositions, after which the melodies go off in different directions. Another similarity is their length, twenty-eight measures of *Adagio* in cut time for the previous mass, twenty-eight measures of *Adagio* in 3/4 time for this one. Both end on a prolonged dominant chord with wavering back and forth between C and D♭. Moreover, both slow sections are darkened by the appearance of tonic minor, diminished-seventh chords and an insistence upon the chord of ♭VI (G♭), along with strident trumpet and drum fanfares in dotted rhythm. There is a sense of menace and latent power in both, suggesting that they too were masses "in time of war" (even though 1801 was a year of uneasy truce). By the time this mass was written, Haydn had a fuller woodwind section at his command. Pairs of oboes, bassoons, and horn joined the pair of clarinets that were his only woodwinds in 1799 (aside from continuo bassoons). The faster section of this new Kyrie is an *Allegro moderato* in 6/8 time. It explores some motifs first heard in the *Adagio* when the alto solo begins singing "Kyrie eleison." There is a clear sonata form at work, with establishment of V, followed by a "Christe eleison" for the soprano solo in plaintive b♭ minor. The return of "Kyrie eleison" in a strong tutti with chorus marks the moment of reprise. The choral sopranos end the movement with a sweep up an octave, partially chromatic, and a pre-cadential lunge up to high B♭ before their final 5 3.

The Gloria begins with a rousing wind and brass fanfare that keeps returning after contrasting sections, like the ritornello of a concerto in the old style. This *Allegro* in cut time moves along swiftly through the text until it reaches "Qui tollis peccata mundi," at which Haydn swings into a dance tune for horns and clarinets in the subdominant, E♭, as if it were another episode preceding yet another appearance of the ritornello. The catch is that this tune was well known to his audience as the saucy contredanse in E♭ sung in the final duet of Adam and Eve in *The Creation*, at the words "The dew-dropping morn, o how she quickens all!" A few pulses must have quickened, too, at hearing this familiar tune sung in church to the words "Qui tollis peccata mundi." Having the horns play it in these circumstances makes Haydn's suggestive leer even more impudent, for the instruments in those days often had the additional signification of cuckoldry. Just as it was the bass Adam who sang of the morning dew in his love duet with Eve, so it is the solo bass who sings the same here to "Who taketh away the sins of the world." Not everyone was amused by Haydn's jesting. Some were scandalized, among them apparently Empress Marie Therese who asked Haydn to recompose the passage in her copy of the mass, which he did. She certainly knew *The Creation* well, having sung the solo soprano part (Eve) in private performance. At a fast tempo the offending passage of eight measures was over at once and then Haydn settled into a long and beautiful projection of the complete text in question, *Adagio* in 3/4 time. Yet that little offending passage was what led to the mass being dubbed "Die Schöpfungsmesse." The sexual indulgence of Adam and Eve in the Garden of Eden was not a story to be laughed at—too much of theology depended on it. Haydn's famous wit in this case skirted impious utterance, in short, blasphemy.

Griesinger reported the incident with economy and explained it with his usual probity and businesslike tone.

> In the mass that Haydn wrote in 1801 it occurred to him in the *Agnus Dei qui tollis peccata mundi* that frail mortals sinned mostly against moderation and purity. So he set the words *qui tollis peccata, peccata mundi* to the trifling melody of the words in *The Creation* "Der thauend Morgen, o wie ermuntert er." But in order that this profane thought should not be too conspicuous, he let the *Miserere* sound in full chorus immediately thereafter. In the copy of the mass that he made for the Empress, he had to alter the place at her request.

The words "qui tollis . . . " are shared by the Agnus Dei and the Gloria, while the infamous citation occurs only in the music of the Gloria, and Griesinger quotes precisely from there by repeating the word "peccata." Dies, not untypically, makes a muddle of the subject by mixing up the Agnus Dei with the offending passage in the Gloria.

The final fast section of the Gloria gets underway at "Quoniam tu solus sanctus." To emphasize the singularity of "Thou *alone*," Haydn sets these words initially in unisons and octaves throughout the chorus and orchestra, *Molto vivace* in common time, a passage in sequence involving minor-second and triadic rises (Example 6.24). The peak tones outline the climb up the scale from the tonic,

EXAMPLE 6.24. *Haydn, "Schöpfungsmesse," Gloria*

B♭ C D, a rise that has been a recurrent feature of the work since the Kyrie. A fugue starts when the tempo speeds up to *Presto*, with the subject first sung by the basses. It is an intriguing theme, with rises of a minor second in an overall falling pattern. To end, after the soloists have made ample contributions to the fray, the chorus reverts to unisons and octaves to sing a last version of the rising minor second idea that extends far beyond its previous statements in a kind of paroxysm. Homophony returns for the final "amens," with sopranos intoning 5 3 at the last, as in the Kyrie.

The Credo begins with a *Vivace* in common time, Haydn's usual choice of meter for the first part of the text. In this case he keeps his orchestra very busy, especially the violins, which sound sixteenth-note passagework against longer tones in the voices, with extended descents in 6/3 chords. The result sounds solid, festive, and rather like the old style of the *Prunkmesse* in C major so favored since Fux and Reutter by the Austro-Bohemian school. The choral sopranos begin with a rise up by step from the tonic so that the most important word, "Deum," is the most accented and prolonged and is set with the typical fall of a third, 5 3. Thus the main idea corresponds with similar rises from the tonic in the Kyrie and Gloria. After various modulations the harmony settles on the chord of d minor, or at least on the tones D and F, which are promptly turned into the third and fifth of a returning B♭. Haydn speeds through the first part of the text, dispatching its many words in fifty-nine measures and a time of about two minutes.

He takes ample time with "Et incarnatus est de Sancto spirito." The orchestra begins it with a leisurely statement, *Adagio* in 3/4 time and in the unexpected key of G. One of the ways to suggest in music the hovering dove that had for centuries been a visual symbol of the Holy Spirit was to imitate the song or movement of a bird in sound. Since his orchestra for this mass had no flute, Haydn played an obbligato solo on the organ using the flute stop. His solo conveys the idea of avian twittering, and as it sounds above the other instruments it seems to hover weightlessly in space. One expects that a solo soprano will narrate the words pertaining to Mary, if only because it was the traditional choice. Here Haydn opts for the solo tenor, who sings in a quasi-dialogue with the frilly flute solo. The bass solo comes in on D at the words "Crucifixus etiam pro nobis," turning the harmony toward g minor but subsiding back to D. At this point the chorus enters with a massive chord of B♭, *forte*, for "sub Pontio Pilato," making the words sound like an ultimatum. The music returns to *piano* and clothes the words "passus et sepultus est" with a rather tortuous chromatic progression ending with a D-major chord low in the chorus, suggesting resolution to either g or G.

"Et resurrexit" brings neither the one nor the other. Rather, it brings B♭ major and furnishes another instance of Haydn's favorite tonal move, V/vi or V/VI followed directly by I, and specifically, B♭ following D. The busy texture of the first part of the Credo returns in this *Allegro* in common time, as does a speedy traversal of the text. Special exception is made for the Last Judgment, as Haydn has done before. Here another third relationship takes place when F becomes the third in a massive outburst of D♭ major. Haydn marks "Et vitam venturi" *più Allegro*. Instead of a fugue he makes do with canons and ends the Credo without the usual intervention of the soloists. The theme of the canons rises up by step from the tonic, recalling the beginning of the Credo. Before the end, the sopranos climb through two octaves up to high B♭ twice. Their last "amen" is sung to 5 3.

The Sanctus begins calmly in B♭ as the clarinets sweetly sing 5 3 in parallel thirds. This *Adagio* in common time is graced by sixteenth-note triplet figurations, played softly, as are the rapid strokes of the timpani. When this lovely music begins to repeat, the choral basses come in singing an octave descent from B♭ followed by the other parts of the chorus singing the word "Sanctus." They start the transition to F with a sudden *forte* chord of V/vi resolving to vi, followed in sequence downward by V/V resolving to V. Through all this and right up to the end of the Sanctus the orchestra keeps up the lacy texture of triplet figurations. A deceptive cadence to D♭ from C lends a darker tint, and the section ends not in F but in f, where the chorus sings "Pleni sunt coeli et terra" to a vigorous *Allegro*. The solo soprano leads in "Osanna in excelsis," a return to B♭, to which the chorus responds singing the same music.

Benedictus begins with another amply-proportioned orchestral prelude. The key is E♭ and the clarinets remain prominent. There is a relaxed, swaying kind of motion to this *Allegretto* in 6/8 time. The minor-second appoggiaturas below the main tones on the strong beats of the measure (one and four) and other dance-like features give the music the character of a slow Ländler. After the soloists begin singing the same music, there are even some occurrences of oom-pah-pah accompaniments; an improvisational character to melodic lines climbing up and down further reinforces the rural dance band impression. Rarely was a setting of the Benedictus more *gemütlich* than this one, and yet the piece also has the sophistication of a rapidly modulating development section in the middle. Haydn integrates the returning "Osanna" text into the main sections of the Benedictus without bringing back any of the original "Osanna" music from the Sanctus.

Agnus Dei opens in G major, providing another third relationship with what came before. It is an *Adagio* in 3/4 time, probably begun by the soloists (the sources are contradictory on this point). The key and tempo duplicate those of the "Et incarnatus est," and there are also some melodic and harmonic similarities. It could be argued that the two texts are related, the "Lamb of God" who is to be sacrificed being of course the same who is born of Mary. The slow, hymnlike theme is stated three times in all, with different continuations, the third ending with a long dominant pedal on D. An increasing familiarity with Haydn's late compositions should enable anyone to guess what will come next. It is predicted specifically in the Agnus Dei of the "Theresienmesse," in many ways the twin of this mass. In both, B♭ major arrives as a *fortissimo* tutti fanfare for "Dona nobis pacem"—there an *Allegro* in 3/4 time, here a related fanfare, *Allegro moderato* in cut time.

Again "Dona nobis pacem" has become not a plea but a positive statement, a point of harmonic arrival that is like a promise fulfilled. Haydn is even more expansive than usual here after the fanfare and choral responses. He begins a fugue in the tenors on a subject that has a running countersubject in eighth notes along with it. Fugues in the Agnus Dei are not frequent. In this case he may be compensating us for the lack of a fugue to finish the Credo. After modulation to the dominant the piece turns quite homophonic, then the fugue begins again and ends triumphantly in tonic B♭, in celebration of which the original tutti fanfare returns followed by the responses to it in the chorus. A series of cadences could well end the mass at this point but they are only the beginning of a mighty coda, one that plumbs more depths by recalling the threatening G♭ from the Kyrie's slow introduction and storms the heights with choral unisons so powerful as to recall the greatest choruses in the late oratorios. The last gesture, after more V - I cadences, with the sopranos singing "pacem" to 5 3, has the chorus in unisons and octaves climbing up and down the tonic triad.

Breitkopf and Härtel published the parts of this and other of Haydn's late masses in 1802. This mass in particular caught the attention of an aged veteran of the tonal art, a doyen of musical life in Leipzig, Johann Adam Hiller, who became Kantor of the Thomaskirche during the 1790s. Hiller is a truly sympathetic figure in the history of music, a great teacher as well as a crystallizing force in the emergence of German Singspiel around 1760. He was nearly four years older than Haydn, and died in mid-1804. Yet he kept up with new music to the end. He took the trouble to score this mass from the parts, then copied his own parts from the score, on which he inscribed "Opus summum viri summi I. Haydn."

Harmoniemesse

Haydn began his last setting of the mass in late 1801 or early 1802. Composing it took him much longer than usual. Griesinger wrote Härtel in a letter dated Vienna, 20 January 1802, that Haydn was again working on a new mass, and repeated the information in a letter of 21 April. On 14 June Haydn wrote from Vienna to Prince Esterházy in Pressburg that he was busy working "very *wearily*, yet still more *anxiously* as to whether it would win him any approval." His words express concerns unusual for him. Confidence in his will or ability to continue may have been at stake. The work was first performed before a distinguished group of visitors to the Esterházy court on St. Mary's day, 8 September, in Eisenstadt's Bergkirche. An account of the festivities preserved in the diary of one of the guests will be quoted and discussed in the next section.

The mass became known as the "Harmoniemesse" because of its large and prominently employed contingent of winds: flute, pairs of oboes, clarinets, bassoons, horns, and trumpets, joined by timpani, the usual strings, and organ. Its key is B♭, where Haydn had come to feel more completely at home than anywhere else. Many ravishing details of harmony and orchestration illuminate the Kyrie. Yet a fundamental directness and simplicity predominate. It has no slow introduction, no long pauses for rhetorical effect, and no flashy fanfares. Its basic sonata form could not be more clearly etched, although treated with the greatest freedom and ingenuity. The orchestra alone states the first phrase, which is smoothly lyrical and led by a trio of solo winds, the strings reinforcing (Example 6.25). The diversion to an ominous G♭, *forte*, in m. 5 is even more prominent than

EXAMPLE 6.25. *Haydn, "Harmoniemesse" (1802), Kyrie*

in the two previous Kyries. As the first cadence approaches, the chorus bursts in with a *forte* tonic unison over a pre-cadential diminished-seventh chord. The effect is startling. One reaction could be that the chorus came in too soon, anticipating resolution. It is left to the orchestra to resolve the chorus's shocking chord to the tonic, softly, whereupon the solo bass enters singing "Kyrie" on B♭ with an octave descent in dotted rhythm.

The orchestra repeats its initial phrase, while the soloists drop in and out of the texture in support of it. As the transition to the second key begins, the soloists commence singing "Christe eleison," thenceforth used freely in exchange with "Kyrie." The second harmonic center of F is more of a presence than any specific secondary melodic idea, everything being derived motivically from the main theme. To reinforce the second key the solo soprano and alto warble in thirds with a string of sixteenth notes up and down, imitated a few measures later by the tenor and bass singing the same by themselves. The effect is pleasant and informal, certainly not severe or liturgical in any formal sense. The seconda parte begins with modulations that range widely, first to the flat side, then to the sharp side, winding down to a chord of D major over a pedal that dwindles to *pianissimo*, functioning as V/vi to tonic B♭, which arrives *forte* as the chorus in unison sings "Kyrie" as an octave descent, like the first entry of the solo bass, signaling the beginning of the reprise. This abrupt return to the tonic is the biggest event in the movement and will recur at the end of the whole mass as its climactic musical event. The reprise ends with a rise up the triad of two octaves to high B♭ in the orchestra, a climb that will also have a bearing on the very end of the mass. This music, for all its seductiveness, challenges the listener in many ways.

Its subtle motivic construction and numerous chromatic shadings are sophisticated enough to help explain why Haydn was apprehensive whether his last mass would be understood or welcomed.

The Gloria begins softly, with an *Allegro* in common time sung by the solo soprano (Example 6.26, mm. 1–8). The conjunct rise from the tonic and fall from

EXAMPLE 6.26. *Haydn, "Harmoniemesse" (1802), Gloria*

the fifth down to the tonic are the same simple materials that suffuse the Kyrie. Here there is a song-like character, a directness of expression in the repeated tones, and the square cut of the melody, with mm. 5–8 rhythmically paralleling mm. 1–4. The open cadence of m. 8 provides a springboard for the chorus to come in *forte* echoing the soprano's solo, except that the equivalent to mm. 5–8 provide instead of a fall to the tonic a rise by a half step up to G and a descending sequence of half-step rises, harmonized by a series of secondary dominants. Going from simple to sophisticated, even in a single phrase, illustrates a fundamental characteristic of this last full-scale composition of the master.

After a rapid treatment of the first part of the text Haydn changes to *Allegretto* in 3/8 time and in E♭, beginning a middle section that lasts nearly three times as long (Example 6.26, mm. 83–102). The alto solo begins it, followed in turn by the other soloists. Like the main melody of the Kyrie, with its falling against rising conjunct third motion (3 2 1 versus 1 2 3), this melody too is a series of rising and falling thirds, but in succession. At "propter magnam" the initial material is beautifully varied, then bursts into flower with a chromatic rise and fall to the cadence at "gloriam tuam." After the solos and an orchestral confirmation of E♭, Haydn moves suddenly, by way of a G♭ sixth chord, to f minor, where the chorus enters singing "Qui tollis peccata mundi miserere nobis." The harmony becomes unstable and reaches several other tonal centers. One particularly lovely moment occurs when the strings softly bring back the variant (Example 6.26, mm. 95–98) of the initial melody but in A♭, against which the soloists sing in pairs and in turn "Suscipe" to a falling octave in dotted rhythm, just as the solo bass first sang "Kyrie." The *Allegretto* section ends in g minor, with a *segue subito* after the last chord.

At "Quoniam tu solus," B♭ returns along with the meter and fast tempo of the initial section, here *Allegro spiritoso*. After an initial homophonic section the tenors begin a fugue to "in gloria Dei Patris," to which the basses sing "amen" in a running countersubject. Eventually there is a return to homophonic texture, also to the fundamental musical premise of the falling conjunct third against a rising version of the same, as well as the downward leap of an octave, features impressed on the ear from the beginning of the Kyrie. Before the very end the soloists make another return, as was their wont, adding some high warbling in rapid notes and in thirds, then the same lower down, also directly related to the Kyrie. The chorus concludes, and the final two V - I progressions are sung by the sopranos as 2 3, 5 3.

The Credo, like the Gloria, follows a general plan of fast outer sections in common time surrounding a slower, more intimate section in triple meter. Orchestra and chorus plunge into the opening *Vivace* together. Haydn selects "unum" for emphasis, partly by repeating the word. The choral unison for the second statement of "Credo" reinforces the concept of unity. An active bass line in continual eighth-note motion lends a solid and retrospective cast to the texture. It is akin to the old Corellian running bass and is no new feature in Haydn's Credo settings. Possibly he connects in his mind Corellian basses with Rome, and hence with the Roman church, the one singled out later in the text as "universal, holy and apostolic." After the chorus illustrates "Descendit de coelis" with descending tonic triads, the orchestra enacts the same over a two octave span from high to low B♭, the opposite from its ascents over the same span near the end of the Kyrie. Haydn had never been timid about depicting verbs of motion in music and he does so here with as much verve as ever.

"Et incarnatus est," sings the soprano solo to an *Adagio* in 3/4 time that opens in E♭. With constant triplet eighth notes, the meter sounds more like the lilting 9/8 of a cradle song. This slowly moving melody is initially sounded by the first clarinet, here truly solo, unlike the beginning of the Kyrie, where it is supported by the violins. The other soloists enter repeating the soprano's words "et homo factus est," the music of which carries the soprano to a cadence on G♭ major. In the same remote realm of G♭, the chorus enters singing "Crucifixus," then quickly modulates as the bass moves up chromatically to C, on which chord it sings "Passus." The lower trio of soloists takes over and completes "Passus et sepultus est," the solo alto on top intoning the traditional chromatic fourth in descent while returning the harmony to E♭. At this juncture the solo soprano returns singing the same words in a soothing fashion, while the first clarinet and first oboe above the voice exchange falling motifs by the measure. Two plagal cadences decorated by the four soloists singing together end the piece softly.

"Et resurrexit" begins *forte* in the chorus and orchestra with a return to the busy texture of the first section. It starts in c minor, a natural link with the end of the previous section in E♭, to which this section works its way back, with fanfare-like eruption of the trumpets and timpani for "judicare vivos." Haydn, as he was struggling to finish this great work, had still not given up totally on the idea of another oratorio, the subject of which was to be the Last Judgment. The weight he lends to the relevant words in his last settings of the Credo can be better understood in this context. He passes through several keys in setting the wordy part of the text that comes next, and this is one of his Credo settings that omits none of its text. At length he brings the music to a stop on a long protracted chord of D major. We should be able to expect what will come next.

The D-major chord is treated as V/vi in tonic B♭, which arrives with an abrupt tutti unison spread throughout the orchestra. It is at the same time the beginning of a fugue in *Vivace* 6/8 time, begun by the basses and followed by the other voices in ascending order, singing "Et vitam venturi." Haydn's partiality for rollicking fugues in 6/8 time was in evidence at the same place in the *Theresienmesse* and demonstrated unforgettably to end "Autumn" in *The Seasons*. This fugue theme is also dance-like, and before the end of it employs the dotted rhythm characteristic of many jigs. So does the closely related "Et vitam venturi" fugue in the *Theresienmesse*. As this fugue continues it becomes more homophonic and there are orchestral interludes. After one of them the soloists make their final entrance, with two soprano soloists singing a countersubject to the fugue theme in thirds, followed by two tenor soloists doing the same. The chorus then brings the Credo quickly to an end.

The Sanctus returns to the mood of the Kyrie and is also an *Adagio* in 3/4 time. It has some motivic similarities too, especially the half-step move in the altos F G♭ F of the soft choral beginning. In both pieces the orchestra is in close dialogue with the chorus. Relatively brief at thirty measures, the Sanctus gives way to an *Allegro* for "Pleni sunt coeli . . . Osanna in excelsis." An orchestral leap down an octave before the first "Osanna" is followed by smaller leaps of the same kind from upbeat to downbeat, and remind us of similar octave descents in the Kyrie and the Gloria. The soloists enter with a descending passage in which the soprano sings half-step rises that match those sung by the sopranos in the first entry of the chorus in the Gloria. Haydn repeats this particularly fine setting of "Osanna" in its entirety, following the Benedictus.

Composers often chose to set the Benedictus as a serene pastorale, perhaps with the intention of conveying that the Lamb of God who is coming in the name of the Lord is also a shepherd tending his flock. This was the case with the Benedictus in the *Schöpfungsmesse* of 1801 and would be so with Beethoven's *Missa solemnis* of twenty years later. In his last mass, Haydn departs from this tradition altogether by writing a *Molto allegro* in common time, for which he chooses the key of F. It gives the impression that whoever is coming in the name of the Lord does so with unseemly haste. The texture is fairly intricate. As the piece begins, the orchestra establishes the quick pace with a walking bass in eighth notes. Frequent use of sixteenth-note passages as more than just decorative filigree impose limits to the speed at which these can be taken and still retain clarity.[61] The chorus enters singing in unison the first statement of the text to the theme announced by the orchestra. It is the first theme of a spacious sonata form movement that requires declaiming the same short text over and over again. The soloists enter with a second theme in the dominant, which they will eventually state in the tonic. The return of the complete "Osanna" in B♭ caps a movement of which it is fully worthy.

The Agnus Dei begins in the bright key of G major as in Haydn's previous mass. The orchestra makes the first statement, an eight-measure phrase in antecedent-consequent form, *Adagio* in 3/4 time. Overlapping its last measure the soloists sing the theme in a simpler, less melodically adorned style. The melody is similar to that which opened the *Adagio* slow movement of Symphony No. 98 in B♭, the movement in which Haydn incorporated an unmistakable quotation from Mozart's last symphony. He reinforces the connections with Mozart here, for his setting of "Agnus Dei" is very close to Mozart's setting of the same text in the "Coronation Mass," K. 317 (see Example 6.19). Quite the same also is the way a subsidiary voice comes out of the orchestra to link the two halves of the vocal phrase. This closeness to Mozart could be used to bolster the claim, often made, that Haydn suspected this mass was his valedictory address, his "hail and farewell."

Haydn's placid setting of the Agnus Dei in G makes its way around a few keys before coming to rest on the triad of D. Once again D plays the role of V/vi in tonic B♭. In this case Haydn clears away the chord of D so there is only the tone D. The orchestra pounces upon it tutti *fortissimi* (only the timpani are held back— they are limited to F and B♭). For this final transformation of D into B♭, Haydn goes slowly, building up a fanfare in which we hear after D, D and F, then B♭ D F, at which point the timpanist does join. "Dona nobis, dona nobis pacem" sings the chorus in a forthright, marching kind of triumphal song. In some ways this is Haydn's most simple and optimistic statement of these words requesting peace, which he had long since been treating as a paean to peace achieved. He has in mind here not just the words and a triumphal ending to the section but to the

---

[61] In his thrilling recording of the six late Masses with the Monteverdi Choir issued in 2002–03 (Philips 975 101–2), John Eliot Gardiner, never known for sluggish tempos, and famous for the opposite, takes the complicated texture into consideration and opts for a tempo fast enough but not so fast as to preclude clarity. Their performance of this Benedictus lasts just under four minutes.

whole mass. The movement is broad-scaled, and the nearly apocalyptic transformation of D into B♭ happens once more before the end. It is signaled by the climb of the sopranos and tenors to high B♭, which they hold for an entire measure, a completion of what had been proposed in more tentative form to end the Kyrie.

The work deserves its nickname of "Woodwind Mass" for in none of the others by Haydn are the winds given so prominent a role, and the term probably emerged from within the Esterházy music personnel. One of the reasons this mass is heard less than some others among Haydn's late ones, especially in churches at an actual service, has to do with its demanding and unusually full orchestration. Even if the nickname were to be read as signifying a cognate expression, "harmony" in the sense of how sounds are woven together, it would still be appropriate, for no other mass by Haydn is more rich and subtle in harmonic treatment. With respect to colorful harmonic progressions as well as great variety in timbral color, it takes up where Haydn left off in *The Seasons*.

Last Years

Princess Marie Hermenegild was well versed in music and trained as a pianist, probably by Haydn, who dedicated sets of piano sonatas (1784) and piano trios (1795) to her. It was only natural that the celebrations of her name day should take on a specifically musical cast with the performances of masses newly composed in her honor. After Haydn's last mass did the honors in 1802 there were a number of name day masses composed by Hummel, Haydn's successor. In 1807, Prince Nicholas commissioned a new mass from Beethoven, who had already dedicated to Marie Hermenegild *Trois Grandes Marches pour le Pianoforte à quatre mains*, Op. 45, of 1804. Beethoven, in an unusually humble vein for him, ended his letter to Prince Nicholas of 26 July 1807, "I shall deliver the Mass to you with timidity, since you, Serene Highness, are accustomed to having the inimitable masterpieces of the great Haydn performed for you."[62] Beethoven traveled to Eisenstadt to direct his beautiful Mass in C for her in 1807. Alas, the performance under his direction turned into a shambles (as was often the case), to the extent that the work was rejected by Prince Nicholas, and ultimately dedicated to someone other than his wife. Luckily we possess an eyewitness account of the festivities attending one of her name day celebrations, not Beethoven's misadventure of 1807, but Haydn's supreme offering to his patroness in 1802. It comes

[62] Alexander Wheelock Thayer, *Thayer's Life of Beethoven*, ed. Elliot Forbes (2 vols., Princeton, 1964), 1:422–44. At the time Beethoven was composing this mass, he copied out two passages from the Gloria of Haydn's *Schöpfungsmesse*. See Lewis Lockwood, *Beethoven: The Music and the Life* (New York, 2003), p. 272 and p. 524, n. 11.

from the diary of Count (later Prince) Louis Starhemberg, one of the brightest and most gifted younger members of the high nobility, whose many accomplishments included playing the flute. His wife was a talented pianist, and in London, where he was Austrian ambassador, they gave weekly musicales in which they sometimes themselves participated as performers.

The Starhembergs, among the oldest and wealthiest of Viennese families, had long distinguished themselves in Austrian military and diplomatic service. Prince Georg Adam von Starhemberg was born in 1733 in London, where his father was Austrian ambassador; his first name honors his godfather George II. He rose steadily in the councils of state and was ambassador to Paris when his son Louis was born in 1762, his godfather being Louis XV. Count Louis held posts in St. Petersburg and The Hague before becoming ambassador in London. In July 1802 he returned briefly to Vienna to visit his elderly father and accepted an invitation from Nicholas II to visit Eisenstadt for the festivities honoring Marie Hermenegild.

The diary entries of Count Louis, like those of Zinzendorf, are in French and require little translation.[63] "Mercredi 8 September, C'était le jour de fête de la Princesse, en conséquence de 10 heures nous allâmes chez elle dans la grande uniforme d'Eisenstadt, puis en grand cortège de beaucoup de voitures à la Messe." "Grande uniforme d'Eisenstadt" means gala dress after the local custom. The ceremony of fetching the Princess and the parade of many carriages from the castle to the Bergkirche were part of the spectacle, probably watched by crowds lining the way. "Messe superbe, nouvelle musique excellente du fameux Haydn et dirigé par lui (il est toujours au service du Prince). Rien de plus beau et de mieux exécuté." We easily forget how experienced and by all accounts superb a music director Haydn was. These skills, acquired over a lifetime's experience as a Kapellmeister, were not the lot of every composer and were not given, for example, to Beethoven.

Celebration of Mass was integrated into a web of secular festivities that probably changed little from year to year. Starhemberg's diary entry, concise and clear, describes them. "Après la messe retour au château et cour plénière des souverains pour leur nombreux sujets, qui vinrent les complimenter. (C'est réellement comme à St. James.)" This kind of reception on a big scale had been largely suppressed in Vienna by the austere Joseph II during the 1780s, when Count Louis came of age. There have been many comparisons of Esterházy's lavish festival ceremonies with those of a royal court, but perhaps none before this with the court of St. James in London, center of an empire.

The dinner that followed the reception was apparently given in the same

---

[63] Andreas Thürheim, *Ludwig, Fürst Starhemberg* (Graz, 1889), pp. 115–17, cited after Landon, *Haydn*, 5:231.

large hall of Eisenstadt castle. "Ensuite diner immense et magnifique, aussi excellent que nombreux, musique pendant le repas." Haydn did not preside over the Tafelmusik as he surely would have done at great events in the early days of his service. On this occasion (and perhaps a few others like it—the evidence is unclear) he sat at the banquet table, maybe not far from Count Louis. "Santé de la Princesse porté par le Prince, et répandu par les fanfares et cannons. Plusiers ensuite, telle que la mienne, et celle de Haydn dinant avec nous et proposé par moi." In other words, the toast Prince Nicholas offered to the health of his wife was followed by fanfares and the booming of cannons. The many subsequent toasts included one to Count Louis, who in his turn proposed a toast to Haydn, "who was dining with us." There is no ambiguity here. Such acceptance for a servant, albeit a famous composer, must have warmed the old man's heart, for whereas he had dined with royalty in England, he can have scarcely done so before this with his own sovereigns.

Count Louis continued with a few words on the ball that followed dinner, showing how it too preserved tradition. "Après le diner on se mit en frac [frock coat] pour le bal de Cour, la princesse Marie l'ouvrit par un menuet à quatre avec sa fille. On ne fit ensuite que valser." Opening a formal ball with a minuet for one or two couples was a practice that went back at least to the court of Louis XIV, and perhaps was still observed at the Bourbon court in Versailles that Count Louis had visited. This residue of the past gave way quickly to the present when the band struck up music for the waltz, and nothing but waltzing ensued, according to this eyewitness.

The celebrations continued the next day in a way that may have been as ritualistic as the rest. "Jeudi 9 September. On parti à 9 heures pour la chasse, après avoir reveillé par les cors." Thus the horns sounded not only throughout the hunt but even as an alarm clock for the noble lords to awaken and don their hunting apparel (an alert also for servants to get the dogs and horses ready). We can picture and hear in our imaginations so much more of what happened during the day thanks to the Hunting Chorus in *The Seasons*, which in its totality celebrated some of the same secular and sacred content as this festival. "Nous eumes ensuite un concert superbe dirigé par Haydn et composé des plus beaux morceaux de la messe de la veille." Here is good precedent for treating Haydn's church music as the main fare of concerts outside sacred precincts or liturgical functions. His last mass is so orchestrally conceived, much of it could be given as a symphony or series of instrumental pieces, without vocal participation. Yet the auditors doubtless would have found it less "superb" if performed without the solo and choral forces that worked so hard to make the premiere a success the day before, and certainly less so if under any other direction. Once again the importance of Haydn as music director appears crucial. He himself emphasized the point when writing to Prince Nicholas from Vienna on 14 June 1802 about some sacred music of his he was requested to send Grand Duke Ferdinand: "I await your command whether I should have both these works copied and sent to Pressburg, where unfortunately they will be performed in my absence and thus lose the greatest part of their worth for lack of finesse."

It would be pleasant to think that Haydn no longer had to appear at gala events in the livery of a princely servant. Such was not the case. Nicholas II could bend only so far in honoring his renowned composer and Kapellmeister. In August of the following year, 1803, when the prince returned from a visit to Paris (the visit Haydn longed to make but never could), he was welcomed by a cantata that Vice-Kapellmeister Johann Fuchs composed to celebrate the event. Haydn appeared in uniform at the head of the band performing it. Marie Hermenegild defrayed all the expenses for this event. In 1804, after Hummel was hired but before Haydn had completely retired, the prince reproached Hummel for not wearing the regular uniform "since every member of the chorus and chamber music, beginning with Herr Kapellmeister Haydn, appears in the regular uniform." There must have been some delinquency in the matter, for in a resolution dated 23 June 1804, the prince went further and specified that "the entire chapel, with male and female singers, will, according to the order that already exists, hold a weekly rehearsal every Thursday morning and are to appear, every individual without exception, in *uniform* in service at the Castle at 10:30 before my presence or that of my wife and children." Mention of female singers should not be interpreted to mean that they had replaced the choirboys as sopranos and altos of the chorus. Hummel's contract stipulated among his duties the training of boy singers in the cappella.

In 1803 Haydn was able to complete two interior movements of a string quartet in d minor. He held back sending them to a publisher for three years in the vain hope that he would be able to complete the work. Not until 1806 did Breitkopf and Härtel publish the two movements, which became known as Op. 103 from André's subsequent print. That he started with two interior movements, an *Andante* and a minuet, can be related to the known cases, discussed above, in which he began composition of a multi-movement work with the minuet. He originally conceived this work as a continuation of the set begun by Op. 77 Nos. 1 and 2. It was his normal practice to include at least one minor-mode quartet in a set. Four pages of sketches survive for the work, plus a one-page draft in score of the minuet. A prominent Haydn scholar has argued that of the two end movements, both of which were in common time (sketched on pp. 2 and 4), the material on p. 2 commencing with multiple-stopped chords was likely for the opening *Allegro*.[64]

---

[64] David Wyn Jones, "A Newly Identified Sketchleaf for Haydn's Quartet in D Minor, 'Opus 103,' " *Haydn-Studien* 8 (2004): 413–17.

The lovely *Andante grazioso* Haydn completed is in B♭ and in 2/4 time. Its initial rounded binary form with repeats raises expectations of variations to follow. What actually follows is a large ternary form: **A**, a quite different **B**, **A'** plus coda. Having descended from the first movement's d (or d-D) to B♭ for the opening **A** section, Haydn descends another major third to G♭ for the beginning of his **B** section. It provides strong contrast with section **A**, where the material was mostly smooth conjunct melodic lines, by offering disjunct triadic material and arpeggios, mainly for the first violin. After modulating to V (D♭), Haydn switches via the enharmonic route to c♯ minor, then modulates through several keys, coming to a stop on D major (V/vi in B♭). With no further connection but this old favorite of the composer, the main section in B♭ returns and concludes with a coda in which the rising arpeggios of **B** are heard at the last. The charming main theme could, with little adaptation, make a nice fit with the text "Benedictus qui venit in nomine Domine."

The *Menuet ma non troppo Presto* in d minor suggests by its tempo marking that the normal minuet had gotten so fast by this time that restraint had to be urged on the performers (some hand other than Haydn's added to the full-score draft the word "Scherzo"). The process of speeding up, long at work in chamber and symphonic music, could not have affected the kind of minuet danced to open formal balls, such as the one in 1802 just described, because the steps would not have allowed a much faster tempo. This minuet in d minor is in the usual rounded binary form with repeats and has regular, moderate sized sections, to which Haydn appended a very long coda, made even longer when he added a full measure of silence that is not in the draft. The Trio is in D major and is contrasted also by its simpler, more *cantabile* style, although both dances use a quite chromatic language. Typical for the second dance are the folklike touches, such as the protracted drones in the bass—open-fifth drones in the cello to end both strains.

As published, the two movements that remain of Haydn's last quartet turned out to be his last composition, possibly excepting only some song arrangements for publication abroad, which may be the work of pupils that was only overseen by the master. How fitting that Haydn's work should end with a minuet, the genre that he, more than anyone else, had for nearly fifty years installed and maintained as a fixture in chamber and orchestral music.

The unfinished quartet comes up for mention in a series of letters from Griesinger in Vienna to Härtel in Leipzig that furnish a little chronicle of Haydn's declining strength.[65] On 25 January 1804, Griesinger relayed that for a specified sum, Haydn would send the publisher various older compositions and "his newest quartet, on which he is working." Seven months later on 22 August: "Haydn

---

[65] Olleson, "Griesinger's Correspondence," 45–51.

has stopped all work because of his health, and a quartet of which he has finished two movements is the offspring to which he now devotes, albeit with difficulty, an occasional quarter of an hour. On the other hand he is occupied with the complete catalogue of his works, which will be sent to you when complete." This became known as the Elssler Catalogue, after Haydn's faithful copyist and servant Johann Elssler. A year later, on 21 August 1805: "He has given up hope of being able to complete the quartet but he has finished with the catalogue." And yet Haydn clung to the unfinished quartet and refused to send it to be printed.

The saga of Haydn's last composition continued on until the spring of 1806, when Griesinger finally got hold of the autograph. He wrote Härtel on 2 April, two days after the composer's seventy-fourth birthday, in a letter that apparently accompanied the piece:

> Here, my friend, is Haydn's swansong, the original of his 83rd [84th] quartet. As an apology for the quartet not being complete Haydn sends you his characteristic visiting card; the words are by Gellert. To be sure Haydn still does not abandon all hope that in a fortunate moment he might be capable of adding a small rondo. We wish it would come to pass but there is not much chance that what Haydn was unable to finish since 1803 could be added now. Would it not be appropriate to print the visiting card instead of the missing rondo? [Count] Fries is in full agreement. Wherever this quartet is played one will see at once from the few words why it is not complete and will therefore be transported by sad feelings [Empfindungen].

The visiting card quoted from the poem "Der Greis" (by Gleim, not Gellert), set as a four-part song in 1796, was No. 5 in Haydn's *Mehrstimmige Gesänge* printed by Breitkopf and Härtel in 1801. The same firm published the visiting-card quotation as Haydn wished to end their edition, brought out by the end of 1806 and entitled *Dernier Quatuor pour 2 violons, viola et violoncelle composé et dédié à Monsieur le Comte Maurice de Fries par Joseph Haydn.*

Griesinger's letter to Härtel dated 2 April 1806 went on to reveal some musings Haydn made on his birthday about music's future. "Its possibilities are boundless, to the extent that what could still come in music is far greater than what has happened already. Ideas often enter his mind whereby the art could be brought much further, but his physical strength no longer permits him to carry them out." By this time, was Haydn even aware that Beethoven had indeed revealed further possibilities?

Personal losses mounted in Haydn's last few years and made his dispirited condition worse. Swieten died in March 1803. Haydn's brother Johann, the tenor in Esterházy service, died on 10 May 1805, news of which came, at least, in a most kindly way. Dies opens his letter of 11 May (Fifth Visit) saying, "By ten o'clock I was there, and learned that the Princess Esterházy had sent word she would visit Haydn in company with the Princess, her daughter." At the beginning of his Sixth Visit, Dies tells the rest of the story.

> Haydn had received the sad news of the death of his brother Johann in Eisenstadt and was most grievously concerned. My readers will be pleased to learn that [the Princesses] . . . wished to give Haydn the news of the death themselves. With delicate care, they feared, and rightly, that such a message of sorrow from any other lips might easily shatter the frail old man, so together, by their own bearing of the news, they took away the bitterness of it, and by their humane behavior perhaps lengthened the days of the venerable Haydn.

Haydn's two sisters surviving childhood had died earlier, in the midst of their own families. There remained only his brother, Michael, to whom he had always been close although they were rarely together after their years as choirboys in St. Stephan's Cathedral. Michael Haydn died at Salzburg on 10 August 1806. The news took a cruelly long time to reach Vienna. After it did, Haydn made provision in his will to take care of the widow. One of Haydn's closest friends, the sculptor Anton Grassi, died a year later and, according to Griesinger, "Haydn took his death on December 30, 1807 very hard." Grassi had been the creator of the life-size bust of the composer in the antique manner that Haydn willed to Count Harrach.

When Haydn was well enough to receive visitors he welcomed them. Many friends, former students, and admirers from afar pressed to pay him their respects, and their visits gave him some of the cheerier moments of his long decline. In 1805 his friend Anton Reicha, along with a host of other visitors, arrived from Paris. In his memoirs Reicha states that he introduced to Haydn Comte Maret-Bassano, Secretary of State, the writer Charles Etienne, Luigi Cherubini, and the violinist Pierre Baillot, "as well as many other persons who were in Vienna at the time of the Battle of Austerlitz."[66] Reicha tactfully omits here that Napoleon made his first incursion into Vienna shortly before defeating the combined armies of Austria and Russia at Austerlitz in Moravia, just north of Vienna, on 2 December 1805, one year to the day after he crowned himself Emperor of the French. The Austrian court had fled. Haydn showed no rancor to the victors. Griesinger wrote that "Haydn had Maret, [General] Soult, and several eminent French officers who were in Vienna at the end of the year 1805 and visited him, inscribe their names in a book; and on days when he felt well, he generally welcomed visits from strangers traveling by." Haydn remained a patriot devoted to Emperor Franz, nevertheless, and is reported to have played his "Kaiserhymne" often and with fervor.

---

[66] *Jiří Vysloužil, Zápisky o Antonínu Rejchovi; Notes sur Antoine Reicha* (Brno, 1970), pp. 12–25, cited after Landon and Jones, *Haydn* (1988), pp. 306–7. The source is not in Landon, *Haydn*.

Cherubini enjoyed Haydn's special favor. When the rumor circulated around Europe in early 1805 that Haydn had died, it was Cherubini who took it upon himself to compose a funeral cantata, presumably for the Loge Olympique in Paris, for which Haydn had written his six Paris Symphonies and for which Cherubini composed two dramatic cantatas.[67] Baron Peter von Braun, who then ran the Viennese court theaters, invited Cherubini to come to Vienna, direct his most celebrated operas, and compose a new one, *Faniska*, which had its premiere in the Kärntnertor Theater on 25 February 1806. Cherubini brought with him a medal for Haydn and an homage from the Conservatoire signed by Méhul, Gossec, Sarette (the director), and Cherubini himself. It is likely that Cherubini played from his scores for the elderly recluse, who certainly knew some music by his visitor. Dies relates that, on his Thirteenth Visit, dated 9 December 1805, he was excoriating Italian composers for writing empty and trivial music in order to provoke a response from Haydn. The master replied that it was not true about some of the recent ones because "several of the Italians have rebelled against the common shopworn ways of their country. They move with ease, as the need arises, in all spheres of harmony, as, for instance, Cherubini." Griesinger quotes Haydn as saying, "When Cherubini looked through several of my manuscripts, he always hit on the places that deserve respect." Earlier in his text, Griesinger had described the parting gift Haydn made the visiting composer. "When Cherubini returned from Vienna to Paris in March 1806, he asked Haydn for one of his original scores. Haydn gave him the score of a symphony that is especially beloved in Paris, and said to him, 'Let me call myself your musical father, and you my son.' Cherubini melted into tears of sadness." The work was the autograph of Symphony No. 103. Countless composers besides Cherubini regarded Haydn as their musical father. They called him "Father Haydn" or "Great Father Haydn," as did Carl Maria von Weber, and more rarely, "Papa Haydn," as did Mozart.

In the aftermath of Austerlitz, Vienna suffered bankruptcy, rampant inflation, and insurrectionary rioting. Haydn's nest egg that he hoped to preserve in order to help his relatives and servants was in danger of dwindling severely because of the rising medical and pharmaceutical expenses he faced. He explained his predicament to Princess Marie Hermenegild during a visit she paid him in 1806. She asked how much he needed, and when he replied by specifying an additional 600 gulden annually, she said, as Haydn told Dies: "Leave it to me." The very next day she returned with a note from her husband authorizing the requested sum. It appears that she often was the angel who softened her husband's rougher edges in treating others. We shall see her shortly as an angel of mercy comforting Haydn during his last public appearance, at a famous performance of *The Creation*.

Marie Hermenegild was the daughter of Franz Joseph I von Liechtenstein,

[67] See chapter 4, p. 358, n. 59.

and was thus a member by birth of the highest-ranking nobility. In 1793 she was painted by Elisabeth Vigée-Lebrun, who was in Vienna at the time. The portrait shows her as the Ariadne of Greek myth, after being abandoned by Theseus on the island of Naxos.[68] She is garbed in plain flowing robes *à l'antique*, and is shown in a pensive mood, with head resting on one arm, at the edge of a cave bordering the sea. The choice of pose could be a tribute to Haydn's widely successful 1790 cantata "Arianna a Naxos," for mezzo-soprano and piano, and perhaps she herself played or sang the piece.

Of the three biographers who were present at Haydn's last public appearance, Griesinger, Dies, and Carpani, it is Dies who best tells the story. In his Twenty-Ninth Visit, dated 5 April 1808, Dies relates the grand event of only eight days earlier.

> The Society of Amateur Concerts gave, under the sponsorship of the Supreme Steward, Prince von Trautmannsdorf, on March 27 the last concert of the year in the University Hall, and thought to conclude most fittingly with Haydn's *Creation*. Carpani had supplied a masterly Italian translation of the text. Haydn was ceremoniously invited to the celebration, at which he was to be the foremost guest, and his health as well as the bright weather permitted him by good fortune to appear at the performance. Prince Esterházy was at court on the day, but sent a carriage to Haydn's house in which Haydn drove slowly to the hall. On his arrival here, he was received by some of the great members of the nobility. The crowd was very large, so that a military guard had to see that order was kept. Now Haydn, sitting on an armchair was borne aloft, and at his entrance into the hall, to the sound of trumpets and timpani, was received by the numerous assemblage and greeted with the joyful cry, "Long live Haydn!"

The hall in question was the Festsaal on the second floor of the handsome new University built by Nicolas Jadot in 1753–56 and located across from the seventeenth-century Jesuit Church just to the east of the cathedral (Figure 6.6).[69] The ceiling is frescoed, and statues decorate each side. Still extant and visitable, the Festsaal is best known from the depiction of the event on 27 March that Marie Hermenegild commissioned from the painter Balthasar Wigand to adorn the lid of a box that she presented to Haydn.[70] Dies continues his description as follows.

> He had taken his place next to the Princess Esterházy. Next to him on the other side sat Fräulein von Kurzbeck. The greatest nobility of that place and from afar had cho-

---

[68] It is preserved in the collections of the reigning Prince of Liechtenstein at Vaduz and is reproduced in Landon, *Haydn*, 4, Plate IV.

[69] On Jadot, the new University (now called the old University), and its Festsaal, see Heartz, "Nicolas Jadot and the Building of the Burgtheater," *Musical Quarterly* 68 (1982): 1–31; 10–11.

[70] There is a good reproduction in color as Plate IV of Landon, *Haydn*, 5.

FIGURE 6.6. Carl Schütz. A view of Nicolas Jadot's New University building, 1790.

sen their places in Haydn's vicinity. It was much feared lest the weak old man catch cold, so he was obliged to keep his hat on. The French Ambassador, Count Andreossy, appeared to notice with pleasure that Haydn was wearing on a ribbon in his buttonhole the gold medal presented to him, in consideration of *The Creation*, by the *Concert des Amateurs* in Paris, and said to him, "You should receive not this medal alone but all the medals awarded in the whole of France."

Perhaps the Count was unaware that Haydn had made a good start in this direction. It would have been out of keeping with Haydn's inherent modesty to wear more than one medal. Dies continued: "Haydn thought he felt a little draft, which the persons sitting around him noticed. Princess Esterházy took her shawl and put it about him. Several ladies followed this example, and Haydn in a few moments was smothered in shawls." Wigand captures the very moment when Marie Hermenegild has risen from her chair with shawl in hand before wrapping it around Haydn. The figure next to her leaning on a cane is Prince Lobkowitz, who was lame. Further attempts to identify individual figures have been made, and one is purported to represent Beethoven, another Salieri.[71] The chorus, orchestra, and soloists are not shown performing. Rather Wigand depicts the moment when four trumpet players raise their bells and sound fanfares, while all eyes turn toward Haydn. One detail not related by Dies concerns the reaction that everywhere greeted the work's most overwhelming moment, "And there was light!" According to Griesinger, "the audience as usual broke into the loudest applause. Haydn made a gesture of the hands heavenward and said, 'It comes from there!'" Haydn's nerves were so strained by the emotions the occasion aroused in him that he had himself carried away in his chair at the end of Part I.

When Dies visited Haydn a week after the event, the master had regained control of his emotions. "He urged me once again in these accounts to assure all the musicians who took part in the performance of *The Creation* of his warmest thanks. In praise of Mademoiselle Fischer, he said, 'She had sung her part [Gabriel] with the utmost grace and so truly that she allowed herself not the least unsuitable addition.'" She was the young daughter of the great bass Ludwig Fischer, Mozart's Osmin, whom Haydn encountered in London.

The Concert des Amateurs in Paris had a special significance for Haydn. Recall that for the Comte d'Ogny and the Masonic lodge Olympique he had written nine symphonies, Nos. 82–87 and 90–92. The famous orchestra of this lodge apparently did not survive the Revolution, nor did its concert series, yet a core of the same performers went on to form the orchestra for the Concerts de la rue Cléry during the Consulate (1799–1804), filled out with notable nonprofessional players.[72] The hall was at 96 Rue Cléry (which begins at the Porte St. Denis), and belonged to Charles Lebrun, the artist and dealer (husband of Elisabeth Vigée-Lebrun) who normally used the hall for his art exhibits. The more common name for this series, particularly in the press, was Concert des Amateurs. Its specialty was Haydn, whose symphonies the Parisian public never tired of hearing. No wonder, then, that the Concert des Amateurs sent the composer a eulogy and a medal (Figure 6.3, second from last). On the face it says simply CONCERT DES AMATEURS A HAYDN while the reverse shows two lyres surrounding a torch, with the words "Le même feu les anime—Professeurs et Amateurs." At the end of 1804, when Lebrun reclaimed the hall for his own use, the concerts moved to the Théâtre Olympique.

In November 1808 the composer-critic Johann Friedrich Reichardt visited Haydn and was welcomed as an old friend—this was not his first visit to Vienna.

---

[71] Albrecht, "The Musicians in Balthasar Wigand's Depiction of the Performance of Haydn's *Die Schöpfung*," 124.

[72] Jean Mongrédien, *French Music from the Enlightenment to Romanticism, 1789–1830*, trans. Sylvain Frémaux (Portland, OR, 1996), pp. 218–26. For a depiction of the hall see the fourth from last illustration in this volume. Navoigille was still the concertmaster (p. 219) as he had been at the Loge Olympique twenty years earlier.

In his *Vertraute Briefe*, Reichardt, as lively and controversial a writer as ever, tells how he was taken to Haydn by Fräulein von Kurzbeck and a Frau von Pereira, and at the end of the visit was shown the treasures.[73] "Then he showed me a whole series of medals, from the Petersburg Musical Society, from the Paris *Concert* for which he had especially composed several symphonies, and from many others."

Reichardt went on to describe what he considered the gem of the collection. "The most interesting was a rather large flat box that Princess Esterházy had ordered with specific instructions to be constructed and decorated." He then describes the lid painting by Wigand just discussed. "In the box there rested a large commonplace book, also black and gold, inscribed with cordial greetings from the Princess and her entire family. 'I must become the first artist to sign it,' said the venerable old man." This precious relic, eventually owned by the Museum of the City of Vienna, did not survive the turbulent events of 1945, except in fragments. Fortunately an exact copy of the lid painting was made earlier.

The Treaty of Pressburg in 1806 forced Austria back to a state of neutrality. By its terms, Austria lost all its Italian possessions. Some of its home provinces were ceded to Bavaria, France's ally. During 1807–8, with the help of large subsidies from Britain, the Austrian military and economy were restored to something like their former conditions, however feeble. In early 1809 Austria attacked Bavaria again, which brought Napoleon back from Spain, where he had suffered reverses. Commanding an army made up mainly of German troops, Napoleon advanced steadily to the east and pursued the Austrian army led by Archduke Charles to the gates of Vienna. By early May, Napoleon, from his headquarters at Schönbrunn Palace, ordered a bombardment of the city on 12 May. Haydn's house was in the path of the invaders and exploding bombs came close to it. Gathering what strength he could muster, Haydn tried to reassure his servants that no harm would come to them. The bombardment lasted twenty-four hours and then stopped when the city capitulated. Napoleon had a guard of honor posted outside Haydn's house, perhaps apprised that Haydn was near death.

Some days later a French Hussar came to pay a visit. According to Griesinger, "Haydn received his last visit on May 17 [Dies: 26 May]. It was from a French army captain, Italian by birth, who wanted to speak to him." Haydn was in bed but had the officer invited in. The rest of the story follows, as told by Griesinger.

> Enthusiastically the soldier described the feelings that Haydn's nearness gave to him, and the great pleasure he owed to the study of his works. At Haydn's request

[73] Johann Friedrich Reichardt, *Vertraute Briefe geschrieben auf einer Reise nach Wien und den österreichischen Staaten zu Ende des Jahres 1808 und zu Anfang 1809* (Amsterdam, 1810), ed. Gustav Gugitz, 2 vols. (Munich, 1915), 1:120–21.

he sang at the clavier in a neighboring room with great perfection the aria from *The Creation*, "Mit Würd' und Hoheit angethan" [In Native Worth and Honor Clad] [see Example 6.13]. Haydn was deeply moved, the officer not less so, they embraced one another, and parted amidst the warmest tears. In a trembling and quite illegible hand the captain wrote down his name. Provided I have deciphered it correctly, it was Clement Sulemy. Duty called him from Haydn's room directly to the Lobau, and from there to the melee of the battle of Aspern, where he was probably killed. Should he still be alive, he can boast of having been the last to give Haydn a few happy moments through music.

Not to be forgotten is the ravishing music that flooded Haydn's mind unbidden, music that he had long since lost the ability to write down.

Haydn died on 31 May 1809.

7
Beethoven in Bonn and in Vienna

Heritage

BEETHOVEN was born in 1770 at Bonn on the Rhine River in a small house that is now a museum and the seat of an Institute devoted to studying the composer and his works. His grandfather, Ludwig or Louis van Beethoven, arrived in Bonn in 1733, attracted by the opulent court of its ruler, Clemens August of Bavaria, archbishop and elector of Cologne. Louis van Beethoven, as he will be called to distinguish him from his grandson, came from Mechelen or Malines in the Duchy of Brabant where he was born in 1712. The son of a tradesman, Louis was trained in music from the age of six in the choir school of St. Rombaut in Malines and became an organist and singer (a bass when he matured). In 1713 Brabant and the other provinces of the Spanish Netherlands were acquired by the Habsburgs and became known as the Austrian Netherlands. From Malines, Louis, not yet twenty, was hired as a singer and choir director at St. Peter's Church in Louvain. From there, continuing his eastward trek, he was appointed to St. Lambert's Cathedral in Liège, seat of a wealthy and independent bishopric of considerable extent. The bishop of Liège was suffragen to the archbishop of Cologne. No more is known of Louis until Clemens August appointed him in March 1733 to the electoral chapel in Bonn.[1] His annual salary was 400 florins,

---

[1] *Thayer's Life of Beethoven*, pp. 42, 45. Forbes, as revisor-editor, wrote large portions anew based on recent research. His edition will be referred to as Thayer-Forbes in this volume. Relying on Belgian scholars,

a large one for that time, especially for so young a musician. It bespeaks high regard for his superior talent and training, as does his gradual rise to the post of Kapellmeister.

Louis van Beethoven married Maria Josepha Poll soon after joining electoral service. From this union came a son, Johann, their only child to survive infancy. Born ca. 1740, Johann entered court service in 1752 as a soprano singer and remained after puberty as a tenor in his father's cappella. There is some evidence that he also taught voice and keyboard in order to eke out a living on his small salary. In 1767 he married a widow, Maria Magdalena Keverich, aged only nineteen, the daughter of a court official responsible for overseeing the kitchen in one of the elector's many palaces. Their first child, baptized Ludwig Maria, died soon after birth in April 1769. Their second was baptized "Ludovicus" on 17 December 1770. Five more children were born subsequently of whom two survived infancy, Caspar Anton Carl (b. 1774) and Nikolaus Johann (b. 1776). Both were to play important parts in the Viennese career of their elder brother.

Elector Clemens August died suddenly in early 1761 at age sixty, exhausted, it was said, from the strains of too active a social life. The electorate and archdiocese was long ruled by princes of the Wittelsbach dynasty in Bavaria. Their rule ceased because there was no suitable replacement and the Wittelsbachs were rapidly dying out. The throne went to Maximilian Friedrich from the Swabian family of Königseck-Rothenfels. As elector of Cologne Max Friedrich was content to leave the actual governing of his states to his first minister, Kaspar Anton von Belderbusch (it was a sage move of Johann van Beethoven to name one of his sons Caspar Anton). The new government was in need of economic prudence after the vast spending programs of Clemens August, and gradually its finances were restored to better condition.

The musical establishment at Bonn under Elector Max Friedrich in the 1760s was modest in size, compared to that of Palatine Elector Carl Theodor at Mannheim, upriver on the Rhine, but it was well run by Kapellmeister Beethoven, who was generally well regarded by his forces and respected in the town. Like the other electoral courts in the Rhineland Bonn kept up with the times by putting on some of the most successful new comic operas from Italy. Thus in the first half of 1764 Bonn saw performances of *Il filosofo di campagna* by Goldoni and Galuppi, and *La buon figliuola* by Goldoni and Piccinni, which has been dubbed the "opera of the decade."[2] Louis and Johann van Beethoven, as bass and tenor

Forbes states that Clemens August was also bishop of Liège. He was not, but his younger brother, Johann Theodor of Bavaria, Cardinal, bishop of Freisung and Regensburg, was, according to *Kurfürst Clemens August, Landesherr und Mäzen des 18. Jahrhunderts.* Catalogue of an exhibition in the Schloss Augustusburg at Brühl (Cologne, 1961), p. 164.

[2] *Music in European Capitals*, p. 158.

soloists, both sang in such productions. The cappella continued to provide singers and players for the theater into and throughout the following decade, and little Ludwig was doubtless on hand to hear some of the productions in which his father sang. He may have seen very little of his grandfather on the other hand, for the Kapellmeister died on 24 December 1773, when the boy had just turned three. Nevertheless it was his grandfather whose memory Beethoven honored throughout his life, not only because of his position and the esteem in which he was held, but also because his father achieved little and turned increasingly to alcohol in his last years. Earlier, Johann taught his son violin and keyboard. The lad made such rapid strides that by the age of ten or thereabouts, he was already participating in some of the theatrical shows at Bonn.

Musical composition was apparently not one of the tasks performed by Louis van Beethoven, although it was expected of a Kapellmeister in the normal course of events. In 1771 Max Friedrich invited Andrea Lucchesi, who had composed several operas and a quantity of sacred music, to Bonn from Venice. Lucchesi was then thirty years of age. When Louis van Beethoven died in late 1773 Johann petitioned to replace him and was refused. Lucchesi became Kapellmeister by decree in May 1774. Shortly later the little Italian troupe Lucchesi brought with him from Italy returned home, with the exception of Gaetano Mattioli, who stayed on as concertmaster of the court orchestra. Revivals of Lucchesi's Venetian operas and some of his new works in Italian composed for Bonn found favor at first, then interest in them waned. Mattioli took over the theatrical directorship in 1777. He in turn was replaced two years later by a new arrival, Christian Gottlob Neefe. Born in Chemnitz in 1748, Neefe had studied law at Leipzig University and music under Hiller, whom he replaced as director of Abel Seyler's theatrical troupe in 1776. In May 1777 the troupe moved to the Rhineland, where Neefe was active also as a composer of Singspiel (premieres of new works by him were given at Frankfurt in 1777 and 1780). In 1779 Neefe joined the Grossman-Hellmut theatrical troupe and moved with them to Bonn. He became young Beethoven's most important teacher and supporter. From 1782 he served the court as organist, in which post his pupil Beethoven deputized for him on occasion. By 1784 Beethoven was appointed second organist at an annual salary of 150 florins.

Neefe was Hiller's favorite student and he continued, sometimes in collaboration with Hiller, to guide German Singspiel in the direction of opéra comique. This genre had high literary standards and vocal demands that did not exceed the abilities of most actors with some musical training—unlike the demands of Italian opera, which required professional singers. In 1791 he summed up his creed by writing, "Modern Italians will have to work with greater effort if they wish to please [music-loving Germany]. As far as music with dialogue and dramatic music as a whole are concerned, preference has generally gone to the French, and with good reason."[3] Neefe died in 1798, having witnessed Mozart's triumphs in Singspiel but lived not long enough to see the success in this genre of his most famous pupil.

Another strength that Neefe brought to Bonn was also important for Beethoven's early development. As a Saxon trained in music at Leipzig by Hiller he carried with him the musical heritage of Johann Sebastian Bach. In the predominantly Catholic Rhineland major works by the Thomaskantor were little known, if known at all. Thanks to Neefe, Beethoven was set to the task of mastering *The Well Tempered Clavier*. Master it he did. Neefe wrote a description of music at Bonn for Cramer's *Magazin der Musik* that was published in the issue dated 2 March 1783. It provides some of the only solid evidence about the training of his most brilliant pupil.

> Ludwig van Beethoven, son of the tenor singer already mentioned, a boy of 11 years [*recte*: going on thirteen] and of most promising talent. He plays the piano very skillfully and with power, reads at sight very well, and I need say no more than that the chief piece he plays is The Well Tempered Clavier of Sebastian Bach, which Herr Neefe put into his hands. Whoever knows this collection of preludes and fugues in all the keys—which might be called the *non plus ultra* of our art—will know what this means.

Continuing to refer to himself in the third person Neefe described his role further, and ventured a prediction.

> So far as his duties permitted, Herr Neefe has also given him instruction in thorough-bass. He is now training him in composition and for his encouragement has had nine variations for the clavier, written by him on a march—by Ernst Christoph Dressler—engraved at Mannheim. This youthful genius is deserving of help to enable him to travel. He would surely become a second Wolfgang Mozart were he to continue as he has begun.

Not mentioned is training in counterpoint, and Neefe may not have had much practice in strict counterpoint himself, hence the pains taken later by Beethoven in Vienna to acquire this discipline. Another of Neefe's attributes was his fine education. He made a good model for the young man. And it should be mentioned also that Neefe was an ardent Freemason, one who had published a collection of *Freimauerlieder* in 1774. This was no impediment in Catholic Bonn, nor was his Calvinist faith.

Bonn under the governance of Elector Max Friedrich and Minister von Belderbusch was considered the most enlightened of the German church states.

---

[3] Thomas Bauman, "Neefe, Christian Gottlob," in *The New Grove Dictionary of Opera*.

Under its last elector, Archduke Maximilian Franz of Austria, the youngest brother of Joseph II, this reputation only grew greater. Maximilian, as he will be called here, was appointed coadjutor of Max Friedrich in 1780, one of the last feats accomplished by his mother, the empress. He acceded to the throne on the death of Max Friedrich in 1784, following which Bonn's already strong political and cultural ties with Vienna became even stronger. These too had a bearing on Beethoven's future.

Beethoven was fortunate to have been born and raised in this small and well-governed state, often praised as one of the loveliest spots along the Rhine. Its beauties strongly appealed to him and he remembered them all his life, as is clear in letters he wrote to friends and acquaintances who remained in Bonn. For example, he wrote Franz Wegeler, perhaps his oldest and closest friend, in a letter dated Vienna, 29 June 1801:

> My fatherland, the beautiful country where I first opened my eyes to the light, still seems to me as lovely and as clearly before my eyes as it was when I left you. In short, the day on which I can meet you again and greet our Father Rhine I shall regard as one of the happiest of my life.

The next section endeavors to take the measure of "Father Rhine" and his valley as they were in the eighteenth century.

A Rhine Journey

Cultural and economic ties as well as geography linked the various political states of the Rhine Valley. This context can be explored from a specific vantage point hitherto neglected in music studies: the letters Leopold Mozart sent home to Salzburg describing the trip he and his family made down the Rhine in the summer of 1763. With his wife Anna Maria and their two surviving children in tow, Leopold planned and led the long journey that would culminate in the display of the two Wunderkinder in Paris and London. He reported back by letters frequently to Leopold Hagenauer, their landlord in Salzburg. Most of his letters were framed so as to entertain a wider audience at home—only a few of them were marked "for you alone." In fact many remarks made by Leopold seemed intended to put him in a good light with his superiors at the court and cathedral and were probably read by a hierarchy that extended all the way up to the elderly prince-archbishop of Salzburg, kindly disposed Sigismund Schrattenbach.

The little family traveled west by way of Munich and Augsburg, Leopold's birthplace, then on to Ulm, about which Leopold had nothing good to say. He found it "horrible, old-fashioned, and such a tastelessly-built place [ein abscheulicher,

FIGURE 7.1. Map of the
Rhineland showing the four
former electorates.

altvätterischer, und so abgeschmackt gebauter Ort]." Particularly distasteful to
him were its half-timbered houses, which he rebuked for showing their beams.
Passing next through Württemberg he found much the same. On the other hand,
the landscape began to please him. About the countryside near Ludwigsburg he
remarked "right and left one sees everywhere water, forests, fields, meadows,
gardens, hills covered with vineyards, and these all tastefully mixed . . . my wife
takes the greatest pleasure in the surroundings we are seeing here in Württemberg." They did not succeed in their desire to perform before Duke Carl Eugen
but they did meet his Kapellmeister, Niccolò Jommelli, giving Leopold a chance
to rail against imported Italian musicians, an implied complaint about the same
in Salzburg. Nevertheless he found the orchestra under Jommelli's direction, and
manned mostly by Italians, to be excellent. Even so it was diminished by what
they heard shortly thereafter in Mannheim, "beyond a doubt the best orchestra in
Germany."

    The Mozarts approached the Rhine Valley by way of Bruchsal, the summer
residence of the prince-bishop of Speyer. Figure 7.1 offers a map showing the four
Electorates alongside the Rhine and three of its tributaries, the Mosel, Main, and

Neckar.[4] Bruchsal is near the bottom of the map. There the bishop had erected a new palace in eighteenth-century style, partly the work of the great architect Balthasar Neumann. This building Leopold heartily endorsed. "The Residence in Bruchsal is worth seeing, its rooms being in the very best taste, not numerous, but so noble, indescribably charming and precious (19 July)." What he describes is generally designated Rococo, or French Style, and there was a lot of it in the Rhineland. His son would later concur, as when he wrote to Leopold in 1778 with praises for the elegant quarter of Nancy built in the mid-eighteenth century, and the new apartments at the Munich Residence.[5] In 1763 the Mozart carriage traveled north to their next stop, Schwetzingen, summer residence of the Palatine elector just south of Mannheim, by the post roads, for the Rhine was not then very navigable over this stretch. Here they were heard by Elector Carl Theodor and his courtiers, whom the children astonished with their playing. Leopold wrote one of his most valuable travelogues when describing the new city of Mannheim in his letter dated 3 August. What pleased him most was the regularity and elegance of the houses, of the whole city for that matter. He contrasted these with their next stop at Worms, seat of another ruling bishop, a town described by Leopold as "old-fashioned and in ruins from the former French wars."

Mainz, where the Main River flows into the Rhine, was then ruled by a powerful elector-archbishop, Friedrich Karl Joseph von Erthal. His palace was magnificently situated overlooking the two rivers' confluence. Leopold praised this view and was well pleased by Mainz, where the children gave several concerts. He was less pleased by the city of Frankfurt on Main, several miles east; for it he resorted to his derogatory term "altvätterlich," and was disappointed by the "Römer" or city hall at its center. Yet Frankfurt was the great center of commerce and trade where money was to be made. The Mozarts left their carriage in Mainz and went by market ship up the Main to Frankfurt, where the children played several concerts. Leopold's letter of 20 August from Frankfurt had much to say about prices, a favorite topic, and financial affairs. Of musical interest in the same letter is Leopold's mention of a good clavichord or spinet he bought from Stein so that the children could keep in practice while traveling ("Ich habe ein artiges Clavierl vom H: Stein in Augsburg gekauft").

The Mozarts next paid their respects to the elector-archbishop of Trier, Clemens Wenceslaus of Saxony, whose residence was at Coblenz and whose archdiocese stretched the length of the Mosel from the French border to the Rhine. In his letter from Coblenz dated 26 September, Leopold describes how they embarked

---

[4] The Electorates had such irregular borders it was not practical to indicate them other than by bold Roman letters. In general they stretched along the four rivers just named. For a more detailed map of southwest Germany see *Music in European Capitals*, fig. 5.1, p. 442.

[5] Daniel Heartz, "Mozart's Sense for Nature," p. 111.

on the 13th with their carriage at Mainz in a ship called a "Jagt" that was three stories tall, with covered decks where merchants plied their wares. They were impeded by strong contrary winds that greatly delayed them, and had to disembark at Bingen, where there were locks for the ship to traverse. When they resumed their voyage they ran into a big storm, causing further delays. "Finally, on Sunday the 17th at noon we reached Coblenz," a very costly trip, Leopold says. "You wonder why we did not go by road and pay less? Because the roads here are so miserable and made worse by being submerged in water by all the bad weather. And this is the reason we must go by river to Bonn and Cologne."

A day after arriving in Coblenz they were received by the elector and the concert offered by the children resulted in a present directly following it of ten Louis d'or. Wolfgang came down with a cold that, combined with the terrible weather, forced Leopold to delay departure for Bonn by several days. On the trip by water to Coblenz they had encountered Count Johann Anton von Pergen, imperial ambassador to the elector of Mainz. Pergen figured above in connection with Haydn. "He took my children by the hand to present them to the elector, which was the reason we got an immediate hearing. Whether we shall meet the elector of Cologne I am very doubtful, for he is now still in Westphalia." The information was correct. Elector Max Friedrich was then paying pastoral visits to the several dioceses of which he was bishop on the east side of the Rhine. The elector of Trier kept in close touch with both his peer rulers of Cologne and Mainz, and was in fact visiting Mainz when the Mozarts first arrived there.

In his long letter from Coblenz of 26 September Leopold revealed details about the mission he believed he was making on behalf of the Archbishop of Salzburg.

> The further I get in these parts the less is made of our court; here, one believes, because this is the place where three ecclesiastic electoral princes convene in one circle, that our archbishop matters no more than, at most, a bishop of Eichstatt, or of Augsburg. I can assure you that they all make big eyes at my stories and pay attention to our performances. They listen with surprise to what I tell them in straight talk.

The idea of Leopold as ambassador of Salzburg without portfolio would probably have amused Archbishop Schrattenbach, who was in fact the ranking German prelate and bore the title *primus Germaniae*.[6] Leopold did not forbear making unflattering comparisons with Salzburg in matters of ecclesiastic propriety.

> I must say that I wondered indeed at the indifference [Lauigkeit], the dirty, negligent [nachlässige] and truly peasant way in which church ceremonies are held in Mainz and Coblenz. No wonder they serve as more of an aggravation than an inspiration to

---

[6] *Haydn, Mozart*, pp. 485–86.

the Lutherans, Calvinists, and Jews, with which these parts are filled . . . in a word, our court is really a second Rome, and our gracious archbishop another Pope!

This was before Leopold actually visited Rome.

Bonn was the Mozarts' next stop. With hopes dashed of receiving a big sum from its absent ruler they stayed there only overnight and the next day. They visited the major sights and the great buildings that Clemens August had erected both in Bonn and in his summer residence at Brühl. Leopold was not about to write home saying what must have been obvious: eighteenth-century Bonn and Brühl were much more impressive than Salzburg, aside from its seventeenth-century cathedral. In one of his longest letters, written from 17 October to 4 November, Leopold was at first rather reserved in his comments.

> We took our own vessel from Coblenz, left at 10 AM and arrived at Bonn in the evening. The Electoral Prince was still in Westphalia. We saw the palace, or residence, Poppelsdorf, and all that there was to see. We went by the post to Cologne stopping at Brühl. There we saw the beautiful palaces of Falkenlust, Augustusburg, the Fasanerey, the Indian House, the so-called Snail's House, etc., and visited everything.

The Augustusburg, planned by two great architects on loan, Balthasar Neumann (from Würzburg) and François de Cuvilliés (from Munich) is a palace of stunning beauty that was restored to pristine condition after World War II. On its contents even Leopold waxed enthusiastic.

> We saw all the precious and rare things that are prized still by the archbishop's subjects and that Electoral Prince Clemens August left behind. They are altogether exceptional, especially the jewels, paintings, statues, and all kinds of invented clocks [musical clocks?]. Among other things the tables in the astonishingly large Concert Room [are noteworthy].[7]

Leopold correctly identified the prince who collected all these riches. He may not have known that Clemens August was also responsible for completing Bonn's Residence, one of the largest in Germany and worthy of a king, the Town Hall, and the rebuilding of Poppelsdorf into a palace, and he was probably unaware that the same Maecenas had lavished money on new buildings in territories he ruled as bishop, including the dioceses of Hildesheim, Münster, Osnabrück, and Paderborn—a large swath of territory across central Germany.

Cologne was a different matter. Clemens August made some attempts to stave off ruin in its great cathedral, yet the edifice remained in bad condition,

---

[7] *Kurfürst Clemens August* (1961). This elaborately illustrated exhibition catalogue of 527 pages devotes color plate 12 to the Concert Room in question.

prompting Leopold to say of it, "the temple of the Lord looks like a stable for horses." The antiphons he heard sung there made him wish to stop the choir-boys' mouths.

From Cologne the Mozarts traveled west to Aachen by the post, over roads that were in horrible shape, worsened by rain. They proceeded via Liège and Louvain to Brussels. Travel conditions improved. Leopold wrote, "From Liège to Paris—consider the astonishing distance!—the post road is paved like the streets of a town and planted on either side with trees like a garden walk . . . You can see at once that this is a country [the Austrian Netherlands] that belongs to Her Majesty the Empress."

Another observer of these parts was Thomas Jefferson, who in 1788 went from Holland to Germany via Cleves, a duchy then held by Prussia: "The transition from ease and opulence to extreme poverty is remarkeable [*sic*] on crossing the line between the Dutch and Prussian territory . . . With the poverty, the fear of slaves is visible on the faces of the Prussian subjects."[8] He crossed the Rhine and entered the duchy of Berg, then governed by Palatine Elector Carl Theodor; he was particularly impressed by the gallery of paintings at Düsseldorf, its capital. He recrossed the river at Cologne, about which he had nothing good to say. On the other hand, Bonn struck him by its magnificence: "The court of England. The palace here is to be seen."[9]

Another traveler of the 1780s to visit the Rhineland and describe it was Kaspar Riesbeck, a German who pretended to be a Frenchman. This passage is better known, having been quoted by Thayer. Riesbeck stressed the flourishing of the three states ruled by archbishop electors, and offered some reasons for it.

> The whole stretch of the country from here [Cologne] to Mainz is one of the richest and most populous in Germany . . . The natural wealth of the soil in comparison with that of other lands, and the easy disposition of its products by means of the Rhine, have no doubt contributed to these results. Nevertheless, great as is the prejudice in Germany against the ecclesiastical governments, they have beyond doubt aided in the blooming development of these regions. In the three ecclesiastical electorates which make up the greater part of this tract of land nothing is known of those tax burdens under which the subjects of so many secular princes of Germany groan. These princes have exceeded the old assessments but slightly. Little is known in their countries of serfdom. The appanage of many princes and princesses do not force them to extortion. They have no inordinate military institution, and do not sell the sons of their farmers; and they have never taken so active a part in the domestic and foreign wars of Germany as the secular princes.[10]

[8] Thomas Jefferson, *Travels*, pp. 288–89.
[9] Jefferson, *Travels*, p. 310.
[10] Johann Kaspar Riesbeck, *Briefe eines reisenden Franzosen über Deutschland an seinen Bruder zu Paris*, 2nd ed. (Leipzig, 1784), 2 vols., 2:387, cited after Thayer-Forbes, pp. 15–16.

One secular ruler who resembled the elector-archbishops in these regards was Carl Theodor of Mannheim, who did not extort great sums from his subjects to support an army, nor sell them to the highest bidders, unlike Duke Carl Eugen of Württemberg.[11] Riesbeck's reference is not to him but likely to the Landgrave of Hesse-Cassel, Frederick II, who sold Hessian troops to England and, for many of them, to ultimate slaughter in the recently concluded War of the American Revolution.

Haydn and Salomon probably traveled by much the same route in December 1790 as did the Mozarts on their Rhine journey of 1763. We know they stopped at Munich on their way west, but nothing else about their trip is documented until they landed in Bonn, where Archbishop Maximilian had prepared a special welcome for Haydn, as we have seen. They probably made some of their Rhine journey by water, putting their coach on vessels that plied the river, as did the Mozarts.

First Compositions

Beethoven's "Dressler" Variations, Werke ohne Opuszahl 63, were apparently an assignment from Neefe, who says he had them published at Mannheim in order to encourage his young pupil. Johann Michael Götz was the music publisher there who had brought out the handsome full score of Holzbauer's *Günther von Schwarzburg* in 1777.[12] His edition is entitled *Variations pour le Clavecin sur une Marche de Dressler composées et dediées à Son Excellence Madame la Comtesse de Wolf-Metternich . . . par un jeune amateur Louis van Beethoven agé de dix ans.* The Countess was the wife of a court official at Bonn and a pupil of Neefe. As for Ernst Christoph Dressler, he was a singer at the court of Hesse-Kassel. His rather grim little march had little to recommend it, yet its treatment by the young composer occasionally rises to a degree of agitation that forecasts the stormy minormode works to come later.[13]

In 1783 another Rhenish music publisher, Heinrich Bossler of Speyer, issued *Drei Sonaten fürs Klavier*, dedicated to Elector Max Friedrich, which has led to them being called the "Electoral Sonatas," WoO 47. Beethoven was in good company also on this publisher's list, augmented a year later by Haydn's three Bossler Sonatas "pour le pianoforte." Haydn's sonatas for his very young Princess were in

---

[11] *Music in European Capitals*, p. 449.

[12] For facsimiles of the title page and dedication, see *Music in European Capitals*, fig. 5.16, p. 591. The indispensable bibliographical tool for Beethoven's compositions remains Georg Kinsky, *Das Werk Beethovens: Thematisch-bibliographisches Verzeichnis seiner sämtlichen vollendeten Kompositionen*, ed. Hans Halm (Munich, 1955); henceforth Kinsky-Halm.

[13] Ludwig Schiedermair, *Der junge Beethoven* (Leipzig, 1925), p. 264, gives an impressive excerpt from Variation 8.

two movements and all in the major mode. Beethoven's pieces were more ambitious, being in three movements and in the keys of E♭, f, and D. No. 1 in E♭ consists of an *Allegro cantabile* in common time, an *Andante* in 2/4 time and in B♭, and a *Rondo vivace* in 6/8 time, a rollicking finale of the hunting type. Sonata No. 2 in f minor opens with a slow introduction, nine measures of *Larghetto maestoso* in cut time, with loud massive chords alternating with a more plaintive sighing melody marked *piano*, followed by an *Allegro assai* in common time that begins by plunging down two octaves by step, an *Andante* in A♭ in 2/4 time, and as a finale, a *Presto* in 2/4 time. Sonata No. 3 in D is the most galant of the set. Its *Allegro* in common time has a theme emphasizing parallel thirds in the right hand, moving smoothly down the scale. The parallel thirds reappear in the theme of the *Menuetto. Sostenuto*, which is in the key of A. The finale is a *Scherzando. Allegro ma non troppo* in 2/4 time. Clear melodic links between the main themes of the three movements enhance the attractiveness of this sonata. The other two also have thematic connections between movements.[14] Use of sudden dynamic changes point to the fortepiano rather than the harpsichord as the composer's choice even at this earliest stage.

Bossler was also the publisher of a periodical, *Blumenlese für Klavierliebhaber*. In an issue dated 1783 there appeared a Lied by Beethoven, "Schilderung eines Mädchen," WoO 107, followed by a *Rondo Allegretto* in C and in 3/8 time, WoO 48. The Rondo has a catchy and quite folklike theme, based on alternating 5 3 1 with 5 4 2, the whole worked into quite a substantial piece of 163 measures. Here the model is clearly the second and last movement of Mozart's Violin and Piano Sonata in G, K. 301, published in the set of six by Sieber at Paris in 1778. The correspondence is evident not only in the theme but also in the way it is treated to rapid alternation of major and minor forms. Beyond looking up to Mozart as a legendary performer, Beethoven obviously took him as a model for composition.

It surely occurred to Beethoven and those around him that he emerged from circumstances not unlike those from which Mozart came. Both were born in small towns that were at the same time capitals of states ruled by prince-archbishops. They were the sons of professional musicians in the service of these rulers' courts, in Beethoven's case both son and grandson. Johann van Beethoven, on the other hand, was very far from being another Leopold Mozart, who taught his two surviving children in every subject, not just music. Nevertheless Beethoven's father was responsible for setting his eldest surviving son on the path to becom-

---

[14] Schiedermair, *Der junge Beethoven*, pp. 226–85, points these out and suggests possible models in the keyboard music of Neefe and that of Abbé Johann Sterkel, a pianist in service to the elector of Mainz. Otto Jahn owned a copy of the 1783 edition, now in the British Library, annotated by Beethoven with additional marks of articulation and fingerings. Michael Ladenburger, "Der junge Beethoven, Komponist und Pianist: Beethovens Handexemplar der Originalausgabe seiner Drei Klaviersonaten, WoO 47," *Bonner Beethoven Studien* 3 (2003): 107–17.

ing a musician. As early as 1777 he organized a concert designed to show off his young son's talents at the keyboard, very Leopold-like indeed, along with those of another of his students, the soprano Mlle Averdonk. In the cases of both great composers, their careers from the start were centered on performing at and writing for the keyboard. In this respect they were quite different from Joseph Haydn. The career Neefe predicted for Beethoven of becoming another Mozart (should he continue to progress) was certainly made with this keyboard-centered conception in mind. The boy Mozart, who astonished listeners in London with his abilities to improvise all sorts of music at the keyboard, was matched by young Beethoven, whose astonishing powers of improvisation at the keyboard were remarked on by many.

Beethoven's main compositional achievement after the Electoral Sonatas of 1783 was a set of three quartets for piano, violin, viola, and cello, WoO 36. These are really just solo sonatas too, or at best and on occasion piano and violin duets with two accompanying lower voices. In the autograph, dated 1785, Beethoven ordered the works C, E♭, D. They were probably meant to be dedicated to the new elector, Maximilian, and to appear in print, but this did not happen. Beethoven kept the autograph, and after his death it was sold to Artaria, who published the works in the order E♭, D, C, which was followed by Kinsky-Halm and is observed here.

Quartet No. 1 in E♭ begins with a slow movement of sixty-nine measures, *Adagio assai* in 2/4 time, a closed composition that is not an introduction. There follows an *Allegro con spirito* in 3/4 time and in the rare key of e♭ minor. The work is rounded out by a theme and variations marked *Tema. Cantabile,* a movement in 2/4 time. This whole work, with its odd sequence of movements, was modeled on a violin and piano sonata by Mozart, K. 379 in G/g in the set of six sonatas dedicated by Mozart to Josepha von Auernhammer and printed by Artaria in 1781. There is also a thematic relationship, beginning with the main theme of the first movements. The indebtedness to Mozart in this case was pointed out as long ago as the 1860s, in the first translation of Thayer into German. It may have been Neefe who brought the work to his pupil's attention and told him to use it as a model. What this and the other quartets lack is Mozart's keen sense of timing and of true dialogue.

Quartet No. 2 in D is patterned on Mozart's K. 380 in E♭ of the Auernhammer set. It begins with an *Allegro moderato* in common time, with chords alternating with unison passages in dotted rhythm. An *Andante con moto* in 3/4 time and in f♯ minor comes next, followed by a *Rondo Allegro* in 6/8 time. For the first movement there exists an autograph earlier version that is more prolix and unfocused than what came later.[15] It took Beethoven a long while to get over a tendency toward verbosity in his music.

[15] Schiedermair, *Der junge Beethoven,* quotes the earlier version as ex. 41, pp. 297–98.

Quartet No. 3 in C bears some marks of having been inspired by K. 296 in C, the second of the Auernhammer sonatas, and is the most interesting of the lot. Its initial *Allegro vivace* in common time begins with an ascending tonic triad stretched over three measures—not very promising. After a scarcely memorable second theme in G, there is a turn to g minor and more subtle discourse (Example 7.1), the sort of clouding over that Mozart was so masterly at (but did not use

EXAMPLE 7.1. *Beethoven, Piano Quartet in C, WoO 36 No. 3 (1785), I*

in K. 296). If this idea sounds familiar it may be because it reappears nearly verbatim in the first movement of Beethoven's Sonata No. 3 in C of Op. 2, published a decade later. Or it may be because Mozart cultivated the same rise by step with a turn to the minor and ensuing melodic sighs, unforgettably in the first movement of the Clarinet Quintet, K. 581 (Example 7.2). Other passages from the opening

EXAMPLE 7.2. *Mozart, Clarinet Quintet, K. 581, I*

movement of the Quartet No. 3 were incorporated into the Sonata in C's opening movement but these amount to no more than filler, the kind of "noodling" at the keyboard in which Beethoven indulged to fill up time when he could think of nothing better to stretch things out. This kind of passagework with little thematic content may well preserve some of the composer's maneuvers while improvising at the piano. The quartet's slow movement, *Adagio con espressione* in 3/4 time and in F, has a theme that shares some features of the *Andante sostenuto* middle movement of Mozart's Sonata in C, K. 296, the first of the 1781 set. Beethoven put his soulful melody in parallel sixths between violin and piano to much more skilled and effective use later in the *Adagio* of the Sonata in f, Op. 2 No. 1. The Quartet in C ends with a *Rondo. Allegro* in cut time.

It was appropriate to the young composer's status as a virtuoso of the keyboard that he should try his hand at writing a piano concerto. There is such a work from 1783–84, the Piano Concerto in E♭, WoO 4. It is in three movements, *Allegro moderato* in common time (263 measures), *Larghetto* in 3/4 time and in B♭ (82 measures), and *Rondo* in 2/4 time (280 measures). The last movement is announced by the soloist with a jolly theme that is like a contredanse. The solo part of this concerto survives, as does a piano arrangement of the orchestral parts. Beethoven made a trip to Holland in late 1783 and may have performed WoO 4 in a concert at The Hague for which he was paid a large sum as a pianist, and at which Carl Stamitz also appeared as a viola soloist (for a much smaller sum).[16]

A FORTNIGHT IN VIENNA

Mozart was the name Neefe invoked in 1783 when predicting a great future for Beethoven. Support was needed for the young master to travel and study abroad, he said, and more specifically, he implied, study with Mozart. The composer on whose works Beethoven mainly patterned his own during this period was Mozart. With the enthronement of Archduke Maximilian as elector and archbishop of Cologne, Vienna came to Bonn so to speak. Vienna could hardly be considered a foreign destination anymore, although it was very far away. It was more like the magnet for the arts, culture, and society toward which gravitated all the scattered lands ruled by Habsburg princes, including the electorate of Cologne. Maximilian had long enjoyed good relations with Mozart, going back at least as far the archduke's visit to Salzburg in 1775, for which occasion Mozart composed *Il re pastore*, K. 208. After Mozart made Vienna his headquarters in 1781 he saw Maximilian often and believed he was in high favor with the prince. He even predicted that he would be named Kapellmeister at Bonn (letter of 23 January 1782). It stands to reason that Maximilian would be forthcoming with the financial support needed for his new court organist to travel to Vienna. At the very least he granted the petition for a leave of absence, to take effect in Lent 1787. He may have written letters of recommendation for Beethoven to take with him. Neither petition nor such letters survive.

On or about 20 March 1787 Beethoven left Bonn. By 1 April he was documented as staying at the tavern "zum schwarzen Adler" in Munich. From there he would have reached Vienna about a week later. He stayed for only two weeks. What has been written about his meeting with Mozart is no more than anecdotal conjecture set down long after the event. If he had a recommendation from Maximilian he likely met Mozart, if only for the presentation of this document. Mozart or Constanze might have been wary of admitting an unprepossessing

---

[16] Luc van Haaselt, "Beethoven in Holland," *Die Musikforschung* 18 (1965): 181–84.

youth of sixteen unless he came recommended by someone in authority. At the time, Mozart was busy finishing his great String Quintet in C, K. 515, entered in his thematic catalogue with a date of 19 April. Leopold Mozart in Salzburg was declining rapidly and Mozart wrote his father the famous letter of consolation at the prospect of death on 4 April (Leopold died at the end of May). Constanze was pregnant with their fourth child. If she and her husband had seen Beethoven at that time she surely would have said something about it later, after Beethoven became famous in Vienna. She was in touch with him professionally in the 1790s.[17] Stadler told Novello that Beethoven did not see Mozart.

The putative encounter with Mozart in 1787 prompted tales from Beethoven's biographers of the 1830s and later. They contradict each other. Ferdinand Ries says, "During his visit to Vienna he received some instruction from Mozart, but the latter, as Beethoven lamented, never played for him."[18] Ignaz von Seyfried told a wild tale of the encounter since discredited.[19] Carl Czerny much later claimed that Beethoven had explained to him that he had heard Mozart play and that he "had a fine but choppy [verhacktes] way of playing, no *legato*." This comment can also be dismissed. Mozart put special emphasis on a smooth *legato* manner of playing with his pupils. He wrote about Mlle Auernhammer that she played well, "yet the true, singing taste in *cantabile* is missing—she chops up everything [nur geht ihr der Wahre feine, singende geschmack in Cantabile, ab; sie verzupft alles]" (letter of 27 June 1781).

Beethoven, had he made the effort, might have met other masters besides Mozart. Kapellmeister Salieri would have been a politic choice, but he was in Paris preparing his opera *Tarare*. His mentor Gluck still lived—he died in late 1787. Haydn was at Esterháza as usual at this time of year, as confirmed by a letter he sent from there to a London publisher dated 7 April 1787. Dittersdorf was in Vienna and at the peak of his public success after the triumph of his *Doktor und Apotheker* for the German troupe in the Kärntnertor Theater in 1786. Its successor, another collaboration with Stephanie, *Die Liebe im Narrenhause*, had its first performance at the same theater on 12 April 1787 and Beethoven could have witnessed it. At the Burgtheater the Italian troupe reopened a day after Easter on 9 April with its first performance of Guglielmi's *L'inganno amoroso*, repeated two days later. On 16 April the Italian troupe revived Paisiello's *Le gare generose*. The repertory of operas and plays in the two imperial theaters was not very different from what visiting theatrical companies were bringing to Bonn at this

---

[17] She asked Beethoven to set a bass under the "Bandl Terzetto," K. 441, according to a letter she wrote Breitkopf and Härtel on 25 May 1799.

[18] Franz Wegeler and Ferdinand Ries, *Biographische Notizen über Ludwig van Beethoven* (Koblenz, 1838), p. 86; cited after Thayer-Forbes, p. 88.

[19] *Ludwig van Beethovens Studien in Generalbasse, Contrapuncte und im der Compositions-Lehre,* ed. Ignaz von Seyfried (Vienna, 1832); Thayer-Forbes, p. 87.

time, although the standards of singing, acting, and production in Vienna were undoubtedly higher, especially in the Burgtheater.

On about 20 April Beethoven left Vienna for the return trip, by way of Munich and Augsburg, where he may have met Stein, the prominent maker of keyboard instruments favored by the Mozarts. He had little or nothing to show from his trip except debts, as Elector Maximilian later complained to Haydn. While he was away his mother became ill; she was very ill by the time he returned, and died on 17 July 1787. Two months later he wrote an apologetic letter, dated Bonn 15 September, to the advocate Joseph Wilhelm Schaden in Augsburg, who had befriended him and loaned him money. In it he describes the death and his own deteriorating health. He begs indulgence as to the loan. "My journey cost me a great deal, and I have not the smallest hopes of earning anything here. Fate is not kind to me here in Bonn [das schiksaal hier in Bonn ist mir nicht günstig]."[20] He must mean his hopes of anything beyond his meager salary of 150 florins per annum as court organist. Does this imply that the trip was undertaken in part to earn money? Did Beethoven expect to concertize in Vienna or on the way to and from it? If he did, his aims were unrealistic. Even so famous a pianist as Mozart could earn little on the road by this time. In the letter he also says that his father wrote with increasing anxiety, urging him to hasten his return home because of his mother's condition. This has been taken to mean that he left Vienna so soon because he knew of his mother's illness, yet this is not what the letter says. The degree of self pity in the letter exposes for the first time a side of Beethoven not likely to win much sympathy. His "unkind fate in Bonn" is best understood as financial worries because of his family situation.

Johann van Beethoven petitioned the elector for aid, and the document was summarized for the prince in this memorandum of 24 July 1787.

> Court Musician makes obedient representation that he has got into a very unfortunate state because of the long-continued sickness of his wife and has already been compelled to sell a portion of his effects and pawn others and that he no longer knows what to do for his sick wife and many children. He prays for the benefaction of an advance of 100 thalers on his salary.

No record exists of action taken on the request. "Many children" is not the exaggeration it may first seem. A daughter, Margareth, was born to Maria Magdalena and Johann in November 1786. She died a year later.

One bright spot in the life of the young composer-pianist in an otherwise dark year was his friendship with the large Von Breuning clan, one of Bonn's

---

[20] Ludwig van Beethoven, *Briefwechsel: Gesamtausgabe*, ed. Sieghard Brandenburg, 7 vols. (Munich, 1996–98), 1:5–6.

most prominent families. Madame von Breuning, widowed in early 1777 and the mother of several talented offspring, was highly respected in Bonn and played a role in its intellectual life. Although she was only a decade older than Beethoven she may in some sense have helped replace the composer's mother, taking him into her family as if he were one of her own children. To the end of his life Beethoven remained close to members of the Breuning family.

Last Bonn Years

At the beginning of 1788 there arrived in Bonn Ferdinand Count Waldstein, who would become one of Beethoven's staunchest patrons. He was eight years older than the composer. As the fourth son of one of Bohemia's noble families he was shunted into a career that was neither military nor ecclesiastic, the usual avenues. He became a knight of the Teutonic Order, the Grand Master of which was Maximilian, with whom he became a close friend, as their extensive correspondence testifies.

In June 1788 Bonn witnessed the ceremonies conducted by Maximilian attending Count Waldstein's initiation into the Teutonic Order. The electoral palace welcomed a grand gathering of rulers from the Rhineland and elsewhere (Figure 7.2). They included the electors of Mainz and Trier, and the new vice-regents of the Austrian Netherlands, Prince Anthony of Saxony and his wife, Archduchess Maria Teresa, Maximilian's niece (whose passage through Prague had been celebrated by a performance of *Figaro* under Mozart's direction). As the Elector of Trier was Clemens Wenceslaus of Saxony, and his sister Princess Kunigunde was also present, this grand family reunion among members of the ruling houses in Dresden and Vienna served to reinforce their alliance.

About this time the Bonn court orchestra consisted of some thirty players. Its leader was Josef Reicha, uncle of first flautist Anton Reicha. Others of note were Franz Ries (violin) and the cousins Andreas Romberg (violin) and Bernard Romberg (cello), both of whom were prolific composers, and Nicolaus Simrock (first horn), later Bonn's most prominent music publisher. Beethoven remained in touch with these musicians long after he left Bonn. With the exception of Josef Reicha, who died in 1795, they were all quite young, and the youngest was Beethoven, who played viola in the orchestra. This band performed in both the chapel and the opera house, which was part of the palace. Neefe was pianist and stage manager for the opera.

In 1788 Maximilian laid plans to form a court theater of his own, rather than relying so much on visiting troupes of actors and singers. He could use the singers of his chapel to a certain extent for opera, as had long been the practice at Bonn. The opera season that opened on 3 January 1789 was ambitious and

FIGURE 7.2. Lorenz Janscha. The electoral palace, Bonn.

wide-ranging in repertory. It began with the big success of Vienna's 1787–88 seasons, *L'Arbore di Diana* by Da Ponte and Martín y Soler, sung in German as *Der Baum der Diana*. Works by Benda, Cimarosa, Nicolas Dezède, Dalayrac, Grétry, Paisiello, and Salieri were staged. Mozart was represented by *Die Entführung*, and one can imagine Beethoven's reaction and his pleasure in playing the viola part, since Mozart's viola parts were generally much more interesting than those of other composers (Haydn excepted). The season ended on 23 May.

The following season commenced on 13 October 1789. There was the usual plethora of works by French and Italian masters, all sung in German. What stands out is Mozart's increased presence. Three performances of *Don Giovanni* and four of *Figaro* took place, both sung in German. Besides these Gluck was represented by *Die Pilgrimme von Mecca*, Dittersdorf by *Doktor und Apotheker*, and the Dresden master Joseph Schuster by *Der Alchymist*. Bonn was not yet in a position to create new operas, as Mannheim had done during its heyday, or as Dresden and Vienna continued to do routinely. Nevertheless it was on a track, with the production of such difficult works as Mozart's Da Ponte operas, which might lead eventually to more ambitious plans. This opera season was cut short when the news of Joseph II's death reached Bonn on 24 February 1790. It reopened for a brief time after Easter.

The next opera season went from 23 October 1790 to 8 March 1791, with the usual closure for the Christmas season. It was during this closure that Haydn and Salomon made their stop at Bonn on the way to London. Salomon was a Bonn native and had been the violin teacher there of Franz Ries. He probably knew several others among both the older members of the chapel and the orchestra that performed a mass by Haydn to honor the great composer. Salomon's connections would have made the banquet that followed all the more convivial. (Lucchesi remained Kapellmeister of the court but with diminished authority, restricted to sacred music).

Anton Reicha set down some of his memories of the Bonn orchestra in an autobiography.[21] His main interest was concentrated on his own music of course. He also throws some light on his close friend and exact contemporary, Beethoven (Reicha was born in January 1770). "At the age of seventeen my symphony for grand orchestra was given, also many Scènes Italiennes for an excellent tenor whom Archduke Maximilian had engaged for the theatre."[22] At another point he describes the rehearsal or performance of this lost symphony: "To see me running from desk to desk, giving my instructions, was a real cause of laughter. One day I became so excited that I pushed the mouthpiece down the throat of the bassoon player, broke a violin bow, and tore the bridge from Beethoven's viola." A longer passage mentions an aria by Mozart sung with orchestra by a soprano identifiable as the Countess Maria Anna Hortensia Hatzfeld, whose singing Neefe praised in his 1783 description of music at Bonn sent to Cramer's *Magazin*.

> At the concerts given by the Elector of Cologne, in which he often took part himself, playing the viola, a young Countess astounded and electrified us with her beautiful singing. One evening she sang the sixth scene, in d minor, from Mozart's *Idomeneo*, which so impressed van Beethoven and myself that we were haunted by its beauty for weeks thereafter. I shall never forget it. Beethoven, who was born at Bonn, was organist at the Court of the Elector. Like Orestes and Pylades, we were constant companions during fourteen years of our youth.

[21] J. G. Prod'homme, "From the Unpublished Autobiography of Antoine Reicha," *Musical Quarterly* 22 (1936): 339–53. The autograph is in the Bibliothèque de l'Opéra, Paris. I have not seen J. Vysloužil, *Zápisky o Antonínu Rejchovi*.

[22] A fine tenor by the name of Luigi Simonetti was a favorite of Elector Maximilian (Thayer-Forbes, 102). In the article on Reicha in *New Grove* is listed an *"Armide* (scene, R. di Calzabigi), c. 1787, lost."

Reicha arrived in Bonn in 1785 and Beethoven left Bonn in late 1792, so that makes possible seven years of youthful friendship, not fourteen. The analogy with Orestes perhaps sprang to Reicha's mind because he was the brother of Electra, whose grand aria in d minor in the first act of *Idomeneo* so stunned the youths. The music of *Idomeneo* was not known widely outside Munich and Vienna in the 1780s. In this case the transmitter was surely Countess Hatzfeld herself, for she had sung the role of Electra in the performance of *Idomeneo* under Mozart's direction in Vienna on 13 March 1786.

Reicha relates another episode that suggests Mozart's piano concertos were well known at Bonn, and that Beethoven was performing them as soloist. It bears also on the perils undergone by the still quite fragile solo instruments of those days under the stress of Beethoven's forceful playing.

> One evening when Beethoven was playing a Mozart piano concerto at the Court, he asked me to turn the pages for him. But I was mostly occupied with wrenching out the strings of the piano which snapped, while the hammers struck among the strings. Beethoven insisted upon finishing the concerto, so back and forth I leaped, jerking out a string, disentangling a hammer, turning a page, and I worked harder than did Beethoven.

With the d minor of Electra's Act I aria still lingering in our ears from the previous tale, it is not difficult to imagine that the piece in question here was the stormy Concerto No. 20 in d, K. 466. Beethoven is known to have especially treasured K. 466 and is thought to have performed it as an entr'acte at the concert performance of *Tito* in the Burgtheater on 31 March 1795, presented by Constanze Mozart. He wrote two cadenzas for K. 466, one each for the first and third movements, WoO 58. They were not for himself to play—he would not have used or needed such—but for his student Ferdinand Ries, either in the years 1802–5, or 1808–9.

The symphonies of Mozart were also known in Bonn. Beethoven copied from one of them, as his sketching shows. Folio 88 recto preserved in the British Library's Autograph Miscellany and known as the "Kafka Sketchbook" can be dated precisely, because it contains sketches for an aria in the 1790 Cantata for the Elevation of Leopold (WoO 88).[23] It shows as well that he was intimately acquainted with Mozart's "Linz" Symphony, K. 425, of 1783. On the folio in ques-

---

[23] Ludwig van Beethoven, *Autograph Miscellany from circa 1786 to 1799: British Museum Additional Manuscript 29801, ff. 39–162 (The Kafka Sketchbook)*, ed. Joseph Kerman, 2 vols. (London, 1970), 2:89, 228. I am greatly indebted to my colleague Professor Kerman for the inscribed copy he gave me of this magnificent publication. He points out in his introduction that Johann Nepomuk Kafka owned the miscellany only a few years before it was acquired by the British Museum, and that its loose sheets do not form a "sketchbook." His edition will be referred to here as "Kafka."

tion he wrote a passage in 6/8 time with the treble in thirds descending in eighth notes against a scalar bass rising in sixteenth notes. He inscribed it, "this whole passage is stolen from the Mozart Symphony in C, where the Andante is in 6/8 time." Example 7.3abc quotes the passage from Mozart's slow movement, followed

EXAMPLE 7.3 a, b, c.

a. *Mozart, Symphony in C, No. 36, "Linz," K. 425, II*

b. *Beethoven, "Kafka" Sketchbook, 2:228. "gestohlen . . ."*

c. *Beethoven, "Beethoven ipse"*

by Beethoven's adaptation, then by a further adaptation. The original passage by Mozart occurs after a pedal point on C just before the reprise. Although not a prominent idea in the movement, it does come as the culmination of a long modulatory passage. There was much to admire in Mozart's deft part-writing (note the arching line given to the violas). In reducing this passage to two parts and making it more pianistic, Beethoven sacrifices the original's subtle attractions. Still, it might have been recognizable by other key members of the Bonn orchestra. Beethoven made it less like Mozart by dropping the parallel thirds and changing the rising bass in sixteenth notes to a simple repetition of the same an octave higher. He then copied it over making little change except to move the second measure of the treble up an octave, and this he marked "Beethoven ipse" (Beethoven himself), perhaps mocking his attempt to improve and at the same time disguise Mozart. By making the Mozart idea unrecognizable he also destroyed its salient beauties.

Commentators on this remarkable example of borrowing, guilt ("stolen"), and disguise have had difficulty identifying the original Mozart passage.[24] The editor of the "Kafka Sketchbook" comes close: "the curious inscription seems to refer to the 'Linz' Symphony, Poco adagio, bar 45f."[25] Beethoven specified the correct tempo: *Andante*. Measure 45 refers to the passage when the rising bass figure is first introduced, without the descending thirds in syncopation.

Haydn's music too was very well known in Bonn. Neefe, in the letter of 3 March 1783 to Cramer, printed in the *Musikalisches Magazin*, aside from extolling the promise of young Beethoven and the merits of Countess Hatzfeld, singled out several other musicians and amateurs. He devoted the most space to a court official in the finance office, Johann Gottfried von Mastiaux, whose passionate love of music led him to assemble a large library of works and a collection of valuable stringed instruments from Italy with which to play them, helped by his five musically trained children and other amateurs from the town. All were welcome to his musicales. A remarkable detail in this encomium is the connection with Joseph Haydn. "He is a devoted amateur of Haydn, with whom he corresponds, and in his large collection of music there are already 80 symphonies, 30 quartets, and 40 trios by that master." These may be round numbers and exaggerated, but even if they are mere approximations, it would mean that Mastiaux had acquired all the symphonies Haydn is known to have composed up to the early 1780s. Before his String Quartets Op. 33 of 1781–82, Haydn did not openly sell his music. Neefe's mention in 1783 of a correspondence with Haydn suggests that Mastiaux was one of several unidentified clients for Op. 33. A letter written by Haydn to Mastiaux in Bonn was once extant but has since been lost.[26]

Haydn was a commanding presence in Bonn's music life. His new works were eagerly acquired not only by Herr von Mastiaux but also by the electoral music library. A local news journal published a review of a concert at court in its issue of 8 April 1787 (Beethoven being in Vienna).

On the 30th of March at court a new composition by Joseph Haydn was performed with great expression under the direction of Concertmaster Reicha. It consisted of seven Adagios on the seven last words of Christ on the Cross. The idea of expressing these subjects through instrumental music alone is singular and bold—only a genius like Haydn would dare so much . . . Our Residence city becomes constantly more attractive to lovers of music through the most gracious support of our dear Elector. He has a great collection of the most beautiful musical works and makes

[24] See Lewis Lockwood, "Beethoven before 1800: The Mozart Legacy," *Beethoven Forum* 3 (1994), 39–53; 40, and his *Beethoven: The Music and the Life* (New York, 2003), pp. 57–58.

[25] Ludwig van Beethoven, *Autograph Miscellany*, ed. Kerman, 2:293 (commentary on folio 88).

[26] Bartha, ed., *Haydn Briefe*, p. 24.

daily efforts to augment it . . . The keyboard is especially loved here and we have a collection of several Hammerclaviers made by [Johann] Stein of Augsburg.[27]

Earlier electors of Cologne had also formed large collections of music. Their usual practice was to replace a predecessor's music collection with an entirely new one. Maximilian did not do this in regard to the already very large music holdings assembled by Max Friedrich, with the result that the electoral library contained an enormous collection of music dating from 1760 on.[28]

THE JOSEPH AND LEOPOLD CANTATAS

News from Vienna of Joseph II's death on 20 February 1790 took four days to reach Bonn (which would have required couriers riding nonstop). Maximilian immediately suspended Carnival celebrations including the opera season and decreed a period of mourning. Bonn's literary society, the *Lesergesellschaft*, of which Count Waldstein was a leading member, organized a memorial session, scheduled to take place on 19 March, the feast of St. Joseph. Eulogius Schneider, professor of Greek and belles lettres at Bonn University, an ardent promoter of enlightened principles, was designated to give the main eulogy. He let it be known at a planning meeting on 28 February that he would like his address to be preceded or followed by a musical piece such as a cantata, a text for which had conveniently been put in his hand that very day by a young local poet (later named as Severin Anton Averdonk, a student of theology). The text, Schneider assured, "was worthy to be set by a master of the tonal art, either one of our members, or someone outside our circle."[29] This text presented a glowing tribute to the Emperor's enlightened actions in the first half of the 1780s, before Joseph clamped down on Freemasonry. In the normal course of events, with the time for composition being a mere three weeks, the Society would have turned to a seasoned local composer such as Neefe or Josef Reicha, both of them members. It was not surprising, on the other hand, given Count Waldstein's rank and prominence in the Society, that the choice fell upon nineteen-year-old Beethoven, who had never attempted anything of the kind, as far as we know. At the Society's subsequent meeting of 17 March the minutes recorded that "for various reasons the proposed cantata cannot be performed." One reason could be that the music was not finished in time, another that what Beethoven had written was unperformable by the forces at hand.

---

[27] Schiedermair, *Der junge Beethoven*, pp. 82–83.

[28] Sieghard Brandenburg, "Die kurfürstliche Musikbibliothek in Bonn und ihre Bestände im 18. Jahrhundert," *Beethoven Jahrbuch* 8 (1971–72): 7–47. The author omits the 1784 inventory, in which Haydn is very well represented. It may be found in Adolf Sandberger, "Die Inventare der Bonner Hofmusik," in Sandberger, *Ausgewählte Aufsätze zur Musikgeschichte*, 2 vols. (Munich, 1921–24), 2:109–30.

[29] Schiedermair, *Der junge Beethoven*, pp. 219–20.

The Funeral Cantata for Joseph, WoO 87, was an ambitious project. Its text required four soloists and four-part chorus. There were two recitative and aria pairs, one each for solo bass and solo soprano, surrounding a central chorus begun by soprano solo, the whole framed by the initial chorus that returns at the end. As Beethoven set the work, the orchestra assumed an important role too. He chose an ensemble of strings and winds, with no trumpets or timpani. In an orchestral introduction of ten measures, *Largo* in 3/4 time and in c minor, the strings sound a measure of unison C, *piano*, in three octaves, with fermatas, to which the winds respond with a measure of the c-minor chord, higher up, with the third on top, also with fermatas. The strings retort with their unison, marked *mezzo forte*, and the winds reply with a four-part diminished chord built up over C. They sound like a cry from the damned in their stygian gloom. Pitiful and hesitant little sobs of the solo flute high above do nothing to contradict such a vision. The exchange between unison strings and wind chords is an idea that recurs, in f minor, to open Act II of *Fidelio*, beginning the portrait of Florestan in the dungeon. This introduction lacks breadth and depth in comparison. Already in its eleventh measure the initial exchange returns. Here in answer to the strings' unison C it is the chorus that enters in harmony singing "Todt! Todt!"

The critical edition (*BW* X, 3) divides the work into seven numbers by separate enumeration of the two big recitatives. They are elaborate, of the obbligato type, but still recitatives. The first begins with a *Presto*, a rumbling bass line in eighth notes suggesting D major, which the aria will eventually establish. Its agitation responds to the evil conjured by the text: "A monster, by the name of Fanaticism, arose from the depths." The aria opens calmly, *Allegro maestoso* in 3/4 time, although accompanied by a nervous figure in dotted rhythm. It depicts the hero who like St. George has come to slay the dragon: "Then came Joseph . . ." Beethoven sets this to a majestic descent through the tonic triad against which there is a nervous figure in dotted rhythm that comes from the preceding recitative—this dragon did not surrender without a fight.

At this stage of his career the composer is better at starting pieces than finishing them. A good example is the next number, No. 4, which is the most inspired of the whole work. The text speaks of mankind climbing out of darkness up to the light. Such a sublime thought deserved a sublime melody and Beethoven conceived one of his greatest in expressing it. Instrumental timbre was again all-important to him, not vocal color. The melody is an oboe solo, an *Andante con moto* in 3/4 time in the key of F major (Example 7.4). It fits the words in a general way by rising, but it is hardly grateful for the solo soprano to begin in the voice's low register, then suddenly switch to an octave higher. The greatest charm of this melody, after its two initial rising fourths in succession, is the poignant dissonance of that high B♭ against A in the bass, and then the smooth

EXAMPLE 7.4. *Beethoven, Joseph Cantata, WoO I, No. 4*

descent.[30] Purists might quibble with doubling or tripling of the third degree here but the sonority in the oboe is magical. Most music lovers will recognize the oboe melody from its occurrence in the Act II finale of *Fidelio*, when Leonora removes Florestan's shackles and stammers "O Gott! welch' ein Augenblick!" Above her soars the sublime oboe melody. She does not sing it, nor does he, although they join the melody's line here and there. Beethoven then introduces the chorus and works up to a very satisfactory closing in F major. The Cantata too brings in the chorus, and after a while they simply come to a stop without projecting a sense of completion. It might be argued that Beethoven intentionally allowed this piece to peter out, as if to say that the vision of mankind's climb toward enlightenment represents a quest that is endless.

The oboe was an inspired choice for this melody, or better, the oboe's timbres inspired the melody. F major is a perfect key for the instrument in more than one way. Its top range is best around high C and the tones just below it, whereas above high C the tones get thinner and thinner. Mozart chose the key of C for his Oboe Concerto, K. 314, of 1777, and the solo enters with a run up the instrument's higher octave to high C, which is held for four measures, then surrounded by upper and lower auxiliary tones. High D is the highest tone Mozart considered advisable for orchestral oboes in his lessons to Thomas Attwood. This limit he observed in his own orchestral writing for oboes, and also for the solo oboe in K. 314. For his Oboe Quartet, K. 370, written at Munich early in 1781 for the stellar oboist Friedrich Ramm, Mozart chose the key of F, and only twice at the very end did he allow Ramm to climb up the tonic triad to high F. He also chose the key of F for another Oboe Concerto, K. 293, but it got no further than the solo's first entrance, starting on a long-held high C. Beethoven too wrote an Oboe Concerto in F during his Bonn years. Incipits of its three movements survive on a sheet in

---

[30] Brahms followed suit with the oboe melody that begins the slow movement in F of his Violin Concerto in D.

the Beethoven Archive at Bonn.[31] The two oboists in electoral service were Georg Libsich and Joseph Welsch.[32] From them the young composer could have learned the instrument's strengths and limitations. His experiences in Bonn, including playing in the court orchestra, endowed him with a fine feeling for the technical and timbral possibilities of all the instruments.

The text as well as the music of the Joseph Cantata reaches a high point in No. 4. In No. 5 the text veers toward the macabre: "He slumbers, relieved of his worldly cares. The night is still, only a shudder of air reaches my cheeks, like a breath from the grave. You, happy grave, conduct him to an eternal crown." Beethoven sets this to another obbligato recitative, this one for soprano, a *Largo* in common time and mostly in d minor. It leads to an aria, No. 6, that begins softly in E♭, *Adagio con affetto* in 3/4 time: "Hier schlummert sein stiller Frieden." Whether peace, or silent peace, can slumber is a question best not posed. On musical grounds the wisdom of a long slumber aria in E♭, moving in slow triple time, coming after another slow-moving piece in triple meter, is dubious. The effect is soporific. At least E♭ makes a fine tonal passageway to the return of c minor for the sudden repeat of the initial chorus ("Attaca subito il Coro"). It too is in triple meter and slow. The chorus, as No. 7, is enlarged by a few measures but otherwise unchanged.

The Joseph Cantata was followed by another work of the same kind. The Leopold Cantata, WoO 88, celebrates the elevation of Joseph's brother to the throne as Leopold II. This poem too is attributed to Averdonk. When one ruler dies and is succeeded by a legitimate heir, custom decreed that celebration prevail over mourning, and quickly—as expressed by the age-old formula "Le roi est mort, vive le roi!"—Bonn was probably less than fully aware of the situation in Vienna. The difficult straits in which Joseph left the Habsburg monarchy boded ill for his successor. Leopold allowed almost no celebration of his accession in Vienna. It was a different matter with his election as emperor. He traveled to Frankfurt for the imperial coronation in October 1790, by which time the monarchy's outlook was somewhat brighter. The event was celebrated by many festive works, and it will be recalled that Mozart's last extensive journey was the ill-starred trip to Frankfurt in search of monetary rewards and a good position. Beethoven's cantata was one of many festive works in 1790 celebrating Leopold's election, and it was presumably ordered by Elector Maximilian, who attended the coronation. Whether the cantata was performed or not, when, and where, remain open questions.

---

[31] Quoted as a musical example in Thayer-Forbes, p. 126. The third movement, *Rondo Allegretto,* has a theme with an ascent by step up to high F for the oboe solo. The second movement is completely sketched in "Kafka," 2:126–27, and also required a run up to high F.

[32] According to an *Almanac de la Cour* for 1791. Michael Ladenburger, "Das böhmische Element im kurkölnischen Musikleben," in Sieghard Brandenburg and Martella Gutíerrez-Denhoff, eds., *Beethoven und Böhmen: Beiträge zu Biographie und Wirkungsgeschichte Beethovens* (Bonn, 1988), pp. 9–42; 19.

The poet of this cantata treated it as a continuation of the Joseph Cantata. Instead of putting the emphasis on joy ("vive le roi!"), Averdonk or whoever wrote it began with words about the departed Joseph: "Er schlummert." Beethoven set them in music that connects with the end of the previous Cantata, beginning in A♭. The name "Leopold" does not occur until fifty-eight measures into the following soprano aria. An ensemble for soprano, tenor, and bass following a recitative for tenor brings up Joseph again, referring to him as "your father." At the close, finally, there is a joyful chorus of celebration in D major, *Un poco allegro e maestoso* in 12/8 time. The meter is unusual and suggests a lively dance such as the tarantella. It switches to *Allegro vivace* in cut time in the final section as the chorus launches into a none-too-successful fugato to the text "Stürzet nieder, Millionen." By an odd coincidence these words, in the form of the question "Do you bow down, you millions?" occur in Schiller's earlier "Ode to Joy" and were famously set by Beethoven in his Ninth Symphony.

All in all the Leopold Cantata fell far short of its predecessor. At the least the choice of Beethoven to compose the second cantata, presumably in the fall of 1790, throws a positive light on the reception of the Joseph Cantata even though it was not performed on the occasion for which it was written. The high level of musical inspiration in parts of the Joseph Cantata, conspicuously lacking in the Leopold Cantata, says something about Beethoven's own reactions to their texts.

Another occasion for possible performance came in the fall of 1791, when Maximilian took his court orchestra along on a journey to Mergentheim on the Tauber. This small territory had for centuries been the seat of the Teutonic Order. It is located south of the Main River and east of Mannheim (see Figure 7.1). In this lovely rural setting, Maximilian, as grand master of the Order, presided over a meeting of its knights and commanders. Beethoven was among the party of twenty-five orchestral musicians, led by Franz Ries in lieu of Josef Reicha, who was ill. They went by boat up the Rhine and Main rivers, leaving Bonn on about 1 September and returning in late October. It was a very jolly trip, according to reports. At Aschaffenburg am Main, where the elector of Mainz had a large summer palace, Beethoven met the pianist and composer Abbé Sterkel, heard him play, and played for him.

Mergentheim, off the beaten track though it was, drew visitors to the ceremonial meetings of the Teutonic Order. Among them in 1791 was the critic Carl Ludwig Junker, who sent a report on the Bonn musicians to Bossler's *Musikalischer Correspondenz* (Speyer, 23 November 1791). Junker praised the orchestra's superb control of dynamics, saying that "this was formerly to be heard only at Mannheim." He knew whereof he spoke for he visited Mannheim in the 1770s, when the famous orchestra was at its peak. Junker devoted a long and discerning paragraph to Beethoven, who did not perform in public as a pianist, apparently because the instrument available was not to his liking—it was a piano made by Franz Jakob Späth, explained Junker, while at Bonn he played one made by Johann Stein. Junker did hear Beethoven in private and extolled his playing, especially his improvisations.

> Even the members of this remarkable orchestra are, without exception, his admirers, and all ears when he plays. Yet he is exceedingly modest and free from all pretension. He, however, acknowledged to me that, upon the journeys which the Elector had enabled him to make, he had seldom found in the playing of the most distinguished virtuosi [including Sterkel?] that excellence which he supposed he had a right to expect. His style of treating the instrument is so different from that usually adopted, that it impresses one with the idea that by a path of his own discovery he has attained that height of excellence where he now stands.[33]

Junker says nothing about Beethoven's cantata. Another source reports that the orchestra rehearsed it at Mergentheim.

Franz Wegeler wrote in his *Biographisches Notizen* about a planned performance at Mergentheim, and also says that the cantata was shown to Haydn in 1792. The piece in question was surely the funeral cantata for Joseph, as dictated by its merits.

> When Haydn first came back from England [summer of 1792] a breakfast was given for him by the Electoral Orchestra at Godesberg, a resort near Bonn. At this occasion Beethoven laid before him a cantata which was noticed especially by Haydn and which made him urge Beethoven to continue his studies. Later [*recte*: earlier] this cantata was supposed to be performed at Mergentheim, but several places were so difficult for the wind players that some musicians complained that they couldn't be played, and the performance was canceled.

Impossibly difficult wind writing is not evident in the single score of the Joseph Cantata that has come down to us, which may of course have been revised further. While the flute part is often high and exposed, it does not seem beyond the capabilities of so fine a flautist as Anton Reicha.

One other work that appears to have had a connection with the Teutonic Knights is the ballet given at the Bonn court on the last Sunday of Carnival, 1791, known by the coined title "Ritterballet." Gotha's *Theater-Kalender* for 1792 called it "a characteristic ballet in old German costume . . . with plot and music invented by Count Waldstein. It honored the main pastimes of our ancestors—war, hunting, courtship, carousing." The score survives, without title or composer, but notated in Beethoven's hand, WoO 1. There is no doubt that he is the composer, although the bow to Count Waldstein in the report may indicate

[33] Thayer-Forbes, p. 103.

he had given advice (cf. Swieten's suggestions to Haydn). The music consists of seven pieces: march, German Song (which returns twice after subsequent numbers, promenade-like), hunting song (with horn calls and in triple meter), love song, drinking song, and German dance, the last bearing the subtitle "Walzer." This suite of pieces adheres to a principal key, D, except for the love song, titled both "Romanze" and "Minnelied," which fluctuates between b minor, D major, and B major, with exotic effect. Mozart's Romance in *Die Entführung* has some features in common with it: triple meter with dotted rhythm, pizzicato strings, and modal surprises. The young composer had a decided talent for balletic invention. His returning German song is not easily forgotten and it apparently haunted Beethoven too, for he wrote a quite similar melody, with rising disjunct thirds in a descending sequence as the finale of his Sonatine in G major, Op. 79, a little retrospective work of 1809.

Two other composite works for Bonn rank with the Joseph Cantata and the ballet score in interest and workmanship. One is the Octet for Winds in E♭ published posthumously as Op. 103 and composed originally in 1792 as Tafelmusik for the Harmonie band of the elector. The other is the String Trio in E♭, also from 1792, a work Beethoven thought well enough of to allow it to be published by Artaria in 1797 as Op. 3. It is of the serenade type with two minuets and patently inspired by Mozart's String Trio in E♭, K. 563. There were also many songs and several sets of variations for piano. Work was under way at Bonn certainly on what would become the piano trios and solo sonatas of Opp. 1–2. They received their final form in Vienna.

DEPARTURE

In October 1792 Mainz fell to the French. Troubled times loomed for the Rhenish electorates. Beethoven left Bonn in early November of the same year and traveled with a companion up the Rhine to Coblenz, then by coach overland to Regensburg and down the Danube to Vienna, where he arrived about ten days after setting out. Maximilian had given him leave of absence again for a *Studienreise* and a small sum for travel expenses; otherwise he was supposed to get along mainly on his salary as court organist. It was expected that he would return to his post at Bonn after a year or so. He never did. By the end of 1794 Maximilian left Bonn for the last time and there no longer was an electorate of Cologne or a court at Bonn.

Beethoven's friends treated his departure as an occasion of note. They created a souvenir album of sentiments and wishes after the fashion of the time to mark the event. The Breuning daughter Eleonore, Beethoven's exact contemporary, to whom he was very close, quoted a passage from Herder about friendship and signed her entry "Bonn, 1 November 1792, your true friend Eleonore Breuning." The most celebrated entry by far was that of Count Waldstein, who expressed his great hopes for the young composer's future, the realization of which hinged on hard work, under Haydn's guidance.

> Dear Beethoven! You are going to Vienna in fulfillment of your long-frustrated wishes. The Genius of Mozart is mourning and weeping over the death of her pupil. She found a refuge but no occupation with the inexhaustible Haydn; through him she wishes to form a union with another. With the help of assiduous labor you shall receive *Mozart's spirit from Haydn's hands.*
> Your true friend Waldstein   Bonn, 29 October 1792

Note that Eleonore shed the "von" from her name and Waldstein shed even more from his.

Count Waldstein indulged his poetic fancy freely in imagining how Mozart and Haydn related to each other, and how Beethoven might relate to both. Neefe sent a more down-to-earth statement to Spazier's *Berliner Musik Zeitung* in September 1793: "In November of last year Ludwig van Beethoven, assistant court organist and now unquestionably one of the foremost piano-players, went to Vienna at the expense of our elector in order to perfect himself further, under Haydn's direction, in the art of composition." Waldstein puts Haydn in the position of being a mere conveyer of Mozart's inspiration, implying that Haydn himself was unable to take full advantage therefrom. More than one thing is askew in his formulation. Beethoven had already received plenty of inspiration from Mozart's music and needed no medium to assist him in finding more. It has been argued above that Haydn also had in many instances been inspired by Mozart's music. Beethoven had profited much from Haydn's music, as could be said of every young composer of the late eighteenth century. He still had more to learn from Haydn, and not just in technical prowess. One difficulty that beset their relationship, aside from great differences in temperament and age, was that Haydn kept exceeding his own great accomplishments throughout Beethoven's first decade in Vienna. Waldstein's use of "inexhaustible" is demeaning of Haydn because it speaks mainly of quantity, without regard to quality.

The Haydn-Beethoven relationship near its beginnings is commented on in a letter that Professor Bartholomeus Fischenich of Bonn University sent to Charlotte von Schiller, wife of the great dramatist. It is dated Bonn, 29 January 1793, by which time Beethoven was barely settled in Vienna, and may refer back to his meeting with Haydn the previous summer at Bonn. Fischenich sent a copy of one of Beethoven's songs to his correspondent along with the letter.

> I am enclosing with this a setting of the "Feuerfarbe" [Op. 52 No. 2] on which I would like to have your opinion. It is by a young man of this place whose musical talents are universally praised and whom the elector has sent to Haydn. He proposes also to compose Schiller's "Freude" [Ode to Joy], and indeed, strophe by strophe. I

expect something perfect for as far as I know him he is wholly devoted to the great and the sublime. Haydn has written here that he would hand over large works to him and soon be forced to quit composing [Haydn hat hierher berichtet, er würde ihm grosse Opern aufgeben, und bald aufhören müssen zu componieren].[34]

The usual translation of "grosse Opern" is "grand opera" although equally likely is the general meaning of the term as the plural of "opus." If Haydn wrote this in reaction to the Joseph Cantata it would make some slight sense. It makes none in terms of the strict counterpoint that Beethoven had begun studying with Haydn in Vienna. It makes no sense either if interpreted as "grand opera." Haydn was finished with that genre and was not in a position to put anyone, including himself, to work at it. If Haydn did indeed send such a remark to Bonn (to the elector?) it would qualify as another example, one of many and a good one, of his verbal jesting. Fischenich's fillip may be no more than an attempt to amuse Frau Schiller. Even so it misfires. Haydn in 1793 had no intention of retiring from composition. He was very busy preparing string quartets and symphonies for his return to London.

First Vienna Years

Upon arrival in Vienna Beethoven took a room on the ground floor of a house in the Alserstrasse, a fashionable district in the Josephstadt. The address was also that of Prince Lichnowsky, who soon took him into his own quarters as a long-term guest, perhaps as a result of a letter of recommendation. Presumably Beethoven also had some prior commitment from Haydn concerning lessons, if only *viva voce*. Beethoven kept an expense account from this time showing that besides the bare necessities, he invested in new clothes and dancing lessons, with a view to cutting a good figure in fashionable society. Another of his first concerns was to rent a piano for his own use. He lodged until May 1795 with the Lichnowskys, who surely had good pianos of their own.

Johann van Beethoven died in Bonn on 18 December 1792, which news may have taken until January to reach his son. By April Beethoven petitioned the elector to renew the part of their joint salary that had gone to his father, which was approved by the Electoral Council in May. About this time Haydn took Beethoven with him to Eisenstadt, where Haydn was to spend the summer. This move is claimed by Johann Schenk in his autobiography and can be verified by other evidence. The same cannot be said of the lessons in counterpoint Schenk says he was giving Beethoven on the side.

---

[34] Schiedermair, *Der junge Beethoven*, pp. 221–22.

All appeared to be going well for Beethoven in Vienna. In his letter of September 1793 to the *Berlinische musikalische Zeitung* Neefe said several reports had reached Bonn that Beethoven was making great progress in his art.[35] Haydn expressed satisfaction with his charge in a letter to Elector Maximilian dated Vienna, 23 November 1793.

> Your Electoral Highness!
> I take the liberty of humbly sending Your Highness a few pieces of music, a quintet, an eight-voiced parthie, an oboe concerto, variations for the piano, and a fugue composed by my dear pupil Beethoven, who was so graciously entrusted to me. They will, I flatter myself, be graciously accepted by Your Highness as evidence of his diligence beyond the scope of his studies proper [in counterpoint]. On the basis of these pieces, expert and amateur alike must admit that Beethoven in time will attain the rank of one of the greatest musical artists in Europe, and I shall be proud to call myself his teacher. I only wish that he might remain with me for some time yet.

What Haydn did not know was that the pieces he submitted were mostly familiar to the elector, having been composed in Bonn. Within the same envelope containing Haydn's letter was a short note from Beethoven begging his ruler's indulgence and continued favor; he claims that he has "used all my mental power to be able to send within the coming year something that more nearly approaches your kindness to me and your nobility than that which was sent to your Electoral Highness by Herr Heiden." The tone is one of barely concealed embarrassment. Rightly so, since the "parthie" was the Wind Octet in E♭ for the elector's own table, and the oboe concerto was another Bonn work. The piano variations could have been any of several earlier works, and the fugue, presumably also for piano, may be the one in "Kafka" (2:130). The quintet has not been identified.

The second part of Haydn's letter, twice as long as the first part, concerned Beethoven's inadequate financial support, saying that he (Haydn) has had to loan his pupil 500 fl. just to keep him from falling into the hands of usurers. Haydn humbly petitioned the elector to allot his subject 1000 florins for the coming year as the minimum that would be needed to pay for "the teachers who are indispensable to him and the expenses which are unavoidable if he is to be admitted to some of the houses here." One of those teachers, besides Haydn, may have been Salieri, with whom Beethoven would begin studying vocal composition and Italian text-setting. If he was to fulfill the prophecy of becoming "a second Mozart" he would obviously have to triumph on the operatic stage as well as in concert.

The elector's reply to Haydn survives as a draft written by an official with corrections made by Maximilian himself. It is dated 23 December 1793.

---

[35] Thayer-Forbes misnames the title as *Berliner Musik Zeitmag.*

The music of young Beethoven you sent me I received with your letter. Since this music, excepting the fugue, was composed here in Bonn before he departed on his second journey to Vienna, I cannot regard it as progress made in Vienna. As far as the allotment that he has had for his subsistence in Vienna is concerned it does indeed amount to only 500 fl. But in addition to those 500 fl. his salary here of 400 fl. has been continuously paid to him. He received 900 fl. for the year. I cannot, therefore, very well see why he is as much in arrears in his finances as you say. Consequently I wonder whether he should not begin his return trip in order to resume his service here. For I very much doubt that he has made any important progress in composition and in the development of his musical taste during his present stay, and I fear that, as in the case of his first journey to Vienna, he will bring back nothing but debts.

Maximilian, like all the children of Maria Theresa, had been trained in music at a young age and was musical enough to recognize what he had heard or not heard before. Yet he may have missed recent refinements of the pieces in question if he looked only at the incipits. In any case his curt reply had the effect of an implied reprimand of Haydn, both in regard to the pieces, and for insufficient knowledge of Beethoven's finances. Whether the elector's reply was actually sent and eventually received is not known.

The elector's reply says nothing about Beethoven's lessons in counterpoint, only mentioning "progress in composition and in the development of his musical taste." Having put himself under Haydn's guidance Beethoven surely expected advice on compositions submitted to his teacher, as well as on his exercises in counterpoint. Free composition was Haydn's favorite kind of teaching. He must have looked over the pieces his new pupil presented to him and offered suggestions for improvements, which perhaps had been made, both in the compositions from Bonn and in any new ones (such as the fugue). Beethoven's note to the Elector, while it does seem apologetic, need not be read as a confession. Haydn included it presumably as a reinforcement to strengthen his own plea for increased support, which was carefully laid out, albeit in the absence of complete information from his pupil.

The same circumstances apply to Haydn's involvement with the two main sets of works Beethoven was preparing for publication, the piano trios of Op. 1 and the solo sonatas of Op. 2. Work on them was under way before Haydn left Vienna for his second trip to London in early 1794, without Beethoven along, as Haydn had once planned. Both sets may have profited from Haydn's advice. The trios were tried out in performance at the residence of Prince Lichnowsky, to whom they are dedicated. Haydn may have heard them then, before his departure. The final revisions were made after he left and perhaps incorporated some of his suggestions. Subscription to Op. 1 was announced in the *Wiener Zeitung* in May 1795, before Haydn's return. To Haydn went the dedication of the sonatas of Op. 2, published in March 1796.

If there were rough moments between teacher and pupil on account of the contretemps with the elector they were weathered. Haydn sensibly transferred the instruction in counterpoint to an expert on the subject, his good friend Albrechtsberger. From him Beethoven is said to have profited greatly and to have submitted to the strict rules that helped him acquire greater technical proficiency. An easy mastery of the rules allowed him to break them as he saw fit. Albrechtsberger, as maestro di cappella of St. Stephen's Cathedral in succession since 1793 to the defunct Leopold Hofmann, was like Haydn an eminent figure in Viennese musical circles. However much Albrechtsberger lamented the decline of the old strict style of church music he remained on friendly terms with Beethoven.[36]

Another dean of musical life in Vienna was Swieten, who figured so importantly in the creative work of both Mozart and Haydn. He saw in Beethoven a possible replacement for Mozart, both as keyboard player and as arranger of music for his concerts. Beethoven's celebrated abilities at performing Bach's *Well Tempered Clavier*, if nothing else, would have brought the young composer to his attention. There is a charming, undated note from Swieten that must come from 1793 or 1794: "To Hr. Beethoven in Alsergasse, No. 45. with Prince Lichnowsky. If there is nothing to hinder next Wednesday I should be glad to see you at my home at half past 8 with your nightcap in your bag. Give me your immediate answer. Swieten." Beethoven later dedicated a breakthrough work of his, Symphony No. 1, to Swieten after first planning to dedicate it to Maximilian, who died just before its publication in 1801.

Maximilian returned from time to time to Vienna even before leaving Bonn for good. It was on a visit he made to Vienna in January 1794 that, according to one clever surmise, Beethoven gave him the thoroughly delightful String Trio in E♭ published as Op. 3, perhaps remembering the days when the elector of Cologne played the viola in Bonn.[37]

Prince Lichnowsky replaced Maximilian as Beethoven's main patron. Dr. Wegeler describes Lichnowsky in his *Notizen* and calls him "a very great patron, yes, a friend of Beethoven's, who took him into his house as a guest, where he remained at least a few years." Wegeler was another refugee who had fled Bonn, although he returned to it and lived there throughout its French years. When he reached Vienna in October 1794 he sought out Beethoven and found him not in the rented room on the ground floor as he expected, but living as a guest of the family. Lichnowsky had been a piano pupil of Mozart's and married Maria Christiane, one of the daughters of Mozart's prime patroness Countess Thun. He was still playing the piano, and struggling to overcome some of the difficulties

[36] Martin Staehelin, "A Veiled Judgment of Beethoven by Albrechtsberger?" in *Beethoven Essays: Studies in Honor of Elliot Forbes*, ed. Lewis Lockwood and Phyllis Benjamin (Cambridge, MA, 1984), pp. 46–52.

[37] The surmise is that of Forbes in Thayer-Forbes, pp. 168–69.

in Beethoven's pieces, according to Wegeler, who also recorded the situation at Lichnowsky's with regard to chamber music.

> There were performances at his house every Friday morning, participated in by four hired musicians—Schuppanzigh, Weiss, Kraft, and another (Link?) [Sina] besides our Friend [Beethoven]; generally also an amateur, Zmeskall. Beethoven always listened with pleasure to the observations of these gentlemen. Thus, to cite a single instance, the famous violoncellist Kraft, in my presence, called his attention to a passage in the finale of the Trio, Op. 1, No. 3, to the fact that it ought to be marked sulla corda G [*recte*: C], and the indication of 4/4 time which Beethoven had marked in the finale of the second Trio, changed to 2/4. Here the new compositions of Beethoven, so far as was feasible, were first performed.[38]

These musicians were young. Kraft was Nikolaus, sixteen, son of Anton Kraft, the Bohemian who was Haydn's first cellist from 1778 to 1790, and it may be recalled that Mozart met father and son at Dresden in April 1789 and performed with them. Nikolaus was a pupil in the Josephstädter Gymnasium from 1792 to 1795, conveniently near the Lichnowskys. Violinist Ignaz Schuppanzigh, eighteen, was at the beginning of a long and close association with Beethoven. He and Kraft, with Beethoven at the piano, first played the Trios of Op. 1, which were published by Artaria in a deluxe edition (Figure 7.3).

Trios, Opus 1, and Sonatas, Opus 2

Each of the three trios for piano, violin, and cello that comprise Op. 1 is conceived on the grand scale of a symphony. Each has that genre's typical four-movement format, fast—slow—dance—fast, the outer movements being in sonata form. To these, No. 2 in G adds a slow introduction to the initial fast movement, a practice found mostly in symphonies and particularly associated with Haydn. Trio No. 1 in E♭ is the slightest of the set and likely the earliest. Whereas there are sketches for the second and third trios in "Kafka" there are none for the first trio. Its sprightly finale, *Presto* in 2/4 time, begins with a leap up a tenth for the pianist's right hand and sounds quite Haydnesque in general character. Yet Haydn probably would have condensed rather than expanded the reprise of this movement in sonata form. One way that Beethoven expands is by tonal slippage. From tonic E♭, toward the end of the finale, the harmony slips up a half tone to E♮ for three statements of the second theme, then the piano pauses while the violin and cello in octaves very softly descend by half steps preparing the return of E♭, where the second theme is stated three more times. There is

---

[38] Thayer-Forbes, p. 171. Franz Weiss (1778–1830) was an excellent violist; the second violin was Ludwig Sina (1778–1857).

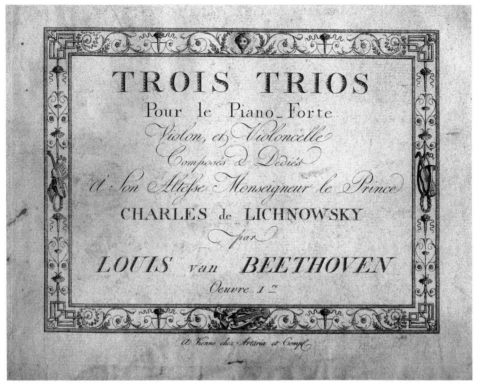

FIGURE 7.3. Title page of Beethoven's Piano Trios, Op. 1.

an expansive coda too, and by the time the movement ends, it has traversed 478 measures. The older composer's finales and first movements are more taut than this, less loose-limbed.

For the dance movements Beethoven writes two scherzos and a minuet. The first two are marked *Allegro assai* and *Allegro* respectively; in Trio No. 3 in c minor he offers a *Menuetto quasi Allegro,* not quite so fast, perhaps because he designated the finale *Prestissimo.* The Trios are well contrasted with their main dances, in No. 1 by being subdued and in the subdominant, in No. 2 by passing from tonic G to b minor and exuding a rather exotic, perhaps Hungarian character, and in No. 3 by passing from tonic minor to tonic major.

Trio No. 1 begins with an *Allegro* in common time stating a broad theme based on the progression I - V/IV - IV - V - I. It would be a regular eight-measure phrase but for an interpolated measure with deceptive cadence to vi, which stretches it to nine measures. An initial move to the subdominant via its dominant was one of Haydn's favorites, used most surpassingly in his late Sonata for Therese Jansen in the same key of E♭. The second theme begins with a repeated chord of three half notes, coming after bursts of sixteenth notes and eighth notes. Getting those half notes to flow quickly and lightly is crucial to the tempo of the whole movement. An *Adagio cantabile* in 3/4 time and in A♭ opens with the same progression as the *Allegro*. The piano first sings its lyric theme alone, then it goes to the violin, with piano and cello accompaniment. The cello states the new material that comes next. Throughout the set Beethoven takes care to insure equality between the partners, in which respect he follows the piano trios of Mozart more than those of Haydn.

Trio No. 2 in G is the most delightful of the set. Its slow introduction, *Adagio* in 3/4 time, takes twenty-seven measures to ground the tonic and move to a preparatory dominant, thus making it possible for the *Allegro vivace* in 2/4 time to begin softly with off-tonic harmony. The main theme is adumbrated in slow motion at the beginning of the *Adagio*, for which there is very good precedent in Haydn's recent symphonies, for instance No. 90 in C and No. 98 in B♭. The second theme is well articulated and has a charming lilt to it. Up to this point the writing for piano has stayed within the abilities of a good amateur pianist. Then comes an awkward, fast triplet figure in descent for the right hand requiring a complicated fingering in order to be played at all—not for amateurs this! In the development Beethoven makes much of the *gruppetto* or turning figure from the beginning of the main theme (both slow and fast versions of it). Fragmentation, so useful a tool in the composer's arsenal of developmental ploys, is already fully in his command here, when the fragment, repeated over and over, results in mounting tension, then blooms into a motif twice as long that begins to resolve the tension. Beethoven took care to sketch this movement and other parts of the development ("Kafka" 2:1–2). The movement is long and has a sizable coda in which the dactylic rhythm of the main theme comes back in augmentation, making it sound like a reference to the slow introduction.

The ravishingly beautiful *Largo con espressione* in 6/8 time drops down a third to E, the major submediant, a tonal move often favored by Haydn, who used it to particularly good effect in the slow movement of his Piano Trio, Hob. XV:25, in G (with the Gypsy rondo). There is a short sketch of a few measures for this *Largo* in "Kafka" and longer sketches for the third and fourth movements. The Scherzo begins off-tonic, like the *Allegro vivace*. Hungarian flavor pervades its Trio and finds company in the *Finale Presto* in 2/4 time (after being at first in 4/4, as the sketch proves). Beginning with the repeated tone G the violin adopts the same rhythm that begins Haydn's Gypsy rondo (*all'ongarese*): ♪|♫♫♪ ♫♫♪|♫. Which piece was composed first cannot be determined. It matters less if both themes reflect a folk rhythm common in Hungarian dance music, as seems to be the case. This sparkling finale ends with the main theme given a new twist, another trait familiar from Haydn.

Trio No. 3 begins softly, *Allegro con brio* in 3/4 time, with a melodic turn around C, a rise to E♭, and a descent to B♮ (cf. Haydn's Symphony No. 53 in c

minor). Two rising sixth chords follow, leading to an augmented-sixth chord over
A♭ in the bass, resolving to V, with fermatas on each chord (Example 7.5). Everything up to the augmented sixth chord is in unisons and octaves for the three

EXAMPLE 7.5. *Beethoven, Piano Trio in c, Op. 1 No. 3, I*

instruments, and *piano* or *pianissimo* (the second rising sixth chord), making for
an eerily subdued first theme. Or is it an introduction? One critic hears these ten
measures as a stretched out, flabby response to the initial tones of Haydn's Symphony No. 95 in c (C G A♭ F♯ G).[39] Both Haydn's and Beethoven's openings could
be regarded as curtains, short in the case of the former, longer in the case of
the latter. Beethoven's main theme would then be the eight-measure antecedent-
consequent that follows from m. 10 on. It is this theme that begins the composer's
sketches for the movement in "Kafka" (2:6). After a not very interesting passage
on a stretched out dominant pedal, the "curtain" idea returns, but beginning on
A♭, with ensuing rising sixth chords outlining E♭. This is followed by a move that
is more intriguing, slippage up a half tone and a rising sixth chord outlining E
major. The passage is already present in the sketch, along with the outlines of the
two diminished chords by way of which Beethoven returns to the flat side. Moving the idea to the beginning of the piece as a curtain may have come later. More
filler material prepares for the arrival of the relative major and the second theme,
or what passes for one, for it is not very distinctive, being merely scalar decoration in eighth notes—the kind of "noodling" common in the composer's piano
quartets of the mid-1780s.

　　Up to this point the pianist has had nothing particularly difficult to play.
That changes with the procession of massive chords on the beat containing as
many as seven tones, then a plethora of sixteenth-note running passages fol-

[39] Douglas Johnson, "Beethoven's Early Sketches in the 'Fischhof' Miscellany: Berlin Autograph 28," 2
vols. (Ph.D. diss., University of California, Berkeley, 1977), pp. 929–31. This passage does not appear in
the abbreviated published version of the thesis (Ann Arbor, MI, 1980).

lowed by octaves in both hands galumphing up and down the keyboard. The quiet passage that follows gives this show away. It is lifted from the second movement of the Piano Quartet in E♭ of 1785 (mm. 76–84) and begins, significantly, with an E♭ sixth chord slipping up a half tone to an E sixth chord. Perhaps this is the original kernel of an idea from which the whole work emanated. It will recur in the finale. Beethoven's recourse to his much earlier piece for what is in fact not much more than a pre-cadential passage of filler material may help explain why this movement gives the impression of a patchwork quilt, at least to this listener.

The seconda parte begins with the curtain theme, developed, leading to two complete statements of the main theme, in F and in A♭. After a long dominant pedal the reprise starts, *fortissimo,* with the curtain theme and an immediate switch to C major, and a halftone move up to D♭ before returning to c minor for a short reference to the main theme. Perhaps it is not the main theme after all? The rest of the material comes back in order, the second theme adjusted to c minor, and after several cadences the movement seems ready to end. At this juncture there sounds, in the piano alone, the main theme, *piano,* its first melodic sigh stretched out by a measure of *Adagio.* The theme is almost all there but is not allowed to end before the rising conjunct tritone motif is stretched out by a modulation that carries it to a sudden climax, *fortissimo,* whence comes the first of several cadences in c minor, soft and sorrowful giving way to loud and energetic.

The *Andante cantabile con Variazioni* in 2/4 time and in E♭ comes as a relief after the stormy first movement. Moreover it gave the public its favorite musical form, as was customary at least once in every set of multi-movement works. The theme is not particularly memorable. A perfectly regular rounded binary form, it is subject to the usual figural variations, one of which is in tonic minor. There are no sketches in "Kafka" for this movement, the only one not sketched there. Perhaps the variation form, with its several routine practices, and Beethoven's great skills at improvising the same, rendered sketching unnecessary. The variations on a *Tema Cantabile* in 2/4 time and in E♭ that constitute the finale of Piano Quartet No. 1 of 1785 make for an interesting comparison with its equivalent, on a rather similar theme, a decade later.

Finale Prestissimo in cut time, like the *Allegro con brio,* begins with a curtain, in this case eight measures ending on the dominant followed by a measure's rest with fermata (Example 7.6, mm. 1–8). Its rocket-like climb by the piano up to high C sounds orchestral—an heir to the "Mannheim rocket" type of beginning. So do the thunderous octaves given the pianist. At breakneck speed, as the tempo and meter demand, these octaves are taxing to perform well and seem more like the stuff of virtuoso concertos than chamber music. The melodic line falls by thirds every two measures, accelerated to one measure (mm. 5–6) by lopping off

EXAMPLE 7.6. *Beethoven, Piano Trio in c, Op. 1 No. 3, III*

the rocket, and descends by step to the leading tone. Then the descent is coun-tered by an angry quick leap of B♮ up to G, a further diminution in time. The fury of this last gesture is operatic and has its equivalent in *Figaro* when an irate Count Almaviva in his Act III aria berates Figaro with "audace!" Long descents in chains of thirds are present in Beethoven from very early to very late. A precedent from 1785 is found in the Piano Quartet No. 1 in D, which begins with four descending third skips. The violin and cello in the example at first do nothing but accompany, then the violin sings the main theme while the piano provides eighth-note rus-tling chords in accompaniment (Example 7.6, mm. 9–20). This main theme with its move from E♭ down to C and G is kin to the same motion in the main theme of the first movement. After a repeat of the main theme by the piano comes a resounding cadence on the tonic, which serves also, by overlapping, to begin the curtain theme again. This time that theme is adjusted to make an abrupt modulation preparing the second key of E♭, which arrives by stating the main theme there in the cello. A second theme proper follows after more dominant preparation. It is smoothly chordal and relatively sedate, moving mostly in half notes. As in the first movement of Trio No. 1, the longer note values here determine the speed of the movement, which has to be very great indeed for this theme to escape sounding stodgy. Abundant cadences on E♭, decorated by arpeggios in the piano part, give way to a distinct closing idea. With references to the main theme over a long pedal on E♭, the prima parte comes to a very quiet ending and is repeated.

The seconda parte gets off to a rousing start by bringing back the curtain, quadruple octaves and all, beginning in f minor, followed immediately by the sedate second theme in F major, then in D♭ major. Development ensues on a portion of this theme. A long pedal on G prepares the reprise. It comes without the curtain, which is never heard again. Instead the main idea takes over, this time very high in the piano and *pianissimo*. The other segments return in order, the second theme now in C major. As the music comes to a near halt on unison G, the strings lower this to F♯, which the piano takes as an invitation to sound the main theme in b minor, *pianissimo*, casting an eerie pall on the proceedings. This is another of the composer's half-tone slippages toward the end of a movement, not the earliest case and far from the last, yet certainly one of the most effective.

The route back to the tonic is soon found and taken. When it finally arrives the tonic is not minor but major. Violin and cello provide several measures of G and E♮ below middle C, *pianissimo*, simply repeating the tones over and over. The piano provides the missing chord member C, and does so with a series of rising scales in eighth notes from its lowest C up to high C. The Trio of such passionate outbursts in c minor thus fades away to near inaudibility in this long *pianissimo*. Rushing scales in C major recall their use in the Trio of the Menuetto, which itself had provided rapid rising arpeggios, prominent from the beginning of the finale and nearly throughout, but banished at the end.

We can imagine the tremendous effect this Trio in c minor must have had upon all who were fortunate enough to hear it at one of Lichnowsky's Friday musicales. This Trio in particular moved in an individual direction, one that distanced Beethoven from Haydn and Mozart. Its outer movements were more forceful, bordering sometimes even on the frenetic. Beethoven held it in special regard, as shown by the free arrangement he made in 1817 of the whole trio as a string quintet, Op. 104, which was then published by Artaria.

Ferdinand Ries, in the *Biographische Notizen* published in 1838, claimed that Haydn advised Beethoven to delay publishing the Trio in c minor as he doubted the public was yet ready to accept it. The claim is not confirmed by any other source and is dubious on grounds of chronology. A judicious analyst of the situation concludes, "Perhaps Haydn did make one or another remark about Beethoven's boldness in publishing such an overwrought work, or about not having expected it to do so well; and maybe Beethoven, in his paranoid way, took offense."[40]

The three solo sonatas of Opus 2 also have four movements each, like the trios. Taken as a whole they are less impressive than the trios, and this may help explain why their composer, who held off so long before allowing any of his works to be labeled "Opus 1," assigned the honor to the trios. Artaria printed the original edition several times over from the same plates.[41] On a later title page he replaced "A Mr Joseph Haydn Maitre de Chapelle de S. A. Monseigneur le Prince Esterhazy" with "A M. Joseph Haydn Docteur en Musique."

Sonata No. 1 in f minor begins with a rising arpeggio to a strong down-beat, like the finale of Trio No. 3 in c. There is a big difference in scale between the two movements, as well as in the pianistic technique required to play them. The Sonata is modest in its demands and in size. The opening *Allegro* in cut time begins a move to the relative major after only eight measures. The prima parte ends at m. 48, the seconda at m. 152, and it is surrounded by repetition signs, as in none of the sonata forms of Op. 1. These differences argue an earlier conception of Op. 2 No. 1. In it there are thick multi-member chords at the end of both parts of the first movement, otherwise they are almost lacking. The *Adagio* in 3/4 time reverts for its theme to the *Adagio con espressione* in F major from the Third Piano Quartet, of 1785. Beethoven perfected this potentially attractive theme by suppressing the fussy dynamic markings and revising m. 4 so that it does not merely repeat the half cadence in m. 2 but leads upward to a better melodic line approaching the full cadence in m. 8. The continuation is also made smoother and less fussy, resulting in a truly singing treble. In the earlier version, the beginning (mm. 1–2) is stated, with the repeats, six times. In the later version there are no repeat signs and the beginning does not recur at all as an exact repetition. Juvenile errors of this kind could have been pointed out by Neefe, and surely this whole sonata was in hand, the finished form of 1796 that is, well before Beethoven began his studies with Haydn. The middle section of the 1796 *Adagio* begins in d minor with a contrasting texture, hand-crossing that allows a deft use of melody on high (r.h.), murmuring accompaniment in the middle (l.h.), and bass tones by crossing over (r.h.). It modulates to C, preparing the return of the first section, embellished. The proportions, as in the *Allegro*, are small: **A** (mm. 1–16); **B** (17–29); **A'** (30–52) plus Coda (52–61).

[40] James Webster, "The Falling-out Between Haydn and Beethoven: The Evidence of the Sources," in *Beethoven Essays: Studies in Honor of Elliot Forbes* (1984), pp. 3–45; 10.
[41] Patricia Stroh, "Evolution of an Edition: The Case of Beethoven's Opus 2. Part I: Punches, Proofs, and Printings: The Seven States of Artaria's First Edition," *Notes* 57 (2000): 289–329.

Menuetto Allegretto comes next, a moderate speed chosen, perhaps, to set off the *Prestissimo* finale (as in the Trio in c minor). Minuet in f and Trio in F are both rather mild-mannered and soft, although both have a loud outburst in the middle of the second strain. The *Prestissimo* in cut time is less than half the length of the one in Trio No. 3 but makes up for this somewhat by repeating the seconda parte. Massive chords used sparingly in the opening *Allegro* see greater use here. The seconda parte begins with an independent lyrical episode that is more like the middle of a large ternary form than the expected development section. There is also a respite from the eighth-note accompaniment in triplets, present throughout much of the finale. The two textures, with and without this accompaniment, are in dialogue during the long retransition that leads to the reprise. The most memorable section is the broad closing theme that comes near the end of both parts, with octaves in the right hand and triplet accompaniment in the left, illustrated here from the seconda parte (Example 7.7). The long chromatic rise of the bass

EXAMPLE 7.7. *Beethoven, Piano Sonata in f minor, Op. 2 No. 1, IV*

provides telling support for the slower descents of a conjunct sixth in the treble, and the dactyls of the last measures already hint at a famous *Allegretto* in the Seventh Symphony. The expressive treble *cantabile* in octaves sounds like a typically Beethovenian *melos*, although its equivalent is not lacking in late Haydn (see Example 5.16).

Sonata No. 2 in A offers very different fare. It counters No. 1's somber mien with lighter textures overall and a sunnier disposition; it also makes more demands on the performer. In the opening *Allegro vivace* in 2/4 time there is a lot of scampering up and down the length of the keyboard, though the most difficult tasks are the stretches of a tenth for the right hand in the development section. A particularly long and impressive rise of the bass, partly chromatic, prepares for the arrival of the second key in both parts. The seconda parte begins in C major as the key signature changes to no sharps or flats, changing back to three sharps at the reprise. As in Sonata No. 1, the seconda parte is repeated. It ends quietly with a tonic pedal.

A *Largo appassionato* in 3/4 time and in D announces a main theme that heralds a more mature kind of movement than the *Adagio* of Sonata No. 1. Whereas that slow movement had a Lied-like quality, this one is more like a hymn, moving in stately procession (treble and supporting chords). A faster walking bass, articulated by short staccato tones so as not to outweigh the main event above, shows an astute use of articulation to control texture and dynamics. The theme is a rounded binary form. After a contrasting section in the relative minor the main theme returns, first unchanged, then adapted to climax with a more expansive cadence. Another contrasting episode consists of the main theme transformed into d minor, modulating to lead to a final return of the main theme in D major, varied slightly at first, then modified to make a more satisfactory end, which is very quiet.

Scherzo Allegretto recaptures the bright, filigree character of the opening movement and has for contrast a flowing trio labeled *Minore*. *Rondo Grazioso* in common time, beginning with a long tonic arpeggio up to high E, from which a wide leap takes the treble back down to middle range. The character is that of an easily flowing gavotte, with a captivating melody. An episode in tonic minor introduces a martial swagger, with dotted rhythm on several offbeats. For this part the three sharps in the signature disappear, returning only for the refrain, introduced this time not by an arpeggio but by a rapid scalar sweep from bottom to top. The episode's swaggering dotted rhythms return for a final stand after the music slips up a half tone from A to B♭. The last word, naturally, goes to the refrain, which ends the movement quietly, like the first and second movements. Only the briefest and least important movement, the Scherzo, is allowed to end with loud chords. The amorous quality so endemic to Mozart's A major may not be in evidence here, yet a certain courtly finesse cannot be denied this rondo finale.

Sonata No. 3 in C shows off the composer as virtuoso of the piano. Its bravura will not be to every listener's taste yet its loosely strung-together assemblage of many sections may convey one of the best impressions we have of young Beethoven's technical skills and improvisatory ramblings at the piano. An *Allegro con brio* in common time begins quite simply, then turns to flashy passagework, marked *fortissimo*, displaying the tonic in arpeggios and scale passages, the section comes to rest on the fifth degree, extended by six measures of mere filler that comes from the first movement of the Piano Quartet in C of 1785. Then follows from the same source the expressive passage in minor quoted above (Example 7.1). A proper second theme in G ensues, then more flashy passagework of the same kind, using the same devices. By the time the prima parte is finished, it has been extended to ninety measures and is repeated. A little closing figure starts the seconda parte. The reprise begins quietly after a long dominant pedal in m. 139. At first the bravura passage is missing but it returns later, and added to it is a fully written-out cadenza after the harmony comes to a stop on I_4^6, as in the first movement of a concerto. This seconda parte, understandably, is not repeated and ends at m. 257.

An *Adagio* in 2/4 time and in the key of E major provides welcome relief from the tiresome theatrics of celebrating C major. In sheer beauty, this movement may not be in a class with the *Largo* in E major from Trio No. 2 in G, but it has some attractions of its own. After only ten measures a secondary idea starts up in tonic minor with a different texture, not block chords like the main theme, but broken-chord figurations in the right hand and plodding longer tones in the left hand. The left hand soon begins crossing over the right to provide a counter melody high above the right hand's figurations, staggered with tones in the bass. The result manages to suggest a three-voiced colloquy not unlike that in the *Largo* of Op. 2 No. 2. The *Scherzo Allegro* is on a larger scale than the dance movements of the previous two sonatas. The first dance has variety in textures, while its trio is mono-textural throughout with arpeggio triplets for the right hand. The best part is a little coda that comes after the repeat of the first dance. The finale, *Allegro assai* in 6/8 time, exploits another of the composer's performing skills: rapid $^6_3$ chords running up the scale, marked staccato (they can scarcely be anything else but detached). Eventually the left hand must perform the same against a long trill in the right hand. The movement is a rondo with a large episode in F major in the middle. No repeats are indicated anywhere in this movement of 312 measures, at the very end of which there is a momentary tonal slippage to A major, turned into a minor, during a long *rallentando*. With a rush, *Tempo Primo* brings back C major and a quick ending, like a fast curtain.

What Haydn thought of these three sonatas cannot be known. By the lights of his own music we can guess that he would have found some parts of them extravagant, others too digressive and overly repetitive. Hearing Beethoven perform them on the other hand must have impressed even Haydn.

There are other indications, besides the dedication of the Sonatas Op. 2, that Haydn and Beethoven still enjoyed friendly relations after Haydn's second return from London. Haydn organized a concert in the small Redoutensaal on 18 December 1795 at which three of his recent symphonies for London were performed. Beethoven joined others selected to complete the program with a performance as soloist of one of his piano concertos, thought to have been No. 2 in B♭, with what was perhaps its original finale, the Rondo in B♭, WoO 6. He had earlier appeared as soloist playing one of his concertos in the Burgtheater on 29 March 1795.

Beethoven composed two sets of dances for orchestra, Twelve Minuets, WoO 7, and Twelve Deutsche Tänze, WoO 8, for a charity ball in the small Redoutensaal on 22 November 1795. This was an annual event sponsored by the Pension Company for Vienna's Visual Artists, with profits going to their widows and orphans. Haydn did the honors by composing these dances, Hob. IX:11–12, gratis in the fall of 1792 after his first return from London. He was followed by Koze-luch in 1793, and in 1794 by Dittersdorf and Eybler. Beethoven, still very young in comparison with the others, surely had Haydn's sponsorship for the task in 1795. Haydn probably attended the ball on 22 November, for which he was given two tickets. Just as Haydn's dances of 1792 were rapidly arranged for keyboard and sold by Artaria, so were Beethoven's three years later. The required com-positions took the same form every year: twelve minuets and twelve German dances. The original scores of Haydn and Beethoven called for the same large band, indeed the full classical orchestra with trumpets, timpani, and clarinets in pairs. There were no viola parts; those who normally played violas on these occa-sions reinforced the violins, which needed to cut through the din from dancers and spectators.

The 1792 and 1795 sets of dances invite a brief comparison, being one of the fields in which the two masters wrote for the same specifications and for the same situation. Haydn's Minuets are shorter, six of them being only sixteen measures in length; all but one have trios. The Minuets by Beethoven are longer, most of them having thirty-two measures, but they have no trios, with a single exception. All these dances are in the major mode, and so are Haydn's trios, except for one. The same applies to the German dances of both composers. Haydn's are almost all sixteen measures in length and have no trios, with one exception. Beethoven's are almost all thirty-two measures in length. Beethoven follows Haydn by put-ting a Coda at the end of his German Dances and here the discrepancy in length is even greater, in 1792 twenty measures, in 1795 137 measures—a sketch sur-vives for this long coda in "Kafka" (2:70). More significantly, Beethoven follows Haydn in choices of key. Almost never do the keys go beyond three sharps or flats, as if there were some rule about this when writing dance music for pub-lic balls. Haydn arranged his Minuets to begin a sequence of keys descending mostly by thirds: D, B♭, G, E, C, F. Beethoven's descend entirely by thirds, more-over using nearly the same keys: D, B♭, G, E♭, C, A. The unspoken rule of no more than three accidentals, broken by Haydn's E, was rectified by Beethoven's E♭. Beethoven pushed the chain of thirds in descent by one link further, down to A, then repeated the sequence, ending on F.

We can read this odd parallelism in key sequence as an act of homage from pupil to teacher, or merely as a sign that Beethoven composed these in a hurry and took a model near at hand to expedite the work. Pianists in Vienna who bought both sets from Artaria must have noticed this particular similarity. Surely Artaria had a large sale of this kind of publication to amateur pianists who could not manage the progressively more difficult sonatas of Op. 2.

Slight as these dances were in comparison with the sonatas of Op. 2, they had their own kind of freshness, variety and melodic inspiration. With contribu-tions like these Beethoven arrived as a composer of fashion in Vienna, writing for a wider public than the aristocratic salons of the few, where chamber music was heard. He was welcomed as another of the masters of public music in the advertisement for a charity masked ball on 22 November 1795 by these words: "The music of the Minuets and German Dances for this ball is once again totally new, composed for the large Redoutensaal by Kapellmeister Salieri, for the small Redoutensaal out of love for artistic colleagues by the master hand of Herr Ludwig van Beethoven." In advertising the piano arrangements Beethoven made of his own dances, Artaria vaunted "the applause with which they were received on 22 November." Beethoven had arrived as a favorite of the Viennese public. He was called upon to write further sets of dances for the public balls and did so. In this quite Viennese vein of orchestral bonbons Beethoven could compete with the best of them, even Mozart and Haydn.

A Journey to Berlin

In February 1796 Beethoven left Vienna on what would become his longest tour, not returning until July. His sponsor was Prince Lichnowsky, in whose entourage he traveled to Prague, and who presented him to some of the many music-loving nobles residing there. A letter dated Prague 19 February 1796 has survived from the composer to his brother Nikolaus Johann, newly arrived in Vienna. It records an unusually positive reaction to his circumstances: "I am getting on well—very well. My art wins for me friends and respect: what more do I want? This time, too, I shall earn considerable sums. I shall remain here a few weeks before I go to *Dresden, Leipzig and Berlin* (his emphasis)." This is the very itinerary that Mozart followed with Lichnowsky in the first part of 1789. Beethoven must have known this from the best possible source—Lichnowsky himself. The journey thus takes on an undeniably symbolic significance, perhaps with Masonic overtones, since Mozart and the Prince were lodge brothers and fervent devotees of the Craft.[42]

Lichnowsky did not go beyond Prague with Beethoven on this trip. He may have traveled to his ancestral castle in Silesia near Troppau, or returned directly to Vienna. In the same letter of 19 February, Beethoven wrote his brother, "Prince Lichnowsky will probably soon return to Vienna; he has already gone from here. If you need money you may go to him boldly, for he still owes me some." It has been surmised the money was owed because he had subscribed for twenty copies of Opus 1, at a hefty cost of 200 ducats. The recipient of the dedication paid the composer an additional sum, and perhaps this was in the form of a promise to be honored. Since Lichnowsky received more dedications from Beethoven than any other person, it follows that he must have been generous in his payments.

---

[42] Jürgen May, "Beethoven und Prince Karl Lichnowsky," *Beethoven Forum* 3 (1994): 29–38; 34. For further on the Mozart-Lichnowsky connections, see the beginning of chapter 3 above.

Reenter Josepha Duschek, the Prague soprano for whom Mozart composed two arias and who sang in his concerts at Dresden and Leipzig in 1789 (Leopold Mozart thought her a siren in more than the musical sense). On 27 November 1796 at a concert in Leipzig she sang "an Italian scena composed for her by Beethoven," according to a printed notice. This is presumed to be the Scena and Aria "Ah! perfido" for soprano and orchestra, eventually printed at Leipzig in 1805 and later assigned Op. 65. The scena, turned by Beethoven into a lively obbligato recitative, has a text that comes from Metastasio's *Achille in Sciro*, while the text of the aria has not been traced. Both sketches and autograph for this piece are written on Viennese paper and presumed to have been composed when Beethoven was in Prague.[43] The orchestra of flute, clarinets in B♭, bassoons, horns in E♭, and strings is expertly handled by Beethoven, as is the voice and compositional style, which is in the best Italian tradition. Since the text is pathetic, his choice of E♭ is appropriate, and so is the form, that of the two-tempo rondò, still the height of fashion in 1796 and just the sort of piece a professional like La Duschek would want to sing. Its languid first part, *Adagio* in 3/4 time, has a theme that returns after contrast, while the second part, *Allegro assai* in common time, has a gavotte-like theme that also returns after contrast. The faster transition between the two parts, which appears later, is unusual. It has been claimed that Beethoven modeled Op. 65 on Mozart's 1787 scena and aria for Duschek "Bella mia fiamma," K. 528.[44] Yet there is little in common between them aside from the form, which Mozart treats more freely still. Scholars still underestimate the sway of the Italian aria in the form and style of the two-tempo rondò, of which there were many hundreds.

Dresden was Beethoven's next stop after Prague. Elector Frederick Augustus III received him well, as he had Mozart. Thanks to his economies, Dresden was recovering its position as a great cultural center. What little is known of Beethoven's visit stems from the correspondence between Court Chamberlain von Schall and Archduke Maximilian in Vienna, who remained well disposed to his former court organist. They show also that Beethoven planned all along to go to Dresden, to which he brought a specific letter of recommendation. On 24 April Schall wrote Maximilian, "The young Beethoven arrived here yesterday. He had letters from Vienna for Count Elz; he will play for the court and then go from here to Leipzig-Berlin. He is said to have improved immensely and to compose well." Perhaps the information in the last sentence came from Maximilian. On 6 May Schall wrote again to Maximilian. "Beethoven has stayed

[43] Beethoven, *Arien, Duett, Terzett*, ed. Ernst Herttrich, *BW* X, 3 (Munich, 1995), Kritischer Bericht, p. 201.
[44] By Helmut Loos, "Beethoven in Prag 1796 und 1797," in Brandenburg and Gutiérrez-Denhoff, eds., *Beethoven und Böhmen*, pp. 63–90; 76.

here about eight days [*recte*: thirteen]. Everyone who heard him play the piano was charmed. Beethoven was granted by the elector of Saxony, a connoisseur in music, the favor to play in the evening all alone without accompaniment for an hour and a half. His Electoral Highness was exceptionally pleased, and gave him a snuffbox of gold." Maximilian answered that he hoped Beethoven would profit more from his journey than did Luigi Simonetti, the tenor who was another of his former court musicians at Bonn. At Leipzig, traces of Beethoven's passage are scant. There are scarcely any mentions, except for those by the often unreliable Rochlitz.

Berlin was apparently the main goal of Beethoven's trip, as it had been for Mozart. There the music-loving sovereign, Frederick William II, still reigned, the one with whom Haydn, Mozart, and Boccherini had dealt. His reign was relatively successful in the 1780s but had turned disastrous by the mid-1790s and was nearing an end—he died in 1797. The cellist Jean-Pierre Duport, whom Mozart encountered in 1789, was still at the head of the court music. He may have been the cellist with whom Beethoven performed at court, and for whom he wrote his two sonatas for piano and cello, Op. 5. A contrary view maintains that it was his brother, the virtuoso cellist Jean-Louis Duport, eight years younger and in the Prussian service only since 1790, with whom Beethoven played at court. Scholars of the cello and its literature are undecided as to which it was.[45]

Artaria printed the two sonatas as Op. 5 in February 1797 with a dedication to Frederick William II. Beethoven sent a copy of the print to Jean-Louis Duport, who thanked him in a letter of 16 September 1798, now lost, expressing a wish to play the sonatas with their composer, which might indicate that he had not yet done so.[46] According to information Beethoven provided to Ferdinand Ries, the king rewarded the composer royally with a gold snuffbox filled with Louis d'or coins. One other composition that can be associated with the two cello sonatas is the fine set of variations for cello and piano Beethoven wrote on "See the conqu'ring hero comes" from Handel's *Judas Maccabeus*, WoO 45. It has been suggested that the Prussian king would have read the choice of theme as reflecting on himself.[47] Since he was the opposite of a "conquering hero" in the wars with France, a dedication to the king could have been read as a travesty. Artaria's 1797 publication of the variations was dedicated to Princess Lichnowsky.

Beethoven chose an unusual format for the two cello sonatas of Op. 5; a long slow introduction ending on V, leading to a large-scale *Allegro* in sonata form, followed only by another lively movement, a rondo, as finale. Perhaps there

---

[45] Mary Cyr and Valerie Walden, "Duport," in *The New Grove Dictionary* (2002).

[46] Lockwood, *Beethoven* (2003), p. 102.

[47] Tia DeNora, *Beethoven and the Construction of Genius: Musical Politics in Vienna, 1792–1803* (Berkeley, 1995), p. 141.

were models for this format in the many cello sonatas of the Duport brothers. It would be surprising if anyone before Beethoven thought to combine an obbligato cello part with a piano sonata in the Viennese classical style. Neither Haydn nor Mozart had, and this may have spurred Beethoven on.

Sonata No. 1 in F begins with an *Adagio sostenuto* in 3/4 time of thirty-four measures, which gives way to an *Allegro* in common time. F is a fine key for the cello, with its low C string, of which Beethoven made good use. The throbbing eighth-note chords as tonic accompaniment get the *Allegro's* main theme off to a good start. It lacks the long breath and power of the great cello theme at the beginning of Beethoven's String Quartet in F, Op. 59 No. 1. The pulsing eighth-note accompaniment is similar, and the tempo and meter are the same. The sequence of two-measure phrases in the sonata's theme falls far short of matching the long buildup of a broad melodic span out of four-measure phrases in the quartet. Thereby is a lesson in the difference between early and middle-period Beethoven. Oddly enough the two movements reach the same total in number of measures: 400. The sonata's *Allegro* lacks the tonal variety of the quartet's *Allegro* although its seconda parte makes a welcome departure from F and C by beginning over in A major, for which event Beethoven changes the key signature momentarily to three sharps. The *Rondo. Allegro vivace* in 6/8 of the sonata's finale aims for more variety too by beginning off-tonic.

Sonata No. 2 in g/G achieves still more tonal variety. Its opening *Adagio sostenuto e espressivo* in common time begins with a meditative dialogue between piano and cello. This slow introduction is so long and intense it verges on being a movement in its own right with a beginning, middle, and end. Beethoven eventually decides to reinforce its function with a dominant pedal preparing for the arrival of the *Allegro molto più tosto presto* in 3/4 time. The cello announces its theme, a gently rising and falling idea. It is especially effective in the reprise, as the cello slips into the first theme against a long descent from on high in parallel thirds by the piano. After this the two instruments divide the main theme's phrases. There is more thematic reciprocity in this sonata than in the first, and finer detailing too. After the second theme, initially in B♭, returns during the reprise in G major, the way back to g minor is forged by a long, rising bass line. Onto an already lengthy movement, with seconda parte repeated, Beethoven adds a big coda, so that the whole reaches an extraordinary total of 553 measures, and at the end returns to G major, making it sound like a dominant. It behaves like one too, with the onset of the finale, *Rondo Allegro* in 2/4 time, for its first chord is that of C major, with E in the treble. The resemblance to the subdominant beginning of the finale in Beethoven's Fourth Piano Concerto has been widely noted. C major is also the place celebrated in the big middle episode of this sonata's ebullient rondo.

Beethoven undertook another concert tour, to Hungary, in the fall of 1796.

He visited Pressburg, then the capital, and Budapest. In a letter dated Pressburg, 19 November 1796 he wrote to the piano maker Andreas Streicher.

> Dear Streicher! The day before yesterday I received your fortepiano, which has turned out to be really excellent. Everyone is anxious to own one, and I—you can have a good laugh but I would be lying did I not tell you that it is too good for me, and why?—because it takes away my freedom to create the tone for myself. But of course this must not deter you from making all your fortepianos in the same way. No doubt there are few people who have whims such as mine. My concert is to be on Wednesday, 23 November.

In another letter from this time to Streicher, undated, Beethoven wrote that many people make the piano sound like a harp, that is to say, plucked. "One may sing on the fortepiano too, provided one is but capable of feeling the music."

By the end of 1796 Beethoven returned to Vienna. He was joined there by his old Bonn friends, the violinist and cellist Andreas and Bernard Romberg, who had been touring in Italy. French military successes in Italy after the Battle of Lodi had flushed a number of Germans from their grand tours of the peninsula and prompted them to return north. Then in Vienna was the youngest Breuning son, Lorenz, who wrote to Dr. Wegeler in Bonn in January 1797, "Beethoven is here again; he played in the Romberg concert. He is the same as of old and I am glad that he and the Rombergs still get along with each other." The following month the Rombergs returned to their positions in the Hamburg orchestra, to which they, along with Anton Reicha, had repaired after Bonn fell.

1797–1798

The early months of 1797 were beset with fears of invasion by the French Army of Italy, which pushed into Austrian territory to the south and west of Vienna, occupying parts of Tyrol, Carniola, and Carinthia. It was this crisis that called forth Haydn's "Kaiserhymne," a moment of national stirring, to which Beethoven contributed two patriotic songs, WoO 121–22, that, unlike Haydn's Hymn, had no popular success. The threat of invasion was averted when a preliminary peace treaty was signed at Leoben, Styria, in March 1797. Austria ceded its former possessions in the Low Countries to France. In the formal Peace Treaty of Campo Formio the following October this was confirmed, along with French acquisition of the entire left bank of the Rhine, including Mainz, Bonn, and Cologne. By his birth at Bonn, Beethoven had rights to French citizenship if he wished to claim them. He did not, but many of his former compatriots in Bonn did, and some were subject to being drafted into the French military. The treaty of peace averted French capture and occupation of Vienna, or rather staved it off until later years, when Emperor Francis foolishly renewed armed hostilities without sufficient preparation.

Beethoven settled down to a relatively calm life in Vienna, where he had many well-paying piano pupils, especially young ladies of noble rank. His health was good, he wrote Dr. Wegeler in Bonn on 29 May 1797. He was composing some of his most charming chamber music at the time. Two works completed by 1797 stand out as examples, Sonata Op. 7 in E♭ and the Quintet Op. 16 for piano, oboe, clarinet, horn, and bassoon, also in E♭. The Quintet had its premiere on 6 April 1797 in a concert of the violinist Schuppanzigh.

Beethoven's Op. 16 is patterned after Mozart's Quintet in E♭, K. 452, composed in 1784 for the same ensemble. In 1797 the autograph of K. 452 was in the possession of one of Beethoven's closest friends in Vienna, the Hungarian nobleman and cellist Nikolaus Zmeskall von Domanovecz. No wonder then that Beethoven had an exact knowledge of K. 452, of which he obviously thought very highly, as did Mozart himself. Each work begins with an imposing slow introduction, Mozart's with a *Largo* leading to an *Allegro moderato,* both in common time. Beethoven starts with a *Grave* in common time brimming with dotted rhythms that gives way to a smoothly flowing *Allegro ma non troppo* in 3/4 time. Particularly lovely in Mozart's *Largo* are the series of descending conjunct sevenths begun by the bassoon, G F E♭ D C B♭ A♭, followed by the horn, clarinet, and oboe in turn with the same descent, each beginning one tone higher than the last. Beethoven made the main theme of his *Allegro* a kind of Ländler version of the same descent, preceded by a leap up of a sixth (Example 7.8). The upbeat leap

EXAMPLE 7.8. *Beethoven, Quintet in E♭ for Piano and Winds, Op. 16, I*

of a sixth followed by the descending conjunct seventh has an even more famous Mozart cousin, in Tamino's "Dies Bildnis ist bezaubernd schön," which is also in E♭. Both composers choose B♭ as the key of their slow movements. Mozart's *Larghetto* in 3/8 time looks back to the sweetness and languor of his Salzburg slow movements of the serenade type, with prominent parallel tenths descending by step. Beethoven begins his *Andante cantabile* in 2/4 time with tender descending tenths too, projected first by the piano. Both make the finale a light and carefree rondo, Mozart's in cut time, Beethoven's with a rollicking rondo refrain in 6/8 time, sounding rather like the finale themes of Mozart's Horn Concertos. These finales make nimble work for the pianist, Mozart's passagework being quite as demanding as Beethoven's. The two works make an ideal study of affinities and differences between their composers.

The Piano Sonata Op. 7 is singular, a rare case for this time of a sonata published by itself instead of in a set. According to Artaria's original edition it was a *Grande Sonate*, dedicated to "Mademoiselle La Comtesse Babette de Keglvics," one of the composer's most advanced piano pupils. It is grand in both conception and size. As in the Op. 2 sonatas Beethoven opted for four movements. In length it matches and outdoes Op. 2 No. 3 in C, while foregoing the bravura clatter of that showpiece. Its grandeur is more interior, and rather calm altogether. The first movement, *Allegro molto e con brio* in 6/8 time, commences softly in slow harmonic rhythm with four measures of static tonic chords. Its main impression is made by the pattern of accented chord followed by nonaccented one. Melodically, the motif climbs the tonic triad: 3 1, 5 3, 8. The answer is also soft but plants an important melodic motif of the rising conjunct third in the bass. When the beginning recurs, *fortissimo*, 3 1 is reharmonized as V_2^6/IV. The main motif suddenly becomes forceful and leads into the bridge to the second key, which takes some time to arrive. When it does, the motif of the smooth conjunct third, rising and falling, comes into its own. The three- and four-voiced chords are beautifully spaced, and on repetition, this theme modifies the treble into a little eighth-note figure that will recur in the finale. A series of mighty cadences begins after a diversion to C major, and the cadential process is stretched out as the texture becomes enlivened with sixteenth-note runs and figurations. This prima part of 136 measures is so rich in ideas no further ones are needed for the development. The first to recur is 5 3 as a secondary dominant pointing to c minor. The development is not very long (52 measures) and leads to a *fortissimo* return of the opening measures. The reprise is stretched out in various ways, at one point by a tonal derailment to F major. There is no repetition of the seconda parte, which ends at m. 362 after a big peroration on the first theme.

Largo con gran espressione proposes the key of C major and a hymn-like theme in 3/4 time. The choice of submediant major for the slow movement, one of Haydn's favorites, brings an air of freshness but does not mask deep kinship with the beginning of the *Allegro*—paired chords with an accent on the first, slurred together. Melodically, the treble, 3 4, 5 3, is also not far from 3 1, 5 3. The most moving moment comes at the very end, when the beginning is reharmonized from I - V_5^6 to V^7/ii - ii$_4^6$ in support of the treble's 3 4. The move is one that Mozart was fond of and used, for example, at the end of the Romance in *Eine kleine Nachtmusik*, K. 525 (a slow movement also in C major). The *Allegro* in 3/4 that follows restores E♭ and is marked *piano* and *dolce*. It restores something else by beginning 5 3 to start a gentle triadic theme, and it ends *forte* with paired chords supporting 3 4, 5 1, the first pair being the harmonic motion V^7/IV - IV$_4^6$ familiar from

the *Allegro*. Then comes an equally long *Minore* in tonic minor in constant triplet motion, followed by the *Allegro da capo*. Beethoven does not call these Minuet
and Trio, although that is what they are in form. They sound more serious than
his typical dance movements of this time and that may explain why. To conclude,
there is a Rondo marked *Poco Allegretto e grazioso*, which is gavotte-like in beginning on the upbeat of 2/4 time. A winding melody drifting down to find resolution certainly displays graciousness, a quality that marks the whole sonata. Its
initial fall, over long-sustained dominant harmony, relates to a similar passage in
the triplet version of the *Allegro*'s second theme (mm. 253–58 of the version in the
reprise). The whole cycle is remarkable for its unified tone, which is both stylistic
and motivic. No sonata of the Op. 2 trilogy dedicated to Haydn quite succeeded
in achieving this feat.

The Serenade in D, Op. 8, for violin, viola, and cello is of a quite different character, sounding like a comic counterpart. Perhaps that was the intention behind
advertising them together in the *Wiener Zeitung* on the same day, 7 October 1797.
The Trio is a real serenade in the traditional Austrian form of several fairly lightweight movements introduced by a march and brought to an end by repetition
of the same march. This preserves the fiction and sometimes the reality that the
players about to do the serenading actually marched into the presence of the
receiving party. For three solo string instruments to produce such a big, pompous sound as this *Marcia Allegro* in common time is already funny and portends a
good show to come, a *commedia dell'arte* skit, perhaps. What in fact comes next is
an *Adagio* in D and in 3/4 time, a mostly elegant and florid solo for the violin that
carries the serenade idea by seeming to sing under the balcony of the beloved.
The viola gets to sing a lot too, and sometimes in duet with the violin in this
miniature sonata form. Next comes a *Menuetto Allegretto*—a Viennese serenade
typically had two minuets. To make things even more Viennese, the violin and
viola play in octaves in the following *Adagio* in 2/4 time and in d minor, a brief
lament such as might be emitted by a maiden in distress. The plaint is mocked in
a *Scherzo Allegro molto* in 2/4 time and in D major, a small dance in binary form
played lightly and staccato, with mighty offbeat triple-stops supplied by the cello.
The *Adagio* returns to plead again, its legato strains now sounding more mournful by contrast. Back comes the mocking Scherzo too, the same as before without
repeats, but it is brought to an abrupt halt with a jolting V/V chord, as if in a recitative. Commanded to cease and desist, as it were, the Scherzo comes to a meek
conclusion, and the *Adagio* sobs its way to an ending in d minor. The piece suggests words, or stage action, but does not need them. Instead of a second minuet
there is a jaunty *Allegretto alla Polacca* in 3/4 time, with accents on the second half
of the first beats. Its key is F major, a nice contrast to all the preceding D/d and
yet following naturally from the previous cadence in d minor. The return to tonic
D major is accomplished by a leisurely theme and variations, *Andante quasi Alle-*

gretto in 2/4 time. The third variation is in an agitated d minor and seems to savor the earlier episode in d. Each instrument gets the theme for an entire variation. To conclude there is a transformation of the theme into 6/8 time and a sudden departure for Bb, a coda that gradually reintroduces D major and is about to conclude when the *Marcia* returns to snatch away the cadence. Since the theme and that of the march are related, this too seems like a natural happening. Beethoven had a knack for conveying gesture as well as mood, talents essential to a pantomime composer.

Critics rarely mention the Serenade Op. 8 and prefer to dwell on the three string trios published as Op. 9 in 1798. Or if mentioned, it is with something like disdain: "With the three String Trios of Opus 9 we come to a higher level . . . These three trios are the best of Beethoven's string chamber music before the Opus 18 quartets."[48] The serious genre is not necessarily at a "higher level" than the comic one, nor is excellence in a lighter genre any less difficult to achieve.

The string trio was a genre, like the cello and piano sonata, in which Haydn and Mozart were not Beethoven's rivals. Haydn cultivated it (for two violins and cello) only in his early period. Mozart wrote only his nonpareil *Divertimento* K. 563 of 1788 for violin, viola, and cello, and we have seen how Beethoven paid tribute to it in his Op. 3 of 1792. Beethoven decided to make a statement with the three Trios of Op. 9. They are in four movements, like the sonatas and piano trios of Opp. 1–2, with which they invite comparison. The set ends with a potent trio in c minor, akin to Op. 1 No. 3.

Trio No. 1 in G confirms the seriousness of the operation with a slow introduction, *Adagio* in common time. In it there are many recurrences of a falling triad, which will become a principal motif in the main theme of the *Allegro con brio*. The follow-up idea, stated by the cello, bears a probably unintended resemblance to the initial utterance of Susanna asking Figaro to notice her hat, "Guarda un po' mio caro Figaro." This idea sees multiple use in the development, then awaits the long coda before reappearing, after the seconda parte has been repeated. The second theme is a curious case of minor-mode understatement, made ominous by staccato and *pianissimo* chords in a hypnotic rhythm, suggesting nothing so much as Verdian conspirators. For the *Adagio, ma non tanto, e cantabile* in 3/4 time, decorated from the outset with triplets, Beethoven resorts to the key of E major (VI), which seems a trifle recherché in these circumstances. After a *Scherzo Allegro* restores the key of G, the finale, a *Presto* sonata form in cut time, rounds out the work. Its first theme is an exercise in species counterpoint, with the eighth note treble theme supported by quarter notes below (Mozart used a similar idea as the finale of his Piano Concerto No. 14 in Eb, K. 449). In the coda, the treble theme appears in augmentation.

---

[48] Lockwood, *Beethoven* (2003), p. 109.

Trio No. 2 in D begins *pianissimo, Allegretto* in 2/4 time, with an idea moving smoothly in four-part harmony, of the kind more likely to be encountered in one of the composer's second themes, answered by the violin alone in a sally up and down an octave, then joined by the other two to form an eight-measure antecedent (3 + 3 + 2). This odd phrase is repeated a tone higher in ii, reaching a half cadence. The last figure heard in the violin is stretched out by fragmentation until there is a resolution on tonic D. With this solid arrival the violin initiates a new idea, a turning figure on the upbeat leading up a third to a downbeat, prophetic of the rising *Allegro con brio* first theme of Symphony No. 2, Op. 36, composed in 1801–2. Later in the prima parte the cello picks up this rising figure and extends it up to the seventh, a passage still more predictive of what is to come in Op. 36. Beethoven chose an *Andante quasi Allegretto* in 6/8 time and in d minor for the second movement, a rondo with three statements of the opening refrain. *Menuetto Allegro* resembles the main theme of the first movement by its first chordal progression and also by moving the initial block up a tone to ii. The finale is a *Rondo Allegro* in cut time that the cello inaugurates with a none-too-promising melody in which mm. 3–4 merely duplicate mm. 1–2. The refrain is too sectionalized into little segments to be of much interest. It is odd that Beethoven chose the refrain form for two of his movements, and the finale is of a stiffness that could mean it comes originally from an earlier time.

Trio No. 3 in c minor begins with a descending "Gypsy scale"—C B♮, A♭ G in unison, *Allegro con spirito* in 6/8 time. From its low G the violin climbs gradually up to A♭, two octaves above, then unleashes a rapid descending scale in sixteenth notes down to middle C, incorporating the cited tones, a descent immediately copied by the viola an octave lower. It is a striking main theme. The unison octave opening is then repeated, but *forte* instead of *piano*. More sixteenth-note flurries lead to loud, accented triple-stopped chords making a half cadence that, upon repetition, is interrupted by a secondary dominant pointing to A♭, which arrives softly but only as a short station on the expected route to the relative major for the second theme. The light meter keeps the music buoyant even when the chords are minor. In texture there is a density that could easily persuade a listener that a quartet of instruments, not a trio, is producing all this. Scarcely a moment of respite is allowed for any of the three players. To end there is an ample coda following the repeat of the seconda parte and the final cadence, which could have brought C major, but resolutely proclaims c minor with an eleven-toned *fortissimo* chord in triple and quadruple stops.

C major is saved for the *Adagio con espressione* in common time, which compares favorably with the similarly hymn-like *Largo con gran espressione* in C major of the Piano Sonata in E♭, Op. 7. This slow movement is more intricate rhythmically and in the demands it makes on all three performers in elaborately decorated passages. The *Scherzo Allegro molto e vivace*, atypically, is in 6/8 time, like the first movement, with which it shares the same c-minor intensity and fierce concentration. Its Trio (not so labeled) offers C major and the simplest music in the whole piece, as a trio traditionally did. Yet its move to E♭ for its second strain's beginning echoes the first big tonal move in the preceding slow movement. Beethoven writes out the return of the Scherzo and adds to it a coda.

Finale Presto in cut time begins with triplets in the violin, a melodic turn up to A♭, then a run by step down to B♮, repeated down an octave, nearly duplicating the descending scale that ends the first theme of the *Allegro*. As in that movement the first tonal departure is for A♭, only later E♭, by way of e♭. The first hint of a turn to C major from c minor comes after the reprise of this terse sonata form. Like the end of the Piano Trio in c minor, Op. 1 No. 3, the final moments are in hushed C major, a *pianissimo* with the violin climbing up to the heavens (Jacob's Ladder?). Beethoven dedicated Op. 9, his last contributions to the genre, to Count Johann Georg von Browne-Camus, an officer in Russian service. He prefaced it with an unusually florid dedication in French praising the Count's munificence and, referring to himself, called the work "la meilleure de ses œuvres."

The solo sonatas that appeared shortly later in 1798 as Op. 10, *Trois Sonates pour le Clavecin ou Pianoforte Composées et Dediées à Madame la Comtesse Browne*, are twins to Op. 9 in some senses. They were printed not by Artaria like the Trios but by the Viennese publisher Joseph Eder and dedicated to the wife of Count Browne. Op. 10 No. 1 is in c minor, as if in continuation of Op. 9 No. 3. The lady in question was presumably a pianist and perhaps one of the composer's many pupils among the nobility. She also received the dedications of two variation sets for piano, WoO 71 and WoO 76, the more interesting being the former on a Russian Dance from Wranitzky's ballet *Das Waldmädchen* (1797). Women continued to garner most of his dedications of works for keyboard, as was the case with Mozart and Haydn.

The Sonata in c, Op. 10 No. 1, reverts to three movements, more typical of keyboard sonatas in general than the four-movement format Beethoven imposed on Op. 2 and Op. 7. In other aspects as well it is less grand than the Sonata in E♭, Op. 7. An *Allegro molto e con brio* in 3/4 time opens the work, written in a thinner texture and with fewer demands on the pianist. The *Adagio molto* in 2/4 time that follows is in A♭, a key that, when joined with the song-like character and coming right after fretful c minor, will make an unforgettable impression in the *Sonate pathétique*, Op. 13. The *Finale Prestissimo* in cut time returns to c minor. It is in sonata form like the first movement (the *Adagio* is one without development). In the reprise the second theme appears in C major, then slips up a half tone to D♭ in the coda. C major prevails at the end, which is another *decrescendo* to the final chord.

Sonata No. 2 in F begins robustly, *Allegro* in 2/4 time, with a series of upbeats pushing to downbeats, as in Op. 2 No. 2, but here with full chords. This movement is more capricious and erratic in its journey, with hints of mockery and sardonic humor. The 8 5 1 motif that ends the prima parte provides the main sustenance of the development, which comes to a stop with a soft V/vi chord. Haydn taught our ears to expect next an elision into I. But Beethoven begins the reprise here not in F but in D (VI) and even changes the key signature to two sharps. He gets through the three four-measure segments of the main theme before there is a pause and a questioning. What has gone awry? F quickly reasserts its place, not with the first segment of the theme, only with the second and third. This charming seconda parte is surrounded by repeat signs. The composer does not shy away from pulling our leg twice. Tonal displacements such as these are frequent in Beethoven and will become more so, yet this may be the first to affect so crucial a spot as the moment of reprise. Nothing in the two remaining movements quite matches the interest of this *Allegro*. The *Allegretto* in 3/4 time in f, with a middle section in D♭, is in dance form but is not remotely like a minuet. The final *Presto* in 2/4 time begins with a point of imitation, as if it were a three-part invention. It restores not only tonic F but the jocular tone of the *Allegro*.

Sonata 3 in D, in four movements and more sweeping in effect, is a bigger work than its two companions. The first movement is a *Presto* in cut time that opens softly with descending octaves falling down a fourth by step from D, then rising an octave and a fifth, during which ascent the octaves turn into double octaves. The descent is made by parallel 6/3 chords marked legato, no easy feat to play at this fast tempo and reminiscent of the same in the finale of Op. 2 No. 3. Much of the subsequent material is derived from the descending conjunct fourth or from contrasting material used as a foil to set it off. The process of development is so prevalent in the prima parte we wonder what else can come in the seconda parte. Beethoven does not disappoint us. He wrenches still more from the basic material, adding a section with hand crossing in wide jumps from the top to the bottom of his keyboard. A truly slow movement follows, *Largo e mesto* in 6/8 time and in d minor, with treble melody in even eighth notes supported by ponderous chords. The effect is lugubrious and is made more anguished by prominent diminished-seventh chords. Two different ones in succession rise to conclude the theme, outdone by the three in succession rising to a climax to conclude the first section (Mozart used the three diminished chords in rising succession like this to conclude Cadenza B of the solemn slow movement in C minor of the "Jenami" Piano Concerto in E♭, K. 271). The *Largo* is in full sonata form without repeats. Quite traditional is the lyrical and lovely *Menuetto Allegro* in D, with Trio in G (more hand crossing). The *Rondo Allegro* in 4/4 time is another of those finales that begin on the subdominant, like that of the Cello Sonata in g/G, Op. 5 No. 2. The questioning nature of the rondo theme never reaches a very firm answer in the way of a thematic-harmonic conclusion until the last moment, when the questions are finally transformed into an answer—a very Haydnesque ploy that is akin to pulling an ace from one's sleeve to end the game.

Other works composed during this rich two-year period are the very entertaining Trio in B♭ for Piano, Clarinet, and Cello, Op. 11, that Beethoven dedicated to Countess Thun (Lichnowsky's mother-in-law) and the comparatively tame Violin and Piano Sonatas, Op. 12, dedicated to Salieri. Of these three sonatas, each in three movements, the second in A is the most sprightly and offers the most interest, although they all pale in comparison with the contemporary sonatas for solo piano. They are said to be indebted to Mozart's works in the genre.[49] Nevertheless they lack gripping ideas, unlike the superb *Sonate pathétique*, Op. 13. Beethoven dedicated this single work, designated like Op. 7 with a number of its own, to Lichnowsky. Sketches for it are found among those for Op. 9 Nos. 1 and 3. It was not published until 1799, by Joseph Eder.

Grande Sonate pathétique, Op. 13, was its original title, the "grand" also applying to Op. 7. It begins with a slow introduction, *Grave* in common time, symphonic in scope, and at the same time very idiomatic for Beethoven's piano. The thick, block chords marked *forte* announcing the key are allowed to fade out to *piano* for the little rising continuation in dotted rhythm that follows, at least on the pianos of that day, but not on modern pianos, with their much greater sustaining power. This exchange continues until the pattern is broken by a sudden modulation to the relative major, which arrives after a sweeping run in quick notes in the right hand. The dynamic contrasts continue, *piano* for the rising pleas answered by *fortissimo* chords at short range. A modulatory passage carries the colloquy back toward c minor, which arrives after another sweeping run from high to low, twice as long as the first, and a *sforzato* A♭ with fermata that is left hanging and must be resolved. There is no further delay as the direction *attacca subito il Allegro* hastens the resolution to c minor for the *Allegro di molto e con brio* in cut time. With its many melodic sighs and "speaking" rhetoric, the *Grave* takes on the character of an operatic scene presaging the anguished aria to follow. The whirlwind that does follow is again very pianistic, with rattling octaves in the left hand ("murky bass") supporting a climb up two octaves from middle to high C, traversing several different harmonies. When the second key arrives, it is scarcely less tense, being a dialogue between high and low achieved by hand crossing right over left, with accompaniment in the middle, not in E♭ but in e♭ minor. On repetition the music sinks down to D♭ and from there gradually attains E♭, with a mighty *crescendo* for another long rise of the treble, this one against a descending

---

[49] By Sieghard Brandenburg. "Beethoven's Opus 12 Violin Sonatas: On the Path to His Personal Style," in Lewis Lockwood and Mark Kroll, eds., *The Beethoven Violin Sonatas: History, Criticism, Performance* (Urbana, 2004), pp. 5–23.

bass, with harmonic filler in the middle, all brilliantly conceived so as to get the most sonority possible out of the instrument.

Beethoven divides the prima parte, which is repeated, from the seconda parte by bringing back four measures of the *Grave*, modulating so as to allow a move up a half tone from E♭ to e minor. He thus initiates a development section that combines first-theme rises with the sighing motif from the *Largo*. In the reprise he works the long closing *crescendo* so as to reach up one tone higher, taking the treble to high F, still the top note on many pianos then. In the coda another four-measure segment of the *Grave* appears before one more whirlwind rise is unleashed and dispersed with emphatic cadential chords, *fortissimo*. The return of the slow introduction at the end brings to mind the first movement of Haydn's "Drumroll" Symphony, No. 103.

An *Adagio cantabile* in 2/4 time takes the middle C on which the treble ended the *Allegro* and makes it the third of A♭ major, the beginning of a lovely, sedate treble melody, commencing C B♭ E♭, against the flowing accompaniment in sixteenth notes. A gentle aura of A♭ and that same middle C after a furious ending of the first movement in c minor will sound again in Symphony No. 5, Op. 67, of several years later. A similar maneuver occurs in Piano Concerto No. 1 in C, Op. 15, transforming C as initial tonic into C as third degree for the *Largo* second movement. The same transformation takes place in the *Adagio cantabile* of the Piano and Violin Sonata in c minor, Op. 30 No. 2. In Op. 13 the *Adagio cantabile* is in a simple ternary form, the middle section beginning in a♭ minor with a distinct accompanimental pattern of triplet sixteenth notes. It is a short section, lengthened in effect by having the triplets held over into the repeat of the main section, thus integrating the two. These triplets last until the end, throughout the coda and up to the penultimate measure. *Rondo Allegro* in cut time returns to c minor yet is more gentle and smoothly flowing throughout than the initial movement. It has a coda, on the other hand, that brings back the emphatic chords of the opening, and to finish, a brief reminder of the blissful *Adagio* melody, now cast as C B♭ A♭.

The two piano sonatas of Op. 14 are lighter counterparts to Op. 13 and are thought to date from the same time. Mollo published them in 1799 with a dedication to Baroness Josephine von Braun (not to be confused with Countess Browne). Sonata No. 1 in E is in three movements. An *Allegro* in common time begins with an accompanied melody that softly climbs in even half notes by step on the first beats, which are followed by rising leaps of a fourth and one of a sixth: 5↑1, 6↑2, 7↑5, 5↑8. The second movement is an *Allegretto* in 3/4 time in tonic minor that takes the form of a minuet with trio (in C major). The third is a *Rondo Allegretto* in cut time that starts with overlapping rising-fourth figures and demonstrates one of the composer's favorite keyboard textures: octaves in the right hand for the melody, with accompanying triplets for the left hand that provide both bass and accompaniment. The first two movements in particular contain a predominance of harmony moving in four-part chords, like an ensemble piece, so it is no surprise that Beethoven opted to arrange the whole as a string quartet (Op. 14 I), moved up half a tone to F to take advantage of open strings, particularly on the viola and cello.[50] Breitkopf and Härtel published it in May 1802 under the title *Quatuor pour deux violons, Alto et Violoncelle, d'après une Sonate composée et dediée à Madame Baronne de Braun par Louis van Beethoven arrangé par lui même.* In a letter to Härtel of 13 July 1802 Beethoven insisted that only the composer could do justice to such an arrangement. This led him to bring up arrangements made by two of his Viennese predecessors of their own keyboard music: "I firmly maintain that only Mozart himself could translate his works from the keyboard to other instruments, and Haydn could do this too—and without wishing to compare myself to those two great men, I claim the same about my keyboard sonatas." The reference to Haydn could be to the orchestral version in Symphony No. 102 of the *Adagio cantabile* of the Piano Trio, Hob. XV:26. Mozart arranged his two-piano Fugue in c minor, K. 426, for string orchestra and appended an *Adagio* introduction, K. 546, the whole of which Beethoven copied out.

Opus 14 No. 2 in G matches its partner in musical interest. The *Allegro* in 2/4 time starts with a nervous upbeat figure that decorates triadic tones with their chromatic lower neighbor tones before verging off into sighing figures. They lead smoothly to V/V and a relaxed second theme in D, with more lower appoggiaturas, sweetened by parallel thirds. It is illustrated above along with its inspiration from Haydn's Quartet in G of Op. 33 (see Examples 4.4 and 4.5). The whole movement presents a model of sonata form that makes it eminently teachable, which is also true of the theme and variations form in the following *Andante* in cut time and in C major. The little march that furnishes its theme makes deft use of contrasting legato and staccato articulations to delineate sections. Its variations are ingenious if simple and retain interest to the end, which comes after *pianissimo* pre-cadential chords with a *fortissimo* wallop (another bow to Haydn?). *Scherzo Allegro assai* in 3/8 time is a skittery lark of a piece, in almost constant hemiola syncopations. It is in clear rondo form. At the very end there are accented lower neighbor-tone appoggiaturas of a minor second, a reminder of how this sonata began.

Beethoven's earlier piano concertos are works that occupied him over several years. As public showcases for him as a performer, they fall in a category different from his piano sonatas and most of his chamber music. He held the concertos back from publication for one thing, and this permitted him to keep tinkering with them, partly so that he could continue advertising them as new at each per-

---

[50] Lewis Lockwood, "Beethoven as Colourist: Another Look at His String Quartet Arrangement of the Piano Sonata, Op. 14 No. 1," in *Haydn, Mozart, and Beethoven*, pp. 175–80.

formance. The work that became Piano Concerto No. 1 in C assumed its final form in 1798 and was published as Op. 15 by Mollo and Company in 1801. The work is actually later than Piano Concerto No. 2 in B♭, which was begun already in Bonn, underwent rewriting for performance at Prague in 1798 and was published by Hoffmeister as Op. 19 after final revisions in 1801. Concerto No. 3 in c minor also had a long gestation. There are jottings for its first and third movements in "Kafka" on the same sheet as sketches for the finale of the Piano Sonata Op. 10 No. 3 in D, which would put them in 1797. It is believed to have reached final form early in 1803 and was published as Op. 37 in 1804. When Beethoven made his first appearance as a piano soloist in the Burgtheater at the concert on 19 March 1795 of the Musicians' Society, he played either Op. 15 or Op. 19. Subsequently he performed often in the fabled hall (Figure 7.4).

Concerto No. 1, Op. 15, calls for the full orchestra of Mozart's largest piano concertos, such as No. 24 in c, K. 491, and No. 25 in C, K. 503. Beethoven opted for the traditional three movements with a slow movement in the middle. The

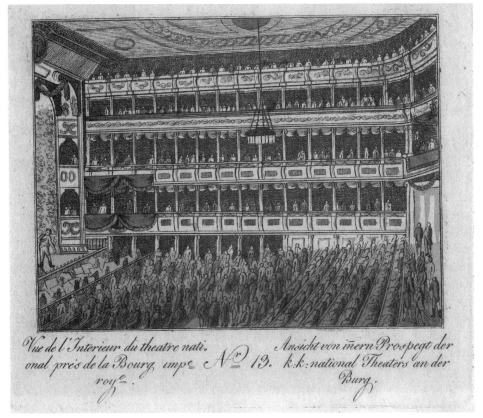

FIGURE 7.4. Interior view of the Burgtheater, ca. 1810/1812.

Allegro con brio in common time marches along with great swagger, notwithstanding its rather humdrum thematic material. Not so common is the second, lyric theme announced by the orchestra, broadly flowing and getting attention for its unusual harmonic placement in E♭, then in f minor, followed by g. To close, there is another theme, drawn out of the fanfare material of the opening. It prepares for the big event: the arrival of the soloist. At first the piano mainly decorates the harmonies with its arpeggios after entering with a soft preparatory passage of its own, which has many parallels in Mozart's concertos (e.g., the first movement of K. 467 in C). The second theme now takes its expected tonality, G, first in the orchestra, scored fully with both winds and strings (Mozart was usually more restrained when orchestrating a second, lyric theme), then for the soloist accompanied by strings. The seconda parte begins by swerving from G to A♭ and from there to the E♭ that was made so prominent in the first exposition. The piano begins a kind of reverie. This too has its parallels in Mozart at the same location within the development. Everything in the reprise is as could have been expected, including the solo cadenza, for which Beethoven left three versions, written somewhat later, after the piano keyboard commonly expanded up beyond high F.

The *Largo* in cut time introduces A♭ as the main key, quite a natural choice after the first movement's motions toward the flat side. Also akin to the *Allegro* is the dactylic beginning of the *Largo*'s main theme, a transformation of C - C C | C into C as third degree in C - C C | D♭, decorated but still clearly perceptible. The move to E♭ for the secondary key area unfolds as expected. To the soloist goes the role of announcing the *Largo*, as it does in the *Rondo. Allegro scherzando* in 2/4 time. The refrain is sharply etched in emphatic rhythms, with many repeated tones, lending it a popular or folklike character, like a country dance. An extended rondo of 571 measures, the finale has some links with sonata form, such as the second theme in the dominant that will eventually sound in the tonic. The soloist moves this tune to E♭, a choice that helps us hear the overall tonal unity of the whole work. From E♭ it undergoes further modulation, leading up to a return of the refrain. What makes this finale a real rondo, besides this recurrent refrain, is the discreet episode the piano proposes in a minor, another country dance by nature, this one with more of a Slavic twang. The finale ends, after a suitable solo cadenza and a tonal displacement up a half tone to B major, with a last statement of the refrain, then a playful coda with rising scales of the piano countered by little descents of the head motif in the winds.

Concerto No. 2 in B♭ has suffered somewhat from comparison to the Concerto in C, notably from the composer's own remark deprecating it to the publisher Hoffmeister as "not one of my best" (letter of 15 January 1801). Its orchestration is more restrained, lacking the clarinets, trumpets, and timpani of Op. 15. It too begins with an *Allegro con brio* in common time, and at the same spot in the first exposition the second key introduced is ♭III (D♭ major). There is likewise a preparatory musing by the piano on its entry before the second exposition begins. An *Adagio* in 3/4 time muses further in the key of the subdominant, E♭, as sanctioned by long tradition. A bracing *Rondo. Molto allegro* in 6/8 time throws *sforzato* accents on the second and fourth beats, producing the effect of a polacca. Before the end, this main theme undergoes transformation into more relaxed rhythm, and there is a momentary tonal slippage, one of the composer's signature devices, before closing. The Rondo in B♭, WoO 6, is thought to have been the concerto's original finale, and it may have been replaced by this movement for the performance at Prague in 1798.

Beethoven had some potent rivals among concert pianists in Vienna. One of the most interesting was Joseph Wölfl, born in 1773 at Salzburg, where he had been a pupil of Leopold Mozart and Michael Haydn. Beethoven met Wölfl at the home of Mozart's patron Raimund Wetzlar, where they staged a piano duel for the entertainment of guests. The event, in March 1799, was taken quite seriously at the time, and later.[51]

At the Turn of the Century

During the years in question there were no sudden changes in Beethoven's habits with regard to composition and promotion of his works. Yet there is a certain sense of growth in the seriousness of the tasks undertaken ca. 1800. Beethoven continued to be a pianist-composer as before. At the same time he set his sights on larger projects that did not involve the piano. Inspired particularly by the string quartets and symphonies of Haydn and Mozart, and driven by ambition to rival his mentors in these prestigious genres, he set to work on the six string quartets that would become Op. 18. After years of futile attempts to compose a symphony, he finished Symphony No. 1, Op. 21. Presented with his first opportunity to write something for the Viennese stage, he composed the music for a full-scale dramatic ballet, *Prometheus*. The works he wrote for piano or centered around the piano became more adventurous than ever.

Beethoven was also branching out in his dealings with publishers, as the demands for his music kept increasing. Besides Artaria, Eder, and Mollo, all in Vienna, he began dealing with the firm that Franz Anton Hoffmeister newly established in Leipzig and also with Breitkopf and Härtel, the most renowned Leipzig house for music publishing, to which Haydn entrusted his *Creation, Seasons,* and other late works. In 1800 Hoffmeister wrote Beethoven in a letter, now

---

[51] DeNora, *Beethoven* (1995) devotes her antepenultimate chapter 7 to the duel. Wölfl left seven piano concertos and was a prolific composer in several other genres.

lost, asking for works he and his partner, Ambrosius Kühnel, could publish. The composer's answer, dated 15 December 1800, was dilatory. It began with excuses for his extremely tardy reply, then continued with a remark inappropriate to the circumstances: "I am very sorry that you, my beloved and worthy Brother, did not let me know sooner, for I could have brought to your market my quartets and also many other works I have already disposed of." Hoffmeister, a prolific composer in his own right, had long been publishing music either alone or with a variety of partners, including Artaria and Eder. His edition of the *Sonate pathétique*, Op. 13, in December 1799 is now thought to have predated Eder's. Hoffmeister was close to Beethoven. They addressed each other as "Brother." This form of address was common between Freemasons, and Hoffmeister is known to have had connections with the Craft.[52] These are the works Beethoven proposed: (1) a septet for winds (Op. 20), with the remark "this septet has been very popular"; (2) a grand symphony for full orchestra (Op. 21); (3) a concerto for pianoforte (Op. 19); and (4) a grand solo sonata (Op. 22). He added "you yourself when replying may fix the prices as well."

Hoffmeister answered promptly and in the affirmative. Beethoven replied on or about 15 January 1801. He named the sums he wanted for each work and went out of his way to praise the sonata while denigrating the concerto: a septet, 20 ducats; a symphony, 20 ducats; a concerto ("not one of my best"), 10 ducats; a grand solo sonata ("Allegro, Adagio, Minuetto, Rondo—this sonata is a first-rate composition"), 20 ducats. It appears that he undervalued the concerto in order to set a high price on the sonata, 20 ducats being an extraordinary sum for any solo sonata. Without waiting for an answer to his proposal he went on to describe the transaction as concluded. "Well that tiresome business has now been settled." The deal was accepted by Hoffmeister, who published all four works.

Beethoven's letters to Hoffmeister, aside from showing a decided talent for doing business, are chatty and contain some revealing asides. In the first he described the money-making potential of the Septet, at the same time insisting that every instrument was written in obbligato style—"I can write nothing that is not obbligato, for I came into the world with an obbligato accompaniment." He could have added, thanks to Joseph Haydn.

Piano Sonatas

The Sonata in B♭, published as Op. 22 in March 1802 with a dedication to Count Browne, was hardly the winner Beethoven claimed. Of its four movements, only

[52] Maynard Solomon, "Beethoven's 'Magazin der Kunst,' " *19th Century Music* 7 (1984): 199–208; 200. The author explores Beethoven's statement in this letter that there ought to be a clearing house where artists could take their works and earn from them only what profits they needed, a remarkably communitarian view for the time. He points out its direct precedents in French revolutionary essays.

the last is undeniably superior in quality. The first movement, *Allegro con brio* in common time, is certainly brilliant and meant to impress by its feats of pianism (the double octaves are comparable to those in Op. 1 No. 3). Its main theme is more show than substance. As a second theme there are thirds descending in a chain of leaps of a third, in dactylic rhythm. On closer acquaintance, the movement seems somewhat lacking in content. The melody that opens the *Adagio con molto espressione* in 9/8 time and in E♭ insists on a long A♮ appoggiatura rising to the chord-tone B♭, the fifth degree, over full tonic harmony. How to make this sound anything but maudlin is a challenge. The melodic line continues in the same vein with matching appoggiaturas rising to other long tones. The *Minuetto*, with a steady eighth-note accompaniment, deploys a pleasant melody. It is short and quite galant, except for the sudden burst of sixteenth-note chords in alternation, with *crescendo*, sounding like an alarm going off. A *Minore* picks up the turning figure from the first dance and makes it into a finger exercise with constant sixteenth notes, in g minor. The finale, *Rondo. Allegretto* in 2/4 time, inverts the turning figure in the minuet to form the agreeable and gracious theme of the refrain, which also has reminders of the half-tone under-appoggiaturas of the *Adagio*. As finely wrought as this refrain is, the rondo with a rather similar theme, composed about the same time in the "Spring" Sonata Op. 24, is finer still.

The Sonata in A♭, Op. 26, is quite unusual in comparison with Op. 22. It is also in four movements but they do not correspond to the normal pattern. There is no sonata-form movement. A very lovely theme and variations begins the procession, marked *Andante con Variazione* in 3/8 time. Its original theme is constructed like a song, **a a' b a'**, with no repeats. Each of the five variations explores a different texture, the last being the most flowing, to which is added a coda. Variation III is in tonic minor and has the seven flats required by this ominous tonality. It literally is an omen here for it foreshadows the march movement in a♭ that will follow after a *Scherzo Allegro molto* in A♭ with a Trio in D♭. Whereas Haydn was no stranger to keyboard sonatas and trios in A♭, Mozart avoided the key, conforming more closely with Italian norms. Galeazzi described A♭ as somber and rare, a♭ as simply impossible: "A♭ is not much used on account of its difficulty. It is somber (*cupo*), lethargic, profound, apt for expressing horror, the silence of the Night, quiet, fear, horror. Its minor is not used because of its surpassing difficulty."[53]

Opus 26 is sometimes called the "Funeral March Sonata" after its third movement, *Marcia funebre sulla morte d'un Eroe*. Like many marches in common time, this one has abundant dotted rhythm, primarily on the weak beats. There is no tempo indication, but the movement must be rather slow, in accordance with its funereal title. The main march is in the same song form as the *Andante* theme and

---

[53] Francesco Galeazzi, *Elementi teorico-pratici di musica*, 2 vols. (Rome, 1791–96), 2:293–95, "I principali caratteri de' Toni moderni."

lacks repeats. A few details, such as the slide in sixteenth notes that leads into the restatement after contrast, and a bass trill, add to the muted horror of the whole. The Trio, which does have repeat signs around its two sections, is just as frightening. It is in A♭ and could portray a march to the scaffold. Both strains begin with rapid, written-out tremolo chords in sixty-fourth notes, marked with *crescendo* from *piano* to *forte*. These should sound like snare drum rolls leading to a stroke on the bass drum at the climaxes. It would not have taken an overheated imagination in those days to have heard in such loud strokes the thud of the guillotine. To the return of the first march is added a poignant coda.

The coda consists of a falling treble line that plunges down nearly an octave by step against a tenor line that rises an octave, while preserving the march rhythm; then the two parts switch and take each other's line. As a contrapuntal device it is quite old—used to end a dramatic scene, as here, it has a respectable pedigree on the Viennese stage. This is how Gluck has the Furies yield to the bard, ending the infernal scene of *Orfeo ed Euridice*, which began astonishing audiences in the Burgtheater in 1762. There is a carryover in the sonata to the movement that comes next, an *Allegro* in 2/4 time in rondo form and in A♭ that deploys nearly constant sixteenth-note motion. It may seem at first no more than a finger exercise, an etude. On further acquaintance one perceives that the refrain uses the same device of rising versus descending lines by step, then inverting them. Its charm defuses the power and intensity of the funeral march yet makes a subtle musical link with its ending.

Beethoven held the *Marcia funebre* in enough esteem to reuse it as an orchestral march for a stage play in 1815. He wisely transposed it to the more orchestrally suitable key of b minor. Another version, for four voices and piano using a specially composed poem, was played at Beethoven's own funeral in 1827. There were many reprints of the original march by itself. The sonata, too, became a favorite, because of the march. In Paris, Pleyel published Op. 26 as a "Grande Sonate avec une Marche funèbre." Beethoven dedicated Op. 26 to Lichnowsky, as he had the *Sonate pathétique*, Op. 13.

What sort of reception would a "Funeral March on the Death of a Hero" have had in Vienna? The age in which Beethoven came to maturity was a heroic one. The French Revolution left no one unmoved by its acts of terror and also of heroism. In Austria the horrors of the Revolution were brought home in particular by the execution of Marie Antoinette in 1793. The youngest daughter of Maria Theresa, she had been particularly close to her brother Maximilian, the youngest son, when they were both children. In contrast to its acts of violence, the Revolution also produced the Declaration of the Rights of Man, repercussions of which were felt everywhere, even in Austria, where the First French Republic was not without its admirers. Legions of heroes died in battle during the 1790s on both sides of the conflict. The musical genre commemorating their deaths was nevertheless connected principally with French Revolutionary Festivals. These civic events often celebrated heroes who had fallen in battle, and one prime musical example, Gossec's *March lugubre,* was so used throughout the 1790s.[54] The funeral march in Op. 26 opened a path for its composer that he would explore fully in the mighty *Marcia funebre* of the "Eroica" Symphony, Op. 55, that followed in 1804.

The political situation at the time of Op. 26 remained in flux. Renewal of the war between France and Austria in 1800 led to two disastrous defeats for the latter, at Marengo in Lombardy during June and at Hohenlinden near Linz, on 3 December 1800. Emperor Francis again was forced to negotiate a settlement. The peace treaty signed at Lunéville in Lorraine on 9 February 1801 led to one of the longer respites from war. Many people took the opportunity to visit Paris again, among them Prince Esterházy, but not the infirm Haydn. Beethoven too intended to go to Paris and seek an appointment there.[55] His intention to dedicate the *Eroica* symphony to Napoleon, or name it "Bonaparte" after him, can be understood as a part of his plan to find a high-level post in France.

An argument has been made that the five solo piano sonatas composed in 1800–1801 form a block that challenges previous norms and makes strides toward new goals.[56] The claim does not suit Op. 22 very well, as argued above, but certainly does fit Op. 26 and the following three solo sonatas. Op. 27 Nos. 1 and 2 are titled "quasi una fantasia." What this meant was a departure from the regular number or order of movements in favor of an unpredictable sequence of pieces, often run together. Op. 28 in D, dubbed "Sonata Pastorale" a few years after first publication, does indeed project pastoral temper and thus would be considered at the time as a "characteristic" sonata.

Opus 27 No. 1 in E♭, the first "Sonata quasi una Fantasia," begins with an *Andante* in common time contrasting right-hand chords with left-hand runs, a pleasant dialogue diverted suddenly by the chords appearing softly in C major, without preparation. The *Andante* ends in E♭ where it began, then gives way at once to an *Allegro* in 6/8 and in C major. Its exuberance quickly peters out with a transition preparing the return of the initial section in E♭, ended by a coda that dies away *pianissimo. Attacca subito l'Allegro* say the directions at this point, launching us at once into an *Allegro molto e vivace* in 3/4 time and in c minor. It has the form and character of a scherzo with trio in A♭ but does not use these designations. At the end of the scherzo there is another *attacca subito* leading to a

[54] Claude V. Palisca, "French Revolutionary Models for Beethoven's *Eroica* Funeral March," in *Music and Context: Essays for John M. Ward,* ed. Anne Dhu Shapiro (Cambridge, MA, 1985), pp. 198–209; 201.

[55] Maynard Solomon, *Beethoven* (New York, 1977), pp. 130–31, 136–37, and Solomon, "Beethoven's *Magazin der Kunst,*" 206.

[56] Lockwood, "Reshaping the Genre: Beethoven's Piano Sonatas from Op. 22 to Op. 28," *Israel Studies in Musicology* 6 (1996): 1–16. The author concludes, "The piano sonata was a field for experimentation of new ways of unfolding ideas."

melodious *Adagio con espressione* in 3/4 time and in A♭. The transition at the end in a cadenza-like passage prepares the return of E♭, arrived at with still another *attacca subito*. This movement, *Allegro vivace* in 2/4 time, begins like a fugue subject with its countersubject in faster notes. What follows is not a fugue but a large homophonic movement on these two ideas. When the end seems nigh, nearly 300 measures later, back comes the *Adagio* theme, although this time in E♭, not A♭, and reduced to only ten measures. The *Adagio* is not quite the end. That is provided by a little *Presto* made from fragments of the subject/countersubject idea. In a flash of motion and color this kaleidoscopic fantasia is over. The impression of hearing Beethoven improvise comes to mind, and perhaps he made up such chameleonic works as this when implored, as he often was, to sit down at the piano. He enjoyed thwarting listeners' expectations.

Opus 27 No. 2 in c♯ minor was destined to become one of the composer's most famous works, posthumously called the "Moonlight Sonata." The evocative title responds to the dreamlike first movement, *Adagio sostenuto* in cut time, with soft accompanying triplets providing the background to sonorous octaves in the bass and a slowly evolving melody in the treble. The effect is as magical as moonlight sometimes can be, by shedding an odd light on familiar objects. No time is left at the end for the moon to set or the mood to dissipate. *Attacca subito il seguente* guarantees that D♭ arrives suddenly with an *Allegretto* in 3/4 time and an iambic melody that, on repetition, turns trochaic by means of notes tied over the bar line. In dance form, it trips off the fingers lightly, in contrast with the solemn and sustained ruminations that came before. Its Trio remains in D♭ and picks out one feature for concentration: notes tied over the bar line. The finale brings back c♯ minor in a *Presto agitato* in common time. This is another study involving sixteenth notes in perpetual motion, as in the finale of Op. 26, although here it is one of great turbulence. Right-hand arpeggios sweep upward to meet punctuating *sforzato* chords. It offers the longest and most substantial movement by far, a big sonata form with prima parte repeated. For all its agitation, it remains a richly melodic experience, superbly crafted. The strongest accents come with an explosive *fortissimo* chord of eight members, a pre-cadential Neapolitan-sixth chord (D major in the reprise). This halts momentarily the flood of sixteenth notes, almost as if commanded by a shout of "Stop!" or some other word that begins with a fricative consonant. The torrent abates only for the closing theme. A long coda is added to the reprise, with some cadenza-like touches and two measures of *Adagio*, consisting only of two pre-cadential whole notes in octaves, G♮ - G♯ in the deep bass, before *Tempo Primo* brings a final burst of motion and a furious ending in c♯ minor.

Beethoven dedicated the sonatas, printed by the newly established firm of Giuseppe Cappi in Vienna, to two different ladies, a distinct oddity for a single opus number. No. 1 bore a dedication to Princess Josephine von Liechtenstein,

No. 2 to Countess Giulietta Guicciardi. Biographers have fastened on the possible connection between the young and not-yet-married Countess with a reference Beethoven made in a letter to Dr. Wegeler in Bonn, dated 16 November 1801, to an unidentified young lady he considered marrying. He described her as "a dear, fascinating maiden who loves me and whom I love . . . unfortunately she is not of my station." Giulietta, then aged seventeen, was one of his piano pupils. She married someone of her own rank two years later.

Opus 28 in D, the "Pastoral" Sonata, deploys from the beginning long pedal tones that evoke rustic pipes and the countryside in general. The *Allegro* in 3/4 time unfurls a soft first theme sung entirely over a tonic pedal in the bass, the first tonal destination being a subdominant 6/4 chord. The second theme area is dominated by a broad trochaic melody with a rustling accompaniment in eighth notes, delicately interwoven with chromatic neighbor notes. Beethoven used this kind of accompaniment often in his writing for piano and had perfected it by the finale of the Sonata for Piano and Cello No. 2. A closing theme that begins with leaping octave reproduces features of the *Allegretto* in Op. 27 No. 2. After repetition of the prima parte the seconda parte starts with a descent of the bass to F♯, which is turned into the leading tone of G major, a resolution that brings the whole first theme in this subdominant area.

With a turn to g minor, the main theme or parts of it are put through their paces in more contrapuntal fashion. Fragmentation of the theme down to just a few tones, repeated measure after measure, leads to a settling down on the pedal tone of F♯, excessively protracted at thirty-eight measures. The chord of F♯, finally diminished to *pianissimo*, brings the movement to a stop. Is this the Haydn strategy of protracting V/vi only to slide smoothly into I for the reprise? Yes and no. This V/vi chord is allowed to resolve, not to I, and not to vi, but to VI, B major, and not to the first theme but to the closing theme. When VI becomes vi, the way is smoothed into the true reprise, in D. At its end the main theme comes back one more time and its closing gesture is repeated many times to end the movement. The following *Andante* in 2/4 time and in d minor is like a little march with a *maggiore* trio in the middle and a subtle coda at the end that echoes the initial rhythm of the trio. Czerny related that this movement was long a favorite of its composer who "played it often for his own pleasure." It has a bearing on the *Larghetto* of Symphony No. 2, discussed below.

The Scherzo that follows makes a single point, one that reinforces a peculiarity of the opening *Allegro*. Marked *Allegro vivace*, it begins by sounding the single tone of F♯ from high to low, the same tone that brought the first movement to a stop. Here, as if demonstrating how many resolutions can come from a single tone, the next thing heard is the keynote D, with F♯ taking its place as a third degree. To begin the second strain F♯ is again the leading tone to G, as in the seconda parte of the opening movement. The Trio consists almost entirely of F♯ as V/

vi resolving to b minor. Preoccupation with this single tone also prefigures Symphony No. 2 in D, Op. 36.

Pastoral mode resumes as well as the keynote in the final Rondo in 6/8 time, marked *Allegro ma non tanto*. Another long tonic pedal supports the refrain, sounded first as an open fifth, making it seem even more rustic. At the end of the movement this bass, being in octaves, is speeded up and made more difficult to play. The tempo change is expressed as *Più allegro quasi presto*. Mercifully, Beethoven allowed the "ma non tanto" to qualify the *Allegro* and everything before the last page of the movement. The wilder dance and whirling sixteenth-note figures in the right hand against the fast octaves in the left make for a brilliant close to this altogether winning sonata.

Beethoven entrusted the publication of Op. 28 to a new Viennese firm, the Bureau d'Arts et d'Industrie. It appeared in August 1802 with a dedication to a leading figure of the Austrian Enlightenment, the long-serving court councilor Joseph von Sonnenfels. We have met him before as Mozart's patron, also as a force for moderation and reform in government, and furthermore as Haydn's lodge brother in True Concord. Earlier still he was encountered as a drama critic, proponent of reform opera, and ardent defender of Gluck's *Alceste*.[57] He was a veritable Prometheus in Vienna's intellectual life. Whether he had the financial resources with which to reward Beethoven for this dedication, or anything else about their connection, remains unknown. It was certainly unusual for the composer to select a dedicatee outside the ranks of the high nobility. True to form, on the other hand, was his dedication of three fine piano and violin sonatas, Op. 30, to Czar Alexander I of Russia, also published by the Bureau d'Arts et d'Industrie. In 1801 the young Alexander mounted the throne over the body of his murdered father Paul I. He quickly became known for his reform ideas, which were never realized. These have been claimed as the reason for Beethoven's dedication, and compared in this light with the dedication to Sonnenfels.[58] More likely, Beethoven was making an early bid for the Czar's favor, with a view to a possible court appointment. Beethoven's payment from the Czar for the dedication was a long time in coming but it was finally made by the Czarina at the Congress of Vienna in 1814.

Another work in pastoral mode, composed about the same time as Op. 28, is the so-called "Spring" Sonata in F, Op. 24, for piano and violin. It was originally paired with the Sonata in a. Both were advertised in the *Wiener Zeitung* of 28 October 1801 as "Deux Sonates pour le Pianoforte avec un violon. Op. 23." They were dedicated to the wealthy banker Count Moritz von Fries. How Op. 24 acquired its sobriquet "Spring," or when, is unclear. The title is apt in any case. The *Allegro* in

---

[57] *Haydn, Mozart*, pp. 228–30.

[58] Solomon, *Beethoven* (1977), p. 136: "He began a series of apparently disinterested dedications of his works to leading adherents of Enlightened positions . . . these unpaid, honorary dedications are all the more significant."

common time commences like a vernal breeze with a melody sung by the violin to the piano's accompaniment (Example 7.9). It begins on the third degree and

EXAMPLE 7.9. *Beethoven, Piano and Violin Sonata in F, Op. 24, "Spring," I*

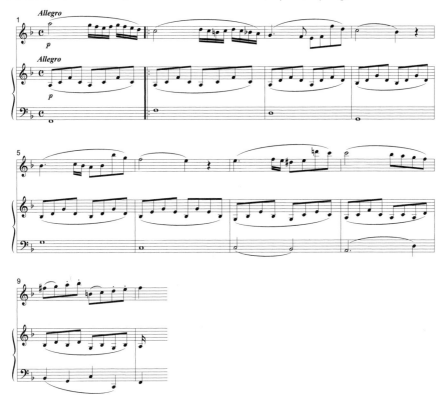

glides down over an octave with ornamented third and fourth beats coming to temporary resting places on vi, then ii. The melodic sighs above both these chords are preceded by octave leaps up and falls by step. Note that the melodic turn on the third beat of m. 1 becomes the melody itself in m. 3, which measure furnishes material for the continuation to the end of this graceful ten-measure theme. The second segment, mm. 5–6, picks up the tone B♭ from the end of the first, and the final segment does likewise with the tone E, giving the melody continuity after the pauses for breath. The phrase is vocal in this sense, although the violin of course needs no pauses for breath. In truth the melody is more instrumental than vocal, as the breathtaking leaps up to high B♭, then up to high D amply demonstrate. The partners switch roles immediately and Beethoven gives the piano's rendition of this theme more elaboration so the leaps upward become rapid runs instead. Violin and piano vie with each other as complete equals although the piano gets idiomatic writing appropriate only to it, such as the thick chordal swells rising up the keyboard and announcing the second key area. Much of the discourse is drawn from the very beginning of the opening theme, whether its rhythmic or melodic shape. Perhaps it occurred to some astute listener in 1802 that the incipit's underlying 3 2 1 motion duplicated the melody with which the chorus welcomed Spring ("Komm holder Lenz") in Haydn's *Seasons*.

The slow movement of Op. 24 is an *Adagio molto espressivo* in 3/4 time and in the key of B♭, the same choice Beethoven was to make for the slow movement of Symphony No. 6 in F Op. 68 ("Sinfonia pastorale") of 1807–8. As in the sonata's opening movement, the emphasis is on long-breathed melody with supporting chordal accompaniment. The kinship with Op. 68's second movement peeps through a little more with the birdlike repeated-note decorations the piano applies to the melody on its return. Still more suggestive is the following section, which moves off tonally, very smoothly, toward distant harmonic realms on the flat side, reaching G♭, as the violin sings the broad main melody above the piano's flowing accompaniment in sixteenth notes. G♭ becomes transformed into f♯ minor beginning the return to B♭. Instead of the expected reprise of the main theme in tonic B♭, Beethoven launches immediately into a coda, which has its own ravishing melody. Coordinated trills at the cadences again suggest birdsong. This movement already has in miniature the avian twitterings and purling brook of Op. 68.

The Scherzo and Rondo of the third and fourth movements are both initiated by themes built from a melodic nucleus of 5 6 5 4 3 2 1, which occurs also in the first theme of the *Allegro*. An exemplary brevity reigns in the Scherzo and Trio, as it had in the *Adagio*, and this seems a far cry from the rambling discourse of much early Beethoven. Since the tempo of the Scherzo is *Allegro molto* it is over very quickly, yet there is still time to make a jest, such as having the violin lag one beat behind the piano, creating tiny dissonances. This persists to the end of the Scherzo, the last two measures being a rhythmic augmentation of the jest that removes the dissonance. Each of the four movements has a high point of interest: in the *Allegro* it was the beautiful main theme itself; in the *Adagio*, the excursion to the far flat side preempting a reprise of the theme in the tonic; in the third movement it is these last two measures, and they give a precise definition of what "Scherzo" means.

The Rondo is in cut time, marked *Allegro ma non tanto*. Its refrain has a theme that is cousin in graciousness to the main theme of the *Allegro*, and is, if anything, a little more flowery because of its frequent melodic turns, and a little more courtly because of its underlying gavotte rhythm. The steady flow of eighth notes in the accompaniment is common to both themes. This theme is more regular than that of the *Allegro* and is built up entirely from four-measure segments. The idea that follows it is even more plainly a gavotte. As for its high point of interest, Beethoven seizes upon the sequence of melodic turns rising to a peak in the refrain, and greatly increases the length and melodic span of the idea, using many chromatic neighbor tones to arrive at the peak, which simultaneously begins a return of the refrain. To increase the wonder of this heart-stopping moment, Beethoven makes it a long *crescendo* to a point of arrival that is suddenly *piano*, a device used so effectively by Mozart. Beethoven later wrote something rather similar in the long chromatic push upwards of the melodic line with many repetitions of the same small figure, arriving finally at the second theme of the Rondo finale of Piano Concerto No. 4 in G, Op. 58. Not to be missed is a parallel between Op. 24 and Op. 28. What was described as the "rustling accompaniment" with chromatic inflections in the first movement of the "Pastoral" Sonata, Op. 28, is used just as effectively to accompany the refrain of Op. 24's finale.

A word is in order about the companion Sonata in a, Op. 23, for piano and violin. It seems dour and astringently contrapuntal compared to the lushly endowed siren before us in Op. 24. In competition with alluring beauties, overt sagacity has rarely won the day, nor does it do so here. Critics have often pointed out that it was the composer's habit to work simultaneously on works of disparate character, of which there is no more cogent demonstration than his Fifth and Sixth Symphonies.

String Quartets, Opus 18

The string quartet, no less than the symphony, had become the measure by which an artist could aspire to be ranked as a composer of instrumental music beside Haydn and Mozart. Beethoven put this test off until he was nearing thirty years of age, although he seemed to approach it in his String Trios, Op. 9. His first goal in Vienna, as previously in Bonn, had been to advance in stature as a pianist-composer on the traces of Mozart. As a pianist he won public recognition especially for performing as a soloist in his first piano concertos and for his improvising. He advanced steadily in his solo piano sonatas and in chamber music with piano, to the point where emphasis was justified on the latter half of the expression "pianist-composer." The solo sonatas since those of Op. 2 were in many senses his most original and inspired compositions, so that at least in this genre he was becoming valued on a par with Mozart. The string quartet presented for him a greater challenge, a more rigorous path to perfection. Rising to the standards set by Haydn in the genre was no easy task even for Mozart, as he confessed while writing his six quartets dedicated to Haydn and remarked later in connection with his "Prussian" quartets. Haydn himself declared his relief at having gotten to the end of composing his six "Prussian" quartets, Op. 50. Perhaps by way of preparing himself for the onerous task Beethoven copied Haydn's Quartet in E♭ from Op. 20 in its entirety. He left no verbal complaints that have survived about laboring on his first six quartets but he spent more than two years composing, revising, and polishing them. They were published by Mollo at Vienna in 1801, in two installments. Prince Franz Joseph Lobkowitz commissioned them, and their dedication went to him.

Quartet No. 1 in F is often selected to be representative of the set of six, with good reason. Although not the first to be composed (Quartet No. 3 in D was written earlier), it is the work that makes the strongest impression, and the only one for which we have a complete early version. Moving it into place as the open-ing work was wise.

An *Allegro con brio* in 3/4 time starts softly with a unison statement combin-ing a turning figure and leap down a fourth, repeated with a leap down a third. The first violin, accompanied by the other instruments, moves up an octave and transforms the head motif so that it rises up a tone instead of leaping down, lead-ing to a smooth half cadence. This constitutes a clear antecedent phrase of eight measures (2 + 2 + 4). The harmonies are consonant and what one would expect (Example 7.10). The consequent begins by repeating the unison opening, *forte*

EXAMPLE 7.10. *Beethoven, String Quartet in F, Op. 18 No. 1, I*

instead of *piano*. Violino primo, unaccompanied at first, continues softly as before but raises the stakes by moving up a third, initiating a long melodic sigh, made more expressive by the diminished-seventh harmony provided by the accom-panying parts. This is repeated up a tone, the melodic sigh now over a differ-ent diminished-seventh chord, and a third time with the first violin reaching up to high C to emit another melodic sigh over more expressive harmony before resolving to the cadence in mm. 19–20. Tension rises in ways that could not have been expected, and the consequent stretches out from eight to twelve measures (2 + 2 + 2 + 2 + 4). (To imagine a regular consequent, try proceeding directly from m. 14 to m. 19.) In the continuation, the turning figure plus melodic sigh are transferred to the second violin in another rising sequence, while the first violin provides commentary using just the turning figure, then rising to a cadence on high F. The texture is dense at the beginning, and it does not become much thinner as it continues, although the harmonic rhythm broadens. After the cello takes the turning figure and ends it with a leap down an octave to its low C, repeated as an ostinato, there commences a move to the second key.

Before the bridge has finished, the harmony slips suddenly from c down a minor third to A♭ for a soft passage, still dominated by the turn and melodic sigh, like everything up to this point. The tonal move to ♭III matches that at the beginning of the First and Second Piano Concertos. When the second theme does arrive, it fights free of the head motif and demonstrates an independent rhythmic character with its syncopations. The head motif slips back, nevertheless, on the second theme's tail, in a little exchange between the cello and first violin, and closes the prima parte as an ostinato for the cello, again using its leap down to low C. On its later occurrences the motif acquires a new whirring form of continual melodic turns in sixteenth notes.

The seconda parte begins, after repetition of the prima parte, as the harmony plunges down a major third from C to A. It often did this in Haydn at the same spot, as we have seen, so it cannot sound very surprising to us and perhaps did not seem so in the Vienna of that time. Not far into the development Beethoven places a contrapuntal working-out based on the head motif plus a diminished-seventh leap down. He makes a canon of the unison or octave from it, at first at the distance of one measure, then at the distance of one beat. The result can sound rather confused (a show less for the ear than the eye?). This is one of the few sections that the composer changed substantially from the earlier version he gave his friend Karl Amenda in 1799 and the printed version of 1801. Amenda and his relationship to Beethoven come in for discussion following this critique of Op. 18 No. 1. The development concludes after a long dominant pedal, with scales rushing up and down the octave from C. After the chord changes from V to V⁷ there is a climactic, headlong rush to begin the reprise, *fortissimo*. This is not the overwhelming release of tension accompanying the onset of the reprise in the first movement of another work in F, the Eighth Symphony, but it shows Beethoven making progress. There is a spacious coda that extracts still more out of the main material. In Amenda's copy the seconda parte is marked for repetition but in the final version it is not.

The *Adagio affetuoso ed appassionato* in 12/8 time and in d minor is a lament expressed with great passion. It takes the shape of a sonata form with no repeat of the prima parte, in which the second theme in the relative major, F, contrasts like a celestial vision of tenderness (especially so when it comes back in D major in the reprise). The movement ends darkly, back in d in a fadeout that suggests a spirit breathing its last sighs. According to Amenda, Beethoven told him he composed the *Adagio* with the tomb scene at the end of *Romeo and Juliet* in mind, and one of the early sketches for it, with the verbal inscription "les derniers soupirs,"seems to bear this out.

Scherzo Allegro restores F major and a sense of urgency as it trips along at a fast pace. Its theme projects another version of the turn motif that saturates the first movement. Some tonal moves also sound familiar from the *Allegro con brio*, such as the plunge from C to A♭ to begin the Scherzo's second strain, or the move from C to D♭ in the Trio. The finale is an *Allegro* in 2/4 time with frequent sixteenth-note triplets, making it sound like a very fast dance in 12/8 meter, such as a tarantella. The main theme or refrain of this sonata rondo offers another version of the turn motif to begin its plunge downward. The second theme starts out in G, then rights itself and moves to the expected key of C. A medial return of the refrain in tonic major confirms that this is a rondo; its sonata-form element consists of a contrasting second theme that eventually returns in the tonic. In the middle there is a development, with hints of a fugato, interrupted by an arrival and stay in D♭. In length if not in weight, the finale matches the opening movement, and it too has a sizable coda.

Karl Amenda was a violinist only ten months younger than Beethoven. He was born in Lepaya on the shore of the Baltic Sea in Courland, Latvia, and had studied theology at Jena University, whence he came to Vienna in 1798 to become a preceptor in the household of Prince Lobkowitz and music teacher to Constanze Mozart's two children. He and Beethoven formed a strong attachment to each other and presumably played together in trying out these new quartets. Their closeness was such that Beethoven gave Amenda a copy of Op. 18 No. 1, and they laid plans for a tour of Italy together as a violin and piano duo, plans that came to naught when Amenda was called home on account of a death in his family in the fall of 1799. They kept up an affectionate correspondence, and its effusive language caused the Victorian Thayer to comment, "Their friendship was of the romantic character once so much the fashion." On the first violin part of the Quartet in F Beethoven wrote, "Dear Amenda: Take this quartet as a small memorial of our friendship, and as often as you play it to yourself remember the days we passed together and the sincere affection felt for you then and which will always be felt by your warm and true friend Ludwig van Beethoven, Vienna, 25 June 1799."

Two years later, on 1 July 1801, Beethoven ended his long letter to Amenda with "Do not lend your quartet to anybody because I have greatly changed it, having just learned how to write quartets properly, as you will observe when you receive them [the printed copies]." These words lead one to believe that there were big changes between the two versions. The final one does show greater attention to the medium's idiomatic possibilities. Otherwise the changes are mostly small and tend toward eliminating some of the fussy dynamic indications with which Beethoven had often overloaded his scores ever since the Piano Quartets of 1785. "I have greatly changed it" is thus something of an exaggeration. Rewriting the contrapuntal section of the first movement's development, it could be argued, made this section even more crabbed than it was in the first place.[59] Nevertheless the general direction of the changes was to simplify, or clarify. Mention has been made of the elimination of the seconda parte's repeat in the first movement. In sum Beethoven made the final version less emphatic and allowed it to speak for itself with fewer fussy dynamic markings.[60]

Quartet No. 2 in G is the jester of the set. Its key was often host to particularly jocular moods, as were, for example, the finale of Mozart's Piano Concerto in G, K. 453, and the first movement of Haydn's Quartet in G from Op. 33. The latter in fact seems to have inspired the entire conception of Op. 18 No. 2. Beethoven begins with an *Allegro* in 2/4 time, the same meter Haydn used, and moves in short, two-measure segments as did Haydn. Moreover there are melodic and harmonic similarities. Haydn's theme keeps sliding from 5 up to 8, which is how his *Vivace assai* both begins and ends (see Example 4.1). Beethoven plays with 5 8 5 in two different octaves and constructs not only the first theme of his *Allegro* therefrom but also the head motif of his Scherzo (Example 7.11ab), and 5 8 begins

EXAMPLE 7.11 a, b. *Beethoven, String Quartet in G, Op. 18 No. 2, I, III*

a.

b.

b. *Scherzo*

the slow movement as well. His finale also begins with the same material as the *Allegro*, with two measures of I followed by two measures of V[7] in outline, but inverted. The playful, light character of all the movements gives this quartet a

[59] Janet M. Levy, *Beethoven's Compositional Choices: The Two Versions of Op. 18 No. 1, First Movement* (Philadelphia, 1982), p. 55 offers the two passages placed one above the other to facilitate comparison.
[60] For more details, see Joseph Kerman, *The Beethoven Quartets* (New York, 1967), pp. 32–34.

personality far removed from that of Op. 18 No. 1. We should not be surprised that Haydn's Op. 33 Quartet in G still hovered in Beethoven's mind after observing how he made use of it in Piano Sonata No. 10 in G, Op. 14 No. 2 (see Examples 4.4 and 4.5).

There are some indications in the abundant sketches for Op. 18 that the composer, from an early stage, had his mind fixed on creating a set of quartets. One reason the surviving sketches are abundant is that he switched at just this time from compiling his ideas on loose leaves to using preassembled sketchbooks, of which the first two, known as "Grasnick 1" and "Grasnick 2," are largely devoted to what became the Op. 18 quartets.[61] The first one he sketched, in "Grasnick 1," was the Quartet in D, after which he jotted down in words "le second qu[atuor] dans une style bien legere excepté le dernier piece."[62] "Quite light" would be an apt description of the Quartet in G, Op. 18 No. 2, including its finale.

In the development of the first movement we might expect the discourse to get a little more serious. An initial turn to the minor there is soon dissipated and replaced by a preparation for E♭ major, which arrives with a massive chord, the first violin playing a quadruple stop. An attempted fugato after this never takes full flight before being swamped by the gamboling banter of the other voice parts. Haydn's first movement makes a big point of a huge E♭ arrival, but only late in the seconda parte. Still the sonorities of this outburst of ♭VI in G major have a similar ring.

Surely, we presume, the slow movement, *Adagio cantabile* in 3/4 time and in C major, will bring with it greater decorum. It does so for a time (unless the showy first violin part, with its fast runs in decoration of a simple melodic line, hints at parody). After only twenty-six measures, the *Adagio* concludes with big cadential gestures in C major. It is replaced by a little dance, *Allegro* in 2/4 time, a rounded binary form with repeats, which brings back the spirit of the initial *Allegro* and thoroughly deflates any serious message from the *Adagio*. Interplay of this comic kind is very Haydnesque and has a parallel in Haydn's Symphony No. 79 in F. For that matter it is closely parallel to the serious *Adagio* beset by frivolity in Beethoven's Serenade in D, Op. 8, for string trio discussed above. In Op. 18 No. 2, the *Adagio* returns to have the last say, yet it is so overcome by fast decorative passages in all the parts as to make it sound even more like parody. At the end, as a little coda, there is a whisper of the impudent dance.

[61] Douglas Johnson, Alan Tyson, and Robert Winter, *The Beethoven Sketchbooks: History, Reconstruction, Inventory,* ed. Douglas Johnson (Berkeley, 1985), pp. 77–88.

[62] Sieghard Brandenburg, "The First Versions of Beethoven's G Major String Quartet, Op. 18 No. 2," *Music and Letters* 58 (1977): 127–52; 145. If this transcription is correct, Beethoven paid little attention to genders in French. "Style" should be masculine and "pièce" feminine. See also Brandenburg, "Beethovens Streichquartette op. 18," in *Beethoven und Böhmen,* ed. Brandenburg and Gutíerrez-Denhoff, pp. 259–309.

The *Scherzo Allegro* is true to type—it is a jest by definition. It was sketched with its main melody nearly in final shape soon after the jottings for the initial *Allegro*, with which it is melodically similar. Its short first strain ends in tonic G, the second strain wanders off by making a big point of V/vi, which is left unresolved at first, then reintroduced more insistently and resolved, not to e (vi) but to C (IV). The Trio takes C for its main key and also begins with a leap from 5 to 8. The finale, *Allegro molto quasi Presto* in 2/4 time, returns to the melos and meter of the initial *Allegro*. It also has a link with the Scherzo: an insistence on V/vi resolving to vi then giving way to IV before returning to the tonic. There is a big section of C major in the middle, in which the main theme is elaborated in canonic form. This feature suggests the medial episode characteristic of a rondo, but in other respects the whole movement is more like a sonata form, although one without repeat signs. A short coda begins softly, with the main idea in C, giving way quickly to tonic G that swells with a *crescendo* up to the final *fortissimo* chords.

Quartet No. 3 in D, unlike Nos. 1 and 2, announces its lyric nature from the start by having the first violin sing a long-breathed melody, *Allegro* in cut time (Example 7.12). The leap up a seventh from A to G is recovered by a gently winding

EXAMPLE 7.12. *Beethoven, String Quartet in D, Op. 18 No. 3, I*

line that descends a tenth before reaching a weak cadence on the third of the tonic, approached by a chromatically raised lower neighbor tone. This particular chromatic spicing is typically galant. The accompanying chords move slowly, one per measure as indicated, and very smoothly. The effect is Mozartian, although the possibility of a Haydn model cannot be dismissed. Haydn's Quartet in D of Op. 20 opened with the leap of a fourth from D to G with resolution to F♯, which at the beginning of the development becomes a leap up a seventh. Both first movements emphasize long legato lines inaugurated by their main themes. Haydn's Op. 20 Quartets were by no means forgotten in Vienna at the turn of the century. Artaria published a new edition of them in 1800–1801 that Haydn dedicated to Beethoven's friend and patron Baron Nikolaus Zmeskall.

The opening theme of the Quartet in D, with its long notes and stepwise motion, provided an ideal subject for canonic treatment. Canons begin at once in the consequent to mm. 1–10, as the viola repeats the opening an octave lower and is imitated a measure later an octave above by the second violin. Then the first violin takes over again, interpolating a much longer descending passage in eighth notes, unaccompanied. This soliloquy is spun out, after the other instruments rejoin the texture, all the way to the cadence in m. 27. Much of what follows involves further imitative treatment of the head motif.

The second movement of Op. 18 No. 3 offers an *Andante con moto* in 2/4 time and in the key of B♭, which produces a muted effect. A songlike and smooth-flowing theme in even eighth notes tinted by delicate chromatic shadings is given first to the second violin, with accompaniment (Example 7.13). An *Allegro* in 3/4 time

EXAMPLE 7.13. *Beethoven, String Quartet in D, Op. 18 No. 3, II*

and in D has all the earmarks of a scherzo but is not called such, and its Trio is called not a Trio but *Minore*. Return of the main dance, usually signaled by "da capo," is written out here and labeled *Maggiore*. Its theme bears an unmistakable resemblance to the Trio of Mozart's String Quartet in A, K. 464. In the second strain Beethoven uses its head motif as the subject of an awkward fugato, one of the few disappointing moments in the work. The theme of the finale, *Presto* in 6/8 time, dances up the seventh from A to G in clear reference to the head motif of the *Allegro*. From this light beginning emerges a sonata form of considerable length and heft.

Quartet No. 4 in c minor answers to the practice of putting at least one minor mode work in a set of quartets, usually tucked in the middle. Perhaps the key was expected too, at least in the close milieu of the Viennese salons where chamber music was regularly heard. Beethoven had already distinguished himself particularly with works in c minor such as the Piano Trio, Op. 1 No. 3, the String Trio, Op. 9 No. 3, and the *Sonate pathétique*, Op. 13.[63] Some critics thought that Op. 18 No. 4 might have been written long before the other quartets, but this view has been discredited. While it does not approach the composer's best works in this key, the work was apparently sketched, however sparsely, at the same time as the other quartets. The first movement, *Allegro ma non tanto* in common time, presents a passionate theme based on melodic sighs that rise in pitch. They keep on rising, in fact, until they have climbed over two octaves, all in the first violin. This is heavy breathing for a main theme but not nearly so effective as the beginning

---

[63] Joseph Kerman, "Beethoven's Minority," in *Haydn, Mozart, and Beethoven*, pp. 151–73, surveys these and other works in c minor within the context of all the composer's minor mode pieces, beginning with the "Joseph" Cantata.

of Op. 18 No. 1 in F, partly because the texture is rather retrospective. The cello keeps up its drumbeat of repeated eighth notes throughout. A sharply contrasting continuation in multiple-stopped chords provides only a short interruption before the first violin is back with more of the same. What seems particularly unwise is that the second theme offers a template of the first, with the same rising melodic sighs but in the relative major (tonic major in the reprise). This saps the development of new possibilities to the extent that it fails to generate much interest or excitement. The movement ends with a return to c minor.

The second movement of Op. 18 No. 4 is a Scherzo in C major, labeled *Andante scherzoso quasi Allegretto*. It is in 3/8 time, in sonata form, and with a lightly tripping staccato main theme, treated fugally. The effect is close in character to the second movement of Symphony No. 1 in C. There follows a *Menuetto. Allegretto* in c minor, with a Trio in A♭. The finale, *Allegro* in 2/4 time and in c minor, trades the seriousness of c minor for the abandon of a Hungarian dance. Haydn's *Rondo all'Ongarese*, the finale of his best-known piano trio, Hob. XV:25, begins with the same melody and rhythm—most likely a traditional gambit—but in major, not minor. Beethoven's rondo is of the old-fashioned kind, consisting of a series of couplets in binary form, with the refrain returning in slightly varied fashion after each. The impression of the whole is that of a Gypsy band, with wild violinistic displays and a *Prestissimo* final appearance for the refrain.

Quartet No. 5 in A takes as a general model the key, movement sequence, types of movement, and more, from the fifth of the six quartets Mozart dedicated to Haydn, K. 464 in A. Their parallels have long been known. Nineteenth-century critics commented on them and also said that Beethoven copied out in score the third and fourth movements of K. 464 (only his copy of the third movement still survives). Table 7.1 outlines the correspondences between the two quartets.

TABLE 7.1 A Mozart-Beethoven Comparison

Mozart, String Quartet in A, K. 464	Beethoven, String Quartet in A, Op. 18 No. 5
Allegro, 3/4, sonata form	*Allegro*, 6/8, sonata form
Menuetto/Trio (in E)	Menuetto/Trio
Andante cantabile, 2/4 in D, variations	*Andante cantabile*, 2/4 in D, variations
Allegro non troppo, cut time, sonata form	*Allegro*, cut time, sonata form

We have seen this kind of overt patterning on Mozart in some of Beethoven's apprentice works when he was still in Bonn. It is rather surprising to encounter it several years after he settled in Vienna. In both initial movements the seconda parte as well as the prima parte is repeated, a practice otherwise mostly discontinued by Beethoven, but it may have been used in this case because his *Allegro*, at 225 measures, is the shortest of the first movements in Op. 18, except for No. 4 in c. Three of Mozart's Haydn quartets have the minuet as a second movement, a practice that was slowly being relinquished in the 1790s by Haydn and others. A case has been made that Beethoven took a lot from K. 464 as to ideas and strategies, while resisting overt thematic resemblances.[64]

The two quartets are closest in the variation movement in 2/4 time, both marked *Andante cantabile* (in the autograph of K. 464 the "cantabile" is crossed out). Mozart spent some effort revising these superb variations, as we can tell from the autograph, in which the order differs from the printed score.[65] The unforgettable last moments when the cello repeats its drumming pattern with emphasis on the fifth degree, A, and the low tonic, D, effect both the rhythm and the cello's low D in Beethoven's last variation. For his ending Beethoven wrote a long coda with the theme appearing in ♭VI (B♭). This has no parallel in Mozart's movement, although the tone B♭ is a prominent goal there.

One of the features in K. 464 that particularly intrigued Beethoven was the sudden hushed passage with diminished-seventh chords in measure-long tones that appears at the end of the first movement, and again in the middle of the finale, purged of diminished chords (with one exception). Beethoven introduced a similarly hushed and mysterious passage in measure-long white notes forming diminished-seventh chords to introduce the second theme section of his finale. When he brings it back, twice, in his seconda parte, it is lacking all but one of the diminished chords. Unlike Mozart, he does not repeat the finale's seconda parte.

Quartet No. 6 in B♭ begins with an *Allegro con brio* in cut time that has a steady stream of eighth notes in the second violin and then in the viola, persisting all the way to the bridge, like a mechanical toy. Against this sonic continuum, the first violin states a triadic theme climbing up over two octaves, with an upbeat turning figure in sixteenth notes (Example 7.14). The triadic rise over a

EXAMPLE 7.14. *Beethoven, String Quartet in B♭, Op. 18 No. 6, I*

sustained tonic brings to mind the beginning of Haydn's sublime Quartet in B♭, Op. 76 No. 4, although that rise is relatively sedate and legato, an *Allegro con spirito* in common time, not cut time, hence half as fast. Beethoven's theme also sounds more pert because of its staccato articulation. The answer to violino pri-

---

[64] Jeremy Yudkin, "Beethoven's 'Mozart' Quartet," *JAMS* 45 (1992): 30–74.

[65] Marius Flothius, "A Close Reading of the Autographs of Mozart's Ten Late Quartets," in *The String Quartets of Haydn, Mozart, and Beethoven: Studies of the Autograph Manuscripts*, ed. Christoph Wolff (Cambridge, MA, 1980), pp. 154–73; 158.

mo's climb is made by the cello, which reiterates the violin's D - B♭, placing the D in accented position. The dialogue of this pair keeps on for several exchanges, before the second violin takes over as the responding partner. Haydn's very late Quartet in G, Op. 77 No. 1, employs a similar texture in its first movement, with the first violin and cello exchanging sallies against a mostly accompanimental middle ground. Haydn composed Op. 77 in 1799, and it was published in 1802. Op. 18 No. 6 was mainly sketched in a source known as "Autograph 19E" that dates from the summer of 1800.[66] Sketches for it mingle with those for the Sonata in B♭, Op. 22. While it may not rely for inspiration on any particular Haydn quartet, Op. 18 No. 6 can be regarded as a distillation from the entire corpus. The first movement hardly has enough different ideas to sustain its seconda parte. Like the first movement of Op. 18 No. 5 it is relatively short, prompting Beethoven to repeat the seconda part here as there. A curious feature of the movement comes directly before the reprise, as motion is suspended and a kind of lethargy sets in. The dominant pedal is so protracted it becomes a tease. Or else the composer dawdles here in order to pad the section, perhaps in order to reach some proportional length on which he had set his mind.

    Adagio ma non troppo, in 2/4 time and in E♭, is an unassuming movement, rather sparse in content and very simple in its overall **A B A'** plan. It moves mostly in four-measure phrases. The unremarkable ideas are heavily decorated with ornamental passagework upon repetition but this makes them no more interesting. **B** is in tonic minor, and its head motif returns in the relative minor to begin a short coda. *Scherzo. Allegro* toys with meter by beginning as if it were in 6/8 time, and for added zest places *sforzato* accents on the weak "sixth" beats which are tied over the bar line (Example 7.15a). The first strain ends on the tonic and the

EXAMPLE 7.15 a, b. *Beethoven, String Quartet in B♭, Op. 18 No. 6*

a. *III*

second strain remains resolutely in the tonic too after a few secondary dominants, thus the interest is mainly rhythmic, and the jest is on the slightly confused listener. The Trio straightens out the rhythmic confusion and mocks the main dance by adopting its tonal scheme and by the first violin's rigid clinging to a rapid dactylic figure on its every beat. Beethoven labored extensively on this movement to get it just the way he wanted.[67]

---

[66] Johnson, Tyson, and Winter, *The Beethoven Sketchbooks* (1985), pp. 96–100.
[67] Douglas Johnson, "Beethoven's Sketches for the Scherzo of the Quartet Op. 18, No. 6," *JAMS* 23 (1970): 385–403.

The finale begins with a surprising return to *Adagio* in 2/4 time, presumably a slow introduction to the main course. Yet it is much more than that. Violino primo announces a falling third 3 1 in dactylic rhythm (Example 7.15b). This

b. *IV*

particular descending third from D to B♭ was a main motif played by the first violin to begin the initial movement and made more prominent in the cello's response (see Example 7.14). From this recollection of how the quartet began, the first violin climbs up to the fifth degree, all over tonic harmony. On reaching F, it is preceded by a turning figure around F, also familiar from the very beginning. The second four-measure phrase repeats the first an octave lower but ends differently as the bass moves down to A, producing a first hint of minor.

Beethoven labeled the finale *La Malinconia*. With this in mind, one's first impression is that this particular melancholy results from the gentle sadness induced by a remembrance of things past. The third four-measure phrase, still *pianissimo*, goes a little further afield, as the cello sinks to G♯/A♭ supporting a diminished-seventh chord marked *crescendo*, sinks further to G, then to F♯, while the first violin pushes up to F♯, anchoring the chord of b minor in 6/4 position, again *pianissimo*. From this improbably distant chord, chaos follows in a wild series of leaps by the treble from low (*forte*) to high (*piano*), harmonized by successive diminished-seventh chords, all three of them. Gentle sadness gives way to pandemonium, a dream becomes a nightmare. *Pianissimo* returns, along with the chords in dactylic rhythm, now over a bass C, supporting another diminished chord. This resolves down to B♮, over which the harmony pauses on V⁷ of E. There is a resolution of sorts accomplished by a fugato in even quarter notes in which the first violin enters last (Example 7.15b, m. 25). Nothing in the entire set of six quartets sounds more like late Beethoven than this. The chromatic crawl initiated by the bass resumes as the treble creeps up a fourth by the quarter note beat, alternating *forte* and *piano* chords as before. The bass follows suit with a slow chromatic rise by the measure, *crescendo*, from low D up to B♭, every one of its ponderous tones preceded by the same melodic turn, which has come to sound less like an ornament than a whiplash. There is very little dominant preparation for the faster movement that follows, and lingering on the last V chord is prohibited by the direction *attacca subito*.

Allegretto quasi Allegro in 3/8 time resurrects the slightly mad 3/8 + 3/8 follies of the Scherzo, also its melodic contour of falling by step to the tonic (Example 7.15b, mm. 45ff.). Its initial skip of a sixth up and recovery by step had just been heard in the harmonically overheated fugato. The mood swing in the *Adagio* gives way to a swing in the opposite direction, toward gleeful abandon. Duets that ensue between the high instruments in thirds, mimicked by the low instruments, recall the tomfoolery of this kind just before the reprise in the first movement, and help explain the harmonic dawdling there. There is no second theme to speak of except these duets in F. After the main idea in F makes a short appearance, it returns along with the whole refrain in tonic B♭. The duets return too, now in B♭, and are followed by the main idea transformed into closing guise, working itself up in a long *crescendo* to a *fortissimo* climax on a protracted diminished-seventh chord. Instead of cadential resolution, Tempo I signals the return of the *Adagio* section, which goes through some of its motions, but it is greatly reduced in length (from 44 measures to 10) and comes to a pause on V of a. A resolution is heard in the return of the *Allegretto* (without *quasi Allegro*) in a, its initial skip of a minor 6th up and recovery further confirming its link with the fugato theme. There is an abrupt stop after four measures, then a measure of silence, followed by two measures of the *Adagio*, preparing the more hopeful key of G; the key is accepted by the *Allegretto* and soon enough transformed into a preparation for B♭, in which the refrain sounds again. An ample coda celebrates the successful outcome. The motion flags only momentarily for an intrusion of *Poco Adagio*, yet using the rondo theme, not that of the original *Adagio*. This delaying tactic is much like the braking actions applied by Haydn at the end of some of his finales. The answer is a *Prestissimo* reaffirmation of the fast theme and a headlong rush to the final chords. A greatly accelerated final statement is familiar from the double-speed Hungarian dance at the end of the Quartet in c minor, which is many times longer than this brief flurry to conclude a quartet that makes a stunning end to the set.

Symphony No. 1 in C Major

On 19 March 1800 Beethoven petitioned the directors of the court theater for permission to give a musical academy on the second of April. One day later permission was granted subject to his paying a sum of six ducats to the theater's fund for the poor.[68] So speedy a process bespeaks a friend in high places. That influential friend may have been Empress Marie Therese, whose name is prominent on the program. On 26 March the concert was announced in the *Wiener Zeitung*.

---

[68] Beethoven, *Briefwechsel*, 1:Nos. 45–46.

The Lenten season, when most concerts of this kind were given, was drawing to a close, and there was the usual rush to take advantage of the time before Holy Week and Easter, after which the theater returned to full time use for opera and other stage works. On 28 March, five days before Beethoven's concert, the benefit concert of trumpeter Anton Weidinger took place, which featured the premiere of Haydn's Trumpet Concerto in E♭, composed specifically for Weidinger. The Musicians' Society gave its two Lenten concerts in the Burgtheater on Palm Sunday and the day after, 7–8 April: a revival of *The Creation* with the same soloists as at its public premiere in the Burgtheater one year earlier. Haydn directed the performances. He remained Vienna's preeminent figure in music.

A handbill for Beethoven's concert has survived in the legacy of the widow of Beethoven's nephew.[69] It was the custom at the time to give the program in some detail on such documents, which were otherwise formulaic, as can be seen by comparing the handbill for 2 April with that of Weidinger's concert on 28 March.[70] The later document begins, in translation, "Today, Wednesday the 2nd of April 1800, in the Imperial-Royal Theater beside the Burg, Herr Ludwig van Beethoven will have the honor of giving a grand musical Academy for his benefit. The pieces to be heard are the following." The items are numbered from one to seven and the only composers represented, besides Beethoven, are Mozart and Haydn.

1. A grand symphony by the late Kapellmeister Mozart.
2. An aria from *The Creation* by Haydn, Kapellmeister of Prince Esterházy, sung by Mlle Saal.
3. A grand concerto for the Piano-Forte, played and composed by Herr Ludwig van Beethoven.
4. A Septet, most humbly and obediently dedicated to Her Majesty the Empress, and composed by Herr Ludwig van Beethoven for four stringed and three wind instruments, played by Herren Schuppanzigh, Schreiber, Schindlecker, Bär, Nickel, Matauschek, and Dietzel.
5. A Duet from Haydn's *Creation* sung by Herr and Mlle Saal.
6. Herr Ludwig van Beethoven will improvise on the Piano-Forte.
7. A new grand Symphony with full orchestra, composed by Herr Ludwig van Beethoven.
   Tickets for boxes and stalls are to be had from Herr van Beethoven at his lodging in the Tiefer Graben No. 241 on the second floor and at the box office. Prices of admission are as usual. The beginning is at half-past six o'clock.

The program is well planned to demonstrate Beethoven's skills, both as a pianist and as a composer of chamber and orchestral music. He must have been working up to it for months. The "new grand Symphony" was his Symphony No. 1 in C major, just finished.

Normally at a benefit concert the beneficiary chose the program as well as which other performers and composers would be represented. All concerts required vocal participation, preferably by soloists, in order to be successful. It

[69] Thayer-Forbes, p. 255. The original is reproduced among other places in Beethoven, *Briefwechsel*, 1:51.
[70] Reproduced in facsimile in Landon, *Haydn*, 4:229.

was wise as well as practical for the choice to fall on Herr Saal and his beautiful daughter Therese to sing excerpts from *The Creation,* which they were already
rehearsing for its revival a few days later. If Beethoven chose the opening symphony by Mozart, which one did he select?

The Mozart symphony could have been No. 36 in C, the "Linz," which fascinated Beethoven, as we have seen, or the "Jupiter," also in C, both good choices
for opening a grand event. Yet an opening symphony in this key might have
loaded the program with too heavy a dose of it. A good program was chosen
in tonal terms as carefully as Haydn planned his *Creation* and *Seasons* to avoid
too much sameness of key. Besides Symphony No. 1 in C to end the program,
recourse was had again to Piano Concerto No. 1 in C. The new Septet in E♭, Op.
20, helped the situation by its diversity of key and also by its lighter character as a
serenade-type of work in several movements for violin, viola, clarinet, horn, bassoon, cello, and contrabass. It was likely Beethoven's doing to include the names
of these individual players on the program, for he insisted on this point in a letter
of January 1801 to the soprano Christine Frank. The most traditional choice for
a concert-opening symphony was one in the most brilliant key of all, D major, a
factor that points to Mozart's "Prague" Symphony, which was also a favorite of
Beethoven's.

After the opening symphony, the program offered variety and novelty. First
it was the turn of the comely Mlle Saal. The aria she sang from *The Creation* was
likely her most substantial one, "On mighty pens," in the key of F, from Part
II. The duet with her father was, of course, that of Adam and Eve from Part III,
"Graceful consort," in E♭. Beethoven took the stage to perform as piano soloist in
his "grand Concerto," followed by the Septet he dedicated to the Empress. She
accepted the dedication of many musical works in manuscript, and doubtless
rewarded their composers well. An anomaly, on the other hand, was so prominent a mention of a dedication as the one on the printed handbill.[71] The Septet did not appear in print, with its formal dedication to her, until June or July
1802. Presumably Marie Therese was present in person at the concert, where she
would have been seated in the imperial box just above the stage, on the right side
of the hall as one faced the stage (see Figure 7.4). At benefit concerts of this kind
the orchestra played from the stage, as Michael Kelly relates in his memoirs (see
Appendix 1).

The high point of the program came at the end: Beethoven's improvisations
and his new symphony for full orchestra. There is no mention of a dedication in
the case of Symphony No. 1. In a letter the composer wrote to Hoffmeister in
June 1801, he gave a precise wording for dedicating the original edition to Elector Maximilian, who lived in quiet exile at Hetzendorf just south of Schönbrunn.

---

[71] John Rice, *Empress Marie Therese and Music at the Viennese Court, 1792–1807* (2003), p. 245.

Maximilian died on 27 June 1801 and only then did Beethoven switch the dedication to Swieten, the "patriarch of music" according to the *Jahrbuch der Tonkunst* (1796). Hoffmeister published the first edition as Op. 21 in December 1801, titled "Grande Simphonie . . . composée et dediée à Son Excellence Monsieur le Baron van Swieten Commandeur de l'ordre roy. de St. Etienne, Conseilleur intime et Bibliothécaire de sa Majesté Imp. et Roy. par Louis van Beethoven" (Figure 7.5).

An anonymous reviewer described the concert in the *Allgemeine Musikalische Zeitung.* The reviewer, who appears to have been an insider with some knowledge of the situation in the Burgtheater, implies that this was not Beethoven's first attempt to give a benefit concert there.

Finally, Herr Beethoven was able for once to obtain the use of the theater, and this was the most interesting Academy held for a long time. He played a new concerto of his own composition, which contains many beautiful things, namely the first two movements. Then a septet by him was performed; it is written with a great deal of taste and feeling. He then improvised with mastery, and at the close a symphony of his composition was performed, which revealed much art, novelty, and wealth of ideas. Only there was too much use of wind instruments, so that it was more like a Harmonie [wind band] than an orchestra.

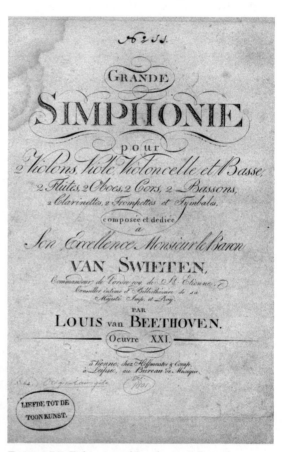

FIGURE 7.5. Title page of Beethoven's Symphony No. 1.

The reviewer called the concerto "new" although the handbill, more trustworthy, does not make this claim, whereas the symphony, which actually was new, was not so described by the reviewer. Many critical complaints before this one had been lodged about the preponderance of wind instruments in music by Mozart and Haydn. Their choice as the only composers on the program besides

Beethoven deserves comment. The typical concert brought works by several composers. Restriction to these few can be read as a signal that Beethoven ranked
himself alongside his illustrious forebears. Perhaps this very concert, Beethoven's
most important one to date, was the turning point at which the public began to
accept the notion that the three composers formed a triumvirate.

In the second part of the review, the critic noted several failings on the part
of the orchestra.

> The orchestra of the Italian Opera showed to very poor advantage. There were quar-
> rels as to who would lead it. Beethoven believed, and rightly, that rather than Herr
> [Giacomo] Conti no one could be better trusted to lead than Herr [Paul] Wranitzky.
> The gentlemen did not want to play under him. The shortcomings of this orches-
> tra noted above[72] were therefore even more evident, especially since Beethoven's
> composition is hard to play. In the accompaniments they did not take the trouble to
> consider the soloist. Of delicacy in accompanying, in following the sequence of the
> feelings of the solo player and so forth, there was not the slightest trace. In the sec-
> ond part of the symphony, they were so condescending that they did not even fol-
> low the beat, so that it was impossible to get any fire into their playing, especially in
> the woodwinds. In such cases, of what avail is their skill?—which one does not in
> the least wish to deny to the majority of the members of this group. What significant
> effect can even the most excellent composition make?

Despite all these flaws, this reviewer called the concert "the most interesting
Academy held for a long time." If the review accurately reflects the orchestra's
performance, standards at Viennese concerts had declined from those of the
previous generation, when critics such as Charles Burney, Friedrich Nicolai,
and Riesbeck marveled at the "nimbleness and precision of Viennese orchestral playing."[73]

Beethoven's sketches in "Kafka" convey the struggles he had when trying
to shape his ideas into a symphony. They show that it was to be a work in C
major and that he relied almost entirely on one-line melodic sketches on these
first attempts, which date from ca. 1795. From the beginning he intended to provide the work with a slow introduction in triple meter. After several tries, there
began to emerge an introduction that would rise from tonic C up to E, then to A.
In another attempt he added dotted rhythm linking these tones.[74] Whether he
knew it or not he was reacting to the beginning of Mozart's "Linz" Symphony,
K. 425, an *Adagio* in 3/4 time of eighteen measures (see Example 1.8). This can

[72] "Lack of goodwill, of unity, of love for the art among the members, frequently poor ensemble, etc. The
general decline since Salieri is blamed on Conti."
[73] *Haydn, Mozart*, pp. 720–21.
[74] Beethoven, *Autograph Miscellany* ["Kafka"], ed. Kerman, 2:166–68; see Kerman's "fourth attempt," p.
167.

come as no surprise since we have seen (in Example 7.3) how the *Andante* of the same symphony lingered in his mind and caused him to worry about unintended plagiarism. In general Beethoven was evidently aiming for a slow introduction less grandiose than those in Haydn's last six London symphonies or in Mozart's Symphonies No. 38 ("Prague") and No. 39 in E♭.

Another idea that appears in the several pages of jottings for the *Allegro* that was to follow the slow introduction betrays a clear anticipation of the move from tonic to supertonic that will eventually emerge in the first theme of the *Allegro con brio* of Op. 21.[75] Following this passage, which moves from I to ii, there is a passage in quarter notes that climbs upward via leaps of a fourth and descents of a third, then wider leaps until it reaches up to high E. Expanded, it will recur in the bridge of the *Allegro con brio* of Op. 21 (Example 7.16a). There is another parallel

EXAMPLE 7.16 a, b.

a. *Beethoven, Symphony No. 1 in C, I, bridge*

with Mozart here, with a work Beethoven knew well and admired, *La clemenza di Tito*, Mozart's last opera. Specifically at issue is Sesto's impassioned obbligato recitative before the ensemble and chorus that ends Act I, as he sees flames mount up and engulf the capital, with a burst of rises of a fourth and descents of a third until reaching high C (Example 7.16b).

b. *Mozart,* La clemenza di Tito, *No. 11*

Another hint of Mozart's *Tito* occurs in the first theme proper of Beethoven's *Allegro con brio*. After statement of the head motif in I and its repetition in ii, the harmony pushes in the direction of V via a progression in which the bass, descending from D to C to B♮, supports the chords ii - ii$^{\flat 6}_{4}$ - V$^{6}_{5}$. Compare this with the progression at the beginning of the *Allegro* in the Overture to *Tito* (Example 7.17ab). Mozart's last opera was very far from being forgotten at the beginning of the nineteenth century; in addition, its superb overture led an independent life of its own.

---

[75] Beethoven, *Autograph Miscellany*, Kerman's "fifth attempt," p. 168, "[Allegro]."

EXAMPLE 7.17 a, b.

a. *Mozart,* La clemenza di Tito, *Overture*

b. *Beethoven, Symphony No. 1 in C, I*

The slow introduction of Symphony No. 1 lasts only twelve measures of *Adagio molto* in common time and is seemingly unrelated to any of the attempts in "Kafka" to compose an introduction. The *Adagio* in Op. 21, though brief, offers rich materials for further use. Most fecund were the resolving seventh chords V⁷/IV - IV, V⁷ - vi, and V⁷/V - V, with treble moving up a half step in each case.[76] The *Allegro con brio* in cut time that follows profits from them and adds others. The second theme begins as a little dialogue between the first flute and first oboe, leading quickly to a reaffirmation of the new key of G, confirmed by a strong tutti passage. A rather mysterious quiet passage comes next, with minor shadings that are reminiscent of the soft bridge passage in the first movement of the Piano Sonata in C, Op. 2 No. 3, borrowed from an earlier Piano Quartet in C (see Example 7.1). Flowing eighth notes are common to both symphony and sonata passages. The closing idea is made mostly from first-theme material.

After repetition of the prima parte, the seconda parte gets under way on a long voyage around the circle of fifths; in terms of the home tonic C, V/ii, V/V, V/I - i, each chord lasting four measures. In terms of roots, these chords are A, D, and G, and the regular segments of four measures continue up a fourth or down a fifth, through C, F, and B♭. At this point the chord is protracted so as to prepare an arrival in E♭. From here the root progression slips upward by step, engendering the chords of E♭, f, and g. These too are four-measure segments that create

---

[76] See Lewis Lockwood, "Beethoven's First Symphony: A Farewell to the Eighteenth Century?" in *Essays in Musicology: A Tribute to Alvin Johnson,* ed. Lewis Lockwood and Edward Roesner (Philadelphia, 1990), pp. 235–46, which concentrates on the slow introduction and ensuing *Allegro con brio.*

the impression of too much regularity in the patterning. The harmonic rhythm doubles a few times to two measures a chord before settling on E♮, suggesting Haydn's old standby V/vi as a way of slipping without resolution directly into the reprise.[77]

Beethoven avoided going directly from V/vi to I by having the winds intone a monophonic connecting passage preparing the return by the tones of V⁷, leading to the reprise, *fortissimo*. He sensed that the movement had been so regular up to this point, monotonously so with its persistent four-measure segments, that a reprise totally regular in its order of recurring material would not be a good idea. Instead he followed the Haydn practice of drastically shortening and rewriting after the main theme. A passage of military bluster celebrating the tonic rise 1 3 5 that followed in the prima parte disappears. The bridge becomes a rapid plunge through the circle of fifths with harmony changing by the measure, and the half-tone rises in the treble extending all the way up an octave and a half. It is the closest thing this symphony has to an event of hair-raising excitement. In due order the second theme returns, adjusted to tonic C, then the mysterious soft and minor passage, followed by the closing material. A coda of ample proportions introduces more secondary dominants and their resolutions on the way to affirming once more the majesty of C major. The final rise up the tonic triad to C, then up to the third above it, then up to the fifth is already sketched in the abortive attempts at a first movement in "Kafka."[78]

To end the movement Beethoven stamped three times, as it were, with the tonic chord, then three more times, in diminution. Anyone looking for Masonic symbolism might find it here, in these three foot-stamping knocks. There was good musical precedent in Haydn, who ended every one of his six symphonies for the Masonic lodge in Paris, Nos. 82–87, with the threefold tonic chord. Beethoven finishes his first movement with twenty-two measures of tonic C major, not so many as he used to end Symphony No. 5, but still emphatic enough to shout "I am Beethoven, and no one else!" To those who would say "overemphatic" one could reply that a composer on so daunting a quest as joining his great predecessors as a symphonist deserves to be given his head.

The *Andante cantabile con moto* in 3/8 time is in the key of F, the subdominant being the most traditional choice for a work in the major mode. It begins with a point of imitation that is fugal, insofar that the second entry of the theme is a tonal answer by the violas and cellos to the theme stated by the second vio-

---

[77] For an argument supporting a direct relationship between Beethoven's development section and that in the first movement of Mozart's "Jupiter" Symphony, see Carl Schachter, "Mozart's Last and Beethoven's First: Echoes of K. 551 in the First Movement of Opus 21," in *Mozart Studies*, ed. Cliff Eisen (Oxford, 1991), pp. 227–51.

[78] Beethoven, *Autograph Miscellany*, 2:171, middle. In this case the ascents are accomplished by runs up the scale, which relate this passage as well to the finales of Op. 21 and of Piano Concerto No. 1 in C, Op. 15.

lins. There is a resemblance to the imitative beginning of the finale in the Piano Sonata in F, Op. 10 No. 2, which also starts with the leap of a fourth from C up to F. Neither movement remains imitative for long before turning homophonic, which this *Andante* does by the time the first violins enter, stating the subject or first theme. It is in sonata form with the prima parte repeated, as in the preceding *Allegro*. The flutes are reduced from two to one, otherwise the full complement of winds returns, including trumpets in C and timpani (C and G), which softly sound pedal tones on C or G. Their use in a slow movement was not common before Mozart and in particular, the timpani's prominent G in rapid dotted rhythms at the end of the prima parte (C in the reprise) points to the *Andante* of the "Linz" Symphony. Before settling on this rumbling timpani pedal, Beethoven includes a passage of secondary dominants at the end of both parts with the trebles rising by half steps, linking this movement with the previous one. It shows how intent the composer was on integrating movements motivically and harmonically, as was often the case with Haydn and Mozart. Berlioz detected in Beethoven's First Symphony "the influence of Mozart, whose ideas he sometimes enlarges, and everywhere imitates with ingenuity."[79] The seconda parte begins by turning the head motif into a statement in c minor, which gives way quickly to D♭ and the dotted rhythms in the strings doubled by the second bassoon, getting the development under way. At the reprise, the imitative treatment of the main theme gains a countersubject in running-sixteenth notes. A nice touch is added by having the two horns in F play the head motif on the third statement of the theme. They also play a prominent part in the coda.

Minuetto Allegro molto e vivace is a real scherzo at a very fast tempo. Beethoven later suggested for it a metronome speed of 118 to the measure of 3/4 time. Did he intend the minuet designation as a joke? He used the same tempo, *Allegro molto e vivace*, for the third movement in 6/8 time of the String Trio in c minor, Op. 9 No. 3, but that he called a Scherzo. In the String Quartets Op. 18, the third movements are marked *Allegro* or *Allegro molto* and designated Scherzo, with the exception of No. 3 in D, which is labeled simply *Allegro*, and No. 5 in A, which is a second-movement Menuetto (after K. 464 by Mozart). Beethoven continued to insert true minuets in several works from this early period, in fact he never gave up the moderate-paced minuet altogether. Haydn had preceded him in requiring some dance movements to be greatly speeded up, such as *Menuet Presto* in his String Quartet in G, Op. 76 No. 1, of 1797, and in his last two completed string quartets, Op. 77. This symphonic minuet, or scherzo, commences by unfolding the rising scale of C major, beginning on the fifth below the tonic and climbing all the way up to high D. It took up the entire first strain, which may be intended

[79] Hector Berlioz, *A travers chants* (Paris, 1862), trans. Ralph de Sola, in *Beethoven by Berlioz: A Critical Appreciation of Beethoven's Nine Symphonies . . .* (Boston, 1975), p. 13.

as another joke. The rising scale of G had already been planted at the end of the slow introduction, prominently placed as the link leading to the *Allegro*. A scant eight measures (first strain) are expanded many times over in the second strain, which goes on some charmingly zany adventures, such as the one that lands it as far away as possible, in the key of D♭, then slinks back to tonic C major by way of soft half-tone rises. The Trio remains in C major and exploits a dialogue between winds softly stating chords and violins issuing flurries of eighth-note passage-work. First in I, then in ii, the chords recall the juxtaposition of these two tonalities so important to the *Allegro con brio*.

The Finale is in 2/4 time, preceded by an *Adagio* of five and a half measures that begins with a prolonged unison G tutti, *fortissimo*. If this sounds familiar it is meant to, for it takes us back to the initial *Adagio*, the first tonal goal of which was a loud chord on G. From this point of departure in the finale, the first violins alone announce the beginnings of a scale rising up from G, tentatively; first only three tones, then adding one more tone to each rise, separated by rests, until there is nearly a complete scale from G to G, ending on F♮, which is prolonged by a fermata. Then comes the complete octave scale from G to G that starts the *Allegro molto e vivace*. The maneuver was compared by Tovey to letting a cat out of a bag. In this case it was stage by stage—first a paw, then a head, etc., etc., until the whole cat is present, tail and all. One's reaction can waver between "how clever!" and "terminally cute!"

The first theme itself sounds like something Haydn might have invented. It has the folklike lilt and repeated-tone patter of many a rondo theme by Haydn. Sonata form more than rondo shapes the finale. Its ties with the first movement emerge also in the theme's prominent V/ii - ii. The second theme is as perky as the first. Scalar motion rising comes back to end the prima parte, after having served in the bridge as descending passages. Repeat of the prima parte is followed by more scalar rises, deflecting the harmony to B♭, initiating a rather routine development. Rising and descending scales are heard against each other, and the rising ones acquire parallel thirds, a move adumbrated in "Kafka." The reprise is regular, except that the second theme first appears in F, then readjusts itself into C major (a subdominant substitution, and not uncommon). When Beethoven halts the movement briefly with two unstable chords protracted by fermatas, a diminished-seventh chord built up over F♯, then V$^6_5$, he is following one of Haydn's signature moves. The coda that ensues rings a few more changes on the material already heard until a march-like concluding section starts in the winds. On come the rising and falling scales in thirds for a final surge. The last gestures are scales leading up to the triumph of 1 3 5 on high, followed by a tumble down to C and the final chords, much like the ending of the *Allegro con brio*.

The symphony as a whole does not reach the level of Haydn and Mozart at their best. All praise to Beethoven, nevertheless, for having the courage to essay a genre that did not come easily to him, and to persevere over four or five years until he was ready to brave public appearance as a symphonist. The work's expanded sonorities and boisterous climaxes swept most but not all auditors off their feet.

An astute judge of Op. 21 was Brahms, who at the end of his life confided these thoughts about it and the Piano Concerto in c minor to a friend.

> Yes, the C minor [Mozart] Concerto: a marvelous work of art and filled with inspired ideas! I also find that, for example, Beethoven's C minor Concerto is much smaller and weaker than Mozart's . . . I admit that the Beethoven concerto is more modern, but it is not as significant! I also see that Beethoven's First Symphony seemed so colossal to its first audiences. It has indeed a new viewpoint! But the last three Mozart symphonies are much more significant. Now and then people realize that this is so.[80]

His interlocutor pursued the argument further by positing the superiority of Mozart's best string quartets over Beethoven's chamber music up to Opus 24, the "Spring" Sonata. Brahms agreed, "Yes, the Razumovsky quartets, the later symphonies, that is another world. One can feel it already in the Second Symphony."

The Creatures of Prometheus

Ballet had been a central feature of entertainments in Vienna's court theaters for several generations before Beethoven's arrival. During the reign of Maria Theresa, full-length ballets independent of opera flourished in the Burgtheater under great choreographers such as Angiolini and Noverre, some of them composed by Gluck.[81] Joseph II suppressed ballet in the 1780s but it was restored by Leopold II and enjoyed a new flourishing in the 1790s, capped by the work of the ballet master and choreographer Salvatore Viganò. The Viganòs were one of several dynasties in the world of dance. Salvatore's father, Onorato, had danced in *Don Juan* (1761) by Angiolini and Gluck; his mother, Maria Ester Boccherini, was *première danseuse* of the troupe in the Burgtheater at that time, before her marriage to Viganò. Salvatore was born at Naples on 25 March 1769, where his parents went to participate in festivities surrounding the marriage of Archduchess Maria Carolina with King Ferdinand of Naples in 1768. He is said to have been taught

[80] Richard Heuberger, *Erinnerungen an Johannes Brahms,* 2nd ed., ed. Kurt Hofmann (Tutzing, 1976), p. 93, cited after Lockwood, *Beethoven* (2003), p. 175.
[81] *Haydn, Mozart,* pp. 179–88, a subject treated more extensively in Bruce Alan Brown, *Gluck and the French Theater in Vienna* (Oxford, 1991), ch. 8.

music by his famous uncle Luigi Boccherini, yet this seems unlikely since the young dancer did not go to Spain until 1789. There he married a Spanish ballerina, Maria Medina. During a very well-paid season as first dancers of the Viennese court in 1794–95, this young couple danced a celebrated fandango during a masked ball in the court theater.[82]

Beethoven was then in Vienna and could have witnessed the event. He had links with the ballet going back to his last years in Bonn, when he composed music for a "Ritterballett," WoO 1. In Vienna this interest showed itself in his selections of music from ballets for themes on which to write keyboard variations. His variations on a "Menuett à la Vigano," WoO 68, has a theme from the ballet *Le nozze disturbate*, music by Jakob Haibel. He wrote variations on a Russian dance from the ballet *Das Waldmädchen*, WoO 71, composed by Paul Wranitzky. After touring widely, Salvatore Viganò returned to Vienna in 1799 as one of two ballet masters at the court theater, with responsibility for staging a new work annually. His Prometheus ballet was the third in this series. It was intended to pay compliment to Empress Marie Therese, who was responsible for Beethoven's being invited to compose the music.[83] Writing the ballet score occupied him intensely in early 1801. The premiere took place in the Burgtheater on 28 March 1801 as a benefit for prima ballerina Maria Casentini.

The ballet, entitled *Die Geschöpfe des Prometheus*, was a "heroic-allegorical" work, according to the handbill. At least, its first act was heroic and a true *ballet en action*. This part was short, compared with the long and allegorical Act II. After the powerful overture, cleverly extracted from the first movement of Symphony No. 1, there comes "Una Tempesta," an agitated piece during which Prometheus flees the wrath of Zeus for having stolen fire from the gods. He takes shelter in a secluded spot, where there are statues of the first man and first woman. He touches them with his torch and they slowly come to life by taking hesitant steps to the alternating *Adagio* and *Allegro* passages of No. 1. They lack all emotion, much to the disappointment of Prometheus, who berates them in No. 2. In No. 3, his anger assuaged, he resolves to take them to Parnassus so that they may be inspired by the arts to a higher consciousness. Sketches for these sections show that Beethoven had in hand both a German and an Italian scenario.[84]

Act II (Nos. 4–16) takes place entirely on Mount Parnassus. It is more pageant than action ballet. The denizens of Parnassus, Apollo and the Nine Muses, the Three Graces, three bards of antiquity—Orpheus, Amphion, Arion—plus other worthies from antique myth appear, including the non-Parnassian Pan and Bacchus.

---

[82] Rice, *Salieri*, pp. 154–55. For the payment record of their salaries see Link, *The National Court Theatre*, p. 444. The couple mostly went their separate ways after this season.

[83] Rice, *Empress Marie Therese*, pp. 248–52.

[84] Gustav Nottebohm, *Zweite Beethoveniana* (Leipzig, 1887), pp. 246–49.

The ballet's plot has been pieced together from diverse sources only in recent times (the original scenario is lost).[85] Viennese audiences initially applauded the work. It received many performances in 1801 and 1802, then disappeared. In comparison with Viganò's most successful creations it was only a modest success. Later, for Milan, he compiled a much longer *Prometeo*, using more of the mythic tale and some of Beethoven's music. The composer himself wrote Hoffmeister on 22 April 1801, "I have made a ballet, but the ballet master did not make the very best of his end of the job."

The procession of wonders and worthies in Act II does, in fact, seem arbitrary. On the other hand, the music is often thrilling, and some of it caught on with the general public in concerts. Beethoven's brother Carl, in a letter to Breitkopf and Härtel dated Vienna 22 January 1803, states that the Overture, Nos. 8, 10, and 16 were often heard at the Augarten concerts. These are the big set pieces of the score. No. 8 is an impressive rondo in martial style, an *Allegro con brio* in common time and in D of 244 measures, a "Danza eroica" executed by Bacchus and the Bacchantes. It is begun by a blazing timpani solo alternating tones 8 and 5, an anticipation of the soft timpani solo in Beethoven's Symphony No. 4, Op. 60. No. 10 is a lovely Pastorale, *Allegro* in 6/8 time and in C major, bedecked with drones and other rustic effects, danced by the god Pan and his followers. No. 16 is the great *Finale. Allegretto* in 2/4 time and in E♭, built upon the composer's favorite dance tune, appearing earlier in the Twelve Contredanses for Orchestra, WoO 14, as No. 7; an episode in G major in the Finale uses No. 11 from these Contredanses. Beethoven also used the dance in E♭ as the subject of his admirable Piano Variations, Op. 35, and lastly for the glorious finale of the Eroica Symphony Op. 55. Opp. 35 and 55 take more than just the theme from the ballet's Finale. On stage this Finale represented festive dances in honor of Prometheus (and by extension of Marie Therese). Its last section was speeded up to *Allegro molto* in cut time and is very like the climactic moments of an opera buffa finale.

Beethoven took care to make tonal connections between the numbers of his score so that the musical effect is less of a hodgepodge than might have emerged from the requirement to string together so many disparate pieces. For example, he connected the end of the overture, in C, to the *Introduzione* by having the horns prolong a soft C into the beginning of the storm and becoming the third of the chord of A♭. This harmonic motion was something like a personal signature with the composer, used famously to begin the slow movement of the *Sonate pathétique*, Op. 13, in c minor and in other works, notably the Violin and Piano Sonata in c minor, Op. 30 No. 2. The three numbers of Act I are in C, F/d minor, with tran-

[85] Constatin Floros, *Beethovens Eroica und Prometheus-Musik* (Wilhelmshaven, 1978), pp. 49–72. There is a valuable essay by the dance historian Stanley Applebaum that introduces the Dover Edition of Beethoven's score (2000).

sition at the end to prepare for the return of F for No. 3. The overall tonal thrust from C to F as from a dominant to a tonic helps make this an easily sensed continuity from the beginning of the overture with V$^6_2$ of F to the closure of Act I in F. Act II with its many dances required a wider variety of keys. It begins in D, with No. 4, and returns to D in the huge "Danza Eroica" of No. 8. The succeeding numbers slip back to C until No. 13, in D, which is the Terzettino for the Grotteschi, a comic dance with abundant accents on weak beats and a folk-song character.

The last three numbers are, from the point of view of the spectacle, the most important of all. For them Beethoven chooses F, B♭, and the long-lasting E♭ of the finale. No. 14 in F is the big solo for the celebrated Signora Casentini, playing the first woman created. It begins with an *Andante* in common time, then switches to an *Adagio* in 3/8 time in which the solo basset horn sings the melody (Example 7.18). When this soloist starts playing triplets to accompany the oboe, some in that

EXAMPLE 7.18. *Beethoven*, The Creatures of Prometheus, *No. 14*

Burgtheater audience surely must have realized that it sounded very like the basset horn solo, *Larghetto* in 3/8 time and in F for Anton Stadler in Vitellia's Rondò, "Non più di fiori," No. 23 in Mozart's *Tito*. Did Stadler himself, who still played in the opera orchestra, take on this basset horn solo in 1801, ten years after *Tito*? The penultimate number in B♭ was a solo for Viganò, in the role of the first man. It was another long, multi-tempo piece, with elaborate concertante parts for clarinet and bassoon, beginning with a passage of fifteen measures during which F is transformed from I to V. The stage is thus set tonally for resolution from B♭, as V, to E♭ for the superb Finale.

An anonymous reviewer in the Viennese journal *Zeitung für die elegante Welt* for 19 May 1801 recapitulated the plot from the lost printed scenario and had this to say, after complaining that La Casentini was not given more opportunities to show her great talents.

> The music did not entirely correspond to hopes either, although it possesses more than ordinary merits. I shall leave undecided whether Herr van Beethoven could achieve what a public such as ours wanted based on such a uniform, not to say monotonous, plot. There is scarcely any doubt that, for a ballet, he wrote music that is too learned and pays insufficient attention to dance. All is laid out too grandly for a divertissement, which is what a ballet should be after all, and fell short of conforming

to the evolving situations; it remains more of a work in fragments than a whole. This began already with the Overture. With every large work an overture has its place and will not fail to make an important effect; but here it was out of place. The solo of Mlle Casentini [No. 14] and the martial dances [No. 8] are where the composer came off the best. One will find in the Dance of Pan [No. 10] reminiscences from other ballets. Yet Herr van Beethoven succeeds to the extent that only his detractors could deny him a truly superior originality, by means of which, admittedly, he often deprived his audience of the charms of soft, pleasing harmonies.[86]

A barbed compliment like the last infers that the critic was more at ease with the pleasant harmonies and less challenging music of a Jakob Haibel or a Paul Wranitzky. In this regard, the reviewer probably spoke for the great majority of ballet lovers.

The most interesting piece of all is the overture, or as Beethoven called it, using the original French spelling also favored by Mozart, *Ouverture*. It is more than just a digest or reformulation of the slow introduction and first *Allegro* of Op. 21. The slow introduction remains as an idea but is switched from duple to triple time. It begins not with a V^7/IV chord resolving softly to IV but with the much bolder stroke of a V^7 chord, *fortissimo*, in third inversion with the seventh in the bass crying out for resolution, V^6_2/IV - IV^6_3. The bass B♭ plunges down a further step to A♭, over which a resounding augmented chord is erected, resolving to V, as the bass descends to G. This tumultuous beginning sounds more like the robust Beethoven of Symphony No. 2 than does the milder-mannered *Adagio* of Op. 21. The same is true of what follows in the overture, a broad hymnic theme in C major softly stated by the strings, doubled by the oboes and horns. The *Allegro molto con brio* begins by following the same harmonic trajectory as found in Op. 21 but does so in running eighth notes, which give the material a more urgent character. Arrival at G for the second theme brings a less contrapuntal idea than that in Op. 21, one that rises up the triad in thirds from D to D, in which respect it resembles the second theme of the overture to *Tito*, with which there is also a similarity in the scoring for high winds. Beethoven's overture is often described as being in sonata form, yet it is far from a regular example of it. There is no repetition of the prima parte, and at the point where the seconda parte begins, the first theme, abbreviated, returns in tonic C major, leading to a short development followed by a reprise that begins not with the first theme but with the second (another point in common with the overture to *Tito*). The overall impression left by the overture is that Beethoven has tightened his material, given it more dramatic impact, and overcome the rather cut-and-dried effect of the first movement of Op. 21.

Beethoven was always laying plans to write for the theater, the operatic stage

---

[86] Floros, *Beethovens Eroica und Prometheus-Musik*, pp. 38–39.

in particular, as his ongoing study with Salieri of Italian text setting confirms. He had long been composing individual arias and songs in both German and Italian. In early 1803 he began work on Schikaneder's libretto "Vestas Feuer." He even moved into the new Theater an der Wien as part of the commission for this work. He soon abandoned the project as an unsuitable subject and turned to large instrumental works such as the "Eroica" Symphony and the "Waldstein" Sonata, Op. 53.

Prometheus caught and enhanced the dramatic fire of which Beethoven was capable. It emboldened him to attempt more daring orchestral feats in Symphony No. 2. Also, experience in theater helped him when he returned to the dramatic stage with his *Leonore* in subsequent years, written in response to the Viennese craze for French rescue operas, especially those by Cherubini.[87] Eventually he would bend the operatic genre to his will, as he did every other genre.

An elaborately scored ballet lacked the appeal of symphonies and concertos for amateur orchestras. Little was to be gained from bringing it out in orchestral parts or in score, but Artaria quickly seized the opportunity to publish a keyboard arrangement, said to be by the composer himself. It appeared in June 1801, entitled *Gli Uomini di Prometeo. Ballo per il Clavicembalo o Piano-Forte. Composto e dedicato a Sua Altezza la Signora Principessa Lichnowsky nata Contessa Thun da Luigi van Beethoven. Opera 24.* After it was realized that Opus 24 had already been assigned by Mollo to the "Spring" Sonata, the keyboard arrangement became Opus 43. Beethoven obviously remained a favorite son of the Lichnowskys and he continued to be indebted to them for many favors. In 1800 they granted him an annuity of 600 florins until he could find a suitable position. To the list of several works dedicated to Prince Lichnowsky he later added Symphony No. 2, published in 1804.

The Year 1802

Beethoven completed his second symphony and Haydn his last mass during 1802, a year of uneasy peace throughout Europe. Napoleon as First Consul of the French Republic had negotiated a concordat with the Vatican promoting a return to the status quo ante relative to affairs between church and state, solemnly promulgated on Easter. The same month, in a letter from Vienna dated 8 April 1802 that Beethoven wrote to his publishers Hoffmeister and Kühnel in Leipzig, he demonstrated how well he kept abreast of current affairs in politics, also how receptive he was to the idea of composing music that would reflect political ferment. The letter began jocularly, with ridicule of a proposal to do just this, then switched to admitting he might accept the idea—for the right price. The publish-

---

[87] Rice, *Salieri*, pp. 565–67, "French Opera in Vienna."

ers proposed that, at the request of an unidentified lady, he write a sonata that would celebrate the French Revolution. She had gone so far as to specify its contents, even the keys to be used. Beethoven replied with the mordant wit sometimes called his "unbuttoned" humor:

> Has the devil got hold of you all gentlemen? You propose that I should write such a Sonata? At the time of the Revolutionary fever maybe that might have been possible, but now, when everything is trying to slip back into the same old rut, now that Bonaparte has concluded his concordat with the Pope, such a Sonata? If it were a *Missa pro sancta maria a tre vocis* or a Vesper, etc, then I would take brush in hand at once, and write a *Credo in unum* with huge pound notes—but Good Lord! such a Sonata in these newfangled Christian times? Ho, ho, there you must leave me out, nothing will come of it. Now in the fastest tempo my answer: the lady can have a Sonata by me, and I am willing to follow her plan as to aesthetic ideas, only without the key scheme. The price is about 50 ducats.

This price for a sonata was so high that the publishers asked their Viennese business partner twice if the composer did not mean 30 ducats.[88] Beethoven drove such a hard bargain it might be doubted that he was serious about accepting the commission. In the same letter he continued by laying down his conditions:

> For that sum she may keep the sonata for her own enjoyment for one year, and neither she nor I will be entitled to publish. After that year is over the sonata will remain exclusively my property, which is to say that I can and will publish it. She can, if she thinks it will do her any honor, request that I dedicate it to her [for an additional sum, it goes without saying].

For his publishers he had a few acerbic remarks about their slowness in bringing out the Sonata in B♭, Op. 22, and the Septet, Op. 20:

> My Sonata is beautifully engraved but you took your sweet time publishing it. Send my Septet into the world a little more quickly, for the rabble [der Pöbel] are impatiently waiting for it, and as you know the Empress has it—and there are scoundrels in the Imperial City just as there are at the Imperial Court. I guarantee you nothing, so make haste.

There followed a complaint about the errors of every sort made in Mollo's engraving of the Op. 18 String Quartets. In a pun on the expression "to engrave" (stechen), Beethoven ended his letter: "I call that *stechen* in truth because my skin is entirely full of pinpricks and fissures."

---

[88] Beethoven, *Briefwechsel Gesamtsausgabe*, 1:106, n. 4.

Beethoven rarely wrote anything touching politics, perhaps because of the prying eyes of the police. His remark about scoundrels in high places is an exception. As for his seeming willingness to write a sonata celebrating the Revolution, it was at least safer to make such a remark in peacetime than in wartime. The composer in any case had been toying with the idea of writing a work about Bonaparte, and dedicated to him. His *Prometheus* already suggested Bonaparte to the minds of people who regarded Napoleon as the Prometheus of the present, a liberator of mankind.[89]

Extra-musical ideas were more common in instrumental music ca. 1800 than was generally admitted by later proponents of "pure" or "absolute" music. Beethoven may have already taken a step in celebrating the Revolution with his "Marcia funebre sulla morte d'un Eroe" in the Sonata in A♭, Op. 26, first published in March 1802. We have seen how the tomb scene in *Romeo and Juliet* was associated with the *Adagio* in d minor of the String Quartet in F, Op. 18 No. 1. The piano sonata in particular led the way to highly charged, message- or image-laden compositions. *Sonata quasi una Fantasia* in c♯, Op. 27 No. 2, subsequently dubbed "Moonlight Sonata," and dedicated to a young lady with whom the composer claimed a romantic liaison, oversteps previous boundaries in both form and content. The Sonata in D, Op. 28, labeled "Pastorale" soon after first publication, anticipates in some respects Symphony No. 6 in F, Op. 68, first published as *Sinfonia Pastorale*, with pertinent titles and descriptions for each of its movements. The "Spring" Sonata in F, Op. 24, generally regarded as a pivotal work both for its excellence and its suggestive, nature-painting qualities, could be considered a preliminary study for the "Scene by the brook" movement of the Pastoral Symphony. As for that Symphony's storm movement, there were parallels in *Prometheus* and in the superb tempest that serves as a finale of the String Quintet in C, Op. 29. In sum, the amount of referential content in the works from Op. 18 to Op. 29, all completed by the end of 1801, was clearly increasing. Thus it is not so surprising that Beethoven appeared ready to compose a work that related to the French Revolution. Hopes were widespread in 1802 that the long period of nearly incessant warfare was over. Gains and losses in the wake of the Revolution could be viewed with more equanimity.

The best of several early portraits of Beethoven was painted by the skilled Danish artist Christian Horneman in 1802 (Figure 7.6). It is a miniature on ivory that the composer ordered to give to his intimate friend Stephan von Breuning.[90]

---

[89] According to Floros, *Beethovens Eroica und Prometheus-Musik*, pp. 45–48, Viganò cited as one of the sources for his *Prometeo* ballet the epic poem *Prometeo* (1797) by Vincenzo Monti, in which Napoleon was hailed as the liberator of Italy.

[90] Peter Clive, *Beethoven and His World: A Biographical Dictionary* (Oxford, 2001), p. 170. Horneman (1765–1844), after study in Copenhagen and in Italy, worked in Germany and Austria. He spent the years 1798–1802 in Vienna.

FIGURE 7.6. Christian Horneman.
Miniature portrait of Beethoven, 1802.

In it Beethoven retains a quite youthful appearance and wears his fine attire with a sense of ease. Particularly striking are his dark hair, eyebrows, and eyes. In the colored original, his eyes are just as dark as his hair, while his coat is of a very deep blue. The fabric of his neckerchief is a luminous white that sets off his pink skin and makes dark areas seem even darker. Horneman chose to place his subject against a slate gray background with a slight lightening effect on the left side of Beethoven's face. He gives Beethoven the air of a fashionable young gentleman, even a nobleman. In Vienna at this time many older gentlemen—and not just Haydn— still wore wigs. Young men on the contrary wore neither wigs, nor powdered hair, nor any other kind of fancy hairdo. Beethoven's locks are shown in their natural state, slightly disheveled, but in an artistic manner. This fashion was considered to be a legacy of Roman antiquity and was even known as "coiffure à la Tito." Horneman manages to lend Beethoven both a sense of ease and a look of determination. The latter matches well with what we know of his iron will to succeed against all odds. He often made life difficult for his closest friends, including Stephan von Breuning, who was four years younger. After a violent quarrel, the two reconciled. In early November 1804 Beethoven wrote his friend, "I know that I tore your heart apart, but the torment within me, which you must have noticed, has sufficiently punished me for that . . . My portrait has long been intended for you."

Torment and serenity alternated in other ways regarding Beethoven. He put the finishing touches on his second symphony during the summer and early fall of 1802 while residing at a cottage in the country. It was located near the village of Heiligenstadt, just north of Vienna, on a stream, the Nestlbach, that flowed from the base of the Kahlenberg to the Danube (see Figure 1.1). At the same time he was finishing two sets of three sonatas apiece, Op. 30 for violin and piano, and Op. 31 for piano solo. Op. 30 No. 2 in c minor is particularly memorable as one of the master's most fiery and concentrated works in this favorite key of his—both outer movements end resolutely in the minor. This side of the composer's musical personality we can align most readily with the Heiligenstadt Testament, his long statement of 1802 expressing torment at the thought of losing his hearing.

The Sonatas of Op. 31 are so individual and innovative that each seems like a little world unto itself.[91] No. 1 in G is high comedy from the start as right and left hands struggle to get their act together. No. 2 in d minor, the "Tempest" Sonata, begins with a slowly unfolding arpeggiated V^6 chord such as might precede the entry of a vocal soloist launching into a recitative. An actual recitative occurs when this chord returns to usher in the reprise, thus confirming the operatic content implied from the beginning. Instrumental recitative was quite frequent in the works of Haydn and Mozart, but this may be its first appearance in a solo sonata within the Viennese School. The theme of the "Tempest" Sonata's finale repeats a leap from the fifth below the tonic up to a third above it then descent by step, 5 ↑ 3 2 1, an idea that is also prominent in the first movement of Mozart's String Quintet in g minor, K. 516 (see example 2.12a, p. 179, m. 30). Sonata No. 3 in E♭ puzzles the ear with a non-tonic beginning, a ii$^6_5$ chord sounding as if we had landed in the middle of a discourse instead of its beginning. Such an opening has to be explained and resolved, and eventually it is. Each of the three sonatas is boldly idiosyncratic, looking more to the future than to the past.

Symphony No. 2 in D Major

Symphony No. 2, Op. 36, is the main fruit of Beethoven's labors in 1801–2 and is considered to be the culminating success of his early period. It proceeded from sketch to draft to finished product with more ease than did Symphony No. 1, partly because the composer felt more at home with the genre after Op. 21 and with orchestral innovations in general after *Prometheus*. Initially he planned the work looking forward to another benefit concert in the Burgtheater to follow, a year after the first one in 1800. The commission to supply the music for a full-length ballet intervened and occupied him intensely in early 1801, after he had already begun the Symphony in D. He recommenced work on the symphony with a view to having it ready for a concert in the court theater during Lent 1802. This did not happen because of a quarrel he had with the vice-director of the Burgtheater, Baron Peter von Braun (to whose wife Josephine, perhaps a pupil, he had dedicated the Sonatas of Op. 14 and the Sonata in F for Piano and Horn, Op. 17). The premiere did not take place until the following Lenten season of 1803, not in the Burgtheater but in the new Theater an der Wien, which was opened on 13 June 1801 under the direction of Emanuel Schikaneder. It was a benefit concert for Beethoven on 5 April 1803 and also included his hastily composed short oratorio *Christus am Ölberge*. The first public performance of Piano Concerto No. 3 in c minor took place then as well.[92]

We have contended that Beethoven's attempts to create a symphonic work in

---

[91] For a telling commentary on the Op. 31 Sonatas, see William Kinderman, *Beethoven* (Berkeley, 1995), pp. 74–79.

[92] As argued persuasively by Leon Plantinga, *Beethoven's Concertos: History, Style, Performance* (New York, 1999), chaps. 6 and 7.

C major with slow introduction bore hints in the sketches that Mozart's "Linz" Symphony in C major was in the back of his mind. The longer slow introduction to Symphony No. 2 in D shows evident signs of inspiration from Mozart's "Prague" Symphony in D, K. 504. An *Adagio* in common time of thirty-six measures opens K. 504, with moments of dark foreboding, such as the outburst of d minor midspan. The discussion of it above in chapter 2 focused on points of contact with the Overture to *Don Giovanni*, composed less than a year later, residing particularly in the sharply etched dynamic alterations between loud and soft, also in certain chromatic rises of the bass common to both. Beethoven's mind, it seems, was not on the Overture but on the slow introduction of Mozart's Symphony. Two dramatic tonal arrivals remain in the ear as a kind of map to Mozart's introduction: that of d minor suddenly taking over from D major, and, as a release from the grip of d minor, the arrival of B♭ major and its subsequent tonicization. Beethoven's *Adagio molto* in 3/4 time comes down to the same two main events, only in reverse order: first the arrival with a jolt of B♭ major, also tonicized at length, and only later, after a little tonal tour ending with a chromatically rising bass line, the return of tonic D. Only, at the most climactic moment, it is not D major, but d minor that sounds out forcefully with a descending tonic triad in dotted rhythm, a moment of tempestuous fury, tutti *unisono* and *fortissimo*. Beethoven's unleashing the full power of the orchestra here gives a hint of what is to come much later in his Symphony No. 9 in d. This startling eruption of another, darker realm lasts but a moment, and then it is gradually back to the celebration of D major, yet it is unforgettable. Both slow introductions end with the customary wait on the dominant pedal to increase expectations of a tonic arrival for the beginning of the *Allegro*.

The instrumentation of K. 504 and of Op. 36 is nearly identical: pairs of flutes, oboes, horns in D, trumpets in D, and timpani on D and A, plus the usual strings. The only difference is that Beethoven adds two clarinets in A that play in all four movements. From the very first sounds there is a tiny difference that matters. Mozart begins on the downbeat with his unison D. Beethoven precedes his unison D with a sixty-fourth note upbeat that makes his downbeat more emphatic and sharply etched. It also prefigures the powerful effect that dotted rhythm, in combination with d minor, will have toward the end of the *Adagio* in the passage just mentioned.

The slow introduction to Op. 36 evolved by way of sketches that show it was not always conceived in triple meter. In the sketchbook known as Landsberg 7 (p. 44), Beethoven experimented with a beginning in duple meter, involving a rise in the treble up the tonic triad to F♯, then a plunge down nearly two octaves to a low A♯ resolving up to B (Example 7.19a).[93] K. 504 was clearly the inspiration for

---

[93] Roger Kamien, "The Slow Introduction to Mozart's Symphony No. 38 in D, K. 504 ('Prague'): A Possible Model for the Slow Introduction of Beethoven's Symphony No. 2 in D, Op. 36," *Israel Studies in Musicology* 5 (1990): 113–30; 116.

both the triadic rise and the plunge to a non-harmonic tone in the bass (Example 7.19b). Mozart brought the winds in over his A♯ low in the strings, and their tones

EXAMPLE 7.19 a, b.

a. *Beethoven, Sketch for beginning of Symphony No. 2*

b. *Mozart, Symphony in D, K. 503, "Prague," I*

completed the chord of V⁶₃/vi with F♯ on top. Thus we have specific evidence, beyond the rather general impressions of similarity between the two introductions already discussed, of a precise modeling at one early stage of composition. The "Prague" Symphony was just too well known, especially in Vienna and Prague, for Beethoven to get away with so blatant a borrowing. Another case of "stolen from Mozart," as he himself noted in "Kafka" with reference to a passage from the "Linz" Symphony, this one would have been noticed unless he covered his tracks and tried another beginning. The prominent V⁶₅/vi with resolution to vi remains in his finished version but it comes in only after the first eight-measure phase that gave him a more lyrical beginning, worked out in triple meter.

The loud unison or chordal tonic followed by a soft lyrical melody to begin a slow introduction is an idea that comes not from Mozart's symphonies but from Haydn's. There are such beginnings for example in Symphony No. 99 in E♭ and Symphony No. 102 in B♭ from the second set of London works, and before them in Symphony No. 93 in D from the first set. The last-named is particularly suggestive because it begins, after the *fortissimo* unisons, with a soft melody in the violins, the first tone of which is the third, F♯ (it was the third that began the melody also in Symphony No. 99). In Symphony No. 94 in G ("Surprise"), the first surprise is that there is no loud outburst before the winds all by themselves commence with a lyrical passage. Thus Beethoven's giving the unaccompanied oboes and bassoons their chance to sing so melodiously was not without precedent.

The melodic line was still more important to Haydn, Mozart, and Beethoven than any other factor, whether rhythmic, harmonic, or contrapuntal, even in their symphonies. One need only look at their sketches to see that they were overwhelmingly concerned with the melodic line first of all. The melody that Beethoven has his first oboe sing at the beginning of the *Adagio,* using the first half of an antecedent-consequent phrase, sounds so sweet and simple with its 3 2 1 melodic motion (against 1 2 3 in the bass) that it might be judged of little consequence. On the contrary, its conjunct melodic motion within the first five tones above the tonic are stamped one way or another on the principal idea of every movement, as shown by their incipits (Example 7.20). The *Allegro con brio* stretches

EXAMPLE 7.20. *Beethoven, Symphony No. 2 in D, Incipits*

the tones 1 2 3 out by following them with 3 4 5. The Larghetto, not cited, exploits the sweetness of the third degree and explores its role in the conjunct descending motion from the fifth degree. The Scherzo and Trio get back to the basics of 3 2 1 and 1 2 3. The Allegro molto makes a raucous jest to begin, then softly rises up by step from the tonic, and then moves back down.

The *Allegro con brio*, pushed along by its many upbeat patterns, sounds as if it is in a great hurry to reach wherever it is going. Just before the bridge passage there is a succession in which the heavily accented chords of d minor give way to B♭ major, the same succession as in the *Adagio* of K. 504. When the second theme does arrive, properly placed in the key of A, it ascends the triad of the new tonic until reaching the fifth, an outline similar to the second theme in the Overture to *Prometheus*, which had its own parallels with Mozart's Overture to *Tito*. It is answered in the *Allegro con brio* with a furious outburst of f♯ minor. The role of this tone and triad is strong throughout the symphony and calls for attention. Before the final cadences in the new key there is a passage in which the massed winds on the offbeat answer the multiple-stopped strings on the downbeat, a rapid exchange that is similar to one in the *Allegro con brio* in D, No. 8, in *Prometheus*. After the prima parte is repeated the seconda parte, beginning with the main theme in d minor, gets going on a long tour around the circle of fifths. The softer second theme makes an appearance in G major, has its ending fragmented and further developed before settling on a back-and-forth between the chords f♯ minor and its dominant C♯. The contest ends with the orchestra settling on the single tone of C♯. From this tone there is a very rapid swerve into the reprise, accomplished by turning C♯ into the third of V⁷ in tonic D. Beethoven makes this sound like a familiar arrival, and it is, because it approximates the last measure of the slow introduction. By the time the thematic material has all reappeared, adjusted to tonic D, three hundred measures have passed. What ensues adds another sixty measures and becomes his most impressive coda up to this time. It is sustained partly by a long chromatic rise in the bass against pedal tones above, a procedure with parallels in similar climactic drives to end the great choruses of Haydn's *Creation* and *Seasons* (see Example 6.12).

The *Larghetto* in 3/8 time is a spacious idyll that answers the "there's not a minute to lose" attitude of the *Allegro con brio* with a demurring "What's the hurry? we've all the time in the world." Beethoven chose its key of A, instead of the more traditional subdominant for a slow movement, in order to take advantage of the two clarinets in A, which lend their suave colors to the whole and play prominent solo roles throughout. Strings alone propose the graceful and smooth main theme. It comes to a half cadence after eight measures, and then the clarinets, not the flutes or oboes, repeat the idea, with string accompaniment. The consequent phrase is just as broad and similarly scored. Next, the clarinets propose a continuation, and it is the violins that respond, not with an echo but a reply that carries the phrase further, rather like two parties in a love duet, reminiscent of a passage in Mozart's first "Prussian" Quartet (see Example 3.1). The second theme goes to the violins, singing a noble melody aloft that is just as smoothly flowing as the main theme, over soft and gentle chords undulating between I and V in the new key of E. Its cadential area is extended with more dialogue between the strings and clarinets doubled by the bassoons, until brought up short by a tutti outburst that has a familiar ring (Example 7.21ab). The orchestral passage

Example 7.21 a, b.

a. *Beethoven, Symphony No. 2 in D, II*

b. *Beethoven, Piano Sonata in D, Op. 28, II*

is quoted here as it appears not in E but back in the home key of A in the reprise, to facilitate comparison with a passage in the middle section of the *Andante* second movement in the Piano Sonata in D ("Pastoral") Op. 28. So close a correspondence between different genres is unusual and alerts us to the possibility of other connections between the Sonata (1801) and the Symphony, which was well under way in 1801. There are several.[94] The prima parte of the *Larghetto* is brought to a close by another theme, no less memorable than the earlier ones, truly a "third theme." This is the one that Schubert approximated in the slow movement of his Grand Duo in C for piano four-hands, D 812.

The relevance of Op. 28 to Op. 36 becomes evident again in the Symphony's Scherzo. It is marked *Allegro*, and the composer later assigned a metronome marking of 100 to the measure, a little less than the 108 he marked the *Menuetto Allegro molto e vivace* of Symphony No. 1. The second strain begins with a burst of B♭ sustained over several measures and then finds its way back to D major by way of d minor, a process bringing to mind the prominence of these sonorities in the slow introduction. The Trio begins properly, with a reduction to a few instruments, namely two oboes and two bassoons. What happens after the double bar, constituting the second strain, could not have been predicted. The strings pay no attention to what has been proposed, and pounce on the tone F♯, loudly and repeatedly. When they leave this single tone it is to proceed up and down the triad of F♯ major and come back to the single tone F♯, which is not resolved. Instead, all the winds, reinforced by a roll on the timpani, sound A. This is a dialogue of a more surly kind than that in the *Larghetto*, with the winds contradicting the strings as if to say, "Not your way, our way!" The winds prevail with the calm return of the first strain, to which the strings then meekly submit by repeating it. In the first movement of the Sonata in D, Op. 28, it may be recalled, the development ended by getting stuck on the tone or the chord of F♯ and at length finding release from its domain only by a relatively sudden move via A toward D major and the reprise. The Sonata's third-movement Scherzo made F♯ an issue by sounding it from high to low to begin the piece, then in the Trio insisting that F♯, as dominant, resolve to b minor over and over. In the Symphony the many

[94] As pointed out by Daniel Coren, "Structural Relations Between Op. 28 and Op. 36," *Beethoven Studies* 2 (1977): 66–83.

meanings of the tone and chord of F♯ go back to m. 8 of the slow introduction, where the two horns in octaves sounded repeated F♯ in a *crescendo* that seems, upon reconsideration, to have been a hortatory warning, a point driven home at the end of the last movement.

The finale is an *Allegro molto* in cut time. In 1817 Beethoven assigned the metronome speed of 152 to the measure, which is so fast as to be unplayable. Either 152 is an error, or it pertains to a whole note, not a half note. The movement has been called Haydnesque, and that it is in a general sense, for without Haydn's countless rondo finales or their levity, often moving us to laughter, there is no imagining how Beethoven could have arrived at the point he did before composing this finale. Yet it has gone beyond Haydn with its rough, not to say coarse, humor. The main theme itself offers evidence enough for this claim. Beginning with a half-tone appoggiatura, F♯ - G, as Beethoven does, elevates the equivalent of a sneer to thematic status (see Example 7.20). Following it with a leap down a tritone, emphasized with a trill on the longer tone, C♯, can only be compared to a snarl. And then the snapping of the descending fifth from E to A is like a burst of anger, in a rhythm compared above to Almaviva's "au-**dá-cé**" hurled at Figaro. So what have we in the space of two very brief measures? A sneer, a sardonic trill, and an angry gesture of defiance. The violins with their pert, chattery tune, smoothly accompanied by the lower strings, try to gloss over the initial outburst with their soft rejoinder. The tutti fights back, finishing the phrase by repeating their angry rhythms, this time made even more emphatic by the timpani's joining in with their sudden D - A, reinforced by the horns and trumpets. The whole movement is made from these elements, the rough humor of which amounts to so abrupt and impolite a beginning that it does not resemble anything Haydn would have cared to invent, although he could be very earthy too—recall the great bassoon joke at the end of the slow movement of Symphony No. 93. One big difference is Beethoven's placing his less than polite proposal in the most exposed spot of all, as the main theme that begins the finale.

Finales that combine sonata form with rondo elements can become large-scale edifices that match the length and weight of opening movements, as Haydn demonstrated in his London Symphonies, especially No. 103 in E♭. The finale of Op. 36 is another such movement. Its sonata form elements consist of a prima parte with modulation to the dominant for a second theme that will eventually return in the tonic during the reprise, which occurs after a wide-ranging development section. Typically with Beethoven, developmental procedures can take over at any point within the large-scale form. They do so directly following the main theme (or refrain) when the basic kernel of 1 2 3 4—in the first violins' rise by step from D and return down in mm. 3–5—gives rise to two new ideas (Example 7.22). The second, longer idea that begins with a dactyl becomes a subject for imitation, first in the strings, then in the winds; it also gets treated to augmentation.

EXAMPLE 7.22. *Beethoven, Symphony No. 2 in D, II*

The bridge follows shortly after this contrapuntal patch, and when the second theme arrives, it is a triadic fall down through an octave, sounding familiar both because of its dactylic beginning and because it seems to answer the second theme of the *Allegro con brio*, which rises through the triad up an octave. Diverging from sonata form is the lack of repetition of the prima parte.

The rondo element consists of multiple returns of the refrain in the tonic, after contrast. The first return, or refrain 2, follows the closing theme of the prima parte. It is not the whole theme here because the consequent phrase turns to d minor and commences the development. That section brings a blustery passage concluding with the tonal impasse of getting stuck in f♯ minor, recalling the development's ending in the *Allegro con brio*. Release comes when F♯ becomes the first note of refrain 3 leading in the reprise (iii⁷ dissolves into V$_5^6$). This time the theme is complete and is followed by the passages that trailed it before, all in tonic D. Then comes refrain 4, strongly reinforcing the rondo character. It dissolves, before completing the theme, into more development by fragmenting the theme, breaking it down to small constituent parts, and repeating those.

The end is near, we sense, when a long tonic pedal succeeds a long dominant pedal. Beethoven stops the frenzy for two measures of V$_5^6$, protracted by fermatas, and dramatized further by a roll on the timpani's A. Instead of resolution, there is the harmonic non sequitur of another such seventh chord, V$_5^6$/vi, softly intoned by the strings with F♯ in the treble (Example 7.23). The interruption by V$_5^6$/vi in

EXAMPLE 7.23. *Beethoven, Symphony No. 2 in D, IV*

the slow introduction, the original spur from Mozart's "Prague" Symphony, now takes on more meaning. Is this the beginning of the coda? It could be, when the nonchalant resolution of the interloping chord gives way to resolution from V to I, not once but twice, followed by more and more emphatic gestures to close the movement. There is even a new take on the impudent head motif, curtly balancing back and forth between I and V—the sort of final trump card that Haydn so often delighted in revealing. But Beethoven is not finished. A mighty *fortissimo* F♯

sounded by the entire orchestra minus the timpani pounds home the point once more. A momentary resolution dances down to b minor, as it did before, followed by a measure of silence. F♯ in the treble moves up to G, supported by V^6_5. This is the last tease. The rest is straightforward tonic D, celebrated in its full glory, to end a symphony that can last as long as thirty-five minutes.

The stentorian F♯ that so rudely brings the finale to a halt for the last time extends its evocative power over the whole symphony and serves as a kind of summary. It was the first melodic tone of the slow introduction sung by the first oboe, even before it was the root of an interrupting secondary dominant. As the chord of f♯ minor it brought the *Allegro con brio* to an uneasy stasis before dissolving into the dominant seventh that immediately resolved into the reprise, much as it did before the reprise (refrain 3) of the finale. In its role as a rude interloper it reminds us of the pesky tone, never explained, in the second strain of the Trio. It made itself felt occasionally in the lovely idyll of the *Larghetto,* and notably in the passage that is so close to one in the "Pastoral" Sonata Op. 28 (Example 7.21ab), a work that functioned as a kind of laboratory experiment on the way to the grander symphonic venture.

Preoccupation with the major mediant chord as an agent that could generate color and mystery was by no means exhausted when Beethoven decided that his Symphony No. 2 was as perfect as he could make it. Citing only two works from the years following Op. 36 should make this point clear. Both have an overall tonic of C major. The "Waldstein" Sonata, Op. 53, takes E major as the location of the first movement's second theme. The Mass in C, Op. 86, lingers with fascination over the chord of E major at both beginning and end (it has, like the end of Op. 36, a last coda that refuses to quit). Or, to take one further example of the magical sonority of the major mediant, there is the first entry of the orchestra in the Piano Concerto No. 4 in G, Op. 58.

Beethoven was aware of how special his second symphony was in raising him up to the plateau of Haydn and Mozart in this magnificent genre. He had his brother Carl offer it for publication to Breitkopf and Härtel in 1802, along with the Piano Concerto in c minor, Op. 37. About the concerto no special case was made, in contrast with Op. 36: "As to the symphony I beg you to act with dispatch, for we would gladly see it in print because it is one of my brother's most outstanding works." This letter, dated 28 March 1802, was written several months before the composer finally signed off on the work. This too shows how special a place it occupied.

Symphony No. 2 was a watershed for its composer, the last of his big works in which he looked to Haydn and Mozart for inspiration. The "Prague" Symphony in particular, Mozart's ultimate one in D major, served as a model for Op. 36, and not just in the weight and proportions of its slow introduction. The complex and extensive fast movements following these introductions were both in common time and celebrated to the maximum this bright, festive and sonorous tonality—the brightest of all, claimed contemporary writers on music. Then there came in both symphonies a gracious movement at a moderate speed in triple time, 3/8 in Op. 36, 6/8 in K. 504. Although they differ in key, both symphonies brim with colorful woodwind passages, and they actually share a similar quality of motion. (Try the aural experiment of splicing Beethoven's "third theme," with its placid, middle-range accompaniment in sixteenth notes, into the second idea of Mozart's *Andante*, which also has a gently murmuring accompaniment in sixteenth notes). Both works are capped by capricious and whirlwind finales in very fast 2/4 time. Beethoven expanded the Mozart model by including a typically vigorous Scherzo as third movement.

Composed in 1803–4, Beethoven's Symphony No. 3 in E♭, the mighty "Eroica," parted company in many ways with Haydn and Mozart. It is on a monumental scale that overwhelmed listeners then, and has ever since commanded the field. In the history of music but few works have provided so epochal a turning point as Beethoven's Third Symphony.

The composer-critic Reichardt, whom we encountered at the end of the previous chapter as one of Haydn's last visitors during the same 1808–9 stay in Vienna, attended a concert at the palace of Count Andrei Rasumovsky devoted to one string quartet apiece by Haydn, Mozart, and Beethoven; which ones he does not say. He described the experience using an architectural metaphor: Haydn built the house and Mozart turned it into a palace. "Beethoven himself was at home in this palace early on and it remained for him only to express his own nature in a unique way; he added daunting towers on which no one could place anything further without breaking his neck."[95] Many another musician reacted similarly to Beethoven's colossal achievement and preferred his earlier music, from the time when Beethoven was still "at home" in the Haydn-Mozart edifice. As late as 1816 the London Philharmonic Society invited Beethoven to compose a symphony "in the style of the first and second symphonies," an offer that deeply offended the composer, who indignantly refused.[96] There can scarcely be more striking confirmation than this that a corner was turned after 1802.

[95] Reichardt, *Vertraute Briefe* (1810), ed. of 1915, 1:185.
[96] Thayer-Forbes, p. 648.

APPENDICES

1

An Irish Tenor
in the Burgtheater

ICHAEL KELLY was born in Dublin in 1762, on either 12 August or Christmas Day. He profited there from good early training in music and in 1779 was shipped to Naples, on the advice of his main teacher, the castrato Rauzzini, in order to perfect his skills. His most important teacher in Italy was another castrato, Giuseppe Aprile, celebrated as a primo uomo throughout Europe and the favorite singer of Jommelli. Aprile was "justly considered as the greatest of all artists," said Kelly in his memoirs, which he dictated to Theodore Hook and saw published shortly before his death on 9 October 1826.[1] One scholar who has dealt with Kelly's autobiography suggests that he may have had a rough diary or notes to go on.[2] Kelly remembered an amazing amount about his life in Italy from 1779 to 1783 and his subsequent four years in Vienna, rarely in chronological order, yet confirmable in many cases. In some other cases he invented what he could not remember, or relied on outside sources. He may have kept much of his life's story in mind by recounting his tales to various listeners over the years. The written result can be faulted for inaccuracies, but no one can claim he was not a good storyteller.

When Kelly sailed for Naples as a lad of seventeen he was accompanied by a treasured possession, an English fortepiano, an indication that he already had wider musical skills than did many singers of the time. After several months

---

[1] Michael Kelly, *Reminiscences*, 2 vols., 2nd ed. (London, 1826; reprint, New York, 1969), 1:82.
[2] Alec Hyatt King, in "Kelly, Michael," *The New Grove Dictionary of Music*.

in Naples, Kelly went to Palermo with Aprile, who was engaged for a season at the opera there. The teaching of Aprile went beyond matters of vocal technique and musical finesse: "He took great pains to explain Metastasio, and other great Italian poets to me, and particularly inculcated a love of truth, and a horror of committing a mean action" (1:92). It was Aprile who secured Kelly his first professional engagement, in the Pergola Theater of Florence. At the parting of their ways Kelly gave his beloved mentor the only treasure he could in repayment, his English fortepiano.

Kelly arrived in the bay of Leghorn (Livorno) after sailing for six days. His first experience ashore is best told in the words of his memoirs.

> After we had been visited by the officers of health I went on shore to shew my passport at the Custom-house: I had on a Sicilian capote, with my hair (of which I had a great quantity, and which, like my complexion, was very fair) floating over it: I was as thin as a walking stick. As I stepped from the boat, I perceived a young lady and gentleman standing on the Mole, making observations; as the former looked at me she laughed, and as I approached, I heard her say to her companion in English, which, of course, she thought I did not understand, "Look at that girl dressed in boy's clothes!" To her astonishment, I answered in the same language, "You are mistaken, Miss, I am a very proper *he* animal, and quite at your service!" We all laughed until we were tired, and became immediately intimate; and these persons, my acquaintance with whom commenced by this jest on the Mole at Leghorn, continued through life the warmest and most attached of my friends. All love and honour to your memories, Stephen and Nancy Storace! (1:94–95).

Nancy Storace, although only fifteen at the time, was the prima buffa of a company that played Leghorn, Lucca, and Parma in 1781. Her brother Stephen, three years older, had been in Italy since 1776, as a student of the San Onofrio Conservatory in Naples. What Kelly says without embarrassment about his rather epicene appearance finds some corroboration in the soft and delicate features given him by portrait artists.[3]

Kelly landed in Venice toward the end of 1782 after various engagements singing in northern Italy and at Graz. During the following Lent he was hired to sing in the performances of an oratorio by Anfossi at the Mendicanti. One day a letter arrived for him from Count Giacomo Durazzo, the Austrian ambassador to Venice, who had once run the theaters in Vienna. Joseph II, through his theater director Count Rosenberg, ordered Durazzo to recruit a company of Italian

---

[3] An example is the anonymous oval portrait of Kelly as a young man illustrated in Geoffrey Brace, *Anna—Susanna: Anna Storace, Mozart's First Susanna: Her Life, Times and Family* (London 1991), following p. 80. See also the frontispiece of S. M. Ellis, *The Life of Michael Kelly: Musician, Actor, and Bon Viveur, 1762–1826* (London, 1930). This likeness is an engraved print after an oil painting by the great portrait artist Sir Thomas Lawrence and depicts Kelly at the age of about twenty-eight.

singers for a comic opera to be installed in the Burgtheater. No expense was to be spared, and only singers of the first class were to be engaged. Although Kelly does not say so, Nancy Storace, who was then singing with great success as the prima buffa of the San Samuele theater, may have brought him to Durazzo's attention. She was engaged, Kelly says, as were "the two best comic singers in Europe, Benucci and Mandini" (1:194).

At the end of Lent, Kelly departed Venice with many letters of introduction from Durazzo to important figures in Vienna, including Field Marshalls Lacy (of Irish descent!) and Loudon, the British ambassador, Robert Keith, and "the illustrious and witty Prince de Ligne." Upon arrival Kelly waited upon the theater's music director, Salieri, bearing with him a letter of recommendation from Ferdinando Bertoni, maestro di coro at the Mendicante. The new troupe opened in the Burgtheater on 22 April 1783, two weeks after arrival. "Storace and Benucci's receptions were perfectly enthusiastic, and I may perhaps be permitted to say, that I had no reason to complain of my own" (1:197). The first opera given was Salieri's *La scuola de' gelosi*, to which Zinzendorf's reaction is quoted above in Chapter 1. Not until 28 May, in a performance of Sarti's *Fra i due litiganti*, did Zinzendorf see fit to mention Kelly: "OKelli chi fait le role de Massoto chanta joliment 'In amor si vuol finezza.'" Kelly was often referred to as "O'Kelly" or some variant thereof. His annual salary began at 1641 florins and stayed about the same until his last year, 1786–87, when he was advanced to 1800 fl; it ranked beneath that of tenors Adamberger and Calvesi but above those of Pugnetti and Dauer.[4] The payment records thus contradict Kelly's claim to having been advanced 100 fl in 1784 by the personal order of Joseph II (1:239).

Kelly's tales of his encounters with Mozart have long been mined by Mozart scholars. They are on the whole credible, and so is his telling of a three-day visit to the country in order to pay his respects to Haydn, in the company of young Antonio Bridi, the Tyrolean tenor and merchant who was a close friend of Mozart. How far Kelly could stray from the truth, on the other hand, is illustrated by what he says of his encounters with Gluck. He relates the story of a grand princely visit to Vienna, during which Gluck's *Alceste* and *Iphigénie en Tauride* were revived in the Burgtheater. Such a visit did take place, and the visitors, incorrectly identified by Kelly, were Grand Duke Paul of Russia and his wife, Maria Feodorovna. It happened in the fall of 1781, more than a year before the arrival of Kelly. There were no other productions of *Alceste* in Vienna after he arrived except the amateur one-night performance with Countess Hatzfeld in the title role he describes attending (12 February 1786), and none at all of *Iphigénie*. Kelly correctly reports that Andrea Bernasconi sang the part of Iphigenia and Adamberger that of Orestes in the festive production, then adds that he sang the role of Pylades (it

---

[4]Link, *The National Court Theatre in Mozart's Vienna*, pp. 408, 412, 415, 421.

was sung by Joseph Souter). Moreover, Kelly claims that he was tutored in part by Gluck himself. He may have imagined his way into the cast of the gala Gluck operas by hearing Adamberger speak of them or reading about them. The reason for concocting this tale emerges at its end, when Gluck invites Kelly to his house and upstairs to his bedroom to see a richly-framed full-length picture of Handel. Gluck then expatiates "with reverential awe" on "the inspired master of our art" and caps his speech by saying "highest praise is due to your country for having distinguished and cherished his gigantic genius" (1:252). This fraud, of the pious and nationalist sort, was only to be expected in a work dedicated with fulsome praises to the reigning British monarch George IV. Kelly perjured himself further by perpetuating the falsehood in his second volume, claiming he was tutored by Gluck in the part of Alceste's husband, Admetus, when in Vienna, a claim that helped him secure this role for himself at the King's Theatre in 1796 (2:81).

Directly after his encounter with Haydn, Kelly tells the story of a visit to Vienna by the London librettist Giovanni Bottarelli, accompanied by his wife, a singer at the public pleasure gardens in London.[5]

> Upon my return [from Eisenstadt] my servant informed me that a lady and gentleman had called upon me, who said they came from England, and requested to see me at their hotel. I called the next morning, and saw the gentleman, who said his name was Botterelli, that he was the Italian poet of the King's Theatre in the Haymarket, and that his wife was an English woman, and a principal singer at Vauxhall, Ranelagh, the Pantheon, Etc. Her object in visiting Vienna was to give a concert, to be heard by the Emperor: and if she gave that satisfaction (which she had no doubt she would), to accept of an engagement at the Royal Theatre; and he added, that she had letters for the first nobility in Vienna. The lady came into the room; she was a very fine woman, and seemed sinking under the weight of her own attractions.—She really had powerful letters of recommendation. (1:219–20).

Her wish was granted. "Everything was done for her;—the orchestra and singers were engaged." No notice of such a concert survives from other sources but perhaps this is because it was set up on such short notice, with the powerful backing of Prince Charles von Liechtenstein and Emperor Joseph himself, according to Kelly. "The concert began to a crowded house but, I must premise, we had no rehearsal. At the end of the first act, the beauteous Syren, led into the orchestra by her caro sposo, placed herself just under the Emperor's box, *the orchestra being on the stage* [my emphasis]." There are some other references to occasions when the orchestra was placed on the stage.[6]

[5] Bottarelli, or Botterelli, as Kelly calls him, had worked on operas with Christian Bach, among others. *Music in European Capitals*, pp. 896ff.
[6] Heartz, "Nicolas Jadot and the Building of the Burgtheater," 28–31.

The emperor, and any guests who accompanied him, customarily took the foremost two boxes in the first tier, on the right side as one faced the stage. These "imperial boxes" are set apart by draperies, as seen in the interior view of the Burgtheater from a print of ca. 1810/1812 (see Figure 7.4). "Just under the Emperor's box" means that she stationed herself at the edge of the stage, as near the emperor as possible. As a master storyteller Kelly deserves to recount his tale to the end without further interruption.

> She requested me to accompany her song on the piano-forte.—I of course consented. Her air and manner spoke "dignity and love." The audience sat in mute and breathless expectation. The doubt was, whether she would melt into their ears in a fine cantabile, or burst upon them with a brilliant bravura. I struck the chords of the symphony—silence reigned—when, to the dismay and astonishment of the brilliant audience, she bawled out, without feeling or remorse, voice or time, or indeed one note in tune, the hunting song of "Tally ho!" in all its pure originality. She continued shrieking out Tally ho! tally ho! in a manner and tone so loud and dissonant, that they were enough to blow off the roof of the house. The audience jumped up terrified; some shrieked with alarm, some hissed, others hooted, and many joined in the unknown yell, in order to propitiate her. The Emperor called me to him, and asked me in Italian (what tally ho! meant)—I replied, I did not know; and literally, at that time, I did *not*.
>
> His Majesty, the Emperor, finding that even *I*, a native of Great Britain, either could not, or would not, explain the purport of the mysterious words, retired with great indignation from the theatre; and the major part of the audience, convinced by His Majesty's sudden retreat that they contained some horrible meaning, followed the Royal example. The ladies hid their faces with their fans, and mothers were heard in the lobbies cautioning their daughters on the way out, never to repeat the dreadful expression of "tally ho," nor venture to ask any of their friends for a translation of it.
>
> The next day, when I saw the husband of "tally ho," he abused the taste of the people of Vienna, and said that the song, which they did not know how to appreciate, had been sung by the celebrated Mrs. Wrighton at Vauxhall, and was a great favourite all over England. Thus, however, ended the exhibition of English taste; and Signora Tally ho! with her Italian poet, went *hunting* elsewhere, and never returned to Vienna, at least during my residence. (1:220–22).

The English hunting call of "Tally ho!" is verbally akin to the cry "Ta-yo!" used in the Hunting Chorus of Haydn's *Seasons* to call the dogs together; the men sing it to rises of a fourth. As sung by the beauteous Mrs. Bottarelli it must have been sufficiently different, since Emperor Joseph did not recognize it. I leave to specialists the pleasure of trying to identify the "Tally-ho!" hunting song supposedly heard at Vauxhall and the other pleasure gardens.

2
Sarti Witnesses
Haydn's Armida

GIUSEPPE SARTI, born at Faenza in late 1729, was one of northern Italy's most eminent composers of opera in the late eighteenth century. As court Kapellmeister at Copenhagen for many years he composed operas in French and Danish as well as in Italian. His international fame was sealed by the huge success of two operas in the early 1780s, one serious, the other comic: *Giulio Sabino* (Venice, 1781) and *Fra i due litiganti il terzo gode* (Milan, 1782). Luigi Cherubini studied with him at this time. In 1784, Sarti traveled by way of Vienna to St. Petersburg, where he replaced Paisiello as Kapellmeister of the Russian court. He remained there, composing operas in French and Russian, but mainly in Italian, with nearly unbroken continuity until 1801. He died the following year at Berlin.

Sarti figures in a letter dated Vienna, 9 June 1784, interrupted and resumed three days later, that Mozart wrote his father about a concert that was to take place in the country at Döbling on the 13th, at which he and his pupil Babette Ployer were to perform on two pianos. Mozart took Paisiello with him in his carriage and reported, "If Maestro Sarti had not been obliged to leave today [the 12th], I would have taken him there too. Sarti is a good, honest fellow! [Rechtschaffner braver Mann!] I played for him at length and finished with variations on one of his arias, which gave him great pleasure." The variations were presumably on "Come un'agnello" from *Fra i due litiganti,* for which the air and two variations for piano survive in Mozart's autograph (K. 460)—the remaining variations, as later published, are of disputed authenticity. This is the same air that Mozart quoted in the Tafelmusik scene of *Don Giovanni*; hearing it struck up by the stage band,

Leporello responds, "e vivano i Litiganti!" Sarti's *Litiganti* held the stage of the Burgtheater from 1783 to 1786 and was revived in 1789. *Giulio Sabino* was performed several times in Vienna during August 1785.

Haydn's *Armida* had its premiere on 26 February 1784 and was repeated twelve times through May, and once in June.[1] Presumably this was the performance Sarti saw as he was traveling east from Vienna close enough to stop at Esterháza. The tale is told by Nicolas-Étienne Framery, who was one of the most active of Parisian music critics, a partisan of Italian opera in the battles between Gluckistes and Piccinistes, and a great admirer of Haydn's music. The year after Haydn died Framery published his *Notice sur Joseph Haydn . . . contenant quelques particularités relatives à sa personne ou à ses ouvrages* (Paris, 1810).[2] His main source was Ignaz Pleyel, who was very well acquainted with Haydn, having been his student in the 1770s and having met his old teacher again as a friend and rival at London in 1791–92. Pleyel paid several visits to the aged master in Vienna after 1800, as did Cherubini. Pleyel's source could also have been Sarti himself. After founding his music publishing house at Paris in 1795, Pleyel established contacts with musicians everywhere. Some of what Framery relates about Haydn is wildly inaccurate but there is often enough truth in his anecdotes to suggest that they cannot be dismissed. Sometimes they ring more true than the tall tales Haydn liked to tell others, surely in jest, like the one about being threatened with castration when he was a choirboy under Reutter in St. Stephan's cathedral.

Framery provides a setting for Sarti's visit to Esterháza by explaining Haydn's multiple duties there.

> The functions that Haydn exercised as Kapellmeister at that time were not limited to composing music. He was also responsible for directing the performance of music by other composers, as requested, whether in the theater or in concerts, and of recruiting and training Italian companies to perform comic and serious operas [d'Opéras bouffons et sérieux]. From the second category, Haydn often performed the *Giulio Sabino* by Sarti, one of the masters whose works he particularly liked, doubtless because the energetic and noble style of this composer had the most in common with the nature of his own talents. And this work, one of Sarti's best and most vigorous, was also one of those to which Haydn gave preference.

This is borne out by the eighteen performances that Haydn led of *Giulio Sabino* in its first production at Esterháza during 1783. It almost goes without saying that Prince Nicholas must have liked the work very well too, for his wishes were paramount as to what was performed and how often.

[1] János Harich, "Das Repertoire des Opernkapellmeisters Joseph Haydn in Esterháza (1780–1790)," *The Haydn Yearbook* 1 (1962): 9–110; 53–54.

[2] Extracts from this work are printed in the original French as an appendix in Landon, *Haydn,* 2:757–63.

In the next paragraph, Framery gets right to his point, without even naming Sarti's destination, except in general terms.

> Called one day to a northern court in order to compose operas, Sarti discovered that he was passing close enough to Esterháza to make a detour, being curious to see a man whose numerous works, especially his symphonies, had made him famous all over Europe. He wished to call on him and offer mutual friendship. He arrived at the prince's palace toward day's end and explained that he wished to speak to the famous Haydn. "For the moment," he is told, "that is impossible; the maestro is directing the opera, which is about to commence, for the prince has just entered his box." "Could I not at least find some place in the corner of the hall?" "Oh, that without any question. We have orders to assign excellent seats to all foreigners." "What is being sung?" "It is *Armida*, of all his works the one the maestro likes the best."

It must also have been the one that Prince Nicholas liked the best, because it was performed many times in the seven years before his death, more than any other opera at Esterháza, whether by Haydn or an Italian master.

The prince's theater was small, seating perhaps three or four hundred, but that would have allowed entrance to much of the castle's population and that of the environs, while still leaving good seats for any visiting foreigners. An idea of the parterre is helpful in imagining the scene that Framery next describes. The prince's box took up the whole back of the auditorium, in front of which were several rows of benches separated by a middle aisle leading up to the orchestra and stage.[3] We resume the narrative just after Sarti learned what opera was being performed.

> This spurred Sarti on all the more since he knew none of Haydn's dramatic music. He asked to be seated as close as possible to the orchestra and obtained his wish. During the whole first act the beauty of the pieces that followed one another astonished, charmed, enchanted him; he applauds with enthusiasm. But as the second act was concluding [with the great act-ending Trio for Armida, Rinaldo, and Ubaldo] he could contain himself no longer. In a sort of delirium he rises and jumps over the benches that separated him from the orchestra, without the permission of those who occupy them, and leaps to embrace the astonished maestro. "It is Sarti who embraces you!"

If we imagine the famous visitor seated somewhere in the middle of the parterre, in the middle of one of the benches, he would have had to jump over only a few before reaching the middle or side aisle, then rushing forward and hurling himself at Haydn, seated at the keyboard.

---

[3] For a diagram of the parterre, see *Haydn, Mozart*, p. 376, Figure 5.5, first segment, "Grundriss zu ebener Erde."

"It is Sarti who embraces you!" he cries out, "Sarti, who wanted to see the great Haydn, to admire his beautiful works, but who had no hopes of admiring one so beautiful as this!" The prince, who, from the back of his box, sees the extraordinary and disorderly commotion, yet could not hear what was said, is alarmed and shouts, "What is it? What is going on? What has happened?" Haydn answers in a loud voice, seized by the same enthusiasm. "It is Giulio Sabino, it is Sarti who has come to see his good friend Joseph." And these two great men, these two friends, who were seeing each other for the first time, embraced and swore a friendship to match the esteem in which they held each other.

The anecdote is so touching, so heartening about the unselfish qualities of both composers, it deserves to be considered true, whether it is or not. In the case of Haydn, it reinforces what is known from many sources about his uncommon generosity of spirit with regard to other composers. It provides another example of how, despite his complaints of being isolated from the world in the Hungarian countryside, the world found its way to him. Such was his renown by the time in question that many musicians, as well as people of higher social status, wished to pay him their respects.

List of Works Cited

Abert, Hermann. *W. A. Mozart. Neubearbeitete und erweiterte Ausgabe von Otto Jahns Mozart.* 2 vols. Leipzig, 1955–56.

Albrecht, Theodore. "Anton Dreyssig (c 1753/4–1820): Mozart's and Beethoven's *Zauberflötist.*" In *Words about Mozart: Essays in Honour of Stanley Sadie,* edited by Dorothea Link with Judith Nagley, 179–92. Woodbridge, Suffolk, 2005.

———. "The Musicians in Balthazar Wigand's Depiction of the Performance of Haydn's *Die Schöpfung,* Vienna, 27 March 1808." *Music in Art* 19 (2004): 123–31.

Allanbrook, Wye Jamison. *Rhythmic gesture in Mozart: "Le nozze di Figaro" & "Don Giovanni."* Chicago, 1983.

Arneth, Alfred, Ritter von. *Beaumarchais und Sonnenfels.* Vienna, 1868.

Arthur, John. " 'N. N.' Revisited: New Light on Mozart's Late Correspondence." In *Haydn, Mozart, and Beethoven: Studies in the Music of the Classical Period: Essays in Honour of Alan Tyson,* edited by Sieghard Brandenburg, 127–45. Oxford, 1998.

———. "Some Chronological Problems in Mozart: the Contribution of Ink-Studies." In *Wolfgang Amadè Mozart: Essays on his Life and Works,* edited by Stanley Sadie, 25–52. Oxford, 1996.

Badura-Skoda, Eva. "Zur Entstehung des Klavierkonzerts in B-dur KV. 456." *Mozart-Jahrbuch 1964*: 193–97.

Barbedette, Henri. "Haydn, sa vie et ses œuvres." *Le Ménestrel* 38 (1871): 27.

Bauman, Thomas. "Coming of Age in Vienna: *Die Entführung aus dem Serail.*" In Daniel Heartz, *Mozart's Operas,* edited by Thomas Bauman, 65–87. Berkeley and Los Angeles, 1990.

———. "Neefe, Christian Gottlob." In *The New Grove Dictionary of Opera,* edited by Stanley Sadie. New York, 1992.

————. *W. A. Mozart: Die Entführung aus dem Serail*. Cambridge, 1987.

Beales, Derek. *Joseph II*. Vol. 1: *In the Shadow of Maria Theresa (1741–1780)*. New York, 1987.

Beethoven, Ludwig van. *Autograph Miscellany from circa 1786 to 1799: British Museum Additional Manuscript 29801, ff. 39–162 (The Kafka Sketchbook)*. Edited by Joseph Kerman. 2 vols. London, 1970.

————. *Briefwechsel: Gesamtausgabe*. Edited by Sieghard Brandenburg. 7 vols. Munich, 1996–98.

————. *Ludwig van Beethoven's Studien im Generalbasse: Contrapuncte und in der Compositions-Lehre*. Edited by Ignaz von Seyfried. Vienna, 1832.

Benton, Rita. *Ignaz Pleyel. A Thematic Catalogue of his Compositions*. New York, 1977.

Berlioz, Hector. *A travers chants* (Paris, 1862). In *Beethoven by Berlioz: A Critical Appreciation of Beethoven's Nine Symphonies . . .* Translated by Ralph de Sola. Boston, 1975.

————. *Critique musicale: 1823–1863*. Edited by H. Robert Cohen and Yves Gérard. 5 vols. Paris, 1996–2004.

Bernard, Paul P. *From the Enlightenment to the Police State: The Public Life of Johann Anton Pergen*. Urbana, IL, 1991.

Blanning, T. C. W. *Reform and Revolution in Mainz, 1743–1803*. Cambridge, 1974.

Bonds, Mark Evan. "The Sincerest Form of Flattery? Mozart's 'Haydn' Quartets and the Question of Influence." *Studi musicali* 22 (1993): 365–409.

Boyden, David D. *The History of Violin Playing from Its Origins to 1761 and Its Relationship to the Violin and Violin Music*. London, 1965.

Brace, Geoffrey. *Anna—Susanna: Anna Storace, Mozart's First Susanna: Her Life, Times and Family*. London, 1991.

Brand, Carl Maria. *Die Messen von Joseph Haydn*. Würzburg, 1941.

Brandenburg, Sieghard. "Beethoven's Opus 12 Violin Sonatas: On the Path to His Personal Style." In *The Beethoven Violin Sonatas: History, Criticism, Performance*, edited by Lewis Lockwood and Mark Kroll, 5–23. Urbana, IL, 2004.

————. "Beethovens Streichquartette op. 18." In *Beethoven und Böhmen: Beiträge zu Biographie und Wirkungsgeschichte Beethovens*, edited by Sieghard Brandenburg and Martella Gutíerrez-Denhoff, 259–309. Bonn, 1988.

————. "Die kurfürstliche Musikbibliothek in Bonn und ihr Bestände im 18. Jahrhundert." *Beethoven Jahrbuch* 8 (1971–72): 7–47.

————. "The First Versions of Beethoven's G Major String Quartet, Op. 18 No. 2." *Music and Letters* 58 (1977): 127–52.

Branscombe, Peter. *W. A. Mozart: Die Zauberflöte*. Cambridge, 1991.

Braunbehrens, Volkmar. *Mozart in Vienna, 1781–1791*. Translated by Timothy Bell. New York, 1986.

Brauneis, Walther. "Mozart's Anstellung am kaiserlichen Hof in Wien: Fakten und Fragen." In *Mozart: Experiment Aufklärung im Wien des ausgehenden 18. Jahrhunderts*, edited by Herbert Lachmayer, 559–72. Ostfildern, 2006.

————. "Wer war Mozarts 'Signora Antonini' in der Prager Uraufführung von 'La clemenza di Tito'? Zur Identifizierung der Antonina Miklaszewicz als Interpretin der

Servilia in der Krönungsoper am 6. September 1791." *Mitteilungen der Interna-tionalen Stiftung Mozarteum* 47 (1999): 32–40.

Brook, Barry S. *La symphonie française dans la seconde moitié du XVIIIe siècle.* 3 vols. Paris, 1962.

Brown, A. Peter. "Haydn's Chaos: Genesis and Genre." *Musical Quarterly* 73 (1989): 18–59.

———. "Joseph Haydn and Leopold Hofmann's 'Street Songs.' " *Journal of the American Musicological Society* 30 (1980): 356–83.

———. *Joseph Haydn's Keyboard Music: Sources and Style.* Bloomington, IN, 1986.

Brown, Bruce Alan. *Gluck and the French Theatre in Vienna.* Oxford, 1991.

———. "Magri in Vienna: The Apprenticeship of a Choreographer." In *The Grotesque Dancer on the Eighteenth-Century Stage: Gennaro Magri and His World,* edited by Rebecca Harris-Warrick and Bruce Alan Brown, 62–90. Madison, WI, 2005.

———. "*Le Pazzie d'Orlando, Orlando Paladino,* and the Uses of Parody." *Italica* 64 (1987): 583–605.

———. "Singing Lessons in Munich." Paper for the Symposium, "L'Europe Galante," at Berkeley, 5 October 2003.

———. *W. A. Mozart: Così fan tutte.* New York, 1995.

———, and John A. Rice. "Salieri's *Così fan tutte.*" *Cambridge Opera Journal* 8 (1996): 17–43.

Buch, David J. "Mozart and the Theater auf der Wieden: New Attributions and Perspec-tives." *Cambridge Opera Journal* 9 (1997): 195–223.

———. "On Mozart's Partial Autograph of the Duet 'Nun liebes Weibchen,' K. 625/592a." *Journal of the Royal Musical Association* 124 (1999): 53–85.

Burney, Charles. *The Letters of Dr. Charles Burney, Volume 1 (1751–1784),* edited by Alvaro Ribeiro. Oxford, 1991.

Cairns, David. *Mozart and His Operas.* Berkeley and Los Angeles, 2006.

Carpani, Giuseppe. *Le Haydine, ovvero, Lettere sulla vita e le opere del celebre maestro Giu-seppe Haydn.* Milan, 1812.

Carr, Bruce. "Banti, Brigida Georgi." In *The New Grove Dictionary of Opera,* edited by Stanley Sadie. New York, 1992.

Castelvecchi, Stefano. "Sentimental and Anti-Sentimental in Le nozze di Figaro." *Journal of the American Musicological Society* 53 (2000): 1–24.

Charlton, David. *French Opera 1730–1830: Meaning and Media.* Aldershot, 2000.

———. *Grétry and the Growth of Opéra-Comique.* Cambridge: New York, 1986.

———. "The 'Romance' and Its Cognates: Narrative, Irony and 'vraisemblance' in Early Opéra-Comique." In *Die Opéra comique und ihr Einfluss auf das europäische Musik-theater im 19. Jahrhundert,* edited by Herbert Schneider and Nicole Wild, 43–92. Hildesheim, 1997.

Clark, Caryl. "Fabricating Magic: Costuming Salieri's *Armida.*" *Early Music* 31 (2003): 451–61.

———. "Orlando paladino." In *The New Grove Dictionary of Opera,* edited by Stanley Sadie. New York, 1992.

Clementi, Muzio. *Epistolario, 1787–1831.* Edited by Remo Giazotto. Milan, 2002.

Clive, Peter. *Beethoven and His World: A Biographical Dictionary.* Oxford, 2001.

Cole, Malcolm S. "Haydn's Symphonic Rondo Finales: Their Structural and Stylistic Evolution." *Haydn Yearbook* 13 (1982): 113–42.

Constant, Pierre. *Histoire du Concert Spirituel, 1725–1790.* Paris, 1975.

Coren, Daniel. "Structural Relations Between Op. 28 and Op. 36." *Beethoven Studies* 2 (1977): 66–83.

Croll, Gerhart. "Remarks on a Mozart Quartet Fragment." In *Haydn Studies: Proceedings of the International Haydn Conference, Washington, D.C., 1975,* edited by Jens Peter Larsen, Howard Serwer and James Webster, 405–7. New York, 1981.

Cyr, Mary, and Valerie Walden. "Duport." In *The New Grove Dictionary of Music and Musicians,* edited by Stanley Sadie and John Tyrrell. New York, 2002.

Da Ponte, Lorenzo. *An Extract from the Life of Lorenzo Da Ponte: With the History of Several Dramas Written by Him, and among Others, Il Figaro, Il Don Giovanni, and La scola degli amanti, Set to Music by Mozart.* New York, 1819.

———. *Memoirs.* Translated by Elisabeth Abbott. Edited by Arthur Livingston. New York, 1959.

Dell'Antonio, Andrew. " 'Il compositore deluso': The Fragments of *Lo sposo deluso.*" In *Wolfgang Amadè Mozart: Essays on His Life and His Music,* edited by Stanley Sadie, 403–12. Oxford, 1996.

DeNora, Tia. *Beethoven and the Construction of Genius: Musical Politics in Vienna, 1792–1803.* Berkeley and Los Angeles, 1995.

Dent, Edward J. *Mozart's Operas: A Critical Study.* 2nd ed. London, 1947.

Derr, Ellwood. "Some Thoughts on the Design of Mozart's Opus 4, the 'Subscription Concertos' (K. 414, 413, and 415)." In *Mozart's Piano Concertos: Text, Context, Interpretation,* edited by Neal Zaslaw, 187–210. Ann Arbor, MI, 1996.

Deutsch, Otto Erich. *Das Freihaustheater auf der Wieden, 1787–1801.* Vienna, 1937.

———. *Mozart: A Documentary Biography.* 2nd ed. Stanford, 1966.

———. *Mozart: Die Dokumente seines Lebens.* Kassel, 1961. [See also Eibl, Joseph Heinz, and Eisen, Cliff.]

———, ed. *Mozart und seine Welt in zeitgenössischen Bilder / Mozart and His World in Contemporary Pictures.* English version by Peter Branscombe. Kassel, 1961.

Dibdin, Charles. *The Musical Tour of Mr. Dibdin.* Sheffield, 1788.

Dies, Albert Christoph. *Biographische Nachrichten von Joseph Haydn.* Vienna, 1810. [See Gotwals, Vernon.]

Durante, Sergio. "The Chronology of Mozart's 'La clemenza di Tito' reconsidered." *Music and Letters* 80 (1999): 560–94.

———. "Le scenografie di Pietro Travaglia per 'La clemenza di Tito' (Praga, 1791): Problemi di identificazione ed implicazioni." *Mozart-Jahrbuch 1994*: 156–69.

Edge, Dexter. "Manuscript Parts as Evidence of Orchestral Size in the Eighteenth-Century Viennese Concerto." In *Mozart's Piano Concertos: Text, Context, Interpretation,* edited by Neal Zaslaw, 427–60. Ann Arbor, MI, 1997.

———. "Mozart's fee for *Così fan tutte.*" *Journal of the Royal Musical Association* 116 (1991): 211–35.

———. "Mozart's Reception in Vienna, 1787–1791." In *Wolfgang Amadè Mozart: Essays on His Life and His Music,* edited by Stanley Sadie, 66–117. Oxford, 1996.

————. "Mozart's Viennese Orchestras." *Early Music* 20 (1992): 64–88.

Eibl, Joseph Heinz, ed. *Mozart, Die Dokumente seines Lebens: Addenda und Corrigenda*. Kassel, 1978.

Einstein, Alfred. *Mozart: His Character, His Work*. Translated by Arthur Mendel and Nathan Broder. New York, 1945.

Eisen, Cliff. *New Mozart Documents: A Supplement to O. E. Deutsch's Documentary Biography*. Stanford, 1991.

————, ed. *Mozart, die Dokumente seines Lebens: Addenda, neue Folge*. NMA X/31/2. Kassel, 1997.

Ellis, Stuart Marsh. *The Life of Michael Kelly: Musician, Actor, and Bon Viveur, 1762–1826*. London, 1930.

Esterházy Archives. "The Acta musícalia of the Esterházy Archives (Nos. 101–52)." *Haydn Yearbook* 15 (1984): 93–180.

Feder, Georg. *Haydns Streichquartette*. Cologne, 1998.

Feldman, Martha. *Opera and Sovereignty: Transforming Myths in Eighteenth-Century Italy*. Chicago, 2007.

Fellerer, Karl Gustav. *Die Kirchenmusik W. A. Mozarts*. Laaber, 1985.

Ferguson, Faye. "*Kritischer Bericht* to *Die Entführung aus dem Serail*, edited by Gerhard Croll. *NMA* II/5/12. Kassel 2002.

Finscher, Ludwig. *Joseph Haydn und seine Zeit*. Laaber, 2000.

Fisher, Stephen C. "Further Thoughts on Haydn's Rondo Finales." *Haydn Yearbook* 17 (1992): 85–107.

Fiske, Roger, and H. Diack Johnstone, eds. *Music in Britain: The Eighteenth Century*. Oxford, 1990.

Floros, Constatin. *Beethovens Eroica und Prometheus-Musik*. Wilhelmshaven, 1978.

Flothius, Marius. "A Close Reading of the Autographs of Mozart's Ten Late Quartets." In *The String Quartets of Haydn, Mozart, and Beethoven: Studies of the Autograph Manuscripts*, edited by Christoph Wolff, 154–73. Cambridge, MA, 1980.

Fraser, Antonia. *Marie Antoinette: The Journey*. New York, 2001.

Freeman, Daniel E. *The Opera Theater of Count Franz Anton von Sporck in Prague*. Stuyvesant, NY, 1992.

Galeazzi, Francesco. *Elementi teorico-pratici di musica*. 2 vols. Rome, 1791–96.

Geiringer, Karl. "From Guglielmi to Haydn: The Transformation of an Opera." In *Report of the Eleventh Congress [of the IMS], Copenhagen 1972*, edited by Henrik Glahn, Søren Sørensen, and Peter Ryom. 2 vols; vol. 1, 391–95. Copenhagen, 1974.

Gerlach, Sonja. "Johann Tost, Geiger und Grosshandlungsgremialist." *Haydn-Studien* 7 (1998): 344–65.

Geyer-Kiefl, Helen. "Guglielmis 'Le Pazzie d'Orlando' und Haydns 'Orlando Paladino.'" In *Bericht über den internationalen Joseph Haydn Kongress 1982*, edited by Eva Badura-Skoda, 403–15. Munich, 1986.

Girdham, Jane. *English Opera in Late Eighteenth-Century London: Stephen Storace at Drury Lane*. Oxford, 1997.

Girdlestone, Cuthbert. *Mozart's Piano Concertos*. 2nd ed. London, 1958.

Goehring, Edmund Joseph. *Three Modes of Perception in Mozart: The Philosophical, Pastoral, and Comic in "Così fan tutte."* Cambridge, 2004.

Goethe, Johann Wolfgang von. *Italian Journey (1786–1788)*. Translated by W. H. Auden and Elizabeth Mayer. San Francisco, 1982.

Gotwals, Vernon. *Joseph Haydn: Eighteenth-Century Gentleman and Genius*. Madison, WI, 1963. [Annotated translation of Dies (1810) and Griesinger (1810).]

Grave, Floyd K., and Margaret G. Grave. *The String Quartets of Joseph Haydn*. Oxford, 2006.

Grétry, André Ernest Modeste. *Memoires, ou, Essais sur la musique*. 3 vols. Paris, 1789–94. Reprint, New York, 1971.

Griesinger, Georg August. *Biographische Notizen über Joseph Haydn*. Leipzig, 1810. [See Gotwals, Vernon.]

———. *"Eben komme ich von Haydn—" Georg August Griesingers Korrespondenz mit Joseph Haydns Verleger Breitkopf & Härtel, 1799–1819*. Edited by Otto Biba. Zurich, 1987.

Gyrowetz, Adalbert. *Biographie des Adalbert Gyrowetz* (Vienna, 1848). Later editions edited by Alfred Einstein (Leipzig, 1915) and R. Fischer-Wildhagen. Stuttgart, 1993.

Haaselt, Luc van. "Beethoven in Holland." *Die Musikforschung* 18 (1965): 181–84.

Haimo, Ethan. *Haydn's Symphonic Forms: Essays in Compositional Logic*. Oxford, 1995.

Halliwell, Ruth. *The Mozart Family: Four Lives in a Social Context*. Oxford, 1998.

Harich, János. "Das Repertoire des Opernkapellmeisters Joseph Haydn in Esterháza (1780–1790)." *Haydn Yearbook* 1 (1962): 9–110.

Haydn, Joseph. *The Battle of the Nile, für Sopran und Klavier, Hob. XXVIb: 4*. Edited by H. C. Robbins Landon. Vienna, 1981.

———. *The Collected Correspondence and London Notebooks of Joseph Haydn*. Edited and translated by H. C. Robbins Landon. London, 1959.

———. *Critical Edition of the Complete Symphonies*. Edited by H. C. Robbins Landon, 12 vols., 2nd ed. Vienna, 1981.

———. *Gesammelte Briefe und Aufzeichnungen*. Edited by Dénes Bartha. Kassel, 1965.

Heartz, Daniel. "Beginnings of the Operatic Romance: Rousseau, Sedaine, and Monsigny." *Eighteenth-Century Studies* 15 (1981–82): 149–82.

———. *From Garrick to Gluck: Essays on Opera in the Age of Enlightenment*. Edited by John A. Rice. Hillsdale, NY, 2004.

———. "Gluck's *Iphigénie en Aulide*: A Prolegomenon." In *Words on Music: Essays in Honor of Andrew Porter on the Occasion of His 75th Birthday*, edited by David Rosen and Claire Brook, 138–51. Hillsdale, NY, 2003.

———. *Haydn, Mozart and the Viennese School, 1740–1780*. New York, 1995.

———. "The Hunting Chorus in Haydn's *Jahreszeiten* and the 'Airs de Chasse' in the *Encyclopédie*." *Eighteenth-Century Studies* 9 (1976): 523–39.

———. "Mozart and Anton Klein." *Mozart Newsletter* 10 (2006): 7–18.

———. "Mozart and Da Ponte." *Musical Quarterly* 79 (1995): 700–19.

———. *Mozart's Operas*. Edited by Thomas Bauman. Berkeley and Los Angeles, 1990.

———. "Mozart's Sense for Nature." *19th Century Music* 15 (1991): 107–15.

———. "Mozarts 'Titus' und die italienische Oper um 1800." *Hamburger Jahrbuch für Musikwissenschaft* 5 (1981): 255–66.

———. *Music in European Capitals: The Galant Style 1720–1780*. New York, 2003.

———. "Nicolas Jadot and the Building of the Burgtheater." *Musical Quarterly* 68 (1982): 1–31.

———. "A Pilgrim's Progress Report Concerning 'Music in the Classic Era.' " In *Music, Libraries, and the Academy: Essays in Honor of Lenore Coral*, edited by James P. Cassaro, 21–29. Middleton, WI, 2007.

———. "Raaff's Last Aria: A Mozartian Idyll in the Spirit of Hasse." *Musical Quarterly* 60 (1974): 517–43.

———. "Susanna's Hat." *Early Music* 19 (1991): 585–89.

———. "Thomas Attwood's Lessons in Composition with Mozart." *Proceedings of the Royal Musical Association* 100 (1973–74): 175–83.

———. "When Mozart Revises: the Case of Guglielmo in *Così fan tutte*." In *Wolfgang Amadè Mozart: Essays on His Life and His Music*, edited by Stanley Sadie, 355–61. Oxford, 1996.

Hertzmann, Erich, and Cecil B. Oldham, eds. *Thomas Attwoods Theorie- und Kompositionstudien bei Mozart*. Completed by Daniel Heartz and Alfred Mann. Kassel, 1965. *NMA* X/30/1. *Kritischer Bericht* by Heartz and Mann (1969).

Heuberger, Richard. *Erinnerungen an Johannes Brahms*. 2nd ed. Edited by Kurt Hofmann. Tutzing, 1976.

Hoboken, Anthony van, ed. *Joseph Haydn: Thematisch-bibliographisches Werkverzeichnis*. 3 vols. Mainz, 1957–78.

Hoffmann, Ernst. *E. T. A. Hoffmann's Musical Writings: Kreisleriana, The Poet and the Composer, Music Criticism*. Edited by David Charlton. Translated by Martyn Clarke. Cambridge, 1989.

Holmes, Edward. *The Life of Mozart*. London, 1845.

Hughes, Rosemary. "Dr. Burney's Championship of Haydn." *Musical Quarterly* 27 (1941): 90–96.

Hunter, Mary. "Rousseau, the Countess, and the Female Domain." In *Mozart Studies 2*, edited by Cliff Eisen, 1–26. New York, 1997.

Hutchings, Arthur. *A Companion to Mozart's Piano Concertos*. London, 1948.

Irving, John. *Mozart: The Haydn Quartets*. Cambridge, 1998.

Jacob, Margaret C. *Living the Enlightenment: Freemasonry and Politics in Eighteenth-Century Europe*. Oxford, 1991.

Jan, Steven. "The Evolution of a 'Memeplex' in Late Mozart: Replicated Structures in Pamina's 'Ach ich fühl's.' " *Journal of the Royal Musical Association* 28 (2003): 330–70.

Jefferson, Thomas. *Travels: Selected Writings, 1784–1789*. Edited by Anthony Brandt. Washington, D.C., 2006.

Johnson, Douglas. "Beethoven's Early Sketches in the 'Fischhof' Miscellany: Berlin Autograph 28." Ph.D. diss., University of California, Berkeley, 1977.

———. "Beethoven's Sketches for the Scherzo of the Quartet Op. 18, No. 6." *Journal of the American Musicological Society* 23 (1970): 385–403.

———, Alan Tyson, and Robert Winter. *The Beethoven Sketchbooks: History, Reconstruction, Inventory*. Edited by Douglas Johnson. Berkeley, 1985.

Johnson, Katherine. *The Masonic Thread in Mozart*. London, 1977.

Kalnein, Wend von. *Architecture in France in the Eighteenth Century*. New Haven, 1995.

Kamien, Roger. "The Slow Introduction to Mozart's Symphony No. 38 in D, K. 504 ('Prague'): A Possible Model for the Slow Introduction of Beethoven's Symphony No. 2 in D, Op. 36." *Israel Studies in Musicology* 5 (1990): 113–30.

Keefe, Simon P. " 'An Entirely Special Manner': Mozart's Piano Concerto No. 14 in E flat, K. 449, and the Stylistic Implications of Confrontation." *Music and Letters* 82 (2002): 559–81.

———. *Mozart's Piano Concertos: Dramatic Dialogue in the Age of Enlightenment*. Rochester, NY, 2001.

Kelly, Michael. *Reminiscences of Michael Kelly, of the King's Theatre and Theatre Royal Drury Lane* . . . 2 vols. London, 1826. Reprint, 1968.

Kerman, Joseph. *The Beethoven Quartets*. New York, 1967.

———. "Beethoven's Minority." In *Haydn, Mozart, and Beethoven: Studies in the Music of the Classical Period: Essays in Honour of Alan Tyson*, edited by Sieghard Brandenburg, 151–73. Oxford, 1998.

Kinderman, William. *Beethoven*. Berkeley and Los Angeles, 1995.

———. "Dramatic Development and Narrative Design in the First Movement of Mozart's Concerto in C Minor, K. 491." In *Mozart's Piano Concertos*, edited by Neal Zaslaw, 285–301. Ann Arbor, MI, 1996.

King, Alec Hyatt. "Kelly, Michael." In *The New Grove Dictionary of Music and Musicians*, edited by Stanley Sadie and John Tyrrell. New York, 2002.

Kinsky, Georg. *Das Werk Beethovens: Thematisch-bibliographisches Verzeichnis seiner sämtlichen vollendeten Kompositionen*. Edited by Hans Halm. Munich, 1955.

Kirnberger, Johann Philipp. *Recueil d'airs de danse caractéristiques* [Berlin, ca. 1777]. Edited by Ulrich Mahlert as *Airs de danse für ein Tasteninstrument*. Wiesbaden, 1995.

Knepler, Georg. *Wolfgang Amadé Mozart*. Translated by J. Bradford Robinson. Cambridge, 1994.

Konrad, Ulrich. "'In seinem Kopfe lag das Werk immer vollendet . . . ': Bemerkungen zu Mozarts Schaffenweise am Beispiel des Klaviertrios B-Dur KV 502." *Mozart-Jahrbuch 1991*: 540–51.

Kozeluch, Leopold. *Konzert D-dur für Klavier und Orchester*. Edited by Raymond Meylan. Wiesbaden, 1963.

Kunze, Stefan. *Mozarts Opern*. Stuttgart: 1984.

Küster, Konrad. *Mozart: A Musical Biography*. Translated by Mary Whittall. Oxford, 1996.

Ladenburger, Michael. "Das böhmische Element im kurkölnischen Musikleben." In *Beethoven und Böhmen: Beiträge zu Biographie und Wirkungsgeschichte Beethovens*. Edited by Sieghard Brandenburg and Martella Gutíerrez-Denhoff, 9–42. Bonn, 1988.

———. "Der junge Beethoven, Komponist und Pianist: Beethovens Handexemplar der Originalausgabe seiner Drei Klaviersonaten, WoO 47." *Bonner Beethoven Studien* 3 (2003): 107–17.

Landon, H. C. Robbins. *Haydn: Chronicle and Works*. 5 vols. Bloomington, IN, 1976–80.

———. *Mozart and Vienna*. New York, 1991.

————. *Mozart: The Golden Years, 1781–1791*. New York, 1989.

————. *Supplement to the Symphonies of Joseph Haydn*. London, 1961.

————, and David Wyn Jones. *Haydn: His Life and Music*. Bloomington, IN, 1988.

Larsen, Jens Peter. "A Haydn Contract." *Musical Times* 117 (1976): 737–38.

————. *Three Haydn Catalogues*. Second revised facsimile ed. New York, 1979.

————, Howard Serwer, and James Webster, eds. *Haydn Studies: Proceedings of the International Haydn Conference, Washington, D.C., 1975*. New York, 1981.

Leeson, Daniel N. "Mozart's *Le Nozze di Figaro*: A Hidden Dramatic Detail." *Eighteenth-Century Music* 1 (2004): 301–4.

————. "A Revisit: Mozart's Serenade for Thirteen Instruments, K. 361 (370a), the 'Gran Partita.'" *Mozart-Jahrbuch 1997*: 181–223.

Levy, Janet M. *Beethoven's Compositional Choices: The Two Versions of Op. 18 No. 1, First Movement*. Philadelphia, 1982.

————. "Gesture, form and syntax in Haydn's music." In *Haydn Studies: Proceedings of the International Haydn Conference, Washington, D.C., 1975*, edited by Jens Peter Larsen, Howard Serwer and James Webster, 355–62. New York, 1981.

Lichtenthal, Peter. "Rondò." In *Dizionario e bibliografia della musica*. 4 vols. Milan, 1826.

Link, Dorothea. "*L'arbore di Diana*: a model for *Così fan tutte*." In *Wolfgang Amadè Mozart: Essays on His Life and His Music*, edited by Stanley Sadie, 362–73. Oxford, 1996.

————. "Mozart's appointment to the Viennese court." In *Words about Mozart: Essays in Honour of Stanley Sadie*, edited by Dorothea Link with Judith Nagley, 153–78. Woodbridge, Suffolk, 2005.

————. *The National Court Theatre in Mozart's Vienna: Sources and Documents, 1783–1792*. Oxford, 1998.

Lippmann, Friedrich. "Mozart, Jommelli, Cimarosa: Zu einigen Arien." *Die Musikforschung* 59 (2006): 31–48.

Lister, Warwick. "The First Performance of Haydn's 'Paris' Symphonies." *Eighteenth-Century Music* 1 (2004): 289–300.

Lockwood, Lewis. "Beethoven as Colourist: Another Look at His String Quartet Arrangement of the Piano Sonata, Op. 14 No. 1." In *Haydn, Mozart, and Beethoven: Studies in the Music of the Classical Period: Essays in Honour of Alan Tyson*, edited by Sieghard Brandenburg, 175–80. Oxford, 1998.

————. "Beethoven before 1800: The Mozart Legacy." *Beethoven Forum* 3 (1994): 39–53.

————. *Beethoven: The Music and the Life*. New York, 2003.

————. "Beethoven's First Symphony: A Farewell to the Eighteenth Century?" In *Essays in Musicology: A tribute to Alvin Johnson*, edited by Lewis Lockwood and Edward Roesner, 235–46. Philadelphia, 1990.

————. "Reshaping the Genre: Beethoven's Piano Sonatas from Op. 22 to Op. 28." *Israel Studies in Musicology* 6 (1996): 1–16.

Loos, Helmut. "Beethoven in Prag 1796 und 1797." In *Beethoven und Böhmen: Beiträge zu Biographie und Wirkungsgeschichte Beethovens*, edited by Sieghard Brandenburg and Martella Gutiérrez-Denhoff, 63–90. Bonn, 1988.

Lorenz, Michael. "Mozarts Haftungserklärung für Freystädtler: Eine Chronologie." *Mozart-Jahrbuch 1998*: 1–20.

Lowinsky, Edward. "On Mozart's Rhythm." *Musical Quarterly* 42 (1956): 162–86.

Lühning, Helga. "Nochmal zum Titus (Erwiderung)." *Die Musikforschung* 28 (1975): 211–14.

———. *Titus-Vertonungen im 18. Jahrhundert: Untersuchungen zur Tradition der Opera seria von Hasse bis Mozart.* Laaber, 1983.

———. "Zur Entstehungsgeschichte von Mozarts 'Titus.' " *Die Musikforschung* 27 (1974): 300–318.

MacIntyre, Bruce C. *Haydn: The Creation.* New York, 1998.

———. *The Viennese Concerted Mass of the Early Classic Period.* Ann Arbor, MI, 1986.

May, Jürgen. "Beethoven und Prince Karl Lichnowsky." *Beethoven Forum* 3 (1994): 29–38.

McClymonds, Marita P. "Haydn and his Contemporaries: 'Armida abbandonata.' " In *Bericht über den internationalen Joseph Haydn Kongress 1982*, edited by Eva Badura-Skoda, 325–52. Munich, 1986.

McFarlane, Meredith, and Simon McVeigh. "The String Quartet in London Concert Life, 1769–1799." In *Concert Life in Eighteenth-Century Britain*, edited by Susan Wollenberg and Simon McVeigh, 161–96. Aldershot, 2004.

McGrann, Jeremiah W. "Of Saints, Name Days, and Turks: Some Background on Haydn's Masses Written for Prince Nikolaus Esterházy II." *Journal of Musicological Research* 17 (1998): 195–210.

McVeigh, Simon. *Concert Life in London from Mozart to Haydn.* Cambridge, 1993.

———. "Freemasonry and Musical Life in London in the Late Eighteenth Century." In *Music in Eighteenth-Century Britain*, edited by David Wyn Jones, 72–100. Aldershot, 2000.

Michtner, Otto. *Das alte Burgtheater als Opernbühne.* Vienna, 1970.

Milhous, Judith, Gabriella Dideriksen, and Robert D. Hume. *The Pantheon Opera and its Aftermath, 1789–1795.* Vol. 2 of *Italian Opera in Late Eighteenth-Century London.* Oxford, 2001.

Mongrédien, Jean. *French Music from the Enlightenment to Romanticism, 1789–1830.* Translated by Sylvain Frémaux. Portland, OR, 1996.

Mörner, Carl-Gabriel Stellan. "Haydniana aus Schweden um 1800." *Haydn-Studien* 2, no. 1 (1969): 1–33.

———. *Johan Wikmanson und die Brüder Silverstolpe: Einige Stockholmer Persönlichkeiten im Musikleben des Gustavianischen Zeitalters.* Stockholm, 1952.

Mount Edgcumbe, Richard, earl of. *Musical Reminiscences.* London, 1824.

Mozart, Leopold. *Versuch einer gründlichen Violinschule.* Translated by Edith Knocker. London, 1948.

Mozart, Wolfgang Amadeus. *Briefe und Aufzeichnungen: Gesamtausgabe.* Edited by Otto Erich Deutsch, Wilhelm A. Bauer, and Joseph Heinz Eibl. 7 vols. Kassel, 1962–75.

Nettl, Paul. "Don Giovanni und Casanova." *Mozart-Jahrbuch 1957*: 108–14.

Niemetschek, Franz Xaver. *Ich kannte Mozart: Die einzige Biographie von einem Augenzeugen.* Edited by Jost Perfahl. Munich, 2005.

Noiray, Michel. "Don Giovanni." In *The Cambridge Mozart Encyclopedia*, edited by Cliff Eisen and Simon P. Keefe, 138–51. Cambridge, 2006.

Nottebohm, Gustav. *Mozartiana*. Leipzig, 1880.

———. *Zweite Beethoveniana*. Leipzig, 1887.

Novello, Vincent, and Mary Novello. *A Mozart Pilgrimage, Being the Travel Diaries of Vincent and Mary Novello in the Year 1829*. Edited by Nerina Medici and Rosemary Hughes. London, 1975.

Olleson, Edward. "Georg August Griesinger's Correspondence with Breitkopf & Härtel." *Haydn Yearbook* 3 (1965): 5–53.

———. "Haydn in the Diaries of Count Karl von Zinzendorf." *Haydn Yearbook* 2 (1963/64): 45–63.

———. "The Origins and Libretto of Haydn's *Creation*." *Haydn Yearbook* 4 (1968): 148–68.

Olleson, Philip. "The London Roman Catholic Embassy Chapels and Their Music in the Eighteenth and Early Nineteenth Centuries." In *Music in Eighteenth-Century Britain*, edited by David Wyn Jones, 101–18. Aldershot, 2000.

Palisca, Claude V. "French Revolutionary Models for Beethoven's *Eroica* Funeral March." In *Music and Context: Essays for John M. Ward*, edited by Anne Dhu Shapiro, 198–209. Cambridge, MA, 1985.

———, ed. *Norton Anthology of Western Music*. 2 vols. New York, 1980.

Pandi, Marianne, and Fritz Schmidt. "Musik zur Zeit Haydns und Beethovens in der Pressburger Zeitung." *Haydn Yearbook* 8 (1971): 165–266.

Papendiek, Charlotte. *Court and Private Life in the Time of Queen Charlotte: Being the Journals of Mrs. Papendiek, Assistant Keeper of the Wardrobe and Reader to Her Majesty*. Edited by Vernon Broughton. 2 vols. London, 1886–87.

Parodi, Elena Biggi. "Francesco Pollini e il suo tempo." *Nuova rivista musicale italiana* 30 (1996): 333–63.

Pezzl, Johann. *Skizze von Wien: Ein Kultur- und Sittenbild aus der josefinischen Zeit*. Edited by Gustav Gugitz and Anton Schlossar. Graz, 1923.

Pichler, Caroline. *Denkwürdigkeiten aus meinem Leben* (Vienna, 1844). Edited by Emil Karl Blümml. 2 vols. Munich, 1914.

Plantinga, Leon. *Beethoven's Concertos. History, Style, Performance*. New York, 1999.

———. *Clementi: His Life and Music*. London, 1977.

Pleyel, Ignaz. *Six String Quartets*, Opus 1. Edited by Simon P. Keefe. The Early String Quartet, vol. 4. Ann Arbor, MI, 2005.

Pohl, Carl Ferdinand. *Joseph Haydn*. 3 vols. Vol. 3 edited by Hugo Botstiber. Leipzig, 1875–82, 1927.

Poštolka, Milan. *Leopold Koželuh: Zivot a dilo*. Prague, 1964.

Price, Curtis. "Italian Opera and Arson in Late Eighteenth-Century London." *Journal of the American Musicological Society* 42 (1989): 55–107.

———, Judith Milhous, and Robert D. Hume. *The King's Theatre, Haymarket, 1778–1791*. Vol. 1 of *Italian Opera in Late Eighteenth-Century London*. Oxford, 1995.

Price, Munro. *The Road from Versailles: Louis XVI, Marie Antoinette, and the Fall of the French Monarchy*. New York, 2002.

Price, Percival. "Chimes." In *The New Grove Dictionary of Music and Musicians*, edited by Stanley Sadie and John Tyrrell. New York, 2002.

Prod'homme, J. G. "From the Unpublished Autobiography of Antoine Reicha." *Musical Quarterly* 22 (1936): 339–53.

Quoy-Bodin, Jean-Luc. "L'Orchestre de la Société Olympique en 1786." *Revue de Musicologie* 70 (1984): 95–105.

Raab, Armin. "Haydns Briefe an den Verleger Boyer." *Haydn-Studien* 8 (2003): 237–52.

Radcliffe, Philip. *Mozart's Concertos.* London, 1978.

Reichardt, Johann Friedrich. "Erinnerung an Mozarts Aufenthalt zu Leipzig." *Berlinische musikalische Zeitung* 1 (1805): 132.

———. *Vertraute Briefe geschrieben auf einer Reise nach Wien und den österreichischen Staaten zu Ende des Jahres 1808 und zu Anfang 1809 (Amsterdam, 1810).* Edited by Gustav Gugitz. 2 vols. Munich, 1915.

Reichart, Sarah Bennet. "The Influence of the Eighteenth-Century Social Dance on the Viennese Classical Style." Ph.D. diss., City University of New York, 1984.

Reinerman, Alan J. "The Papacy, Austria, and the anti-French struggle in Italy, 1792–97." In *Austria in the Age of the French Revolution,* edited by Kinley Brauer and William E. Wright, 47–68. Minneapolis, 1990.

Rice, John A. *Antonio Salieri and Viennese Opera.* Chicago, 1998.

———. *Empress Marie Therese and Music at the Viennese Court, 1792–1807.* Cambridge, 2003.

———. "Mozart and His Singers: The Case of Marchetti Fantozzi, the First Vitellia." *Opera Quarterly* 11 (1995): 31–52.

———. "The Musical Bee: References to Mozart and Cherubini in Hummel's 'New Year' Concerto." *Music and Letters* 77 (1996): 401–24.

———. "Sarti's *Giulio Sabino,* Haydn's *Armida,* and the Arrival of Opera Seria at Esterháza." *Haydn Yearbook* 15 (1984): 181–98.

———. *The Temple of Night at Schönau: Architecture, Music, and Theater in a Late Eighteenth-Century Viennese Garden.* Philadelphia, 2006.

———. *W. A. Mozart, La clemenza di Tito.* Cambridge, 1991.

Richards, Annette. *The Free Fantasia and the Musical Picturesque.* Cambridge, 2001.

Riesbeck, Johann Kaspar. *Briefe eines reisenden Franzosen über Deutschland an seinen Bruder zu Paris.* 2nd ed. 2 vols. Leipzig, 1784.

Rifkin, Joshua. "Ein unbekanntes Haydn-Zitat bei Mozart." *Haydn Studies* 2 (1969–70): 317.

Rosen, Charles. *The Classical Style: Haydn, Mozart, Beethoven.* New York, 1971.

Rosenbaum, Joseph Carl. *The Diaries of Joseph Carl Rosenbaum, 1770–1829.* Edited by Else Radant. *Haydn Yearbook* 5 (1968).

Rosenthal, Albi, and Alan Tyson, eds. *Mozart: Eigenhändiges Werkverzeichnis Faksimile.* London, 1991.

Rumph, Stephen. "Unveiling Cherubino." *Eighteenth-Century Music* 4 (2007): 131–40.

Rushton, Julian. "Viennese Amateur or London Professional? A Reconsideration of Haydn's Tragic Cantata *Arianna a Naxos.*" In *Music in Eighteenth-Century Austria,* edited by David Wyn Jones, 232–45. Cambridge, 1991.

Sadie, Stanley, ed. *Wolfgang Amadè Mozart: Essays on His Life and His Music.* Oxford, 1996.

Sandberger, Adolf. "Die Inventare der Bonner Hofmusik." In *Ausgewählte Aufsätze zur Musikgeschichte*. 2 vols., 2:109–30. Munich, 1921–24.

Schachter, Carl. "Mozart's Last and Beethoven's First: Echoes of K. 551 in the First Movement of Opus 21." In *Mozart Studies*, edited by Cliff Eisen, 227–51. New York, 1991.

Schiedermair, Ludwig. *Der junge Beethoven*. Leipzig, 1925.

Schloss Augustusburg. *Kurfürst Clemens August, Landesherr und Mäzen des 18. Jahrhunderts: Ausstellung in Schloss Augustusburg zu Bruhl, 1961*. Cologne, 1961.

Schmid, Ernst Fritz. "Joseph Haydn und Carl Philipp Emanuel Bach." *Zeitschrift für Musikwissenschaft* 14 (1932): 299–330.

Schneider, Herbert. "Le mythe du vaisseau *Le Vengeur* de 1794 à 1951: Textes—Images—Musique." *Acta Musicologica* 77 (2005): 71–121.

———. "Vaudeville-Finale in Haydns Opern und ihre Vorgeschichte." In *Bericht über den internationalen Joseph Haydn Kongress 1982*, edited by Eva Badura-Skoda, 302–9. Munich, 1986.

Schönfeld, Johann Ferdinand, Ritter von. *Jahrbuch der Tonkunst von Wien und Prag*. München, 1796.

———. "A Yearbook of the Music of Vienna and Prague, 1796." In *Haydn and His World*, edited by Elaine Sisman, translated by Kathrine Talbot, 289–320. Princeton, 1997.

Schroeder, David P. *Haydn and the Enlightenment: The Late Symphonies and Their Audience*. Oxford, 1990.

Schuler, Heinz. "'Mozart von der Wohltätigkeit: Die Mitglieder der gerechten und vollkommenen St-Johannes-Freimaurer-Loge 'Zur Wohltätigkeit' im Orient von Wien." *Mitteilungen der Internationalen Stiftung Mozarteum* 36 (1988): 1–56.

Seeger, Horst. "Zur musikhistorischen Bedeutung der Haydn-Biographie von Albert Christoph Dies (1810)." *Beiträge zur Musikwissenschaft* 1, no. 3 (1959): 24–31.

Sisman, Elaine. *Mozart: The "Jupiter" Symphony*. Cambridge, 1993.

Solomon, Maynard. *Beethoven*. New York, 1977.

———. "Beethoven's 'Magazin der Kunst.'" *19th Century Music* 7 (1984): 199–208.

———. *Mozart: A Life*. New York, 1995.

———. "Mozart's Journey to Berlin." *Journal of Musicology* 12 (1994): 76–84.

———. "The Rochlitz Anecdotes: Issues of Authenticity in Early Mozart Biography." In *Mozart Studies*, edited by Cliff Eisen, 1–59. New York, 1991.

Somfai, László. "A Bold Enharmonic Modulatory Model in Joseph Haydn's String Quartets." In *Studies in Eighteenth-Century Music: A Tribute to Karl Geiringer on His Seventieth Birthday*, edited by H. C. Robbins Landon and Roger E. Chapman, 370–81. New York, 1970.

———. *Joseph Haydn: His Life in Contemporary Pictures*. London, 1969.

———. *The Keyboard Sonatas of Joseph Haydn: Instruments and Performance Practice, Genres and Styles*. Translated by the author with Charlotte Greenspan. Chicago, 1995.

———. "Learned Style in Two Late String Quartet Movements by Haydn." *Studia Musicologica* 28 (1986): 326–49.

Spink, Ian. "Haydn at St. Paul's—1791 or 1792?" *Early Music* 33 (2005): 273–80.

Spitzer, John, and Neal Zaslaw. *The Birth of the Orchestra: History of an Institution, 1650–1815.* Oxford, 2004.

Staehelin, Martin. "A Veiled Judgment of Beethoven by Albrechtsberger?" In *Beethoven Essays: Studies in Honor of Elliot Forbes,* edited by Lewis Lockwood and Phyllis Benjamin, 46–52. Cambridge, MA, 1984.

Steblin, Rita. *A History of Key Characteristics in the Eighteenth and Early Nineteenth Centuries.* Ann Arbor, MI, 1983.

Stroh, Patricia. "Evolution of an Edition: The Case of Beethoven's Opus 2. Part I: Punches, Proofs, and Printings: The Seven States of Artaria's First Edition." *Notes* 57 (2000): 289–329.

Sutcliffe, W. Dean. "The Haydn Piano Trio: Textual Facts and Textural Principles." In *Haydn Studies,* edited by W. Dean Sutcliffe, 246–90. Cambridge, 1998.

———. *Haydn: String Quartets, Op. 50.* Cambridge, 1992.

Taïeb, Patrick. "*La Chasse du Jeune Henri* (Méhul, 1797). Une analyse historique," *Revue de Musicologie* 83 (1997): 205–46.

Temperley, Nicholas. *Haydn: The Creation.* Cambridge, 1991.

Thayer, Alexander Wheelock. *Thayer's Life of Beethoven.* Edited by Elliot Forbes. 2 vols. Princeton, 1964.

Thürheim, Andreas. *Ludwig, Fürst Starhemberg.* Graz, 1889.

Till, Nicholas. *Mozart and the Enlightenment: Truth, Virtue, and Beauty in Mozart's Operas.* London, 1992.

Tovey, Donald Francis. *Essays in Musical Analysis.* 6 vols. London, 1935–39.

Tyson, Alan. *Mozart. Studies of the Autograph Scores.* Cambridge, MA, 1987.

———. "The 1786 Prague Version of Mozart's 'Le nozze di Figaro.' " *Music and Letters* 69 (1988): 321–33.

Verti, Roberto, ed. *Un almanacco drammatico: L'Indice de' teatrali spettacoli, 1764–1823.* 2 vols. Pesaro, 1996.

Vincent, Edgar. *Nelson: Love and Fame.* New Haven, 2003.

Volek, Tomislav. "Über den Ursprung von Mozarts Oper 'La Clemenza di Tito.' " *Mozart-Jahrbuch 1959*: 274–86.

———, and Jitřenka Pešková. *Mozart's Don Giovanni.* Exhibition catalogue. Prague, 1987.

Vysloužil, Jiří. *Zápisky o Antonínu Reijchovi; Notes sur Antoine Reicha.* Brno, 1970 .

Wagner, Karl, ed. *Abbé Maximilian Stadler: Seine "Materialien zur Geschichte der Musik unter den österreichischen Regenten," ein Beitrag zum musikalischen Historismus im vormärzlichen Wien.* Schriftenreihe der Internationalen Stiftung Mozarteum 6. Salzburg, 1974.

Waldoff, Jessica. *Recognition in Mozart's Operas.* Oxford, 2006.

Wangermann, Ernst. *The Austrian Achievement, 1700–1800.* London, 1973.

———. *From Joseph II to the Jacobin Trials.* 2nd ed. Oxford, 1969.

Webster, James. "The Falling-out Between Haydn and Beethoven: The Evidence of the Sources." In *Beethoven Essays: Studies in Honor of Elliot Forbes,* edited by Lewis Lockwood and Phyllis Benjamin, 3–45. Cambridge, MA, 1984.

————. *Haydn's "Farewell" Symphony and the Idea of Classical Style: Through-Composition and Cyclic Integration in His Instrumental Music.* Cambridge, 1991.

Wegeler, Franz, and Ferdinand Ries. *Biographische Notizen über Ludwig van Beethoven.* Koblenz, 1838.

Wheelock, Gretchen A. *Haydn's Ingenious Jesting with Art: Contexts of Musical Wit and Humor.* New York, 1992.

White, Chappel. *From Vivaldi to Viotti: A History of the Early Classical Violin Concerto.* Philadelphia, 1992.

Wiesand, Reinhard. "Ein 'einfaches Sekundariestück, ohne individuelle Züge'? Tradition und Erfindung in der Arie 'Torna di Tito a latò.' " *Mozart-Jahrbuch 1984/85*: 134–44.

Will, Richard. *The Characteristic Symphony in the Age of Haydn and Beethoven.* Cambridge, 2002.

Wolff, Christoph, ed. *The String Quartets of Haydn, Mozart, and Beethoven: Studies of the Autograph Manuscripts.* Cambridge, MA, 1980.

Woodfield, Ian. *Opera and Drama in Eighteenth-Century London: The King's Theatre, Garrick, and the Business of Performance.* Cambridge, 2001.

————. "Reflections on Mozart's 'Non so più cosa son, cosa faccio.' " *Eighteenth-Century Music* 3 (2006): 133–39.

————. *Salomon and the Burneys: Private Patronage and a Public Career.* Aldershot, 2003.

Wyn Jones, David. "A Newly Identified Sketchleaf for Haydn's Quartet in D Minor, 'Opus 103.' " *Haydn-Studien* 8 (2004): 413–17.

————, ed. *Music in Eighteenth-Century Austria.* Cambridge, 1991.

————, ed. *Music in Eighteenth-Century Britain.* Aldershot, 2000.

Yudkin, Jeremy. "Beethoven's 'Mozart' Quartet." *Journal of the American Musicological Society* 45 (1992): 30–74.

Zahn, Robert von. "Haydns Aufenthalt in Hamburg 1795." *Haydn-Studien* 6, no. 4 (1994): 309–12.

Zaslaw, Neal. "Mozart's Incidental Music to *Lanassa* and His *Thamos* Motets." In *Music, Libraries, and the Academy: Essays in Honor of Lenore Coral.* Edited by James P. Cassaro, 55–63. Middleton, WI, 2007.

————, ed. *Mozart's Piano Concertos. Text, Context, Interpretation.* Ann Arbor, MI, 1996.

————, with William Cowdery, eds. *The Compleat Mozart. A Guide to the Musical Works of Wolfgang Amadeus Mozart.* New York, 1990.

Credits

Figs. 1.4, 1.5, 1.6, 1.7, 3.1, 3.7: International Stiftung Mozarteum, Salzburg, Austria. Fig. 2.2: by permission of the Houghton Library, Harvard University, Cambridge, MA. Fig. 2.4: Národni Galerie, Prague, Czech Republic. Fig. 4.2: Széchényi National Library, Theater Collection. Budapest, Hungary. Fig. 4.4: by courtesy of Fürst Oettingen-Wallerstein, Harburg, Germany. Fig. 4.7: The Jean Gray Hargrove Music Library, University of California, Berkeley, CA. Fig. 5.1: Cambridge University Press, London. Fig. 5.2: Royal College of Music, Picture Collection, London. Figs. 5.5, 6.2: British Library London. Fig. 5.6: Albertina Museum, Vienna, Austria. Fig. 7.2: Beethoven Haus, Bonn, Germany. Figs. 7.3, 7.4. 7.5: reproduced with permission of the Ira F. Brilliant Center for Beethoven Studies, San José State University, San Jose, CA. Fig. 7.6: Beethoven Haus, Collection H. C. Bodmer, Bonn, Germany.

Index

Note: Page numbers in *italics* denote illustrations or musical examples; page numbers in **boldface** indicate major discussions of the works.

3 4
Strasse
Korneuburg
S. Veith
S. Voit
Unt Krinzendorf
Ob. Krinzendorf
Höflein
Bisamberg
Langenzersdorf
Strebersdorf
Jedlersee
Dullndorf
S. Jacob
S. Mörten
Kirrling
Lederbach
Klosterneuburg
Guging
Weidling
Kirchbach
Wädlingbach
Kahlenberg
Leop: Berg
Riede Berg
Kahlenbergerdörfel
Kobenzl
Himmel
Josephidorf
Jedlersdorf am Spit
Orbesbach
Nusdorf
Heiligstadt
Sifring
Grinzing
Neustift
Salmansdorf
Mauerbach
Galizibberg
Pötzleinsdorf
Gersthof
Döbling
Alsterbach
Dornbach
Weinhaus
Neuwaldeck
Währing
Hernals
Leopoldstadt
Hadersdorf
Breitensee
Hüteldorf
Baumgarten
Presbaum
Purkersdorf
M: Brun
das Reich
Neulerchenfeld
Josephstadt
Weidlingau
Auhof
S. Veit
Penzing
Hakking
Hietzing
Schönbrun
Grundorf
Nicola
Wien Fl.
WIEN
Glacis
Lainz
Speising
Maidling
Gumpendorf
Magdalenengrund
Geschlossener Park
Hetzendorf
Mauer
Engelburg
Laab
Altmansdorf
Favoritte
Rennweg
Landstrass
Erdberg
Breitenfurt
Kalchsburg
Ob. Ziesing
Mon Pery
Erla
Steinhof
Inzersdorf
Rodaun
Unter
Atzgersdorf
Perchtoldsdorf
Siebenhirten
Schellhof
Roth Neusiedl
Ob. Laach
Kaltenleutgeben
Gisteibel
Porthof
Vösendorf
Hennersdorf
Leopoldsdorf
Klederin
Vildeg
Brun
Lichtenstein
Altes Schlos
Sparbach
Kalch Ofen
Garn
Priel
Kinzensdorf
Lanzendorf
Achau
S. Johanstein
Mödling
Pittermansdorf
Neudorf
Rasschenhof
Klausen
Mödling Bach
Baulnerbach oder Schwacha Fl.
Gaden
Thalling
Laxenburg
Guntramsdorf
Strasse nach Steyer mark
Zachsenburg
Strassnach Hungarn
Tristing
48
3 4